Lecture Notes in Computer Science　　　10770

Commenced Publication in 1973
Founding and Former Series Editors:
Gerhard Goos, Juris Hartmanis, and Jan van Leeuwen

Editorial Board

More information about this series at http://www.springer.com/series/7410

Michel Abdalla · Ricardo Dahab (Eds.)

Public-Key Cryptography – PKC 2018

21st IACR International Conference
on Practice and Theory of Public-Key Cryptography
Rio de Janeiro, Brazil, March 25–29, 2018
Proceedings, Part II

 Springer

Editors
Michel Abdalla (iD)
CNRS and École Normale Supérieure
Paris
France

Ricardo Dahab
University of Campinas
Campinas, SP
Brazil

ISSN 0302-9743   ISSN 1611-3349   (electronic)
Lecture Notes in Computer Science
ISBN 978-3-319-76580-8   ISBN 978-3-319-76581-5   (eBook)
https://doi.org/10.1007/978-3-319-76581-5

Library of Congress Control Number: 2018934351

LNCS Sublibrary: SL4 – Security and Cryptology

Printed on acid-free paper

This Springer imprint is published by the registered company Springer International Publishing AG part of Springer Nature
The registered company address is: Gewerbestrasse 11, 6330 Cham, Switzerland

Preface

The 21st IACR International Conference on Practice and Theory of Public-Key Cryptography (PKC 2018) was held March 25–29, 2018, in Rio de Janeiro, Brazil. The conference is sponsored by the International Association for Cryptologic Research (IACR) and focuses on all technical aspects of public-key cryptography.

These proceedings consist of two volumes including 49 papers that were selected by the Program Committee from 186 submissions. Each submission was assigned to at least three reviewers while submissions co-authored by Program Committee members received at least four reviews. Following the initial reviewing phase, the submissions were discussed over a period of five weeks. During this discussion phase, the Program Committee used quite intensively a recent feature of the review system, which allows Program Committee members to anonymously ask questions to the authors.

The reviewing and selection process was a challenging task and I am deeply grateful to the Program Committee members and external reviewers for their hard and thorough work. Many thanks also to Shai Halevi for his assistance with the Web submission and review software and for his constant availability.

The conference program also included invited talks by Elette Boyle (IDC Herzliya, Israel) and Hugo Krawczyk (IBM Research, USA). I would like to thank both of them as well as all the other speakers for their contributions to the program.

Finally, I would like to thank Ricardo Dahab, the general chair, for organizing a great conference and all the conference attendees for making this a truly intellectually stimulating event through their active participation.

March 2018   Michel Abdalla

PKC 2018

21st International Conference on Practice and Theory of Public-Key Cryptography

Rio de Janeiro, Brazil
March 25–29, 2018

Sponsored by
The International Association of Cryptologic Research

General Chair

Ricardo Dahab   University of Campinas, Brazil

Program Chair

Michel Abdalla   CNRS and École Normale Supérieure, France

Program Committee

Shweta Agrawal	Indian Institute of Technology, Madras, India
Prabhanjan Ananth	UCLA and MIT, USA
Diego Aranha	University of Campinas, Brazil
Mihir Bellare	University of California, San Diego, USA
Chris Brzuska	Hamburg University of Technology, Germany
Dario Catalano	Università di Catania, Italy
Jie Chen	East China Normal University, China
Yilei Chen	Boston University, USA
Céline Chevalier	Université Panthéon-Assas Paris 2, France
Kai-Min Chung	Academia Sinica, Taiwan
Dana Dachman-Soled	University of Maryland, USA
Bernardo David	Tokyo Institute of Technology, Japan
Léo Ducas	CWI Amsterdam, The Netherlands
Nico Döttling	FAU Erlangen-Nürnberg, Germany
Pierre-Alain Fouque	Rennes 1 University, France
Sergey Gorbunov	University of Waterloo, Canada
Aurore Guillevic	Inria, France
Carmit Hazay	Bar-Ilan University, Israel
Julia Hesse	Karlsruhe Institute of Technology, Germany
Zahra Jafargholi	Aarhus University, Denmark
Tibor Jager	Paderborn University, Germany
Bhavana Kanukurthi	Indian Institute of Science, India
Markulf Kohlweiss	Microsoft Research and University of Edinburgh, UK

Adeline Langlois	CNRS and Rennes 1 University, France
Payman Mohassel	Visa Research, USA
Ryo Nishimaki	NTT Secure Platform Labs, Japan
Alain Passelègue	UCLA, USA
Arpita Patra	Indian Institute of Science, India
Antigoni Polychroniadou	Cornell University, USA
Carla Ràfols Salvador	Universitat Pompeu Fabra, Spain
Alessandra Scafuro	North Carolina State University, USA
Christian Schaffner	University of Amsterdam & QuSoft, The Netherlands
Gil Segev	Hebrew University, Israel
Jae Hong Seo	Myongji University, South Korea
Qiang Tang	New Jersey Institute of Technology, USA
Mehdi Tibouchi	NTT Secure Platform Laboratories, Japan
Bogdan Warinschi	University of Bristol, UK
Mor Weiss	Northeastern University, USA

Additional Reviewers

Masayuki Abe
Shashank Agrawal
Erdem Alkım
Nuttapong Attrapadung
Saikrishna Badrinarayanan
Shi Bai
Christian Bardertscher
Hridam Basu
Balthazar Bauer
Carsten Baum
Pascal Bemmann
Fabrice Benhamouda
David Bernhard
Pauline Bert
Olivier Blazy
Guillaume Bonnoron
Niek Bouman
Florian Bourse
Jacqueline Brendel
Ran Canetti
Guilhem Castagnos
Suvradip Chakraborty
Nishanth Chandran
Sanjit Chatterjee

Binyi Chen
Long Chen
Rongmao Chen
Yu Chen
Nai-Hui Chia
Arka Rai Choudhuri
Ashish Choudhury
Peter Chvojka
Michele Ciampi
Ran Cohen
Sandro Coretti
Craig Costello
Geoffroy Couteau
Jan Czajkowski
Anders Dalskov
Luca De Feo
Jean Paul Degabriele
David Derler
Apoorvaa Deshpande
Mario Di Raimondo
Luis J. Dominguez Perez
Rafael Dowsley
Yfke Dulek
Lisa Eckey

Andrew Ellis
Lucas Enloe
Naomi Ephraim
Thomas Espitau
Leo Fan
Xiong Fan
Antonio Faonio
Prastudy Fauzi
Armando Faz-Hernández
Rex Fernando
Houda Ferradi
Claus Fieker
Dario Fiore
Marc Fischlin
Benjamin Fuller
Philippe Gaborit
Nicolas Gama
Chaya Ganesh
Romain Gay
Kai Gellert
Ran Gelles
Nicholas Genise
Paul Germouty
Essam Ghadafi
Satrajit Ghosh
Irene Giacomelli
Huijing Gong
Junqing Gong
Alonso González
Conrado Porto Lopes Gouvêa
Rishab Goyal
Paul Grubbs
Siyao Guo
Divya Gupta
Kyoohyung Han
Javier Herranz
Justin Holmgren
Kristina Hostakova
Zhengan Huang
Andreas Huelsing
Robin Hui
Shih-Han Hung

Aaron Hutchinson
Ilia Iliashenko
Sorina Ionica
Malika Izabachène
Michael Jacobson
Joseph Jaeger
Aayush Jain
Christian Janson
Stacey Jeffery
Saqib Kakvi
Shuichi Katsumata
Natasha Kharchenko
Sam Kim
Taechan Kim
Elena Kirshanova
Fuyuki Kitagawa
Susumu Kiyoshima
Konrad Kohbrok
Lisa Kohl
Ilan Komargodski
Stephan Krenn
Ashutosh Kumar
Rafael Kurek
Eyal Kushilevitz
Russell Lai
Kim Laine
Mario Larangeira
Changmin Lee
Hyung Tae Lee
Kwangsu Lee
Moon Sung Lee
Nikos Leonardos
Iraklis Leontiadis
Qinyi Li
Benoît Libert
Weikai Lin
Feng-Hao Liu
Shengli Liu
Tianren Liu
Alex Lombardi
Vadim Lyubashevsky
Fermi Ma

Gilles Macario-Rat
Varun Madathil
Bernardo Magri
Monosij Maitra
Christian Majenz
Hemanta K. Maji
Giulio Malavolta
Mary Maller
Mark Manulis
Giorgia Azzurra Marson
Takahiro Matsuda
Sogol Mazaheri
Thierry Mefenza
Peihan Miao
Ian Miers
Ameer Mohammed
Paz Morillo
Fabrice Mouhartem
Pratyay Mukherjee
Pierrick Méaux
Gregory Neven
Khoa Nguyen
David Niehues
Luca Nizzardo
Sai Lakshmi Bhavana Obbattu
Cristina Onete
Michele Orrù
Emmanuela Orsini
Jheyne N. Ortiz
Daniel Escudero Ospina
Maris Ozols
Jiaxin Pan
Tapas Pandit
Dimitris Papadopoulos
Filip Pawlega
Thomas Peters
Doung Hieu Phan
Cecile Pierrot
Zaira Pindado
Oxana Poburinnaya
Chen Qian
Elizabeth Quaglia
Liz Quaglia
Ananth Raghunathan
Srinivasan Raghuraman
Somindu C. Ramanna

Divya Ravi
Guénaël Renault
Peter Rindal
Miruna Rosca
Lior Rotem
Kai Samelin
Pratik Sarkar
Sajin Sasy
John Schanck
Peter Scholl
Dominique Schröder
Adam Sealfon
Sruthi Sekar
Nicolas Sendrier
Barak Shani
Abhishek Shetty
Javier Silva
Mark Simkin
Luisa Siniscalchi
Daniel Slamanig
Ben Smith
Fang Song
Eduardo Soria-Vazquez
Akshayaram Srinivasan
Ron Steinfeld
Mario Strefler
Christoph Striecks
Atsushi Takayasu
Benjamin Hong Meng Tan
Emmanuel Thomé
Sri Aravinda Thyagarajan
Ni Trieu
Rotem Tsabary
Jorge L. Villar
Dhinakaran Vinayagamurthy
Satyanarayana Vusirikala
Riad S. Wahby
Kun-Peng Wang
Mingyuan Wang
Xiao Wang
Yuyu Wang
Yohei Watanabe
Weiqiang Wen
Benjamin Wesolowski
David Wu
Keita Xagawa

Fan Xiong
Sophia Yakoubov
Shota Yamada
Takashi Yamakawa
Avishay Yanai
Rupeng Yang
Arkady Yerukhimovich
Eylon Yogev
Zuoxia Yu

Aaram Yun
Mohammad Zaheri
Mark Zhandry
Daode Zhang
Jiang Zhang
Kai Zhang
Ren Zhang
Linfeng Zhou

Sponsoring Institutions

Accenture Digital (https://www.accenture.com/br-pt/digital-index)
ERC CryptoCloud (http://www.di.ens.fr/users/pointche/cryptocloud.php)
Scyphir Unipessoal, LDA (http://scyphir.pt)

Contents – Part II

Lattices

Contents – Part I

Signatures

SOFIA: $\mathcal{MQ}$-Based Signatures in the QROM

Ming-Shing Chen[1,2]($\boxtimes$), Andreas Hülsing[3]($\boxtimes$), Joost Rijneveld[4]($\boxtimes$),
Simona Samardjiska[4]($\boxtimes$), and Peter Schwabe[4]($\boxtimes$)

[1] Department of Electrical Engineering, National Taiwan University,
Taipei, Taiwan
mschen@crypto.tw
[2] Research Center for Information Technology Innovation,
Academia Sinica, Taipei, Taiwan
[3] Department of Mathematics and Computer Science,
Technische Universiteit Eindhoven, Eindhoven, The Netherlands
andreas@huelsing.net
[4] Digital Security Group, Radboud University, Nijmegen, The Netherlands
joost@joostrijneveld.nl, simonas@cs.ru.nl, peter@cryptojedi.org

Abstract. We propose SOFIA, the first $\mathcal{MQ}$-based signature scheme provably secure in the quantum-accessible random oracle model (QROM). Our construction relies on an extended version of Unruh's transform for 5-pass identification schemes that we describe and prove secure both in the ROM and QROM.

Based on a detailed security analysis, we provide concrete parameters for SOFIA that achieve 128-bit post-quantum security. The result is SOFIA-4-128 with parameters carefully optimized to minimize signature size and maximize performance. SOFIA-4-128 comes with an implementation targeting recent Intel processors with the AVX2 vector-instruction set; the implementation is fully protected against timing attacks.

Keywords: Post-quantum cryptography · Multivariate cryptography 5-pass identification schemes · QROM · Unruh's transform Vectorized implementation

1 Introduction

At Asiacrypt 2016 [11], we presented a post-quantum signature scheme called MQDSS, obtained by applying a generalized Fiat-Shamir transform to a 5-pass identification schemes (IDS) with security based on the hardness of solving a system of multivariate quadratic equations ($\mathcal{MQ}$ problem). Unlike previous $\mathcal{MQ}$

This work was supported by the Netherlands Organization for Scientific Research (NWO) under Veni 2013 project 13114, by the European Commission through the ICT Programme under contract ICT-645622 PQCRYPTO and by the Faculty of Computer Science and Engineering at the "Ss. Cyril and Methodius" University.

© International Association for Cryptologic Research 2018
M. Abdalla and R. Dahab (Eds.): PKC 2018, LNCS 10770, pp. 3–33, 2018.
https://doi.org/10.1007/978-3-319-76581-5_1

signature schemes, MQDSS comes with a reduction from a random instance of $\mathcal{MQ}$; it does not need additional assumptions on the hardness of related problems like the Isomorphism of Polynomials (IP) [29] or MinRank [13,20].

Unfortunately, the security reduction of MQDSS is in the random oracle model and highly non-tight, while our ultimate goal is (as stated in [11]) a scheme with a tight reduction from $\mathcal{MQ}$ in the quantum random oracle model (QROM) or even in the standard model. In this paper, we take a step closer towards such a scheme. More specifically, we propose SOFIA, a digital signature scheme that is provably EU-CMA secure in the QROM if the $\mathcal{MQ}$ problem is hard and allows for a tight reduction in the ROM (albeit not in the QROM).

To achieve this, we start from Unruh's transform [33] for transforming Σ-protocols to NIZK proofs (and signatures) in the QROM. The reason for a different transform comes from the inherent problems of the Fiat-Shamir transform (and also the generalization to 5-pass schemes) in the QROM. Namely, the proof technique introduced by Pointcheval and Stern [30] requires rewinding of the adversary and adaptively programming the random oracle. Not only does this cause problems in the QROM, but it also produces non-tight proofs in the ROM. Unruh's transform avoids these problems by adopting and tweaking an idea from Fischlin's transform [21] that solves the rewinding problem.

Recently, Kiltz, Loss, and Pan [27] considered a generalization of the Fiat-Shamir transform to 5-pass schemes, and provided a tight reduction in the ROM. However, the technique faces similar issues when it comes to the QROM such as adaptive programming of the random oracles. Hence, no proof in the QROM is known. Therefore, it is not applicable for SOFIA. In concurrent work, Kiltz, Lyubashevsky, and Schaffner [28] provide a viable alternative to Unruh's transform in the QROM. The authors prove security of the Fiat-Shamir transform in the QROM, using the additional assumption of "lossiness" of the IDS. While this requires modifications in the IDS and re-parametrization of MQDSS, it seems promising future work to see whether one can obtain a more efficient scheme with a QROM proof this way.

MQDSS builds on a 5-pass $\mathcal{MQ}$-based IDS from [31]. While [31] also introduces a 3-pass IDS, we showed in [11] that the 5-pass scheme leads to smaller signatures due to a smaller soundness error. Hence, we do not simply apply the Unruh transform to the 3-pass IDS but extend it such that it applies to any 5-pass IDS with binary second challenge (named $q2$-IDS in [11]) and thus to the $\mathcal{MQ}$-based 5-pass IDS from [31]. We prove that the signature scheme resulting from the application of the transform is post-quantum EU-CMA secure (PQ-EU-CMA) in the QROM. This proof follows a two-step approach: We first give a (tight) proof in the ROM, and then discuss the changes necessary to carry over to the QROM. We then instantiate the construction with the $\mathcal{MQ}$-based 5-pass IDS by Sakumoto, Shirai, and Hiwatari [31] and provide various optimizations particularly suited for this specific IDS. These optimizations almost halve the size of the signature compared to the non-optimized generic transform.

We instantiate SOFIA with carefully optimized parameters aiming at the 128-bit post-quantum security level; we refer to this instance as SOFIA-4-128. A comparison with MQDSS-31-64 from [11], which targets the same security level, shows that the improvements in security guarantees come at a cost: with 123 KiB, SOFIA-4-128 signatures are about a factor of 3 larger than MQDSS-31-64 signatures and our optimized SOFIA-4-128 software takes about a factor of 3 longer for both signing and verification than the optimized one for MQDSS-31-64. However, like MQDSS, SOFIA features extremely short keys; specifically, SOFIA-4-128 public keys have 64 bytes and the secret keys have 32 bytes.

SOFIA is not the first concrete signature scheme with a proof in the QROM. Notably, TESLA-2 [1] is a lattice-based signature scheme with a reduction in the QROM, while Picnic-10-38 [10] is the result of constructing a signature scheme from a symmetric primitive using the transform by Unruh [33] that was mentioned above. Relying on even more conservative assumptions, the hash-based signature scheme SPHINCS-256 [6] has a tight proof in the standard model. Although SOFIA-4-128 remains faster than SPHINCS-256 (which is, because of its standard model assumptions, arguably the 'scheme to beat'), we do significantly exceed its 40 KiB signature size. Conversely, but on a similar note, SOFIA-4-128 outperforms Picnic-10-38 both in terms of signing speed and signature size. TESLA-2 remains the 'odd one out' with its small signatures but much larger keys; it strongly depends on context whether this is an upside or a problem. See Table 3 for a numeric overview of the comparison.

Organization of the paper. Section 2 gives the necessary background on identification schemes and signature schemes. Section 3 presents the extended Unruh transform to support $q2$ identification schemes. Section 4 revisits the 5-pass identification scheme introduced in [31]. Section 5 introduces the SOFIA signature scheme and finally Section 6 explains our parameter choices for SOFIA-4-128 and gives details of our optimized implementation.

Availability of software. We place all software presented in this paper into the public domain to maximize re-usability of our results. It is available for download at https://joostrijneveld.nl/papers/sofia.

2   Preliminaries

In the following we provide basic definitions used throughout this work. We are concerned with post-quantum security, i.e., a setting where honest parties use classical computers but adversaries might have access to a quantum computer. Therefore, we adapt some common security notions accordingly, modeling adversaries as quantum algorithms.

Digital signatures. In this work we are concerned with the construction of digital-signature schemes. Due to space limitations, we omit the standard definitions for digital signatures and their security. They are included in the full version of the paper.

Identification schemes. An identification scheme (IDS) is a protocol that allows a prover $\mathcal{P}$ to prove its identity to a verifier $\mathcal{V}$. More formally:

Definition 2.1 (Identification scheme). *An identification scheme with security parameter k, denoted $\mathsf{IDS}(1^k)$, is a triplet of PPT algorithms $\mathsf{IDS} = (\mathsf{KGen}, \mathcal{P}, \mathcal{V})$ such that the key generation algorithm KGen is a probabilistic algorithm that outputs a key pair $(\mathsf{sk}, \mathsf{pk})$, and $\mathcal{P}$ and $\mathcal{V}$ are interactive algorithms, executing a common protocol. The prover $\mathcal{P}$ takes as input a secret key sk and the verifier $\mathcal{V}$ takes as input a public key pk. At the conclusion of the protocol, $\mathcal{V}$ outputs a bit b with $b = 1$ indicating "accept" and $b = 0$ indicating "reject".*

For correctness of an IDS, we require that for all $(\mathsf{pk}, \mathsf{sk}) \leftarrow \mathsf{KGen}()$ we have where $\langle \mathcal{P}(\mathsf{sk}), \mathcal{V}(\mathsf{pk}) \rangle$ refers to the common execution of the protocol between $\mathcal{P}$ with input sk and $\mathcal{V}$ on input pk. We denote by $\mathsf{trans}(\langle \mathcal{P}(\mathsf{sk}), \mathcal{V}(\mathsf{pk}) \rangle)$ the transcript of messages exchanged during this execution.

In this work we are concerned with canonical 5-pass IDS, where the prover and the verifier exchange two challenges and replies. More formally:

Definition 2.2 (Canonical 5-pass identification schemes). *Consider $\mathsf{IDS} = (\mathsf{KGen}, \mathcal{P}, \mathcal{V})$, a 5-pass identification scheme with two challenge spaces C_1 and C_2. We call IDS a canonical 5-pass identification scheme if the prover can be split into three subroutines $\mathcal{P} = (\mathcal{P}_0, \mathcal{P}_1, \mathcal{P}_2)$ and the verifier into three subroutines $\mathcal{V} = (\mathsf{ChS}_1, \mathsf{ChS}_2, \mathsf{Vf})$ such that:*

$\mathcal{P}_0(\mathsf{sk})$ computes the initial commitment com sent as the first message and a state fstate fed forward to $\mathcal{P}_1$. ChS_1 computes the first challenge message $\mathsf{ch}_1 \leftarrow_R \mathsf{C}_1$, sampling at random from the challenge space C_1. $\mathcal{P}_1(\mathsf{fstate}, \mathsf{ch}_1)$ computes the first response resp_1 of the prover (and updates the state fstate) given access to the state and the first challenge. ChS_2 computes the second challenge message $\mathsf{ch}_2 \leftarrow_R \mathsf{C}_2$. $\mathcal{P}_2(\mathsf{fstate}, \mathsf{ch}_2)$ computes the second response resp_2 of the prover given access to the state and the second challenge. $\mathsf{Vf}(\mathsf{pk}, \mathsf{com}, \mathsf{ch}_1, \mathsf{resp}_1, \mathsf{ch}_2, \mathsf{resp}_2)$ upon access to the public key and the whole transcript outputs $\mathcal{V}$'s final decision.

Note that the state forwarded among the prover algorithms can contain all inputs to previous prover algorithms if they are needed later. We also assume that the verifier keeps all sent and received messages to feed them to Vf.

We will consider a particular type of 5-pass identification protocols where the size of the two challenge spaces is restricted to q and 2.

Definition 2.3 ($q2$-Identification scheme). *A $q2$-Identification scheme IDS with security parameter $k \in \mathbb{N}$ is a canonical 5-pass identification scheme where for the challenge spaces C_1 and C_2 it holds that $|\mathsf{C}_1| = q$ and $|\mathsf{C}_2| = 2$. Moreover, the probability that the commitment com takes a given value is $\leq 2^{-k}$, where the probability is taken over the random choice of the input and the used randomness.*

Our goal is to construct signature schemes from identification schemes. It is well known that passively secure identification schemes suffice for this. In this setting, security is defined in terms of two properties: special soundness and honest-verifier zero-knowledge (HVZK). To prove security of our signature scheme, we will make use of the existence of so called $q2$-extractor which is a variant of special soundness.

Definition 2.4 ((computational) PQ-HVZK). *Let* $k \in \mathbb{N}$, $\mathsf{IDS}(1^k) = (\mathsf{KGen}, \mathcal{P}, \mathcal{V})$ *an identification scheme with security parameter* k. *We say that* IDS *is computational post-quantum honest-verifier zero-knowledge (PQ-HVZK) if there exists a probabilistic polynomial time algorithm* $\mathcal{S}$, *called the simulator, such that for any polynomial time quantum algorithm* $\mathcal{A}$ *and* $(\mathsf{pk}, \mathsf{sk}) \leftarrow \mathsf{KGen}()$:

$$\mathrm{Succ}^{pq-hvzk}_{\mathsf{IDS}(1^k)}(\mathcal{A}) =$$

$$|\Pr\left[1 \leftarrow \mathcal{A}\left(\mathsf{sk}, \mathsf{pk}, \mathsf{trans}(\langle \mathcal{P}(\mathsf{sk}), \mathcal{V}(\mathsf{pk})\rangle)\right)\right] - \Pr\left[1 \leftarrow \mathcal{A}\left(\mathsf{sk}, \mathsf{pk}, \mathcal{S}(\mathsf{pk})\right)\right]| = \mathrm{negl}(k).$$

Intuitively it must be hard for any cryptographic scheme to derive a valid secret key given a public key. To formally capture this intuition, we need to define what valid means. For this we define the notion of a key relation.

Definition 2.5 (Key relation). *Let* IDS *be a $q2$-Identification scheme and R a relation. We say* IDS *has key relation R iff R is the minimal relation such that*

$$\forall(\mathsf{pk}, \mathsf{sk}) \leftarrow \mathsf{KGen}() : (\mathsf{pk}, \mathsf{sk}) \in R$$

Now that we have defined what valid means, we can define key-one-wayness.

Definition 2.6 (PQ-KOW). *Let* $k \in \mathbb{N}$ *be the security parameter,* $\mathsf{IDS}(1^k)$ *be a $q2$-Identification scheme with key relation R. We call IDS post-quantum key-one-way (PQ-KOW) (with respect to key relation R) if for all quantum polynomial time algorithms* $\mathcal{A}$,

$$\mathrm{Succ}^{pq-kow}_{\mathsf{IDS}(1^k)}(\mathcal{A}) = \Pr\left[(\mathsf{pk}, \mathsf{sk}) \leftarrow \mathsf{KGen}(), \mathsf{sk}' \leftarrow \mathcal{A}(\mathsf{pk}) : (\mathsf{pk}, \mathsf{sk}') \in R\right] = \mathrm{negl}(k)$$

In [11] it was shown that in general, for $q2$-Identification Schemes, it is not possible to efficiently extract a matching secret key from two related transcripts alone (as in the case of 3-pass schemes fulfilling special soundness). In order to capture the nature of these schemes and provide sufficient conditions for efficient extraction, we proposed the definition of a $q2$-Extractor. In the following we give a slightly refined definition that uses the notion of key relation to capture what kind of secret key the extractor returns.

Definition 2.7 ($q2$-Extractor). *Let* $\mathsf{IDS}(1^k)$ *be a $q2$-Identification scheme with key relation R. We say that* $\mathsf{IDS}(1^k)$ *has a $q2$-Extractor if there exists a polynomial time algorithm* $\mathcal{K}_{IDS}$, *the extractor, that, given a public key* pk *and four valid transcripts with respect to* pk

$$\begin{aligned} \mathsf{trans}^{(1)} &= (\mathsf{com}, \mathsf{ch}_1, \mathsf{resp}_1, \mathsf{ch}_2, \mathsf{resp}_2), \quad \mathsf{trans}^{(3)} = (\mathsf{com}, \mathsf{ch}_1', \mathsf{resp}_1', \mathsf{ch}_2, \mathsf{resp}_2), \\ \mathsf{trans}^{(2)} &= (\mathsf{com}, \mathsf{ch}_1, \mathsf{resp}_1, \mathsf{ch}_2', \mathsf{resp}_2'), \quad \mathsf{trans}^{(4)} = (\mathsf{com}, \mathsf{ch}_1', \mathsf{resp}_1', \mathsf{ch}_2', \mathsf{resp}_2'), \end{aligned} \quad (1)$$

where $\mathsf{ch}_1 \neq \mathsf{ch}_1'$ *and* $\mathsf{ch}_2 \neq \mathsf{ch}_2'$, *outputs a secret key* sk *such that* $(\mathsf{pk}, \mathsf{sk}) \in R$ *with non-negligible success probability in* k.

3   From $q2$-IDS to Signatures in the QROM

In [11], we showed that the Fiat-Shamir transform can be generalized to the case of 5-pass IDS whose ChS_2 is bounded to two elements. We showed that the Pointcheval-Stern proof [30] can be extended to this case, and the obtained signature scheme can be shown EU-CMA secure in the random oracle model. This result is further extended to any $2n+1$ round identification scheme that fulfills a certain kind of special soundness in [15]. However, similar to the standard Fiat-Shamir transform, these proofs rely on the forking lemma, which introduces two serious problems in the post-quantum setting: rewinding of the adversary, and adaptively programming the random oracle. While it is known how to deal with the latter [33], the former seems to become a real show stopper [3]. The only known way (at the time of writting[1]) to fix the Fiat-Shamir transform in the QROM setting is using oblivious commitments [14], which are a certain kind of trapdoor commitments, effectively avoiding rewinding at the cost of introducing the necessity of a trapdoor function. This makes the solution not applicable in our setting as there are no known trapdoor functions with a reduction from the $\mathcal{MQ}$-problem.

In [33], Unruh proposes a different transform, based on Fischlin's transform [21], that turns 3-pass zero-knowledge proofs into non-interactive ones in the QROM. In addition, Unruh shows how to use his transform to obtain a signature scheme. The transform essentially works by "unrolling" Fischlin's transform and then applying a few tweaks. This works, as Fischlin's transform already avoids rewinding. The basic idea is to let the signer generate several transcripts for a commitment. This is iterated for several initial commitments. Next, the signer "blinds" all responses in the transcripts by applying a length-preserving hash. All the obtained data is hashed together with the public key and the message to obtain a challenge vector. This challenge vector determines one transcript per commitment that has to be unblinded, i.e., for which the response must be included in the signature. The signature consists of all the transcripts with "blinded" responses and the unblinded responses for the transcripts identified by the challenge vector. The reasoning behind the transform is that without knowing the secret key, a forger cannot know sufficiently many valid openings to be able to include all the challenged responses. On the other hand, a security reduction can replace the length-preserving hash (modeled as QRO) by an invertible function (e.g. a QPRP). That way, a reduction can "unblind" the remaining responses in the signature by inverting the function. Now, it can be argued that an adversary with non-negligible success probability must have known several valid transcripts for at least one commitment. The unblinding reveals those transcripts and they can be used to run the extractor.

Here, we show that a similar transform can be applied to 5-pass IDS with a binary second challenge (i.e., $q2$-IDS). Basically, we treat the second challenge-response round like the first. However, as we have a binary second challenge, we ask that for each first challenge, a transcript for both values of the second

---

[1] Very recently, Kiltz et al. [28] proposed the use of "lossy" IDS which enabled them to prove security of the Fiat-Shamir transform in the QROM.

challenge is generated. The main difference between the security reduction of Unruh's transform and our extension to $q2$-IDS is a more involved argument to show that we get sufficiently many valid transcripts that follow the pattern needed to extract a valid secret key. As this argument is essentially independent of the RO, we first give a proof in the classical ROM. This also allows us to show that the reduction is tight in the ROM. Afterwards we describe how things change in the QROM along the lines of Unruh's QROM proof. This is where the reduction becomes loose. It remains an interesting open question whether this is a fundamental issue with QROM reductions or the existing techniques are just not sufficiently evolved, yet.

3.1 Extending Unruh's Transform to $q2$-IDS

Let $\mathsf{IDS} = (\mathsf{KGen}, \mathcal{P}, \mathcal{V})$ be a $q2$-IDS, with $\mathcal{P} = (\mathcal{P}_0, \mathcal{P}_1, \mathcal{P}_2)$, $\mathcal{V} = (\mathsf{ChS}_1, \mathsf{ChS}_2, \mathsf{Vf})$, and let $r, t \in \mathbb{N}$ be two parameters, where $2 \leqslant t \leqslant q$. Moreover let $\mathrm{H}_1 : \{0,1\}^{|\mathsf{resp}_1|} \to \{0,1\}^{|\mathsf{resp}_1|}$, $\mathrm{H}_2 : \{0,1\}^{|\mathsf{resp}_2|} \to \{0,1\}^{|\mathsf{resp}_2|}$, and $\mathcal{H} : \{0,1\}^* \to \{0,1\}^{\lceil \log 2t \rceil r}$ be hash functions, later modeled as random oracles. We define the following digital signature scheme $(\mathsf{KGen}, \mathsf{Sign}, \mathsf{Vf})$. The key generation algorithm just runs $\mathsf{IDS.KGen}()$. Signature and verification algorithms are given in Figs. 1 and 2.

For ease of exposition, we will use the notation $T(j, i, b)$ for a string that has the format of a transcript of the IDS (not necessarily a valid transcript), corresponding to the j-th round of the non-interactive protocol, with i and b being the indices of the corresponding challenges ch_1 and ch_2, i.e.

$$T(j, i, b) := (\mathsf{com}^{(j)}, \mathsf{ch}_1^{(i,j)}, \mathsf{resp}_1^{(i,j)}, \mathsf{ch}_2 = b, \mathsf{resp}_2^{(i,j,b)}),$$

where $j \in \{1, \ldots, r\}$, $i \in \{1, \ldots, t\}$, $b \in \{0, 1\}$.

Sign(sk, M)

For $j \in \{1, \ldots, r\}$ **do**

$\quad$ $(\mathsf{state}^{(j)}, \mathsf{com}^{(j)}) \leftarrow \mathcal{P}_0(\mathsf{sk})$

$\quad$ **For** $i \in \{1, \ldots, t\}$ **do**

$\quad\quad$ $\mathsf{ch}_1^{(i,j)} \leftarrow_R \mathsf{ChS}_1 \setminus \{\mathsf{ch}_1^{(1,j)}, \ldots, \mathsf{ch}_1^{(i-1,j)}\}$

$\quad\quad$ $(\mathsf{state}^{(i,j)}, \mathsf{resp}_1^{(i,j)}) \leftarrow \mathcal{P}_1(\mathsf{state}^{(j)}, \mathsf{ch}_1^{(i,j)})$

$\quad\quad$ $\mathsf{cr}_1^{(i,j)} \leftarrow \mathrm{H}_1(\mathsf{resp}_1^{(i,j)})$

$\quad\quad$ $\mathsf{resp}_2^{(i,j,0)} \leftarrow \mathcal{P}_2(\mathsf{state}^{(i,j)}, \mathsf{ch}_2 = 0), \mathsf{resp}_2^{(i,j,1)} \leftarrow \mathcal{P}_2(\mathsf{state}^{(i,j)}, \mathsf{ch}_2 = 1)$

$\quad\quad$ $\mathsf{cr}_2^{(i,j,0)} \leftarrow \mathrm{H}_2(\mathsf{resp}_2^{(i,j,0)}), \mathsf{cr}_2^{(i,j,1)} \leftarrow \mathrm{H}_2(\mathsf{resp}_2^{(i,j,1)})$

$\quad\quad$ $\mathsf{trans}_{\mathsf{full}}(j) := \mathsf{com}^{(j)}, \left\{ \mathsf{ch}_1^{(i,j)}, \mathsf{cr}_1^{(i,j)}, (\mathsf{cr}_2^{(i,j,0)}, \mathsf{cr}_2^{(i,j,1)}) \right\}_{i=1}^{t}$

$\mathsf{md} \leftarrow \mathcal{H}\left(\mathsf{pk}, M, \{\mathsf{trans}_{\mathsf{full}}(j)\}_{j=1}^{r} \right)$

Read md as vector $((I_1, B_1), \ldots, (I_r, B_r))$

$\mathsf{trans}_{\mathsf{red}}(j) := \mathsf{com}^{(j)}, \left\{ \mathsf{ch}_1^{(i,j)}, \mathsf{cr}_1^{(i,j)}, (\mathsf{cr}_2^{(i,j,0)}, \mathsf{cr}_2^{(i,j,1)}) \right\}_{i \neq I_j, i=1}^{t}$

$\sigma := \left(\mathsf{md}, \left\{ \mathsf{trans}_{\mathsf{red}}(j), \mathsf{ch}_1^{(I_j,j)}, \mathsf{resp}_1^{(I_j,j)}, \mathsf{resp}_2^{(I_j,j,B_j)}, \mathsf{cr}_2^{(I_j,j,\neg B_j)} \right\}_{j=1}^{r} \right)$

Fig. 1. Signature generation.

$\mathsf{Vf}(\mathsf{pk}, \sigma, \mathbf{M})$

Read md as vector $((I_1, B_1), \ldots, (I_r, B_r))$

For $j \in \{1, \ldots, r\}$ **do**

$\quad \mathsf{cr}_1^{(I_j, j)} \leftarrow \mathsf{H}_1(\mathsf{resp}_1^{(I_j, j)}), \quad \mathsf{cr}_2^{(I_j, j, B_j)} \leftarrow \mathsf{H}_2(\mathsf{resp}_2^{(I_j, j, B_j)})$

$\mathsf{md}' \leftarrow \mathcal{H}\left(\mathsf{pk}, M, \{\mathsf{trans}_{\mathsf{full}}(j)\}_{j=1}^r\right)$

Check that $\mathsf{md}' \stackrel{?}{=} \mathsf{md}$

For $j \in \{1, \ldots, r\}$ **do**

$\quad$ Check that $\mathsf{ch}_1^{(1,j)}, \ldots \mathsf{ch}_1^{(t,j)}$ are all distinct

$\quad$ Check $1 \stackrel{?}{=} b \leftarrow \mathsf{Vf}(\mathsf{pk}, \mathsf{com}^{(j)}, \mathsf{ch}_1^{(I_j, j)}, \mathsf{resp}_1^{(I_j, j)}, B_j, \mathsf{resp}_2^{(I_j, j, B_j)})$

If all checks succeed, output **success**.

Fig. 2. Verification.

3.2 PQ-EU-CMA-Security in the ROM

In the following, we first establish post-quantum security under key-only attacks (PQ-KOA). More specifically, we will show that a successful KOA-forger $\mathcal{A}$ can be used to extract a valid secret key for the underlying IDS. Afterwards, we will extend the result to existential unforgeability under chosen message attacks.

PQ-KOW $\Rightarrow$ PQ-KOA. The following lemma gives an exact relation between the key-one-wayness of the identification scheme and the security of the proposed signature scheme under key-only attacks.

Lemma 3.1. *Let* $k, t, r \in \mathbb{N}$ *be the parameters of the signature scheme from Figs. 1 and 2, using a q2-IDS that has a key relation* R, *a q2-extractor, and is PQ-KOW secure. Let* $\mathcal{A}$ *be a quantum algorithm that implements a KOA forger which given only the public key* pk *outputs a valid message-signature pair* (M, σ) *with probability* ϵ. *Then, in the random oracle model there exists an algorithm* $\mathcal{M}^{\mathcal{A}}$ *that given oracle access to any such* $\mathcal{A}$ *breaks the KOW security of* IDS *in essentially the same running time as the given* $\mathcal{A}$ *and with success probability*

$$\epsilon' \geq \epsilon - (q_{\mathcal{H}} + 1)2^{-r \log \frac{2t}{t+1}}. \tag{2}$$

Moreover, $\mathcal{M}^{\mathcal{A}}$ *only manipulates the random oracles* $\mathsf{H}_1, \mathsf{H}_2$ *and leaves* $\mathcal{H}$ *untouched.*

Proof. We show how to construct such an algorithm $\mathcal{M}^{\mathcal{A}}$. On input of an IDS public key pk, $\mathcal{M}^{\mathcal{A}}$ first runs $\mathcal{A}(\mathsf{pk})$. Let $\mathcal{E}_A$ be the event that $\mathcal{A}$ outputs a valid message-signature pair (M, σ) with

$$\sigma = \left(\mathsf{md}, \left\{\mathsf{trans}_{\mathsf{red}}(j), \mathsf{ch}_1^{(I_j, j)}, \mathsf{resp}_1^{(I_j, j)}, \mathsf{resp}_2^{(I_j, j, B_j)}, \mathsf{cr}_2^{(I_j, j, \neg B_j)}\right\}_{j=1}^r\right).$$

Then $\mathcal{E}_A$ implies that for every $j \in \{1, \ldots, r\}$, $T(j, I_j, B_j)$ is a valid transcript of IDS and the Verifier Vf accepts. Now, our goal is to use the q2-extractor to extract. This means, we need to obtain four valid transcripts $T(j, i_1, 0)$, $T(j, i_1, 1)$, $T(j, i_2, 0)$, $T(j, i_2, 1)$ for some $j \in \{1, \ldots, r\}$. To this end, $\mathcal{M}^{\mathcal{A}}$ simulates the random oracles H_1 and H_2 for $\mathcal{A}$ in the common way. The important point is that this way $\mathcal{M}^{\mathcal{A}}$ learns all of $\mathcal{A}$'s queries together with the given responses. Hence, when given $\mathcal{A}$'s forgery, $\mathcal{M}^{\mathcal{A}}$ can open all blinded responses in the signature.

Now, $\mathcal{M}^{\mathcal{A}}$ will only fail to extract if among all the $2tr$ opened transcripts of the signature, there are no four valid transcripts with the above pattern. Consider the event $\mathcal{E}_{\neg\text{ext}}$ which describes this case.

$\mathcal{E}_{\neg\text{ext}}$: $\forall j \in \{1, \ldots, r\}$, and $\forall i_1, i_2 \in \{1, \ldots, t\}$, $i_1 \neq i_2$, at least one of $T(j, i_1, 0)$, $T(j, i_1, 1)$, $T(j, i_2, 0)$, $T(j, i_2, 1)$ is not a valid transcript of the IDS.

We will upper bound $\Pr[(\mathcal{E}_A \cap \mathcal{E}_{\neg\text{ext}})]$ and thereby lower bound $\mathcal{M}^{\mathcal{A}}$'s success probability. Let (M, σ) be $\mathcal{A}$'s output under the event $(\mathcal{E}_A \cap \mathcal{E}_{\neg\text{ext}})$. First, (M, σ) must be valid because of $\mathcal{E}_A$. Now, consider the set $\mathcal{S}_{\neg\text{ext}}$ of tuples $\left(\text{pk}, M, \{\text{trans}_{\text{full}}(j)\}_{j=1}^{r} \right)$, such that for every $j \in \{1, \ldots, r\}$ there is at most one I_j^* with $T(j, I_j^*, 0)$ and $T(j, I_j^*, 1)$ being valid transcripts of IDS. It is clear that $\mathcal{A}$'s output under the event $\mathcal{E}_A \cap \mathcal{E}_{\neg\text{ext}}$ must come from $\mathcal{S}_{\neg\text{ext}}$. Indeed, if a tuple does not satisfy the given condition, then there exist at least two indices I_j^*, I_j^{**} such that $T(j, I_j^*, 0)$, $T(j, I_j^*, 1)$, $T(j, I_j^{**}, 0)$, $T(j, I_j^{**}, 1)$ are valid transcripts of IDS, which is in contradiction to the event $\mathcal{E}_{\neg\text{ext}}$.

Let $\left(\text{pk}, M, \{\text{trans}_{\text{full}}(j)\}_{j=1}^{r} \right)$ be such a tuple. Then the indexes that define the required openings in σ are obtained as the output of the random oracle $\mathcal{H}$ on input of the tuple, i.e. $((I_1, B_1), \ldots, (I_r, B_r)) \leftarrow \mathcal{H} \left(\text{pk}, M, \{\text{trans}_{\text{full}}(j)\}_{j=1}^{r} \right)$. In order for the signature to pass verification, for each $j \in \{1, \ldots, r\}$, the transcript $T(j, I_j, B_j)$ must be valid. Given the conditions of $\mathcal{E}_{\neg\text{ext}}$, for each $j \in \{1, \ldots, r\}$, there are at most $t + 1$ valid transcripts per j. Hence for the entire $((I_1, B_1), \ldots, (I_r, B_r))$ at most $(t + 1)^r$ possible values. Thus, the probability for the adversary to produce a valid signature from such a tuple is $\frac{(t+1)^r}{(2t)^r} = 2^{-r \log \frac{2t}{t+1}}$.

Now let $q_{\mathcal{H}}$ be the number of queries of the adversary to the oracle $\mathcal{H}$. Then

$$\Pr(\mathcal{E}_A \cap \mathcal{E}_{\neg\text{ext}}) \leq (q_{\mathcal{H}} + 1) 2^{-r \log \frac{2t}{t+1}},$$

as $\mathcal{A}$ can try at most $q_{\mathcal{H}}$ tuples to obtain a valid signature and output a signature based on a new tuple otherwise. Towards obtaining a bound on $\mathcal{M}^{\mathcal{A}}$'s success probability, note that $\mathcal{M}^{\mathcal{A}}$ succeeds in the event $(\mathcal{E}_A \cap \neg\mathcal{E}_{\neg\text{ext}})$, and

$$\Pr(\mathcal{E}_A \cap \neg\mathcal{E}_{\neg\text{ext}}) = \Pr(\mathcal{E}_A) - \Pr(\mathcal{E}_A \cap \mathcal{E}_{\neg\text{ext}}) \geq \epsilon - (q_{\mathcal{H}} + 1) 2^{-r \log \frac{2t}{t+1}}.$$

This proves the claimed bound. $\qquad\square$

PQ-KOA $\Rightarrow$ PQ-EU-CMA. Given the above lemma, it suffices to reduce PQ-KOA to PQ-EU-CMA security to eventually prove PQ-EU-CMA security of the proposed scheme, i.e. we have to show that we can answer an adversary's signature queries without knowledge of a secret key. This is done in the following lemma. Afterwards we can derive the main theorem of the section.

Lemma 3.2. *Let $k, t, r \in \mathbb{N}$ be the parameters of the signature scheme from Figs. 1 and 2 above, using a q2-IDS that is PQ-HVZK. Let $\mathcal{A}$ be a quantum algorithm that breaks the PQ-EU-CMA security of the signature scheme with probability ϵ. Then, in the random oracle model there exists an algorithm $\mathcal{M}^{\mathcal{A}}$ that breaks the PQ-KOA security of the signature scheme in essentially the same running time as $\mathcal{A}$ and with success probability*

$$\epsilon' \geq \epsilon(1 - q_{\mathsf{Sign}} q_{\mathcal{H}} 2^{-rk}). \tag{3}$$

Moreover, $\mathcal{M}^{\mathcal{A}}$ only manipulates the random oracle $\mathcal{H}$ and leaves $\mathrm{H}_1, \mathrm{H}_2$ untouched.

Proof. We show how to construct $\mathcal{M}^{\mathcal{A}}$ that on input a public key pk of the signature scheme (which is also a public key for IDS), access to a HVZK-simulator $\mathcal{S}_{\mathsf{IDS}}$ for IDS and the random oracles $\mathrm{H}_1, \mathrm{H}_2, \mathcal{H}$, breaks the KOA security of the signature scheme. The running time and success probability of $\mathcal{M}^{\mathcal{A}}$ are essentially the same as that of $\mathcal{A}$ up to a negligible difference.

Upon receiving the public key pk, $\mathcal{M}^{\mathcal{A}}$ runs $\mathcal{A}(\mathsf{pk})$, simulating all signature and random oracle queries for $\mathcal{A}$. Whenever $\mathcal{A}$ queries H_1 or H_2, $\mathcal{M}^{\mathcal{A}}$ simply forwards the query to his respective RO. For $\mathcal{H}$, $\mathcal{M}^{\mathcal{A}}$ keeps a local list $\mathcal{L}_{\mathcal{H}}$. Whenever $\mathcal{A}$ queries $\mathcal{H}$, $\mathcal{M}^{\mathcal{A}}$ first checks $\mathcal{L}_{\mathcal{H}}$ and returns the stored answer if one exists. Otherwise, $\mathcal{M}^{\mathcal{A}}$ forwards the query to his oracle $\mathcal{H}$ and stores the query together with the result in $\mathcal{L}_{\mathcal{H}}$ before returning the response. Whenever $\mathcal{A}$ makes a signature query on a message M, $\mathcal{M}^{\mathcal{A}}$ does the following:

1. Samples $\tilde{\mathsf{md}} \leftarrow_R \{0,1\}^{\lceil \log 2t \rceil r}$ and interprets it as challenge string, i.e., $((I_1, B_1), \ldots, (I_r, B_r)) := \tilde{\mathsf{md}}$.
2. Runs the HVZK-simulator $\mathcal{S}_{\mathsf{IDS}}$ r times to obtain r valid transcripts of IDS:

$$\left\{ \left(\mathsf{com}^{(j)}, \mathsf{ch}_1^{(I_j, j)}, \mathsf{resp}_1^{(I_j, j)}, \mathsf{ch}_2^{(j)}, \mathsf{resp}_2^{(I_j, j, B_j)} \right) \right\}_{j=1}^{r},$$

   and uses them as the challenged transcripts $T(j, I_j, B_j)$ for $j \in \{1, \ldots, r\}$.
3. Blinds the responses $\mathsf{resp}_1^{(I_j, j)}$ and $\mathsf{resp}_2^{(I_j, j, B_j)}$ for every $j \in \{1, \ldots, r\}$:

$$\mathsf{cr}_1^{(I_j, j)} \leftarrow \mathrm{H}_1(\mathsf{resp}_1^{(I_j, j)}), \quad \mathsf{cr}_2^{(I_j, j, B_j)} \leftarrow \mathrm{H}_2(\mathsf{resp}_2^{(I_j, j, B_j)}).$$

4. For all $j \in \{1, \ldots, r\}$, and all $(i, b) \in \{1, \ldots, t\} \times \{0, 1\} \setminus \{(I_j, B_j)\}_{j=1}^{r}$,
   - samples a first challenge $\mathsf{ch}_1^{(i,j)} \leftarrow_R \mathsf{ChS}_1 \setminus \{\mathsf{ch}_1^{(I_j, j)}, \mathsf{ch}_1^{(1,j)}, \ldots, \mathsf{ch}_1^{(i-1,j)}\}$,
   - samples fake responses $\mathsf{resp}_1^{(i,j)} \leftarrow_R \mathsf{RespS}_1$, $\mathsf{resp}_2^{(i,j,b)} \leftarrow_R \mathsf{RespS}_2$,,
   - blinds the fake responses $\mathsf{cr}_1^{(i,j)} \leftarrow \mathrm{H}_1(\mathsf{resp}_1^{(i,j)})$, $\mathsf{cr}_2^{(i,j,b)} \leftarrow \mathrm{H}_2(\mathsf{resp}_2^{(i,j,b)})$,
   - sets $\mathsf{trans}_{\mathsf{full}}(j) := \mathsf{com}^{(j)}, \left\{ \mathsf{ch}_1^{(i,j)}, \mathsf{cr}_1^{(i,j)}, (\mathsf{cr}_2^{(i,j,0)}, \mathsf{cr}_2^{(i,j,1)}) \right\}_{i=1}^{t}$.
5. Checks if there is already an entry for $\left(\mathsf{pk}, M, \{\mathsf{trans}_{\mathsf{full}}(j)\}_{j=1}^{r} \right)$ in $\mathcal{L}_{\mathcal{H}}$. If so, $\mathcal{M}^{\mathcal{A}}$ aborts. Otherwise, $\mathcal{M}^{\mathcal{A}}$ stores $\left(\left(\mathsf{pk}, M, \{\mathsf{trans}_{\mathsf{full}}(j)\}_{j=1}^{r} \right), \tilde{\mathsf{md}} \right)$ in $\mathcal{L}_{\mathcal{H}}$.

6. Outputs the signature

$$\sigma = \left(\mathsf{md}, \left\{ \mathsf{trans}_{\mathsf{red}}(j), \mathsf{ch}_1^{(I_j,j)}, \mathsf{resp}_1^{(I_j,j)}, \mathsf{resp}_2^{(I_j,j,B_j)}, \mathsf{cr}_2^{(I_j,j,\neg B_j)} \right\}_{j=1}^{r} \right),$$

where $\mathsf{trans}_{\mathsf{red}}(j) := \mathsf{com}^{(j)}, \left\{ \mathsf{ch}_1^{(i,j)}, \mathsf{cr}_1^{(i,j)}, (\mathsf{cr}_2^{(i,j,0)}, \mathsf{cr}_2^{(i,j,1)}) \right\}_{i \neq I_j, i=1}^{t}.$

Finally, $\mathcal{M}^{\mathcal{A}}$ outputs whatever $\mathcal{A}$ outputs.

Now, $\mathcal{M}^{\mathcal{A}}$ must succeed with probability at most differing from $\mathcal{A}$'s success probability by a negligible additive term as long as it does not abort (to be more precise, the term is $rq_{\mathsf{Sign}}\mathsf{Succ}_{\mathsf{IDS}(1^k)}^{pq-hvzk}(\mathcal{A})$). This is the case because otherwise $\mathcal{A}$ could be used to break the PQ-HVZK property of the used IDS. All RO queries follow the correct distribution and so do the signatures. An abort only occurs if $\mathcal{A}$ queried $\mathcal{H}$ before on the value for which $\mathcal{M}^{\mathcal{A}}$ wants to program. The value has the form $\left(\mathsf{pk}, M, \{\mathsf{trans}_{\mathsf{full}}(j)\}_{j=1}^{r} \right)$ with $\mathsf{trans}_{\mathsf{full}}(j) := \mathsf{com}^{(j)}, \left\{ \mathsf{ch}_1^{(i,j)}, \mathsf{cr}_1^{(i,j)}, (\mathsf{cr}_2^{(i,j,0)}, \mathsf{cr}_2^{(i,j,1)}) \right\}_{i=1}^{t}.$ The $\{\mathsf{trans}_{\mathsf{full}}(j)\}_{j=1}^{r}$ term has at least rk bits of entropy as the commitments have at least k bits of entropy according to the definition of $q2$-IDS and there is one commitment for each of the r rounds. This is merely a very loose (but more than sufficient) lower bound on the entropy as the blinded responses also add additional entropy. Hence, if $\mathcal{A}$ makes a total of $q_{\mathcal{H}}$ queries for $\mathcal{H}$ and q_{Sign} signature queries, an abort occurs with probability $\Pr[abort] \leq q_{\mathsf{Sign}}q_{\mathcal{H}}2^{-rk}$.

Hence, $\mathcal{M}^{\mathcal{A}}$ succeeds with probability $\epsilon' \geq \epsilon(1 - q_{\mathsf{Sign}}q_{\mathcal{H}}2^{-rk})$.   □

PQ-KOW $\Rightarrow$ PQ-EU-CMA. Combining the two previous lemmas we obtain the following theorem.

Theorem 3.3. *Let $k, t, r \in \mathbb{N}$ be the parameters of the signature scheme from Figs. 1 and 2 above using a q2-IDS IDS that is PQ-HVZK and has a PQ-q2-extractor. Let $\mathcal{A}$ be a PQ-EU-CMA forger that succeeds with probability ϵ. Then, there exists an algorithm $\mathcal{M}^{\mathcal{A}}$, that in the random oracle model breaks the PQ-KOW security of IDS in essentially the same running time as $\mathcal{A}$ and with success probability*

$$\epsilon' \geq \epsilon - \epsilon q_{\mathsf{Sign}}q_{\mathcal{H}}2^{-rk} - (q_{\mathcal{H}} + 1)2^{-r\log\frac{2t}{t+1}}. \tag{4}$$

Proof. Suppose there exists a PQ-EU-CMA forger $\mathcal{A}$ that succeeds with non-negligible probability ϵ. We construct a PQ-KOW adversary $\mathcal{C}$ for the $q2$-IDS as follows. $\mathcal{C}$ runs $\mathcal{A}(\mathsf{pk})$, to construct a key-only forger $\mathcal{M}^{\mathcal{A}}$ as in Lemma 3.2, that succeeds with probability (3). Now as in Lemma 3.1, $\mathcal{C}$ can extract a valid secret key sk, in approximately the same time, and with only negligibly smaller probability (see (2)). This concatenation of the two reductions is possible as the reduction from Lemma 3.2 only manipulates random oracle $\mathcal{H}$, while the one from Lemma 3.1 only touches H_1, H_2. In total the success probability of $\mathcal{C}$ is exactly (4), and the running time of $\mathcal{C}$ is essentially the same as that of $\mathcal{A}$.   □

3.3   PQ-EU-CMA Security in the QROM

We now show that with only slight changes, the two lemmas above also hold in the QROM. We do this in reverse order, starting with the PQ-KOA to PQ-EU-CMA reduction as it is the easier case. As already the QROM proofs in Unruh's work which we build on are non-tight, we only give our arguments in the asymptotic regime.

PQ-KOA $\Rightarrow$ PQ-EU-CMA. We will first revisit the reduction from PQ-KOA to PQ-EU-CMA. We show the following lemma:

Lemma 3.4. *Let $k, t, r \in \mathbb{N}$ be the parameters of the signature scheme from Figs. 1 and 2 above, using a q2-IDS that is PQ-HVZK. Let $\mathcal{A}$ be a quantum algorithm that breaks the PQ-EU-CMA security of the signature scheme with probability ϵ. Then, in the quantum-accessible random oracle model there exists a quantum algorithm $\mathcal{M}^{\mathcal{A}}$ that breaks the PQ-KOA security of the signature scheme in essentially the same running time as $\mathcal{A}$ and with success probability*

$$\epsilon' \geq \epsilon(1 - \mathrm{negl}(k)). \tag{5}$$

Moreover, $\mathcal{M}^{\mathcal{A}}$ only manipulates the random oracle $\mathcal{H}$ and leaves H_1, H_2 untouched.

Proof (Sketch). The proof in the ROM above also applies in the QROM with essentially a single change. The queries to H_1 and H_2 are still just forwarded by $\mathcal{M}^{\mathcal{A}}$ without interaction. This works without any issues in the QROM given that $\mathcal{M}^{\mathcal{A}}$ is now a quantum algorithm (which is unavoidable in the QROM). The only issue is the way $\mathcal{M}^{\mathcal{A}}$ handles $\mathcal{H}$. It is not possible anymore for $\mathcal{M}^{\mathcal{A}}$ to learn $\mathcal{A}$'s queries to $\mathcal{H}$ and thereby not possible to abort. However, we only added the abort condition above for clarity: in the classical case $\mathcal{M}^{\mathcal{A}}$ could also simply always program $\mathcal{H}$. Then $\mathcal{A}$'s success probability might change if $\mathcal{M}^{\mathcal{A}}$ programmed on an input previously queried by $\mathcal{A}$. However, we still obtain the same bound on the probability. In the QROM, Unruh showed in [33, Corollary 11] that this adaptive programming only negligibly changes $\mathcal{A}$'s success probability (the exact argument for our specific case is exactly the one made in the first game hop of the proof of Theorem 15 in [33]). From this it follows that $\mathcal{M}^{\mathcal{A}}$'s success probability still only negligibly deviates from that of $\mathcal{A}$. $\square$

PQ-KOW $\Rightarrow$ PQ-KOA. Now we revisit the reduction from PQ-KOW to PQ-KOA in the quantum-accessible ROM. While we still do this in the asymptotic regime, we make the parts of the reduction loss explicit which depend on the parameters r, t of the scheme. This is to support parameter selection in later sections.

Lemma 3.5. *Let $k, t, r \in \mathbb{N}$ be the parameters of the signature scheme from Figs. 1 and 2 above, using a q2-IDS that has a key relation R, a q2-extractor, and is PQ-KOW secure. Let $\mathcal{A}$ be a quantum algorithm that implements a KOA forger which given only the public key pk outputs a valid message-signature pair*

(M, σ) *with probability ϵ. Then, in the quantum-accessible random oracle model there exists a quantum algorithm $\mathcal{M}^{\mathcal{A}}$ that given oracle access to any such $\mathcal{A}$ breaks the KOW security of* IDS *in essentially the same running time as the given $\mathcal{A}$ and with success probability*

$$\epsilon' \geq \epsilon - 2(q_{\mathcal{H}} + 1)2^{-(r \log \frac{2t}{t+1})/2}. \tag{6}$$

Moreover, $\mathcal{M}^{\mathcal{A}}$ only manipulates the random oracles H_1, H_2 and leaves $\mathcal{H}$ untouched.

Proof (Sketch). A QROM version of our proof is obtained by essentially following the proof of Lemma 17 in [33]. The changes in the proof above are as follows. First, $\mathcal{M}^{\mathcal{A}}$ cannot learn $\mathcal{A}$'s RO queries to H_1 and H_2 by simulating these the classical way, anymore. Instead, $\mathcal{M}^{\mathcal{A}}$ simulates these oracles using one quantum PRP (QPRP) per oracle with a random secret key per QPRP. QPRPs exist as shown in [38] and they are quantum indistinguishable from random functions. Now, $\mathcal{M}^{\mathcal{A}}$ can open the blinded responses in the signature by inverting the QPRP using the secret key. Second, the analysis of $\Pr(\mathcal{E}_A \cap \mathcal{E}_{\neg\text{ext}})$ changes. As we have shown, the probability of a tuple from $\mathcal{E}_{\neg\text{ext}}$ to lead to a valid signature is $2^{-r \log \frac{2t}{t+1}}$. We can now follow the analysis in [33] that reduces distinguishing the constant zero function from a Bernoulli distributed boolean function to finding a tuple in $\mathcal{E}_{\neg\text{ext}}$ that leads to a valid signature. Thereby we get the claimed bound:

$$\Pr(\mathcal{E}_A \cap \mathcal{E}_{\neg\text{ext}}) \leq 2(q_{\mathcal{H}} + 1)2^{-(r \log \frac{2t}{t+1})/2}. \qquad \square$$

PQ-KOW $\Rightarrow$ PQ-EU-CMA. Putting the above two lemmas together allows us to state the following theorem.

Theorem 3.6. *Let $k, t, r \in \mathbb{N}$ be the parameters of the signature scheme above using a q2-IDS* IDS *that is computational honest-verifier zero-knowledge and has a q2-extractor. Let $\mathcal{A}$ be a PQ-EU-CMA forger that succeeds with probability ϵ. Then, there exists a quantum algorithm $\mathcal{M}^{\mathcal{A}}$, that in the quantum-accessible random oracle model breaks the PQ-KOW security of* IDS *in essentially the same running time as $\mathcal{A}$ and with success probability*

$$\epsilon' \geq (\epsilon - 2(q_{\mathcal{H}} + 1)2^{-(r \log \frac{2t}{t+1})/2})(1 - \text{negl}(k)).$$

4   The Sakumoto-Shirai-Hiwatari 5-Pass IDS Scheme

In [31], Sakumoto, Shirai, and Hiwatari proposed two new identification schemes, a 3-pass and a 5-pass IDS, based on the intractability of the $\mathcal{MQ}$ problem. Unlike previous public key schemes, their solution provably relies only on the $\mathcal{MQ}$ problem (and the security of the commitment scheme), and not on other related problems in multivariate cryptography such as the Isomorphism of Polynomials (IP) [29], the related Extended IP [17] and IP with partial knowledge [32] problems or the MinRank problem [13,20]. Let us quickly recall the $\mathcal{MQ}$ problem.

Definition 4.1 ($\mathcal{MQ}$ problem (search version)). *Let* $m, n, q \in \mathbb{N}$, $\mathbf{x} = (x_1, \ldots, x_n)$ *and let* $\mathcal{MQ}(n, m, \mathbb{F}_q)$ *denote the family of vectorial functions* $\mathbf{F} : \mathbb{F}_q^n \to \mathbb{F}_q^m$ *of degree 2 over* $\mathbb{F}_q$:

$$\mathcal{MQ}(n, m, \mathbb{F}_q) = \{\mathbf{F}(\mathbf{x}) = (f_1(\mathbf{x}), \ldots, f_m(\mathbf{x})) | f_s(\mathbf{x}) = \sum_{i,j} a_{i,j}^{(s)} x_i x_j + \sum_i b_i^{(s)} x_i |_{s=1}^m \}.$$

An instance $\mathcal{MQ}(\mathbf{F}, \mathbf{v})$ *of the* $\mathcal{MQ}$ *(search) problem is defined as:*
  Given $\mathbf{F} \in \mathcal{MQ}(n, m, \mathbb{F}_q)$, $\mathbf{v} \in \mathbb{F}_q^m$ *find, if any,* $\mathbf{s} \in \mathbb{F}_q^n$ *such that* $\mathbf{F}(\mathbf{s}) = \mathbf{v}$.

The decisional version of the $\mathcal{MQ}$ problem is NP−complete [23]. It is widely believed that the $\mathcal{MQ}$ problem is intractable even for quantum computers in the average case, i.e., that there exists no polynomial-time quantum algorithm that given $\mathbf{F} \leftarrow_R \mathcal{MQ}(n, m, \mathbb{F}_q)$ and $\mathbf{v} = \mathbf{F}(\mathbf{s})$ (for random $\mathbf{s} \leftarrow_R \mathbb{F}_q^n$) outputs a solution $\mathbf{s}'$ to the $\mathcal{MQ}(\mathbf{F}, \mathbf{v})$ problem with non-negligible probability.

We will later also need the $\mathcal{MQ}$ relation $R_{\mathcal{MQ}}$ which is the relation of $\mathcal{MQ}$ instances and solutions:

Definition 4.2 ($\mathcal{MQ}$ relation). *The* $\mathcal{MQ}$ *relation is the binary relation:*
$R_{\mathcal{MQ}(m,n,q)} \subseteq (\mathcal{MQ}(n, m, \mathbb{F}_q) \times \mathbb{F}_q^m) \times \mathbb{F}_q^n : ((\mathbf{F}, \mathbf{v}), \mathbf{s}) \in R_{\mathcal{MQ}(m,n,q)}$ *iff* $\mathbf{F}(\mathbf{s}) = \mathbf{v}$.

We will omit m, n, q whenever they are clear from the context.

In [31], Sakumoto, Shirai, and Hiwatari propose a clever splitting technique, using the so-called polar form of the function $\mathbf{F}$ which is the function $\mathbf{G}(\mathbf{x}, \mathbf{y}) = \mathbf{F}(\mathbf{x} + \mathbf{y}) - \mathbf{F}(\mathbf{x}) - \mathbf{F}(\mathbf{y})$. Using the polar form and its bilinearity, it becomes possible to split a secret into two shares, such that none of the shares on its own leaks anything about the secret. From this result, they showed how to construct zero knowledge arguments of knowledge for the $\mathcal{MQ}$ problem, using a statistically hiding and computationally binding commitment scheme. They present a 3- and a 5-pass protocol with differing performance properties. Later, in [11], the security properties of the 5-pass scheme were reexamined to provide the minimal requirements for Fiat-Shamir type signatures from 5-pass IDS. For completeness and better readability we provide the description of the 5-pass IDS, together with the properties that we will use.

Let $(\mathsf{pk}, \mathsf{sk}) = ((\mathbf{F}, \mathbf{v}), \mathbf{s}) \in R_{\mathcal{MQ}}$ be the public and private keys of the prover. Without loss of generality, let the elements from $\mathbb{F}_q$ be $\alpha_1, \ldots, \alpha_q$. The 5-pass IDS from [31] is given in Fig. 3.

Theorem 4.3. *The 5-pass identification scheme from* [31] *(see Fig. 3)*

1. *is computationally PQ-HVZK when the commitment scheme Com is computationally hiding,*
2. *has key relation* $R_{\mathcal{MQ}(m,n,q)}$,
3. *is PQ-KOW if the* $\mathcal{MQ}$ *search problem is hard on average, and*
4. *has a q2-Extractor if the commitment scheme Com is computationally binding against quantum polynomial time algorithms.*

$\mathcal{P}(\mathsf{pk}, \mathsf{sk})$ $\mathcal{V}(\mathsf{pk})$

//*setup*

$\mathbf{r}_0, \mathbf{t}_0 \leftarrow_R \mathbb{F}_q^n, \mathbf{e}_0 \leftarrow_R \mathbb{F}_q^m$

$\mathbf{r}_1 \leftarrow \mathbf{s} - \mathbf{r}_0$

//*commit*

$c_0 \leftarrow Com(\mathbf{r}_0, \mathbf{t}_0, \mathbf{e}_0)$

$c_1 \leftarrow Com(\mathbf{r}_1, \mathbf{G}(\mathbf{t}_0, \mathbf{r}_1) + \mathbf{e}_0)$ $\mathsf{com} = (c_0, c_1) \longrightarrow$ //*challenge 1*

                                        $I \leftarrow_R \{1, \ldots, q\}$

//*first response* $\longleftarrow \mathsf{ch}_1 = I$

$\mathbf{t}_1 \leftarrow \alpha_I \mathbf{r}_0 - \mathbf{t}_0$

$\mathbf{e}_1 \leftarrow \alpha_I \mathbf{F}(\mathbf{r}_0) - \mathbf{e}_0$

                    $\mathsf{resp}_1 = (\mathbf{t}_1, \mathbf{e}_1) \longrightarrow$ //*challenge 2*

//*second response* $\longleftarrow \mathsf{ch}_2$ $\mathsf{ch}_2 \leftarrow_R \{0, 1\}$

If $\mathsf{ch}_2 = 0$, $\mathsf{resp}_2 \leftarrow \mathbf{r}_0$

Else $\mathsf{resp}_2 \leftarrow \mathbf{r}_1$ $\mathsf{resp}_2 \longrightarrow$ //*verify*

                              If $\mathsf{ch}_2 = 0$, parse $\mathsf{resp}_2 = \mathbf{r}_0$, check

                              $c_0 \stackrel{?}{=} Com(\mathbf{r}_0, \alpha_I \mathbf{r}_0 - \mathbf{t}_1, \alpha_I \mathbf{F}(\mathbf{r}_0) - \mathbf{e}_1)$

                              Else, parse $\mathsf{resp}_2 = \mathbf{r}_1$, check

                              $c_1 \stackrel{?}{=} Com(\mathbf{r}_1, \alpha_I(\mathbf{v} - \mathbf{F}(\mathbf{r}_1)) - \mathbf{G}(\mathbf{t}_1, \mathbf{r}_1) - \mathbf{e}_1)$

Fig. 3. The 5-pass IDS by Sakumoto, Shirai, and Hiwatari.

A stronger result of the first statement in the classical case was shown in [31], namely that the 5-pass IDS is statistically honest-verifier zero-knowledge when the commitment scheme Com is statistically hiding. Relaxing the requirements of Com to computationally hiding, weakens the result to computationally HVZK, since now, it is possible to distinguish (albeit only with negligible probability) whether the commitment was produced in a valid run of the protocol. This easily transfers to the post-quantum setting, if Com is computationally hiding against quantum PPT algorithms.

The second statement holds by construction. The third statement follows from the second. The $q2$-Extractor essentially follows from a proof in [11]. In [11] the existence of a $q2$-Extractor was proven under the condition that the commitment scheme is computationally binding. The proof shows that there exists a PPT algorithm that given four valid transcripts of the IDS with the correct pattern always either extracts a secret key or outputs two valid openings for the commitment. Hence, as long as the used commitment scheme achieves the traditional definition of computationally binding also against quantum polynomial time algorithms, the 5-pass IDS from [31] has a $q2$-Extractor (as the probability to output two valid openings must be negligible).

5 Instantiation from the Sakumoto-Shirai-Hiwatari 5-Pass IDS

In the previous sections, we have defined a signature scheme as the result of a transformed $q2$-IDS scheme. Here, we define it instantiated with the 5-pass identification scheme proposed in [31].

5.1 SOFIA

We define the signature scheme in generic terms by describing the required parameters and the functions KGen, Sign and Vf, and defer giving concrete parameters m, n, r, t and $\mathbb{F}_q$ for a specific security parameter k to the next section, where we also instantiate the pseudorandom generators (PRGs) and extendable output functions (XOFs). For now, we only need to fix $2 \leqslant t \leqslant q$ elements of the field $\mathbb{F}_q$. Without loss of generality, we denote them by $\alpha_1, \ldots, \alpha_t$.

Key generation. The SOFIA key generation algorithm formally just samples a $\mathcal{MQ}$ relation. Practically, the algorithm is realized as shown in Fig. 4. The secret key is used as a seed to derive the following values: $S_{\mathbf{F}}$, a seed from which the system parameter $\mathbf{F}$ is expanded; $\mathbf{s}$, the secret input to the $\mathcal{MQ}$ function; $S_{\mathbf{rte}}$, a seed that is used to sample all vectors $r_0^{(i)}$, $t_0^{(i)}$ and $e_0^{(i)}$. Note that $S_{\mathbf{rte}}$ is not yet needed during key generation, but is required during signing.

KGen()

$\mathsf{sk} \leftarrow_R \{0, 1\}^k$
$S_{\mathbf{F}}, \mathbf{s}, S_{\mathbf{rte}} \leftarrow \mathrm{PRG}_{\mathsf{sk}}(\mathsf{sk}), \mathbf{F} \leftarrow \mathrm{XOF}_{\mathbf{F}}(S_{\mathbf{F}}), \mathbf{v} \leftarrow \mathbf{F}(\mathbf{s})$
$\mathsf{pk} := (S_{\mathbf{F}}, \mathbf{v})$
Return $(\mathsf{pk}, \mathsf{sk})$

Fig. 4. SOFIA key generation.

Signature generation. For the signing procedure, we assume as input a message $M \in \{0, 1\}^*$ and a secret key sk. The signing procedure is given in Fig. 5. Note that the scheme definition includes several optimizations to reduce the signature size. We discuss these later in this section.

The signer begins by effectively performing KGen() to obtain pk and $\mathbf{F}$, and then iterates through r rounds of the transformed identification scheme to obtain the transcript. He then uses this as input for $\mathrm{XOF}_{\mathsf{trans}}$ to derive a sequence of indices $((I_1, B_1), \ldots, (I_r, B_r))$, which effectively dictate the responses that should be included unblinded in the signature.

Verification. Upon receiving a message M, a signature σ, and a public key $\mathsf{pk} = (S_{\mathbf{F}}, \mathbf{v})$, the verifier begins by obtaining the system parameter $\mathbf{F}$ and parsing the signature σ as defined by its construction in Sign(). The verification routine that follows is listed in Fig. 6.

Optimizations. There are several optimizations that can be applied to signatures resulting from a transformed $q2$-IDS. Some of them are specific for SOFIA and some are more general; similar and related optimizations were suggested in [10, 11, 33].

Sign(sk, M)

$S_{\mathbf{F}}, \mathbf{s}, S_{\mathbf{rte}} \leftarrow \text{PRG}_{\text{sk}}(\text{sk}), \quad \mathbf{F} \leftarrow \text{XOF}_{\mathbf{F}}(S_{\mathbf{F}})$

pk $:= (S_{\mathbf{F}}, \mathbf{F}(\mathbf{s}))$

$\mathbf{r}_0^{(1)}, \ldots, \mathbf{r}_0^{(r)}, \mathbf{t}_0^{(1)}, \ldots, \mathbf{t}_0^{(r)}, \mathbf{e}_0^{(1)}, \ldots, \mathbf{e}_0^{(r)} \leftarrow \text{PRG}_{\mathbf{rte}}(S_{\mathbf{rte}}, M)$

For $j \in \{1, \ldots, r\}$ **do**

   $\mathbf{r}_1^{(j)} \leftarrow \mathbf{s}^{(j)} - \mathbf{r}_0^{(j)}$

   $c_0^{(j)} \leftarrow Com(\mathbf{r}_0^{(j)}, \mathbf{t}_0^{(j)}, \mathbf{e}_0^{(j)}), \quad c_1^{(j)} \leftarrow Com(\mathbf{r}_1^{(j)}, \mathbf{G}(\mathbf{t}_0^{(j)}, \mathbf{r}_1^{(j)}) + \mathbf{e}_0^{(j)})$

   com$^{(j)} := (c_0^{(j)}, c_1^{(j)})$

   For $i \in \{1, \ldots, t\}$ **do**

      $\mathbf{t}_1^{(i,j)} \leftarrow \alpha_i \mathbf{r}_0^{(j)} - \mathbf{t}_0^{(j)}, \quad \mathbf{e}_1^{(i,j)} \leftarrow \alpha_i \mathbf{F}(\mathbf{r}_0^{(j)}) - \mathbf{e}_0^{(j)}$

      $\text{resp}_1^{(i,j)} := (\mathbf{t}_1^{(i,j)}, \mathbf{e}_1^{(i,j)}), \quad \text{cr}_1^{(i,j)} \leftarrow \text{H}_1(\text{resp}_1^{(i,j)})$

   $\text{resp}_2^{(j,0)} := \mathbf{r}_0^{(j)}, \text{resp}_2^{(j,1)} := \mathbf{r}_1^{(j)}$

   $\text{cr}_2^{(j,0)} \leftarrow \text{H}_2(\text{resp}_2^{(j,0)}), \text{cr}_2^{(j,1)} \leftarrow \text{H}_2(\text{resp}_2^{(j,1)})$

   $\text{trans}_{\text{full}}(j) := (\text{com}^{(j)}, \left\{ \text{cr}_1^{(i,j)} \right\}_{i=1}^{t}, \text{cr}_2^{(j,0)}, \text{cr}_2^{(j,1)})$

md $\leftarrow \mathcal{H}\left(\text{pk}, M, \{\text{trans}_{\text{full}}(j)\}_{j=1}^{r} \right)$

$((I_1, B_1), \ldots, (I_r, B_r)) \leftarrow \text{XOF}_{\text{trans}}(\text{md})$

$\text{trans}_{\text{red}}(j) := (c_{\neg B_j}^{(j)}, \left\{ \text{cr}_1^{(i,j)} \right\}_{i \neq I_j, i=1}^{t}, \text{cr}_2^{(j, \neg B_j)})$

Return $\left(\text{md}, \left\{ \text{trans}_{\text{red}}(j), \alpha_{I_j}, \text{resp}_1^{(I_j, j)}, \text{resp}_2^{(j, B_j)} \right\}_{j=1}^{r} \right)$

Fig. 5. SOFIA signature generation.

Vf(pk, σ, M)

$\mathbf{F} \leftarrow \text{XOF}_{\mathbf{F}}(S_{\mathbf{F}})$

$((I_1, B_1), \ldots, (I_r, B_r)) \leftarrow \text{XOF}_{\text{trans}}(\text{md})$

For $j \in \{1, \ldots, r\}$ **do**

   $\text{cr}_1^{(I_j, j)} \leftarrow \text{H}_1(\text{resp}_1^{(I_j, j)}), \quad \text{cr}_2^{(I_j, B_j)} \leftarrow \text{H}_2(\text{resp}_2^{(I_j, B_j)})$

For $j \in \{1, \ldots, r\}$ **do**

   If $B_j = 0$ **then**

      $\mathbf{r}_0^{(j)} := \text{resp}_2^{(I_j, B_j)}$

      $c_0^{(j)} \leftarrow Com(\mathbf{r}_0^{(j)}, \alpha_{I_j} \mathbf{r}_0^{(j)} - \mathbf{t}_1^{(I_j, j)}, \alpha_{I_j} \mathbf{F}(\mathbf{r}_0^{(j)}) - \mathbf{e}_1^{(I_j, j)})$

   Else

      $\mathbf{r}_1^{(j)} := \text{resp}_2^{(I_j, B_j)}$

      $c_1^{(j)} \leftarrow Com(\mathbf{r}_1^{(j)}, \alpha_{I_j}(\mathbf{v} - \mathbf{F}(\mathbf{r}_1^{(j)})) - \mathbf{G}(\mathbf{t}_1^{(I_j, j)}, \mathbf{r}_1^{(j)}) - \mathbf{e}_1^{(I_j, j)})$

md$' \leftarrow \mathcal{H}\left(\text{pk}, M, \{\text{trans}_{\text{full}}(j)\}_{j=1}^{r} \right)$

Return md$' = $ md

Fig. 6. SOFIA signature verification.

Excluding unnecessary blindings. The signature contains blindings of all computed responses, as well as a selection of opened responses $\mathsf{resp}_1^{(I_j,j)}$ and $\mathsf{resp}_2^{(j,B_j)}$. It is redundant to include the values $\mathsf{cr}_1^{(I_j,j)}$ and $\mathsf{cr}_2^{(j,B_j)}$, as these can be recomputed based on the opened responses. This optimization was actually proposed in the generic Unruh transform [33], and applies to any construction similar to Unruh's and ours. However, for the verifier to know which responses were actually opened, they must be able to reproduce the indices $((I_1, B_1), \ldots, (I_r, B_r))$, which are derived from the transcript, and without the blinded responses, this transcript is incomplete. To solve this circular dependency, we could include the selected indices in the signature. However, for typical parameters (see Section 6.1), we can do this more efficiently by breaking $\mathsf{XOF}_{\mathsf{trans}}$ into two parts, composing it of a hash function over the transcript $\mathcal{H}$ and an extendable output function XOF_{IB} to derive the indices from the hash output. We then include $\mathcal{H}\left(\mathsf{pk}, M, \{\mathsf{trans}_{\mathsf{full}}(j)\}_{j=1}^r\right)$ as part of the signature, so that the verifier can reconstruct the indices, blind the corresponding responses, construct $\mathsf{trans}_{\mathsf{full}}$, and recompute the same hash for comparison.

Fixed challenge-space definition. Following the generic description of the signature, the selected $\alpha^{(i,j)}$ are included in the signature. Depending on the specific choice of t and q, it may be more efficient to include the challenges $\alpha^{(i,j)}$ that were *not* selected. However, there is no reason not to take this a step further and simply fix a challenge space ChS_1 of t elements. That way, all the α's from ChS_1 will be selected and there is no need to include them in the signature. This not only reduces the signature size, but also simplifies the implementation.

Excluding unnecessary second responses. The underlying IDS from [31] has a specific property, namely that the second responses do not depend on the previous state (that is, on the first challenge and response). Therefore, regardless of the value of α, the second responses are always the same. For this reason, they need to be included only once per commitment (rather than repeating the same value t times). Combined with the previous optimization, this implies that one of the second responses will be opened, and the other will be included blinded.

Omitting commitments. The check that the verifier performs for each round consists of recomputing $c_{B_j}^{(j)}$, and comparing it to one of the commits supplied by the signer. Similar to the above, and as already suggested in [31], the signer can omit the commits that the verifier will recompute. A hash over all commits could be included instead, which the verifier can reconstruct using the commits $c_{B_j}^{(j)}$ he recomputes and the commits $c_{\neg B_j}^{(j)}$ the signer includes. However, it turns out that this hash is not necessary either: as these commitments are part of the transcript and the verifier is already checking the correctness of the transcript as per the first optimization, the correctness of the recomputed commitments is implicitly checked when comparing the two hashes md and md'.

No need for additional randomness in the commitments. Commitments must be randomized in order for them to be hiding. This is typically done by including a randomization string. In our case, $r_0^{(j)}$, $t_0^{(j)}$ and $e_0^{(j)}$ are all randomly chosen, already providing sufficient randomness in both $c_0^{(j)}$ and $c_1^{(j)}$.

While constructing this scheme, we attempted several other variations. Notably, we explored opening for multiple α-challenges, but that led to no improvement in the number of rounds, and, in some cases, to a contradiction of the zero-knowledge property. Variants that employ a form of internal parallelization by committing to multiple values for t_0 do reduce the number of rounds, but increase the size of the transcript disproportionately.

Altogether, the above optimizations are crucial: they add up to around 126 KiB, more than halving the signature size of the scheme that results from the transform.

5.2   Security of SOFIA

In Section 3 we described an extension of Unruh's transform to $q2$-IDS and have proven that it provides PQ-EU-CMA security in the QROM for *any* underlying $q2$-IDS with a $q2$-extractor, the HVZK property, and PQ-key-one-wayness. This, of course, implies that this transform can immediately be applied to the 5-pass $\mathcal{MQ}$ IDS from [31], to give an $\mathcal{MQ}$ signature secure in the QROM.

As discussed in the previous subsection, some optimizations can significantly improve the performance of the scheme. They deviate from the generic construction, however, causing a need for some changes in the security proof. Fortunately, only minor changes are required. We specify the following theorem.

Theorem 5.1. *Let $k \in \mathbb{N}$ be the security parameter. The signature scheme SOFIA is post-quantum existentially unforgeable under adaptive chosen message attacks in the quantum-accessible random oracle model if the following conditions are satisfied:*

- *The search version of the $\mathcal{MQ}$ problem is intractable in the average case,*
- *the hash functions $\mathcal{H}$, H_1, H_2 as well as the extendable output functions XOF_F and XOF_{trans} are modeled as quantum-accessible random oracles,*
- *the commitment function Com is computationally binding and computationally hiding against quantum adversaries, and has $O(k)$ bits of output entropy,*
- *the pseudorandom generators, PRG_{rte}, PRG_{sk} have outputs computationally indistinguishable from random for any polynomial-time quantum adversary.*

Proof. First let's consider a signature scheme obtained by applying the optimizations from the previous section on the signature scheme from Figs. 1 and 2. We will refer to it as the optimized scheme throughout this proof. We will show that this optimized scheme is PQ-EU-CMA secure, if the underlying $q2$-IDS satisfies the conditions from Theorem 4.3. We will assume some additional properties of the IDS, that represent a special case of $q2$-IDS schemes. The optimized scheme is characterized by the following optimizations.

- We fix the challenge space ChS_1 to t elements. Note that this change does not influence the security arguments at all.
- We assume that the underlying IDS of the optimized scheme is such that the second response does not depend on the first challenge and response, but only on the second challenge and the initial output by the prover $\mathcal{P}_0$. In this case, in the signature generation, instead of calculating the second response as $\mathsf{resp}_2^{(i,j,\mathsf{ch}_2)} \leftarrow \mathcal{P}_2(\mathsf{fstate}^{(i,j)}, \mathsf{ch}_2)$ for every $i \in \{1, \ldots, t\}$, we calculate it once per round as $\mathsf{resp}_2^{(j,\mathsf{ch}_2)} \leftarrow \mathcal{P}_2(\mathsf{fstate}^{(j)}, \mathsf{ch}_2)$. The full transcript is now $\{\mathsf{trans}_{\mathsf{full}}(j)\}_{j=1}^r$, with $\mathsf{trans}_{\mathsf{full}}(j) = \mathsf{com}^{(j)}, \left\{ \mathsf{ch}_1^{(i,j)}, \mathsf{cr}_1^{(i,j)} \right\}_{i=1}^t, (\mathsf{cr}_2^{(j,0)}, \mathsf{cr}_2^{(j,1)})$. The reduced transcript $\mathsf{trans}_{\mathsf{red}}(j)$ that is included in the signature is influenced similarly.
- Assuming that the underlying IDS is such that $\mathsf{com} = (c_0, c_1)$, we omit from the signature the commitment c_{ch_2} that the verifier recomputes, depending on the challenge ch_2. This alters the content of $\mathsf{trans}_{\mathsf{red}}(j)$ but not of $\mathsf{trans}_{\mathsf{full}}(j)$.

It is straight forward to verify that Lemma 3.1 (and in the QROM, Lemma 3.5) still hold for the optimized scheme. We only removed duplicate information from the signature, which the reduction can recompute. The exact probability of abort in Lemma 3.2 might change as we remove some values from $\{\mathsf{trans}_{\mathsf{full}}(j)\}_{j=1}^r$, maybe reducing its entropy. However, the given bound does not change as it only depends on the amount of entropy coming from the commitments, which remains unchanged. Thus, the claims of Lemma 3.2 remain valid.

Next, recall (cf. Theorem 4.3) that, under the assumption of intractability of the $\mathcal{MQ}$ problem on average, and assuming computationally binding and computationally hiding properties of Com, the 5-pass IDS from [31] is PQ-KOW, is HVZK, and has a $q2$-Extractor. Furthermore, it satisfies the particular properties that the optimized scheme above requires. Thus applying the optimized transform on the Sakumoto-Shirai-Hiwatari 5-pass IDS scheme, we obtain a PQ-EU-CMA secure signature (cf. Theorems 3.3 and 3.6).

To complete the proof, we note that using a standard game hopping argument, it is straightforward to show that the success probability of a PQ-EU-CMA adversary against SOFIA is negligibly close to the success probability of a PQ-EU-CMA adversary against the optimized scheme from the Sakumoto-Shirai-Hiwatari 5-pass IDS scheme when the outputs of $\mathrm{PRG}_{\mathsf{rte}}$ and $\mathrm{PRG}_{\mathsf{sk}}$ are post-quantum computationally indistinguishable from random. $\qquad\square$

6   SOFIA-4-128

Having described the scheme in general terms, we now provide concrete parameters that allow us to specify a specific instance, which we will refer to as SOFIA-4-128. We present an optimized software implementation and list the results, in particular in comparison to MQDSS-31-64. All benchmarks mentioned below were obtained on a single core of an Intel Core i7-4770K (Haswell) CPU, following the standard practice of disabling TurboBoost and hyper-threading. We compiled the code using gcc 4.9.2-10, with -O3 and -march = native.

6.1 Parameters

The previous section assumed a number of parameters and functions. Notably, we must define $\mathbb{F}_q$, the field in which we perform the arithmetic, and n and m, the number of variables and equations defining the $\mathcal{MQ}$ problem. The number of rounds r is determined by t (i.e. the number of responses $\mathsf{resp}_1^{(i,j)}$, bounded by q in SOFIA) and the targeted security level, using Theorem 3.6.

For MQDSS-31-64, the choice of $\mathbb{F}_{31}$ was motivated by the fact that it brings the soundness error close to $\frac{1}{2}$ while providing convenient characteristics for fast implementation [11]. For SOFIA-4-128, our primary focus is on optimizing for signature size while still maintaining efficiency. To do so, we compute signature sizes for a wide range of candidates, and investigate several in more detail by implementing and measuring the resulting $\mathcal{MQ}$ evaluation functions. In particular, we look at the results of $\mathcal{MQ}(128, 128, \mathbb{F}_4)$, $\mathcal{MQ}(96, 96, \mathbb{F}_7)$ and $\mathcal{MQ}(72, 72, \mathbb{F}_{16})$, and compare to $\mathcal{MQ}(64, 64, \mathbb{F}_{31})$ from [11]. Of these, $\mathcal{MQ}(128, 128, \mathbb{F}_4)$ is the decisive winner, resulting in the smallest signatures while still providing decent performance. This is also the minimum amongst all candidate systems we looked at – it is not merely beating $\mathbb{F}_7$ and $\mathbb{F}_{16}$, but also less common options such as $\mathbb{F}_5$ and $\mathbb{F}_8$. See Table 2 for benchmarks of single evaluation functions and the related signature sizes. Note that, as the number of rounds r does not depend on the choice of $\mathbb{F}_q$ but merely on t, the signing time scales proportionally.

Parameters for $\mathcal{MQ}(\mathbf{m}, \mathbf{n}, \mathbb{F}_\mathbf{q})$. A straightforward method for solving systems of m quadratic equations in n variables over $\mathbb{F}_q$ is by performing exhaustive search on all possible q^n values for the variables, and testing whether they satisfy the system. Currently, [9] provide the fastest enumeration algorithm for systems over $\mathbb{F}_2$, needing $4 \log n \cdot 2^n$ operations. The techniques from [9] can be extended to other fields $\mathbb{F}_q$ with the same expected complexity of $\Theta(\log_q n \cdot q^n)$.

In addition, there exist algebraic techniques that analyze the properties of the ideal generated by the given polynomials. The most important are the algorithms from the F4/F5 family [4,8,18,19], and the variants of the XL algorithm [12,16,35,36]. Although different in description, the two families bear many similarities, which results in similar complexity [37].

In the Boolean case, today's state of the art algorithms BooleanSolve [5] and FXL [35], provide improvement over exhaustive search, with an asymptotic complexity of $\Theta(2^{0.792n})$ and $\Theta(2^{0.875n})$ for $m = n$, respectively. Practically, the improvement is visible for polynomials with more than 200 variables. A very recent algorithm, the Crossbred algorithm [26] over $\mathbb{F}_2$, is likely to further improve the asymptotic complexity, as the authors report that it passes the exhaustive search barrier already for 37 Boolean variables. Unfortunately, at the time of writing, the preprint does not include a detailed complexity analysis that we can use (the authors of [26] confirmed that the complexity analysis is an ongoing work, and will soon be made public).

The current best known algorithms, BooleanSolve [5], FXL [35,36], the Crossbred algorithm [26] and the Hybrid approach [8] all combine algebraic techniques with exhaustive search. This immediately allows for improvement in their quantum version using Grover's quantum search algorithm [25], provided the cost of running them on a quantum computer does not diminish the gain from Grover. Unfortunately, the current literature lacks analysis of the quantum version of these algorithms. To the best of our knowledge, a detailed analysis has only been done for pure enumeration using Grover's search [34], showing that a system of n equations in n variables can be solved using $\Theta(n \cdot 2^{n/2})$ operations.

In what follows we will analyze the complexity of the quantum versions of the Hybrid approach and BooleanSolve, and use the results as a reference point in choosing parameters for $\mathcal{MQ}(m, n, \mathbb{F}_q)$ that provide 128 bit post-quantum security. A similar analysis can be made using the algorithms from the XL family.

First of all, we note that $m = n$ is the best choice in terms of hardness of the $\mathcal{MQ}$ problem. Indeed, if there are more equations than variables, they provide more information about the solution, so finding one becomes easier. On the other hand, if there are more variables than equations, we can simply fix $n - m$ variables and reduce the problem to a smaller one, with m variables.

Let $\mathbf{F} = (f_1, \ldots, f_m), f_i \in \mathbb{F}_q[x_1, \ldots, x_n]$. Without loss of generality, the equation system that we want to solve is $\mathbf{F}(\mathbf{x}) = \mathbf{0}$.

The main complexity in both the Hybrid approach and BooleanSolve comes from performing linear algebra on a Macaulay matrix $Mac_D(\mathbf{F})$ of degree D (with rows formed by the coefficients of monomials of uf_i of maximal degree D). The degree D should be big enough so that a Gröbner basis of the ideal generated by the polynomials can be obtained by performing linear algebra on the Macaulay matrix. The smallest such D is called the degree of regularity D_{reg}, and for semi-regular systems (which is a very plausible assumption for randomly generated polynomials) it is given by $D_{reg}(n, m) = 1 + deg(HS_q(t))$, where

$$HS_q(t) = \left[\frac{(1 - t^2)^m}{(1 - t)^n} \right]_+, \text{ for } q > 2, \text{ and } HS_2(t) = \left[\frac{(1 + t)^n}{(1 + t^2)^m} \right]_+,$$

and the $+$ subscript denotes that the series has been truncated before the first non-positive coefficient. Since D_{reg} determines the size of the matrix, and thus the complexity of the linear algebra performed on it, both algorithms first fix k among the n variables in order to reduce the complexity of the costliest computational step. Now the linear algebra step is instead performed on $Mac_{D_{reg}}(\tilde{\mathbf{F}})$, where $\tilde{\mathbf{F}} = (\tilde{f}_1, \ldots, \tilde{f}_m)$ and $\tilde{f}_i(x_1, \ldots, x_{n-k}) = f_i(x_1, \ldots, x_{n-k}, a_{n-k+1}, \ldots, a_n)$, for some $(a_{n-k+1}, \ldots, a_n) \in \mathbb{F}_2^k$. The value of k is chosen such that the overall complexity is minimized.

Given the linear algebra constant $2 \leqslant \omega \leqslant 3$, the complexity of the Hybrid approach for solving systems of n equations in n variables over $\mathbb{F}_q$ is

$$C_{Hyb}(n, k) = Guess(q, k) \cdot C_{F5}(n - k, n), \tag{7}$$

where $C_{F5}(n,m) = \Theta\left(\left(m\binom{n+D_{reg}(n,m)-1}{D_{reg}(n,m)}\right)^{\omega}\right)$, is the complexity of computing a Gröbner basis of a system of m equations in n variables, $m \geqslant n$, using the F5 algorithm [19], $Guess(q,k) = \log_q(k)q^k$ in the classical case and $Guess(q,k) = \log_q(k)q^{k/2}$ in the quantum case using Grover's algorithm. Here, we assume a rather optimistic factor of $\log_q(k)$ in the quantum case, i.e., it is the same as in the classical case, as opposed to the factor k from [34].

In the case of $\mathbb{F}_2$, the BooleanSolve algorithm performs better than the Hybrid approach. It reduces the problem to testing the consistency of a related linear system

$$\mathbf{u} \cdot Mac_{D_{reg}}(\tilde{\mathbf{F}}) = (0, \ldots, 0, 1) \tag{8}$$

If the system is consistent, then the original system does not have a solution. This allows for pruning of all the inconsistent branches corresponding to some $a \in \mathbb{F}_2^k$. A simple exhaustive search is then performed on the remaining branches. It can be shown that the running time of the algorithm is dominated by the first part of the algorithm in both the classical and the quantum version, although in the quantum case the difference is not as big, as a consequence of the reduced complexity of the first part. Therefore, for simplicity, we omit the exhaustive search on the remaining branches from our analysis. The complexity of the Boolean-Solve algorithm is given by

$$C_{Bool}(n,k) = Guess(2,k) \cdot C_{cons}(Mac_{D_{reg}}(\tilde{\mathbf{F}})), \tag{9}$$

where $Guess(2,k)$ is defined the same as in the Hybrid approach, and

$$C_{cons}(Mac_{D_{reg}}(\tilde{\mathbf{F}})) = \Theta(N^2 \log^2 N \log \log N), \quad N = \sum_{i=0}^{D_{reg}(n-k,n)} \binom{n}{i}$$

is the complexity of testing consistency of the matrix (8), using the sparse linear algebra algorithm from [24].

Table 1 below provides estimates of the minimum requirements for 128 bit post-quantum security of $\mathcal{MQ}(n,n,\mathbb{F}_q)$ with regards to BooleanSolve and the Hybrid Approach using Grover's search, as well as plain use of Grover's search. In the estimates we used $\omega = 2.3$, which is smaller than the best known value $\omega = 2.3728639$ [22]. We provide the optimal number of fixed variables in brackets, where actually this number does not equal the number of variables in the initial system. When this is the case, the optimal strategy is to simply use Grover (fix all variables), which we denote with G. Note that since any system of n variables over $\mathbb{F}_{2^s}$ can be efficiently transformed into a system of sn variables over $\mathbb{F}_2$, we have scaled the results for BooleanSolve for larger $\mathbb{F}_{2^s}$ accordingly.

As mentioned earlier, a new algebraic method for equations over $\mathbb{F}_2$, the Crossbred algorithm, was proposed very recently [26]. The main idea of this approach is to first perform some operations on the Macaulay matrix of degree $D_{reg}(n-k,n)$ of the given system, and fix variables only afterwards. In particular, the algorithm first tries to find enough linearly independent elements

Table 1. Lower bound on number of variables n for 128 bit post quantum security against the quantum versions of Hybrid approach [8] and BooleanSolve [5]. In brackets is the number of fixed variables. G denotes that the best strategy is to fix all variables, i.e. plain Grover search.

	$\mathbb{F}_2$	$\mathbb{F}_3$	$\mathbb{F}_4$	$\mathbb{F}_5$	$\mathbb{F}_7$	$\mathbb{F}_8$
BooleanSolve	221 (200)	/	111	/	/	56
Hybrid	G	G	G	G	G	84 (57)
Grover	251	158	126	108	90	84
	$\mathbb{F}_{11}$	$\mathbb{F}_{13}$	$\mathbb{F}_{16}$	$\mathbb{F}_{17}$	$\mathbb{F}_{31}$	$\mathbb{F}_{32}$
BooleanSolve	/	/	28	/	/	14
Hybrid	77 (51)	73 (43)	69 (40)	69 (40)	61 (30)	60 (21)
Grover	73	68	63	62	51	51

in the kernel of a submatrix of $Mac_{D_{reg}(n-k,n)}$, corresponding to monomials of specialized degree in the variables that will later remain in the system (i.e. will not be fixed). These can then be used to form new polynomials in the $n - k$ remaining variables of total small degree d, which added to $Mac_d(\tilde{\mathbf{F}})$ will result in working with a much smaller Macaulay matrix. The advantage here comes from using sparse linear algebra algorithms on $Mac_{D_{reg}(n-k,n)}$ for the first part and dense linear algebra only on the smaller Macaulay matrix in the second part. An external specialization of variables is also possible, but this does not bring any improvement classically, and we have verified for some parameters (including ours) that this is the case also quantumly. Even more, the algorithm can be split into two distinct parts: thus, the first part, that is more memory demanding can always be performed on a classical computer, and the second part which can make use of Grover's algorithm can be performed on a quantum computer. Since [26] does not contain a complexity analysis, we refrain from claiming exact security requirements based on the quantum version of the algorithm. Nevertheless, following the description of the algorithm we have estimated the security of our chosen instance $\mathcal{MQ}(128, 128, \mathbb{F}_4)$. We analyzed both the quantum version of the algorithm over $\mathbb{F}_2$ as described in [26] and the quantum version over $\mathbb{F}_4$.

In both cases, as long as the number of the remaining $n - k$ variables is small, the sparse linear algebra part takes much less time, since in this case $D_{reg}(n - k, n)$ is also small. It turns out that actually it is more efficient to work with a Mac_D, with $D > D_{reg}(n - k, n)$, but not too large so that the cost of the first part becomes significant. The complexity thus, is dominated by enumeration of k variables in a system in n variables of degree D over $\mathbb{F}_4$, and checking whether the obtained system has a valid solution. Clearly, a quantum version of this part using Grover can quadraticly speed up the enumeration, however there will be some additional cost for the Grover oracle.

Our analysis showed that for our parameters, the version over $\mathbb{F}_4$ is much more efficient. Not counting the evaluation cost of the polynomials and any additional cost of the Grover oracle, the quantum algorithm against

$\mathcal{MQ}(128, 128, \mathbb{F}_4)$ takes at least 2^{117} operations for the best found trade-off of parameters of the algorithm. Very likely, the additional cost we did not take into account would be much bigger than 2^{11} operations. In total, we can safely assume that a system of 128 variables over $\mathbb{F}_4$ provides 128-bit security against the quantum version of Crossbred algorithm. We will include a more detailed analysis for the quantum version once a classical complexity analysis of [26] is available.

Number of rounds r and blinded responses t per round. The choice of t provides a trade-off between size and speed; a larger t implies a smaller error, resulting in less rounds, but more included blinded responses per round (the additional computational cost of which is insignificant). Interestingly, $t = 3$ provides the minimal size, followed by $t = 4$, and, only then, $t = 2$. The decrease in rounds quickly diminishes, making $t = 3$ and $t = 4$ the most attractive choices. Note that t is naturally bounded by q, making these the *only* options for $\mathbb{F}_4$.

Table 2. Benchmarks for varying parameter sets.

	Cycles[b]	Size $t = 3, r = 438$	Size $t = 4, r = 378$
$\mathcal{MQ}(128, 128, \mathbb{F}_4)$	21 412	123.22 KiB	129.97 KiB
$\mathcal{MQ}(96, 96, \mathbb{F}_7)$	36 501	129.00 KiB[a]	136.20 KiB[a]
$\mathcal{MQ}(72, 72, \mathbb{F}_{16})$	25 014	136.91 KiB	144.73 KiB
$\mathcal{MQ}(64, 64, \mathbb{F}_{31})$	6 616 [11]	149.34 KiB[a]	158.15 KiB[a]

[a] Assumes optimally packing the elements of $\mathbb{F}_q$, which may not be practical.
[b] For single evaluation. In practice, batching provides a speedup. See Section 6.2.

Given the above considerations (and with a prospect of some convenience of implementation), we select the parameters $n = m = 128$, $q = 4$ and $t = 3$. For a security level of 128 bits post-quantum security, it follows from Theorem 3.6 that we must select r such that $2^{-(r \log \frac{2t}{t+1})/2} < 2^{-128}$. This implies $r = 438$.

Required functions. Before being able to implement the scheme, we must still define several of the functions we have assumed to exist. In particular, we need: a string commitment function Com; pseudorandom generators $\mathrm{PRG}_{\mathsf{sk}}$ and $\mathrm{PRG}_{\mathbf{rte}}$; extendable output functions $\mathrm{XOF}_{\mathbf{F}}$ and XOF_{IB}; permutation functions H_1 and H_2; and a cryptographic hash function $\mathcal{H}$.

We instantiate the extendable output functions, the string commitment functions, the permutations and the hash function with SHAKE-128 [7]. This applies trivially, except for XOF_{IB}, of which the output domain is a series of ternary and binary indices (as $t = 3$). We resolve this by applying rejection sampling to the output of SHAKE-128 to derive the ternary challenges. Note that this does not enable a timing attack, as the input to SHAKE-128 is public. For $\mathrm{XOF}_{\mathbf{F}}$, we achieve a significant speedup by dividing its output in four separate pieces, generating each of them with a domain-separated call to cSHAKE-128 [7]. For the application of $\mathcal{H}$ to the public key, the message and the transcript, collision resilience is achieved by absorbing the transcript into the SHAKE-128 state first, as the included randomness prevents internal collisions.

We also instantiate PRG_{rte} and PRG_{sk} with SHAKE-128, but note that implementations can make different choices without breaking compatibility. In fact, for the optimized Haswell implementation discussed in the next section, we instantiate PRG_{rte} with AES in counter mode, using the AES-NI instruction set.

6.2 Implementation

As part of this work, we provide a C reference implementation and an implementation optimized for AVX2. The focus of this section is the evaluation of the $\mathcal{MQ}$ function, given the abovementioned parameter set $\mathcal{MQ}(128, 128, \mathbb{F}_4)$. The rest of the scheme depends on fairly straight-forward operations (such as multiplying vectors of $\mathbb{F}_4$ elements by a constant scalar) and applications of existing implementations of AES-CTR and SHAKE-128 The used AES-CTR and SHAKE-128 implementations are in the public domain and run in constant time.

Before discussing the computation, we note that the chosen parameters lend themselves to a very natural data representation. Throughout the entire scheme, we interpret 256 bit vectors as vectors of 128 bitsliced $\mathbb{F}_4$ elements: the low 128 bits make up the lower bits of the two-bit elements, and the high 128 bits make up the higher bits of each element. This makes operations such as scalar multiplication very convenient in C code, as this can be easily expressed as logical operations on bit sequences, but provides an even more important benefit for AVX2 assembly code. Notably, one vector of $\mathbb{F}_4$ elements fits exactly into one 256 bit vector register, with the lower bits now fitting into the low lane and the higher bits into the high lane. Whereas other parameter sets could result in having to consider crossing the lanes, in this case the separation is very natural.

When sampling elements in $\mathbb{F}_4$ from the output of SHAKE-128 or AES-CTR, we can freely interpret the random data to be in bitsliced representation. Similarly, we include the elements in the signature in this representation, as signature verification enjoys precisely the same benefits. Throughout the entire scheme, there is no point at which we need to actually perform a bitslicing operation.

As a side effect of this choice of representation, it is very natural to perform the $\mathcal{MQ}$ evaluation in constant time. While bigger underlying fields might have implied approaches based on lookup tables, for vectors over $\mathbb{F}_4$ it is much faster to perform the evaluation using bitsliced field arithmetic.

Evaluating $\mathcal{MQ}$. For a given input $\mathbf{x}$, we split the evaluation into two phases: computing all quadratic monomial terms $x_i x_j$, and composing them to evaluate the quadratic polynomials.

Computing the quadratic terms. To perform the first step, we use a similar approach as was used in [11]. It can be viewed as a combination of their approach for $\mathbb{F}_2$ and for $\mathbb{F}_{31}$, as we now operate on a single register that contains all input elements, but view each lane as 16 separate single-byte registers. Using vpshufb instructions, the elements can be easily arranged such that all multiplications can be performed using only a minimal number of rotations. We used the script from [11] as a starting point to generate the arrangement.

A bitsliced multiplication in $\mathbb{F}_4$ can be efficiently performed using only a few logical operations. The inputs to these multiplications are a register containing $\mathbf{x}$ and a register containing some rotated arrangement of $\mathbf{x}$. However, some of these operations require the low and high lanes of the vector registers to interact, which is typically costly. As $\mathbf{x}$ is constant, we speed up these multiplications by rewriting them as shown below, and presetting two registers that contain $[\mathbf{x}_{high}|\mathbf{x}_{high}]$ and $[\mathbf{x}_{high} \oplus \mathbf{x}_{low}|\mathbf{x}_{low}]$, respectively. Note that all of these operations are not performed on single bits, but rather on 128 bit vector lanes. The multiplication of 128 elements then requires only two vpand instructions, one vperm instruction, and a vpxor to combine the results.

$$c_{high} = (a_{high} \wedge (b_{low} \oplus b_{high})) \oplus (a_{low} \wedge b_{high})$$
$$c_{low} = (a_{low} \wedge b_{low}) \oplus (a_{high} \wedge b_{high})$$

Multiplying, and accumulating results. We focus on two approaches to perform the second and most costly part of the evaluation, in which all of the above monomials need to be multiplied with coefficients from $\mathbf{F}$ and summed into the output vector. They are best described as iterating either 'horizontally' or 'vertically' through the required multiplications. For the vertical approach, we iterate over all[2] registers of monomials, broadcasting each of the monomials to each of the 128 possible positions (using rotations), before multiplying with a sequence of coefficients from $\mathbf{F}$ and adding into an accumulator. Alternatively, we iterate over the output elements in the outer-most loop. For each output element, we iterate over all registers of monomials, perform the multiplications and horizontally sum the results by making use of the popcnt instruction.

Intuitively, the latter approach may seem like more work (notably because it requires more loads from memory), but in practice it turns out to be faster for our parameters. The main reason for this is that by maintaining multiple separate accumulators, loaded monomials can be re-used while still maintaining chains of logic operations that operate on independent results (as the accumulators are only joined together later), which leads to highly efficient scheduling.

For both cases, delaying part of the multiplication in $\mathbb{F}_4$ provides a significant speedup. This is done by computing both $[\hat{\mathbf{x}}_{high} \wedge \mathbf{f}_{high}|\hat{\mathbf{x}}_{low} \wedge \mathbf{f}_{low}]$ and $[\hat{\mathbf{x}}_{low} \wedge \mathbf{f}_{high}|\hat{\mathbf{x}}_{high} \wedge \mathbf{f}_{low}]$, with $\mathbf{f}$ from $\mathbf{F}$ and $\hat{\mathbf{x}}$ a sequence of quadratic monomials, and accumulating these results separately. After accumulating, all multiplications and reductions can be completed at once, eliminating the duplicate operations that would otherwise be performed for each of the 65 multiplications.

---

[2] There are $\frac{n \cdot (n+1)}{2} = 8256$ such monomials, which results in $64\frac{1}{2}$ 256-bit sequences. We round up to 65 by zeroing out half of the high and half of the low lane. To still get results that are compatible with implementations on other platforms, we create similar gaps in the stream of random values used to construct $\mathbf{F}$, ensuring that the same random elements are still used for the same coefficients.

Evaluating $\mathcal{MQ}$ instances in parallel. As each of the coefficients in **F** is used only once, loading these elements from memory causes a considerable burden. Since **F** is constant for each evaluation, however, a significant speedup can be achieved by processing multiple instances of the $\mathcal{MQ}$ function in parallel. This applies in particular to the vertical approach, as its critical section leaves some registers unused. Horizontally, there is a trade-off with registers used for parallel accumulators, but there is still considerable gain from parallelizing evaluations.

For SOFIA-4-128, the signer evaluates $r = 438$ instances of **F** and its polar form **G** on completely independent inputs, which can be trivially batched.

Parallel SHAKE-128 and cSHAKE-128. As will be apparent in the next section, many cycles are spent computing the Keccak permutation (as part of either SHAKE-128 or cSHAKE-128). Some of the main culprits are the commitments, the blinding of responses and the expansion of **F**. While the Keccak permutation does not provide internal parallelism, it is straightforward to compute four instances in parallel in a 256 bit vector register. This allows us to seriously speed up the many commitments and blindings, as these are all fully independent and can be grouped together across rounds. Deriving **F** can be parallelized by splitting it in four domain-separated cSHAKE-128 calls operating on the same seed, as was alluded to in Section 6.1.

Benchmarks. Evaluating the $\mathcal{MQ}$ function horizontally in batches of three turns out to give the fastest results, measuring in at 17 558 cycles per evaluation. Evaluating vertically costs 18 598 cycles. The cost for evaluating the polar form is not significantly different, differing by approximately a hundred cycles from regular $\mathcal{MQ}$. Generating the monomial terms $x_i y_j + x_j y_i$ is somewhat more costly, but this is countered by the fact that the linear terms cancel out.

To generate a signature, we spend 21 305 472 cycles. Of this, 15 420 520 cycles can be attributed to evaluating $\mathcal{MQ}$, and 43 954 to AES-CTR. The remainder is almost entirely accounted for by the various calls to SHAKE-128 and cSHAKE-128 for the commitments, blindings and randomness expansion. In particular, expanding **F** costs 1 120 782 cycles. Note, however, that if many signatures are to be generated, this expansion only needs to be done once and **F** can be kept in memory across subsequent signatures. Verification costs 15 492 686 cycles, and key generation costs 1 157 112; key generation is dominated by expansion of **F**.

The keys of SOFIA-4-128 are very small by nature, with the secret key consisting of only a single 32 byte seed, and the 64 byte public key being made up of a seed and a single $\mathcal{MQ}$ output.

The natural candidate for comparison is MQDSS-31-64 [11]. While MQDSS has a proof in the ROM, we focus further comparison on post-quantum schemes that have proofs in the QROM or standard model. See Table 3, below; as mentioned in the introduction, we include SPHINCS-256 [6] (standard model), Picnic-10-38 [10] (QROM) and TESLA-2 [2] (QROM). Since [2] does not implement the TESLA-2 parameter set, we include TESLA-1 (ROM) for context.

Table 3. Benchmark overview.

	$|\sigma|$ (bytes)	$|pk|$, $|sk|$ (bytes)	Keygen (cycles)	Signing (cycles)	Verification (cycles)
SOFIA-4-128[a]	126 176	64 32	1 157 112	21 305 472	15 492 686
MQDSS-31-64[a]	40 952	72 64	1 826 612	8 510 616	5 752 612
SPHINCS-256[b]	41 000	1056 1088	3 237 260	51 636 372	1 451 004
Picnic-10-38[c,d]	195 458	64 32	$\approx$36 000	$\approx$112 716k	$\approx$58 680 000
TESLA-1[a]	2 444	11 653k 6 769k	?[e]	143 402 231	19 284 672
TESLA-2[f]	$\geq$4.0k^g	$\geq$21 799k^g $\geq$7 700k^g	?[f]	?[f]	?[f]

[a] Benchmarked on an Intel Core-i7-4770K (Haswell).   [b] Benchmarked on an Intel Xeon E3-1275 (Haswell).   [c] Benchmarked on an Intel Core-i7-4790 (Haswell).   [d] Converted from milliseconds at 3.6 GHz.   [e] The benchmarks in [2] omit key generation. In [10], a measurement of approximately 173 billion cycles is reported for the preceding TESLA-768 [1] scheme, which uses a similar key generation operation but is instantiated with smaller parameters. [f] The TESLA-2 parameter set is not implemented in [2]; no benchmarks are available. [g] "Sizes are theoretic sizes for fully compressed keys and signatures" [2].

References

1. Alkim, E., Bindel, N., Buchmann, J., Dagdelen, O.: TESLA: tightly-secure efficient signatures from standard lattices. Cryptology ePrint Archive, report 2015/755 (2015)
2. Alkim, E., Bindel, N., Buchmann, J., Dagdelen, Ö., Eaton, E., Gutoski, G., Krämer, J., Pawlega, F.: Revisiting TESLA in the quantum random oracle model. In: Lange, T., Takagi, T. (eds.) PQCrypto 2017. LNCS, vol. 10346, pp. 143–162. Springer, Cham (2017). https://doi.org/10.1007/978-3-319-59879-6_9
3. Ambainis, A., Rosmanis, A., Unruh, D.: Quantum attacks on classical proof systems: the hardness of quantum rewinding. In: FOCS, pp. 474–483 (2014)
4. Bardet, M., Faugère, J., Salvy, B.: On the complexity of the F5 Gröbner basis algorithm. J. Symbolic Comput. **70**, 49–70 (2015)
5. Bardet, M., Faugère, J., Salvy, B., Spaenlehauer, P.: On the complexity of solving quadratic Boolean systems. J. Complex. **29**(1), 53–75 (2013)
6. Bernstein, D.J., Hopwood, D., Hülsing, A., Lange, T., Niederhagen, R., Papachristodoulou, L., Schneider, M., Schwabe, P., Wilcox-O'Hearn, Z.: SPHINCS: practical stateless hash-based signatures. In: Oswald, E., Fischlin, M. (eds.) EUROCRYPT 2015. LNCS, vol. 9056, pp. 368–397. Springer, Heidelberg (2015). https://doi.org/10.1007/978-3-662-46800-5_15
7. Bertoni, G., Daemen, J., Peeters, M., Van Assche, G.: The Keccak reference (2011)
8. Bettale, L., Faugère, J., Perret, L.: Solving polynomial systems over finite fields: improved analysis of the hybrid approach. In: Proceedings of the 37th International Symposium on Symbolic and Algebraic Computation - ISSAC 2012, pp. 67–74. ACM (2012)
9. Bouillaguet, C., Chen, H.-C., Cheng, C.-M., Chou, T., Niederhagen, R., Shamir, A., Yang, B.-Y.: Fast exhaustive search for polynomial systems in $\mathbb{F}_2$. In: Mangard, S., Standaert, F.-X. (eds.) CHES 2010. LNCS, vol. 6225, pp. 203–218. Springer, Heidelberg (2010). https://doi.org/10.1007/978-3-642-15031-9_14
10. Chase, M., Derler, D., Goldfeder, S., Orlandi, C., Ramacher, S., Rechberger, C., Slamanig, D., Zaverucha, G.: Post-quantum zero-knowledge and signatures from symmetric-key primitives. Cryptology ePrint Archive, report 2017/279 (2017)

11. Chen, M.-S., Hülsing, A., Rijneveld, J., Samardjiska, S., Schwabe, P.: From 5-pass $\mathcal{MQ}$-based identification to $\mathcal{MQ}$-based signatures. In: Cheon, J.H., Takagi, T. (eds.) ASIACRYPT 2016. LNCS, vol. 10032, pp. 135–165. Springer, Heidelberg (2016). https://doi.org/10.1007/978-3-662-53890-6_5

12. Courtois, N., Klimov, A., Patarin, J., Shamir, A.: Efficient algorithms for solving overdefined systems of multivariate polynomial equations. In: Preneel, B. (ed.) EUROCRYPT 2000. LNCS, vol. 1807, pp. 392–407. Springer, Heidelberg (2000). https://doi.org/10.1007/3-540-45539-6_27

13. Courtois, N.T.: Efficient zero-knowledge authentication based on a linear algebra problem MinRank. In: Boyd, C. (ed.) ASIACRYPT 2001. LNCS, vol. 2248, pp. 402–421. Springer, Heidelberg (2001). https://doi.org/10.1007/3-540-45682-1_24

14. Dagdelen, Ö., Fischlin, M., Gagliardoni, T.: The Fiat–Shamir transformation in a quantum world. In: Sako, K., Sarkar, P. (eds.) ASIACRYPT 2013. LNCS, vol. 8270, pp. 62–81. Springer, Heidelberg (2013). https://doi.org/10.1007/978-3-642-42045-0_4

15. Dagdelen, Ö., Galindo, D., Véron, P., El Yousfi Alaoui, S.M., Cayrel, P.-L.: Extended security arguments for signature schemes. Des. Codes Crypt. **78**(2), 441–461 (2016)

16. Diem, C.: The XL-algorithm and a conjecture from commutative algebra. In: Lee, P.J. (ed.) ASIACRYPT 2004. LNCS, vol. 3329, pp. 323–337. Springer, Heidelberg (2004). https://doi.org/10.1007/978-3-540-30539-2_23

17. Ding, J., Hu, L., Yang, B.-Y., Chen, J.-M.: Note on design criteria for rainbow-type multivariates. Cryptology ePrint Archive, report 2006/307 (2006)

18. Faugère, J.-C.: A new efficient algorithm for computing Gröbner bases (F4). J. Pure Appl. Algebra **139**, 61–88 (1999)

19. Faugère, J.-C.: A new efficient algorithm for computing Gröbner bases without reduction to zero (F5). In: Proceedings of the 2002 International Symposium on Symbolic and Algebraic Computation - ISSAC 2002, pp. 75–83. ACM (2002)

20. Faugère, J.-C., Levy-dit-Vehel, F., Perret, L.: Cryptanalysis of MinRank. In: Wagner, D. (ed.) CRYPTO 2008. LNCS, vol. 5157, pp. 280–296. Springer, Heidelberg (2008). https://doi.org/10.1007/978-3-540-85174-5_16

21. Fischlin, M.: Communication-efficient non-interactive proofs of knowledge with online extractors. In: Shoup, V. (ed.) CRYPTO 2005. LNCS, vol. 3621, pp. 152–168. Springer, Heidelberg (2005). https://doi.org/10.1007/11535218_10

22. Gall, F.L.: Powers of tensors and fast matrix multiplication. In: Proceedings of the 39th International Symposium on Symbolic and Algebraic Computation - ISSAC 2014, 296–303. ACM (2014)

23. Garey, M.R., Johnson, D.S.: Computers and Intractability: A Guide to the Theory of NP-Completeness. W.H. Freeman and Company, London (1979)

24. Giesbrecht, M., Lobo, A., Saunders, B.D.: Certifying inconsistency of sparse linear systems. In: Proceedings of the 1998 International Symposium on Symbolic and Algebraic Computation - ISSAC 1998, pp. 113–119 (1998)

25. Grover, L.K.: A fast quantum mechanical algorithm for database search. In: Proceedings of the Twenty-eighth Annual ACM Symposium on Theory of Computing - STOC 1996, pp. 212–219. ACM (1996)

26. Joux, A., Vitse, V.: A crossbred algorithm for solving Boolean polynomial systems. Cryptology ePrint Archive, report 2017/372 (2017)

27. Kiltz, E., Loss, J., Pan, J.: Tightly-secure signatures from five-move identification protocols. In: Takagi, T., Peyrin, T. (eds.) ASIACRYPT 2017. LNCS, vol. 10626, pp. 68–94. Springer, Cham (2017). https://doi.org/10.1007/978-3-319-70700-6_3

28. Kiltz, E., Lyubashevsky, V., Schaffner, C.: A concrete treatment of Fiat-Shamir signatures in the quantum random-oracle model. Cryptology ePrint Archive, report 2017/916 (2017)
29. Patarin, J.: Hidden Fields Equations (HFE) and Isomorphisms of Polynomials (IP): two new families of asymmetric algorithms. In: Maurer, U. (ed.) EUROCRYPT 1996. LNCS, vol. 1070, pp. 33–48. Springer, Heidelberg (1996). https://doi.org/10.1007/3-540-68339-9_4
30. Pointcheval, D., Stern, J.: Security proofs for signature schemes. In: Maurer, U. (ed.) EUROCRYPT 1996. LNCS, vol. 1070, pp. 387–398. Springer, Heidelberg (1996). https://doi.org/10.1007/3-540-68339-9_33
31. Sakumoto, K., Shirai, T., Hiwatari, H.: Public-key identification schemes based on multivariate quadratic polynomials. In: Rogaway, P. (ed.) CRYPTO 2011. LNCS, vol. 6841, pp. 706–723. Springer, Heidelberg (2011). https://doi.org/10.1007/978-3-642-22792-9_40
32. Thomae, E.: About the security of multivariate quadratic public key schemes. Ph.D. thesis, Ruhr-University Bochum, Germany (2013)
33. Unruh, D.: Non-interactive zero-knowledge proofs in the quantum random oracle model. In: Oswald, E., Fischlin, M. (eds.) EUROCRYPT 2015. LNCS, vol. 9057, pp. 755–784. Springer, Heidelberg (2015). https://doi.org/10.1007/978-3-662-46803-6_25
34. Schwabe, P., Westerbaan, B.: Solving binary $\mathcal{MQ}$ with Grover's algorithm. In: Carlet, C., Hasan, M.A., Saraswat, V. (eds.) SPACE 2016. LNCS, vol. 10076, pp. 303–322. Springer, Cham (2016). https://doi.org/10.1007/978-3-319-49445-6_17
35. Yang, B.-Y., Chen, J.-M.: Theoretical analysis of XL over small fields. In: Wang, H., Pieprzyk, J., Varadharajan, V. (eds.) ACISP 2004. LNCS, vol. 3108, pp. 277–288. Springer, Heidelberg (2004). https://doi.org/10.1007/978-3-540-27800-9_24
36. Yang, B.-Y., Chen, J.-M.: All in the XL family: theory and practice. In: Park, C., Chee, S. (eds.) ICISC 2004. LNCS, vol. 3506, pp. 67–86. Springer, Heidelberg (2005). https://doi.org/10.1007/11496618_7
37. Yeh, J.Y.-C., Cheng, C.-M., Yang, B.-Y.: Operating degrees for XL vs. F_4/F_5 for generic $\mathcal{MQ}$ with number of equations linear in that of variables. In: Fischlin, M., Katzenbeisser, S. (eds.) Number Theory and Cryptography. LNCS, vol. 8260, pp. 19–33. Springer, Heidelberg (2013). https://doi.org/10.1007/978-3-642-42001-6_3
38. Zhandry, M.: A note on quantum-secure PRPs. Cryptology ePrint Archive, report 2016/1076 (2016)

A Unified Framework
for Trapdoor-Permutation-Based
Sequential Aggregate Signatures

Craig Gentry[1], Adam O'Neill[2(✉)], and Leonid Reyzin[3]

[1] Cryptography Research Group, Thomas J. Watson Research Center,
Yorktown Heights, NY, USA
cbgentry@us.ibm.com
[2] Department of Computer Science, Georgetown University,
3700 Reservoir Road NW, Washington, D.C. 20057, USA
adam@cs.georgetown.edu
[3] Department of Computer Science, Boston University,
111 Cummington St., Boston, MA 02215, USA
reyzin@cs.bu.edu
https://researcher.watson.ibm.com/researcher/view.php?person=us-cbgentry,
http://cs.georgetown.edu/adam, http://cs.bu.edu/reyzin

Abstract. We give a framework for trapdoor-permutation-based sequential aggregate signatures (SAS) that unifies and simplifies prior work and leads to new results. The framework is based on *ideal ciphers over large domains*, which have recently been shown to be realizable in the random oracle model. The basic idea is to replace the random oracle in the full-domain-hash signature scheme with an ideal cipher. Each signer in sequence applies the ideal cipher, keyed by the message, to the output of the previous signer, and then inverts the trapdoor permutation on the result. We obtain different variants of the scheme by varying additional keying material in the ideal cipher and making different assumptions on the trapdoor permutation. In particular, we obtain the first scheme with lazy verification and signature size independent of the number of signers that does not rely on bilinear pairings.

Since existing proofs that ideal ciphers over large domains can be realized in the random oracle model are lossy, our schemes do not currently permit practical instantiation parameters at a reasonable security level, and thus we view our contribution as mainly conceptual. However, we are optimistic tighter proofs will be found, at least in our specific application.

Keywords: Aggregate signatures · Trapdoor permutations
Ideal cipher model

1 Introduction

AGGREGATE SIGNATURES AND THEIR VARIANTS. Aggregate signature schemes (AS), introduced by Boneh et al. [6] (BGLS), allow n signatures on different

© International Association for Cryptologic Research 2018
M. Abdalla and R. Dahab (Eds.): PKC 2018, LNCS 10770, pp. 34–57, 2018.
https://doi.org/10.1007/978-3-319-76581-5_2

messages produced by n different signers to be combined by any third party into a single short signature for greater efficiency, while maintaining the same security as n individual signatures. In this paper we are concerned with the more restricted *sequential* aggregate signatures (SAS), introduced by Lysyan-skaya *et al.* (LMRS) [22] and further studied by [1,5,7,17,21,24]. These schemes, while still maintaining the same security, require signers themselves to compute the aggregated signature in order, with the output of each signer (so-called "aggregate-so-far") used as input to the next during the signing process. This restriction turns out to be acceptable in several important applications of aggregate signatures, such as PKI certification chains and authenticated network routing protocols (*e.g.*, BGPsec).

TDP-BASED SAS. Existing SAS constructions are usually based on trapdoor permutations (TDPs) [1,7,22,24] or bilinear pairings [1,5,17,21]. In this paper, we focus on improving and simplifying TDP-based SAS schemes, which are all in the random oracle (RO) model. We describe existing constructions below, and illustrate them in Fig. 1.

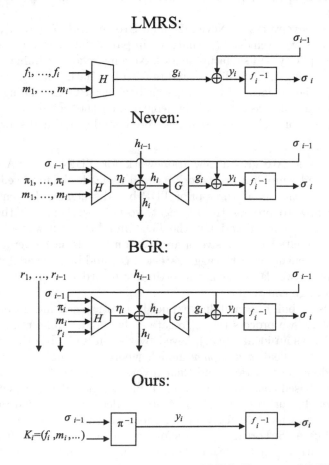

Fig. 1. Our framework, compared to LMRS, Neven, and BGR.

The first TDP-based SAS scheme, by Lysyanskaya *et al.* [22] (LMRS), is very similar to the full-domain-hash (FDH) signature scheme of Bellare and Rogaway [2]. Recall that in FDH, the hash function is modeled as a random oracle whose range is equal to the domain of the TDP, and the signer simply hashes the message and inverts the TDP on the hash output. In LMRS, the signer exlcusive-ors the previous signer's output together with the hash of the message before inverting the TDP. This procedure enabled the verifier to verify in reverse order of signing, because exclusive-or could be undone to obtain the previous signer's (alleged) output.

Unfortunately, this very simple construction is not secure, and two additional checks are used in LMRS to achieve security: first, each signer must ensure that the public keys of all preceding signers are "certified"—*i.e.*, specify permutations; and second, each signer must verify the signature received from the previous signers before applying the signing operation. These two checks prevented fast signing; ideally, each signer would be able to sign independently of others, and verify when time permitted (this option is called "lazy verification" and was observed by Brogle *et al.* [7] to be crucial in authenticated network routing protocols).

In two successive works by Neven [24] and Brogle *et al.* [7] (BGR), these two additional checks were removed (permitting, in particular, lazy verification), but at a cost to simplicity and signature length. Neven's scheme eliminated the first check by introducing a Feistel-like structure with two hash functions, at the cost of lengthening the signature by a single hash value; BGR, building on top of Neven, eliminated the second check by lengthening the signature further by a short per-signer value. These two schemes were complex and had subtle security proofs.

OUR FRAMEWORK. We give a new framework for TDP-based SAS schemes, which unifies and simplifies prior work as well as leads to improved constructions. We observe that in all three prior TDP-based schemes, the central design question was how to process the aggregate-so-far together with the message before applying the hard direction of the TDP; in all three, it was accomplished using some combination of exclusive-or and random-oracle hash operations which were designed to ensure that the aggregate-so-far could be recovered during verification. In other words, achieving invertibility in order to enable verification was a major design constraint.

Our idea is to build invertibility explicitly into the scheme. In our scheme, pictured in Fig. 1, we process the aggregate-so-far via a public random permutation (modeled as an ideal cipher), kcyed by the message. In other words, our schemes are in the ideal *ideal cipher* model, where algorithms have access to a family of random permutations and their inverses. This model is typically used for blockcipher-based constructions, where a blockcipher like AES is modeled as an ideal cipher. In our work, the domain of the ideal cipher is that of the trapdoor permutation, which is usually much larger than the block-length of a typical block cipher like AES. Fortunately, as shown by a series of works [10,12–14] we can replace arbitrary-length ideal ciphers by using 8 rounds of Feistel network, and obtain the same security in the random oracle as in the ideal cipher model using indifferentiability arguments [23].

OUR RESULTS. Our framework not only simplifies prior work, but gives rise to more efficient aggregate signatures. Specifically, we obtain:

- A scheme that, like Neven's, does not require certified TDPs, but may permit shorter signatures than Neven's scheme, of length equal to the length of the TDP output.[1]
- A scheme that, like BGR, permits lazy verification, but retains constant-size signatures. This scheme is based on a stronger assumption of adaptive tag-based TDPs [20] instead of plain TDPs.

If one prefers to stay with plain TDPs, we also obtain a scheme that permits lazy verification and, like BGR, has signatures that grow with the number of signers, but still the signatures have the potential to be shorter than in BGR (with the same caveat as above). We do not compare computational costs of our scheme vs. Neven's and BGR's because the only difference is the (small) number of additional hashes, which is negligible compared to the cost of evaluating the TDP.

MAIN TECHNIQUE: CHAIN-TO-ZERO LEMMA. The security proofs for all our schemes are enabled by a lemma we prove about an ideal cipher keyed by descriptions of functions. We emphasize that the functions are unrelated to the ideal cipher itself, and that the cipher keyed by a function description results in permutation that is unrelated to the function. This lemma, which we call "Chain-to-Zero Lemma," states the following.

Let π_k denote the ideal cipher with key k. Recall that accessing π and π^{-1} requires querying an oracle. Let f and g denote functions with the same domain and range as π; the function descriptions will also be used as keys for π (again, we emphasize that the resulting permutations π_f and π_g have nothing to do with f and g as functions). Suppose for some a, $\pi_g(a) = b$, $f(b) = c$, and $\pi_f(c) = d$. We will say that a, b is *linked* to c, d. In our schemes, linking corresponds to consecutive steps of the verification algorithm.

A sequence of values in which each pair is linked to the next pair defines a *chain*. Signature verification will make sure that the last element of a chain is 0. The Chain-to-Zero Lemma says that if the last element of the chain is 0, then with overwhelming probability it was formed via queries to π^{-1} rather than to π. In our security proofs, this lemma means that we can program the relevant queries to π^{-1}, and therefore a forgery can be used to break the underlying TDP.

RSA-BASED INSTANTIATIONS. The schemes we obtain via our framework are proven secure under claw-freeness of the underlying TDP, or adaptive claw-freeness in the tag-based TDPs case. For plain-TDP-based schemes, this means

---

[1] For a comparison at the same security level, one must take into account losses in the security proofs. Unfortunately, the proofs of [10,12–14] are lossy, so currently we have to use a much larger domain size of the ideal cipher than the TDP output. However, we are optimistic tighter proofs will be found; see open problems below.

that we can use RSA assuming standard one-wayness. For the tag-based TDP scheme, we can use RSA under a stronger assumption called the instance-independent RSA assumption [25]. This instantiation hashes to the exponent (an idea originating from [18]), so verification is more expensive than for standard RSA.

PERSPECTIVE AND OPEN PROBLEMS. Compared to prior work, our framework pushes much of the complexity of security proofs to indifferentiability arguments that a Feistel network realizes an ideal cipher, and allows working with an ideal cipher as a clean abstraction. We point out two interesting directions for future work:

- Known proofs that a Feistel network is indifferentiable from an ideal cipher are lossy in the sense that the security guarantees obtained are weaker for a fixed domain size. We conjecture that a weaker property suffices to prove our Chain-to-Zero Lemma and can be realized via a tight proof. We leave proving or disproving this conjecture as an interesting direction for future work (and perhaps fewer Feistel rounds).
- The RSA-based instantiation of our tag-based TDP scheme has an expensive verification algorithm that performs a full exponentiation modulo N, and its security relies on a very strong assumption about RSA. It would be interesting to remove either of these drawbacks. We conjecture that one can actually prove a negative result here, namely that plain TDPs cannot be used to realize constant-size lazy-verifying SAS schemes in the RO model, in a black-box way.

Finally, we mention that an open problem is removing the use of ROs in TDP-based SAS schemes, although our framework does not shed any light on this issue.

2 Preliminaries

2.1 Notation and Conventions

ALGORITHMS. If A is an algorithm then $y \leftarrow A(x_1, \ldots, x_n; r)$ means we run A on inputs $x_1, \ldots, x_n$ and coins r and denote the output by y. By $y \leftarrow^{\$} A(x_1, \ldots, x_n)$ we denote the operation of picking r at random and letting $y \leftarrow A(x_1, \ldots, x_n; r)$. By $\Pr[P(x) : \ldots]$ we denote the probably that $P(x)$ holds after the elided experiment is executed. Unless otherwise indicated, an algorithm may be randomized. "PPT" stands for "probabilistic polynomial time" and "PT" stands for "polynomial time." The security parameter is denoted $k \in \mathbb{N}$. If we say that an algorithm is efficient we mean that it is PPT. All algorithms we consider are efficient unless indicated otherwise.

STRINGS AND VECTORS. We denote by $\{0,1\}^*$ the set of all (binary) strings, by $\{0,1\}^n$ the set of all strings of length $n \in N$, and by $\{0,1\}^{\geq n}$ the set of all strings of length *at least* $n \in \mathbb{N}$. If a, b are strings then $a \| b$ denotes an encoding from which a and b are uniquely recoverable. Vectors are denoted in boldface, for example $\mathbf{x}$. We sometimes use set notation with vectors, so that the notation $\mathbf{x} \leftarrow \mathbf{x} \cup \{x\}$ means that the next empty position in $\mathbf{x}$ is assigned x. If X is a random variable over some (finite) probability space then $\mathbf{E}[X]$ denotes its expectation.

TABLES. We use the term "table" to refer to an associative array implicitly initialized to empty. We use the pseudocode "Record $x = T[y]$ in the X-table" to mean that x is put at index y in table T. We use the pseudocode "X-table entry $x = T[y]$" to refer to x as the value at index y in table T.

SIMPLIFYING CONVENTIONS. We implicitly assume that an honestly generated secret key contains the matching public key. In experiments, we assume that an adversarially-provided public key can be parsed into the requisite form, and that if it contains a description of a function f then f is PT. This does *not* mean we assume public keys certified by a CA. Indeed, our requirement can be met by running f via inputting it and its input to some PT algorithm F, say universal machine that executes f on its input for a fixed amount of time; if f halts with some output then F outputs it as well, otherwise F outputs a default value. For simplicity, we also assume trapdoor permutations have domain $\{0,1\}^k$ but discuss RSA-based instantiations in Appendix A and Sect. 7.

2.2 Claw-Freeness

CLAW-FREE TRAPDOOR PERMUTATIONS. A *trapdoor permutation (TDP) gener-ator* $\mathcal{F}$ on input 1^k outputs a pair (f, f^{-1}, g) describing permutations f, g on $\{0,1\}^k$, and f^{-1} describing the inverse of f. For a claw-finding algorithm C and every $k \in \mathbb{N}$, define its *CF-advantage* against $\mathcal{F}$ as

$$\mathbf{Adv}^{\mathrm{cf}}_{\mathcal{F},C}(k) = \Pr\left[f(x) = g(x') \, : \, (f, f^{-1}, g) \leftarrow_{\$} \mathcal{F}; \; (x, x') \leftarrow_{\$} C(f, g) \right].$$

We say that $\mathcal{F}$ is a *claw-free* if $\mathbf{Adv}^{\mathrm{cf}}_{\mathcal{F},C}(\cdot)$ is negligible for every PPT C.

The permutation g is only used for security proofs. In our constructions, we will ignore g and write $(f, f^{-1}) \leftarrow_{\$} \mathcal{F}(1^k)$, corresponding to the standard notion of trapdoor permutations.

(ADAPTIVE) CLAW-FREE TAG-BASED TDPS. A *tag-based trapdoor permutation (TB-TDP) generator* $\mathcal{F}_{tag}$ with tag-space $\{0,1\}^\tau$ on input 1^k outputs a pair $(f_{tag}, f^{-1}_{tag}, g_{tag})$ describing functions of two inputs: $t \in \{0,1\}^\tau$ (called the *tag*) and $x \in \{0,1\}^k$. For every tag $t \in \{0,1\}^\tau$, $f_{tag}(t, \cdot), g_{tag}(t, \cdot)$ are permutations and $f^{-1}_{tag}(t, \cdot)$ is the inverse of $f_{tag}(t, \cdot)$. For a claw-finding algorithm C and every $k \in \mathbb{N}$, define its *ACF-advantage* against $\mathcal{F}_{tag}$ as

$$\mathbf{Adv}^{\mathrm{acf}}_{\mathcal{F},C}(k) = \Pr[f(t, x) = g(t, x') \, : \, (f, f^{-1}, g) \leftarrow_{\$} \mathcal{F}_{tag}(1^k); \; t \leftarrow_{\$} \{0,1\}^k;$$
$$(x, x') \leftarrow_{\$} C^{f^{-1}(\cdot, \cdot)}(f, g, t)]$$

where we require that C does not make a query of the form $f^{-1}(t, \cdot)$ to its oracle. We say that $\mathcal{F}$ is *adaptive claw-free* if $\mathbf{Adv}^{\mathrm{cf}}_{\mathcal{F},C}(\cdot)$ is negligible for every such PPT C.

Intuitively, $\mathcal{F}$ is adaptive claw-free if it is hard to find a claw even given access to an inversion oracle for f that may be called on tags other than the challenge tag. The notion of adaptive claw-freeness is new to this work. It is an extension of the notion of adaptive one-wayness introduced by Kiltz et al. [20].

INSTANTIATIONS. Dodis and Reyzin [16] show that any homomorphic or randomly self-reducible trapdoor permutation, in particular RSA [26] is claw-free (with a tight security reduction to one-wayness).

The notion of adaptive one-wayness for trapdoor permutations) (and more generally trapdoor functions) was introduced by Kiltz *et al.* [20]. They show that RSA gives rise to an adaptive one-way tag-based TDP under the instance-independent RSA assumption (II-RSA). In Appendix A we show that the same construction yields an adaptive claw-free tag-based TDP. In the construction, computing the forward direction is slower than for standard RSA, as it performs an exponentiation where the exponent is the length of the modulus rather than a small constant.

2.3   Random Oracle Model

In the *random oracle model* [2] all parties (all algorithms and adversaries) have oracle access to a function ("the random oracle") $H\colon \{0,1\}^* \to \{0,1\}^*$ where for every $x \in \{0,1\}^*$ the value of $H(x)$ is chosen uniformly at random of some desired output length. By using standard domain separation, it is equivalent to give all parties oracle access to an unlimited number of independent random oracles $H_1, H_2, \ldots \colon \{0,1\}^* \to \{0,1\}^*$. It is a well-known heuristic proposed by [2] to instantiate these oracles in practice via functions constructed appropriately from a cryptographic hash function.

2.4   Ideal Cipher Model

In the version of the *ideal cipher model* [27] we consider, all parties (again, all algorithms and adversaries) have oracle access to two functions ("the ideal cipher"):

$$\pi\colon \{0,1\}^* \times \{0,1\}^{\geq k} \to \{0,1\}^{\geq k} \quad \text{and} \quad \pi^{-1}\colon \{0,1\}^* \times \{0,1\}^{\geq k} \to \{0,1\}^{\geq k},$$

where the first is such that for each $K \in \{0,1\}^*$ and each input length $n \geq k$, $\pi(K, \cdot)$ is an independent random permutation on $\{0,1\}^n$. The second is such that for each $K \in \{0,1\}^*$ and each input length $n \geq k$, $\pi^{-1}(K, \cdot)$ is the inverse of $\pi(K, \cdot)$ on $\{0,1\}^n$. Such a model has typically been used to analyze blockcipher-based constructions in the symmetric-key setting (see, *e.g.*, [4]), where the key length is fixed to the key length of the blockcipher and the input length is fixed to the block length.

Our constructions are in the public-key setting, the key length will be unbounded, and the input length will be at least as long as the input length of a trapdoor permutation (say 2048 bits in the case of RSA). To implement such an ideal cipher in the random oracle model, one can use a Feistel network. Indeed, in their seminal work, Coron *et al.* [10] show that a 14-round Feistel network, where the round functions are independent random oracles, is indifferentiable in the sense of Maurer *et al.* [23] from a random permutation, which can then be used to implement the ideal cipher in a straightforward way. Essentially, indifferentiability implies that any reduction using the random permutation can be translated to one in the random oracle model. A subsequent sequence of works [12–14] show that 8 rounds is sufficient; the minimal number of rounds is still open but known to be at least six. Unfortunately, none of these works are "tight" in the sense that the resulting reduction in the random oracle model will be very loose. An interesting question for future work is whether a weaker notion than indifferentiability from an ideal cipher suffices in our constructions.

3 Sequential Aggregate Signatures

Sequential aggregate signatures (SAS) were introduced by Lysyanskaya *et al.* [22] and were subsequently studied by [1,5,7,17,21,24]. Following the work of Brogle *et al.* [7] and Fischlin *et al.* [17] (and in particular using terminology of the latter) we classify SAS schemes into two types: *general* and *history-free*. In a history-free scheme, the signing algorithm uses only on the current signer's secret key, the message, and the aggregate-so-far. In a general scheme, it may also use the public keys and messages of the *previous* signers.

3.1 The General Case

SYNTAX. A *(general) sequential aggregate signature* (SAS) scheme is a tuple SAS = (Kg, AggSign, AggVer) of algorithms defined as follows. The *key-generation* algorithm Kg on input 1^k outputs a public-key pk and matching secret-key sk. The *aggregate signing* algorithm AggSign on inputs a secret key sk_i, message m_i, aggregate-so-far σ_{i-1} and a list of pairs of public keys and messages $((pk_1, m_1), \ldots, (pk_{i-1}, m_{i-1}))$ outputs a new aggregate signature σ_i. The *aggregate verification* algorithm AggVer on inputs a list of public keys and messages $(pk_1, m_1), \ldots, (pk_i, m_i)$ and an aggregate signature σ_i outputs a bit.

SECURITY. The security notion we use is the same as that in [7,24] and originates from [1], who strengthen the original notion of [22] to allow repeating public keys (which they call "unrestricted" SAS). To a general SAS scheme SAS and a forger F we associate for every $k \in \mathbb{N}$ a *(general) SAS-unforgeability* experiment $\mathbf{Exp}_{\mathsf{SAS},F}^{\mathrm{sas\text{-}uf}}(k)$ that runs in three phases:

- *Setup:* The experiment generates $(pk, sk) \leftarrow_\$ \mathsf{Kg}(1^k)$.
- *Attack:* Next, the experiment runs F on input pk with oracle access to AggSign$(sk, \cdot, \cdot, \cdot)$.

- *Forgery:* Eventually, F halts with output parsed as $(pk_1, m_1), \ldots,$ $(pk_n, m_n), \sigma$. The experiment outputs 1 iff: (1) $\mathsf{AggVer}((pk_1, m_1), \ldots,$ $(pk_n, m_n), \sigma)$ outputs 1, (2) $pk_{i^*} = pk$ for some $1 \leq i^* \leq n$, and (3) F did not make an oracle query of the form $\mathsf{AggSign}(sk, m_{i^*}, ((pk_1, m_1),$ $\ldots, (pk_{i^*-1}, m_{i^*-1})))$.

Define the *(general) SAS-unforgeability advantage* of F as

$$\mathbf{Adv}_{\mathsf{SAS}, F}^{\text{sas-uf}}(k) = \Pr\left[\, \mathbf{Exp}_{\mathsf{SAS}, F}^{\text{sas-uf}}(k) \text{ outputs } 1 \,\right].$$

3.2   The History-Free Case

SYNTAX. A *history-free sequential aggregate signature* (HF-SAS) scheme is a tuple $\mathsf{HF\text{-}SAS} = (\mathsf{Kg}, \mathsf{AggSign}, \mathsf{AggVer})$ of algorithms defined as follows. The *key-generation* algorithm Kg on input 1^k outputs a public-key pk and matching secret-key sk. The *history-free aggregate signing* algorithm $\mathsf{AggSign}$ on inputs sk, m, σ' outputs a new aggregate signature σ. The *aggregate verification* algorithm AggVer on inputs a list of public key and messages $(pk_1, m_1), \ldots, (pk_i, m_i)$ and aggregate signature σ outputs a bit.

SECURITY. Security in the history-free case is more restrictive on what is considered to be a forgery by the adversary than in the general case. In particular, we follow Brogle *et al.* [7] in our formulation of security here but leave investigation of a stronger security model due to Fischlin *et al.* [17] for furtur work. (As noted by [7], this strengthening is not needed in applications such as BGPsec.) To an HF-SAS scheme HF-SAS and a forger F be a forger we associate for every $k \in \mathbb{N}$ a *history-free SAS unforgeability* experiment $\mathbf{Exp}_{\mathsf{SAS}, F}^{\text{hf-sas-uf}}(k)$ that runs in three phases:

- *Setup:* The experiment generates $(pk, sk) \leftarrow_{\$} \mathsf{Kg}(1^k)$.
- *Attack:* Next, the experiment runs F on input pk with oracle access to $\mathsf{AggSign}(sk, \cdot, \cdot)$.
- *Forgery:* Eventually, F halts with output parsed as $(pk_1, m_1), \ldots,$ $(pk_n, m_n), \sigma$. The experiment outputs 1 iff: (1) $\mathsf{AggVer}((pk_1, m_1), \ldots,$ $(pk_n, m_n), \sigma)$ outputs 1, (2) $pk_{i^*} = pk$ for some $1 \leq i^* \leq n$, and (3) F did not make an oracle query of the form $\mathsf{AggSign}(sk, m_{i^*}, \cdot)$.

Define the *history-free SAS-unforgeability advantage* of F as

$$\mathbf{Adv}_{\mathsf{HF\text{-}SAS}, F}^{\text{hf-sas-uf}}(k) = \Pr\left[\, \mathbf{Exp}_{\mathsf{HF\text{-}SAS}, F}^{\text{hf-sas-uf}}(k) \text{ outputs } 1 \,\right].$$

3.3   Message Recovery

We also consider sequential aggregate signature schemes with *message recovery*, following [3,24]. The goal is to save on bandwidth. Here we replace the verification algorithm by a recovery algorithm, which we view as taking as inputs a list of public keys and an aggregate signature and outputting either a list of messages, with the intended meaning that the verifier accepts each message as authentic under the respective public key, or $\perp$, indicating the aggregate signature is rejected.

4 Our Basic Schemes

We give three basic schemes: a general scheme (where the signing algorithm uses the public keys and messages of the previous signers in addition to the current signer's secret key and message), and two history-free schemes (where the signing algorithm uses only the current signer's secret key and message). In this section we only present the constructions and security theorems. We postpone the proofs since we later give our main lemma that unifies the proofs.

4.1 SAS₁: A General Scheme

Let $\mathcal{F}$ be a trapdoor permutation generator. Define $\mathsf{SAS}_1[\mathcal{F}] = (\mathsf{Kg}, \mathsf{AggSign}, \mathsf{AggVer})$ in the ideal cipher model with input length of π and π^{-1} fixed to $k \in \mathbb{N}$, and where $\mathsf{Kg}(1^k)$ outputs (f, f^{-1}) generated via $\mathcal{F}(1^k)$ and:

Alg $\mathsf{AggSign}(f_i^{-1}, m_i, \sigma_{i-1}, (f_1, m_1), \ldots,$
$(f_{i-1}, m_{i-1}))$:
    //This is for the ith signer in the sequence:
    If $\mathsf{AggVer}((f_1, m_1), \ldots, (f_{i-1}, m_{i-1}), \sigma_{i-1})$
      outputs 0 then
        Return $\perp$
    If $i = 1$ then $\sigma_{i-1} \leftarrow 0^k$
    $x_{i-1} \leftarrow \sigma_{i-1}$; $K_i \leftarrow f_1 \| m_1 \| \ldots \| f_i \| m_i$
    $y_i \leftarrow \pi^{-1}(K_i, x_{i-1})$; $x_i \leftarrow f_i^{-1}(y_i)$; $\sigma_i \leftarrow x_i$
    Return σ_i

Alg $\mathsf{AggVer}((f_1, m_1), \ldots,$
$(f_n, m_n), \sigma)$:
    $x_n \leftarrow \sigma$
    For $i = n$ down to 1 do:
      $y_i \leftarrow f_i(x_i)$
      $K \leftarrow f_1 \| m_1 \| \ldots \| f_i \| m_i$
      $x_{i-1} \leftarrow \pi(K_i, y_i)$
    If $x_0 = 0^k$ then return 1
    Else return 0

Theorem 1. *Suppose $\mathcal{F}$ is claw-free. Then $\mathsf{SAS}_1[\mathcal{F}]$ is aggregate-unforgeable in the ideal cipher model. In particular, suppose there is a forger F against $\mathsf{SAS}_1[\mathcal{F}]$ making at most q_π ideal cipher queries and at most q_S signing queries. Then there is a claw-finding algorithm C against $\mathcal{F}$ such that for every $k \in \mathbb{N}$*

$$\mathbf{Adv}^{\text{sas-ufcma}}_{\mathsf{SAS}_1[\mathcal{F}], F}(k) \leq \left(\frac{1}{1/(e(q_S + 1)) - q_\pi/2^k} \right) \cdot \mathbf{Adv}^{\text{cf}}_{\mathcal{F}, C}(k) + q_\pi^2/2^k.$$

The running-time of C is that of F plus minor bookkeeping.

4.2 SAS₂: A History-Free Scheme with Randomized Signing

Let $\mathcal{F}$ be a trapdoor permutation generator and $\rho = \rho(k)$ be an integer parameter. Define $\mathsf{SAS}_2[\mathcal{F}] = (\mathsf{Kg}, \mathsf{AggSign}, \mathsf{AggVer})$ where $\mathsf{Kg}(1^k)$ outputs (f, f^{-1}) generated via $\mathcal{F}(1^k)$ and:

Algorithm $\mathsf{AggSign}(f_i^{-1}, m_i, \sigma_{i-1})$:
//This is for the ith signer in the sequence:
If $i = 1$ then $x_0 \leftarrow 0^k$ and $r_0 \leftarrow \varepsilon$
Else $(x_{i-1}, \mathbf{r}_{i-1}) \leftarrow \sigma_{i-1}$
$r_i \leftarrow_{\$} \{0,1\}^{\rho}$; $K_i \leftarrow f_i \| m_i \| r_i$
$y_i \leftarrow \pi^{-1}(K_i, x_{i-1})$
$x_i \leftarrow f_i^{-1}(y_i)$; Append r_i to $\mathbf{r}_{i-1}$
$\sigma_i \leftarrow (x_i, \mathbf{r}_i)$
Return σ_i

Algorithm $\mathsf{AggVer}((f_1, m_1),$
$\dots, (f_n, m_n), \sigma)$:
$(\sigma_n, (r_1, \dots, r_n)) \leftarrow \sigma$
$x_n \leftarrow \sigma_n$
For $i = n$ down to 1 do:
$\quad y_i \leftarrow f_i(x_i)$
$\quad K \leftarrow f_i \| m_i \| r_i$
$\quad x_{i-1} \leftarrow \pi(K_i, y_i)$
If $x_0 = 0^k$ then return 1
Else return 0

Theorem 2. *Suppose $\mathcal{F}$ is claw-free. Then $\mathsf{SAS}_2[\mathcal{F}]$ is aggregate-unforgeable in the ideal cipher model. In particular, suppose there is a forger F against $\mathsf{SAS}_2[\mathcal{F}]$ making at most q_H queries to H, at most q_π queries to the ideal cipher, and at most q_S signing queries. Then there is a claw-finding algorithm C against $\mathcal{F}$ such that for every $k \in \mathbb{N}$*

$$\mathbf{Adv}^{\text{hf-sas-ufcma}}_{\mathsf{SAS}_2[\mathcal{F}], F}(k) \leq \frac{2^{\rho+k}}{(2^\rho - q_S^2)(2^k - q_\pi^2)} \cdot \mathbf{Adv}^{\text{cf}}_{\mathcal{F}, C}(k) + q_\pi^2/2^k.$$

The running-time of C is that of F plus minor bookkeeping.

4.3 SAS₃: A History-Free Scheme with Deterministic Signing

To get intuition, we first sketch how to forge against $\mathsf{SAS}_2[\mathcal{F}]$ when randomness r_i is simply omitted. Let $K_i = f_i \| m_i$ be the ideal cipher key that the i-th signer "thinks" it is using. Let $K_i' = f_i \| m_i'$ be the ideal cipher key derived from a message m_i' that it will be duped into signing, and let x_{i-1}' be the real aggregate-so-far. We show how to derive a corresponding fake aggregate-so-far x_{i-1}. Let $y_i = \pi^{-1}(K_i, x_{i-1})$ be the value that the i-th signer will apply f_i^{-1} to. We want to make $y_i = \pi^{-1}(K_i', x_{i-1}')$, so that the i-th signer is duped. But this is easy: In order to force $y_i = \pi^{-1}(K_i', x_{i-1}')$, we only have to choose $\pi^{-1}(K_i, x_{i-1}) = \pi^{-1}(K_i', x_{i-1}')$ and therefore $x_{i-1} = \pi(K_i, \pi^{-1}(K_i', x_{i-1}'))$. In essence, to solve this issue we make f_i depend on m_i as well.

Our construction. Let $\mathcal{F}_{tag}$ be a tag-based trapdoor permutation with tag-space $\{0,1\}^\tau$. Let $H \colon \{0,1\}^* \to \{0,1\}^\tau$ be a hash function modeled as a random oracle. Define $\mathsf{SAS}_3[\mathcal{F}] = (\mathsf{Kg}, \mathsf{AggSign}, \mathsf{AggVer})$ where $\mathsf{Kg}(1^k)$ outputs (f, f^{-1}) generated via $\mathcal{F}_{tag}(1^k)$ and:

Algorithm AggSign($f_i^{-1}, m_i, \sigma_{i-1}$):

//This is for the ith signer in the sequence:

$x_{i-1} \leftarrow \sigma_{i-1}$

If $i = 1$ then $\sigma_{i-1} \leftarrow 0^k$

$K_i \leftarrow f_i \| m_i$

$y_i \leftarrow \pi^{-1}(K_i, x_{i-1})$

$t_i \leftarrow H(f_i \| m_i)$

$x_i \leftarrow f_i^{-1}(t_i, y_i)$

Return $\sigma_i = x_i$

Algorithm AggVer($((f_1, m_1),$
$\dots, (f_n, m_n), \sigma)$:

$x_n \leftarrow \sigma$

For $i = n$ down to 1 do:

  $t_i \leftarrow H(f_i \| m_i)$

  $y_i \leftarrow f_i(t_i x_i)$

  $K \leftarrow f_i \| m_i \| r_i$

  $x_{i-1} \leftarrow \pi(K_i, y_i)$

If $x_0 = 0^k$ then return 1

Else return 0

Theorem 3. *Suppose $\mathcal{F}_{tag}$ is adaptive claw-free. Then $\mathsf{SAS}_3[\mathcal{F}]$ is aggregate-unforgeable in the ideal cipher and random oracle models. In particular, suppose there is a forger F against $\mathsf{SAS}_3[\mathcal{F}]$ making at most q_H queries to the random oracle and at most q_π queries to the ideal cipher. Then there is a claw-finding algorithm C against $\mathcal{F}_{tag}$ such that for every $k \in \mathbb{N}$*

$$\mathbf{Adv}^{\text{hf-sas-ufcma}}_{\mathsf{SAS}_3[\mathcal{F}], F}(k) \leq \frac{2^{k+\tau}}{(2^k - q_\pi^2)(2^\tau - q_H)} \cdot \mathbf{Adv}^{\text{acf}}_{\mathcal{F}_{tag}, C}(k) + q_\pi^2/2^k.$$

The running-time of C is that of F plus minor bookkeeping.

5 The Chain-to-Zero Lemma

Here we give a main lemma that will unify security analyses of our schemes.

THE SETTING. Consider an adversary A executing in the ideal cipher model where the input and output length of the ideal cipher is fixed to $k \in \mathbb{N}$, and where a key of the ideal cipher also describes a function $f: \{0,1\}^k \to \{0,1\}^k$ unrelated to the function $\pi: f \times \{0,1\}^k \to \{0,1\}^k$. That is, A may submit a query to π of the form f, y to receive a random $x \in \{0,1\}^k$, or a query f, x to π^{-1} to receive a random $y \in \{0,1\}^k$.[2] For simplicity, we assume that A does not make the same query twice or ask redundant queries, *i.e.*, does not ask for $\pi^{-1}[f, x]$ if it already asked for $\pi[f, y]$ for some y and got x in response, or vice versa.

LINKING. We say that π-table entry $x_1 = \pi[f_2, y_2]$ is *linked to* π-table entry $x_0 = \pi[f_1, y_1]$ if $f_1(x_1) = y_1$. For intuition, one can think of a π-table entry $x_0 = \pi[f_1, y_1]$ as indicating that f_1 applied to something (which in our constructions correspond to an aggregate-so-far) yielded y_1; this entry is linked if the "something" is also stored in the π-table. See Fig. 2 for a depiction. We inductively define a π-table entry $x = \pi[f, y]$ to be *chained to zero* if $x = 0^k$ or it is linked to an entry that is chained to zero. The *length of the chain* is defined naturally, where a chain consisting of a single entry $0^k = \pi[f_1, y_1]$ has length one. We say that π-table entry $x = \pi[f, y]$ is a *forward query* if it is defined upon A making a π query. Similarly, we say that π-table entry $x = \pi[f, y]$ is a *backward query* if it is defined upon A making a π^{-1} query.

---

[2] In the game, we denote by "y" an input to π and by "x" its output for consistency with our constructions in Sect. 4.

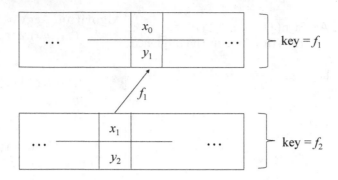

Fig. 2. A link between ideal cipher entries.

Lemma 4 (Chain-to-Zero Lemma). *Consider an execution A in which it makes at most q queries. Define BAD_π to be the event that some forward query gets chained to zero. Then $\Pr[\mathsf{BAD}_\pi] \leq q^2/2^k$.*

In the proof we will make use of the following claims.

Claim. Let $f \colon \{0,1\}^k \to \{0,1\}^k$. Consider choosing random $y_1, \ldots, y_q \in \{0,1\}^k$, and let $Y_{\max}$ be the random variable giving the maximum over i of the size of the pre-image set of $f^{-1}(y_i)$. Then $\mathbf{E}[Y_{\max}] = q$.

Proof. Let Y_i be the random variable giving the size of the pre-image set of $f^{-1}(y_i)$. We compute

$$\mathbf{E}[Y_{\max}] \;=\; \sum_{x=0}^{\infty} \Pr[Y_{\max} > x] \;\leq\; \sum_{x=0}^{\infty}\sum_{i=1}^{q} \Pr[Y_i > x] \;=\; \sum_{i=1}^{q} \mathbf{E}[Y_i] \;=\; q.$$

Above, for the first (in)equality we the fact that for a nonnegative integer-valued random variable X, $\mathbf{E}[X] = \sum_{x=0}^{\infty} \Pr[X > x]$. For the second inequality we use a union bound. For the last (in)equality we use that $E[Y_i] = 1$, because the expectation is simply the sum all pre-image set sizes divided by the total number of points. ∎

Now define Coll_1 to be the event that a forward query $x_i = \pi[f_{i+1}, y_{i+1}]$ is such that it is linked to some already existing backward query $x_{i-1} = \pi[f_i, y_i]$, and Coll_2 to be the event that a backward query $x_{i-1} = \pi[f_i, y_i]$ is such that it is linked to some already existing query $x_i = \pi[f_{i+1}, y_{i+1}]$ (either forward or backward). Define $\mathsf{Coll} = \mathsf{Coll}_1 \vee \mathsf{Coll}_2$.

Claim. In an execution A as above in which it makes at most q queries, we have $\Pr[\mathsf{Coll}] \leq q^2/2^k$.

Proof. We say that a forward query *collides* if satisfies the condition for Coll_1, and similarly for a backward query and Coll_2. After at most j backward queries have been made, define the random variable P_j to give the maximum over all such queries of the size of the pre-image set $f^{-1}(y)$. We claim that after i queries, the probability a forward query collides is at most $i/2^k$. This is because for such a forward query $x = \pi[f, y]$, we have

$$\Pr[x = \pi[f, y] \text{ collides}] \leq \sum_{j=1}^{\infty} j \cdot \Pr[P_i = j] \cdot 2^{-k} = \mathbf{E}[P_i] \cdot 2^{-k} \leq i \cdot 2^{-k},$$

where the last inequality is by the claim above.

Now if $x_{i-1} = \pi[f_i, y_i]$ is a backward query then y_i is random and independent, while for any existing query $x_i = \pi[f_{i+1}, y_{i+1}]$ we know $f_i(x_i)$ is already defined before y_i is chosen. So the probability $f_i(x_i) = y_i$ is 2^{-k}.

Hence, by a union bound the total probability of collision is at most $q^2/2^k$. ∎

We are now ready to prove our main lemma.

Proof (of Lemma 4). By a conditioning argument, we have

$$\Pr[\mathsf{BAD}_\pi] \leq \Pr[\mathsf{BAD}_\pi \mid \overline{\mathsf{Coll}}] + \Pr[\mathsf{Coll}]$$
$$\leq \Pr[\mathsf{BAD}_\pi \mid \overline{\mathsf{Coll}}] + q^2/2^k$$

using Claim 5.

Now if BAD_π occurs there are two possibilities, either some forward query $x = \pi[f, y]$ gets chained to zero by a chain of length $i = 1$, or it gets chained to zero by a chain of length $i > 1$. If $i = 1$ this would mean that $x = 0^k$. Since x is random and independent, the probability of this is 2^{-k}. Summing over all possible queries, the probability that any forward query gets chained to zero by a chain of length one is at most $q/2^k$.

Now suppose forward query $x_i = \pi[f_{i+1}, y_{i+1}]$ gets chained to zero by a chain of length $i > 1$. Then there are two possibilities: this query is chained to zero immediately when it is defined, or later.

The first possibility would require that there is a π-table entry $x_{i-1} = \pi[f_i, y_i]$ such that $f_i(x_i) = y_i$ and the entry is already chained to zero by a chain of length $i - 1$. By induction on i, $x_{i-1} = \pi[f_i, y_i]$ is a backward query, so it would cause a collision.

For the second possibility, consider a query that completes the chain from $x_{i-1} = \pi[f_i, y_i]$ to zero. At the time it is asked, all the other entries in the chain are already fixed. That query itself must be chained to zero via a chain of length j, for some $1 \leq j \leq i - 1$, so let us denote it by $x_{j-1} = \pi[f_j, y_j]$. The query number $j+1$ in the chain, which we denote by $x_j = \pi[f_{j+1}, y_{j+1}]$, must be linked to query number j, i.e., it must hold that $f_j(x_j) = y_j$. Because query number $j - 1$ must be chained to zero, again by (strong) induction on i it must be a backward query, so it would cause a collision.

This completes the proof. ∎

Remark 5. The Chain-to-Zero Lemma can be extended in the following way. Instead of functions $f\colon \{0,1\}^k \to \{0,1\}^k$ we allow functions $f\colon \{0,1\}^n \to \{0,1\}^n$, for any $n \geq k$, choose x and y in the game's pseudocode for answering A's queries of length n defined in the query, and define $x = \pi[f,y]$ to be *chained to zero* if $x = 0^k z^{n-k}$ for any $z \in \{0,1\}^{n-k}$, where n is the input length of f. The statement of the lemma remains unchanged.

6   Proofs for the Basic Schemes

Here we give security proofs of our basic schemes, using the Chain-to-Zero Lemma. To simplify the proofs, we assume that no query of forger F to the ideal cipher is asked twice (even in reverse direction) and that all queries needed in a signing query and for verifying the final forgery are already asked.

6.1   Proof of Theorem 1

We give a simpler proof that loses a factor q_π in the reduction rather than q_S; the improved reduction can be obtained via application of Coron's technique using biased coin flipping [9].

CLAW FINDER. Claw-finding algorithm C is given in Fig. 3.

ANALYSIS. Let's consider executions of the general SAS-unforgeability experiment with F and of the claw-finding experiment with C over a common set of random coin sequences, where the same coins are used for choices common across both experiments. Using the terminology of Sect. 5, in the execution of C in its claw-finding experiment let BAD_π be the event that any forward query is chained to zero and ABORT be the event that C aborts. Let FORGE be the event that F produces a valid forgery in its general SAS-unforgeability experiment. Then we have

$$\mathbf{Adv}^{\mathrm{cf}}_{\mathcal{F},C}(k) \geq \Pr\left[\mathsf{FORGE} \wedge \overline{\mathsf{ABORT}} \wedge \overline{\mathsf{BAD}_\pi}\right]$$
$$= \Pr\left[\mathsf{FORGE} \mid \overline{\mathsf{ABORT}} \wedge \overline{\mathsf{BAD}_\pi}\right] \cdot \Pr\left[\overline{\mathsf{ABORT}} \mid \overline{\mathsf{BAD}_\pi}\right] \cdot$$
$$\Pr\left[\overline{\mathsf{BAD}_\pi}\right].$$

The first inequality above is due to the fact that on coin sequences where C does not abort, the execution of F in its experiment and when run by C is identical. Hence, on such coin sequences F also forges in its execution by C.

Now by the Chain-to-Zero Lemma (Lemma 4), we have

$$\Pr\left[\overline{\mathsf{BAD}_\pi}\right] \geq 1 - q_\pi^2/2^k.$$

Next we claim that

$$\Pr\left[\overline{\mathsf{ABORT}} \mid \overline{\mathsf{BAD}_\pi}\right] \geq 1/q_\pi.$$

To see this, note that there are two places C could abort: answering a signing query, or after receiving the final forgery. In answering a signing query, we know

Algorithm $C(f^*, g^*)$:
  $ctr \leftarrow 0$; $ctr^* \leftarrow_\$ \{1, \ldots, q_\pi\}$
  Run F on input f^*, answering its queries as follows:
    On π-query $f_1 \| m_1 \| \ldots \| f_i \| m_i, y$ do:
      $x \leftarrow_\$ \{0, 1\}^k$
      Record $\pi[f_1 \| m_1 \| \ldots \| f_i \| m_i, y] = x$ in the π-table ; Return x
    On π^{-1}-query $f_1 \| m_1 \| \ldots \| f_i \| m_i, x$ do:
      If $f_i = f^*$ then
        $ctr \leftarrow ctr + 1$
        If $ctr = ctr^*$ then
          $x' \leftarrow_\$ \{0, 1\}^k$; $y \leftarrow g^*(x')$; Record $g^*[x'] = y$ in the g^*-table
          Record $\pi[f_1 \| m_1 \| \ldots \| f_i \| m_i, y] = x$ in the π-table ; Return y
      Else
          $x' \leftarrow_\$ \{0, 1\}^k$; $y \leftarrow f^*(x')$; Record $f^*[x'] = y$ in the f^*-table
          Record $\pi[f_1 \| m_1 \| \ldots \| f_i \| m_i, y] = x$ in the π-table ; Return y
    On signing query $m_i, \sigma_{i-1}, (f_1, m_1), \ldots, (f_{i-1}, m_{i-1})$ do:
      If $\mathsf{AggVer}((f_1, m_1), \ldots, (f_{i-1}, m_{i-1}), \sigma_{i-1})$ outputs 0 then return $\bot$
      $x_{i-1} \leftarrow \sigma_{i-1}$; $y_i \leftarrow \pi^{-1}[f_1 \| m_1 \ldots f_{i-1} \| m_{i-1} \| f^* \| m_i, x_{i-1}]$
      If y_i is not in the f^*-table then abort
      Else let x_i be the index of y_i in the f^*-table
      Return $\sigma = x_i$
  Let $(f_1^*, m_1^*), \ldots, (f_n^*, m_n^*), \sigma^*$ be the output of F
  If $\mathsf{AggVer}((f_1^*, m_1^*), \ldots, (f_n^*, m_n^*), \sigma^*)$ outputs 0 then return $\bot$
  If there does not exist $1 \le i^* \le n$ such that $f_{i^*}^* = f^*$ then return $\bot$
  $x_n^* \leftarrow \sigma^*$
  For $i = n$ down to $i^* + 1$ do:
    $y_i^* \leftarrow f_i^*(x_i^*)$
    $x_{i-1}^* \leftarrow \pi[f_1^* \| m_1^* \| \ldots \| f_i^* \| m_i^*, y_i^*]$
  $y_{i^*}^* \leftarrow f^*(x_{i^*}^*)$
  If $y_{i^*}^*$ is not in the g^*-table then abort
  Else let x_{i^*}' be the index of $y_{i^*}^*$ in the g^*-table
  Return $(x_{i^*}^*, x_{i^*}')$

Fig. 3. Claw-finder C for the proof of Theorem 1.

that the aggregate-so-far must verify (otherwise C returns $\bot$), so π-table entry $x_{i-1} = \pi[f_1 \| m_1 \| \ldots \| f^* \| m_i, y_i]$ is chained to zero, and since we are conditioning on $\overline{\mathsf{BAD}_\pi}$ it must be a backward query. Similarly, upon receiving the F's final output, if it is a valid forgery then π-table entry $x_{i^*-1}^* = \pi[f_1^* \| m_1^* \| \ldots \| f^* \| m_{i^*}^*, y_{i^*}^*]$ must also be a backward query. So if C chooses ctr^* to be such that $x_{i^*-1}^* = \pi[f_1^* \| m_1^* \| \ldots \| f^* \| m_{i^*}^*, y_{i^*}^*]$ was defined on the ctr^*-th query, then C does not abort. This happens with probability at least $1/q_\pi$ since ctr^* is random and independent.

To complete the proof, we claim that

$$\Pr\left[\,\mathsf{FORGE} \mid \overline{\mathsf{ABORT}} \;\wedge\; \overline{\mathsf{BAD}_\pi}\,\right] \geq \mathbf{Adv}^{\mathrm{sas\text{-}ufcma}}_{\mathsf{SAS}_1[\mathcal{F}],F}(k) - q_\pi^2/2^k.$$

To see this, first note that $\overline{\mathsf{ABORT}}$ is independent of FORGE because the random choices made by C in determining whether to abort in its claw-finding experiment do not affect whether F forges in its SAS-unforgeability experiment. Thus

$$\Pr\left[\,\mathsf{FORGE} \mid \overline{\mathsf{ABORT}} \;\wedge\; \overline{\mathsf{BAD}_\pi}\,\right] = \Pr\left[\,\mathsf{FORGE} \mid \overline{\mathsf{BAD}_\pi}\,\right].$$

Now

$$
\begin{aligned}
\Pr\left[\,\mathsf{FORGE} \mid \overline{\mathsf{BAD}_\pi}\,\right]
&= \frac{\Pr[\,\mathsf{FORGE}\,] - \Pr[\,\mathsf{FORGE} \mid \mathsf{BAD}_\pi\,] \cdot \Pr[\,\mathsf{BAD}_\pi\,]}{\Pr\left[\,\overline{\mathsf{BAD}_\pi}\,\right]} \\
&\geq \Pr[\,\mathsf{FORGE}\,] - \Pr[\,\mathsf{BAD}_\pi\,] \\
&\geq \Pr[\,\mathsf{FORGE}\,] - q_\pi^2/2^k \\
&= \mathbf{Adv}^{\mathrm{sas\text{-}ufcma}}_{\mathsf{SAS}_1[\mathcal{F}],F}(k) - q_\pi^2/2^k.
\end{aligned}
$$

Combining the above, we have

$$\mathbf{Adv}^{\mathrm{cf}}_{\mathcal{F},C}(k) \geq \left(\mathbf{Adv}^{\mathrm{sas\text{-}ufcma}}_{\mathsf{SAS}_1[\mathcal{F}],F}(k) - q_\pi^2/2^k\right) \cdot \left(1/q_\pi - q_\pi/2^k\right)$$

and rearranging yields the theorem. ∎

6.2   Proof of Theorem 2

CLAW FINDER. Claw-finding algorithm C is given in Fig. 4.

ANALYSIS. Again, let's consider executions of the general SAS-unforgeability experiment with F and of the claw-finding experiment with C over a common set of random coin sequences with the same coins used for common choices across both experiments. Using the terminology of Sect. 5, in the execution of C in its claw-finding experiment let BAD_π be the event that any forward query gets chained to zero. Also in the execution of C in its experiment, let BAD_r be the event that π-table entry $\pi[f\|m\|r,y]$ defined when C answers signing query of F was previously defined. Let FORGE be the event that F produces a valid forgery in its experiment. We claim that

$$
\begin{aligned}
\mathbf{Adv}^{\mathrm{cf}}_{\mathcal{F},C}(k)
&\geq \Pr\left[\,\mathsf{FORGE} \wedge \overline{\mathsf{BAD}_r} \wedge \overline{\mathsf{BAD}_\pi}\,\right] \\
&= \Pr\left[\,\mathsf{FORGE} \mid \overline{\mathsf{BAD}_r} \wedge \overline{\mathsf{BAD}_\pi}\,\right] \cdot \Pr\left[\,\overline{\mathsf{BAD}_r} \mid \overline{\mathsf{BAD}_\pi}\,\right] \cdot \Pr\left[\,\overline{\mathsf{BAD}_\pi}\,\right] \\
&\geq \Pr\left[\,\mathsf{FORGE} \mid \overline{\mathsf{BAD}_r} \wedge \overline{\mathsf{BAD}_\pi}\,\right] \cdot \Pr\left[\,\overline{\mathsf{BAD}_r} \mid \overline{\mathsf{BAD}_\pi}\,\right] \cdot \left(1 - q_\pi^2/2^k\right)
\end{aligned}
$$

Above, the first inequality is because on a coin sequences on which F forges in its experiment and on which no π-table entry defined when C answers a signing query in its experiment was previously defined, the executions of both

Algorithm $C(f^*, g^*)$:

Run F on input f^*, answering its queries as follows:

On π-query $f\|m\|r, y$ do:

$\quad x \leftarrow_\$ \{0,1\}^k$

$\quad$ Record $\pi[f\|m\|r, y] = x$ in the π-table

$\quad$ Return x

On π^{-1} query $f\|m\|r, x$ do:

$\quad x' \leftarrow_\$ \{0,1\}^k \,; \, y \leftarrow g^*(x')$

$\quad$ Record $g^*[x'] = y$ in the g^*-table

$\quad$ Record $\pi[f\|m\|r, y] = x$ in the π-table

$\quad$ Return y

On signing query m, σ do:

$\quad (x_{i-1}, \mathbf{r}) \leftarrow \sigma \,; \, r \leftarrow_\$ \{0,1\}^\rho$

$\quad x_i \leftarrow_\$ \{0,1\}^k \,; \, y_i \leftarrow f(x)$

$\quad$ Record $\pi[f\|m\|r, x_{i-1}] = y_i$ in the π-table

$\quad \mathbf{r} \leftarrow \mathbf{r} \cup \{r\} \,; \, \sigma \leftarrow (x_i, \mathbf{r})$

$\quad$ Return σ

Let $(f_1^*, m_1^*), \ldots, (f_n^*, m_n^*), \sigma^*$ be the output of F

If $\mathsf{AggVer}((f_1^*, m_1^*), \ldots, (f_n^*, m_n^*), \sigma^*)$ outputs 0 then return $\bot$

If there does not exist $1 \le i^* \le n$ such that $f_{i^*}^* = f^*$ then return $\bot$

$(x_n^*, \mathbf{r}^*) \leftarrow \sigma^*$

For $i = n$ down to $i^* + 1$ do:

$\quad y_i^* \leftarrow f_i^*(x_i^*)$

$\quad x_{i-1}^* \leftarrow \pi[f_i^*\|m_i^*\|r_i^*, y_i^*]$

$y_{i^*}^* \leftarrow f^*(x_{i^*}^*)$

Let x_{i^*}' be the index of y_{i^*} in the g^*-table

Return $(x_{i^*}^*, x_{i^*}')$

Fig. 4. Claw-finder C for the proof of Theorem 2.

experiments are identical. Hence, on such coin sequences F also forges in its execution by C. Moreover, since the final output of F is a valid forgery, we know that π-table entry $x_{i^*-1}^* = \pi[f^*\|m_{i^*}^*\|r_{i^*}^*, y_{i^*}]$ is chained to zero. Since we are conditioning on $\overline{\mathsf{BAD}_\pi}$, the query on which the above π-table entry is defined must be a backward query, and since C populates the g^*-table on backwards queries, on such executions it can successfully find a claw. Finally, the last line is by the Chain-to-Zero Lemma.

Now we claim $\Pr\left[\mathsf{BAD}_r \mid \overline{\mathsf{BAD}_\pi}\right] \le q_S^2/2^\rho$. This is because on each signing query r is chosen independently at random, in other words BAD_r and BAD_π are independent, and the probability that $x = \pi[(f, m, r), y]$ is already defined on a given signing query is at most $q_S/2^\rho$. Summing over all signing queries yields the claim.

Finally, we compute

$$\Pr\left[\text{FORGE} \mid \overline{\text{BAD}_r} \wedge \overline{\text{BAD}_\pi}\right] =$$
$$\frac{\Pr\left[\text{FORGE}\right] - \Pr\left[\text{FORGE} \mid \text{BAD}_r \wedge \text{BAD}_\pi\right] \cdot \Pr\left[\text{BAD}_r \wedge \text{BAD}_\pi\right]}{\Pr\left[\overline{\text{BAD}_r} \wedge \overline{\text{BAD}_\pi}\right]}$$
$$\geq \Pr\left[\text{FORGE}\right] - \Pr\left[\text{BAD}_r \wedge \text{BAD}_\pi\right]$$
$$\geq \Pr\left[\text{FORGE}\right] - \Pr\left[\text{BAD}_\pi\right]$$
$$= \mathbf{Adv}_{\text{SAS}_1[\mathcal{F}],F}^{\text{sas-ufcma}}(k) - q_\pi^2/2^k.$$

where the last line uses the Chain-to-Zero Lemma. Combining terms yields the theorem. ∎

6.3   Proof of Theorem 3

CLAW FINDER. Claw-finding algorithm C is given in Fig. 5.

ANALYSIS. Again, let's consider executions of the history-free SAS-unforgeability experiment with F and of the adaptive claw-finding experiment with C over a common set of random coin sequences, where the same coins are used choices common across both experiments. And, in the execution of C, let BAD_π be the event that any forward query is chained to zero. Let ABORT be the event that C aborts. Let FORGE be the event that F produces a valid forgery in its experiment. Then we have

$$\mathbf{Adv}_{\mathcal{F},C}^{\text{acf}}(k) \geq \Pr\left[\text{FORGE} \wedge \overline{\text{ABORT}} \wedge \overline{\text{BAD}_\pi}\right]$$
$$= \Pr\left[\text{FORGE} \mid \overline{\text{ABORT}} \wedge \overline{\text{BAD}_\pi}\right] \cdot \Pr\left[\overline{\text{ABORT}} \mid \overline{\text{BAD}_\pi}\right] \cdot$$
$$\Pr\left[\overline{\text{BAD}_\pi}\right].$$

The first inequality above is due to the fact that on coin sequences where C does not abort and no forward query made by F gets chained to zero, the execution of F in its experiment and when run by C is identical. Hence, on such coin sequences F also forges in its execution by C.

Now by the Chain-to-Zero Lemma (Lemma 4), we have

$$\Pr\left[\overline{\text{BAD}_\pi}\right] \geq 1 - q_\pi^2/2^k.$$

Next we claim that

$$\Pr\left[\overline{\text{ABORT}} \mid \overline{\text{BAD}_\pi}\right] \geq 1/q_H \cdot (1 - q_H/2^\tau).$$

To see this, note that there are three places C could abort: answering a hash query, answering a signing query, or after receiving the final forgery. Note that on each hash query where the "Else" is executed, we $t = t^*$ with probability $1/2^\tau$ since t and t^* are independent and random. Upon receiving the F's final output, if it is a valid forgery then π-table entry $x_{i^*-1}^* = \pi[f^* \| m_{i^*}^*, y_{i^*}^*]$ must be chained to zero and hence be a backward query. So if C chooses ctr^* to be

Algorithm $C^{f^*_{inv}(\cdot,\cdot)}(f^*, g^*, t^*)$:

  $ctr \leftarrow 0$; $ctr^* \leftarrow_\$ \{1, \ldots, q_H\}$

  Run F on input f^* as follows:

    On H-query $f\|m$ do:

      If $f = f^*$ then

        $ctr \leftarrow ctr + 1$

        If $ctr = ctr^*$ then $t \leftarrow t^*$

      Else $t \leftarrow_\$ \{0,1\}^k$; If $t = t^*$ then abort

      Record $H[f\|m] = t$ in the H-table ; Return t

    On π-query $f\|m, y$ do:

      $x \leftarrow_\$ \{0,1\}^k$

      Record $\pi[f\|m, y] = x$ in the π-table ; Return x

    On π^{-1} query $f\|m, x$ do:

      $x' \leftarrow_\$ \{0,1\}^k$; $y \leftarrow g^*(t^*, x')$

      Record $g^*[t^*, x'] = y$ in the g^*-table

      Record $\pi[f\|m, y] = x$ in the π-table ; Return y

    On signing query m, σ do:

      If $H[f^*\|m] = t^*$ then abort

      $x_{i-1} \leftarrow \sigma$

      $t_i \leftarrow H[f^*\|m]$; $y_i \leftarrow \pi[x_{i-1}]$; $x_i \leftarrow f^*_{inv}(t_i, y_i)$

      Return $\sigma = x_i$

  Let $(f^*_1, m^*_1), \ldots, (f^*_n, m^*_n), \sigma$ be the output of F

  If $\mathsf{AggVer}((f^*_1, m^*_1), \ldots, (f^*_n, m^*_n), \sigma^*)$ outputs 0 then return $\perp$

  If there does not exist $1 \leq i^* \leq n$ such that $f^*_{i^*} = f^*$ then return $\perp$

  $x^*_n \leftarrow \sigma^*$

  For $i = n$ down to $i^* + 1$ do:

    $t^*_i \leftarrow H[f^*_i\|m^*_i]$

    $y^*_i \leftarrow f^*_i(t^*_i, x^*_i)$

    $x^*_{i-1} \leftarrow \pi[f^*_i\|m^*_i, y^*_i]$

  $t^*_{i^*} \leftarrow H[f^*_{i^*}\|m^*_{i^*}]$

  $y^*_{i^*} \leftarrow f^*(t^*_{i^*}, x^*_{i^*})$

  If $y^*_{i^*}$ is not in the g^*-table then abort

  Let x'_{i^*} be the index of $y^*_{i^*}$ in the g^*-table

  Return $(x^*_{i^*}, x'_{i^*})$

Fig. 5. Adaptive Claw-finder C for the proof of Theorem 3.

such that $x^*_{i^*-1} = \pi[f^*\|m^*_{i^*}, y^*_{i^*}]$ was defined on the ctr^*-th query, then C does not abort. This happens with probability at least $1/q_H$ since ctr^* is random and independent.

To complete the proof, we claim that

$$\Pr\left[\, \mathsf{FORGE} \mid \overline{\mathsf{ABORT}} \wedge \overline{\mathsf{BAD}_\pi} \,\right] \geq \mathbf{Adv}^{\mathrm{sas\text{-}ufcma}}_{\mathsf{SAS}_1[\mathcal{F}], F}(k) - q^2_\pi / 2^k.$$

To see this, first note that $\overline{\mathsf{ABORT}}$ is independent of FORGE because the random choices made by C in determining whether to abort in its claw-finding experiment do not affect whether F forges in its SAS-unforgeability experiment. Thus

$$\Pr\left[\,\mathsf{FORGE} \mid \overline{\mathsf{ABORT}} \wedge \overline{\mathsf{BAD}_\pi}\,\right] \;=\; \Pr\left[\,\mathsf{FORGE} \mid \overline{\mathsf{BAD}_\pi}\,\right].$$

Now

$$
\begin{aligned}
\Pr\left[\,\mathsf{FORGE} \mid \overline{\mathsf{BAD}_\pi}\,\right] \;&=\; \frac{\Pr\left[\,\mathsf{FORGE}\,\right] - \Pr\left[\,\mathsf{FORGE} \mid \mathsf{BAD}_\pi\,\right]\cdot \Pr\left[\,\mathsf{BAD}_\pi\,\right]}{\Pr\left[\,\overline{\mathsf{BAD}_\pi}\,\right]} \\
&\geq\; \Pr\left[\,\mathsf{FORGE}\,\right] - \Pr\left[\,\mathsf{BAD}_\pi\,\right] \\
&\geq\; \Pr\left[\,\mathsf{FORGE}\,\right] - q_\pi^2/2^k \\
&=\; \mathbf{Adv}^{\mathsf{sas\text{-}ufcma}}_{\mathsf{SAS}_1[\mathcal{F}],F}(k) - q_\pi^2/2^k
\end{aligned}
$$

as claimed. Combining the above, we have

$$\mathbf{Adv}^{\mathsf{cf}}_{\mathcal{F},C}(k) \;\geq\; \left(\mathbf{Adv}^{\mathsf{sas\text{-}ufcma}}_{\mathsf{SAS}_1[\mathcal{F}],F}(k) - q_\pi^2/2^k\right) \cdot \left(1/q_H - q_\pi^2/2^k\right)$$

and rearranging yields the theorem. $\blacksquare$

7   Extensions

We extend our basic schemes in a few ways. First, we add message recovery to them, so that we save on bandwidth. Second, we handle non-binary domains, as is needed for RSA-based instantiations.

7.1   Adding Message Recovery

To add message recovery to any of our schemes, the first signer can, instead of using the all-zeros string (of k-bits in length) as the first "aggregate-so-far," use n zero bits followed $n - k$ bits of the message for n equal to security parameter (here we abuse notation and use n as the security parameter, say 128, while k is the length of the modulus, say 2048). The security proofs are identical except that they use the extension of the Chain-to-Zero Lemma discussed in Remark 5. This gives us only security parameters number of bits of bandwidth overhead from the signature for sufficiently long messages. One issue is that the public keys of the signers still contribute to bandwidth overhead. It would be interesting for future work to treat message recovery for sequential aggregate signatures in the identity-based setting, which avoids public keys, as considered by [5].

7.2   Handling Non-binary Domains

Our RSA-based instantiations in Appendix A have domain not $\{0,1\}^k$ but $\mathbb{Z}_N$ for per-signer N. The problem is that we may have a signer with modulus N_i and a subsequent signer with modulus N_{i+1} such that $N_{i+1} < N_i$. To handle this, there are two options. The first option is to append the fractional bit to the aggregate-so-far, so that the aggregate-so-far may grow by a bit per signer. This is quite modest growth, and in many applications such as S-BGP the number of signers is typically small. For highly bandwidth constrained applications, another option is to first convert the instantiation into one that does have a binary domain by using the technique of Hayashi et al. [19]. The idea is to exponentiate twice, reflecting the intermediate result about N. The downside is that this increases the cost of verification and signing by a factor of two.

Acknowledgements. We thank the anonymous reviewers of PKC 2018 for their helpful feedback, as well as Dana Dachman-Soled and Sharon Goldberg for helpful discussions. Adam O'Neill is supported in part by NSF grant 1650419. Leonid Reyzin is supported in part by NSF grant 1422965.

A   RSA-Based Instantiations

We first define a general parameter generation algorithm used in our constructions. An RSA [26] parameter generation algorithm is an algorithm RSAGen that on input 1^k outputs (N, p, q, e, d) where $N = pq$, p and q are $m/2$-bit primes for some $m = m(k)$, and $ed = 1 \bmod \phi(N)$.

RSA TRAPDOOR PERMUTATION. An RSA trapdoor permutation generator $\mathcal{F}_{rsa}$ on input 1^k returns $f_{rsa} = (N, e)$, $f_{rsa}^{-1} = (N, d)$ where $(N, e, d, p, q) \leftarrow_\$ \mathsf{RSAGen}(1^k)$. On input $x \in \mathbb{Z}_N^*$ algorithm f_{rsa} outputs $x^e \bmod N$ and on input $y \in \mathbb{Z}_N^*$ algorithm f_{rsa}^{-1} outputs $y^d \bmod N$. Dodis and Reyzin [16] show that the RSA trapdoor permutation generator is claw-free under the standard assumption it is one-way.

RSA TAG-BASED TRAPDOOR PERMUTATION. An RSA tag-based trapdoor permutation generator from Kiltz et al. [20] works as follows. Let $H: \{0,1\}^\tau \rightarrow \{0,1\}^\eta$ for some $\eta \in \mathbb{N}$ be a hash function. Define the tag-based trapdoor permutation generator $\mathcal{F}_{rsa\text{-}tag}$ with tag-space $\{0,1\}^\tau$ that on input 1^k outputs

$$f_{rsa\text{-}tag} = N; \ f_{rsa\text{-}tag}^{-1} = (p, q)$$

for where $(N, p, q, e, d) \leftarrow_\$ \mathsf{RSAGen}$. On inputs $t \in \{0,1\}^\tau, x \in \mathbb{Z}_N^*$, algorithm $f_{rsa\text{-}tag}$ outputs $x^{H(t)} \bmod N$. On inputs $t \in \{0,1\}^\tau, y \in \mathbb{Z}_N^*$, algorithm $f_{rsa\text{-}tag}^{-1}$ computes $d \leftarrow H(t)^{-1} \bmod \phi(N)$ and outputs $y^d \bmod N$. Kiltz et al. [20] show that this tag-based trapdoor permutation generator is adaptive one-way assuming the *instance-independent RSA assumption* [8,20,25] holds and H is *division-intractable* [18]. This is plausible if $\eta = m$ (the modulus length) [11]. The same proof strategy of Dodis and Reyzin [16] works in the adaptive case and we thus obtain that this tag-based trapdoor permutation generator is adaptive claw-free under the same assumptions.

References

1. Bellare, M., Namprempre, C., Neven, G.: Unrestricted aggregate signatures. In: Arge, L., Cachin, C., Jurdziński, T., Tarlecki, A. (eds.) ICALP 2007. LNCS, vol. 4596, pp. 411–422. Springer, Heidelberg (2007). https://doi.org/10.1007/978-3-540-73420-8_37
2. Bellare, M., Rogaway, P.: Random Oracles are practical: a paradigm for designing efficient protocols. In: Ashby, V. (ed.) ACM CCS 1993, pp. 62–73. ACM Press, November 1993
3. Bellare, M., Rogaway, P.: The exact security of digital signatures-how to sign with RSA and rabin. In: Maurer, U. (ed.) EUROCRYPT 1996. LNCS, vol. 1070, pp. 399–416. Springer, Heidelberg (1996). https://doi.org/10.1007/3-540-68339-9_34
4. Black, J., Rogaway, P., Shrimpton, T.: Black-box analysis of the block-cipher-based hash-function constructions from PGV. In: Yung, M. (ed.) CRYPTO 2002. LNCS, vol. 2442, pp. 320–335. Springer, Heidelberg (2002). https://doi.org/10.1007/3-540-45708-9_21
5. Boldyreva, A., Gentry, C., O'Neill, A., Yum, D.H.: Ordered multisignatures and identity-based sequential aggregate signatures, with applications to secure routing. In: Ning, P., di Vimercati, S.D.C., Syverson, P.F. (eds.) ACM CCS 2007, pp. 276–285. ACM Press, October 2007
6. Boneh, D., Gentry, C., Lynn, B., Shacham, H.: Aggregate and verifiably encrypted signatures from bilinear maps. In: Biham, E. (ed.) EUROCRYPT 2003. LNCS, vol. 2656, pp. 416–432. Springer, Heidelberg (2003). https://doi.org/10.1007/3-540-39200-9_26
7. Brogle, K., Goldberg, S., Reyzin, L.: Sequential aggregate signatures with lazy verification from trapdoor permutations. In: Wang, X., Sako, K. (eds.) ASIACRYPT 2012. LNCS, vol. 7658, pp. 644–662. Springer, Heidelberg (2012). https://doi.org/10.1007/978-3-642-34961-4_39
8. Chevallier-Mames, B., Joye, M.: Chosen-ciphertext secure RSA-type cryptosystems. In: Pieprzyk, J., Zhang, F. (eds.) ProvSec 2009. LNCS, vol. 5848, pp. 32–46. Springer, Heidelberg (2009). https://doi.org/10.1007/978-3-642-04642-1_5
9. Coron, J.-S.: On the exact security of full domain hash. In: Bellare, M. (ed.) CRYPTO 2000. LNCS, vol. 1880, pp. 229–235. Springer, Heidelberg (2000). https://doi.org/10.1007/3-540-44598-6_14
10. Coron, J.-S., Holenstein, T., Künzler, R., Patarin, J., Seurin, Y., Tessaro, S.: How to build an ideal cipher: the indifferentiability of the Feistel construction. J. Cryptol. **29**(1), 61–114 (2016)
11. Coron, J.-S., Naccache, D.: Security analysis of the gennaro-halevi-rabin signature scheme. In: Preneel, B. (ed.) EUROCRYPT 2000. LNCS, vol. 1807, pp. 91–101. Springer, Heidelberg (2000). https://doi.org/10.1007/3-540-45539-6_7
12. Dachman-Soled, D., Katz, J., Thiruvengadam, A.: 10-round feistel is indifferentiable from an ideal cipher. In: Fischlin, M., Coron, J.-S. (eds.) EUROCRYPT 2016. LNCS, vol. 9666, pp. 649–678. Springer, Heidelberg (2016). https://doi.org/10.1007/978-3-662-49896-5_23
13. Dai, Y., Steinberger, J.: Indifferentiability of 10-round Feistel networks. Cryptology ePrint Archive, Report 2015/874 (2015). http://eprint.iacr.org/2015/874
14. Dai, Y., Steinberger, J.: Indifferentiability of 8-round feistel networks. In: Robshaw, M., Katz, J. (eds.) CRYPTO 2016. LNCS, vol. 9814, pp. 95–120. Springer, Heidelberg (2016). https://doi.org/10.1007/978-3-662-53018-4_4

15. Diffie, W., Hellman, M.E.: New directions in cryptography. IEEE Trans. Inf. Theory **22**(6), 644–654 (1976)
16. Dodis, Y., Reyzin, L.: On the power of claw-free permutations. In: Cimato, S., Persiano, G., Galdi, C. (eds.) SCN 2002. LNCS, vol. 2576, pp. 55–73. Springer, Heidelberg (2003). https://doi.org/10.1007/3-540-36413-7_5
17. Fischlin, M., Lehmann, A., Schröder, D.: History-free sequential aggregate signatures. In: Visconti, I., De Prisco, R. (eds.) SCN 2012. LNCS, vol. 7485, pp. 113–130. Springer, Heidelberg (2012). https://doi.org/10.1007/978-3-642-32928-9_7
18. Gennaro, R., Halevi, S., Rabin, T.: Secure hash-and-sign signatures without the random Oracle. In: Stern, J. (ed.) EUROCRYPT 1999. LNCS, vol. 1592, pp. 123–139. Springer, Heidelberg (1999). https://doi.org/10.1007/3-540-48910-X_9
19. Hayashi, R., Okamoto, T., Tanaka, K.: An RSA family of trap-door permutations with a common domain and its applications. In: Bao, F., Deng, R., Zhou, J. (eds.) PKC 2004. LNCS, vol. 2947, pp. 291–304. Springer, Heidelberg (2004). https://doi.org/10.1007/978-3-540-24632-9_21
20. Kiltz, E., Mohassel, P., O'Neill, A.: Adaptive trapdoor functions and chosen-ciphertext security. In: Gilbert, H. (ed.) EUROCRYPT 2010. LNCS, vol. 6110, pp. 673–692. Springer, Heidelberg (2010). https://doi.org/10.1007/978-3-642-13190-5_34
21. Lu, S., Ostrovsky, R., Sahai, A., Shacham, H., Waters, B.: Sequential aggregate signatures and multisignatures without random Oracles. In: Vaudenay, S. (ed.) EUROCRYPT 2006. LNCS, vol. 4004, pp. 465–485. Springer, Heidelberg (2006). https://doi.org/10.1007/11761679_28
22. Lysyanskaya, A., Micali, S., Reyzin, L., Shacham, H.: Sequential aggregate signatures from trapdoor permutations. In: Cachin, C., Camenisch, J.L. (eds.) EUROCRYPT 2004. LNCS, vol. 3027, pp. 74–90. Springer, Heidelberg (2004). https://doi.org/10.1007/978-3-540-24676-3_5
23. Maurer, U., Renner, R., Holenstein, C.: Indifferentiability, impossibility results on reductions, and applications to the random Oracle methodology. In: Naor, M. (ed.) TCC 2004. LNCS, vol. 2951, pp. 21–39. Springer, Heidelberg (2004). https://doi.org/10.1007/978-3-540-24638-1_2
24. Neven, G.: Efficient sequential aggregate signed data. In: Smart, N. (ed.) EUROCRYPT 2008. LNCS, vol. 4965, pp. 52–69. Springer, Heidelberg (2008). https://doi.org/10.1007/978-3-540-78967-3_4
25. Paillier, P., Villar, J.L.: Trading one-wayness against chosen-ciphertext security in factoring-based encryption. In: Lai, X., Chen, K. (eds.) ASIACRYPT 2006. LNCS, vol. 4284, pp. 252–266. Springer, Heidelberg (2006). https://doi.org/10.1007/11935230_17
26. Rivest, R.L., Shamir, A., Adleman, L.M.: A method for obtaining digital signature and public-key cryptosystems. Commun. Assoc. Comput. Mach. **21**(2), 120–126 (1978)
27. Shannon, C.E.: Communication theory of secrecy systems. Bell Syst. Tech. J. **28**(4), 656–715 (1949)

Constant-Size Group Signatures
from Lattices

San Ling, Khoa Nguyen, Huaxiong Wang, and Yanhong Xu$^{(\boxtimes)}$

Division of Mathematical Sciences, School of Physical and Mathematical Sciences,
Nanyang Technological University, Singapore, Singapore
{lingsan,khoantt,hxwang,xu0014ng}@ntu.edu.sg

Abstract. Lattice-based group signature is an active research topic in
recent years. Since the pioneering work by Gordon, Katz and Vaikuntanathan (Asiacrypt 2010), ten other schemes have been proposed, providing various improvements in terms of security, efficiency and functionality. However, in all known constructions, one has to fix the number N
of group users in the setup stage, and as a consequence, the signature
sizes are dependent on N.

In this work, we introduce the first constant-size group signature from
lattices, which means that the size of signatures produced by the scheme
is independent of N and only depends on the security parameter λ. More
precisely, in our scheme, the sizes of signatures, public key and users'
secret keys are all of order $\widetilde{\mathcal{O}}(\lambda)$. The scheme supports dynamic enroll-
ment of users and is proven secure in the random oracle model under
the Ring Short Integer Solution (RSIS) and Ring Learning With Errors
(RLWE) assumptions. At the heart of our design is a zero-knowledge
argument of knowledge of a valid message-signature pair for the Ducas-
Micciancio signature scheme (Crypto 2014), that may be of independent
interest.

Keywords: Lattice-based cryptography
Constant-size group signatures · Zero-knowledge proofs
Ducas-Micciancio signature

1 Introduction

Group signature, introduced by Chaum and van Heyst [18], is a fundamental
anonymity primitive which allows members of a group to sign messages on behalf
of the whole group. Yet, users are kept accountable for the signatures they issue
since a tracing authority can identify them should the need arise. These two
appealing features allow group signatures to find applications in various real-
life scenarios, such as digital right management, anonymous online communications, e-commerce systems, and much more. On the theoretical front, designing
secure and efficient group signature schemes is interesting and challenging, since
those advanced constructions usually require a sophisticated combination of carefully chosen cryptographic ingredients: digital signatures, encryption schemes,

© International Association for Cryptologic Research 2018
M. Abdalla and R. Dahab (Eds.): PKC 2018, LNCS 10770, pp. 58–88, 2018.
https://doi.org/10.1007/978-3-319-76581-5_3

and zero-knowledge protocols. Numerous group signature schemes have been proposed in the last quarter-century, some of which produce very short signatures [2,8]. In the setting of bilinear groups, many schemes [1,12,28,40] achieved constant-size signatures, which means that the group signatures only contain $\mathcal{O}(1)$ number of group ts. In other words, the signature sizes in those schemes only depend on the security parameter and are independent of the number N of group users. In the lattice setting, however, none of the existing constructions achieved this feature.

LATTICE-BASED GROUP SIGNATURES. Lattice-based cryptography has been an exciting research area since the seminal works of Regev [55] and Gentry et al. [24]. Lattices not only allow to build powerful primitives (e.g., [23,25]) that have no feasible instantiations in conventional number-theoretic cryptography, but they also provide several advantages over the latter, such as conjectured resistance against quantum adversaries and faster arithmetic operations. Along with other primitives, lattice-based group signature has received noticeable attention in recent years. The first scheme was introduced by Gordon et al. [26] whose solution produced signature size linear in the number of group users N. Camenisch et al. [16] then extended [26] to achieve anonymity in the strongest sense. Later, Laguillaumie et al. [32] put forward the first scheme with the signature size logarithmic in N, at the cost of relatively large parameters. Simpler and more efficient solutions with $\mathcal{O}(\log N)$ signature size were subsequently given by Nguyen et al. [52] and Ling et al. [42]. Libert et al. [37] obtained substantial efficiency improvements via a construction based on Merkle trees which eliminates the need for GPV trapdoors [24]. More recently, a scheme supporting message-dependent opening (MDO) feature [56] was proposed in [39]. All the schemes mentioned above are designed for static groups, and all have signature sizes dependent on N.

Three lattice-based group signatures that have certain dynamic features were proposed by Langlois et al. [33], Libert et al. [35], and Ling et al. [43]. The first one is a scheme with verifier-local revocation (VLR) [9], which means that only the verifiers need to download the up-to-date group information. The second one addresses the orthogonal problem of dynamic user enrollments, which was formalized by Kiayias and Yung [31] and by Bellare et al. [5]. The third one is a fully dynamic scheme that supports both features, following Bootle et al.'s model [10]. Again, all these three schemes have signature size $\mathcal{O}(\log N)$.

In all existing works on lattice-based group signatures, for various reasons, one has to fix the number $N = \mathsf{poly}(\lambda)$, where λ is the security parameter, in the setup stage. For the schemes from [16,26,32,33,35,39,42,52] - which are based on full-fledged lattice-based ordinary signatures [11,17,24], this is due to the fact that their security reductions have to guess a target user with probability $1/N$, and cannot go through unless N is known in advance. For the schemes from [37,43] - which associate group users with leaves in lattice-based Merkle hash trees - this is because the size N of the trees has to be determined so that the setup algorithm succeeds. As a consequence, the parameters of those schemes, including the signature sizes, are unavoidably dependent on N.

This state-of-affairs is somewhat unsatisfactory, considering that the constant-size feature has been achieved in the pairing setting. This inspires us to investigate the problem of designing constant-size lattice-based group signatures.

OUR RESULTS AND TECHNIQUES. We introduce the first constant-size group signature scheme from lattices. Here, by "constant-size", we mean that the signature size is independent of the number of group users N, as in the context of pairing-based group signatures [12,28]. The crucial difference between our scheme and previous works on lattice-based group signatures is that we do not have to fix N in the setup phase. As a result, the execution of the scheme is totally independent of N. The sizes of the public key, users' signing keys and signatures are of order $\widetilde{\mathcal{O}}(\lambda)$. A comparison between our schemes and previous works, in terms of asymptotic efficiency and functionality, is given in Table 1.

The scheme operates in Bellare et al.'s model for partially dynamic groups [5], and is proven secure under the hardness of the Ring Short Integer Solution (RSIS) and the Ring Learning With Errors (RLWE) problems. As for all known lattice-based group signatures, our security analysis is in the random oracle model.

Table 1. Comparison of known lattice-based group signatures, in terms of asymptotic efficiency and functionality. The comparison is done based on two governing parameters: security parameter λ and the maximum expected number of group users $N = 2^{\ell}$. Among the listed schemes, the LNW-II [42] scheme and ours are the only ideal-lattice-based constructions, while other schemes rely on various SIS and LWE assumptions in the general-lattice setting.

Scheme	Sig. size	Group PK size	Signer's SK size	Functionality
GKV [26]	$\widetilde{\mathcal{O}}(\lambda^2 \cdot N)$	$\widetilde{\mathcal{O}}(\lambda^2 \cdot N)$	$\widetilde{\mathcal{O}}(\lambda^2)$	static
CNR [16]	$\widetilde{\mathcal{O}}(\lambda^2 \cdot N)$	$\widetilde{\mathcal{O}}(\lambda^2)$	$\widetilde{\mathcal{O}}(\lambda^2)$	static
LLLS [32]	$\widetilde{\mathcal{O}}(\lambda \cdot \ell)$	$\mathcal{O}(\lambda^2 \cdot \ell)$	$\widetilde{\mathcal{O}}(\lambda^2)$	static
LLNW [33]	$\widetilde{\mathcal{O}}(\lambda \cdot \ell)$	$\widetilde{\mathcal{O}}(\lambda^2 \cdot \ell)$	$\widetilde{\mathcal{O}}(\lambda \cdot \ell)$	VLR
NZZ [52]	$\widetilde{\mathcal{O}}(\lambda + \ell^2)$	$\widetilde{\mathcal{O}}(\lambda^2 \cdot \ell^2)$	$\widetilde{\mathcal{O}}(\lambda^2)$	static
LNW-I [42]	$\widetilde{\mathcal{O}}(\lambda \cdot \ell)$	$\widetilde{\mathcal{O}}(\lambda^2 \cdot \ell)$	$\widetilde{\mathcal{O}}(\lambda)$	static
LNW-II [42]	$\widetilde{\mathcal{O}}(\lambda \cdot \ell)$	$\widetilde{\mathcal{O}}(\lambda \cdot \ell)$	$\widetilde{\mathcal{O}}(\lambda) + \ell$	static
LLNW [37]	$\widetilde{\mathcal{O}}(\lambda \cdot \ell)$	$\widetilde{\mathcal{O}}(\lambda^2 + \lambda \cdot \ell)$	$\widetilde{\mathcal{O}}(\lambda \cdot \ell)$	static
LLM+ [35]	$\widetilde{\mathcal{O}}(\lambda \cdot \ell)$	$\widetilde{\mathcal{O}}(\lambda^2 \cdot \ell)$	$\widetilde{\mathcal{O}}(\lambda)$	partially dynamic
LMN [39]	$\widetilde{\mathcal{O}}(\lambda \cdot \ell)$	$\widetilde{\mathcal{O}}(\lambda^2 \cdot \ell)$	$\widetilde{\mathcal{O}}(\lambda)$	MDO
LNWX [43]	$\widetilde{\mathcal{O}}(\lambda \cdot \ell)$	$\widetilde{\mathcal{O}}(\lambda^2 + \lambda \cdot \ell)$	$\widetilde{\mathcal{O}}(\lambda) + \ell$	fully dynamic
Ours	$\widetilde{\mathcal{O}}(\lambda)$	$\widetilde{\mathcal{O}}(\lambda)$	$\widetilde{\mathcal{O}}(\lambda)$	partially dynamic

Our scheme relies on the RSIS-based signature scheme by Ducas and Micciancio [20], which exploits the "confined guessing" technique [7] in the ring setting to achieve short public key. We employ the stateful and adaptively secure version of the scheme, described in [21], which suffices for building group signatures and which allows to work with even shorter key.

The scheme follows the usual sign-then-encrypt-then-prove approach for constructing group signatures. Each user generates a secret-public key pair $(\mathbf{x}, p)$ and becomes a certified group member once receiving a Ducas-Micciancio signature on his public key p. When generating group signatures, the user first encrypts his public key p to ciphertext $\mathbf{c}$ via a CCA-secure encryption scheme obtained by applying the Naor-Yung transformation [51] to a variant of the RLWE-based scheme by Lyubashevsky et al. [47]. Then he proves in zero-knowledge that: (i) he has a valid secret key $\mathbf{x}$ corresponding to p; (ii) he possesses a Ducas-Micciancio signature on p; and (iii) $\mathbf{c}$ is a correct ciphertext of p. The protocol is then transformed into a signature via the Fiat-Shamir heuristic [22].

To instantiate the above approach, we design a zero-knowledge argument of knowledge of a valid message-signature pair for the Ducas-Micciancio signature, which is based on Stern's framework [57]. We observe that a similar protocol for the Boyen signature [11] was proposed by Ling et al. [42], but their method is suboptimal in terms of efficiency. We thus propose a refined technique that allows to achieve better communication cost, and hence, shorter signature size. We believe that our protocol is of independent interest. Indeed, apart from group signatures, zero-knowledge protocols for valid message-signature pairs are essential ingredients for designing various privacy-enhancing constructions, such as anonymous credentials [15], compact e-cash [14,38], policy-based signatures [3,19], and much more.

On the practical front, as all known lattice-based group signatures, our scheme is not truly practical. Even though the scheme produces signatures of constant size $\widetilde{\mathcal{O}}(\lambda)$, due to a large poly-logarithmic factor contained in the $\widetilde{\mathcal{O}}$ notation, the signature size is too big to be really useful in practice. We, however, hope that our result will inspire more efficient constructions in the near future.

2 Background

NOTATIONS. The set $\{1, \ldots, n\}$ is denoted by $[n]$. If S is a finite set, then $x \xleftarrow{\$} S$ means that x is chosen uniformly at random from S. When concatenating column vectors $\mathbf{x} \in \mathbb{R}^m$ and $\mathbf{y} \in \mathbb{R}^k$, for simplicity, we use the notation $(\mathbf{x}\|\mathbf{y}) \in \mathbb{R}^{m+k}$ instead of $(\mathbf{x}^\top \| \mathbf{y}^\top)^\top$.

2.1 Rings, RSIS and RLWE

Let $q \geq 3$ be a positive integer and let $\mathbb{Z}_q = [-\frac{q-1}{2}, \frac{q-1}{2}]$. Consider rings of the form $R = \mathbb{Z}[X]/(\Phi_{2n}(X))$ and $R_q = (R/qR)$, where n is a power of 2 and $\Phi_{2n}(X) = X^n + 1$ is the cyclotomic polynomial of degree n.

We will use the coefficient embedding $\tau : R_q \rightarrow \mathbb{Z}_q^n$ that maps ring element $v = v_0 + v_1 \cdot X + \ldots + v_{n-1} \cdot X^{N-1} \in R_q$ to vector $\tau(v) = (v_0, v_1, \ldots, v_{n-1})^\top \in \mathbb{Z}_q^n$. We will also use the ring homomorphism $\mathsf{rot} : R_q \rightarrow \mathbb{Z}_q^{n \times n}$ that maps $a \in R_q$ to matrix $\mathsf{rot}(a) = [\tau(a) \mid \tau(a \cdot X) \mid \ldots \mid \tau(a \cdot X^{n-1})] \in \mathbb{Z}_q^{n \times n}$ (see, e.g., [49,58]). These functions allow us to interpret the product $y = a \cdot v$ over R_q as the matrix-vector product $\tau(y) = \mathsf{rot}(a) \cdot \tau(v) \bmod q$.

When working with vectors over R_q, we often abuse the notations rot and τ. If $\mathbf{A} = [a_1 \mid \ldots \mid a_m] \in R_q^{1 \times m}$, then we denote by $\text{rot}(A)$ the matrix

$$\text{rot}(\mathbf{A}) = \left[\text{rot}(a_1) \mid \ldots \mid \text{rot}(a_m)\right] \in \mathbb{Z}_q^{n \times mn}.$$

If $\mathbf{v} = (v_1, \ldots, v_m)^\top \in R_q^m$, then we let $\tau(\mathbf{v}) = (\tau(v_1) \| \ldots \| \tau(v_m)) \in \mathbb{Z}_q^{mn}$. Note that, if $y = \mathbf{A} \cdot \mathbf{v}$ over R_q, then we have $\tau(y) = \text{rot}(\mathbf{A}) \cdot \tau(\mathbf{v}) \bmod q$.

For $a = a_0 + a_1 \cdot X + \ldots + a_{n-1} \cdot X^{N-1} \in R$, we define $\|a\|_\infty = \max_i(|a_i|)$. Similarly, for vector $\mathbf{b} = (b_1, \ldots, b_m)^\top \in R^m$, we define $\|\mathbf{b}\|_\infty = \max_j(\|b_j\|_\infty)$.

We now recall the average-case problems RSIS and RLWE associated with the rings R, R_q, as well as their hardness results.

Definition 1 [44,45,54]. *The* $\text{RSIS}_{n,m,q,\beta}$ *problem is as follows. Given a uniformly random* $\mathbf{A} = [a_1 \mid \ldots \mid a_m] \in R_q^{1 \times m}$, *find a non-zero vector* $\mathbf{x} = (x_1, \ldots, x_m)^\top \in R^m$ *such that* $\|\mathbf{x}\|_\infty \leq \beta$ *and* $\mathbf{A} \cdot \mathbf{x} = a_1 \cdot x_1 + \ldots + a_m \cdot x_m = 0$.

For $m > \frac{\log q}{\log(2\beta)}$, $\gamma = 16\beta mn \log^2 n$, and $q \geq \frac{\gamma\sqrt{n}}{4 \log n}$, the $\text{RSIS}_{n,m,q,\beta}$ problem is at least as hard as SVP_γ^∞ in any ideal in the ring R (see, e.g., [44]).

Definition 2 [46]. *Let* $n, m \geq 1$, $q \geq 2$, *and let* χ *be a probability distribution on* R. *For* $s \in R_q$, *let* $A_{s,\chi}$ *be the distribution obtained by sampling* $a \xleftarrow{\$} R_q$ *and* $e \hookleftarrow \chi$, *and outputting the pair* $(a, a \cdot s + e) \in R_q \times R_q$. *The* $\text{RLWE}_{n,m,q,\chi}$ *problem (the Hermite-Normal-Form version) asks to distinguish* m *samples chosen according to* $A_{s,\chi}$ *(for* $s \hookleftarrow \chi$*) and* m *samples chosen according to the uniform distribution over* $R_q \times R_q$.

Let $q = \text{poly}(n)$ be a prime power. Let $B = \widetilde{\mathcal{O}}(n^{5/4})$ be an integer and χ be a B-bounded distribution on R, i.e., it outputs samples $e \in R$ such that $\|e\|_\infty \leq B$ with overwhelming probability in n. Then, for $\gamma = n^2(q/B)(nm/\log(nm))^{1/4}$, the $\text{RLWE}_{n,m,q,\chi}$ problem is at least as hard as SVP_γ^∞ in any ideal in the ring R, via a polynomial-time quantum reduction (see, e.g., [34,46,48,53]).

2.2   Decompositions

We next recall the integer decomposition technique from [41]. For any $B \in \mathbb{Z}_+$, define $\delta_B := \lfloor \log_2 B \rfloor + 1 = \lceil \log_2(B + 1) \rceil$ and the sequence $B_1, \ldots, B_{\delta_B}$, where $B_j = \lfloor \frac{B + 2^{j-1}}{2^j} \rfloor$, for each $j \in [1, \delta_B]$. As observed in [41], it satisfies $\sum_{j=1}^{\delta_B} B_j = B$ and any integer $v \in [0, B]$ can be decomposed to $\text{idec}_B(v) = (v^{(1)}, \ldots, v^{(\delta_B)})^\top \in \{0,1\}^{\delta_B}$ such that $\sum_{j=1}^{\delta_B} B_j \cdot v^{(j)} = v$. This decomposition procedure is described in a deterministic manner as follows:

1. $v' := v$
2. For $j = 1$ to δ_B do:
    (i) If $v' \geq B_j$ then $v^{(j)} := 1$, else $v^{(j)} := 0$;
    (ii) $v' := v' - B_j \cdot v^{(j)}$.
3. Output $\text{idec}_B(v) = (v^{(1)}, \ldots, v^{(\delta_B)})^\top$.

In this work, we will employ the above decomposition procedure when working with polynomials in the ring R_q. Specifically, for $B \in [1, \frac{q-1}{2}]$, we define the injective function rdec_B that maps $a \in R_q$ such that $\|a\|_\infty \leq B$ to $\mathbf{a} \in R^{\delta_B}$ such that $\|\mathbf{a}\|_\infty \leq 1$, which works as follows.

1. Let $\tau(a) = (a_0, \ldots, a_{n-1})^\top$. For each i, let $\sigma(a_i) = 0$ if $a_i = 0$; $\sigma(a_i) = -1$ if $a_i < 0$; and $\sigma(a_i) = 1$ if $a_i > 0$.
2. $\forall i$, compute $\mathbf{w}_i = \sigma(a_i) \cdot \mathsf{idec}_B(|a_i|) = (w_{i,1}, \ldots, w_{i,\delta_B})^\top \in \{-1, 0, 1\}^{\delta_B}$.
3. Form the vector $\mathbf{w} = (\mathbf{w}_0\| \ldots \|\mathbf{w}_{n-1}) \in \{-1, 0, 1\}^{n\delta_B}$, and let $\mathbf{a} \in R^{\delta_B}$ be such that $\tau(\mathbf{a}) = \mathbf{w}$.
4. Output $\mathsf{rdec}_B(a) = \mathbf{a}$.

When working with vectors of ring elements, e.g., $\mathbf{v} = (v_1, \ldots, v_m)^\top$ such that $\|\mathbf{v}\|_\infty \leq B$, then we let $\mathsf{rdec}_B(\mathbf{v}) = (\mathsf{rdec}_B(v_1)\| \ldots \|\mathsf{rdec}_B(v_m)) \in R^{m\delta_B}$.

Now, $\forall m, B \in \mathbb{Z}_+$, we define matrices $\mathbf{H}_B \in \mathbb{Z}^{n \times n\delta_B}$ and $\mathbf{H}_{m,B} \in \mathbb{Z}^{nm \times nm\delta_B}$ as

$$
\mathbf{H}_B = \begin{bmatrix} B_1 \ldots B_{\delta_B} & & \\ & \ddots & \\ & & B_1 \ldots B_{\delta_B} \end{bmatrix}, \quad \text{and} \quad \mathbf{H}_{m,B} = \begin{bmatrix} \mathbf{H}_B & & \\ & \ddots & \\ & & \mathbf{H}_B \end{bmatrix}.
$$

Then we have

$$
\tau(a) = \mathbf{H}_B \cdot \tau(\mathsf{rdec}_B(a)) \bmod q \quad \text{and} \quad \tau(\mathbf{v}) = \mathbf{H}_{m,B} \cdot \tau(\mathsf{rdec}_B(\mathbf{v})).
$$

For simplicity of presentation, when $B = \frac{q-1}{2}$, we will use the notation rdec instead of $\mathsf{rdec}_{\frac{q-1}{2}}$, and $\mathbf{H}$ instead of $\mathbf{H}_{\frac{q-1}{2}}$.

2.3 A Variant of the Ducas-Micciancio Signature Scheme

We recall a variant of the Ducas-Micciancio signature scheme [20,21], which is to used to design a (partially) dynamic group signature scheme as in the model of Bellare et al. [5]. Specifically, we use it to enroll new users.

In their papers, Ducas and Micciancio proposed two versions of signature schemes from ideal lattices: non-stateful and stateful. Note that in a group signature scheme, there are at most polynomial number of users. Therefore, it is reasonable to assume there are at most polynomial number of signature queries to the Ducas-Micciancio signature scheme. Under this assumption, the stateful version not only reduces the security loss of the proof, but also allows better parameters ([21, Sect. 4.1]), compared with the non-stateful version. We also note that in a group signature scheme, the signature scheme used to enroll users should be adaptively secure. To achieve adaptive security, we thus embed the chameleon hash function [21, Appendix B.3] into the above non-adaptively secure version.

Now we summarize the stateful and adaptively secure version of Ducas-Micciancio signature scheme below. Following [20,21], throughout this work, let $c > 1$ be some real constant and $\alpha_0 \geq 1/(c-1)$. Let $d \geq \log_c(\omega(\log n))$ be an integer and $\{c_0, c_1 \cdots, c_d\}$ be a strictly increasing integer sequence with $c_0 = 0$ and $c_i = \lfloor \alpha_0 c^i \rfloor$ for $i \in [d]$. Define $\mathcal{T}_i = \{0,1\}^{c_i}$ for $i \in [d]$. For a tag $t = (t_0, t_1 \ldots, t_{c_d-1})^\top \in \mathcal{T}_d$, let $t_{[i]} = (t_{c_{i-1}}, \ldots, t_{c_i-1})^\top$. Then we can check that $t = (t_{[1]} \| t_{[2]} \| \ldots \| t_{[d]})$. Identify each tag $t \in \mathcal{T}_d$ as $t(X) = \sum_{j=0}^{c_d-1} t_j X^j \in R$ and $t_{[i]}$ as $t_{[i]}(X) = \sum_{j=c_{i-1}}^{c_i-1} t_j X^j \in R$.

This variant works with the following parameters. Given the security parameter λ, the key generation algorithm works as follows.

- Choose parameter $n = \mathcal{O}(\lambda)$ being a power of 2, and modulus $q = 3^k$ for some positive integer k. Let $R = \mathbb{Z}[X]/(X^n + 1)$ and $R_q = R/qR$.
- Also, let $\ell = \lfloor \log \frac{q-1}{2} \rfloor + 1$, $m \geq 2\lceil \log q \rceil + 2$, and $\overline{m} = m + k$.
- Let integer d and sequence $c_0, \ldots, c_d$ as described above. Let $\beta = \widetilde{\mathcal{O}}(n)$ be a integer.
- Let $S \in \mathbb{Z}$ be a state initialized to 0.

The verification key consists of the following:

$$\mathbf{A}, \mathbf{F}_0 \in R_q^{1 \times \overline{m}}; \mathbf{A}_{[0]}, \ldots, \mathbf{A}_{[d]} \in R_q^{1 \times k}; \mathbf{F}, \mathbf{F}_1 \in R_q^{1 \times \ell}; u \in R_q$$

while the signing key is a Micciancio-Peikert [50] trapdoor matrix $\mathbf{R} \in R_q^{m \times k}$.

To sign a message $p \in R_q$, let $\mathbf{p} = \mathsf{rdec}(p) \in R^\ell$ whose coefficients are in the set $\{-1, 0, 1\}$. The signer then proceeds as follows.

- Set the tag $t = (t_0, t_1 \ldots, t_{c_d-1})^\top \in \mathcal{T}_d$, where $S = \sum_{j=0}^{c_d-1} 2^j \cdot t_j$, and compute $\mathbf{A}_t = [\mathbf{A} | \mathbf{A}_{[0]} + \sum_{i=1}^d t_{[i]} \mathbf{A}_{[i]}] \in R_q^{1 \times (\overline{m}+k)}$. Update S to $S + 1$.
- Sample $\mathbf{r} \in R^{\overline{m}}$ such that $\|\mathbf{r}\|_\infty \leq \beta$.
- Let $y = \mathbf{F}_0 \cdot \mathbf{r} + \mathbf{F}_1 \cdot \mathbf{p} \in R_q$ and $u_p = \mathbf{F} \cdot \mathsf{rdec}(y) + u \in R_q$.
- Using the trapdoor matrix $\mathbf{R}$, generate a ring vector $\mathbf{v} \in R^{\overline{m}+k}$ such that $\mathbf{A}_t \cdot \mathbf{v} = u_p$ and $\|\mathbf{v}\|_\infty \leq \beta$.
- Output the tuple $(t, \mathbf{r}, \mathbf{v})$ as a signature for $p \in R_q$.

To verify a signature tuple $(t, \mathbf{r}, \mathbf{v})$ on message $p \in R_q$, the verifier computes the matrix $\mathbf{A}_t$ as above and checks the following conditions hold or not. If yes, he outputs 1. Otherwise, he outputs 0.

$$\begin{cases} \mathbf{A}_t \cdot \mathbf{v} = \mathbf{F} \cdot \mathsf{rdec}(\mathbf{F}_0 \cdot \mathbf{r} + \mathbf{F}_1 \cdot \mathsf{rdec}(p)) + u, \\ \|\mathbf{r}\|_\infty \leq \beta, \ \|\mathbf{v}\|_\infty \leq \beta. \end{cases}$$

Remark 1. We remark that $\mathbf{p} = \mathsf{rdec}(p) \in R^\ell$ and $\mathsf{rdec}(y) \in R^\ell$ are ring vectors with coefficients in the set $\{-1, 0, 1\}$ while Ducas-Micciancio signature scheme handles ring vectors with binary coefficients. However, this does not affect the security of the Ducas-Micciancio signature scheme.

Lemma 1 [20,21]. *If we assume there are at most polynomial number of signature queries and the* $\mathsf{RSIS}_{n,\overline{m},q,\widetilde{\mathcal{O}}(n^2)}$ *problem is hard, then the above variant of Ducas-Micciancio signature scheme is existentially unforgeable against adaptive chosen message attacks.*

2.4   Zero-Knowledge Argument Systems and Stern-Like Protocols

We will work with statistical zero-knowledge argument systems, namely, interactive protocols where the zero-knowledge property holds against *any* cheating verifier, while the soundness property only holds against *computationally
bounded* cheating provers. More formally, let the set of statements-witnesses
$R = \{(y, w)\} \in \{0, 1\}^* \times \{0, 1\}^*$ be an NP relation. A two-party game $\langle \mathcal{P}, \mathcal{V} \rangle$ is
called an interactive argument system for the relation R with soundness error e
if the following conditions hold:

- Completeness. If $(y, w) \in R$ then $\Pr[\langle \mathcal{P}(y, w), \mathcal{V}(y) \rangle = 1] = 1$.
- Soundness. If $(y, w) \notin R$, then $\forall$ PPT $\widehat{\mathcal{P}}$: $\Pr[\langle \widehat{\mathcal{P}}(y, w), \mathcal{V}(y) \rangle = 1] \le e$.

An argument system is called statistical zero-knowledge if there exists a PPT
simulator $\mathcal{S}(y)$ having oracle access to any $\widehat{\mathcal{V}}(y)$ and producing a simulated
transcript that is statistically close to the one of the real interaction between
$\mathcal{P}(y, w)$ and $\widehat{\mathcal{V}}(y)$. A related notion is argument of knowledge, which requires
the witness-extended emulation property. For protocols consisting of 3 moves
(*i.e.*, commitment-challenge-response), witness-extended emulation is implied
by *special soundness* [27], where the latter assumes that there exists a PPT
extractor which takes as input a set of valid transcripts with respect to all possible values of the "challenge" to the same "commitment", and outputs w' such
that $(y, w') \in R$.

Stern-like protocols. The statistical zero-knowledge arguments of knowledge
presented in this work are Stern-like [57] protocols. In particular, they are Σ-
protocols in the generalized sense defined in [6, 29] (where 3 valid transcripts are
needed for extraction, instead of just 2). The basic protocol consists of 3 moves:
commitment, challenge, response. If a statistically hiding and computationally
binding string commitment scheme, such as the KTX scheme [30], is employed
in the first move, then one obtains a statistical zero-knowledge argument of
knowledge (ZKAoK) with perfect completeness, constant soundness error $2/3$.
In many applications, the protocol is repeated $\kappa = \omega(\log \lambda)$ times to make the
soundness error negligibly small in λ.

An abstraction of Stern's protocol. We recall an abstraction of Stern's
protocol, proposed in [35]. Let K, L, q be positive integers, where $L \ge K$ and
$q \ge 2$, and let VALID be a subset of $\{-1, 0, 1\}^L$. Suppose that $\mathcal{S}$ is a finite set
such that one can associate every $\phi \in \mathcal{S}$ with a permutation Γ_ϕ of L elements,
satisfying the following conditions:

$$\begin{cases} \mathbf{w} \in \mathsf{VALID} \iff \Gamma_\phi(\mathbf{w}) \in \mathsf{VALID}, \\ \text{If } \mathbf{w} \in \mathsf{VALID} \text{ and } \phi \text{ is uniform in } \mathcal{S}, \text{ then } \Gamma_\phi(\mathbf{w}) \text{ is uniform in } \mathsf{VALID}. \end{cases} \quad (1)$$

We aim to construct a statistical ZKAoK for the following abstract relation:

$$R_{\text{abstract}} = \{(\mathbf{M}, \mathbf{u}), \mathbf{w} \in \mathbb{Z}_q^{K \times L} \times \mathbb{Z}_q^K \times \mathsf{VALID} : \mathbf{M} \cdot \mathbf{w} = \mathbf{u} \bmod q.\}$$

The conditions in (1) play a crucial role in proving in ZK that $\mathbf{w} \in \mathsf{VALID}$: To do so, the prover samples $\phi \xleftarrow{\$} \mathcal{S}$ and let the verifier check that $\Gamma_\phi(\mathbf{w}) \in \mathsf{VALID}$, while the latter cannot learn any additional information about $\mathbf{w}$ thanks to the randomness of ϕ. Furthermore, to prove in ZK that the linear equation holds, the prover samples a masking vector $\mathbf{r}_w \xleftarrow{\$} \mathbb{Z}_q^L$, and convinces the verifier instead that $\mathbf{M} \cdot (\mathbf{w} + \mathbf{r}_w) = \mathbf{M} \cdot \mathbf{r}_w + \mathbf{u} \bmod q$.

The interaction between prover $\mathcal{P}$ and verifier $\mathcal{V}$ is described in Fig. 1. The protocol employs a statistically hiding and computationally binding string commitment scheme COM (e.g., the RSIS-based scheme from [30]).

---

1. **Commitment:** Prover samples $\mathbf{r}_w \xleftarrow{\$} \mathbb{Z}_q^L$, $\phi \xleftarrow{\$} \mathcal{S}$ and randomness ρ_1, ρ_2, ρ_3 for COM. Then he sends $\mathrm{CMT} = \big(C_1, C_2, C_3\big)$ to the verifier, where

$$C_1 = \mathsf{COM}(\phi, \mathbf{M} \cdot \mathbf{r}_w \bmod q; \rho_1), \quad C_2 = \mathsf{COM}(\Gamma_\phi(\mathbf{r}_w); \rho_2),$$
$$C_3 = \mathsf{COM}(\Gamma_\phi(\mathbf{w} + \mathbf{r}_w \bmod q); \rho_3).$$

2. **Challenge:** The verifier sends a challenge $Ch \xleftarrow{\$} \{1, 2, 3\}$ to the prover.
3. **Response:** Depending on Ch, the prover sends RSP computed as follows:
   - $Ch = 1$: Let $\mathbf{t}_w = \Gamma_\phi(\mathbf{w})$, $\mathbf{t}_r = \Gamma_\phi(\mathbf{r}_w)$, and $\mathrm{RSP} = (\mathbf{t}_w, \mathbf{t}_r, \rho_2, \rho_3)$.
   - $Ch = 2$: Let $\phi_2 = \phi$, $\mathbf{w}_2 = \mathbf{w} + \mathbf{r}_w \bmod q$, and $\mathrm{RSP} = (\phi_2, \mathbf{w}_2, \rho_1, \rho_3)$.
   - $Ch = 3$: Let $\phi_3 = \phi$, $\mathbf{w}_3 = \mathbf{r}_w$, and $\mathrm{RSP} = (\phi_3, \mathbf{w}_3, \rho_1, \rho_2)$.

Verification: Receiving RSP, the verifier proceeds as follows:

- $Ch = 1$: Check that $\mathbf{t}_w \in \mathsf{VALID}$, $C_2 = \mathsf{COM}(\mathbf{t}_r; \rho_2)$, $C_3 = \mathsf{COM}(\mathbf{t}_w + \mathbf{t}_r \bmod q; \rho_3)$.

- $Ch = 2$: Check that $C_1 = \mathsf{COM}(\phi_2, \mathbf{M} \cdot \mathbf{w}_2 - \mathbf{u} \bmod q; \rho_1)$, $C_3 = \mathsf{COM}(\Gamma_{\phi_2}(\mathbf{w}_2); \rho_3)$.

- $Ch = 3$: Check that $C_1 = \mathsf{COM}(\phi_3, \mathbf{M} \cdot \mathbf{w}_3; \rho_1)$, $C_2 = \mathsf{COM}(\Gamma_{\phi_3}(\mathbf{w}_3); \rho_2)$.

In each case, the verifier outputs 1 if and only if all the conditions hold.

Fig. 1. Stern-like ZKAoK for the relation R_{abstract}.

Theorem 1 [35]. *Assume that* COM *is a statistically hiding and computationally binding string commitment scheme. Then, the protocol in Fig. 1 is a statistical* ZKAoK *with perfect completeness, soundness error* $2/3$, *and communication cost* $\mathcal{O}(L \log q)$. *In particular:*

- *There exists a polynomial-time simulator that, on input* $(\mathbf{M}, \mathbf{u})$, *outputs an accepted transcript statistically close to that produced by the real prover.*
- *There exists a polynomial-time knowledge extractor that, on input a commitment* CMT *and 3 valid responses* $(\mathrm{RSP}_1, \mathrm{RSP}_2, \mathrm{RSP}_3)$ *to all 3 possible values of the challenge* Ch, *outputs* $\mathbf{w}' \in \mathsf{VALID}$ *such that* $\mathbf{M} \cdot \mathbf{w}' = \mathbf{u} \bmod q$.

The proof of the Theorem 1, appeared in [35], employs standard simulation and extraction techniques for Stern-like protocols (e.g., [30,36,41]). The details are available in the full version.

Looking ahead, all the relations we consider in this work (Sects. 3.2 and 4.2), will be reduced to instances of the above abstract protocol.

3   ZKAoK for the Ducas-Micciancio Signature Scheme

This section presents our statistical zero-knowledge argument of knowledge for a valid message-signature pair for the Ducas-Micciancio signature scheme [20, 21]. In the process, we will need to prove knowledge of a witness vector of the "mixing" form

$$\big(\mathbf{z} \parallel t_0 \cdot \mathbf{z} \parallel \ldots \parallel t_{c_d-1} \cdot \mathbf{z}\big), \tag{2}$$

where $\mathbf{z} \in \{-1,0,1\}^{\mathfrak{m}}$ and $\mathbf{t} = (t_0, \ldots, t_{c_d-1})^\top \in \{0,1\}^{c_d}$ for some positive integers $\mathfrak{m}$ and c_d.

We note that, in their ZK protocol for the Boyen signature [11], Ling et al. [42] also derived a vector of similar form. To handle such a vector in the Stern's framework [57], Ling et al. used a permutation in the symmetric group $\mathcal{S}_{3\mathfrak{m}}$ to hide the value of $\mathbf{z}$ and a permutation in the symmetric group $\mathcal{S}_{2c_d}$ to hide the value of $\mathbf{t}$. As a consequence, the cost of communicating the permutations from the prover to the verifier is $3\mathfrak{m} \log \mathfrak{m} + 2c_d \log c_d$ bits. This is sub-optimal, because the cost is much larger than the number of secret bits.

In Sect. 3.1, we put forward a refined permuting technique in which the total cost for the permutations is exactly the total bit-size of $\mathbf{z}$ and $\mathbf{t}$. We then employ this technique as a building block for our ZK protocol in Sect. 3.2.

3.1   A Refined Permuting Technique

We first observe that the coefficients of the vector described in (2) are highly correlated: most of them are products of t_i and z_j, where both t_i and z_j do appear at other positions. Thus, to prove the well-formedness of such a vector, we have to solve two sub-problems: (i) proving that a secret integer z is an element of the set $\{-1,0,1\}$; (ii) proving that a secret integer y is the product of secret integers $t \in \{0,1\}$ and $z \in \{-1,0,1\}$. Furthermore, these sub-protocols must be compatible and extendable, so that we can additionally prove that the *same* t and z satisfy other relations.

Technique for proving that $z \in \{-1,0,1\}$. For any integer a, let us denote by $[a]_3$ the integer $a' \in \{-1,0,1\}$ such that $a' = a \bmod 3$. For integer $z \in \{-1,0,1\}$, we define the 3-dimensional vector $\mathsf{enc}_3(z)$ as follows:

$$\mathsf{enc}_3(z) = \big([z+1]_3, [z]_3, [z-1]_3\big)^\top \in \{-1,0,1\}^3.$$

Namely, $\mathsf{enc}_3(-1) = (0,-1,1)^\top$, $\mathsf{enc}_3(0) = (1,0,-1)^\top$ and $\mathsf{enc}_3(1) = (-1,1,0)^\top$.

Now, for any integer $e \in \{-1, 0, 1\}$, define the permutation π_e that transforms vector $\mathbf{v} = (v^{(-1)}, v^{(0)}, v^{(1)})^\top \in \mathbb{Z}^3$ into vector

$$\pi_e(\mathbf{v}) = (v^{([-e-1]_3)}, v^{([-e]_3)}, v^{([-e+1]_3)})^\top.$$

We then observe that, for any $z, b \in \{-1, 0, 1\}$, the following equivalence holds.

$$\mathbf{v} = \mathsf{enc}_3(z) \iff \pi_e(\mathbf{v}) = \mathsf{enc}_3([z + e]_3). \tag{3}$$

In the framework of Stern's protocol, the above technique in fact allows us to prove knowledge of $z \in \{-1, 0, 1\}$, where z may satisfy other relations. To do this, we first extend z to $\mathbf{v} = \mathsf{enc}_3(z)$. Then, to show that $\mathbf{v}$ is a well-formed extension, we pick a uniformly random $e \xleftarrow{\$} \{-1, 0, 1\}$, and send $\pi_e(\mathbf{v})$ to the verifier. Thanks to the equivalence observed in (3), when seeing that $\pi_e(\mathbf{v}) = \mathsf{enc}_3([z + e]_3)$, the verifier should be convinced that $\mathbf{v} = \mathsf{enc}_3(z)$, which implies that $z \in \{-1, 0, 1\}$. Meanwhile, since e acts as a "one-time pad", the value of z is completely hidden from the verifier. Furthermore, to prove that z satisfies other relations, we can use the same "one-time pad" e at other appearances of z. An example of that is to prove that z is involved in a product $t \cdot z$, which we now present.

Technique for proving that $y = t \cdot z$. For any $b \in \{0, 1\}$, we denote by $\bar{b}$ the bit $1 - b$. The addition operation modulo 2 is denoted by $\oplus$.

For any $t \in \{0, 1\}$ and $z \in \{-1, 0, 1\}$, we construct the 6-dimensional integer vector $\mathsf{ext}(t, z) \in \{-1, 0, 1\}^6$ as follows:

$$\mathsf{ext}(t, z) = \left(\bar{t} \cdot [z + 1]_3, \; t \cdot [z + 1]_3, \; \bar{t} \cdot [z]_3, \; t \cdot [z]_3, \; \bar{t} \cdot [z - 1]_3, \; t \cdot [z - 1]_3 \right)^\top.$$

Now, for any $b \in \{0, 1\}$ and $e \in \{-1, 0, 1\}$, we define the permutation $\psi_{b,e}(\cdot)$ that transforms vector

$$\mathbf{v} = \left(v^{(0,-1)}, v^{(1,-1)}, v^{(0,0)}, v^{(1,0)}, v^{(0,1)}, v^{(1,1)} \right)^\top \in \mathbb{Z}^6$$

into vector

$$\psi_{b,e}(\mathbf{v}) = \left(v^{(b,[-e-1]_3)}, v^{(\bar{b},[-e-1]_3)}, v^{(b,[-e]_3)}, v^{(\bar{b},[-e]_3)}, v^{(b,[-e+1]_3)}, v^{(\bar{b},[-e+1]_3)} \right)^\top.$$

We then observe that the following equivalence holds for any $t, b \in \{0, 1\}$ and any $z, e \in \{-1, 0, 1\}$.

$$\mathbf{v} = \mathsf{ext}(t, z) \iff \psi_{b,e}(\mathbf{v}) = \mathsf{ext}(t \oplus b, [z + e]_3). \tag{4}$$

Example 1. Let $t = 1$ and $z = -1$. Then we have

$$\mathbf{v} = \mathsf{ext}(t, z) = (0, 0, 0, -1, 0, 1)^\top = (v^{(0,-1)}, v^{(1,-1)}, v^{(0,0)}, v^{(1,0)}, v^{(0,1)}, v^{(1,1)})^\top.$$

Suppose that $b = 0$ and $e = 1$, then

$$\psi_{b,e}(\mathbf{v}) = (v^{(0,1)}, v^{(1,1)}, v^{(0,-1)}, v^{(1,-1)}, v^{(0,0)}, v^{(1,0)})^\top = (0, 1, 0, 0, 0, -1)^\top,$$

which is equal to $\mathsf{ext}(1, 0) = \mathsf{ext}(1 \oplus 0, [-1 + 1]_3)$.

In the framework of Stern's protocol, the above technique will be used to prove that $y = t \cdot z$, as follows. We first extend y to $\mathbf{v} = \mathsf{ext}(t, z)$. Then, to prove that $\mathbf{v}$ is well-formed, we sample $b \xleftarrow{\$} \{0,1\}$, $e \xleftarrow{\$} \{-1,0,1\}$, and demonstrate to the verifier that $\psi_{b,e}(\mathbf{v}) = \mathsf{ext}(t \oplus b, [z+e]_3)$. Thanks to the equivalence observed in (4), the verifier should be convinced that $\mathbf{v}$ is well-formed, implying that the original integer y does have the form $t \cdot z$. Meanwhile, the random integers b, e essentially act as "one-time pads" that perfectly hide the values of t and z, respectively. Moreover, if we want to prove that the same t, z appear elsewhere, we can use the same b, e at those places.

Next, we will describe the somewhat straightforward generalizations of the above two core techniques, which enable us to prove knowledge of vector $\mathbf{z} \in \{-1,0,1\}^m$ as well as vector of the form (2). Based on the above discussions, one can see that the target is to obtain equivalences similar to (3) and (4), which are useful in Stern's framework.

Proving that $\mathbf{z} \in \{-1,0,1\}^m$. For any vector $\mathbf{a} \in \mathbb{Z}^m$, we will also use the notation $[\mathbf{a}]_3$ to denote the vector $\mathbf{a}' \in \{-1,0,1\}^m$ such that $\mathbf{a}' = \mathbf{a} \bmod 3$.

For $\mathbf{z} = (z_1, \ldots, z_m)^\top \in \{-1,0,1\}^m$, we define the following extension:

$$\mathsf{enc}(\mathbf{z}) = \big(\mathsf{enc}_3(z_1)\| \ldots \|\mathsf{enc}_3(z_m)\big) \in \{-1,0,1\}^{3m}.$$

For any vector $\mathbf{e} = (e_1, \ldots, e_m)^\top \in \{-1,0,1\}^m$, we define the permutation $\Pi_{\mathbf{e}}$ that acts as follows. When applied to vector $\mathbf{v} = (\mathbf{v}_1\| \ldots \|\mathbf{v}_m) \in \mathbb{Z}^{3m}$ consisting of m blocks of size 3, it transforms $\mathbf{v}$ into vector:

$$\Pi_{\mathbf{e}}(\mathbf{v}) = \big(\pi_{e_1}(\mathbf{v}_1)\| \ldots \|\pi_{e_m}(\mathbf{v}_m)\big).$$

It then follows from (3) that the following holds for any $\mathbf{z}, \mathbf{e} \in \{-1,0,1\}^m$.

$$\mathbf{v} = \mathsf{enc}(\mathbf{z}) \Longleftrightarrow \Pi_{\mathbf{e}}(\mathbf{v}) = \mathsf{enc}([\mathbf{z} + \mathbf{e}]_3). \tag{5}$$

Handling a "mixing" vector. We now tackle the "mixing" vector discussed earlier, i.e.,

$$\mathbf{y} = \big(\mathbf{z} \,\|t_0 \cdot \mathbf{z}\| \ldots \|t_{c_d-1} \cdot \mathbf{z}\big).$$

For any $\mathbf{z} = (z_1, \ldots, z_m)^\top \in \{-1,0,1\}^m$ and $\mathbf{t} = (t_0, \ldots, t_{c_d-1})^\top \in \{0,1\}^{c_d}$, we define vector $\mathsf{mix}(\mathbf{t}, \mathbf{z}) \in \{-1,0,1\}^{3m+6mc_d}$ of the form:

$$\big(\mathsf{enc}(\mathbf{z})\|\mathsf{ext}(t_0, z_1)\| \ldots \|\mathsf{ext}(t_0, z_m)\| \ldots \|\mathsf{ext}(t_{c_d-1}, z_1)\| \ldots \|\mathsf{ext}(t_{c_d-1}, z_m)\big),$$

which is an extension of vector $\mathbf{y}$. Next, for $\mathbf{b} = (b_0, \cdots, b_{c_d-1})^\top \in \{0,1\}^{c_d}$ and $\mathbf{e} = (e_1, \ldots, e_m) \in \{-1,0,1\}^m$, we define the permutation $\Psi_{\mathbf{b},\mathbf{e}}$ that acts as follows. When applied to vector

$$\mathbf{v} = \big(\mathbf{v}_{-1}\|\mathbf{v}_{0,1}\| \ldots \|\mathbf{v}_{0,m}\| \ldots \|\mathbf{v}_{c_d-1,1}\| \ldots \|\mathbf{v}_{c_d-1,m}\big) \in \mathbb{Z}^{3m+6mc_d},$$

where block $\mathbf{v}_{-1}$ has length $3m$ and each block $\mathbf{v}_{i,j}$ has length 6, it transforms $\mathbf{v}$ into vector

$$\Psi_{\mathbf{b},\mathbf{e}}(\mathbf{v}) = \big(\Pi_{\mathbf{e}}(\mathbf{v}_{-1})\| \ \psi_{b_0,e_1}(\mathbf{v}_{0,1})\| \cdots \|\psi_{b_0,e_m}(\mathbf{v}_{0,m})\| \cdots \|$$
$$\psi_{b_{c_d-1},e_1}(\mathbf{v}_{c_d-1,1})\| \cdots \|\psi_{b_{c_d-1},e_m}(\mathbf{v}_{c_d-1,m})\big).$$

Then, observe that the following desirable equivalence holds for all $\mathbf{t},\mathbf{b} \in \{0,1\}^{c_d}$ and $\mathbf{z},\mathbf{e} \in \{-1,0,1\}^m$.

$$\mathbf{v} = \mathsf{mix}(\mathbf{t},\mathbf{z}) \iff \Psi_{\mathbf{b},\mathbf{e}}(\mathbf{v}) = \mathsf{mix}(\mathbf{t} \oplus \mathbf{b}, [\mathbf{z}+\mathbf{e}]_3). \tag{6}$$

3.2   Zero-Knowledge Protocol for the Ducas-Micciancio Signature

We now present our statistical ZKAoK of a valid message-signature pair for the Ducas-Micciancio signature scheme. Let $n,q,m,k,\overline{m},\ell,\beta,d,c_0,\ldots,c_d$ as specified in Sect. 2.3. The protocol can be summarized as follows.

– The public input consists of

$$\mathbf{A},\mathbf{F}_0 \in R_q^{1\times\overline{m}}; \ \ \mathbf{A}_{[0]},\ldots,\mathbf{A}_{[d]} \in R_q^{1\times k}; \ \ \mathbf{F},\mathbf{F}_1 \in R_q^{1\times\ell}; \ \ u \in R_q.$$

– The prover's secret input consists of message $p \in R_q$ and signature $(t,\mathbf{r},\mathbf{v})$, where

$$\begin{cases} t = (t_0,\ldots,t_{c_1-1},\ldots,t_{c_{d-1}},\ldots,t_{c_d-1})^\top \in \{0,1\}^{c_d}; \\ \mathbf{r} \in R^{\overline{m}}; \ \mathbf{v} = (\mathbf{s}\|\mathbf{z}) \in R^{\overline{m}+k}; \ \mathbf{s} \in R^{\overline{m}}; \ \mathbf{z} \in R^k; \end{cases}$$

– The prover's goal is to prove in zero-knowledge that $\|\mathbf{r}\|_\infty \le \beta$, $\|\mathbf{v}\|_\infty \le \beta$, and that the equation

$$\mathbf{A}\cdot\mathbf{s} + \mathbf{A}_{[0]}\cdot\mathbf{z} + \sum_{i=1}^{d} \mathbf{A}_{[i]}\cdot t_{[i]}\cdot\mathbf{z} = \mathbf{F}\cdot\mathbf{y} + u \tag{7}$$

holds for $\big\{t_{[i]} = \sum_{j=c_{i-1}}^{c_i-1} t_j\cdot X^j\big\}_{i=1}^{d}$ and

$$\mathbf{y} = \mathsf{rdec}\,(\mathbf{F}_0\cdot\mathbf{r} + \mathbf{F}_1\cdot\mathsf{rdec}(p)) \in R^\ell. \tag{8}$$

Our strategy is to reduce the considered statement to an instance of the abstract protocol from Sect. 2.4. The reduction consists of 2 steps.

DECOMPOSING-UNIFYING. In the first step, we will employ the decomposition techniques from Sect. 2.2 together with the notations rot and τ from Sect. 2.1 to transform Eqs. (7) and (8) into one equation of the form $\mathbf{M}_0\cdot\mathbf{w}_0 = \mathbf{u} \bmod q$, where $\mathbf{M}_0,\mathbf{u}$ are public, and the coefficients of vector $\mathbf{w}_0$ are in the set $\{-1,0,1\}$.

Let $\mathbf{s}^\star = \tau(\mathsf{rdec}_\beta(\mathbf{s})) \in \{-1,0,1\}^{n\overline{m}\delta_\beta}$, $\mathbf{z}^\star = \tau(\mathsf{rdec}_\beta(\mathbf{z})) \in \{-1,0,1\}^{nk\delta_\beta}$ and $\mathbf{r}^\star = \tau(\mathsf{rdec}_\beta(\mathbf{r})) \in \{-1,0,1\}^{n\overline{m}\delta_\beta}$. Then, we observe that, Eq. (7) is equivalent to,

$$[\mathsf{rot}(\mathbf{A}_{[0]}) \cdot \mathbf{H}_{k,\beta}] \cdot \mathbf{z}^\star + \sum_{i=1}^d \sum_{j=c_{i-1}}^{c_i-1} [\mathsf{rot}(\mathbf{A}_{[i]} \cdot X^j) \cdot \mathbf{H}_{k,\beta}] \cdot t_j \cdot \mathbf{z}^\star +$$
$$[\mathsf{rot}(\mathbf{A}) \cdot \mathbf{H}_{\overline{m},\beta}] \cdot \mathbf{s}^\star - [\mathsf{rot}(\mathbf{F})] \cdot \tau(\mathbf{y}) = \tau(u) \bmod q,$$

and Eq. (8) is equivalent to

$$[\mathsf{rot}(\mathbf{F}_0) \cdot \mathbf{H}_{\overline{m},\beta}] \cdot \mathbf{r}^\star + [\mathsf{rot}(\mathbf{F}_1)] \cdot \tau(\mathsf{rdec}(p)) - [\mathbf{H}] \cdot \tau(\mathbf{y}) = \mathbf{0} \bmod q.$$

Now, using basic algebra, we can manipulate the two derived equations: rearranging the secret vectors and combining them, as well as concatenating the public matrices (namely, those written inside $[\cdot]$) accordingly. As a result, we obtain an unifying equation of the form:

$$\mathbf{M}_0 \cdot \mathbf{w}_0 = \mathbf{u} \bmod q,$$

where $\mathbf{u} = (\tau(u)\|\mathbf{0}) \in \mathbb{Z}_q^{2n}$ and $\mathbf{M}_0$ are public, and $\mathbf{w}_0 = (\mathbf{w}_1\|\mathbf{w}_2)$, with

$$\begin{cases} \mathbf{w}_1 = (\mathbf{z}^\star\|t_0 \cdot \mathbf{z}^\star\| \ \ldots \| \ t_{c_d-1} \cdot \mathbf{z}^\star) \in \{-1,0,1\}^{(k\delta_\beta + c_d k\delta_\beta)n}; \\ \mathbf{w}_2 = (\mathbf{s}^\star\| \ \mathbf{r}^\star\| \ \tau(\mathbf{y})\| \ \tau(\mathsf{rdec}(p))) \in \{-1,0,1\}^{(\overline{m}\delta_\beta + \ell)2n}. \end{cases}$$

EXTENDING-PERMUTING. In this second step, we will transform the equation $\mathbf{M}_0 \cdot \mathbf{w}_0 = \mathbf{u} \bmod q$ obtained in the first step into an equation of the form $\mathbf{M} \cdot \mathbf{w} = \mathbf{u} \bmod q$, where the secret vector $\mathbf{w}$ satisfies the conditions required by the abstract protocol. In the process, we will employ the techniques introduced in Sect. 3.1.

Specifically, we extend the blocks of vector $\mathbf{w}_0 = (\mathbf{w}_1\|\mathbf{w}_2)$ as follows.

$$\mathbf{w}_1 \mapsto \mathbf{w}_1' = \mathsf{mix}(t, \mathbf{z}^\star) \in \{-1,0,1\}^{L_1}; \qquad (9)$$
$$\mathbf{w}_2 \mapsto \mathbf{w}_2' = \mathsf{enc}(\mathbf{w}_2) \in \{-1,0,1\}^{L_2}.$$

Then we form vector $\mathbf{w} = (\mathbf{w}_1'\|\mathbf{w}_2') \in \{-1,0,1\}^L$, where

$$L = L_1 + L_2; \ L_1 = (k\delta_\beta + 2c_d k\delta_\beta)3n; \ L_2 = (\overline{m}\delta_\beta + \ell)6n.$$

At the same time, we insert suitable zero-columns to matrix $\mathbf{M}_0$ to obtain matrix $\mathbf{M} \in \mathbb{Z}_q^{2n\times L}$ such that $\mathbf{M} \cdot \mathbf{w} = \mathbf{M}_0 \cdot \mathbf{w}_0$.

Up to this point, we have transformed the considered relations into one equation of the desired form $\mathbf{M} \cdot \mathbf{w} = \mathbf{u} \bmod q$. We now specify the set VALID that contains the obtained vector $\mathbf{w}$, the set $\mathcal{S}$ and permutations $\{\Gamma_\phi : \phi \in \mathcal{S}\}$, such that the conditions in (1) hold.

Define VALID as the set of all vectors $\mathbf{v}' = (\mathbf{v}_1'\|\mathbf{v}_2') \in \{-1,0,1\}^L$, satisfying the following:

- There exist $t \in \{0,1\}^{c_d}$ and $\mathbf{z}^\star \in \{-1,0,1\}^{nk\delta_\beta}$ such that $\mathbf{v}'_1 = \mathsf{mix}(t, \mathbf{z}^\star)$.
- There exists $\mathbf{w}_2 \in \{-1,0,1\}^{(\overline{m}\delta_\beta+\ell)2n}$ such that $\mathbf{v}'_2 = \mathsf{enc}(\mathbf{w}_2)$.

Clearly, our vector $\mathbf{w}$ belongs to this tailored set VALID.

Now, let $\mathcal{S} = \{0,1\}^{c_d} \times \{-1,0,1\}^{nk\delta_\beta} \times \{-1,0,1\}^{(\overline{m}\delta_\beta+\ell)2n}$, and associate every element $\phi = (\mathbf{b}, \mathbf{e}, \mathbf{f}) \in \mathcal{S}$ with permutation Γ_ϕ that acts as follows. When applied to vector $\mathbf{v}^\star = (\mathbf{v}_1^\star \| \mathbf{v}_2^\star) \in \mathbb{Z}^L$, where $\mathbf{v}_1^\star \in \mathbb{Z}^{L_1}$ and $\mathbf{v}_2^\star \in \mathbb{Z}^{L_2}$, it transforms $\mathbf{v}^\star$ into vector

$$\Gamma_\phi(\mathbf{v}^\star) = \big(\Psi_{\mathbf{b},\mathbf{e}}(\mathbf{v}_1^\star) \;\|\; \Pi_{\mathbf{f}}(\mathbf{v}_2^\star)\big).$$

Based on the equivalences observed in (5) and (6), it can be checked that VALID, $\mathcal{S}$ and Γ_ϕ satisfy the conditions specified in (1). In other words, we have reduced the considered statement to an instance of the abstract protocol from Sect. 2.4.

The interactive protocol. Given the above preparations, our interactive protocol works as follows.

- The public input consists of matrix $\mathbf{M}$ and vector $\mathbf{u}$, which are built from $\mathbf{A}$, $(\mathbf{A}_{[0]}, \ldots, \mathbf{A}_{[d]}, \mathbf{F}, \mathbf{F}_0, \mathbf{F}_1, u)$, as discussed above.
- The prover's witness is vector $\mathbf{w} \in \mathsf{VALID}$, which is obtained from the original witnesses $(p, t, \mathbf{r}, \mathbf{v})$, as described above.

Both parties then run the protocol of Fig. 1. The protocol uses the KTX string commitment scheme COM, which is statistically hiding and computationally binding under the (R)SIS assumption. We therefore obtain the following result, as a corollary of Theorem 1.

Theorem 2. *Assume that* COM *is a statistically hiding and computationally binding string commitment scheme. Then the protocol described above is a statistical* ZKAoK *of a valid message-signature pair for the Ducas-Micciancio signature scheme, with perfect completeness, soundness error* $2/3$ *and communication cost* $\widetilde{\mathcal{O}}(\lambda)$.

Proof. For simulation, we simply run the simulator of Theorem 1. As for extraction, we invoke the knowledge extractor of Theorem 1 to obtain a vector $\mathbf{w}' \in \mathsf{VALID}$ such that $\mathbf{M} \cdot \mathbf{w}' = \mathbf{u} \bmod q$. Then, by "backtracking" the transformations being done, we can extract from $\mathbf{w}'$ a satisfying witness $(p', t', \mathbf{r}', \mathbf{v}')$ for the considered statement.

The perfect completeness, soundness error and communication cost of the protocol directly follow from those of the abstract protocol in Sect. 2.4. In particular, the communication cost is:

$$\mathcal{O}(L \cdot \log q) = \mathcal{O}\big((k\delta_\beta + 2c_d k\delta_\beta)3n \cdot \log q + (\overline{m}\delta_\beta + \ell)6n \cdot \log q\big) = \mathcal{O}(n \cdot \log^4 n) = \widetilde{\mathcal{O}}(\lambda),$$

for the setting of parameters for the Ducas-Micciancio signature in Sect. 2.3. $\square$

4   Constant-Size Group Signatures from Lattices

In Sect. 4.1, we recall the syntax, correctness and security requirements of the (partially) dynamic group signatures, as in the model of Bellare et al. [5]. In Sect. 4.2, we describe our main zero-knowledge argument, which will be used as a building block in our group signature scheme constructed in Sect. 4.3.

4.1   Dynamic Group Signatures

In this section, we recall the syntax, correctness and security definitions of the (partially) dynamic group signatures, as put forward by Bellare et al. [5]. A dynamic group signature scheme involves a trusted party who generates the initial keys, an authority named issuer, an authority named opener and a set of users who are potential group members. The scheme consists of the following polynomial-time algorithms.

GKg(λ): Given the security parameter λ, the trusted party runs this algorithm to generate a triple (gpk, ik, ok). The issue key ik is given to the issuer, the opening key ok is given to the opener and the group public key gpk is made public.

UKg(λ): A user who intends to be a group member runs this algorithm to obtain a personal key pair (upk, usk). It is assumed that upk is public.

⟨Join, Iss⟩: This is an interactive protocol run by the issuer and a user. If it completes successfully, the issuer registers this user to the group and this user becomes a group member. The final state of the Join is the secret signing key gsk_i while the final state of the Iss is the registration information $\mathbf{reg}[i]$ stored in the registration table $\mathbf{reg}$.

Sign(gpk, gsk_i, M): A group member, using his group signing key gsk_i, runs this algorithm to obtain a signature Σ on message M.

Verify(gpk, M, Σ): This algorithm outputs 1/0 indicating whether or not Σ is a valid signature on message M, with respect to the group public key gpk.

Open(gpk, ok, $\mathbf{reg}$, M, Σ): Given gpk, a message-signature pair (M, Σ) and ok, the opener, who has read-access to the registration table $\mathbf{reg}$, runs this algorithm to obtain a pair (i, Π_{open}), where $i \in \mathbb{N} \cup \{\perp\}$. In case $i = \perp$, $\Pi_{\text{open}} = \perp$.

Judge(gpk, M, Σ, i, upk_i, Π_{open}): This algorithm outputs 1/0 to check whether or not Π_{open} is a proof that i produced Σ, with respect to the group public key gpk and message M.

Now we recall the correctness and security definitions of dynamic group signatures below.

Correctness requires that for any signature generated by honest group members, the following should hold: the signature should be valid; the opening algorithm, given the message and signature, should correctly identify the signer; the proof returned by the opening algorithm should be accepted by the judge.

Full Anonymity requires that it is infeasible to recover the identity of a signer from a signature, even if the adversary is given access to the opening oracle. As pointed out by [4,5], it is sufficient that the adversary is unable to distinguish which of two signers of its choice signed a targeted message of its choice.

Traceability requires that every valid signature should be traced to some group member and the opener is able to generate a proof accepted by the judge.

Non-frameability requires that the adversary is unable to generate a proof, which is accepted by the judge, that an honest user generated a valid signature unless this user really did generate this signature.

Formal definitions of correctness and security requirements are available in the full version.

4.2 The Underlying Zero-Knowledge Argument System

Before describing our group signature scheme in Sect. 4.3, let us first present the statistical ZKAoK that will be invoked by the signer when generating group signatures. The protocol is an extension of the one for the Ducas-Micciancio signature from Sect. 3.2, for which the prover additionally convinces the verifier of the following two facts.

1. He knows a secret key $\mathbf{x} \in R^m$ corresponding to the public key $p \in R_q$, which satisfies $\|\mathbf{x}\|_\infty \leq 1$ and $\mathbf{B} \cdot \mathbf{x} = p$. Here, $\mathbf{B} \in R_q^{1 \times m}$ is a public matrix.

2. He has correctly encrypted the vector $\mathsf{rdec}(p) \in R^\ell$ to a given ciphertext $(\mathbf{c}_{1,1}, \mathbf{c}_{1,2}, \mathbf{c}_{2,1}, \mathbf{c}_{2,2}) \in (R_q^\ell)^4$, under public key $(\mathbf{a}, \mathbf{b}_1, \mathbf{b}_2) \in (R_q^\ell)^3$. To this end, he proves that equations

$$\mathbf{c}_{i,1} = \mathbf{a} \cdot g_i + \mathbf{e}_{i,1}, \quad \mathbf{c}_{i,2} = \mathbf{b}_i \cdot g_i + \mathbf{e}_{i,2} + \lfloor q/4 \rfloor \cdot \mathsf{rdec}(p), \tag{10}$$

hold for B-bounded randomness $g_1, g_2 \in R$, and $\mathbf{e}_{1,1}, \mathbf{e}_{2,1}, \mathbf{e}_{1,2}, \mathbf{e}_{2,2} \in R^\ell$.

As the transformations for the "Ducas-Micciancio layer" have been established in Sect. 3.2, in the following, we only specify the transformations with respect to the newly appeared relations.

We will first apply the decomposition techniques in Sect. 2.2 to the secret objects.

- Let $\mathbf{x}^\star = \tau(\mathbf{x}) \in \{-1, 0, 1\}^{nm}$.
- For $i \in \{1, 2\}$, compute $\mathbf{g}_i^\star = \tau(\mathsf{rdec}_B(g_i)) \in \{-1, 0, 1\}^{n\delta_B}$.
- For $i \in \{1, 2\}$, compute $\mathbf{e}_{i,1}^\star = \tau(\mathsf{rdec}_B(\mathbf{e}_{i,1}))$ and $\mathbf{e}_{i,2}^\star = \tau(\mathsf{rdec}_B(\mathbf{e}_{i,2}))$. Note that they are vectors in $\{-1, 0, 1\}^{n\ell\delta_B}$.

Then the equation $\mathbf{B} \cdot \mathbf{x} = p$ can be translated as

$$[\mathsf{rot}(\mathbf{B})] \cdot \mathbf{x}^\star - [\mathbf{H}] \cdot \tau(\mathsf{rdec}(p)) = \mathbf{0}^n \bmod q. \tag{11}$$

Meanwhile, let $\mathbf{a} = (a_1, \ldots, a_\ell)^\top$, $\{\mathbf{b}_i = (b_{i,1}, \ldots, b_{i,\ell})^\top\}_{i=1,2}$, then Eq. (10) can be rewritten as, for $i = 1, 2$,

$$\begin{bmatrix} \mathrm{rot}(a_1) \cdot \mathbf{H}_B \\ \vdots \\ \mathrm{rot}(a_\ell) \cdot \mathbf{H}_B \end{bmatrix} \cdot \mathbf{g}_i^\star + [\mathbf{H}_{\ell,B}] \cdot \mathbf{e}_{i,1}^\star = \tau(\mathbf{c}_{i,1}) \bmod q; \quad (12)$$

$$\begin{bmatrix} \mathrm{rot}(b_{i,1}) \cdot \mathbf{H}_B \\ \vdots \\ \mathrm{rot}(b_{i,\ell}) \cdot \mathbf{H}_B \end{bmatrix} \cdot \mathbf{g}_i^\star + [\mathbf{H}_{\ell,B}] \cdot \mathbf{e}_{i,2}^\star + \lfloor q/4 \rfloor \cdot \tau(\mathrm{rdec}(p)) = \tau(\mathbf{c}_{i,2}) \bmod q. \quad (13)$$

Before proceeding further, let us recall that, in the protocol for the Ducas-Micciancio signature from Sect. 3.2, at the end of the Decomposing-Unifying step, we did combine the secret objects into vectors $\mathbf{w}_1, \mathbf{w}_2$ of the form:

$$\begin{cases} \mathbf{w}_1 = (\mathbf{z}^\star \| t_0 \cdot \mathbf{z}^\star \| \cdots \| t_{c_d-1} \cdot \mathbf{z}^\star) \in \{-1,0,1\}^{(k\delta_\beta + c_d k \delta_\beta)n}; \\ \mathbf{w}_2 = (\mathbf{s}^\star \| \mathbf{r}^\star \| \tau(\mathbf{y}) \| \tau(\mathrm{rdec}(p))) \in \{-1,0,1\}^{(\overline{m}\delta_\beta + \ell)2n}. \end{cases}$$

Since vector $\tau(\mathrm{rdec}(p))$ has been counted as a block of vector $\mathbf{w}_2$, we now combine the newly appeared secret vectors in Eqs. (11), (12) and (13) into vector

$$\mathbf{w}_3 = (\, \mathbf{x}^\star \| \mathbf{g}_1^\star \| \mathbf{g}_2^\star \| \mathbf{e}_{1,1}^\star \| \mathbf{e}_{1,2}^\star \| \mathbf{e}_{2,1}^\star \| \mathbf{e}_{2,2}^\star \,) \in \{-1,0,1\}^{nm+2n\delta_B+4n\ell\delta_B},$$

and let $\mathbf{w}_4 = (\mathbf{w}_2\|\mathbf{w}_3) \in \{-1,0,1\}^{L_4'}$, for $L_4' = (\overline{m}\delta_\beta+\ell)2n+nm+2n\delta_B+4n\ell\delta_B$.

Next, we extend $\mathbf{w}_4$ to vector $\mathbf{w}_4' = \mathrm{enc}(\mathbf{w}_4) \in \{-1,0,1\}^{L_4}$, where $L_4 = 3L_4'$, and form the vector

$$\widetilde{\mathbf{w}} = (\mathbf{w}_1'\|\mathbf{w}_4') \in \{-1,0,1\}^{\widetilde{L}},$$

where $\mathbf{w}_1' = \mathrm{mix}(t, \mathbf{z}^\star) \in \{-1,0,1\}^{L_1}$ is the "mixing vector" obtained in (9), and $\widetilde{L} = L_1 + L_4$.

We remark that, by suitably concatenating/extending the matrices and vectors derived from the public input, we can obtain public matrix $\widetilde{\mathbf{M}}$ and public vector $\widetilde{\mathbf{u}}$ such that $\widetilde{\mathbf{M}} \cdot \widetilde{\mathbf{w}} = \widetilde{\mathbf{u}} \bmod q$. Having obtained this desired equation, we now proceed as in Sect. 3.2.

Define $\widetilde{\mathrm{VALID}}$ as the set of all vectors $\mathbf{v}' = (\mathbf{v}_1'\|\mathbf{v}_4') \in \{-1,0,1\}^{\widetilde{L}}$, satisfying the following:

- There exist $t \in \{0,1\}^{c_d}$ and $\mathbf{z}^\star \in \{-1,0,1\}^{nk\delta_\beta}$ such that $\mathbf{v}_1' = \mathrm{mix}(t, \mathbf{z}^\star)$.
- There exists $\mathbf{w}_4 \in \{-1,0,1\}^{L_4'}$ such that $\mathbf{v}_4' = \mathrm{enc}(\mathbf{w}_4)$.

It can be seen that vector $\widetilde{\mathbf{w}}$ belongs to $\widetilde{\mathrm{VALID}}$.

Now, let $\widetilde{\mathcal{S}} = \{0,1\}^{c_d} \times \{-1,0,1\}^{nk\delta_\beta} \times \{-1,0,1\}^{L_4'}$, and associate every element $\phi = (\mathbf{b}, \mathbf{e}, \mathbf{f}) \in \mathcal{S}$ with permutation $\widetilde{\Gamma}_\phi$ that acts as follows. When applied to vector $\mathbf{v}^\star = (\mathbf{v}_1^\star\|\mathbf{v}_4^\star) \in \mathbb{Z}^{\widetilde{L}}$, where $\mathbf{v}_1^\star \in \mathbb{Z}^{L_1}$ and $\mathbf{v}_2^\star \in \mathbb{Z}^{L_4}$, it transforms $\mathbf{v}^\star$ into vector

$$\widetilde{\Gamma}_\phi(\mathbf{v}^\star) = (\Psi_{\mathbf{b},\mathbf{e}}(\mathbf{v}_1^\star)\|\Pi_{\mathbf{f}}(\mathbf{v}_4^\star)).$$

Based on the equivalences observed in (5) and (6), it can be checked that $\widetilde{\mathsf{VALID}}$, $\widetilde{\mathcal{S}}$ and $\widetilde{\Gamma}_\phi$ satisfy the conditions specified in (1). In other words, we have reduced the considered statement to an instance of the abstract protocol from Sect. 2.4.

The interactive protocol. Given the above preparations, our interactive protocol works as follows.

– The public input consists of matrix $\widetilde{\mathbf{M}}$ and vector $\widetilde{\mathbf{u}}$, which are built from $\mathbf{A}, (\mathbf{A}_{[0]}, \ldots, \mathbf{A}_{[d]}, \mathbf{F}, \mathbf{F}_0, \mathbf{F}_1, u)$, and $\mathbf{B}, \mathbf{c}_{1,1}, \mathbf{c}_{1,2}, \mathbf{c}_{2,1}, \mathbf{c}_{2,2}, \mathbf{a}, \mathbf{b}_1, \mathbf{b}_2$, as discussed in Sect. 3.2 and above.
– The prover's witness is vector $\widetilde{\mathbf{w}} \in \widetilde{\mathsf{VALID}}$, which is obtained from the original witnesses $(p, t, \mathbf{r}, \mathbf{v}, \mathbf{x}, g_1, g_2, \mathbf{e}_{1,1}, \mathbf{e}_{2,1}, \mathbf{e}_{1,2}, \mathbf{e}_{2,2})$, as described in Sect. 3.2 and above.

Both parties then run the protocol of Fig. 1. The protocol uses the KTX string commitment scheme COM, which is statistically hiding and computationally binding under the (R)SIS assumption. We therefore obtain the following result, as a corollary of Theorem 1.

Theorem 3. *Assume that* COM *is a statistically hiding and computationally binding string commitment scheme. Then the protocol described above is a statistical* ZKAoK *for the considered statement, with perfect completeness, soundness error* $2/3$ *and communication cost* $\widetilde{\mathcal{O}}(\lambda)$.

Proof. For simulation, we simply run the simulator of Theorem 1. As for extraction, we invoke the knowledge extractor of Theorem 1 to obtain a vector $\widetilde{\mathbf{w}}' \in \widetilde{\mathsf{VALID}}$ such that $\widetilde{\mathbf{M}} \cdot \widetilde{\mathbf{w}}' = \widetilde{\mathbf{u}} \bmod q$. Then, by "backtracking" all the transformations being done, we can extract from vector $\widetilde{\mathbf{w}}'$ a satisfying witness $(p', t', \mathbf{r}', \mathbf{v}', \mathbf{x}', g_1', g_2', \mathbf{e}_{1,1}', \mathbf{e}_{2,1}', \mathbf{e}_{1,2}', \mathbf{e}_{2,2}')$ for the considered statement.

The perfect completeness, soundness error and communication cost of the protocol directly follow from those of the abstract protocol in Sect. 2.4. In particular, the communication cost is:

$$\mathcal{O}(\widetilde{L} \cdot \log q) = \mathcal{O}\big((k\delta_\beta + c_d k\delta_\beta)n \cdot \log q + ((\overline{m}\delta_\beta + \ell)n + nm + n\delta_B + n\ell\delta_B) \cdot \log q\big),$$

which is of order $\mathcal{O}(n \cdot \log^4 n) = \widetilde{\mathcal{O}}(\lambda)$, for the setting of parameters we use in the group signature scheme of Sect. 4.3. $\square$

4.3   Description of Our Scheme

In the description below, the Ducas-Micciancio signature scheme [20, 21] as described in Sect. 2.3 is used to design a group signature scheme for (partially) dynamic groups. Group public key consists of three parts: (i) a verification key from the Ducas-Micciancio signature scheme, (ii) *two* public keys of an extended version of LPR encryption scheme [47] and (iii) a public matrix $\mathbf{B}$ for users to generate their short secret vectors together with public syndromes as user key pairs. The issue key is the corresponding signing key of the verification key while the opening key is *any one* of the corresponding secret keys of the two public keys.

When a user joins the group, it first generates a short vector together with a public syndrome using matrix **B**. It then interacts with the issuer. The issuer signs the public syndrome of this user using the issue key. If the interaction completes successfully, the user obtains a signature on his syndrome from the issuer while the issuer registers this user to the group.

Once registered as a group member, the user can sign messages on behalf of the group. When signing a message, it first encrypts the public syndrome twice using the two public keys. The user then generates a ZKAoK of his syndrome, of the signature on the syndrome obtained from the issuer, of the short vector corresponding to his syndrome and of randomness used in the encryptions of the syndrome. This ZKAoK protocol is repeated $\kappa = \omega(\log \lambda)$ times to achieve negligible soundness error and made non-interactive via Fiat-Shamir transform [22]. The signature then consists of the NIZKAoK Π_{gs} and the two ciphertexts of the syndrome. Note that the ZK argument together with double encryption enables CCA-security of the underlying encryption scheme, which is known as the Naor-Yung transformation [51]. This enables full anonymity of our group signature scheme.

When one needs to know the validity of a signature, one simply verifies Π_{gs}. In case of dispute, the opener can decrypt the syndrome using his opening key. To prevent corrupted opening, the opener is required to generate a NIZKAoK of correct opening Π_{open}. Only when Π_{open} is a valid proof, will the judger accept the opening result. Details of the scheme are described below.

GKg(λ): Given the security parameter λ, the trusted party proceeds as follows.
- Choose parameter $n = \mathcal{O}(\lambda)$ being a power of 2, and modulus $q = \widetilde{\mathcal{O}}(n^4)$, where $q = 3^k$ for some positive integer k. Let $R = \mathbb{Z}[X]/(X^n + 1)$ and $R_q = R/qR$.
  Also, let $\ell = \lfloor \log \frac{q-1}{2} \rfloor + 1$, $m \geq 2\lceil \log q \rceil + 2$, and $\overline{m} = m + k$.
- Choose integer d and sequence $c_0, \ldots, c_d$ as described in Sect. 2.3.
- Choose integer bounds $\beta = \widetilde{\mathcal{O}}(n)$, $B = \widetilde{\mathcal{O}}(n^{5/4})$, and let χ be a B-bounded distribution over R.
- Let $\mathcal{H}_{\text{FS}} : \{0,1\}^* \rightarrow \{1,2,3\}^\kappa$, where $\kappa = \omega(\log \lambda)$, be a collision-resistant hash function, to be modelled as a random oracle in the Fiat-Shamir transformations [22].
- Let COM be the statistically hiding and computationally binding commitment scheme from [30], to be used in our zero-knowledge argument systems.
- Draw a uniformly random matrix $\mathbf{B} \in R_q^{1 \times m}$.
- Generate verification key

$$\mathbf{A}, \mathbf{F}_0 \in R_q^{1 \times \overline{m}}; \mathbf{A}_{[0]}, \ldots, \mathbf{A}_{[d]} \in R_q^{1 \times k}; \mathbf{F}, \mathbf{F}_1 \in R_q^{1 \times \ell}; u \in R_q$$

and signing key $\mathbf{R} \in R_q^{m \times k}$ for the Ducas-Micciancio signature scheme, as described in Sect. 2.3.

- Initialize the Naor-Yung double-encryption mechanism [51] with an extended version of the LPR encryption scheme [47] that allows to encrypt $\{-1, 0, 1\}$ ring vectors of length ℓ. Specifically, sample $s_1, s_2 \hookleftarrow \chi$, $\mathbf{e}_1, \mathbf{e}_2 \hookleftarrow \chi^\ell$, $\mathbf{a} \xleftarrow{\$} R_q^\ell$, and compute

$$\mathbf{b}_1 = \mathbf{a} \cdot s_1 + \mathbf{e}_1 \in R_q^\ell; \quad \mathbf{b}_2 = \mathbf{a} \cdot s_2 + \mathbf{e}_2 \in R_q^\ell.$$

Set the public parameter pp, the group public key gpk, the issue key ik and the opening key ok as follows:

$$\mathsf{pp} = \{n, q, k, R, R_q, \ell, m, \overline{m}, \chi, d, c_0, \ldots, c_d, B, \beta, \kappa, \mathcal{H}_{\mathsf{FS}}, \mathsf{COM}, \mathbf{B}\},$$

$$\mathsf{gpk} = \{\mathsf{pp}, \mathbf{A}, \{\mathbf{A}_{[j]}\}_{j=0}^d, \mathbf{F}, \mathbf{F}_0, \mathbf{F}_1, u, \mathbf{a}, \mathbf{b}_1, \mathbf{b}_2\},$$

$$\mathsf{ik} = \mathbf{R}, \ \mathsf{ok} = (s_1, \mathbf{e}_1).$$

The trusted party then makes gpk public and sends ik to the issuer and ok to the opener.

Assume that after receiving ik from the trusted party, the issuer initializes his internal state $S = 0$ and the registration table **reg**.

UKg(gpk): The user samples $\mathbf{x} \in R^m$, whose coefficients are uniformly random in the set $\{-1, 0, 1\}$. Then he computes $p = \mathbf{B} \cdot \mathbf{x} \in R_q$. Set $\mathsf{upk} = p$ and $\mathsf{usk} = \mathbf{x}$.

$\langle\mathsf{Join}, \mathsf{Iss}\rangle$: When receiving the joining request from a user with public key $\mathsf{upk} = p$, the issuer verifies that upk was not previously used by a registered user, and aborts if this is not the case. Otherwise, he proceeds as follows.

- Set the tag $t = (t_0, t_1 \ldots, t_{c_d-1})^\top \in \mathcal{T}_d$, where $S = \sum_{j=0}^{c_d-1} 2^j \cdot t_j$, and compute $\mathbf{A}_t = [\mathbf{A}|\mathbf{A}_{[0]} + \sum_{i=1}^d t_{[i]}\mathbf{A}_{[i]}] \in R_q^{1 \times (\overline{m}+k)}$.

- Using the signing key $\mathbf{R}$, generate a Ducas-Micciancio signature $(t, \mathbf{r}, \mathbf{v})$ on message $\mathsf{rdec}(p) \in R^\ell$ - whose coefficients are in $\{-1, 0, 1\}$. As described in Sect. 2.3, one has $\mathbf{r} \in R^{\overline{m}}$, $\mathbf{v} \in R^{\overline{m}+k}$ and

$$\begin{cases} \mathbf{A}_t \cdot \mathbf{v} = \mathbf{F} \cdot \mathsf{rdec}(\mathbf{F}_0 \cdot \mathbf{r} + \mathbf{F}_1 \cdot \mathsf{rdec}(p)) + u, \\ \|\mathbf{r}\|_\infty \leq \beta, \ \|\mathbf{v}\|_\infty \leq \beta. \end{cases} \quad (14)$$

The issuer then sends the triple $(t, \mathbf{r}, \mathbf{v})$ to the user. The latter sets his group signing key as $\mathsf{gsk} = (t, \mathbf{r}, \mathbf{v}, \mathbf{x})$ while the former stores $\mathbf{reg}[S] = p$ and updates S to $S + 1$.

Sign(gpk, gsk_i, M): To sign a message $M \in \{0, 1\}^*$ using $\mathsf{gsk} = (t, \mathbf{r}, \mathbf{v}, \mathbf{x})$, the group member who has public key $p \in R_q$ proceeds as follows.

- Encrypt the ring vector $\mathsf{rdec}(p) \in R_q^\ell$ with coefficients in $\{-1, 0, 1\}$ twice. Namely, for each $i \in \{1, 2\}$, sample $g_i \hookleftarrow \chi$, $\mathbf{e}_{i,1} \hookleftarrow \chi^\ell$, and $\mathbf{e}_{i,2} \hookleftarrow \chi^\ell$ and compute

$$\begin{aligned} \mathbf{c}_i &= (\mathbf{c}_{i,1}, \mathbf{c}_{i,2}) \\ &= (\mathbf{a} \cdot g_i + \mathbf{e}_{i,1}, \mathbf{b}_i \cdot g_i + \mathbf{e}_{i,2} + \lfloor q/4 \rfloor \cdot \mathsf{rdec}(p)) \in R_q^\ell \times R_q^\ell. \end{aligned}$$

– Generate a NIZKAoK Π_{gs} to demonstrate the possession of a valid tuple

$$\zeta = (t, \mathbf{r}, \mathbf{v}, \mathbf{x}, p, g_1, g_2, \mathbf{e}_{1,1}, \mathbf{e}_{2,1}, \mathbf{e}_{1,2}, \mathbf{e}_{2,2}) \tag{15}$$

such that

(i) The conditions from (14) hold.

(ii) $\mathbf{c}_1$ and $\mathbf{c}_2$ are both correct encryptions of $\mathsf{rdec}(p)$ with B-bounded randomness $g_1, \mathbf{e}_{1,1}, \mathbf{e}_{1,2}$ and $g_2, \mathbf{e}_{2,1}, \mathbf{e}_{2,2}$, respectively.

(iii) $\|\mathbf{x}\|_\infty \leq 1$ and $\mathbf{B} \cdot \mathbf{x} = p$.

This is done by running the argument system described in Sect. 4.2. The protocol is an extension of the one for the Ducas-Micciancio signature from Sect. 3.2, in which the prover additionally proves statements (ii) and (iii). The protocol is repeated $\kappa = \omega(\log \lambda)$ times to achieve negligible soundness error and made non-interactive via Fiat-Shamir heuristic [22] as a triple $\Pi_{\mathsf{gs}} = (\{\mathrm{CMT}_i\}_{i=1}^{\kappa}, \mathrm{CH}, \{\mathrm{RSP}_i\}_{i=1}^{\kappa})$ where $\mathrm{CH} = \mathcal{H}_{\mathsf{FS}}(M, \{\mathrm{CMT}_i\}_{i=1}^{\kappa}, \xi)$ with

$$\xi = (\mathbf{A}, \mathbf{A}_{[0]}, \dots, \mathbf{A}_{[d]}, \mathbf{F}, \mathbf{F}_0, \mathbf{F}_1, u, \mathbf{B}, \mathbf{a}, \mathbf{b}_1, \mathbf{b}_2, \mathbf{c}_1, \mathbf{c}_2) \tag{16}$$

– Output the group signature $\Pi = (\Pi_{\mathsf{gs}}, \mathbf{c}_1, \mathbf{c}_2)$.

Verify(gpk, M, Σ): Given the inputs, this algorithm proceeds as follows.

1. Parse Σ as $\Sigma = (\{\mathrm{CMT}_i\}_{i=1}^{\kappa}, (Ch_1, \dots, Ch_\kappa), \{\mathrm{RSP}\}_{i=1}^{\kappa}, \mathbf{c}_1, \mathbf{c}_2)$. If $(Ch_1, \dots, Ch_\kappa) \neq \mathcal{H}_{\mathsf{FS}}(M, \{\mathrm{CMT}_i\}_{i=1}^{\kappa}, \xi)$, then return 0, where ξ is as in (16).

2. For each $i \in [\kappa]$, run the verification phase of the protocol in Sect. 4.2 to check the validity of RSP_i with respect to CMT_i and Ch_i. If any of the conditions does not hold, then return 0.

3. Return 1.

Open(gpk, ok, $\mathbf{reg}, M, \Sigma$): Let ok $= (s_1, \mathbf{e}_1)$ and $\Sigma = (\Pi_{\mathsf{gs}}, \mathbf{c}_1, \mathbf{c}_2)$. This algorithm then does the following.

1. Use s_1 to decrypt $\mathbf{c}_1 = (\mathbf{c}_{1,1}, \mathbf{c}_{1,2})$ as follows.

   (a) It computes

   $$\mathbf{p}'' = \frac{\mathbf{c}_{1,2} - \mathbf{c}_{1,1} \cdot s_1}{\lfloor q/4 \rfloor}.$$

   (b) For each coefficient of $\mathbf{p}''$,
   - if it is closer to 0 than to -1 and 1, then round it to 0;
   - if it is closer to -1 than to 0 and 1, then round it to -1;
   - if it is closer to 1 than to 0 and -1, then round it to 1.

   (c) Denote the rounded $\mathbf{p}''$ as $\mathbf{p}' \in R_q^\ell$ with coefficients in $\{-1, 0, 1\}$.

   (d) Let $p' \in R_q$ such that $\tau(p') = \mathbf{H} \cdot \tau(\mathbf{p}')$. Recall that $\mathbf{H} \in \mathbb{Z}_q^{n \times n\ell}$ is the decomposition matrix for elements of R_q (see Sect. 2.2).

2. If $\mathbf{reg}$ does not include an entry p', then return $(\perp, \perp)$.

3. Otherwise, generate a NIZKAoK Π_{open} to demonstrate the possession of a tuple $(s_1, \mathbf{e}_1, \mathbf{y}) \in R_q \times R_q^\ell \times R_q^\ell$

$$\begin{cases} \|s_1\|_\infty \leq B; \ \|\mathbf{e}_1\|_\infty \leq B; \ \|\mathbf{y}\|_\infty \leq \lceil q/10 \rceil; \\ \mathbf{a} \cdot s_1 + \mathbf{e}_1 = \mathbf{b}_1; \\ \mathbf{c}_{1,2} - \mathbf{c}_{1,1} \cdot s_1 = \mathbf{y} + \lfloor q/4 \rfloor \cdot \mathsf{rdec}(p'). \end{cases} \tag{17}$$

We remark that conditions in (17) involve only linear secret objects with bounded norms, and can be handled using the Stern-like techniques from Sects. 3.2 and 4.2. As a result, we can obtain a statistical ZKAoK for the considered statement. The protocol is repeated $\kappa = \omega(\log \lambda)$ times to achieve negligible soundness error and made non-interactive via the Fiat-Shamir heuristic as a triple $\Pi_{\text{Open}} = (\{\text{CMT}_i\}_{i=1}^\kappa, \text{CH}, \{\text{RSP}\}_{i=1}^\kappa)$, where

$$\text{CH} = \mathcal{H}_{\text{FS}}(\{\text{CMT}_i\}_{i=1}^\kappa, \mathbf{a}, \mathbf{b}_1, M, \Sigma, p') \in \{1, 2, 3\}^\kappa. \tag{18}$$

4. Output (p', Π_{Open}).

Judge($\mathsf{gpk}, M, \Sigma, p', \Pi_{\text{open}}$): If Verify algorithm outputs 0, then this algorithm returns 0. Otherwise, this algorithm then verifies the argument Π_{Open} w.r.t. common input $(\mathbf{a}, \mathbf{b}_1, M, \Sigma, p')$, in a similar manner as in algorithm Verify. If Π_{open} does not verify, then return 0; otherwise, return 1.

4.4   Analysis of the Scheme

EFFICIENCY. We first analyze the efficiency of the scheme described in Sect. 4.3, with respect to security parameter λ.

– The public key gpk has bit-size $\mathcal{O}(\lambda \cdot \log^2 \lambda) = \widetilde{\mathcal{O}}(\lambda)$.
– The signing key gsk_i has bit-size $\mathcal{O}(\lambda \cdot \log^2 \lambda) = \widetilde{\mathcal{O}}(\lambda)$.
– The size of a signature Σ is dominated by that of the Stern-like NIZKAoK Π_{gs}, which is $\mathcal{O}(\widetilde{L} \cdot \log q) \cdot \omega(\log \lambda)$, where $\widetilde{L}$ denotes the bit-size of a vector $\widetilde{\mathbf{w}} \in \overline{\mathsf{VALID}}$ as described in Sect. 4.2. Recall $\mathcal{O}(\widetilde{L} \cdot \log q) = \mathcal{O}(\lambda \cdot \log^4 \lambda)$. As a result, Σ has bit-size $\mathcal{O}(\lambda \cdot \log^4 \lambda) \cdot \omega(\log \lambda) = \widetilde{\mathcal{O}}(\lambda)$.
– The Stern-like NIZKAoK Π_{open} has bit-size $\mathcal{O}(\lambda \cdot \log^3 \lambda) \cdot \omega(\log \lambda) = \widetilde{\mathcal{O}}(\lambda)$.

CORRECTNESS. The correctness of the above group signature scheme relies on the following facts: (i) the underlying argument systems to generate Π_{gs} and Π_{open} are perfectly complete; (ii) the underlying encryption scheme, which is an extended version of LPR encryption scheme [47] is correct.

Specifically, for an honest user, when he signs a message on behalf of the group, he is able to demonstrate the possession of a valid tuple ζ of the form (15). With probability 1, Π_{gs} is accepted by the Verify algorithm, which is implied by the perfect completeness of the argument system to generate Π_{gs}. As for the correctness of the Open algorithm, note that

$$\begin{aligned}
\mathbf{c}_{1,1} - \mathbf{c}_{1,2} \cdot s_1 &= \mathbf{b}_1 \cdot g_1 + \mathbf{e}_{1,2} + \lfloor q/4 \rfloor \cdot \mathsf{rdec}(p) - (\mathbf{a} \cdot g_1 + \mathbf{e}_{1,1}) \cdot s_1 \\
&= (\mathbf{a} \cdot s_1 + \mathbf{e}_1) \cdot g_1 + \mathbf{e}_{1,2} + \lfloor q/4 \rfloor \cdot \mathsf{rdec}(p) - (\mathbf{a} \cdot g_1 + \mathbf{e}_{1,1}) \cdot s_1 \\
&= \mathbf{e}_1 \cdot g_1 + \mathbf{e}_{1,2} - \mathbf{e}_{1,1} \cdot s_1 + \lfloor q/4 \rfloor \cdot \mathsf{rdec}(p)
\end{aligned}$$

where $\|\mathbf{e}_1\|_\infty \leq B$, $\|s_1\|_\infty \leq B$, $\|g_1\|_\infty \leq B$, $\|\mathbf{e}_{1,1}\|_\infty \leq B$, $\|\mathbf{e}_{1,2}\|_\infty \leq B$. Recall $B = \widetilde{\mathcal{O}}(n^{5/4})$ and $q = \widetilde{\mathcal{O}}(n^4)$. Hence we have:

$$\|\mathbf{e}_1 \cdot g_1 + \mathbf{e}_{1,2} - \mathbf{e}_{1,1} \cdot s_1\|_\infty \leq 2n \cdot B^2 + B = \widetilde{\mathcal{O}}(n^{3.5}) \leq \lceil \tfrac{q}{10} \rceil = \widetilde{\mathcal{O}}(n^4).$$

With probability 1, the rounding procedure described in the Open algorithm recovers $\mathsf{rdec}(p)$ and hence outputs p, which is the actual signer. Thus the opener is able to identify the signer of a signature and hence correctness of the Open algorithm holds.

As the opener correctly recovers $\mathsf{rdec}(p)$ and p, it possesses a valid tuple $(s_1, \mathbf{e}_1, \mathbf{y})$ satisfying conditions in (17). It then follows from the perfect completeness of the argument system to generate Π_{open}, the judge will accept the opening result outputted by the opener and hence correctness of the Judge algorithm holds.

SECURITY. In Theorem 4, we prove that our scheme satisfies the security requirements of the Bellare et al. model [5]. For the proof of non-frameability, we will use the following simple lemma.

Lemma 2. *Let $\mathbf{B} \in R_q^{1 \times m}$, where $m \geq 2\lceil \log q \rceil + 2$. If $\mathbf{x}$ is a uniformly random element of R^m such that $\|\mathbf{x}\|_\infty \leq 1$, then with probability at least $1 - 2^{-n}$, there exists another $\mathbf{x}' \in R^m$ such that $\|\mathbf{x}'\|_\infty \leq 1$ and $\mathbf{B} \cdot \mathbf{x} = \mathbf{B} \cdot \mathbf{x}' \in R_q$.*

Proof. Note that there are in total 3^{nm} elements $\mathbf{x} \in R^m$ such that $\|\mathbf{x}\|_\infty \leq 1$. Among them, there exist at most $q^n - 1$ elements that do not have $\mathbf{x}'$ such that $\mathbf{B} \cdot \mathbf{x} = \mathbf{B} \cdot \mathbf{x}'$. Hence, the probability that a uniformly random $\mathbf{x}$ has a corresponding $\mathbf{x}'$ for which $\mathbf{B} \cdot \mathbf{x} = \mathbf{B} \cdot \mathbf{x}'$ is at least

$$\frac{3^{nm} - q^n + 1}{3^{nm}} = 1 - \frac{q^n - 1}{3^{nm}} > 1 - \frac{q^n}{2^n q^n} = 1 - 2^{-n}.$$

$\square$

Theorem 4. *Assume that the Stern-like argument systems used in Sect. 4.3 are simulation-sound. Then, in the random oracle model, the given group signature scheme satisfies full anonymity, traceability and non-frameability under the RLWE and RSIS assumptions.*

In the random oracle model, the proof of Theorem 4 relies on the following facts:

1. The Stern-like zero-knowledge argument systems being used are simulation-sound;

2. The underlying encryption scheme, which is an extended version of the LPR encryption scheme [47], via the Naor-Yung transformation [51], is IND-CCA secure;
3. The variant of Ducas-Micciancio signature scheme described in Sect. 2.3 with at most polynomial number of signature queries is existentially unforgeable against adaptive chosen message attacks [20,21];
4. For a properly generated user key pair $(\mathbf{x}, p)$, it is infeasible to find $\mathbf{x}' \in R_q^m$ such that $\|\mathbf{x}'\|_\infty \le 1$, $\mathbf{x}' \ne \mathbf{x}$ and $\mathbf{B} \cdot \mathbf{x}' = p$.

The proof of Theorem 4 is established by Lemmas 3–5 given below.

Lemma 3. *Assume that the* RLWE$_{n,\ell,q,\chi}$ *problem is hard. Then the given group signature scheme is fully anonymous in the random oracle model.*

The detailed proof of Lemma 3 is available in the full version.

Lemma 4. *Assume that the* RSIS$^\infty_{n,\overline{m},q,\widetilde{\mathcal{O}}(n^2)}$ *problem is hard. Then the given group signature scheme is traceable in the random oracle model.*

Proof. We prove traceability by contradiction. Suppose that $\mathcal{A}$ succeeds with non-negligible advantage ϵ. Then we build a PPT algorithm $\mathcal{B}$ that, with non-negligible probability, breaks the unforgeability of the Ducas-Micciancio signature scheme from Sect. 2.3, which is based on the hardness of the RSIS$^\infty_{n,\overline{m},q,\widetilde{\mathcal{O}}(n^2)}$ problem. It then follows that our construction is traceable.

When given the verification key of the Ducas-Micciancio signature scheme, the simulator $\mathcal{B}$ runs the experiment $\mathbf{Exp}^{\text{trace}}_{\text{GS},\mathcal{A}}(\lambda)$ faithfully. $\mathcal{B}$ can answer all oracle queries made by $\mathcal{A}$ except when $\mathcal{A}$ queries the *send to issuer* SndToI oracle or *add user* AddU oracle. However, $\mathcal{B}$ can resort to his oracle queries of the signature scheme. In these two cases, $\mathcal{B}$ enrolls the corresponding user to the group. When $\mathcal{A}$ halts, it outputs $(M^*, \Pi^*_{\text{gs}}, \mathbf{c}_1^*, \mathbf{c}_2^*)$. With non-negligible probability ϵ, $\mathcal{A}$ wins the experiment. Parse $\Pi^*_{\text{gs}} = (\{\text{CMT}^*_i\}^\kappa_{i=1}, \text{CH}^*, \{\text{RSP}^*_i\}^\kappa_{i=1})$. Let

$$\xi^* = (\mathbf{A}, \mathbf{A}_{[0]}, \ldots, \mathbf{A}_{[d]}, \mathbf{F}, \mathbf{F}_0, \mathbf{F}_1, u, \mathbf{B}, \mathbf{a}, \mathbf{b}_1, \mathbf{b}_2, \mathbf{c}_1^*, \mathbf{c}_2^*).$$

Then $\text{CH}^* = \mathcal{H}_{\text{FS}}(M^*, \{\text{CMT}^*_i\}^\kappa_{i=1}, \xi^*)$ and RSP^*_i is a valid response w.r.t. CMT^*_i and CH^*_i for $i \in [\kappa]$ by the fact that $\mathcal{A}$ wins and hence $(\Pi^*_{\text{gs}}, \mathbf{c}_1^*, \mathbf{c}_2^*)$ is a valid signature on message M^*.

We claim that $\mathcal{A}$ had queried $(M^*, \{\text{CMT}^*_i\}^\kappa_{i=1}, \xi^*)$ to the hash oracle $\mathcal{H}_{\text{FS}}$ with overwhelming probability. Otherwise, the probability of guessing correctly the value of $\mathcal{H}_{\text{FS}}(M^*, \{\text{CMT}^*_i\}^\kappa_{i=1}, \xi^*)$ is at most $3^{-\kappa}$, which is negligible. Therefore, with probability $\epsilon' = \epsilon - 3^{-\kappa}$, $\mathcal{A}$ had queried the hash oracle $\mathcal{H}_{\text{FS}}$. Denote by $\theta^* \in \{1, 2, \ldots, Q_H\}$ the index of this specific query, where Q_H is the total number of hash queries made by $\mathcal{A}$.

Algorithm $\mathcal{B}$ then runs at most $32 \cdot Q_H/\epsilon'$ executions of $\mathcal{A}$. For each new run, it is exactly the same as the original run until the point of θ^*-th query to the hash oracle $\mathcal{H}_{\text{FS}}$. From this point on, $\mathcal{B}$ replies $\mathcal{A}$'s hash queries with uniformly random and independent values for each new run. This guarantees that the input of θ^*-th query $\mathcal{A}$ made to $\mathcal{H}_{\mathsf{FS}}$ is the tuple $\left(M^*, \{\mathrm{CMT}_i^*\}_{i=1}^\kappa, \xi^*\right)$ for each new run while the output of this hash query is uniformly random and independent for each new run. To this point, by the forking lemma of Brickell et al. [13], with probability $\geq 1/2$, $\mathcal{B}$ obtains 3-fork involving the same tuple $\left(M^*, \{\mathrm{CMT}_i^*\}_{i=1}^\kappa, \xi^*\right)$ with pairwise distinct hash values $\mathrm{CH}_{\theta^*}^{(1)}, \mathrm{CH}_{\theta^*}^{(2)}, \mathrm{CH}_{\theta^*}^{(3)} \in \{1,2,3\}^\kappa$ and corresponding valid responses $\mathrm{RSP}_{\theta^*}^{(1)}, \mathrm{RSP}_{\theta^*}^{(2)}, \mathrm{RSP}_{\theta^*}^{(3)}$. A simple calculation shows that with probability $1 - (\frac{7}{9})^\kappa$, we have $\{\mathrm{CH}_{\theta^*,j}^{(1)}, \mathrm{CH}_{\theta^*,j}^{(2)}, \mathrm{CH}_{\theta^*,j}^{(3)}\} = \{1,2,3\}$ for some $j \in \{1,2,\ldots,\kappa\}$.

Therefore, $\mathrm{RSP}_{\theta^*,j}^{(1)}, \mathrm{RSP}_{\theta^*,j}^{(2)}, \mathrm{RSP}_{\theta^*,j}^{(3)}$ are 3 valid responses for all the challenges $1,2,3$ w.r.t. the same commitment CMT_j^*. Since COM is computationally binding, $\mathcal{B}$ is able to extract the witness

$$t^* \in \mathcal{T}_d; \mathbf{r}^* \in R_q^{\overline{m}}; \mathbf{v}^* \in R_q^{\overline{m}+k}; \mathbf{p}^* \in R_q^\ell,$$

such that $\|\mathbf{r}^*\|_\infty \leq \beta$, $\|\mathbf{v}^*\|_\infty \leq \beta$, $\|\mathbf{p}^*\|_\infty \leq 1$ and

$$\mathbf{A}_{t^*} \cdot \mathbf{v}^* = \mathbf{F} \cdot \mathrm{rdec}(\mathbf{F}_0 \cdot \mathbf{r}^* + \mathbf{F}_1 \cdot \mathbf{p}^*) + u,$$

and $\mathbf{c}_1^*, \mathbf{c}_2^*$ are correct encryptions of $\mathbf{p}^*$.

Since $\mathcal{A}$ wins the game, either we have (i) the Open algorithm outputs $(\perp, \perp)$ or (ii) the Open algorithm output $(p', \Pi_{\mathsf{open}}^*)$ with $p' \neq \perp$ but the Judge algorithm rejects the opening result.

Case (i) implies that, if $\mathbf{c}_1^*$ is decrypted to $\mathbf{p}'$ and $p' \in R_q$ such that $\tau(p') = \mathbf{H} \cdot \tau(\mathbf{p}') \in \mathbb{Z}_q^n$, then p' is not in the registration table. From the extraction, we know that $\mathbf{c}_1^*$ will be decrypted to $\mathbf{p}^*$ by the correctness of our encryption scheme. Therefore, the *intermediate* opening result $\mathbf{p}'$ is equal to $\mathbf{p}^*$. On the other hand, the fact that p' is not in the registration table implies that $\mathcal{B}$ did not enroll p' to the group, that is, $\mathcal{B}$ did not query p' to his challenger when $\mathcal{A}$ made the AddU oracle queries or SndToI oracle queries. To summarize, $\mathcal{B}$ did not query signature on p' and $\mathcal{B}$ extracts a signature $(t^*, \mathbf{r}^*, \mathbf{v}^*)$ on $\mathbf{p}^* = \mathbf{p}'$ such that $\tau(p') = \mathbf{H} \cdot \tau(\mathbf{p}')$. Therefore $(\mathbf{p}^*, t^*, \mathbf{r}^*, \mathbf{v}^*)$ is a valid forgery of the Ducas-Micciancio signature scheme.

Case (ii) implies that, if $\mathbf{c}_1^*$ is decrypted to $\mathbf{p}'$ and $p' \in R_q$ such that $\tau(p') = \mathbf{H} \cdot \tau(\mathbf{p}') \in \mathbb{Z}_q^n$, then p' is in the registration table and Π_{open}^* generated by $\mathcal{B}$ is not accepted by the Judge algorithm. From the extraction, we know that $\mathbf{c}_1^*$ will be decrypted to $\mathbf{p}^*$ by the correctness of our encryption scheme. Therefore, the *intermediate* opening result $\mathbf{p}'$ is equal to $\mathbf{p}^*$. On the other hand, we claim that $\mathrm{rdec}(p') \neq \mathbf{p}' = \mathbf{p}^*$. Otherwise, $\mathrm{rdec}(p') = \mathbf{p}' = \mathbf{p}^*$, then $\mathcal{B}$ possesses valid witness to generate the proof Π_{open}^*. By the perfect completeness of the underlying argument system generating Π_{open}^*, it will be accepted by the judge algorithm with probability 1. This is a contradiction and hence we obtain $\mathrm{rdec}(p') \neq \mathbf{p}' = \mathbf{p}^*$. Recall that in the $\langle \mathsf{Join}, \mathsf{Iss} \rangle$ algorithm, the issuer only generates signature on $\mathrm{rdec}(p')$. So $\mathcal{B}$ only queries the signature on $\mathrm{rdec}(p')$ and hence $(\mathbf{p}^*, t^*, \mathbf{r}^*, \mathbf{v}^*)$ is a valid forgery of the Ducas-Micciancio signature scheme.

Therefore, with probability at least $\frac{1}{2} \cdot (\epsilon - 3^{-\kappa})(1 - (\frac{7}{9})^\kappa)$, which is non-negligible, $\mathcal{B}$ breaks the unforgeability of the Ducas-Micciancio signature scheme. This concludes the proof. $\qquad\square$

Lemma 5. *Assume that the* $\mathsf{RSIS}_{n,m,q,1}^{\infty}$ *problem is hard. Then the given group signature scheme is non-frameable in the random oracle model.*

Proof. We prove non-frameability by contradiction. Suppose that $\mathcal{A}$ succeeds with non-negligible advantage ϵ. Then we build a PPT algorithm $\mathcal{B}$ that solves a $\mathsf{RSIS}_{n,m,q,1}$ instance $\mathbf{B} \in R_q^{1 \times m}$ with non-negligible probability.

After $\mathcal{B}$ is given a RSIS instance matrix $\mathbf{B}$, it runs the experiment $\mathbf{Exp}_{\mathsf{GS},\mathcal{A}}^{\mathsf{nf}}$ faithfully. $\mathcal{B}$ can answer all the oracle queries made by $\mathcal{A}$ since $\mathcal{B}$ knows all the keys. When $\mathcal{A}$ halts, it outputs $(M^*, \Pi_{\mathsf{gs}}^*, \mathbf{c}_1^*, \mathbf{c}_2^*, p^*, \Pi_{\mathsf{open}}^*)$. With non-negligible probability ϵ, $\mathcal{A}$ wins the experiment.

The fact that $\mathcal{A}$ wins the game implies $(M^*, \Pi_{\mathsf{gs}}^*, \mathbf{c}_1^*, \mathbf{c}_2^*)$ is a valid message-signature pair that was not queried before. By the same extraction technique as in Lemma 4, we can extract witness $\mathbf{x}' \in R_q^m$ and $\mathbf{p}' \in R_q^{\ell}$ such that $\mathbf{x}', \mathbf{p}'$ have coefficients in $\{-1, 0, 1\}$, $\mathbf{B} \cdot \mathbf{x}' = p'$ with $\tau(p') = \mathbf{H} \cdot \tau(\mathbf{p}')$ and $\mathbf{c}_1^*, \mathbf{c}_2^*$ are correct encryptions of $\mathbf{p}'$. By the correctness of the encryption scheme being used, $\mathbf{c}_1^*$ will be decrypted to $\mathbf{p}'$.

The fact that $\mathcal{A}$ wins the game also implies $(p^*, \Pi_{\mathsf{open}}^*)$ is accepted by the Judge algorithm. It follows from the soundness of the argument system used to generate Π_{open}^* that $\mathbf{c}_1^*$ will be decrypted to $\mathsf{rdec}(p^*)$. Therefore, we have $\mathbf{p}' = \mathsf{rdec}(p^*)$ and hence $p' = p^*$. Note that $\mathcal{A}$ wins the game also implies that p^* is an honest user with $\mathsf{gsk} \neq \bot$ and $\mathcal{A}$ did not query the user secret key $\mathbf{x}^*$ that corresponds to p^*. Thus we obtain: $\mathbf{B} \cdot \mathbf{x}' = p' = p^* = \mathbf{B} \cdot \mathbf{x}^*$, where $\mathbf{x}^*$ has coefficients in $\{-1, 0, 1\}$. By Lemma 2, $\mathbf{x}' \neq \mathbf{x}^*$ with probability at least $1/2$. In the case they are not equal, we obtain a non-zero vector $\mathbf{y} = \mathbf{x}' - \mathbf{x}^*$ such that $\mathbf{B} \cdot \mathbf{y} = 0$ and $\|\mathbf{y}\|_{\infty} = 1$.

Therefore, with probability at least $\frac{1}{2} \cdot (\epsilon - 3^{-\kappa})(1 - (\frac{7}{9})^{\kappa}) \cdot \frac{1}{2}$, which is non-negligible, $\mathcal{B}$ solves a $\mathsf{RSIS}_{n,m,q,1}$ instance $\mathbf{B} \in R_q^{1 \times m}$. This concludes the proof. $\qquad\square$

Acknowledgements. The authors would like to thank Benoît Libert and the anonymous reviewers of PKC 2018 for helpful comments and discussions. The research is supported by Singapore Ministry of Education under Research Grant MOE2016-T2-2-014(S).

References

1. Ateniese, G., Camenisch, J., Hohenberger, S., de Medeiros, B.: Practical group signatures without random oracles. IACR Cryptology ePrint Archive 2005/385 (2005)

2. Ateniese, G., Camenisch, J., Joye, M., Tsudik, G.: A practical and provably secure coalition-resistant group signature scheme. In: Bellare, M. (ed.) CRYPTO 2000. LNCS, vol. 1880, pp. 255–270. Springer, Heidelberg (2000). https://doi.org/10.1007/3-540-44598-6_16

3. Bellare, M., Fuchsbauer, G.: Policy-based signatures. In: Krawczyk, H. (ed.) PKC 2014. LNCS, vol. 8383, pp. 520–537. Springer, Heidelberg (2014). https://doi.org/10.1007/978-3-642-54631-0_30

4. Bellare, M., Micciancio, D., Warinschi, B.: Foundations of group signatures: formal definitions, simplified requirements, and a construction based on general assumptions. In: Biham, E. (ed.) EUROCRYPT 2003. LNCS, vol. 2656, pp. 614–629. Springer, Heidelberg (2003). https://doi.org/10.1007/3-540-39200-9_38
5. Bellare, M., Shi, H., Zhang, C.: Foundations of group signatures: the case of dynamic groups. In: Menezes, A. (ed.) CT-RSA 2005. LNCS, vol. 3376, pp. 136–153. Springer, Heidelberg (2005). https://doi.org/10.1007/978-3-540-30574-3_11
6. Benhamouda, F., Camenisch, J., Krenn, S., Lyubashevsky, V., Neven, G.: Better zero-knowledge proofs for lattice encryption and their application to group signatures. In: Sarkar, P., Iwata, T. (eds.) ASIACRYPT 2014. LNCS, vol. 8873, pp. 551–572. Springer, Heidelberg (2014). https://doi.org/10.1007/978-3-662-45611-8_29
7. Böhl, F., Hofheinz, D., Jager, T., Koch, J., Striecks, C.: Confined guessing: new signatures from standard assumptions. J. Cryptol. **28**(1), 176–208 (2015)
8. Boneh, D., Boyen, X., Shacham, H.: Short group signatures. In: Franklin, M. (ed.) CRYPTO 2004. LNCS, vol. 3152, pp. 41–55. Springer, Heidelberg (2004). https://doi.org/10.1007/978-3-540-28628-8_3
9. Boneh, D., Shacham, H.: Group signatures with verifier-local revocation. In: ACM CCS 2004, pp. 168–177. ACM (2004)
10. Bootle, J., Cerulli, A., Chaidos, P., Ghadafi, E., Groth, J.: Foundations of fully dynamic group signatures. In: Manulis, M., Sadeghi, A.-R., Schneider, S. (eds.) ACNS 2016. LNCS, vol. 9696, pp. 117–136. Springer, Cham (2016). https://doi.org/10.1007/978-3-319-39555-5_7
11. Boyen, X.: Lattice mixing and vanishing trapdoors: a framework for fully secure short signatures and more. In: Nguyen, P.Q., Pointcheval, D. (eds.) PKC 2010. LNCS, vol. 6056, pp. 499–517. Springer, Heidelberg (2010). https://doi.org/10.1007/978-3-642-13013-7_29
12. Boyen, X., Waters, B.: Full-domain subgroup hiding and constant-size group signatures. In: Okamoto, T., Wang, X. (eds.) PKC 2007. LNCS, vol. 4450, pp. 1–15. Springer, Heidelberg (2007). https://doi.org/10.1007/978-3-540-71677-8_1
13. Brickell, E., Pointcheval, D., Vaudenay, S., Yung, M.: Design validations for discrete logarithm based signature schemes. In: Imai, H., Zheng, Y. (eds.) PKC 2000. LNCS, vol. 1751, pp. 276–292. Springer, Heidelberg (2000). https://doi.org/10.1007/978-3-540-46588-1_19
14. Camenisch, J., Hohenberger, S., Lysyanskaya, A.: Compact E-cash. In: Cramer, R. (ed.) EUROCRYPT 2005. LNCS, vol. 3494, pp. 302–321. Springer, Heidelberg (2005). https://doi.org/10.1007/11426639_18
15. Camenisch, J., Lysyanskaya, A.: An efficient system for non-transferable anonymous credentials with optional anonymity revocation. In: Pfitzmann, B. (ed.) EUROCRYPT 2001. LNCS, vol. 2045, pp. 93–118. Springer, Heidelberg (2001). https://doi.org/10.1007/3-540-44987-6_7
16. Camenisch, J., Neven, G., Rückert, M.: Fully anonymous attribute tokens from lattices. In: Visconti, I., De Prisco, R. (eds.) SCN 2012. LNCS, vol. 7485, pp. 57–75. Springer, Heidelberg (2012). https://doi.org/10.1007/978-3-642-32928-9_4
17. Cash, D., Hofheinz, D., Kiltz, E., Peikert, C.: Bonsai trees, or how to delegate a lattice basis. In: Gilbert, H. (ed.) EUROCRYPT 2010. LNCS, vol. 6110, pp. 523–552. Springer, Heidelberg (2010). https://doi.org/10.1007/978-3-642-13190-5_27
18. Chaum, D., van Heyst, E.: Group signatures. In: Davies, D.W. (ed.) EUROCRYPT 1991. LNCS, vol. 547, pp. 257–265. Springer, Heidelberg (1991). https://doi.org/10.1007/3-540-46416-6_22
19. Cheng, S., Nguyen, K., Wang, H.: Policy-based signature scheme from lattices. Des. Codes Crypt. **81**(1), 43–74 (2016)

20. Ducas, L., Micciancio, D.: Improved short lattice signatures in the standard model. In: Garay, J.A., Gennaro, R. (eds.) CRYPTO 2014. LNCS, vol. 8616, pp. 335–352. Springer, Heidelberg (2014). https://doi.org/10.1007/978-3-662-44371-2_19

21. Ducas, L., Micciancio, D.: Improved short lattice signatures in the standard model. IACR Cryptology ePrint Archive 2014/495 (2014)

22. Fiat, A., Shamir, A.: How to prove yourself: practical solutions to identification and signature problems. In: Odlyzko, A.M. (ed.) CRYPTO 1986. LNCS, vol. 263, pp. 186–194. Springer, Heidelberg (1987). https://doi.org/10.1007/3-540-47721-7_12

23. Gentry, C.: Fully homomorphic encryption using ideal lattices. In: STOC 2009, pp. 169–178. ACM (2009)

24. Gentry, C., Peikert, C., Vaikuntanathan, V.: Trapdoors for hard lattices and new cryptographic constructions. In: STOC 2008, pp. 197–206. ACM (2008)

25. Gorbunov, S., Vaikuntanathan, V., Wee, H.: Predicate encryption for circuits from LWE. In: Gennaro, R., Robshaw, M. (eds.) CRYPTO 2015. LNCS, vol. 9216, pp. 503–523. Springer, Heidelberg (2015). https://doi.org/10.1007/978-3-662-48000-7_25

26. Gordon, S.D., Katz, J., Vaikuntanathan, V.: A group signature scheme from lattice assumptions. In: Abe, M. (ed.) ASIACRYPT 2010. LNCS, vol. 6477, pp. 395–412. Springer, Heidelberg (2010). https://doi.org/10.1007/978-3-642-17373-8_23

27. Groth, J.: Evaluating security of voting schemes in the universal composability framework. In: Jakobsson, M., Yung, M., Zhou, J. (eds.) ACNS 2004. LNCS, vol. 3089, pp. 46–60. Springer, Heidelberg (2004). https://doi.org/10.1007/978-3-540-24852-1_4

28. Groth, J.: Fully anonymous group signatures without random oracles. In: Kurosawa, K. (ed.) ASIACRYPT 2007. LNCS, vol. 4833, pp. 164–180. Springer, Heidelberg (2007). https://doi.org/10.1007/978-3-540-76900-2_10

29. Jain, A., Krenn, S., Pietrzak, K., Tentes, A.: Commitments and efficient zero-knowledge proofs from learning parity with noise. In: Wang, X., Sako, K. (eds.) ASIACRYPT 2012. LNCS, vol. 7658, pp. 663–680. Springer, Heidelberg (2012). https://doi.org/10.1007/978-3-642-34961-4_40

30. Kawachi, A., Tanaka, K., Xagawa, K.: Concurrently secure identification schemes based on the worst-case hardness of lattice problems. In: Pieprzyk, J. (ed.) ASIACRYPT 2008. LNCS, vol. 5350, pp. 372–389. Springer, Heidelberg (2008). https://doi.org/10.1007/978-3-540-89255-7_23

31. Kiayias, A., Yung, M.: Secure scalable group signature with dynamic joins and separable authorities. Int. J. Secur. Netw. 1(1), 24–45 (2006)

32. Laguillaumie, F., Langlois, A., Libert, B., Stehlé, D.: Lattice-based group signatures with logarithmic signature size. In: Sako, K., Sarkar, P. (eds.) ASIACRYPT 2013. LNCS, vol. 8270, pp. 41–61. Springer, Heidelberg (2013). https://doi.org/10.1007/978-3-642-42045-0_3

33. Langlois, A., Ling, S., Nguyen, K., Wang, H.: Lattice-based group signature scheme with verifier-local revocation. In: Krawczyk, H. (ed.) PKC 2014. LNCS, vol. 8383, pp. 345–361. Springer, Heidelberg (2014). https://doi.org/10.1007/978-3-642-54631-0_20. http://eprint.iacr.org/2014/033

34. Langlois, A., Stehlé, D.: Worst-case to average-case reductions for module lattices. Des. Codes Crypt. 75(3), 565–599 (2015)

35. Libert, B., Ling, S., Mouhartem, F., Nguyen, K., Wang, H.: Signature schemes with efficient protocols and dynamic group signatures from lattice assumptions. In: Cheon, J.H., Takagi, T. (eds.) ASIACRYPT 2016. LNCS, vol. 10032, pp. 373–403. Springer, Heidelberg (2016). https://doi.org/10.1007/978-3-662-53890-6_13

36. Libert, B., Ling, S., Mouhartem, F., Nguyen, K., Wang, H.: Zero-knowledge arguments for matrix-vector relations and lattice-based group encryption. In: Cheon, J.H., Takagi, T. (eds.) ASIACRYPT 2016. LNCS, vol. 10032, pp. 101–131. Springer, Heidelberg (2016). https://doi.org/10.1007/978-3-662-53890-6_4

37. Libert, B., Ling, S., Nguyen, K., Wang, H.: Zero-knowledge arguments for lattice-based accumulators: logarithmic-size ring signatures and group signatures without trapdoors. In: Fischlin, M., Coron, J.-S. (eds.) EUROCRYPT 2016. LNCS, vol. 9666, pp. 1–31. Springer, Heidelberg (2016). https://doi.org/10.1007/978-3-662-49896-5_1

38. Libert, B., Ling, S., Nguyen, K., Wang, H.: Zero-knowledge arguments for lattice-based PRFs and applications to E-cash. In: Takagi, T., Peyrin, T. (eds.) ASIACRYPT 2017. LNCS, vol. 10626, pp. 304–335. Springer, Cham (2017). https://doi.org/10.1007/978-3-319-70700-6_11

39. Libert, B., Mouhartem, F., Nguyen, K.: A lattice-based group signature scheme with message-dependent opening. In: Manulis, M., Sadeghi, A.-R., Schneider, S. (eds.) ACNS 2016. LNCS, vol. 9696, pp. 137–155. Springer, Cham (2016). https://doi.org/10.1007/978-3-319-39555-5_8

40. Libert, B., Peters, T., Yung, M.: Short group signatures via structure-preserving signatures: standard model security from simple assumptions. In: Gennaro, R., Robshaw, M. (eds.) CRYPTO 2015. LNCS, vol. 9216, pp. 296–316. Springer, Heidelberg (2015). https://doi.org/10.1007/978-3-662-48000-7_15

41. Ling, S., Nguyen, K., Stehlé, D., Wang, H.: Improved zero-knowledge proofs of knowledge for the ISIS problem, and applications. In: Kurosawa, K., Hanaoka, G. (eds.) PKC 2013. LNCS, vol. 7778, pp. 107–124. Springer, Heidelberg (2013). https://doi.org/10.1007/978-3-642-36362-7_8

42. Ling, S., Nguyen, K., Wang, H.: Group signatures from lattices: simpler, tighter, shorter, ring-based. In: Katz, J. (ed.) PKC 2015. LNCS, vol. 9020, pp. 427–449. Springer, Heidelberg (2015). https://doi.org/10.1007/978-3-662-46447-2_19

43. Ling, S., Nguyen, K., Wang, H., Xu, Y.: Lattice-based group signatures: achieving full dynamicity with ease. In: Gollmann, D., Miyaji, A., Kikuchi, H. (eds.) ACNS 2017. LNCS, vol. 10355, pp. 293–312. Springer, Cham (2017). https://doi.org/10.1007/978-3-319-61204-1_15

44. Lyubashevsky, V., Micciancio, D.: Generalized compact knapsacks are collision resistant. In: Bugliesi, M., Preneel, B., Sassone, V., Wegener, I. (eds.) ICALP 2006. LNCS, vol. 4052, pp. 144–155. Springer, Heidelberg (2006). https://doi.org/10.1007/11787006_13

45. Lyubashevsky, V., Micciancio, D., Peikert, C., Rosen, A.: SWIFFT: a modest proposal for FFT hashing. In: Nyberg, K. (ed.) FSE 2008. LNCS, vol. 5086, pp. 54–72. Springer, Heidelberg (2008). https://doi.org/10.1007/978-3-540-71039-4_4

46. Lyubashevsky, V., Peikert, C., Regev, O.: On ideal lattices and learning with errors over rings. In: Gilbert, H. (ed.) EUROCRYPT 2010. LNCS, vol. 6110, pp. 1–23. Springer, Heidelberg (2010). https://doi.org/10.1007/978-3-642-13190-5_1

47. Lyubashevsky, V., Peikert, C., Regev, O.: On ideal lattices and learning with errors over rings. J. ACM **60**(6), 43:1–43:35 (2013)

48. Lyubashevsky, V., Peikert, C., Regev, O.: A toolkit for ring-LWE cryptography. In: Johansson, T., Nguyen, P.Q. (eds.) EUROCRYPT 2013. LNCS, vol. 7881, pp. 35–54. Springer, Heidelberg (2013). https://doi.org/10.1007/978-3-642-38348-9_3

49. Micciancio, D.: Generalized compact knapsacks, cyclic lattices, and efficient one-way functions. Comput. Complex **16**(4), 365–411 (2007)
50. Micciancio, D., Peikert, C.: Trapdoors for lattices: simpler, tighter, faster, smaller. In: Pointcheval, D., Johansson, T. (eds.) EUROCRYPT 2012. LNCS, vol. 7237, pp. 700–718. Springer, Heidelberg (2012). https://doi.org/10.1007/978-3-642-29011-4_41
51. Naor, M., Yung, M.: Public-key cryptosystems provably secure against chosen ciphertext attacks. In: ACM 1990, pp. 427–437. ACM (1990)
52. Nguyen, P.Q., Zhang, J., Zhang, Z.: Simpler efficient group signatures from lattices. In: Katz, J. (ed.) PKC 2015. LNCS, vol. 9020, pp. 401–426. Springer, Heidelberg (2015). https://doi.org/10.1007/978-3-662-46447-2_18
53. Peikert, C., Regev, O., Stephens-Davidowitz, N.: Pseudorandomness of ring-LWE for any ring and modulus. In: STOC 2017, pp. 461–473. ACM (2017)
54. Peikert, C., Rosen, A.: Efficient collision-resistant hashing from worst-case assumptions on cyclic lattices. In: Halevi, S., Rabin, T. (eds.) TCC 2006. LNCS, vol. 3876, pp. 145–166. Springer, Heidelberg (2006). https://doi.org/10.1007/11681878_8
55. Regev, O.: On lattices, learning with errors, random linear codes, and cryptography. In: ACM 2005, pp. 84–93. ACM (2005)
56. Sakai, Y., Emura, K., Hanaoka, G., Kawai, Y., Matsuda, T., Omote, K.: Group signatures with message-dependent opening. In: Abdalla, M., Lange, T. (eds.) Pairing 2012. LNCS, vol. 7708, pp. 270–294. Springer, Heidelberg (2013). https://doi.org/10.1007/978-3-642-36334-4_18
57. Stern, J.: A new paradigm for public key identification. IEEE Trans. Inf. Theory **42**(6), 1757–1768 (1996)
58. Xagawa, K.: Improved (hierarchical) inner-product encryption from lattices. IACR Cryptology ePrint Archive 2015/249 (2015)

Attribute-Based Signatures
for Unbounded Circuits in the ROM
and Efficient Instantiations from Lattices

Ali El Kaafarani[1] and Shuichi Katsumata[2]($\boxtimes$)

[1] University of Oxford, Oxford, UK
ali.elkaafarani@maths.ox.ac.uk
[2] National Institute of Advanced Industrial Science and Technology (AIST),
The University of Tokyo, Tokyo, Japan
shuichi_katsumata@it.k.u-tokyo.ac.jp

Abstract. Attribute-based signature (ABS), originally introduced by Maji et al. (CT-RSA'11), represents an essential mechanism to allow for fine-grained authentication. A user associated with an attribute x can sign w.r.t. a given public policy C only if his attribute satisfies C, i.e., $C(x) = 1$. So far, much effort on constructing bilinear map-based ABS schemes have been made, where the state-of-the-art scheme of Sakai et al. (PKC'16) supports the very wide class of *unbounded* circuits as policies. However, construction of ABS schemes without bilinear maps are less investigated, where it was not until recently that Tsabary (TCC'17) showed a lattice-based ABS scheme supporting *bounded* circuits as policies, at the cost of weakening the security requirement.

In this work, we affirmatively close the gap between ABS schemes based on bilinear maps and lattices by constructing the first lattice-based ABS scheme for *unbounded circuits* in the random oracle model. We start our work by providing a generic construction of ABS schemes for unbounded-circuits in the rand om oracle model, which in turn implies that one-way functions are sufficient to construct ABS schemes. To prove security, we formalize and prove a generalization of the Forking Lemma, which we call *"general multi-forking lemma with oracle access"*, capturing the situation where the simulator is interacting with some algorithms he *cannot* rewind, and also covering many features of the recent lattice-based ZKPs. This, in fact, was a formalization lacking in many existing anonymous signatures from lattices so far (e.g., group signatures). Therefore, this formalization is believed to be of independent interest. Finally, we provide a concrete instantiation of our generic ABS construction from lattices by introducing a new Σ-protocol, that highly departs from the previously known techniques, for proving possession of a valid signature of the lattice-based signature scheme of Boyen (PKC'10).

1 Introduction

1.1 Background

Attribute-based signature (ABS) was introduced by [MPR11] as a versatile tool allowing a signer to *anonymously* authenticate a message M w.r.t. a public

© International Association for Cryptologic Research 2018
M. Abdalla and R. Dahab (Eds.): PKC 2018, LNCS 10770, pp. 89–119, 2018.
https://doi.org/10.1007/978-3-319-76581-5_4

signing policy C only if the signer has a signing key associated to an attribute $x \in \{0,1\}^*$ that satisfies C, i.e., $C(x) = 1$. An attribute-based signature scheme reveals no information on the signer's identity or the attribute other than the fact that the signature is valid, hence the anonymity property of ABS schemes. One of the central research themes on ABS is to expand the expressiveness of the class of policies that can be supported by the schemes. In the bilinear map setting, there has been a long line of interesting works, including ABS schemes for threshold policy (e.g., [HLLR12]), boolean formula (e.g., [MPR11, OT11, OT13, EGK14]) and the current state-of-the-art; *unbounded circuits* [SAH16].[1]

On the other hand, the constructions of ABS schemes without bilinear maps, in particular ABS schemes from lattices, are much less investigated. To the best of our knowledge, there are only two major works concerning lattice-based ABS schemes [EE16, Tsa17]. El Bansarkhani et al. [EE16] construct a lattice-based ABS scheme for boolean formulas using a non-interactive zero-knowledge (NIZK) proof system as the main building block, following one of the most promising ways of constructing ABS schemes [MPR11, EGK14, SAH16]. Informally, a signature for a signer with attribute $\mathbf{x}$ is simply a zero-knowledge proof attesting to the fact that he has a certificate corresponding to the attribute $\mathbf{x}$ issued by the authority and that the policy C associated to the message M satisfies $C(\mathbf{x}) = 1$. Although this approach has been very effective in the bilinear map setting where [SAH16] were able to obtain ABS schemes for *unbounded circuits*, this has not been the case for lattices. One of the main reasons behind this is the lack of efficient lattice-based NIZK proof systems for a wide enough language. In particular, we only have efficient NIZK proof systems tailored for specific languages, such as proving possession of a solution to the short integer solution (SIS) problem or the learning with errors (LWE) problem [LNSW13], proving possession of a valid signature of the Boyen digital signature scheme [Boy10, LLNW14, LNW15] and so on, which in general does not seem strong enough for constructing ABS schemes. Recently, [YAL+17] showed (informally) how to construct lattice-based NIZK proof systems for languages accepted by monotone span programs, however, this still does not seem strong enough to use as a building block for ABS schemes supporting *unbounded* circuits as policies.

Tsabary [Tsa17] constructs lattice-based ABS schemes following a different approach; they show equivalence between a homomorphic signature (HS) scheme and a (message-policy) ABS scheme. Therefore, based on the HS construction of Gorbunov et al. [GVW15], they achieve a lattice-based ABS scheme for *bounded circuits* that does not make use of NIZK proof systems.[2] Here, by bounded, we mean that the required hardness assumptions on the LWE and/or SIS problems

---

[1] In our paper, we only consider *message-policy* ABS schemes. Recall that using universal circuits, we can convert message-policy ABS schemes into *key-policy* ABS schemes [BF14], where the functionality of the secret keys and messages are reversed.

[2] We note that the ABS scheme presented in [Tsa17] does not fulfill the standard security requirements of (message-policy) ABS schemes as originally defined in [MPR11]; achieving either unforgeability or anonymity in its full capacity comes at the cost of getting a much weaker version of the other, i.e., one has to choose between single-key-selective-unforgeability, or leaking information about the signing key.

grow exponentially in the depth of the circuit, e.g., to base the security of the ABS scheme under a polynomial LWE assumption, we need to restrict the depth of the circuit to be $O(\log \lambda)$, where λ is the security parameter. However, it seems challenging to improve their techniques to ABS schemes for unbounded circuits, due to the inherent noise-growth incurred by the homomorphic operations of matrices while computing the circuit gate-by-gate. The only known method of overcoming these $O(\log \lambda)$ depth barrier concerning homomorphic operations is the bootstrapping technique of fully homomorphic encryptions [Gen09], however, it is still an open problem whether there is a signature analogue of this technique.

1.2 Our Contribution

In this paper, we affirmatively close the gap between the state-of-the-art ABS schemes based on bilinear maps and lattices by constructing the first lattice-based ABS scheme for *unbounded circuits* in the random oracle model. We start by providing a general construction of ABS schemes supporting unbounded-circuits as policies. We then give an instantiation in the lattice setting showing that all the building blocks required by our generic construction is obtainable from lattices. We stress that, despite the expressiveness of the signing policy, we manage to prove the security of our scheme under surprisingly mild SIS and LWE assumptions with polynomial modulus size $q = \tilde{O}(\ell\lambda^{1.5})$, where ℓ denotes the length of the inputs to the circuits. Specifically, the required hardness assumptions are independent of the depth of the circuits that express the policies. Furthermore, the sizes of the public parameter, signing keys and signatures are $\tilde{O}(\ell\lambda^2)$, $\tilde{O}(\lambda)$ and $\tilde{O}((\ell\lambda+|C|)\lambda^2)$, respectively, where $|C|$ is the size of the circuit (i.e., policy) associated to the message.

To this end we prepare two new tools equipped for the lattice setting: we provide a generalization of the forking lemma of [PS00] which we call the *general multi-forking lemma with oracle access* and further construct a new lattice-based NIZK proof system for proving possession of a valid Boyen signature [Boy10] that departs from the previously known techniques (e.g., [LLNW14, LNW15]). Below, we give a more detailed overview of the techniques we used in our work.

Generic Construction of ABS for Unbounded Circuits. We propose a generic construction of ABS schemes supporting unbounded depth circuits as policies in the random oracle model[3], which employs the following primitives as its building blocks; a commitment scheme, a digital signature scheme and a Σ-protocol for a sufficiently wide relation. As a separate theoretical contribution, since all of the above primitives are implied from one-way functions, our result implies that one-way functions are sufficient to construct an ABS scheme for unbounded circuits in the random oracle model. Here, the random oracle is used only to convert the underlying Σ-protocol into a NIZK proof system via the Fiat-Shamir transformation [FS86].

At a high level, the generic construction of our ABS scheme follows closely the bilinear map based construction of [SAH16] (which is non-generic and proven in

---

[3] In this paper, we only consider circuits that do not have random oracle gates.

the standard model). We briefly review the construction in slightly more detail; first, the attribute authority issues a signature σ on an attribute $\mathbf{x} \in \{0,1\}^{\ell}$ to certify that a signer is indeed authorized to sign a message on behalf of that attribute. Then, to sign anonymously, the signer produces a zero-knowledge proof attesting to the following two facts:

(I) the signature σ issued by the authority is valid, and
(II) the corresponding secret attribute $\mathbf{x}$ satisfies the circuit C associated to the message M.

However, in spite of the similarities shared with the construction of [SAH16], the security proof of our construction requires a rather sensitive and technical analysis, which calls for new tools. This difficulty mainly stems from the fact that security proofs relying on the Fiat-Shamir-based NIZK proof systems are often times not as simple as the construction appears to be and in some cases the intuition may fail, e.g., [BPW12, BFW16].

Our proof of security of the generic ABS scheme relies on our generalization of the forking lemma of [PS00], which we call the *general multi-forking lemma with oracle access*. Our forking lemma can be seen as a generalization and a simplification of the general forking lemma of [BN06] and the improved forking lemma of [BPVY00]. In particular, we analyze the output behavior of an algorithm when run multiple times on related inputs, instead of when only run twice as in [BN06], while also providing it with oracle access to a deterministic algorithm. Recall that the original forking lemma of [PS00] applies to Fiat-Shamir type signature schemes and roughly states that, if there exists a valid forger $\mathcal{A}$, then one can rewind $\mathcal{A}$ initialized with the same randomness tape to find two accepting transcripts with the same commitment but different challenges, leading, via the special soundness property of Σ-protocols, to extract the secret signing key from the transcripts and hence a proof of security of the signature scheme in the random oracle model.

First, we require the forking lemma to analyze the output behavior of an algorithm on multiple runs to capture the situation arising in the recent lattice-based NIZK proof systems (e.g., [LNSW13, LLNW14, LNW15]) where the extractor of the underlying Σ-protocol requires more than two valid transcripts to extract a witness. Although the improved forking lemma of [BPVY00] captures this multiplicity of the forking lemma of a particular El Gamal-type signature scheme, it seems hard to apply in situations like ours where we are not dealing with regular signature schemes. Our forking lemma, similar to the one of [BN06], divorces the probabilistic essence of the forking lemma from any particular application context. Furthermore, our forking lemma provides worst-case rather than expected-time guarantees; the improved forking lemma of [BPVY00] roughly states that an expected $O(1/\epsilon)$ repeated executions of a forger $\mathcal{A}$ with advantage ϵ is required to extract a valid witness. We believe this feature to be more suitable for standard assumptions that are defined for PPT algorithms, as also stated in [BN06].

Second, and more importantly, our forking lemma allows the algorithm $\mathcal{A}$ that can be rewinded, to have oracle access to some algorithm $\mathcal{O}$ that *cannot* be rewinded. This is a useful feature for the forking algorithm to have in situations where the simulator cannot rewind all the algorithms which he is interacting with. This may be easiest to explain with a concrete example; in particular, when we reduce the eu-cma security of the underlying digital signature scheme to the security of our ABS scheme, the simulator (which is the eu-cma adversary) simulates the view of an ABS security game to the ABS adversary $\mathcal{A}$, and answers the queries made by $\mathcal{A}$ using its eu-cma challenger $\mathcal{O}$. At some point when $\mathcal{A}$ outputs a forgery for the ABS security game, the simulator hopes to extract the witness from the forgery and use it to win his own eu-cma security game. However, for this particular situation, the problem with all the previous forking lemmas is that the simulator will not be able to run the forking algorithm in the specified way; the simulator *can* rewind $\mathcal{A}$ to a particular point where the fork happens, however, the simulator *cannot* rewind the eu-cma challenger $\mathcal{O}$ in the same way, since it is outside the simulator's (i.e., eu-cma adversary's) control. Then, since the behavior of $\mathcal{A}$ is implicitly dependent on the behavior of the eu-cma challenger, the standard forking lemma does not provide meaningful analysis of the output of $\mathcal{A}$ on multiple runs. We therefore present a general multi-forking lemma *with oracle access* to capture these situations where the simulator is restricted to rewinding only some of the algorithms he is interacting with. We note that in case one is willing to use some algebraic problem such as the SIS or LWE problem as the underlying hardness assumption, these situations do not show up, since once given a fixed problem instance, the simulator can reuse it in every run to simulate the view to $\mathcal{A}$.

Finally, one of the benefits of using the Fiat-Shamir-based NIZK proof system is that we do not have to rely on the dummy attribute technique of those ABS schemes based on Goth-Sahai NIZK proof systems [MPR11,SAH16] to prove adaptive unforgeability and hence obtaining a more efficient signing algorithm. At a high level, this is because Fiat-Shamir based NIZK proof systems can be simulation-sound and extractable at the same time, whereas Goth-Sahai NIZK proof systems can only be instantiated to have one of the two properties. Therefore, during the proof of adaptive unforgeability, since the simulator needs to set up the common reference string in the extractable mode to extract a witness from the forgery, the simulator has to rely on these extra dummy attributes, which are never used in the actual scheme, to simulate signatures (i.e., proofs).

Instantiation from Lattices. To instantiate our generic ABS construction from lattices, we require three primitives: a signature scheme, a commitment scheme, and a Σ-protocol for a relation capturing the aforementioned items (I) and (II). As for the signature scheme, we can use the simple and efficient lattice-based signature scheme of Boyen [Boy10], which has been extensively studied in the lattice-based NIZK literatures. In particular, Ling et al. [LNSW13] provides an efficient Σ-protocol for proving possession of a valid Boyen signature (i.e., item (I)). However, unfortunately, it is not known whether the Σ-protocol of Ling et al. can be extended to prove circuit satisfiability, which is what we require in item (II), and in fact, recent subsequent results of [LLM+16,YAL+17] suggest that they are not powerful enough to capture circuit satisfiability. On the other hand, Xie et al. [XXW13] provides a lattice-based Σ-protocol for proving NP relations via arithmetic circuit satisfiability, which is what we exactly require in item (II), however, it does not seem possible to simply combine the two different types of Σ-protocols of [LNSW13, XXW13].

To this end, in this paper we present a new Σ-protocol for proving possession of a valid Boyen signature by expressing the verification algorithm of the Boyen signature as a simple arithmetic circuit that is compatible with the Σ-protocol of Xie et al. Specifically, since both items (I) and (II) can now be represented as arithmetic circuits, we can use the Σ-protocol of Xie et al. to obtain our desired Σ-protocol. The main observation is that, most operations that show up in lattice-based cryptography are composed of simple arithmetic operations such as matrix multiplications, and therefore naturally leads to simple arithmetic circuit representations. For our particular case, the verification algorithm of the Boyen signature scheme essentially boils down to checking two simple conditions; whether a vector $\mathbf{z}$ satisfies $\|\mathbf{z}\|_\infty \leq \beta$ and $\mathbf{A}\mathbf{z} = \mathbf{u} \bmod q$, where we intentionally dismiss the message for simplicity. As it can be seen, the latter equation is readily expressed by a very simple arithmetic circuit. On the other hand, the first inequality requires some extra work, however, this too can be expressed as an simple arithmetic circuit without much overhead by efficiently encoding predicates such as $x \stackrel{?}{\in} \{-1, 0, 1\}$ into arithmetic circuits.

2   Preliminaries

2.1   Commitment Schemes with Gap Openings

We define a standard commitment scheme that supports an additional notion we call *gap openings*. This additional notion will make it conceptually easier when we combine it with gap-Σ-protocols, which we later define. Informally, a commitment scheme with a gap opening is a standard commitment scheme where there may exist additional valid openings that are never created during the commitment algorithm.

Definition 1 (Commitments). *A commitment scheme with message space $\mathcal{M}$ and commitment space $\mathcal{C}$ is a triple of PPT algorithms* (C.Gen, C.Com, C.Open) *of the following form:*

C.Gen(1^λ) $\rightarrow$ pk: *The key generation algorithm takes as input the security parameter 1^λ and outputs a public commitment key* pk.

C.Com(pk, M) $\rightarrow$ (c, d): *The commitment algorithm takes as inputs the commitment key* pk *and message* M $\in \mathcal{M}$, *and outputs a commitment/opening pair (c, d). We denote $\mathcal{D}_{\mathsf{Com}}(\mathsf{pk}, \mathsf{M})$ as the set of all possible outputs of this algorithm under fixed* pk *and* M.

C.Open(pk, M, c, d) $\rightarrow$ $1\backslash 0$: *The* deterministic *opening algorithm takes as inputs the commitment key* pk, *message* M *and commitment/opening pair (c, d) as inputs and outputs 1 or 0. We denote $\mathcal{D}_{\mathsf{G\text{-}Com}}(\mathsf{pk}, \mathsf{M})$ as the set of all possible pairs (c, d) this algorithm outputs 1 under fixed* pk *and* M.

Here, we require the commitment scheme to satisfy the following correctness notion: for all $M \in \mathcal{M}$, $pk \leftarrow C.Gen(1^\lambda), (c, d) \leftarrow C.Com(pk, M)$ *we have* $C.Open(pk, M, c, d) = 1$.

It is clear that we have $\mathcal{D}_{Com}(pk, M) \subseteq \mathcal{D}_{G\text{-}Com}(pk, M)$ for all pk and $M \in \mathcal{M}$. We say the commitment scheme has a *gap-opening* when $\mathcal{D}_{Com} \subset \mathcal{D}_{G\text{-}Com}$. We require the following security notions for a commitment scheme:

Binding. We call the scheme unconditionally (resp. computationally) binding if for all (resp. PPT) algorithm $\mathcal{A}$, we have the following:

$$\Pr[pk \leftarrow C.Gen(1^\lambda); (c, M, M', d, d') \leftarrow \mathcal{A}(pk) :$$
$$C.Open(pk, M, c, d) = C.Open(pk, M', c, d') = 1 \wedge M \neq M'] \leq negl(\lambda)$$

Note that even though such a pair (c, d) may never be outputted by the commitment algorithm C.Com, the binding property must hold even for adversaries that output $(c, d) \in \mathcal{D}_{G\text{-}Com}(pk, M) \backslash \mathcal{D}_{Com}(pk, M)$.

Hiding. We call the scheme unconditionally (resp. computationally) hiding if for all (resp. PPT) algorithm $\mathcal{A}$ and any message $M \in \mathcal{M}$, we have the following:[4]

$$\Pr[pk \leftarrow C.Gen(1^\lambda); \; b \leftarrow \{0, 1\}; \; c_0 \leftarrow \mathcal{C}; \; (c_1, d) \leftarrow C.Com(pk, M);$$
$$b' \leftarrow \mathcal{A}(pk, M, c_b) : b = b'] \leq 1/2 + negl(\lambda)$$

2.2   Digital Signature Schemes

In this paper, we use *deterministic* digital signature schemes; a scheme where the randomness of the signing algorithm is derived from the secret key and message. We briefly recall the standard syntax and security notions, and refer the full version for the exact definition. A deterministic digital signature scheme is a tuple of PPT algorithms (S.KeyGen, S.Sign, S.Verify), such that the key generation algorithm S.KeyGen outputs a verification key vk and a signing key sk. The *deterministic* signing algorithm S.Sign on input the signing key sk and a message x outputs a signature σ, and the verification algorithm S.Verify verifies the signature σ using the verification key vk. We consider the standard security notion of existential unforgeability under an adaptive chosen message attack (eu-cma).

2.3   Arithmetic Circuit Representation

Here, we explain how we represent an arithmetic circuit. Let C be an arithmetic circuit over a ring R having ℓ input wires, one output wire and N gates. Here the gates are labelled by either + (addition) or × (product) gates. The input wires are indexed by $1, \cdots, \ell$, the internal wires are indexed by $\ell+1, \cdots, \ell+N-1$ and

---

[4] We assume that the commitment space $\mathcal{C}$ is efficiently sampleable. Namely, as long as the hiding property holds, $\mathcal{C}$ may be larger than the set of all possible commitments. These situations come up in many of the lattice-based commitment schemes.

the output wire has index $\ell + N$. We assume each gate takes only two incoming wires with multiple fan-out wires, where all the fan-out wires are indexed with the same index. We specify the topology of an arithmetic circuit by a function topo : $\{\ell+1, \cdots, \ell+N\} \to \{+, \times\} \times \{1, \cdots, \ell+N-1\} \times \{1, \cdots, \ell+N-1\}$. They map a non-input wire to its first and second incoming wires in which these three wires are connected by either a gate labelled by $+$ or $\times$. For $(\star, i_1, i_2) \leftarrow \mathsf{topo}(i)$, we require that $i_1, i_2 < i$ where $\star \in \{+, \times\}$.

2.4 Attribute-Based Signature Scheme

An attribute-based signature scheme supporting the class of arithmetic circuits $\mathcal{C} = \{\mathcal{C}_\lambda\}_{\lambda \in \mathbb{N}}$ and message space $\{0,1\}^*$ is defined by the following four probabilistic polynomial time algorithms (Setup, KeyGen, Sign, Verify):

Setup($1^\lambda, 1^\ell$) $\to$ (mpk, msk): The setup algorithm takes as input the security parameter 1^λ and the input length 1^ℓ of the circuits in $\mathcal{C}_\ell$, and outputs the master public key mpk and the master secret key msk.

KeyGen(mpk, msk, $\mathbf{x}$) $\to$ sk$_\mathbf{x}$: The signing key generation algorithm takes as input the master public key mpk, the master secret key msk and an attribute $\mathbf{x} \in \{0,1\}^\ell$, and outputs a signing key sk$_\mathbf{x}$.

Sign(mpk, sk$_\mathbf{x}$, C, M) $\to$ Σ: The signing algorithm takes as input the master public key mpk, a secret key sk$_\mathbf{x}$ associated with an attribute $\mathbf{x}$, a circuit $C \in \mathcal{C}_\ell$ and a message M $\in \{0,1\}^*$, and outputs a signature σ.

Verify(mpk, M, C, Σ) $\to$ Valid/Invalid: The verification algorithm takes as input the master public key mpk, a message M, a circuit C and a signature Σ, and outputs Valid or Invalid.

Correctness. We require the following correctness condition to hold: for all $\lambda, \ell \in \mathbb{N}$, $\mathbf{x} \in \{0,1\}^\ell$, $C \in \mathcal{C}_\ell$ such that $C(\mathbf{x}) = 1$, it holds with all but negligible probability that Verify(mpk, M, C, Sign(mpk, sk$_\mathbf{x}$, C, M)) = Valid, where the probability is taken over the randomness used in (mpk, msk) $\leftarrow$ Setup($1^\lambda, 1^\ell$) and sk$_\mathbf{x}$ $\leftarrow$ KeyGen(mpk, msk, $\mathbf{x}$).

We require two types of security notions for attribute-based signature schemes.

Definition 2 (Privacy). *The security notion of privacy for an attribute-based signature scheme is defined by the following game between a challenger and an adversary $\mathcal{A}$:*

Setup. *The challenger runs* (mpk, msk) $\leftarrow$ Setup($1^\lambda, 1^\ell$) *and gives* (mpk, msk) *to $\mathcal{A}$.*

Challenge. *$\mathcal{A}$ outputs a message* M $\in \{0,1\}^*$, *two attributes* $\mathbf{x}_0, \mathbf{x}_1 \in \{0,1\}^\ell$ *and a circuit* $C \in \mathcal{C}_\ell$ *such that* $C(\mathbf{x}_0) = C(\mathbf{x}_1) = 1$ *to the challenger. The challenger first runs* sk$_{\mathbf{x}_\beta}$ $\leftarrow$ KeyGen(mpk, msk, $\mathbf{x}_\beta$) *for* $\beta = 0, 1$. *Then, it picks a random bit* $b \leftarrow \{0,1\}$ *and returns to $\mathcal{A}$ the signature* $\Sigma^* \leftarrow$ Sign(mpk, sk$_{\mathbf{x}_b}$, C, M) *along with the two secret keys* (sk$_{\mathbf{x}_0}$, sk$_{\mathbf{x}_1}$).

Forgery. *Finally, $\mathcal{A}$ outputs a guess* $b' \in \{0,1\}$ *for b.*

The advantage of $\mathcal{A}$ is defined as $|\Pr[b' = b] - 1/2|$. We say that the attribute-based signature scheme is computationally private *if the advantage of any PPT algorithm $\mathcal{A}$ is negligible. We say it is* unconditionally private *if the advantage of any (possibly inefficient) algorithm $\mathcal{A}$ is negligible.*

Definition 3 (Unforgeability). *The security notion of adaptively unforgeable for an attribute-based signature scheme is defined by the following game between a challenger and an adversary $\mathcal{A}$:*

Setup. *The challenger runs* $(\mathsf{mpk}, \mathsf{msk}) \leftarrow \mathsf{Setup}(1^\lambda, 1^\ell)$ *and gives* mpk *to $\mathcal{A}$.*
Queries. *$\mathcal{A}$ may adaptively make the following queries to the challenger:*

- **Signing.** *$\mathcal{A}$ submits a signing query on any attribute, message and circuit tuple $(\mathbf{x}, \mathsf{M}, C)$ such that $C(\mathbf{x}) = 1$ to the challenger. The challenger runs $\mathsf{sk}_{\mathbf{x}} \leftarrow \mathsf{KeyGen}(\mathsf{mpk}, \mathsf{msk}, \mathbf{x})$. Then, it returns the signature $\Sigma \leftarrow \mathsf{Sign}(\mathsf{mpk}, \mathsf{sk}_{\mathbf{x}}, C, \mathsf{M})$ to $\mathcal{A}$.*
- **Key reveal.** *$\mathcal{A}$ submits a key reveal query on any attribute $\mathbf{x}$ to the challenger. The challenger returns the signing key $\mathsf{sk}_{\mathbf{x}} \leftarrow \mathsf{KeyGen}(\mathsf{mpk}, \mathsf{msk}, \mathbf{x})$ to $\mathcal{A}$.*

Forgery. *Finally, $\mathcal{A}$ outputs a signature $(\mathsf{M}^*, C^*, \Sigma^*)$.*

The adversary $\mathcal{A}$ wins the game if the following three conditions hold:

(i) $\mathsf{Verify}(\mathsf{mpk}, \mathsf{M}^*, C^*, \Sigma^*) = \mathsf{Valid}$,
(ii) *Adversary $\mathcal{A}$ did not submit a key reveal query for $\mathbf{x}$ such that $C^*(\mathbf{x}) = 1$,*
(iii) *Adversary $\mathcal{A}$ did not submit a signing query on $(\mathbf{x}, \mathsf{M}^*, C^*)$ for any $\mathbf{x}$ such that $C^*(\mathbf{x}) = 1$.*

The advantage of $\mathcal{A}$ is defined as the probability of $\mathcal{A}$ winning the above game. We say that the attribute-based signature scheme is adaptively unforgeable *if the advantage of any PPT algorithm $\mathcal{A}$ is negligible.*

2.5   General Multi-forking Lemma with Oracle Access

Here we state and prove an extended version of the forking lemma of [PS00], which will play a central role in our proof of security of our ABS scheme. Our forking lemma analyzes the output behavior of an algorithm $\mathcal{A}$ when run multiple times on related inputs, instead of when only run twice, while also providing it with oracle access to a *deterministic* algorithm $\mathcal{O}$.

Lemma 1 (General Multi-forking Lemma with Oracle Access). *Fix an integer $q \geq 1$ and a set $\mathcal{H}$ of size $h \geq 2$. Let $\mathcal{A}$ be a randomized algorithm that has oracle access to some* deterministic *algorithm $\mathcal{O}$, where on input $\mathsf{par}, h_1, \cdots, h_q$, algorithm $\mathcal{A}$ returns a pair; the first element is an integer in the range $0, \cdots, q$*

and the second element is what we refer to as a side output. *Let* IG *be a randomized algorithm called the* input generator. *The accepting probability of* $\mathcal{A}$, *denoted* acc, *is defined as the probability that* $J \geq 1$ *in the experiment below:*

$$(\mathsf{par}, \overline{\mathsf{par}}) \leftarrow \mathsf{IG}; \; h_1, \cdots, h_q \leftarrow \mathcal{H}; \; (J, \sigma) \leftarrow \mathcal{A}^{\mathcal{O}(\overline{\mathsf{par}}, \cdot)}(\mathsf{par}, h_1, \cdots, h_q).$$

For a positive integer $\ell \geq 2$, *the* forking algorithm $\mathsf{F}_{\mathcal{A}, \ell}^{\mathcal{O}(\overline{\mathsf{par}}, \cdot)}$ *associated to* $\mathcal{A}^{\mathcal{O}(\overline{\mathsf{par}}, \cdot)}$ *is a randomized oracle algorithm that takes input* par *and proceeds as in Fig. 1, where* $\{\epsilon_k\}_{k \in [\ell]}$ *denotes an arbitrary set of strings. Let*

$$\mathsf{frk} = \Pr[(\mathsf{par}, \overline{\mathsf{par}}) \leftarrow \mathsf{IG}; \; (b, \{\sigma_k\}_{k \in [\ell]}) \leftarrow \mathsf{F}_{\mathcal{A}, \ell}^{\mathcal{O}(\overline{\mathsf{par}}, \cdot)}(\mathsf{par}) \; : \; b = 1].$$

Then,

$$\mathsf{frk} \geq \mathsf{acc} \cdot \left(\left(\frac{\mathsf{acc}}{q} \right)^{\ell - 1} - \frac{f(\ell)}{h} \right), \tag{1}$$

where $f(\ell)$ *is some universal positive valued function that only depends on the value* ℓ.

Algorithm $\mathsf{F}_{\mathcal{A}, \ell}^{\mathcal{O}(\overline{\mathsf{par}}, \cdot)}(\mathsf{par})$
Pick coin ρ for $\mathcal{A}$ at random.
$h_1^{(1)}, \cdots, h_q^{(1)} \leftarrow \mathcal{H}$
$(I^{(1)}, \sigma^{(1)}) \leftarrow \mathcal{A}^{\mathcal{O}(\overline{\mathsf{par}}, \cdot)}(\mathsf{par}, h_1^{(1)}, \cdots, h_q^{(1)}; \rho)$
if $I^{(1)} = 0$ **then return** $(0, \{\epsilon_k\}_{k \in [\ell]})$
for $k = 2$ **to** ℓ **do**
$\quad h_{I^{(1)}}^{(k)}, \cdots, h_q^{(k)} \leftarrow \mathcal{H}$
$\quad (I^{(k)}, \sigma^{(k)}) \leftarrow \mathcal{A}^{\mathcal{O}(\overline{\mathsf{par}}, \cdot)}(\mathsf{par}, h_1^{(1)}, \cdots, h_{I^{(1)}-1}^{(1)}, h_{I^{(1)}}^{(k)}, \cdots h_q^{(k)}; \rho)$
if $I^{(1)} = I^{(k)}$ and $h_{I^{(1)}}^{(k)} \neq h_{I^{(1)}}^{(k')}$ for all $k, k' \in [\ell]$ **then**
$\quad$ **return** $(1, \{\sigma^{(k)}\}_{k \in [\ell]})$
else
$\quad$ **return** $(0, \{\epsilon_k\}_{k \in [\ell]})$.

Fig. 1. Description of the forking algorithm $\mathsf{F}_{\mathcal{A}, \ell}^{\mathcal{O}(\overline{\mathsf{par}}, \cdot)}$.

Proof. For any input $x = (\mathsf{par}, \overline{\mathsf{par}})$, denote $\mathsf{acc}(x)$ as the probability that $J \geq 1$ in the following experiment:

$$h_1, \cdots, h_q \leftarrow H; \; (J, \sigma) \leftarrow \mathcal{A}^{\mathcal{O}(\overline{\mathsf{par}}, \cdot)}(\mathsf{par}, h_1, \cdots, h_q).$$

Also, let $\mathsf{frk}(x) = \Pr[(b, \{\sigma_k\}_{k \in [\ell]}) \leftarrow \mathsf{F}_{\mathcal{A}, \ell}^{\mathcal{O}(\overline{\mathsf{par}}, \cdot)}(\mathsf{par}) \; : \; b = 1]$. We claim that there exists some universal positive valued function $f(\ell)$ such that for all x,

$$\mathsf{frk}(x) \geq \mathsf{acc}(x) \cdot \left(\left(\frac{\mathsf{acc}(x)}{q} \right)^{\ell - 1} - \frac{f(\ell)}{h} \right). \tag{2}$$

By taking the expectation of $\mathsf{frk}(x)$ over $x = (\mathsf{par}, \overline{\mathsf{par}}) \leftarrow \mathsf{IG}$ and using the fact $\mathbb{E}[\mathsf{acc}(x)^\ell] \geq \mathbb{E}[\mathsf{acc}(x)]^\ell$ (which follows from Jensen's inequality), we obtain Eq. (1). Therefore, to prove the claim, we must prove Eq. (2). Now, for any input x, with the probabilities taken over the coin tosses of $\mathsf{F}_{\mathcal{A},\ell}^{\mathcal{O}(\overline{\mathsf{par}},\cdot)}(\mathsf{par})$, $\mathsf{frk}(x)$ is equivalent to the following.

$$\Pr\left[(I^{(1)} = I^{(k)} \text{ for all } k \in [\ell]) \wedge (I^{(1)} \geq 1) \wedge (h_{I^{(1)}}^{(k)} \neq h_{I^{(1)}}^{(k')} \text{ for all } k, k' \in [\ell])\right]$$

$$\geq \Pr\left[(I^{(1)} = I^{(k)} \text{ for all } k \in [\ell]) \wedge (I^{(1)} \geq 1)\right]$$

$$- \Pr\left[(I^{(1)} \geq 1) \wedge (h_{I^{(1)}}^{(k)} = h_{I^{(1)}}^{(k')} \text{ for some } k, k' \in [\ell])\right]$$

$$= \Pr\left[(I^{(1)} = I^{(k)} \text{ for all } k \in [\ell]) \wedge (I^{(1)} \geq 1)\right] - \Pr\left[(I^{(1)} \geq 1)\right] \cdot \left(1 - \prod_{k=1}^{\ell-1} \frac{h-k}{h}\right)$$

Here, we can rewrite $1 - \prod_{k=1}^{\ell-1} \frac{h-k}{h} = \frac{1}{h} \cdot \left(\sum_{k=0}^{\ell-2} \alpha_k(\ell) \cdot \frac{1}{h^k}\right)$, where $(\alpha_k(\ell))_{k=0}^{\ell-2}$ are functions that only depend on ℓ. Since $h \geq 1$, we can always upper bound the right hand side by $f(\ell)/h$ using some positive valued function $f(\ell)$ that only depends on ℓ, where for example, we can use $f(\ell) = (\ell-1) \cdot \max\{|\alpha_k(\ell)|\}_{k=0}^{\ell-2}$. Here, note that $f(\ell)$ is some universal function that depends neither on $\mathcal{A}$ nor $\mathcal{O}$. Therefore, we can further rewrite the inequality as follows:

$$\mathsf{frk}(x) \geq \Pr\left[(I^{(1)} = I^{(k)} \text{ for all } k \in [\ell]) \wedge (I^{(1)} \geq 1)\right] - \frac{\mathsf{acc}(x) \cdot f(\ell)}{h}.$$

Hence, it remains to show that $\Pr\left[(I^{(1)} = I^{(k)} \text{ for all } k \in [\ell]) \wedge (I^{(1)} \geq 1)\right] \geq \mathsf{acc}(x)^\ell/q^{\ell-1}$. Let $\mathcal{R}$ denote the set from which $\mathcal{A}$ draws its random coins. For each $i \in [q]$, let $X_i : \mathcal{R} \times \mathcal{H}^{i-1} \to [0,1]$ be defined by setting $X_i(\rho, h_1, \cdots, h_{i-1})$ to

$$\Pr[h_i, \cdots, h_q \leftarrow \mathcal{H} \; ; \; (J, \sigma) \leftarrow \mathcal{A}^{\mathcal{O}(\overline{\mathsf{par}},\cdot)}(\mathsf{par}, h_1, \cdots, h_q; \rho) \; : \; J = i]$$

for all $\rho \in \mathcal{R}$ and $h_1, \cdots, h_{i-1} \in \mathcal{H}$. Here, regard X_i as a random variable over the uniform distribution on its domain. Then,

$$\Pr\left[(I^{(1)} = I^{(k)} \text{ for all } k \in [\ell]) \wedge (I^{(1)} \geq 1)\right] = \sum_{i=1}^{q} \Pr\left[I^{(k)} = i \text{ for all } k \in [\ell]\right]$$

$$= \sum_{i=1}^{q} \left(\Pr[I^{(1)} = i] \cdot \prod_{k=2}^{\ell} \Pr[I^{(k)} = i \mid I^{(1)} = i]\right) \tag{3}$$

$$= \sum_{i=1}^{q} \sum_{\rho, h_1, \cdots, h_{i-1}} X_i(\rho, h_1, \cdots, h_{i-1})^\ell \cdot \frac{1}{|\mathcal{R}| \cdot |\mathcal{H}|^{i-1}}$$

$$= \sum_{i=1}^{q} \mathbb{E}[X_i^\ell] \quad \geq \quad \sum_{i=1}^{q} \mathbb{E}[X_i]^\ell. \tag{4}$$

Here Eq. (3) follows from independence of $I^{(k)}$ and $I^{(k')}$ for $k, k' \in [2, \ell]$, and Eq. (4) follows from Jensen's inequality where we use the fact that $f(x) = x^\ell$ is a convex function. Finally, using Holder's inequality, we obtain

$$\sum_{i=1}^{q} \mathbb{E}[X_i]^\ell \geq \frac{1}{q^{\ell-1}} \cdot \left(\sum_{i=1}^{q} \mathbb{E}[X_i] \right)^\ell = \frac{1}{q^{\ell-1}} \cdot \mathsf{acc}(x)^\ell.$$

This completes the proof of Eq. (1), hence concluding our claim.

Remark. As can be checked from the proof, we can set the function $f(\ell)$ so that in case $\ell = 2$, we have $f(2) = 1$. Therefore, by setting the deterministic oracle $\mathcal{O}$ to be an oracle that outputs nothing, the above lemma implies the general forking lemma of [BN06].

3 Gap-Σ-Protocols and Non-interactive Zero-Knowledge Proofs

Before presenting the main tools we use in this paper, we first recall the definition of languages and relations. A *language* $\mathcal{L} \subseteq \{0,1\}^*$ is said to have polynomial time recognizable *relation* $\mathcal{R} \subseteq \{0,1\}^* \times \{0,1\}^*$ if $\mathcal{L} = \{x \mid \exists \text{w s.t.} (x, w) \in \mathcal{R}\}$ where $|w| \leq \mathsf{poly}(|x|)$. We call the string w a *witness* to the *statement* $x \in \mathcal{L}$.

3.1 Gap-Σ-Protocols

Σ-protocols are a special type of 3-round interactive proof systems that is also a proof of knowledge. Below, we define (a special type of) the *gap-Σ-protocol*, which is a generalization of the standard Σ-protocol where we allow the extracted witness to lie in a slightly larger space than the actual witness being proven during the protocol. Furthermore, the special soundness is defined for cases where more than 2 valid transcripts are required to extract a witness. These non-standard formalizations are required, since most of the lattice-based Σ-protocols are not captured by the standard formalizations.

Definition 4 (Gap-Σ-protocols). *Let m be an integer constant and t an integer-valued function of the security parameter. Let $(\mathcal{P}, \mathcal{V})$ be a two-party protocol, where $\mathcal{V}$ is PPT, and let $\mathcal{L}, \mathcal{L}' \subseteq \{0,1\}^*$ be languages with witness relations $\mathcal{R}, \mathcal{R}'$ such that $\mathcal{R} \subseteq \mathcal{R}'$. Then $(\mathcal{P}, \mathcal{V})$ is called a gap-$\Sigma_{m,t}$-protocol for relations $(\mathcal{R}, \mathcal{R}')$ with challenge space $\mathcal{C} = \{0, 1, \cdots, m - 1\}^t$, if it satisfies the following conditions:*

- **3-move form:** *The protocol is of the following form:*

  - *The prover $\mathcal{P}$, on input $(x, w) \in \mathcal{R}$, sends a commitment α to $\mathcal{V}$.*
  - *The verifier $\mathcal{V}$ samples a challenge $\beta \leftarrow \mathcal{C}$ and sends it to $\mathcal{P}$.*
  - *The prover $\mathcal{P}$ sends a response γ to $\mathcal{V}$, and $\mathcal{V}$ decides to accept of reject based on the protocol transcript (α, β, γ).*

The protocol transcript (α, β, γ) *is called a* valid transcript *if the verifier* $\mathcal{V}$ *accepts the protocol run.*

- **Completeness:** *Whenever* $(x, w) \in \mathcal{R}$, $\mathcal{V}$ *accepts with probability 1.*
- **Soundness:** *If* $(x, w) \notin \mathcal{R}$, *then any cheating (possibly inefficient) prover* $\mathcal{P}^*$ *succeeds with probability at most* $(\frac{m-1}{m})^t$. *We call this value the* soundness error.
- **Special gap-soundness:** *There exists a PPT algorithm* $\mathcal{E}$ *(the knowledge extractor) which takes* m *valid transcripts* $\{(\alpha, \beta_i, \gamma_i)\}_{i \in [m]}$ *for some statement* $x \in \mathcal{L}$, *where there exists at least one index* $j \in [t]$ *such that* $\{\beta_{i,j}\}_{i \in [m]} = \{0, 1, \cdots, m-1\}$ *as inputs, and outputs* w *such that* $(x, w) \in \mathcal{R}'$. *Here* $\beta_{i,j}$ *denotes the* j-th *value of the string* β_i. *Note that the knowledge extractor outputs a witness in the* gap *relation.*
- **Special honest-verifier zero-knowledge (HVZK):** *There exists a PPT algorithm* $\mathcal{S}$ *(the HVZK simulator) taking* $x \in \mathcal{L}$ *as input, that outputs* (α, β, γ) *whose distribution is indistinguishable from an accepting protocol transcript generated by a real protocol run. Although no guarantees on the outputs are made, the simulator* $\mathcal{S}$ *is also defined over the inputs* $x \notin \mathcal{L}$.

We call the gap-$\Sigma_{m,t}$-protocol computationally (resp. statistically) special HVZK if the simulated transcript is computationally (resp. statistically) indistinguishable from a real transcript.

Lastly, we say the gap-Σ-protocol has high-commitment entropy *if for all* $(x, w) \in \mathcal{R}$ *and* α, *the probability that an honestly generated commitment by* $\mathcal{P}$ *takes on the value* α *is negligible.*

We omit the subscript (m, t) of the gap-$\Sigma_{m,t}$-protocol whenever it is irrelevant to the context. Occasionally, we omit t and simply write gap-Σ_m-protocol to emphasize that the soundness error is negligible in the security parameter. We note that the standard Σ-protocol is a special case of the gap-Σ-protocol where $m = 2, \mathcal{R} = \mathcal{R}'$. In this case the soundness error will simply be 2^{-t} and special gap-soundness implies special soundness, since if there exists an index $j \in [t]$ for which the binary strings (i.e., the challenges) differ, then it implies that the two challenges are different. Finally, we assume without loss of generality that all of the gap-Σ-protocols we consider in this paper have high-commitment entropy, since the condition can be easily met by appending a super-logarithmic number of public random bits to the commitments.

Often times, the gap in the relations allows for much more efficient schemes, and do not affect their usefulness in practice as long as $\mathcal{R}'$ is still a sufficiently hard relation, e.g., [FO97, DF02, AJLA+12, BCK+14]. We note that for simplicity, in this paper we only consider gap-Σ-protocols that are complete with probability 1. Namely, our formalization does not capture those gap-Σ-protocols that are based on the rejection sampling technique such as [Lyu09, Lyu12, BCK+14].[5]

---

[5] Note that we intentionally disregard [BKLP15] from our work. Although they offer an attractive rejection sampling-based gap-Σ-protocol for proving arbitrary arithmetic operations that are more efficient than those of [XXW13] which we use in Sect. 5,

Finally, we formally describe the Fiat-Shamir transformation [FS86] which is a technique to make any (gap-)Σ-protocol into a non-interactive proof system by using a cryptographic hash function.

Definition 5. *Let $(\mathcal{P}, \mathcal{V})$ be a gap-Σ-protocol with relation $(\mathcal{R}, \mathcal{R}')$, and $H(\cdot)$ a hash function with range equal to the verifier's challenge space $\mathcal{C}$. The Fiat-Shamir transformation of gap-Σ is the non-interactive proof system $(\mathcal{P}^H, \mathcal{V}^H)$ defined as follows:*

$\mathcal{P}^H(x, w)$: *Run $\mathcal{P}(x, w)$ to obtain a commitment α, and compute $\beta \leftarrow H(x, \alpha)$. Then complete the run of $\mathcal{P}$ with β as the challenge to get the response γ. Finally output the pair (α, γ)*

$\mathcal{V}^H(x, \alpha, \gamma)$: *Compute $\beta = H(x, \alpha)$ and return the output of $\mathcal{V}(\alpha, \beta, \gamma)$.*

3.2   Non-interactive Zero-Knowledge Proof Systems

We formalize the notion of non-interactive zero-knowledge (NIZK) proof systems in the *explicitly programmable* random oracle model [Wee09], where the zero-knowledge (ZK) simulator is allowed to explicitly program the random oracle. We follow the notations provided in [FKMV12] for presentation. Namely, we model the ZK simulator of a NIZK proof system as a stateful PPT algorithm $\mathcal{S}$ that can operate in two modes: $(h, \mathsf{st}) \leftarrow \mathcal{S}(1, \mathsf{st}, q)$ takes care of answering random oracle queries, and $(\pi, \mathsf{st}) \leftarrow \mathcal{S}(2, \mathsf{st}, x)$ simulates the proof. Here, the calls to $\mathcal{S}(1, \cdots)$ and $\mathcal{S}(2, \cdots)$ share the common state st that is updated after each invocation of the simulator. Furthermore, we define three algorithms $\mathcal{S}_1, \mathcal{S}_2, \hat{\mathcal{S}}_2$ that run simulator $\mathcal{S}$ internally: $\mathcal{S}_1(q)$ returns the first output of $(h, \mathsf{st}) \leftarrow \mathcal{S}(1, \mathsf{st}, q)$, $\mathcal{S}_2(x, w)$ ignores the second input w and returns the first output of $(\pi, \mathsf{st}) \leftarrow \mathcal{S}(2, \mathsf{st}, x)$ if and only if $(x, w) \in \mathcal{R}$ (or equivalently $x \in \mathcal{L}$), and $\hat{\mathcal{S}}_2(x)$ is essentially the same as $\mathcal{S}_2(x, w)$ except that it does not take a second input w and is also defined for inputs such that $x \notin \mathcal{L}$. Observe that $\mathcal{S}_2$ and $\hat{\mathcal{S}}_2$ are identical for inputs $x \in \mathcal{L}$, and unlike $\mathcal{S}_2$, $\hat{\mathcal{S}}_2$ may be invoked to simulate proofs for invalid statements.

Definition 6 (Non-interactive Zero-Knowledge Proof System). *Let $\mathcal{R}$ be a relation with an associated language $\mathcal{L}_\mathcal{R}$. We say a non-interactive proof system $(\mathcal{P}, \mathcal{V})$ is a statistical NIZK proof system for language $\mathcal{L}_\mathcal{R}$ with a (PPT) ZK simulator $\mathcal{S}$ in the random oracle model, if for any algorithm $\mathcal{D}$ we have*

$$\left| \Pr[\mathcal{D}^{H(\cdot), \mathcal{P}^H(\cdot, \cdot)}(1^\lambda) = 1] - \Pr[\mathcal{D}^{\mathcal{S}_1(\cdot), \mathcal{S}_2(\cdot, \cdot)}(1^\lambda) = 1] \right| = \mathsf{negl}(\lambda),$$

where $H(\cdot)$ is modeled as a random oracle, and both $\mathcal{P}$ and $\mathcal{S}_2$ output $\bot$ if $(x, w) \notin \mathcal{R}$. It is called a computational NIZK proof system in case the above holds only for all PPT algorithms $\mathcal{D}$.

---

we were not able to verify the correctness of their proof sketch. In particular, the knowledge extractor for the protocol for proving multiplicative relations could not be constructed as stated in their paper.

It is a well known fact that in the random oracle model, the Fiat-Shamir transformation of any Σ-protocol is a NIZK proof system. It is straightforward to prove that it is also the case for gap-Σ-protocols, as we state in the following lemma.

Lemma 2 (Fiat-Shamir NIZK Proof Systems). *Let $(\mathcal{P}, \mathcal{V})$ be a gap-Σ-protocol with relation $(\mathcal{R}, \mathcal{R}')$ that is computationally (resp. statistically) special HVZK, and $H(\cdot)$ a hash function with range equal to the verifier's challenge space $\mathcal{C}$. Then, in the random oracle model, the non-interactive proof system $(\mathcal{P}^H, \mathcal{V}^H)$ obtained by the Fiat-Shamir transformation of gap-Σ is a computational (resp. statistical) non-interactive zero-knowledge proof system for the language $\mathcal{L}_{\mathcal{R}}$.*

Proof (Proof sketch.). To prove that the proof system $(\mathcal{P}^H, \mathcal{V}^H)$ is a NIZK proof system for the language $\mathcal{L}_{\mathcal{R}}$, it suffices to show that there exists a ZK simulator $\mathcal{S}$ as in the above Definition 6. Below, we construct $\mathcal{S}$ by invoking the HVZK simulator $\mathcal{S}_\Sigma$ of the underlying gap-Σ-protocol $(\mathcal{P}, \mathcal{V})$:

- $\mathcal{S}(1, \mathsf{st}, q = (x, \alpha)) \rightarrow (h = \beta, \mathsf{st})$: To answer random oracle queries, it searches the table $\mathcal{T}_H$ kept in the state st whether an output for $q = (x, \alpha)$ is already defined. If so it returns the previously defined assigned value. If not, it samples a uniformly random value $\beta \leftarrow \mathcal{C}$ and stores $(q = (x, \alpha), h = \beta)$ in the table. Note that this corresponds to algorithm $\mathcal{S}_1$.
- $\mathcal{S}(2, \mathsf{st}, x) \rightarrow (\pi = (\alpha, \beta, \gamma), \mathsf{st})$: To simulate a proof for the statement $x \in \mathcal{L}_{\mathcal{R}}$, it runs the HVZK simulator $\mathcal{S}_\Sigma$ on input x to obtain a proof (α, β, γ). Then, it updates the table $\mathcal{T}_H$ by adding $(q = (x, \alpha), h = \beta)$. If $\mathcal{T}_H$ happens to be already defined on input $q = (x, \alpha)$, $\mathcal{S}$ aborts. This completely specifies algorithm $\mathcal{S}_2$ as required. Observe that the simulator $\mathcal{S}$ can also be run on statements $x \notin \mathcal{L}_{\mathcal{R}}$ using the above method, since $\mathcal{S}_\Sigma$ is well-defined for $x \in \mathcal{L}$ as well. In particular, the above description for $\mathcal{S}$ also specifies algorithm $\hat{\mathcal{S}}_2$ as well.

Since, we only consider gap-Σ-protocols with high-commitment entropy, the probability of simulator $\mathcal{S}$ aborting is negligible, which ends the proof sketch.

In the following, we use the above algorithm $\mathcal{S}$ as the ZK simulator for a NIZK proof system $(\mathcal{P}^H, \mathcal{V}^H)$ based on the Fiat-Shamir transformation of a gap-Σ-protocol $(\mathcal{P}, \mathcal{V})$. Note that we do not explicitly define the soundness property of the NIZK proof system, since this property will be implicitly implied when we construct a knowledge extractor during the security proof.

4   Generic Construction of Attribute-Based Signatures

Preparation. Before presenting our construction, we describe the relations and languages we require for our NIZK proof system. Our construction relies on a gap-Σ-protocol for the relations $(\mathcal{R}_{\mathsf{ABS}}, \mathcal{R}'_{\mathsf{ABS}})$ defined below and employs the Fiat-Shamir transformation provided in Definition 5 to turn it in into a NIZK proof system. In the following, x_i for $i \in [\ell + 1, \ell + N - 1]$ denotes the values assigned to the i-th (internal) wire of C on input $\mathbf{x} = (x_1, \cdots, x_\ell)$ and $\mathsf{vk_{Sign}}$, $\mathsf{pk_{Com}}$ denotes the verification key and public commitment key of the underlying digital signature scheme and commitment scheme, respectively. Then the relation $\mathcal{R}_{\mathsf{ABS}}$ is defined as follows:

$$\mathcal{R}_{\mathsf{ABS}} = \left\{ \left(\mathsf{statement} = \left(\mathsf{vk_{Sign}}, \mathsf{pk_{Com}}, C \in \mathcal{C}_\ell, c_\sigma, (c_i)_{i=1}^{\ell + |C| - 1} \right), \right.\right.$$
$$\left.\left. \mathsf{witness} = \left(\mathbf{x} = (x_1, \cdots, x_\ell), \sigma, d_\sigma, (d_i)_{i=1}^{\ell + |C| - 1} \right) \right) \right|$$

the committed values in $c_\sigma, (c_i)_{i=1}^{\ell + |C| - 1}$ satisfy the following conditions:

- $\mathsf{S.Verify}(\mathsf{vk_{Sign}}, \mathbf{x}, \sigma) = 1$
- $x_i = x_{i_1} \star_i x_{i_2}$ for $i \in [\ell + 1, \ell + |C| - 1]$ for $(\star_i, i_1, i_2) \leftarrow \mathsf{topo}_C(i)$
- $1 = x_{(\ell + |C|)_1} \star_{\ell + |C|} x_{(\ell + |C|)_2}$ for $(\star_{\ell + |C|}, i_{(\ell + |C|)_1}, i_{(\ell + |C|)_2}) \leftarrow \mathsf{topo}_C(\ell + |C|)$
- $(c_\sigma, d_\sigma) \in \mathcal{D}_{\mathsf{Com}}(\mathsf{pk_{Com}}, \sigma)$ and $(c_i, d_i) \in \mathcal{D}_{\mathsf{Com}}(\mathsf{pk_{Com}}, x_i)$ for $i \in [\ell + |C| - 1]\}$

Here, recall that $\mathcal{D}_{\mathsf{Com}}(\mathsf{pk_{Com}}, M)$ is the set of all possible outputs of the commitment algorithm $\mathsf{C.Com}(\mathsf{pk_{Com}}, M)$. We simply define the corresponding language $\mathcal{L}_{\mathsf{ABS}}$ as the language induced by the relation $\mathcal{R}_{\mathsf{ABS}}$. Furthermore, the gap-relation $\mathcal{R}'_{\mathsf{ABS}}$ is defined analogously to $\mathcal{R}_{\mathsf{ABS}}$ except that we replace the last condition as follows:

- $(c_\sigma, d_\sigma) \in \mathcal{D}_{\mathsf{G\text{-}Com}}(\mathsf{pk_{Com}}, \sigma) \wedge (c_i, d_i) \in \mathcal{D}_{\mathsf{G\text{-}Com}}(\mathsf{pk_{Com}}, x_i)$ for $i \in [\ell + |C| - 1]$

The only difference between the two relations are the condition on the commitment and opening pairs. In the latter, it is only required that the pairs are in the set $\mathcal{D}_{\mathsf{G\text{-}Com}}(\cdot)$ and not in the more restricted set $\mathcal{D}_{\mathsf{Com}}(\cdot)$. Recall that $\mathcal{D}_{\mathsf{G\text{-}Com}}(\mathsf{pk_{Com}}, M)$ is the set of all commitment and opening pairs that the opening algorithm outputs 1 on message M. As we noted in Sect. 3.1, we require this gap-relation $\mathcal{R}'_{\mathsf{ABS}}$ purely for technical reasons, since in many of the lattice-based Σ-protocols we can only extract witnesses that lie in a slightly larger space than the actual witnesses being proven in the actual protocol. Similarly to above, we define the language $\mathcal{L}'_{\mathsf{ABS}}$ as the language induced by the relation $\mathcal{R}'_{\mathsf{ABS}}$.

For simplicity, in the following we omit $\mathsf{vk_{Sign}}$ and $\mathsf{pk_{Com}}$ from the statement, since they are fixed by the Setup algorithm and all signers use the same $\mathsf{vk_{Sign}}$ and $\mathsf{pk_{Com}}$.

Construction. Here, we provide our attribute-based signature scheme for unbounded (arithmetic) circuits. In the following, assume a digital signature scheme $(\mathsf{S.KeyGen}, \mathsf{S.Sign}, \mathsf{S.Verify})$, a commitment scheme $(\mathsf{C.Gen}, \mathsf{C.Com}, \mathsf{C.Open})$ and a NIZK proof system for the relation $\mathcal{R}_{\mathsf{ABS}}$.

$\mathsf{Setup}(1^\lambda, 1^\ell)$: On input the security parameter 1^λ and the input length 1^ℓ for the family of circuits $\mathcal{C}_\ell$, generate a verification key and a signing key $(\mathsf{vk_{Sign}}, \mathsf{sk_{Sign}}) \leftarrow \mathsf{S.KeyGen}(1^\lambda, 1^\ell)$ and a public commitment key $\mathsf{pk_{Com}} \leftarrow \mathsf{C.Gen}(1^\lambda)$. Then output

$$\mathsf{mpk} = (\mathsf{vk_{Sign}}, \mathsf{pk_{Com}}, H(\cdot), G(\cdot)) \quad \text{and} \quad \mathsf{msk} = (\mathsf{sk_{Sign}}).$$

Here, $H(\cdot)$ and $G(\cdot)$ are hash functions used by the NIZK proof system and by algorithm Sign, respectively, which are programmed as random oracles in the security reduction. Further, we assume the output space of $G(\cdot)$ to be $\{0,1\}^{\ell}$.[6]

KeyGen(mpk, msk, $\mathbf{x}$): On input $\mathbf{x} = (x_1 \cdots, x_\ell) \in \{0,1\}^{\ell}$, create a signature on the attribute $\mathbf{x} \in \{0,1\}^{\ell}$ by running $\sigma \leftarrow$ S.Sign(sk$_{\mathsf{Sign}}$, $\mathbf{x}$). Then, output the secret key as sk$_{\mathbf{x}} = (\mathbf{x}, \sigma)$.

Sign(mpk, sk$_{\mathbf{x}}$, C, M): On input message M $\in \{0,1\}^{*}$ and circuit $C \in \mathcal{C}_\ell$ with an associating topology topo$_C$ proceed as follows:

1. Compute $\mathbf{h} = (h_1, \cdots, h_\ell) \leftarrow G(\mathsf{M}, C)$[7] and create a new circuit $\hat{C} \in \mathcal{C}_\ell$ with two dummy gates connected to each of the input wires of C. Namely, to the input wires $i \in [\ell]$ of C, we add a series composition of two addition gates where one gate adds h_i and the other gate adds $-h_i$; on input x_i to the i-th input wire of $\hat{C}$, it first evaluates to $x_i + h_i$ and then evaluates back to x_i, on which point it gets fed to the i-th (input) wire of C. Here, the value $\mathbf{h}$ is hard-wired into $\hat{C}$, and is considered as one of the internal wires. Further, let N be the number of gates $|\hat{C}|$.

2. Compute the assignment to each non-input wires in $\hat{C}(x_1, \cdots, x_\ell)$: for all $i \in [\ell+1, \ell+(N-1)]$, compute $(\star_i, i_1, i_2) \leftarrow \mathsf{topo}(i)$ where $\star_i \in \{+, \times\}$, and denote the newly created values $(x_i)_{i=\ell+1}^{\ell+N-1}$ in ascending order as

$$\begin{cases} x_i = x_{i_1} + x_{i_2} & \text{if } \star_i = + \\ x_i = x_{i_1} \cdot x_{i_2} & \text{if } \star_i = \times \end{cases}.$$

3. Create a commitment $(c_\sigma, d_\sigma) \leftarrow$ C.Com(pk$_{\mathsf{Com}}$, σ) of the signature σ. Furthermore, for all $i \in [\ell+N-1]$, create a commitment $(c_i, d_i) \leftarrow$ C.Com(pk$_{\mathsf{Com}}$, x_i) that commits to the value of each wire in $\hat{C}$ (except for the output wire).

4. Generate a NIZK proof π proving that the committed values satisfy relation $\mathcal{R}_{\mathsf{ABS}}$. Concretely, it generates a proof for the following conditions.[8]

   - The attribute $\mathbf{x} = (x_1, \cdots, x_\ell)$ committed to $(c_i)_{i=1}^{\ell}$ and the signature σ committed to c_σ satisfy the following verification equation:

$$\mathsf{S.Verify}(\mathsf{vk}_{\mathsf{Sign}}, \mathbf{x}, \sigma) = 1. \tag{5}$$

   - For all $i \in [\ell+1, \ell+N-1]$, the value x_i committed to c_i satisfy the following equation:

$$\begin{cases} x_i = x_{i_1} + x_{i_2} & \text{if } \star_i = + \\ x_i = x_{i_1} \cdot x_{i_2} & \text{if } \star_i = \times \end{cases}. \tag{6}$$

---

[6] Here, we do not explicitly define the input and output space of the hash functions, since it may differ according to the underlying NIZK proof system being used.

[7] Here, we assume that we can encode C uniquely into a binary string.

[8] Note that we intentionally dismiss the conditions $(c, d) \in \mathcal{D}_{\mathsf{Com}}(\mathsf{pk}_{\mathsf{Com}}, \star)$ as in the overview, i.e., proving knowledge of a valid opening, since they will be implicitly proven by the fact that the committed messages satisfy Eqs. (5–7).

- The values $x_{(\ell+N)_1}$ and $x_{(\ell+N)_2}$ committed to $c_{(\ell+N)_1}$ and $c_{(\ell+N)_2}$, respectively, satisfy the following equation:

$$\begin{cases} 1 = x_{(\ell+N)_1} + x_{(\ell+N)_2} & \text{if } \star_{\ell+N} = + \\ 1 = x_{(\ell+N)_1} \cdot x_{(\ell+N)_2} & \text{if } \star_{\ell+N} = \times \end{cases}. \tag{7}$$

5. Finally, output $\Sigma = \left(c_\sigma, (c_i)_{i=1}^{\ell+N-1}, \pi\right)$.

Verify(mpk, M, C, Σ): Compute $\mathbf{h} \leftarrow G(\mathsf{M}, C)$ and construct the circuit $\hat{C}$ as in Step 1 of the Sign algorithm. Then, verify the proof with respect to the circuit $\hat{C}$. Output Valid if the proof is verified valid, and output Invalid otherwise.

Correctness. Observe that $\hat{C}(\mathbf{x}) = C(\mathbf{x})$ for all M, $\mathbf{x}$. Therefore, the correctness of the scheme follows simply from the correctness of the underlying NIZK proof system. In particular, a signer that has a certified attribute $\mathbf{x}$ such that $C(\mathbf{x}) = 1$ can properly generate a proof proving Eqs. (5–7).

4.1 Security Analysis

Theorem 1 (Privacy). *Assume a statistically hiding commitment scheme with gap-openings and a statistically special HVZK gap-Σ-protocol for relations $(\mathcal{R}_{\mathsf{ABS}}, \mathcal{R}'_{\mathsf{ABS}})$. Then, converting the gap-Σ-protocol into a Fiat-Shamir NIZK proof system, the above attribute-based signature scheme is statistically private in the random oracle model. In case either the hiding property or the special HVZK property only holds computationally, then we obtain computational privacy.*

The proof follows naturally from the zero-knowledge property of the NIZK proof system, and is deferred the full version.

Theorem 2 (Adaptive Unforgeability). *Assume a computationally hiding and a statistically binding commitment scheme with gap openings, a computationally special HVZK gap-Σ_m-protocol[9] for relations $(\mathcal{R}_{\mathsf{ABS}}, \mathcal{R}'_{\mathsf{ABS}})$ and an eu-cma secure (deterministic) digital signature scheme. Then, by converting the gap-Σ_m-protocol into a Fiat-Shamir NIZK proof system, the above attribute-based signature scheme is adaptively unforgeable in the random oracle model.*

Proof. Assume there exists a PPT adversary $\mathcal{B}_{\mathsf{ABS}}$ that wins the adaptive unforgeability game with advantage $\epsilon = \epsilon(\lambda)$. Furthermore, let $Q_H = Q_H(\lambda)$ be the number of unique random oracle queries $\mathcal{B}_{\mathsf{ABS}}$ makes to $H(\cdot)$ that is bounded by some polynomial in the security parameter λ. Our proof proceeds in a sequence of games, where X_i denotes the event the adversary wins in Game_i. Our final goal is to construct an adversary $\mathcal{B}_{\mathsf{Sign}}$ that breaks the eu-cma security of the underlying digital signature scheme by using $\mathcal{B}_{\mathsf{ABS}}$. For our Fiat-Shamir NIZK proof system, we use the ZK simulator $\mathcal{S}$ that we have defined in Lemma 2.

---

[9] Here, recall that we write gap-Σ_m-protocol, when we make explicit of the fact that m valid transcripts are requried for special gap-soundness to hold. Furthermore, this notation also implies that the soundness error is negligible (See Sect. 3.1).

Game$_{real}$: This game is identical to the real adaptive unforgeability game where all the random oracle queries to $H(\cdot)$ and $G(\cdot)$ are answered randomly by the challenger. At the end of the game, $\mathcal{B}_{ABS}$ outputs a valid forged signature $(\mathsf{M}^*, C^*, \Sigma^*)$ with probability $\Pr[X_{real}] = \epsilon$.

Game$_1$: In this game, we change the way the challenger answers the random oracle queries to $H(\cdot)$ and the signing queries. Namely, we use the ZK simulator $\mathcal{S}$ associated to the NIZK proof system to answer these. Recall that simulator $\mathcal{S}$ has two modes for running the two oracles $\mathcal{S}_1$ and $\hat{\mathcal{S}}_2$. When $\mathcal{B}_{ABS}$ submits a random oracle query to $H(\cdot)$, the challenger relays this to oracle $\mathcal{S}_1$ and returns the value outputted by $\mathcal{S}_1$ to $\mathcal{B}_{ABS}$. Here, the random oracle queries to $G(\cdot)$ are answered by the Game$_1$ challenger as in the previous game. Furthermore, when $\mathcal{B}_{ABS}$ submits a signing query on an attribute, message and circuit tuple $(\mathbf{x}, \mathsf{M}, C)$ such that $C(\mathbf{x}) = 1$, it first runs $\mathsf{sk}_{\mathbf{x}} = (\mathbf{x}, \sigma) \leftarrow \mathsf{KeyGen}(\mathsf{mpk}, \mathsf{msk}, \mathbf{x})$ and constructs the circuit $\hat{C}$ with N gates using $\mathbf{h} \leftarrow G(\mathsf{M}, C)$ as in Step 1 of the Sign algorithm. Then it proceeds with Step 2 and 3 to create commitments $\big(c_\sigma, (c_i)_{i=1}^{\ell+N-1}\big)$ along with valid openings $\big(d_\sigma, (d_i)_{i=1}^{\ell+N-1}\big)$. Finally, it invokes $\hat{\mathcal{S}}_2$ on input the statement $\big(\hat{C}, c_\sigma, (c_i)_{i=1}^{\ell+N-1}\big) \in \mathcal{L}_{ABS}$[10] and obtains a proof π, and returns the signature $\Sigma = \big(c_\sigma, (c_i)_{i=1}^{\ell+N-1}, \pi\big)$ to $\mathcal{B}_{ABS}$. Here, the simulated proofs of $\hat{\mathcal{S}}_2$ are distributed negligibly close to the actual proofs in Game$_{real}$ by the definition of the NIZK proof system (See Definition 6), and the fact that the oracles $\mathcal{S}_2$ and $\hat{\mathcal{S}}_2$ are equivalent in case the statement to be proven is in the language. Hence, $|\Pr[X_{real}] - \Pr[X_1]| = \mathsf{negl}(\lambda)$.

Game$_2$: In this game, we change the way the challenger creates the commitment for the signature σ produced during the signing query. In the previous game, when $\mathcal{B}_{ABS}$ submitted a signing query on an attribute, message and circuit tuple $(\mathbf{x}, \mathsf{M}, C)$ such that $C(\mathbf{x}) = 1$, the challenger created a proper commitment c_σ for the signature σ following Step 3 of the Sign algorithm, i.e., $(c_\sigma, d_\sigma) \leftarrow \mathsf{Com}(\mathsf{pk}_{\mathsf{Com}}, \sigma)$. In this game, however, the Game$_2$ challenger will instead sample a random value c in the commitment space $\mathcal{C}_{\mathsf{Com}}$ and sets $c_\sigma = c$. Then, as in Game$_2$, it invokes $\hat{\mathcal{S}}_2$ on input $\big(\hat{C}, c_\sigma, (c_i)_{i=1}^{\ell+N-1}\big)$ and obtains a proof π, and returns the signature $\Sigma = \big(c_\sigma, (c_i)_{i=1}^{\ell+N-1}, \pi\big)$ to $\mathcal{B}_{ABS}$. Here, recall that oracle $\hat{\mathcal{S}}_2$ is defined to simulate proofs for false statements that are not in the language $\mathcal{L}_{ABS}$ as well. Then, the differences in the view of the adversary in Game$_1$ and Game$_2$ are computationally indistinguishable due to the computationally hiding property of the commitment scheme.[11] In other words, we have $|\Pr[X_1] - \Pr[X_2]| = \mathsf{negl}(\lambda)$.

Game$_3$: In this game, we add an additional winning condition for adversary $\mathcal{B}_{ABS}$ to satisfy. Namely, when $\mathcal{B}_{ABS}$ outputs a forgery $(\mathsf{M}^*, C^*, \Sigma^*)$, the Game$_3$

---

[10] Recall we ignore the public parameters $\mathsf{vk}_{\mathsf{Sign}}$ and $\mathsf{pk}_{\mathsf{Com}}$ from the statement for simplicity.

[11] More formally, we create q_{sign} hybrid games and swap the commitments of the signature to a random value in the commitment space one hybrid game at a time until we have swapped every signature commitments into the desired random form, where q_{sign} is the number of signature queries $\mathcal{B}_{ABS}$ makes.

challenger checks if the random oracle $G(\cdot)$ was ever queried on a message-circuit pair $(\mathsf{M}, C) \neq (\mathsf{M}^*, C^*)$ such that $\hat{C} = \hat{C}^*$. Note that this implies $G(\mathsf{M}, C) = G(\mathsf{M}^*, C^*)$. Hereafter, we say $\mathcal{B}_{\mathsf{ABS}}$ wins if and only if in addition to the winning condition of the previous game, there are no such message-circuit pairs. Since, the output values of the random oracle $G(\cdot)$ are uniformly random over $\{0,1\}^\ell$ for $\ell = \mathsf{poly}(n)$, the probability that a collision occurs for different message-circuit pairs is negligible. Hence, $|\Pr[X_2] - \Pr[X_3]| = \mathsf{negl}(\lambda)$. Below, we denote $\epsilon_3 = \Pr[X_3]$.

In the following, we define the algorithms $\mathcal{A}$ and $\mathcal{O}$ to be used in the forking algorithm $\mathsf{F}_{\mathcal{A},m}^{\mathcal{O}(\overline{\mathsf{par}},\cdot)}$ of the generfal multi-forking lemma with oracle access (See Lemma 1). Looking ahead, the forking algorithm will be used by adversary $\mathcal{B}_{\mathsf{Sign}}$ to win the eu-cma security of the underlying digital signature scheme.

To provide the full description of algorithms $\mathcal{A}$ and $\mathcal{O}$, we first define the input generator IG, the set $\mathcal{H}$ and the integer q, which are required to define the inputs for $\mathcal{A}$ and $\mathcal{O}$. First, the input generator IG outputs $(\mathsf{par}, \overline{\mathsf{par}})$ where par constitutes of the verification key $\mathsf{vk}_{\mathsf{Sign}}$, public commitment key $\mathsf{pk}_{\mathsf{Com}}$ and any extra auxiliary parameters required to specify the ABS scheme (e.g., the family of circuits), and $\overline{\mathsf{par}}$ is simply the signing key $\mathsf{sk}_{\mathsf{Sign}}$. Here, $\mathsf{vk}_{\mathsf{Sign}}, \mathsf{sk}_{\mathsf{Sign}}$ and $\mathsf{pk}_{\mathsf{Com}}$ are generated by running $(\mathsf{vk}_{\mathsf{Sign}}, \mathsf{sk}_{\mathsf{Sign}}) \leftarrow \mathsf{S.KeyGen}(1^\lambda, 1^\ell)$ and $\mathsf{pk}_{\mathsf{Com}} \leftarrow \mathsf{C.Gen}(1^\lambda)$. Furthermore, we define the set $\mathcal{H}$ to be the verifier's challenge space $\mathcal{C}_\Sigma$ of the underlying gap-Σ_m-protocol, and set q as Q_H; the number of unique random oracle queries made to $H(\cdot)$ by $\mathcal{B}_{\mathsf{ABS}}$. To summarize, $\mathcal{A}$ will be given par and $h_1, \cdots, h_{Q_H} \in \mathcal{H}$ as input.

We next specify how algorithms $\mathcal{A}$ and $\mathcal{O}$ run. First, the deterministic algorithm $\mathcal{O}$ is simply defined as the signing algorithm of the underlying deterministic digital signature scheme; $\mathcal{O}(\overline{\mathsf{par}}, \cdot) = \mathsf{S.Sign}(\mathsf{sk}_{\mathsf{Sign}}, \cdot)$. Here, $\mathcal{O}$ is deterministic since the signing algorithm is deterministic once fixed a signing key $\mathsf{sk}_{\mathsf{Sign}}$. Next, we define $\mathcal{A}$ as the randomized algorithm that simulates Game_3 and outputs a small modification of the forgery returned by $\mathcal{B}_{\mathsf{ABS}}$. We first explain how $\mathcal{A}$ simulates Game_3: $\mathcal{A}$ essentially runs the Game_3 challenger, $\mathcal{B}_{\mathsf{ABS}}$ and the ZK simulator $\mathcal{S}$ internally, with two conceptual changes concerning the Game_3 challenger and the ZK simulator $\mathcal{S}$. In particular the Game_3 challenger is modified to an algorithm which we call the Game_3' challenger, so that it does not run $(\mathsf{vk}_{\mathsf{Sign}}, \mathsf{sk}_{\mathsf{Sign}}) \leftarrow \mathsf{S.KeyGen}(1^\lambda, 1^\ell)$ anymore. Instead of generating $(\mathsf{vk}_{\mathsf{Sign}}, \mathsf{sk}_{\mathsf{Sign}})$ on its own, the Game_3' challenger is provided with $\mathsf{vk}_{\mathsf{Sign}}$ by $\mathcal{A}$, and no longer possesses $\mathsf{sk}_{\mathsf{Sign}}$. Whenever the Game_3' challenger requires to run the signing algorithm $\mathsf{S.Sign}(\mathsf{sk}_{\mathsf{Sign}}, \cdot)$, $\mathcal{A}$ simply invokes $\mathcal{O}(\overline{\mathsf{par}}, \cdot) = \mathsf{S.Sign}(\mathsf{sk}_{\mathsf{Sign}}, \cdot)$, which it has oracle access to, and returns whatever output by $\mathcal{O}$ to the Game_3' challenger. Furthermore, the ZK simulator $\mathcal{S}$ (See Lemma 2) is modified in a way so that it does not sample a random value $h_i \leftarrow \mathcal{C}_\Sigma$ when invoked on a random oracle query to $H(\cdot)$. Concretely, on the i-th unique random oracle query to $H(\cdot)$, it simply outputs the value h_i provided by $\mathcal{A}$.[12] This is only a conceptual change,

---

[12] More formally, we can think the state st provided to the ZK simulator $\mathcal{S}$ includes $(h_i)_{i=1}^{Q_H}$, assuming without loss of generality that $\mathcal{S}$ knows the bound on the number of query made by $\mathcal{B}_{\mathsf{ABS}}$.

since $\mathcal{C}_\Sigma = \mathcal{H}$ and h_i are sampled uniformly over $\mathcal{H}$. Therefore, the above changes do not alter the view of $\mathcal{B}_{\mathsf{ABS}}$. Hence the advantage of $\mathcal{B}_{\mathsf{ABS}}$ winning the game simulated by $\mathcal{A}$ is exactly the same as of Game_3. Finally, we describe the output of $\mathcal{A}$. In particular, at the end of the simulation of Game_3, $\mathcal{B}_{\mathsf{ABS}}$ outputs a valid forgery $(\mathsf{M}^*, C^*, \Sigma^*)$ where $\Sigma^* = \left(c_\sigma^*, (c_i^*)_{i=1}^{\ell+N-1}, \pi^*\right)$ with probability ϵ_3. In the following let χ^* denote the statement $(\hat{C}^*, c_\sigma^*, (c_i^*)_{i=1}^{\ell+N-1})$, where $\hat{C}^*$ is the circuit with N gates constructed from C^* in Step 1 of the Sign algorithm. Since this is a valid forgery, we must have $\chi^* \in \mathcal{L}_{\mathsf{ABS}}$. Given the forgery of $\mathcal{B}_{\mathsf{ABS}}$, $\mathcal{A}$ first parses the proof π^* as (α^*, γ^*), where α^*, γ^* are the commitment and response of the underlying gap-Σ_m-protocol (See Definition 5), respectively. $\mathcal{A}$ then checks whether $H(\cdot)$ was queried on (χ^*, α^*). If not it outputs $(0, \epsilon_1)$. Otherwise, there exists an index $i^* \in [Q_H]$ for which the challenge $H(\chi^*, \alpha^*)$ is set to h_{i^*}. In this case, it outputs $(i^*, (\alpha^*, h_{i^*}, \gamma^*, \chi^*, \mathsf{M}^*, C^*))$. Now, since $\mathcal{A}$ simulates Game_3 perfectly and the probability of $\mathcal{B}_{\mathsf{ABS}}$ outputting a valid forgery without knowledge of the output of $H(\chi^*, \alpha^*)$ (i.e., the challenge) is negligible, we have

$$\mathsf{acc} = \Pr\left[(i^*, (\alpha^*, h_{i^*}, \gamma^*, \chi^*, \mathsf{M}^*, C^*)) \leftarrow \mathcal{A}^{\mathcal{O}(\overline{\mathsf{par}}, \cdot)}(\mathsf{par}, h_1, \cdots, h_{Q_H}) \; : \; i^* \geq 1\right]$$
$$\geq \epsilon_3 - \mathsf{negl}(\lambda), \tag{8}$$

where the probability is taken over the choice of $(\mathsf{par}, \overline{\mathsf{par}})$, $(h_i)_{i=1}^{Q_H}$ and the randomness used by $\mathcal{A}$.

Finally we construct an adversary $\mathcal{B}_{\mathsf{Sign}}$ against the eu-cma security of the underlying digital signature scheme using the forking algorithm $\mathsf{F}_{\mathcal{A},m}^{\mathcal{O}(\overline{\mathsf{par}}, \cdot)}$. In particular the advantage of $\mathcal{B}_{\mathsf{Sign}}$ will be $\epsilon_3^m / Q_H^{m-1} - \mathsf{negl}(\lambda)$ for a constant m. Hence, assuming the eu-cma security of the digital signature scheme, ϵ_3 is negligible. Therefore, since $\epsilon = \epsilon_3 \pm \mathsf{negl}(\lambda)$, we conclude that ϵ is negligible, thus completing the proof. Below, let $\mathcal{C}_{\mathsf{Sign}}$ be the challenger for the eu-cma game of the underlying digital signature scheme. Also, let $\mathsf{vk}_{\mathsf{Sign}}$ be the verification key given to $\mathcal{B}_{\mathsf{Sign}}$ and $\mathsf{sk}_{\mathsf{Sign}}$ be the signing key used by $\mathcal{C}_{\mathsf{Sign}}$ to answer the signature queries. In particular, $\mathcal{C}_{\mathsf{Sign}}$ uses the signing algorithm $\mathsf{S.Sign}(\mathsf{sk}_{\mathsf{Sign}}, \cdot)$ to answer signature queries made be $\mathcal{B}_{\mathsf{ABS}}$. Now, given $\mathsf{vk}_{\mathsf{Sign}}$, $\mathcal{B}_{\mathsf{Sign}}$ runs $\mathsf{pk}_{\mathsf{Com}} \leftarrow \mathsf{C.Gen}(1^\lambda)$ and prepares par, i.e., the input to $\mathcal{A}$ provided by the input generator IG. This can be done efficiently since par constitutes only of public values: $\mathsf{vk}_{\mathsf{Sign}}, \mathsf{pk}_{\mathsf{Com}}$ and some other public auxiliary parameters specifying the ABS scheme. Since the forking algorithm only requires oracle access to the deterministic algorithm $\mathcal{O}(\overline{\mathsf{par}}, \cdot) = \mathsf{S.Sign}(\mathsf{sk}_{\mathsf{Sign}}, \cdot)$, which is provided by $\mathcal{C}_{\mathsf{Sign}}$, $\mathcal{B}_{\mathsf{Sign}}$ can properly run the forking algorithm $\mathsf{F}_{\mathcal{A},m}^{\mathcal{O}(\overline{\mathsf{par}}, \cdot)}(\mathsf{par})$ as specified. Note that $\mathsf{par}, \overline{\mathsf{par}}$ are distributed exactly as the output of the input generator IG defined above. Now, due to the general multi-forking lemma with oracle access (Lemma 1), we obtain the following pairs with probability frk:

$$\left(1, \; \{\alpha^{(k)}, h^{(k)}, \gamma^{(k)}, \chi^{(k)}, \mathsf{M}^{(k)}, C^{(k)}\}_{k \in [m]}\right), \tag{9}$$

where $\chi^{(k)} = \left(\hat{C}^{(k)}, c_\sigma^{(k)}, (c_i^{(k)})_{i=1}^{\ell+N-1}\right)_{k\in[m]}$. Here, by Eq. (1) of Lemma 1, we have

$$\mathsf{frk} \geq \mathsf{acc} \cdot \left(\left(\frac{\mathsf{acc}}{Q_H}\right)^{m-1} - \frac{f(m)}{|\mathcal{C}_\Sigma|}\right) = \frac{\mathsf{acc}^m}{Q_H^{m-1}} - \mathsf{negl}(\lambda), \tag{10}$$

where $\mathcal{C}_\Sigma$ is the output range of $H(\cdot)$ that is super-polynomially large, m is a constant representing the number of valid transcripts we require to extract a witness and $f(m)$ is a universal positive valued function that only depends on m, i.e., a constant value when viewed as a funtion on the security parameter λ. Now, we argue that for all $k \in [m]$, the values of the commitments $\alpha^{(k)}$ and statements $\chi^{(k)}$ are equivalent, respectively. Let $i^* \in [Q_H]$ be the index outputted by $\mathcal{A}$ in the first run inside the forking algorithm $\mathsf{F}_{\mathcal{A},m}^{\mathcal{O}(\overline{\mathsf{par}},\cdot)}(\mathsf{par})$. Then, up until the i^*-th unique random oracle query to $H(\cdot)$, the behavior of $\mathcal{B}_{\mathsf{ABS}}$ is the same for every run, since we fix the randomness being used by the challenger Game_3', $\mathcal{B}_{\mathsf{ABS}}$ and the ZK simulator $\mathcal{S}$. This implies that whatever submitted by $\mathcal{B}_{\mathsf{ABS}}$ on the i^*-th unique random oracle query to $H(\cdot)$, which is the pair $(\alpha^{(k)}, \chi^{(k)})$, must be the same in every run. Let us denote this as $(\alpha^*, \chi^* = (\hat{C}^*, c_\sigma^*, (c_i^*)_{i=1}^{\ell+N-1}))$. Therefore, by running $\mathsf{F}_{\mathcal{A},m}^{\mathcal{O}(\overline{\mathsf{par}},\cdot)}(\mathsf{par})$, $\mathcal{B}_{\mathsf{Sign}}$ obtains m valid transcript of the form $\left(\alpha^*, h^{(k)}, \gamma^{(k)}, \chi^*, \mathsf{M}^*, C^*\right)_{k\in[m]}$ where M^*, C^* are the same in every run as well, due to the winning condition we added in Game_3 and the fact that $\hat{C}^*$ is the same in every run.

Next, we show that $\mathcal{B}_{\mathsf{Sign}}$ can properly extract a witness from the valid transcripts using the knowledge extractor of the underlying gap-Σ_m-protocol (See special gap-soundness of Definition 4). Recall that the range of the random oracle $H(\cdot)$ is $\mathcal{C}_\Sigma = \{0, 1, \cdots, m-1\}^t$ for some constant m and an integer-valued function t that is poly-logarithmic in the security parameter λ. Now, by Definition 4, in order to extract a witness there needs to exist at least one index $j \in [t]$ such that $\{h_j^{(k)}\}_{k\in[m]} = \{0, 1, \cdots, m-1\}$. Since each $h^{(k)}$ are sampled uniformly random over $\mathcal{C}_H = \{0, 1, \cdots, m-1\}^t$, the probability of no such $j \in [t]$ existing is $(1 - \frac{m!}{m^m})^t$, which is negligible in the security parameter for our choices of m, t. Therefore, with all but negligible probability, $\mathcal{B}_{\mathsf{Sign}}$ is able to extract a witness $(\mathbf{x}^*, \sigma^*, d_\sigma^*, (d_i^*)_{i=1}^{\ell+N-1})$ in the gap-language $\mathcal{L}_{\mathsf{ABS}}'$ from the m valid transcripts. Furthermore, since we use a statistically binding commitment scheme, the $(\mathbf{x}^*, \sigma^*)$ pair extracted from the transcripts are the actual pairs used by $\mathcal{B}_{\mathsf{ABS}}$ to create a forgery, with all but negligible probability.

Finally, we show that $(\mathbf{x}^*, \sigma^*)$ is a valid signature forgery that allows $\mathcal{B}_{\mathsf{Sign}}$ to win the eu-cma game between the challenger $\mathcal{C}_{\mathsf{Sign}}$. Namely, we show that $\mathbf{x}^*$ was never queried as the key reveal query by $\mathcal{B}_{\mathsf{ABS}}$ in all of the m runs of $\mathcal{A}$. Note that the only situation $\mathcal{A}$ invokes the signing oracle $\mathcal{O}(\overline{\mathsf{par}}, \cdot) = \mathsf{S.Sign}(\mathsf{sk}_{\mathsf{Sign}}, \cdot)$ is when $\mathcal{B}_{\mathsf{ABS}}$ submits a key reveal query to the Game_3' challenger. This is because we altered the game in Game_2 so that the ZK simulator is used to answer the signing queries made by $\mathcal{B}_{\mathsf{ABS}}$. Now, since $\mathcal{B}_{\mathsf{ABS}}$ outputs a valid forgery we have $\hat{C}^*(\mathbf{x}^*) = 1$. Then, by the way we construct $\hat{C}^*(\mathbf{x}^*)$ in Step 1 of the Sign algorithm, we have

$C(\mathbf{x}^*) = 1$ as well. On the other hand, due to the winning condition of $\mathcal{B}_{\mathsf{ABS}}$, $\mathcal{B}_{\mathsf{ABS}}$ must have never made a key reveal query on $\mathbf{x}^*$ such that $C^*(\mathbf{x}^*) = 1$ (in any of the runs). Therefore, we conclude that $\mathbf{x}^*$ was never queried to the Game_3' challenger by $\mathcal{B}_{\mathsf{ABS}}$ in any of the runs of $\mathcal{A}$; $(\mathbf{x}^*, \sigma^*)$ is a valid forgery. Hence, combining Eqs. (8) and (10), the advantage of $\mathcal{B}_{\mathsf{Sign}}$ is $\epsilon_3^m / Q_H^{m-1} - \mathsf{negl}(\lambda)$.

4.2 Implications

Since a computationally hiding and statistically binding commitment scheme, a deterministic digital signature scheme and a computationally special HVZK Σ-protocols for any NP-language are all implied from one-way functions (See for example [Nao91, Rom90, PSV06]), we obtain the following lemma as an implication of our above result:

Lemma 3. *If one-way functions exist, then there exist computationally private and adaptive unforgeable attribute-based signature schemes for unbounded circuits in the random oracle model.*

5   ABS for Unbounded Circuits from Lattices

In this section, we provide an efficient instantiation of our generic ABS construction for unbounded circuits from lattices. In particular, we prepare a lattice-based signature scheme and a commitment scheme with gap-openings, and construct an associating lattice-based gap-Σ-protocol for the relation $\mathcal{R}_{\mathsf{ABS}}$. We believe our gap-$\Sigma$-protocol for proving possession of a valid signature, which departs from the previously known stern-type protocol of [LNSW13], to have applications in other contexts such as group signatures.

5.1 Preparing Tools

We present the underlying lattice-based digital signature scheme and commitment scheme with gap-openings that we use as building blocks for our lattice-based ABS scheme.

Digital Signature Scheme. Here, we review the lattice-based digital signature scheme of Boyen [Boy10] with an improved security reduction by [MP12]. Below, we provide a deterministic version of Boyen's signature scheme, where the signing algorithm uses a PRF for generating the required randomness. We defer the formal definition of lattices and PRFs to the full version. In the following, by lattice convention, we use the dimension of the lattice n to denote the security parameter.

Theorem 3. *Let n, m, q be positive integers such that $m \geq 2n \log q$. Let α, β be positive reals such that $\alpha = \Omega(\sqrt{\ell n \log q} \log n)$ and $\beta = \alpha\omega(\sqrt{\log m})$. Then, the following algorithms* (S.KeyGen, S.Sign, S.Verify) *form a deterministic digital signature scheme with message space $\mathcal{M} = \{0,1\}^\ell$ that is eu-cma secure under hardness of the $\mathsf{SIS}_{n,m,q,\ell\tilde{O}(n)}^\infty$ problem.*

S.KeyGen($1^n, 1^\ell$): *It samples a matrix* $\mathbf{A} \in \mathbb{Z}_q^{n \times m}$ *with a trapdoor* $\mathbf{T_A} \in \mathbb{Z}^{m \times m}$ *using algorithm* TrapGen($1^n, 1^m, q$). *It also samples matrices* $\mathbf{A}_i \leftarrow \mathbb{Z}_q^{n \times m}$ *for* $i \in [0, \ell]$, *a vector* $\mathbf{u} \in \mathbb{Z}_q^n$ *and generates a seed for a PRF by running* $r \leftarrow$ PRF.Gen(1^n). *Finally it outputs the verification key* vk *and signing key* sk *as*

$$\mathsf{vk} = (\mathbf{A}, \mathbf{A}_0, \cdots, \mathbf{A}_\ell, \mathbf{u}), \quad \mathsf{sk} = (\mathbf{T_A}, r).$$

S.Sign($\mathsf{sk}, \mathbf{x}$): *On input the message* $\mathbf{x} \in \{0,1\}^\ell$, *it first constructs the matrix* $\mathbf{A_x} = \mathbf{A}_0 + \sum_{i=1}^{\ell} x_i \mathbf{A}_i \in \mathbb{Z}_q^{n \times m}$, *where* x_i *is the i-th bit of* $\mathbf{x}$. *Then using* $\mathbf{T_A}$, *it samples a short vector* $\mathbf{z} \in \mathbb{Z}^{2m}$ *such that* $[\mathbf{A}|\mathbf{A_x}]\mathbf{z} = \mathbf{u} \mod q$ *using algorithm* SampleLeft($\mathbf{A}, \mathbf{A_x}, \mathbf{u}, \mathbf{T_A}, \alpha$), *where the output of* PRF.Eval($r, \mathbf{x}$) *is used as the randomness. Finally, it outputs* $\sigma = \mathbf{z}$ *as the signature.*

S.Verify($\mathsf{vk}, \mathbf{x}, \sigma$): *It first checks that* $\mathbf{x} \in \{0,1\}^\ell$. *Next, it checks whether* $[\mathbf{A}|\mathbf{A_x}]\mathbf{z} = \mathbf{u} \mod q$ *and* $\|\mathbf{z}\|_\infty \leq \beta$. *It outputs 1 if all the above check passes, otherwise it outputs 0.*

Commitment Scheme. Here, we present the commitment scheme of [XXW13] with minor modification. In the following let $[\cdot||\cdot]$ denote the vertical concatenation of vectors.

Theorem 4. *Let* $n, \bar{m}, q$ *be positive integers such that* $\bar{m} \geq 3n$, q *a prime. Further, let* γ, γ' *be positive reals such that* $q \geq (4\gamma + 1)^2$ *and* $\gamma \geq \gamma' \omega(\log n)$.[13] *Then, the following algorithms* (C.Gen, C.Com, C.Open) *form a computationally hiding and statistically binding commitment scheme with gap openings under the hardness of the* $\mathsf{LWE}_{n, \bar{m}, q, D_{\mathbb{Z}, \gamma}}$ *problem. Here the message space* $\mathcal{M}$ *is* $\mathbb{Z}_q$ *and the commitment space* $\mathcal{C}$ *is* $\mathbb{Z}_q^{\bar{m}}$.

C.Gen(1^n): *It samples* $\mathbf{B} \leftarrow \mathbb{Z}_q^{(n+1) \times \bar{m}}$ *and outputs* $\mathsf{pk} = \mathbf{B}$.

C.Com(pk, M): *For a message* $\mathsf{M} \in \mathbb{Z}_q$, *it samples a random vector* $\mathbf{s} \leftarrow \mathbb{Z}_q^n$. *Then, it samples* $\mathbf{e} \leftarrow D_{\mathbb{Z}^{\bar{m}}, \gamma'}$ *until* $\|\mathbf{e}\|_\infty \leq \gamma$ *holds.*[14] *Finally, it outputs* $(c, d) = (\mathbf{B}^\top[\mathbf{s}||\mathsf{M}] + \mathbf{e} \mod q, (\mathbf{s}, \mathbf{e}))$.

C.Open($\mathsf{pk}, \mathsf{M}, c, d$): *It first checks if* $\mathsf{M} \in \mathbb{Z}_q$. *It then parses* $d = (\mathbf{s}, \mathbf{e})$ *and checks if* $c = \mathbf{B}^\top[\mathbf{s}||\mathsf{M}] + \mathbf{e} \mod q$ *and* $\|\mathbf{e}\|_\infty \leq 2\gamma$ *hold. If all the check passes it outputs 1, otherwise it outputs 0.*

Observe that the above commitment scheme has gap-openings; although the commitment algorithm C.Com only samples vectors $\mathbf{e}$ such that $\|\mathbf{e}\|_\infty \leq \gamma$, the opening algorithm C.Open accepts $\mathbf{e}$ such that $\gamma < \|\mathbf{e}\|_\infty \leq 2\gamma$ as well.

Furthermore, [XXW13] provides three gap-Σ-protocols for proving useful relations over committed values: Σ_{Open} for proving knowledge of a valid opening and $\Sigma_{\mathsf{Add}}, \Sigma_{\mathsf{Mult}}$[15] for proving arithmetic relations (over $\mathbb{Z}_q$) of committed values.

---

[13] Here, we use Lemma 4 of [LLNW14] instead of Lemma 1 of [XXW13] to optimize the required parameters of the commitment scheme.

[14] For our parameter selection, this procedure will end in a constant number of trials with all but negligible probability.

[15] In their paper, they present two protocols for proving arithmetic relations, however, in our paper we only consider the more efficient protocol in [XXW13], Sect. 4.3.

We additionally construct one useful gap-Σ-protocol $\Sigma_{\mathsf{EqTo\star}}$ for proving that a commitment opens to a specific value. The details of the construction are provided in the full version. Then, the above commitment scheme is equipped with the following four *basic* gap-Σ-protocols.

Theorem 5. *The commitment scheme with gap openings in Theorem 4 has associating computationally special HVZK gap-Σ-protocols ($\Sigma_{\mathsf{Open}}, \Sigma_{\mathsf{EqTo\star}}, \Sigma_{\mathsf{Add}}, \Sigma_{\mathsf{Mult}}$) for the following four relations:*

$$\mathcal{R}_{\mathsf{Open}} = \{(\mathsf{pk}, c), (\mathsf{M}, d) \mid (c, d) \in \mathcal{D}_{\mathsf{Com}}(\mathsf{pk}, \mathsf{M})\},$$
$$\mathcal{R}_{\mathsf{EqTo\star}} = \{(\mathsf{pk}, c, \mathsf{M}), d \mid (c, d) \in \mathcal{D}_{\mathsf{Com}}(\mathsf{pk}, \mathsf{M})\},$$
$$\mathcal{R}_{\mathsf{Add}} = \{(\mathsf{pk}, (c_i)_{i=1}^3), ((\mathsf{M}_i, d_i)_{i=1}^3) \mid \mathsf{M}_3 = \mathsf{M}_1 + \mathsf{M}_2$$
$$\wedge\ (c_i, d_i) \in \mathcal{D}_{\mathsf{Com}}(\mathsf{pk}, \mathsf{M}_i)\ for\ i \in [3]\},$$
$$\mathcal{R}_{\mathsf{Mult}} = \{(\mathsf{pk}, (c_i)_{i=1}^3), ((\mathsf{M}_i, d_i)_{i=1}^3) \mid \mathsf{M}_3 = \mathsf{M}_1 \cdot \mathsf{M}_2$$
$$\wedge\ (c_i, d_i) \in \mathcal{D}_{\mathsf{Com}}(\mathsf{pk}, \mathsf{M}_i)\ for\ i \in [3]\}.$$

The gap-relations ($\Sigma'_{\mathsf{Open}}, \Sigma'_{\mathsf{EqTo\star}}, \Sigma'_{\mathsf{Add}}, \Sigma'_{\mathsf{Mult}}$) are defined similarly except that the set $\mathcal{D}_{\mathsf{G\text{-}Com}}$ is used instead of $\mathcal{D}_{\mathsf{Com}}$.

The above gap-Σ-protocols of [XXW13] additionally require internally a standard commitment scheme, which is used by the prover in the first round to send a commitment to the verifier. Although, we can use the commitment scheme of [XXW13] provided above, we use the more efficient lattice-based commitment scheme of Kawachi et al. [KTX08] to instantiate the gap-Σ-protocols. In this case, the communication costs of $\Sigma_{\mathsf{Open}}, \Sigma_{\mathsf{EqTo\star}}$ are $\omega(\bar{m} \log q \log \gamma \log n)$ and $\Sigma_{\mathsf{Add}}, \Sigma_{\mathsf{Mult}}$ are $\omega(\bar{m} \log^3 q \log \gamma \log n)$.

Remark 1. The above four basic gap-Σ-protocols can be composed in parallel to obtain a gap-Σ-protocol for larger relations, e.g., provided with commitments $(c_i)_{i=1}^4$ of the values $(\mathsf{M}_i)_{i=1}^4$ satisfying $\mathsf{M}_4 = \sum_{i=1}^3 \mathsf{M}_i$, we can prove this relation by creating one extra auxiliary commitment c_{aux} for $\mathsf{M}_{\mathsf{aux}} = \mathsf{M}_1 + \mathsf{M}_2$ and running two Σ_{Add} in parallel for the statement pairs $(\mathsf{pk}, c_1, c_2, c_{\mathsf{aux}})$ and $(\mathsf{pk}, c_{\mathsf{aux}}, c_3, c_4)$.

5.2 ABS for Unbounded Circuits Based on Lattices

To instantiate the generic ABS construction in Sect. 4 from lattices, it is sufficient to prove that the above digital signature scheme and commitment scheme are equipped with a gap-Σ-protocol for the relation $\mathcal{R}_{\mathsf{ABS}}$. Therefore, below we aim at constructing a gap-Σ protocol for proving Eqs. (5)–(7) in our ABS construction, where the attribute $\mathbf{x}$ and Boyen signatures σ are committed using the commitment scheme of [XXW13]. Here, taking the above Remark 1 into consideration, a gap-Σ-protocol for proving Eqs. (6) and (7), which are essentially proving that the circuit is computed correctly, can be constructed by simply composing the basic gap-Σ-protocols $\Sigma_{\mathsf{EqTo\star}}, \Sigma_{\mathsf{Add}}, \Sigma_{\mathsf{Mult}}$ in parallel. In more detail, we use Σ_{Add} and Σ_{Mult} to prove that we computed each gates correctly, and use $\Sigma_{\mathsf{EqTo\star}}$ to prove that the value associated to the output wire is equal to 1. Therefore, in the following, we only focus on how to construct a gap-Σ-protocol for proving Eq. (5); we construct a gap-Σ-protocol for proving possession of a valid Boyen-signature using $\Sigma_{\mathsf{EqTo\star}}, \Sigma_{\mathsf{Add}}, \Sigma_{\mathsf{Mult}}$. Here, we stress that we cannot simply use the gap-Σ-protocol for proving possession of a valid Boyen-signature of [LNSW13] for our purpose, since their protocol does not allow us to efficiently prove possession of messages satisfying complex arithmetic relations.[16] In other words, since Eqs. (5) and (6) share the same witness $\mathbf{x} = (x_1, \cdots, x_\ell)$, we will not be able to combine the different types of gap-Σ-protocols of [LNSW13] and [XXW13] to construct a gap-Σ protocol for the relation $\mathcal{R}_{\mathsf{ABS}}$.

To summarize, our goal is to construct a gap-Σ-protocol for proving possession of a valid Boyen signature $\sigma = \mathbf{z} = [z_1, \cdots, z_{2m}]^\top \in \mathbb{Z}^{2m}$, where $\mathbf{x} = (x_1, \cdots, x_\ell) \in \{0,1\}^\ell$ is viewed as the message, provided the verification key $\mathsf{vk_{Sign}}$ and the commitments to the signature σ and message $\mathbf{x}$. Then, since the basic gap-Σ-protocols of Theorem 4 allows for parallel composition, our desired gap-Σ-protocol for the relation $\mathcal{R}_{\mathsf{ABS}}$ is obtained by composing the gap-Σ protocol for the Boyen signature with the gap-Σ-protocols for Eqs. (6) and (7) together. Below, we assume the commitment c_σ of the signature is provided in the form $(\bar{c}_k)_{k\in[2m]}$ where each $\bar{c}_i$ is a commitment of the k-th element $z_k \in \mathbb{Z}$ of $\mathbf{z}$ (viewed as an element in $\mathbb{Z}_q$), and the commitment of the message $c_\mathbf{x}$ is provided in the form $(c_i)_{i\in[\ell]}$ where each c_i is a commitment of the value $x_i \in \{0,1\}$. Now, due to the verification algorithm of the Boyen signature scheme, proving a signature is valid is equivalent to proving the following three statements:

$$\mathbf{x} \in \{0,1\}^\ell \iff x_i \in \{0,1\} \text{ for } i \in [\ell], \tag{11}$$

$$\|\mathbf{z}\|_\infty \leq \beta \iff |z_k| \leq \beta \text{ for } k \in [2m], \tag{12}$$

$$\left[\mathbf{A}|\mathbf{A}_0 + \sum_{i=1}^\ell x_i \mathbf{A}_i\right]\mathbf{z} = \mathbf{u} \mod q. \tag{13}$$

Below we construct gap-Σ-protocols respectively for the above equations by converting each of them into an arithmetic circuit, and using the basic gap-Σ-protocols provided in Theorem 4 as building blocks to prove the satisfiability of each circuit.

Gap-Σ-Protocol for Proving Eq. (11). It is sufficient to prove that for every $i \in [\ell]$, the commitment $c_i \leftarrow \mathsf{C.Com}(\mathsf{pk}, x_i)$ opens to either 0 or 1. To do so, we first create auxiliary commitments $c_{\mathsf{zero}} \leftarrow \mathsf{C.Com}(\mathsf{pk}, 0)$ and $g_i \leftarrow \mathsf{C.Com}(\mathsf{pk}, x_i^2)$ for $i \in [\ell]$. Then using the commitments $(c_i)_{i\in[\ell]}$ and the auxiliary commitments, and combining the basic gap-Σ-protocols $\Sigma_{\mathsf{EqTo\star}}, \Sigma_{\mathsf{Add}}$ and Σ_{Mult} together, we construct a gap-Σ-protocol for proving the following statement for all $i \in [\ell]$:

$$c_{\mathsf{zero}} \text{ opens to } 0 \quad \wedge \quad x_i^2 = x_i \cdot x_i \quad \wedge \quad 0 = x_i^2 - x_i$$

---

[16] The subsequent works of [LLM+16, YAL+17] allow proving possession of a valid Boyen-signature while also proving possession of messages satisfying some simple arithmetic relations. However, their protocols are not strong enough to prove arbitrary circuits in zero-knowledge.

Since all arithmetic operations are over the finite field $\mathbb{Z}_q$, the only x_i that satisfy the above relations are $x_i = 0$ or 1. Therefore, the above gap-Σ-protocol indeed proves Eq. (11). The total communication cost is $\omega(\ell \bar{m} \log^3 q \log \gamma \log n)$.[17]

Gap-Σ-Protocol for Proving Eq. (12). Here, for simplicity of the protocol, we assume that β can be written as $2^\zeta - 1$ for some positive integer ζ. Equivalently, $\zeta = \log(\beta+1)$. This does not harm the efficiency nor the security of the signature scheme by much, since given any β, there always exists a value of the form $2^\zeta - 1$ in between β and 2β.

First, we prepare some notations. For $k \in [2m]$, let $z_{k,j}$ be the j-th bit of the binary representation of $z_k \in \mathbb{Z}$ for $j \in [\zeta]$. Note that, we extend the standard binary decomposition to negative integers as well in the obvious way. In particular, we can bit decompose any $z_k \in [-\beta, \beta]$ as $z_k = \sum_{j=1}^{\zeta} 2^{j-1} z_{k,j}$, where $z_{k,j} \in \{-1, 0, 1\}$.[18] Further, set $w_{k,j} = 2^{j-1} z_{k,j}$ for $j \in [\zeta]$ and $w_{k,[j']} = \sum_{j=1}^{j'} w_{k,j}$ for $j' \in [2, \zeta]$. Finally, define $w_{k,[1]} = w_{k,1}$. Next, create the following auxiliary commitments for $k \in [2m]$: $c_{\mathsf{zero}} \leftarrow \mathsf{C.Com}(\mathsf{pk}, 0)$, $c_{\mathsf{coeff},j} \leftarrow \mathsf{C.Com}(\mathsf{pk}, 2^{j-1})$, $\bar{c}_{k,j,\mu} \leftarrow \mathsf{C.Com}(\mathsf{pk}, z_{k,j}^\mu)$, $h_{k,j} \leftarrow \mathsf{C.Com}(\mathsf{pk}, w_{k,j})$ for $\mu \in [3]$, $j \in [\zeta]$, and $h_{k,[j']} \leftarrow \mathsf{C.Com}(\mathsf{pk}, w_{k,[j']})$ for $j' \in [2, \zeta]$. Then, using the commitments $(\bar{c}_k)_{k \in [2m]}$, the auxiliary commitments and composing the gap-Σ-protocols $\Sigma_{\mathsf{EqTo\star}}$, Σ_{Add} and Σ_{Mult} together, we construct a gap-Σ-protocol for the following statement for all $k \in [2m], j \in [\zeta]$ and $j' \in [2, \zeta]$:[19]

$$c_{\mathsf{zero}} \text{ opens to } 0 \wedge c_{\mathsf{coeff},j} \text{ opens to } 2^j \wedge z_{k,j}^2 = z_{k,j} \cdot z_{k,j} \wedge z_{k,j}^3 = z_{k,j}^2 \cdot z_{k,j} \wedge$$
$$0 = z_{k,j}^3 - z_{k,j} \wedge w_{k,j} = 2^{j-1} \cdot z_{k,j} \wedge w_{k,[j']} = w_{k,j'} + w_{k,[j'-1]} \wedge 0 = z_k - w_{k,[\zeta]}.$$

We check that the above statement is equivalent to Eq. (12), i.e., each z_k satisfy $|z_k| \leq \beta$ for all $k \in [2m]$. First, since q is a prime, the only $z_{k,j}$ satisfying $z_{k,j}^3 - z_{k,j} = 0$ over $\mathbb{Z}_q$ are $-1, 0, 1$. Hence, the above statement proves that $z_{k,j} \in \{-1, 0, 1\}$. Furthermore, when $z_{k,j} \in \{-1, 0, 1\}$, we have $|z_k| \leq \sum_{j=1}^{\zeta} 2^{j-1} |z_{k,j}| \leq 2^{\zeta-1} = \beta$. Therefore, if the above statement holds, then we must have $|z_k| \leq \beta$ for all $k \in [2m]$. The total communication cost is $\omega(m\bar{m} \log \beta \log^3 q \log \gamma \log n)$.

Gap-Σ-Protocol for Proving Eq. (13). We first prepare some notations. Let $a_{s,k}$ (resp., $a_{i,s,k}$) denote the (s, k_1)-th (resp., $(s, k_2 - m)$-th) entry of $\mathbf{A}$ (resp., $\mathbf{A}_i$) $\in \mathbb{Z}_q^{n \times m}$, for $s \in [n]$, $k_1 \in [m]$ (resp., $k_2 \in [m+1, 2m]$) and $i \in [0, \ell]$. Then, observe that we can rewrite Eq. (13) using the following equations for $s \in [n]$:

---

[17] Note that $\omega(f(X))$ denotes any function that grows asymptotically faster than $f(X)$, e.g., $\log^2(X) = \omega(\log(X))$.

[18] A subtly is that unlike standard bit decomposition, the bit representation is not unique anymore, e.g., 11 can be decomposed as $(1, 1, 0, 1)$ or $(-1, 0, 1, 1)$. However, this will not affect our following argument.

[19] Since we prove c_{zero} opens to 0 in the above gap-Σ-protocol for proving Eq. (11), we will not require this when we compose the gap-Σ-protocols together. The same holds for the aforementioned gap-Σ-protocol for proving Eq. (13).

$$\sum_{k_1=1}^{m} a_{s,k_1} \cdot z_{k_1} + \sum_{k_2=m+1}^{2m} \left(a_{0,s,k_2} + \sum_{i=1}^{\ell} x_i \cdot a_{i,s,k_2} \right) \cdot z_{k_2} = u_s \qquad (14)$$

Next, we prepare some auxiliary values for $s \in [n]$ in order to prove the above equations using the gap-Σ-protocols $\Sigma_{\text{EqTo}\star}$, Σ_{Add} and Σ_{Mult}: $w_{i,s,k_2} = x_i \cdot a_{i,s,k_2}$, $w_{[i'],s,k_2} = \sum_{i=1}^{i'} w_{i,s,k_2}$, $a_{s,k_2} = a_{0,s,k_2} + w_{[\ell],s,k_2}$ for $i \in [\ell]$, $i' \in [2,\ell]$, $k_2 \in [m+1,2m]$, $b_{s,k} = a_{s,k} \cdot z_k$ for $k \in [2m]$, $b_{s,[k']} = \sum_{k_1=1}^{k'} b_{s,k_1}$ for $k' \in [2,m]$, $b_{s,[k']} = \sum_{k_2=m+1}^{k'} b_{s,k_2}$ for $k' \in [m+2,2m]$ and $t_s = b_{s,[m]} + b_{s,[2m]}$. Further define $w_{[1],s,k_2} = w_{1,s,k_2}$, $b_{s,[1]} = b_{s,1}$ and $b_{s,[m+1]} = b_{s,m+1}$. Next, we create auxiliary commitments for the related values for $s \in [n]$: $c_{\text{mat},s,k_1} \leftarrow \text{C.Com}(\text{pk}, a_{s,k_1})$, $c_{\text{mat},i,s,k_2} \leftarrow \text{C.Com}(\text{pk}, a_{i,s,k_2})$ for $i \in [0,\ell]$, $k_1 \in [m]$, $k_2 \in [m+1,2m]$, $\omega_{i,s,k_2} \leftarrow \text{C.Com}(\text{pk}, w_{i,s,k_2})$, $\omega_{[i'],s,k_2} \leftarrow \text{C.Com}(\text{pk}, w_{[i'],s,k_2})$, $\alpha_{s,k_2} \leftarrow \text{C.Com}(\text{pk}, a_{s,k_2})$ for $i \in [\ell]$, $i' \in [2,\ell]$, $k_2 \in [m+1,2m]$, $\beta_{s,k} \leftarrow \text{C.Com}(\text{pk}, b_{s,k})$ for $k \in [2m]$, $\beta_{s,[k']} \leftarrow \text{C.Com}(\text{pk}, b_{s,[k']})$ for $k' \in [2,m] \cup [m+2,2m]$. Then, using the commitment $(c_i)_{i=1}^{\ell}$, $(\bar{c}_k)_{k \in [2m]}$, the auxiliary commitments and composing the gap-Σ-protocols $\Sigma_{\text{EqTo}\star}$, Σ_{Add} and Σ_{Mult} together, we construct a gap-Σ-protocol for the following statement for all $s \in [n]$, $i \in [\ell]$, $i' \in [2,\ell]$, $k_1 \in [m]$, $k_2 \in [m+1,2m]$, $k \in [2m]$, $k' \in [2,m] \cup [m+2,2m]$:

c_{zero} opens to 0 $\land$

$c_{\text{mat},s,k_1}, c_{\text{mat},0,s,k_2}, c_{\text{mat},i,s,k_2}$ opens to $a_{s,k}, a_{0,s,k}, a_{i,s,k}$, respectively $\land$

$w_{i,s,k_2} = x_i \cdot a_{i,s,k_2} \land w_{[i'],s,k_2} = w_{i',s,k_2} + w_{[i'-1],s,k_2} \land$

$a_{s,k_2} = a_{0,s,k_2} + w_{[\ell],s,k_2} \land b_{s,k} = a_{s,k} \cdot z_k \land b_{s,[k']} = b_{s,k'} + b_{s,[k'-1]} \land$

$t_s = b_{s,[m]} + b_{s,[2m]} \land 0 = u_s - t_s$

The above statement can be checked that it is equivalent to proving Eq. (14) for $s \in [n]$. The total communication cost is $\omega(\ell n m \bar{m} \log^3 q \log \gamma \log n)$.

Gap-Σ-Protocol for $\mathcal{R}_{\text{ABS}}$. To summarize, we obtain a gap-Σ-protocol for proving possession of a valid Boyen signature by composing the gap-Σ-protocols for proving Eqs. (11–13) together. Then, by composing this protocol with the aforementioned gap-Σ-protocols for proving Eqs. (6) and (7), we obtain our desired gap-Σ-protocol for the relation $\mathcal{R}_{\text{ABS}}$ where the total communication cost is $\omega((m(\ell n + \log \beta) + |C|) \bar{m} \log^3 q \log \gamma \log n)$. Here, $|C|$ is size of the circuit (i.e., policy) associated to the message. Thus, we obtain our lattice-based ABS scheme for *unbounded circuits* in the random oracle model by instantiating the generic ABS construction in Sect. 4 with our gap-Σ protocol for $\mathcal{R}_{\text{ABS}}$.

Acknowledgement. We would like to thank the anonymous reviewers of PKC 2018 for insightful comments. In particular, we are grateful for Yusuke Sakai and Takahiro Matsuda for the helpful discussions and feedback on this work. The first author was funded by a research grant from the UK Government. The second author was partially supported by JST CREST Grant Number JPMJCR1302 and JSPS KAKENHI Grant Number 17J05603.

References

[AJLA+12] Asharov, G., Jain, A., López-Alt, A., Tromer, E., Vaikuntanathan, V., Wichs, D.: Multiparty computation with low communication, computation and interaction via threshold FHE. In: Pointcheval, D., Johansson, T. (eds.) EUROCRYPT 2012. LNCS, vol. 7237, pp. 483–501. Springer, Heidelberg (2012). https://doi.org/10.1007/978-3-642-29011-4_29

[BCK+14] Benhamouda, F., Camenisch, J., Krenn, S., Lyubashevsky, V., Neven, G.: Better zero-knowledge proofs for lattice encryption and their application to group signatures. In: Sarkar, P., Iwata, T. (eds.) ASIACRYPT 2014. LNCS, vol. 8873, pp. 551–572. Springer, Heidelberg (2014). https://doi.org/10.1007/978-3-662-45611-8_29

[BF14] Bellare, M., Fuchsbauer, G.: Policy-based signatures. In: Krawczyk, H. (ed.) PKC 2014. LNCS, vol. 8383, pp. 520–537. Springer, Heidelberg (2014). https://doi.org/10.1007/978-3-642-54631-0_30

[BFW16] Bernhard, D., Fischlin, M., Warinschi, B.: On the hardness of proving CCA-security of signed ElGamal. In: Cheng, C.-M., Chung, K.-M., Persiano, G., Yang, B.-Y. (eds.) PKC 2016. LNCS, vol. 9614, pp. 47–69. Springer, Heidelberg (2016). https://doi.org/10.1007/978-3-662-49384-7_3

[BKLP15] Benhamouda, F., Krenn, S., Lyubashevsky, V., Pietrzak, K.: Efficient zero-knowledge proofs for commitments from learning with errors over rings. In: Pernul, G., Ryan, P.Y.A., Weippl, E. (eds.) ESORICS 2015. LNCS, vol. 9326, pp. 305–325. Springer, Cham (2015). https://doi.org/10.1007/978-3-319-24174-6_16

[BN06] Bellare, M., Neven, G.: Multi-signatures in the plain public-key model and a general forking lemma. In: CCS, pp. 390–399. ACM (2006)

[Boy10] Boyen, X.: Lattice mixing and vanishing trapdoors: a framework for fully secure short signatures and more. In: Nguyen, P.Q., Pointcheval, D. (eds.) PKC 2010. LNCS, vol. 6056, pp. 499–517. Springer, Heidelberg (2010). https://doi.org/10.1007/978-3-642-13013-7_29

[BPVY00] Brickell, E., Pointcheval, D., Vaudenay, S., Yung, M.: Design validations for discrete logarithm based signature schemes. In: Imai, H., Zheng, Y. (eds.) PKC 2000. LNCS, vol. 1751, pp. 276–292. Springer, Heidelberg (2000). https://doi.org/10.1007/978-3-540-46588-1_19

[BPW12] Bernhard, D., Pereira, O., Warinschi, B.: How not to prove yourself: pitfalls of the fiat-shamir heuristic and applications to helios. In: Wang, X., Sako, K. (eds.) ASIACRYPT 2012. LNCS, vol. 7658, pp. 626–643. Springer, Heidelberg (2012). https://doi.org/10.1007/978-3-642-34961-4_38

[DF02] Damgård, I., Fujisaki, E.: A statistically-hiding integer commitment scheme based on groups with hidden order. In: Zheng, Y. (ed.) ASIACRYPT 2002. LNCS, vol. 2501, pp. 77–85. Springer, Heidelberg (2002). https://doi.org/10.1007/3-540-36178-2_8

[EE16] El Bansarkhani, R., El Kaafarani, A.: Post-quantum attribute-based signatures from lattice assumptions. Cryptology ePrint Archive, report 2016/823 (2016)

[EGK14] El Kaafarani, A., Ghadafi, E., Khader, D.: Decentralized traceable attribute-based signatures. In: Benaloh, J. (ed.) CT-RSA 2014. LNCS, vol. 8366, pp. 327–348. Springer, Cham (2014). https://doi.org/10.1007/978-3-319-04852-9_17

[FKMV12] Faust, S., Kohlweiss, M., Marson, G.A., Venturi, D.: On the non-malleability of the Fiat-Shamir transform. In: Galbraith, S., Nandi, M. (eds.) INDOCRYPT 2012. LNCS, vol. 7668, pp. 60–79. Springer, Heidelberg (2012). https://doi.org/10.1007/978-3-642-34931-7_5

[FO97] Fujisaki, E., Okamoto, T.: Statistical zero knowledge protocols to prove modular polynomial relations. In: Kaliski, B.S. (ed.) CRYPTO 1997. LNCS, vol. 1294, pp. 16–30. Springer, Heidelberg (1997). https://doi.org/10.1007/BFb0052225

[FS86] Fiat, A., Shamir, A.: How to prove yourself: practical solutions to identification and signature problems. In: Odlyzko, A.M. (ed.) CRYPTO 1986. LNCS, vol. 263, pp. 186–194. Springer, Heidelberg (1987). https://doi.org/10.1007/3-540-47721-7_12

[Gen09] Gentry, C.: Fully homomorphic encryption using ideal lattices. In: STOC, pp. 169–169. ACM (2009)

[GVW15] Gorbunov, S., Vaikuntanathan, V., Wichs, D.: Leveled fully homomorphic signatures from standard lattices. In: STOC, pp. 469–477. ACM (2015)

[HLLR12] Herranz, J., Laguillaumie, F., Libert, B., Ràfols, C.: Short attribute-based signatures for threshold predicates. In: Dunkelman, O. (ed.) CT-RSA 2012. LNCS, vol. 7178, pp. 51–67. Springer, Heidelberg (2012). https://doi.org/10.1007/978-3-642-27954-6_4

[KTX08] Kawachi, A., Tanaka, K., Xagawa, K.: Concurrently secure identification schemes based on the worst-case hardness of lattice problems. In: Pieprzyk, J. (ed.) ASIACRYPT 2008. LNCS, vol. 5350, pp. 372–389. Springer, Heidelberg (2008). https://doi.org/10.1007/978-3-540-89255-7_23

[LLM+16] Libert, B., Ling, S., Mouhartem, F., Nguyen, K., Wang, H.: Zero-knowledge arguments for matrix-vector relations and lattice-based group encryption. In: Cheon, J.H., Takagi, T. (eds.) ASIACRYPT 2016. LNCS, vol. 10032, pp. 101–131. Springer, Heidelberg (2016). https://doi.org/10.1007/978-3-662-53890-6_4

[LLNW14] Langlois, A., Ling, S., Nguyen, K., Wang, H.: Lattice-based group signature scheme with verifier-local revocation. In: Krawczyk, H. (ed.) PKC 2014. LNCS, vol. 8383, pp. 345–361. Springer, Heidelberg (2014). https://doi.org/10.1007/978-3-642-54631-0_20

[LNSW13] Ling, S., Nguyen, K., Stehlé, D., Wang, H.: Improved zero-knowledge proofs of knowledge for the ISIS problem, and applications. In: Kurosawa, K., Hanaoka, G. (eds.) PKC 2013. LNCS, vol. 7778, pp. 107–124. Springer, Heidelberg (2013). https://doi.org/10.1007/978-3-642-36362-7_8

[LNW15] Ling, S., Nguyen, K., Wang, H.: Group signatures from lattices: simpler, tighter, shorter, ring-based. In: Katz, J. (ed.) PKC 2015. LNCS, vol. 9020, pp. 427–449. Springer, Heidelberg (2015). https://doi.org/10.1007/978-3-662-46447-2_19

[Lyu09] Lyubashevsky, V.: Fiat-Shamir with aborts: applications to lattice and factoring-based signatures. In: Matsui, M. (ed.) ASIACRYPT 2009. LNCS, vol. 5912, pp. 598–616. Springer, Heidelberg (2009). https://doi.org/10.1007/978-3-642-10366-7_35

[Lyu12] Lyubashevsky, V.: Lattice signatures without trapdoors. In: Pointcheval, D., Johansson, T. (eds.) EUROCRYPT 2012. LNCS, vol. 7237, pp. 738–755. Springer, Heidelberg (2012). https://doi.org/10.1007/978-3-642-29011-4_43

[MP12] Micciancio, D., Peikert, C.: Trapdoors for lattices: simpler, tighter, faster, smaller. In: Pointcheval, D., Johansson, T. (eds.) EUROCRYPT 2012. LNCS, vol. 7237, pp. 700–718. Springer, Heidelberg (2012). https://doi.org/10.1007/978-3-642-29011-4_41

[MPR11] Maji, H.K., Prabhakaran, M., Rosulek, M.: Attribute-based signatures. In: Kiayias, A. (ed.) CT-RSA 2011. LNCS, vol. 6558, pp. 376–392. Springer, Heidelberg (2011). https://doi.org/10.1007/978-3-642-19074-2_24

[Nao91] Naor, M.: Bit commitment using pseudorandomness. J. Cryptol. 151–158 (1991)

[OT11] Okamoto, T., Takashima, K.: Efficient attribute-based signatures for non-monotone predicates in the standard model. In: Catalano, D., Fazio, N., Gennaro, R., Nicolosi, A. (eds.) PKC 2011. LNCS, vol. 6571, pp. 35–52. Springer, Heidelberg (2011). https://doi.org/10.1007/978-3-642-19379-8_3

[OT13] Okamoto, T., Takashima, K.: Decentralized attribute-based signatures. In: Kurosawa, K., Hanaoka, G. (eds.) PKC 2013. LNCS, vol. 7778, pp. 125–142. Springer, Heidelberg (2013). https://doi.org/10.1007/978-3-642-36362-7_9

[PS00] Pointcheval, D., Stern, J.: Security arguments for digital signatures and blind signatures. J. Cryptol. 361–396 (2000)

[PSV06] Pass, R., Shelat, A., Vaikuntanathan, V.: Construction of a non-malleable encryption scheme from any semantically secure one. In: Dwork, C. (ed.) CRYPTO 2006. LNCS, vol. 4117, pp. 271–289. Springer, Heidelberg (2006). https://doi.org/10.1007/11818175_16

[Rom90] Rompel, J.: One-way functions are necessary and sufficient for secure signatures. In: STOCS, pp. 387–394. ACM (1990)

[SAH16] Sakai, Y., Attrapadung, N., Hanaoka, G.: Attribute-based signatures for circuits from bilinear map. In: Cheng, C.-M., Chung, K.-M., Persiano, G., Yang, B.-Y. (eds.) PKC 2016. LNCS, vol. 9614, pp. 283–300. Springer, Heidelberg (2016). https://doi.org/10.1007/978-3-662-49384-7_11

[Tsa17] Tsabary, R.: An equivalence between attribute-based signatures and homomorphic signatures, and new constructions for both. Cryptology ePrint Archive, report 2017/723 (to appear in TCC 2017)

[Wee09] Wee, H.: Zero knowledge in the random oracle model, revisited. In: Matsui, M. (ed.) ASIACRYPT 2009. LNCS, vol. 5912, pp. 417–434. Springer, Heidelberg (2009). https://doi.org/10.1007/978-3-642-10366-7_25

[XXW13] Xie, X., Xue, R., Wang, M.: Zero knowledge proofs from Ring-LWE. In: Abdalla, M., Nita-Rotaru, C., Dahab, R. (eds.) CANS 2013. LNCS, vol. 8257, pp. 57–73. Springer, Cham (2013). https://doi.org/10.1007/978-3-319-02937-5_4

[YAL+17] Yang, R., Au, M., Lai, J., Xu, Q., Yu, Z.: Lattice-based techniques for accountable anonymity: composition of abstract sterns protocols and weak PRF with efficient protocols from LWR. Cryptology ePrint Archive, report 2017/781 (2017)

Structure-Preserving Signatures

Improved (Almost) Tightly-Secure Structure-Preserving Signatures

Charanjit S. Jutla[1], Miyako Ohkubo[2], and Arnab Roy[3(✉)]

[1] IBM T. J. Watson Research Center, Yorktown Heights, NY, USA
csjutla@us.ibm.com
[2] Security Fundamentals Laboratories, CSR, NICT, Tokyo, Japan
m.ohkubo@nict.go.jp
[3] Fujitsu Laboratories of America, Sunnyvale, CA, USA
aroy@us.fujitsu.com

Abstract. Structure Preserving Signatures (SPS) allow the signatures and the messages signed to be further encrypted while retaining the ability to be proven valid under zero-knowledge. In particular, SPS are tailored to have *structure* suitable for Groth-Sahai NIZK proofs. More precisely, the messages, signatures, and verification keys are required to be elements of groups that support efficient bilinear-pairings (*bilinear groups*), and the signature verification consists of just evaluating one or more bilinear-pairing product equations. Since Groth-Sahai NIZK proofs can (with zero-knowledge) prove the validity of such pairing product equations, it leads to interesting applications such as blind signatures, group signatures, traceable signatures, group encryption, and delegatable credential systems.

In this paper, we further improve on the SPS scheme of Abe, Hofheinz, Nishimaki, Ohkubo and Pan (CRYPTO 2017) while maintaining only an $O(\lambda)$-factor security reduction loss to the SXDH assumption. In particular, we compress the size of the signatures by almost 40%, and reduce the number of pairing-product equations in the verifier from fifteen to seven. Recall that structure preserving signatures are used in applications by encrypting the messages and/or the signatures, and hence these optimizations are further amplified as proving pairing-product equations in Groth-Sahai NIZK system is not frugal. While our scheme uses an important novel technique introduced by Hofheinz (EuroCrypt 2017), i.e. *structure-preserving adaptive partitioning*, our approach to building the signature scheme is different and this leads to the optimizations mentioned. Thus we make progress towards an open problem stated by Abe et al. (CRYPTO 2017) to design more compact SPS-es with smaller number of group elements.

Keywords: Structure-preserving signatures · Bilinear pairings
SXDH · Matrix-DDH · Groth-Sahai · Cramer-Shoup · QA-NIZK

© International Association for Cryptologic Research 2018
M. Abdalla and R. Dahab (Eds.): PKC 2018, LNCS 10770, pp. 123–152, 2018.
https://doi.org/10.1007/978-3-319-76581-5_5

1   Introduction

Structure-Preserving Signatures (SPS), introduced in [AFG+10], allow the signatures and the messages signed to be further encrypted while retaining the ability to be proven valid under zero-knowledge. In particular, SPS are tailored to have *structure* suitable for Groth-Sahai NIZK proofs [GS12]. More precisely, the messages, signatures, and verification keys are required to be elements of groups that support efficient bilinear-pairings (*bilinear groups*), and the signature verification consists of just evaluating one or more bilinear-pairing product equations. Since GS-NIZK proofs can (with zero-knowledge) prove the validity of such pairing product equations, it leads to interesting applications such as blind signatures [AO09, AFG+10], group signatures [AHO10], traceable signatures [ACHO11], group encryption [CLY09], and delegatable credential systems [Fuc11].

While there is a long sequence of works starting with Groth in 2006 [Gro06], and with the formalization of definition of SPS in [AFG+10], recently there have been major efficiency improvements in terms of signature size, number of pairing-product equations and verification time [KPW15, LPY15, JR17]. With the exception of [HJ12], most of these works that are based on static assumptions such as SXDH or k-LIN, incur a security reduction loss of factor $O(q)$ or even $O(q^2)$, where q is the number of signature queries. Recently, in a remarkable work, Abe et al. [AHN+17] show a SPS scheme which is quite compact and yet has only a $O(\lambda)$ factor security loss, where λ is the security parameter[1]. The security is based on the SXDH assumption in asymmetric bilinear-pairing groups, which is essentially the decisional Diffie-Hellman (DDH) assumption in each of the two asymmetric groups.

In this work, we further improve on the SPS scheme of [AHN+17] while maintaining only a $O(\lambda)$-factor security reduction loss. In particular, we compress the size of the signatures by almost 40% of that in [AHN+17], and reduce the number of pairing-product equations in the verifier from fifteen to seven (see Table 1 for more details). Recall, structure-preserving signatures are used in applications by encrypting the messages and/or the signatures, and hence these optimizations are further amplified as proving pairing-product equations in Groth-Sahai NIZK system is not frugal. While our scheme uses an important novel technique introduced in [AHN+17], i.e. *structure-preserving adaptive partitioning*, our approach to building the signature scheme is different and this leads to the optimizations mentioned. It was mentioned as an open problem in [AHN+17] to design more compact SPSes with smaller number of group elements.

At a high level, signature schemes usually encrypt a secret and prove in zero-knowledge that such a secret is encrypted in the signature. Since we consider security under chosen-message attacks (EUF-CMA), this entails some type of simulation-soundness requirement on the zero-knowledge proof. For example, the encryption scheme may then be required to be CCA2. In the standard model,

---

[1] The work of [HJ12] only encountered a constant factor security loss. However, the scheme produces signatures that require hundreds of group elements.

Table 1. Comparison with existing SPS schemes with table adapted from [AHN+17]. (n_1, n_2) denotes n_1 $\mathbb{G}_1$ elements and n_2 $\mathbb{G}_2$ elements. The table gives message, signature and public key sizes and finally the security loss in the reduction to the listed assumption(s). For [HJ12], the parameter d limits number of signing to 2^d. The parameters q and λ represent the number of signing queries and the security parameter, respectively.

	$|M|$	$|\sigma|$	$|pk|$	Sec. loss	Assumption
[HJ12]	1	$10d + 6$	13	8	DLIN
[ACD+12]	$(n_1, 0)$	$(7, 4)$	$(5, n_1 + 12)$	$O(q)$	SXDH, XDLIN
[ACD+12]	(n_1, n_2)	$(8, 6)$	$(n_2 + 6, n_1 + 13$	$O(q)$	SXDH, XDLIN
[LPY15]	$(n_1, 0)$	$(10, 1)$	$(16, 2n_1 + 5)$	$O(q)$	SXDH, XDLIN
[KPW15]	(n_1, n_2)	$(7, 3)$	$(n_2 + 1, n_1 + 7)$	$O(q^2)$	SXDH
[KPW15]	$(n_1, 0)$	$(6, 1)$	$(0, n_1 + 6)$	$O(q^2)$	SXDH
[JR17]	$(n_1, 0)$	$(5, 1)$	$(0, n_1 + 6)$	$O(q \log q)$	SXDH
[AHN+17]	$(n_1, 0)$	$(13, 12)$	$(18, n_1 + 11)$	$O(\lambda)$	SXDH
[AHN+17]	(n_1, n_2)	$(14, 14)$	$(n_2 + 19, n_1 + 12)$	$O(\lambda)$	SXDH
This paper	$(n_1, 0)$	$(11, 6)^{a,b}$	$(7, n_1 + 16)$	$O(\lambda)$	SXDH
This paper	(n_1, n_2)	$(12, 8)$	$(n_2 + 8, n_1 + 17)$	$O(\lambda)$	SXDH

[a] Based on the optimization in Sect. 5.2; otherwise $(11, 7)$.
[b] The batched-pairing optimization of Sect. 5.3 has $(12, 7)$.

CCA2 encryption schemes have more or less followed two paradigms: (a) The Naor-Yung paradigm [NY90] of double CPA encryption, and a simulation-sound NIZK proof that the double encryption is valid [Sah99], or (b) An augmented ElGamal Encryption (reminiscent of [Dam92]) along with a hash proof that the augmentation is valid [CS98]. However until very recently, known solutions to both these approaches have had two limitations, i.e. these schemes were inherently tag-based and hence not amenable to structure-preservation, and further they had at least $O(q)$-factor security loss in reduction to standard assumptions. In the context of signature schemes, IBEs and CCA2-encryption, a recent flurry of works [CW13,BKP14,LPJY15,AHY15,GHKW16,Hof17], starting with Chen and Wee's almost tightly-secure IBE scheme [CW13], do manage to handle the second concern but these works (except one) rely on tag-based approaches[2], and hence do not lead to (almost) tightly-secure SPS. The one exception being the recent work [AHN+17] mentioned above. The work [AHN+17] however does build on earlier string of works in obtaining tight-security, and in particular it enhances a technique of [Hof17], *called adaptive-partitioning*, so as to enable structure-preservation.

---

[2] A tag is usually either computed using a 1-1 or collision-resistant function or is chosen afresh at random. In some cases it is clear that the resulting scheme is not SPS, but there are cases of the latter variety [KPW15,LPY15,JR17] that lead to SPS, but where it is not clear if a tight reduction can be obtained or not.

We now briefly discuss message-space partitioning techniques, which is used in both [AHN+17] and our new SPS. Chen and Wee consider partitioning the message space (resp. identity space in IBEs) repeatedly into two sets based on a bit derived from the message or a tag. In this iterative reduction process, they adjust signatures for messages in one of the two sets so that after logarithmic number of steps (say, in the size of the tag space) all modified signatures hide the secret. The partitioning scheme is however based on the message or tag, and hence this does not lead to structure-preserving signatures. Hofheinz [Hof17] introduced "adaptive partitioning" in which the partitioning is decided dynamically based on an encrypted partitioning-bit embedded in the signature. This leads to public-keys that are constant sized (as opposed to $O(\lambda)$-sized), but the strategy is still "tag"-based, and hence not structure-preserving.

In [AHN+17], simulation-soundness (for the Naor-Yung encryption paradigm) is achieved using Groth-Sahai NIZK proofs for "OR"-systems. The scheme has almost tight-security reduction due to adaptive partitioning and yet it is structure-preserving as tags (or hashes) are not used. Very concisely, the public-key contains a commitment to a bit x which is initially set to zero. Each signature also contains an encryption of a bit y, which is set arbitrarily in the scheme (i.e. real world). The "OR" system proves that either $y == x$ or the double encryptions of the secret are consistent. Simulation-soundness is achieved by ensuring that inconsistent double encryptions are only generated in signatures where the simulator was able to ensure $y = x$. This requires an intricate sequence of reduction steps where y^i (i.e. y in i-th signature) is first set to M_j^i (i.e. the j-bit in the message M^i) and x is set to be the complement of a guess of y^* (i.e. adversary's y). Since $x \neq y^*$ with probability at least half, this enforces soundness of consistency of double encryption, and the result follows by complexity leveraging. The security argument also requires enacting a strategy of "dynamically" augmenting/strengthening the language that is verified.

In our work, we advantageously use simple split-CRS[3] (quasi-adaptive) QA-NIZK for affine languages introduced in [JR13], wherein the verifier CRS does not depend on the affine component of an affine language. This greatly simplifies the security proof while also yielding smaller signatures and verification (PPE) equation sizes. In particular, we do not employ the strategy of augmenting/strengthening the language that is verified, but more or less follow the strategy of obtaining signature schemes using augmented ElGamal encryption along with hash proofs. Moreover, using the enhanced adaptive partitioning technique of [AHN+17] we are able to do this without using tags or hashes of messages and hence our scheme is structure-preserving and simultaneously (almost) tightly-secure. The strategy of obtaining SPS from split-CRS QA-NIZK for affine languages was first used in [JR17], but that scheme incurred an $O(q \log q)$-factor loss in security in reduction to the SXDH assumption. Another advantage of using the split-CRS QA-NIZK of [JR13] is that it is also true-simulation sound (i.e. it is

---

[3] In a split-CRS QA-NIZK, the CRS can be split into two parts, a prover CRS and a verifier CRS. to prove a statement only the prover CRS is required, and to verify a statement and its proof only the verifier CRS is required.

unbounded simulation-sound when the simulator only issues proofs on true state-ments), and this allows us to give an SPS that does not need discrete logarithm of message (group) elements. This was required in the construction of [AHN+17], and thus the final scheme required boot-strapping using a Partial One-time Sig-nature (POS) scheme (or more complicated GS-NIZK proofs of PPEs). Moreover, while [AHN+17] also use the POS for boosting an SPS for a single coordinate message to an SPS for vector messages, we directly construct our SPS for mes-sage vectors, which saves us a couple of elements in the signature. We leverage the constant size of QA-NIZKs to achieve this saving. In order to maintain $O(\lambda)$ security we first map the message vector to an $O(\lambda)$-length bit-string and then let the reduction games hop through each bit position of this bit-string.

Our scheme also utilizes Groth-Sahai NIZK proofs for "OR"-systems. In par-ticular, we follow [AHN+17] by having a commitment to bit x in the public-key, and including an encryption of bit y in each signature. The "OR" system now proves that either $x == y$ or the augmentation in augmented ElGamal encryp-tion is correct. In other words, the signature contains $\rho = g^r$, $\hat{\rho} = g^{br}$, and an (ElGamal) encryption of a secret k_0 using randomness r (and ElGamal secret key d). In Cramer-Shoup CCA2-encryption scheme the hash proof system proves that ρ and $\hat{\rho}$ are consistent, i.e. $\hat{\rho} = \rho^b$ where g^b is in the public-key. Here we prove the same using Groth-Sahai NIZK and further only as a consequent of $x \neq y$. At a high level, the security reduction works iteratively as follows (for simplicity, assume that the discrete log m of each message M is available to the simulator): in each round j, y^i is set to m_j^i. Next x is guessed to be the comple-ment of y^*. With probability half the guess is correct, and then only in messages where $y_j^i == x$ the simulator uses a DDH challenge to replace $d = d_1 + b \cdot d_2$ by $d' = d_1 + b' \cdot d_2$. This of course requires soundness of $\hat{\rho}^* = (\rho^*)^b$, which would indeed hold because the guess x is not equal to y^*, and further one can easily switch between Groth-Sahai binding and hiding commitments as all "OR"-proofs in signed messages always remain true. The security proof requires careful use of pairwise independence to replace k_0 by a random function of the prefix of the message bits $m_{\leq j}^i$, but otherwise uses standard arguments.

We now briefly remark about the efficiency implications of tight-security reductions. For standard bilinear pairings groups, this point has been well argued in [AHN+17], where for instance the authors point out that the next standard level of security for pairings friendly groups from 128-bit security is 192-bits or 256-bits. Moreover, as SPS schemes are just building blocks for applications, the loss in efficiency is amplified. The authors point out that computing a pairing in the 192-bit security level is slowed by a factor of 6 to 12 as compared to those in 128-bit security levels. As shown in Table 2, with batching of pairings computations in the various pairing-product equations required for signature verification, both [AHN+17] and our new construction has only at most 2.5 factor more pairings than the most efficient [JR17] non-tight scheme. Thus, our scheme (or the [AHN+17] scheme) running at 128-bit security can verify 2.5 to 4.5 times faster than [JR17] running at 192-bit security. Moreover, our new scheme has signatures that are shorter than [AHN+17] by a factor of 2/3 (see Table 1).

Table 2. Comparison of factors relevant to computational efficiency in SPS schemes with smaller signature sizes. Third column indicates the no. of scalar multiplications in $\mathbb{G}_1, \mathbb{G}_2$ for signing. Multi-scalar multiplications are counted with a weight 1.5. For [JR17] a constant pairing is included. Column "Batched" shows the no. of pairings in a verification when pairing product equations are aggregated by batch verification techniques [BFI+10].

	$\lvert M \rvert$	#(s.mult) in signing	#(PPEs)	#(Pairings) Plain	Batched
[KPW15]		$(6,1)$	3	$n_1 + 11$	$n_1 + 10$
[JR17]		$(6,1)$	2	$n_1 + 8$	$n_1 + 6$
[AHN+17]	$(n_1, 0)$	$(15,15)$	15	$n_1 + 57$	$n_1 + 16$
This paper		$(13.5, 7.5)$	7	$n_1 + 33$	$n_1 + 22$
This paper, Sect. 5.3		$(15, 8.5)$	10	$n_1 + 39$	$n_1 + 16$
[KPW15]		$(8, 3.5)$	4	$n_1 + n_2 + 15$	$n_1 + n_2 + 14$
[AHN+17]	(n_1, n_2)	$(17.5, 16)$	16	$n_1 + n_2 + 61$	$n_1 + n_2 + 18$
This paper		$(15, 8.5)$	8	$n_1 + n_2 + 4$	$n_1 + n_2 + 24$
This paper, Sect. 5.3		$(16.5, 9.5)$	11	$n_1 + n_2 + 43$	$n_1 + n_2 + 18$

2 Preliminaries

We will consider cyclic groups $\mathbb{G}_1, \mathbb{G}_2$ and $\mathbb{G}_T$ of prime order q, with an efficient bilinear map $e : \mathbb{G}_1 \times \mathbb{G}_2 \to \mathbb{G}_T$. Group elements $\mathbf{g}_1$ and $\mathbf{g}_2$ will typically denote generators of the group $\mathbb{G}_1$ and $\mathbb{G}_2$ respectively. Following [EHK+13], we will use the notations $[a]_1, [a]_2$ and $[a]_T$ to denote $a\mathbf{g}_1, a\mathbf{g}_2$, and $a \cdot e(\mathbf{g}_1, \mathbf{g}_2)$ respectively and use additive notations for group operations. When talking about a general group $\mathbb{G}$ with generator $\mathbf{g}$, we will just use the notation $[a]$ to denote $a\mathbf{g}$. The notation generalizes to vectors and matrices in a natural component-wise way.

For two vector or matrices A and B, we will denote the product $A^\top B$ as $A \cdot B$. The pairing product $e([A]_1, [B]_2)$ evaluates to the matrix product $[AB]_T$ in the target group with pairing as multiplication and target group operation as addition.

We recall the *Matrix Decisional Diffie-Hellman* or MDDH assumptions from [EHK+13]. A matrix distribution $\mathcal{D}_{l,k}$, where $l > k$, is defined to be an efficiently samplable distribution on $\mathbb{Z}_q^{l \times k}$ which is full-ranked with overwhelming probability. The $\mathcal{D}_{l,k}$-MDDH assumption in group $\mathbb{G}$ states that with samples $\mathbf{A} \leftarrow \mathcal{D}_{l,k}, \mathbf{s} \leftarrow \mathbb{Z}_q^k$ and $\mathbf{s}' \leftarrow \mathbb{Z}_q^l$, the tuple $([\mathbf{A}], [\mathbf{As}])$ is computationally indistinguishable from $([\mathbf{A}], [\mathbf{s}'])$. A matrix distribution $\mathcal{D}_{k+1,k}$ is simply denoted by $\mathcal{D}_k$.

2.1 Quasi-Adaptive NIZK Proofs

A witness relation is a binary relation on pairs of inputs, the first called a word and the second called a witness. Each witness relation R defines a corresponding language L which is the set of all words x for which there exists a witness w, such that $R(x, w)$ holds.

We will consider Quasi-Adaptive NIZK proofs [JR13] for a probability distribution $\mathcal{D}$ on a collection of (witness-) relations $\mathcal{R} = \{R_\rho\}$ (with corresponding languages L_ρ). Recall that in a quasi-adaptive NIZK, the CRS can be set after the language parameter has been chosen according to $\mathcal{D}$. Please refer to [JR13] for detailed definitions.

For our SPS construction we will also need a property called true-simulation-soundness and an extension of QA-NIZKs called strong split-CRS QA-NIZK. We recall the definitions of these concepts below.

Definition 1 (Strong Split-CRS QA-NIZK [JR13]). *We call a tuple of efficient algorithms* $(\mathsf{pargen}, \mathsf{crsgen}_v, \mathsf{crsgen}_p, \mathsf{prover}, \mathsf{verifier})$ *a* **strong split-CRS QA-NIZK** *proof system for an ensemble of distributions* $\{\mathcal{D}_\eta\}$ *on collection of witness-relations* $\mathcal{R}_\eta = \{R_\rho\}$ *with associated parameter language* $\mathcal{L}_{par}$ *if there exists probabilistic polynomial time simulators* $(\mathsf{crssim}_v, \mathsf{crssim}_p, \mathsf{sim})$, *such that for all non-uniform PPT adversaries* $\mathcal{A}_1, \mathcal{A}_2, \mathcal{A}_3$, *and* $\eta \leftarrow \mathsf{pargen}(1^\lambda)$, *we have:*

Quasi-Adaptive Completeness:

$$\Pr\left[\begin{array}{l}(\mathrm{CRS}_v, st) \leftarrow \mathsf{crsgen}_v(\eta), \ \rho \leftarrow \mathcal{D}_\eta \\ \mathrm{CRS}_p \leftarrow \mathsf{crsgen}_p(\eta, \rho, st) \\ (x, w) \leftarrow \mathcal{A}_1(\eta, \mathrm{CRS}_v, \mathrm{CRS}_p, \rho) \\ \pi \leftarrow \mathsf{prover}(\mathrm{CRS}_p, x, w)\end{array} : \begin{array}{c}\mathsf{ver}(\mathrm{CRS}_v, x, \pi) = 1 \text{ if} \\ R_\rho(x, w)\end{array}\right] = 1$$

Quasi-Adaptive Soundness:

$$\Pr\left[\begin{array}{l}(\mathrm{CRS}_v, st) \leftarrow \mathsf{crsgen}_v(\eta), \ \rho \leftarrow \mathcal{D}_\eta \\ \mathrm{CRS}_p \leftarrow \mathsf{crsgen}_p(\eta, \rho, st) \\ (x, \pi) \leftarrow \mathcal{A}_2(\eta, \mathrm{CRS}_v, \mathrm{CRS}_p, \rho)\end{array} : \begin{array}{c}\mathsf{ver}(\mathrm{CRS}_v, x, \pi) = 1 \text{ and} \\ \mathbf{not} \ (\exists w : R_\rho(x, w))\end{array}\right] \approx 0$$

Quasi-Adaptive Zero-Knowledge:

$$\Pr\left[\begin{array}{l}(\mathrm{CRS}_v, st) \leftarrow \mathsf{crsgen}_v(\eta) \\ \rho \leftarrow \mathcal{D}_\eta \\ \mathrm{CRS}_p \leftarrow \mathsf{crsgen}_p(\eta, \rho, st)\end{array} : \mathcal{A}_3^{\mathsf{prover}(\mathrm{CRS}_p, \cdot, \cdot)}(\eta, \mathrm{CRS}_v, \mathrm{CRS}_p, \rho) = 1\right]$$

$$\approx$$

$$\Pr\left[\begin{array}{l}(\mathrm{CRS}_v, \mathsf{trap}, st) \leftarrow \mathsf{crssim}_v(\eta) \\ \rho \leftarrow \mathcal{D}_\eta \\ \mathrm{CRS}_p \leftarrow \mathsf{crssim}_p(\eta, \rho, st)\end{array} : \mathcal{A}_3^{\mathsf{sim}^*(\mathsf{trap}, \cdot, \cdot)}(\eta, \mathrm{CRS}_v, \mathrm{CRS}_p, \rho) = 1\right],$$

where $\mathsf{sim}^*(\mathsf{trap}, x, w) = \mathsf{sim}(\mathsf{trap}, x)$ *for* $(x, w) \in R_\rho$ *and both oracles (i.e.* prover *and* sim^**) output failure if* $(x, w) \notin R_\rho$.

Definition 2 (True-Simulation-Sound [Har11]). *A QA-NIZK is called* **true-simulation-sound** *if soundness holds even when an adaptive adversary has access to simulated proofs on language members. More precisely, for all PPT* $\mathcal{A}$,

$$\Pr\left[\begin{array}{l}(\mathrm{CRS}, \mathsf{trap}) \leftarrow \mathsf{crssim}(\eta, \rho) \\ (x, \pi) \leftarrow \mathcal{A}^{\mathsf{sim}(\mathrm{CRS}, \mathsf{trap}, \cdot, \cdot)}(\mathrm{CRS}, \rho)\end{array} : \begin{array}{c}x \notin L_\rho \text{ and} \\ \mathsf{ver}(\mathrm{CRS}, x, \pi) = 1\end{array}\right] \approx 0,$$

where the experiment aborts if the oracle is called with some $x \notin L_\rho$.

In this paper, we use a strong split-CRS QA-NIZK (pargen, crsgen$_v$, crsgen$_p$, prover, verifier) for affine linear subspace languages $\{L_{[\mathbf{M}]_1, [\mathbf{a}]_1}\}$, consisting of words of the form $[\mathbf{Mx} + \mathbf{a}]_1$, with parameters sampled from a robust and efficiently witness-samplable distribution $\mathcal{D}$ over the associated parameter language $\mathcal{L}_{\mathrm{par}}$ and with soundness under a $\mathcal{D}_k$-MDDH assumption. Robustness means that the top square matrix of $\mathbf{M}$ is full-ranked with overwhelming probability. The construction is described in [JR17], with a single element proof under the SXDH assumption.

2.2   Groth-Sahai NIWI Proofs

The Groth-Sahai NIWI (non-interactive witness-indistinguishable) and NIZK Proof system provides highly efficient proofs for groups with efficient bilinear pairings [GS12]. We refer the reader to the cited paper for detailed definitions, constructions and proofs. Here we give a brief overview. As usual, and in line with Sect. 2.1, a non-interactive proof system for a witness relation R consists of four probabilistic polynomial time algorithms: pargen, crsgen, prover, ver. Groth-Sahai proof system satisfies perfect completeness and soundness. Moreover, it satisfies *composable witness indistinguishability*. This requires that there be an efficient probabilistic algorithm crssim such that for all non-uniform polynomial time adversaries $\mathcal{A}$ we have *CRS indistinguishability*, i.e.,

$$\Pr\left[\eta \leftarrow \mathsf{pargen}(1^\lambda), \mathsf{crs} \leftarrow \mathsf{crsgen}(\eta) \; : \; \mathcal{A}(\mathsf{crs}) = 1\right]$$
$$\approx \Pr\left[\eta \leftarrow \mathsf{pargen}(1^\lambda), \mathsf{simcrs} \leftarrow \mathsf{crssim}(\eta) \; : \; \mathcal{A}(\mathsf{simcrs}) = 1\right],$$

and for all adversaries $\mathcal{A}$ we also have (perfect *witness-indistinguishability*)

$$\Pr[\eta \leftarrow \mathsf{pargen}(1^\lambda), \mathsf{simcrs} \leftarrow \mathsf{crssim}(\eta); \; (x, w_0, w_1) \leftarrow \mathcal{A}(\mathsf{simcrs});$$
$$\pi \leftarrow \mathsf{prover}(\mathsf{simcrs}, x, w_0) \; : \; \mathcal{A}(\pi) = 1]$$
$$= \Pr[\eta \leftarrow \mathsf{pargen}(1^\lambda), \mathsf{simcrs} \leftarrow \mathsf{crssim}(\eta); \; (x, w_0, w_1) \leftarrow \mathcal{A}(\mathsf{simcrs});$$
$$\pi \leftarrow \mathsf{prover}(\mathsf{simcrs}, x, w_1) \; : \; \mathcal{A}(\pi) = 1],$$

where we require that both (x, w_0) and (x, w_1) are in R.

Groth-Sahai system is a commit and prove system, i.e. all free variables are first committed to, and then equations are proven w.r.t. the variables in the commitment. In other words prover above may have two components, one a randomized commitment algorithm and another an actual prover. An integer (or $\mathbb{Z}_q$) variable can be committed to in either group $\mathbb{G}_1$ or $\mathbb{G}_2$. These randomized commitments algorithms are denoted by $\mathsf{com}_1(\mathsf{crs}, x; r)$ or $\mathsf{com}_2(\mathsf{crs}, x; r)$. In the context of Groth-Sahai NIWI proofs, the algorithm crsgen is referred to as BG, i.e. binding generator, since such crs lead to binding commitments. The algorithm crssim is referred to as HG, i.e. hiding generator, as such simcrs lead to hiding commitments.

The GS proof system is itself structure-preserving for proving satisfiability of linear multi-scalar equations and a non-linear quadratic equation. It is also known that its CRS indistinguishability is tightly reduced to the SXDH assumption [GS12]. The maximum (absolute-value) of the difference in the two probabilities (over all efficient adversaries) will be denoted by $\mathrm{ADV}^{\mathrm{CRSIND}}$. More details about the actual commitment schemes can be found in Sect. 5.2. For full details the reader is referred to [GS12].

2.3 Public-Key Encryption Schemes

Let GEN be an algorithm that, on input security parameter λ, outputs par that includes parameters of pairing groups.

Definition 3 (Public-key encryption). *A Public-Key Encryption scheme (PKE) consists of proabilistic polynomial-time algorithms* $\mathsf{PKE} := (\mathsf{Gen}, \mathsf{Enc}, \mathsf{Dec})$:

- *Key generation algorithm* $\mathsf{Gen}(\mathsf{par})$ *takes* $\mathsf{par} \leftarrow \mathsf{GEN}(1^\lambda)$ *as input and generates a pair of public and secret keys* $(\mathsf{pk}, \mathsf{sk})$. *Message space* $\mathcal{M}$ *is determined by* pk.
- *Encryption algorithm* $\mathsf{Enc}(\mathsf{pk}, \mathsf{M})$ *returns a ciphertext* ct.
- *Decryption algorithm* $\mathsf{Dec}(\mathsf{sk}, \mathsf{ct})$ *is deterministic and returns a message* M.

For correctness, it must hold that, for all $\mathsf{par} \leftarrow \mathsf{GEN}(1^\lambda)$, $(\mathsf{pk}, \mathsf{sk}) \leftarrow \mathsf{Gen}(\mathsf{par})$, *messages* $\mathsf{M} \in \mathcal{M}$, *and* $\mathsf{ct} \leftarrow \mathsf{Enc}(\mathsf{pk}, \mathsf{M})$, $\mathsf{Dec}(\mathsf{sk}, \mathsf{ct}) = \mathsf{M}$.

Definition 4 (IND-mCPA Security [BBM00]). *A PKE scheme* PKE *is indistinguishable against multi-instance chosen-plaintext attack (IND-mCPA-secure) if for any* $q_e \geq 0$ *and for all* PPT *adversaries* $\mathcal{A}$ *with access to oracle* $\mathcal{O}_e$ *at most* q_e *times the following advantage function* $\mathsf{Adv}_{\mathsf{PKE}}^{\mathsf{mcpa}}(\mathcal{A})$ *is negligible,*

$$\mathsf{Adv}_{\mathsf{PKE}}^{\mathsf{mcpa}}(\mathcal{A}) := \left| \Pr\left[b' = b \, \middle| \, \begin{array}{l} \mathsf{par} \leftarrow \mathsf{GEN}(1^\lambda); (\mathsf{pk}, \mathsf{sk}) \leftarrow \mathsf{Gen}(\mathsf{par}); \\ b \leftarrow \{0,1\}; b' \leftarrow \mathcal{A}^{\mathcal{O}_e(\cdot, \cdot)}(\mathsf{pk}) \end{array} \right] - \frac{1}{2} \right|,$$

where $\mathcal{O}_e(\mathsf{M}_0, \mathsf{M}_1)$ *runs* $\mathsf{ct}^* \leftarrow \mathsf{Enc}(\mathsf{pk}, \mathsf{M}_b)$, *and returns* ct^* *to* $\mathcal{A}$.

There exist public-key encryption schemes that are structure-preserving, IND-mCPA secure, and have tight reductions based on compact assumptions. Examples are ElGamal encryption [ElG84] and Linear encryption [BBS04] based on the DDH assumption and the Decision Linear assumption, respectively.

2.4 Structure-Preserving Signatures

Definition 5 (Structure-Preserving Signature). *A structure-preserving signature scheme SPS is defined as a triple of probabilistic polynomial time (PPT) algorithms* $SPS = (\mathsf{Gen}, \mathsf{Sign}, \mathsf{Verify})$:

- *The probabilistic key generation algorithm* $\mathsf{Gen}(par)$ *returns the public/secret key* (pk, sk), *where* $pk \in \mathbb{G}^{n_{pk}}$ *for some* $n_{pk} \in poly(\lambda)$. *We assume that pk implicitly defines a message space* $M := \mathbb{G}^n$ *for some* $n \in poly(\lambda)$.
- *The probabilistic signing algorithm* $\mathsf{Sign}(sk, [m])$ *returns a signature* $\sigma \in \mathbb{G}^{n_\sigma}$ *for* $n_\sigma \in poly(\lambda)$.

– *The deterministic verification algorithm* $\mathsf{Verify}(pk, [m], \sigma)$ *only consists of pairing product equations and returns 1 (accept) or 0 (reject).*

Perfect correctness holds if for all $(pk, sk) \leftarrow \mathsf{Gen}(par)$ *and all messages* $[m] \in M$ *and all* $\sigma \leftarrow \mathsf{Sign}(sk, [m])$ *we have* $\mathsf{Verify}(pk, [m], \sigma) = 1.$

Definition 6 (Existential Unforgeability against Chosen Message Attack). *To an adversary A and scheme SPS we associate the advantage function:*

$$\mathrm{ADV}_{SPS}^{CMA}(A) := \Pr \left[\begin{array}{l} (pk, sk) \leftarrow \mathsf{Gen}(par) \\ ([m^*], \sigma^*) \leftarrow A^{SignO(\cdot)}(pk) \end{array} : \begin{array}{l} [m^*] \notin Q_{msg} \text{ and} \\ \mathsf{Verify}(pk, [m^*], \sigma^*) = 1 \end{array} \right]$$

where $SignO([m])$ *runs* $\sigma \leftarrow \mathsf{Sign}(sk, [m])$, *adds the vector* $[m]$ *to* Q_{msg} *(initialized with* $\emptyset$*) and returns* σ *to A. An SPS is said to be (unbounded) EUF-CMA-secure if for all PPT adversaries A,* $\mathrm{ADV}_{SPS}^{CMA}(A)$ *is negligible.*

3   The New (Almost) Tightly-Secure SPS Scheme

The new scheme is conveniently described in Fig. 1. While a brief overview of the new scheme was given in the introduction, we now describe it in more detail.

As a first step, we follow the signature scheme of [JR13] (which itself is built on Cramer-Shoup CCA2-encryption) where the split-CRS QA-NIZK for affine languages is used. The affine component is a secret k_0 which is only part of the prover CRS of the QA-NIZK and is not part of the verifier CRS (and hence public key of SPS). The secret k_0 or its group representation is encrypted using an augmented ElGamal encryption scheme. In other words, the signer picks r, computes $s = br$, and outputs $\rho = [r]_1$, and $\hat{\rho} = [s]_1$, where b is a secret key (normally, in a Cramer-Shoup style CCA-secure encryption scheme $[b]_1$ would be part of the public key). Since, we cannot use tags (for example by hashing $\rho, \hat{\rho}$) in a structure-preserving scheme, the last component of the augmented ElGamal encryption γ is just computed as $[k_0]_1 + d\rho + \mathbf{k} \cdot \boldsymbol{\mu}$, where $\mathbf{k}$ is another vector of secret keys of length n, $\boldsymbol{\mu} \in \mathbb{G}_1^n$ is a length n (adversarially supplied) input message and '$\cdot$' denotes inner product.

The signer provides a QA-NIZK Π_3 that γ and $\hat{\rho}$ are well-formed, as the language L_3 (see Fig. 1) is an affine subspace language. However, so far the signature components constructed are malleable, as we do not use tags. To this end, the signer also encrypts a bit z using another ElGamal encryption with keys (pke, ske). Call the encryption ζ. The bit z is just set to zero. However, in addition, the signer proves using a Groth-Sahai NIWI that either z is same as x (where x is a bit committed in the public key) or $s = br$. To this end, it also provides a Groth Sahai commitment to br (i.e. t in Fig. 1). Since, for the Groth-Sahai proof s and t must also be committed using Groth-Sahai commitments (named c_s and c_t), the signer must prove that these relate to the same r in the augmented ElGamal encryption. This is achieved by proving a QA-NIZK for the linear subspace language L_1 (see Fig. 1). Finally, it must also be proven that

Gen $(q, \mathbb{G}_1, \mathbb{G}_2, \mathbb{G}_T, e, [1]_1, [1]_2, n)$:
Sample crs as a Groth-Sahai NIWI BG-CRS.
Sample $(\mathsf{CRS}_p^i, \mathsf{CRS}_v^i, \mathsf{trap}_i) \leftarrow \Pi_i.\mathsf{crssim}()$ for $i = 1, 2, 3$.

Sample $r_x \leftarrow \mathbb{Z}_q$. Set $x = 1$ and $c_x = com_2(crs, x; r_x)$.
Sample $(b, k_0, d) \leftarrow \mathbb{Z}_q^3$, $\mathbf{k} \leftarrow \mathbb{Z}_q^n$ and $(pke, ske) \leftarrow ElGamal.Gen(\mathbb{G}_2)$.

Set $pk := (crs, \mathsf{CRS}_v^1, \mathsf{CRS}_v^2, \mathsf{CRS}_v^3, c_x)$.
Set $sk := (b, k_0, \mathbf{k}, d, \mathsf{trap}_1, \mathsf{trap}_2, \mathsf{trap}_3, pke, r_x)$.

Return (pk, sk).

Sign $(sk, \boldsymbol{\mu} \in \mathbb{G}_1^n)$:
Sample $(r, r_s, r_t, r_z) \leftarrow \mathbb{Z}_q^4$.
Set $s = t = br$, $c_s = com_1(crs, s; r_s)$ and $c_t = com_1(crs, t; r_t)$.
Let $\rho = [r]_1$, $\hat{\rho} = [s]_1$, $\gamma = \mathbf{k} \cdot \boldsymbol{\mu} + [k_0 + dr]_1$.

Set $z = 0$, $c_z = com_2(crs, z; r_z)$ and sample $\zeta \leftarrow ElGamal.Enc(pke, z)$.

Let $\pi := \Pi.\mathsf{prover}(crs, (c_s, c_t, c_z, c_x), (r_s, r_t, r_z, r_x))$.
Let $\pi_1 := \Pi_1.\mathsf{sim}(\mathsf{trap}_1, (\rho, c_t, \hat{\rho}, c_s))$.
Let $\pi_2 := \Pi_2.\mathsf{sim}(\mathsf{trap}_2, (\zeta, c_z))$.
Let $\pi_3 := \Pi_3.\mathsf{sim}(\mathsf{trap}_3, (\boldsymbol{\mu}, \rho, \hat{\rho}, \gamma))$.

Return $\sigma := (\rho, \hat{\rho}, \gamma, \zeta, c_s, c_t, c_z, \pi, \pi_1, \pi_2, \pi_3) \in \mathbb{G}_1^{11} \times \mathbb{G}_2^7$.

Verify $(pk, \boldsymbol{\mu}, \sigma)$:
Check all the NIZK proofs:
$\Pi.\mathsf{ver}(crs, (c_s, c_t, c_z, c_x), \pi)$ and $\Pi_1.\mathsf{ver}(\mathsf{CRS}_v^1, (\rho, \hat{\rho}, c_t, c_s), \pi_1)$ and
$\Pi_2.\mathsf{ver}(\mathsf{CRS}_v^2, (\zeta, c_z), \pi_2)$ and $\Pi_3.\mathsf{ver}(\mathsf{CRS}_v^3, (\boldsymbol{\mu}, \rho, \hat{\rho}, \gamma), \pi_3)$.

Languages:

Π is a GS-NIZK for $L \overset{\text{def}}{=} \{(c_s, c_t, c_z, c_x) \mid \exists (s, t, z, x, r_s, r_t, r_z, r_x) : (s-t)(z-x) = 0$ and $c_s = com_1(s; r_s)$ and $c_t = com_1(t; r_t)$ and $c_z = com_2(z; r_z)$ and $c_x = com_2(x; r_x)\}$.

Π_1 is a QA-NIZK for $L_1 \overset{\text{def}}{=} \{(\rho, c_t, \hat{\rho}, c_s) \mid \exists (r, s, r_t, r_s) : \rho = [r]_1$ and $c_t = com_1(br; r_t)$ and $\hat{\rho} = [s]_1$ and $c_s = com_1(s; r_s)\}$, with parameters (b, com_1).

Π_2 is a QA-NIZK for $L_2 \overset{\text{def}}{=} \{(\zeta, c_z) \mid \exists (z, r_e, r_z) : \zeta = ElGamal.Enc(pke, [z]_2; r_e)$ and $c_z = com_2(z; r_z)\}$, with parameters (com_2, pke).

Π_3 is a QA-NIZK for $L_3 \overset{\text{def}}{=} \{(\boldsymbol{\mu}, \rho, \hat{\rho}, \gamma) \mid \exists (\mathbf{m}, r) : \boldsymbol{\mu} = [\mathbf{m}]_1$ and $\rho = [r]_1$ and $\hat{\rho} = [br]_1$ and $\gamma = [\mathbf{k} \cdot \mathbf{m} + k_0 + dr]_1\}$, with parameters $(b, \mathbf{k}, k_0, d)$.

Fig. 1. Structure preserving signature SPS_{SXDH}

the ElGamal encryption of z, i.e. ζ is indeed that of z used in the Groth-Sahai "OR" proof. This can be proven by either a Groth-Sahai proof or a QA-NIZK for language L_2.

Thus, the signer produces the following signature on $\boldsymbol{\mu}$:

$$(\rho, \hat{\rho}, \gamma, \zeta, c_s, c_t, c_z, \pi, \pi_1, \pi_2, \pi_3) \in \mathbb{G}_1^{11} \times \mathbb{G}_2^7$$

The verification of the signature just involves checking all the proofs, i.e. the Groth-Sahai "OR" proof π for language L, and the three QA-NIZK proofs π_1, π_2, π_3 for languages L_1, L_2, L_3.

The (almost) tight security of this scheme is proved in the next section. The crux of the proof is in Lemmas 1 and 2. The hybrid games for these lemmas are summarized in Figs. 3 and 4. Further, the main transitions in the various hybrid games in these two lemmas are depicted in Figs. 5 and 6.

4   Security of the SPS Scheme

In this section we state and prove the security of the scheme SPS_{SXDH} described in Fig. 1.

Theorem 1. *For any efficient adversary $\mathcal{A}$, which makes at most Q signature queries before attempting a forgery, its probability of success in the EUF-CMA game against the scheme SPS_{SXDH} is at most*

$$\text{ADV}_{\Pi_3}^{\text{TSS}} + 12L(\text{ADV}_{\Pi_1}^{\text{TSS}} + \text{ADV}_{\Pi_2}^{\text{TSS}}) + 8L \cdot \text{ADV}_{\text{SXDH}}$$

$$+ (12L + 1)\text{ADV}_{\Pi}^{\text{CRSIND}} + 2L \cdot \text{ADV}_{ElGamal}^{mCPA} + \frac{6L + (q_s + 1)^2 + 1}{q}$$

Here L is the least integer greater than the bit size of q, and q_s is an upper bound on the number of signature queries issued by the adversary.

Remark 1. $\text{ADV}_{\Pi_i}^{\text{TSS}}$ of a QA-NIZK Π_i reduces to SXDH by a factor of $(n - t)$ where the (affine) linear subspace language is of dimension t within a full space of dimension n. Also, $\text{ADV}_{\Pi}^{\text{CRSIND}}$ of a Groth-Sahai NIZK Π reduces to SXDH by a factor of 1. Thus the overall reduction in Theorem 1 to SXDH is $O(\lambda)$.

Proof. We go through a sequence of Games $\mathbf{G_0}$ to $\mathbf{G_3}$ which are described below and summarized in Fig. 2. In the following, $\text{Prob}_i[X]$ will denote probability of predicate X holding in probability space defined in game $\mathbf{G_i}$ and WIN_i will denote the winning condition for the adversary in game $\mathbf{G_i}$.

Game $\mathbf{G_0}$: This game exactly replicates the real construction to the adversary. So the adversary's advantage in $\mathbf{G_0}$ (defined as WIN_0 below) is the EUF-CMA advantage we seek to bound.

$$\text{WIN}_0 \overset{\triangle}{=} (\boldsymbol{\mu}^* \notin \mathcal{M}) \text{ and } \text{Verify}(pk, \boldsymbol{\mu}^*, \sigma^*)$$

Game $\mathbf{G_0'}$: In Game $\mathbf{G_0'}$, the challenger lazily simulates (by maintaining a table) a random function RP from $\mathbb{G}_1^n$ to L-bit strings. Define COL to be the predicate which returns true when there is a collision, i.e., when any pair of message vectors from the set of signature queries union the adversarial response message at the

$\mathsf{Gen}() : \cdots$

Games 0-1 $crs \leftarrow \text{GS-NIWI-BG}$

Games 2-3 $simcrs \leftarrow \text{GS-NIWI-HG}$

Sample $\beta \leftarrow \{0,1\}$, $r_x \leftarrow \mathbb{Z}_q$

Set $x = 1$

Games 0-1 $c_x = com_2(crs, x; r_x)$

Games 2-3 $c_x = com_2(simcrs, 0; r_x)$

Sample $d \leftarrow \mathbb{Z}_q$

$\mathsf{Sign}(sk, \boldsymbol{\mu}^i \in \mathbb{G}_1^n) :$

Sample $\rho^i \leftarrow \mathbb{G}_1$.

Simulate a random function $\text{RP} : \mathbb{G}_1^n \to \{0,1\}^L$. Let $\nu^i = \text{RP}(\boldsymbol{\mu}^i)$.

Set $z^i = 0$

Games 0-1 $c_z^i = com_2(crs, z^i; r_z^i)$

Games 2-3 $c_z^i = com_2(simcrs, 0; r_z^i)$

Let $(\hat{\rho}^i, \gamma^i) :=$

Games 0-2 $(b\rho^i, \ \mathbf{k} \cdot \boldsymbol{\mu}^i + [k_0]_1 + d\rho^i)$

Game 3 $(b\rho^i, \ \mathbf{k} \cdot \boldsymbol{\mu}^i + [\text{RF}_L(\nu^i)]_1 + d\rho^i)$

$\cdots$

$\mathsf{WIN} \triangleq$

Games 0'-3   **if** COL (as defined in the text) **return true; else**

$\sigma^* = (\rho^*, \hat{\rho}^*, \gamma^*, \zeta^*, c_s^*, c_t^*, c_z^*, \pi^*, \pi_1^*, \pi_2^*, \pi_3^*) :$

$(\boldsymbol{\mu}^* \notin \mathcal{M})$ **and** $\mathsf{Verify}(pk, \boldsymbol{\mu}^*, \sigma^*)$

Games 1-3   **and** $\gamma^* == \mathbf{k} \cdot \boldsymbol{\mu}^* + [k_0]_1 + d\rho^*$

Games 1-3   **and** $\hat{\rho}^* == b\rho^*$

Fig. 2. Top level games and winning conditions

end get mapped to the same output L-bit string. In this game, the adversary is allowed to win outright if COL is true at the end:

$$\mathsf{WIN}_0' \triangleq COL \text{ or } ((\boldsymbol{\mu}^* \notin \mathcal{M}) \text{ and } \mathsf{Verify}(pk, \boldsymbol{\mu}^*, \sigma^*))$$

The difference in advantage is at most the collision probability, which is bounded by $(q_s + 1)^2/q$.

Game G_1: The challenge-response in this game is the same as G_0. The winning condition is now defined as:

$$\text{WIN}_1 \overset{\triangle}{=} COL \text{ or}$$
$$\text{WIN}_0 \text{ and } \sigma^* = (\rho^*, \hat{\rho}^*, \gamma^*, \cdots) \text{ s.t.}$$
$$(\gamma^* = \mathbf{k} \cdot \boldsymbol{\mu}^* + [k_0]_1 + d \cdot \rho^*)$$
$$\text{and } (\hat{\rho}^* == b\rho^*)$$

The difference in advantages of the adversary is upper bounded by the unbounded true-simulation-soundness of Π_3:

$$|\text{Prob}_1[\text{WIN}_1] - \text{Prob}_0[\text{WIN}_0]| \leq \text{ADV}_{\Pi_3}^{\text{TSS}} \tag{1}$$

Game G_2: In this game, the Groth-Sahai CRS is generated as a hiding CRS, i.e., *simcrs*. Moreover, since all zero is a solution of the equation $(s-t)(z-x) = 0$, by witness-indistinguishability property of Groth-Sahai under the hiding CRS, all proofs and commitments can be generated with all zero witness (i.e., $(s, t, z, x) = (0, 0, 0, 0)$). The winning condition WIN_2 remains the same as WIN_1.

$$|\text{Prob}_2[\text{WIN}_2] - \text{Prob}_1[\text{WIN}_1]| \leq \text{ADV}_{\Pi}^{\text{CRSIND}} \tag{2}$$

Game G_3: In this game, the challenger also lazily maintains a function RF_L mapping L-bit strings to $\mathbb{Z}_q$. The function RF_L has the property that it is a random and independent function from L-bit strings to $\mathbb{Z}_q$ except possibly at one value in the domain (on which the challenger has defined RF_L) where the value of RF_L can be k_0. In G_3, each signature component γ^i is generated as $\mathbf{k} \cdot \boldsymbol{\mu}^i + [\text{RF}_L(\text{RP}(\boldsymbol{\mu}^i))]_1 + d\rho^i$, instead of $\mathbf{k} \cdot \boldsymbol{\mu}^i + [k_0]_1 + d\rho^i$. For ease of exposition, we will denote $\text{RP}(\boldsymbol{\mu}^i)$ as ν^i. The winning condition WIN_3 remains the same as WIN_2.

Lemma 1. $|Prob_3[\text{WIN}_3] - Prob_2[\text{WIN}_2]| \leq$

$$12L(\text{ADV}_{\Pi_1}^{\text{TSS}} + \text{ADV}_{\Pi_2}^{\text{TSS}}) + 8L \cdot \text{ADV}_{\text{SXDH}}$$

$$+ 12L \cdot \text{ADV}_{\Pi}^{\text{CRSIND}} + 2L \cdot \text{ADV}_{ElGamal}^{mCPA} + \frac{6L}{q}$$

We will prove this Lemma in Sect. 4.1. We now claim that $\text{Prob}_3[\text{WIN}_3] \leq 1/q$. To prove this claim, we observe that k_0 is absent from the public key as well as from all the signature responses, except at most one response by property of RF_L and RP and the conjunct COL, which ensures that no RP collision occurred. Let's say this is the j-th query. For all queries $i \neq j$, we observe that $RF_L(\mu^i)$ is uniformly random and independent of both k and k_0. So all the γ^is, for $i \neq j$, might as well be sampled independently randomly.

Coming back to the special j-th query, we claim that $[k_0]_1 + \mathbf{k} \cdot \boldsymbol{\mu}^*$ is uniformly random and independent of $[k_0]_1 + \mathbf{k} \cdot \boldsymbol{\mu}_j$, given that $\boldsymbol{\mu}^* \neq \boldsymbol{\mu}_j$. This linear algebra fact is most conveniently seen by the following information- theoretic argument: Let $\alpha \stackrel{\text{def}}{=} [k_0]_1 + \mathbf{k} \cdot \boldsymbol{\mu}_j$ and $\beta \stackrel{\text{def}}{=} [k_0]_1 + \mathbf{k} \cdot \boldsymbol{\mu}^*$. Now sample $\mathbf{k} \leftarrow \mathbb{Z}_q^n$, and $k' \leftarrow \mathbb{Z}_q$ independently and randomly. Set k_0 such that $[k_0]_1 = [k']_1 - \mathbf{k} \cdot \boldsymbol{\mu}_j$. Then, k_0 is still distributed randomly and independently. Then we have $\alpha = [k']_1$ and $\beta = [k']_1 + \mathbf{k} \cdot (\boldsymbol{\mu}^* - \boldsymbol{\mu}_j)$. Thus α is uniformly random and independent of k, while β has an independent uniformly random distribution due to the additional term $\mathbf{k} \cdot (\boldsymbol{\mu}^* - \boldsymbol{\mu}_j)$, where $\mathbf{k}$ is uniformly random and $\boldsymbol{\mu}^* - \boldsymbol{\mu}_j$ is non-zero. Thus the probability of the adversary producing $\gamma^* - d \cdot \rho^* = \mathbf{k}\boldsymbol{\mu}^* + [k_0]_1$ is bounded in probability by $1/q$:

$$\text{Prob}_3[\text{WIN}_3] \leq 1/q.$$

4.1   Proof of Lemma 1

To prove Lemma 1, we go through a series of L games, each of which has several sub-games. We will identify $\mathbf{G_2}$ with $\mathbf{G_{2,1,0}}$ and $\mathbf{G_3}$ with $\mathbf{G_{2,L,10}}$. These games are summarized in Fig. 3 with a table of transitions given in Fig. 5.

In the following, we will consider various functions RF_j, $j \in [0 \dots L]$. RF_j maps j-bit length strings to $\mathbb{Z}_q$. Define $\text{RF}_0(\epsilon) = k_0$, where ϵ denotes the empty string. We will maintain the induction hypothesis (over $j \in [0 \dots L]$) that the function RF_j is a random function from its domain to its range except possibly for at most one string in the domain where its value is k_0. Clearly, the base case holds ($j = 0$).

Game $\mathbf{G_{2,j,0}}$: For all signature responses i, let $\nu^i|_{j-1}$ be the $(j-1)$-length prefix of ν^i. We generate γ^i as $\mathbf{k} \cdot \boldsymbol{\mu}^i + [\text{RF}_{j-1}(\nu^i|_{j-1})]_1 + d\rho^i$.

In the base case, i.e., when $j = 1$, $\mathbf{G_{2,j,0}}$ is indeed the same as $\mathbf{G_2}$ by definition of $\text{RF}_0(\epsilon)$. For the inductive case, we defer the proof of equivalence of $\mathbf{G_{2,j,0}}$ and $\mathbf{G_{2,j-1,10}}$ till the description of the latter game.

Game $\mathbf{G_{2,j,1}}$: We also sample $(d_1, d_2) \leftarrow \mathbb{Z}_q^2$ and substitute d with $d_1 + d_2 b$, instead of sampling it from random. Consequently, we change the winning condition's γ^*-test conjunct to $\gamma^* == \mathbf{k} \cdot \boldsymbol{\mu}^* + [k_0]_1 + d_1\rho^* + d_2\hat{\rho}^*$, which is same as the earlier winning condition as the winning condition also has the conjunct $\hat{\rho}^* = b\rho^*$. Also set z^i to be $\nu_k^i = \text{RP}(\boldsymbol{\mu}^i)_k$, the k-th bit of output of applying the simulated random function to the query message $\boldsymbol{\mu}^i$.

Difference in advantage is the IND-mCPA security of the ElGamal encryption scheme, in switching all the z^i plaintexts. Rest of the changes are information theoretic as x is committed with a hiding CRS and d has the same distribution.

Game $\mathbf{G_{2,j,2}}$: The challenger samples a bit β randomly from $\{0, 1\}$. In the winning condition we introduce a predicate called *CheckAbort* which behaves as follows: it returns true and forces the adversary to lose outright if the decryption of ζ^* is zero or one and equals β. In the case that decryption of ζ^* is not zero or one, then it still forces the adversary to lose at random with probability half. If

$$\mathsf{Gen}() : \cdots$$

Games (2,j,3-7)	$crs \leftarrow$ GS-NIWI-BG
Games (2,j,0-2, 8-10)	$simcrs \leftarrow$ GS-NIWI-HG

Sample $\beta \leftarrow \{0,1\}$, $r_x \leftarrow \mathbb{Z}_q$

Games (2,j,0-2,10)	Set $x = 1$
Games (2,j,3-9)	Set $x = 1 - \beta$
Games (2,j,3-7)	$c_x = com_2(crs, x; r_x)$
Games (2,j,0-2, 8-10)	$c_x = com_2(simcrs, 0; r_x)$

Games (2,j,0, 7-10)	Sample $d \leftarrow \mathbb{Z}_q$
Games (2,j,1-6)	Sample $(d_1, d_2) \leftarrow \mathbb{Z}_q^2$

$$\mathsf{Sign}(sk, \boldsymbol{\mu}^i \in \mathbb{G}_1^n) :$$

Sample $\rho^i \leftarrow \mathbb{G}_1$.

Simulate a random function RP $: \mathbb{G}_1^n \to \{0,1\}^L$. Let $\nu^i = \mathrm{RP}(\boldsymbol{\mu}^i)$.

Game (2,j,0,10)	Set $z^i = 0$
Games (2,j,1-9)	Set $z^i = \nu_j^i$
Games (2,j,3-7)	$c_z^i = com_2(crs, z^i; r_z^i)$
Games (2,j,0-2, 8-10)	$c_z^i = com_2(simcrs, 0; r_z^i)$

Let $(\hat{\rho}^i, \gamma^i) :=$

Games (2,j,0)	$\left(b\rho^i, \ \mathbf{k} \cdot \boldsymbol{\mu}^i + [\mathrm{RF}_{j-1}(\nu^i|_{j-1})]_1 + d\rho^i \right)$
Games (2,j,1-4)	$\left(b\rho^i, \ \mathbf{k} \cdot \boldsymbol{\mu}^i + [\mathrm{RF}_{j-1}(\nu^i|_{j-1})]_1 + d_1\rho^i + d_2\hat{\rho}^i \right)$
Games (2,j,5-6)	$\left(b\rho^i, \ \mathbf{k} \cdot \boldsymbol{\mu}^i + \begin{bmatrix} \mathrm{RF}_{j-1}(\nu^i|_{j-1}), \text{ if } (\nu_j^i == \beta) \\ \mathrm{RF}'_{j-1}(\nu^i|_{j-1}), \text{ if } (\nu_j^i \neq \beta) \end{bmatrix}_1 + d_1\rho^i + d_2\hat{\rho}^i \right)$
Games (2,j,7-10)	$\left(b\rho^i, \ \mathbf{k} \cdot \boldsymbol{\mu}^i + [\mathrm{RF}_j(\nu^i|_j)]_1 + d\rho^i \right)$

$\cdots$

	WIN $\triangleq$ **if** (COL) **return true; else**
Games (2,j,2-8)	**if** $CheckAbort$(as defined in the text) **return false; else**
	$\sigma^* = (\rho^*, \hat{\rho}^*, \gamma^*, \zeta^*, c_s^*, c_t^*, c_z^*, \pi^*, \pi_1^*, \pi_2^*, \pi_3^*) :$
	$(\mu^* \notin \mathcal{M})$ **and** Verify(pk, μ^*, σ^*)
	and
Games (2,j,0,7-10)	$\gamma^* == \mathbf{k} \cdot \boldsymbol{\mu}^* + [k_0]_1 + d\rho^*$
Games (2,j,1-6)	$\gamma^* == \mathbf{k} \cdot \boldsymbol{\mu}^* + [k_0]_1 + d_1\rho^* + d_2\hat{\rho}^*$
Games (2,j,0-3,6-10)	**and** $\hat{\rho}^* == b\rho^*$

Fig. 3. Going from Game 2 to 3

the *CheckAbort* predicate does not force a loss for the adversary, then the rest of the winning condition remains the same as the previous game.

Since β is information theoretically hidden from the adversary, the adversary's advantage goes down by exactly a factor of 2.

Game $G_{2,j,3}$: The challenger sets $x = 1 - \beta$. It goes back to binding-CRS crs for Π. Thus, z^i as set above is used in GS-commitment c_z^i to z^i.

Since $s^i = t^i$ for all i, by Groth-Sahai witness-indistinguishability the difference in the adversary's advantage is at most $\mathrm{ADV}_\Pi^{\mathrm{CRSIND}}$. (Note that Groth-Sahai NIWI has perfect composable witness-indistinguishability.)

Game $G_{2,j,4}$: The challenger removes the conjunct $\hat{\rho}^* == b\rho^*$ from the winning condition.

We first check that QA-NIZK Π_1 and Π_2 are in true-simulation mode, i.e., the simulator for these QA-NIZK is only issuing simulated proofs on true statements. For Π_1 it is indeed the case as $s = b \cdot r = t$. For Π_2 it is also true, since the GS commitment of z^i is same as z^i encrypted in ζ^i. Now, since $\mathsf{dec}(\zeta^*) \neq x$ is in the scope of this removed conjunct, by true-simulation soundness of Π_2, $z^* \neq x$ is also in the scope of the removed conjunct. This implies by soundness of the NIWI that $s^* = t^*$. Next, by true-simulation soundness of Π_1, $\hat{\rho}^* = b\rho^*$. Thus this conjunct is indeed redundant and can be removed. The difference in advantage is at most $\mathrm{ADV}_{\Pi_1}^{\mathrm{TSS}} + \mathrm{ADV}_{\Pi_2}^{\mathrm{TSS}}$.

Game $G_{2,j,5}$: We change the computation of γ^i from

$$\mathbf{k} \cdot \boldsymbol{\mu}^i + [\mathrm{RF}_{j-1}(\nu^i|_{j-1})]_1 + d_1\rho^i + d_2\hat{\rho}^i$$

to

$$\mathbf{k} \cdot \boldsymbol{\mu}^i + \left[\begin{matrix} \mathrm{RF}_{j-1}(\nu^i|_{j-1}), \text{if}(\nu_j^i == \beta) \\ \mathrm{RF}'_{j-1}(\nu^i|_{j-1}), \text{if}(\nu_j^i \neq \beta) \end{matrix} \right]_1 + d_1\rho^i + d_2\hat{\rho}^i.$$

Here RF'_j is another independent random function from j-bit strings to $\mathbb{Z}_q$.

Lemma 2. $|Prob_{2,j,4}[\mathsf{WIN}_{2,j,4}] - Prob_{2,j,5}[\mathsf{WIN}_{2,j,5}]| \leq$

$$4(\mathrm{ADV}_{\Pi_1}^{\mathrm{TSS}} + \mathrm{ADV}_{\Pi_2}^{\mathrm{TSS}}) + 4 \cdot \mathrm{ADV}_{\mathrm{SXDH}} + 4 \cdot \mathrm{ADV}_\Pi^{\mathrm{CRSIND}} + \frac{3}{q}$$

We will prove this Lemma in the next subsection using another sequence of hybrid games.

Game $G_{2,j,6}$: We now start rolling the games back. In this game we add back the condition $\hat{\rho}^* == b\rho^*$ into the winning condition.

Since $z^* \neq x$ in the scope of this clause, the difference in advantage is $\mathrm{ADV}_{\Pi_1}^{\mathrm{TSS}} + \mathrm{ADV}_{\Pi_2}^{\mathrm{TSS}}$ due to the true-simulation soundness of the QA-NIZKs and the perfect soundness of GS-NIZK Π.

Game $G_{2,j,7}$: Challenger (lazily) defines RF_j as follows:

$$\mathrm{RF}_j(\nu^i|_j) \overset{\text{def}}{=} \left\{ \begin{matrix} \mathrm{RF}_{j-1}(\nu^i|_{j-1}), \text{ if } (\nu_j^i = \beta) \\ \mathrm{RF}'_{j-1}(\nu^i|_{j-1}), \text{if}(\nu_j^i \neq \beta) \end{matrix} \right\}$$

Since RF' is random and independent of RF, the induction hypothesis related to RF continues to hold: if τ is the only $(j-1)$-bit string on which $RF_{j-1}(\tau)$ equals k_0, then $(\tau;\beta)$ is the only j-bit string on which RF_j equals k_0.

The challenger also goes back to sampling d from random, instead of setting it to $d_1 + bd_2$. γ^i is now computed as $(\mathbf{k} \cdot \boldsymbol{\mu}^i + [RF_j(\nu^i|_j)]_1 + d\rho^i)$. It also changes the winning condition γ^*-conjunct to $\gamma^* == \mathbf{k} \cdot \boldsymbol{\mu}^* + [k_0]_1 + d\rho^*$, which holds as $\hat{\rho}^* = b\rho^*$.

Changes in this game are statistically indistinguishable from the previous and hence the advantage of the adversary remains the same.

Game $\mathbf{G_{2,j,8}}$: The challenger goes back to generating the hiding CRS for Π. Further, the Groth-Sahai NIWI proofs and commitments are now generated using all zero witnesses (i.e., using 0 in place of x and z^i).

The difference in adversary's advantage is at most $\mathrm{ADV}_{\Pi}^{\mathrm{CRSIND}}$.

Game $\mathbf{G_{2,j,9}}$: In the winning condition, we remove the *CheckAbort* disjunct where the adversary lost outright in the previous games, i.e., if the decryption of ζ^* was $0/1$ and equaled β, or with probability half if the decryption was non-$0/1$.

Since β is information theoretically hidden from the adversary, the adversary's advantage goes up by exactly a factor of 2.

Game $\mathbf{G_{2,j,10}}$: The challenger sets $z^i = 0$, which also changes the El-Gamal encryption of z^i. It also sets x back to 1.

The difference in adversary's advantage is the IND-mCPA security of the ElGamal encryption scheme, in switching all the z^i plaintexts. Rest of the changes are statistically indistinguishable as x is committed with a hiding CRS.

We now observe that game $\mathbf{G_{2,j,10}}$ is same as $\mathbf{G_{2,j+1,0}}$ for $j < L$ and same as $\mathbf{G_3}$ for $j = L$. This concludes our proof.

4.2   Proof of Lemma 2

The various hybrid games to prove this lemma are depicted in Fig. 4 with a table of transitions given in Fig. 6.

Game $\mathbf{G_0}$: The game $\mathbf{H_0}$ is defined to exactly the same as game $\mathbf{G_{2,j,4}}$.

Game $\mathbf{H_1}$: In this game, the challenger generates the Groth-Sahai NIWI-CRS as simcrs, i.e., using the simulator CRS generator. Further, for each query i, if ν_j^i is not equal to β, then instead of just picking r^i, the challenger picks r_1^i and r_2^i at random, and sets $\rho^i = \rho_1^i + \rho_2^i = [r_1^i + r_2^i]_1$. Similarly, it sets $s^i = t^i = b(r_1^i + r_2^i)$, and thus $\hat{\rho}^i = b[r_1^i + r_2^i]_1$ and a similar change in the generation of γ^i. Finally, in generating the Groth-Sahai commitments and proof Π, the challenger uses all zero witnesses.

By the witness-indistinguishability property of GS-NIWI, and since rest of the game is statistically the same as the previous game, the adversary's advantage of winning is at most $\mathrm{ADV}_{\Pi}^{\mathrm{CRSIND}}$.

Game $\mathbf{H_2}$: In this game, the adversary also picks a b' randomly and independently from $\mathbb{Z}_q$. Next, for each query i, if ν_j^i is not equal to β, then the challenger

$\text{Gen}() : \cdots$

Games $H_{0,3-5,10-14}$ $crs \leftarrow \text{GS-NIWI-BG}$
Games $H_{1-2,6-9}$ $crs \leftarrow \text{GS-NIWI-HG}$

$\text{Sign}(sk,\ \boldsymbol{\mu}^i \in \mathbb{G}_1): \quad \cdots$

Let $(\hat{\rho}^i, \gamma^i) :=$

Games (2,j,4)
$$\left(b\rho^i,\ \mathbf{k} \cdot \boldsymbol{\mu}^i + [RF_{j-1}(\nu^i|_{j-1})]_1 + d_1\rho^i + d_2\hat{\rho}^i \right)$$

Game H_0
$$\left(\begin{array}{ll} b\rho^i,\ \mathbf{k} \cdot \boldsymbol{\mu}^i + [RF_{j-1}(\nu^i|_{j-1})]_1 + d_1\rho^i + d_2\hat{\rho}^i, & \text{if } (\nu^i_j == \beta) \\ b\rho^i,\ \mathbf{k} \cdot \boldsymbol{\mu}^i + [RF_{j-1}(\nu^i|_{j-1})]_1 + d_1\rho^i + d_2\hat{\rho}^i, & \text{if } (\nu^i_j \neq \beta) \end{array} \right)$$

Game H_1
$$\left(\begin{array}{ll} b\rho^i,\ \mathbf{k} \cdot \boldsymbol{\mu}^i + [RF_{j-1}(\nu^i|_{j-1})]_1 + d_1\rho^i + d_2\hat{\rho}^i, & \text{if } (\nu^i_j == \beta) \\ b(\rho^i_1 + \rho^i_2),\ \mathbf{k} \cdot \boldsymbol{\mu}^i + [RF_{j-1}(\nu^i|_{j-1})]_1 + (d_1 + d_2 b)\rho^i_1 + (d_1 + d_2 b)\rho^i_2, & \text{if } (\nu^i_j \neq \beta) \end{array} \right)$$

Game H_2, H_3
$$\left(\begin{array}{ll} b\rho^i,\ \mathbf{k} \cdot \boldsymbol{\mu}^i + [RF_{j-1}(\nu^i|_{j-1})]_1 + d_1\rho^i + d_2\hat{\rho}^i, & \text{if } (\nu^i_j == \beta) \\ b\rho^i_1 + b'\rho^i_2,\ \mathbf{k} \cdot \boldsymbol{\mu}^i + [RF_{j-1}(\nu^i|_{j-1})]_1 + (d_1 + d_2 b)\rho^i_1 + (d_1 + d_2 b')\rho^i_2, & \text{if } (\nu^i_j \neq \beta) \end{array} \right)$$

Game H_4, H_5, H_6
$$\left(\begin{array}{ll} b\rho^i,\ \mathbf{k} \cdot \boldsymbol{\mu}^i + [RF_{j-1}(\nu^i|_{j-1})]_1 + d\rho^i, & \text{if } (\nu^i_j == \beta) \\ b\rho^i_1 + b'\rho^i_2,\ \mathbf{k} \cdot \boldsymbol{\mu}^i + [RF_{j-1}(\nu^i|_{j-1})]_1 + d\rho^i_1 + d'\rho^i_2, & \text{if } (\nu^i_j \neq \beta) \end{array} \right)$$

Game H_7
$$\left(\begin{array}{ll} b\rho^i,\ \mathbf{k} \cdot \boldsymbol{\mu}^i + [RF_{j-1}(\nu^i|_{j-1})]_1 + d\rho^i, & \text{if } (\nu^i_j == \beta) \\ b\rho^i_1 + b\rho^i_2,\ \mathbf{k} \cdot \boldsymbol{\mu}^i + [RF_{j-1}(\nu^i|_{j-1})]_1 + d\rho^i_1 + d'\rho^i_2, & \text{if } (\nu^i_j \neq \beta) \end{array} \right)$$

Game H_8
$$\left(\begin{array}{ll} b\rho^i,\ \mathbf{k} \cdot \boldsymbol{\mu}^i + [RF_{j-1}(\nu^i|_{j-1})]_1 + d\rho^i, & \text{if } (\nu^i_j == \beta) \\ b\rho^i_1 + b\rho^i_2,\ \mathbf{k} \cdot \boldsymbol{\mu}^i + [RF'_{j-1}(\nu^i|_{j-1})]_1 + d\rho^i_1 + d'\rho^i_2, & \text{if } (\nu^i_j \neq \beta) \end{array} \right)$$

Game H_9, H_{10}
$$\left(\begin{array}{ll} b\rho^i,\ \mathbf{k} \cdot \boldsymbol{\mu}^i + [RF_{j-1}(\nu^i|_{j-1})]_1 + d\rho^i, & \text{if } (\nu^i_j == \beta) \\ b\rho^i_1 + b'\rho^i_2,\ \mathbf{k} \cdot \boldsymbol{\mu}^i + [RF'_{j-1}(\nu^i|_{j-1})]_1 + d\rho^i_1 + d'\rho^i_2, & \text{if } (\nu^i_j \neq \beta) \end{array} \right)$$

Game H_{11}, H_{12}
$$\left(\begin{array}{ll} b\rho^i,\ \mathbf{k} \cdot \boldsymbol{\mu}^i + [RF_{j-1}(\nu^i|_{j-1})]_1 + d_1\rho^i + d_2\hat{\rho}^i, & \text{if } (\nu^i_j == \beta) \\ b\rho^i_1 + b'\rho^i_2,\ \mathbf{k} \cdot \boldsymbol{\mu}^i + [RF'_{j-1}(\nu^i|_{j-1})]_1 + (d_1 + d_2 b)\rho^i_1 + (d_1 + d_2 b')\rho^i_2, & \text{if } (\nu^i_j \neq \beta) \end{array} \right)$$

Game H_{13}
$$\left(\begin{array}{ll} b\rho^i,\ \mathbf{k} \cdot \boldsymbol{\mu}^i + [RF_{j-1}(\nu^i|_{j-1})]_1 + d_1\rho^i + d_2\hat{\rho}^i, & \text{if } (\nu^i_j == \beta) \\ b(\rho^i_1 + \rho^i_2),\ \mathbf{k} \cdot \boldsymbol{\mu}^i + [RF'_{j-1}(\nu^i|_{j-1})]_1 + (d_1 + d_2 b)\rho^i_1 + (d_1 + d_2 b)\rho^i_2, & \text{if } (\nu^i_j \neq \beta) \end{array} \right)$$

Game H_{14}
$$\left(\begin{array}{ll} b\rho^i,\ \mathbf{k} \cdot \boldsymbol{\mu}^i + [RF_{j-1}(\nu^i|_{j-1})]_1 + d_1\rho^i + d_2\hat{\rho}^i, & \text{if } (\nu^i_j == \beta) \\ b\rho^i,\ \mathbf{k} \cdot \boldsymbol{\mu}^i + [RF'_{j-1}(\nu^i|_{j-1})]_1 + d_1\rho^i + d_2\hat{\rho}^i, & \text{if } (\nu^i_j \neq \beta) \end{array} \right)$$

Games (2,j,5)
$$\left(b\rho^i,\ \mathbf{k} \cdot \boldsymbol{\mu}^i + \left[\begin{array}{l} RF_{j-1}(\nu^i|_{j-1}), \text{ if } (\nu^i_j == \beta) \\ RF'_{j-1}(\nu^i|_{j-1}), \text{ if } (\nu^i_j \neq \beta) \end{array} \right]_1 + d_1\rho^i + d_2\hat{\rho}^i \right)$$

$\cdots$

$\text{WIN} \triangleq$ **if** (COL) **return true; else if** $(CheckAbort)$ **return false; else**

$\sigma^* = (\rho^*, \hat{\rho}^*, \gamma^*, \zeta^*, c^*_s, c^*_t, c^*_z, \pi^*, \pi^*_1, \pi^*_2, \pi^*_3):$

$(\boldsymbol{\mu}^* \notin \mathcal{M})$ **and** $\text{Verify}(pk,\ \boldsymbol{\mu}^*,\ \sigma^*)$
and

Games $H_0\text{-}H_3, H_{11}\text{-}H_{14}$ $\gamma^* == \mathbf{k} \cdot \boldsymbol{\mu}^* + [k_0]_1 + d_1\rho^* + d_2\hat{\rho}^*$
Games $H_4\text{-}H_{10}$ $\gamma^* == \mathbf{k} \cdot \boldsymbol{\mu}^* + [k_0]_1 + d\rho^*$
Games $H_3\text{-}H_4, H_{10}\text{-}H_{11}$ **and** $\hat{\rho}^* == b\rho^*$

Fig. 4. Going from game $(2, j, 4)$ to $(2, j, 5)$.

picks r^i_1 and r^i_2 at random, and sets $\rho^i = [r^i_1 + r^i_2]_1$. It sets $s^i = br^i_1 + b'r^i_2$, $t^i = b(r^i_1 + r^i_2)$. It sets $\hat{\rho}^i = b[r^i_1]_1 + b'[r^i_2]_1$ and a similar change in generation of γ^i (see Fig. 4).

We now prove that the absolute value of the difference of the advantage in adversary's winning probability in $\mathbf{H_2}$ and $\mathbf{H_1}$ is at most the maximum advantage of winning in an SXDH game. In other words,

$$|\text{Prob}_{\mathbf{H_2}}(\text{WIN}_{\mathbf{H_2}}) - \text{Prob}_{\mathbf{H_1}}(\text{WIN}_{\mathbf{H_1}})| \leq \text{ADV}_{\text{SXDH}}.$$

#	crs	β	x	z^i	witness	d	If $\nu^i_j \neq \beta$: γ^i	If $\nu^i_j = \beta$: γ^i	forgery check	abort	reduction
2.j.0	HG	-	1	$\boxed{0}$	$\hat{\rho} = b\rho$	d	$\mathbf{k}\cdot\boldsymbol{\mu}^i + [\mathrm{RF}_{j-1}(\nu^i\|_{j-1})]_1 + d\rho^i)$	$\mathbf{k}\cdot\boldsymbol{\mu}^i + [\mathrm{RF}_{j-1}(\nu^i\|_{j-1})]_1 + d\rho^i)$	$\gamma^* = \mathbf{k}\cdot\boldsymbol{\mu}^* + [k_0]_1 + d\rho^* \wedge \hat{\rho}^* = b\rho^*$	-	
2.j.1	HG	-	1	$\boxed{\nu^i_j}$	$\hat{\rho} = b\rho$	$\boxed{(d_1, d_2)}$	$\boxed{\mathbf{k}\cdot\boldsymbol{\mu}^i + [\mathrm{RF}_{j-1}(\nu^i\|_{j-1})]_1 + d_1\rho^i + d_2\hat{\rho}^i}$	$\boxed{\mathbf{k}\cdot\boldsymbol{\mu}^i + [\mathrm{RF}_{j-1}(\nu^i\|_{j-1})]_1 + d_1\rho^i + d_2\hat{\rho}^i}$	$\boxed{\gamma^* = \mathbf{k}\cdot\boldsymbol{\mu}^* + [k_0]_1 + d_1\rho^* + d_2\hat{\rho}^*} \wedge \hat{\rho}^* = b\rho^*$	-	IND-mCPA
2.j.2	HG	$\boxed{\beta}$	1	ν^i_j	$\hat{\rho} = b\rho$	(d_1, d_2)	$\mathbf{k}\cdot\boldsymbol{\mu}^i + [\mathrm{RF}_{j-1}(\nu^i\|_{j-1})]_1 + d_1\rho^i + d_2\hat{\rho}^i$	$\mathbf{k}\cdot\boldsymbol{\mu}^i + [\mathrm{RF}_{j-1}(\nu^i\|_{j-1})]_1 + d_1\rho^i + d_2\hat{\rho}^i$	$\gamma^* = \mathbf{k}\cdot\boldsymbol{\mu}^* + [k_0]_1 + d_1\rho^* + d_2\hat{\rho}^* \wedge \hat{\rho}^* = b\rho^*$	$\boxed{Dec(\zeta^*) = \beta}$	down by a factor of 2
2.j.3	BG	β	$\boxed{1-\beta}$	ν^i_j	$\hat{\rho} = b\rho$	(d_1, d_2)	$\mathbf{k}\cdot\boldsymbol{\mu}^i + [\mathrm{RF}_{j-1}(\nu^i\|_{j-1})]_1 + d_1\rho^i + d_2\hat{\rho}^i$	$\mathbf{k}\cdot\boldsymbol{\mu}^i + [\mathrm{RF}_{j-1}(\nu^i\|_{j-1})]_1 + d_1\rho^i + d_2\hat{\rho}^i$	$\gamma^* = \mathbf{k}\cdot\boldsymbol{\mu}^* + [k_0]_1 + d_1\rho^* + d_2\hat{\rho}^* \wedge \hat{\rho}^* = b\rho^*$	$Dec(\zeta^*) = \beta$	crsind
2.j.4	BG	β	$1-\beta$	ν^i_j	$\boxed{x = z}$	(d_1, d_2)	$\mathbf{k}\cdot\boldsymbol{\mu}^i + [\mathrm{RF}_{j-1}(\nu^i\|_{j-1})]_1 + d_1\rho^i + d_2\hat{\rho}^i$	$\mathbf{k}\cdot\boldsymbol{\mu}^i + [\mathrm{RF}_{j-1}(\nu^i\|_{j-1})]_1 + d_1\rho^i + d_2\hat{\rho}^i$	$\gamma^* = \mathbf{k}\cdot\boldsymbol{\mu}^* + [k_0]_1 + d_1\rho^* + d_2\hat{\rho}^* \wedge \boxed{}$	$Dec(\zeta^*) = \beta$	TSS
2.j.5	BG	β	$1-\beta$	ν^i_j	$x = z$	(d_1, d_2)	$\boxed{\mathbf{k}\cdot\boldsymbol{\mu}^i + [\mathrm{RF}'_{j-1}(\nu^i\|_{j-1})]_1 + d_1\rho^i + d_2\hat{\rho}^i}$	$\boxed{\mathbf{k}\cdot\boldsymbol{\mu}^i + [\mathrm{RF}_{j-1}(\nu^i\|_{j-1})]_1 + d_1\rho^i + d_2\hat{\rho}^i}$	$\gamma^* = \mathbf{k}\cdot\boldsymbol{\mu}^* + [k_0]_1 + d_1\rho^* + d_2\hat{\rho}^*$	$Dec(\zeta^*) = \beta$	Lemma 2
2.j.6	BG	β	$1-\beta$	ν^i_j	$\hat{\rho} = b\rho$	(d_1, d_2)	$\mathbf{k}\cdot\boldsymbol{\mu}^i + [\mathrm{RF}'_{j-1}(\nu^i\|_{j-1})]_1 + d_1\rho^i + d_2\hat{\rho}^i$	$\mathbf{k}\cdot\boldsymbol{\mu}^i + [\mathrm{RF}_{j-1}(\nu^i\|_{j-1})]_1 + d_1\rho^i + d_2\hat{\rho}^i$	$\gamma^* = \mathbf{k}\cdot\boldsymbol{\mu}^* + [k_0]_1 + d_1\rho^* + d_2\hat{\rho}^* \wedge \boxed{\hat{\rho}^* = b\rho^*}$	$Dec(\zeta^*) = \beta$	TSS
2.j.7	BG	β	$1-\beta$	ν^i_j	$\hat{\rho} = b\rho$	$\boxed{d}$	$\boxed{\mathbf{k}\cdot\boldsymbol{\mu}^i + [\mathrm{RF}_j(\nu^i\|_j)]_1 + d\rho^i)}$	$\boxed{\mathbf{k}\cdot\boldsymbol{\mu}^i + [\mathrm{RF}_j(\nu^i\|_j)]_1 + d\rho^i)}$	$\boxed{\gamma^* = \mathbf{k}\cdot\boldsymbol{\mu}^* + [k_0]_1 + d\rho^*} \wedge \hat{\rho}^* = b\rho^*$	$Dec(\zeta^*) = \beta$	stat.ind
2.j.8	$\boxed{\mathrm{HG}}$	β	$1-\beta$	ν^i_j	$\hat{\rho} = b\rho$	d	$\mathbf{k}\cdot\boldsymbol{\mu}^i + [\mathrm{RF}_j(\nu^i\|_j)]_1 + d\rho^i)$	$\mathbf{k}\cdot\boldsymbol{\mu}^i + [\mathrm{RF}_j(\nu^i\|_j)]_1 + d\rho^i)$	$\gamma^* = \mathbf{k}\cdot\boldsymbol{\mu}^* + [k_0]_1 + d\rho^* \wedge \hat{\rho}^* = b\rho^*$	$Dec(\zeta^*) = \beta$	crsind
2.j.9	HG	β	$1-\beta$	ν^i_j	$\hat{\rho} = b\rho$	d	$\mathbf{k}\cdot\boldsymbol{\mu}^i + [\mathrm{RF}_j(\nu^i\|_j)]_1 + d\rho^i)$	$\mathbf{k}\cdot\boldsymbol{\mu}^i + [\mathrm{RF}_j(\nu^i\|_j)]_1 + d\rho^i)$	$\gamma^* = \mathbf{k}\cdot\boldsymbol{\mu}^* + [k_0]_1 + d\rho^* \wedge \hat{\rho}^* = b\rho^*$	$\boxed{}$	up by a factor of 2
2.j.10	HG	β	$\boxed{1}$	$\boxed{0}$	$\hat{\rho} = b\rho$	d	$\mathbf{k}\cdot\boldsymbol{\mu}^i + [\mathrm{RF}_j(\nu^i\|_j)]_1 + d\rho^i)$	$\mathbf{k}\cdot\boldsymbol{\mu}^i + [\mathrm{RF}_j(\nu^i\|_j)]_1 + d\rho^i)$	$\gamma^* = \mathbf{k}\cdot\boldsymbol{\mu}^* + [k_0]_1 + d\rho^* \wedge \hat{\rho}^* = b\rho^*$		IND-mCPA

Fig. 5. Summary of the game transitions in Lemma 1.

#	crs	β	witness	If $\nu^i_j \neq \beta$: $\hat{\rho}^i$	If $\nu^i_j \neq \beta$: γ^i	If $\nu^i_j = \beta$: $\hat{\rho}^i$	If $\nu^i_j = \beta$: γ^i	forgery check	abort	reduction
2.j.4	BG	β	$x = z$	$b\rho^i$	$\mathbf{k}\cdot\boldsymbol{\mu}^i + [\mathrm{RF}_{j-1}(\nu^i\|_{j-1})]_1 + d_1\rho^i + d_2\hat{\rho}^i$	$b\rho^i$	$\mathbf{k}\cdot\boldsymbol{\mu}^i + [\mathrm{RF}_{j-1}(\nu^i\|_{j-1})]_1 + d_1\rho^i + d_2\hat{\rho}^i$	$\gamma^* = \mathbf{k}\cdot\boldsymbol{\mu}^* + [k_0]_1 + d_1\rho^* + d_2\hat{\rho}^*$	$Dec(\zeta^*) = \beta$	
$\mathbf{H_0}$	BG	β	$x = z$	$b\rho^i$	$\mathbf{k}\cdot\boldsymbol{\mu}^i + [RF_{j-1}(\nu^i\|_{j-1})]_1 + d_1\rho^i + d_2\hat{\rho}^i$	$b\rho^i$	$\mathbf{k}\cdot\boldsymbol{\mu}^i + [RF_{j-1}(\nu^i\|_{j-1})]_1 + d_1\rho^i + d_2\hat{\rho}^i$	$\gamma^* = \mathbf{k}\cdot\boldsymbol{\mu}^* + [k_0]_1 + d_1\rho^* + d_2\hat{\rho}^*$	$Dec(\zeta^*) = \beta$	
$\mathbf{H_1}$	$\underline{\mathrm{HG}}$	β	$x = z$	$\underline{b(\rho^i_1 + \rho^i_2)}$	$\mathbf{k}\cdot\boldsymbol{\mu}^i + [RF_{j-1}(\nu^i\|_{j-1})]_1 + \underline{(d_1 + d_2b)\rho^i_1 + (d_1 + d_2b)\rho^i_2}$	$b\rho^i$	$\mathbf{k}\cdot\boldsymbol{\mu}^i + [RF_{j-1}(\nu^i\|_{j-1})]_1 + d_1\rho^i + d_2\hat{\rho}^i$	$\gamma^* = \mathbf{k}\cdot\boldsymbol{\mu}^* + [k_0]_1 + d_1\rho^* + d_2\hat{\rho}^*$	$Dec(\zeta^*) = \beta$	crsind
$\mathbf{H_2}$	HG	β	$x = z$	$\underline{b\rho^i_1 + b'\rho^i_2}$	$\mathbf{k}\cdot\boldsymbol{\mu}^i + [RF_{j-1}(\nu^i\|_{j-1})]_1 + \underline{(d_1 + d_2b)\rho^i_1 + (d_1 + d_2b')\rho^i_2}$	$b\rho^i$	$\mathbf{k}\cdot\boldsymbol{\mu}^i + [RF_{j-1}(\nu^i\|_{j-1})]_1 + d_1\rho^i + d_2\hat{\rho}^i$	$\gamma^* = \mathbf{k}\cdot\boldsymbol{\mu}^* + [k_0]_1 + d_1\rho^* + d_2\hat{\rho}^*$	$Dec(\zeta^*) = \beta$	SXDH
$\mathbf{H_3}$	$\underline{\mathrm{BG}}$	β	$x = z$	$b\rho^i_1 + b'\rho^i_2$	$\mathbf{k}\cdot\boldsymbol{\mu}^i + [RF_{j-1}(\nu^i\|_{j-1})]_1 + (d_1 + d_2b)\rho^i_1 + (d_1 + d_2b')\rho^i_2$	$b\rho^i$	$\mathbf{k}\cdot\boldsymbol{\mu}^i + [RF_{j-1}(\nu^i\|_{j-1})]_1 + d_1\rho^i + d_2\hat{\rho}^i$	$\gamma^* = \mathbf{k}\cdot\boldsymbol{\mu}^* + [k_0]_1 + d_1\rho^* + d_2\hat{\rho}^* \wedge \underline{\hat{\rho}^* = b\rho^*}$	$Dec(\zeta^*) = \beta$	crsind, TSS
$\mathbf{H_4}$	BG	β	$x = z$	$b\rho^i_1 + b'\rho^i_2$	$\mathbf{k}\cdot\boldsymbol{\mu}^i + [RF_{j-1}(\nu^i\|_{j-1})]_1 + \underline{d\rho^i_1 + d'\rho^i_2}$	$b\rho^i$	$\mathbf{k}\cdot\boldsymbol{\mu}^i + [RF_{j-1}(\nu^i\|_{j-1})]_1 + \underline{d\rho^i}$	$\underline{\gamma^* = \mathbf{k}\cdot\boldsymbol{\mu}^* + [k_0]_1 + d\rho^*} \wedge \hat{\rho}^* = b\rho^*$	$Dec(\zeta^*) = \beta$	stat.ind
$\mathbf{H_5}$	BG	β	$x = z$	$b\rho^i_1 + b'\rho^i_2$	$\mathbf{k}\cdot\boldsymbol{\mu}^i + [RF_{j-1}(\nu^i\|_{j-1})]_1 + d\rho^i_1 + d'\rho^i_2$	$b\rho^i$	$\mathbf{k}\cdot\boldsymbol{\mu}^i + [RF_{j-1}(\nu^i\|_{j-1})]_1 + d\rho^i$	$\gamma^* = \mathbf{k}\cdot\boldsymbol{\mu}^* + [k_0]_1 + d\rho^* \wedge$ ______	$Dec(\zeta^*) = \beta$	TSS
$\mathbf{H_6}$	$\underline{\mathrm{HG}}$	β	$x = z$	$b\rho^i_1 + b'\rho^i_2$	$\mathbf{k}\cdot\boldsymbol{\mu}^i + [RF_{j-1}(\nu^i\|_{j-1})]_1 + d\rho^i_1 + d'\rho^i_2$	$b\rho^i$	$\mathbf{k}\cdot\boldsymbol{\mu}^i + [RF_{j-1}(\nu^i\|_{j-1})]_1 + d\rho^i$	$\gamma^* = \mathbf{k}\cdot\boldsymbol{\mu}^* + [k_0]_1 + d\rho^*$	$Dec(\zeta^*) = \beta$	crsind
$\mathbf{H_7}$	HG	β	$x = z$	$b\rho^i_1 + \underline{b\rho^i_2}$	$\mathbf{k}\cdot\boldsymbol{\mu}^i + [RF_{j-1}(\nu^i\|_{j-1})]_1 + d\rho^i_1 + d'\rho^i_2$	$b\rho^i$	$\mathbf{k}\cdot\boldsymbol{\mu}^i + [RF_{j-1}(\nu^i\|_{j-1})]_1 + d\rho^i$	$\gamma^* = \mathbf{k}\cdot\boldsymbol{\mu}^* + [k_0]_1 + d\rho^*$	$Dec(\zeta^*) = \beta$	SXDH
$\mathbf{H_8}$	HG	β	$x = z$	$b\rho^i_1 + b\rho^i_2$	$\mathbf{k}\cdot\boldsymbol{\mu}^i + \underline{[RF'_{j-1}(\nu^i\|_{j-1})]_1} + d\rho^i_1 + d'\rho^i_2$	$b\rho^i$	$\mathbf{k}\cdot\boldsymbol{\mu}^i + [RF_{j-1}(\nu^i\|_{j-1})]_1 + d\rho^i$	$\gamma^* = \mathbf{k}\cdot\boldsymbol{\mu}^* + [k_0]_1 + d\rho^*$	$Dec(\zeta^*) = \beta$	stat.ind
$\mathbf{H_9}$	HG	β	$x = z$	$b\rho^i_1 + \underline{b'\rho^i_2}$	$\mathbf{k}\cdot\boldsymbol{\mu}^i + [RF'_{j-1}(\nu^i\|_{j-1})]_1 + d\rho^i_1 + d'\rho^i_2$	$b\rho^i$	$\mathbf{k}\cdot\boldsymbol{\mu}^i + [RF_{j-1}(\nu^i\|_{j-1})]_1 + d\rho^i$	$\gamma^* = \mathbf{k}\cdot\boldsymbol{\mu}^* + [k_0]_1 + d\rho^*$	$Dec(\zeta^*) = \beta$	SXDH
$\mathbf{H_{10}}$	$\underline{\mathrm{BG}}$	β	$x = z$	$b\rho^i_1 + b'\rho^i_2$	$\mathbf{k}\cdot\boldsymbol{\mu}^i + [RF'_{j-1}(\nu^i\|_{j-1})]_1 + d\rho^i_1 + d'\rho^i_2$	$b\rho^i$	$\mathbf{k}\cdot\boldsymbol{\mu}^i + [RF_{j-1}(\nu^i\|_{j-1})]_1 + d\rho^i$	$\gamma^* = \mathbf{k}\cdot\boldsymbol{\mu}^* + [k_0]_1 + d\rho^* \wedge \underline{\hat{\rho}^* = b\rho^*}$	$Dec(\zeta^*) = \beta$	crsind, TSS
$\mathbf{H_{11}}$	BG	β	$x = z$	$b\rho^i_1 + b'\rho^i_2$	$\mathbf{k}\cdot\boldsymbol{\mu}^i + [RF'_{j-1}(\nu^i\|_{j-1})]_1 + \underline{(d_1 + d_2b)\rho^i_1 + (d_1 + d_2b')\rho^i_2}$	$b\rho^i$	$\mathbf{k}\cdot\boldsymbol{\mu}^i + [RF_{j-1}(\nu^i\|_{j-1})]_1 + \underline{d_1\rho^i + d_2\hat{\rho}^i}$	$\underline{\gamma^* = \mathbf{k}\cdot\boldsymbol{\mu}^* + [k_0]_1 + d_1\rho^* + d_2\hat{\rho}^*} \wedge \hat{\rho}^* = b\rho^*$	$Dec(\zeta^*) = \beta$	stat.ind
$\mathbf{H_{12}}$	BG	β	$x = z$	$b\rho^i_1 + b'\rho^i_2$	$\mathbf{k}\cdot\boldsymbol{\mu}^i + [RF'_{j-1}(\nu^i\|_{j-1})]_1 + (d_1 + d_2b)\rho^i_1 + (d_1 + d_2b')\rho^i_2$	$b\rho^i$	$\mathbf{k}\cdot\boldsymbol{\mu}^i + [RF_{j-1}(\nu^i\|_{j-1})]_1 + d_1\rho^i + d_2\hat{\rho}^i$	$\gamma^* = \mathbf{k}\cdot\boldsymbol{\mu}^* + [k_0]_1 + d_1\rho^* + d_2\hat{\rho}^* \wedge$ ______	$Dec(\zeta^*) = \beta$	TSS
$\mathbf{H_{13}}$	BG	β	$x = z$	$\underline{b(\rho^i_1 + \rho^i_2)}$	$\mathbf{k}\cdot\boldsymbol{\mu}^i + [RF'_{j-1}(\nu^i\|_{j-1})]_1 + (d_1 + d_2b)\rho^i_1 + \underline{(d_1 + d_2b)\rho^i_2}$	$b\rho^i$	$\mathbf{k}\cdot\boldsymbol{\mu}^i + [RF_{j-1}(\nu^i\|_{j-1})]_1 + d_1\rho^i + d_2\hat{\rho}^i$	$\gamma^* = \mathbf{k}\cdot\boldsymbol{\mu}^* + [k_0]_1 + d_1\rho^* + d_2\hat{\rho}^*$	$Dec(\zeta^*) = \beta$	SXDH
$\mathbf{H_{14}}$	BG	β	$x = z$	$\underline{b\rho^i_1}$	$\mathbf{k}\cdot\boldsymbol{\mu}^i + [RF'_{j-1}(\nu^i\|_{j-1})]_1 + \underline{d_1\rho^i + d_2\hat{\rho}^i}$	$b\rho^i$	$\mathbf{k}\cdot\boldsymbol{\mu}^i + [RF_{j-1}(\nu^i\|_{j-1})]_1 + d_1\rho^i + d_2\hat{\rho}^i$	$\gamma^* = \mathbf{k}\cdot\boldsymbol{\mu}^* + [k_0]_1 + d_1\rho^* + d_2\hat{\rho}^*$	$Dec(\zeta^*) = \beta$	WI
2.j.5	BG	β	$x = z$	$b\rho^i_1$	$\mathbf{k}\cdot\boldsymbol{\mu}^i + [RF'_{j-1}(\nu^i\|_{j-1})]_1 + d_1\rho^i + d_2\hat{\rho}^i$	$b\rho^i$	$\mathbf{k}\cdot\boldsymbol{\mu}^i + [RF_{j-1}(\nu^i\|_{j-1})]_1 + d_1\rho^i + d_2\hat{\rho}^i$	$\gamma^* = \mathbf{k}\cdot\boldsymbol{\mu}^* + [k_0]_1 + d_1\rho^* + d_2\hat{\rho}^*$	$Dec(\zeta^*) = \beta$	

Fig. 6. Summary of the game transitions in Lemma 2.

To this end, for each Adversary $\mathcal{A}$ playing against the challenger in games $\mathbf{H_1}$ and $\mathbf{H_2}$, we will build another adversary $\mathcal{B}$ that plays against the SXDH challenge. Say, the adversary $\mathcal{B}$ receives an SXDH challenge $(\mathbf{g}, \mathbf{x}, \mathbf{y}, \mathbf{w})$, all elements in $\mathbb{G}_1$, where either $\mathbf{w}$ is a real DDH element, i.e., $\mathbf{w} = (\log_\mathbf{g} \mathbf{x})(\log_\mathbf{g} \mathbf{y})\mathbf{g}$ or $\mathbf{w}$ is a fake DDH element, i.e., is random and independent of the other three elements.

Adversary $\mathcal{B}$ next emulates the challenger $\mathcal{C}$ against $\mathcal{A}$ as follows. It starts emulating $\mathcal{C}$ by letting the first element of the challenge being the group generator for $\mathbb{G}_1$. Next, it emulates rest of $\mathcal{C}$ perfectly, except for queries i where ν_j^i is not equal to β. In this case, it picks r_1^i and r_2^i at random, and sets $\rho^i = r_1^i \mathbf{g} + r_2^i \mathbf{x}$. It sets $\hat{\rho}^i = r_1^i \mathbf{y} + r_2^i \mathbf{w}$. It does not need to set s^i and t^i, as these quantities are only needed in GS commitments and proof, but in game $\mathbf{H_1}$ we switched to all zero witnesses. The quantity γ^i is also generated using the just defined ρ^i and $\hat{\rho}^i$ (as well as d_1 and d_2). Also, the CRS of the QA-NIZK Π_1 which includes b in its language parameter, can also be simulated using the group element $\mathbf{x}$ only.

Now, it is easy to check that if the SXDH challenge was real, then $\mathcal{B}$ emulated game $\mathbf{H_1}$ to $\mathcal{A}$, and if the SXDH challenge was fake, then $\mathcal{B}$ emulated $\mathbf{H_2}$ to $\mathcal{A}$. This proves the claim above.

Game $\mathbf{H_3}$: In this game, the Challenger goes back to generating the GS-NIWI CRS as crs, i.e., using the binding CRS generator. It also generates all GS-commitments and proofs using real witnesses, i.e., s^i, t^i, z^i and x. it also re-introduces the conjunct $\hat{\rho}^* == b\rho^*$ in the winning condition.

We now show that the adversary's advantage in winning in $\mathbf{H_3}$ is different from its advantage in winning in game $\mathbf{H_2}$ by

$$\text{ADV}_{\Pi_1}^{\text{TSS}} + \text{ADV}_{\Pi_2}^{\text{TSS}} + \text{ADV}_{\Pi}^{\text{CRSIND}}.$$

We first prove that the real witnesses, i.e., s^i, t^i, z^i and x satisfy the equation $(s - t)(z - x) == 0$. Indeed, if $z_j^i = \nu_j^i$ is equal to $\beta = 1 - x$, i.e., $z_j^i \neq x$, then the challenger generated $s^i = t^i$, thus the quadratic equation holds. On the other hand, $z_j^i = x$, in which case also the quadratic equation holds. Thus, by witness-indistinguishability, the adversary's advantage in distinguishing between the two games is at most $\text{ADV}_{\Pi}^{\text{CRSIND}}$.

Next, we prove that the other conjuncts in the winning condition already imply $\hat{\rho}^* == b\rho^*$. To ascertain this, we must first check that the QA-NIZK Π_1 and Π_2 are in true-simulation mode. For cases such that ν_j^i is equal to β, this is true as $t^i = s^i$. In the other cases, note that challenger sets $\hat{\rho}^i = b[r_1^i]_1 + b'[r_2^i]_1 = [s^i]_1$. Also $t^i = b(r^i)$, where $r^i = r_1^i + r_2^i$, and $\rho^i = [r^i]_1$. Thus, the two QA-NIZK are indeed in true-simulation mode. Then, by the true-simulation soundness of these two, and the perfect soundness of the Groth-Sahai NIWI it follows that $\hat{\rho}^* == b\rho^*$ is implied by the other conjuncts in the winning condition: since $\text{dec}(\zeta^*) \neq x$ holds by true-simulation soundness of Π_2, $z^* \neq x$ also holds. This implies by soundness of the NIWI that $s^* = t^*$. Next, by true-simulation soundness of Π_1, $\hat{\rho}^* = b\rho^*$. This completes the proof of the claim.

Game $\mathbf{H_4}$: In this game, instead of pikcing d_1 and d_2 at random, the challenger picks d, d' uniformly and randomly. Note d, d' are independent of b and b'.

The challenger changes the γ^*-test conjunct in the winning condition by replacing $d_1\rho^* + d_2\hat{\rho}^*$ by $d\rho^*$. Further, in each signature query output it modifies the computation of γ^i as follows: if $\nu_j^i == \beta$ then $d_1\rho^i + d_2\hat{\rho}^i$ is replaced by $d\rho^i$. Otherwise, it replaces $(d_1 + d_2 b)\rho_1^i + (d_1 + d_2 b')\rho_2^i$ by $(d)\rho_1^i + (d')\rho_2^i$, where $\rho_1^i = [r_1^i]_1$ and $\rho_2^i = [r_2^i]_1$.

First note that since $\hat{\rho}^* = b\rho^*$ is a conjunct in the winning condition, replacing $d_1\rho^* + d_2\hat{\rho}^*$ by $d\rho^*$ is equivalent if $d_1 + bd_2$ is replaced by d. It is easy to see (by pairwise independence) that the adversary's view in the two games $\mathbf{H_3}$ and $\mathbf{H_4}$ is statistically indistinguishable, except if $b = b'$ which happens with probability at most $1/q$.

Game $\mathbf{H_5}$: In this game the challenger again removes the conjunct $\hat{\rho}^* = b\rho^*$ from the winning condition.

We again, first check that the QA-NIZK Π_1 and Π_2 are in true-simulation mode. This is indeed the case, as the only change from game $\mathbf{H_3}$ to $\mathbf{H_4}$ was in γ^i computation which is not used in Π_1 and Π_2. Then by the same argument as given in $\mathbf{H_3}$ indistinguishability from $\mathbf{H_2}$, the adversary's advantage is different from advantage in game $\mathbf{H_4}$ by at most $\mathrm{ADV}_{\Pi_1}^{\mathrm{TSS}} + \mathrm{ADV}_{\Pi_2}^{\mathrm{TSS}}$.

Game $\mathbf{H_6}$: In this game the challenger again generates the GS-NIWI CRS as simcrs, i.e., using the hinding CRS generator. Further, all GS commitments and proofs use the all zero witnesses.

The adversary's advantage in game $\mathbf{H_6}$ is different from its advantage in $\mathbf{H_5}$ by at most $\mathrm{ADV}_{\Pi}^{\mathrm{CRSIND}}$.

Game $\mathbf{H_7}$: In this game, the adversary need not pick b'. Next, for each query i, if ν_j^i is not equal to β, then the challenger picks r_1^i and r_2^i at random, and sets $\rho^i = [r_1^i + r_2^i]_1$. It sets $s^i = t^i = b(r_1^i + r_2^i)$, Note s^i and t^i are not used in the GS commitments or proof. It sets $\hat{\rho}^i = b[r_1^i]_1 + b[r_2^i]_1$. There is no change in the generation of γ^i as it uses d and d'.

By a reduction argument similar to that given for games $\mathbf{H_1}$ and $\mathbf{H_2}$, the adversary's advantage in distinguishing between $\mathbf{H_6}$ and $\mathbf{H_7}$ is at most $\mathrm{ADV}_{\mathrm{SXDH}}$.

Game $\mathbf{H_8}$: In this game the Challenger lazily defines another random and independent function RF'_{j-1} from $(j-1)$-bit strings to $\mathbb{Z}_q$. Then, for all i such that ν_j^i is not equal to β, it replaces in the computation of γ^i, the function RF_{j-1} by RF'_{j-1}.

Since in each query i, r_1^i and r_2^i are chosen afresh randomly and independently, and since all other terms (i.e., other that γ^i) use one linear combination of r_1^i and r_2^i, namely $r_1^i + r_2^i$, and γ^i uses a different linear combination, namely $dr_1^i + d'r_2^i$, then conditioned on $d \neq d'$, the transcripts in games $\mathbf{H_7}$ and $\mathbf{H_8}$ are statistically identical. The probability of $d = d'$ is just $1/q$, and hence that is the statistical distance between the distributions of the transcripts in $\mathbf{H_7}$ and $\mathbf{H_8}$. Thus, this is also an upper bound on the difference in adversary's advantage in the two games.

Game $\mathbf{H_9}$: In this game, the adversary also picks a b' randomly and independently from $\mathbb{Z}_q$. Next, for each query i, if ν_j^i is not equal to β, then the challenger picks r_1^i and r_2^i at random, and sets $\rho^i = [r_1^i + r_2^i]_1$. It sets $s^i = br_1^i + b'r_2^i$, $t^i = b(r_1^i + r_2^i)$. Note s^i and t^i are not used in the GS commitments or proof. It sets $\hat{\rho}^i = b[r_1^i]_1 + b'[r_2^i]_1$. There is no change in generation of γ^i (see Fig. 4).

Again, by a similar reduction argument to SXDH assumption, the difference in adversary's advantage in games $\mathbf{H_9}$ and $\mathbf{H_8}$ is at most ADV_{SXDH}.

Game $\mathbf{H_{10}}$: In this game, the challenger generates the GS-NIWI CRS as crs, i.e., using the binding CRS generator. It also uses the real witnesses, i.e. s^i, t^i, x and z^i in generating the GS commitments and proof. In this game, the challenger also re-introduces the conjunct $\hat{\rho}^* == b\rho^*$.

First note that the witnesses s^i, t^i, z^i, x do satisfy the quadratic equation for all queries i, by an argument similiar to that given for games $\mathbf{H_3}$ and $\mathbf{H_2}$. Then by repeating the argument there, we also conclude that $\hat{\rho}^* == b\rho^*$ is implied by other conjuncts. Thus, the difference in adversary's advantage is at most

$$\text{ADV}_{\Pi_1}^{\text{TSS}} + \text{ADV}_{\Pi_2}^{\text{TSS}} + \text{ADV}_{\Pi}^{\text{CRSIND}}.$$

Game $\mathbf{H_{11}}$: In this game, the challenger picks d_1, d_2 randomly and independently (instead of picking d, d') and setting $d = d_1 + bd_2$ and $d' = d_1 + b'd_2$. The challenger also changes the γ^*-test in the winning condition by replacing $d\rho^*$ by $d_1\rho^* + d_2\hat{\rho}^*$. Further, similar changes are made in the computation of γ^i (see Fig. 4).

With the conjunct $\hat{\rho}^* == b\rho^*$ in place in the winning condition, the new winning condition is equivalent to the previous winning condition. Moreover, conditioned on $b \neq b'$, the distribution of d and d' remains same as in game $\mathbf{H_{10}}$. Thus, the difference in adversary's advantage is at most $1/q$.

Game $\mathbf{H_{12}}$: In this game, the challenger drops the conjunct $\hat{\rho}^* == b\rho^*$ from the winning condition.

Again, by arguments similar to that given for games $\mathbf{H_2}$ and $\mathbf{H_3}$ the difference in adversary's advantage is at most $\text{ADV}_{\Pi_1}^{\text{TSS}} + \text{ADV}_{\Pi_2}^{\text{TSS}}$.

Game $\mathbf{H_{13}}$: In this game the challenger does not pick b'. The challenger picks r_1^i and r_2^i at random, and sets $\rho^i = [r_1^i + r_2^i]_1$. Similarly, it sets $s^i = t^i = b(r_1^i + r_2^i)$, and thus $\hat{\rho}^i = b[r_1^i + r_2^i]_1$ and a similar change in generation of γ^i (see Fig. 4).

This is essentially the rewind of going from game $\mathbf{H_1}$ to $\mathbf{H_2}$. Hence, by a similar argument, the difference in adversary's advantage in games $\mathbf{H_{13}}$ and $\mathbf{H_{12}}$ is at most ADV_{SXDH}.

Game $\mathbf{H_{14}}$: In this game, even for i such that ν_j^i is not equal to β, the challenger just picks r^i, and defines $\rho^i = [r^i]_1$, $s^i = t^i = br^i$, and $\hat{\rho}^i = [s^i]_1$.

There is no statistical difference in the two games $\mathbf{H_{14}}$ and $\mathbf{H_{13}}$. Now, note that game $\mathbf{H_{14}}$ is identical to game $\mathbf{G_{2,j,5}}$. This completes the proof.

5   Extensions and Optimizations

We begin this section by extending our construction to messages with elements in both groups. We then describe an optimization which reduces one group element from the ElGamal encryption of z. Next, we describe another optimization that moves some of the QA-NIZK proofs to Groth-Sahai proofs. While this may lead to slightly larger signature sizes, it reduces the size of the public-key and consequently may benefit in batching the various pairings in the verification step.

5.1   Bilateral Message Vectors

We use the same technique employed by [AHN+17] to extend our SPS to sign bilateral messages, i.e., messages (μ_1, μ_2) in $\mathbb{G}_1^{n_1} \times \mathbb{G}_2^{n_2}$. Essentially, we sign μ_2 using a Partial One-Time signature scheme (POS) [BS07] of Abe et al. [ACD+16] which has a one-time public key opk consisting of one element of $\mathbb{G}_1$ and one-time signature $osig$ consisting of 2 elements of $\mathbb{G}_2$. The public key opk is appended to the message vector μ_1 making it $(n_1 + 1)$-elements long. Then SPS_{SXDH} is used to sign the extended $\mathbb{G}_1$ vector. The final signature consists of $(opk, osig)$ and the SPS_{SXDH} signature. Thus the signature has 1 $\mathbb{G}_1$ and 2 $\mathbb{G}_2$ additional elements. The public key is extended by $(n_2 + 1)$ $\mathbb{G}_1$ elements and 1 $\mathbb{G}_2$ element due to the POS public key and an additional SPS_{SXDH} public key for the extra dimension in $\mathbb{G}_1$.

5.2   Double Groth-Sahai Commitments to Replace ElGamal

In the SPS scheme described in Fig. 1, the signer needs to provide an ElGamal encryption ζ of z, as well as a Groth-Sahai (binding) commitment c_z to z (both in $\mathbb{G}_2$). Under the SXDH assumption, this requires a total of four group elements. Note, the encryption of z just needs to be IND-mCPA secure, and not CCA-secure.

While in the proof of security in Sect. 4, the challenger *does* need to decrypt ζ^* in some hybrid games (namely, games $(2, j, 2\text{–}8)$), it is the case that the security proof *does not* need to employ IND-mCPA security in those hybrid games (which is only needed in games $(2, j, 0\text{–}1)$ and $(2, j, 9\text{–}10)$).

So, it is worthwhile investigating if a double Groth-Sahai commitment which shares randomness might achieve the same IND-mCPA goal: the decryption to be performed using a trapdoor for the second commitment, which will not be used in NIWI proofs. At this point, we briefly describe Groth-Sahai commitments (under SXDH assumption).

Let $\mathbf{g}$ be a generator of group $\mathbb{G}_2$ (a cyclic group of order q, with identity $\mathcal{O}$). The commitment public-key pk is of the form

$$u_1 = (\mathbf{g}, Q = \chi\mathbf{g}), u_2 = (\mathcal{U}, \mathcal{V}).$$

where χ is chosen at random from $\mathbb{Z}_q^*$. Note both u_1 and u_2 are in $\mathbb{G}_2^2$ which is a $\mathbb{Z}_q$-module. The second element u_2 can be chosen in two different ways: $u_2 = \psi u_1$ or $u_2 = \psi u_1 + (\mathcal{O}, \mathbf{g})$. The former choice of u_2 gives a perfectly hiding commitment key, whereas the latter choice of u_2 gives a perfectly binding commitment key (as we will see), and the two choices are indistinguishable under the DDH assumption in $\mathbb{G}_2$.

Commitments $\text{com}(pk, x; r_x)$ to $x \in \mathbb{Z}_q$ using randomness $r_x \in \mathbb{Z}_q$ work as follows:

$$\text{com} = (r_x, x) \cdot (u_1, u_2),$$

where the latter "·" is an inner product.

On a hiding key pk, we have $u_2 = \psi u_1$ and hence u is in the span of $\langle u_1 \rangle$, consequently, we get a perfectly hiding commitment. On a binding key pk, the commitment just becomes an El-Gamal encryption of $x\mathbf{g}$ with randomness $r_x + x\psi$, with secret key χ.

While so far we have described the standard Groth-Sahai commitments, we now describe the alternate double Groth-Sahai commitment. In the double commitment, the public key is expanded to have $u_1' = \chi' u_1$, where χ' is a random and independent value from $\mathbb{Z}_q$. The value u_2' is again defined in terms of u_1' but using the same factor ψ as used for u_2. Thus, $u_2' = \psi u_1$ (hiding) or $u_2' = \psi u_1 + (\mathcal{O}, \mathbf{g})$ (binding).

Now double commitments $\text{dcom}(pk, x; r_x)$ is just $\langle c = (r_x, x) \cdot (u_1, u_2), c' = (r_x, x) \cdot (u_1', u_2') \rangle$.

On a hiding key pk, we have that four-vector $(u_2; u_2')$ is in span of four-vector (u_1, u_1') (being a ψ-multiple). And hence dcom is a hiding commitment of x. In the binding setting, both commitments are ElGamal encryptions of x, first with secret key χ and the second with secret key χ' (with common randomness $(r_x + x\psi)$.

We also have the freedom to make one of the first public key hiding and the second binding. However, the double commitment is not hiding in this mixed case. But, if there are other values that are only committed using the first public key (i.e. do not use double commitment) then those commitments are still hiding. Thus, e.g. in the SPS scheme, both x and z^i are committed in the group $\mathbb{G}_2$. Now, for each z^i we will use double commitment, whereas for x we will only commit using (u_1, u_2). If this latter is in hiding mode and (u_1', u_2') is in binding mode, then c_x is a hiding commitment, and c_z for all i is not hiding. Moreover, if (x, z) and (x', z) are both witnesses for ρ satisfying a witness-relation R, then the commitments (in this mixed mode) and the proofs are still witness indistinguishable. This is easily seen (under SXDH assumption) because for each commitment there is a unique proof satisfying the verification Equation [GS12].

Coming back to the SPS scheme of Fig. 1, we first replace the ElGamal encryption ζ of z by a double commitment of z using the above expanded public key in $\mathbb{G}_2$. Note, only x and z are GS-committed in $\mathbb{G}_2$. Next, the QA-NIZK Π_2 now has the language

$$L_2 \overset{\text{def}}{=} \left\{ \begin{array}{l} (c_z, c_z') \mid \exists(z, r_z) : c_z = \text{com}_2(z; r_z) \text{ and} \\ c_z' = \langle r_z \mathbf{g} + z[\psi]_2, \ r_z(\chi' \mathbf{g}) + z((\chi'\psi + 1)\mathbf{g}) \rangle \end{array} \right\}$$

Note $(\mathbf{g}, \psi\mathbf{g}, \chi'\mathbf{g}, (\chi'\psi + 1)\mathbf{g})$ are public parameters, and the above language is thus a linear-subspace language, and a single group element QA-NIZK proof can be given.

Next, note that decryption of ζ^* which is required in games $(2, j, 2\text{--}8)$ can be performed using secret key χ'. The property that this is a good decryption of ζ^* holds only if the QA-NIZK $\varPi_2$ is sound and the double commitment is in binding mode; this in turn requires that $\varPi_2$ be in true-simulation mode. This property is only required in games $(2, j, 4\text{--}6)$, so the double commitments must be in binding mode in these games. The only games where the challenger needs to hide z and/or x lie outside these games. However, there are games where z is being decrypted using χ', and yet we need to transition between hiding and binding modes in $\mathbb{G}_2$. In particular, in games $(2, j, 1\text{--}3)$ and similarly in games $(2, j, 8\text{--}10)$. So instead, now consider an intermediate game between $(2, j, 1)$ and $(2, j, 2)$ where the commitment pk for $\mathbb{G}_2$ is moved to being mixed, i.e. binding for χ' and hiding for χ. In this, the adversary's advantage changes by at most $\mathrm{ADV}_{\varPi}^{\mathrm{CRSIND}}$. Next, in game $(2, j, 2)$, the challenger introduces decryption using χ'. In game $(2, j, 3)$ the challenger moves the first public key of the double commitment also to binding mode (after setting $x = 1 - \beta$). This incurs another penalty of $\mathrm{ADV}_{\varPi}^{\mathrm{CRSIND}}$. Hence forth, till game $(2, j, 8)$ the double commitment remains binding. The argument is reversed in games $(2, j, 8\text{--}10)$.

While this only saves one group element from the SPS scheme, it is worth recalling that savings can multiply in applications requiring SPS.

5.3   Mixing Groth-Sahai and QA-NIZK Proofs

While the scheme in Fig. 1 is optimized for the size of the signature, its public key can be larger because of the use of QA-NIZK. In this section, we note that some of the QA-NIZK (or parts) can be replaced by Groth-Sahai NIZK proofs without much increase in size of the signatures.

The QA-NIZK $\varPi_2$ can easily be replaced to be a GS NIZK which just checks the multi-scalar equation that $\zeta = (\zeta_a, \zeta_b)$ satisfy $z\mathbf{g}_2 + ske\ \zeta_a - \zeta_b = 0$, where z is committed in c_z and commitment of El-Gamal secret-key ske is in the public-key of SPS. The GS proof of this multi-scalar equation is only one group element (see e.g. Eq. (22) in [AHN+17]).

Next, the QA-NIZK $\varPi_1$ can be split into two parts, (i) one proving that ρ and c_t are related, which should remain a QA-NIZK –as this can be costly as a GS proof, and (ii) the other proving the $\hat{\rho}$ is $[s]_1$, which is just one group element as a GS proof. The QA-NIZK $\varPi_3$ remains as it is since true-simulation soundness is required.

So, this scheme requires an extra group element in the proof as $\varPi_1$ has been split. However, this scheme cannot use the optimization of Sect. 5.2. As for the proof of Theorem 1, note that the proof just employed the GS NIWI property, whereas now we must use the GS NIZK property, for proving $\hat{\rho} = [s]_1$. Fortunately, for such equations it is quite straightforward to convert Groth-Sahai NIWI to NIZK (for more details see [GS12]).

5.4   Sharing Groth-Sahai and QA-NIZK Public-Key Components

Note that the Groth-Sahai CRS (for each group) consists of four group elements (under the SXDH assumption), these being $u_1 = (\mathbf{g}, Q = \chi\mathbf{g})$, and $u_2 = (\mathcal{U}, \mathcal{V})$ as described above in Sect. 5.2.

The verifier CRS size of a QA-NIZK depends on the language (i.e. the number of its defining parameters), but some components of the CRS can be general group parameters and can be shared with GS CRS. From [JR14] recall that in a QA-NIZK for language with parameters $\mathbf{A}$ the prover and verifier CRS, i.e. $\mathbf{CRS}_p$ and $\mathbf{CRS}_v$ are defined as

$$\mathbf{CRS}_p := \mathbf{A} \cdot \begin{bmatrix} \mathsf{D} \\ \mathsf{R} \end{bmatrix} \qquad \mathbf{CRS}_v = \begin{bmatrix} \mathsf{D\ B} \\ \mathsf{R\ B} \\ -\mathsf{B} \end{bmatrix} \cdot \mathsf{g}$$

where B is a $k \times k$ matrix in the k-lin setting, and D and R are simulation trapdoors. Since SXDH is the k-lin setting with $k = 1$, B is just a single element. Moreover, this B matrix can be shared among all the QA-NIZK (in the same group). In fact, it can also be made the same as one component of the GS CRS, namely $\mathcal{U} = \psi\mathsf{g}$.

5.5   Batching Pairings in Pairing-Product-Equations

We first analyze the size of the public key in the scheme of Fig. 1, especially considering the sharing mentioned in Sect. 5.4. Now the 2 Groth-Sahai CRSes are of total size $(4, 4)$, including group generators and $\mathcal{U}$ that can be shared for QA-NIZK. The QA-NIZK Π_1 verifier CRS is then of size $(0, 6)$. The QA-NIZK Π_2 verifier CRS is of size $(4, 0)$ (or, $(3, 0)$ considering the optimization in Sect. 5.2). The QA-NIZK Π_3 verifier CRS is of size $(0, n_1 + 4)$. Since the commitment to x is of size $(0, 2)$, the public key is of size $(8, n_1 + 16)$ (or $(7, n_1 + 16)$ with optimization).

As for batch-verification, the number of pairing computations for verification can be reduced to pairing with $\mathbf{g}_1, \mathbf{g}_2, \mathcal{U}_1, \mathcal{U}_2, c_x, c_z$, and the elements in the QA-NIZK verification CRSes (other than those shared with GS CRS), which amounts to a total of $(8 + 14 + n_1 + 1) = n_1 + 23$ pairings.

If we use the scheme of Sect. 5.3 then the number of pairings reduce to $(8 + 7 + n_1 + 1) = n_1 + 16$ pairings (where one of these pairings is a constant pairing from the affine split-CRS QA-NIZK).

References

[ACD+12] Abe, M., Chase, M., David, B., Kohlweiss, M., Nishimaki, R., Ohkubo, M.: Constant-size structure-preserving signatures: generic constructions and simple assumptions. In: Wang, X., Sako, K. (eds.) ASIACRYPT 2012. LNCS, vol. 7658, pp. 4–24. Springer, Heidelberg (2012). https://doi.org/10.1007/978-3-642-34961-4_3

[ACD+16] Abe, M., Chase, M., David, B., Kohlweiss, M., Nishimaki, R., Ohkubo, M.: Constant-size structure-preserving signatures: generic constructions and simple assumptions. J. Cryptol. **29**(4), 833–878 (2016)

[ACHO11] Abe, M., Chow, S.S.M., Haralambiev, K., Ohkubo, M.: Double-trapdoor anonymous tags for traceable signatures. In: Lopez, J., Tsudik, G. (eds.) ACNS 2011. LNCS, vol. 6715, pp. 183–200. Springer, Heidelberg (2011). https://doi.org/10.1007/978-3-642-21554-4_11

[AFG+10] Abe, M., Fuchsbauer, G., Groth, J., Haralambiev, K., Ohkubo, M.:
Structure-preserving signatures and commitments to group elements. In:
Rabin, T. (ed.) CRYPTO 2010. LNCS, vol. 6223, pp. 209–236. Springer,
Heidelberg (2010). https://doi.org/10.1007/978-3-642-14623-7_12

[AHN+17] Abe, M., Hofheinz, D., Nishimaki, R., Ohkubo, M., Pan, J.: Compact
structure-preserving signatures with almost tight security. In: Katz, J.,
Shacham, H. (eds.) CRYPTO 2017. LNCS, vol. 10402, pp. 548–580.
Springer, Cham (2017). https://doi.org/10.1007/978-3-319-63715-0_19

[AHO10] Abe, M., Haralambiev, K., Ohkubo, M.: Signing on elements in bilinear groups for modular protocol design. IACR Cryptology ePrint Archive
2010:133 (2010)

[AHY15] Attrapadung, N., Hanaoka, G., Yamada, S.: A framework for identity-
based encryption with almost tight security. In: Iwata, T., Cheon, J.H.
(eds.) ASIACRYPT 2015, Part I. LNCS, vol. 9452, pp. 521–549. Springer,
Heidelberg (2015). https://doi.org/10.1007/978-3-662-48797-6_22

[AO09] Abe, M., Ohkubo, M.: A framework for universally composable non-
committing blind signatures. In: Matsui, M. (ed.) ASIACRYPT 2009.
LNCS, vol. 5912, pp. 435–450. Springer, Heidelberg (2009). https://doi.
org/10.1007/978-3-642-10366-7_26

[BBM00] Bellare, M., Boldyreva, A., Micali, S.: Public-key encryption in a multi-user
setting: security proofs and improvements. In: Preneel, B. (ed.) EURO-
CRYPT 2000. LNCS, vol. 1807, pp. 259–274. Springer, Heidelberg (2000).
https://doi.org/10.1007/3-540-45539-6_18

[BBS04] Boneh, D., Boyen, X., Shacham, H.: Short group signatures. In: Franklin,
M. (ed.) CRYPTO 2004. LNCS, vol. 3152, pp. 41–55. Springer, Heidelberg
(2004). https://doi.org/10.1007/978-3-540-28628-8_3

[BFI+10] Blazy, O., Fuchsbauer, G., Izabachène, M., Jambert, A., Sibert, H.,
Vergnaud, D.: Batch Groth–Sahai. In: Zhou, J., Yung, M. (eds.) ACNS
2010. LNCS, vol. 6123, pp. 218–235. Springer, Heidelberg (2010). https://
doi.org/10.1007/978-3-642-13708-2_14

[BKP14] Blazy, O., Kiltz, E., Pan, J.: (Hierarchical) identity-based encryption
from affine message authentication. In: Garay, J.A., Gennaro, R. (eds.)
CRYPTO 2014, Part I. LNCS, vol. 8616, pp. 408–425. Springer, Heidelberg (2014). https://doi.org/10.1007/978-3-662-44371-2_23

[BS07] Bellare, M., Shoup, S.: Two-tier signatures, strongly unforgeable signatures, and Fiat-Shamir without random oracles. In: Okamoto, T., Wang,
X. (eds.) PKC 2007. LNCS, vol. 4450, pp. 201–216. Springer, Heidelberg
(2007). https://doi.org/10.1007/978-3-540-71677-8_14

[CLY09] Cathalo, J., Libert, B., Yung, M.: Group encryption: non-interactive realization in the standard model. In: Matsui, M. (ed.) ASIACRYPT 2009.
LNCS, vol. 5912, pp. 179–196. Springer, Heidelberg (2009). https://doi.
org/10.1007/978-3-642-10366-7_11

[CS98] Cramer, R., Shoup, V.: A practical public key cryptosystem provably
secure against adaptive chosen ciphertext attack. In: Krawczyk, H. (ed.)
CRYPTO 1998. LNCS, vol. 1462, pp. 13–25. Springer, Heidelberg (1998).
https://doi.org/10.1007/BFb0055717

[CW13] Chen, J., Wee, H.: Fully, (almost) tightly secure IBE and dual system
groups. In: Canetti, R., Garay, J.A. (eds.) CRYPTO 2013, Part II. LNCS,
vol. 8043, pp. 435–460. Springer, Heidelberg (2013). https://doi.org/10.
1007/978-3-642-40084-1_25

[Dam92]   Damgård, I.: Towards practical public key systems secure against chosen
ciphertext attacks. In: Feigenbaum, J. (ed.) CRYPTO 1991. LNCS, vol.
576, pp. 445–456. Springer, Heidelberg (1992). https://doi.org/10.1007/3-
540-46766-1_36

[EHK+13] Escala, A., Herold, G., Kiltz, E., Ràfols, C., Villar, J.: An algebraic
framework for Diffie-Hellman assumptions. In: Canetti, R., Garay, J.A.
(eds.) CRYPTO 2013. LNCS, vol. 8043, pp. 129–147. Springer, Heidelberg
(2013). https://doi.org/10.1007/978-3-642-40084-1_8

[ElG84]   ElGamal, T.: A public key cryptosystem and a signature scheme based on
discrete logarithms. In: Blakley, G.R., Chaum, D. (eds.) CRYPTO 1984.
LNCS, vol. 196, pp. 10–18. Springer, Heidelberg (1985). https://doi.org/
10.1007/3-540-39568-7_2

[Fuc11]   Fuchsbauer, G.: Commuting signatures and verifiable encryption. In:
Paterson, K.G. (ed.) EUROCRYPT 2011. LNCS, vol. 6632, pp. 224–245.
Springer, Heidelberg (2011). https://doi.org/10.1007/978-3-642-20465-
4_14

[GHKW16] Gay, R., Hofheinz, D., Kiltz, E., Wee, H.: Tightly CCA-secure encryption
without pairings. In: Fischlin, M., Coron, J.-S. (eds.) EUROCRYPT 2016,
Part I. LNCS, vol. 9665, pp. 1–27. Springer, Heidelberg (2016). https://
doi.org/10.1007/978-3-662-49890-3_1

[Gro06]   Groth, J.: Simulation-sound NIZK proofs for a practical Language and
constant size group signatures. In: Lai, X., Chen, K. (eds.) ASIACRYPT
2006. LNCS, vol. 4284, pp. 444–459. Springer, Heidelberg (2006). https://
doi.org/10.1007/11935230_29

[GS12]   Groth, J., Sahai, A.: Efficient non-interactive proof systems for bilinear
groups. SIAM J. Comput. 41(5), 1193–1232 (2012)

[Har11]   Haralambiev, K.: Efficient cryptographic primitives for non-interactive
zero-knowledge proofs and applications. Ph.D thesis. New York University (2011)

[HJ12]   Hofheinz, D., Jager, T.: Tightly secure signatures and public-key encryption. In: Safavi-Naini, R., Canetti, R. (eds.) CRYPTO 2012. LNCS, vol.
7417, pp. 590–607. Springer, Heidelberg (2012). https://doi.org/10.1007/
978-3-642-32009-5_35

[Hof17]   Hofheinz, D.: Adaptive partitioning. In: Coron, J.-S., Nielsen, J.B. (eds.)
EUROCRYPT 2017, Par II. LNCS, vol. 10212, pp. 489–518. Springer,
Cham (2017). https://doi.org/10.1007/978-3-319-56617-7_17

[JR13]   Jutla, C.S., Roy, A.: Shorter quasi-adaptive NIZK proofs for linear subspaces. In: Sako, K., Sarkar, P. (eds.) ASIACRYPT 2013, Part I. LNCS,
vol. 8269, pp. 1–20. Springer, Heidelberg (2013). https://doi.org/10.1007/
978-3-642-42033-7_1

[JR14]   Jutla, C.S., Roy, A.: Switching lemma for bilinear tests and constant-
size NIZK proofs for linear subspaces. In: Garay, J.A., Gennaro, R. (eds.)
CRYPTO 2014, Part II. LNCS, vol. 8617, pp. 295–312. Springer, Heidelberg (2014). https://doi.org/10.1007/978-3-662-44381-1_17

[JR17]   Jutla, C.S., Roy, A.: Improved structure preserving signatures under standard bilinear assumptions. In: Fehr, S. (ed.) PKC 2017, Part II. LNCS,
vol. 10175, pp. 183–209. Springer, Heidelberg (2017). https://doi.org/10.
1007/978-3-662-54388-7_7

[KPW15] Kiltz, E., Pan, J., Wee, H.: Structure-preserving signatures from standard
         assumptions, revisited. In: Gennaro, R., Robshaw, M. (eds.) CRYPTO
         2015, Part II. LNCS, vol. 9216, pp. 275–295. Springer, Heidelberg (2015).
         https://doi.org/10.1007/978-3-662-48000-7_14

[KW15]   Kiltz, E., Wee, H.: Quasi-adaptive NIZK for linear subspaces revisited. In:
         Oswald, E., Fischlin, M. (eds.) EUROCRYPT 2015, Part II. LNCS, vol.
         9057, pp. 101–128. Springer, Heidelberg (2015). https://doi.org/10.1007/
         978-3-662-46803-6_4

[LPJY15] Libert, B., Peters, T., Joye, M., Yung, M.: Compactly hiding linear spans.
         In: Iwata, T., Cheon, J.H. (eds.) ASIACRYPT 2015, Part I. LNCS, vol.
         9452, pp. 681–707. Springer, Heidelberg (2015). https://doi.org/10.1007/
         978-3-662-48797-6_28

[LPY15] Libert, B., Peters, T., Yung, M.: Short group signatures via structure-
         preserving signatures: standard model security from simple assumptions.
         In: Gennaro, R., Robshaw, M. (eds.) CRYPTO 2015, Part II. LNCS, vol.
         9216, pp. 296–316. Springer, Heidelberg (2015). https://doi.org/10.1007/
         978-3-662-48000-7_15

[NY90]   Naor, M., Yung, M.: Public-key cryptosystems provably secure against
         chosen ciphertext attacks. In: 22nd ACM STOC, pp. 427–437. ACM Press,
         May 1990

[Sah99] Sahai, A.: Non-malleable non-interactive zero knowledge and adaptive
         chosen-ciphertext security. In: 40th FOCS, pp. 543–553. IEEE Computer
         Society Press, October 1999

Weakly Secure Equivalence-Class Signatures from Standard Assumptions

Georg Fuchsbauer[1,2(✉)] and Romain Gay[1,2]

[1] Inria, Paris, France
[2] École normale supérieure, CNRS, PSL Research University, Paris, France
{fuchsbau,rgay}@di.ens.fr

Abstract. Structure-preserving signatures on equivalence classes, or equivalence-class signatures for short (EQS), are signature schemes defined over bilinear groups whose messages are vectors of group elements. Signatures are perfectly randomizable and given a signature on a vector, anyone can derive a signature on any multiple of the vector; EQS thus sign projective equivalence classes. Applications of EQS include the first constant-size anonymous attribute-based credentials, efficient round-optimal blind signatures without random oracles and efficient access-control encryption.

To date, the only existing instantiation of EQS is proven secure in the generic-group model. In this work we show that by relaxing the definition of unforgeability, which makes it efficiently verifiable, we can construct EQS from standard assumptions, namely the Matrix-Diffie-Hellman assumptions. We then show that our unforgeability notion is sufficient for most applications.

Keywords: Structure-preserving signatures on equivalence classes · Standard assumptions

1 Introduction

SPS. Structure-preserving signature (SPS) schemes [AFG+10] are defined over bilinear groups, which are described by three prime-order groups $\mathbb{G}_1$, $\mathbb{G}_2$, $\mathbb{G}_T$ and a bilinear map (pairing) $e: \mathbb{G}_1 \times \mathbb{G}_2 \to \mathbb{G}_T$. Public keys, messages and signatures of SPS schemes all consist of elements from $\mathbb{G}_1$ and $\mathbb{G}_2$ and signatures are verified by comparing evaluations of pairings applied to elements of the key, the message and the signature. The primary motivation for the introduction of SPS was their smooth interoperability with the Groth-Sahai (GS) proof system [GS08], which provides efficient non-interactive zero-knowledge (NIZK) proofs proving knowledge of group elements that satisfy sets of pairing-product equations.

Together, SPS and GS proofs enable proving knowledge of signatures, keys and/or messages, and thereby modular constructions of privacy-preserving cryptographic protocols. A long line of research [AGHO11, ACD+12, AGOT14, BFF+15, AKOT15, KPW15, Gro15, Gha16, JR17, AHN+17] has led to schemes

© International Association for Cryptologic Research 2018
M. Abdalla and R. Dahab (Eds.): PKC 2018, LNCS 10770, pp. 153–183, 2018.
https://doi.org/10.1007/978-3-319-76581-5_6

with improved efficiency, additional properties as well as schemes that are proven secure under standard computational hardness assumptions. Randomizable SPS [AGHO11] allow for more efficient schemes in that parts of the signature can, after randomization, be given in the clear. However, for privacy-preserving applications, they still inherently require hiding the message and using NIZK proofs.

EQS. Structure-preserving signatures on equivalence classes, or *equivalence-class signatures* (EQS) for short, allow similar applications to SPS. Unlike the latter, they achieve them without requiring *any* NIZK proofs on top, thereby yielding more efficient schemes. Intuitively, this is because not only their signatures but also the *messages* can be randomized. Equivalence-class signatures were introduced by Hanser and Slamanig [HS14]. Their initial instantiation was only secure against random-message attacks [Fuc14], which is insufficient for the intended applications. With Fuchsbauer [FHS14] they subsequently presented a scheme that satisfies the stronger notion of unforgeability under chosen-message attacks (EUF-CMA) in the generic group model. They also strengthened the model of EQS, which later enabled further applications [FHS15].

As for regular SPS, the messages in an EQS system are vectors of group elements $[\mathbf{m}]_1 \in \mathbb{G}_1^\ell$ (which in our notation stands for $(m_1 \cdot P_1, \ldots, m_\ell \cdot P_1)$ with P_1 being a generator of $\mathbb{G}_1$). EQS provide an additional algorithm that, given a signature σ for message $[\mathbf{m}]_1$, allows to adapt σ to a signature for the message $[\mu \cdot \mathbf{m}]_1$ for any $\mu \in \mathbb{Z}_p^*$ without access to the signing key. A signature therefore actually signs all multiples of a message at once (as a signature can be adapted to any of them). In other words, signatures or on *equivalence classes* of the equivalence relation "$\sim$" on the message space $(\mathbb{G}_1^*)^\ell$ defined as $[\mathbf{m}]_1 \sim [\mathbf{n}]_1$ $\Leftrightarrow \exists s \in \mathbb{Z}_p^* : \mathbf{m} = s \cdot \mathbf{n}$.

The definition of EQS moreover requires that signatures are randomizable, in that adaptation to a new representative leads to a signature that is distributed like a fresh signature for the new representative. The DDH assumption in group $\mathbb{G}_1$ implies that given a message $[\mathbf{m}]_1 \in (\mathbb{G}_1^*)^\ell$, then $[\mu \cdot \mathbf{m}]_1$ for a random μ is indistinguishable from $[\mathbf{m}']_1$ for a random $\mathbf{m}'$. For EQS signatures DDH thus implies that given a message signature pair $([\mathbf{m}]_1, \sigma)$, an adapted signature on a random representative $([\mu \cdot \mathbf{m}]_1, \sigma')$ looks like a *fresh* signature on a *random* message.

It is the latter property that is central in applications that use EQS instead of SPS+GS-proofs. Instead of having users give (costly) zero-knowledge proofs that they possess a signature to protect their privacy, it suffices to use an EQS scheme and have the user *randomize* the message and adapt the signature every time they show it. (We discuss applications of EQS in more detail below.)

Existential unforgeability under chosen-message attacks (EUF-CMA) for EQS is defined with respect to equivalence classes: an adversary that can query signatures for messages $[\mathbf{m}_i]_1$ of its choice should be incapable of returning a signature for a message $[\mathbf{m}^*]_1$ such that $[\mathbf{m}^*]_1$ is not a multiple of any $[\mathbf{m}_i]_1$. (Note that this winning condition cannot be efficiently decided, as this would amount to breaking DDH.)

The first EQS scheme by FHS [FHS14] signs messages from $(\mathbb{G}_1^*)^\ell$ and signatures consist of 3 group elements. The authors show that this size is optimal by relying on an impossibility result [AGO11] for SPS. Security of the FHS scheme was proved directly in the generic-group model, which amounts to an interactive assumption. The same authors [FHS15] later provided a scheme from a *non*-interactive q-type assumption; the assumption is that the FHS scheme is secure against random-message attacks (where instead of a signing oracle the adversary is given signatures for q randomly chosen messages). They then build a scheme on top of the original scheme and prove EUF-CMA security. However, the signatures of their scheme are *not* randomizable, which is required for all applications of EQS.

The construction of an EQS scheme (which is randomizable) from any non-interactive assumption is still an open problem.

Applications of EQS. The first application of EQS was to anonymous (attribute-based) credentials [CL03, CL04, BCKL08, BCC+09, Fuc11], yielding the first construction for which the cost of showing a credential is independent of the number of possessed, or showed, or existing attributes. In most schemes a credential is a signature from the credential-issuing authority on a message representing the user's attributes. When the user wishes to present her credential, previous constructions require her to give a zero-knowledge proof of possessing a valid signature from the organization. Using EQS [FHS14] these proofs can be avoided: the user randomizes the message of its credential by multiplying it with a random value $\mu \leftarrow_R \mathbb{Z}_p^*$, adapts the authority's EQS signature on it and presents message and signature *in the clear*. By DDH and the properties of EQS, this pair looks like a fresh signature on a random message, which yields unlinkable user anonymity. (See Sect. 5 for more details of this construction.) Derler, Hanser and Slamanig later added the possibility of revoking users to the credential scheme [DHS15].

Fuchsbauer et al. [FHS15] used EQS to construct the first round-optimal blind signature scheme without random oracles nor CRS nor trusted setup with blindness against fully malicious signers. In order to obtain a blind signature, the user commits to her message as $[c]_1$, picks $\mu \leftarrow_R \mathbb{Z}_p^*$ and obtains an EQS signature from the signer on the randomized message $(\mu \cdot [c]_1, [\mu]_1)$. The blind signature is then an adapted signature to $([c]_1, [1]_1)$ together with an opening of $[c]_1$ to the message. While unforgeability relies on EUF-CMA of EQS and the binding property of the commitment, blindness is proved under an interactive variant of the DDH assumption.

In follow-up work [FHKS16], the authors changed the used commitment scheme from perfectly hiding to perfectly binding, which enabled them to prove blindness under a *non-interactive* (B)DDH-type assumption. (Another construction with blindness under a non-interactive assumption was also given by Hanzlik and Kluczniak [HK17].)

EQS were also used to construct verifiably encrypted signatures [HRS15] and group signatures without encryption [DS16] (see Sect. 6 for more on this).

Access-control encryption. Access-control encryption [DHO16] is a recently introduced primitive that models information flow between senders and receivers. Whereas all forms of encryption only prevent unauthorized receivers from obtaining information, access-control encryption (ACE) additionally prevents unauthorized senders from *distributing* information.

ACE considers a relation on a set of senders and receivers that specifies who is allowed to send information to whom. To prevent unauthorized sending, all messages are sent via an authority, called the *sanitizer*, who can tweak the messages before broadcasting it; (the sanitizer should however not obtain information about sender, receiver or content of a message).

Access-control encryption was introduced by Damgård et al. [DHO16] and two papers have recently improved on it: Badertscher et al. [BMM17] strengthen the security model by requiring chosen-ciphertext security and non-malleability of messages, and Kim and Wu [KW17] give the first construction from standard assumptions for general policies. The only existing efficient constructions are for restricted classes of policies; the most efficient scheme is the one by Fuchsbauer et al. [FGKO17] based on EQS.

In their construction any receiver Bob has a public key $[k]_1$ for ElGamal encryption. If Alice is allowed to send messages to Bob, she obtains an EQS signature σ on $([1]_1, [k]_1)$ from the authority, which serves as a certificate. When Alice wants to send a message to Bob, she first picks $s, r \leftarrow_R \mathbb{Z}_p^*$ and adapts σ to the new representative $([s]_1, s \cdot [k]_1)$. She then sends this new message/signature pair together with an ElGamal encryption $([r]_1, r \cdot [k]_1 + [m]_1)$ of her message $[m]_1$ to the sanitizer. The latter verifies the adapted signature and, if correct, picks $t \leftarrow_R \mathbb{Z}_p^*$ and sends the following to Bob: $([r]_1 + t \cdot [s]_1, [r \cdot k + m]_1 + t \cdot [s \cdot k]_1)$, which is a re-randomized encryption of $[m]_1$ under $[k]_1$.

Note that if the pair that the sanitizer uses to randomize the ciphertext was *not* a multiple of $([1]_1, [k]_1)$, then Bob would receive an encryption of a random message. Now EUF-CMA of EQS guarantees that the only way Alice can provide a signature on such a multiple is if she received a certificate for Bob's key; that is, if she is allowed to send messages to Bob. On the other hand, by the EQS randomization properties, the sanitizer does not learn anything about the intended receiver (nor the encrypted message), since $([s]_1, s \cdot [k]_1)$ and the ElGamal ciphertext look like random group elements to it.

Our contribution

In this work we present the first equivalence-class signature scheme based on standard assumptions; in particular the family of Matrix-Diffie-Hellman assumptions [EHK+13], which encompasses well-known assumptions such as the decision-linear assumption [BBS04]. In order to achieve this, we need to make two modifications to the model of EQS: the first one is syntactical and the second one concerns the definition of unforgeability.

Syntax. Whereas in the original EQS model [HS14, FHS14] there is only one type of signatures, we distinguish between signatures that were output by the signing algorithm, and which can be adapted and perfectly randomized on the one hand; and signatures that have been randomized on the other. The latter type cannot be randomized any further.

We note that we are not aware of *any* applications where signatures that have been randomized need to be randomized again by an entity that does not know the original signature. In the application to credential systems, the first (randomizable) signature type would correspond to the credential that is stored by the user, whereas the second (smaller) type corresponds to *credential proofs*, that is, the object presented by the user when proving possession of a credential. For access control encryption, signatures of the first type are part of an encryption key, and randomized signatures are issued as part of a ciphertext produced from this encryption key. For the round-optimal blind signatures [FHS15], the user receives a (randomizable) signature from the signer, adapts it (to the second type) and includes it in her blind signature.

Security. We relax the notion of unforgeability considered in the original work [HS14, FHS14] and make it an *efficiently verifiable* notion. When the adversary queries its signing oracle for a signature on a message $[\mathbf{m}]$, we require it to present the discrete logarithm of its elements, that is, a query is of the form $\mathbf{m} \in (\mathbb{Z}_p^*)^\ell$. After the adversary has output a purported forgery on a message $[\mathbf{m}^*]_1$ (without giving its logarithm), the experiment can efficiently check whether it is contained in one of the classes defined by the queried messages. We call our weakened notion *existential unforgeability under chosen* open *message attacks* (EUF-CoMA).

In Sects. 4–6 we then argue that for most applications of EQS this security notion is sufficient, as constructions building on EQS either only require EUF-CoMA or they can be made to with very minor modifications. In particular, we show this for *all* applications of EQS in the literature, except for the one to round-optimal blind signatures.

Our scheme. Our scheme builds upon the affine MAC by Blazy et al. [BKP14], which we first turn into a structure-preserving and "linear" MAC, that is, a MAC that allows for deriving a tag of a message $\mu \cdot [\mathbf{m}]_1$ from a tag for $[\mathbf{m}]_1 \in \mathbb{G}_1^\ell$ for any scalar $\mu \in \mathbb{Z}_p^*$. We then build upon Kiltz and Wee's [KW15] method of transforming a MAC into a signature, which has also been used in [KPW15] in the context of structure-preserving signatures. (Details on our scheme are provided in a technical overview at the beginning of Sect. 3.)

Overall, we obtain an EQS whose EUF-CoMA security is based on the bilateral variant of the DLIN assumption (where the challenge is given in both groups $\mathbb{G}_1$ and $\mathbb{G}_2$), and DDH in $\mathbb{G}_2$. More generally, we use the Matrix Decisional Diffie-Hellman (MDDH) assumption [EHK+13], and its computational variant, the Kernel Matrix Diffie-Hellman (KMDH) assumption [MRV16], both of which are parameterized by a distribution of full-rank $\ell \times k$ matrices for some specified dimensions $\ell, k \in \mathbb{N}^*$, $\ell > k$, and which capture most known standard assumptions in pairing groups, such as DLIN and DDH which correspond to particular matrix distributions (of size $\ell := 3$ by $k := 2$ for DLIN, and $\ell := 2$ by $k := 1$ for DDH).

We adopt this matrix viewpoint for a more general and overall cleaner exposition of our construction. In particular, we give a construction that is secure under the $\mathcal{D}_{2k,k}$-MDDH assumption for any matrix distribution $\mathcal{D}_{2k,k}$ with $k \geq 2$, and the $\mathcal{D}_{k'}$-KerMDH assumption for any matrix distribution $\mathcal{D}_{k'}$ for $k' \geq 1$. We summarize the concrete efficiency of our scheme depending on the choices of k and k' in Table 1.

Table 1. Efficiency and security of our scheme for messages from $(\mathbb{G}_1^*)^\ell$ from general assumptions (middle) and for the most efficient setting $k := 2$, $k' := 1$ (right).

Signature size	$\big(2k\ell + (k'+1)\big)|\mathbb{G}_1| + 2k|\mathbb{G}_2|$	$(4\ell + 2)|\mathbb{G}_1| + 4|\mathbb{G}_2|$
Public key size	$k'(k' + 1 + 2k\ell)|\mathbb{G}_2|$	$(4\ell + 2)|\mathbb{G}_2|$
Secret key size	$2k(k'+1)\ell + 2k^2$ $\mathbb{Z}_p$ elements	$8(\ell+1)$ $\mathbb{Z}_p$ elements
Pairing to verify	$4\ell k + k' + 1$	$8\ell + 2$
Assumption	$\mathcal{D}_{2k,k}$-MDDH, $\mathcal{D}_{k'}$-KerMDH in $\mathbb{G}_2$	$\mathcal{D}_{4,2}$-MDDH and $\mathcal{D}_1$-KerMDH in $\mathbb{G}_2$

Concrete assumptions. Suppose we choose the matrix distribution $\mathcal{D}_{4,2}$ to be the uniform distribution $\mathcal{U}_{4,2}$ over all invertible matrices in $\mathbb{Z}_p^{4\times 2}$, and $\mathcal{D}_1$ to be the DDH distribution over $\mathbb{Z}_p^2$ defined as $\{(1, a) : a \leftarrow_{\mathrm{R}} \mathbb{Z}_p\}$. Then, $\mathcal{U}_{4,2}$-MDDH reduces to the bilateral variant of the DLIN assumption (Lemma 1), and $\mathcal{D}_1$-KerMDH in $\mathbb{G}_2$ reduces to DDH in $\mathbb{G}_2$ (Lemma 2). Thus, we obtain an EQS signature scheme whose EUF-CoMA security is based on DDH in $\mathbb{G}_2$ and bilateral DLIN (which is comparable to the original DLIN [BBS04], which was for symmetric bilinear groups).

2   Preliminaries

2.1   Notations

We denote by $x \leftarrow_{\mathrm{R}} \mathcal{B}$ the process of sampling an element x from set $\mathcal{B}$ uniformly at random. We denote by λ the security parameter, and by $\mathsf{negl}(\cdot)$ any negligible function of λ. For any $k, \ell \in \mathbb{N}^*$ such that $\ell > k$, and any matrix $\mathbf{A} \in \mathbb{Z}_p^{\ell \times k}$, we write $\mathsf{orth}(\mathbf{A}) := \{\mathbf{A}^\perp \in \mathbb{Z}_p^{\ell \times (\ell-k)} \mid \mathbf{A}^\top \mathbf{A}^\perp = \mathbf{0}$ and $\mathbf{A}^\perp$ has full rank$\}$.

2.2   Pairing Groups

Let GGen be a probabilistic polynomial-time (PPT) algorithm that on input 1^λ returns a description $\mathcal{PG} = (p, \mathbb{G}_1, \mathbb{G}_2, \mathbb{G}_T, e, P_1, P_2)$ of asymmetric bilinear groups where $\mathbb{G}_1$, $\mathbb{G}_2$, $\mathbb{G}_T$ are cyclic groups of order p for a 2λ-bit prime p, P_1 and P_2 are generators of $\mathbb{G}_1$ and $\mathbb{G}_2$, respectively, and $e : \mathbb{G}_1 \times \mathbb{G}_2 \to \mathbb{G}_T$ is an efficiently computable (non-degenerate) bilinear map. Define $P_T := e(P_1, P_2)$, which is a generator of $\mathbb{G}_T$. We use implicit representation of group elements. Namely, for $s \in \{1, 2, T\}$ and $a \in \mathbb{Z}_p$, we define $[a]_s = aP_s \in \mathbb{G}_s$ as the implicit representation of a in $\mathbb{G}_s$. More generally, for a matrix $\mathbf{A} = (a_{ij}) \in \mathbb{Z}_p^{m \times n}$ we define $[\mathbf{A}]_s$ as the implicit representation of $\mathbf{A}$ in $\mathbb{G}_s$:

$$[\mathbf{A}]_s := \begin{pmatrix} a_{11}P & \dots & a_{1n}P \\ \vdots & & \vdots \\ a_{m1}P & \dots & a_{mn}P \end{pmatrix} \in \mathbb{G}_s^{m \times n}$$

Note that from $[a]_s \in \mathbb{G}_s$ it is generally hard to compute the value a (discrete logarithm problem in $\mathbb{G}_s$). Further, from $[b]_T \in \mathbb{G}_T$, it is hard to compute the value $[b]_1 \in \mathbb{G}_1$ and $[b]_2 \in \mathbb{G}_2$ (pairing inversion problem). Obviously, given $[a]_s \in \mathbb{G}_s$ and a scalar $x \in \mathbb{Z}_p$, one can efficiently compute $[ax]_s \in \mathbb{G}_s$. Further, given $[a]_1, [a]_2$, one can efficiently compute $[ab]_T$ using the pairing e. For two matrices $\mathbf{A}$, $\mathbf{B}$ with matching dimensions define $[\mathbf{A}]_1 \bullet [\mathbf{B}]_2 := [\mathbf{AB}]_T \in \mathbb{G}_T$, which can be computed efficiently using the pairing $e\colon \mathbb{G}_1 \times \mathbb{G}_2 \to \mathbb{G}_T$.

2.3   Matrix Diffie-Hellman Assumptions

We first recall the definitions of the Matrix Decisional Diffie-Hellman (MDDH) Assumption [EHK+13].

Definition 1 (Matrix Distribution). *Let $k, \ell \in \mathbb{N}^*$, such that $\ell > k$. We call $\mathcal{D}_{\ell,k}$ a matrix distribution if it outputs matrices in $\mathbb{Z}_p^{\ell \times k}$ of full rank k in polynomial time (w.l.o.g. we assume the first k rows of $\mathbf{A} \leftarrow_R \mathcal{D}_{\ell,k}$ form an invertible matrix). We write $\mathcal{D}_k := \mathcal{D}_{k+1,k}$.*

We define a bilateral variant of the Matrix Decisional Diffie-Hellman (MDDH) assumption. Namely, [EHK+13] originally defines the $\mathcal{D}_{\ell,k}$-MDDH assumption in $\mathbb{G}_s$ for any $s \in \{1,2,T\}$ to be distinguishing the two distributions: $([\mathbf{A}]_s, [\mathbf{Ar}]_s)$ and $([\mathbf{A}]_s, [\mathbf{u}]_s)$, whereas we use the bilateral variant which consists in distinguishing the two distributions: $([\mathbf{A}]_1, [\mathbf{A}]_2, [\mathbf{Ar}]_1, [\mathbf{Ar}]_2)$ and $([\mathbf{A}]_1, [\mathbf{A}]_2, [\mathbf{u}]_1, [\mathbf{u}]_2)$ where $\mathbf{A} \leftarrow_R \mathcal{D}_{\ell,k}$, $\mathbf{r} \leftarrow_R \mathbb{Z}_p^k$ and $\mathbf{u} \leftarrow_R \mathbb{Z}_p^\ell$, for asymmetric pairings. Note that the bilateral variant is provably no weaker (in the generic group model) than the unilateral variant in symmetric bilinear groups. Bilateral variant of the DLIN assumption in asymmetric pairings has already been used in prior works [LPJY15, AC17].

Definition 2 ($\mathcal{D}_{\ell,k}$-Matrix Decisional Diffie-Hellman Assumption ($\mathcal{D}_{\ell,k}$-MDDH)). *Let $\lambda, k, \ell \in \mathbb{N}^*$ such that $\ell > k \geq 2$, and let $\mathcal{D}_{\ell,k}$ be a matrix distribution. We say that the $\mathcal{D}_{\ell,k}$-Matrix Decisional Diffie-Hellman ($\mathcal{D}_{\ell,k}$-MDDH) Assumption holds relative to GGen if for all PPT adversaries $\mathcal{A}$,*

$$\mathsf{Adv}^{\mathrm{MDDH}}_{\mathsf{GGen},\mathcal{D}_{\ell,k},\mathcal{A}}(\lambda) := \Big| \Pr\left[\mathcal{A}\left(\mathcal{PG}, \{[\mathbf{A}]_s, [\mathbf{Ar}]_s\}_{s \in \{1,2\}}\right) = 1\right]$$
$$- \Pr\left[\mathcal{A}\left(\mathcal{PG}, \{[\mathbf{A}]_s, [\mathbf{u}]_s\}_{s \in \{1,2\}}\right) = 1\right] \Big| = \mathsf{negl}(\lambda),$$

where the probability is taken over $\mathcal{PG} := (p, \mathbb{G}_1, \mathbb{G}_2, \mathbb{G}_T, e, P_1, P_2) \leftarrow_R \mathsf{GGen}(1^\lambda)$, $\mathbf{A} \leftarrow_R \mathcal{D}_k, \mathbf{r} \leftarrow_R \mathbb{Z}_p^k, \mathbf{u} \leftarrow_R \mathbb{Z}_p^\ell$.

Let $Q \geq 1$. For $\mathbf{W} \leftarrow_R \mathbb{Z}_p^{k \times Q}, \mathbf{U} \leftarrow_R \mathbb{Z}_p^{\ell \times Q}$, we consider the Q-fold $\mathcal{D}_{\ell,k}$-MDDH Assumption in $\mathbb{G}_s$, which consists in distinguishing the distributions $\{[\mathbf{A}]_s, [\mathbf{AW}]_s\}_{s \in \{1,2\}}$ from $\{[\mathbf{A}]_s, [\mathbf{U}]_s\}_{s \in \{1,2\}}$. That is, a challenge for the Q-fold $\mathcal{D}_{\ell,k}$-MDDH assumption consists of Q independent challenges of the $\mathcal{D}_k$-MDDH assumption (with the same $\mathbf{A}$ but different randomness $\mathbf{w}$).

Definition 3 (Uniform distribution). *Let $k, \ell \in \mathbb{N}^*$, with $\ell > k$. We denote by $\mathcal{U}_{\ell,k}$ the uniform distribution over all full-rank $\ell \times k$ matrices over $\mathbb{Z}_p$.*

Among all possible matrix distributions $\mathcal{D}_{\ell,k}$, the uniform matrix distribution $\mathcal{U}_{\ell',k}$ is the hardest possible instance.

Lemma 1 ($\mathcal{D}_{\ell,k}$-MDDH   implies Q-fold $\mathcal{U}_{\ell',k}$-MDDH [EHK+13, GHKW16]). *Let* $k, \ell, \ell', Q \in \mathbb{N}^*$, *such that* $\ell > k$, $\ell' > k$, *and let* $\mathcal{D}_{\ell,k}$ *be a matrix distribution. For any PPT adversary* $\mathcal{A}$, *there exists a PPT adversary* $\mathcal{B}$ *such that* $\mathsf{Adv}^{Q\text{-MDDH}}_{\mathsf{GGen},\mathcal{U}_{\ell',k},\mathcal{A}}(\lambda) \leq \mathsf{Adv}^{\text{MDDH}}_{\mathsf{GGen},\mathcal{D}_{\ell,k},\mathcal{B}}(\lambda) + \frac{1}{p-1}$.

Now we recall the definition of the $\mathcal{D}_k$-Kernel Matrix Decisional Diffie-Hellman assumption [MRV16], a natural computational analog of the $\mathcal{D}_k$-Matrix Decisional Diffie-Hellman assumption.

Definition 4 ($\mathcal{D}_k$-Kernel Matrix Diffie-Hellman ($\mathcal{D}_k$-KerMDH) assumption [MRV16]). *Let* $\lambda, k \in \mathbb{N}^*$, *and* $\mathcal{D}_k$ *be a matrix distribution. We say that the* $\mathcal{D}_k$*-Kernel Matrix Diffie-Hellman ($\mathcal{D}_k$-KerMDH) assumption holds relative to* GGen *in* $\mathbb{G}_s$ *for* $s \in \{1,2\}$, *if for all PPT adversaries* $\mathcal{A}$,

$$\mathsf{Adv}^{\text{KerMDH}}_{\mathsf{GGen},\mathcal{D}_k,\mathbb{G}_s,\mathcal{A}}(\lambda) := \Pr\left[\mathbf{c} \in \mathsf{orth}(\mathbf{A}) \mid [\mathbf{c}]_{3-s} \leftarrow \mathcal{A}(\mathcal{PG}, [\mathbf{A}]_s)\right] = \mathsf{negl}(\lambda),$$

where the probability is taken over $\mathcal{PG} := (p, \mathbb{G}_1, \mathbb{G}_2, \mathbb{G}_T, e, P_1, P_2) \leftarrow_{\mathrm{R}} \mathsf{GGen}(1^\lambda)$, *and* $\mathbf{A} \leftarrow_{\mathrm{R}} \mathcal{D}_k$.

Note that the winning condition is efficiently checkable using the pairing: $\mathbf{c} \in \mathsf{orth}(\mathbf{A}) \Leftrightarrow e([\mathbf{A}]_s, [\mathbf{c}]_{3-s}) = [\mathbf{0}]_T$.

For any matrix distribution $\mathcal{D}_k$, the $\mathcal{D}_k$-KerMDH assumption is weaker than its decisional counterpart:

Lemma 2 ($\mathcal{D}_k$-MDDH $\Rightarrow \mathcal{D}_k$-KerMDH [MRV16]). *Let* $k \in \mathbb{N}^*$, *and let* $\mathcal{D}_k$ *be a matrix distribution. For any PPT adversary* $\mathcal{A}$, *there exists a PPT adversary* $\mathcal{B}$ *such that* $\mathsf{Adv}^{\text{KerMDH}}_{\mathsf{GGen},\mathcal{D}_k,\mathbb{G}_s,\mathcal{A}}(\lambda) \leq \mathsf{Adv}^{\text{MDDH}}_{\mathsf{GGen},\mathcal{D}_k,\mathbb{G}_s,\mathcal{B}}(\lambda)$.

2.4   Equivalence-Class Signatures

We recall the definition of *structure preserving signatures on equivalence classes* from [FHS14], which we call equivalence-class signatures for short.

Let us denote $\mathsf{Span}([\mathbf{m}]_1) := \{[\mu\cdot\mathbf{m}]_1 \mid \mu \in \mathbb{Z}_p\}$ and $(\mathbb{G}_1^\ell)^* := \mathbb{G}_1^\ell \setminus \{[\mathbf{0}]_1 \in \mathbb{G}_1^\ell\}$. Let $\lambda, \ell \in \mathbb{N}^*$ and $\mathcal{PG} := (p, \mathbb{G}_1, \mathbb{G}_2, \mathbb{G}_T, e, P_1, P_2)$ be an output of $\mathsf{GGen}(1^\lambda)$. An EQS scheme signs an equivalence class $\mathsf{Span}([\mathbf{m}]_1)$ for $[\mathbf{m}]_1 \in (\mathbb{G}_1^\ell)^*$, and it allows to derive from a signature for $[\mathbf{m}]_1$ a fresh signature for any vector in $\mathsf{Span}([\mathbf{m}]_1)$ without access to the secret key.

Our definition slightly differs from that of [FHS14], as we make a syntactical difference between signatures output by the signing algorithm, which can be re-randomized, and (final) signatures that have been re-randomized and cannot be re-randomized again. In [FHS14], these are the same object, but in our scheme, re-randomizable signatures are vectors of group elements of different dimension than final signatures. We call the re-randomizable signature pre-signature, and final signatures simply signatures. Note that the re-randomizability is crucial to obtain signature adaptation, defined below.

Definition 5 (EQS). *An equivalence-class signature scheme consists of the following PPT algorithms:*

- Setup$(\mathcal{PG})$, *on input a pairing group* $\mathcal{PG} \leftarrow_R \mathsf{GGen}(1^\lambda)$, *outputs a secret key sk and a public key pk, which implicitly defines a pre-signature space* $\mathcal{R}$ *and a signature space* $\mathcal{S}$.
- Sign$(sk, [\mathbf{m}]_1 \in (\mathbb{G}_1^\ell)^*)$, *on input the secret key sk and a representative* $[\mathbf{m}]_1 \in (\mathbb{G}_1^\ell)^*$ *of the equivalence class* Span$([\mathbf{m}]_1)$, *outputs a pre-signature* ρ *that is valid for the representative* $[\mathbf{m}]_1$.
- Adapt$(pk, \rho \in \mathcal{R}, \mu \in \mathbb{Z}_p^*)$, *on input the public key pk, a pre-signature* $\rho \in \mathcal{R}$, *and a scalar* $\mu \in \mathbb{Z}_p^*$, *outputs an updated signature* $\sigma \in \mathcal{S}$ *for the same equivalence class. If* ρ *is valid for representative* $[\mathbf{m}]_1$, *then* σ *is valid for representative* $[\mu \cdot \mathbf{m}]_1$ *of the same equivalence class.*
- Ver$(pk, [\mathbf{m}]_1 \in (\mathbb{G}_1^\ell)^*, \sigma \in \mathcal{S})$, *on input the public key pk,* $[\mathbf{m}]_1 \in (\mathbb{G}_1^\ell)^*$, *and a signature* $\sigma \in \mathcal{S}$, *outputs 1 if the signature is valid for* $[\mathbf{m}]_1$ *under pk, and 0 otherwise.*
- VerKey(sk, pk), *is a deterministic algorithm that on input the secret key sk and the public key pk checks their consistency and outputs 1 in case the check is successful, 0 otherwise.*

Although there is no algorithm to verify pre-signatures, one can easily do so by first adapting them using $\mu := 1$ and then applying Ver to the result.

Remark 1. We note that we are not aware of any application of EQS where a signature that has been re-randomized by some entity A needs to be re-randomized again by another entity B. (Even in the application to blind signatures in [FHS15], the user only needs to adapt once.) In such applications, having signatures of different types would pose a problem.

EQS schemes that adhere to the type above can thus be used in all applications: a user obtains a (pre-)signature of type $\mathcal{R}$ and uses it to derive randomizations (and possibly adaptations to other messages) from it.

Correctness. An EQS (Setup, Sign, Adapt, Ver, VerKey) satisfies correctness if the following hold:

- $\Pr[\mathsf{VerKey}(sk, pk) = 1]$, where the probability is taken over $(sk, pk) \leftarrow_R$ Setup(1^λ);
- for all $[\mathbf{m}]_1 \in (\mathbb{G}_1^\ell)^*$, $\mu \in \mathbb{Z}_p^*$: $\Pr[\mathsf{Ver}(pk, [\mu \cdot \mathbf{m}]_1, \sigma) = 1] = 1$, where the probability is taken over $(sk, pk) \leftarrow$ Setup(1^λ), $\rho \leftarrow$ Sign$(sk, [\mathbf{m}]_1)$, $\sigma \leftarrow_R$ Adapt(pk, ρ, μ).

We define a new unforgeability notion, which is weaker than the original EUF-CMA security definition from [FHS14] (which we restate below for completeness), but still suffices for many applications, as we show in Sects. 5 and 6. An advantage of our new definition is that it is efficiently decidable whether the adversary has won the security game, contrary to EUF-CMA as originally defined.

EUF-CMA. An EQS scheme $\mathsf{EQS} := (\mathsf{Setup}, \mathsf{Sign}, \mathsf{Adapt}, \mathsf{Ver}, \mathsf{VerKey})$ satisfies existential unforgeability under chosen-message attacks (EUF-CMA) if for all PPT adversaries $\mathcal{A}$,

$$\mathsf{Adv}_{\mathsf{EQS},\mathcal{A}}^{\mathrm{EUF\text{-}CMA}}(\lambda) := \Pr\left[\mathsf{Exp}_{\mathsf{EQS}}^{\mathrm{EUF\text{-}CMA}}(1^\lambda, \mathcal{A}) = 1\right] = \mathsf{negl}(\lambda),$$

with game $\mathsf{Exp}_{\mathsf{EQS}}^{\mathrm{EUF\text{-}CMA}}(1^\lambda, \mathcal{A})$ defined as follows:

Game Definition	Oracle Definition
$\mathsf{Exp}_{\mathsf{EQS}}^{\mathrm{EUF\text{-}CMA}}(1^\lambda, \mathcal{A})$:	$\mathsf{SignO}([\mathbf{m}]_1)$:
$\mathcal{PG} \leftarrow \mathsf{GGen}(1^\lambda)$	$\mathcal{Q}_{\mathsf{sign}} := \mathcal{Q}_{\mathsf{sign}} \cup \{[\mathbf{m}]_1\}$
$\mathcal{Q}_{\mathsf{sign}} := \emptyset$	$\rho := \mathsf{Sign}(sk, [\mathbf{m}]_1)$
$(sk, pk) \leftarrow_{\mathrm{R}} \mathsf{Setup}(\mathcal{PG})$	Return ρ.
$([\mathbf{m}^\star]_1, \sigma^\star) \leftarrow \mathcal{A}^{\mathsf{SignO}(\cdot)}(pk)$	
Return 1 iff $\mathsf{Ver}(pk, [\mathbf{m}^\star]_1, \sigma^\star) = 1$ and	
$[\mathbf{m}^\star]_1 \notin \bigcup_{[\mathbf{m}]_1 \in \mathcal{Q}_{\mathsf{sign}}} \mathsf{Span}([\mathbf{m}]_1)$.	

It is still an open problem to construct an EQS scheme that achieves standard EUF-CMA under standard assumptions.

We now state our new notion, which we call *Existential UnForgeability under Chosen Open Message Attacks* (EUF-CoMA). The only difference to EUF-CMA is that the adversary has to give the discrete logarithm of messages $\mathbf{m} \in \mathbb{Z}_p^\ell$ instead of $[\mathbf{m}]_1$ to SignO.

EUF-CoMA. An EQS scheme $\mathsf{EQS} := (\mathsf{Setup}, \mathsf{Sign}, \mathsf{Adapt}, \mathsf{Ver}, \mathsf{VerKey})$ satisfies existential unforgeability under chosen open message attacks if for all PPT adversaries $\mathcal{A}$,

$$\mathsf{Adv}_{\mathsf{EQS},\mathcal{A}}^{\mathrm{EUF\text{-}CoMA}}(\lambda) := \Pr\left[\mathsf{Exp}_{\mathsf{EQS}}^{\mathrm{EUF\text{-}CoMA}}(1^\lambda, \mathcal{A}) = 1\right] = \mathsf{negl}(\lambda),$$

with game $\mathsf{Exp}_{\mathsf{EQS}}^{\mathrm{EUF\text{-}CoMA}}(1^\lambda, \mathcal{A})$ defined as follows:

Game Definition	Oracle Definition
$\mathsf{Exp}_{\mathsf{EQS}}^{\mathrm{EUF\text{-}CoMA}}(1^\lambda, \mathcal{A})$:	$\mathsf{SignO}(\mathbf{m})$:
$\mathcal{PG} \leftarrow \mathsf{GGen}(1^\lambda)$	$\mathcal{Q}_{\mathsf{sign}} := \mathcal{Q}_{\mathsf{sign}} \cup \{\mathbf{m}\}$
$\mathcal{Q}_{\mathsf{sign}} := \emptyset$	$\rho := \mathsf{Sign}(sk, [\mathbf{m}]_1)$
$(sk, pk) \leftarrow_{\mathrm{R}} \mathsf{Setup}(\mathcal{PG})$	Return ρ.
$([\mathbf{m}^\star]_1, \sigma^\star) \leftarrow \mathcal{A}^{\mathsf{SignO}(\cdot)}(pk)$	
Return 1 iff $\mathsf{Ver}(pk, [\mathbf{m}^\star]_1, \sigma^\star) = 1$ and	
$[\mathbf{m}^\star]_1 \notin \bigcup_{\mathbf{m} \in \mathcal{Q}_{\mathsf{sign}}} \mathsf{Span}([\mathbf{m}]_1)$.	

Remark 2 (Decidability of breaks). As opposed to the original definition [FHS14], our variant allows to efficiently check whether an adversary has won, since for all $\mathbf{m} \in \mathcal{Q}_{\mathsf{sign}}$, one can efficiently check whether $[\mathbf{m}^\star]_1 \in \mathsf{Span}([\mathbf{m}]_1)$ (or equivalently

$\det[\mathbf{m}^\star \| \mathbf{m}]_1 = 0)$ when given $\mathbf{m} \in \mathbb{Z}_p^\ell$ directly as follows: check whether for some $i \in [\ell]$: $m_i \cdot [m_1^\star]_1 \neq m_1 \cdot [m_i^\star]_1$.

Signature-Adaptation. An scheme $\mathsf{EQS} := (\mathsf{Setup}, \mathsf{Sign}, \mathsf{Adapt}, \mathsf{Ver}, \mathsf{VerKey})$ perfectly adapts signatures if for all $(sk, pk, [\mathbf{m}]_1, \mu)$ with

$$\mathsf{VerKey}(sk, pk) = 1, \ [\mathbf{m}]_1 \in (\mathbb{G}_1^\ell)^*, \ \mu \in \mathbb{Z}_p^*,$$

the following are identically distributed:

$$\Big(\rho := \mathsf{Sign}(sk, [\mathbf{m}]_1), \mathsf{Adapt}(pk, \rho, \mu) \Big) \quad \text{and}$$

$$\Big(\rho := \mathsf{Sign}(sk, [\mathbf{m}]_1), \mathsf{Adapt}(pk, \mathsf{Sign}(sk, [\mu \cdot \mathbf{m}]_1), 1) \Big).$$

3 EQS from Standard Assumptions

In this section we present our EQS scheme and prove it secure under the Matrix Diffie-Hellman assumption.

Overview of the construction. We first build a private-key variant of EQS, that is, a MAC on equivalence classes. Our starting point is a modification of the affine MAC by Blazy et al. [BKP14, Sect. 3.3], which we make linear instead of affine. This then allows anyone to multiply the tag of $[\mathbf{m}]_1 \in \mathbb{G}_1^\ell$ to obtain a tag of any vector in $\mathsf{Span}([\mathbf{m}]_1)$. We start with recalling the MAC from [BKP14], which is based on the $\mathcal{D}_k$-MDDH assumption:

$$\text{BKP: } sk := \big(\mathbf{k}_0 \leftarrow_{\text{R}} \mathbb{Z}_p^{k+1}, \mathbf{K}_1 \leftarrow_{\text{R}} \mathbb{Z}_p^{\ell \times (k+1)}, \mathbf{A} \leftarrow_{\text{R}} \mathcal{D}_k \big)$$

$$\mathsf{Tag}(sk, [\mathbf{m}]_1) := \big([(\mathbf{k}_0^\top + \mathbf{m}^\top \mathbf{K}_1)\mathbf{t}]_1, [\mathbf{t}]_1 := [\mathbf{Au}]_1 \big) \text{ with } \mathbf{u} \leftarrow_{\text{R}} \mathbb{Z}_p^k.$$

A first idea to make this MAC an "equivalence-class MAC" would be to omit $\mathbf{k}_0$:

$$\text{First attempt: } sk := \big(\mathbf{K} \leftarrow_{\text{R}} \mathbb{Z}_p^{\ell \times (k+1)}, \mathbf{A} \leftarrow_{\text{R}} \mathcal{D}_k \big)$$

$$\mathsf{Tag}(sk, [\mathbf{m}]_1) := \big([\mathbf{m}^\top \mathbf{Kt}]_1, [\mathbf{t}]_1 := [\mathbf{Au}]_1 \big) \text{ with } \mathbf{u} \leftarrow_{\text{R}} \mathbb{Z}_p^k.$$

Note that now it suffices to multiply $[\mathbf{m}^\top \mathbf{Kt}]_1$ by any scalar $\mu \in \mathbb{Z}_p^*$ to obtain a tag for $[\mu \cdot \mathbf{m}]_1$. One problem with this first attempt though is correctness: our goal is a structure-preserving MAC, where the verification takes as input a message $[\mathbf{m}]_1 \in \mathbb{G}_1^\ell$, and not $\mathbf{m} \in \mathbb{Z}_p^\ell$, as for BKP's MAC. Thus, we put the vector $[\mathbf{t}]_2$ in source group $\mathbb{G}_2$, and a tag $\tau := ([t_0]_1, [\mathbf{t}]_2)$ is considered valid for message $[\mathbf{m}]_1$ if $[\mathbf{m}^\top]_1 \mathbf{K} \bullet [\mathbf{t}]_2 = [t_0]_1 \bullet [1]_2$, where the product "$\bullet$" is computed using the pairing $e \colon \mathbb{G}_1 \times \mathbb{G}_2 \to \mathbb{G}_T$. Note that this change requires to use the $\mathcal{D}_k$-MDDH assumption for $k \geq 2$, for instance DLIN, which allows to switch vectors $\{[\mathbf{Au}]_s\}_{s \in \{1,2\}}$ given in *both* source groups $\mathbb{G}_1$ and $\mathbb{G}_2$ to uniformly random over these groups.

   Still, we run into another problem when reducing the unforgeability of the MAC to MDDH: the reduction needs to compute tags for messages $[\mathbf{m}]_1$, given an MDDH challenge $\{[\mathbf{t}]_s\}_{s \in \{1,2\}}$. This is not possible, since each tag contains

$[\mathbf{m}^\top \mathbf{Kt}]_1$, in source group $\mathbb{G}_1$. One solution is to put the latter in the target group: $[\mathbf{m}^\top \mathbf{Kt}]_T$ (note that correctness is maintained since we can simply check $[\mathbf{m}^\top]_1 \mathbf{K} \bullet [\mathbf{t}]_2 = [\mathbf{m}^\top \mathbf{Kt}]_T$), thereby allowing the reduction to simulate tags. However, looking ahead, this will pose problems when going from MAC to signature, since for signatures the public key contains group elements and not $\mathbb{Z}_p$ elements.

Another solution is to require the adversary against unforgeability of the MAC to know the discrete logarithm of its challenge messages, that is, the signing oracle takes as input $\mathbf{m} \in \mathbb{Z}_p^\ell$ instead of $[\mathbf{m}]_1 \in \mathbb{G}_1^\ell$ (cf. Definition 5). This way, the reduction (from unforgeability to MDDH), given $\mathbf{m} \in \mathbb{Z}_p^\ell$ and its MDDH challenge $\{[\mathbf{t}]_s\}_{s \in \{1,2\}}$, can compute tags.

Successful attempt for MAC: $sk := \left(\mathbf{K} \leftarrow_{\mathrm{R}} \mathbb{Z}_p^{\ell \times (k+1)}, \mathbf{A} \leftarrow_{\mathrm{R}} \mathcal{D}_k \text{ for } k \geq 2\right)$

$$\mathsf{Tag}(sk, [\mathbf{m}]_1) := \left([\mathbf{m}^\top \mathbf{Kt}]_1, [\mathbf{t}]_2 := [\mathbf{Au}]_2\right) \text{ with } \mathbf{u} \leftarrow_{\mathrm{R}} \mathbb{Z}_p^k.$$

In order to transform the MAC into a signature, we use techniques similar to those used by Kiltz and Wee [KW15]. We first write the key $\mathbf{K}^\top := (\mathbf{k}_1 \| \cdots \| \mathbf{k}_\ell) \in \mathbb{Z}_p^{(k+1) \times \ell}$, and any tag for a message $[\mathbf{m}]_1$, as

$$\mathsf{Tag}(sk, [\mathbf{m}]_1) := \left(\left[\sum_{i \in [\ell]} m_i \mathbf{k}_i^\top \mathbf{t}\right]_1, [\mathbf{t}]_2\right).$$

Then we carry out the transformation $\mathbf{k}_i \in \mathbb{Z}_p^{k+1} \to \mathbf{K}_i \in \mathbb{Z}_p^{(k+1) \times (k'+1)}$, which allows us to publish $([\mathbf{B}]_2, \{[\mathbf{K}_i \mathbf{B}]_2\}_{i \in [\ell]})$ as the public key, where $\mathbf{B} \leftarrow_{\mathrm{R}} \mathcal{D}_{k'}$. To prove security, we first argue that the $\mathbf{K}_i$ have some entropy that is computationally inaccessible from $[\mathbf{K}_i \mathbf{B}]_2$, based on the KerMDH assumption with respect to $[\mathbf{B}]_2$. That entropy is then used to perform the security proof of the private-key variant of our scheme. To make signatures verifiable, we include the vectors $[m_i \mathbf{t}]_1$ for all $i \in [\ell]$ as part of the signature, and verify them as follows:

$sk := \left(\{\mathbf{K}_i \leftarrow_{\mathrm{R}} \mathbb{Z}_p^{(k+1) \times (k'+1)}\}_{i \in [\ell]}, \mathbf{A} \leftarrow_{\mathrm{R}} \mathcal{D}_k \text{ for } k \geq 2\right)$

$pk := \left([\mathbf{B}]_2, \{[\mathbf{K}_i \mathbf{B}]_2\}_{i \in [\ell]}\right)$

$\sigma := \left(\left[\sum_{i \in [\ell]} m_i \mathbf{K}_i^\top \mathbf{t}\right]_1, \{[m_i \mathbf{t}]_1\}_{i \in [\ell]}, [\mathbf{t}]_2\right)$ where $\mathbf{t} := \mathbf{Au}$, and $\mathbf{u} \leftarrow_{\mathrm{R}} \mathbb{Z}_p^k$

$\mathsf{Ver}(pk, [\mathbf{m}]_1, \sigma):$ checks $\sum_{i=1}^\ell [m_i \mathbf{t}^\top]_1 \bullet [\mathbf{K}_i \mathbf{B}]_2 = \left[\sum_{i \in [\ell]} m_i \mathbf{t}^\top \mathbf{K}_i\right]_1 \bullet [\mathbf{B}]_2.$

Note that the verification also needs to check that the $[m_i \mathbf{t}]_1$ are consistent with $[\mathbf{t}]_2$ and $[\mathbf{m}]_1$, that is, for all $i \in [\ell]: [m_i \mathbf{t}]_1 \bullet [1]_2 = [m_i]_1 \bullet [\mathbf{t}]_2$, and that $[\mathbf{t}]_2 \neq [\mathbf{0}]_2$, to avoid trivial forgeries. As for the MAC, it is easy to change a signature for $[\mathbf{m}]_1$ to a signature for $[\mu \cdot \mathbf{m}]_1$ for any $\mu \in \mathbb{Z}_p^*$, only knowing pk.

Finally, we want to make it possible to re-randomize signatures (so that it is impossible to trace back the original signature from a fresh one): we change $[\mathbf{t}]_2 := [\mathbf{Au}]_2$ to $[\mathbf{S}]_2 := [\mathbf{AU}]_2$, where $\mathbf{A} \leftarrow_{\mathrm{R}} \mathcal{D}_k$, $\mathbf{u} \leftarrow_{\mathrm{R}} \mathbb{Z}_p^k$, and $\mathbf{U} \leftarrow_{\mathrm{R}} \mathsf{GL}_k$. Here, GL_k denotes all invertible matrices in $\mathbb{Z}_p^{k \times k}$. This way, a fresh MDDH vector can be obtained by multiplying $[\mathbf{S}]_2$ by a random vector $\mathbf{r} \leftarrow_{\mathrm{R}} \mathbb{Z}_p^k$.

For technical reasons (which we explain in step "Game$_{i.3}$ to Game$_{i.4}$" on page 20) we actually require a matrix distribution $\mathcal{D}_{2k,k}$ for $\mathbf{A} \leftarrow_{\mathrm{R}} \mathcal{D}_{2k,k}$, with

---

Setup($\mathcal{PG}$):

$\mathbf{A} \leftarrow_{\mathrm{R}} \mathcal{D}_{2k,k}$, $\mathbf{B} \leftarrow_{\mathrm{R}} \mathcal{D}_{k'}$, for all $i \in [\ell]$: $\mathbf{K}_i \leftarrow_{\mathrm{R}} \mathbb{Z}_p^{2k \times (k'+1)}$

Return $pk := \left([\mathbf{B}]_2, \{[\mathbf{K}_i\mathbf{B}]_2\}_{i\in[\ell]}\right)$ and $sk := \left(\mathbf{A}, \{\mathbf{K}_i\}_{i\in[\ell]}\right)$

Sign($sk, [\mathbf{m}]_1 \in (\mathbb{G}_1^\ell)^*$):

$\mathbf{U} \leftarrow_{\mathrm{R}} \mathsf{GL}_k$, $\mathbf{S} := \mathbf{AU}$, for all $i \in [\ell]$: $[\mathbf{S}_i]_1 := [m_i]_1\mathbf{S}$, $[\mathbf{S}_{\ell+1}]_1 := \sum_{i=1}^\ell [m_i]_1 \mathbf{K}_i^\top \mathbf{S}$

Return $\rho := \left(\{[\mathbf{S}_i]_1\}_{i\in[\ell+1]}, [\mathbf{S}]_2\right)$

Adapt($pk, \rho := \left(\{[\mathbf{S}_i]_1\}_{i\in[\ell+1]}, [\mathbf{S}]_2\right), \mu \in \mathbb{Z}_p^*$):

$\mathbf{r} \leftarrow_{\mathrm{R}} (\mathbb{Z}_p^k)^*$, $[\mathbf{s}]_2 := [\mathbf{S}]_2\mathbf{r}$, for all $i \in [\ell+1]$: $[\mathbf{s}_i]_1 := \mu[\mathbf{S}_i]_1\mathbf{r}$

Return $\sigma := \left(\{[\mathbf{s}_i]_1\}_{i\in[\ell+1]}, [\mathbf{s}]_2\right)$

Ver $\left(pk, [\mathbf{m}]_1, \sigma := \left(\{[\mathbf{s}_i]_1\}_{i\in[\ell+1]}, [\mathbf{s}]_2\right)\right)$:

Return 1 if the followings conditions are true:

o $[\mathbf{s}]_2 \neq [\mathbf{0}]_2$

o $\forall i \in [\ell] : [\mathbf{s}_i]_1 \bullet [1]_2 = [m_i]_1 \bullet [\mathbf{s}]_2$

o $\sum_{i=1}^\ell [\mathbf{s}_i^\top]_1 \bullet [\mathbf{K}_i\mathbf{B}]_2 = [\mathbf{s}_{\ell+1}^\top]_1 \bullet [\mathbf{B}]_2$

Return 0 otherwise

Fig. 1. EQS scheme that satisfies EUF-CoMA based on the $\mathcal{D}_{2k,k}$-MDDH (for $k \geq 2$) and $\mathcal{D}_{k'}$-KerMDH (for $k' \geq 1$) assumptions.

$k \geq 2$, instead of $\mathcal{D}_k$. The size of the matrices $\mathbf{K}_i$ needs to be changed accordingly. Our scheme is given in Fig. 1.

Comparison with linearly homomorphic SPS. Note that the linear homomorphism property of our signatures is limited to produce signatures in the same equivalence class. In particular, when Sign is invoked first on $[\mathbf{m}]_1 \in (\mathbb{G}_1^\ell)^*$, then on another input $[\mathbf{m}']_1 \in (\mathbb{G}_1^\ell)^*$ it produces a signature with fresh randomness, that cannot be combined with the signature generated previously on input $[\mathbf{m}]_1$. In that respect, EQS differ from linearly homomorphic structure-preserving signatures, such as those from [KPW15].

Theorem 1 (EUF-CoMA). *If the $\mathcal{D}_{2k,k}$-MDDH and $\mathcal{D}_{k'}$-KerMDH assumptions hold relative to* GGen, *then the EQS scheme in Fig. 1 satisfies EUF-CoMA. In particular, for any PTT adversary $\mathcal{A}$, there exist PPT adversaries $\mathcal{B}_1$ and $\mathcal{B}_2$ such that:*

$$\mathsf{Adv}_{\mathsf{EQS},\mathcal{A}}^{EUF\text{-}CoMA}(\lambda)$$

$$\leq \mathsf{Adv}_{\mathsf{GGen},\mathcal{D}_{k'},\mathcal{B}_1}^{\mathrm{KerMDH}}(\lambda) + 2Q_{\mathsf{Sign}} \cdot \mathsf{Adv}_{\mathsf{GGen},\mathcal{D}_{2k,k},\mathcal{B}_2}^{\mathrm{MDDH}}(\lambda) + \frac{3kQ_{\mathsf{Sign}}+1}{p}.$$

Game$_0$, | Game$_1$, | Game$_2$ |:

$\mathcal{Q}_{\mathsf{sign}} := \emptyset$, $\mathbf{A} \leftarrow_{\mathsf{R}} \mathcal{D}_{2k,k}$, $\mathbf{B} \leftarrow_{\mathsf{R}} \mathcal{D}_{k'}$, pick $\mathbf{b}^{\perp} \in \mathsf{orth}(\mathbf{B})$

for all $i \in [\ell]$: $\mathbf{K}_i \leftarrow_{\mathsf{R}} \mathbb{Z}_p^{2k \times (k'+1)}$, $\mathbf{k}_i \leftarrow_{\mathsf{R}} \mathbb{Z}_p^{k+1}$

$pk := ([\mathbf{B}]_2, \{[\mathbf{K}_i\mathbf{B}]_2\}_{i \in [\ell]})$

$([\mathbf{m}^{\star}]_1, \sigma^{\star}) \leftarrow \mathcal{A}^{\mathsf{SignO}(\cdot)}(pk)$

Return 1 if $\mathsf{VerO}([\mathbf{m}^{\star}]_1, \sigma^{\star}) = 1$ and $[\mathbf{m}^{\star}]_1 \notin \bigcup_{\mathbf{m} \in \mathcal{Q}_{\mathsf{sign}}} \mathsf{Span}([\mathbf{m}]_1)$

Return 0 otherwise

$\mathsf{VerO}\Big([\mathbf{m}^{\star}]_1, \sigma^{\star} := (\{[\mathbf{s}_i]_1\}_{i \in [\ell+1]}), [\mathbf{s}]_2\Big)$:

Return 1 if the following conditions are true:

- $[\mathbf{s}]_2 \neq [\mathbf{0}]_2$
- $\forall i \in [\ell]$: $[\mathbf{s}_i]_1 \bullet [1]_2 = [m_i^{\star}]_1 \bullet [\mathbf{s}]_2$
- $\sum_{i=1}^{\ell} [\mathbf{s}_i^{\top}]_1 \bullet [\mathbf{K}_i\mathbf{B}]_2 = [\mathbf{s}_{\ell+1}^{\top}]_1 \bullet [\mathbf{B}]_2$

  and $\sum_{i=1}^{\ell} [\mathbf{s}_i^{\top}]_1 \big(\mathbf{K}_i + \mathbf{k}_i(\mathbf{b}^{\perp})^{\top}\big) = [\mathbf{s}_{\ell+1}^{\top}]_1$

Return 0 otherwise

$\mathsf{SignO}(\mathbf{m} \in (\mathbb{Z}_p^{\ell})^{*})$:

$\mathcal{Q}_{\mathsf{sign}} := \mathcal{Q}_{\mathsf{sign}} \cup \{\mathbf{m}\}$, $\mathbf{U} \leftarrow_{\mathsf{R}} \mathsf{GL}_k$, $\mathbf{S} := \mathbf{A}\mathbf{U}$

For all $i \in [\ell]$: $\mathbf{S}_i := [m_i]_1\mathbf{S}$

$[\mathbf{S}_{\ell+1}]_1 := \sum_{i=1}^{\ell} [m_i]_1\mathbf{K}_i^{\top}\mathbf{S} + \sum_{i=1}^{\ell} [m_i]_1\mathbf{b}^{\perp}\mathbf{k}_i^{\top}\mathbf{S}$

Return $\rho := ([\mathbf{S}]_2, \{[\mathbf{S}_i]_1\}_{i \in [\ell+1]})$

Fig. 2. Game$_0$ through Game$_2$, for the proof of Theorem 1. In each procedure, the components inside a solid (gray) frame are only present in the games marked by a solid (gray) frame.

Proof of Theorem 1. We use hybrids Game$_1$ through Game$_3$ defined in Fig. 2. We denote by Adv$_i$ the advantage of $\mathcal{A}$ in Game$_i$, that is $\Pr[\mathsf{Game}_i(1^{\lambda}, \mathcal{A}) = 1]$, where the probability is taken over the random coins of Game$_i$ and $\mathcal{A}$. Note that Game$_0$ is $\mathsf{Exp}_{\mathsf{EQS}}^{\mathsf{EUF\text{-}CoMA}}(1^{\lambda}, \mathcal{A})$.

From Game$_0$ to Game$_1$: We change the verification oracle, using the $\mathcal{D}_{k'}$-KerMDDH assumption on $[\mathbf{B}]_2$. A pair $([\mathbf{m}]_1, \sigma = (\{[\mathbf{s}_i]_1\}_{i \in [\ell+1]}, [\mathbf{s}]_2))$ that passes VerO in Game$_0$ but not in Game$_1$ is such that $\big(\sum_{i=1}^{\ell} \mathbf{s}_i^{\top}\mathbf{K}_i - \mathbf{s}_{\ell+1}^{\top}\big)\mathbf{B} = 0$, and $\big(\sum_{i=1}^{\ell} \mathbf{s}_i^{\top}\mathbf{K}_i - \mathbf{s}_{\ell+1}^{\top}\big) \neq \mathbf{0}^{\top}$. We can thus build a PPT algorithm $\mathcal{B}_1$ such that:

$$|\mathsf{Adv}_0 - \mathsf{Adv}_1| \leq \mathsf{Adv}_{\mathsf{GGen}, \mathcal{D}_{k'}, \mathcal{B}_1}^{\mathsf{KerMDH}}(\lambda)$$

as follows. $\mathcal{B}_1$ gets a challenge $[\mathbf{B}]_2$ for $\mathbf{B} \leftarrow_R \mathcal{D}_{k'}$, picks $\mathbf{A} \leftarrow_R \mathcal{D}_{2k,k}$ and $\mathbf{K}_i \leftarrow_R \mathbb{Z}_p^{2k \times (k'+1)}$ with which it simulates $\mathcal{A}$'s view. When $\mathcal{A}$ outputs a forgery $\left([\mathbf{m}]_1, \sigma := \left(\{[\mathbf{s}_i]_2\}_{i \in [\ell+1]}, [\mathbf{s}]_1\right)\right)$, $\mathcal{B}$ computes and returns $\sum_{i=1}^{\ell} [\mathbf{s}_i^\top]_1 \mathbf{K}_i - [\mathbf{s}_{\ell+1}^\top]_1$, which breaks the KerMDDH assumption whenever Game_0 and Game_1 differed.

From Game_1 to Game_2: These two games are in fact equivalently distributed: for all $\mathbf{k}_i \in \mathbb{Z}_p^{2k}$, $\mathbf{b}^\perp \in \mathrm{orth}(\mathbf{B})$, the two following distributions are the same:

$$\mathbf{K}_i \leftarrow_R \mathbb{Z}_p^{2k \times (k'+1)} \quad \text{and} \quad \mathbf{K}_i + \boxed{\mathbf{k}_i \mathbf{b}^\perp}, \text{ with } \mathbf{K}_i \leftarrow_R \mathbb{Z}_p^{2k \times (k'+1)}.$$

Now any occurrence of $\mathbf{K}_i$ in Game_1 is replaced by $\mathbf{K}_i + \mathbf{k}_i \mathbf{b}^\perp$ in Game_2. Note that the extra term $\mathbf{k}_i \mathbf{b}^\perp$ does not appear in pk, since $(\mathbf{K}_i + \mathbf{k}_i \mathbf{b}^\perp)\mathbf{B} = \mathbf{K}_i \mathbf{B}$.

Game_2: We bound Adv_2 using a core lemma (Lemma 3), which essentially proves EUF-CoMA of a private-key variant of our EQS. Namely, we build a PTT adversary $\mathcal{A}'$ such that

$$\mathsf{Adv}_2 \leq \mathsf{Adv}_{\mathcal{A}'}^{\mathsf{core}}(\lambda),$$

where $\mathsf{Adv}_{\mathcal{A}'}^{\mathsf{core}}(\lambda) := \Pr[\mathsf{Exp}_{\mathsf{core}}(1^\lambda, \mathcal{A}') = 1]$ and $\mathsf{Exp}_{\mathsf{core}}(1^\lambda, \mathcal{A}')$ is defined in Fig. 3. Using the core lemma, we then get that there exists a PPT algorithm $\mathcal{B}_2$ such that:

$$\mathsf{Adv}_2 \leq 2Q_{\mathsf{Sign}} \cdot \mathsf{Adv}_{\mathsf{GGen}, \mathcal{D}_{2k,k}, \mathcal{B}_2}^{\mathsf{MDDH}}(\lambda) + \frac{3kQ_{\mathsf{Sign}} + 1}{p}.$$

We now describe the adversary $\mathcal{A}'$ playing in the security game $\mathsf{Exp}_{\mathsf{core}}$ in Fig. 3. It first gets the public key $\mathcal{PG} \leftarrow_R \mathsf{GGen}(1^\lambda)$, then samples $\mathbf{B} \leftarrow_R \mathcal{D}_{k'}$, picks $\mathbf{b}^\perp \in \mathrm{orth}(\mathbf{B})$, $\mathbf{K}_i \leftarrow_R \mathbb{Z}_p^{2k \times (k'+1)}$ for all $i \in [\ell]$, and runs $\mathcal{A}$ on input $pk := \left([\mathbf{B}]_2, \{[\mathbf{K}_i \mathbf{B}]_2\}_{i \in [\ell]}\right)$.

Then, to simulate oracle SignO in Game_2 for query $\mathbf{m} \in (\mathbb{Z}_p^\ell)^*$, $\mathcal{A}'$ queries its own oracle $\mathsf{TagO}(\mathbf{m})$ to obtain $([\mathbf{t}_0]_1, [\mathbf{T}]_1, [\mathbf{T}]_2)$. It sets $[\mathbf{S}]_2 := [\mathbf{T}]_2$, and computes for all $i \in [\ell]$: $[\mathbf{S}_i]_1 := m_i[\mathbf{T}]_1$, and $[\mathbf{S}_{\ell+1}]_1 := \sum_{i=1}^{\ell} m_i \mathbf{K}_i^\top [\mathbf{T}]_1 + \mathbf{b}^\perp[\mathbf{t}_0^\top]_1$. Note that with $\mathbf{K}^\top =: (\mathbf{k}_1 \| \cdots \| \mathbf{k}_\ell)$ we have $\mathbf{t}_0^\top = \sum_{i \in [\ell]} m_i \mathbf{k}_i^\top \mathbf{T}$, thus the values $\mathbf{k}_i$ in the simulation of Game_2 are implicitly defined by $\mathbf{K}$ from Fig. 3, chosen by $\mathcal{A}'$'s challenger. $\mathcal{A}'$ returns $\sigma := \left(\{[\mathbf{S}_i]_1\}_{i \in [\ell+1]}, [\mathbf{S}]_2\right)$ to $\mathcal{A}$.

Finally, when $\mathcal{A}$ sends its forgery $\left([\mathbf{m}^\star]_1, \sigma^\star := \left(\{[\mathbf{s}_i]_1\}_{i \in [\ell+1]}, [\mathbf{s}]_2\right)\right)$, $\mathcal{A}'$ uses it to create a forgery on its own as follows. First, $\mathcal{A}'$ checks that

$$[\mathbf{s}]_2 \neq [\mathbf{0}]_2 \tag{1}$$

$$\forall i \in [\ell] : [\mathbf{s}_i]_1 \bullet [1]_2 = [m_i^\star]_1 \bullet [\mathbf{s}]_2 \tag{2}$$

$$\exists [\mathbf{t}_0]_1 \in \mathbb{G}_1 : [\mathbf{s}_{\ell+1}^\top]_1 - \sum_{i=1}^{\ell} [\mathbf{s}_i^\top]_1 \mathbf{K}_i = (\mathbf{b}^\perp)^\top \cdot [\mathbf{t}_0]_1 \tag{3}$$

Note that $\mathcal{A}'$ can efficiently check (3) since it knows $\mathbf{b}^\perp \in \mathbb{Z}_p^{k'+1}$. Indeed, given any vector $[\mathbf{x}]_1 \in \mathbb{G}_1^n$ and $\mathbf{y} \in \mathbb{Z}_p^n$ for some $n \in \mathbb{N}^*$, one can efficiently compute $[\det(\mathbf{x}\|\mathbf{y})]_1$ since this only requires computing exponentiations in $\mathbb{G}_1$.

$\mathsf{Exp}_{\mathrm{core}}(1^\lambda, \mathcal{A}')$:

$\mathcal{Q}_{\mathrm{tag}} := \emptyset$, $pk := \mathcal{PG} \leftarrow_{\mathrm{R}} \mathsf{GGen}(1^\lambda)$, $\mathbf{A} \leftarrow \mathcal{D}_{2k,k}$, $\mathbf{K} \leftarrow_{\mathrm{R}} \mathbb{Z}_p^{\ell \times 2k}$, $sk := (\mathbf{A}, \mathbf{K})$

$([\mathbf{m}^\star]_1, \tau^\star) \leftarrow \mathcal{A}'^{\mathsf{TagO}(\cdot)}(pk)$

Return 1 if $\mathsf{VerO}([\mathbf{m}^\star]_1, \tau^\star) = 1$ and $[\mathbf{m}^\star]_1 \notin \bigcup_{\mathbf{m} \in \mathcal{Q}_{\mathrm{tag}}} \mathsf{Span}([\mathbf{m}]_1)$, 0 otherwise

---

$\mathsf{VerO}([\mathbf{m}^\star]_1, \tau^\star)$:

Parse $\tau^\star := ([t_0]_1, [\mathbf{t}]_2) \in \mathbb{G}_1 \times \mathbb{G}_2^{2k}$

Return 1 if $[\mathbf{t}]_2 \neq [\mathbf{0}]_2$ and $[\mathbf{m}^{\star\top}]_1 \mathbf{K} \bullet [\mathbf{t}]_2 = [t_0]_1 \bullet [1]_2$

Return 0 otherwise

$\mathsf{TagO}(\mathbf{m} \in (\mathbb{Z}_p^\ell)^\star)$:

$\mathcal{Q}_{\mathrm{tag}} := \mathcal{Q}_{\mathrm{tag}} \cup \{\mathbf{m}\}$, $\mathbf{U} \leftarrow_{\mathrm{R}} \mathsf{GL}_k$, $\mathbf{T} := \mathbf{AU}$, $t_0^\top := \mathbf{m}^\top \mathbf{KT}$

Return $\tau := ([t_0]_1, [\mathbf{T}]_1, [\mathbf{T}]_2)$

Fig. 3. Experiment for Lemma 3.

Note that if the forgery submitted by $\mathcal{A}$ is successful, it must satisfy (1), (2), and the following equation (cf. Fig. 2):

$$\sum_{i=1}^{\ell} [\mathbf{s}_i^\top]_1 (\mathbf{K}_i + \mathbf{k}_i(\mathbf{b}^\perp)^\top) = [\mathbf{s}_{\ell+1}^\top]_1 \tag{4}$$

which implies (3), with $[t_0]_1 := \sum_{i=1}^{\ell} [\mathbf{s}_i^\top]_1 \cdot \mathbf{k}_i$.

Thus, if either (1), (2) or (3) fails, then $\mathcal{A}$ produced an unsuccessful forgery and $\mathcal{A}'$ can abort.

Otherwise, $\mathcal{A}$ can efficiently compute $[t_0]_1 \in \mathbb{G}_1$ satisfying (3), from $(\mathbf{b}^\perp)^\top \cdot [t_0]_1$ and $\mathbf{b}^\perp$: let $i \in [k'+1]$ be such that the i-th coordinate of $\mathbf{b}^\perp$ is non-zero (recall $\mathbf{b}^\perp \neq \mathbf{0}$); then $[t_0]_1$ is the i-th coordinate of $(\mathbf{b}^\perp)^\top \cdot [t_0]_1$ divided by the i-th coordinate of $\mathbf{b}^\perp$. Finally, $\mathcal{A}'$ sets $[\mathbf{t}]_2 := [\mathbf{s}]_2$, and returns the forgery $([\mathbf{m}^\star]_1, ([t_0]_1, [\mathbf{t}]_2))$ in $\mathsf{Exp}_{\mathrm{core}}$.

When $\mathcal{A}$ submits a successful forgery $([\mathbf{m}^\star]_1, \sigma^\star := (\{[\mathbf{s}_i]_1\}_{i \in [\ell+1]}, [\mathbf{s}]_2))$, it satisfies (1), (2). Moreover, it satisfies (4), which means the value computed by $\mathcal{A}'$ is

$$[t_0]_1 := \sum_{i=1}^{\ell} [\mathbf{s}_i^\top]_1 \cdot \mathbf{k}_i. \tag{5}$$

This implies that the forgery produced by $\mathcal{A}'$ is also successful, since it satisfies

$$[\mathbf{t}]_2 \neq [\mathbf{0}]_2 \quad \text{by (1), and}$$

$$\sum_{i=1}^{\ell} [m_i^\star]_1 \mathbf{k}_i^\top \bullet [\mathbf{t}]_2 = [t_0]_1 \bullet [1]_2 \quad \text{by (2) and (5).}$$

This concludes the proof that $\mathsf{Adv}_2 \leq \mathsf{Adv}_{\mathcal{A}'}^{\mathrm{core}}(\lambda)$. $\qquad\square$

To prove the above theorem, we use the following core lemma, which essentially proves the security of a private-key variant of our EQS scheme.

Lemma 3 (Core lemma). *For an adversary $\mathcal{A}'$ and a security parameter $\lambda \in \mathbb{N}^*$, let $\mathsf{Adv}_{\mathcal{A}'}^{\mathrm{core}}(\lambda) := \Pr[\mathsf{Exp}_{core}(1^\lambda, \mathcal{A}') = 1]$, with $\mathsf{Exp}_{core}(1^\lambda, \mathcal{A}')$ depicted in Fig. 3. Then for any PPT adversary $\mathcal{A}'$, there exists a PPT algorithm $\mathcal{B}$ such that:*

$$\mathsf{Adv}_{\mathcal{A}'}^{\mathrm{core}}(\lambda) \leq 2kQ_{\mathsf{Tag}} \cdot \mathsf{Adv}_{\mathsf{GGen}, \mathcal{D}_{2k,k}, \mathcal{B}}^{\mathrm{MDDH}}(\lambda) + \frac{3kQ_{\mathsf{Tag}} + 1}{p},$$

where Q_{Tag} is the number of tag queries.

Proof of Lemma 3. We use hybrids $\mathsf{Game}_{i.1}$ for $i \in [Q_{\mathsf{Sign}} + 1]$, and $\mathsf{Game}_{i.2}$, $\mathsf{Game}_{i.3}$ for $i \in [Q_{\mathsf{Sign}}]$, described in Fig. 4, and we denote by Adv_i the advantage of $\mathcal{A}'$ in Game_i, that is $\Pr[\mathsf{Game}_i(1^\lambda, \mathcal{A}') = 1]$, where the probability is taken over the random coins of Game_i and $\mathcal{A}'$.

$\mathsf{Game}_{1.1}$ is $\mathsf{Exp}_{core}(1^\lambda, \mathcal{A}')$.

From $\mathsf{Game}_{i.1}$ to $\mathsf{Game}_{i.2}$: We switch the matrices $[\mathbf{T}]_1$ and $[\mathbf{T}]_2$ computed by TagO on its i-th query to uniformly random over $\mathbb{Z}_p^{2k \times k}$, using the $\mathcal{D}_{2k,k}$-MDDH assumption. Namely, we show that for all $i \in [Q_{\mathsf{Tag}}]$, there is a PPT algorithm $\mathcal{B}_{i.1}$ such that

$$|\mathsf{Adv}_{i.1} - \mathsf{Adv}_{i.2}| \leq k \cdot \mathsf{Adv}_{\mathsf{GGen}, \mathcal{D}_{2k,k}, \mathbb{G}_2, \mathcal{B}_{i.1}}^{\mathrm{MDDH}}(\lambda) + \frac{k}{p}.$$

First, we argue that the distribution $\mathbf{U} \leftarrow_{\mathrm{R}} \mathsf{GL}_k$ and $\mathbf{U} \leftarrow_{\mathrm{R}} \mathbb{Z}_p^{k \times k}$ are $\frac{k}{p}$-close. Then, we use the k-fold $\mathcal{D}_{2k,k}$-MDDH assumption (which reduces to its 1-fold variant with a security loss of k, via a hybrid argument) to switch $\{[\mathbf{A}]_s, [\mathbf{AU}]_s\}_{s \in \{1,2\}}$ to $\{[\mathbf{A}]_s, [\mathbf{T}]_s\}_{s \in \{1,2\}}$ where $\mathbf{T} \leftarrow_{\mathrm{R}} \mathbb{Z}_p^{2k \times k}$. We give a precise description of the reduction $\mathcal{B}_{i.1}'$ to the k-fold $\mathcal{D}_{2k,k}$-MDDH assumption below. Finally, we use the basis $(\mathbf{A}|\mathbf{A}^\perp)$ of $\mathbb{Z}_p^{2k}$, where $\mathbf{A}^\perp \in \mathsf{orth}(\mathbf{A})$, and $(\mathbf{A}^\perp)^\top \mathbf{A}^\perp = \mathsf{Id}_{k \times k}$, the identity matrix in $\mathbb{Z}_p^{k \times k}$, which allows us to write $\mathbf{T} \leftarrow_{\mathrm{R}} \mathbb{Z}_p^{2k \times k}$ as $\mathbf{T} := \mathbf{AU} + \mathbf{A}^\perp \mathbf{V}$, with $\mathbf{U}, \mathbf{V} \leftarrow_{\mathrm{R}} \mathbb{Z}_p^{k \times k}$.

We now describe adversary $\mathcal{B}_{i.1}'$ playing against the k-fold $\mathcal{D}_{2k,k}$-MDDH assumption. Given a challenge $\left(\mathcal{PG}, \{[\mathbf{A}]_s, [\mathbf{Z}]_s\}_{s \in \{1,2\}}\right)$, where $[\mathbf{Z}]_s \in \mathbb{G}_s^{2k \times k}$ is either of the form $[\mathbf{AU}]_s$ for $\mathbf{U} \leftarrow_{\mathrm{R}} \mathbb{Z}_p^{k \times k}$ or uniformly random over $\mathbb{G}_s^{2k \times k}$, $\mathcal{B}_{i.1}'$ samples $\mathbf{K} \leftarrow_{\mathrm{R}} \mathbb{Z}_p^{\ell \times 2k}$, which it uses to simulate VerO. To simulate $\mathsf{TagO}(\mathbf{m} \in \mathbb{Z}_p^\ell)$ on its ν-th query, it does the following:

- if $\nu < i$: $\mathcal{B}_{i.1}'$ samples $\mathbf{U} \leftarrow_{\mathrm{R}} \mathsf{GL}_k$, $\mathbf{t}_0 \leftarrow_{\mathrm{R}} \mathbb{Z}_p^k$, computes $[\mathbf{T}]_s := [\mathbf{A}]_s \mathbf{U}$ for all $s \in \{1, 2\}$, and returns $([\mathbf{t}_0]_1, [\mathbf{T}]_1, [\mathbf{T}]_2)$ to $\mathcal{A}'$.
- if $\nu = i$: $\mathcal{B}_{i.1}'$ sets $[\mathbf{T}]_s := [\mathbf{Z}]_s$ for all $s \in \{1, 2\}$, computes $[\mathbf{t}_0^\top]_1 := \mathbf{m}^\top \mathbf{K}[\mathbf{T}]_1$, and returns $([\mathbf{t}_0]_1, [\mathbf{T}]_1, [\mathbf{T}]_2)$ to $\mathcal{A}'$.
- if $\nu > i$: $\mathcal{B}_{i.1}'$ samples $\mathbf{U} \leftarrow_{\mathrm{R}} \mathsf{GL}_k$, computes $[\mathbf{T}]_s := [\mathbf{A}]_s \mathbf{U}$ for all $s \in \{1, 2\}$, $[\mathbf{t}_0^\top]_1 := \mathbf{m}^\top \mathbf{K}[\mathbf{T}]_1$, and returns $([\mathbf{t}_0]_1, [\mathbf{T}]_1, [\mathbf{T}]_2)$ to $\mathcal{A}'$.

$\boxed{\text{Game}_{i.1},}\; \boxed{\text{Game}_{i.2},\; \boxed{\text{Game}_{i.3}}\;,\; \overline{\vphantom{|}\;\text{Game}_{i.4}\;}}$:

$\mathcal{Q}_{\text{tag}} := \emptyset$, $pk := \mathcal{PG} \leftarrow_{\text{R}} \mathsf{GGen}(1^\lambda)$, $\mathbf{A} \leftarrow \mathcal{D}_{2k,k}$, $\mathbf{K} \leftarrow_{\text{R}} \mathbb{Z}_p^{\ell \times 2k}$, $sk := (\mathbf{A}, \mathbf{K})$

$\boxed{\text{Pick } \mathbf{A}^\perp \in \text{orth}(\mathbf{A}) \text{ such that } (\mathbf{A}^\perp)^\top \mathbf{A}^\perp = \mathsf{Id}_{k \times k}}$

$([\mathbf{m}^\star]_1, \tau^\star) \leftarrow \mathcal{A}^{\mathsf{TagO}(\cdot)}(pk)$

Return 1 if $\mathsf{VerO}([\mathbf{m}^\star]_1, \tau^\star) = 1$ and $[\mathbf{m}^\star]_1 \notin \bigcup_{\mathbf{m} \in \mathcal{Q}_{\text{tag}}} \mathsf{Span}([\mathbf{m}]_1)$, 0 otherwise

---

$\mathsf{VerO}([\mathbf{m}^\star]_1, \tau^\star := ([t_0]_1, [\mathbf{t}]_2)):$

Return 1 if $[\mathbf{t}]_2 \neq [\mathbf{0}]_2$ and $[\mathbf{m}^{\star\top}]_1 \mathbf{K} \bullet [\mathbf{t}]_2 = [t_0]_1 \bullet [1]_2$

Return 0 otherwise

$\mathsf{TagO}(\mathbf{m}):$

On the ν'th query, $\mathcal{Q}_{\text{tag}} := \mathcal{Q}_{\text{tag}} \cup \{\mathbf{m}\}$, then:

If $\nu < i$: $\mathbf{U} \leftarrow_{\text{R}} \mathsf{GL}_k$, $\mathbf{T} := \mathbf{AU}$, $\mathbf{t}_0 \leftarrow_{\text{R}} \mathbb{Z}_p^k$

If $\nu = i$: $\mathbf{U} \leftarrow_{\text{R}} \mathsf{GL}_k$, $\mathbf{T} := \mathbf{AU}$, $\boxed{\mathbf{U}, \mathbf{V} \leftarrow_{\text{R}} \mathbb{Z}_p^{k \times k}, \; \mathbf{T} := \mathbf{AU} + \mathbf{A}^\perp \mathbf{V}}$

$\boxed{\mathbf{w} \leftarrow_{\text{R}} \mathbb{Z}_p^k, \; \mathbf{t}_0^\top := \mathbf{m}^\top \mathbf{KT} + \mathbf{w}^\top \mathbf{V}}$, $\overline{\; \mathbf{t}_0 \leftarrow_{\text{R}} \mathbb{Z}_p^k \;}$

If $\nu > i$: $\mathbf{U} \leftarrow_{\text{R}} \mathsf{GL}_k$, $\mathbf{T} := \mathbf{AU}$, $\mathbf{t}_0^\top := \mathbf{m}^\top \mathbf{KT}$

Return $\tau := ([\mathbf{t}_0]_1, [\mathbf{T}]_1, [\mathbf{T}]_2,)$

Fig. 4. $\text{Game}_{i.1}$ for $i \in [\mathcal{Q}_{\text{tag}} + 1]$ and $\text{Game}_{i.2}$, $\text{Game}_{i.3}$ for $i \in [\mathcal{Q}_{\text{tag}}]$ in the proof of Lemma 3. In each procedure, the components inside a solid (dotted, gray) frame are only present in the games marked by a solid (dotted, gray) frame. In particular, the $\boxed{\text{solid}}$ frame is present in all games except $\text{Game}_{i.1}$.

From $\text{Game}_{i.2}$ to $\text{Game}_{i.3}$: We show that

$$|\mathsf{Adv}_{i.2} - \mathsf{Adv}_{i.3}| = 0.$$

To do so, first consider the *selective* variant of these games, that is, $\text{Game}_{i.2}^\star$ and $\text{Game}_{i.3}^\star$, which are as $\text{Game}_{i.2}$ and $\text{Game}_{i.3}$ except that the adversary has to commit to the forgery message $[\mathbf{m}^\star]_1$ beforehand. We will then show that $|\mathsf{Adv}_{i.2}^\star - \mathsf{Adv}_{i.3}^\star| = 0$. Using complexity leveraging,[1] we obtain $\mathsf{Adv}_{i.2}^\star = p^{-\ell} \cdot \mathsf{Adv}_{i.2}$ and $\mathsf{Adv}_{i.2}^\star = p^{-\ell} \cdot \mathsf{Adv}_{i.2}$, which allows to conclude.

---

[1] Complexity leveraging is a technique that allows to prove adaptive from selective security: the reduction (playing in the selective game) simply guesses the (adaptive) adversary's forgery at the beginning of the game and aborts if its guess later turns out wrong. The security loss of the reduction is therefore inversely proportional to the number of guesses (here: number of messages, i.e. p^ℓ).

We now prove that $|\mathsf{Adv}^\star_{i.2} - \mathsf{Adv}^\star_{i.3}| = 0$. We use the fact that the distributions:

$$\mathbf{K} \leftarrow_{\mathrm{R}} \mathbb{Z}_p^{\ell \times 2k} \quad \text{and} \quad \mathbf{K} + \boxed{\mathbf{M}^\perp \mathbf{Z}(\mathbf{A}^\perp)^\top} \text{ with } \mathbf{K} \leftarrow_{\mathrm{R}} \mathbb{Z}_p^{\ell \times 2k},$$

are identical, where $\mathbf{M}^\perp \in \mathrm{orth}(\mathbf{m}^{\star\top})$, that is, $\mathbf{M}^\perp \in \mathbb{Z}_p^{\ell \times (\ell-1)}$ is a full-rank matrix such that $\mathbf{m}^{\star\top}\mathbf{M}^\perp = \mathbf{0}$; $\mathbf{Z} \leftarrow_{\mathrm{R}} \mathbb{Z}_p^{(\ell-1)\times 2k}$; and $\mathbf{A}^\perp \in \mathrm{orth}(\mathbf{A})$ such that $(\mathbf{A}^\perp)^\top \mathbf{A}^\perp = \mathsf{Id}_{k \times k}$.

Since $\mathbf{K}$ is distributed like $\mathbf{K} + \mathbf{M}^\perp \mathbf{Z}(\mathbf{A}^\perp)^\top$, we replace the former by the latter in $\mathsf{Game}^\star_{i.2}$ and then show that the resulting game is distributed like $\mathsf{Game}^\star_{i.3}$.

We start with the oracle $\mathsf{VerO}([\mathbf{m}^\star]_1, \tau^\star := ([t_0]_1, [\mathbf{t}]_2,))$, which checks:

$$[\mathbf{m}^{\star\top}]_1(\mathbf{K} + \boxed{\mathbf{M}^\perp \mathbf{Z}(\mathbf{A}^\perp)^\top}) \bullet [\mathbf{t}]_2 = [\mathbf{m}^{\star\top}]_1 \mathbf{K} \bullet [\mathbf{t}]_2 \overset{?}{=} [t_0]_1 \bullet [1]_2,$$

where the first equality always holds, since $\mathbf{m}^{\star\top}\mathbf{M}^\perp = \mathbf{0}$.

Let us now analyze the TagO queries. For the first $i-1$ queries, the output of TagO is independent of $\mathbf{K}$.

Consider the i-th query $[\mathbf{m}]_1 \in (\mathbb{G}_1^\ell)^*$ to the TagO oracle. We have:

$$t_0^\top := \mathbf{m}^\top \mathbf{K}\mathbf{T} + \boxed{\mathbf{m}^\top \mathbf{M}^\perp \mathbf{Z}(\mathbf{A}^\perp)^\top(\mathbf{A}\mathbf{U} + \mathbf{A}^\perp \mathbf{V})} = \mathbf{m}^\top \mathbf{K}\mathbf{T} + \boxed{\mathbf{m}^\top \mathbf{M}^\perp \mathbf{Z}\mathbf{V}},$$

where for the last equality we used $(\mathbf{A}^\perp)^\top \mathbf{A} = \mathbf{0}$ and $(\mathbf{A}^\perp)^\top \mathbf{A}^\perp = \mathsf{Id}_{k \times k}$. Moreover, if the adversary wins the game then $\mathbf{m}^\top \mathbf{M}^\perp \neq \mathbf{0}$, as otherwise $\mathbf{m}$ is a multiple of $\mathbf{m}^\star$, thus the latter is not a valid forgery. Now $\mathbf{m}^\top \mathbf{M}^\perp \neq \mathbf{0}$ implies that $\mathbf{m}^\top \mathbf{M}^\perp \mathbf{Z}$ is identically distributed to $\mathbf{w}^\top \leftarrow_{\mathrm{R}} \mathbb{Z}_p^{1 \times 2k}$, as in $\mathsf{Game}_{i.3}$.

For the remaining TagO queries, $\mathsf{TagO}(\mathbf{m})$ computes $t_0^\top := \mathbf{m}^\top(\mathbf{K} + \boxed{\mathbf{M}^\perp \mathbf{Z}(\mathbf{A}^\perp)^\top})\mathbf{A}\mathbf{U} = \mathbf{m}^\top \mathbf{K}\mathbf{A}\mathbf{U}$, since $(\mathbf{A}^\perp)^\top \mathbf{A} = \mathbf{0}$.

All in all, we have thus shown that the modified game (which is distributed like $\mathsf{Game}^\star_{i.2}$) is distributed equivalently to $\mathsf{Game}^\star_{i.3}$.

From $\mathsf{Game}_{i.3}$ to $\mathsf{Game}_{i.4}$: We show that these two games are statistically close. This follows from the fact that with probability at least $1 - \frac{k}{p}$ over the choice of $\mathbf{V} \leftarrow_{\mathrm{R}} \mathbb{Z}_p^{k \times k}$, $\mathbf{V}$ is invertible. In that case, $\mathbf{w}^\top \mathbf{V}$ for $\mathbf{w} \leftarrow_{\mathrm{R}} \mathbb{Z}_p^k$ is uniformly random over $\mathbb{Z}_p^{1 \times k}$, which means the vector $\mathbf{t}_0$ computed by TagO on its i-th query is itself uniformly random over $\mathbb{Z}_p^k$, as in $\mathsf{Game}_{i.4}$.

We note that for this step is was crucial that V is a $k \times k$ matrix. For the definition of $\mathbf{T}$ from $\mathsf{Game}_{i.2}$ on, we therefore require that $\mathbf{A}^\perp \in \mathbb{Z}_p^{2k \times k}$, which is what forced us to choose $\mathbf{A} \in \mathbb{Z}_p^{2k \times k}$ (rather than $\mathbf{A} \in \mathbb{Z}_p^{(k+1)\times k}$).

From $\mathsf{Game}_{i.4}$ to $\mathsf{Game}_{i+1.1}$: We switch back the matrices $[\mathbf{T}]_1$ and $[\mathbf{T}]_2$ computed by TagO on its i-th query to $[\mathbf{A}\mathbf{U}]_1$ and $[\mathbf{A}\mathbf{U}]_2$ with $\mathbf{U} \leftarrow_{\mathrm{R}} \mathsf{GL}_k$, using the k-fold $\mathcal{D}_{2k,k}$-MDDH assumption. This transition is similar to the transition from $\mathsf{Game}_{i.1}$ to $\mathsf{Game}_{i.2}$. We defer to the latter for further details.

$\mathsf{Game}_{Q_{tag}+1.1}$: We show that $\mathsf{Adv}_{Q_{tag}+1.1} = \frac{1}{p}$. In this game there is no information leaked about $\mathbf{K}$ prior to $\mathcal{A}'$'s query to VerO, since all the tags generated by TagO contain a uniformly random vector $[\mathbf{t}_0]_1 \leftarrow_R \mathbb{G}_1^k$. Therefore, the vector $[\mathbf{m}^{\star\top}]_1\mathbf{K}$ computed by $\mathsf{VerO}([\mathbf{m}^\star]_1, \tau^\star := ([\mathbf{t}_0]_1, [\mathbf{t}]_2))$ is uniformly random over $\mathbb{G}_1^{1\times 2k}$, which means $[\mathbf{m}^{\star\top}]_1\mathbf{K} \bullet [\mathbf{t}]_2$ is uniformly random over $\mathbb{G}_T$, independent of $[\mathbf{t}_0]_1$, when $[\mathbf{t}]_2 \neq [\mathbf{0}]_2$. Thus, we have: $\mathsf{Adv}_{Q_{tag}+1.1} = \frac{1}{p}$. □

4 Application to Access Control Encryption

Access Control Encryption. Damgård et al. [DHO16] introduced the notion of access control encryption (ACE), which allows to control the information flow between senders and receivers. In their model each sender $i \in \{0,1\}^n$ has an encryption key ek_i, and each receiver $j \in \{0,1\}^n$ has a decryption key dk_j; the system specifies an access control policy $P\colon \{0,1\}^n \times \{0,1\}^n \to \{0,1\}$, and communication is allowed from sender i to receiver j iff $P(i,j) = 1$. Thus, ACE restricts both what information is being received (this is captured by a so-called *No-Read rule*), and what can be sent (captured by a so-called *No-Write rule*). To prevent sending of information by unauthorized senders (No-Write rule), it is necessary to assume that messages are relayed via a special party, called the *sanitizer*, which is assumed to be honest (it will behave according to the protocol specification) but curious (it will try to learn additional information by colluding with other parties in the system).

More precisely, the No-Read rule stipulates that given all encryptions keys, if the sanitizer colludes with a set of unauthorized receivers $\mathcal{J} \subset \{0,1\}^n$, it should not be able to learn any information from an encryption by sender $i \in \{0,1\}^n$ if $P(i,j) = 0$ for all $j \in \mathcal{J}$. In particular, both the underlying plaintext and the identity of i should remain hidden. The No-Write rule roughly says that a collusion of senders $\mathcal{I} \subset \{0,1\}^n$ and receivers $\mathcal{J} \subset \{0,1\}^n$ such that $P(i,j) = 0$ for all $i \in \mathcal{I}$, $j \in \mathcal{J}$ that tries to exchange information will be prevented from doing so by the (in this case honest) sanitizer. (If the sanitizer is corrupt then it can always distribute information and thereby break the No-Write rule.) We recall the formal definitions below for completeness.

Construction from EQS. Fuchsbauer et al. [FGKO17] built the first pairing-based ACE for predicates such as equality $(P(i,j) = 1 \Leftrightarrow i = j)$ and range $(P(i,j) = 1 \Leftrightarrow i \leq j)$, whose ciphertexts contain $O(n)$ group elements. The work introducing the concept [DHO16] had built ACE from indistinguishability obfuscation for general circuits and gave an inefficient construction from DDH with ciphertexts of size $O(2^n)$.

One construction from [FGKO17] generically uses EQS, which they instantiated with the scheme from [FHS14] and thus relies on an interactive assumption. When replacing their EQS with our scheme from Sect. 3, we obtain another efficient ACE. We need to show that the relaxed unforgeability notion satisfied by our EQS (namely EUF-CoMA; Definition 5) suffices for the security of the ACE. We note that the resulting ACE (as for [FGKO17]), does *not* require a private key for the sanitizer, unlike the original schemes from [DHO16].

Related works. Recent work [KW17] builds ACE for *arbitrary* access control policies based on standard assumptions (such as DDH or LWE), using (single-key) general-purpose functional encryption and predicate encryption. Our scheme has the advantage of being much more efficient, although specialized to the equality and range predicates. In [BMM17], the authors define new, stronger security notions for ACE and give constructions that achieve them under standard assumptions for the equality predicate, which can be lifted to a disjunction of equalities and to predicates such a range, as shown in [FGKO17].

In the rest of this section, we first recall the definition of ACE from [FGKO17] and the construction for the equality predicate [FGKO17, Construction 2]. We then give a proof of its security when the underlying EQS is only EUF-CoMA. ACE for range can then be obtained from the ACE for equality generically, as shown in [FGKO17].

Definition 6 (ACE). *An* access control encryption *(ACE) [FGKO17] scheme is defined by the following PPT algorithms:*

- Setup($1^\lambda, P$), *on input the security parameter $\lambda \in \mathbb{N}$ and a policy $P \colon \{0,1\}^n \times \{0,1\}^n \to \{0,1\}$, outputs a master secret key* msk *and public parameters* pp *(which implicitly define the message space $\mathcal{M}$ and ciphertext spaces $\mathcal{C}, \mathcal{C}'$).*
- Gen(msk, i, t) *is a* deterministic *algorithm that on input the master secret key* msk*, an identity $i \in \{0,1\}^n$ and a type $t \in \{\mathsf{sen}, \mathsf{rec}\}$, specifying whether i is a sender or a receiver, outputs a key k. We use the following notation for the types of keys:*
  - $ek_i \leftarrow$ Gen(msk, $i,$ sen) *and call it an* encryption key *for $i \in \{0,1\}^n$,*
  - $dk_j \leftarrow$ Gen(msk, $j,$ rec) *and call it a* decryption key *for $j \in \{0,1\}^n$.*
- Enc(ek_i, m), *on input an encryption key ek_i and a message $m \in \mathcal{M}$, outputs a ciphertext $c \in \mathcal{C}$.*
- San(pp, c), *on input the public parameters* pp *and a ciphertext $c \in \mathcal{C}$, outputs a sanitized ciphertext $c' \in \mathcal{C}'$.*
- Dec(dk_j, c') *is a* deterministic *algorithm that on input a decryption key dk_j, a ciphertext $c' \in \mathcal{C}'$, outputs a message $m \in \mathcal{M} \cup \{\bot\}$.*

Definition 7 (Correctness). *For all $m \in \mathcal{M}$, $i, j \in \{0,1\}^n$ with $P(i,j) = 1$:*

$$\Pr\left[\mathsf{Dec}\big(dk_j, \mathsf{San}(pp, \mathsf{Enc}\,(ek_i, m))\big) = m\right] \geq 1 - \mathsf{negl}(\lambda),$$

where the probability is taken over $(pp, msk) \leftarrow$ Setup($1^\lambda, P$), $ek_i \leftarrow$ Gen(msk, $i,$ sen), and $dk_j \leftarrow$ Gen(msk, $j,$ rec).

Complementary to correctness, we require that it is detectable when decryption does not succeed, formalized as follows.

Definition 8 (Detectability). *For all $m \in \mathcal{M}$, $i, j \in \{0,1\}^n$ with $P(i,j) = 0$:*

$$\Pr\left[\mathsf{Dec}\big(dk_j, \mathsf{San}(pp, \mathsf{Enc}\,(ek_i, m))\big) = \bot\right] \geq 1 - \mathsf{negl}\,(\lambda),$$

where the probability is taken over $(pp, msk) \leftarrow$ Setup($1^\lambda, P$), $ek_i \leftarrow$ Gen(msk, $i,$ sen), and $dk_j \leftarrow$ Gen(msk, $j,$ rec).

No-Read Rule. An access control encryption scheme ACE := (Setup, Gen, Enc, San, Dec) is said to satisfy the No-Read rule if for all PPT adversaries $\mathcal{A}$,

$$\mathsf{Adv}_{\mathsf{ACE},\mathcal{A}}^{\mathsf{No\text{-}Read}}(\lambda) := \Pr\left[\mathsf{Exp}_{\mathsf{ACE}}^{\mathsf{No\text{-}Read}}(1^\lambda, \mathcal{A}) = 1\right] - \tfrac{1}{2} = \mathsf{negl}(\lambda),$$

where the game $\mathsf{Exp}_{\mathsf{ACE}}^{\mathsf{No\text{-}Read}}(1^\lambda, \mathcal{A})$ is defined as follows:

Game Definition	Oracle Definition
$\mathsf{Exp}_{\mathsf{ACE}}^{\mathsf{No\text{-}Read}}(1^\lambda, \mathcal{A})$:	$\mathcal{O}_G(j, t)$:
$\mathcal{Q}_{\mathsf{key}} := \emptyset$	$\mathcal{Q}_{\mathsf{key}} := \mathcal{Q}_{\mathsf{key}} \cup \{(j,t)\}$
$(pp, msk) \leftarrow \mathsf{Setup}(1^\lambda, P)$	Return $k \leftarrow \mathsf{Gen}(msk, j, t)$
$(m_0, m_1, i_0, i_1) \leftarrow \mathcal{A}^{\mathcal{O}_G(\cdot), \mathcal{O}_E(\cdot)}(pp)$	
$b \leftarrow \{0,1\}$; $c \leftarrow \mathsf{Enc}(\mathsf{Gen}(msk, i_b, \mathsf{sen}), m_b)$	$\mathcal{O}_E(i, m)$:
$b' \leftarrow \mathcal{A}^{\mathcal{O}_G(\cdot), \mathcal{O}_E(\cdot)}(c)$	$ek_i \leftarrow \mathsf{Gen}(msk, i, \mathsf{sen})$
Return 1 iff $b' = b$, $|m_0| = |m_1|$, $i_0, i_1 \in \{0,1\}^n$ and	Return $c \leftarrow \mathsf{Enc}(ek_i, m)$
$\forall (j, \mathtt{rec}) \in \mathcal{Q}_{\mathsf{key}}$, $P(i_0, j) = P(i_1, j) = 0$	

Recall that Gen is assumed to be a deterministic algorithm, which is why the experiment need not do any bookkeeping of already-generated keys.

No-Write Rule. An access control encryption scheme ACE := (Setup, Gen, Enc, San, Dec) is said to satisfy the No-Write rule if for all PPT adversaries $\mathcal{A}$,

$$\mathsf{Adv}_{\mathsf{ACE},\mathcal{A}}^{\mathsf{No\text{-}Write}}(\lambda) := \Pr\left[\mathsf{Exp}_{\mathsf{ACE}}^{\mathsf{No\text{-}Write}}(1^\lambda, \mathcal{A}) = 1\right] - \tfrac{1}{2} = \mathsf{negl}(\lambda),$$

where the game $\mathsf{Exp}_{\mathsf{ACE}}^{\mathsf{No\text{-}Write}}(1^\lambda, \mathcal{A})$ is defined as follows:

Game Definition	Oracle Definition
$\mathsf{Exp}_{\mathsf{ACE}}^{\mathsf{No\text{-}Write}}(1^\lambda, \mathcal{A})$:	$\mathcal{O}_S(j, t)$:
$\mathcal{Q}_{\mathsf{sen}}, \mathcal{Q}_{\mathsf{rec}} := \emptyset$	$\mathcal{Q}_t := \mathcal{Q}_t \cup \{j\}$
$(pp, msk) \leftarrow \mathsf{Setup}(1^\lambda, P)$	Return $k \leftarrow \mathsf{Gen}(msk, j, t)$
$b \leftarrow \{0,1\}$; $m' \leftarrow \mathcal{M}$	
$(c^{(0)}, i') \leftarrow \mathcal{A}^{\mathcal{O}_S(\cdot), \mathcal{O}_E(\cdot)}(pp)$	$\mathcal{O}_R(j, t)$:
$c^{(1)} \leftarrow \mathsf{Enc}(\mathsf{Gen}(msk, i', \mathsf{sen}), m')$	if $t = \mathtt{rec}$, $\mathcal{Q}_{\mathsf{rec}} := \mathcal{Q}_{\mathsf{rec}} \cup \{j\}$
$b' \leftarrow \mathcal{A}^{\mathcal{O}_R(\cdot), \mathcal{O}_E(\cdot)}(\mathsf{San}(pp, c^{(b)}))$	Return $dk \leftarrow \mathsf{Gen}(msk, j, \mathtt{rec})$
Return 1 iff $b' = b$, $i' \in \mathcal{Q}_{\mathsf{sen}}$, $\mathsf{San}(pp, c^{(0)}) \neq \bot$	
and $\forall i \in \mathcal{Q}_{\mathsf{sen}}, j \in \mathcal{Q}_{\mathsf{rec}}$, $P(i, j) = 0$	$\mathcal{O}_E(i, m)$:
	$ek_i \leftarrow \mathsf{Gen}(msk, i, \mathsf{sen})$
	Return $c \leftarrow \mathsf{San}(pp, \mathsf{Enc}(ek_i, m))$

Remark 3 (Definition of the No-Write experiment). Oracle $\mathcal{O}_S$ needs to keep track of encryption query, since an encryption ek_i for i such that $P(i, j) = 1$ for some $j \in \mathcal{Q}_{\mathsf{rec}}$ would allow $\mathcal{A}$ to produce a ciphertext $c^{(0)}$ that once sanitized,

could be decrypted using dk_j, unlike $c^{(1)}$, thus trivially breaking the game. However, encryption keys queried after the adversary committed to $c^{(0)}$ are useless in breaking No-Write, as they do not allow for extracting meaningful information from $c^{(0)}$ by the No-Read rule.

Note that $\mathcal{O}_E$ needs to return a sanitized ciphertext, since an unsanitized ciphertext would allow the following attack: an adversary queries $ek_{i'}$, dk_j for arbitrary $i', j \in \{0,1\}^n$ such that $P(i',j) = 0$, then gets $\mathsf{Enc}(ek_i, m)$ from $\mathcal{O}_E(i, m)$ for arbitrary message m and $i \in \{0,1\}^n$ such that $P(i,j) = 1$. It then sets $c^{(0)} := \mathsf{Enc}(ek_i, m)$ and sends $(c^{(0)}, i)$ to the No-Write experiment. By correctness, sanitized $c^{(0)}$ could be decrypted using dk_j. By detectability, decryption of sanitized $c^{(1)}$ with dk_j will output $\perp$ with overwhelming probability.

ACE for Equality. An overview of the ACE by Fuchsbauer et al. [FGKO17, Construction 2] was given in the introduction (page 4); we recall it in Fig. 5. For ease of readability, we used randomized notion in the definition of Gen but emphasize that all randomness is derived deterministically from the PRF key K. Plugging in our new EQS from Sect. 3 yields an ACE for equality, disjunction of equality, and for range, as we show that EUF-CoMA of our EQS is sufficient to prove security of the ACE.

Correctness and **detectability** follow by inspection.

No-Read rule. The proof does not rely on the EUF-CMA security of the used EQS scheme and can be found in [FGKO17, Theorem 3]. We provide a sketch of the proof here. The proof goes through a sequence of hybrids, where in the first hybrid, we change the way the challenge ciphertext is computed: instead of containing a signature of the form $\sigma' \leftarrow \mathsf{EQS.Adapt}(vk, \mathsf{Sign}(sk, [1, dk_{i_b}]_1, s))$, it is computed as $\sigma' \leftarrow \mathsf{EQS.Adapt}(vk, \mathsf{Sign}(sk, [s, s \cdot dk_{i_b}]_1, 1))$. By the perfect adaptation of the signatures of the EQS, this does not change the distribution of the adversary's view.

Then, we use the DDH assumption in $\mathbb{G}_1$ to switch the vectors $[s, s \cdot dk_{i_b}]_1$ and $[r, r \cdot dk_{i_b} + m]_1$ one after the other to uniformly random elements from $\mathbb{G}_1^2$. The underlying plaintext and identity of the sender are then perfectly hidden. We can do so since by definition of the security game, the adversary is not allowed to query the decryption key dk_{i_b} (which the simulator does not know when relying on DDH during the game hops).

No-Write rule. Since our EQS achieves a weaker unforgeability notion, we need to show that it is still sufficient for the ACE to satisfy the No-Write rule. The proof follows closely the one from [FGKO17], which first replaces the pseudorandomness used in Gen by real randomness. Consider the following event E: the adversary $\mathcal{A}$ returns $c^{(0)} = ([c_0]_1, [c_1]_1, [c_2]_1, [c_3]_1, \sigma')$, which contains a successful EQS forgery. That is, $([c_2, c_3]_1, \sigma')$ passes the verification and $[c_2, c_3]_1$ is not a multiple of any $[1, dk_j]$ for $j \in \mathcal{Q}_{\mathsf{sen}}$ (where $\mathcal{Q}_{\mathsf{sen}}$ is the set of identities queried to $\mathcal{O}_S(\cdot, \mathsf{sen})$).

$\mathsf{Setup}(1^\lambda, P)$:

$\mathcal{PG} \leftarrow \mathsf{GGen}(1^\lambda)$; $(sk, vk) \leftarrow \mathsf{EQS.Setup}(\mathcal{PG})$; pick a PRF key K

Return $pp := (\mathcal{PG}, vk)$ and $msk := (sk, K)$

$\mathsf{Gen}(msk = (sk, K), i, t)$:

Use K to pseudorandomly generate all needed randomness

$dk_i \leftarrow_{\mathrm{R}} \mathbb{Z}_p$

If $t = \mathbf{rec}$ then return dk_i

$pk_i := [dk_i]_1$; $\sigma_i \leftarrow \mathsf{EQS.Sign}(sk, [1, dk_i]_1)$

Return $ek_i := (pk_i, \sigma_i)$

$\mathsf{Enc}(ek_i = (pk_i, \sigma_i), [m]_1 \in \mathbb{G}_1)$:

$r \leftarrow_{\mathrm{R}} \mathbb{Z}_p$; $[c_0]_1 := [r]_1$; $[c_1]_1 := r \cdot pk_i + [m]_1$

$s \leftarrow_{\mathrm{R}} \mathbb{Z}_p^*$; $[c_2]_1 := [s]_1$; $[c_3]_1 := s \cdot pk_i$; $\sigma' \leftarrow \mathsf{EQS.Adapt}(vk, \sigma_i, s)$

Return $([c_0]_1, [c_1]_1, [c_2]_1, [c_3]_1, \sigma')$

$\mathsf{San}\Big(pp, ([c_0]_1, [c_1]_1, [c_2]_1, [c_3]_1, \sigma')\Big)$:

If $\mathsf{EQS.Ver}(vk, [c_2, c_3]_1, \sigma') = 0$ then return $\bot$.

Else, $t \leftarrow_{\mathrm{R}} \mathbb{Z}_p$; $[c_0']_1 := [c_0]_1 + t \cdot [c_2]_1$; $[c_1']_1 := [c_1]_1 + t \cdot [c_3]_1$

Return $([c_0']_1, [c_1']_1)$

$\mathsf{Dec}\big(dk_i, ([c_0']_1, [c_1']_1)\big)$:

Return $[c_1']_1 - dk_i \cdot [c_0']_1$

Fig. 5. ACE for equality, using an EQS (EQS.Setup, EQS.Sign, EQS.Adapt, EQS.Ver, EQS.VerKey) and a PRF that takes a key K and outputs an element in $\mathbb{Z}_p$.

We (1) bound the probability of event E happening using the EUF-CoMA security of the EQS, and we (2) show that $\Pr[\mathsf{Exp}_{\mathsf{ACE}}^{\mathrm{No\text{-}Write}}(1^\lambda, \mathcal{A}) = 1 \mid \neg E] - \frac{1}{2}$ is negligible, using the DDH assumption in $\mathbb{G}_1$ and the KEA [BP04].

(1) The reduction $\mathcal{B}$ playing the EUF-CoMA game of the EQS simulates the No-Write experiment for $\mathcal{A}$ as follows. Whenever $\mathcal{A}$ makes a query containing an identity i for the first time, $\mathcal{B}$ samples $dk_i \leftarrow_{\mathrm{R}} \mathbb{Z}_p$. If it is a **sen** query, $\mathcal{B}$ queries its signing oracle SignO on $(1, dk_i) \in \mathbb{Z}_p^2$ to obtain σ_i and returns $ek_i := ([dk_i]_1, \sigma_i)$. Note that since the reduction picks the secret keys dk_i itself, it knows the discrete logarithms of the message being signed by the EQS: thus EUF-CoMA is sufficient. When $\mathcal{A}$ returns $\big(c^{(0)} := ([c_0]_1, [c_1]_1, [c_2]_1, [c_3]_1, \sigma'), i'\big)$, $\mathcal{B}$ then returns $([c_2, c_3]_1, \sigma')$ as its forgery. This is a successful forgery exactly when E happens.

(2) $\Pr[\mathsf{Exp}_{\mathsf{ACE}}^{\mathrm{No\text{-}Write}}(1^\lambda, \mathcal{A}) \to 1 \mid \neg E]$ is bounded exactly as in the original proof [FGKO17, Theorem 4]. It requires KEA relative to GGen, which states

that for every PPT algorithm $\mathcal{A}$, which given $(p, \mathbb{G}_1, \mathbb{G}_2, \mathbb{G}_T, e, P_1, P_2) \leftarrow$ GGen(1^λ) and a random $[r]_1 \leftarrow_R \mathbb{G}_1$, outputs $[s]_1, [r \cdot s]_1$ for some $s \in \mathbb{Z}_p$, there exists a PPT extractor which, when given the coins of $\mathcal{A}$, extracts s with non-negligible probability.

5 Application to Attribute-Based Credentials

Their main application of EQS in the work introducing the concept [HS14, FHS14] is an anonymous (multi-show) attribute-based credential (ABC) scheme, for which the authors introduce set commitment schemes with randomizable commitments.

ABCs. Credential schemes that we consider here let users obtain *credentials* for certain *attributes* that they possess from an *organization*. The users can then later *show* that they possess a credential for any subset of their attributes. Unforgeability requires that no user can show possession of attributes for which he was not issued a credential (moreover, users cannot combine their attributes). Anonymity requires that different showings of the same credential are unlinkable (credentials are thus *multi-show*) and that moreover, nothing is leaked about the contained attributes that are not shown. This property should hold even against a malicious organization. (See [FHS14] for the formal definitions.)

FHS's construction. Besides EQS, the second ingredient to constructing ABCs is a *set commitment scheme* that the authors introduce. These let one commit to sets and, besides regular commitment opening, one can open a commitment to any subset of the committed elements, without revealing anything about the committed elements that were not opened. Their construction is similar to polynomial commitments [KZG10] and it is perfectly hiding. The size of a commitment key is linear in the maximum size of the committed sets, whereas a commitment consists of a single group element from $\mathbb{G}_1^*$ and openings are in $\mathbb{Z}_p^*$. Openings to subsets (which hide the remaining elements) are in $\mathbb{G}_1^*$. Moreover, if $[c]_1$ is a commitment with opening ρ, then $s \cdot [c]_1$ is a commitment to the same set with opening $s \cdot \rho$.

Let us sketch the ABC scheme from [FHS14]:

1. A credential for a user consists of a commitment $[c]_1$ to the user's attributes, and an EQS signature σ by the organization on $([c]_1, [r \cdot c]_1, [1]_1)$; it also contains the opening ρ of $[c]_1$ and the value r.
2. When being issued a credential, the user chooses $\rho, r \leftarrow_R \mathbb{Z}_p^*$ and sends $[c]_1$ and $r \cdot [c]_1$ to obtain σ. In addition, the user gives an interactive zero-knowledge proof of knowledge (zkPoK) [CDM00] of ρ and the organization proves knowledge of its signing key.
3. When showing a credential, the user picks $s \leftarrow_R \mathbb{Z}_p^*$ and shows an adaptation of σ to $(s \cdot [c]_1, s \cdot [r \cdot c]_1, [s]_1)$. The user also presents an opening of the randomized commitment $s \cdot [c]_1$ to the subset of showed attributes.

Unforgeability of the ABC is showed [FHS14] by reducing a forgery to either a forgery of an EQS signature or a "forgery" of a subset opening of the commitment. After a slight modification of the issuing protocol, it suffices that the used EQS scheme satisfies our EUF-CoMA notion of unforgeability:

2'. Credentials are obtained as in [FHS14] (see 2. above), except that the user gives a zkPoK of ρ and r.

In the proof of anonymity, these zkPoK are simulated anyway, so additionally proving knowledge of r does not break anything. In the proof of unforgeability, the simulation can now extract the value r in addition to ρ, which together with the randomness used to set up the commitment key completely define the logarithm of a tuple $([c]_1, [rc]_1, [1]_1)$. In the reduction of ABC unforgeability to EQS unforgeability, the simulator can thus make its signature queries using the logarithms $(c, r \cdot c, 1)$ instead of the group elements $([c]_1, [r \cdot c]_1, [1]_1)$. An EQS that is secure under our definition is thus sufficient for the application to anonymous ABCs.

ABCs with revocation. Derler et al. [DHS15] extend the protocol from [HS14] (which considers a trusted setup of parameters and achieves thus weaker security than the scheme from [FHS14]) to incorporate revocation of users.

It is easily seen that our slight modifications carry over to their protocol: extend the interactive proof of knowledge done by the user when obtaining a credential, so that the simulator in the unforgeability game can extract the logarithm of the message sent by the user. Again, EUF-CoMA of the EQS scheme then suffices to prove security.

6   Further Applications

For completeness, let us mention two more applications that only require our relaxed definition of unforgeability.

6.1   Group Signatures Without Encryption

Inspired by the construction of ABC from EQS, Derler and Slamanig [DS16] use EQS to construct a dynamic (users can join at any point) group-signature scheme, which they show satisfies the formal model by Bellare et al. [BSZ05]. In particular, the scheme is fully (i.e. CCA2-) anonymous (that is, in the anonymity game the adversary has access to an opening oracle). The scheme (roughly) works as follows:

- When joining the group, a user first chooses $q, r \leftarrow_R \mathbb{Z}_p^*$. The value r will be linked to the user's identity and she creates an encryption of $[r]_2$ under the opener's public key, which she sends to the issuer together with $([q \cdot r]_1, [q]_1)$. She also proves that the ciphertext encrypts the correct value. The issuer replies with an EQS signature on the sent pair, from which the user derives a signature on $([r]_1, [1]_1)$, which serves as the signing key.

– When making a group signature, the user randomizes her key to $([\rho \cdot r]_1, [\rho]_1)$ and makes a "signature of knowledge" proving knowledge of the randomizer ρ.

As for the construction of a credential scheme from EQS in the previous section, a minor modification of the scheme suffices so that we can use EQS schemes that are EUF-CoMA secure: during issuing we require the user to make a zero-knowledge proof of knowledge of r and q. In the proof of *traceability* (which is the security notion that relies on unforgeability the EQS scheme), the reduction can extract these values and thus make an open-message query (qr, q) to its signing oracle.

6.2   Verifiably Encrypted Signatures

Hanser et al. [HRS15] use EQS to construct verifiably encrypted signatures. In their scheme, messages are elements from $\mathbb{Z}_p$ (rather than group elements) and they are signed by picking $s \leftarrow_R \mathbb{Z}_p^*$ and producing an EQS signature on $(s \cdot [m]_1, [s]_1, [1]_1)$. The arbiter's public key (who can decrypt verifiably encrypted signatures in case of dispute) is $[a]_1$ and a verifiably encrypted signature is defined as an EQS signature on $([m \cdot s \cdot a]_1, [s \cdot a]_1, [a]_1)$.

In the games defining the different security notions the adversary can either query signatures on messages $m \in \mathbb{Z}_p^*$ or verifiably encrypted signatures under the arbiter's public key. Since the latter is trusted in all notions, the security reduction always knows the discrete logarithms of the message for which it needs to produce an EQS signature; an EUF-CoMA-secure EQS scheme is thus sufficient.

7   Conclusion

We have presented the first EQS scheme from standard assumptions and showed that the relaxed unforgeability notion that it achieves is sufficient for *all* applications that have been considered in the literature, *except* the one to round-optimal blind signatures.

Acknowledgements. We would like to thank the anonymous reviewers for their valuable comments that greatly helped to improve the paper. The first author is supported by the French ANR EfTrEC project (ANR-16-CE39-0002). The second author is partially supported by ERC Project aSCEND (639554), and a Google PhD fellowship.

References

[AC17]   Agrawal, S., Chase, M.: FAME: fast attribute-based message encryption. In: ACM CCS 2017, pp. 665–682. ACM Press (2017)

[ACD+12] Abe, M., Chase, M., David, B., Kohlweiss, M., Nishimaki, R., Ohkubo, M.: Constant-size structure-preserving signatures: generic constructions and simple assumptions. In: Wang, X., Sako, K. (eds.) ASIACRYPT 2012. LNCS, vol. 7658, pp. 4–24. Springer, Heidelberg (2012). https://doi.org/10.1007/978-3-642-34961-4_3

[AFG+10] Abe, M., Fuchsbauer, G., Groth, J., Haralambiev, K., Ohkubo, M.: Structure-preserving signatures and commitments to group elements. In: Rabin, T. (ed.) CRYPTO 2010. LNCS, vol. 6223, pp. 209–236. Springer, Heidelberg (2010). https://doi.org/10.1007/978-3-642-14623-7_12

[AGHO11] Abe, M., Groth, J., Haralambiev, K., Ohkubo, M.: Optimal structure-preserving signatures in asymmetric bilinear groups. In: Rogaway, P. (ed.) CRYPTO 2011. LNCS, vol. 6841, pp. 649–666. Springer, Heidelberg (2011). https://doi.org/10.1007/978-3-642-22792-9_37

[AGO11] Abe, M., Groth, J., Ohkubo, M.: Separating short structure-preserving signatures from non-interactive assumptions. In: Lee, D.H., Wang, X. (eds.) ASIACRYPT 2011. LNCS, vol. 7073, pp. 628–646. Springer, Heidelberg (2011). https://doi.org/10.1007/978-3-642-25385-0_34

[AGOT14] Abe, M., Groth, J., Ohkubo, M., Tibouchi, M.: Unified, minimal and selectively randomizable structure-preserving signatures. In: Lindell, Y. (ed.) TCC 2014. LNCS, vol. 8349, pp. 688–712. Springer, Heidelberg (2014). https://doi.org/10.1007/978-3-642-54242-8_29

[AHN+17] Abe, M., Hofheinz, D., Nishimaki, R., Ohkubo, M., Pan, J.: Compact structure-preserving signatures with almost tight security. In: Katz, J., Shacham, H. (eds.) CRYPTO 2017. LNCS, vol. 10402, pp. 548–580. Springer, Cham (2017). https://doi.org/10.1007/978-3-319-63715-0_19

[AKOT15] Abe, M., Kohlweiss, M., Ohkubo, M., Tibouchi, M.: Fully structure-preserving signatures and shrinking commitments. In: Oswald, E., Fischlin, M. (eds.) EUROCRYPT 2015. LNCS, vol. 9057, pp. 35–65. Springer, Heidelberg (2015). https://doi.org/10.1007/978-3-662-46803-6_2

[BBS04] Boneh, D., Boyen, X., Shacham, H.: Short group signatures. In: Franklin, M. (ed.) CRYPTO 2004. LNCS, vol. 3152, pp. 41–55. Springer, Heidelberg (2004). https://doi.org/10.1007/978-3-540-28628-8_3

[BCC+09] Belenkiy, M., Camenisch, J., Chase, M., Kohlweiss, M., Lysyanskaya, A., Shacham, H.: Randomizable proofs and delegatable anonymous credentials. In: Halevi, S. (ed.) CRYPTO 2009. LNCS, vol. 5677, pp. 108–125. Springer, Heidelberg (2009). https://doi.org/10.1007/978-3-642-03356-8_7

[BCKL08] Belenkiy, M., Chase, M., Kohlweiss, M., Lysyanskaya, A.: P-signatures and noninteractive anonymous credentials. In: Canetti, R. (ed.) TCC 2008. LNCS, vol. 4948, pp. 356–374. Springer, Heidelberg (2008). https://doi.org/10.1007/978-3-540-78524-8_20

[BFF+15] Barthe, G., Fagerholm, E., Fiore, D., Scedrov, A., Schmidt, B., Tibouchi, M.: Strongly-optimal structure preserving signatures from type II pairings: synthesis and lower bounds. In: Katz, J. (ed.) PKC 2015. LNCS, vol. 9020, pp. 355–376. Springer, Heidelberg (2015). https://doi.org/10.1007/978-3-662-46447-2_16

[BKP14] Blazy, O., Kiltz, E., Pan, J.: (Hierarchical) identity-based encryption from affine message authentication. In: Garay, J.A., Gennaro, R. (eds.) CRYPTO 2014. LNCS, vol. 8616, pp. 408–425. Springer, Heidelberg (2014). https://doi.org/10.1007/978-3-662-44371-2_23

[BMM17] Badertscher, C., Matt, C., Maurer, U.: Strengthening access control encryption. In: Takagi, T., Peyrin, T. (eds.) ASIACRYPT 2017. LNCS, vol. 10624, pp. 502–532. Springer, Cham (2017). https://doi.org/10.1007/978-3-319-70694-8_18

[BP04] Bellare, M., Palacio, A.: The knowledge-of-exponent assumptions and 3-round zero-knowledge protocols. In: Franklin, M. (ed.) CRYPTO 2004. LNCS, vol. 3152, pp. 273–289. Springer, Heidelberg (2004). https://doi.org/10.1007/978-3-540-28628-8_17

[BSZ05] Bellare, M., Shi, H., Zhang, C.: Foundations of group signatures: the case of dynamic groups. In: Menezes, A. (ed.) CT-RSA 2005. LNCS, vol. 3376, pp. 136–153. Springer, Heidelberg (2005). https://doi.org/10.1007/978-3-540-30574-3_11

[CDM00] Cramer, R., Damgård, I., MacKenzie, P.: Efficient zero-knowledge proofs of knowledge without intractability assumptions. In: Imai, H., Zheng, Y. (eds.) PKC 2000. LNCS, vol. 1751, pp. 354–372. Springer, Heidelberg (2000). https://doi.org/10.1007/978-3-540-46588-1_24

[CL03] Camenisch, J., Lysyanskaya, A.: A signature scheme with efficient protocols. In: Cimato, S., Persiano, G., Galdi, C. (eds.) SCN 2002. LNCS, vol. 2576, pp. 268–289. Springer, Heidelberg (2003). https://doi.org/10.1007/3-540-36413-7_20

[CL04] Camenisch, J., Lysyanskaya, A.: Signature schemes and anonymous credentials from bilinear maps. In: Franklin, M. (ed.) CRYPTO 2004. LNCS, vol. 3152, pp. 56–72. Springer, Heidelberg (2004). https://doi.org/10.1007/978-3-540-28628-8_4

[DHO16] Damgård, I., Haagh, H., Orlandi, C.: Access control encryption: enforcing information flow with cryptography. In: Hirt, M., Smith, A. (eds.) TCC 2016. LNCS, vol. 9986, pp. 547–576. Springer, Heidelberg (2016). https://doi.org/10.1007/978-3-662-53644-5_21

[DHS15] Derler, D., Hanser, C., Slamanig, D.: A new approach to efficient revocable attribute-based anonymous credentials. In: Groth, J. (ed.) IMACC 2015. LNCS, vol. 9496, pp. 57–74. Springer, Cham (2015). https://doi.org/10.1007/978-3-319-27239-9_4

[DS16] Derler, D., Slamanig, D.: Fully-anonymous short dynamic group signatures without encryption. Cryptology ePrint Archive, Report 2016/154 (2016). http://eprint.iacr.org/2016/154

[EHK+13] Escala, A., Herold, G., Kiltz, E., Ràfols, C., Villar, J.: An algebraic framework for Diffie-Hellman assumptions. In: Canetti, R., Garay, J.A. (eds.) CRYPTO 2013. LNCS, vol. 8043, pp. 129–147. Springer, Heidelberg (2013). https://doi.org/10.1007/978-3-642-40084-1_8

[FGKO17] Fuchsbauer, G., Gay, R., Kowalczyk, L., Orlandi, C.: Access control encryption for equality, comparison, and more. In: Fehr, S. (ed.) PKC 2017. LNCS, vol. 10175, pp. 88–118. Springer, Heidelberg (2017). https://doi.org/10.1007/978-3-662-54388-7_4

[FHKS16] Fuchsbauer, G., Hanser, C., Kamath, C., Slamanig, D.: Practical round-optimal blind signatures in the standard model from weaker assumptions. In: Zikas, V., De Prisco, R. (eds.) SCN 2016. LNCS, vol. 9841, pp. 391–408. Springer, Cham (2016). https://doi.org/10.1007/978-3-319-44618-9_21

[FHS14] Fuchsbauer, G., Hanser, C., Slamanig, D.: Structure-preserving signatures on equivalence classes and constant-size anonymous credentials. Cryptology ePrint Archive, Report 2014/944 (2014). http://eprint.iacr.org/2014/944, to appear at Journal of Cryptology

[FHS15] Fuchsbauer, G., Hanser, C., Slamanig, D.: Practical round-optimal blind signatures in the standard model. In: Gennaro, R., Robshaw, M. (eds.) CRYPTO 2015. LNCS, vol. 9216, pp. 233–253. Springer, Heidelberg (2015). https://doi.org/10.1007/978-3-662-48000-7_12

[Fuc11] Fuchsbauer, G.: Commuting signatures and verifiable encryption. In: Paterson, K.G. (ed.) EUROCRYPT 2011. LNCS, vol. 6632, pp. 224–245. Springer, Heidelberg (2011). https://doi.org/10.1007/978-3-642-20465-4_14

[Fuc14] Fuchsbauer, G.: Breaking existential unforgeability of a signature scheme from Asiacrypt 2014. Cryptology ePrint Archive, Report 2014/892 (2014). http://eprint.iacr.org/2014/892

[Gha16] Ghadafi, E.: Short structure-preserving signatures. In: Sako, K. (ed.) CT-RSA 2016. LNCS, vol. 9610, pp. 305–321. Springer, Cham (2016). https://doi.org/10.1007/978-3-319-29485-8_18

[GHKW16] Gay, R., Hofheinz, D., Kiltz, E., Wee, H.: Tightly CCA-secure encryption without pairings. In: Fischlin, M., Coron, J.-S. (eds.) EUROCRYPT 2016. LNCS, vol. 9665, pp. 1–27. Springer, Heidelberg (2016). https://doi.org/10.1007/978-3-662-49890-3_1

[Gro15] Groth, J.: Efficient fully structure-preserving signatures for large messages. In: Iwata, T., Cheon, J.H. (eds.) ASIACRYPT 2015. LNCS, vol. 9452, pp. 239–259. Springer, Heidelberg (2015). https://doi.org/10.1007/978-3-662-48797-6_11

[GS08] Groth, J., Sahai, A.: Efficient non-interactive proof systems for bilinear groups. In: Smart, N. (ed.) EUROCRYPT 2008. LNCS, vol. 4965, pp. 415–432. Springer, Heidelberg (2008). https://doi.org/10.1007/978-3-540-78967-3_24

[HK17] Hanzlik, L., Kluczniak, K.: Two-move and setup-free blind signatures with perfect blindness. In: Proceedings of the 4th ACM International Workshop on ASIA Public-Key Cryptography, APKC 2017, pp. 1–11. ACM, New York (2017)

[HRS15] Hanser, C., Rabkin, M., Schröder, D.: Verifiably encrypted signatures: security revisited and a new construction. In: Pernul, G., Ryan, P.Y.A., Weippl, E. (eds.) ESORICS 2015. LNCS, vol. 9326, pp. 146–164. Springer, Cham (2015). https://doi.org/10.1007/978-3-319-24174-6_8

[HS14] Hanser, C., Slamanig, D.: Structure-preserving signatures on equivalence classes and their application to anonymous credentials. In: Sarkar, P., Iwata, T. (eds.) ASIACRYPT 2014. LNCS, vol. 8873, pp. 491–511. Springer, Heidelberg (2014). https://doi.org/10.1007/978-3-662-45611-8_26

[JR17] Jutla, C.S., Roy, A.: Improved structure preserving signatures under standard bilinear assumptions. In: Fehr, S. (ed.) PKC 2017. LNCS, vol. 10175, pp. 183–209. Springer, Heidelberg (2017). https://doi.org/10.1007/978-3-662-54388-7_7

[KPW15] Kiltz, E., Pan, J., Wee, H.: Structure-preserving signatures from standard assumptions, revisited. In: Gennaro, R., Robshaw, M. (eds.) CRYPTO 2015. LNCS, vol. 9216, pp. 275–295. Springer, Heidelberg (2015). https://doi.org/10.1007/978-3-662-48000-7_14

[KW15] Kiltz, E., Wee, H.: Quasi-adaptive NIZK for linear subspaces revisited. In: Oswald, E., Fischlin, M. (eds.) EUROCRYPT 2015. LNCS, vol. 9057, pp. 101–128. Springer, Heidelberg (2015). https://doi.org/10.1007/978-3-662-46803-6_4

[KW17] Kim, S., Wu, D.J.: Access control encryption for general policies from standard assumptions. In: Takagi, T., Peyrin, T. (eds.) ASIACRYPT 2017. LNCS, vol. 10624, pp. 471–501. Springer, Cham (2017). https://doi.org/10.1007/978-3-319-70694-8_17

[KZG10] Kate, A., Zaverucha, G.M., Goldberg, I.: Constant-size commitments to polynomials and their applications. In: Abe, M. (ed.) ASIACRYPT 2010. LNCS, vol. 6477, pp. 177–194. Springer, Heidelberg (2010). https://doi.org/10.1007/978-3-642-17373-8_11

[LPJY15] Libert, B., Peters, T., Joye, M., Yung, M.: Compactly hiding linear spans. In: Iwata, T., Cheon, J.H. (eds.) ASIACRYPT 2015. LNCS, vol. 9452, pp. 681–707. Springer, Heidelberg (2015). https://doi.org/10.1007/978-3-662-48797-6_28

[MRV16] Morillo, P., Ràfols, C., Villar, J.L.: The kernel matrix Diffie-Hellman assumption. In: Cheon, J.H., Takagi, T. (eds.) ASIACRYPT 2016. LNCS, vol. 10031, pp. 729–758. Springer, Heidelberg (2016). https://doi.org/10.1007/978-3-662-53887-6_27

Functional Encryption

Simple and Generic Constructions of Succinct Functional Encryption

Fuyuki Kitagawa[1], Ryo Nishimaki[2](✉) , and Keisuke Tanaka[1]

[1] Tokyo Institute of Technology, Tokyo, Japan
{kitagaw1,keisuke}@is.titech.ac.jp
[2] Secure Platform Laboratories, NTT Corporation, Tokyo, Japan
nishimaki.ryo@lab.ntt.co.jp

Abstract. We propose simple and generic constructions of succinct functional encryption. Our key tool is exponentially-efficient indistinguishability obfuscator (XIO), which is the same as indistinguishability obfuscator (IO) except that the size of an obfuscated circuit (or the running-time of an obfuscator) is *slightly* smaller than that of a brute-force canonicalizer that outputs the entire truth table of a circuit to be obfuscated. A "compression factor" of XIO indicates how much XIO compresses the brute-force canonicalizer. In this study, we propose a significantly simple framework to construct succinct functional encryption via XIO and show that XIO is a powerful enough to achieve cutting-edge cryptography. In particular, we prove the followings:

- Single-key weakly succinct secret-key functional encryption (SKFE) is constructed from XIO (even with a bad compression factor) and one-way function.
- Single-key weakly succinct public-key functional encryption (PKFE) is constructed from XIO with a good compression factor and public-key encryption.
- Single-key weakly succinct PKFE is constructed from XIO (even with a bad compression factor) and identity-based encryption.

Our new framework has side benefits. Our constructions do not rely on any number theoretic or lattice assumptions such as decisional Diffie-Hellman and learning with errors assumptions. Moreover, all security reductions incur only polynomial security loss. Known constructions of weakly succinct SKFE or PKFE from XIO with polynomial security loss rely on number theoretic or lattice assumptions.

1 Introduction

1.1 Background

In cryptography, it is one of major research topics to construct more complex cryptographic primitives from simpler ones in a *generic* way. Here, "generic" means that we use only general cryptographic tools such as one-way function and

F. Kitagawa—This work was done while the author was visiting NTT Secure Platform Laboratories as a summer internship student.

© International Association for Cryptologic Research 2018
M. Abdalla and R. Dahab (Eds.): PKC 2018, LNCS 10770, pp. 187–217, 2018.
https://doi.org/10.1007/978-3-319-76581-5_7

public-key encryption. For such a generic construction, we do not use any specific or concrete algebraic assumptions such as the factoring, decisional Diffie-Hellman (DDH), learning with errors (LWE) assumptions. Generic constructions are useful in cryptography because they do not rely on any specific structure of underlying primitives. It means that even if a specific number theoretic assumption is broken, say the DDH, a generic construction based on public-key encryption is still secure since there are many instantiations of public-key encryption from other assumptions. Moreover, generic constructions are useful to deeply understand the nature of cryptographic primitives.

Many generic constructions have been proposed. For example, one-way functions imply pseudo-random function (PRF) [32], and many other primitives. However, we understand little of how to construct functional encryption [13,45] in a generic way despite its usefulness as explained below.

Functional encryption is a generalization of public-key encryption and enables us to generate functional keys that are tied with a certain function f. Given such a functional key, we can obtain $f(x)$ by decryption of ciphertext $\mathsf{Enc}(x)$ where x is a plaintext. Functional encryption is a versatile cryptographic primitive since it enables us to achieve not only fine-grained access control systems over encrypted data but also indistinguishability obfuscation (IO) [3,8,11,27].

IO converts computer programs into those that hide secret information in the original programs while preserving their functionalities. An obvious application of IO is protecting softwares from reverse engineering. Moreover, IO enables us to achieve many cutting-edge cryptographic tasks that other standard cryptographic tools do (or can) not achieve such as (collusion-resistant) functional encryption, program watermarking, and deniable encryption [21,27,47]. We basically focus on functional encryption and IO for all circuits in this study.

Many concrete functional encryption and IO constructions have been proposed since the celebrated invention of a candidate graded encoding system by Garg et al. [26]. However, regarding designing secure functional encryption and IO, we are still at the "embryonic" stage[1]. A few candidates of graded encoding schemes have been proposed [24,26,30]. However, basically speaking, all are attacked, and most applications (including functional encryption) that use graded encoding schemes are also insecure [5,18–20,22,23,43]. As an exception, a few IO constructions are still standing [25,28][2].

The purpose of this study is that we shed new light on how to achieve functional encryption and IO.

The number of functional keys and the size of encryption circuit. In fact, the hardness of constructing functional encryption depends on certain features of

---

[1] We borrow this term from the talk by Amit Sahai at MIT, "State of the IO: Where we stand in the quest for secure obfuscation" http://toc.csail.mit.edu/node/981.

[2] Martin Albrecht and Alex Davidson maintain the status of graded encoding schemes and IO constructions at http://malb.io/are-graded-encoding-schemes-broken-yet.html.

functional encryption such as the number of issuable functional keys and cipher-texts and the size of encryption circuit.

We say "single-key" if only one functional key can be issued. We also say q-key or bounded collusion-resistant when a-priori bounded q functional keys can be issued. If q is an a-priori unbounded polynomial, then we say "collusion-resistant". It is known that a single-key secret-key and public-key functional encryption (SKFE and PKFE) are constructed from standard one-way function and public-key encryption, respectively [46]. It is also known that a bounded collusion-resistant PKFE (resp. SKFE) is constructed from public-key encryption (resp. one-way function) and pseudo-random generator computed by polynomial degree circuits [34]. However, it is not known whether collusion-resistant functional encryption is constructed without expensive cryptographic tools such as graded encoding systems [24,26,30] or IO [26].

It is also known that we can construct collusion-resistant PKFE from single-key weakly succinct PKFE [29,40]. The notion of succinctness for functional encryption schemes [3,11][3] means the size of encryption circuit is independent of the function-size. Weak succinctness means the size of the encryption circuit is $s^\gamma \cdot \text{poly}(\lambda, n)$ where λ is a security parameter, s is the size of f that is embedded in a functional key, n is the length of a plaintext, and γ is a constant such that $0 < \gamma < 1$. The results of Garg and Srinivasan [29] and Li and Micciancio [40] mean that we can arbitrarily increase the number of issuable functional keys by using succinctness. Moreover, succinct SKFE and PKFE are constructed from collusion-resistant SKFE and PKFE, respectively [4]. Thus, it is also a difficult task to construct succinct functional encryption schemes without graded encoding systems or IO.

The succinctness of functional encryption is also key feature to achieve IO. Ananth and Jain [3] and Bitansky and Vaikuntanathan [11] show that a sub-exponentially secure single-key weakly succinct PKFE implies IO.

These facts indicate that it is a challenging task to achieve either collusion-resistance or succinctness.

Running time of obfuscator. Not only the encryption-time of functional encryption but also the size of obfuscated circuits and the running time of obfuscators are important measures.

Lin et al. [41] introduced the notion of exponentially-efficient indistinguishability obfuscator (XIO), which is a weaker variant of IO. XIO is almost the same as IO, but the size of the obfuscated circuits is $\text{poly}(\lambda, |C|) \cdot 2^{\gamma n}$ where λ is a security parameter, C is a circuit to be obfuscated, n is the length of input for C, and a compression factor γ is some value such that $0 < \gamma < 1$. We note that the running time of XIO on an input a circuit of n-bit inputs can be 2^n. They prove that if we assume that there exists XIO for circuits and the LWE problem is hard, then there exists single-key weakly succinct PKFE (and IO if sub-exponential security is additionally assumed).

---

[3] In some papers, the term "compactness" is used for this property, but we use the term by Bitansky and Vaikuntanathan [11] in this study.

Bitansky et al. [9] extend the notion of XIO and define strong XIO (SXIO). If the running time of the obfuscator is $\text{poly}(\lambda, |C|) \cdot 2^{\gamma n}$, then we say it is SXIO. Bitansky et al. show that sub-exponentially secure SXIO and public-key encryption imply IO. In addition, they prove that single-key weakly succinct PKFE is constructed from SXIO, public-key encryption, and weak PRF in NC^1, which is implied by the DDH [44] or LWE assumptions [7].

Thus, (S)XIO is useful enough to achieve weakly succinct functional encryption and IO. In this study, we discuss more applications of SXIO to functional encryption. In particular, we discuss significantly simple and generic constructions of weakly succinct functional encryption by using SXIO.

From SKFE to PKFE. Bitansky et al. [9] also prove that SXIO is constructed from collusion-resistant SKFE. Thus, we can construct weakly succinct PKFE from a weaker primitive than PKFE by the results of Lin et al. and Bitansky et al., though it is not known whether we can construct collusion-resistant SKFE from standard cryptographic primitives.

The works of Lin et al. and Bitansky et al. are advancements on how to construct succinct PKFE from weaker primitives. In particular, Bitansky et al. provide a nice generic framework for constructing weakly succinct PKFE from SKFE and public-key encryption. However, their technique is very complicated. Moreover, they still use the DDH or LWE assumptions to achieve weakly succinct PKFE *with polynomial security loss*. Thus, it is not known whether we can construct weakly succinct PKFE with polynomial security loss from SKFE and public-key encryption in a generic way.

1.2   Our Contributions

The primary contribution of this study is that we propose a *significantly simple and generic framework* to construct single-key weakly succinct functional encryption *by using SXIO*. In particular, our constructions are significantly simpler than those by Bitansky et al. [9]. More specifically, we prove the following theorems via our framework:

Main theorem 1 (informal): A single-key weakly succinct PKFE is implied by public-key encryption and SXIO with a *sufficiently small* compression factor.

Main theorem 2 (informal): A single-key weakly succinct PKFE is implied by identity-based encryption and SXIO with a compression factor that is only *slightly smaller than* 1.

Main theorem 3 (informal): A single-key weakly succinct SKFE is implied by one-way function and SXIO with a compression factor that is only *slightly smaller than* 1.

Readers might find that the technique (see the overview in Sect. 1.3) in our framework is a little bit straightforward and a combination of (minor variants of) well-known or implicitly known techniques. However, we stress that *it is not a disadvantage but the advantage of our study*. We reveal that such a simple combination of known techniques yields highly non-trivial results above for the first time. We believe that our simple technique is useful to construct better functional encryption (and IO). In fact, Kitagawa, Nishimaki, and Tanaka extend our technique and obtain an IO construction based only on SKFE [37]. As side benefits of our new framework, our functional encryption schemes have advantages over previous constructions. In particular, the third main theorem is totally new. We highlight that all these new theorems incur *only polynomial* security loss and *do not rely on any specific number theoretic or lattice assumption*. These are advantages over the constructions of Lin et al. and Bitansky et al. [9,41] and the secondary contributions of this study. We explain details of our results below.

Implication of first and second theorems. There are transformations from a single-key weakly succinct PKFE scheme to a collusion-resistant one with polynomial security loss [29,40]. Thus, by combining the first or second theorems with the transformation, we obtain two collusion-resistant PKFE schemes *with polynomial security loss*. One is based on public-key encryption and collusion-resistant (non-succinct) SKFE since collusion-resistant (non-succinct) SKFE implies SXIO with an arbitrarily small constant compression factor [9]. The other is based on identity-based encryption and single-key weakly succinct SKFE since single-key weakly succinct SKFE implies SXIO with a compression factor that is slightly smaller than 1 [10]. Note that we can also obtain IO constructions from the same building blocks if we assume that they are sub-exponentially secure by using the result of Ananth and Jain [3] or Bitansky and Vaikuntanathan [11].

As well as one-way function and public-key encryption, identity-based encryption [48] is also a standard cryptographic primitive since there are many instantiations of identity-based encryption based on widely believed number theoretic assumptions and lattice assumptions [12,31]. Thus, our second result indicates that all one needs is to *slightly compress* the brute-force canonicalizer that outputs an entire truth table of a circuit to be obfuscated to construct single-key weakly succinct (or collusion-resistant) PKFE and IO.

Advantages over previous constructions. We look closer at previous works for comparison. Readers who are familiar with the previous works on PKFE can skip this part and jump into the part about implication of the third theorem.

Lin et al. [41]: They construct single-key weakly succinct PKFE from XIO and single-key succinct PKFE for *Boolean* circuits. It is known that a single key succinct PKFE for Boolean circuits is constructed from the LWE assumption [33].

Both their construction and ours are generic constructions using (S)XIO. However, their construction additionally needs single-key succinct PKFE for Boolean circuits. We have only one instantiation of such PKFE based on the LWE assumption while our additional primitives (i.e., public-key encryption and identity-based encryption) can be instantiated based on wide range of assumptions. This is the advantage of our construction over that of Lin et al.

Bitansky et al. [9]: They construct single-key weakly succinct PKFE from SXIO and public-key encryption with $2^{O(d)}$ security loss where d is the depth of a circuit. They introduce decomposable garbled circuit, which is an extension of Yao's garbled circuit [49], to achieve succinctness [9]. Decomposable garbled circuit is implied by one-way function. However, it has two disadvantages. One is that it incurs the $2^{O(d)}$ security loss. The other is that its security proof is complex.

When we construct single-key weakly succinct (or collusion-resistant) PKFE only with *polynomial security loss*, the exponential security loss in the depth of circuits is a big issue. Thus, Bitansky et al. need weak PRF in NC^1 to achieve single-key weakly succinct (or collusion-resistant) PKFE with polynomial security loss due to the $2^{O(d)}$ security loss [9, Sect. 5.3][4]. If our goal is constructing IO, then the $2^{O(d)}$ security loss is not an issue in the sense that we need sub-exponential security of PKFE to achieve IO [3,11], and we can cancel the $2^{O(d)}$ security loss by complexity leveraging.

Decomposable garbled circuit is a useful tool for Bitansky et al.'s construction. However, the definition is complicated and it is not easy to understand the security proof. Our unified design strategy significantly simplifies a construction of single-key weakly succinct PKFE based on SXIO. In fact, our constructions use decomposable *randomized encoding* [6,35], but decomposable randomized encoding is a simple tool and *does not incur $2^{O(d)}$ security loss*.

Using identity-based encryption. We show that we can relax the requirements on SKFE to achieve PKFE and IO if we are allowed to use identity-based encryption.

Our construction of PKFE using identity-based encryption needs SXIO with compression factor slightly smaller than 1 that is implied by single-key (weakly) succinct SKFE while the constructions using public-key encryption need SXIO with sufficiently small compression factor that is implied by collusion-resistant SKFE. It is not known whether single-key (weakly) succinct SKFE implies collusion-resistant SKFE though the opposite is known [4]. Of course, regarding additional assumptions (public-key encryption and identity-based encryption), the existence of identity-based encryption is a stronger assumption than that of public-key encryption. However, identity-based encryption is a standard cryptographic primitive and the assumption is reasonably mild since many instantiations of identity-based encryption are known [12,31]. Readers who are familiar with the construction of Bitansky et al. might think the second theorem is easily obtained from the result of Bitansky et al., which actually uses an identity-based encryption scheme constructed from SXIO and public-key encryption as a building block.[5] This is not the case because their construction uses an SXIO *three times in a nested manner*

---

[4] They use a bootstrapping technique by Ananth et al. [1], which transforms functional encryption for NC^1 into one for P/poly.

[5] Note that our requirements on an identity-based encryption scheme is the same as theirs on their identity-based encryption scheme.

to construct their single-key weakly succinct PKFE scheme. They construct a single-key weakly succinct PKFE scheme for Boolean functions by using SXIO and identity-based encryption, and then transform it into a single-key weakly succinct PKFE scheme for non-Boolean functions by using SXIO again. Therefore, even if we replace their identity-based encryption scheme based on SXIO and public-key encryption with an assumption that there exists identity-based encryption, their construction still requires the use of SXIO *two times in a nested manner*, and due to this nested use, it still needs SXIO with sufficiently small compression factor.

Thus, the advantages of our single-key weakly succinct PKFE schemes over Bitansky et al.'s construction are as follows:

- Our single-key weakly succinct PKFE scheme does not incur $2^{O(d)}$ security loss thus does not need weak PRF in NC^1 (implied by the DDH or LWE assumptions) to support all circuits.
- Our PKFE schemes and proofs are much simpler.
- We can use single-key weakly succinct SKFE instead of collusion-resistant SKFE (if we use identity-based encryption instead of public-key encryption).

Komargodski and Segev [39]: Komargodski and Segev construct IO for *circuits with inputs of poly-logarithmic length and sub-polynomial size* from a quasi-polynomially secure and collusion-resistant SKFE scheme for P/poly. They also construct PKFE for *circuits with inputs of poly-logarithmic length and sub-polynomial size* from a quasi-polynomially secure and collusion-resistant SKFE scheme for P/poly and *sub-exponentially secure* one-way function. Their reduction incurs super-polynomial security loss. Thus, the advantages of our single-key weakly succinct PKFE schemes and IO over Komargodski and Segev's construction are as follows:
    - Our PKFE schemes support all circuits. (When constructing IO by combining previous results [3,11], the construction also supports all circuits.)
    - We can use single-key weakly succinct SKFE instead of collusion-resistant SKFE (if we use identity-based encryption).
    - Our PKFE schemes are with polynomial security loss and do not need sub-exponentially secure one-way function (though we additionally use a public-key primitive).

We summarize differences between these previous constructions of single-key weakly succinct (or collusion-resistant) PKFE schemes and ours in Table 1.

Implication of third theorem. We can obtain interesting by-products from the third theorem.

By-product 1: We show that single-key weakly succinct SKFE is equivalent to one-way function and SXIO since it is known that such SKFE implies SXIO with a compression factor that is slightly smaller than 1 [10].

Table 1. Comparison with previous constructions. OWF, PKE, IBE, GC, dGC, and dRE denote one-way function, public-key encryption, identity-based encryption, garbled circuit, decomposable garbled circuit, and decomposable randomized encoding, respectively. Underlines denote disadvantages. In "supported circuit" column, $C_{\log\text{-input}}^{\text{sub-poly}}$ means circuits with inputs of poly-logarithmic length and sub-polynomial size.

	Ingredients for 1-key weakly succinct (or collusion-resistant) PKFE	Supported circuits
[41]	1-key weakly succinct SKFE, LWE	P/poly
[9]	collusion-resistant SKFE, PKE, dGC, PRF in NC^1(DDH or LWE)	P/poly
[39]	collusion-resistant SKFE, sub-exponentially secure OWF	$C_{\log\text{-input}}^{\text{sub-poly}}$
1st thm.	collusion-resistant SKFE, PKE, dRE	P/poly
2nd thm.	1-key weakly succinct SKFE, IBE, GC, dRE	P/poly

By-product 2: We show that the existence of output-compact updatable randomized encoding with unbounded number of updates [2] and one-way function is equivalent to that of single-key weakly succinct SKFE. Previously, it is known that the existence of output-compact updatable randomized encoding with unbounded number of updates and *the hardness of the LWE problem* imply the existence of single-key weakly succinct SKFE [2]. It is also known that single-key weakly succinct SKFE implies output-compact updatable randomized encoding with unbounded number of updates. Thus, we replace the LWE assumption in the results by Ananth, Cohen, and Jain [2] with one-way function.

1.3   Overview of Our Construction Technique

Our core schemes are q-key weakly collusion-succinct functional encryption schemes for a-priori fixed polynomial q that are constructed from SXIO and an additional cryptographic primitive (one-way function, public-key encryption, or identity-based encryption). Weak collusion-succinctness means the size of the encryption circuit is *sub-linear in the number of issuable functional keys*. See Definition 3 for more details on succinctness. It is known that weakly collusion-succinct functional encryption is transformed into weakly-succinct one [4,11].

We explain our ideas to achieve q-key weakly collusion-succinct functional encryption schemes below.

Our main idea in one sentence. We compress parallelized encryption circuits of a non-succinct scheme based on standard cryptographic primitives by using SXIO to achieve weak collusion-succinctness.

Starting point. A naive idea to construct a q-key functional encryption scheme from a single-key non-succinct functional encryption scheme is running q single-key non-succinct functional encryption schemes in parallel where q is a polynomial fixed in advance. A master secret/public key consist of q master secret/public keys of the single-key scheme, respectively. A ciphertext consists of q ciphertexts of a plaintext x under q master secret or public keys. This achieves q-key functional encryption.[6] However, this simply parallelized scheme is clearly not weakly collusion-succinct since the size of the encryption circuit is linear in q. Note that a single-key non-succinct functional encryption scheme is constructed from a standard cryptographic primitive (such as one-way function, public-key encryption) [34,46].

Compressing by SXIO. Our basic idea is compressing the encryption circuit of the simply parallelized scheme by using SXIO. Instead of embedding all q keys in an encryption circuit, our encryption algorithm obfuscates a circuit that generates the i-th master secret/public key of the simply parallelized scheme and uses it to generate a ciphertext under the i-th key where i is an input to the circuit.

For simplicity, we consider the SKFE case. We set a pseudo-random function (PRF) key K as a master secret key. For a plaintext x, our weakly collusion-succinct encryption algorithm generates a circuit $\mathsf{E}'[K,x]$ that takes as an input an index $i \in [q]$, generates the i-th master secret key MSK_i by using the hard-wired K and the index i, and outputs a ciphertext $\mathsf{Enc}(\mathsf{MSK}_i, x)$ of the single-key scheme[7]. A ciphertext of our scheme is $\mathsf{sxi}\mathcal{O}(\mathsf{E}'[K,x])$. In $\mathsf{E}'[K,x]$, each master secret key is generated in an on-line manner by using the PRF (it is determined only by K and input i). The encryption circuit size of each $\mathsf{Enc}(\mathsf{MSK}_i, x)$ is independent of q because it is the encryption algorithm of the single-key scheme. The input space of $\mathsf{E}'[K,x]$ is $[q]$. Thus, the time needed to generate the ciphertext $\mathsf{sxi}\mathcal{O}(\mathsf{E}'[K,x])$ is $\mathrm{poly}(\lambda, |x|, |f|) \cdot q^\gamma$ from the efficiency guarantee of SXIO. This achieves weak collusion-succinctness. The size depends on $|f|$, but it is not an issue since our goal at this step is not (weak) succinctness. The security is proved using the standard punctured programming technique [47].

Extension to public-key setting. We achieve a q-key weakly collusion-succinct PKFE by a similar idea to the SKFE case. Only one exception is that we need an SXIO to generate not only a ciphertext but also *a master public-key* to prevent the size of a master public-key from linearly depending on q. That is, a master public-key is an obfuscated circuit that outputs a master public-key of a single-key scheme by using a PRF key. We give the simplified description of this setup circuit (denoted by S) below for clarity. For the formal description of S, see Fig. 2 in Sect. 3.2. If we do not use $\mathsf{sxi}\mathcal{O}(\mathsf{S})$ as the master public key, we must use $\{\mathsf{MPK}_i\}_{i\in[q]}$ as the master public-key and embed them in a *public* encryption circuit E'' since we cannot make PRF key K public. This leads to linear dependence on q of the encryption time.

Encryption circuit E'' is almost the same as E' in the SKFE construction except that $\mathsf{MPK} = \mathsf{sxi}\mathcal{O}(\mathsf{S})$ is hardwired to generate a master public-key in an on-line manner. Similarly to the SKFE construction, a ciphertext is $\mathsf{sxi}\mathcal{O}(\mathsf{E}'')$.

---

[6] In fact, the functional key generation algorithm takes an additional input called index and is stateful. We ignore this issue here. However, in fact, this issue does not matter at all. See Remark 2 in Sect. 2 regarding this issue.

[7] We ignore the issue regarding randomness of the ciphertext in this section.

// Description of (simplified) S	// Description of (simplified) E''
Hard-Coded Constants: K. **Input:** $i \in [q]$	**Hard-Coded Constants:** MPK, x. **Input:** $i \in [q]$
1. Compute $r_{\mathsf{Setup}}^i \leftarrow \mathsf{F}_K(i)$. 2. Compute $(\mathsf{MPK}_i, \mathsf{MSK}_i) \leftarrow$ $\quad \mathsf{Setup}(1^\lambda; r_{\mathsf{Setup}}^i)$. 3. Return MPK_i.	1. Parse $\mathsf{sxi}\mathcal{O}(\mathsf{S}) \leftarrow \mathsf{MPK}$. 2. Compute $\mathsf{MPK}_i \leftarrow \mathsf{sxi}\mathcal{O}(\mathsf{S})(i)$ 3. Return $\mathsf{CT}_i \leftarrow \mathsf{Enc}(\mathsf{MPK}_i, x)$.

This incurs two applications of SXIO in a nested manner (i.e., we obfuscate a circuit in which another obfuscated circuit is hard-wired). Although the input space of E'' is $[q]$ and the size of the encryption circuit of the single-key scheme is independent of q, the size of $\mathsf{sxi}\mathcal{O}(\mathsf{E}'')$ polynomially depends on $\mathsf{sxi}\mathcal{O}(\mathsf{S})$. Thus, a better compression factor of SXIO for S is required to ensure the weak collusion-succinctness of the resulting scheme. Such better SXIO is implied by *collusion-resistant* (non-succinct) SKFE [9]. See Sect. 3.2 for details of the efficiency analysis.

Using power of identity-based encryption. To overcome the nested applications of SXIO, we directly construct a q-key weakly collusion-succinct PKFE from SXIO, identity-based encryption, and garbled circuit. The main idea is the same. Our starting point is the single-key non-succinct PKFE scheme of Sahai and Seyalioglu [46], which is based on a public-key encryption scheme PKE. We use a universal circuit $U(\cdot, x)$ in which a plaintext x is hard-wired and takes as an input a function f, which will be embedded in a functional key. Let $s := |f|$. The scheme of Sahai and Seyalioglu is as follows.

Setup: A master public-key consists of $2s$ public-keys of PKE, $\{\mathsf{pk}_0^j, \mathsf{pk}_1^j\}_{j \in [s]}$.

Functional Key: A functional key for f consists of s secret-keys of PKE, $\{\mathsf{sk}_{f_j}^j\}_{j \in [s]}$ where $f = f_1 \ldots f_s$ and f_j is a single bit for every $j \in [s]$.

Encryption: A ciphertext of a plaintext x consists of a garbled circuit of $U(\cdot, x)$ and encryptions of $2s$ labels of the garbled circuit under pk_b^j for all $j \in [s]$ and $b \in \{0, 1\}$.

Decryption: We obtain labels corresponding to f by using $\{\mathsf{sk}_{f_j}^j\}_{j \in [s]}$ and evaluate the garbled $U(\cdot, x)$ with those labels.

We can replace PKE with an identity-based encryption scheme IBE by using identities in $[s] \times \{0, 1\}$. That is, $\{\mathsf{pk}_0^j, \mathsf{pk}_1^j\}_{j \in [s]}$ is aggregated into a master public-key of IBE. A functional key for f consists of secret keys for identities $(1, f_1), \ldots, (s, f_s)$. In addition, encryptions of $2s$ labels consist of $2s$ ciphertexts for identities (j, b) for all $j \in [s]$ and $b \in \{0, 1\}$. We parallelize this by extending the identity space into $[q] \times [s] \times \{0, 1\}$ to achieve a q-key scheme. We need compression to achieve weak collusion-succinctness since simple parallelization incurs the linearity in q.

Our encryption algorithm obfuscates the following circuit $\widetilde{\mathsf{E}}$ by using an SXIO. A master public-key of IBE and plaintext x are hard-wired in $\widetilde{\mathsf{E}}$. Given index i, $\widetilde{\mathsf{E}}$ generates a garbled circuit of $U(\cdot, x)$ with $2s$ labels and outputs the garbled circuit and encryptions of the $2s$ labels under appropriate identities. Identities consist of $(i, j, f_j) \in [q] \times [s] \times \{0, 1\}$ for every $j \in [s]$. A ciphertext of our scheme is $\mathsf{sxi}\mathcal{O}(\widetilde{\mathsf{E}})$. Therefore, if secret keys for identities $\{(i, j, f_j)\}_{j \in [s]}$ are given as functional keys, then we can obtain labels only for f from corresponding ciphertexts of IBE output by $\mathsf{sxi}\mathcal{O}(\widetilde{\mathsf{E}})$ on the input i, and compute $U(f, x) = f(x)$.

A master public-key and encryption circuit of the identity-based encryption are succinct in the sense that their size is sub-linear in $|\mathcal{ID}|$ where $\mathcal{ID}$ is the identity space of IBE. That is, the size depends on $|\mathcal{ID}|^\alpha$ for sufficiently small constant α.[8] In addition, the input space of $\widetilde{\mathsf{E}}$ is just $[q]$ and the garbled circuit part of $\widetilde{\mathsf{E}}$ is independent of q. Therefore, the time needed to generate a ciphertext $\mathsf{sxi}\mathcal{O}(\widetilde{\mathsf{E}})$ is sub-linear in q from the efficiency property of SXIO. Thus, the scheme is weakly collusion-succinct.

In fact, this PKFE construction is similar to that of Bitansky et al. [9], but we do not need decomposable garbled circuit because our goal is achieving weak collusion-succinctness, which allows encryption circuits to polynomially depend on the size of f (our goal is *not weak succinctness* at this stage). Thus, a standard garbled circuit is sufficient for our construction. Moreover, SXIO with a bad compression factor is sufficient since we use an SXIO only once.

Uniting pieces. It is known that public-key encryption (resp. one-way function) implies single-key non-succinct PKFE (resp. SKFE) [34,46] and bounded-key weakly collusion-succinct PKFE (resp. SKFE) implies single-key weakly succinct PKFE (resp. SKFE) [4,11]. Thus, via our weakly collusion-succinct PKFE (resp. SKFE), we can obtain single-key weakly succinct PKFE (resp. SKFE) based on SXIO and standard cryptographic primitives. Figure 1 illustrates our first and third informal theorems.

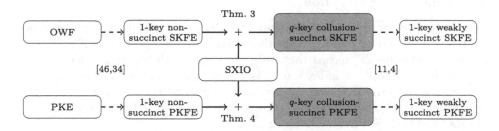

Fig. 1. Illustration of our first and third theorems. Dashed lines denote known constructions. Purple boxes denote our core schemes. We ignore puncturable PRF in this figure. It is implied by one-way function. (Color figure online)

---

[8] When we say identity-based encryption, we assume that it satisfies this type of succinctness. In fact, most identity-based encryption schemes based on number theoretic or lattice assumptions satisfy it.

Concurrent and independent work. Lin and Tessaro [42] prove that a collusion-resistant PKFE scheme for P/poly is constructed from any single-key PKFE scheme for P/poly (e.g., a PKFE scheme based on public-key encryption proposed by Gorbunov et al. [34]) and IO for $\omega(\log \lambda)$-bit-input circuits.

Their construction is similar to that of our single-key weakly succinct PKFE scheme for P/poly from public-key encryption and SXIO. One notable difference is that they use IO for $\omega(\log \lambda)$-bit-input circuits while we use SXIO for P/poly based on collusion-resistant SKFE for P/poly with polynomial security loss, which is a weaker tool than theirs.

Organization. This paper consists of the following parts. In Sect. 2, we provide preliminaries and basic definitions. In Sect. 3, we present our constructions of weakly collusion-succinct functional encryption schemes based on SXIO and standard cryptographic primitives. In Sect. 4, we provide a statement about how to transform weakly collusion-succinct functional encryption schemes into single-key weakly succinct functional encryption schemes. In Sect. 5, we summarize our results.

2   Preliminaries

We now define some notations and cryptographic primitives. We omit some notations and definitions due to limited space.

If $\mathcal{X}^{(b)} = \{X_\lambda^{(b)}\}_{\lambda \in \mathbb{N}}$ for $b \in \{0, 1\}$ are two ensembles of random variables indexed by $\lambda \in \mathbb{N}$, we say that $\mathcal{X}^{(0)}$ and $\mathcal{X}^{(1)}$ are computationally indistinguishable if for any PPT distinguisher $\mathcal{D}$, there exists a negligible function $\mathsf{negl}(\lambda)$, such that $\Delta := |\Pr[\mathcal{D}(X_\lambda^{(0)}) = 1] - \Pr[\mathcal{D}(X_\lambda^{(1)}) = 1]| \le \mathsf{negl}(\lambda)$. We write $\mathcal{X}^{(0)} \stackrel{c}{\approx}_\delta \mathcal{X}^{(1)}$ to denote that the advantage Δ is bounded by δ.

2.1   Functional Encryption

Secret-Key Functional Encryption (SKFE). We introduce the syntax of an index based variant SKFE scheme that we call an *index based SKFE (iSKFE)* scheme. "Index based" means that, to generate the i-th functional decryption key, we need to feed an index i to a key generation algorithm. For a single-key scheme, an iSKFE scheme is just a standard SKFE scheme in which the key generation algorithm does not take an index as an input since the index is always fixed to 1. See Remark 2 for details.

Definition 1 (Index Based Secret-key Functional Encryption). *Let* $\mathcal{M} := \{\mathcal{M}_\lambda\}_{\lambda \in \mathbb{N}}$ *be a message domain,* $\mathcal{Y} := \{\mathcal{Y}_\lambda\}_{\lambda \in \mathbb{N}}$ *a range,* $\mathcal{I} := [q_k(\lambda)]$ *an index space where* q_k *is a fixed polynomial, and* $\mathcal{F} := \{\mathcal{F}_\lambda\}_{\lambda \in \mathbb{N}}$ *a class of functions* $f : \mathcal{M} \to \mathcal{Y}$. *An iSKFE scheme for* $\mathcal{M}, \mathcal{Y}, \mathcal{I},$ *and* $\mathcal{F}$ *is a tuple of algorithms* $\mathsf{SKFE} = (\mathsf{Setup}, \mathsf{iKG}, \mathsf{Enc}, \mathsf{Dec})$ *where:*

- $\mathsf{Setup}(1^\lambda)$ *takes as input the security parameter and outputs a master secret key* MSK.

- iKG(MSK, f, i) *takes as input* MSK, *a function* $f \in \mathcal{F}$, *and an index* $i \in \mathcal{I}$, *and outputs a secret key* sk_f *for* f.
- Enc(MSK, x) *takes as input* MSK *and a message* $x \in \mathcal{M}$ *and outputs a ciphertext* CT.
- Dec(sk_f, CT) *takes as input* sk_f *for* $f \in \mathcal{F}$ *and* CT *and outputs* $y \in \mathcal{Y}$, *or* $\perp$.

Correctness: *We require* Dec(iKG(MSK, f, i), Enc(MSK, x)) $= f(x)$ *for any* $x \in \mathcal{M}$, $f \in \mathcal{F}$, $i \in \mathcal{I}$, *and* MSK $\leftarrow$ Setup(1^λ).

Next, we introduce selective-message message privacy [17].

Definition 2 (Selective-Message Message Privacy). *Let* SKFE *be an iSKFE scheme whose message space, function space, and index space are* $\mathcal{M}$, $\mathcal{F}$, *and* $\mathcal{I}$, *respectively. We define the selective-message message privacy experiment* $\mathsf{Exp}_{\mathcal{A}}^{\mathsf{sm\text{-}mp}}(1^\lambda, b)$ *between an adversary* $\mathcal{A}$ *and a challenger as follows.*

1. $\mathcal{A}$ *is given* 1^λ *and sends* $(x_0^{(1)}, x_1^{(1)}), \cdots, (x_0^{(q_m)}, x_1^{(q_m)})$ *to the challenger, where* q_m *is an a-priori unbounded polynomial of* λ.
2. *The challenger chooses* MSK $\leftarrow$ Setup(1^λ) *and a challenge bit* $b \leftarrow \{0, 1\}$.
3. *The challenger generates* $\mathsf{CT}^{(j)} \leftarrow$ Enc(MSK, $x_b^{(j)}$) *for* $j \in [q_m]$ *and sends them to* $\mathcal{A}$.
4. $\mathcal{A}$ *is allowed to make arbitrary function queries at most* $|\mathcal{I}| = q_k$ *times. For the* ℓ-*th key query* $f_\ell \in \mathcal{F}$ *from* $\mathcal{A}$, *the challenger generates* $\mathsf{sk}_{f_\ell} \leftarrow$ iKG(MSK, f_ℓ, ℓ) *and returns* sk_{f_ℓ} *to* $\mathcal{A}$.
5. $\mathcal{A}$ *outputs* $b' \in \{0, 1\}$. *The experiment output* b' *if* $f_\ell(x_0^{(j)}) = f_\ell(x_1^{(j)})$ *for all* $j \in [q_m]$ *and* $\ell \in [q_k]$, *where* q_k *is the number of key queries made by* $\mathcal{A}$; *otherwise* $\perp$.

We say that SKFE *is* q_k-*selective-message message private (or selectively secure for short) if for any PPT* $\mathcal{A}$, *it holds that*

$$\mathsf{Adv}_{\mathcal{A}}^{\mathsf{sm\text{-}mp}}(\lambda) := |\Pr[\mathsf{Exp}_{\mathcal{A}}^{\mathsf{sm\text{-}mp}}(1^\lambda, 0) = 1] - \Pr[\mathsf{Exp}_{\mathcal{A}}^{\mathsf{sm\text{-}mp}}(1^\lambda, 1) = 1]| \leq \mathsf{negl}(\lambda).$$

We further say that SKFE *is* (q_k, δ)-*selective-message message private, for some concrete negligible function* $\delta(\cdot)$, *if for any PPT* $\mathcal{A}$ *the above advantage is smaller than* $\delta(\lambda)^{\Omega(1)}$.

Remark 1 (Regarding the number of key queries). Let FE be a functional encryption scheme. If q_k is an unbounded polynomial, then we say FE is a *collusion-resistant* functional encryption. If q_k is a bounded polynomial (i.e., fixed in advance), then we say FE is a *bounded collusion-resistant* functional encryption. If $q_k = 1$, we say FE is a *single-key* functional encryption. In this study, our constructions are bounded collusion-resistant.

Remark 2 (Regarding an index for algorithm iKG*).* Our definitions of functional encryptions slightly deviates from the standard ones (e.g., the definition by Ananth and Jain [3] or Brakerski and Segev [17]). Our key generation algorithm takes not only a master secret key and a function but also an index, which is used to bound the number of functional key generations. This index should be different for each functional key generation. One might think this is a limitation, but this is not the case in this study because our goal is constructing single-key PKFE. For a single-key scheme, $|\mathcal{I}| = 1$ and we do not need such an index. Index based bounded collusion-resistant functional encryption schemes are just intermediate tools in this study. In fact, such an index has been introduced by Li and Micciancio in the context of PKFE [40].[9]

Next, we introduce notions regarding efficiency, called succinctness for functional encryption schemes.

Definition 3 (Succinctness of Functional Encryption [11]). *For a class of functions $\mathcal{F} = \{\mathcal{F}_\lambda\}$ over message domain $\mathcal{M} = \{\mathcal{M}_\lambda\}$, we let $n(\lambda)$ be the input length of the functions in $\mathcal{F}$, $s(\lambda) = \max_{f \in \mathcal{F}_\lambda} |f|$ the upper bound on the circuit size of functions in $\mathcal{F}_\lambda$, and $d(\lambda) = \max_{f \in \mathcal{F}_\lambda} \mathsf{depth}(f)$ the upper bound on the depth, and a functional encryption scheme is*

- *succinct if the size of the encryption circuit is bounded by $\mathrm{poly}(n, \lambda, \log s)$, where poly is a fixed polynomial.*
- *weakly succinct if the size of the encryption circuit is bounded by $s^\gamma \cdot \mathrm{poly}(n, \lambda)$, where poly is a fixed polynomial, and $\gamma < 1$ is a constant.*
- *weakly collusion-succinct if the size of the encryption circuit is bounded by $q^\gamma \cdot \mathrm{poly}(n, \lambda, s)$, where q is the upper bound of issuable functional keys in bounded-key schemes (that is, the size of the index space of the scheme), poly is a fixed polynomial, and $\gamma < 1$ is a constant.*

We call γ the compression factor. The following theorem states that one can construct IO from any single-key weakly succinct PKFE. We recall that single-key iPKFE is also single-key PKFE, and vice versa.

Theorem 1 [11]. *If there exists a single-key sub-exponentially weakly selectively secure weakly succinct PKFE scheme for P/poly, then there exists an indistinguishability obfuscator for P/poly.*

2.2   Indistinguishability Obfuscation

Definition 4 (Indistinguishability Obfuscator). *A PPT algorithm $i\mathcal{O}$ is an IO for a circuit class $\{\mathcal{C}_\lambda\}_{\lambda \in \mathbb{N}}$ if it satisfies the following two conditions.*

Functionality: *For any security parameter $\lambda \in \mathbb{N}$, $C \in \mathcal{C}_\lambda$, and input x, we have that $\Pr[C'(x) = C(x) : C' \leftarrow i\mathcal{O}(C)] = 1$.*

---

[9] The security definition of Li and Micciancio for index based functional encryption and ours is slightly different. Their definition allows an adversary to use indices for key generation in an arbitrary order. On the other hand, our definition does not allow it. The difference comes from the fact that their goal is constructing collusion-resistant functional encryption while our goal is constructing single-key functional encryption. By restricting an adversary to use indices successively from one, we can describe security proofs more simply.

Indistinguishability: *For any PPT distinguisher* D *and for any pair of circuits* $C_0, C_1 \in \mathcal{C}_\lambda$ *such that for any input* x, $C_0(x) = C_1(x)$ *and* $|C_0| = |C_1|$, *it holds that* $|\Pr[D(i\mathcal{O}(C_0)) = 1] - \Pr[D(i\mathcal{O}(C_1)) = 1]| \leq \mathsf{negl}(\lambda)$. *We further say that* $i\mathcal{O}$ *is* δ-*secure, for some concrete negligible function* $\delta(\cdot)$, *if for any PPT* D *the above advantage is smaller than* $\delta(\lambda)^{\Omega(1)}$.

Definition 5 (Strong   Exponentially-Efficient   Indistinguishability Obfuscation). *Let* $\gamma < 1$ *be a constant. An algorithm* $\mathsf{sxi}\mathcal{O}$ *is a* γ-*compressing SXIO for a circuit class* $\{\mathcal{C}_\lambda\}_{\lambda \in \mathbb{N}}$ *if it satisfies the functionality and indistinguishability in Definition 4 and the following efficiency requirement:*

Non-trivial time efficiency: *We require that the running time of* $\mathsf{sxi}\mathcal{O}$ *on input* $(1^\lambda, C)$ *is at most* $2^{n\gamma} \cdot \mathsf{poly}(\lambda, |C|)$ *for any* $\lambda \in \mathbb{N}$ *and any circuit* $C \in \{\mathcal{C}_\lambda\}_{\lambda \in \mathbb{N}}$ *with input length* n.

Remark 3. In this paper, when we write "SXIO for P/poly", we implicitly mean that SXIO for polynomial-size circuits with inputs of logarithmic length. This follows the style by Bitansky et al. [9] though Lin et al. [41] use the circuit class $\mathsf{P}^{\log}/\mathsf{poly}$ to denote the class of polynomial-size circuits with inputs of logarithmic length. The reason why we use the style is that we can consider the polynomial input length if we do not care about the polynomial running time of $\mathsf{sxi}\mathcal{O}$ and the input length n obviously must be logarithmic for the *polynomial* running time of $\mathsf{sxi}\mathcal{O}$ from the definition.

3   Collusion-Succinct Functional Encryption from SXIO

In our bounded-key weakly collusion-succinct iSKFE and iPKFE schemes, we use single-key non-succinct SKFE and PKFE schemes that are implied from one-way function and public-key encryption, respectively.

Theorem 2 [34][10]. *If there exists a* δ-*secure one-way function, then there exists a* $(1, \delta)$-*selectively-secure and non-succinct SKFE scheme for* P/poly. *If there exists a* δ-*secure public-key encryption, then there exists a* $(1, \delta)$-*selectively-secure and non-succinct PKFE scheme for* P/poly.

Throughout this paper, let n and s be the length of a message x and size of a function f of a functional encryption scheme, respectively as in Definition 3.

3.1   Collusion-Succinct SKFE from SXIO and One-Way Function

We put only our theorem in this section due to limited space. We can understand an essence of the theorem from the construction in the next section.

---

[10] More precisely, Gorbunov et al. prove that we can construct *adaptively* secure schemes, in which adversaries are allowed to declare a target message pair after the function query phase. However, selective security is sufficient for our purpose.

Theorem 3. *If there exists non-succinct* $(1, \delta)$*-selective-message message private SKFE for* P/poly *and* δ*-secure* $\widetilde{\gamma}$*-compressing SXIO for* P/poly *where* $0 < \widetilde{\gamma} < 1$ *(*$\widetilde{\gamma}$ *might be close to 1), then there exists weakly collusion-succinct* (q, δ)*-selective-message message private iSKFE for* P/poly *with compression factor* γ' *such that* $0 < \widetilde{\gamma} < \gamma' < 1$*, where* q *is an a-priori fixed polynomial of* λ*.*

3.2   Collusion-Succinct PKFE from SXIO and Public-Key Encryption

In this section, we discuss how to construct a bounded-key weakly collusion-succinct iPKFE scheme from an SXIO and PKE scheme.

Overview and proof strategy. Before we proceed to details, we give a main idea for our iPKFE scheme.

Analogously to SKFE setting in Sect. 3.1, to achieve collusion-succinctness, we consider to set a ciphertext as a circuit obfuscated by SXIO that can generate q ciphertexts of a single-key non-succinct scheme. We need to maintain q encryption keys succinctly. In the SKFE setting, we maintain q master secret-keys as one puncturable PRF key. However, we cannot directly use this solution in the PKFE setting. If we do so in the PKFE setting, since the puncturable PRF key should be the master secret-key, an encryptor cannot use it. Thus, we need some mechanism that makes all master public-keys of single-key non-succinct schemes available to an encryptor maintaining them succinctly.

To generate a *succinct* master public-key, we generate a setup circuit (denoted by S_{1fe} in our scheme) that outputs i-th master public-key of a single-key non-succinct scheme corresponding to an input i, and obfuscate the circuit by SXIO as explained in Sect. 1.3. An encryptor embeds $MPK := sxi\mathcal{O}(S_{1fe})$ into an encryption circuit and outputs an obfuscation of this encryption circuit as a ciphertext. This encryption circuit is hardwired a plaintext x and can output ciphertexts under all q master public-keys like the encryption circuit in Sect. 3.1.

Our solution means that we must obfuscate a circuit in which an obfuscated circuit is hardwired (nested applications of SXIO). The nested application still increases the size of a ciphertext. However, if the compression factor of SXIO for S_{1fe} is sufficiently small, we can achieve weak collusion-succinctness.

In the security proof, we use the security of a single-key non-succinct scheme to change a ciphertext of x_0 under each master public-key into that of x_1 via the punctured programming approach as the SKFE case. However, in the reduction to the single-key security, a target master public-key should be given from the security experiment. This means that we must embed the target master public-key into the setup circuit instead of generating it in an on-line manner. Thus, we must apply the punctured programming technique to the setup circuit too before the reduction to the single-key security. This is what the first hybrid step in the security proof does. The rest of the proof is almost the same as that of our iSKFE scheme.

Setup Circuit $\mathsf{S}_{1\mathsf{fe}}[K](i)$

Hardwired: puncturable PRF key K.
Input: index $i \in [q]$.
Padding: circuit is padded to size $\mathsf{pad}_\mathsf{S} := \mathsf{pad}_\mathsf{S}(\lambda, n, s, q)$, which is determined in analysis.

1. Compute $r_i \leftarrow \mathsf{F}_K(i)$.
2. Compute $(\mathsf{MPK}_i, \mathsf{MSK}_i) \leftarrow 1\mathsf{FE}.\mathsf{Setup}(1^\lambda; r_i)$ and output MPK_i.

Fig. 2. Description of $\mathsf{S}_{1\mathsf{fe}}[K]$.

Our construction. The construction of an iPKFE scheme qFE whose index space is $[q]$ from an SXIO and public-key encryption scheme is as follows, where q is a fixed polynomial of λ. Let $1\mathsf{FE} = (1\mathsf{FE}.\mathsf{Setup}, 1\mathsf{FE}.\mathsf{KG}, 1\mathsf{FE}.\mathsf{Enc}, 1\mathsf{FE}.\mathsf{Dec})$ be a single-key non-succinct PKFE scheme and $(\mathsf{PRF}.\mathsf{Gen}, \mathsf{F}, \mathsf{Punc})$ a puncturable PRF.

$\mathsf{qFE}.\mathsf{Setup}(1^\lambda)$:
- Generate $K \leftarrow \mathsf{PRF}.\mathsf{Gen}(1^\lambda)$ and $\mathsf{S}_{1\mathsf{fe}}[K]$ defined in Fig. 2.
- Return $(\widehat{\mathsf{MPK}}, \widehat{\mathsf{MSK}}) := (\mathsf{sxi}\mathcal{O}(\mathsf{S}_{1\mathsf{fe}}), K)$.

$\mathsf{qFE}.\mathsf{iKG}(\widehat{\mathsf{MSK}}, f, i)$:
- Parse $K := \widehat{\mathsf{MSK}}$.
- Compute $r_i \leftarrow \mathsf{F}_K(i)$ and $(\mathsf{MSK}_i, \mathsf{MPK}_i) \leftarrow 1\mathsf{FE}.\mathsf{Setup}(1^\lambda; r_i)$.
- Compute $\mathsf{sk}_f^i \leftarrow 1\mathsf{FE}.\mathsf{KG}(\mathsf{MSK}_i, f)$ and return $\widehat{\mathsf{sk}}_f \leftarrow (i, \mathsf{sk}_f^i)$.

$\mathsf{qFE}.\mathsf{Enc}(\widehat{\mathsf{MPK}}, x)$:
- Generate $K' \leftarrow \mathsf{PRF}.\mathsf{Gen}(1^\lambda)$ and $\mathsf{E}_{1\mathsf{fe}}[\widehat{\mathsf{MPK}}, K', x]$ defined in Fig. 3.
- Return $\widehat{\mathsf{CT}} \leftarrow \mathsf{sxi}\mathcal{O}(\mathsf{E}_{1\mathsf{fe}}[\widehat{\mathsf{MPK}}, K', x])$.

$\mathsf{qFE}.\mathsf{Dec}(\widehat{\mathsf{sk}}_f, \widehat{\mathsf{CT}})$:
- Parse $(i, \mathsf{sk}_f^i) := \widehat{\mathsf{sk}}_f$.
- Compute the circuit $\widehat{\mathsf{CT}}$ on input i, that is $\mathsf{CT}_i \leftarrow \widehat{\mathsf{CT}}(i)$.
- Return $y \leftarrow 1\mathsf{FE}.\mathsf{Dec}(\mathsf{sk}_f^i, \mathsf{CT}_i)$.

Theorem 4. *If there exists $(1, \delta)$-selectively-secure non-succinct PKFE for P/poly and δ-secure γ-compressing SXIO for P/poly where γ is an arbitrarily small constant such that $0 < \gamma < 1$, then there exists (q, δ)-selectively-secure weakly collusion-succinct iPKFE for P/poly with compression factor β, where q is an a-priori fixed polynomial of λ, and β is a constant such that $0 < \beta < 1$ specified later.*

Proof of Theorem 4. We start with the security proof, then move on to analyzing succinctness.

Encryption Circuit $\mathsf{E}_{1\mathsf{fe}}[\widehat{\mathsf{MPK}}, K', x](i)$

Hardwired: circuit $\widehat{\mathsf{MPK}}$, puncturable PRF key K', and message x.
Input: index $i \in [q]$.
Padding: circuit is padded to size $\mathsf{pad}_\mathsf{E} := \mathsf{pad}_\mathsf{E}(\lambda, n, s, q)$, which is determined in analysis.

1. Compute the circuit $\widehat{\mathsf{MPK}}$ on input i, that is $\mathsf{MPK}_i \leftarrow \widehat{\mathsf{MPK}}(i)$.
2. Compute $r_i' \leftarrow \mathsf{F}_{K'}(i)$ and output $\mathsf{CT}_i \leftarrow \mathsf{1FE.Enc}(\mathsf{MPK}_i, x; r_i')$.

Fig. 3. Description of $\mathsf{E}_{1\mathsf{fe}}[\widehat{\mathsf{MPK}}, K', x]$.

Security Proof. Let us assume that the underlying primitives are δ-secure. Let $\mathcal{A}$ be an adversary attacking the selective security of qFE. We define a sequence of hybrid games.

Hyb_0: The first game is the original selective security experiment for $b = 0$, that is $\mathsf{Expt}_\mathcal{A}^{\mathsf{sel}}(1^\lambda, 0)$. $\mathcal{A}$ first selects the challenge messages (x_0^*, x_1^*) and receives the master public key $\widehat{\mathsf{MPK}} := \mathsf{sxi}\mathcal{O}(\mathsf{S}_{1\mathsf{fe}}[K])$ and target ciphertext $\mathsf{sxi}\mathcal{O}(\mathsf{E}_{1\mathsf{fe}}[\widehat{\mathsf{MPK}}, K', x_0^*])$. Next, $\mathcal{A}$ adaptively makes q function queries $f_1, \ldots, f_q$ such that $f_i(x_0^*) = f_i(x_1^*)$ for all $i \in [q]$ and receives functional keys $\widehat{\mathsf{sk}}_{f_1}, \ldots, \widehat{\mathsf{sk}}_{f_q}$.

$\mathsf{Hyb}_1^{i^*}$: Let $i^* \in [q]$. We generate $\widehat{\mathsf{MPK}}$ as obfuscated $\mathsf{S}_{1\mathsf{fe}}^*$ described in Fig. 4. In this hybrid game, we set $r_{i^*} \leftarrow \mathsf{F}_K(i^*)$, $K\{i^*\} \leftarrow \mathsf{Punc}(K, i^*)$ and $(\mathsf{MPK}_{i^*}, \mathsf{MSK}_{i^*}) \leftarrow \mathsf{1FE.Setup}(1^\lambda; r_{i^*})$.
When $i^* = 1$, the behavior of $\mathsf{S}_{1\mathsf{fe}}^*$ is the same as that of $\mathsf{S}_{1\mathsf{fe}}$ since the hardwired MPK_1 in $\mathsf{S}_{1\mathsf{fe}}^*$ is the same as the output of $\mathsf{S}_{1\mathsf{fe}}$ on the input 1. Their size is also the same since we pad circuit $\mathsf{S}_{1\mathsf{fe}}$ to have the same size as $\mathsf{S}_{1\mathsf{fe}}^*$. Then, we can use the indistinguishability guarantee of $\mathsf{sxi}\mathcal{O}$ and it holds that $\mathsf{Hyb}_0 \overset{\mathsf{c}}{\approx}_\delta \mathsf{Hyb}_1^1$.

$\mathsf{Hyb}_2^{i^*}$: The challenge ciphertext is generated by obfuscating $\mathsf{E}_{1\mathsf{fe}}^*$ described in Fig. 5. In this hybrid game, we set $r_{i^*}' \leftarrow \mathsf{F}_K(i^*)$, $K'\{i^*\} \leftarrow \mathsf{Punc}(K', i^*)$, $\mathsf{CT}_{i^*} \leftarrow \mathsf{1FE.Enc}(\mathsf{MPK}_{i^*}, x_0^*; r_{i^*}')$, and $\mathsf{MPK}_{i^*} \leftarrow \widehat{\mathsf{MPK}}(i^*)$.
When $i^* = 1$, the behavior of $\mathsf{E}_{1\mathsf{fe}}^*$ is the same as that of $\mathsf{E}_{1\mathsf{fe}}$ since the hardwired CT_1 in $\mathsf{E}_{1\mathsf{fe}}^*$ is the same as the output of $\mathsf{E}_{1\mathsf{fe}}$ on the input 1. Moreover, both circuits have the same size by padding pad_E. Then, we can use the indistinguishability guarantee of $\mathsf{sxi}\mathcal{O}$ and it holds that $\mathsf{Hyb}_1^1 \overset{\mathsf{c}}{\approx}_\delta \mathsf{Hyb}_2^1$.
In addition, for $i^* \geq 2$, the behavior of $\mathsf{E}_{1\mathsf{fe}}^*$ does not change between $\mathsf{Hyb}_1^{i^*}$ and $\mathsf{Hyb}_2^{i^*}$. Thus, $\mathsf{Hyb}_1^{i^*} \overset{\mathsf{c}}{\approx}_\delta \mathsf{Hyb}_2^{i^*}$ holds for every $i^* \in \{2, \cdots, q\}$ due to the security guarantee of $\mathsf{sxi}\mathcal{O}$.

$\mathsf{Hyb}_3^{i^*}$: We change $r_{i^*} = \mathsf{F}_K(i^*)$ and $r_{i^*}' = \mathsf{F}_{K'}(i^*)$ into uniformly random r_{i^*} and r_{i^*}'. Due to the pseudo-randomness at punctured points of puncturable PRF, it holds that $\mathsf{Hyb}_2^{i^*} \overset{\mathsf{c}}{\approx}_\delta \mathsf{Hyb}_3^{i^*}$ for every $i^* \in [q]$.

Setup Circuit $\mathsf{S}^*_{\mathsf{1fe}}[K\{i^*\}, \mathsf{MPK}_{i^*}](i)$

Hardwired: puncturable PRF key $K\{i^*\}$ and 1FE master public-key MPK_{i^*}.
Input: index $i \in [q]$.
Padding: circuit is padded to size $\mathsf{pad}_\mathsf{S} := \mathsf{pad}_\mathsf{S}(\lambda, n, s, q)$, which is determined in analysis.

1. If $i = i^*$, output MPK_{i^*}.
2. Else, compute $r_i \leftarrow \mathsf{F}_{K\{i^*\}}(i)$.
3. Compute $(\mathsf{MPK}_i, \mathsf{MSK}_i) \leftarrow \mathsf{1FE.Setup}(1^\lambda; r_i)$ and output MPK_i.

Fig. 4. Circuit $\mathsf{S}^*_{\mathsf{1fe}}[K\{i^*\}, \mathsf{MPK}_{i^*}]$. The description depends on i^*, but we use the notion $\mathsf{S}^*_{\mathsf{1fe}}$ instead of $\mathsf{S}^{i^*}_{\mathsf{1fe}}$ for simpler notations.

Encryption Circuit $\mathsf{E}^*_{\mathsf{1fe}}[\widehat{\mathsf{MPK}}, K'\{i^*\}, x^*_0, x^*_1, \mathsf{CT}_{i^*}](i)$

Hardwired: master public key $\widehat{\mathsf{MPK}}$ (that is an obfuscated circuit), puncturable PRF key $K'\{i^*\}$, messages x^*_0, x^*_1, and ciphertext CT_{i^*}.
Input: index $i \in [q]$.
Padding: circuit is padded to size $\mathsf{pad}_\mathsf{E} := \mathsf{pad}_\mathsf{E}(\lambda, n, s, q)$, which is determined in analysis.

1. If $i = i^*$, output CT_{i^*}.
2. Else, compute $r'_i \leftarrow \mathsf{F}_{K'}(i)$ and the circuit $\widehat{\mathsf{MPK}}$ on input i, that is $\mathsf{MPK}_i \leftarrow \widehat{\mathsf{MPK}}(i)$.
   If $i > i^*$: Output $\mathsf{CT}_i \leftarrow \mathsf{1FE.Enc}(\mathsf{MPK}_i, x^*_0; r'_i)$.
   If $i < i^*$: Output $\mathsf{CT}_i \leftarrow \mathsf{1FE.Enc}(\mathsf{MPK}_i, x^*_1; r'_i)$.

Fig. 5. Circuit $\mathsf{E}^*_{\mathsf{1fe}}[\widehat{\mathsf{MPK}}, K'\{i^*\}, x^*_0, x^*_1, \mathsf{CT}_{i^*}]$. The description depends on i^*, but we use the notion $\mathsf{E}^*_{\mathsf{1fe}}$ instead of $\mathsf{E}^{i^*}_{\mathsf{1fe}}$ for simpler notations.

$\mathsf{Hyb}^{i^*}_4$: We change CT_{i^*} from $\mathsf{1FE.Enc}(\mathsf{MPK}_{i^*}, x^*_0)$ to $\mathsf{1FE.Enc}(\mathsf{MPK}_{i^*}, x^*_1)$. In $\mathsf{Hyb}^{i^*}_3$ and $\mathsf{Hyb}^{i^*}_4$, we do not need randomness to generate MPK_{i^*} and CT_{i^*}. We just hardwire MPK_{i^*} and CT_{i^*} into $\mathsf{S}^*_{\mathsf{1fe}}$ and $\mathsf{E}^*_{\mathsf{1fe}}$, respectively. Therefore, for every $i^* \in [q]$, $\mathsf{Hyb}^{i^*}_3 \approx_\delta \mathsf{Hyb}^{i^*}_4$ follows from the selective security of 1FE under the master public key MPK_{i^*}.

$\mathsf{Hyb}^{i^*}_5$: We change r^*_i and r'_{i^*} into $r_{i^*} = \mathsf{F}_K(i^*)$ and $r'_{i^*} = \mathsf{F}_{K'}(i^*)$. We can show $\mathsf{Hyb}^{i^*}_4 \approx_\delta \mathsf{Hyb}^{i^*}_5$ for every $i^* \in [q]$ based on the pseudo-randomness at punctured point of puncturable PRF.

From the definition of $\mathsf{S}^*_{\mathsf{1FE}}$, $\mathsf{E}^*_{\mathsf{1FE}}$, and $\mathsf{Hyb}^{i^*}_1$, the behaviors of $\mathsf{S}^*_{\mathsf{1FE}}$ and $\mathsf{E}^*_{\mathsf{1FE}}$ in $\mathsf{Hyb}^{i^*}_5$ and $\mathsf{Hyb}^{i^*+1}_1$ are the same. Thus, $\mathsf{Hyb}^{i^*}_5 \approx_\delta \mathsf{Hyb}^{i^*+1}_1$ holds for every $i^* \in [q-1]$ due to the security guarantee of sxi$\mathcal{O}$. It also holds that $\mathsf{Hyb}^q_5 \approx_\delta \mathsf{Expt}^{\mathsf{sel}}_\mathcal{A}(1^\lambda, 1)$ based on the security guarantee of sxi$\mathcal{O}$. This completes the security proof.

Padding Parameter. The proof of security relies on the indistinguishability of obfuscated $\mathsf{S}_{\mathsf{1fe}}$ and $\mathsf{S}^*_{\mathsf{1fe}}$ defined in Figs. 2 and 4, and that of obfuscated $\mathsf{E}_{\mathsf{1fe}}$ and

E^*_{1fe} defined in Figs. 3 and 5. Accordingly, we set $\mathsf{pad}_S := \max(|S_{1fe}|, |S^*_{1fe}|)$ and $\mathsf{pad}_E := \max(|E_{1fe}|, |E^*_{1fe}|)$.

The circuits S_{1fe} and S^*_{1fe} compute a puncturable PRF over domain $[q]$ and a key pair of 1FE, and may have punctured PRF keys and a master public key hardwired. The circuits E_{1fe} and E^*_{1fe} run the circuit $\widehat{MPK}$ and compute a puncturable PRF over domain $[q]$ and a ciphertext of 1FE, and may have punctured PRF keys and a hard-wired ciphertext. Note that the size of instances of 1FE is independent of q. Thus, it holds that

$$\mathsf{pad}_S \leq \mathrm{poly}(\lambda, n, s, \log q) \qquad \text{and} \qquad \mathsf{pad}_E \leq \mathrm{poly}(\lambda, n, s, \log q, |\widehat{MPK}|).$$

Weak Collusion-Succinctness. To clearly analyze the size of qFE.Enc, we suppose that SXIO used to obfuscate S_{1fe} and that used to obfuscate E_{1fe} are different.

Let γ' be the compression factor of the SXIO for S_{1fe}. The input space for S_{1fe} is $[q]$. Therefore, by the efficiency guarantee of SXIO, we have

$$|\mathsf{sxi}\mathcal{O}(S_{1fe})| < q^{\gamma'} \cdot \mathrm{poly}(\lambda, n, s, \log q).$$

Let γ be the compression factor of the SXIO for E_{1fe}. The input space of E_{1fe} is also $[q]$. The size of the encryption circuit qFE.Enc (dominated by generating the obfuscated E_{1fe}) is

$$q^{\gamma} \cdot \mathrm{poly}(\lambda, n, s, \log q, |\mathsf{sxi}\mathcal{O}(S_{1fe})|) < q^{\gamma + c\gamma'} \cdot \mathrm{poly}(\lambda, n, s),$$

where c is some constant.

We assume there exists SXIO with an arbitrarily small compression factor. Thus, by setting γ' as $\gamma' < \frac{1-\gamma}{c}$, we can ensure that $\beta := \gamma + c\gamma' < 1$, that is qFE is weakly collusion-succinct.

This completes the proof of Theorem 4.   ∎

3.3   Collusion-Succinct PKFE from SXIO and Identity-Based Encryption

In this section, we directly construct a weakly collusion-succinct and weakly selectively secure iPKFE scheme from an SXIO and identity-based encryption scheme.

Our construction. The construction of a weakly collusion-succinct and weakly selectively secure q-key iPKFE scheme qFE for any fixed polynomial q of λ is based on an SXIO, identity-based encryption scheme[11], and garbled circuit which is implied by a one-way function. Our collusion-succinct iPKFE scheme

---

[11] We stress that the size of the encryption circuit of an identity-based encryption scheme is $|\mathcal{ID}|^{\alpha} \cdot \mathrm{poly}(\lambda, \ell)$ where ℓ is the length of plaintext, $\mathcal{ID}$ is the identity-space, and α is a constant such that $0 < \alpha < 1$. Most identity-based encryption schemes based on concrete assumptions have such succinct encryption circuits. In our scheme, $\mathcal{ID}$ is just a polynomial size.

Garbling with encrypted labels circuit $\mathsf{EL}_{\mathsf{gc}}[\mathsf{MPK}_{\mathsf{ibe}}, K, x]$

Hardwired: public parameter of IBE $\mathsf{MPK}_{\mathsf{ibe}}$, puncturable PRF key K, and plaintext x.
Input: index $i \in [q]$.
Padding: circuit is padded to size $\mathsf{pad}_{\mathsf{EL}} := \mathsf{pad}_{\mathsf{EL}}(\lambda, s, q)$, which is determined in analysis.

1. Compute $r_{\mathsf{gc}} \leftarrow \mathsf{F}_K(i\|1\|2)$.
2. Compute $(\widetilde{U}, \{L_{j,\alpha}\}_{j \in [s], \alpha \in \{0,1\}}) \leftarrow \mathsf{Grbl}(1^\lambda, U(\cdot, x); r_{\mathsf{gc}})$.
3. For every $j \in [s]$ and $\alpha \in \{0,1\}$, compute $r_{i\|j\|\alpha} \leftarrow \mathsf{F}_K(i\|j\|\alpha)$ and $\mathsf{CT}^{j,\alpha} \leftarrow \mathsf{IBE.Enc}(\mathsf{MPK}_{\mathsf{ibe}}, (i, j, \alpha), L_{j,\alpha}; r_{i\|j\|\alpha})$.
4. Return $(\widetilde{U}, \{\mathsf{CT}^{j,\alpha}\}_{j \in [s], \alpha \in \{0,1\}})$.

Fig. 6. The description of $\mathsf{EL}_{\mathsf{gc}}$. $U(\cdot, x)$ is a universal circuit in which x is hardwired as the second input.

is *weakly selectively* secure because we use function descriptions as identities of identity-based encryption, and the selective security of identity-based encryption requires adversaries to submit a target identity at the beginning of the game.

We assume that we can represent every function f by a s bit string $(f[1], \cdots, f[s])$ where $s = \mathsf{poly}(\lambda)$. Let $\mathsf{IBE} = (\mathsf{IBE.Setup}, \mathsf{IBE.KG}, \mathsf{IBE.Enc}, \mathsf{IBE.Dec})$ be an identity-based encryption scheme whose identity space is $[q] \times [s] \times \{0,1\}$, $\mathsf{GC} = (\mathsf{Grbl}, \mathsf{Eval})$ a garbled circuit, and $(\mathsf{PRF.Gen}, \mathsf{F}, \mathsf{Punc})$ a PRF whose domain is $[q] \times [s] \times \{0,1,2\}$.

$\mathsf{qFE.Setup}(1^\lambda)$:
- Generate $(\mathsf{MPK}_{\mathsf{ibe}}, \mathsf{MSK}_{\mathsf{ibe}}) \leftarrow \mathsf{IBE.Setup}(1^\lambda)$.
- Set $\mathsf{MPK} := \mathsf{MPK}_{\mathsf{ibe}}$ and $\mathsf{MSK} := \mathsf{MSK}_{\mathsf{ibe}}$ and return $(\mathsf{MPK}, \mathsf{MSK})$.

$\mathsf{qFE.iKG}(\mathsf{MSK}, f, i)$:
- Parse $\mathsf{MSK}_{\mathsf{ibe}} \leftarrow \mathsf{MSK}$ and $(f[1], \cdots, f[s]) := f$.
- For every $j \in [s]$, compute $\mathsf{SK}^j \leftarrow \mathsf{IBE.KG}(\mathsf{MSK}_{\mathsf{ibe}}, (i, j, f[j]))$.
- Return $\mathsf{sk}_f := (i, f, \{\mathsf{SK}^j\}_{j \in [s]})$.

$\mathsf{qFE.Enc}(\mathsf{MPK}, x)$:
- Parse $\mathsf{MPK}_{\mathsf{ibe}} \leftarrow \mathsf{MPK}$ and choose $K \leftarrow \mathsf{PRF.Gen}(1^\lambda)$.
- Return $\mathsf{CT}_{\mathsf{fe}} \leftarrow \mathsf{sxi}\mathcal{O}(\mathsf{EL}_{\mathsf{gc}}[\mathsf{MPK}_{\mathsf{ibe}}, K, x])$. $\mathsf{EL}_{\mathsf{gc}}$ is defined in Fig. 6.

$\mathsf{qFE.Dec}(\mathsf{sk}_f, \mathsf{CT}_{\mathsf{fe}})$:
- Parse $(i, f, \{\mathsf{SK}^j\}_{j \in [s]}) \leftarrow \mathsf{sk}_f$.
- Compute the circuit $\mathsf{CT}_{\mathsf{fe}}$ on input i, that is $(\widetilde{U}, \{\mathsf{CT}^{j,\alpha}\}_{j \in [s], \alpha \in \{0,1\}}) \leftarrow \mathsf{CT}_{\mathsf{fe}}(i)$.
- For every $j \in [s]$, compute $L_j \leftarrow \mathsf{IBE.Dec}(\mathsf{SK}^j, \mathsf{CT}^{j, f[j]})$.
- Return $y \leftarrow \mathsf{Eval}(\widetilde{U}, \{L_j\}_{j \in [s]})$.

Theorem 5. *If there exists δ-selectively-secure succinct identity-based encryption with α-compression (α is a sufficiently small constant) and δ-secure $\widetilde{\gamma}$-compressing SXIO for P/poly for a constant $\widetilde{\gamma}$ such that $0 < \widetilde{\gamma} < 1$ ($\widetilde{\gamma}$ might be close to 1), then there exists weakly collusion-succinct (q, δ)-weakly-selectively secure iPKFE for circuits of size at most s with compression factor β, where s and q are a-priori fixed polynomials of λ and β is a constant such that $\widetilde{\gamma} < \beta < 1$ specified later.*

Proof of Theorem 5. We start with the security proof then moving to analyzing succinctness.

Security Proof. Let us assume that the underlying primitives are δ-secure. Let $\mathcal{A}$ be an adversary attacking weakly selective security of qFE. We define a sequence of hybrid games.

Hyb_0: The first game is the original weakly selective security experiment for $b = 0$, that is $\mathsf{Expt}_{\mathcal{A}}^{\mathsf{sel}^*}(1^\lambda, 0)$. In this game, $\mathcal{A}$ first selects the challenge messages (x_0^*, x_1^*) and queries q functions $f_1, \ldots, f_q$ such that $f_i(x_0^*) = f_i(x_1^*)$ for all $i \in [q]$. Then $\mathcal{A}$ obtains an encryption of x_0^*, the master public key, and functional keys $\mathsf{sk}_{f_1}, \ldots, \mathsf{sk}_{f_q}$.

$\mathsf{Hyb}_1^{i^*}$: Let $i^* \in [q]$. The challenge ciphertext is generated by obfuscating $\mathsf{EL}_{\mathsf{gc}}^*$ described in Fig. 7. In this hybrid game, we set $r_{\mathsf{gc}}^* \leftarrow \mathsf{F}_K(i^* \| 1 \| 2)$, $r_{i^* \| j \| \alpha}^* \leftarrow \mathsf{F}_K(i^* \| j \| \alpha)$ for all $j \in [s]$ and $\alpha \in \{0, 1\}$, $K\{S^*\} \leftarrow \mathsf{Punc}(K, S^*)$ where $S^* := \left\{ i^* \| 1 \| 2, \{i^* \| j \| \alpha\}_{j \in [s], \alpha \in \{0,1\}} \right\}$, $(\widetilde{U}^*, \{L_{j,\alpha}^*\}_{j \in [s], \alpha \in \{0,1\}}) \leftarrow \mathsf{Grbl}(1^\lambda, U(\cdot, x_0^*); r_{\mathsf{gc}}^*)$, and $\mathsf{CT}_{i^*}^{j,\alpha} \leftarrow \mathsf{IBE.Enc}(\mathsf{MPK}_{\mathsf{ibe}}, (i^*, j, \alpha), L_{j,\alpha}; r_{i^* \| j \| \alpha}^*)$ for all $j \in [s]$ and $\alpha \in \{0, 1\}$. Hereafter, we use $r_{j \| \alpha}^*$ instead of $r_{i^* \| j \| \alpha}^*$ for ease of notation.

When $i^* = 1$, the behaviors of $\mathsf{EL}_{\mathsf{gc}}$ and $\mathsf{EL}_{\mathsf{gc}}^*$ are the same from the definition of $\mathsf{EL}_{\mathsf{gc}}^*$, and so are their size since we pad circuit $\mathsf{EL}_{\mathsf{gc}}$ to have the same size as $\mathsf{EL}_{\mathsf{gc}}^*$. Then, we can use the indistinguishability guarantee of sxi$\mathcal{O}$, and it holds that $\mathsf{Hyb}_0 \overset{\mathsf{c}}{\approx}_\delta \mathsf{Hyb}_1^1$.

$\mathsf{Hyb}_2^{i^*}$: We change $r_{\mathsf{gc}}^* = \mathsf{F}_K(i^* \| 1 \| 2)$ and $r_{j \| \alpha}^* = \mathsf{F}_K(i^* \| j \| \alpha)$ into uniformly random r_{gc}^* and $r_{j \| \alpha}^*$ for all $j \in [s]$ and $\alpha \in \{0, 1\}$. Due to the pseudo-randomness at punctured points of puncturable PRF, it holds that $\mathsf{Hyb}_1^{i^*} \overset{\mathsf{c}}{\approx}_\delta \mathsf{Hyb}_2^{i^*}$ for every $i^* \in [q]$.

$\mathsf{Hyb}_3^{i^*}$: For ease of notation, let $f^* := f_{i^*}$ and $\bar{f}$ be the complement of f, that is, $(\bar{f}[1], \ldots, \bar{f}[s]) := (1 - f[1], \ldots, 1 - f[s])$. Moreover, we omit each randomness for IBE.Enc since it is uniformly random at this hybrid game. For every $j \in [s]$, we change

- normal ciphertexts $\mathsf{CT}_{i^*}^{j, \bar{f}^*[j]} \leftarrow \mathsf{IBE.Enc}(\mathsf{MPK}_{\mathsf{ibe}}, (i^*, j, \bar{f}^*[j]), L_{j, \bar{f}^*[j]})$ into

- junk ciphertexts $\mathsf{CT}_{i^*}^{j, \bar{f}^*[j]} \leftarrow \mathsf{IBE.Enc}(\mathsf{MPK}_{\mathsf{ibe}}, (i^*, j, \bar{f}^*[j]), 0^{\ell(\lambda)})$, where ℓ is a polynomial denoting the length of labels output by Grbl.

That is, for identities which *do not correspond* to the i^*-th function queried by $\mathcal{A}$, we do not encrypt labels of garbled circuit. We do not change $\mathsf{CT}_{i^*}^{j, f^*[j]}$ for all $j \in [s]$. Note that all $f_1, \ldots, f_q$ are known in advance since we consider weakly selective security. $\mathcal{A}$ is *not* given secret keys of IBE for identity $(i^*, j, \bar{f}^*[j])$, so it is hard for $\mathcal{A}$ to detect this change. We show $\mathsf{Hyb}_2^{i^*} \overset{\mathsf{c}}{\approx}_\delta \mathsf{Hyb}_3^{i^*}$ more formally in Lemma 1 by using the selective security of IBE.

Garbling with encrypted labels circuit

$$\mathsf{EL}^*_{\mathsf{gc}}[\mathsf{MPK}_{\mathsf{ibe}}, K\{S^*\}, x_0^*, x_1^*, (\widetilde{U}^*, \{\mathsf{CT}_{i^*}^{j,\alpha}\}_{j\in[s],\alpha\in\{0,1\}})]$$

Hardwired: punctured PRF key $K\{S^*\}$ where $S^* := \{i^*\|1\|2, \{i^*\|j\|\alpha\}_{j\in[s],\alpha\in\{0,1\}}\}$,

   public parameter of IBE $\mathsf{MPK}_{\mathsf{ibe}}$, messages x_0^*, x_1^*, and $(\widetilde{U}^*, \{\mathsf{CT}_{i^*}^{j,\alpha}\}_{j\in[s],\alpha\in\{0,1\}})$.

Input: index $i \in [q]$.

Padding: circuit is padded to size $\mathsf{pad}_{\mathsf{EL}} := \mathsf{pad}_{\mathsf{EL}}(\lambda, s, q)$, which is determined in analysis.

1. If $i = i^*$, then output $(\widetilde{U}^*, \{\mathsf{CT}_{i^*}^{j,\alpha}\}_{j\in[s],\alpha\in\{0,1\}})$.
2. Else, compute $r_{\mathsf{gc}} \leftarrow \mathsf{F}(K, i\|1\|2)$.
   If $i > i^*$, compute $(\widetilde{U}, \{L_{j,\alpha}\}_{j\in[s],\alpha\in\{0,1\}}) \leftarrow \mathsf{Grbl}(1^\lambda, U(\cdot, x_0^*); r_{\mathsf{gc}})$.
   If $i < i^*$, compute $(\widetilde{U}, \{L_{j,\alpha}\}_{j\in[s],\alpha\in\{0,1\}}) \leftarrow \mathsf{Grbl}(1^\lambda, U(\cdot, x_1^*); r_{\mathsf{gc}})$.
3. For every $j \in [s]$ and $\alpha \in \{0,1\}$, compute $r_{i\|j\|\alpha} \leftarrow \mathsf{F}(K, i\|j\|\alpha)$ and $\mathsf{CT}_i^{j,\alpha} \leftarrow \mathsf{IBE.Enc}(\mathsf{MPK}_{\mathsf{ibe}}, (i, j, \alpha), L_{j,\alpha}; r_{i\|j\|\alpha})$.
4. Return $(\widetilde{U}, \{\mathsf{CT}_i^{j,\alpha}\}_{j\in[s],\alpha\in\{0,1\}})$.

Fig. 7. The description of $\mathsf{EL}^*_{\mathsf{gc}}$. The description depends on i^*, but we use the notion $\mathsf{EL}^*_{\mathsf{gc}}$ instead of $\mathsf{EL}^{i^*}_{\mathsf{gc}}$ for simpler notations. $U(\cdot, x)$ is a universal circuit in which x is hardwired as the second input.

Lemma 1. *It holds that* $\mathsf{Hyb}_2^{i^*} \approx^c_\delta \mathsf{Hyb}_3^{i^*}$ *for all* $i^* \in [q]$ *if* IBE *is selectively secure.*

Proof. First, we define more hybrid games H_{j^*} for $j^* \in \{0, \cdots, s\}$ as follows.

H_{j^*}: This is the same as $\mathsf{Hyb}_2^{i^*}$ except that for $j \leq j^*$, $\mathsf{CT}_{i^*}^{j,\bar{f}^*[j]} \leftarrow \mathsf{IBE.Enc}(\mathsf{MPK}_{\mathsf{ibe}}, i^*\|j\| \bar{f}^*[j], 0^\ell)$. We see that H_0 and H_s are the same as $\mathsf{Hyb}_2^{i^*}$ and $\mathsf{Hyb}_3^{i^*}$, respectively.

We show that $\mathsf{H}_{j^*-1} \approx^c_\delta \mathsf{H}_{j^*}$ holds for all $j^* \in [s]$. This immediately implies the lemma.

We construct an adversary $\mathcal{B}$ in the selective security game of IBE as follows. To simulate the weakly selective security game of iPKFE, $\mathcal{B}$ runs $\mathcal{A}$ attacking qFE and receives a message pair (x_0^*, x_1^*) and function queries $f_1, \cdots, f_q$. $\mathcal{B}$ simulates the game of qFE as follows.

Setup and Encryption: $\mathcal{B}$ sets $\mathsf{id}^* := i^*\|j^*\| \bar{f}^*[j^*]$ as the target identity to the challenger of IBE. Note that $f^* = f_{i^*}$.
   To set challenge messages of IBE, $\mathcal{B}$ computes $(\widetilde{U}^*, \{L_{j,\alpha}^*\}_{j\in[s],\alpha\in\{0,1\}}) \leftarrow \mathsf{Grbl}(1^\lambda, U(\cdot, x_0^*))$ and sets $m_0^* := L_{j^*,\bar{f}^*[j^*]}^*$ and $m_1^* := 0^{\ell(\lambda)}$. $\mathcal{B}$ sends id^* and (m_0^*, m_1^*) to the challenger of IBE, and receives $\mathsf{MPK}_{\mathsf{ibe}}$ and $\mathsf{CT}_{i^*}^{j^*,\bar{f}^*[j^*]}$ as the master public-key and target ciphertext of IBE. $\mathcal{B}$ sets $\mathsf{MPK} := \mathsf{MPK}_{\mathsf{ibe}}$. To simulate ciphertexts of qFE, $\mathcal{B}$ does the followings.
   – For all $j \leq j^* - 1$, $\mathcal{B}$ computes $\mathsf{CT}_{i^*}^{j,f^*[j]} \leftarrow \mathsf{IBE.Enc}(\mathsf{MPK}_{\mathsf{ibe}}, i^*\| j\|f^*[j], L_{j,f^*[j]})$ and $\mathsf{CT}_{i^*}^{j,\bar{f}^*[j]} \leftarrow \mathsf{IBE.Enc}(\mathsf{MPK}_{\mathsf{ibe}}, i^*\|j\| \bar{f}^*[j]), 0^\ell)$.

- For $j = j^*$, $\mathcal{B}$ computes $\mathsf{CT}_{i^*}^{j^*,f^*[j^*]} \leftarrow \mathsf{IBE.Enc}(\mathsf{MPK}_{\mathsf{ibe}}, i^*\|j^*\|f^*[j^*], L_{j^*,f^*[j^*]})$.
- For all $j \geq j^* + 1$ and $\alpha \in \{0,1\}$, $\mathcal{B}$ computes $\mathsf{CT}_{i^*}^{j,\alpha} \leftarrow \mathsf{IBE.Enc}(\mathsf{MPK}_{\mathsf{ibe}}, i^*\|j\|\alpha), L_{j,\alpha})$.

By using these ciphertexts $\{\mathsf{CT}_{i^*}^{j,\alpha}\}_{j\in[s],\alpha\in\{0,1\}}$, $\mathcal{B}$ constructs program $\mathsf{EL}_{\mathsf{gc}}^*$ and sets $\mathsf{CT}_{\mathsf{fe}}^* := \mathsf{sxi}\mathcal{O}(\mathsf{EL}_{\mathsf{gc}}^*)$ as the target ciphertext of qFE.

Key Generation: Then, $\mathcal{B}$ queries identities $(i,1,f_i[1]),\ldots,(i,s,f_i[s])$ for all $i \in [q]$ to the challenger of IBE, receives $\mathsf{SK}_i^j \leftarrow \mathsf{IBE.KG}(\mathsf{MSK}_{\mathsf{ibe}}, i\|j\|f_i[j])$, and sets $\mathsf{SK}_{f_i} := (i,f_i,\{\mathsf{SK}_i^j\}_{j\in[s]})$ for all $i \in [q]$. Note that $\mathcal{B}$ does not have to query the challenge identity $(i^*\|j^*\|\bar{f}^*[j^*])$.

Now $\mathcal{B}$ sets all values for $\mathcal{A}$ and sends MPK, $\mathsf{CT}_{\mathsf{fe}}^*$, and $\{\mathsf{SK}_{f_i}\}_{i\in[q]}$ to $\mathcal{A}$. If $\mathcal{B}$ is given $\mathsf{CT}_{i^*}^{j^*,\bar{f}^*[j^*]} = \mathsf{IBE.Enc}(\mathsf{MPK}_{\mathsf{ibe}}, i^*\|j^*\|\bar{f}^*[j^*]), L_{j^*,\bar{f}^*[j^*]})$, then $\mathcal{B}$ perfectly simulates H_{j^*-1}. If $\mathcal{B}$ is given $\mathsf{CT}_{i^*}^{j^*,\bar{f}^*[j^*]} = \mathsf{IBE.Enc}(\mathsf{MPK}_{\mathsf{ibe}}, i^*\|j^*\|\bar{f}^*[j^*], 0^{\ell(\lambda)})$, then $\mathcal{B}$ perfectly simulates H_{j^*}. Therefore, the advantage of $\mathcal{A}$ between H_{j^*-1} and H_{j^*} is bounded by that of $\mathcal{B}$ attacking IBE and it holds that $\mathsf{H}_{j^*-1} \overset{c}{\approx}_\delta \mathsf{H}_{j^*}$. This completes the proof of the lemma. ∎

$\mathsf{Hyb}_4^{i^*}$: We change $(\widetilde{U}^*, \{L_{j,\alpha}^*\}_{j\in[s],\alpha\in\{0,1\}}) \leftarrow \mathsf{Grbl}(1^\lambda, U(\cdot, x_0^*))$ into a simulated output $(\widetilde{U}^*, \{L_{j,f^*[j]}^*\}_{j\in[s]}) \leftarrow \mathsf{Sim.GC}(1^\lambda, y^*))$ where $y^* := f^*(x_0^*) = f^*(x_1^*)$. By the requirement of the game, $f^*(x_0^*) = f^*(x_1^*)$ holds. In this game, $\{L_{j,\bar{f}^*[j]}^*\}_{j\in[s]}$ are not generated since the simulator of GC does not generate them. This is not a problem since for such labels, junk ciphertexts are generated as in $\mathsf{Hyb}_3^{i^*}$. It holds that $\mathsf{Hyb}_3^{i^*} \overset{c}{\approx}_\delta \mathsf{Hyb}_4^{i^*}$ for every $i^* \in [q]$ due to the security of the garbled circuit.

$\mathsf{Hyb}_5^{i^*}$: We change the simulated garbled circuit, junk ciphertexts, and punctured PRF keys hardwired into $\mathsf{EL}_{\mathsf{gc}}^*$ back into the real garbled circuit, normal IBE ciphertexts, and un-punctured PRF keys. In this hybrid game, we set $r_{\mathsf{gc}}^* = F_K(i^*\|1\|2)$, $r_{j\|\alpha}^* = F_K(i^*\|j\|\alpha)$ for all $j \in [s]$ and $\alpha \in \{0,1\}$, $(\widetilde{U}^*, \{L_{j,\alpha}^*\}_{j\in[s],\alpha\in\{0,1\}}) \leftarrow \mathsf{Grbl}(1^\lambda, U(\cdot, x_1^*); r_{\mathsf{gc}}^*)$, and $\mathsf{CT}_{i^*}^{j,\alpha} \leftarrow \mathsf{IBE.Enc}(\mathsf{MPK}_{\mathsf{ibe}}, (i^*,j,\alpha), L_{j,\alpha}; r_{j\|\alpha}^*)$. We can show $\mathsf{Hyb}_4^{i^*} \overset{c}{\approx}_\delta \mathsf{Hyb}_5^{i^*}$ for every $i^* \in [q]$ in a reverse manner.

It holds $\mathsf{Hyb}_5^{i^*} \overset{c}{\approx}_\delta \mathsf{Hyb}_1^{i^*+1}$ for every $i^* \in [q-1]$ by the definition of $\mathsf{EL}_{\mathsf{gc}}^*$ and $\mathsf{sxi}\mathcal{O}$. That is, $\mathsf{Expt}_{\mathcal{A}}^{\mathsf{sel}^*}(1^\lambda, 0) = \mathsf{Hyb}_0 \overset{c}{\approx}_\delta \mathsf{Hyb}_1^1 \overset{c}{\approx}_\delta \cdots \overset{c}{\approx}_\delta \mathsf{Hyb}_5^q \overset{c}{\approx}_\delta \mathsf{Expt}_{\mathcal{A}}^{\mathsf{sel}^*}(1^\lambda, 1)$ holds. This completes the security proof.

Padding Parameter. The proof of security relies on the indistinguishability of obfuscated $\mathsf{EL}_{\mathsf{gc}}$ and $\mathsf{EL}_{\mathsf{gc}}^*$ defined in Figs. 6 and 7, respectively. Accordingly, we set $\mathsf{pad}_{\mathsf{EL}} := \max(|\mathsf{EL}_{\mathsf{gc}}|, |\mathsf{EL}_{\mathsf{gc}}^*|)$.

The circuits $\mathsf{EL}_{\mathsf{gc}}$ and $\mathsf{EL}_{\mathsf{gc}}^*$ compute a puncturable PRF over domain $[q]$, $2s$ IBE ciphertexts, and garbled circuit of $U(\cdot, x)$, and may have punctured PRF keys and a hard-wired ciphertext. Note that the size of set S^* of punctured points of PRF in $\mathsf{EL}^*_{\mathsf{gc}}$ is logarithmic in q. Note also that $|\mathcal{ID}| = 2qs$. Thus, due to the efficiency of IBE, it holds that

$$\mathsf{pad}_{\mathsf{EL}} \leq 2s \cdot (2qs)^\alpha \cdot \mathrm{poly}(\lambda) + \mathrm{poly}(\lambda, s, \log q) \leq q^\alpha \cdot \mathrm{poly}(\lambda, s),$$

where α is a constant such that $0 < \alpha < 1$.

Weak Collusion-Succinctness. The input space for $\mathsf{EL}_{\mathsf{gc}}$ is $[q]$. Thus, by the efficiency guarantee of SXIO, the size of the encryption circuit $\mathsf{qFE}.\mathsf{Enc}$ (dominated by generating an obfuscated $\mathsf{EL}_{\mathsf{gc}}$) is

$$q^{\widetilde{\gamma}} \cdot \mathrm{poly}(\lambda, \mathsf{pad}_{\mathsf{EL}}) < q^{\widetilde{\gamma}+c\alpha} \cdot \mathrm{poly}(\lambda, s),$$

where $\widetilde{\gamma}$ is a constant such that $0 < \widetilde{\gamma} < 1$ and c is some constant.

By using an identity-based encryption scheme whose compression factor α satisfies $\alpha < \frac{1-\widetilde{\gamma}}{c}$, we ensure that $\beta := \widetilde{\gamma} + c\alpha < 1$, that is qFE is weakly collusion succinct. This completes the proof of Theorem 5.   ∎

4 Weak Succinctness from Collusion-Succinctness

We state only the theorem due to limited space.

Theorem 6. *If there exists weakly collusion-succinct (μ, δ)-weakly-selectively secure iPKFE (resp. iSKFE) for circuits of size at most $s = s(\lambda)$ with $n = n(\lambda)$ inputs with encryption circuit of size $\mu^\gamma \cdot \mathrm{poly}(\lambda, n, s)$ where $\mu = s \cdot \mathrm{poly}_{\mathsf{RE}}(\lambda, n)$ and $\mathrm{poly}_{\mathsf{RE}}$ is a fixed polynomial determined by RE, then there exists weakly succinct $(1, \delta)$-weakly-selectively secure PKFE (resp. SKFE) for circuits of size at most $s = s(\lambda)$ with encryption circuit of size $s^{\gamma'} \cdot \mathrm{poly}(\lambda, n)$, where γ' is a fixed constant such that $\gamma < \gamma' < 1$.*

We can obtain this theorem by slightly modifying the analysis of the transformation by Bitansky and Vaikuntanathan [11, Proposition IV.1].

5 Putting it Altogether

Before summarizing our results, we introduce the following theorems regarding SKFE and SXIO obtained by the results of Brakerski et al. [16] and Bitansky et al. [9,10]. Note that poly denotes an unspecified polynomial below.

Theorem 7 [9,16]. *If there exists (poly, δ)-selective-message message private and non-succinct SKFE for P/poly, then there exists δ-secure and γ-compressing SXIO for P/poly where γ is an arbitrary constant such that $0 < \gamma < 1$. (γ could be sufficiently small)*

Theorem 8 [10]. *If there exists $(1, \delta)$-selective-message message private and weakly succinct SKFE for P/poly, then there exists δ-secure and $\widetilde{\gamma}$-compressing SXIO for P/poly where $\widetilde{\gamma}$ is a constant such that $1/2 \leq \widetilde{\gamma} < 1$.*

We also introduce the following result shown by Garg and Srinivasan [29] stating that we can transform single-key PKFE into collusion-resistant one strengthening selective security and succinctness.

Theorem 9 [29]. *If there exists a $(1, \delta)$-weakly-selectively secure and weakly succinct PKFE scheme for $\mathsf{P/poly}$, then there exists a (poly, δ)-selectively secure and succinct PKFE scheme for $\mathsf{P/poly}$.*

5.1   Transformation from SKFE to PKFE

By Theorems 2, 4, 6 and 7, we obtain the following theorem. We note that Theorem 4 requires a sufficiently small compression factor for SXIO.

Theorem 10. *If there exists δ-secure plain public-key encryption and (poly, δ)-selective-message message private and non-succinct SKFE for $\mathsf{P/poly}$, then there exists $(1, \delta)$-selectively secure and weakly succinct PKFE for $\mathsf{P/poly}$.*

From this theorem and Theorem 9, we obtain the following corollary stating that collusion-resistant PKFE is constructed from collusion-resistant SKFE if we additionally assume public-key encryption.

Corollary 1. *If there exists δ-secure plain public-key encryption and (poly, δ)-selective-message message private and non-succinct SKFE for $\mathsf{P/poly}$, then there exists (poly, δ)-selectively secure and succinct PKFE for $\mathsf{P/poly}$.*

We stress that the transformations above incur only *polynomial security loss.*

We next see that single-key weakly-succinct SKFE is also powerful enough to yield PKFE if we additionally assume identity-based encryption. By Theorems 5, 6 and 8, we obtain the following theorem since Theorem 5 just requires that the compression factor of SXIO $\widetilde{\gamma}$ is slightly smaller than 1 (no need to be sufficiently small).

Theorem 11. *If there exists δ-secure identity-based encryption and $(1, \delta)$-selective-message message private and weakly succinct SKFE for $\mathsf{P/poly}$, then there exists $(1, \delta)$-weakly-selectively secure and weakly succinct PKFE for $\mathsf{P/poly}$.*

We stress that the transformation above incurs only polynomial security loss. We note the following two facts. It was not known whether $(1, \delta)$-selective-message message private and weakly succinct SKFE for $\mathsf{P/poly}$ implies (poly, δ)-selective-message message private SKFE for $\mathsf{P/poly}$ or not before the recent work of Kitagawa et al. [38]. Moreover, the transformation of Kitagawa et al. incurs *quasi-polynomial* security loss.

By combining this theorem with Theorem 9, we obtain the following corollary stating that we can construct collusion-resistant PKFE from single-key weakly succinct SKFE if we additionally assume identity-based encryption.

Corollary 2. *If there exists δ-selectively-secure identity-based encryption and $(1, \delta)$-selectively-secure weakly succinct SKFE for $\mathsf{P/poly}$, then there exists (poly, δ)-selectively secure and succinct PKFE for $\mathsf{P/poly}$.*

We stress that the transformation above incurs only polynomial security loss. Figure 8 illustrates our results stated above.

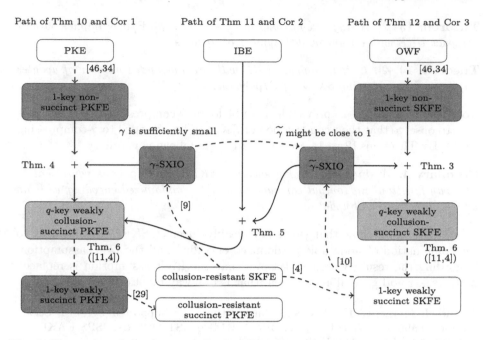

Fig. 8. Illustration of our theorems. Dashed lines denote known facts or trivial implications. White boxes denote our ingredients or goal. Purple boxes denote our key schemes. Green boxes denote our intermediate tools. *All transformations in this figure incur only polynomial security loss.* γ-SXIO (resp. $\widetilde{\gamma}$-SXIO) denotes SXIO with compression factor γ (resp. $\widetilde{\gamma}$), which is *sufficiently small* constant of less than 1 (resp. *arbitrary* constant of less than 1). We ignore garbled circuit, puncturable PRF, and decomposable RE in this figure. They are implied by one-way function. (Color figure online)

5.2 Equivalence of SKFE, SXIO, and Updatable RE

By Theorems 2, 3 and 6, we obtain the following theorem.

Theorem 12. *If there exists δ-secure one-way function and δ-secure and $\widetilde{\gamma}$-compressing SXIO for P/poly for a constant $\widetilde{\gamma}$ such that $0 < \widetilde{\gamma} < 1$ ($\widetilde{\gamma}$ might be close to 1), then there exists $(1, \delta)$-selective-message message private and weakly succinct SKFE for P/poly.*

By combining this theorem and Theorem 8, we obtain the following corollary stating that the existence of single-key weakly-succinct SKFE is equivalent to those of SXIO and one-way function. Note that single-key weakly succinct SKFE for P/poly trivially implies one-way function.

Corollary 3. *A single-key weakly succinct SKFE for P/poly is equivalent to one-way function and $\widetilde{\gamma}$-compressing SXIO for P/poly such that $0 < \widetilde{\gamma} < 1$ ($\widetilde{\gamma}$ might be close to 1).*

We can also obtain equivalence of these primitives and updatable randomized encoding (URE). We introduce the following results related to URE shown by Ananth et al. [2].

Theorem 13 [2]. *A single-key weakly succinct SKFE for* P/poly *implies output-compact URE with an unbounded number of updates.*

Theorem 14 [2]. *Output-compact URE with an unbounded number of updates implies a $\widetilde{\gamma}$-compressing SXIO for* P/poly *where $\frac{1}{2} \leq \widetilde{\gamma} < 1$.*

Note that Ananth et al. prove Theorem 14 for a $\widetilde{\gamma}$-compressing XIO, but it is easy to observe that their construction of XIO can be extended to $\widetilde{\gamma}$-compressing SXIO. By Theorems 12 to 14, we can obtain the following corollary.

Corollary 4. *A single-key weakly succinct SKFE for* P/poly *is equivalent to one-way function and output-compact updatable randomized encoding with an unbounded number of updates.*

Ananth et al. show that single-key weakly-succinct SKFE is equivalent to the combination of updatable randomized encoding and the LWE assumption. Regarding the result, Corollary 4 shows that the LWE assumption is replaced with weaker and general assumption, that is one-way function.

Acknowledgement. The first and third authors are supported by NTT Secure Platform Laboratories, JST CREST JPMJCR14D6, JST OPERA, JSPS KAKENHI JP16H01705, JP16J10322, JP17H01695.

References

1. Ananth, P., Brakerski, Z., Segev, G., Vaikuntanathan, V.: From selective to adaptive security in functional encryption. In: Gennaro, R., Robshaw, M. (eds.) CRYPTO 2015. LNCS, vol. 9216, pp. 657–677. Springer, Heidelberg (2015). https://doi.org/10.1007/978-3-662-48000-7_32
2. Ananth, P., Cohen, A., Jain, A.: Cryptography with updates. In: Coron, J.-S., Nielsen, J.B. (eds.) EUROCRYPT 2017. LNCS, vol. 10211, pp. 445–472. Springer, Cham (2017). https://doi.org/10.1007/978-3-319-56614-6_15
3. Ananth, P., Jain, A.: Indistinguishability obfuscation from compact functional encryption. In: Gennaro, R., Robshaw, M. (eds.) CRYPTO 2015. LNCS, vol. 9215, pp. 308–326. Springer, Heidelberg (2015). https://doi.org/10.1007/978-3-662-47989-6_15
4. Ananth, P., Jain, A., Sahai, A.: Indistinguishability obfuscation from functional encryption for simple functions. Cryptology ePrint Archive, Report 2015/730
5. Apon, D., Döttling, N., Garg, S., Mukherjee, P.: Cryptanalysis of indistinguishability obfuscations of circuits over GGH13. In: ICALP 2017 (2017)
6. Applebaum, B., Ishai, Y., Kushilevitz, E.: Computationally private randomizing polynomials and their applications. Comput. Complex. **15**(2), 115–162 (2006)
7. Banerjee, A., Peikert, C., Rosen, A.: Pseudorandom functions and lattices. In: Pointcheval, D., Johansson, T. (eds.) EUROCRYPT 2012. LNCS, vol. 7237, pp. 719–737. Springer, Heidelberg (2012). https://doi.org/10.1007/978-3-642-29011-4_42
8. Barak, B., Goldreich, O., Impagliazzo, R., Rudich, S., Sahai, A., Vadhan, S.P., Yang, K.: On the (im)possibility of obfuscating programs. J. ACM **59**(2), 6 (2012)

9. Bitansky, N., Nishimaki, R., Passelègue, A., Wichs, D.: From cryptomania to obfustopia through secret-key functional encryption. In: Hirt, M., Smith, A. (eds.) TCC 2016. LNCS, vol. 9986, pp. 391–418. Springer, Heidelberg (2016). https://doi.org/10.1007/978-3-662-53644-5_15

10. Bitansky, N., Nishimaki, R., Passelègue, A., Wichs, D.: From cryptomania to obfustopia through secret-key functional encryption. Cryptology ePrint Archive, Report 2016/558 (2016)

11. Bitansky, N., Vaikuntanathan, V.: Indistinguishability obfuscation from functional encryption. In: 56th FOCS, pp. 171–190 (2015)

12. Boneh, D., Franklin, M.K.: Identity-based encryption from the weil pairing. SIAM J. Comput. **32**(3), 586–615 (2003)

13. Boneh, D., Sahai, A., Waters, B.: Functional encryption: definitions and challenges. In: Ishai, Y. (ed.) TCC 2011. LNCS, vol. 6597, pp. 253–273. Springer, Heidelberg (2011). https://doi.org/10.1007/978-3-642-19571-6_16

14. Boneh, D., Waters, B.: Constrained pseudorandom functions and their applications. In: Sako, K., Sarkar, P. (eds.) ASIACRYPT 2013. LNCS, vol. 8270, pp. 280–300. Springer, Heidelberg (2013). https://doi.org/10.1007/978-3-642-42045-0_15

15. Boyle, E., Goldwasser, S., Ivan, I.: Functional signatures and pseudorandom functions. In: Krawczyk, H. (ed.) PKC 2014. LNCS, vol. 8383, pp. 501–519. Springer, Heidelberg (2014). https://doi.org/10.1007/978-3-642-54631-0_29

16. Brakerski, Z., Komargodski, I., Segev, G.: Multi-input functional encryption in the private-key setting: stronger security from weaker assumptions. In: Fischlin, M., Coron, J.-S. (eds.) EUROCRYPT 2016. LNCS, vol. 9666, pp. 852–880. Springer, Heidelberg (2016). https://doi.org/10.1007/978-3-662-49896-5_30

17. Brakerski, Z., Segev, G.: Function-private functional encryption in the private-key setting. In: Dodis, Y., Nielsen, J.B. (eds.) TCC 2015. LNCS, vol. 9015, pp. 306–324. Springer, Heidelberg (2015). https://doi.org/10.1007/978-3-662-46497-7_12

18. Chen, Y., Gentry, C., Halevi, S.: Cryptanalyses of candidate branching program obfuscators. In: Coron, J.-S., Nielsen, J.B. (eds.) EUROCRYPT 2017. LNCS, vol. 10212, pp. 278–307. Springer, Cham (2017). https://doi.org/10.1007/978-3-319-56617-7_10

19. Cheon, J.H., Fouque, P.-A., Lee, C., Minaud, B., Ryu, H.: Cryptanalysis of the new CLT multilinear map over the integers. In: Fischlin, M., Coron, J.-S. (eds.) EUROCRYPT 2016. LNCS, vol. 9665, pp. 509–536. Springer, Heidelberg (2016). https://doi.org/10.1007/978-3-662-49890-3_20

20. Cheon, J.H., Han, K., Lee, C., Ryu, H., Stehlé, D.: Cryptanalysis of the multilinear map over the integers. In: Oswald, E., Fischlin, M. (eds.) EUROCRYPT 2015. LNCS, vol. 9056, pp. 3–12. Springer, Heidelberg (2015). https://doi.org/10.1007/978-3-662-46800-5_1

21. Cohen, A., Holmgren, J., Nishimaki, R., Vaikuntanathan, V., Wichs, D.: Watermarking cryptographic capabilities. In: 48th ACM STOC, pp. 1115–1127 (2016)

22. Coron, J.-S., Gentry, C., Halevi, S., Lepoint, T., Maji, H.K., Miles, E., Raykova, M., Sahai, A., Tibouchi, M.: Zeroizing without low-level zeroes: new MMAP attacks and their limitations. In: Gennaro, R., Robshaw, M. (eds.) CRYPTO 2015. LNCS, vol. 9215, pp. 247–266. Springer, Heidelberg (2015). https://doi.org/10.1007/978-3-662-47989-6_12

23. Coron, J.-S., Lee, M.S., Lepoint, T., Tibouchi, M.: Zeroizing attacks on indistinguishability obfuscation over CLT13. In: Fehr, S. (ed.) PKC 2017. LNCS, vol. 10174, pp. 41–58. Springer, Heidelberg (2017). https://doi.org/10.1007/978-3-662-54365-8_3

24. Coron, J.-S., Lepoint, T., Tibouchi, M.: Practical multilinear maps over the integers. In: Canetti, R., Garay, J.A. (eds.) CRYPTO 2013. LNCS, vol. 8042, pp. 476–493. Springer, Heidelberg (2013). https://doi.org/10.1007/978-3-642-40041-4_26

25. Fernando, R., Rasmussen, P.M.R., Sahai, A.: Preventing CLT attacks on obfuscation with linear overhead. In: Takagi, T., Peyrin, T. (eds.) ASIACRYPT 2017. LNCS, vol. 10626, pp. 242–271. Springer, Cham (2017). https://doi.org/10.1007/978-3-319-70700-6_9

26. Garg, S., Gentry, C., Halevi, S.: Candidate multilinear maps from ideal lattices. In: Johansson, T., Nguyen, P.Q. (eds.) EUROCRYPT 2013. LNCS, vol. 7881, pp. 1–17. Springer, Heidelberg (2013). https://doi.org/10.1007/978-3-642-38348-9_1

27. Garg, S., Gentry, C., Halevi, S., Raykova, M., Sahai, A., Waters, B.: Candidate indistinguishability obfuscation and functional encryption for all circuits. In: 54th FOCS, pp. 40–49. IEEE Computer Society Press (2013)

28. Garg, S., Miles, E., Mukherjee, P., Sahai, A., Srinivasan, A., Zhandry, M.: Secure obfuscation in a weak multilinear map model. In: Hirt, M., Smith, A. (eds.) TCC 2016. LNCS, vol. 9986, pp. 241–268. Springer, Heidelberg (2016). https://doi.org/10.1007/978-3-662-53644-5_10

29. Garg, S., Srinivasan, A.: Single-Key to multi-key functional encryption with polynomial loss. In: Hirt, M., Smith, A. (eds.) TCC 2016. LNCS, vol. 9986, pp. 419–442. Springer, Heidelberg (2016). https://doi.org/10.1007/978-3-662-53644-5_16

30. Gentry, C., Gorbunov, S., Halevi, S.: Graph-induced multilinear maps from lattices. In: Dodis, Y., Nielsen, J.B. (eds.) TCC 2015. LNCS, vol. 9015, pp. 498–527. Springer, Heidelberg (2015). https://doi.org/10.1007/978-3-662-46497-7_20

31. Gentry, C., Peikert, C., Vaikuntanathan, V.: Trapdoors for hard lattices and new cryptographic constructions. In: 40th ACM STOC, pp. 197–206. ACM Press (2008)

32. Goldreich, O., Goldwasser, S., Micali, S.: How to construct random functions. J. ACM **33**(4), 792–807 (1986)

33. Goldwasser, S., Kalai, Y.T., Popa, R.A., Vaikuntanathan, V., Zeldovich, N.: Reusable garbled circuits and succinct functional encryption. In: STOC 2013, pp. 555–564 (2013)

34. Gorbunov, S., Vaikuntanathan, V., Wee, H.: Functional encryption with bounded collusions via multi-party computation. In: Safavi-Naini, R., Canetti, R. (eds.) CRYPTO 2012. LNCS, vol. 7417, pp. 162–179. Springer, Heidelberg (2012). https://doi.org/10.1007/978-3-642-32009-5_11

35. Ishai, Y., Kushilevitz, E.: Randomizing polynomials: a new representation with applications to round-efficient secure computation. In: 41st FOCS, pp. 294–304 (2000)

36. Kiayias, A., Papadopoulos, S., Triandopoulos, N., Zacharias, T.: Delegatable pseudorandom functions and applications. In: ACM CCS 2013, pp. 669–684 (2013)

37. Kitagawa, F., Nishimaki, R., Tanaka, K.: Indistinguishability obfuscation for all circuits from secret-key functional encryption. Cryptology ePrint Archive, Report 2017/361 (2017)

38. Kitagawa, F., Nishimaki, R., Tanaka, K.: From single-key to collusion-resistant secret-key functional encryption by leveraging succinctness. Cryptology ePrint Archive, Report 2017/638 (2017)

39. Komargodski, I., Segev, G.: From minicrypt to obfustopia via private-key functional encryption. In: Coron, J.-S., Nielsen, J.B. (eds.) EUROCRYPT 2017. LNCS, vol. 10210, pp. 122–151. Springer, Cham (2017). https://doi.org/10.1007/978-3-319-56620-7_5

40. Li, B., Micciancio, D.: Compactness vs collusion resistance in functional encryption. In: Hirt, M., Smith, A. (eds.) TCC 2016. LNCS, vol. 9986, pp. 443–468. Springer, Heidelberg (2016). https://doi.org/10.1007/978-3-662-53644-5_17

41. Lin, H., Pass, R., Seth, K., Telang, S.: Indistinguishability obfuscation with non-trivial efficiency. In: Cheng, C.-M., Chung, K.-M., Persiano, G., Yang, B.-Y. (eds.) PKC 2016. LNCS, vol. 9615, pp. 447–462. Springer, Heidelberg (2016). https://doi.org/10.1007/978-3-662-49387-8_17

42. Lin, H., Tessaro, S.: Indistinguishability obfuscation from trilinear maps and block-wise local PRGs. Cryptology ePrint Archive, Report 2017/250 (2017)

43. Miles, E., Sahai, A., Zhandry, M.: Annihilation attacks for multilinear maps: crypt-analysis of indistinguishability obfuscation over GGH13. In: Robshaw, M., Katz, J. (eds.) CRYPTO 2016. LNCS, vol. 9815, pp. 629–658. Springer, Heidelberg (2016). https://doi.org/10.1007/978-3-662-53008-5_22

44. Naor, M., Reingold, O.: Number-theoretic constructions of efficient pseudo-random functions. J. ACM **51**(2), 231–262 (2004)

45. O'Neill, A.: Definitional issues in functional encryption. Cryptology ePrint Archive, Report 2010/556 (2010)

46. Sahai, A., Seyalioglu, H.: Worry-free encryption: functional encryption with public keys. In: ACM CCS 2010, pp. 463–472. ACM Press (2010)

47. Sahai, A., Waters, B.: How to use indistinguishability obfuscation: deniable encryption, and more. In: 46th ACM STOC, pp. 475–484. ACM Press (2014)

48. Shamir, A.: Identity-based cryptosystems and signature schemes. In: Blakley, G.R., Chaum, D. (eds.) CRYPTO 1984. LNCS, vol. 196, pp. 47–53. Springer, Heidelberg (1985). https://doi.org/10.1007/3-540-39568-7_5

49. Yao, A.C.-C.: How to generate and exchange secrets (extended abstract). In: 27th FOCS, pp. 162–167. IEEE Computer Society Press, October 1986

Making Public Key Functional Encryption
Function Private, Distributively

Xiong Fan[1](✉) and Qiang Tang[2]

[1] Cornell University, Ithaca, NY, USA
xfan@cs.cornell.edu
[2] New Jersey Institute of Technology, Newark, NJ, USA
qiang@njit.edu

Abstract. We put forth a new notion of distributed public key functional encryption. In such a functional encryption scheme, the secret key for a function f will be split into shares sk_i^f. Given a ciphertext ct that encrypts a message x, a secret key share sk_i^f, one can evaluate and obtain a shared value y_i. Adding all the shares up can recover the actual value of $f(x)$, while partial shares reveal nothing about the plaintext. More importantly, this new model allows us to establish *function privacy* which was not possible in the setting of regular public key functional encryption. We formalize such notion and construct such a scheme from any public key functional encryption scheme together with learning with error assumption.

We then consider the problem of hosting services in the untrusted cloud. Boneh, Gupta, Mironov, and Sahai (Eurocrypt 2014) first studied such application and gave a construction based on indistinguishability obfuscation. Their construction had the restriction that the number of corrupted clients has to be bounded and known. They left an open problem how to remove such restriction. We resolve this problem by applying our function private (distributed) public key functional encryption to the setting of hosting service in multiple clouds. Furthermore, our construction provides a much simpler and more flexible paradigm which is of both conceptual and practical interests.

Along the way, we strengthen and simplify the security notions of the underlying primitives, including function secret sharing.

1 Introduction

Cloud computing has the advantages that the cloud servers provide infrastructure and resources that can hold data, do computation for the clients, and even host service on behalf of the individual vendor (also called service providers). Despite those appealing features, major concerns of deploying such a computing

X. Fan—This material is based upon work supported by IBM under Agreement 4915013672. Any opinions, findings, and conclusions or recommendations expressed in this material are those of the author(s) and do not necessarily reflect the views of the sponsors.

M. Abdalla and R. Dahab (Eds.): PKC 2018, LNCS 10770, pp. 218–244, 2018.
https://doi.org/10.1007/978-3-319-76581-5_8

paradigm are the security and privacy considerations, as data owner does not have control of the outsourced data.

Functional encryption [BSW11,O'N10] provides a powerful tool to enable such versatile "outsourcing" without leaking the actual data. In particular, a data owner can first encrypt his data x and store the ciphertext ct on the cloud server, and then issue a secret key sk_f to the cloud for a functionality f that the data owner would like the cloud to compute. Decrypting ct using sk_f yields only $f(x)$ and nothing else. For instance, the client would like to request the cloud to apply a transformation T to all his files that satisfies a certain condition described by a predicate P. This can be easily done by defining a following function $g(\cdot)$, where $g(x) = T(x)$, if $P(x) = 1$; otherwise, $g(x) = x$; the data owner can simply send such a decryption key sk_g to the cloud and enable the cloud to carry on the transformation given only the encrypted files. Those mechanisms could potentially enable a very powerful paradigm shift in computing. For example, content providers can simply focus on producing the data while offloading all the content management and delivery functionalities to the cloud provider. Concretely, Netflix streaming services have been migrated to Amazon cloud [net]. In particular, Netflix could codify their algorithm (such as the recommendation system) f to be sk_f and let Amazon cloud process all the subscriber requests expressed as ciphertext.

In many cases, hiding data only is not enough for those applications, as the function itself may already leak critical or proprietary information. In the above example, other content providers such as Hulu also hosts their service in the Amazon cloud [hul], the recommendation system might be one of the competing advantages of those content vendors. If not protected properly, one service provider has great interests to infer information about the competing vendor's proprietary program via the cloud. For this reason, *function privacy* was first proposed by Shen, Shi, Waters in the setting of private key predicate encryption in [SSW09]. It requires that a decryption key sk_f does not leak anything about the function f.

It is easy to see that for a public key functional encryption, standard function privacy cannot be possible as it is. Since the attacker who has a key sk_f, can generate ciphertext on the fly, and thus obtain values of $f(x_1), \ldots, f(x_n)$ for the plaintext $x_1, \ldots, x_n$ of his choices. As a result, majority of research along this line have been carried in two paths: (i) study function privacy in the setting of private key functional encryption such as the elegant work of Brakerski and Segev [BS15]. (ii) study weakened notion of function privacy by requiring that the function comes from high-entropy distribution [AAB+13], and those are studied only in special cases of identity based encryption [BRS13a] and subspace-membership encryption [BRS13b].[1]

Private key functional encryption is very useful for data owner to do outsourcing, however it is not convenient for sharing applications in which multiple clients may want to freely encode inputs, i.e., a public encryption operation is needed. While putting entropy restriction on the functions is a natural choice for

---

[1] Except the nice work of Agrawal et al. [AAB+13] which considered both above cases.

feasibility of function privacy in specific scenarios, it is not clear how could the weakened notion be applied in the general setting. In this paper, we are trying to answer the following question:

Can we find a realistic model that allows us to approach function privacy for general public key functional encryption?

1.1   Our Contributions

Circumventing impossibility via a distributed model. We initiate the study of public key, distributed functional encryption. In such a cryptographic primitive, the secret key of a function f will be split into shares sk_i^f and distributed to different parties. Given a secret key share, and a ciphertext ct that encrypts a message x, one can evaluate locally using sk_i^f and obtains $\mathsf{Dec}(\mathsf{sk}_i^f, \mathsf{Enc}(x)) = y_i$. Once all the evaluation shares $\{y_1, \ldots, y_n\}$ are obtained, everyone can reconstruct the actual evaluation $f(x)$. This new model of distributed functional encryption naturally generalizes the notion of threshold decryption to the setting of functional encryption, and enables the joint efforts to recover an evaluation for a plaintext from a ciphertext (i.e., computing $f(x)$ from the ciphertext ct), and when the number function shares are not enough, nothing will be revealed about $f(x)$.

More interestingly, such a new model offers an opportunity to bypass the impossibility of function privacy in the setting of public key functional encryption. Intuitively, given only a share sk_i^f (or multiple shares as long as it is below the threshold), the adversary can only learn y_i which may not be enough to determine $f(x)$. Formalizing such intuition, we give formal definitions of public key distributed functional encryption, and transform any public key functional encryption into a distributed version supporting both message privacy and function privacy via function secret sharing [BGI15, BGI16, KZ16]. Our construction can be instantiated from any functional encryption together with Learning With Error assumption [Reg05] where the construction of function secret sharing is based on, and reconstruction from shares $\{y_1, \ldots, y_n\}$ can be done by simply summing them up.

We remark here that our notion of distributed functional encryption is different from the decentralized key generation of functional encryption [CGJS15]. The latter mainly considers how to distribute the master key setup; while we consider how to split each function into secret key shares, and use such a model as a basis for studying function privacy. We also emphasize that the goal in this work is to achieve results generically from functional encryption itself directly, instead of from stronger primitives such as indistinguishability obfuscation (iO). With the help of iO or its stronger variant, differing-inputs obfuscation, we know how to construction multi-input functional encryption [GGG+14] and also function secret sharing [KZ16], there might be alternative ways to construct distributed public key functional encryption, which we will not explore in this paper.

Hosting service in multiple clouds securely and efficiently. One of the most appealing and widely deployed applications of cloud computing is to hosting service in the cloud. Boneh, Gupta, Mironov, and Sahai gave the first formal study of such an application [BGMS15]. The security considerations in this application scenario include protecting program (service) information and clients' inputs against a untrusted cloud and protecting program (service) information and authorization procedure against untrusted clients. Their construction relied on indistinguishability obfuscation (iO), and had to restrict the number of colluded/corrupted clients for both security. They left as an open problem how to get rid of such a restriction. As one major application of our function private functional encryption, we demonstrate how to tackle this challenge in the model of hosting service in multiple clouds.

Let us elaborate via a concrete example: the popular augmented-reality game Pokémon Go server was hosted at Google Cloud [pok]. The whole game as a computer program is deployed in Google cloud servers, and players directly interact with Google cloud to play the game once they are registered. The players try to catch various level Poke Monsters depending on the locations. Thus the level and location of the monsters contained in the game program need to be hidden. At the same time, the business model for such a game is to sell virtual goods, thus the program that hosts the service in the cloud will have to authenticate those in-game equipments. If such function is not protected well, when the cloud is corrupted, such authentication could either be bypassed or even completely reaped. On the other hand, there were also huge number of security concerns about the server collecting user private information when playing the game.

The above example highlights the need of *securely* hosting service in the cloud, and the service may be provided to millions of clients. One simple observation we would like to highlight in the paper is that our public key functional encryption with function privacy is already very close to the powerful notion of virtual black-box obfuscation (VBB) [BGI+01]. Taking a "detour" from using iO as in [BGMS15] to using VBB, and then "instantiating" it using our functional encryption yields a new way of securely hosting service in multiple clouds, and enables us to achieve much stronger security notions that have no restriction on the number of corrupted clients. From a high level, to host a service described as a function f in the cloud, the service provider runs our distributed functional encryption key generation algorithm and generates shares sk_i^f for each cloud.

It is not hard to see from the above description, as our construction following such a paradigm, we can easily extend the functionalities by encode the original functionality f into other program g to support more advanced properties and more complex access control.

Moreover, as our distributed functional encryption only relies on a regular functional encryption instead of a general iO, this new paradigm may potentially lead efficient constructions that can be actually instantiated. For example, if a service provider only hosts a couple of functionalities in the cloud, we do not have to use the full power of general functional encryption, instead we can use the bounded collusion functional encryption [GVW12] which could be further optimized for particular functions.

Last, as our reconstruction procedure only requires an addition, it gives minimum overhead to the client.

Strengthened and simplified security models, and modular constructions. We note that since the application of hosting service in the cloud is complex, several underlying building blocks such as function secret sharing as given are not enough for our applications. We carefully decoupled the complex security notions of [BGMS15] which handles two properties for each notion. This simplification helps us identify necessary enhancements of the security notions of the underlying building blocks, which in turn, enables us to have a smooth modular construction for the complex object.

Consider the security of the program against untrusted clouds when the service is hosted in two clouds. A corrupted cloud has one share of the program, on the mean time, the cloud may pretend to be a client and send requests to the other cloud for service. This means that considering function privacy against adversaries that has only partial shares is not enough. We should further allow the adversary to query the rest of function shares to reconstruct values for a bunch of points. The desired security notion now is that the adversary should learn nothing more than the values she already obtained as above. For this reason, we propose a CCA-type of definition for function privacy. To tackle this, we revisited the security of function secret sharing and study a CCA-type of security notion for it (the existing work only considered the CPA version).

Consider the security of the program against untrusted clients. Now a legitimate client can send requests and get evaluated at arbitrary points. To ensure the security of the program which comes from the function privacy in our construction, it naturally requires a simulation style definition. While IND style of function privacy was considered in most of previous works, even for private key functional encryption [BS15], we propose to study a simulation based definition with the CCA-type of enhancement mentioned above.

We show that the simple construction of function secret sharing from Spooky Encryption [DHRW16] actually satisfies the stronger notions, and we can safely apply it to construct our distributed functional encryption and eventually lead to the secure service hosting in multiple clouds.

1.2 Related Work

As mentioned above, despite the great potential of function privacy, our understanding of it is limited. Shen, Shi and Waters [SSW09] initiated the research on predicate privacy of attribute-based encryption in private key setting. Boneh, Raghunathan and Segev [BRS13a,BRS13b] initiated function privacy research in public key setting. They constructed function-private public-key functional encryption schemes for point functions (identity-based encryption) and for subspace membership (generalization of inner-product encryption). However, their framework assumes that the functions come from a distribution of sufficient entropy.

In an elegant work [AAB+15], Agrawal et al. presented a general framework of security that captures both data and function hiding, both public key and symmetric key settings, and show that it can be achieved in the generic group model for Inner Product FE [KSW08]. Later, in the private-key setting, Brakerski and Segev [BS15] present a generic transformation that yields a function-private functional encryption scheme, starting with any non-function-private scheme for a sufficiently rich function class.

In [BGMS15], Boneh et al. provide the first formalizations of security for a secure cloud service scheme. They also provide constructions of secure cloud service schemes assuming indistinguishability obfuscation, one-way functions, and non-interactive zero-knowledge proofs.

2   Preliminaries

Notation. Let λ be the security parameter, and let PPT denote probabilistic polynomial time. We say a function $\mathsf{negl}(\cdot) : \mathbb{N} \to (0,1)$ is negligible, if for every constant $c \in \mathbb{N}$, $\mathsf{negl}(n) < n^{-c}$ for sufficiently large n. We say two distributions D_1, D_2 over a finite universe $\mathcal{U}$ are ϵ-close if their statistical distance $\frac{1}{2}||D_1 - D_2||_1$ are at most ϵ, and denoted as $D_1 \approx D_2$.

2.1   Signature Scheme

In this part, we recall the syntax and security definition of a signature scheme. A signature scheme $\Sigma = (\mathsf{Setup}, \mathsf{Sign}, \mathsf{Verify})$ can be described as

- $(\mathsf{sk}, \mathsf{vk}) \leftarrow \mathsf{Setup}(1^\lambda)$: On input security parameter λ, the setup algorithm outputs signing key sk and verification key vk.
- $\sigma \leftarrow \mathsf{Sign}(\mathsf{sk}, m)$: On input signing key sk and message m, the signing algorithm outputs signature σ for message m.
- 1 or 0 $\leftarrow \mathsf{Verify}(\mathsf{vk}, m, \sigma)$: On input verification key vk, message m and signature σ, the verification algorithm outputs 1 if the signature is valid. Otherwise, output 0.

For the security definition of signature scheme, we use the following experiment to describe it. Formally, for any PPT adversary $\mathcal{A}$, we consider the experiment $\mathbf{Expt}_{\mathcal{A}}^{\mathsf{sig}}(1^\lambda)$:

1. Challenger runs $\mathsf{Setup}(1^\lambda)$ to obtain $(\mathsf{vk}, \mathsf{sk})$ and sends vk to adversary $\mathcal{A}$.
2. Adversary $\mathcal{A}$ sends signing queries $\{m_i\}_{i \in [Q]}$ to challenger. For $i \in [Q]$, challenger computes $\sigma_i \leftarrow \mathsf{Sign}(\mathsf{sk}, m_i)$ and sends $\{\sigma_i\}_{i \in [Q]}$ to adversary $\mathcal{A}$.
3. Adversary $\mathcal{A}$ outputs a forgery pair (m^*, σ^*).

We say adversary $\mathcal{A}$ wins experiment $\mathbf{Expt}_{\mathcal{A}}^{\mathsf{sig}}(1^\lambda)$ if m^* is not queried before and $\mathsf{Verify}(\mathsf{vk}, m^*, \sigma^*) = 1$.

Definition 1 (Existential Unforgeability). *We say a signature scheme Σ is existentially unforgeable if no PPT adversary $\mathcal{A}$ can win the experiment* $\mathbf{Expt}_{\mathcal{A}}^{\mathsf{sig}}(1^\lambda)$ *with non-negligible probability.*

2.2 Functional Encryption

We recall the syntax and ind-based security of functional encryption introduced in [BSW11]. A functional encryption scheme FE for function ensemble $\mathcal{F}$ consists of four algorithms defined as follows:

- (pp, msk) $\leftarrow$ Setup(1^λ): On input the security parameter λ, the setup algorithm outputs public parameters pp and master secret key msk.
- sk_f $\leftarrow$ Keygen(msk, f): On input the master secret key msk and a function f, the key generation algorithm outputs a secret key sk_f for function f.
- ct $\leftarrow$ Enc(pp, μ): On input the public parameters pp and a message μ, the encryption algorithm outputs a ciphertext ct.
- $f(\mu)$ $\leftarrow$ Dec(sk_f, ct): On input a secret key sk_f for function f and a ciphertext ct for plaintext μ, the decryption algorithm outputs $f(\mu)$.

Definition 2 (Correctness). *A functional encryption scheme* FE *is correct if for any* (pp, msk) $\leftarrow$ Setup(1^λ), *any* $f \in \mathcal{F}$, *and* $\mu \in$ domain(f), *it holds that*

$$\Pr[\mathsf{Dec}(\mathsf{Keygen}(\mathsf{msk}, f), \mathsf{Enc}(\mathsf{pp}, \mu)) \neq f(\mu)] = \mathsf{negl}(\lambda)$$

where the probability is taken over the coins in algorithms Keygen *and* Enc.

Security Definition. We present the security of functional encryption scheme FE for function ensemble $\mathcal{F}$ by first describing an experiment $\mathbf{Expt}_{\mathcal{A}}^{\mathsf{FE}}(1^\lambda)$ between an adversary $\mathcal{A}$ and a challenger in the following:

Setup: The challenger runs (msk, pp) $\leftarrow$ Setup(1^λ) and sends pp to adversary $\mathcal{A}$.

Key query phase I: Proceeding adaptively, the adversary $\mathcal{A}$ submits function $f_i \in \mathcal{F}$ to challenger. The challenger then sends back sk_f $\leftarrow$ Keygen(msk, f_i) to adversary $\mathcal{A}$.

Challenge phase: The adversary submits the challenge pair (μ_0^*, μ_1^*), with the restriction that $f_i(\mu_0^*) = f_i(\mu_1^*)$ for all functions f_i queried before. The challenger first chooses a random bit $b \in \{0, 1\}$ and sends back ct* $\leftarrow$ Enc(pp, μ_b) to adversary $\mathcal{A}$.

Key query phase II: The adversary $\mathcal{A}$ may continue his function queries $f_i \in \mathcal{F}$ adaptively with the restriction that $f_i(\mu_0^*) = f_i(\mu_1^*)$ for all function queries f_i.

Guess: Finally, the adversary $\mathcal{A}$ outputs his guess b' for the bit b.

We say the adversary wins the experiment if $b' = b$.

Definition 3 (Ind-based Data Privacy). *A functional encryption scheme* FE = (Setup, Keygen, Enc, Dec) *for a family of function* $\mathcal{F}$ *is secure if no* PPT *adversary* $\mathcal{A}$ *can win the experiment* $\mathbf{Expt}_{\mathcal{A}}^{\mathsf{FE}}(1^\lambda)$ *with non-negligible probability.*

2.3 Spooky Encryption

We recall the definition of spooky encryption, introduced in [DHRW16] in this part. A public key encryption scheme consists a tuple (Gen, Enc, Dec) of polynomial-time algorithms. The key-generation algorithm Gen gets as input a security parameter λ and outputs a pair of public/secret keys (pk, sk). The encryption algorithm Enc takes as input the public key pk and a bit m and output a ciphertext ct, whereas the decryption algorithm Dec gets as input the secret key sk and ciphertext ct, and outputs the plaintext m. The basic correctness guarantee is that $\Pr[\mathsf{Dec}_{\mathsf{sk}}(\mathsf{Enc}(\mathsf{pk}, m)) = m] \geq 1 - \mathsf{negl}(\lambda)$, where the probability is over the randomness of all these algorithms. The security requirement is that for any PPT adversary $(\mathcal{A}_1, \mathcal{A}_2)$ it holds that

$$\Pr_{b\leftarrow\{0,1\}}[(m_0, m_1) \leftarrow \mathcal{A}_1(\mathsf{pk}), \mathcal{A}_2(\mathsf{pk}, \mathsf{ct}_b) = 1] \leq \frac{1}{2} + \mathsf{negl}(\lambda)$$

where $(\mathsf{pk}, \mathsf{sk}) \leftarrow \mathsf{Gen}(1^\lambda)$, $\mathsf{ct}_b \leftarrow \mathsf{Enc}(\mathsf{pk}, m_b)$ and require $|m_0| = |m_1|$.

Definition 4 (Spooky Encryption). *Let* (Gen, Enc, Dec) *be a public key encryption and* Eval *be a polynomial-time algorithm that takes as input a (possibly randomized) circuit C with $n = n(\lambda)$ inputs and n outputs, $C : (\{0,1\}^*)^n \to (\{0,1\}^*)^n$, and also n pairs of (public key, ciphertext), and outputs n ciphertext.*

Let $\mathcal{C}$ be a class of such circuits, we say that $\Pi = $ (Gen, Enc, Dec, Eval) is a $\mathcal{C}$-spooky encryption scheme if for any security parameter λ, any randomized circuit $C \in \mathcal{C}$, and any input $\boldsymbol{x} = (x_1, \ldots, x_n)$ for C, the following distributions are close upto a negligible distance in λ

$$C(x_1, \ldots, x_n) \approx \mathsf{SPOOK}[C, \boldsymbol{x}] \triangleq$$
$$\{(\mathsf{Dec}(\mathsf{sk}_1, \mathsf{ct}'_1), \ldots, \mathsf{Dec}(\mathsf{sk}_n, \mathsf{ct}'_n)) : (\mathsf{ct}'_1, \ldots, \mathsf{ct}'_n) \leftarrow \mathsf{Eval}(C, \{(\mathsf{pk}_i, \mathsf{ct}_i)\}_i)\}$$

where for $i \in [n]$, $(\mathsf{pk}_i, \mathsf{sk}_i) \leftarrow \mathsf{Gen}(1^\lambda)$, $\mathsf{ct}_i \leftarrow \mathsf{Enc}(\mathsf{pk}_i, m_i)$.

A special case of spooky encryption, named additive-function-sharing (AFS) spooky encryption, allows us to take encryptions $\mathsf{ct}_i \leftarrow \mathsf{Enc}(\mathsf{pk}_i, x_i)$ under n independent keys of inputs $x_1, \ldots, x_n$ to an n-argument function f, and produce new ciphertext under the same n keys that decrypts to additive secret shares of $y = f(x_1, \ldots, x_n)$. Formally, the definition is the following

Definition 5 (AFS-Spooky). *Let $\Pi = $ (Gen, Enc, Dec, Eval) be a scheme where (Gen, Enc, Dec) is a semantically secure public key encryption. We say Π is leveled ϵ-AFS-spooky if Π satisfies*

- *If for any boolean circuit C computing an n-argument function $f :$ $(\{0,1\}^*)^n \to \{0,1\}$, and any input $(x_1, \ldots, x_n)$ for C, it holds that*

$$\Pr[\sum_{i=1}^{n} y_i = C(x_1, \ldots, x_n) : (\mathsf{ct}'_1, \ldots, \mathsf{ct}'_n) \leftarrow \mathsf{Eval}(C, \{(\mathsf{pk}_i, \mathsf{ct}_i)\}_i)]$$

  where for $i \in [n]$, $(\mathsf{pk}_i, \mathsf{sk}_i) \leftarrow \mathsf{Gen}(1^\lambda)$, $\mathsf{ct}_i \leftarrow \mathsf{Enc}(\mathsf{pk}_i, x_i)$, $y_i = \mathsf{Dec}(\mathsf{sk}_i, \mathsf{ct}'_i)$.
- *Any $n - 1$ of the shares y_i above are distributed ϵ-close to uniform.*
- *We say Π is leveled if the Gen algorithm receives an additional depth parameter 1^d, and the conditions above hold only for circuit of depth upto d.*

Spooky Encryption with CRS. We say that $(\mathsf{Gen}, \mathsf{Enc}, \mathsf{Dec}, \mathsf{Spooky.Eval})$ is a $\mathcal{C}$-*spooky encryption scheme with CRS*, if Definitions 4 and 5 are satisfied if we allow all algorithms (and the adversary) to get as input also a public uniformly distributed common random string.

In [DHRW16], the authors showed how to construction ϵ-AFS-Spooky Encryption with CRS from Learning With Error assumption (LWE) [Reg05]. Their results can be summarized below:

Theorem 1 [DHRW16]. *Assuming the hardness of LWE assumption, there exists a leveled ϵ-AFS-spooky encryption scheme.*

3   Distributed Public Key FE with Function Privacy

In this section, we give a detailed study of distributed functional encryption (DFE), and specifically a simplified DFE notion, n-out-of-n threshold functional encryption. In an (n, n)-DFE scheme, during key generation, we split a secret key corresponding to the function into n secret key shares $\{\mathsf{sk}_i^f\}_{i=1}^n$, and by running partial decryption on sk_i^f and a ciphertext ct, we can obtain a share s_i of $f(x)$, where ct is an encryption of message x. There is also a reconstruction process that outputs $f(x)$ on n shares $\{s_i\}_{i=1}^n$. We then define security, including *function privacy* and *data privacy*, with respect to (n, n)-DFE.

To achieve a secure DFE satisfying our security definitions, we rely on a building block, named function secret sharing [BGI15, BGI16]. We strengthen the security definition of FSS in comparison with that in [BGI15, BGI16], and show that a construction[2] based on spooky encryption satisfies our generalized security definition.

3.1   Syntax and Security Definition

We first describe the syntax $\mathsf{DFE} = (\mathsf{DFE.Setup}, \mathsf{DFE.Keygen}, \mathsf{DFE.Enc}, \mathsf{DFE.PartDec}, \mathsf{DFE.Reconstruct})$:

- $\mathsf{DFE.Setup}(1^\lambda, n, \mathcal{F})$: On input security parameter λ, threshold parameter n and function ensemble $\mathcal{F}$, the setup algorithm produces $(\mathsf{pp}, \mathsf{msk})$ for the whole system.
- $\mathsf{DFE.Keygen}(f, \mathsf{msk})$: On input a function $f \in \mathcal{F}$ and the secret key sk_i of this authority, the key generation algorithm outputs n secret key shares $\{\mathsf{sk}_i^f\}_{i \in [n]}$ for the function f.
- $\mathsf{DFE.Enc}(\mathsf{pp}, m)$: On input the public parameters pp and a message m, the encryption algorithm outputs a ciphertext ct.
- $\mathsf{DFE.PartDec}(\mathsf{ct}, \mathsf{sk}_i^f)$: On input a ciphertext ct and a secret key share sk_i^f for function f, the partial decryption algorithm outputs a decryption share s_i.

---

[2] We remark that the construction was first sketched in [DHRW16]. Here we generalize it and provide a formal security proof for the stronger notions.

- DFE.Reconstruct(pp, $\{s_i\}_{i=1}^n$): On input the public parameters pp and decryption shares $\{s_i\}_{i=1}^n$ for the same ciphertext, the reconstruction algorithm outputs $f(m)$.

Definition 6 (Correctness). *An (n,n)-DFE scheme is correct if for any* $(\text{pp}, \text{msk}) \leftarrow \text{DFE.Setup}(1^\lambda, 1^n)$, *any* $f \in \mathcal{F}$, *and any* $m \in \text{domain}(f)$, *it holds*

$$\Pr[\text{DFE.Reconstruct}(\text{pp}, \{\text{DFE.PartDec}(\text{ct}, \text{sk}_i^f)\}_{i=1}^n) \neq f(m)] = \text{negl}(\lambda)$$

where $\text{ct} \leftarrow \text{DFE.Enc}(\text{pp}, m), \text{sk}_i^f \leftarrow \text{DFE.Keygen}(f, \text{msk})$ *and the probability is taken over the coins in algorithms* DFE.Keygen *and* DFE.Enc.

Security Definition of DFE. As mentioned before, we consider both the data privacy and function privacy for DFE. For completeness, we give both IND-based and simulation based notions for function privacy. As we know, simulation based data privacy is infeasible [AGVW13], thus we only give a Ind based definition. It would be an interesting open problem to consider an alternative model that simulation based data privacy for functional encryption become feasible, e.g., [GVW12] The detailed definitions are below.

Definition 7 (Ind-based function privacy). *We first describe an experiment* $\text{Expt}_{\mathcal{A}}^{\text{DFE-func}}(1^\lambda)$ *between an adversary $\mathcal{A}$ and a challenger as follows:*

- *Setup: The challenger runs $(\text{msk}, \text{pp}) \leftarrow \text{DFE.Setup}(1^\lambda, 1^n)$ and sends pp to adversary $\mathcal{A}$.*
- *Key query phase I: Proceeding adaptively, the adversary $\mathcal{A}$ submits function $f_j \in \mathcal{F}$ to challenger. The challenger then sends back $\{\text{sk}_i^{f_j}\}_{i=1}^n \leftarrow \text{DFE.Keygen}(\text{msk}, f_j)$ to adversary $\mathcal{A}$.*
- *Challenge phase: The adversary submits the challenge function pair (f_0^*, f_1^*) that are not queried before. The challenger first chooses a random bit $b \in \{0,1\}$ and computes $\{\text{sk}_i^{f_b^*}\}_{i \in [n]} \leftarrow \text{DFE.Keygen}(\text{msk}, f_b^*)$. Then challenge selects random $n-1$ keys $\{\text{sk}_i^{f_b^*}\}_{i \in S}$ and sends them to adversary $\mathcal{A}$.*
- *Key query phase II: Proceeding adaptively, the adversary $\mathcal{A}$ continues querying function $f_j \in \mathcal{F}$ with the restriction that $f_j \neq f_0^*$ and $f_j \neq f_1^*$. The challenger then sends back $\{\text{sk}_i^{f_j}\}_{i=1}^n \leftarrow \text{DFE.Keygen}(\text{msk}, f_j)$ to adversary $\mathcal{A}$.*
- *Guess: Finally, the adversary $\mathcal{A}$ outputs his guess b' for the bit b.*

We say the adversary wins the experiment if $b' = b$.

A distributed functional encryption scheme Π for a family of function $\mathcal{F}$ is function private if no PPT *adversary $\mathcal{A}$ can win the experiment $\text{Expt}_{\mathcal{A}}^{\text{DFE-func}}(1^\lambda)$ with non-negligible probability.*

In the simulation-based definition of function privacy, we additionally allow adversary to query oracle $\text{DFE.Dec}(\text{sk}_n^{f^*}, \cdot)$, where $\text{sk}_n^{f^*}$ is the only secret key share for challenge function f^* that is not given to adversary. We then show that our sim-based function privacy implies ind-based function privacy as defined above. The detail is as follows:

Definition 8 (Sim-based function privacy). *Let Π be a distributed functional encryption scheme for a function family $\mathcal{F}$. Consider a PPT adversary $\mathcal{A} = (\mathcal{A}_1, \mathcal{A}_2)$ and simulator $\mathcal{S} = (\mathcal{S}_1, \mathcal{S}_2, \mathcal{S}_3)^3$. We say the function secret sharing scheme Π is simulation-secure if the following two distribution ensembles (over the security parameter λ) are computationally indistinguishable:*

Real Distribution:
1. $(\mathsf{pp}, \mathsf{msk}) \leftarrow \mathsf{DFE.Setup}(1^\lambda, n)$.
2. $(f^*, \tau) \leftarrow \mathcal{A}_1^{\mathsf{DFE.Keygen}(\mathsf{msk}, \cdot)}(\mathsf{pp})$.
3. $\{\mathsf{sk}_i^{f^*}\}_{i=1}^n \leftarrow \mathsf{DFE.Keygen}(\mathsf{msk}, f^*)$.
4. $\alpha \leftarrow \mathcal{A}_2^{\mathsf{DFE.Keygen}(\mathsf{msk}, \cdot), \mathsf{DFE.Dec}(\mathsf{sk}_n^{f^*}, \cdot)}(\mathsf{pp}, \{\mathsf{sk}_i^{f^*}\}_{i=S}^{n-1}, \tau)$.
5. *Output* $(\mathsf{pp}, f^*, \tau, \alpha)$.

Ideal Distribution:
1. $\mathsf{pp} \leftarrow \mathcal{S}_1(1^\lambda, n)$.
2. $(f^*, \tau) \leftarrow \mathcal{A}_1^{\mathcal{S}_2(\cdot)}(\mathsf{pp})$.
3. $\{\mathsf{sk}_{f_i^*}\}_{i=1}^n \leftarrow \mathcal{S}_2(|f^*|)$.
4. $\alpha \leftarrow \mathcal{A}_2^{\mathcal{S}_2(\cdot), \mathcal{S}_3^{f^*}(\cdot)}(\mathsf{pp}, \{\mathsf{sk}_i^{f^*}\}_{i=1}^{n-1}, \tau)$.
5. *Output* $(\mathsf{pp}, f^*, \tau, \alpha)$.

where on query $\mathsf{ct} = \mathsf{Enc}(\mathsf{pp}, x)$ made by adversary $\mathcal{A}_2$, simulator $\mathcal{S}_3^{f^*}(\cdot)$ makes a query to the oracle f^*.

Remark 1. We note that if a DFE construction satisfies sim-based function privacy, then we can show that it also satisfies ind-based function privacy. The challenger in the ind-based experiment $\mathbf{Expt}_{\mathcal{A}}^{\mathsf{DFE\text{-}func}}(1^\lambda)$ first uses simulation $\mathcal{S}_1(1^\lambda, n)$ to generate pp. For key queries f_i, challenger responses by computing $\{\mathsf{sk}_{f_{ij}}\}_{j=1}^n \leftarrow \mathcal{S}_2(f_i)$. For challenge function (f_0^*, f_1^*), the challenger chooses a random bit b (let $f^* = f_b^*$) and computes $\{\mathsf{sk}_{f^*}\}_{i=1}^n \leftarrow \mathcal{S}_2(f^*)$. Then by sim-based function privacy as defined above, the responses for key queries simulated by $\mathcal{S}_2$ are indistinguishable from real execution and the bit b is chosen from random, thus we show that it also satisfies ind-based function privacy.

Next, we adapt the standard ind-based data privacy for a DFE scheme.

Definition 9 (Ind-based data privacy). *We first describe an experiment $\mathbf{Expt}_{\mathcal{A}}^{\mathsf{DFE\text{-}data}}(1^\lambda)$ between a challenger and an adversary $\mathcal{A}$ as below:*

- **Setup:** *The challenger runs $(\mathsf{msk}, \mathsf{pp}) \leftarrow \mathsf{DFE.Setup}(1^\lambda, 1^n)$ and sends pp to adversary $\mathcal{A}$.*
- **Key query phase I:** *Proceeding adaptively, the adversary $\mathcal{A}$ submits function $f_j \in \mathcal{F}$ to challenger. The challenger then sends back $\{\mathsf{sk}_i^{f_j}\}_{i=1}^n \leftarrow \mathsf{DFE.Keygen}(\mathsf{msk}, f_j)$ to adversary $\mathcal{A}$.*

---

3 Looking ahead, we abuse the notation of S_2 in the ideal distribution, by allowing it taking two kinds of inputs: 1. the description of function f, 2. the size of function f.

- **Challenge phase:** *Adversary submits the challenge message pair (m_0^*, m_1^*) with the restriction that $f_i(m_0) = f_i(m_1)$ for all queried f_i. The challenger first chooses a random bit $b \in \{0, 1\}$ and computes $\mathsf{ct} \leftarrow \mathsf{DFE.enc}(\mathsf{pp}, m_b)$. Then send ct to adversary.*
- **Key query phase II:** *The same as* **Key query phase I** *with the restriction that the query f_i satisfies $f_i(m_0) = f_i(m_1)$.*
- **Guess:** *Finally, the adversary $\mathcal{A}$ outputs his guess b' for the bit b.*

We say the adversary wins the experiment if $b' = b$.

A distributed functional encryption scheme Π for a family of function $\mathcal{F}$ is data private if no PPT adversary $\mathcal{A}$ can win the experiment $\mathbf{Expt}_{\mathcal{A}}^{\mathsf{DFE\text{-}data}}(1^\lambda)$ with non-negligible probability.

3.2   Building Block: Function Secret Sharing

A function secret sharing scheme provides a method to split this function into a set of separate keys, where each key enable it to efficiently generate a share of evaluation $f(x)$, and yet each key individually does not reveal information about the details of function f. In [BGI15, BGI16], Boyle et al. formalized the syntax and security definition of function secret sharing. In this part, we first revisit the definition of function secret sharing along with a new security definition.

Syntax and Security Definition A (n, n)-function secret sharing scheme for a function family $\mathcal{F}$ consists of algorithms (FSS.Setup, FSS.ShareGen, FSS.Reconstruct) described as follows:

- FSS.Setup($1^\lambda, n, \mathcal{F}$): Given the security parameter λ, the parameter n of the secret sharing system and the description of function family $\mathcal{F}$, the setup outputs the public parameters pp.
- FSS.ShareGen(pp, f): Given pp and a function $f \in \mathcal{F}$, the share generation algorithm outputs n shares of function f as $\{f_i\}_{i=1}^n$.
- FSS.Reconstruct(pp, $\{f_i(x)\}_{i=1}^n$): Given an input x, evaluating each function share f_i on x, we obtain n output shares $\{f_i(x)\}_{i=1}^n$. The reconstruction algorithm then aggregates all the share values $\{f_i(x)\}_{i=1}^n$ and outputs $f(x)$.

Definition 10 (Correctness). *We say that an (n, n)-function secret sharing scheme FSS for function family $\mathcal{F}$ is correct, if for any function $f \in \mathcal{F}$, $\forall x \in \mathsf{dom}(f)$, $\mathsf{pp} \leftarrow \mathsf{FSS.Setup}(1^\lambda, n, \mathcal{F})$, we have*

$$f(x) = \mathsf{FSS.Reconstruct}(\mathsf{pp}, \{f_i(x)\}_{i=1}^n)$$

where $\{f_i\}_{i=1}^n \leftarrow \mathsf{FSS.ShareGen}(\mathsf{pp}, f)$.

Security definition of FSS. In [BGI15, BGI16], Boyle et al. proposed a ind-based security definition. In their security definition, adversary is given $n-1$ shares of function f_b, where f_b is chosen randomly from (f_0, f_1) of adversary's choice. It requires that adversary cannot guess bit b correctly with overwhelming probability. We enhance the security of FSS by modeling it as simulation-based CCA-type one. More specifically, in additional to the $n-1$ shares of challenge function f^*, the adversary is given oracle access to the function share generation algorithm of his choice (different from challenge function f^*). Moreover, the adversary is given oracle access to the share that she is not holding for f^*. The security requires that adversary cannot tell real execution from simulated one. The detailed definition is below.

Definition 11 (CCA-type of Security, Sim-based). *Let Π be a function secret sharing scheme for a function family $\mathcal{F}$. Consider a* PPT *adversary $\mathcal{A} = (\mathcal{A}_1, \mathcal{A}_2)$ and simulator $\mathcal{S} = (\mathcal{S}_1, \mathcal{S}_2, \mathcal{S}_3)^4$. We say the function secret sharing scheme Π is simulation-secure if the following two distribution ensembles (over the security parameter λ) are computationally indistinguishable:*

Real Distribution:
  1. $\mathsf{pp} \leftarrow \mathsf{FSS.Setup}(1^\lambda, n, \mathcal{F})$.
  2. $(f^*, \tau) \leftarrow \mathcal{A}_1^{\mathsf{FSS.ShareGen}(\mathsf{pp}, \cdot)}(\mathsf{pp})$
  3. $\{f_i^*\}_{i=1}^n \leftarrow \mathsf{FSS.ShareGen}(\mathsf{pp}, f^*)$
  4. $\alpha \leftarrow \mathcal{A}_2^{\mathsf{FSS.ShareGen}(\mathsf{pp}, \cdot), f_n^*(\cdot)}(\mathsf{pp}, \{f_i^*\}_{i=1}^{n-1}, \tau)$
  5. *Output* $(\mathsf{pp}, f^*, \tau, \alpha)$.

Ideal Distribution:
  1. $\mathsf{pp} \leftarrow \mathcal{S}_1(1^\lambda, n, \mathcal{F})$.
  2. $(f^*, \tau) \leftarrow \mathcal{A}_1^{\mathcal{S}_2(\cdot)}(\mathsf{pp})$.
  3. $\{f_i^*\}_{i=1}^{n-1} \leftarrow \mathcal{S}_2(|f^*|)$
  4. $\alpha \leftarrow \mathcal{A}_2^{\mathcal{S}_2(\cdot), \mathcal{S}_3^{f^*}(\{f_i^*\}_{i=1}^{n-1}, \cdot)}(\mathsf{pp}, \{f_i^*\}_{i=1}^{n-1}, \tau)$.
  5. *Output* $(\mathsf{pp}, f^*, \tau, \alpha)$.

where on query x made by adversary $\mathcal{A}_2$, simulator $\mathcal{S}_3^{f^*(\cdot)}(\cdot)$ makes a single query to oracle $f^*(\cdot)$ on x.

FSS Construction. Let $\mathsf{SP} = (\mathsf{SP.Gen}, \mathsf{SP.Enc}, \mathsf{SP.Dec}, \mathsf{SP.Eval})$ be a $\mathcal{F}$-AFS-spooky encryption as defined in Definition 4. To make the description simpler, we add a temporary algorithm, $\hat{f}_i(x) \leftarrow \mathsf{LocalEval}(\hat{f}_i, x)$, which locally evaluates x using the i-th share $\hat{f}_i$. The construction of function secret sharing scheme $\Pi = (\mathsf{FSS.Setup}, \mathsf{FSS.ShareGen}, \mathsf{FSS.Reconstruct})$ for $\mathrm{poly}(\lambda)$-depth circuit family $\mathcal{F}$ is the following:

---

[4] Looking ahead, we overload the notation of S_2 in the ideal distribution, by allowing it to take two kinds of inputs: 1. the description of a function f; 2. the size of a function f.

- FSS.Setup($1^\lambda, n, \mathcal{F}$): The setup algorithm outputs public parameter pp $=$ $(n, \mathcal{F})$ for the system.
- FSS.ShareGen(pp, f): On input a function $f \in \mathcal{F}$, the share generation algorithm first generates a n-out-of-n secret sharing $\{f_i\}_{i=1}^n$ of the description of f, and for $i \in [n]$ computes $(\mathsf{SP.pk}_i, \mathsf{SP.sk}_i) \leftarrow \mathsf{SP.Gen}(1^\lambda)$. Then for $i \in [n]$, encrypt the description share using spooky encryption $\mathsf{SP.Enc}(\mathsf{pk}_i, f_i)$. Output the i-th share of function f as $f_i = (\mathsf{SP.sk}_i, \{\mathsf{SP.pk}_i\}_{i=1}^n, \{\mathsf{SP.Enc}(\mathsf{SP.pk}_i, f_i)\}_{i=1}^n)$.
- FSS.LocalEval(f_i, x): On input the i-th share f_i, which is composed of the items $(\mathsf{SP.sk}_i, \{\mathsf{SP.pk}_i\}_{i=1}^n, \{\mathsf{SP.Enc}(\mathsf{SP.pk}_i, f_i)\}_{i=1}^n)$, and a value x, run the spooky evaluation $\{c_i\}_{i=1}^n = \mathsf{SP.Eval}(C_x, \{\mathsf{SP.Enc}(\mathsf{SP.pk}_i, f_i)\}_{i=1}^n)$, where the circuit $C_x(\cdot)$ is defined in Fig. 1.
Then output $s_i = \mathsf{SP.Dec}(\mathsf{SP.sk}_i, c_i)$.
- FSS.Reconstruct(pp, $\{s_i\}_{i=1}^n$): Given the n shares $\{s_i\}_{i=1}^n$ of function $f(x)$, the reconstruction algorithm outputs $f(x) = \sum_{i=1}^n s_i$.

Hardcode: value x.   **Input**: $\{\mathsf{SP.Enc}(\mathsf{SP.pk}_i, f_i)\}_{i=1}^n$.

1. Compute $\hat{f} = \sum_{i=1}^n \mathsf{SP.Enc}(\mathsf{SP.pk}_i, f_i)$.
2. Compute $\hat{f}(x)$.

Fig. 1. Description of function $C_x(\cdot)$

Correctness Proof. The correctness of our FSS construction is proved using properties of $\mathcal{F}$-AFS-spooky encryption as defined in Definition 4.

Lemma 1. *Our FSS construction described above is correct (c.f. Definition 10).*

Proof. Assuming wlog that the evaluate algorithm is deterministic, we obtain the same $\{c_i\}_{i=1}^n = \mathsf{SP.Eval}(C_x, \{\mathsf{SP.Enc}(\mathsf{SP.pk}_i, f_i)\}_{i=1}^n)$ in algorithm FSS.LocalEval($\hat{f}_i, x$), for $i \in [n]$. By the correctness of $\mathcal{F}$-AFS-spooky encryption as stated in Definition 4, we have $\sum_{i=1}^n s_i = C_x(\{f_i\}_{i=1}^n) = f(x)$, where $s_i = \mathsf{SP.Dec}(\mathsf{SP.sk}_i, c_i)$.

Security Proof. In this part, we show that our construction of FSS is secure as defined in Definition 11. Intuitively, for function queries other than the challenge one, the simulation computes in the exactly same method as the real execution. For the challenge function, we rely on the semantic security and psedurandomness of $n - 1$ evaluations of challenge function shares on any input, provided by the underlying spooky encryption to show the indistinguishability between real and simulated executions. The proof detail is the following.

Theorem 2. *Let* SP *be a secure $\mathcal{F}$-AFS-spooky encryption as defined in Definition 4. Our construction of FSS described above is secure (c.f. Definition 11).*

Proof. We first describe the simulation algorithm $\mathcal{S} = (\mathcal{S}_1, \mathcal{S}_2, \mathcal{S}_3)$ that are used in the proof.

- $\mathcal{S}_1(1^\lambda, n, \mathcal{F})$: Run FSS.Setup$(1^\lambda, n, \mathcal{F})$ to obtain pp and output pp.
- $\mathcal{S}_2(\text{inp})$: On input $\text{inp} = f_i$ or $\text{inp} = |f^*|$:
  - On input function f_i, first look for $(f_i, \{f_{ij}\}_{j=1}^n)$ in local storage. If found, output $(f_i, \{f_{ij}\}_{j=1}^n)$. Otherwise, compute $\{f_{ij}\}_{j=1}^n \leftarrow$ FSS.ShareGen(pp, f_i) and store $(f_i, \{f_{ij}\}_{j=1}^n)$ locally. Then output $(f_i, \{f_{ij}\}_{j=1}^n)$.
  - On input size $|f^*|$, first choose $n-1$ bit strings t_i of size $|f^*|$. For $i \in [n]$ computes $(\text{SP.pk}_i, \text{SP.sk}_i) \leftarrow$ SP.Gen(1^λ). Then for $i \in [n-1]$, encrypt the description share using spooky encryption $\text{ct}_i \leftarrow$ SP.Enc(pk_i, t_i), and $\text{ct}_n \leftarrow$ SP.Enc$(\text{pk}_i, 0^{|f^*|})$. Output $f_j^* = (\text{SP.sk}_j, \{\text{SP.pk}_i\}_{i=1}^n, \{\text{ct}_i\}_{i=1}^n)$ for $j \in [n-1]$.
- $\mathcal{S}_3^{f^*}(\{f_i^*\}_{i \in S}, x)$: On input $n-1$ shares $\{f_i^*\}_{i \in S}$ and x, for $i \in S$, compute $y_i \leftarrow$ FSS.LocalEval(f_i^*, x). Then call the oracle f on input x to obtain $y = f^*(x)$. Output $y_n = y - \sum_{i \in S} y_i$.

The view of adversary includes $(\text{pp}, f^*, \tau, \alpha)$, where (τ, α) are states that incorporate adversary's queries to FSS.ShareGen$(\text{pp}, \cdot)$ (or $\mathcal{S}_2$) and $f_{i \notin [S]}^*$ (or $\mathcal{S}_3$). As we described above, $\mathcal{S}_1(1^\lambda, n, \mathcal{F})$ computes FSS.Setup$(1^\lambda, n, \mathcal{F})$ as a subroutine, so the output pp is identical in these two procedures. For each function query f_i, $\mathcal{S}_2(f_i)$ calls FSS.ShareGen(pp, f_i) as a subroutine, so the output of $\mathcal{S}_2(f_i)$ is identical to that of FSS.ShareGen(pp, f_i). For challenge function query $\mathcal{S}_2(|f^*|)$, the shares given to adversary are $f_j^* = (\text{SP.sk}_j, \{\text{SP.pk}_i\}_{i=1}^n, \{\text{ct}_i\}_{i=1}^n)$ for $j \in [n-1]$. By the semantic security of underlying spooky encryption, ct_n remains secure. By the second property of spooky encryption (c.f. Definition 4), any $n-1$ of the shares y_i above are distributed ϵ-close to uniform, where $y_i = $ FSS.LocalEval(f_i^*, x) for any x.

Lastly, on query x, in the real execution, adversary gets back $y_n = f_n^*(x)$, while in the ideal execution, he gets back $y_n = y - \sum_{i \in S} y_i$, where $y_i \leftarrow$ FSS.LocalEval(f_i^*, x). Also by property of spooky encryption as stated in Definition 5, the $n-1$ shares $\{y_i\}$ are distributed ϵ-close to uniform. Thus, y_n in the ideal execution is a valid share and is identical to that in real execution.

3.3   Instantiation of DFE from FSS

Let FSS = (FSS.Setup, FSS.ShareGen, FSS.LocalEval, FSS.Reconstruct) be a function secret sharing scheme for function ensemble $\mathcal{F}$, and FE = (FE.Setup, FE.Keygen, FE.Enc, FE.Dec) be a functional encryption. The description of DFE scheme DFE = (Setup, Keygen, Enc, PartDec, Reconstruct) is as follows:

- DFE.Setup$(1^\lambda, n)$: Run the FSS setup algorithm FSS.pp $\leftarrow$ FSS..Setup$(1^\lambda, n)$ and the FE setup algorithm (FE.pp, FE.msk) $\leftarrow$ FE.Setup(1^λ). Output the public parameters pp and master secret key msk as

$$\text{pp} = (\text{FSS.pp}, \text{FE.pp}), \quad \text{msk} = \text{FE.msk}$$

- DFE.Enc(pp, m): Run the FE encryption algorithm ct $\leftarrow$ FE.Enc(FE.pp, m). Output ciphertext ct.
- DFE.Keygen(msk, f): Given a function $f \in \mathcal{F}$ and msk, the key generation algorithm first runs the share generation algorithm in FSS as $\{f_i\}_{i=1}^n \leftarrow$ FSS.ShareGen(FSS.msk, f), and then compute the key shares by running the FE key generation as $\mathsf{sk}_i^f \leftarrow$ FE.Keygen(FE.msk, C_i), for $i \in [n]$, where the function $C_i(\cdot)$ is defined as in Fig. 2.
  Output the secret key shares $\{\mathsf{sk}_i^f\}_{i=1}^n$.
- DFE.PartDec(ct, sk_i^f): Given the i-th secret key share sk_i^f, compute and output $s_i = $ FE.Dec(sk_i^f, ct).
- DFE.Reconstruct(pp, $\{s_i\}_{i=1}^n$): Output the reconstructed result as $f(m) = \sum_{i=1}^n s_i$.

Hardcode: function share f_i **Input:** value x.

Compute and output $c_i = $ FSS.LocalEval(f_i, x)

Fig. 2. Description of function $C_i(\cdot)$

Correctness Proof. The correctness proof of our DFE construction follows directly from the correctness of FSS and FE. First by the correctness of FSS scheme FSS, the output of circuit C_i (c.f. Fig. 2) satisfies $\sum_{i=1}^n c_i = f(m)$. Secondly, by correctness of functional encryption scheme FE, the output of $s_i = $ FE.Dec(sk_f^i, ct), where sk_f^i is secret key for circuit C_i satisfies $s_i = c_i$. Therefore in DFE.Keygen(msk, f), we also get $f(m) = \sum_{i=1}^n s_i$.

Security Proof. In this part, we show that our construction of DFE satisfies (sim-based) function privacy and data privacy as defined above. The function privacy of our DFE construction mainly is based on the sim-based security of FSS (c.f. Definition 11), thus in our proof below, we use the simulation algorithm of FSS to setup the system and answer adversary's queries. The data privacy of our DFE construction directly follows the ind-based data privacy of underlying functional encryption (c.f. Definition 3).

Theorem 3. *Let* FSS *be function secret sharing scheme satisfying security as defined in Definition 11, our construction of DFE described above is function private (c.f. Definition 8).*

Proof. We first describe the simulation algorithm $\mathcal{S} = (\mathcal{S}_1, \mathcal{S}_2, \mathcal{S}_3)$ based on the simulation algorithms of FSS, (FSS.$\mathcal{S}_1$, FSS.$\mathcal{S}_2$) (as described in the proof of Theorem 2), that are used in the proof.

- $\mathcal{S}_1(1^\lambda, n)$: Run the FSS simulated setup algorithm FSS.pp $\leftarrow$ FSS.$\mathcal{S}_1(1^\lambda, n)$ and the FE setup algorithm (FE.pp, FE.msk) $\leftarrow$ FE.Setup(1^λ). Send pp $=$ (FSS.pp, FE.pp) to adversary.

- $\mathcal{S}_2(f)$: On input function query f, first look for $(f, \{\mathsf{sk}_i^f\}_{i=1}^n)$ in local storage. If found, send $(f_i, \{\mathsf{sk}_i^f\}_{i=1}^n)$ to adversary. Otherwise, $\mathcal{S}_2$ runs the simulation algorithm $\mathsf{FSS}.\mathcal{S}_2(f)$ of FSS to obtain $\{f_i\}_{i=1}^n$ as shares of function f. Then for $i \in [n]$, compute $\mathsf{sk}_i^f \leftarrow \mathsf{FE.Keygen}(\mathsf{msk}, f_i)$ and store $(f, \{\mathsf{sk}_i^f\}_{i=1}^n)$ locally. Send $(f, \{\mathsf{sk}_i^f\}_{i=1}^n)$ to adversary.
- $\mathcal{S}_3^{f^*}(\{\mathsf{sk}_i^{f^*}\}_{i=1}^{n-1}, \mathsf{ct})$: On input ciphertext query ct, first compute $x = \mathsf{FE.Dec}(\mathsf{sk}_{\mathsf{id}}, \mathsf{ct})$, where $\mathsf{sk}_{\mathsf{id}} \leftarrow \mathsf{FE.Keygen}(\mathsf{msk}, \mathsf{id})$ and id denotes the identity function. Then for $i \in [n-1]$, compute $s_i = \mathsf{FE.Dec}(\mathsf{sk}_i^{f^*}, \mathsf{ct})$. Output $s_n = f(x) - \sum_{i=1}^{n-1} s_i$.

In the following, we show, that adversary's view $(\mathsf{pp}, f^*, \tau, \alpha)$, where (τ, α) are states that incorporate adversary's queries to $\mathsf{DFE.Keygen}$ (or $\mathcal{S}_2$) and $\mathsf{DFE.Dec}(\mathsf{sk}_n^{f^*}, \cdot)$ (or $\mathcal{S}_3$), are indistinguishable in the two executions. As described above, $\mathcal{S}_1$ computes the FSS simulated setup $\mathsf{FSS}.\mathcal{S}_1$ and a real $\mathsf{FE.Setup}$ as subroutines, by the security of underlying FSS scheme, we have the distribution of public parameters in real and ideal executions are statistically close. Similarly, by the security of underlying FSS scheme, the function shares $\{f_i\}_{i=1}^n \leftarrow \mathsf{FSS}.\mathcal{S}_2(f)$ computed in simulation $\mathcal{S}_2(f)$ is indistinguishable from that in the real execution $\mathsf{DFE.Keygen}(f)$, thus the responses for key queries in the real and ideal executions are indistinguishable. Lastly, the output $s_n = \mathcal{S}_3^{f^*}(\{\mathsf{sk}_i^{f^*}\}_{i=1}^{n-1}, \mathsf{ct})$, where $\mathsf{ct} = \mathsf{FE.enc}(\mathsf{pp}, x)$, satisfies $\sum_{i=1}^n s_i = f(x)$, where $s_i = \mathsf{FE.Dec}(\mathsf{sk}_i^{f^*}, \mathsf{ct})$ can be computed by the adversary himself. In conclusion, the view of adversary in real execution is indistinguishable from that in the ideal execution.

Theorem 4. *Let* FE *be functional encryption scheme satisfying ind-based data privacy as defined in Definition 3, our construction of DFE described above is data private (c.f. Definition 9).*

Proof. The ciphertext in our DFE construction is indeed a FE ciphertext, thus by ind-based data privacy of FE scheme, our construction of DFE is data private.

4   Hosting Services Securely in Multiple Clouds

In [BGMS15], the authors consider a setting of hosting service in untrusted clouds: there exist three parties: *Service provider* who owns a program and setups the whole system, *cloud server* where the program is hosted, and arbitrary many *clients*. Intuitively speaking, the service provider wants to host the program P on a cloud server, and additionally it wants to authenticate clients who pay for the service provided by program P. This authentication should allow a legitimate user to access the program hosted on the cloud server and compute output on inputs of his choice. Moreover, the program P could contain proprietary information, thus needs to be kept confidential. The authors in [BGMS15] also require that the scheme satisfies some essential properties:

Weak client: The amount of work performed by client should only depends on the size of input and security parameter, but independent of the running time of program P.

Delegation: The work performed by the service provider includes one-time setup of the whole system and authentication clients. The amount of work in one-time setup phase should be bounded by a fixed polynomial in the program size, while the amount of work incurred in authentication should only depend on the security parameter.

Polynomial slowdown: The running time of encoded program (running on cloud server) is bounded by a fixed polynomial in the running time of program P.

Boneh et al. give a construction based on indistinguishability obfuscation, and their construction suffers from a restriction that the number of corrupted clients should be pre-fixed [BGMS15]. In this section, we generalize the above model by distributing encoded program shares to multiple cloud servers and resolve the open problem that to remove the restriction on number of corrupted clients from [BGMS15].

In our Distributed Secure Cloud Service (DSCS) scheme, the service provider generates a set of encoded program shares for program P, and then hosts each encoded program share on one cloud server. Any authenticated users can access the encoded program shares hosted multiple cloud servers and compute output on inputs of his choice. We also require that our DSCS scheme satisfied the above three properties.

4.1   Syntax and Security Definitions

The Distributed Secure Cloud Service scheme consists of algorithms DSCS = (DSCS.Prog, DSCS.Auth, DSCS.Inp, DSCS.Eval, DSCS.Reconstruct) with details as follows:

- DSCS.Prog($1^\lambda, n, P$): On input the security parameter λ, the threshold parameter n and a program P, it returns the distributed encoded program $\{\tilde{P}_i\}_{i=1}^n$ and a secret sk to be useful in authentication.
- DSCS.Auth(id, sk): On input the identity id of a client and the secret sk, it produces an authentication token token$_{id}$ for the client.
- DSCS.Inp(token$_{id}, x$): On input the authentication token token$_{id}$ and an input x, it outputs an encoded input $\tilde{x}$ and α which is used by the client to later decode the evaluated results.
- DSCS.Eval($\tilde{P}_i, \tilde{x}$): On input the encoded program $\tilde{P}_i$ and input $\tilde{x}$, it produces the encoded distributed result $\tilde{y}_i = \tilde{P}_i(\tilde{x})$.
- DSCS.Reconstruct($\{\tilde{P}_i(\tilde{x})\}_{i=1}^n$): On input the evaluated result $\{\tilde{P}_i(\tilde{x})\}_{i=1}^n$, it reconstructs the result $P(x)$.

Similar to the analysis in [BGMS15], the procedure goes as follows: the service provider first runs the procedure Prog($1^\lambda, P$) to obtain the distributed encoded program $\{\tilde{P}_i\}_{i=1}^n$ and the secret σ. Then for $i \in [n]$, it will send $\tilde{P}_i$ to cloud server i. Later, the service provider will authenticate users using σ. A client with identity id, who has been authenticated, will encode his input using procedure $\mathsf{Inp}(1^\lambda, \sigma_{\mathsf{id}}, x)$. The client will send $\tilde{x}$ to cloud i, for $i \in [n]$. For $i \in [n]$, the cloud will evaluate the program $\tilde{P}_i$ on encoded input $\tilde{x}$ and return the result $P_i(x)$. Finally, the client can run $\mathsf{Reconstruct}(\{P_i(x)\}_{i=1}^n)$ to obtain the result $P(x)$.

Security definitions. In [BGMS15], the authors consider two cases for security definition, namely *untrusted cloud security* and *untrusted client security*. We generalize their security definition to the DSCS setting. More specifically, we decouple the case of untrusted cloud security into two subcases, *program privacy* and *input privacy* in untrusted cloud security. And in untrusted client security, we enhance it by allowing the set of corrupt clients colluding with some corrupt servers. In various security definitions below, we assume that the service provider is uncompromisd.

For program privacy in untrusted cloud case, the service provider first setup the whole system based on program (P_0, P_1) submitted by adversary. In the system, the adversary can corrupts a set of servers and also has access to authentication and encoding oracles, but he cannot tell which program P_b is used to setup the system. The only restriction here is that P_0 and P_1 are of the same size.

Definition 12 (Untrusted Cloud Security – Program Privacy). *For the program privacy case in untrusted cloud setting, we first describe the following experiment* $\mathbf{Expt}^{\mathsf{prog}}(1^\lambda)$ *between a challenger and adversary* $\mathcal{A}$:

- **Setup:** *The adversary sends challenge programs* (P_0, P_1) *to challenger. The challenger choose a random bit* $b \in \{0,1\}$ *and obtains the challenge encoded program* $(\{\tilde{P}_i\}_{i=1}^n, \mathsf{sk}) \leftarrow \mathsf{DSCS}.\mathsf{Prog}(1^\lambda, n, P_b)$ *and sends* $\{\tilde{P}_i\}_{i=1}^{n-1}$ *to adversary* $\mathcal{A}$.
- **Query phase:** *Proceeding adaptively, the adversary* $\mathcal{A}$ *can submit the following two kinds of queries:*
  - **Authentication query:** $\mathcal{A}$ *sends identity* id_i *to challenger. The challenger computes* $\mathsf{token}_{\mathsf{id}_i} \leftarrow \mathsf{DSCS}.\mathsf{Auth}(\mathsf{id}, \mathsf{sk})$ *and sends back* $\mathsf{token}_{\mathsf{id}_i}$.
  - **Input query:** $\mathcal{A}$ *sends* (x, id) *to challenger. The challenger computes* $\mathsf{ct} \leftarrow \mathsf{DSCS}.\mathsf{Inp}(\mathsf{token}_{\mathsf{id}}, x)$, *where* $\mathsf{token}_{\mathsf{id}_i} \leftarrow \mathsf{DSCS}.\mathsf{Auth}(\mathsf{id}, \mathsf{sk})$. *Then send back* ct.
- **Guess:** *Finally, the adversary* $\mathcal{A}$ *outputs his guess* b' *for the bit* b.

We say the adversary wins the experiment if $b' = b$.

A DSCS scheme is program private in untrusted cloud setting if no PPT *adversary* $\mathcal{A}$ *can win the experiment* $\mathbf{Expt}^{\mathsf{prog}}(1^\lambda)$ *with non-negligible probability.*

For input privacy in untrusted cloud security, the service provider first sets up the whole system using program P submitted by adversary. Then in the system, the adversary corrupts all servers, and additionally has access to authentication oracles, but he cannot distinguish the encryption of two message (m_0, m_1), where $P(m_0) = P(m_1)$. Put simply, beyond the evaluation of program, he learns nothing about the underlying message.

Definition 13 (Untrusted Cloud Security – Input Privacy). *For the input privacy case in untrusted cloud setting, we first describe the following experiment* $\mathbf{Expt}^{\mathsf{inp}}(1^\lambda)$ *between a challenger and adversary* $\mathcal{A}$:

- **Setup:** *The adversary sends challenge program* P *to challenger. The challenger runs* $(\{\tilde{P}_i\}_{i=1}^n, \mathsf{sk}) \leftarrow \mathsf{DSCS.Prog}(1^\lambda, n, P)$ *and sends* $\{\tilde{P}_i\}_{i=1}^n$ *to adversary* $\mathcal{A}$.
- **Authentication query phase I:** *Proceeding adaptively, the adversary* $\mathcal{A}$ *sends identity* id_i *to challenger. The challenger computes* $\mathsf{token}_{\mathsf{id}_i} \leftarrow \mathsf{DSCS.Auth}(\mathsf{id}, \mathsf{sk})$ *and sends back* $\mathsf{token}_{\mathsf{id}_i}$.
- **Challenge phase:** *Adversary submits the challenge message pair* $(m_0, m_1, \mathsf{id}^*)$ *with the constraint that* $P(m_0) = P(m_1)$. *The challenger first chooses a random bit* $b \in \{0, 1\}$ *and computes* $\mathsf{ct} \leftarrow \mathsf{DSCS.Inp}(\mathsf{token}_{\mathsf{id}}, m_b)$, *where* $\mathsf{token}_{\mathsf{id}_i^*} \leftarrow \mathsf{DSCS.Auth}(\mathsf{id}^*, \mathsf{sk})$. *Then send* ct *to adversary.*
- **Authentication query phase II:** *The same as* **Authentication query phase I** *with the restriction that the query* id_i *does not equal* id^* *in the challenge phase*
- **Guess:** *Finally, the adversary* $\mathcal{A}$ *outputs his guess* b' *for the bit* b.

We say the adversary wins the experiment if $b' = b$.

A DSCS scheme is data private in untrusted cloud setting if no PPT *adversary* $\mathcal{A}$ *can win the experiment* $\mathbf{Expt}^{\mathsf{inp}}(1^\lambda)$ *with non-negligible probability.*

Remark 2. We note that in the above data privacy definition, the challenge phase can be access multiple times as long as the query pair $(m_0, m_1, \mathsf{id}_i^*)$ satisfies $P(m_0) = P(m_1)$, and challenger use the same random bit b in generating the challenge ciphertext.

For untrusted client security, a collection of corrupt clients with the help of a subset of corrupt servers do not learn anything beyond the program's output with respect to their identities on certain inputs of their choice, and if a client is not authenticated, it learns nothing.

Definition 14 (Untrusted Client Security). *Let* DSCS *be the secure Distributed Secure Cloud Service scheme as described above. We say the scheme satisfies untrusted client security if the following holds. Let* $\mathcal{A}$ *be a* PPT *adversary who corrupts* ℓ *clients* $I = \{\mathsf{id}_1, \ldots, \mathsf{id}_\ell\}$. *Consider any program* P, *let* $Q = \mathrm{poly}(\lambda)$. *The experiment described below requires one additional procedure* decode. *Based on these two procedures, we define simulator* $\mathcal{S} = (\mathcal{S}_1, \mathcal{S}_2)$. *Consider the following two experiments:*

The experiment $\mathsf{Real}(1^\lambda)$ *is as follows:*
1. $(\{\tilde{P}\}_{i=1}^n, \mathsf{sk}) \leftarrow \mathsf{DSCS.Prog}(1^\lambda, n, P)$.
2. *For all* $i \in [\ell]$, $\mathsf{token}_{\mathsf{id}_i} \leftarrow \mathsf{DSCS.Auth}(\mathsf{id}_i, \mathsf{sk})$.
3. *For* $i \in [Q]$, $\mathcal{A}(\{\tilde{P}_i\}_{i=1}^{n-1})$ *adaptively sends an encoding* $\tilde{x}_i$, *using identity* id, *and gets back response*

$$\tilde{y}_{ij} = \tilde{P}_j(x_i) \leftarrow \mathsf{DSCS.Eval}(\tilde{P}_j, \tilde{x}_i), \forall j \in [n]$$

4. *Output* $(\{\tilde{P}\}_{i=1}^{n-1}, \{\mathsf{token}_{\mathsf{id}_i}\}_{i \in [\ell]}, \{\tilde{y}_{ij}\})$.

The experiment $\mathsf{Ideal}^\mathsf{P}(1^\lambda)$ *is as follows:*
1. $\{\tilde{P}'_i\}_{i=1}^n \leftarrow \mathcal{S}_1(1^\lambda, n)$.
2. *For all* $i \in [\ell]$, $\mathsf{token}_{\mathsf{id}_i} \leftarrow \mathcal{S}_2(\mathsf{id}_i)$
3. *For* $i \in [Q]$, $\mathcal{A}(\{\tilde{P}\}_{i=1}^{n-1})$ *adaptively sends an encoding* $\tilde{x}_i$, *using identity* id,
    - *If* $\mathsf{id} \notin I$, *then return* $\tilde{y}_{ij} = \perp$ *for* $j \in [n]$.
    - *Otherwise, compute* $x_i = \mathsf{decode}(\sigma, \tilde{x}_i)$. *Then the simulator sends* (id, x_i) *to oracle* P *and obtains* $y_i = P(\mathsf{id}, x_i)$. *Simulator then sends shares* $\{y_{ij}\}_{j \in [n]}$ *of* y_i *to adversary* $\mathcal{A}$.
4. *Output* $(\{\tilde{P}\}_{i=1}^{n-1}, \{\mathsf{token}_{\mathsf{id}_i}\}_{i \in [\ell]}, \{\tilde{y}_{ij}\})$.

Then we have $\mathsf{Real}(1^\lambda) \overset{c}{\approx} \mathsf{Sim}^\mathsf{P}(1^\lambda)$.

4.2   Our DSCS Construction

Let $\mathsf{DFE} = (\mathsf{DFE.Setup}, \mathsf{DFE.Keygen}, \mathsf{DFE.Enc}, \mathsf{DFE.PartDec}, \mathsf{DFE.Reconstruct})$ be a distributed functional encryption and $\Sigma = (\Sigma.\mathsf{Setup}, \Sigma.\mathsf{Sign}, \Sigma.\mathsf{Verify})$ be an existential unforgeable signature scheme. We describe our construction for DSCS as follows:

- $\mathsf{DSCS.Prog}(1^\lambda, n, P)$: First run

$$(\mathsf{DFE.pp}, \mathsf{DFE.msk}) \leftarrow \mathsf{DFE.Setup}(1^\lambda, n), \quad (\Sigma.\mathsf{sk}, \Sigma.\mathsf{vk}) \leftarrow \Sigma.\mathsf{Setup}(1^\lambda)$$

Then let the augmented program P_{aug} be

And compute $\{\mathsf{sk}_i^{P_{\mathsf{aug}}}\}_{i=1}^n \leftarrow \mathsf{DFE.Keygen}(\mathsf{DFE.msk}, P_{\mathsf{aug}})$. For $i \in [n]$, define the distributed encoded program $\tilde{P}_i$[5] as

Output $\{\tilde{P}_i\}_{i=1}^n$ and secret $\mathsf{sk} = (\Sigma.\mathsf{sk}, \mathsf{DFE.pp})$.
- $\mathsf{DSCS.Auth}(\mathsf{id}, \mathsf{sk})$: First parse $\mathsf{sk} = (\Sigma.\mathsf{sk}, \mathsf{DFE.pp})$, and then compute $\sigma_{\mathsf{id}} \leftarrow \Sigma.\mathsf{Sign}(\Sigma.\mathsf{sk}, \mathsf{id})$. Output $\mathsf{token}_{\mathsf{id}} = (\sigma_{\mathsf{id}}, \mathsf{DFE.pp})$.
- $\mathsf{DSCS.Inp}(\mathsf{token}_{\mathsf{id}}, x)$: First parse $\mathsf{token}_{\mathsf{id}} = (\sigma_{\mathsf{id}}, \mathsf{DFE.pp})$, then compute $\mathsf{ct} \leftarrow \mathsf{DFE.Enc}(\mathsf{DFE.pp}, \sigma_{\mathsf{id}} || x)$. Output ciphertext $\tilde{x} = \mathsf{ct}$.
- $\mathsf{DSCS.Eval}(\tilde{P}_i, \tilde{x})$: Compute and output $\tilde{y}_i = \tilde{P}_i(\tilde{x})$.
- $\mathsf{DSCS.Reconstruct}(\{\tilde{y}_i\}_{i=1}^n)$: Compute and output $y = \mathsf{DFE.Reconstruct}(\{\tilde{y}_i\}_{i \in [n]})$.

Correctness Proof. The correctness proof of our DSCS construction follows directly from the correctness of underlying distributed functional encryption scheme DFE and signature scheme Σ. As we described above, in the distributed encoded program $\tilde{P}_i$, it outputs $\perp$ for an invalid signature, otherwise outputs $\tilde{y}_i = \mathsf{DFE.PartDec}(\mathsf{sk}_i^{P_{\mathsf{aug}}}, \mathsf{ct})$, where $\mathsf{ct} = \mathsf{DFE.Enc}(\mathsf{DFE.pp}, \sigma_{\mathsf{id}} || x)$. By correctness of DFE, the output of $\mathsf{DSCS.Reconstruct}(\{\tilde{y}_i\}_{i=1}^n)$ is $P(x)$.

---

[5] We note that the distributed encoded program $\tilde{P}_i$ does not require obfuscation.

Security Proof. In this part, we show that our DSCS construction satisfies untrusted cloud security (program and data privacy) and untrusted client security as defined above. Intuitively, the program privacy in untrusted cloud setting can reduce to the ind-based function privacy of underlying DFE scheme, thus in the proof we construction a reduction that reduces the program privacy property to the ind-based function privacy of DFE scheme. The data privacy in untrusted cloud setting can be based on ind-based data privacy of DFE scheme, so similarly we show a reduction that bounds this two properties together. Lastly, the untrusted client security is based on the sim-based function privacy of DFE scheme. Therefore, we use the simulation algorithms of DFE to do the simulation for our DSCS construction. The detailed proofs are as follows.

Theorem 5. *Let distributed functional encryption* DFE *satisfy ind-based function privacy (c.f. Definiton 7), then our DSCS construction described above satisfies program privacy in untrusted cloud setting (c.f. Definition 12).*

Proof. We describe a reduction $\mathcal{B}$ against the ind-based function privacy of underlying DFE scheme. If the adversary $\mathcal{A}$ can win the experiment $\mathbf{Expt}_{\mathcal{A}}^{\mathsf{DFE\text{-}func}}(1^\lambda)$ as defined in Definition 7, then reduction $\mathcal{B}$ can also win the experiment $\mathbf{Expt}^{\mathsf{prog}}(1^\lambda)$ as defined in Definition 12. The description of reduction $\mathcal{B}$ is as follows:

- **Setup:** $\mathcal{B}$ interacts with the challenger of DFE to obtain DFE.pp and computes $(\Sigma.\mathsf{vk}, \Sigma.\mathsf{sk}) \leftarrow \Sigma.\mathsf{Setup}(1^\lambda)$. Then $\mathcal{B}$ invokes adversary $\mathcal{A}$ to get the challenge programs (P^0, P^1). Next, $\mathcal{B}$ sends the augmented program $(P^0_{\mathsf{aug}}, P^1_{\mathsf{aug}})$ (as described in Fig. 3) to the challenger of DFE, and the challenger sends back $\{\mathsf{sk}_i^{P^b_{\mathsf{aug}}}\}_{i=1}^n$. Lastly, $\mathcal{B}$ sends $\{\tilde{P}_i\}_{i=1}^{n-1}$ to adversary, where $\{\tilde{P}_i\}_{i=1}^n$ are constructed as in Fig. 4 using $\{\mathsf{sk}_i^{P^b_{\mathsf{aug}}}\}_{i=1}^n$ as input.
- **Identity query:** On input identity query id_i, $\mathcal{B}$ computes $\sigma_{\mathsf{id}} \leftarrow \Sigma.\mathsf{Sign}(\Sigma.\mathsf{sk}, \mathsf{id})$ and sends back $\mathsf{token}_{\mathsf{id}} = (\sigma_{\mathsf{id}}, \mathsf{DFE.pp})$ to adversary $\mathcal{A}$.
- **Input query:** On input (x, id), $\mathcal{B}$ computes $\mathsf{ct} \leftarrow \mathsf{DSCS.Inp}(\mathsf{token}_{\mathsf{id}}, x)$, where $\mathsf{token}_{\mathsf{id}_i} \leftarrow \mathsf{DSCS.Auth}(\mathsf{id}, \mathsf{sk})$. Then send back ct.
- **Guess:** $\mathcal{B}$ receives adversary $\mathcal{A}$'s guess b'. And $\mathcal{B}$ outputs b' as his guess for the DFE experiment $\mathbf{Expt}^{\mathsf{DFE\text{-}func}}(1^\lambda)$.

Hardcode: DFE.pp, $\Sigma.\mathsf{vk}$ and program P **Input:** signature σ, value x and id.

1. If $\Sigma.\mathsf{Verify}(\sigma, \mathsf{id}, \Sigma.\mathsf{vk}) = 0$, output $\bot$.
2. Compute and output $P(x)$.

Fig. 3. Description of augmented program P_{aug}

Hardcode: $\mathsf{sk}_i^{P_{\mathsf{aug}}}$ and algorithm DFE.Dec.   **Input:** ciphertext ct.

Compute and output $\mathsf{DFE.PartDec}(\mathsf{sk}_i^{P_{\mathsf{aug}}}, \mathsf{ct})$.

Fig. 4. Description of distributed encoded program $\tilde{P}_i$

We now argue that the adversary's view $(\{\tilde{P}_i\}_{i=1}^{n-1}, \{\text{token}_{\text{id}}\}, \{\text{ct}\})$ in real execution is identical here as produced by reduction $\mathcal{B}$. This follows obviously, as $\{\tilde{P}_i\}_{i=1}^n$ is generated in the same way with the help of the challenge of DFE, token_{id} is valid signature of identity id. The ciphertexts $\{\text{ct}\}$ are generated in the same way in both executions. Therefore, a correct guess b' from adversary $\mathcal{A}$ is a correct guess for experiment $\mathbf{Expt}^{\text{DFE-func}}(1^\lambda)$.

Theorem 6. *Let distributed functional encryption* DFE *satisfy ind-based data privacy (c.f. Definiton 9), then our DSCS construction described above satisfies input privacy in untrusted cloud setting (c.f. Definition 13).*

Proof. We describe a reduction $\mathcal{B}$ against the ind-based data privacy of underlying DFE scheme. If the adversary $\mathcal{A}$ can win the experiment $\mathbf{Expt}^{\text{DFE-data}}(1^\lambda)$ as defined in Definition 9, then reduction $\mathcal{B}$ can also win the experiment $\mathbf{Expt}^{\text{inp}}(1^\lambda)$ as defined in Definition 13. The description of reduction $\mathcal{B}$ is as follows:

- **Setup;** $\mathcal{B}$ interacts with the challenger of DFE to obtain DFE.pp and computes $(\Sigma.\text{vk}, \Sigma.\text{sk}) \leftarrow \Sigma.\text{Setup}(1^\lambda)$. Then $\mathcal{B}$ invokes adversary $\mathcal{A}$ to get the program P. Next, $\mathcal{B}$ sends the augmented program P_{aug} (as described in Fig. 3) to the challenger of DFE, and the challenger sends back $\{\text{sk}_i^{P_{\text{aug}}}\}_{i=1}^n$. Lastly, $\mathcal{B}$ sends $\{\tilde{P}_i\}_{i=1}^n$ to adversary, where $\{\tilde{P}_i\}_{i=1}^n$ are constructed as in Fig. 4.
- **Authentication query phase I:** On input identity query id_i, $\mathcal{B}$ computes $\sigma_{\text{id}} \leftarrow \Sigma.\text{Sign}(\Sigma.\text{sk}, \text{id})$ and sends back $\text{token}_{\text{id}} = (\sigma_{\text{id}}, \text{DFE.pp})$ to adversary $\mathcal{A}$.
- **Challenge phase:** On input (m_0, m_1, id^*) from adversary, where $P(m_0) = P(m_1)$, $\mathcal{B}$ first computes $\sigma_{\text{id}^*} \leftarrow \Sigma.\text{Sign}(\Sigma.\text{sk}, \text{id}^*)$, and sends $(m_0||\sigma_{\text{id}^*}, m_1|| \sigma_{\text{id}^*})$ to challenger, and receives challenge ciphertext ct^*.
- **Authentication query phase II:** Same as Authentication query phase I.
- **Guess:** $\mathcal{B}$ receives adversary $\mathcal{A}$'s guess b'. And $\mathcal{B}$ outputs b' as his guess for the DFE experiment $\mathbf{Expt}^{\text{DFE-data}}(1^\lambda)$.

We now argue that the adversary's view $(\{\tilde{P}_i\}_{i=1}^n, \{\text{token}_{\text{id}}\}, \text{ct}^*)$ in real execution is identical here as produced by reduction $\mathcal{B}$. This follows obviously, as $\{\tilde{P}_i\}_{i=1}^n$ is generated in the same way with the help of the challenge of DFE, token_{id} is valid signature of identity id. For the challenge ciphertext ct^*, since $P'(m_0||\sigma_{\text{id}^*}) = P'(m_1||\sigma_{\text{id}^*})$, so the query $(m_0||\sigma_{\text{id}^*}, m_1||\sigma_{\text{id}^*})$ is a valid one. Therefore, a correct guess b' from adversary $\mathcal{A}$ is a correct guess for experiment $\mathbf{Expt}^{\text{DFE-data}}(1^\lambda)$.

Theorem 7. *Let distributed functional encryption* DFE *satisfy sim-based function privacy (c.f. Definition 8) and* Σ *be an existential unforgeable signature scheme (c.f. Definition 1), then our DSCS construction described above satisfies untrusted client security (c.f. Definition 14).*

Proof. Based on the simulation algorithms of distributed functional encryption $(\text{DFE}.\mathcal{S}_1, \text{DFE}.\mathcal{S}_2, \text{DFE}.\mathcal{S}_3)$ (c.f. Definition 8), we first describe the simulation algorithms $(\mathcal{S}_1, \mathcal{S}_2)$ and procedure decode as follows:

- $\mathcal{S}_1(1^\lambda, n)$: The simulation $\mathcal{S}_1$ first runs $\text{DFE}.\mathcal{S}_1(1^\lambda, n)$ to obtain DFE.pp, and $\Sigma.\text{Setup}(1^\lambda)$ to obtain $(\Sigma.\text{vk}, \Sigma.\text{sk})$. Then $\mathcal{S}_1$ chooses a random program P' of the same size as P, and computes $\{\mathsf{sk}_i^{P'_\mathsf{aug}}\}_{i=1}^n \leftarrow \mathsf{DFE}.\mathcal{S}_2(P'_\mathsf{aug})$, where P'_aug is the augmented program of P' (c.f. Fig. 3). Then compute $\{\tilde{P}'_i\}_{i=1}^n$ as described in Fig. 4 and send back $\{\tilde{P}'_i\}_{i=1}^{n-1}$ to adversary.

- $\mathcal{S}_2(\mathsf{id}_i)$: On input identity id_i, $\mathcal{S}_2$ computes $\sigma_{\mathsf{id}_i} \leftarrow \mathit{\Sigma}.\mathsf{Sign}(\mathit{\Sigma}.\mathsf{sk}, \mathsf{id}_i)$. Send back $\mathsf{token}_{\mathsf{id}_i} = (\sigma_{\mathsf{id}_i}, \mathsf{DFE}.\mathsf{pp})$.
- $\mathsf{decode}(\tilde{x}_i, \mathsf{id})$: On input ciphertext $\tilde{x}$ and identity id, it first computes $\{\mathsf{sk}_i^{\mathsf{Ind}}\}_{i=1}^n \leftarrow \mathsf{DFE}.\mathcal{S}_2(\mathsf{Ind})$, where Ind denotes the identity function, i.e. $\mathsf{Ind}(x) = x$, for any x. Then compute $x_i \| \sigma_{\mathsf{id}} = \mathsf{DFE}.\mathsf{Reconstruct}(\mathsf{DFE}.\mathsf{pp}, \{s_j\}_{j=1}^n)$, where $s_j = \mathsf{DFE}.\mathsf{PartDec}(\tilde{x}_i, \mathsf{sk}_j^{\mathsf{Ind}})$ for $j \in [n]$. Output $\perp$ if $\mathit{\Sigma}.\mathsf{Verify}(\mathit{\Sigma}.\mathsf{vk}, \mathsf{id}, \sigma_{\mathsf{id}}) = 0$. Otherwise, choose $n - 1$ random values $\{y_{ij}\}_{j=1}^{n-1}$, then query $\mathsf{DFE}.\mathcal{S}_3^P$ on input $(x_i, \{y_{ij}\}_{j=1}^{n-1})$ to get y_{in}. Lastly, send back $\{y_{ij}\}_{j=1}^n$ back to adversary.

In the following, we show that adversary's view $(\{\tilde{P}\}_{i=1}^{n-1}, \{\mathsf{token}_{\mathsf{id}_i}\}_{i\in[\ell]}, \{\tilde{y}_{ij}\})$ in the two executions are indistinguishable. By the sim-based function privacy of DFE, $\{\tilde{P}\}_{i=1}^{n-1}$ in the two executions are indistinguishable. The tokens $(\{\mathsf{token}_{\mathsf{id}_i}\}_{i\in[\ell]}$ are computed identically in the two execution, thus they are indistinguishable in two executions. For query $(\tilde{x}_i, \mathsf{id})$, by the unforgeability of signature scheme $\mathit{\Sigma}$, if the underlying plaintext of $\tilde{x}_i$ does not contain a valid signature of id, then both executions output $\perp$ for query $(\tilde{x}_i, \mathsf{id})$. Otherwise, by the sim-based function privacy of DFE, the output $\{y_{ij}\}_{j=1}^n$ returned by simulation $\mathsf{DFE}.\mathcal{S}_3^P$ is indistinguishable from that in the real execution. Therefore, we reach the conclusion that our DSCS construction satisfies untrusted client security.

Additional properties. We remark that there are multiple additional properties we can consider for the application of hosting service in a cloud.

First, we can inherit the two extra properties of *verifiability* and *persistent memory* mentioned briefly in [BGMS15]. The *verifiability* requires that the validity of the results returned by the server can be checked, same as [BGMS15], we can rely on the technology of verifiable computation [GHRW14]. *Persistent memory* property is to consider the server can maintain a state for each client across different invocations. We can do the same as in [BGMS15] except the client needs to return the aggregated value back after each invocation.

Furthermore, we remark that as our construction is very simple and easy to extend, we can further support many other properties as well. Here we only list two examples. (i) Our current version and previous work [BGMS15] only puts the authentication on the client, once authorized, the client can query the cloud unlimitedly. If the service provider wants to post more fine grained control on each input data, we can further enable this by embedding the access structure into the function. (ii) We can further support *client anonymity* that the server (even all of them collude) cannot recognize whether two queries are from the same client. Currently, the client will submit the authentication token together with the data. It is easy to see that if we replace the token with an anonymous credential, we can have the additional anonymity.

5   Conclusion and Open Problems

We study the problem of public key functional encryption in a distributed model. Such a model enables us to circumvent the impossibility of function privacy in public key functional encryption. We formulated such a new primitive and gave a construction from functional secret sharing, which can be obtained from learning with error assumption. We showcased the power of our new primitive by applying it to host services in multiple clouds.

One important observation of our distributed public key functional encryption is that achieving function privacy in this alternative model yields the power of virtual black-box obfuscation (essentially), which could potentially help circumvent other theoretic impossibilities in a distributed model. Another observation that may benefit application is that our construction is generic that upgrades any functional encryption. In some applications, we may only need a functional encryption for a special class of functions, which could have efficient constructions. This in turn yields potentially practical solutions for a class of important problems, such as encrypted search [SSW09], and copyright protection [KT15].

We leave the exploration of those interesting questions as open problems.

References

[AAB+13] Agrawal, S., Agrawal, S., Badrinarayanan, S., Kumarasubramanian, A., Prabhakaran, M., Sahai, A.: Functional encryption and property preserving encryption: new definitions and positive results. Cryptology ePrint Archive, report 2013/744 (2013). http://eprint.iacr.org/2013/744

[AAB+15] Agrawal, S., Agrawal, S., Badrinarayanan, S., Kumarasubramanian, A., Prabhakaran, M., Sahai, A.: On the practical security of inner product functional encryption. In: Katz, J. (ed.) PKC 2015. LNCS, vol. 9020, pp. 777–798. Springer, Heidelberg (2015). https://doi.org/10.1007/978-3-662-46447-2_35

[AGVW13] Agrawal, S., Gorbunov, S., Vaikuntanathan, V., Wee, H.: Functional encryption: new perspectives and lower bounds. In: Canetti and Garay [CG13], pp. 500–518

[BGI+01] Barak, B., Goldreich, O., Impagliazzo, R., Rudich, S., Sahai, A., Vadhan, S., Yang, K.: On the (Im)possibility of obfuscating programs. In: Kilian, J. (ed.) CRYPTO 2001. LNCS, vol. 2139, pp. 1–18. Springer, Heidelberg (2001). https://doi.org/10.1007/3-540-44647-8_1

[BGI15] Boyle, E., Gilboa, N., Ishai, Y.: Function secret sharing. In: Oswald and Fischlin [OF15], pp. 337–367

[BGI16] Boyle, E., Gilboa, N., Ishai, Y.: Function secret sharing: improvements and extensions. In: Weippl, E.R., Katzenbeisser, S., Kruegel, C., Myers, A.C., Halevi, S., (eds.), ACM CCS 16, pp. 1292–1303. ACM Press, October 2016

[BGMS15] Boneh, D., Gupta, D., Mironov, I., Sahai, A.: Hosting services on an untrusted cloud. In: Oswald and Fischlin [OF15], pp. 404–436

[BRS13a] Boneh, D., Raghunathan, A., Segev, G.: Function-private identity-based encryption: hiding the function in functional encryption. In: Canetti and Garay [CG13], pp. 461–478

[BRS13b] Boneh, D., Raghunathan, A., Segev, G.: Function-private subspace-membership encryption and its applications. In: Sako, K., Sarkar, P. (eds.) ASIACRYPT 2013. LNCS, vol. 8269, pp. 255–275. Springer, Heidelberg (2013). https://doi.org/10.1007/978-3-642-42033-7_14

[BS15] Brakerski, Z., Segev, G.: Function-private functional encryption in the private-key setting. In: Dodis, Y., Nielsen, J.B. (eds.) TCC 2015. LNCS, vol. 9015, pp. 306–324. Springer, Heidelberg (2015). https://doi.org/10.1007/978-3-662-46497-7_12

[BSW11] Boneh, D., Sahai, A., Waters, B.: Functional encryption: definitions and challenges. In: Ishai, Y. (ed.) TCC 2011. LNCS, vol. 6597, pp. 253–273. Springer, Heidelberg (2011). https://doi.org/10.1007/978-3-642-19571-6_16

[CG13] Canetti, R., Garay, J.A. (eds.): CRYPTO 2013. LNCS, vol. 8043. Springer, Heidelberg (2013). https://doi.org/10.1007/978-3-642-40084-1

[CGJS15] Chandran, N., Goyal, V., Jain, A., Sahai, A.: Functional encryption: decentralised and delegatable. Cryptology ePrint Archive, report 2015/1017 (2015). http://eprint.iacr.org/2015/1017

[DHRW16] Dodis, Y., Halevi, S., Rothblum, R.D., Wichs, D.: Spooky encryption and its applications. In: Robshaw, M., Katz, J. (eds.) CRYPTO 2016, Part III. LNCS, vol. 9816, pp. 93–122. Springer, Heidelberg (2016). https://doi.org/10.1007/978-3-662-53015-3_4

[GGG+14] Goldwasser, S., Gordon, S.D., Goyal, V., Jain, A., Katz, J., Liu, F.-H., Sahai, A., Shi, E., Zhou, H.-S.: Multi-input functional encryption. In: Nguyen, P.Q., Oswald, E. (eds.) EUROCRYPT 2014. LNCS, vol. 8441, pp. 578–602. Springer, Heidelberg (2014). https://doi.org/10.1007/978-3-642-55220-5_32

[GHRW14] Gentry, C., Halevi, S., Raykova, M., Wichs, D.: Outsourcing private RAM computation. In: 55th FOCS, pp. 404–413. IEEE Computer Society Press, October 2014

[GVW12] Gorbunov, S., Vaikuntanathan, V., Wee, H.: Functional encryption with bounded collusions via multi-party computation. In: Safavi-Naini, R., Canetti, R. (eds.) CRYPTO 2012. LNCS, vol. 7417, pp. 162–179. Springer, Heidelberg (2012). https://doi.org/10.1007/978-3-642-32009-5_11

[hul] Hulu's move into live television makes Amazon a surprise winner. http://fortune.com/2017/08/15/hulu-live-tv-amazon-aws/

[KSW08] Katz, J., Sahai, A., Waters, B.: Predicate encryption supporting disjunctions, polynomial equations, and inner products. In: Smart, N. (ed.) EUROCRYPT 2008. LNCS, vol. 4965, pp. 146–162. Springer, Heidelberg (2008). https://doi.org/10.1007/978-3-540-78967-3_9

[KT15] Kiayias, A., Tang, Q.: Traitor deterring schemes: using bitcoin as collateral for digital content. In: Ray, I., Li, N., Kruegel, C. (eds.), ACM CCS 15, pp. 231–242. ACM Press, October 2015

[KZ16] Komargodski, I., Zhandry, M.: Cutting-edge cryptography through the lens of secret sharing. In: Kushilevitz, E., Malkin, T. (eds.) TCC 2016. LNCS, vol. 9563, pp. 449–479. Springer, Heidelberg (2016). https://doi.org/10.1007/978-3-662-49099-0_17

[net] Completing the netflix cloud migration. https://media.netflix.com/en/company-blog/completing-the-netflix-cloud-migration

[OF15] Oswald, E., Fischlin, M. (eds.): EUROCRYPT 2015, Part II. LNCS, vol. 9057. Springer, Heidelberg (2015). https://doi.org/10.1007/978-3-662-46803-6

[O'N10] O'Neill, A.: Definitional issues in functional encryption. IACR Cryptology ePrint Archive 2010:556 (2010)

[pok]   Bringing pokémon go to life on Google cloud. https://cloudplatform. googleblog.com/2016/09/bringing-Pokemon-GO-to-life-on-Google-Cloud. html

[Reg05] Regev, O.: On lattices, learning with errors, random linear codes, and cryptography. In: Gabow, H.N., Fagin, R. (eds.) 37th ACM STOC, pp. 84–93. ACM Press, May 2005

[SSW09] Shen, E., Shi, E., Waters, B.: Predicate Privacy in Encryption Systems. In: Reingold, O. (ed.) TCC 2009. LNCS, vol. 5444, pp. 457–473. Springer, Heidelberg (2009). https://doi.org/10.1007/978-3-642-00457-5_27

Full-Hiding (Unbounded) Multi-input Inner Product Functional Encryption from the k-Linear Assumption

Pratish Datta[✉], Tatsuaki Okamoto, and Junichi Tomida

NTT Secure Platform Laboratories, Tokyo 180-8585, Japan
{datta.pratish,okamoto.tatsuaki,tomida.junichi}@lab.ntt.co.jp

Abstract. This paper presents two *non-generic* and *practically efficient* private key *multi-input functional encryption* (MIFE) schemes for the multi-input version of the *inner product* functionality that are the *first* to achieve simultaneous message and function privacy, namely, the *full-hiding* security for a non-trivial multi-input functionality under *well-studied* cryptographic assumptions. Our MIFE schemes are built in bilinear groups of prime order, and their security is based on the standard *k-Linear* (k-LIN) assumption (along with the existence of semantically secure symmetric key encryption and pseudorandom functions). Our constructions support polynomial number of encryption slots (inputs) without incurring any super-polynomial loss in the security reduction. While the number of encryption slots in our first scheme is apriori bounded, our second scheme can withstand an *arbitrary* number of encryption slots. Prior to our work, there was no known MIFE scheme for a non-trivial functionality, even without function privacy, that can support an unbounded number of encryption slots without relying on any heavy-duty building block or little-understood cryptographic assumption.

Keywords: Multi-input functional encryption · Inner products Full-hiding security · Unbounded arity · Bilinear maps

1 Introduction

Functional encryption (FE) [12,36] is a new vision of modern cryptography that aims to overcome the potential limitation of the traditional encryption schemes, namely, the so called "all-or-nothing" control over decryption capabilities, i.e., parties holding the legitimate decryption key can recover the entire message encrypted within a ciphertext, whereas others can learn nothing. Specifically, FE offers additional flexibility by supporting restricted decryption keys which enable decrypters to learn specific functions of encrypted messages, without revealing any additional information. More precisely, an FE scheme for a function family $\mathcal{F}$ involves a setup authority which holds a master secret key and publishes public system parameters. An encrypter uses the public parameters (along with a secret encryption key provided by the setup authority in case of a private key

© International Association for Cryptologic Research 2018
M. Abdalla and R. Dahab (Eds.): PKC 2018, LNCS 10770, pp. 245–277, 2018.
https://doi.org/10.1007/978-3-319-76581-5_9

scheme) to encrypt its message m belonging to some supported message space $\mathcal{M}$, creating a ciphertext CT. A decrypter may obtain a private decryption key SK corresponding to some function $f \in \mathcal{F}$ from the setup authority provided the authority deems that the decrypter is entitled for that key. Such a decryption key SK corresponding to certain decryption function f can be used to decrypt a ciphertext CT encrypting some message m to recover $f(m)$. The basic security requirement for an FE scheme is the privacy of encrypted messages against collusion of decrypters, i.e., an arbitrary number of decrypters cannot jointly retrieve any more information about an encrypted message beyond the union of what they each can learn individually.

Multi-input functional encryption (MIFE), introduced by Goldwasser et al. [23], is a generalization of FE to the setting of multi-input functions. An MIFE scheme has several encryption slots, and messages can be encrypted to different slots independently. A MIFE decryption key for an n-input function f simultaneously decrypts a set of n ciphertexts, each of which is encrypted with respect to one of the n input slots associated with f, to unveil the joint evaluation of f on the n messages encrypted within those n ciphertexts. Just like single-input FE the primary security requirement for an MIFE scheme as well is the privacy of encrypted messages against collusion attacks. However, unlike single-input FE, the formalization of this security notion in case of MIFE is somewhat subtle. In their pioneering work, Goldwasser et al. [23] presented a rigorous framework to formally capture message privacy for MIFE, both in the public key and in the private key regimes.

MIFE is particularly useful in scenarios where informations, which need to be processed together during decryption, become available at different points of time or are supplied by different parties. In fact, MIFE can be employed in a wide range of applications pertaining to computation and mining over encrypted data coming from multiple sources. Examples include executing search queries over encrypted data-bases, processing encrypted streaming data, non-interactive differentially private data releases, multi-client delegation of computations to external servers, and many more. All of these applications are in fact relevant in both the public key and the private key regimes.

In view of its countless practical applications, a series of recent works have attempted to construct MIFE schemes based on various cryptographic tools. These constructions can be broadly classified into two categories. The first line of research has tried to build MIFE schemes for general multi-input functionalities, e.g., arbitrary polynomial-size circuits [6,13,23,24,28] or Turing machines [7]. Unfortunately however, all such MIFE constructions rely on highly strong cryptographic primitives like indistinguishability obfuscation [8,20], single-input FE for general circuits [20,21], or multilinear maps [17,19], neither of which is currently instantiable using efficient building blocks or under well-studied cryptographic assumptions. Consequently, a second line of research have emerged whose focus is to design concretely efficient MIFE schemes based on standard assumptions for specific multi-input functionalities, e.g., comparison [15,16,31] or multi-input inner product [3,27,30]. However, majority of the existing works on MIFE have concentrated merely on achieving the basic security notion, namely, message confidentiality.

Unfortunately, message confidentiality is not sufficient in several advanced applications of FE, rather privacy also needs to be ensured for the functions for which the decryption keys are issued. This is especially important in situations where the decryption functions themselves contain sensitive informations. Consider the following scenario: Suppose a hospital subscribes to an external cloud server for storing medical records of its patients. In order to ensure confidentiality of the records and, at the same time, remotely perform various computations on the outsourced data from time to time, a promising choice for the hospital is to use an FE scheme to encrypt the records locally prior to uploading to the cloud server. Now, suppose the hospital wishes to retrieve the list of all patients who is receiving treatment for a certain chronic disease from the cloud server. For this, the hospital needs to provide the cloud server a decryption key for the corresponding functionality. However, if the FE scheme used by the hospital possesses no function privacy, then the cloud server would get to know the functionality from the decryption key provided by the hospital. Thus, after performing the assigned computation, if the cloud server notices the name of some celebrity in the obtained list of patients, it would at once understand that the particular celebrity is suffering from such a chronic disease, and it may leak the information to the media possibly for financial gain. This is clearly undesirable from the privacy point of view.

In order to address such scenarios, several recent works have studied the notion of function privacy in the context of FE, both in the single-input setting [4,9–11,14,18,25,27,32,33,38,39] and in the multi-input setting [6,13,28,32]. Intuitively, function privacy demands that the decryption keys leak no additional information about the functions embedded within them, beyond what is revealed through decryption. However, it has been observed that the extent to which function privacy can be realized differs dramatically between the public key and the private key regimes. In fact, in the public key setting, where anyone can encrypt messages, only a weak form of function privacy can be realized [10,11,25]. More precisely, in order to capture function privacy for FE in the public key setting, the framework must assume that the functions come from a certain high-entropy distribution. On the contrary, function-private FE (both the single-input and the multi-input versions) has been shown to possess great potentials in the private key setting, not only as a stand-alone feature, but also as a very useful building block [5,6,28,29,32,33]. Consequently, the research on function-private FE has been focused primarily on the private key setting. However, despite of its immense theoretical and practical significance, so far, there are only a handful of function-private FE schemes available in the literature that can be implemented in practice [9,18,27,32,33,39], and all of them have been designed for single-input functions, precisely, inner products. In case of function-private MIFE, the only known concrete construction is the recent one due to Lin [32]. She has constructed a private key function-private MIFE scheme for computing inner products of arbitrary polynomial degree, where standard inner product is a degree 2 function. However, her construction employs multilinear maps, and thus is currently uninstantiable in practice.

In this work, our goal is to design practical private key function-private MIFE scheme supporting a polynomial number of encryption slots, incurring only polynomial loss in the security reduction. Goldwasser et al. [23] have already shown that private key MIFE for general functionalities supporting a polynomial number of encryption slots is equivalent to full-fledged indistinguishability obfuscation. Hence, it seems impossible to design such highly expressive MIFE scheme without a sub-exponential security loss [22]. In fact, all existing private key MIFE schemes for general functionalities [6,13,23,28] do suffer from at least a quasi-polynomial security loss to support even a poly-logarithmic number of encryption slots. Hence, we concentrate on a specific multi-input functionality that has a wide range of real-life applications, namely, the natural multi-input generalization of the inner product functionality. This functionality has been first considered by Abdalla et al. [3]. Concretely, a multi-input inner product function $f_{\{\vec{y}_\iota\}_{\iota \in S}}$ is associated with a set S of encryption slot indices and vectors $\vec{y}_\iota \in \mathbb{Z}^m$ for all $\iota \in S$. It takes as input a set of vectors $\{\vec{x}_\iota\}_{\iota \in S}$ with the same index set S, where $\vec{x}_\iota \in \mathbb{Z}^m$ for all $\iota \in S$, and outputs $\sum_{\iota \in S} \vec{x}_\iota \cdot \vec{y}_\iota$, where $\vec{x}_\iota \cdot \vec{y}_\iota$ represents the inner product of the vectors $\vec{x}_\iota$ and $\vec{y}_\iota$ over $\mathbb{Z}$. It is required that the norm of each component inner product $\vec{x}_\iota \cdot \vec{y}_\iota$ is smaller than some upper bound $\mathscr{B}$. Observe that this functionality is different from the high-degree inner product functionality considered by Lin [32]. The multi-input inner product functionality captures various important computations arising in the context of data-mining, e.g., computing weighted mean of informations supplied by different parties. Please refer to [3] for a comprehensive exposure of the practical significance of the multi-input inner product functionality.

Abdalla et al. [3] have presented an MIFE scheme for the multi-input inner product functionality described above in the private key setting, using bilinear groups of prime order. Their construction supports a fixed polynomial number of encryption slots and multi-input inner product functions associated with a fixed index set S of polynomial size, as well as incurs only a polynomial loss in the security reduction. Precisely, the index set S in their construction is of the form $S = [n] = \{1, \ldots, n\}$, where n is the number of encryption slots – a polynomial determined at the time of setup, for the multi-input inner product functions. Their construction achieves adaptive message privacy against arbitrary collusion, as per the framework of Goldwasser et al. [23], in the standard model under the well-studied k-$Linear$ (k-LIN) assumption [37]. Prior to the work of Abdalla et al. [3], two independent works, namely, [27,30] were able to realize a two-input variant of their result, of which [27] achieved it in the generic group model. However, none of these constructions guarantee function privacy. In fact, in their paper [3], Abdalla et al. have posed the construction of a function-private MIFE scheme for the multi-input inner product functionality based on the k-LIN assumption in prime order bilinear groups as an open problem.

Our Contribution

In this paper we solve the above open problem. More specifically, we construct two *concretely efficient* standard-model private key MIFE schemes for the multi-input inner product functionality in prime order bilinear groups that are the *first* to achieve *function privacy* under *well-studied* cryptographic assumptions. In fact, our constructions achieve the unified notion of message and function privacy, namely, the *full-hiding* security, formulated by Brakerski et al. [13] in the context of private key MIFE by combining the corresponding notion in the context of private key single-input FE [4,14] with the framework for message privacy of MIFE [23], under the k-LIN assumption (along with the existence of semantically secure symmetric key encryption and pseudorandom functions). Both of our constructions support polynomial number of encryption slots and are free from any super-polynomial loss in the security reduction. Our MIFE schemes withstands any polynomial number of decryption key queries and any polynomial number of ciphertext queries for each encryption slot. We employ the elegant technique of dual pairing vector spaces (DPVS) introduced by Okamoto and Takashima [34,35], and are implementable using both symmetric and asymmetric bilinear groups. Just like [3], our first construction supports an apriori fixed number of encryption slots and a fixed slot index set for the multi-input inner product functions. These limitations are removed in our second construction. More precisely, our second construction is capable of supporting an apriori *unbounded* number of encryption slots and multi-input inner product functions with *arbitrary* slot index sets of any polynomial size. In fact, this construction is the *first* MIFE scheme for a non-trivial functionality with an unbounded number of encryption slots, built using efficient cryptographic tools and under well-studied complexity assumptions. The only prior MIFE construction which achieves this feature [7] has been designed using heavy machineries and relies on little-understood cryptographic assumption like public-coin differing input obfuscation [26]. Moreover, the MIFE construction of [7] has been developed in public key setting and possesses no function privacy.

Our MIFE constructions are very efficient. When instantiated under the Symmetric External Diffie-Hellman (SXDH) assumption ($k = 1$ version of the k-LIN assumption) and a symmetric key encryption (SKE) whose secret key size is λ bits, the ciphertexts of our bounded MIFE scheme consist of $2m + 3$ group elements and a λ-bit string, while the decryption keys consist of $n(2m + 3)$ group elements. We would like to mention that these group elements are encrypted by SKE. The master secret key comprises of $n(2m+3)^2$ elements of the underlying finite field and n λ-bit strings. The encryption incurs one encryption of SKE and $2m+3$ exponentiations, while key generation algorithm incurs one encryption of SKE and $n(2m+3)$ exponentiations. On the other hand, the decryption algorithm involves $(n + 1)$ executions of the decryption algorithm of SKE and $n(2m + 3)$ pairing operations followed by an exhaustive search step over a polynomial-size range of possible values. Here, m and n respectively denote the length of the vectors and the size of the index set associated with the multi-input inner product functionality. Observe that these figures are already in close compliance with the n-fold extension of the most efficient standard-model full-hiding single-input FE construction for inner products known till date, namely, the scheme by Lin [32] (which is also designed under the SXDH assumption). The exhaustive search step in the decryption algorithm is reminiscent of all currently known bilinear-map-based FE constructions for inner products, both in the single-input and in the multi-input settings. In unbounded scheme, the ciphertext size and decryption key size are the same as bounded scheme, while the master secret key consists of two pseudorandom function (PRF) keys and $(2m + 3)^2$ elements of the underlying finite field. The encryption incurs two PRF evaluations and $2m + 3$ exponentiations, while the key generation algorithm incurs n executions of the encryption algorithm of SKE, $2n$ PRF evaluations, and $n(2m + 3)$ exponentiations. The decryption algorithm, on the other hand, involves n executions of the decryption algorithm of SKE and $n(2m + 3)$ pairing operations followed by an exhaustive search step similar to the bounded scheme.

Our Techniques

We now explain the principal ideas underlying our MIFE constructions for the multi-input inner product functionality. In order to simplify the exposition, we ignore many technicalities in this overview.

Our bounded-arity scheme: Since, the multi-input inner product functionality is a multi-input generalization of its single-input version, a natural first step is to explore whether we can obtain a private key full-hiding n-input MIFE scheme for inner products by executing n parallel copies of a private key full-hiding FE scheme for inner products. The most efficient such scheme available in the literature is the one due to Lin [32], which is based on the SXDH assumption. However, the construction is built upon the Decisional-Diffie-Hellman (DDH)-based construction of Abdalla et al. [1] and is not readily amenable to the general k-LIN assumption. Moreover, the construction is built in a two step approach, namely, first constructing an FE scheme for inner products achieving only a weaker form of function privacy, and then bootstrapping to the full-hiding security by using the conversion of Lin and Vaikuntanathan [33]. We want to avoid such an approach, rather our goal is to design a direct construction of full-hiding MIFE for multi-input inner products. So, we start with the full-hiding single-input inner-product FE scheme proposed by Tomida et al. [39]. This construction is direct, and while originally presented under a variant of the Decisional Linear (DLIN) assumption, seems naturally generalizable to the k-LIN assumption. Further, in terms of efficiency, this construction is next to the construction of Lin [32] among the standard-model private key function-private FE constructions available in the literature [9,18,32,39]. Besides, this construction has the flexibility of being implementable in both symmetric and asymmetric bilinear groups.

First, let us briefly review the construction and proof idea of Tomida et al. [39]. We assume familiarity with the DPVS framework for the rest of this section. (The background on DPVS is provided in Sect. 2.3.) The master secret key MSK in the construction of Tomida et al. [39] consists of a pair of dual orthogonal bases $(\mathbb{B}, \mathbb{B}^*)$ of a $(2m + 5)$-dimensional DPVS, where m is the length of the ciphertext and decryption key vectors. Out of the $2m + 5$ dimensions, $m + 4$ dimensions are utilized in the real construction, while the rest are used in performing various hybrid transitions in the security proof. Note that the use of such hidden dimensions is a powerful feature of the DPVS framework, and it has been proven to be instrumental in deducing various complex security proofs in the literature. The ciphertext CT of [39] encrypting an m-dimensional vector $\vec{x}$ is given by $\mathrm{CT} = (\vec{x}, \vec{0}^m, \vec{0}^2, \varphi_1, \varphi_2, 0)_{\mathbb{B}}$, where $\varphi_1, \varphi_2 \xleftarrow{\mathsf{U}} \mathbb{F}_q$. On the other hand, the decryption key SK corresponding to some m-dimensional vector $\vec{y}$ is of the form $\mathrm{SK} = (\vec{y}, \vec{0}^m, \gamma_1, \gamma_2, \vec{0}^2, 0)_{\mathbb{B}^*}$, where $\gamma_1, \gamma_2 \xleftarrow{\mathsf{U}} \mathbb{F}_q$. Here, $(\vec{v})_{\mathbb{W}}$, for any vector $\vec{v}$ with entries in $\mathbb{F}_q$ and any basis $\mathbb{W}$ of a DPVS, signifies the linear combination of the members of $\mathbb{W}$ using the entries of $\vec{v}$ as coefficients. The decryption algorithm works by computing $e(\mathrm{CT}, \mathrm{SK})$ followed by performing an exhaustive search step over a specified polynomial-size range to determine the output. The correctness readily follows by the dual orthogonality property of $(\mathbb{B}, \mathbb{B}^*)$.

Recall that in the full-hiding security experiment for single-input inner product FE [4,14], first the challenger $\mathcal{B}$ sets up the system and samples a random bit $\beta \xleftarrow{\mathsf{U}} \{0, 1\}$. Next, the adversary $\mathcal{A}$ is allowed to adaptively make any polynomial number of ciphertext and decryption key queries to $\mathcal{B}$. In order to make a ciphertext query, $\mathcal{A}$ submits a pair of message vectors $(\vec{x}_0, \vec{x}_1)$ to $\mathcal{B}$, while to make a decryption key query, $\mathcal{A}$ submits a pair of vectors $(\vec{y}_0, \vec{y}_1)$ to $\mathcal{B}$. Depending on the random bit β, $\mathcal{B}$ returns respectively an encryption of $\vec{x}_\beta$ and a decryption key for vector $\vec{y}_\beta$ to the adversary in response to the respective queries. Finally, the adversary has to correctly guess the random bit β to win the experiment. The restriction on the queries of $\mathcal{A}$ is that for all pairs of vectors $(\vec{x}_0, \vec{x}_1)$ for which a ciphertext query is made and for all pairs of vectors $(\vec{y}_0, \vec{y}_1)$ for which a decryption key query is made, it should hold that $\vec{x}_0 \cdot \vec{y}_0 = \vec{x}_1 \cdot \vec{y}_1$.

In order to prove security of the construction of [39] in the above full-hiding model, the following hybrid transitions are performed: The initial hybrid is the real full-hiding experiment with the challenge bit $\beta = 0$, i.e., where the forms of the ciphertexts and decryption keys returned to $\mathcal{A}$ are respectively $\mathrm{CT}^* = (\vec{x}_0, \vec{0}^m, \vec{0}^2, \varphi_1, \varphi_2, 0)_{\mathbb{B}}$ and $\mathrm{SK}^* = (\vec{y}_0, \vec{0}^m, \gamma_1, \gamma_2, \vec{0}^2, 0)_{\mathbb{B}^*}$, while the final hybrid corresponds to the real full-hiding experiment with $\beta = 1$, i.e., where the forms of the ciphertexts and decryption keys returned to the adversary are of the form $\mathrm{CT}^* = (\vec{x}_1, \vec{0}^m, \vec{0}^2, \varphi_1, \varphi_2, 0)_{\mathbb{B}}$ and $\mathrm{SK}^* = (\vec{y}_1, \vec{0}^m, \gamma_1, \gamma_2, \vec{0}^2, 0)_{\mathbb{B}^*}$ respectively. Towards achieving this change, first, applying a combination of a computational change using the DLIN assumption, in conjunction with a conceptual transformation of the underlying bases, the form of the ciphertexts are altered one by one to $\mathrm{CT}^* = (\vec{x}_0, \vec{x}_1, \vec{0}^2, \varphi_1, \varphi_2, 0)_{\mathbb{B}}$. In the next step, applying another combination of computational and conceptual changes, the form of the queried decryption keys are changed one by one to the form $\mathrm{SK}^* = (\vec{0}^m, \vec{y}_1, \gamma_1, \gamma_2, \vec{0}^2, 0)_{\mathbb{B}^*}$. This is the most subtle transition step, and this is where we have to rely crucially on the restriction of the security model. More precisely, observe that before altering the decryption keys, decrypting the queried ciphertexts using the queried decryption keys result in $\vec{x}_0 \cdot \vec{y}_0$, whereas after the transformation, the decryption results are $\vec{x}_1 \cdot \vec{y}_1$. However, thanks to the restriction of the full-hiding security experiment, we can ensure that the decryption results in the two cases are the same, and thus the change cannot be detected through decryption. After this step, the forms of ciphertexts and decryption keys are further altered respectively to $\text{CT}^* = (\vec{x}_1, \vec{x}_0, \vec{0}^2, \varphi_1, \varphi_2, 0)_{\mathbb{B}}$ and $\text{SK}^* = (\vec{y}_1, \vec{0}^m, \gamma_1, \gamma_2, \vec{0}^2, 0)_{\mathbb{B}^*}$, with the help of another conceptual basis transformation. Once this step is executed, the forms of the queried ciphertexts are changed to $\text{CT}^* = (\vec{x}_1, \vec{0}^m, \vec{0}^2, \varphi_1, \varphi_2, 0)_{\mathbb{B}}$ using a reverse transformation to the one used in the first step. Observe that this last step takes us to the experiment corresponding to $\beta = 1$.

Let us now consider an MIFE scheme for the n-input inner product functionality obtained by an n-fold extension of the above single-input scheme. More precisely, consider an n-input MIFE scheme having the following specifications: The master secret key MSK consists of n independently generated master secret keys for the single-input scheme, i.e., $\text{MSK} = \{\text{MSK}_\iota = (\mathbb{B}_\iota, \mathbb{B}_\iota^*)\}_{\iota \in [n]}$. The ciphertext of some vector $\vec{x}_\iota$ with respect to index $\iota \in [n]$ is simply a single-input FE ciphertext for $\vec{x}_\iota$ with respect to MSK_ι, i.e., the ciphertext has the form $\text{CT}_\iota = (\iota, c_\iota = (\vec{x}_\iota, \vec{0}^m, \vec{0}^2, \varphi_{\iota,1}, \varphi_{\iota,2}, 0)_{\mathbb{B}_\iota})$, where $\varphi_{\iota,1}, \varphi_{\iota,2} \xleftarrow{\text{U}} \mathbb{F}_q$. On the other hand, a decryption key associated with a set of n vectors $\{\vec{y}_\iota\}_{\iota \in [n]}$ is given by a set of n decryption keys $\{\text{SK}_\iota\}_{\iota \in [n]}$, where SK_ι is the single-input FE secret key for $\vec{y}_\iota$ with respect to MSK_ι, i.e., $\text{SK} = \{k_\iota = (\vec{y}_\iota, \vec{0}^m, \gamma_{\iota,1}, \gamma_{\iota,2}, \vec{0}^2, 0)_{\mathbb{B}_\iota^*}\}_{\iota \in [n]}$, where $\gamma_{\iota,1}, \gamma_{\iota,2} \xleftarrow{\text{U}} \mathbb{F}_q$ for all $\iota \in [n]$. To decrypt a set of n ciphertexts $\{\text{CT}_\iota\}_{\iota \in [n]}$ using a decryption key SK, one first computes $\prod_{\iota \in [n]} e(c_\iota, k_\iota)$, and then performs an exhaustive search step. It is easy to see that the correctness follows analogously to the single-input case.

However, one can readily observe that the above n-input extension is not secure. In particular, the construction leaks partial information. Precisely, notice that for each $\iota \in [n]$, one can easily recover $\vec{x}_\iota \cdot \vec{y}_\iota$ by computing $e(c_\iota, k_\iota)$, whereas ideally one should only be able to learn $\sum_{\iota \in [n]} \vec{x}_\iota \cdot \vec{y}_\iota$. Abdalla et al. [3] also faced a similar challenge while constructing their MIFE scheme by building on a single input inner product FE scheme. In order to overcome this problem, they introduced additional randomness within ciphertexts and decryption keys. Precisely, in order to generate a ciphertext for vector $\vec{x}_\iota$ with respect to index $\iota \in [n]$, they encrypted the vector $(\vec{x}_\iota, z_\iota)$, where $z_1, \ldots, z_n \xleftarrow{\text{U}} \mathbb{F}_q$ are included within the master secret key. Similarly, while preparing a decryption key for a set of n vectors $\{\vec{y}_\iota\}_{\iota \in [n]}$, they sampled a random value $r \xleftarrow{\text{U}} \mathbb{F}_q$, and generated single-input FE decryption keys for the vectors $(\vec{y}_\iota, r)$ for all $\iota \in [n]$, and additionally create the component $k_T = g_T^{\sum_{\iota \in [n]} z_\iota r}$. We attempt to apply their trick to our setting. More precisely, we modify our MIFE construction as follows: We add one additional dimension in the dual orthogonal bases $(\mathbb{B}_\iota, \mathbb{B}_\iota^*)$ for each $\iota \in [n]$, i.e., they are now $(2m + 6)$-dimensional. A ciphertext encrypting the vector $\vec{x}_\iota$ with respect to index $\iota \in [n]$ is of the form

$\text{CT}_\iota = (\iota, \boldsymbol{c}_\iota = (\overrightarrow{x}_\iota, \overrightarrow{0}^m, z_\iota, \overrightarrow{0}^2, \varphi_{\iota,1}, \varphi_{\iota,2}, 0)_{\mathbb{B}_\iota})$, where $z_1, \ldots, z_n \xleftarrow{\mathsf{U}} \mathbb{F}_q$ are parts of MSK, and the decryption key corresponding to a set of n vectors $\{\overrightarrow{y}_\iota\}_{\iota \in [n]}$ is given by $\text{SK} = (\{\boldsymbol{k}_\iota = (\overrightarrow{y}_\iota, \overrightarrow{0}^m, r, \gamma_{\iota,1}, \gamma_{\iota,2}, \overrightarrow{0}^2, 0)_{\mathbb{B}_\iota^*}\}_{\iota \in [n]}, k_T = g_T^{\sum_{\iota \in [n]} z_\iota r})$.

Decryption works by first computing $[\prod_{\iota \in [n]} e(\boldsymbol{c}_\iota, \boldsymbol{k}_\iota)]/k_T = g_T^{\sum_{\iota \in [n]} \overrightarrow{x}_\iota \cdot \overrightarrow{y}_\iota}$, and then performing an exhaustive search step to recover $\sum_{\iota \in [n]} \overrightarrow{x}_\iota \cdot \overrightarrow{y}_\iota$.

Let us now consider the security of the modified construction. For simplicity, assume that the adversary queries a single decryption key and a single ciphertext for each of the n encryption slots. The full-hiding security model for private key MIFE [13] is an extension of its single-input counter part, but is significantly more complicated compared to it. Analogous to the single-input case, in this multi-input security model, in order to make a ciphertext query for the ιth slot, the adversary has to submit a pair of vectors $(\overrightarrow{x}_{\iota,0}, \overrightarrow{x}_{\iota,1})$, whereas for making a decryption key query, the adversary has to submit a pair of sets of n vectors $(\{\overrightarrow{y}_{\iota,0}\}_{\iota \in [n]}, \{\overrightarrow{y}_{\iota,1}\}_{\iota \in [n]})$. However, unlike the single-input setting, now the restriction on the queries is that $\sum_{\iota \in [n]} \overrightarrow{x}_{\iota,0} \cdot \overrightarrow{y}_{\iota,0} = \sum_{\iota \in [n]} \overrightarrow{x}_{\iota,1} \cdot \overrightarrow{y}_{\iota,1}$. Let us try to argue security of our modified construction by taking a similar path to that taken by Tomida et al. [39]. We start with the case where the challenge bit $\beta = 0$, i.e., when the ciphertexts and decryption key returned to the adversary have the form $\text{CT}_\iota^* = (\iota, \boldsymbol{c}_\iota^* = (\overrightarrow{x}_{\iota,0}, \overrightarrow{0}^m, z_\iota, \overrightarrow{0}^2, \varphi_{\iota,1}, \varphi_{\iota,2}, 0)_{\mathbb{B}_\iota})$, for $\iota \in [n]$, and $\text{SK}^* = (\{\boldsymbol{k}_\iota^* = (\overrightarrow{y}_{\iota,0}, \overrightarrow{0}^m, r, \gamma_{\iota,1}, \gamma_{\iota,2}, \overrightarrow{0}^2, 0)_{\mathbb{B}_\iota^*}\}_{\iota \in [n]}, k_T = g_T^{\sum_{\iota \in [n]} z_\iota r})$. Just like [39], first, using a combination of computational changes using the DLIN assumption, in conjunction with a conceptual transformation to the underlying bases, we can alter the forms of all the ciphertexts to $\text{CT}_\iota^* = (\iota, \boldsymbol{c}_\iota^* = (\overrightarrow{x}_{\iota,0}, \overrightarrow{x}_{\iota,1}, z_\iota, \overrightarrow{0}^2, \varphi_{\iota,1}, \varphi_{\iota,2}, 0)_{\mathbb{B}_\iota})$. After this step is done, we would have to change the form of the queried decryption key SK^* so that the first $2m$ coefficients of each $\boldsymbol{k}_\iota^*$ become $(\overrightarrow{0}^m, \overrightarrow{y}_{\iota,1})$. In order to achieve this change, we first perform a computational change to $\boldsymbol{k}_\iota^*$, for each $\iota \in [n]$, with the help of the DLIN assumption to $\boldsymbol{k}_\iota^* = (\overrightarrow{y}_{\iota,0}, \overrightarrow{0}^m, r, \gamma_{\iota,1}, \gamma_{\iota,2}, \overrightarrow{0}^2, \omega_\iota)_{\mathbb{B}_\iota^*}$, where $\omega_\iota \xleftarrow{\mathsf{U}} \mathbb{F}_q$ for all $\iota \in [n]$. Next, we need to perform a conceptual transformation to the underlying bases in each slot so that the first two m blocks of each $\boldsymbol{k}_\iota^*$ gets interchanged. However, this conceptual change would generate the term $\overrightarrow{x}_{\iota,0} \cdot \overrightarrow{y}_{\iota,0} - \overrightarrow{x}_{\iota,1} \cdot \overrightarrow{y}_{\iota,1}$ in the $(2m + 6)^{\text{th}}$ coefficient of each ciphertext CT_ι. In the single-input case, such a term vanishes by the restriction on the ciphertext and decryption key queries. But, unlike the single-input case, now $\overrightarrow{x}_{\iota,0} \cdot \overrightarrow{y}_{\iota,0}$ is not guaranteed to be equal to $\overrightarrow{x}_{\iota,1} \cdot \overrightarrow{y}_{\iota,1}$ for all $\iota \in [n]$, and hence the term in the $(2m + 6)^{\text{th}}$ coefficient does not vanish.

In order to overcome this problem, we modify the above construction by introducing a different randomness in each of the n component of the decryption key rather than using a same shared randomness across all the n components. More precisely, a decryption key corresponding to a set of n vectors $\{\overrightarrow{y}_\iota\}_{\iota \in [n]}$ has the form $\text{SK} = (\{\boldsymbol{k}_\iota = (\overrightarrow{\boldsymbol{y}}_\iota, \overrightarrow{0}^m, r_\iota, \gamma_{\iota,1}, \gamma_{\iota,2}, \overrightarrow{0}^2, 0)_{\mathbb{B}_\iota^*}\}_{\iota\in[n]}, k_T = g_T^{\sum\limits_{\iota\in[n]} z_\iota r_\iota}$), where $r_\iota \xleftarrow{\text{U}} \mathbb{F}_q$ for all $\iota \in [n]$. First, observe that this modification does not affect the correctness. Now, with this modification, we can resolve the above problem as follows: In the above conceptual change step, we transform the underlying bases in such a way that not only the first two m blocks of each $\boldsymbol{k}_\iota^*$ gets interchanged, but also each r_ι gets altered to $\widetilde{r}_\iota$, where $\widetilde{r}_\iota = r_\iota + [\overrightarrow{\boldsymbol{x}}_{\iota,0} \cdot \overrightarrow{\boldsymbol{y}}_{\iota,0} - \overrightarrow{\boldsymbol{x}}_{\iota,1} \cdot \overrightarrow{\boldsymbol{y}}_{\iota,1}]/z_\iota$. Observe that the $\widetilde{r}_\iota$'s are also distributed uniformly and independently over $\mathbb{F}_q$ since r_ι's are so. Also, this new basis transformation will create the additional term $[\overrightarrow{\boldsymbol{x}}_{\iota,1} \cdot \overrightarrow{\boldsymbol{y}}_{\iota,1} - \overrightarrow{\boldsymbol{x}}_{\iota,0} \cdot \overrightarrow{\boldsymbol{y}}_{\iota,0}]$ in the $(2m+6)^{\text{th}}$ coefficient of the queried ciphertext in each slot that would cancel out the term $[\overrightarrow{\boldsymbol{x}}_{\iota,0} \cdot \overrightarrow{\boldsymbol{y}}_{\iota,0} - \overrightarrow{\boldsymbol{x}}_{\iota,1} \cdot \overrightarrow{\boldsymbol{y}}_{\iota,1}]$. Further, notice that $\sum\limits_{\iota\in[n]} z_\iota \widetilde{r}_\iota = \sum\limits_{\iota\in[n]} z_\iota r_\iota$ by the restriction of the full-hiding security experiment of the multi-input setting, namely, $\sum\limits_{\iota\in[n]} \overrightarrow{\boldsymbol{x}}_{\iota,0} \cdot \overrightarrow{\boldsymbol{y}}_{\iota,0} = \sum\limits_{\iota\in[n]} \overrightarrow{\boldsymbol{x}}_{\iota,1} \cdot \overrightarrow{\boldsymbol{y}}_{\iota,1}$.

Note that our actual construction and security proof, which is presented under the general k-LIN assumption, is more subtle. In our actual construction, we observe that replacing the z_ι values with the scalar 1 and choosing the r_ι values associated with a decryption key under the restriction that $\sum\limits_{\iota\in[n]} r_\iota = 0$ is sufficient to argue the security proof. As a result of this modification, we are able to remove the k_T component from the decryption keys. Also, in the actual construction, we reduce the dimension of the underlying bases further by making a more careful use of the randomness.

Our unbounded-arity scheme: In our bounded-arity scheme, the setup algorithm makes n random dual orthogonal bases for n-input case, and stores them as a master secret key. The first problem is how to make these bases unboundedly from a master secret key, whose size is independent from n. Considering that our scheme is private-key MIPE, to get an idea of making them from a pseudorandom function is not difficult. That is, we prepare a randomly chosen pseudorandom function key as a master secret key in a setup phase, and in encryption or key generation, we can generate dual orthogonal bases from the pseudorandom function with its input being the slot index when they are needed. Actually, this naive idea works in a conditional full-hiding security model, where for each decryption key, all indices included in the decryption keys are queried in ciphertext query. The crucial point is that, for some decryption key queried by the adversary, if all indices that are included in the decryption key are queried in ciphertext query, then all corresponding vectors must satisfy some restrictions to avoid a trivial attack. Concretely, for each decryption key SK_S for a index set S and vectors $\{\overrightarrow{\boldsymbol{y}}_\iota\}_{\iota\in S}$, all vectors $\overrightarrow{\boldsymbol{x}}_\iota$ for slot $\iota \in S$ queried in ciphertext query, satisfy the following restriction s.t. $\sum\limits_{\iota\in S} \overrightarrow{\boldsymbol{x}}_{\iota,0} \cdot \overrightarrow{\boldsymbol{y}}_{\iota,0} = \sum\limits_{\iota\in S} \overrightarrow{\boldsymbol{x}}_{\iota,1} \cdot \overrightarrow{\boldsymbol{y}}_{\iota,1}$. When we construct our bounded-arity scheme, we first construct a scheme that is secure in the conditional full-hiding security model, and then we convert it into one that has full-hiding security with no conditions by a generic transformation, similarly to Abdalla et al. [3]. We leverage such a restriction in the proof of the underlying scheme.

In the conversion, we prepare a random bit string k_ι for each index. Next, we encrypt all decryption keys and ciphertexts of the underlying scheme with SKE using $K = \bigoplus_{\iota=1}^{n} k_\iota$ as a secret key. Then, we append the random bit string k_ι to ciphertexts for index ι. By the construction, if there exist some indices that are not queried in ciphertext query, an adversary cannot compute K and all ciphertexts and decryption keys are completely hidden from the adversary. Therefore we can exclude such a situation and focus on the conditional full-hiding security model. However, this generic transformation does not work in the unbounded arity-case, because a set of ciphertexts (or indices) needed for decryption differs by each decryption key. Then we do not know how to convert an unbounded-arity scheme secure under the conditional full-hiding security model into one with full-hiding security.

To solve this problem, we introduce a new construction and new proof techniques. Our solution inherits the spirit of the above technique due to Abdalla et al. [3], but is not completely generic. The basic scheme is that making use of pseudorandom functions as mentioned earlier. Then we introduce another pseudorandom function, which takes an index of slots ι as an input and outputs a random bit string k_ι, which is assigned for each index. Those bit strings are appended to corresponding ciphertexts like the above generic transformation, but we do not encrypt ciphertexts with SKE, or even cannot because it is impossible to decide which indices are needed for decryption in the unbounded case. Instead we encrypt each decryption key with SKE, using the all bit strings corresponding to the index set of decryption key, as a secret key of SKE in some way. We can see that if there are some indices which are not queried in ciphertext query (we call such indices as absent indices), then the decryption keys which contain absent indices will be completely hidden from the adversary. It is because to obtain the secret keys of SKE, the adversary needs all bit strings k_ι (or ciphertexts) for the corresponding indices.

In this construction, however, we cannot use a generic transformation because ciphertexts are not encrypted with SKE. Instead we consider a series of hybrids in the same manner as bounded-arity case for the security proof. During the hybrids, we encounter the problem that there are some decryption keys that have absent indices, and therefore these decryption keys and ciphertexts might not satisfy the restriction as explained above. To solve the problem, we leverage the power of SKE, and it enables us to go the hybrids ahead. More precisely, for the decryption keys that have absent indices, we use the power of SKE, and for the other decryption keys, we use the power of the basic scheme. But here, if we define the secret key of SKE to encrypt a decryption key for a set S as $\bigoplus_{\iota \in S} k_\iota$, likely to the generic transformation of the bounded case, we realize that we cannot make a reduction algorithm for SKE. This problem is mainly due to the flexibleness of decryption keys, that is, a set, which can be associated with secret keys, is not determined in the scheme. Observe that in the bounded case, the set is determined as $\{1, \ldots, n\}$. Consider the case where the adversary has a decryption key for a set $\{1, 2, 3\}$ (say K_{123}), one for $\{1, 2\}$ (say K_{12}) and a ciphertext for index 3. Then the adversary cannot compute the secret key for these decryption keys, i.e., $K_{123} = \bigoplus_{\iota=1}^{3} k_{\iota}$ and $K_{12} = \bigoplus_{\iota=1}^{2} k_{\iota}$. However, the adversary has k_3, which is appended to the ciphertext for index 3, and knows $K_{123} = K_{12} \oplus k_3$. This correlation becomes a obstacle for the reduction. To circumvent this obstacle, we introduce another encrypting method. That is, we iteratively encrypt a decryption key with SKE, making each bit strings k_{ι} be a secret key. Then such a correlation does not appear over every decryption key.

The final difficulty is that the adversary asks for decryption keys and ciphertexts in *adaptive manner*. Consequently, the challenger cannot know which type a queried decryption key will be, one that has absent indices or one does not, at the point where the decryption key is queried. Then we need to carefully construct reduction algorithms and evaluate successful probabilities of the reductions.

Concurrent Work

Concurrently and independently to our work, Abdalla et al. [2] have also considered the problem of constructing function-private MIFE scheme for the multi-input inner product functionality supporting a polynomial number of encryption slots under standard assumption. They have first presented a semi-generic scheme that achieves the full-hiding security only in a selective sense. They have subsequently overcome the selective restriction in a concrete instantiation of their semi-generic construction. However, similar to our first MIFE scheme, their construction can only support an apriori fixed number of encryption slots and a fixed slot index set for the multi-input inner product functions. Their concrete adaptively full-hiding MIFE scheme is built in prime order bilinear group setting under the k-MDDH assumption, which subsumes the k-LIN assumption used in our construction. When instantiated under the SXDH assumption, while our construction contains $4n(m^2 - 1)$ more field elements in the master secret key, it involves 2 and $2n + 1$ less group elements in ciphertexts and decryption keys respectively compared to their scheme. On the other hand, our scheme incurs 2 and $2n + 1$ less exponentiations in encryption and key generation procedures respectively, as well as requires $2n$ less pairing operations during decryption compared to theirs. Recall that m and n respectively denote the length of the vectors and the size of the index set associated with the multi-input inner product functionality.

2   Preliminaries

In this section we present various definitions and decisional problems used in this paper.

2.1   Notations

Let $\lambda \in \mathbb{N}$ denotes the security parameter and 1^{λ} be its unary encoding. Let $\mathbb{N}$ and $\mathbb{Z}$ denote the set of all positive integers and the set of all integers respectively, while $\mathbb{F}_q$, for any prime power $q \in \mathbb{N}$, denotes the finite field of integers modulo p.

For $s \in \mathbb{N}$ and $t \in \mathbb{N} \cup \{0\}$ (with $t < s$), we let $[s] = \{1, \ldots, s\}$ and $[t, s] = \{t, \ldots, s\}$. For any set Z, $z \xleftarrow{\mathsf{U}} Z$ represents the process of uniformly sampling an element z from the set Z, and $|Z|$ signifies the size or cardinality of Z. For a probabilistic algorithm $\mathcal{R}$, we denote by $\varkappa = \mathcal{R}(\Theta; \Phi)$ the output of $\mathcal{R}$ on input Θ and the content of the random tape being Φ, while $\varkappa \xleftarrow{\mathsf{R}} \mathcal{R}(\Theta)$ represents the process of sampling $\varkappa$ from the output distribution of $\mathcal{R}$ on input Θ with a uniform random tape. On the other hand, for any deterministic algorithm $\mathcal{D}$, $\varkappa = \mathcal{D}(\Theta)$ denotes the output of $\mathcal{D}$ on input Θ. We use the abbreviation PPT to mean probabilistic polynomial-time. We assume that all the algorithms are given the unary representation 1^λ of the security parameter λ as input and will not write 1^λ explicitly as input of the algorithms when it is clear from the context. For any finite field $\mathbb{F}_q$ and $m \in \mathbb{N}$, let $\vec{v}$ denotes a vector $(v^{(1)}, \ldots, v^{(m)}) \in \mathbb{Z}^m$ or $\mathbb{F}_q^m$, where $v^{(j)} \in \mathbb{Z}$ or $\mathbb{F}_q$ respectively, for all $j \in [m]$. The all zero vectors in $\mathbb{F}_q^m$ will be denoted by $\vec{0}^m$. For any two vectors $\vec{v}, \vec{w} \in \mathbb{Z}^m$ or $\mathbb{F}_q^m$, $\vec{v} \cdot \vec{w}$ stands for the inner product of the vectors $\vec{v}$ and $\vec{w}$ over the integers, i.e., $\vec{v} \cdot \vec{w} = \sum_{j \in [m]} v^{(j)} w^{(j)} \in \mathbb{Z}$. For any multiplicative cyclic group $\mathbb{G}$ of order q and any generator $g \in \mathbb{G}$, let $\boldsymbol{u}$ represents the m-dimensional vector of group elements $(g^{v^{(1)}}, \ldots, g^{v^{(m)}}) \in \mathbb{G}^m$, for some $\vec{v} \in \mathbb{F}_q^m$. By $\mathbf{1}_\mathbb{G}^m$ we denote the m-dimensional vector $(1_\mathbb{G}, \ldots, 1_\mathbb{G}) \in \mathbb{G}^m$, where $1_\mathbb{G}$ represents the identity element of the group $\mathbb{G}$. We use $A = (a_{j,t})$ to represent a matrix with entries $a_{j,t} \in \mathbb{F}_q$. By A^T we will signify the transpose of the matrix A, while by A^* the matrix $(A^{-1})^\mathsf{T}$. Let $\mathsf{GL}(\ell, \mathbb{F}_q)$ denotes the set of all $\ell \times \ell$ invertible matrices over $\mathbb{F}_q$. A function $\mathsf{negl} : \mathbb{N} \to \mathbb{R}^+$ is said to be *negligible* if for every $c \in \mathbb{N}$, there exists $T \in \mathbb{N}$ such that for all $\lambda \in \mathbb{N}$ with $\lambda > T$, $|\mathsf{negl}(\lambda)| < 1/\lambda^c$.

2.2   Some Essential Cryptographic Tools

Definition 2.1 (Pseudorandom Functions: PRFs): A pseudorandom function family $\mathcal{F} = \{\mathcal{F}_\lambda\}_{\lambda \in \mathbb{N}}$ with key space $\mathcal{K} = \{\mathcal{K}_\lambda\}_{\lambda \in \mathbb{N}}$, domain $\mathcal{X} = \{\mathcal{X}_\lambda\}_{\lambda \in \mathbb{N}}$, and range $\mathcal{Y} = \{\mathcal{Y}_\lambda\}_{\lambda \in \mathbb{N}}$ is a function family that consists of functions $F_\lambda : \mathcal{K}_\lambda \times \mathcal{X}_\lambda \to \mathcal{Y}_\lambda$. Let $\mathcal{R}_\lambda$ be a set of functions consists of all functions whose domain and range are $\mathcal{X}_\lambda$ and $\mathcal{Y}_\lambda$ respectively. For all PPT adversary $\mathcal{A}$, the following condition holds;

$$\mathsf{Adv}_\mathcal{A}^{\mathrm{PRF}}(\lambda) = \left| \Pr[1 \xleftarrow{\mathsf{R}} \mathcal{A}^{F(K, \cdot)}] - \Pr[1 \xleftarrow{\mathsf{R}} \mathcal{A}^{R(\cdot)}] \right| \leq \mathsf{negl}(\lambda),$$

where $F \in \mathcal{F}_\lambda$, $K \xleftarrow{\mathsf{U}} \mathcal{K}_\lambda$, and $R \xleftarrow{\mathsf{U}} \mathcal{R}_\lambda$.

Definition 2.2 (Symmetric Key Encryption: SKE): A symmetric key encryption consists of a tuple of three PPT algorithms (SKE.KeyGen, SKE.Encrypt, SKE.Decrypt). SKE.KeyGen takes 1^λ as an input and outputs a secret key K. SKE.Encrypt takes a secret key K and a message m and outputs a ciphertext c. SKE.Decrypt takes a secret key K and a ciphertext c and outputs a message m'. Correctness of SKE is that

$$\Pr[m = m' | K \xleftarrow{\mathsf{R}} \mathsf{SKE.KeyGen}, m' = \mathsf{SKE.Decrypt}(K, \mathsf{SKE.Encrypt}(K, m))] = 1.$$

A semantically secure symmetric key encryption scheme satisfies the following condition. For all PPT adversary $\mathcal{A}$,

$$\mathsf{Adv}_{\mathcal{A}}^{\mathsf{SKE}}(\lambda) = \left| \Pr[1 \xleftarrow{\mathsf{R}} \mathcal{A}^{\mathcal{O}_0(\cdot)}] - \Pr[1 \xleftarrow{\mathsf{R}} \mathcal{A}^{\mathcal{O}_1(\cdot)}] \right| \leq \mathsf{negl}(\lambda),$$

where an oracle $\mathcal{O}_{\beta \in \{0,1\}}$ chooses a random secret key K as $K \xleftarrow{\mathsf{R}} \mathsf{SKE.KeyGen}$ and when it takes a pair of messages (m_0, m_1), it returns $\mathsf{SKE.Encrypt}(K, m_\beta)$.

2.3   Bilinear Groups and Dual Pairing Vector Spaces

Definition 2.3 (Bilinear Group): A bilinear group $\mathsf{params}_{\mathbb{G}} = (q, \mathbb{G}_1, \mathbb{G}_2, \mathbb{G}_T, g_1, g_2, e)$ is a tuple of a prime integer $q \in \mathbb{N}$; cyclic multiplicative groups $\mathbb{G}_1, \mathbb{G}_2, \mathbb{G}_T$ of order q each with polynomial-time computable group operations; generators $g_1 \in \mathbb{G}_1$, $g_2 \in \mathbb{G}_2$; and a polynomial-time computable non-degenerate bilinear map $e : \mathbb{G}_1 \times \mathbb{G}_2 \to \mathbb{G}_T$, i.e., e satisfies the following two properties:

- *Bilinearity*: $e(g_1^\zeta, g_2^\eta) = e(g_1, g_2)^{\zeta\eta}$ for all $\zeta, \eta \in \mathbb{F}_q$.
- *Non-degeneracy*: $e(g_1, g_2) \neq 1_{\mathbb{G}_T}$, where $1_{\mathbb{G}_T}$ denotes the identity element of the group $\mathbb{G}_T$.

Definition 2.4 (Dual Pairing Vector Spaces: DPVS [34,35]): A dual pairing vector space (DPVS) $\mathsf{params}_{\mathbb{V}} = (q, \mathbb{V}_1, \mathbb{V}_2, \mathbb{G}_T, \mathbb{A}_1, \mathbb{A}_2, e)$ by the direct product of a bilinear group $\mathsf{params}_{\mathbb{G}} = (q, \mathbb{G}_1, \mathbb{G}_2, \mathbb{G}_T, g_1, g_2, e)$ is a tuple of a prime integer q; m-dimensional vector spaces $\mathbb{V}_\chi = \mathbb{G}_\chi^m$ over $\mathbb{F}_q$, for $\chi \in [2]$, under vector addition '$\boxplus$' and scalar multiplication '$\circ$' defined componentwise; canonical bases $\mathbb{A}_\chi = \{\boldsymbol{a}_{\chi,j} = (\overbrace{1_{\mathbb{G}_\chi}, \ldots, 1_{\mathbb{G}_\chi}}^{j-1}, g_\chi, \overbrace{1_{\mathbb{G}_\chi}, \ldots, 1_{\mathbb{G}_\chi}}^{m-j})\}_{j \in [m]}$ of $\mathbb{V}_\chi$, for $\chi \in [2]$, where $1_{\mathbb{G}_\chi}$ is the identity element of the group $\mathbb{G}_\chi$, for $\chi \in [2]$; and a pairing $e : \mathbb{V}_1 \times \mathbb{V}_2 \to \mathbb{G}_T$ defined by $e(\boldsymbol{v}, \boldsymbol{w}) = \prod_{j \in [m]} e(g_1^{v^{(j)}}, g_2^{w^{(j)}}) \in \mathbb{G}_T$, for all $\boldsymbol{v} = (g_1^{v^{(1)}}, \ldots, g_1^{v^{(q)}}) \in \mathbb{V}_1$, $\boldsymbol{w} = (g_2^{w^{(1)}}, \ldots, g_2^{w^{(q)}}) \in \mathbb{V}_2$. Observe that the newly defined map e is also non-degenerate bilinear, i.e., e satisfies the following two properties:

- *Bilinearity*: $e(\mu \circ \boldsymbol{v}, \eta \circ \boldsymbol{w}) = e(\boldsymbol{v}, \boldsymbol{w})^{\mu\eta}$, for $\mu, \eta \in \mathbb{F}_q$, $\boldsymbol{v} \in \mathbb{V}_1$, and $\boldsymbol{w} \in \mathbb{V}_2$.
- *Non-degeneracy*: If $e(\boldsymbol{v}, \boldsymbol{w}) = 1_{\mathbb{G}_T}$ for all $\boldsymbol{w} \in \mathbb{V}_2$, then $\boldsymbol{v} = 1_{\mathbb{G}_1}^m$.

We will often omit the symbol '$\circ$' for scalar multiplication and abuse '$+$' for the vector addition '$\boxplus$' when it is clear from the context. For any set $\mathbb{W} = \{\boldsymbol{w}_1, \ldots, \boldsymbol{w}_m\}$ of vectors in $\mathbb{V}_\chi$, for $\chi \in [2]$, and any vector $\vec{v} \in \mathbb{F}_q^m$, let $(\vec{v})_{\mathbb{W}}$ represents the vector in $\mathbb{V}_\chi$ formed by the linear combination of the members of $\mathbb{W}$ with the entries of $\vec{v}$ as the coefficients, i.e., $(\vec{v})_{\mathbb{W}} = \sum_{j \in [m]} v^{(j)} \boldsymbol{w}_j \in \mathbb{V}_\chi$. Also, for any vector $\boldsymbol{v} \in \mathbb{V}_\chi$, for $\chi \in [2]$, and any matrix $A = (a_{j,t})$ with entries $a_{j,t} \in \mathbb{F}_q$, for $j, t \in [m]$, we denote by $\boldsymbol{v}A$ the m-dimensional vector $(g_\chi^{\sum_{j \in [m]} a_{j,1} v^{(j)}}, \ldots, g_\chi^{\sum_{j \in [m]} a_{j,m} v^{(j)}}) \in \mathbb{V}_\chi$. The DPVS generation algorithm $\mathcal{G}_{\mathsf{DPVS}}$

$\mathcal{G}_{\mathrm{OB}}(m, \mathsf{params}_{\mathbb{V}}, \nu)$: This algorithm takes as input the unary encoded security parameter 1^λ, a dimension value $m \in \mathbb{N}$, a m-dimensional DPVS $\mathsf{params}_{\mathbb{V}} = (q, \mathbb{V}_1, \mathbb{V}_2, \mathbb{G}_T, \mathbb{A}_1, \mathbb{A}_2, e) \xleftarrow{\mathsf{R}} \mathcal{G}_{\mathrm{DPVS}}(m, \mathsf{params}_{\mathbb{G}} = (q, \mathbb{G}_1, \mathbb{G}_2, \mathbb{G}_T, g_1, g_2, e))$, along with a random value $\nu \xleftarrow{\mathsf{U}} \mathbb{F}_q \backslash \{0\}$, and performs the following operations:

1. It first samples random $B = (b_{j,t}) \xleftarrow{\mathsf{U}} \mathsf{GL}(m, \mathbb{F}_q)$.
2. Next, it computes $B^\star = (b^*_{j,t}) = \nu B^*$.
3. For all $j \in [m]$, let $\vec{b}_j$ and $\vec{b}^*_j$ represent the jth row-vectors of B and $B^\star$ respectively. It computes $\boldsymbol{b}_j = (\vec{b}_j)_{\mathbb{A}_1}, \boldsymbol{b}^*_j = (\vec{b}^*_j)_{\mathbb{A}_2}$, for $j \in [m]$, and sets

$$\mathbb{B} = \{\boldsymbol{b}_1, \dots, \boldsymbol{b}_m\}, \mathbb{B}^* = \{\boldsymbol{b}^*_1, \dots, \boldsymbol{b}^*_m\}.$$

Clearly $\mathbb{B}$ and $\mathbb{B}^*$ form bases of the vector spaces $\mathbb{V}_1 = \mathbb{G}_1^m$ and $\mathbb{V}_2 = \mathbb{G}_2^m$ respectively. Also, note that $\mathbb{B}$ and $\mathbb{B}^*$ are dual orthogonal in the sense that for all $j, j' \in [m]$,

$$e(\boldsymbol{b}_j, \boldsymbol{b}^*_{j'}) = \begin{cases} g_T, & \text{if } j = j' \\ 1_{\mathbb{G}_T}, & \text{otherwise} \end{cases},$$

where $g_T = e(g_1, g_2)^\nu$.
4. It returns $(\mathbb{B}, \mathbb{B}^*)$.

Fig. 1. Dual orthogonal basis generator $\mathcal{G}_{\mathrm{OB}}$

takes input the unary encoded security parameter 1^λ, a dimension value $m \in \mathbb{N}$, along with a bilinear group $\mathsf{params}_{\mathbb{G}} = (q, \mathbb{G}_1, \mathbb{G}_2, \mathbb{G}_T, g_1, g_2, e) \xleftarrow{\mathsf{R}} \mathcal{G}_{\mathrm{BPG}}()$, and outputs a description $\mathsf{params}_{\mathbb{V}} = (q, \mathbb{V}_1, \mathbb{V}_2, \mathbb{G}_T, \mathbb{A}_1, \mathbb{A}_2, e)$ of DPVS with m-dimensional $\mathbb{V}_1$ and $\mathbb{V}_2$.

We now describe random *dual orthogonal* basis generator $\mathcal{G}_{\mathrm{OB}}$ [34,35] in Fig. 1. This algorithm would be utilized as a sub-routine in our constructions.

2.4 Complexity Assumptions

Assumption 1 (k-Linear: k-LIN [37]): Fix a number $\chi \in [2]$. The k-LIN problem is to guess a bit $\hat{\beta} \xleftarrow{\mathsf{U}} \{0,1\}$ given $\varepsilon_{\hat{\beta}} = (\mathsf{params}_{\mathbb{G}}, g_\chi^{\xi_1}, \dots, g_\chi^{\xi_k}, g_\chi^{\delta_1 \xi_1}, \dots, g_\chi^{\delta_k \xi_k}, \Re_{\hat{\beta}})$; where $\mathsf{params}_{\mathbb{G}} = (q, \mathbb{G}_1, \mathbb{G}_2, \mathbb{G}_T, g_1, g_2, e) \xleftarrow{\mathsf{R}} \mathcal{G}_{\mathrm{BPG}}()$; $\xi_1, \dots, \xi_k, \sigma \xleftarrow{\mathsf{U}} \mathbb{F}_q \backslash \{0\}$; $\delta_1, \dots, \delta_k \xleftarrow{\mathsf{U}} \mathbb{F}_q$; and $\Re_{\hat{\beta}} = g_\chi^{\sum_{j \in [k]} \delta_j}$ or $g_\chi^{\sigma + \sum_{j \in [k]} \delta_j}$ according as $\hat{\beta} = 0$ or 1. The k-LIN assumption states that for any PPT algorithm $\mathcal{A}$, for any security parameter λ, the advantage of $\mathcal{F}$ in deciding the k-LIN problem,

$$\mathsf{Adv}_{\mathcal{A}}^{k\text{-LIN}}(\lambda) = \left| \Pr[1 \xleftarrow{\mathsf{R}} \mathcal{A}(\varepsilon_0)] - \Pr[1 \xleftarrow{\mathsf{R}} \mathcal{A}(\varepsilon_1)] \right| \leq \mathsf{negl}(\lambda),$$

for some negligible function negl.

We now define a set of decisional problems. We rely on the hardness of these problems for deriving security of our constructions. We justify the reducibility of the hardness of these problems to that of the k-LIN problem in the full version of this paper.

Definition 2.5 (Problem 1): Problem 1 is to guess a bit $\hat{\beta} \xleftarrow{\text{U}} \{0,1\}$ given $\varrho_{\hat{\beta}} = (\text{params}_{\mathbb{V}}, g_T, \{\widehat{\mathbb{B}}_\iota, \widehat{\mathbb{B}}_\iota^*\}_{\iota \in [n]}, \{\Upsilon_{\iota,\hat{\beta}}\}_{\iota \in [n]})$; where $\text{params}_{\mathbb{G}} = (q, \mathbb{G}_1, \mathbb{G}_2, \mathbb{G}_T,$ $g_1, g_2, e) \xleftarrow{\text{R}} \mathcal{G}_{\text{BPG}}()$; $\text{params}_{\mathbb{V}} = (q, \mathbb{V}_1, \mathbb{V}_2, \mathbb{G}_T, \mathbb{A}_1, \mathbb{A}_2, e) \xleftarrow{\text{R}} \mathcal{G}_{\text{DPVS}}(2m +$ $2k + 1, \text{params}_{\mathbb{G}})$; $\nu \xleftarrow{\text{U}} \mathbb{F}_q \backslash \{0\}$; $g_T = e(g_1, g_2)^\nu$; $(\mathbb{B}_\iota, \mathbb{B}_\iota^*) \xleftarrow{\text{R}} \mathcal{G}_{\text{OB}}(2m +$ $2k + 1, \text{params}_{\mathbb{V}}, \nu)$; $\widehat{\mathbb{B}}_\iota = \{\boldsymbol{b}_{\iota,1}, \ldots, \boldsymbol{b}_{\iota,2m+1}, \boldsymbol{b}_{\iota,2m+k+1}, \ldots, \boldsymbol{b}_{\iota,2m+2k}\}$, $\widehat{\mathbb{B}}_\iota^* =$ $\{\boldsymbol{b}_{\iota,1}^*, \ldots, \boldsymbol{b}_{\iota,2m+k}^*\}$, for $\iota \in [n]$; $\alpha_1, \ldots, \alpha_k \xleftarrow{\text{U}} \mathbb{F}_q$; $\mathfrak{F} \xleftarrow{\text{U}} \mathbb{F}_q \backslash \{0\}$; and $\Upsilon_{\iota,\hat{\beta}} =$ $(\overrightarrow{0}^{2m+k}, \alpha_1, \ldots, \alpha_k, 0)_{\mathbb{B}_\iota}$ or $(\overrightarrow{0}^{2m+k}, \alpha_1, \ldots, \alpha_k, \mathfrak{F})_{\mathbb{B}_\iota}$ according as $\hat{\beta} = 0$ or 1. For any PPT algorithm $\mathcal{A}$, the advantage of $\mathcal{A}$ in deciding Problem 1 is defined as

$$\text{Adv}_{\mathcal{A}}^{\text{P1}}(\lambda) = \left| \Pr[1 \xleftarrow{\text{R}} \mathcal{A}(\varrho_0)] - \Pr[1 \xleftarrow{\text{R}} \mathcal{A}(\varrho_1)] \right|.$$

Definition 2.6 (Problem 1*): Problem 1* is to guess a bit $\hat{\beta} \xleftarrow{\text{U}} \{0,1\}$ given $\varrho_{\hat{\beta}} = (\text{params}_{\mathbb{V}}, g_T, \{\widehat{\mathbb{B}}_\iota, \widehat{\mathbb{B}}_\iota^*\}_{\iota \in [n]}, \{\Upsilon_{\iota,\hat{\beta}}\}_{\iota \in [n]})$; where $\text{params}_{\mathbb{G}} =$ $(q, \mathbb{G}_1, \mathbb{G}_2, \mathbb{G}_T, g_1, g_2, e) \xleftarrow{\text{R}} \mathcal{G}_{\text{BPG}}()$; $\text{params}_{\mathbb{V}} = (q, \mathbb{V}_1, \mathbb{V}_2, \mathbb{G}_T, \mathbb{A}_1, \mathbb{A}_2, e) \xleftarrow{\text{R}}$ $\mathcal{G}_{\text{DPVS}}(2m + 2k + 1, \text{params}_{\mathbb{G}})$; $\nu \xleftarrow{\text{U}} \mathbb{F}_q \backslash \{0\}$; $g_T = e(g_1, g_2)^\nu$; $(\mathbb{B}_\iota, \mathbb{B}_\iota^*) \xleftarrow{\text{R}} \mathcal{G}_{\text{OB}}(2m +$ $2k + 1, \text{params}_{\mathbb{V}}, \nu)$, for $\iota \in [n]$; $\widehat{\mathbb{B}}_\iota = \{\boldsymbol{b}_{\iota,1}, \ldots, \boldsymbol{b}_{\iota,2m+1}, \boldsymbol{b}_{\iota,2m+k+1}, \ldots, \boldsymbol{b}_{\iota,2m+2k}\}$, $\widehat{\mathbb{B}}_\iota^* = \{\boldsymbol{b}_{\iota,1}^*, \ldots, \boldsymbol{b}_{\iota,2m+k}^*, \boldsymbol{b}_{\iota,2m+2k+1}^*\}$, for $\iota \in [n]$; $\alpha_1, \ldots, \alpha_k \xleftarrow{\text{U}} \mathbb{F}_q$; $\mathfrak{F} \xleftarrow{\text{U}} \mathbb{F}_q \backslash \{0\}$; and $\Upsilon_{\iota,\hat{\beta}} = (\overrightarrow{0}^{2m}, \alpha_1, \ldots, \alpha_k, \overrightarrow{0}^k, 0)_{\mathbb{B}_\iota^*}$ or $(\overrightarrow{0}^{2m}, \alpha_1, \ldots, \alpha_k, \overrightarrow{0}^k, \mathfrak{F})_{\mathbb{B}_\iota^*}$ according as $\hat{\beta} = 0$ or 1, for $\iota \in [n]$. For any PPT algorithm $\mathcal{A}$, the advantage of $\mathcal{A}$ in deciding Problem 1* is defined as

$$\text{Adv}_{\mathcal{A}}^{\text{P1}*}(\lambda) = \left| \Pr[1 \xleftarrow{\text{R}} \mathcal{A}(\varrho_0)] - \Pr[1 \xleftarrow{\text{R}} \mathcal{A}(\varrho_1)] \right|.$$

2.5   Notion of Full-Hiding Multi-input Inner Product Functional Encryption

Definition 2.7 (Multi-input Inner Product Functionality): An unbounded-arity multi-input inner product function family $\mathcal{F}_\lambda^{m,\mathscr{B}} = \{\mathcal{F}_S^{m,\mathscr{B}}\}$, for some $m, \mathscr{B} \in \mathbb{N}$, consists of the sub-families $\mathcal{F}_S^{m,\mathscr{B}}$ of bounded-arity multi-input inner product functions, where each subfamily $\mathcal{F}_S^{m,\mathscr{B}}$ is parameterized with an index set $S \subseteq [t(\lambda)]$ for any polynomial t, and contains functions $f_{\{\overrightarrow{y}_\iota\}_{\iota \in S}} : (\mathbb{Z}^m)^{|S|} \rightarrow \mathbb{Z}$ associated with sets of vectors $\{\overrightarrow{y}_\iota\}_{\iota \in S}$ such that each vector $\overrightarrow{y}_\iota \in \mathbb{Z}^m$, where $f_{\{\overrightarrow{y}_\iota\}_{\iota \in S}}(\{\overrightarrow{x}_\iota\}_{\iota \in S}) = \sum_{\iota \in S} \overrightarrow{x}_\iota \cdot \overrightarrow{y}_\iota$, for all sets of vectors $\{\overrightarrow{x}_\iota\}_{\iota \in S}$ such that each vector $\overrightarrow{x}_\iota \in \mathbb{Z}^m$ and the norm of the inner product $|\overrightarrow{x}_\iota \cdot \overrightarrow{y}_\iota| \leq \mathscr{B}$ for all $\iota \in S$.

Without loss of generality, when dealing with MIFE for some bounded-arity multi-input inner product function family $\mathcal{F}_S^{m,\mathscr{B}}$, we consider the associated index set S to be $[n]$, and denote the function family as $\mathcal{F}_n^{m,\mathscr{B}}$, where $n = |S|$.

Definition 2.8 (Full-Hiding Private Key Bounded-Arity Multi-input Inner Product Functional Encryption: FH-MIPE): A full-hiding private key bounded-arity multi-input inner product functional encryption scheme for an inner product function family $\mathcal{F}_n^{m,\mathscr{B}}$ consists of the following polynomial-time algorithms:

FH-MIPE.Setup($m, n, \mathscr{B}$): This algorithm takes as input the unary encoded security parameter 1^λ, along with the length $m \in \mathbb{N}$ of vectors, the arity $n \in \mathbb{N}$ of the multi-input inner product functionality, and the bound $\mathscr{B} \in \mathbb{N}$ on the size of each component inner products. It generates a master secret key MSK and the corresponding public parameters PP. Observe that we are considering private key setting and hence PP is not sufficient to encrypt. It merely includes some public informations required for decryption, e.g., the group description in a bilinear-map-based construction.

FH-MIPE.KeyGen(PP, MSK, $\{\vec{y}_\iota\}_{\iota \in [n]}$): On input the public parameters PP, the master secret key MSK, along with a set of n vectors $\{\vec{y}_\iota\}_{\iota \in [n]}$ such that $\vec{y}_\iota \in \mathbb{Z}^m$ for all $\iota \in [n]$, this algorithm outputs a decryption key SK.

FH-MIPE.Encrypt(PP, MSK, $\iota, \vec{x}_\iota$): This algorithm upon input the public parameters PP, the master secret key MSK, an index $\iota \in [n]$, and a vector $\vec{x}_\iota \in \mathbb{Z}_p^m$, outputs a ciphertext CT_ι, which includes the index ι in the clear.

FH-MIPE.Decrypt(PP, SK, $\{\text{CT}_\iota\}_{\iota \in [n]}$): On input the public parameters PP, a decryption key SK, along with a set of n ciphertexts $\{\text{CT}_\iota\}_{\iota \in [n]}$, where for all $\iota \in [n]$, CT_ι is a ciphertext prepared for the ιth index, this algorithm either outputs a value $\Lambda \in \mathbb{Z}$ or the distinguished symbol $\perp$ indicating failure.

The algorithm FH-MIPE.Decrypt is deterministic while all the others are probabilistic. The algorithms satisfy the following correctness and security requirements.

■ **Correctness:** An FH-MIPE scheme is correct if for any security parameter $\lambda \in \mathbb{N}$, any polynomial n in λ, any $m, \mathscr{B} \in \mathbb{N}$, any two sets of n vectors $\{\vec{x}_\iota\}_{\iota \in [n]}, \{\vec{y}_\iota\}_{\iota \in [n]}$ such that $\vec{x}_\iota, \vec{y}_\iota \in \mathbb{Z}^m$ with $|\vec{x}_\iota \cdot \vec{y}_\iota| \leq \mathscr{B}$ for all $\iota \in [n]$, we have

$$\Pr\big[\text{FH-MIPE.Decrypt}(\text{PP}, \text{SK}, \{\text{CT}_\iota\}_{\iota \in [n]}) = \sum_{\iota \in [n]} \vec{x}_\iota \cdot \vec{y}_\iota :$$

$$(\text{PP}, \text{MSK}) \xleftarrow{\text{R}} \text{FH-MIPE.Setup}(m, n, \mathscr{B});$$

$$\text{SK} \xleftarrow{\text{R}} \text{FH-MIPE.KeyGen}(\text{PP}, \text{MSK}, \{\vec{y}_\iota\}_{\iota \in [n]});$$

$$\{\text{CT}_\iota \xleftarrow{\text{R}} \text{FH-MIPE.Encrypt}(\text{PP}, \text{MSK}, \iota, \vec{x}_\iota)\}_{\iota \in [n]}\big] \geq 1 - \text{negl}(\lambda),$$

for some negligible function negl.

■ **Full-Hiding Security:** The (indistinguishability-based) full-hiding security notion for a private key bounded-arity FH-MIPE scheme is formalized through the experiment $\mathsf{Expt}_{\mathcal{A}}^{\text{FH-MIPE}}(\beta)$, for random $\beta \xleftarrow{\mathsf{U}} \{0,1\}$, which involves a PPT adversary $\mathcal{A}$ and a PPT challenger $\mathcal{B}$. The experiment is described below:

Setup: $\mathcal{B}$ generates $(\text{PP}, \text{MSK}) \xleftarrow{\mathsf{R}} \mathsf{FH\text{-}MIPE.Setup}(m, n, \mathscr{B})$ and provides PP to $\mathcal{A}$.

Query Phase: $\mathcal{A}$ is allowed to adaptively make any polynomial number of queries of the following two types in arbitrary order:

- *Decryption key query*: In response to the ith decryption key query of $\mathcal{A}$ corresponding to a pair of sets of vectors $(\{\vec{y}_{\iota,i,0}\}_{\iota \in [n]}, \{\vec{y}_{\iota,i,1}\}_{\iota \in [n]})$ such that $\vec{y}_{\iota,i,0}, \vec{y}_{\iota,i,1} \in \mathbb{Z}^m$ for all $\iota \in [n]$, $\mathcal{B}$ forms a decryption key $\text{SK}_i^* \xleftarrow{\mathsf{R}} \mathsf{FH\text{-}MIPE.KeyGen}(\text{PP}, \text{MSK}, \{\vec{y}_{\iota,i,\beta}\}_{\iota \in [n]})$ and hands SK_i^* to $\mathcal{A}$.

- *Ciphertext query*: To answer a ciphertext query of $\mathcal{A}$ for the ιth index corresponding to a pair of vectors $(\vec{x}_{\iota,t_\iota,0}, \vec{x}_{\iota,t_\iota,1}) \in (\mathbb{Z}^m)^2$, $\mathcal{B}$ prepares a ciphertext $\text{CT}_{\iota,t_\iota}^* \xleftarrow{\mathsf{R}} \mathsf{FH\text{-}MIPE.Encrypt}(\text{PP}, \text{MSK}, \vec{x}_{\iota,t_\iota,\beta})$ and gives $\text{CT}_{\iota,t_\iota}^*$ to $\mathcal{A}$.

Let the total number of decryption key query made by $\mathcal{A}$ be $q_{\text{KEY}}(\geq 0)$ and the total number of ciphertext query made for the ιth index be $q_{\text{CT},\iota}(\geq 0)$. The restrictions on the queries of $\mathcal{A}$ are that if $q_{\text{CT},\iota} \geq 1$ for all $\iota \in [n]$, then for all $i \in [q_{\text{KEY}}]$ and for all $(t_1, \ldots, t_n) \in [q_{\text{CT},1}] \times \ldots \times [q_{\text{CT},n}]$, we must have

$$\sum_{\iota \in [n]} \vec{x}_{\iota,t_\iota,0} \cdot \vec{y}_{\iota,i,0} = \sum_{\iota \in [n]} \vec{x}_{\iota,t_\iota,1} \cdot \vec{y}_{\iota,i,1}. \tag{2.1}$$

Guess: $\mathcal{A}$ eventually outputs a guess bit $\beta' \in \{0,1\}$, which is the output of the experiment.

A private key FH-MIPE scheme is said to be full-hiding if for any PPT adversary $\mathcal{A}$, for any security parameter λ, the advantage of $\mathcal{A}$ in the above experiment,

$$\mathsf{Adv}_{\mathcal{A}}^{\text{FH-MIPE}}(\lambda) = \left| \Pr[\mathsf{Expt}_{\mathcal{A}}^{\text{FH-MIPE}}(0) = 1] - \Pr[\mathsf{Expt}_{\mathcal{A}}^{\text{FH-MIPE}}(1) = 1] \right| \leq \mathsf{negl}(\lambda),$$

for some negligible function negl.

Definition 2.9 (Full-Hiding Unbounded Private Key Multi-input Inner Product Functional Encryption: FH-UMIPE): An unbounded full-hiding private key multi-input inner product functional encryption scheme for an inner product function family $\mathcal{F}_{\lambda}^{m,\mathscr{B}}$ consists of the following polynomial-time algorithms:

$\mathsf{FH\text{-}UMIPE.Setup}(m, \mathscr{B})$: This algorithm takes as input the unary encoded security parameter 1^λ, along with the length $m \in \mathbb{N}$ of vectors, and the bound $\mathscr{B} \in \mathbb{N}$ of each inner product values. It generates a master secret key MSK and the corresponding public parameters PP. It publishes PP, while keeps MSK to itself.

FH-UMIPE.KeyGen($\mathrm{PP}, \mathrm{MSK}, S, \{\vec{y}_\iota\}_{\iota \in S}$): On input the public parameters PP, the master secret key MSK, a set of indices $S \subseteq [t(\lambda)]$ where t is any polynomial, along with an $|S|$-tuple of vectors $\{\vec{y}_\iota\}_{\iota \in S} \in (\mathbb{Z}^m)^{|S|}$, this algorithm provides a decryption key SK_S including the set S explicitly.

FH-UMIPE.Encrypt($\mathrm{PP}, \mathrm{MSK}, \iota, \vec{x}_\iota$): On input the public parameters PP, the master secret key MSK, an index $\iota \in [2^\lambda]$, and a vector $\vec{x}_\iota \in \mathbb{Z}^m$, outputs a ciphertext CT_ι, which includes the index ι in the clear.

FH-UMIPE.Decrypt($\mathrm{PP}, \mathrm{SK}_S, \{\mathrm{CT}_\iota\}_{\iota \in S}$): On input the public parameters PP, a decryption key SK_S associated with S, along with a tuple of $|S|$ ciphertexts $\{\mathrm{CT}_\iota\}_{\iota \in S}$, where CT_ι is a ciphertext prepared for the index ι, a decrypter either outputs a value $\Lambda \in \mathbb{N}$ or the distinguished symbol $\bot$ indicating failure.

The algorithm FH-UMIPE.Decrypt is deterministic while all the others are probabilistic. The algorithms satisfy the following correctness and security requirements.

■ **Correctness:** An FH-UMIPE scheme is correct if for any $m, \mathscr{B}, \lambda \in \mathbb{N}$, any set of indices $S \subseteq [t(\lambda)]$, where t is any polynomial, any two $|S|$-tuples of vectors $\{\vec{x}_\iota\}_{\iota \in S}, \{\vec{y}_\iota\}_{\iota \in S} \in (\mathbb{Z}^m)^{|S|}$ with $|\vec{x}_\iota \cdot \vec{y}_\iota| \leq \mathscr{B}$ for all $\iota \in S$, we have

$$\Pr\big[\mathsf{FH\text{-}UMIPE.Decrypt}(\mathrm{PP}, \mathrm{SK}_S, \{\mathrm{CT}_\iota\}_{\iota \in S}) = \sum_{\iota \in S} \vec{x}_\iota \cdot \vec{y}_\iota :$$

$$(\mathrm{PP}, \mathrm{MSK}) \xleftarrow{\mathsf{R}} \mathsf{FH\text{-}UMIPE.Setup}(m, \mathscr{B});$$

$$\mathrm{SK}_S \xleftarrow{\mathsf{R}} \mathsf{FH\text{-}UMIPE.KeyGen}(\mathrm{PP}, \mathrm{MSK}, S, \{\vec{y}_\iota\}_{\iota \in S});$$

$$\{\mathrm{CT}_\iota \xleftarrow{\mathsf{R}} \mathsf{FH\text{-}UMIPE.Encrypt}(\mathrm{PP}, \iota, \vec{x}_\iota)\}_{\iota \in S}\big] \geq 1 - \mathsf{negl}(\lambda)$$

■ **Full-Hiding Security:** The (indistinguishability-based) full-hiding security notion for a private key FH-UMIPE scheme is formalized through the experiment $\mathsf{Expt}_{\mathcal{A}}^{\mathrm{FH\text{-}UMIPE}}(\beta)$, for random $\beta \xleftarrow{\mathsf{U}} \{0, 1\}$, which involves a PPT adversary $\mathcal{A}$ and a PPT challenger $\mathcal{B}$. The experiment is described below:

Setup: $\mathcal{B}$ generates $(\mathrm{PP}, \mathrm{MSK}) \xleftarrow{\mathsf{R}} \mathsf{FH\text{-}UMIPE.Setup}(m, \mathscr{B})$ and gives PP to $\mathcal{A}$.

Query Phase: $\mathcal{A}$ is allowed to adaptively make any polynomial number of queries of the following two types in arbitrary order:

- *Decryption key query*: In response to the ith decryption key query of $\mathcal{A}$ corresponding to a set of indices $S_i \subseteq [t(\lambda)]$ for any polynomial t and a pair of $|S_i|$-tuples of vectors $\{\vec{y}_{\iota,i,0}, \vec{y}_{\iota,i,1}\}_{\iota \in S_i} \in ((\mathbb{Z}^m)^{|S_i|})^2$, $\mathcal{B}$ forms a decryption key $\mathrm{SK}_{S_i,i}^* \xleftarrow{\mathsf{R}} \mathsf{FH\text{-}UMIPE.KeyGen}(\mathrm{PP}, \mathrm{MSK}, S_i, \{\vec{y}_{\iota,i,\beta}\}_{\iota \in S_i})$ and hands $\mathrm{SK}_{S_i,i}^*$ to $\mathcal{A}$.

- *Ciphertext query*: To answer a ciphertext query of $\mathcal{A}$ for the ιth index corresponding to a pair of vectors $(\vec{x}_{\iota,t_\iota,0}, \vec{x}_{\iota,t_\iota,1}) \in (\mathbb{Z}^m)^2$, $\mathcal{B}$ prepares a ciphertext $\mathrm{CT}_{\iota,t_\iota}^* \xleftarrow{\mathsf{R}} \mathsf{UFH.MIPE.Encrypt}(\mathrm{PP}, \mathrm{MSK}, \vec{x}_{\iota,t_\iota,\beta})$ and gives $\mathrm{CT}_{\iota,t_\iota}^*$ to $\mathcal{A}$.

Let the total number of decryption key query made by $\mathcal{A}$ be $q_{\text{KEY}}(\geq 0)$ and the total number of ciphertext query made for the ιth index be $q_{\text{CT},\iota}(\geq 0)$. The restrictions on the queries of $\mathcal{A}$ are that for each $i \in [q_{\text{KEY}}]$, if $q_{\text{CT},\iota} \geq 1$ for all $\iota \in S_i$, then for all $\{t_\iota\}_{\iota \in S_i} \in \prod_{\iota \in S_i}[q_{\text{CT},\iota}]$ we must have $\sum_{\iota \in S_i} \vec{x}_{\iota,t_\iota,0} \cdot \vec{y}_{\iota,i,0} = \sum_{\iota \in S_i} \vec{x}_{\iota,t_\iota,1} \cdot \vec{y}_{\iota,i,1}$.

Guess: $\mathcal{A}$ eventually outputs a guess bit $\beta' \in \{0,1\}$, which is the output of the experiment.

A private key FH-UMIPE scheme is said to be full-hiding if for any PPT adversary $\mathcal{A}$, for any security parameter λ, the advantage of $\mathcal{A}$ in the above experiment,

$$\text{Adv}_{\mathcal{A}}^{\text{FH-UMIPE}}(\lambda) = \left| \Pr[\text{Expt}_{\mathcal{A}}^{\text{FH-UMIPE}}(0) = 1] - \Pr[\text{Expt}_{\mathcal{A}}^{\text{FH-UMIPE}}(1) = 1] \right| \leq \text{negl}(\lambda),$$

for some negligible function negl.

3 The Proposed Full-Hiding Bounded Multi-input Inner Product Functional Encryption Scheme

In this section, we present our FH-MIPE scheme.

3.1 Construction

FH-MIPE.Setup$(m, n, \mathscr{B})$: This algorithm takes as input the unary encoded security parameter 1^λ, the length $m \in \mathbb{N}$ of vectors, the arity $n \in \mathbb{N}$ of the multi-input inner product functionality, and the bound $\mathscr{B} \in \mathbb{N}$ on each component inner product. It proceeds as follows:

1. First, it generates a bilinear group $\text{params}_{\mathbb{G}} = (q, \mathbb{G}_1, \mathbb{G}_2, \mathbb{G}_T, g_1, g_2, e) \xleftarrow{\text{R}} \mathcal{G}_{\text{BPG}}()$ with $q \gg n\mathscr{B}$.

2. Next, it creates $\text{params}_{\mathbb{V}} = (q, \mathbb{V}_1, \mathbb{V}_2, \mathbb{G}_T, \mathbb{A}_1, \mathbb{A}_2, e) \xleftarrow{\text{R}} \mathcal{G}_{\text{DPVS}}(2m + 2k + 1, \text{params}_{\mathbb{G}})$.

3. Then, it samples random $\nu \xleftarrow{\text{U}} \mathbb{F}_q \backslash \{0\}$, and computes $g_T = e(g_1, g_2)^\nu$.

4. After that, for $\iota \in [n]$, it generates $(\mathbb{B}_\iota = \{\boldsymbol{b}_{\iota,1}, \ldots, \boldsymbol{b}_{\iota,2m+2k+1}\}, \mathbb{B}_\iota^* = \{\boldsymbol{b}_{\iota,1}^*, \ldots, \boldsymbol{b}_{\iota,2m+2k+1}^*\}) \xleftarrow{\text{R}} \mathcal{G}_{\text{OB}}(2m + 2k + 1, \text{params}_{\mathbb{V}}, \nu)$ and sets

$$\widehat{\mathbb{B}}_\iota = \{\boldsymbol{b}_{\iota,1}, \ldots, \boldsymbol{b}_{\iota,m}, \boldsymbol{b}_{\iota,2m+1}, \boldsymbol{b}_{\iota,2m+k+1}, \ldots, \boldsymbol{b}_{\iota,2m+2k}\},$$
$$\widehat{\mathbb{B}}_\iota^* = \{\boldsymbol{b}_{\iota,1}^*, \ldots, \boldsymbol{b}_{\iota,m}^*, \boldsymbol{b}_{\iota,2m+1}^*, \ldots, \boldsymbol{b}_{\iota,2m+k}^*\}.$$

5. It publishes the public parameters $\text{PP} = (\text{params}_{\mathbb{V}}, g_T)$, while sets the master secret key $\text{MSK} = \{\widehat{\mathbb{B}}_\iota, \widehat{\mathbb{B}}_\iota^*\}_{\iota \in [n]}$.

FH-MIPE.KeyGen$(\text{PP}, \text{MSK}, \{\vec{y}_\iota\}_{\iota \in [n]})$: On input the public parameters PP, the master secret key MSK, along with a set of n vectors $\{\vec{y}_\iota\}_{\iota \in [n]}$ such that $\vec{y}_\iota \in \mathbb{F}_q^m$, this algorithm executes the following steps:

1. First, it samples random $r_\iota, \gamma_{\iota,1}, \ldots, \gamma_{\iota,k-1} \xleftarrow{\mathsf{U}} \mathbb{F}_q$, for $\iota \in [n]$, subject to the restriction that $\sum_{\iota \in [n]} r_\iota = 0$.

2. Next, for each $\iota \in [n]$, it computes

$$
\begin{aligned}
\boldsymbol{k}_\iota &= \sum_{j \in [m]} y_\iota^{(j)} \boldsymbol{b}_{\iota,j}^* + r_\iota \boldsymbol{b}_{\iota,2m+1}^* + \sum_{j \in [k-1]} \gamma_{\iota,j} \boldsymbol{b}_{\iota,2m+1+j}^* \\
&= (\vec{y}_\iota, \vec{0}^m, r_\iota, \gamma_{\iota,1}, \ldots, \gamma_{\iota,k-1}, \vec{0}^k, 0)_{\mathbb{B}_\iota^*},
\end{aligned}
$$

by making use of $\widehat{\mathbb{B}}_\iota^*$ extracted from MSK.

3. It outputs the decryption key $\mathrm{SK} = \{\boldsymbol{k}_\iota\}_{\iota \in [n]}$.

FH-MIPE.Encrypt($\mathrm{PP}, \mathrm{MSK}, \iota, \vec{x}_\iota$): Taking as input the public parameters PP, the master secret key MSK, an index $\iota \in [n]$, along with a vector $\vec{x}_\iota \in \mathbb{F}_q^m$, this algorithm performs the following steps:

1. It selects random $\varphi_{\iota,1}, \ldots, \varphi_{\iota,k} \xleftarrow{\mathsf{U}} \mathbb{F}_q$, and computes

$$
\begin{aligned}
\boldsymbol{c}_\iota &= \sum_{j \in [m]} x_\iota^{(j)} \boldsymbol{b}_{\iota,j} + \boldsymbol{b}_{\iota,2m+1} + \sum_{j \in [k]} \varphi_{\iota,j} \boldsymbol{b}_{\iota,2m+k+j} \\
&= (\vec{x}_\iota, \vec{0}^m, 1, \vec{0}^{k-1}, \varphi_{\iota,1}, \ldots, \varphi_{\iota,k}, 0)_{\mathbb{B}_\iota},
\end{aligned}
$$

by utilizing $\widehat{\mathbb{B}}_\iota$ extracted from MSK.

2. It outputs the ciphertext $\mathrm{CT}_\iota = (\iota, \boldsymbol{c}_\iota)$.

FH-MIPE.Decrypt($\mathrm{PP}, \mathrm{SK}, \{\mathrm{CT}_\iota\}_{\iota \in [n]}$): This algorithm takes as input the public parameters PP, a decryption key $\mathrm{SK} = \{\boldsymbol{k}_\iota\}_{\iota \in [n]}$, and a set of n ciphertexts $\{\mathrm{CT}_\iota = (\iota, \boldsymbol{c}_\iota)\}_{\iota \in [n]}$. It does the following:

1. It first computes $L_T = \prod_{\iota \in [n]} e(\boldsymbol{c}_\iota, \boldsymbol{k}_\iota)$.

2. Then, it attempts to determine a value $\Lambda \in \mathbb{Z}$ such that $g_T^\Lambda = L_T$ by performing an exhaustive search over a specified polynomial-size range of possible values. If it succeeds, then it outputs Λ. Otherwise, it outputs $\bot$ indicating failure.

We emphasize that the polynomial running time of our decryption algorithm is guaranteed by restricting the output to lie within a fixed polynomial-size range. Note that similar exhaustive search step is used to determine the output in the decryption algorithm of all bilinear-map-based IPE constructions (both single and multi-input) available in the literature.

Remark 3.1: We would like to mention here that the FH-MIPE scheme described above can be proven to achieve the full-hiding security only when the adversary makes at least one ciphertext query for each of the n encryption indices, i.e., the restriction Eq. (2.1) is applicable. However, using a semantically secure SKE scheme, one can generically transform any FH-MIPE scheme that achieves full-hiding security under such restriction to one that achieves the full-hiding security even when the adversary makes no ciphertext query for some of the encryption slots. The transformation is rather straightforward and is presented in the full version of this paper.

■ **Correctness:** The correctness of the above FH-MIPE construction can be verified as follows: Observe that for any set of n ciphertexts $\{\mathrm{CT}_\iota = (\iota, \boldsymbol{c}_\iota)\}_{\iota \in [n]}$, where $\mathrm{CT}_\iota = (\iota, \boldsymbol{c}_\iota)$ encrypts some vector $\vec{x}_\iota \in \mathbb{F}_q^m$ with respect to the index ι, for $\iota \in [n]$, and any decryption key $\mathrm{SK} = \{\boldsymbol{k}_\iota\}_{\iota \in [n]}$ corresponding to a set of n vectors $\{\vec{y}_\iota\}_{\iota \in [n]}$ such that $\vec{y}_\iota \in \mathbb{F}_q^m$ for all $\iota \in [n]$, we have

$$L_T = \prod_{\iota \in [n]} e(\boldsymbol{c}_\iota, \boldsymbol{k}_\iota) = g_T^{\sum\limits_{\iota \in [n]} \vec{x}_\iota \cdot \vec{y}_\iota} .$$

This follows from the expressions of $\boldsymbol{c}_\iota, \boldsymbol{k}_\iota$, for $\iota \in [n]$, in conjunction with the fact that for each $\iota \in [n]$, $\mathbb{B}_\iota$ and $\mathbb{B}_\iota^*$ are dual orthogonal bases. Thus, if $\sum\limits_{\iota \in [n]} \vec{x}_\iota \cdot \vec{y}_\iota$ is contained within the specified polynomial-size range of possible values that the decryption algorithm searches, then the decryption algorithm would definitely output $\Lambda = \sum\limits_{\iota \in [n]} \vec{x}_\iota \cdot \vec{y}_\iota$ as desired.

3.2 Security

Theorem 3.1 (Security of our FH-MIPE Scheme): *Assume that the k-LIN problem is hard. Then, the FH-MIPE construction described above achieves full-hiding security under the restriction that the adversary makes at least one ciphertext query for each encryption index. Additionally, assuming the existance of a semantically secure SKE scheme, we can generically convert the above FH-MIPE scheme to one that achieves full-hiding security without any restriction on the number of ciphertext queries per encryption slot. More formally, for any PPT adversary $\mathcal{A}$ against the full-hiding security of the FH-MIPE construction obtained by generically converting the above FH-MIPE scheme with the help of an SKE scheme, there exists a PPT algorithm $\mathcal{B}_1$ against the k-LIN problem and a PPT adversary $\mathcal{B}_2$ against the simantic security of SKE such that for any security parameter λ, we have*

$$\mathsf{Adv}_{\mathcal{A}}^{\mathrm{FH\text{-}MIPE}}(\lambda) \leq [4 \sum_{\iota \in [n]} q_{\mathrm{CT},\iota} + 2q_{\mathrm{KEY}}]\mathsf{Adv}_{\mathcal{B}_1}^{k\text{-}\mathrm{LIN}}(\lambda) + \mathsf{Adv}_{\mathcal{B}_2}^{\mathrm{SKE}}(\lambda).$$

Proof: Here, we only proof the hull-hiding security of the above FH-MIPE scheme under the restriction that the adversary makes at least one ciphertext query per encryption slot. The proof is structured as a hybrid argument over a series of experiments which differ in the construction of the decryption keys and/or ciphertexts queried by the adversary $\mathcal{A}$ in the full-hiding security model described in Definition 2.8. In the first hybrid experiment, the queried decryption keys and ciphertexts are constructed as those in the security experiment $\mathsf{Expt}_{\mathcal{A}}^{\mathrm{FH\text{-}MIPE}}(0)$. We then progressively change the ciphertexts and decryption keys in multiple hybrid steps to those in the security experiment $\mathsf{Expt}_{\mathcal{A}}^{\mathrm{FH\text{-}MIPE}}(1)$. We prove that each hybrid is indistinguishable from the previous one, thus proving the full-hiding security of the above FH-MIPE construction. Let q_{KEY} be the number of $\mathcal{A}$'s decryption key queries and $q_{\mathrm{CT},\iota}$ (≥ 1), for $\iota \in [n]$, be the number of $\mathcal{A}$'s ciphertext queries for the ιth index. As noted earlier, we consider $q_{\mathrm{CT},\iota} \geq 1$ for all $\iota \in [n]$. The hybrid experiments are described below. In these hybrids, a part framed by a box indicates those terms which were modified in the transition from the previous game. The sequence of hybrid experiments follow:

▶ **Sequence of Hybrid Experiments**

Hyb$_0$: This experiment corresponds to the experiment $\mathsf{Expt}_{\mathcal{A}}^{\mathrm{FH\text{-}MIPE}}(0)$ described in Definition 2.8, i.e., the full-hiding security experiment where the random bit used by the challenger $\mathcal{B}$ to generate queried ciphertexts and decryption keys is $\beta = 0$. More precisely, for all $\iota \in [n], t_\iota \in [q_{\mathrm{CT},\iota}]$, in response to the t_ι^{th} ciphertext query of $\mathcal{A}$ with respect to index ι corresponding to pair of vectors $(\overrightarrow{x}_{\iota,t_\iota,0}, \overrightarrow{x}_{\iota,t_\iota,1}) \in (\mathbb{F}_q^m)^2$, $\mathcal{B}$ returns $\mathrm{CT}_{\iota,t_\iota}^* = (\iota, \boldsymbol{c}_{\iota,t_\iota}^*)$, where

$$\boldsymbol{c}_{\iota,t_\iota}^* = (\overrightarrow{x}_{\iota,t_\iota,0}, \overrightarrow{0}^m, 1, \overrightarrow{0}^{k-1}, \varphi_{\iota,t_\iota,1}, \ldots, \varphi_{\iota,t_\iota,k}, 0)_{\mathbb{B}_\iota}, \tag{3.1}$$

and for all $i \in [q_{\mathrm{KEY}}]$, to answer the ith decryption key query of $\mathcal{A}$ corresponding to pair of sets of n vectors $(\{\overrightarrow{y}_{\iota,i,0}\}_{\iota \in [n]}, \{\overrightarrow{y}_{\iota,i,1}\}_{\iota \in [n]})$ such that $\overrightarrow{y}_{\iota,i,0}, \overrightarrow{y}_{\iota,i,1} \in \mathbb{F}_q^m$, $\mathcal{B}$ generates $\mathrm{SK}_i^* = \{\boldsymbol{k}_{\iota,i}^*\}_{\iota \in [n]}$, where

$$\boldsymbol{k}_{\iota,i}^* = (\overrightarrow{y}_{\iota,i,0}, \overrightarrow{0}^m, r_{\iota,i}, \gamma_{\iota,i,1}, \ldots, \gamma_{\iota,i,k-1}, \overrightarrow{0}^k, 0)_{\mathbb{B}_\iota^*}, \text{ for } \iota \in [n]. \tag{3.2}$$

Here, $\mathsf{params}_{\mathbb{G}} = (q, \mathbb{G}_1, \mathbb{G}_2, \mathbb{G}_T, g_1, g_2, e) \xleftarrow{\mathrm{R}} \mathcal{G}_{\mathrm{BPG}}()$; $\mathsf{params}_{\mathbb{V}} = (q, \mathbb{V}_1, \mathbb{V}_2, \mathbb{G}_T, \mathbb{A}_1, \mathbb{A}_2, e) \xleftarrow{\mathrm{R}} \mathcal{G}_{\mathrm{DPVS}}(2m + 2k + 1, \mathsf{params}_{\mathbb{G}})$; $\nu \xleftarrow{\mathrm{U}} \mathbb{F}_q \backslash \{0\}$; $(\mathbb{B}_\iota, \mathbb{B}_\iota^*) \xleftarrow{\mathrm{R}} \mathcal{G}_{\mathrm{OB}}(2m + 2k + 1, \mathsf{params}_{\mathbb{V}}, \nu)$, for $\iota \in [n]$; and $\varphi_{\iota,t_\iota,1}, \ldots, \varphi_{\iota,t_\iota,k}, r_{\iota,i}, \gamma_{\iota,i,1}, \ldots, \gamma_{\iota,i,k-1} \xleftarrow{\mathrm{U}} \mathbb{F}_q$ for all $\iota \in [n], t_\iota \in [q_{\mathrm{CT},\iota}], i \in [q_{\mathrm{KEY}}]$, such that $\sum_{\iota \in [n]} r_{\iota,i} = 0$ for all $i \in [q_{\mathrm{KEY}}]$.

Hyb$_1$ Sequence

Hyb$_{1,\iota^*,\mu_{\iota^*},1}$ $(\iota^* \in [n], \mu_{\iota^*} \in [q_{\mathrm{CT},\iota^*}])$: $\mathsf{Hyb}_{1,0,q_{\mathrm{CT},0},3}$ coincides with Hyb_0. This experiment is the same as $\mathsf{Hyb}_{1,\iota^*-1,q_{\mathrm{CT},\iota^*-1},3}$, if $\mu_{\iota^*} = 1$, or $\mathsf{Hyb}_{1,\iota^*,\mu_{\iota^*}-1,3}$, if $\mu_{\iota^*} > 1$, with the only exception that in response to the $\mu_{\iota^*}^{\mathrm{th}}$ ciphertext query of $\mathcal{A}$ with respect to index ι^* corresponding to pair of vectors $(\overrightarrow{x}_{\iota^*,\mu_{\iota^*},0}, \overrightarrow{x}_{\iota^*,\mu_{\iota^*},1}) \in (\mathbb{F}_q^m)^2$, $\mathcal{B}$ returns $\mathrm{CT}_{\iota^*,\mu_{\iota^*}}^* = (\iota^*, \boldsymbol{c}_{\iota^*,\mu_{\iota^*}}^*)$, where

$$\boldsymbol{c}_{\iota^*,\mu_{\iota^*}}^* = (\overrightarrow{x}_{\iota^*,\mu_{\iota^*},0}, \overrightarrow{0}^m, 1, \overrightarrow{0}^{k-1}, \varphi_{\iota^*,\mu_{\iota^*},1}, \ldots, \varphi_{\iota^*,\mu_{\iota^*},k}, \boxed{\rho_{\iota^*,\mu_{\iota^*}}})_{\mathbb{B}_{\iota^*}}. \tag{3.3}$$

Here, $\rho_{\iota^*,\mu_{\iota^*}} \xleftarrow{\mathrm{U}} \mathbb{F}_q \backslash \{0\}$, and the other variables are formed as in $\mathsf{Hyb}_{1,\iota^*-1,q_{\mathrm{CT},\iota^*-1},3}$ or $\mathsf{Hyb}_{1,\iota^*,\mu_{\iota^*}-1,3}$ according as $\mu_{\iota^*} = 1$ or $\mu_{\iota^*} > 1$.

Hyb$_{1,\iota^*,\mu_{\iota^*},2}$ $(\iota^* \in [n], \mu_{\iota^*} \in [q_{\mathrm{CT},\iota^*}])$: This experiment is analogous to $\mathsf{Hyb}_{1,\iota^*,\mu_{\iota^*},1}$ except that to answer the $\mu_{\iota^*}^{\mathrm{th}}$ ciphertext query of $\mathcal{A}$ with respect to index ι^* corresponding to pair of vectors $(\vec{x}_{\iota^*,\mu_{\iota^*},0}, \vec{x}_{\iota^*,\mu_{\iota^*},1}) \in (\mathbb{F}_q^m)^2$, $\mathcal{B}$ generates $\mathrm{CT}^*_{\iota^*,\mu_{\iota^*}} = (\iota^*, \boldsymbol{c}^*_{\iota^*,\mu_{\iota^*}})$, where

$$\boldsymbol{c}^*_{\iota^*,\mu_{\iota^*}} = (\vec{x}_{\iota^*,\mu_{\iota^*},0}, \boxed{\vec{x}_{\iota^*,\mu_{\iota^*},1}}, 1, \vec{0}^{k-1}, \varphi_{\iota^*,\mu_{\iota^*},1}, \ldots, \varphi_{\iota^*,\mu_{\iota^*},k}, \rho_{\iota^*,\mu_{\iota^*}})_{\mathbb{B}_{\iota^*}}. \quad (3.4)$$

Here, all the variables are created as in $\mathsf{Hyb}_{1,\iota^*,\mu_{\iota^*},1}$.

$\mathsf{Hyb}_{1,\iota^*,\mu_{\iota^*},3}$ $(\iota^* \in [n], \mu_{\iota^*} \in [q_{\mathrm{CT},\iota^*}])$: This experiment is exactly identical to $\mathsf{Hyb}_{1,\iota^*,\mu_{\iota^*},2}$ with the only exception that in response to the $\mu_{\iota^*}^{\mathrm{th}}$ ciphertext query of $\mathcal{A}$ with respect to the index ι^* corresponding to pair of vectors $(\vec{x}_{\iota^*,\mu_{\iota^*},0}, \vec{x}_{\iota^*,\mu_{\iota^*},1}) \in (\mathbb{F}_q^m)^2$, $\mathcal{B}$ returns $\mathrm{CT}^*_{\iota^*,\mu_{\iota^*}} = (\iota^*, \boldsymbol{c}^*_{\iota^*,\mu_{\iota^*}})$, where

$$\boldsymbol{c}^*_{\iota^*,\mu_{\iota^*}} = (\vec{x}_{\iota^*,\mu_{\iota^*},0}, \vec{x}_{\iota^*,\mu_{\iota^*},1}, 1, \vec{0}^{k-1}, \varphi_{\iota^*,\mu_{\iota^*},1}, \ldots, \varphi_{\iota^*,\mu_{\iota^*},k}, \boxed{0})_{\mathbb{B}_{\iota^*}}. \quad (3.5)$$

Here, all the variables are created as in $\mathsf{Hyb}_{1,\iota^*,\mu_{\iota^*},2}$.

Hyb_2 Sequence

$\mathsf{Hyb}_{2,\upsilon,1}$ $(\upsilon \in [q_{\mathrm{KEY}}])$: $\mathsf{Hyb}_{2,0,3}$ coincides with $\mathsf{Hyb}_{1,n,q_{\mathrm{CT},n},3}$. This experiment is analogous to $\mathsf{Hyb}_{2,\upsilon-1,3}$ with the only exception that in response to the υth decryption key query of $\mathcal{A}$ corresponding to the pair of sets of n vectors $(\{\vec{y}_{\iota,\upsilon,0}\}_{\iota\in[n]}, \{\vec{y}_{\iota,\upsilon,1}\}_{\iota\in[n]})$ such that $\vec{y}_{\iota,\upsilon,0}, \vec{y}_{\iota,\upsilon,1} \in \mathbb{F}_q^m$ for all $\iota \in [n]$, $\mathcal{B}$ gives back $\mathrm{SK}^*_\upsilon = \{\boldsymbol{k}^*_{\iota,\upsilon}\}_{\iota\in[n]}$, where

$$\boldsymbol{k}^*_{\iota,\upsilon} = (\vec{y}_{\iota,\upsilon,0}, \vec{0}^m, r_{\iota,\upsilon}, \gamma_{\iota,\upsilon,1}, \ldots, \gamma_{\iota,\upsilon,k-1}, \vec{0}^k, \boxed{\omega_{\iota,\upsilon}})_{\mathbb{B}^*_\iota}, \text{ for } \iota \in [n]. \quad (3.6)$$

Here, $\omega_{\iota,\upsilon} \xleftarrow{\mathsf{U}} \mathbb{F}_q \backslash \{0\}$ for all $\iota \in [n]$, such that $\sum\limits_{\iota\in[n]} \omega_{\iota,\upsilon} = 0$, and all the other variables are generated as in $\mathsf{Hyb}_{2,\upsilon-1,3}$.

$\mathsf{Hyb}_{2,\upsilon,2}$ $(\upsilon \in [q_{\mathrm{KEY}}])$: This experiment is identical to $\mathsf{Hyb}_{2,\upsilon,1}$ except that in response to the υth decryption key query of $\mathcal{A}$ corresponding to the pair of sets of n vectors $(\{\vec{y}_{\iota,\upsilon,0}\}_{\iota\in[n]}, \{\vec{y}_{\iota,\upsilon,1}\}_{\iota\in[n]})$ such that $\vec{y}_{\iota,\upsilon,0}, \vec{y}_{\iota,\upsilon,1} \in \mathbb{F}_q^m$, $\mathcal{B}$ returns $\mathrm{SK}^*_\upsilon = \{\boldsymbol{k}^*_{\iota,\upsilon}\}_{\iota\in[n]}$, where

$$\boldsymbol{k}^*_{\iota,\upsilon} = (\boxed{\vec{0}^m, \vec{y}_{\iota,\upsilon,1}, \widetilde{r}_{\iota,\upsilon}}, \gamma_{\iota,\upsilon,1}, \ldots, \gamma_{\iota,\upsilon,k-1}, \vec{0}^k, \omega_{\iota,\upsilon})_{\mathbb{B}^*_\iota}, \text{ for } \iota \in [n]. \quad (3.7)$$

Here, $\widetilde{r}_{\iota,\upsilon} \xleftarrow{\mathsf{U}} \mathbb{F}_q$ for all $\iota \in [n]$, such that $\sum\limits_{\iota\in[n]} \widetilde{r}_{\iota,\upsilon} = 0$, and all the variables are generated as in $\mathsf{Hyb}_{2,\upsilon,1}$.

$\mathsf{Hyb}_{2,\upsilon,3}$ $(\upsilon \in [q_{\mathrm{KEY}}])$: This experiment is analogous to $\mathsf{Hyb}_{2,\upsilon,2}$ except that to answer the υth decryption key query of $\mathcal{A}$ corresponding to the pair of sets of n vectors $(\{\vec{y}_{\iota,\upsilon,0}\}_{\iota\in[n]}, \{\vec{y}_{\iota,\upsilon,1}\}_{\iota\in[n]})$ such that $\vec{y}_{\iota,\upsilon,0}, \vec{y}_{\iota,\upsilon,1} \in \mathbb{F}_q^m$, $\mathcal{B}$ gives back $\mathrm{SK}^*_\upsilon = \{\boldsymbol{k}^*_{\iota,\upsilon}\}_{\iota\in[n]}$, where

$$\boldsymbol{k}^*_{\iota,\upsilon} = (\vec{0}^m, \vec{y}_{\iota,\upsilon,1}, \widetilde{r}_{\iota,\upsilon}, \gamma_{\iota,\upsilon,1}, \ldots, \gamma_{\iota,\upsilon,k-1}, \vec{0}^k, \boxed{0})_{\mathbb{B}^*_\iota}, \text{ for } \iota \in [n]. \quad (3.8)$$

Here, all the variables are generated as in $\mathsf{Hyb}_{2,\upsilon,2}$.

Hyb$_3$: This experiment is identical to Hyb$_{2,q_{\text{KEY}},3}$ with the only exception that for all $\iota \in [n], t_\iota \in [q_{\text{CT},\iota}]$, in response to the t_ι^{th} ciphertext query of $\mathcal{A}$ with respect to index ι corresponding to pair of vectors $(\overrightarrow{x}_{\iota,t_\iota,0}, \overrightarrow{x}_{\iota,t_\iota,1}) \in (\mathbb{F}_q^m)^2$, $\mathcal{B}$ returns $\text{CT}^*_{\iota,t_\iota} = (\iota, \boldsymbol{c}^*_{\iota,t_\iota})$, where

$$\boldsymbol{c}^*_{\iota,t_\iota} = (\boxed{\overrightarrow{x}_{\iota,t_\iota,1}, \overrightarrow{x}_{\iota,t_\iota,0}}, 1, \overrightarrow{0}^{k-1}, \varphi_{\iota,t_\iota,1}, \ldots, \varphi_{\iota,t_\iota,k}, 0)_{\mathbb{B}_\iota}, \tag{3.9}$$

and for all $i \in [q_{\text{KEY}}]$, to answer the ith decryption key query of $\mathcal{A}$ corresponding to pair of sets of n vectors $(\{\overrightarrow{y}_{\iota,i,0}\}_{\iota \in [n]}, \{\overrightarrow{y}_{\iota,i,1}\}_{\iota \in [n]})$ such that $\overrightarrow{y}_{\iota,i,0}, \overrightarrow{y}_{\iota,i,1} \in \mathbb{F}_q^m$, $\mathcal{B}$ generates $\text{SK}^*_i = \{\boldsymbol{k}^*_{\iota,i}\}_{\iota \in [n]}$, where

$$\boldsymbol{k}^*_{\iota,i} = (\boxed{\overrightarrow{y}_{\iota,i,1}, \overrightarrow{0}^m}, \widetilde{r}_{\iota,i}, \gamma_{\iota,i,1}, \ldots, \gamma_{\iota,i,k-1}, \overrightarrow{0}^k, 0)_{\mathbb{B}^*_\iota}, \text{ for } \iota \in [n]. \tag{3.10}$$

Here, all the variables are generated as in Hyb$_{2,q_{\text{KEY}},3}$.

Hyb$_4$: This experiment corresponds to the experiment $\text{Expt}_{\mathcal{A}}^{\text{FH-MIPE}}(1)$ described in Definition 2.8, i.e., the full-hiding security experiment where the random bit used by $\mathcal{B}$ to generate the ciphertexts and decryption keys queried by $\mathcal{A}$ is $\beta = 1$.

► **Analysis**

Let us now denote by $\text{Adv}_{\mathcal{A}}^{(h)}(\lambda)$ the advantage of the adversary $\mathcal{A}$, i.e., $\mathcal{A}$'s probability of outputting 1 in Hyb$_h$, for $h \in \{0, \{1, \iota^*, \mu_{\iota^*}, \jmath\}_{\iota^* \in [n], \mu_{\iota^*} \in [q_{\text{CT},\iota^*}], \jmath \in [3]}, \{2, \upsilon, \jmath\}_{\upsilon \in [q_{\text{KEY}}], \jmath \in [3]}, 3, 4\}$. Then, by the definitions of hybrids, we clearly have $\text{Adv}_{\mathcal{A}}^{(0)}(\lambda) \equiv \Pr[\text{Expt}_{\mathcal{A}}^{\text{FH-MIPE}}(0) = 1]$, $\text{Adv}_{\mathcal{A}}^{(1,0,q_{\text{CT}},0,3)}(\lambda) \equiv \text{Adv}_{\mathcal{A}}^{(0)}(\lambda)$, $\text{Adv}_{\mathcal{A}}^{(2,0,3)}(\lambda) \equiv \text{Adv}_{\mathcal{A}}^{(1,n,q_{\text{CT}},n,3)}(\lambda)$, and $\text{Adv}_{\mathcal{A}}^{(4)}(\lambda) \equiv \Pr[\text{Expt}_{\mathcal{A}}^{\text{FH-MIPE}}(1) = 1]$. Also, observe that the transition from Hyb$_3$ to Hyb$_4$ is essentially the reverse transition of the Hyb$_1$ sequence of hybrids with $\overrightarrow{x}_{\iota^*,\mu_{\iota^*},0}$ and $\overrightarrow{x}_{\iota^*,\mu_{\iota^*},1}$ interchanged. Therefore, it follows that

$$\begin{aligned}
\text{Adv}_{\mathcal{A}}^{\text{FH-MIPE}}(\lambda) \leq 2 \sum_{\iota^* \in [n]} & \left[|\text{Adv}_{\mathcal{A}}^{(1,\iota^*-1,q_{\text{CT}},\iota^*-1,3)}(\lambda) - \text{Adv}_{\mathcal{A}}^{(1,\iota^*,1,1)}(\lambda)| \right. \\
& + \sum_{\mu_{\iota^*} \in [2,q_{\text{CT}},\iota^*]} |\text{Adv}_{\mathcal{A}}^{(1,\iota^*,\mu_{\iota^*}-1,3)}(\lambda) - \text{Adv}_{\mathcal{A}}^{(1,\iota^*,\mu_{\iota^*},1)}(\lambda)| \\
& + \sum_{\mu_{\iota^*} \in [q_{\text{CT}},\iota^*], \jmath \in [2,3]} |\text{Adv}_{\mathcal{A}}^{(1,\iota^*,\mu_{\iota^*},\jmath-1)}(\lambda) - \text{Adv}_{\mathcal{A}}^{(1,\iota^*,\mu_{\iota^*},\jmath)}(\lambda)| \right] \\
& + \sum_{\upsilon \in [q_{\text{KEY}}]} \left[|\text{Adv}_{\mathcal{A}}^{(2,\upsilon-1,3)}(\lambda) - \text{Adv}_{\mathcal{A}}^{(2,\upsilon,1)}(\lambda)| \right. \\
& + \sum_{\jmath \in [2,3]} |\text{Adv}_{\mathcal{A}}^{(2,\upsilon,\jmath-1)}(\lambda) - \text{Adv}_{\mathcal{A}}^{(2,\upsilon,\jmath)}(\lambda)| \right] \\
& + |\text{Adv}_{\mathcal{A}}^{(2,q_{\text{KEY}},3)}(\lambda) - \text{Adv}_{\mathcal{A}}^{(3)}(\lambda)|.
\end{aligned} \tag{3.11}$$

The fact that each term on the RHS of Eq. (3.11) is negligible is formally argued in a sequence of lemmas presented in the full version of this paper. This completes the proof of Theorem 3.1. □

4   The Proposed Full-Hiding Unbounded Multi-input Inner Product Functional Encryption Scheme

In this section, we present our FH-UMIPE scheme.

4.1   Construction

For the simplicity, we consider the scheme based on the SXDH(1-Lin) in this section. However, it is clear that we can instantiate our FH-UMIPE scheme from k-Lin assumption. We also consider the case where the vector length m is polynomial in λ. Let $F_1 : \{0,1\}^\lambda \times \{0,1\}^\lambda \to \mathbb{F}_q^{(2m+3) \times (2m+3)}$ and $F_2 : \{0,1\}^\lambda \times \{0,1\}^\lambda \to \{0,1\}^\lambda$ be pseudorandom functions and (SKE.KeyGen, SKE.Encrypt, SKE.Decrypt) be a semantically secure secret key encryption scheme whose secret key space is $\{0,1\}^\lambda$. We require that SKE.KeyGen outputs a randomly chosen λ-bit string as a secret key K, i.e., $K \xleftarrow{\mathsf{U}} \{0,1\}^\lambda$. We abuse the notation such that for a set of N vectors of M dimensional DPVS $\mathbb{D} = (\boldsymbol{d}_1, \ldots, \boldsymbol{d}_N)$ and $W \in \mathsf{GL}(M, \mathbb{F}_q)$, $\mathbb{B} = \mathbb{D}W$ denotes $\mathbb{B} = (\boldsymbol{d}_1 W, \ldots, \boldsymbol{d}_N W)$.

FH-UMIPE.Setup$(m, \mathscr{B})$: It takes as input the unary encoded security parameter 1^λ, the length $m \in \mathbb{N}$ of vectors, and the bound $\mathscr{B} \in \mathbb{N}$. It proceeds as follows:

1. First, it generates a bilinear group $\mathsf{params}_\mathbb{G} = (q, \mathbb{G}_1, \mathbb{G}_2, \mathbb{G}_T, g_1, g_2, e) \xleftarrow{\mathsf{R}} \mathcal{G}_{\mathrm{BPG}}()$ with q a λ-bit prime.

2. Next, it forms $\mathsf{params}_\mathbb{V} = (q, \mathbb{V}_1, \mathbb{V}_2, \mathbb{G}_T, \mathbb{A}_1, \mathbb{A}_2, e) \xleftarrow{\mathsf{R}} \mathcal{G}_{\mathrm{DPVS}}(2m + 3, \mathsf{params}_\mathbb{G})$, samples $\nu \xleftarrow{\mathsf{U}} \mathbb{F}_q \backslash \{0\}$, computes $g_T = e(g_1, g_2)^\nu$, generates $(\mathbb{D}, \mathbb{D}^*) \xleftarrow{\mathsf{R}} \mathcal{G}_{\mathrm{OB}}(2m + 3, \mathsf{params}_\mathbb{V}, \nu)$, and samples PRF keys $K_1, K_2 \xleftarrow{\mathsf{U}} \{0,1\}^\lambda$. Then it sets $\widehat{\mathbb{D}} = (\boldsymbol{d}_1, \ldots, \boldsymbol{d}_m, \boldsymbol{d}_{2m+1}, \boldsymbol{d}_{2m+2}), \widehat{\mathbb{D}}^* = (\boldsymbol{d}_1^*, \ldots, \boldsymbol{d}_m^*, \boldsymbol{d}_{2m+1}^*)$.

3. It publishes the public parameters $\mathrm{PP} = (\mathsf{params}_\mathbb{V}, g_T)$, while keeps the master secret key $\mathrm{MSK} = (K_1, K_2, \widehat{\mathbb{D}}, \widehat{\mathbb{D}}^*)$.

FH-UMIPE.KeyGen$(\mathrm{PP}, \mathrm{MSK}, S, \{\vec{y}_\iota\}_{\iota \in S})$: On input the public parameters PP, the master secret key MSK, a set of indices $S \subseteq [t(\lambda)]$ for any polynomial t, along with a $|S|$-tuple of vectors $\{\vec{y}_\iota\}_{\iota \in S} \in (\mathbb{Z}^m)^{|S|}$, this algorithm executes the following steps:

1. First, it creates random dual orthogonal bases for the index $\iota \in S$ as follows;

$$W_\iota = F_1(K_1, \iota), \quad \mathbb{B}_\iota^* = \mathbb{D}^* W_\iota^*.$$

If W_ι for some $\iota \in S$ is not a regular matrix, then it outputs $\bot$ and halts.

2. Next, for each $\iota \in S$, it computes decryption keys similarly to the bounded case;

$$\{r_\iota\}_{\iota \in S} \xleftarrow{\mathsf{U}} \mathbb{F}_q \text{ s.t. } \sum_{\iota \in S} r_\iota = 0, \quad \boldsymbol{k}_\iota = (\vec{y}_\iota, \vec{0}^m, r_\iota, \vec{0}^2)_{\mathbb{B}_\iota^*}.$$

3. Let s_j be the jth element of S in ascending order. Then it iteratively encrypts the decryption keys by symmetric key encryption as

$$C_1 = \text{SKE.Encrypt}(F_2(K_2, s_1), \{\boldsymbol{k}_\iota\}_{\iota \in S}),$$
$$C_2 = \text{SKE.Encrypt}(F_2(K_2, s_2), C_1),$$

$$\vdots$$

$$C_{|S|} = \text{SKE.Encrypt}(F_2(K_2, s_{|S|}), C_{|S|-1}),$$

and outputs $\text{SK}_S = (C_{|S|}, S)$ as a decryption key for FH-UMIPE.

FH-UMIPE.Encrypt($\text{PP}, \text{MSK}, \iota, \vec{x}_\iota$): Taking as input the public parameters PP, the master secret key MSK, an index $\iota \in [2^\lambda]$, along with a vector $\vec{x}_\iota \in \mathbb{Z}^m$, this algorithm performs the following steps:

1. First, it creates random dual orthogonal bases for the index ι as follows;

$$W_\iota = F_1(K_1, \iota), \quad \mathbb{B}_\iota = \mathbb{D}W_\iota.$$

If W_ι is not a regular matrix, then it outputs $\bot$ and halts.

2. Otherwise, it selects random $\kappa_\iota \xleftarrow{\text{U}} \mathbb{F}_q$, computes

$$\boldsymbol{c}_\iota = (\vec{x}_\iota, \vec{0}^m, 1, \kappa_\iota, 0)_{\mathbb{B}_\iota}, \quad k_\iota = F_2(K_2, \iota),$$

and outputs the ciphertext $\text{CT}_\iota = (\boldsymbol{c}_\iota, k_\iota, \iota)$.

FH-UMIPE.Decrypt($\text{PP}, \text{SK}_S, \{\text{CT}_\iota\}_{\iota \in S}$): A decrypter takes as input the public parameters PP, a decryption key SK_S for a set S, and a tuple of $|S|$ ciphertexts $\{\text{CT}_\iota\}_{\iota \in S}$. It does the following:

1. It first decrypts decryption keys as follows;

$$C'_{|S|-1} = \text{SKE.Decrypt}(k_{s_{|S|}}, C_{|S|}),$$

$$\vdots$$

$$C'_1 = \text{SKE.Decrypt}(k_{s_2}, C'_2),$$
$$\{\boldsymbol{k}'_\iota\}_{\iota \in S} = \text{SKE.Decrypt}(k_{s_1}, C'_1).$$

2. Next, it computes $L_T = \prod\limits_{\iota \in S} e(\boldsymbol{c}_\iota, \boldsymbol{k}'_\iota)$.

3. Then, it attempts to determine a value $\Lambda \in \mathbb{N}$ such that $g_T^\Lambda = L_T$ by performing an exhaustive search over a specified polynomial-size range of possible values. If it succeeds, then it outputs Λ. Otherwise, it outputs $\bot$ indicating failure.

■ **Correctness:** The correctness of our unbounded scheme is presented in the full version of this paper.

4.2 Security

Theorem 4.1 (Security of Our *FH-UMIPE* Scheme): *Assume that F_1 and F_2 are pseudorandom functions, SKE is semantically secure symmetric key encryption, and SXDH problem is hard, then our FH-UMIPE construction achieves full-hiding security. More formally, for any PPT adversary $\mathcal{A}$ against the full-hiding security of the proposed FH-UMIPE construction, there exists a PPT algorithm $\mathcal{B}_1$ against the SXDH problem, $\mathcal{B}_2$ against the symmetric key encryption scheme, and $\mathcal{B}_3$ and $\mathcal{B}_4$ against the pseudorandom functions such that for any security parameter λ, we have*

$$\mathsf{Adv}_{\mathcal{A}}^{\text{FH-UMIPE}}(\lambda) \leq [4 \sum_{\iota \in [2^\lambda]} q_{\text{CT},\iota} + 2q_{\text{KEY}}]\mathsf{Adv}_{\mathcal{B}_1}^{\text{SXDH}}(\lambda) + n_{max}q_{\text{KEY}}\mathsf{Adv}_{\mathcal{B}_2}^{\text{SKE}}(\lambda)$$
$$+ 2\mathsf{Adv}_{\mathcal{B}_3}^{\text{PRF1}}(\lambda) + 2\mathsf{Adv}_{\mathcal{B}_4}^{\text{PRF2}}(\lambda),$$

where $q_{\text{CT},\iota}$ is the total number of ciphertext query for the index ι, q_{KEY} is the total number of decryption key query, and n_{max} is the maximum index of a decryption key that $\mathcal{A}$ queries, i.e., $S_i \subseteq [n_{max}]$ for all $i \in [q_{\text{SK}}]$.

Proof: The proof of Theorem 4.1 is structured as a hybrid argument over a series of experiments which differ in the construction of the decryption keys and/or ciphertexts queried by the adversary $\mathcal{A}$ in the full-hiding security model described in Definition 2.9. The hybrid transition is proceeded in the similar way to the bounded scheme, that is, first we gradually change the ciphertext form from $(\vec{x}_{\iota,0}, \vec{0}^m, 1, \kappa_\iota, 0)_{\mathbb{B}_\iota}$ to $(\vec{x}_{\iota,0}, \vec{x}_{\iota,1}, 1, \kappa_\iota, 0)_{\mathbb{B}_\iota}$. Next, we change the decryption key form from $(\vec{y}_{\iota,0}, \vec{0}^m, r_\iota, \vec{0}^2)_{\mathbb{B}_\iota^*}$ to $(\vec{0}^m, \vec{y}_{\iota,1}, r_\iota, \vec{0}^2)_{\mathbb{B}_\iota^*}$. Then, switch the first m coefficients with the second m coefficients and restore the ciphertexts. The proof of the ciphertexts part is almost same as that of the bounded scheme, while the decryption key part is more complicated than the bounded one. The hybrid experiments are described below. In these hybrids, a part framed by a box indicates those terms which were modified in the transition from the previous game. The sequence of hybrid experiments follow:

▶ Sequence of Hybrid Experiments

Hyb$_0$: We denote the jth element of S_i in ascending order by $s_{i,j}$. This experiment is the same as $\mathsf{Expt}_{\mathcal{A}}^{\text{FH-UMIPE}}(0)$ defined in Definition 2.9. That is, when the challenger receives $(\vec{x}_{\iota,t_\iota,0}, \vec{x}_{\iota,t_\iota,1})$ from $\mathcal{A}$ as a t_ι^{th} ciphertext query for index ι, it returns $\text{CT}_{\iota,t_\iota}^* = (c_{\iota,t_\iota}^*, k_\iota, \iota)$, where

$$W_\iota = F_1(K_1, \iota), \quad \mathbb{B}_\iota = \mathbb{D}W_\iota,$$
$$\kappa_{\iota,t_\iota} \xleftarrow{\mathsf{U}} \mathbb{F}_q, \quad c_{\iota,t_\iota}^* = (\vec{x}_{\iota,t_\iota,0}, \vec{0}^m, 1, \kappa_{\iota,t_\iota}, 0)_{\mathbb{B}_\iota}, \quad k_\iota = F_2(K_2, \iota).$$

On the other hand, when the challenger receives $(S_i, \{\vec{y}_{\iota,i,0}, \vec{y}_{\iota,i,1}\}_{\iota \in S_i})$ for i^{th} decryption key query, it returns $\text{SK}^*_{S_i,i} = (C_{|S_i|}, S_i)$, where

$$r_{\iota,i} \xleftarrow{\mathsf{U}} \mathbb{F}_q \ \text{s.t.} \ \sum_{\iota \in S_i} r_{\iota,i} = 0, \ \ W_\iota = F_1(K_1, \iota), \ \ \mathbb{B}^*_\iota = \mathbb{D}^* W^*_\iota,$$

$$k^*_{\iota,i} = (\vec{y}_{\iota,i,0}, \vec{0}^m, r_{\iota,i}, \vec{0}^2)_{\mathbb{B}^*_\iota} \ \text{ for } \iota \in S_i,$$

$$C_{|S_i|} = \mathsf{SKE.Encrypt}(F_2(K_2, s_{i,|S_i|}), \dots, \mathsf{SKE.Encrypt}(F_2(K_2, s_{i,1}), \{k^*_{\iota,i}\}_{\iota \in S_i}) \dots).$$

Hyb$_1$: In this hybrids, we replace pseudorandom functions $F_i(K_i, \cdot)$ for $i \in \{1, 2\}$ with random functions $R_i(\cdot) \xleftarrow{\mathsf{U}} \mathcal{R}_{i,\lambda}$, where $\mathcal{R}_{i,\lambda}$ is a set of functions consists of all functions that have the same domain and range as F_i. Observe that all dual orthogonal bases used in the ciphertexts and decryption keys queried by $\mathcal{A}$ are completely independent and random ones by each index after Hyb$_1$.

Hyb$_2$: The all replies for the ciphertext queries are changed as follows;

$$W_\iota = R_1(\iota), \ \ \mathbb{B}_\iota = \mathbb{D} W_\iota,$$

$$\kappa_{\iota,t_\iota} \xleftarrow{\mathsf{U}} \mathbb{F}_q, \ \ c^*_{\iota,t_\iota} = (\vec{x}_{\iota,t_\iota,0}, \boxed{\vec{x}_{\iota,t_\iota,1}}, 1, \kappa_{\iota,t_\iota}, 0)_{\mathbb{B}_\iota}, \ \ k_\iota = R_2(\iota),$$

and returns $\text{CT}^*_{\iota,t_\iota} = (c^*_{\iota,t_\iota}, k_\iota, \iota)$.

Hyb$_3$ Sequence

Hyb$_{3,v}$ ($v \in [q_{\text{KEY}}]$): Hyb$_{3,0}$ is the same as Hyb$_2$. The challenger replies to the first v decryption key queries, i.e., the ith decryption key query for all $i \le v$, as

$$r_{\iota,i} \xleftarrow{\mathsf{U}} \mathbb{F}_q \ \text{s.t.} \ \sum_{\iota \in S_i} r_{\iota,i} = 0, \ \ W_\iota = R_1(\iota), \ \ \mathbb{B}^*_\iota = \mathbb{D}^* W^*_\iota,$$

$$k^*_{\iota,i} = (\vec{0}^m, \boxed{\vec{y}_{\iota,i,1}}, r_{\iota,i}, \vec{0}^2)_{\mathbb{B}^*_\iota} \ \text{ for } \iota \in S_i,$$

$$C_{|S_i|} = \mathsf{SKE.Encrypt}(R_2(s_{i,|S_i|}), \dots, \mathsf{SKE.Encrypt}(R_2(s_{i,1}), \{k^*_{\iota,i}\}_{\iota \in S_i}) \dots),$$

and returns $\text{SK}^*_{S_i,i} = (C_{|S_i|}, S_i)$. For the other decryption key queries, the challenger replies the same way as Hyb$_2$.

Hyb$_4$: In this hybrid, we switch the coefficients of 1 to m^{th} vector with those of $m + 1$ to $2m^{\text{th}}$ vector in both decryption key side and ciphertext side. Namely, the replies for the ciphertext queries are $\text{CT}^*_{\iota,t_\iota} = (c^*_{\iota,t_\iota}, k_\iota, \iota)$, where

$$W_\iota = R_1(\iota), \ \ \mathbb{B}_\iota = \mathbb{D} W_\iota,$$

$$\kappa_{\iota,t_\iota} \xleftarrow{\mathsf{U}} \mathbb{F}_q, \ \ c^*_{\iota,t_\iota} = (\boxed{\vec{x}_{\iota,t_\iota,1}, \vec{x}_{\iota,t_\iota,0}}, 1, \kappa_{\iota,t_\iota}, 0)_{\mathbb{B}_\iota}, \ \ k_\iota = R_2(\iota),$$

and the replies for the decryption key queries are $\text{SK}^*_{S_i,i} = (C_{|S_i|}, S_i)$, where

$$r_{\iota,i} \xleftarrow{\mathsf{U}} \mathbb{F}_q \ \text{s.t.} \ \sum_{\iota \in S_i} r_{\iota,i} = 0, \ \ W_\iota = R_1(\iota), \ \ \mathbb{B}^*_\iota = \mathbb{D}^* W^*_\iota,$$

$$k^*_{\iota,i} = (\boxed{\vec{y}_{\iota,i,1}, \vec{0}^m}, r_{\iota,i}, \vec{0}^2)_{\mathbb{B}^*_\iota} \ \text{ for } \iota \in S_i,$$

$$C_{|S_i|} = \mathsf{SKE.Encrypt}(R_2(s_{i,|S_i|}), \dots, \mathsf{SKE.Encrypt}(R_2(s_{i,1}), \{k^*_{\iota,i}\}_{\iota \in S_i}) \dots).$$

Hyb$_5$: This hybrid is the same as $\mathsf{Expt}_{\mathcal{A}}^{\text{FH-UMIPE}}(1)$ defined in Definition 2.9. That is, the replies for the ciphertext queries are $\text{CT}_{\iota,t_\iota}^* = (\boldsymbol{c}_{\iota,t_\iota}^*, k_\iota, \iota)$, where

$$W_\iota = \boxed{F_1(K_1, \iota)}, \quad \mathbb{B}_\iota = \mathbb{D}W_\iota,$$

$$\kappa_{\iota,t_\iota} \xleftarrow{\mathsf{U}} \mathbb{F}_q, \quad \boldsymbol{c}_{\iota,t_\iota}^* = (\overrightarrow{x}_{\iota,t_\iota,1}, \boxed{\overrightarrow{0}^m}, 1, \kappa_{\iota,t_\iota}, 0)_{\mathbb{B}_\iota}, \quad \boxed{k_\iota = F_2(K_2, \iota)},$$

and the replies for the decryption key queries are $\text{SK}_{S_i,i}^* = (C_{|S_i|}, S_i)$, where

$$r_{\iota,i} \xleftarrow{\mathsf{U}} \mathbb{F}_q \text{ s.t. } \sum_{\iota \in S_i} r_{\iota,i} = 0, \quad \boxed{W_\iota = F_1(K_1, \iota)}, \quad \mathbb{B}_\iota^* = \mathbb{D}^* W_\iota^*,$$

$$k_{\iota,i}^* = (\overrightarrow{y}_{\iota,i,1}, \overrightarrow{0}^m, r_{\iota,i}, \overrightarrow{0}^2)_{\mathbb{B}_\iota^*} \quad \text{for } \iota \in S_i,$$

$$C_{|S_i|} = \mathsf{SKE.Encrypt}(\boxed{F_2(K_2, s_{i,|S_i|})}, \ldots, \mathsf{SKE.Encrypt}(\boxed{F_2(K_2, s_{i,1})}, \{k_{\iota,i}^*\}_{\iota \in S_i}) \ldots).$$

▶ **Analysis**

Let us now denote by $\mathsf{Adv}_{\mathcal{A}}^{(h)}(\lambda)$ the advantage of the adversary $\mathcal{A}$, i.e., $\mathcal{A}$'s probability of outputting 1 in Hyb$_h$. Then, we can see that

$$\mathsf{Adv}_{\mathcal{A}}^{\text{FH-UMIPE}}(\lambda) \leq |\mathsf{Adv}_{\mathcal{A}}^{(0)}(\lambda) - \mathsf{Adv}_{\mathcal{A}}^{(1)}(\lambda)| + |\mathsf{Adv}_{\mathcal{A}}^{(1)}(\lambda) - \mathsf{Adv}_{\mathcal{A}}^{(2)}(\lambda)|$$

$$+ \sum_{\upsilon=1}^{q_{\text{KEY}}} |\mathsf{Adv}_{\mathcal{A}}^{(3,\upsilon-1)}(\lambda) - \mathsf{Adv}_{\mathcal{A}}^{(3,\upsilon)}(\lambda)| \tag{4.1}$$

$$+ |\mathsf{Adv}_{\mathcal{A}}^{(3,q_{\text{KEY}})}(\lambda) - \mathsf{Adv}_{\mathcal{A}}^{(4)}(\lambda)| + |\mathsf{Adv}_{\mathcal{A}}^{(4)}(\lambda) - \mathsf{Adv}_{\mathcal{A}}^{(5)}(\lambda)|.$$

The fact that each term on the RHS of Eq. (4.1) is negligible is formally argued in a sequence of lemmas in the full version of this paper. This completes the proof of Theorem 4.1.   □

References

1. Abdalla, M., Bourse, F., De Caro, A., Pointcheval, D.: Simple functional encryption schemes for inner products. In: Katz, J. (ed.) PKC 2015. LNCS, vol. 9020, pp. 733–751. Springer, Heidelberg (2015). https://doi.org/10.1007/978-3-662-46447-2_33
2. Abdalla, M., Catalano, D., Fiore, D., Gay, R., Ursu, B.: Multi-input functional encryption for inner products: function-hiding realizations and constructions without pairings. Cryptology ePrint Archive, Report 2017/972 (2017)
3. Abdalla, M., Gay, R., Raykova, M., Wee, H.: Multi-input inner-product functional encryption from pairings. In: Coron, J.-S., Nielsen, J.B. (eds.) EUROCRYPT 2017. LNCS, vol. 10210, pp. 601–626. Springer, Cham (2017). https://doi.org/10.1007/978-3-319-56620-7_21
4. Agrawal, S., Agrawal, S., Badrinarayanan, S., Kumarasubramanian, A., Prabhakaran, M., Sahai, A.: Function private functional encryption and property preserving encryption: New definitions and positive results. Cryptology ePrint Archive, Report 2013/744 (2013)

5. Ananth, P., Brakerski, Z., Segev, G., Vaikuntanathan, V.: From selective to adaptive security in functional encryption. In: Gennaro, R., Robshaw, M. (eds.) CRYPTO 2015. LNCS, vol. 9216, pp. 657–677. Springer, Heidelberg (2015). https://doi.org/10.1007/978-3-662-48000-7_32

6. Ananth, P., Jain, A.: Indistinguishability obfuscation from compact functional encryption. In: Gennaro, R., Robshaw, M. (eds.) CRYPTO 2015. LNCS, vol. 9215, pp. 308–326. Springer, Heidelberg (2015). https://doi.org/10.1007/978-3-662-47989-6_15

7. Badrinarayanan, S., Gupta, D., Jain, A., Sahai, A.: Multi-input functional encryption for unbounded arity functions. In: Iwata, T., Cheon, J.H. (eds.) ASIACRYPT 2015. LNCS, vol. 9452, pp. 27–51. Springer, Heidelberg (2015). https://doi.org/10.1007/978-3-662-48797-6_2

8. Barak, B., Goldreich, O., Impagliazzo, R., Rudich, S., Sahai, A., Vadhan, S., Yang, K.: On the (im)possibility of obfuscating programs. In: Kilian, J. (ed.) CRYPTO 2001. LNCS, vol. 2139, pp. 1–18. Springer, Heidelberg (2001). https://doi.org/10.1007/3-540-44647-8_1

9. Bishop, A., Jain, A., Kowalczyk, L.: Function-hiding inner product encryption. In: Iwata, T., Cheon, J.H. (eds.) ASIACRYPT 2015. LNCS, vol. 9452, pp. 470–491. Springer, Heidelberg (2015). https://doi.org/10.1007/978-3-662-48797-6_20

10. Boneh, D., Raghunathan, A., Segev, G.: Function-private identity-based encryption: hiding the function in functional encryption. In: Canetti, R., Garay, J.A. (eds.) CRYPTO 2013. LNCS, vol. 8043, pp. 461–478. Springer, Heidelberg (2013). https://doi.org/10.1007/978-3-642-40084-1_26

11. Boneh, D., Raghunathan, A., Segev, G.: Function-private subspace-membership encryption and its applications. In: Sako, K., Sarkar, P. (eds.) ASIACRYPT 2013. LNCS, vol. 8269, pp. 255–275. Springer, Heidelberg (2013). https://doi.org/10.1007/978-3-642-42033-7_14

12. Boneh, D., Sahai, A., Waters, B.: Functional encryption: definitions and challenges. In: Ishai, Y. (ed.) TCC 2011. LNCS, vol. 6597, pp. 253–273. Springer, Heidelberg (2011). https://doi.org/10.1007/978-3-642-19571-6_16

13. Brakerski, Z., Komargodski, I., Segev, G.: Multi-input functional encryption in the private-key setting: stronger security from weaker assumptions. In: Fischlin, M., Coron, J.-S. (eds.) EUROCRYPT 2016. LNCS, vol. 9666, pp. 852–880. Springer, Heidelberg (2016). https://doi.org/10.1007/978-3-662-49896-5_30

14. Brakerski, Z., Segev, G.: Function-private functional encryption in the private-key setting. In: Dodis, Y., Nielsen, J.B. (eds.) TCC 2015. LNCS, vol. 9015, pp. 306–324. Springer, Heidelberg (2015). https://doi.org/10.1007/978-3-662-46497-7_12

15. Cash, D., Liu, F.H., O'Neill, A., Zhang, C.: Reducing the leakage in practical order-revealing encryption. Cryptology ePrint Archive, Report 2016/661 (2016)

16. Chenette, N., Lewi, K., Weis, S.A., Wu, D.J.: Practical order-revealing encryption with limited leakage. In: Peyrin, T. (ed.) FSE 2016. LNCS, vol. 9783, pp. 474–493. Springer, Heidelberg (2016). https://doi.org/10.1007/978-3-662-52993-5_24

17. Coron, J.-S., Lepoint, T., Tibouchi, M.: Practical multilinear maps over the integers. In: Canetti, R., Garay, J.A. (eds.) CRYPTO 2013. LNCS, vol. 8042, pp. 476–493. Springer, Heidelberg (2013). https://doi.org/10.1007/978-3-642-40041-4_26

18. Datta, P., Dutta, R., Mukhopadhyay, S.: Functional encryption for inner product with full function privacy. In: Cheng, C.-M., Chung, K.-M., Persiano, G., Yang, B.-Y. (eds.) PKC 2016. LNCS, vol. 9614, pp. 164–195. Springer, Heidelberg (2016). https://doi.org/10.1007/978-3-662-49384-7_7

19. Garg, S., Gentry, C., Halevi, S.: Candidate multilinear maps from ideal lattices. In: Johansson, T., Nguyen, P.Q. (eds.) EUROCRYPT 2013. LNCS, vol. 7881, pp. 1–17. Springer, Heidelberg (2013). https://doi.org/10.1007/978-3-642-38348-9_1

20. Garg, S., Gentry, C., Halevi, S., Raykova, M., Sahai, A., Waters, B.: Candidate indistinguishability obfuscation and functional encryption for all circuits. SIAM J. Comput. **45**, 882–929 (2016)

21. Garg, S., Gentry, C., Halevi, S., Zhandry, M.: Functional encryption without obfuscation. In: Kushilevitz, E., Malkin, T. (eds.) TCC 2016. LNCS, vol. 9563, pp. 480–511. Springer, Heidelberg (2016). https://doi.org/10.1007/978-3-662-49099-0_18

22. Garg, S., Gentry, C., Sahai, A., Waters, B.: Witness encryption and its applications. In: symposium on Theory of computing-STOC 2013, pp. 467–476. ACM (2013)

23. Goldwasser, S., Gordon, S.D., Goyal, V., Jain, A., Katz, J., Liu, F.-H., Sahai, A., Shi, E., Zhou, H.-S.: Multi-input functional encryption. In: Nguyen, P.Q., Oswald, E. (eds.) EUROCRYPT 2014. LNCS, vol. 8441, pp. 578–602. Springer, Heidelberg (2014). https://doi.org/10.1007/978-3-642-55220-5_32

24. Goyal, V., Jain, A., O'Neill, A.: Multi-input functional encryption with unbounded-message security. In: Cheon, J.H., Takagi, T. (eds.) ASIACRYPT 2016. LNCS, vol. 10032, pp. 531–556. Springer, Heidelberg (2016). https://doi.org/10.1007/978-3-662-53890-6_18

25. Iovino, V., Tang, Q., Zebrowski, K.: On the power of public-key functional encryption with function privacy. Cryptology ePrint Archive, Report 2015/470 (2015)

26. Ishai, Y., Pandey, O., Sahai, A.: Public-coin differing-inputs obfuscation and its applications. In: Dodis, Y., Nielsen, J.B. (eds.) TCC 2015. LNCS, vol. 9015, pp. 668–697. Springer, Heidelberg (2015). https://doi.org/10.1007/978-3-662-46497-7_26

27. Kim, S., Lewi, K., Mandal, A., Montgomery, H.W., Roy, A., Wu, D.J.: Function-hiding inner product encryption is practical. Cryptology ePrint Archive, Report 2016/440 (2016)

28. Komargodski, I., Segev, G.: From minicrypt to obfustopia via private-key functional encryption. In: Coron, J.-S., Nielsen, J.B. (eds.) EUROCRYPT 2017. LNCS, vol. 10210, pp. 122–151. Springer, Cham (2017). https://doi.org/10.1007/978-3-319-56620-7_5

29. Komargodski, I., Segev, G., Yogev, E.: Functional encryption for randomized functionalities in the private-key setting from minimal assumptions. In: Dodis, Y., Nielsen, J.B. (eds.) TCC 2015. LNCS, vol. 9015, pp. 352–377. Springer, Heidelberg (2015). https://doi.org/10.1007/978-3-662-46497-7_14

30. Lee, K., Lee, D.H.: Two-input functional encryption for inner products from bilinear maps. Cryptology ePrint Archive, Report 2016/432 (2016)

31. Lewi, K., Wu, D.J.: Order-revealing encryption: new constructions, applications, and lower bounds. In: ACM SIGSAC Conference on Computer and Communications Security-CCS 2016, pp. 1167–1178. ACM (2016)

32. Lin, H.: Indistinguishability obfuscation from SXDH on 5-linear maps and locality-5 PRGs. In: Katz, J., Shacham, H. (eds.) CRYPTO 2017. LNCS, vol. 10401, pp. 599–629. Springer, Cham (2017). https://doi.org/10.1007/978-3-319-63688-7_20

33. Lin, H., Vaikuntanathan, V.: Indistinguishability obfuscation from DDH-like assumptions on constant-degree graded encodings. In: Foundations of Computer Science-FOCS 2016, pp. 11–20. IEEE (2016)

34. Okamoto, T., Takashima, K.: Hierarchical predicate encryption for inner-products. In: Matsui, M. (ed.) ASIACRYPT 2009. LNCS, vol. 5912, pp. 214–231. Springer, Heidelberg (2009). https://doi.org/10.1007/978-3-642-10366-7_13

35. Okamoto, T., Takashima, K.: Fully secure functional encryption with general relations from the decisional linear assumption. In: Rabin, T. (ed.) CRYPTO 2010. LNCS, vol. 6223, pp. 191–208. Springer, Heidelberg (2010). https://doi.org/10.1007/978-3-642-14623-7_11

36. O'Neill, A.: Definitional issues in functional encryption. Cryptology ePrint Archive, Report 2010/556 (2010)

37. Shacham, H.: A cramer-shoup encryption scheme from the linear assumption and from progressively weaker linear variants. Cryptology ePrint Archive, Report 2007/074 (2007)

38. Shen, E., Shi, E., Waters, B.: Predicate privacy in encryption systems. In: Reingold, O. (ed.) TCC 2009. LNCS, vol. 5444, pp. 457–473. Springer, Heidelberg (2009). https://doi.org/10.1007/978-3-642-00457-5_27

39. Tomida, J., Abe, M., Okamoto, T.: Efficient functional encryption for inner-product values with full-hiding security. In: Bishop, M., Nascimento, A.C.A. (eds.) ISC 2016. LNCS, vol. 9866, pp. 408–425. Springer, Cham (2016). https://doi.org/10.1007/978-3-319-45871-7_24

Foundations

Local Non-malleable Codes
in the Bounded Retrieval Model

Dana Dachman-Soled, Mukul Kulkarni, and Aria Shahverdi[✉]

University of Maryland, College Park, USA
danadach@ece.umd.edu, mukul@terpmail.umd.edu, ariash@umd.edu

Abstract. In a recent result, Dachman-Soled et al. (TCC '15) proposed a new notion called locally decodable and updatable non-malleable codes, which informally, provides the security guarantees of a non-malleable code while also allowing for efficient random access. They also considered locally decodable and updatable non-malleable codes that are *leakage-resilient*, allowing for adversaries who continually leak information in addition to tampering.

The bounded retrieval model (BRM) (cf. Alwen et al. (CRYPTO '09) and Alwen et al. (EUROCRYPT '10)) has been studied extensively in the setting of leakage resilience for cryptographic primitives. This threat model assumes that an attacker can learn information about the secret key, subject only to the constraint that the overall amount of leaked information is upper bounded by some value. The goal is then to construct cryptosystems whose secret key length grows with the amount of leakage, but whose runtime (assuming random access to the secret key) is *independent* of the leakage amount.

In this work, we combine the above two notions and construct local non-malleable codes in the split-state model, that are secure against *bounded retrieval* adversaries. Specifically, given leakage parameter ℓ, we show how to construct an efficient, 3-split-state, locally decodable and updatable code (with CRS) that is secure against one-time leakage of any polynomial time, 3-split-state leakage function whose output length is at most ℓ, and one-time tampering via any polynomial-time 3-split-state tampering function. The locality we achieve is polylogarithmic in the security parameter.

1 Introduction

Non-malleable codes were introduced by Dziembowski et al. [39] as a relaxation of error-correcting codes, and are useful in settings where privacy—but not necessarily correctness—is desired. Informally, a coding scheme is *non-malleable* against a tampering function if by tampering with the codeword, the function

D. Dachman-Soled—This work is supported in part by an NSF CAREER Award #CNS-1453045, by a research partnership award from Cisco and by financial assistance award 70NANB15H328 from the U.S. Department of Commerce, National Institute of Standards and Technology.

M. Abdalla and R. Dahab (Eds.): PKC 2018, LNCS 10770, pp. 281–311, 2018.
https://doi.org/10.1007/978-3-319-76581-5_10

either keeps the underlying message unchanged or changes it to an unrelated message. The main application of non-malleable codes proposed in the literature is achieving security against leakage and tampering attacks on memory (so-called *physical attacks* or *hardware attacks*) [57,58], although non-malleable codes have also found applications in other areas of cryptography [25,26,46] and theoretical computer science [21].

In this work, we go beyond considering non-malleable codes in the context of physical and/or hardware attacks and consider the problem of providing data assurance in a *network* environment. Our main focus is on providing privacy and integrity for large amounts of dynamic data (such as a large medical database with many authorized users), while allowing for efficient, random access to the data. We are interested in settings where *all* persistent data is assumed vulnerable to attack and there is no portion of memory that is assumed to be fully protected. We protect against *bounded-retrieval* adversaries, who may "leak" (i.e. download) large amounts of data, as long as the total amount leaked is bounded a priori.

In the following, we provide context for the contribution of this work by discussing (1) the limitations of standard non-malleable codes, (2) the recent notion of locally decodable and updatable non-malleable codes (LDUNMC) [29] (for settings where large amounts of dynamic data must be protected) and (3) the reason previous constructions of LDUNMC fall short in our setting.

Drawbacks of standard non-malleable codes. Standard non-malleable codes are useful for protecting small amounts of secret data stored on a device (e.g. cryptographic secret key) but unfortunately are not suitable in settings where, say, an entire database must be protected. This is due to the fact that non-malleable codes do not allow for random access: Once the database is encoded via a non-malleable code, in order to access just a single location, the entire database must first be decoded, requiring a linear scan over the database. Similarly, to update a single location, the entire database must be decoded, updated and re-encoded.

Locally decodable and updatable non-malleable codes (LDUNMC). In a recent result, [29] proposed a new notion called LDUNMC, which informally speaking, provides the security guarantees of a non-malleable code while also allowing for efficient random access (i.e. allowing to decode/update a particular position i of the underlying message via $\mathsf{DEC}^C(i)/\mathsf{UPDATE}^C(i)$). In more detail, we consider a database $D = D_1, \ldots, D_n$ consisting of n blocks, and an encoding algorithm $\mathsf{ENC}(D)$ that outputs a codeword $C = C_1, \ldots, C_{\hat{n}}$ consisting of $\hat{n}$ blocks. As introduced by Katz and Trevisan [54], local decodability means that in order to retrieve a single block of the underlying database, one does not need to read through the whole codeword but rather, one can access just a few locations of the codeword. In 2014, Chandran et al. [17] introduced the notion of local updatability, which means that in order to update (or "re-encode") a single block of the underlying database, one only needs to update a few blocks of the codeword.

As observed by [29], achieving these locality properties requires a modification of the definition of non-malleability: Suppose a tampering function f only modifies one block of the codeword, then it is likely that the output of the decoding algorithm, DEC, remains unchanged in most locations. (Recall DEC gets as input an index $i \in [n]$ and will only access a few blocks of the codeword to recover the i-th block of the database, so it may not detect the modification.) In this case, the (overall) decoding of the tampered codeword $f(C)$ (i.e. $(\mathsf{DEC}^{f(C)}(1), \ldots, \mathsf{DEC}^{f(C)}(n)))$ can be highly related to the original message, which intuitively means it is highly malleable.

To handle this, [29] consider a more fine-grained experiment. They require that for any tampering function f (within some class), there exists a simulator that computes a vector of decoded messages D^* and a set of indices $\mathcal{I} \subseteq [n]$. Here $\mathcal{I}$ denotes the coordinates of the underlying messages that have been tampered with. If $\mathcal{I} = [n]$, then the simulator thinks that the decoded messages are D^*, which should be unrelated to the original messages. On the other hand, if $\mathcal{I} \subsetneq [n]$, the simulator thinks that all the indices not in $\mathcal{I}$ remain unchanged, while those in $\mathcal{I}$ become $\bot$. More formally, the output of the experiment is as follows:

1. If $\mathcal{I} = [n]$ then output the simulator's output D^*, else
2. If $\mathcal{I} \neq [n]$ then for all $i \in \mathcal{I}$, set $D'(i) = \bot$ and for $i \notin \mathcal{I}$, set $D'(i) = D(i)$, where $D(i)$ is the ith block of current underlying message D. Output D'.

This means the tampering function can do one of the following:

1. It destroys block(s) of the underlying messages—i.e. causes DEC to output $\bot$ on those blocks—while keeping the other blocks unchanged, OR
2. If it modifies a block of the underlying message to a valid encoding, then it must have modified *all* blocks to encodings of unrelated messages, thus destroying the original message.

It turns out, as shown by [29], that the above is sufficient for achieving tamper-resilience for RAM computations. Specifically, the above (together with an ORAM scheme) yields a compiler for any RAM program with the guarantee that any adversary who gets input/output access to the compiled RAM program Π running on compiled database D and can additionally apply tampering functions $f \in \mathcal{F}$ to the database D adaptively throughout the computation, learns no more than what can be learned given only input/output access to Π running on database D. Dachman-Soled et al. in [29] considered LDUNMC that are also *leakage-resilient*, thus allowing for adversaries who continually leak information about D in addition to tampering.

Drawbacks of LDUNMC. The final construction in [29] achieved a leakage resilient, LDUNMC in the *split-state* and *relative leakage* model. In the split-state model, the codeword C is divided into sections called split-states and it is assumed that adversarial tampering and leakage on each section is *independent*. In the relative leakage model, the amount of information the adversary can leak is at most ℓ bits, and *all parameters of the system* (including complexity of

DEC/UPDATE) scale with ℓ. Thus, a main drawback of the construction of [29] is that, since their result is in the relative leakage model, the efficiency of the DEC/UPDATE procedures scales with the amount of leakage ℓ allowed from one of the two split-states, which gives rise to the following dilemma: If the amount of leakage, ℓ, is allowed to be large, e.g. $\ell := \Omega(n) \cdot \log |\hat{\Sigma}|$ bits, where $\log |\hat{\Sigma}|$ is the number of bits in each block of the codeword, then *locality* is compromised, since DEC/UPDATE must now have complexity that scales with $\Omega(n) \cdot \log |\hat{\Sigma}|$ and thus will need to read/write to at least $\Omega(n)$ data blocks. On the other hand, if it is required that DEC/UPDATE have locality at most polylog(n), then it means that leakage of at most ℓ bits, where $\ell := c \cdot \mathrm{polylog}(n) \cdot \log |\hat{\Sigma}|$, for some $c < 1$, can be tolerated. In this work—motivated by a network setting, in which the adversary typically corrupts a server and modifies memory while downloading large amounts of data—we allow the adversary's leakage budget to be much larger than the complexity of DEC/UPDATE. We do assume that if an adversary surpasses its budget, its behavior will be detected and halted by network security monitors. Thus, an adversary cannot simply download the entire encoded database (in which case security would be impossible to achieve) without being caught.

1.1   Our Contributions and Results

Our first contribution is the conceptual contribution of introducing the notion of locally decodable and updatable non-malleable codes in the BRM, which we believe to be well-motivated, for the reasons discussed above.

We then construct LDUNMC in the split-state model, that are secure against *bounded retrieval* adversaries. The bounded retrieval model (BRM) (cf. [9,10]) has been studied extensively in the setting of leakage resilience for cryptographic primitives (e.g. public key encryption, digital signatures and identification schemes). This threat model assumes that an attacker can repeatedly and adaptively learn information about the secret key, subject only to the constraint that the overall amount of leaked information is upper bounded by some value. Cryptosystems in the BRM have the property that while the secret key length grows with the amount of leakage, the runtime (assuming random access to the secret key) is *independent* of the leakage amount. Thus, the parameters of interest in a bounded retrieval model cryptosystem are the following: (1) The leakage parameter ℓ, which gives the upper bound on the overall amount of leakage; (2) The locality t of the scheme which determines the number of locations of the secret key that must be accessed to perform an operation (e.g. decryption or signing); and (3) The relative leakage $\alpha := \ell/|\mathsf{sk}|$, which gives the ratio of the amount of leakage to secret key length. Since we consider bounded retrieval adversaries in the context of locally decodable and updatable codes, our threat model differs from the standard BRM threat model in the following ways:

- We consider the protection of arbitrary data (not limited to the secret key of a cryptosystem).

- We allow adversarial tampering in addition to bounded leakage and do not assume that any portion of memory is tamper-proof[1].
- We assume that both leakage and tampering are *split-state*, i.e. that the leakage/tampering functions are applied independently to different sections of memory.

In our setting, we retain the same parameters of interest ℓ, t, α as above, with the only differences that each split-state must be able to tolerate at least ℓ bits of leakage and the overall relative leakage, α is taken to be the minimum relative leakage over all split-states, where the relative leakage for each split-state is computed as the maximum amount of allowed leakage for that split-state (which may be greater than ℓ) divided by the size of that split-state.

   We additionally restrict ourselves to a one-time tampering and leakage model (we discuss below the difficulties of extending to a fully continuous setting), where the experiment proceeds as follows: The adversary interacts with a challenger in an arbitrary polynomial number of rounds and may adaptively choose two rounds i, j where $i \leq j$, specifying a single leakage function $g \in \mathcal{G}$ in round i and a single tampering function $f \in \mathcal{F}$ in round j. The adversary gets to observe the leakage in round i before specifying tampering function f in round j. At the end of the experiment, the entire decoding of the (corrupted) codeword in each round is released in addition to the leakage obtained in each round. Our security requirement follows the ideal/real paradigm and requires that a simulator can simulate the output of the leakage as well as the decoding of *each position in each round*, without knowing the underlying encoded message. More precisely, as in the definition of [29], in each round the simulator outputs a vector of decoded data D^* along with a set of indices $\mathcal{I} \subseteq [n]$. Here $\mathcal{I}$ denotes the coordinates of the underlying messages that have been tampered with. If $\mathcal{I} = [n]$, then the simulator must output a complete vector of decoded messages D^*. On the other hand, if $\mathcal{I} \subsetneq [n]$, the simulator gets to output "same" for all messages not in $\mathcal{I}$, while those in $\mathcal{I}$ become $\perp$. When the output of the real and ideal experiments are compared, positions designated as "same" are replaced with either the original data in that position or with the most recent value placed in that position by an update instruction. We next state our main result:

Theorem 1 (Informal). *Under standard assumptions we have that for security parameter $\lambda \in \mathbb{N}$ and $\ell := \ell(\lambda)$, there exists an efficient, 3-split-state, LDUNMC (with CRS) in the bounded retrieval model that is secure against one-time tampering and leakage for tampering class $\mathcal{F}$ and leakage class $\mathcal{G}$, where*

- $\mathcal{F}$ *consists of all efficient, 3-split-state functions $f = (f_1, f_2, f_3)$.*
- $\mathcal{G}$ *consists of all efficient, 3-split-state functions $g = (g_1, g_2, g_3)$, such that g_1, g_2, g_3 each output at most ℓ bits.*

The scheme has locality $t := t(\lambda) \in \mathrm{polylog}(\lambda)$ and relative leakage $\alpha := \alpha(\lambda) \in \frac{1}{8} - o(1)$.

---

[1] [37] also allowed for tampering in the BRM setting, but required portions of memory to be completely tamper-proof.

In fact, the number of bits leaked from the third split-state can be much larger than ℓ and, in particular, will depend on the total size of the data being stored. The above theorem guarantees that, regardless of the size of the database, the relative leakage (for all three split-states) will be at least $\frac{1}{8} - o(1)$.

The above theorem can be instantiated assuming the existence of collision-resistant hash functions with subexponential security, NIZK with simulation sound extractability and identity-based hash proof systems, which can be realized from a variety of assumptions including standard assumptions in bilinear groups and lattices.

To obtain our result of a RAM-compiler against 3-split-state adversaries in the BRM, we note that using the same construction and proof of Theorem 4.6 in [29], we obtain a tamper and leakage resilient compiler TLR-RAM = (CompMem, CompNext) that is one-time tamper and leakage resilient w.r.t. function families $\mathcal{F}, \mathcal{G}$ above, given an ORAM compiler that is access-pattern hiding and a one-time non-malleable and leakage resilient LDUNMC w.r.t. function families $\mathcal{F}, \mathcal{G}$ as above. Moreover, the locality of the final compiled program, is $t \cdot t'$, where t is the locality of the underlying LDUNMC and t' is the locality of the underlying ORAM.

Applications. Our encoding scheme can be used to protect data privacy and integrity while a RAM program is being computed on it in situations where: (1) the data is stored across at least 3 servers, (2) the attacker can corrupt all servers and launch a fully coordinated attack, (3) the attacker cannot download too much data from any of the servers at once. (3) can be justified either by assuming that the attacker has limited storage capacity or that an attacker who tries to download too much data will be detected by network security monitors. The advantage of using our approach of LDUNMC versus simply using encryption to achieve privacy and a Merkle tree to achieve integrity is that our approach allows tampering and leakage on *all* persistent data, whereas the former approach requires certain parts of memory (e.g. the parts storing the secret keys for encryption/decryption and the root of the Merkle tree) to be leak and tamper-free.

Difficulty of achieving continual tampering and leakage in the BRM setting. In order to achieve continual security in the BRM model an attacker must be prevented from running an attack in which it internally simulates the *decode* algorithm by leaking the required information from the appropriate split-state each time a read request is issued (this would trivially break privacy). The overall leakage of such an attack is bounded—and so it will always qualify as a BRM attack—since the local decodability property guarantees that only a small number of locations will be read. Indeed, our construction is vulnerable to such an attack: We store the first part of the secret key in one split-state, the second part of the secret key in a second split-state and ciphertexts in the third split-state. An attacker can first leak a target ciphertext from the third split-state, learn the locations required for decryption from the first split-state, leak those locations, then learn the locations required for decryption from the second split-state and leak those locations. It is unlikely (over the coins of update) that during this three-round attack any of the relevant locations in the first and second split-states are overwritten by the updater, since the few locations accessed by an update are randomly distributed. Thus, after three rounds of leakage the attacker has sufficient information to decrypt the target ciphertext. We leave open the question of whether such an attack can be generalized to show an impossibility result for continual LDUNMC in the BRM.

1.2 Techniques

Our construction proceeds in three stages:

Leakage Only (2-split-state construction). Here the attacker submits a single split-state leakage function $g := (g_1, g_2)$ and is not allowed to tamper. To achieve security, we encrypt the database block-by-block using a CPA-secure public key encryption (PKE) scheme in the BRM model. The codeword then has two split-states: The first contains the secret key and the second contains the ciphertexts. The locality and relative leakage of the scheme will be the same as that of the underlying encryption scheme. Even though the leakage is on both the secret key and ciphertexts, regular PKE in the BRM is sufficient since the leakage $g := (g_1, g_2)$ on both split-states is submitted simultaneously.

Leakage and Partial Tampering (2-split-state construction). Here the attacker submits a split-state leakage function $g := (g_1, g_2)$ followed by a split-state tampering function $f = (f_1, f_2)$, where f_1 is required to be the *identity function*. In terms of the previous construction, this means that the attacker gets to tamper with the ciphertexts only, but not the secret key. A first attempt to extend the previous construction is to use a CCA-secure PKE scheme in the BRM instead of a CPA-secure scheme. This will allow the simulator to use the CCA oracle to decrypt any encrypted blocks of the database that have been modified via tampering, thus ruling out mauling attacks on any individual block. Unfortunately, it does not prevent mauling attacks across blocks. Namely, some encrypted blocks can be replaced with fresh valid encryptions while others remain the same, leading to a valid, decoded database which is different, but correlated to the original data. To prevent this, we tie together the encrypted blocks in the database using a Merkle tree and store the Merkle tree in the second split-state along with the ciphertexts. During decode and update, we check that the relevant ciphertext block is consistent with the Merkle root. Unfortunately, this still does not work since the tampering function f_2 can be used to update the Merkle tree and root to be consistent with the modified ciphertexts at the leaves. Therefore, we additionally store a secret key for a signature scheme in the BRM model in the first split-state and include a signature on the root of the Merkle tree in the second split-state, which is verified during each decode and update. Note, however, that existentially unforgeable signatures are impossible in the BRM model, since an attacker can always use its leakage query g_1 to learn a signature on a new message. Nevertheless, so-called *entropic* signatures are possible [10, 11][2]. Entropic signatures guarantee unforgeability for message distributions that have high entropy, even conditioned on the adversary's view after receiving the output of g_1 but before receiving the output of g_2. Thus, to argue non-malleability we show that either (1) The ciphertexts contained in the second split-state are *all* low entropy, conditioned on the adversary's view after receiving the output of g_1 but before receiving the output of g_2. In this case, it means that $\mathcal{I} = [n]$, i.e. all the ciphertexts have been modified and so the decryption across all blocks will lead to an unrelated database or (2) At least one ciphertext has high entropy, conditioned on the adversary's view after receiving the output of g_1 but before receiving the output of g_2. In this case, we argue that the root of the Merkle tree has high entropy and so an adversary who produces a forged signature violates the entropic security of the BRM signature scheme. We refer reader to the full version of the paper [27] for further details.

Full Leakage and Tampering (3-split-state construction). When trying to extend the above construction to allow tampering on the secret (and public) keys, it becomes clear that the entire secret key cannot be stored in a single split-state due to the following trivial attack: The adversary leaks a single ciphertext from the second split-state using leakage function g_2 and subsequently tampers with the first split-state using a tampering function f_1 such that f_1 does nothing if the leaked ciphertext decrypts to 0, and otherwise erases the entire contents of the first split-state. Such an attack clearly breaks non-malleability, since the entire codeword will decode properly if the leaked block contained a 0, and decode to $\bot$ otherwise. To overcome this attack, we introduce a third split-state: We store the secret keys across the first two split-states and store the public keys and ciphertexts in the third. We also replace the CCA-secure public key encryption scheme in the BRM with a new primitive we introduce called *CCA secure SS-BRM public key encryption*, which may be of independent interest (See Subsect. 2.2 for the definition and the full version of the paper [27] for a construction and security proof). Given leakage parameter ℓ, such an encryption scheme stores the secret key in a split-state and guarantees CCA security even under ℓ bits of split-state leakage both before and *after* seeing the challenge ciphertext. The final construction is as follows: The first split-state stores the first part of secret key of the SS-BRM PKE scheme, the secret key of the BRM signature scheme, and a Merkle tree of the former two keys with root R_1. The second split-state stores the second part of the secret key of the SS-BRM PKE scheme, and a Merkle tree of the key with root R_2. The third split-state contains the ciphertexts, Merkle tree and signature on the root as in the previous construction and, in addition, stores a simulation-sound NIZK proof of knowledge

---

[2] The constructions cited above are in the random oracle model. However, as discussed in the full version of the paper [27], the primitive we require is slightly weaker than regular entropic signatures in the BRM and can be constructed in a straightforward manner in the standard model, without use of random oracles. For conceptual simplicity we present our constructions and state our theorems in terms of the existence of entropic signatures in the BRM.

of the pre-images of R_1 and R_2, with *local* verifiability (this is the reason a CRS is necessary). The property of local verifiability is necessary to ensure locality of decode/update and is achieved by using a probabilistically checkable proof (PCP) on top of a regular NIZK. Note that while computation of the PCP is expensive, this need only be done a single time, during the encode procedure, but the proof remains static during decode/update. Decode/update proceed as in the previous construction and additionally, during each decode/update, the proof is verified using the local verifier. Each time a location is accessed in the first or second split-state during decode/update, the corresponding locations in the Merkle tree of the first and second split-state are checked and compared with the R_1 and R_2 values contained in the proof statement in the third split-state. If they do no match, an error is outputted. In the security proof, we reduce a leakage/tampering adversary A to an adversary A' against the SS-BRM PKE scheme. To achieve this, when A submits its tampering query $f = (f_1, f_2, f_3)$, A' will use its post challenge leakage query to output a bit corresponding to each leaf block in the first and second split-state indicating whether the block is consistent with the corresponding Merkle root, R_1 or R_2. Now in order to decode and update there are two cases, if the hash values R_1 or R_2 change, then the statement of the NIZK changes and a candidate encryption and signature secret key can be extracted from the proof. If the public keys, R_1 and R_2 do not change, then the candidate encryption and signature secret keys are the original keys and the CCA oracle can be used for decryption. In addition, during each decode/update, before the candidate secret keys are used to perform the decryption or signing operation, the post-challenge leakage is used to verify that the corresponding blocks needed to perform the operation are consistent with the R_1 and R_2 values contained in the proof. If yes, the candidate key is used to decrypt or sign. If not, then an error is produced. See Sect. 3.

On 2 vs 3 split-states. A natural question is whether we can reduce the number of split-states to 2, which would be optimal. Towards answering this question, recall our newly introduced notion *CCA secure SS-BRM public key encryption*, (described in the previous section), which given leakage parameter ℓ, stores the secret key in a split-state and guarantees CCA security even under ℓ bits of split-state leakage before and *after* seeing the challenge ciphertext. This notion gives rise to a 3-split-state construction of LDUNMC in the BRM model, since each split-state of the key and the ciphertext must be stored separately. We note that our construction of CCA secure SS-BRM public key encryption, given in the full version [27] achieves a stronger notion of security, where the secret key $\mathsf{sk} := \mathsf{sk}_1 \| \mathsf{sk}_2$ is split into two parts and two phases of leakage are allowed: In the first phase, leakage is allowed on sk_1 and on (sk_2, c), where c is the challenge ciphertext. Then, the challenge ciphertext is given to the adversary and an additional leakage query is allowed on sk_1 and on sk_2. While this notion seems useful for achieving 2-split-state construction of LDUNMC in the BRM model, since sk_1 can be stored in one split-state and (sk_2, c) in the other, this approach does not work for our construction (as we elaborate below). We therefore choose to present the simpler notion of *CCA secure SS-BRM public key encryption* in

Subsect. 2.2 and we refer reader to the full version of the paper [27] for the construction/security proof.

The above does not help in reducing our construction from 3 to 2 split-states since our proof requires one of the split-states (which contains the ciphertexts, the Merkle tree, the signature on the root and the simulation-sound NIZK proof of knowledge) to be *entirely public*, and thus must be stored in a separate state, apart from both sk_1 and sk_2. This allows us to fully simulate the entire contents of the split-state after the tampering function has been applied, which enables us to use the NIZK knowledge extractor to extract the encryption and signature secret keys from the (tampered) NIZK proof (as described previously). We cannot rely on the BRM security of the encryption/signature scheme to instead *leak* the extracted witness, since the witness corresponds to the encryption and signature secret keys, which are required to be larger than the allowed leakage bound, ℓ, in order for security of the encryption/signature scheme to be possible.

1.3 Related Work

Non-malleable Codes. The concept of non-malleability, introduced by Dolev et al. [34] has been applied widely in cryptography, in both the computational and information-theoretic setting. Error-correcting codes and early works on tamper resilience [45,50] gave rise to the study of non-malleable codes. The notion of non-malleable codes was formalized in the seminal work of Dziembowski et al. [39]. Split state classes of tampering functions introduced by Liu and Lysyanskaya [62], have subsequently received much attention with a sequence of improvements achieving reduced number of states, improved rate, or other desirable features [1–3,7,20,36,56]. Recently [6,12,13,19,41] gave efficient constructions of non-malleable codes for "non-compartmentalized" tampering function classes. Other works on non-malleable codes and memory tampering attacks include [4,5,16,23,42,51–53].

There are also several inefficient, existential or randomized constructions for much more general classes of functions in addition to those above [22,39,44]. Choi et al. [24], in the context of designing UC secure protocols via tamperable hardware tokens, consider a variant of non-malleable codes which has *deterministic* encoding and decoding. In contrast, our work relies on both randomized encoding and decoding, as does the recent work of [12]. Chandran et al. [17] introduced the notion of locally updatable and locally decodable codes. This was extended by Dachman-Soled et al. [29] who introduced the notion of *locally decodable and updatable non-malleable codes* with the application of constructing compilers that transform any RAM machine into a RAM machine secure against leakage and tampering. This application was also studied by Faust et al. [43]. Recently, Chandran et al. [18] studied information-theoretic local non-malleable codes. Dachman-Soled et al. [28] gave tight upper and lower bounds on the construction of LDUNMC.

Memory Leakage Attacks. Recently, the area of *Leakage Resilient Cryptography* has received much attention by the community. Here, the goal is to design cryptographic primitives resistant to arbitrary side-channel attacks, permitting the adversary to learn information about the secret key adaptively, as long as the *total amount* of leaked information is bounded by some leakage parameter ℓ. The majority of the results are in the *Relative Leakage Model*, which allows the systems parameters to depend on ℓ with aim of making ℓ as large as possible relative to the length of the secret key. Akavia et al. [8] started the study of side-channel attacks in the *public-key* setting by showing Regev's encryption scheme [67] is leakage resilient in the relative leakage model. Naor and Segev [63] constructed new public-key schemes based on non-lattice assumptions, which allowed for more leakage and achieved CCA security. Katz and Vaikuntanathan [55] subsequently developed signature schemes in the relative leakage model.

The Bounded Retrieval Model (BRM). Introduced in [30,35], the model assumes a bound ℓ on the overall amount of information learned by the adversary during the lifetime of the system (usually by setting ℓ very large). This model differs from the relative leakage model since it ensures that all the system parameters, except the length of the secret key, are independent of ℓ. Dziembowski [35], constructed a symmetric key authenticated key agreement protocol in Random Oracle model for the BRM setting, which was subsequently extended to standard model [15]. Password authentication and secret sharing in the BRM, was studied in [30], and [38] respectively. *Non-interactive* symmetric key encryption schemes using partially compromised keys were constructed by [66] implicitly and by [31] explicitly. The first public key cryptosystems in the BRM were provided by [10] who built leakage-resilient identification schemes, leakage-resilient signature schemes (in the random oracle model), and provided tools for converting schemes in relative leakage model to the BRM. Recently, Faonio et al. [40] presented a construction of another weaker variant of leakage resilient signature schemes (introduced by [65]); in BRM using random oracles. The first PKE scheme in the BRM was provided by [9] based on assumptions like lattices, quadratic residuosity and bilinear maps. Alwen et al. [11] provide an excellent survey of various leakage resilient primitives in BRM.

2 Preliminaries

In this section we introduce the preliminaries on local non-malleable codes, RAM and bounded retrieval model.

2.1 Preliminaries on Local Non-malleable Codes

In this section we first review the notion of decodable and updatable codes. We then present one time tampering and leakage experiment.

Definition 1 (Locally Decodable and Updatable Code). *Let $\Sigma, \hat{\Sigma}$ be sets of strings, and $n, \hat{n}, p, q$ be some parameters. An $(n, \hat{n}, p, q)$ locally decodable and updatable coding scheme consists of three algorithms $(\mathsf{ENC}, \mathsf{DEC}, \mathsf{UPDATE})$ with the following syntax:*

- *The encoding algorithm* ENC *(perhaps randomized) takes input an n-block (in Σ) database and outputs an $\hat{n}$-block (in $\hat{\Sigma}$) codeword.*
- *The (local) decoding algorithm* DEC *takes input an index in $[n]$, reads at most p blocks of the codeword, and outputs a block of the database in Σ. The overall decoding algorithm simply outputs* (DEC(1), DEC(2), ..., DEC(n)).
- *The (local) updating algorithm* UPDATE *(perhaps randomized) takes inputs an index in $[n]$ and a string in $\Sigma \cup \{\epsilon\}$, and reads/writes at most q blocks of the codeword. Here the string ϵ denotes the procedure of refreshing without changing anything.*

Let $C \in \hat{\Sigma}^{\hat{n}}$ be a codeword. For convenience, we denote $\mathsf{DEC}^C, \mathsf{UPDATE}^C$ *as the processes of reading/writing individual blocks of the codeword, i.e. the codeword oracle returns or modifies an individual block upon a query. Recall that C is a random access memory where the algorithms can read/write to the memory C at individual different locations.*

Definition 2 (Correctness). *An $(n, \hat{n}, p, q)$ locally decodable and updatable coding scheme (with respect to $\Sigma, \hat{\Sigma}$) satisfies the following properties. For any database $D = (D_1, D_2, \ldots, D_n) \in \Sigma^n$, let $C = (C_1, C_2, \ldots, C_{\hat{n}}) \leftarrow \mathsf{ENC}(D)$ be a codeword output by the encoding algorithm. Then we have:*

- *for any index $i \in [n], \Pr[\mathsf{DEC}^C(i) = D_i] = 1$, where the probability is over the randomness of the encoding algorithm.*
- *for any update procedure with input $(i, v) \in [n] \times \Sigma \cup \{\epsilon\}$ and for all $j \in \mathbb{N}$, let $C^{(j+1)}$ be the resulting codeword by running $\mathsf{UPDATE}^{C^{(j)}}(i, v)$. Then we have $\Pr[\mathsf{DEC}^{C^{(j+1)}}(i) = v] = 1$, where the probability is over the encoding and update procedures. Moreover, the decodings of the other positions remain unchanged.*

Following [29], our definition includes a third party called the *updater*, who reads the underlying messages and decides how to update the codeword. This notion captures the RAM program computing on the underlying, unencoded data. The adversary learns the location that the updater updated the messages, but not the content of the updated messages.

Our experiment is interactive and consists of rounds: The adversary adaptively chooses two rounds i, j such that $i \leq j$, submits a leakage function in round i, gets its output and then submits a tampering function in round j. We assume WLOG that at the end of each round, the updater runs UPDATE, and the codeword will be somewhat updated and refreshed. The security experiment then considers the decoding of the entire message after each round.

Definition 3 (One Time Tampering and Leakage Experiment). *Let λ be the security parameter, $\mathcal{F}, \mathcal{G}$ be some families of functions. Let (ENC, DEC, UPDATE) be an $(n, \hat{n}, p, q)$-locally decodable and updatable coding scheme with respect to $\Sigma, \hat{\Sigma}$. Let $\mathcal{U}$ be an updater that takes input a database $D \in \Sigma^n$ and outputs an index $i \in [n]$ and $v \in \Sigma \cup \{\epsilon\}$. Flags Leaked and Tampered will be set to 0 and let r be the total number of rounds. Then for any blocks of databases*

$D = (D_1, D_2, \ldots, D_n) \in \Sigma^n$, and any (non-uniform) adversary $\mathcal{A}$, any updater $\mathcal{U}$ define the following experiment **TamperLeak**$_{\mathcal{A},\mathcal{U},D}$:

- Let $D^{(0)} = D$. The challenger first computes an initial encoding $C^{(0)} \leftarrow$ ENC(D).
- Then the following procedure repeats, at each round j, recall $C^{(j)}$ be the current codeword and $D^{(j)}$ be the underlying database:
  - The updater computes $(i^{(j)}, v) \leftarrow \mathcal{U}(D^{(j)})$ for the challenger. The challenger runs UPDATE$^{C^{(j)}}(i^{(j)}, v)$.
  - $\mathcal{A}$ sends either a tampering function $f \in \mathcal{F}$ and/or a leakage function $g \in \mathcal{G}$ or $\bot$ to the challenger.
  - if Leaked is 0 and g is sent by $\mathcal{A}$, the challenger sends back a leakage $\ell = g(C^{(j+1)})$ and sets Leaked to 1.
  - if Leaked is 1, Tampered is 0 and f is sent by $\mathcal{A}$, the challenger replaces the codeword with $f(C^{(j+1)})$ and sets Tampered to 1.
  - if Leaked is 1, Tampered is 1, ignore any function sent by $\mathcal{A}$.
  - We define $D^{(j+1)} \overset{\text{def}}{=} \left(\text{DEC}^{C^{(j+1)}}(1), \ldots, \text{DEC}^{C^{(j+1)}}(n) \right)$. Where $C^{(j+1)}$ is the tampered codeword.
  - $\mathcal{A}$ may terminate the procedure at any point.
- Let r be the total number of rounds. At the end, the experiment outputs $\left(\ell, D^{(0)}, \ldots, D^{(r)} \right)$.

Definition 4 (One Time Non-malleability and Leakage Resilience against Attacks). *An $(n, \hat{n}, p, q)$-locally decodable and updatable coding scheme with respect to $\Sigma, \hat{\Sigma}$ is non-malleable against $\mathcal{F}$ and leakage resilient against $\mathcal{G}$ if for all* PPT *(non-uniform) adversaries $\mathcal{A}$, and* PPT *updater $\mathcal{U}$, there exists some* PPT *(non-uniform) simulator $\mathcal{S}$ such that for any $D = (D_1, \ldots, D_n) \in \Sigma^n$, **TamperLeak**$_{\mathcal{A},\mathcal{U},D}$ is (computationally) indistinguishable to the following ideal experiment* **Ideal**$_{\mathcal{S},\mathcal{U},D}$:

- The experiment proceeds in rounds. Let $D^{(0)} = D$ be the initial database.
- At each round j, the experiment runs the following procedure:
  - At the beginning of each round, the updater runs $(i^{(j)}, v) \leftarrow \mathcal{U}(D^{(j)})$ and sends the index $i^{(j)}$ to the simulator. If $v = \epsilon$, set $D^{(j+1)} := D^{(j)}$ otherwise the experiment updates $D^{(j+1)}$ as follows: $D^{(j+1)} := D^{(j)}$ for all coordinates except $i^{(j)}$, and set $D^{(j+1)}[i^{(j)}] := v$.
  - $\mathcal{S}$ outputs $(\mathcal{I}^{(j+1)}, \boldsymbol{w}^{(j+1)})$, where $\mathcal{I}^{(j+1)} \subseteq [n]$.
  - Define

$$D^{(j+1)} = \begin{cases} \boldsymbol{w}^{(j+1)} & \text{if } \mathcal{I}^{(j+1)} = [n] \\ D^{(j+1)}|_{\mathcal{I}^{(j+1)}} := \bot, D^{(j+1)}|_{\bar{\mathcal{I}}^{(j+1)}} := D^{(j+1)}|_{\bar{\mathcal{I}}^{(j+1)}} & \text{otherwise} \end{cases}$$

  where $\boldsymbol{x}|_{\mathcal{I}}$ denotes the coordinates $\boldsymbol{x}[v]$ where $v \in \mathcal{I}$, and bar denotes complement.
- Let r be the total number of rounds. $\mathcal{S}$ outputs ℓ and the experiment outputs $\left(\ell, D^{(0)}, \ldots, D^{(r)} \right)$.

2.2   Preliminaries on RAM and Primitives in the BRM

We define random access machine, public key encryption in BRM and signature schemes in the BRM and introduce a new construction called Split-State Public Key Encryption in Bounded Retrieval Model (SS-BRM-PKE).

Preliminaries on Random Access Machines. We consider RAM programs to be interactive stateful systems $\langle \Pi, \mathsf{state}, D \rangle$, where Π denotes a next instruction function, state denotes the current state stored in registers, and D denotes the content of memory. Upon input state and a value d, the next instruction function outputs the next instruction I and an updated state state'. The initial state of the RAM machine, state, is set to $(\mathsf{start}, *)$. We denote by $\mathsf{A}^D(x)$, the execution of RAM algorithm A with random access to array D and explicit input x. We define operator *Access* which outputs the access patterns of $\mathsf{A}^D(x)$, and denote by $\boldsymbol{I}$ the locations in D accessed by $\mathsf{A}^D(x)$. Thus, we write $\boldsymbol{I} \xleftarrow{Access} \mathsf{A}^D(x)$.

Public Key Encryption in the BRM. A public key encryption scheme $(\mathcal{E})$ in the BRM consists of the algorithms (KeyGen, Encrypt, Decrypt), which are all parameterized by a security parameter λ and a leakage parameter ℓ. The syntax and correctness property of an encryption scheme follow the standard notion of public-key encryption. We define the following CPA game, with leakage ℓ, between an adversary $\mathcal{A}$ and a challenger.

- **Key Generation:** The challenger computes $(\mathsf{pk}, \mathsf{sk}) \leftarrow \mathsf{KeyGen}(1^\lambda, 1^\ell)$ and gives pk to the adversary $\mathcal{A}$.
- **Leakage:** The adversary $\mathcal{A}$ selects a PPT function $g : \{0,1\}^* \rightarrow \{0,1\}^\ell$ and gets $g(\mathsf{sk})$ from the challenger.
- **Challenge:** The adversary $\mathcal{A}$ selects two messages m_0, m_1. The challenger chooses $b \leftarrow \{0,1\}$ uniformly at random and gives $c \leftarrow \mathsf{Encrypt}^{\mathsf{pk}}(m_b)$ to the adversary $\mathcal{A}$.
- **Output:** The adversary $\mathcal{A}$ outputs a bit $b' \in \{0,1\}$. We say that $\mathcal{A}$ wins the game if $b' = b$.

For any adversary $\mathcal{A}$, the advantage of $\mathcal{A}$ in the above game is defined as $\mathbf{Adv}_{\mathcal{E},\mathcal{A}}^{\mathrm{CPA}}(\lambda, \ell) \stackrel{\text{def}}{=} |\Pr[\mathcal{A} \text{ wins}] - \frac{1}{2}|$.

Definition 5 (Leakage-Resilient PKE). *[9] A public-key encryption scheme $\mathcal{E}$ is leakage-resilient, if for any polynomial $\ell(\lambda)$ and any PPT adversary $\mathcal{A}$, we have $\mathbf{Adv}_{\mathcal{E},\mathcal{A}}^{\mathrm{CPA}}(\lambda, \ell(\lambda)) = \mathsf{negl}(\lambda)$.*

Definition 6 (PKE in the BRM). *[9]   We say that a leakage-resilient PKE scheme is a **PKE in the BRM**, if the public-key size, ciphertext size, encryption-time and decryption-time (and the number of secret-key bits read by decryption) are independent of the leakage-bound ℓ. More formally, **there exist** polynomials $\mathsf{pksize}, \mathsf{ctsize}, \mathsf{encT}, \mathsf{decT}$, such that, **for any** polynomial ℓ and any $(\mathsf{pk}, \mathsf{sk}) \leftarrow \mathsf{KeyGen}(1^\lambda, 1^\ell)$, $m \in \mathcal{M}$, $c \leftarrow \mathsf{Encrypt}^{\mathsf{pk}}(m)$, the scheme satisfies:*

1. Public-key size is $|\mathsf{pk}| \leq O(\mathsf{pksize}(\lambda))$, ciphertext size is $|c| \leq O(\mathsf{ctsize}(\lambda, |m|))$.

2. *Run-time of* $\mathsf{Encrypt}^{\mathsf{pk}}(m)$ *is* $\leq O(\mathsf{encT}(\lambda, |m|))$.
3. *Run-time of* $\mathsf{Decrypt}^{\mathsf{sk}}(c)$, *and the number of bits of* sk *accessed is* $\leq$ $O(\mathsf{decT}(\lambda, |m|))$.

*The **relative-leakage** of the scheme is* $\alpha \stackrel{def}{=} \frac{\ell}{|\mathsf{sk}|}$.

Alwen et al. [9] give a generic transformation to construct a CCA-secure PKE scheme in the BRM using Naor-Young "double encryption" paradigm.

Signature Scheme in BRM. Consists of three algorithms: $(\mathsf{Gen}, \mathsf{Sign}, \mathsf{Verify})$. Attacker is separated into two parts, first part, $\mathcal{A}_1$, will interact with leakage oracle and signing oracle and output an arbitrary hint for the second part, $\mathcal{A}_2$. $\mathcal{A}_2$ only accesses signature oracle and tries to forge the signature of a message. The Entropic Unforgeability attack Game EUG_ℓ^λ is as follows:

1. Challenger select $(\mathsf{vk}, help, \mathsf{sk}_\sigma) \leftarrow \mathsf{Gen}(1^\lambda)$ and gives vk to $\mathcal{A}_1$.
2. Adversary $\mathcal{A}_1$ is given access to signing oracle $\mathcal{S}_{\mathsf{sk}_\sigma}(\cdot)$ and leakage oracle $\mathcal{O}_{\mathsf{sk}_\sigma}^{\lambda,\ell}(.)$ and outputs a hint $v \in \{0,1\}^*$.
3. Adversary $\mathcal{A}_2$ is given access to hint v and signing oracle $\mathcal{S}_{\mathsf{sk}_\sigma}(\cdot)$ and outputs message, signature pair (m, σ).

We define the advantage of the attacker $\mathcal{A} = (\mathcal{A}_1, \mathcal{A}_2)$ to be the probability that $\mathsf{Verify}^{\mathsf{vk}}(m, \sigma) = 1$ and that the signing oracle was never queried with m.

Definition 7 (Signature Scheme). *[10] Let $View_{\mathcal{A}_1}$ be a random variable denoting the view of $\mathcal{A}_1$ which includes its random coin and the responses it gets from signing oracle and leakage oracle. Let $MSG_{\mathcal{A}_2}$ be a random variable of the messages output by $\mathcal{A}_2$ in EUG_ℓ^λ. Adversary $\mathcal{A} = (\mathcal{A}_1, \mathcal{A}_2)$ is entropic if $\tilde{H}_\infty(MSG_{\mathcal{A}_2} \mid View_{\mathcal{A}_1}) \geq \lambda$ for security parameter λ. We say a signature scheme is entropically unforgeable with leakage ℓ if the advantage of adversary $\mathcal{A}$ in EUG_ℓ^λ is negligible in λ.*

Remark 1. Entropic signatures in the BRM can be constructed in the random oracle (RO) model (cf. [10,11]). Combining a signature scheme in the relative leakage model (with additional properties) such as [55] with the leakage amplification techniques of [10], it may be possible to construct entropic signatures in the BRM without RO. However, as discussed in full version of the paper [27], the primitive we require is slightly weaker than regular entropic signatures in the BRM and can be constructed in a straightforward manner in the standard model, without RO. Nevertheless, for conceptual simplicity we present our constructions and state our theorems in terms of the existence of entropic signatures in the BRM.

Split-State Public Key Encryption in the BRM (SS-BRM-PKE). We define a new primitive called as Split-State Public Key Encryption in Bounded Retrieval Model (SS-BRM-PKE) with the following properties:

1. The secret key sk is stored in the split-state $\mathsf{sk}_1 \| \mathsf{sk}_2$ and the adversary is allowed to obtain leakage on sk_1 and sk_2 independently.

2. The encryption scheme is secure in the bounded retrieval model, as defined in Definition 6 with respect to the split-state leakage.
3. The encryption scheme is chosen plaintext attack (CPA)-secure even in the presence of adversary who can observe the access pattern of the blocks of pk and $sk_1 \| sk_2$ accessed during encryption and decryption procedure.
4. The scheme is CPA-secure against an adversary getting additional split-state leakage (bounded) on the secret key, even *after* receiving the ciphertext.

Formally, a public key encryption scheme ($\mathcal{E}$) in the SS-BRM consists of the algorithms (KeyGen, Encrypt, Decrypt), which are all parameterized by a security parameter λ and a leakage parameter ℓ. The syntax and correctness property of an encryption scheme follow the standard notion of public-key encryption. We define the following semantic-security game (SS-BRM-PKE-CPA) with leakage ℓ between an adversary $\mathcal{A}$ and a challenger.

- **Key Generation:** The challenger computes $(pk, sk_1 \| sk_2) \leftarrow KeyGen(1^\lambda, 1^\ell)$ and gives pk to the adversary $\mathcal{A}$.
- **Message Commitment:** The adversary $\mathcal{A}$ selects two messages m_0, m_1.
- **Pre-challenge Leakage:** The adversary $\mathcal{A}$ selects a PPT function $g := (g_1, g_2) : \{0,1\}^* \times \{0,1\}^* \rightarrow \{0,1\}^\ell \times \{0,1\}^\ell$ and gets $L_1 := g_1(sk_1), L_2 := g_2(sk_2)$ from the challenger.
- **Challenge:** The challenger chooses $b \leftarrow \{0,1\}$ uniformly at random and gives $c \leftarrow Encrypt^{pk}(m_b)$ to the adversary $\mathcal{A}$.
- **Encryption Access Patterns:** The challenger also sends the access pattern $(i^{(1)}, i^{(2)}, \ldots, i^{(t)})$ corresponding to the encryption procedure, to $\mathcal{A}$.
- **Post-challenge Leakage:** The adversary $\mathcal{A}$ selects a PPT function $g' := (g'_1, g'_2) : \{0,1\}^* \times \{0,1\}^* \rightarrow \{0,1\}^\ell \times \{0,1\}^\ell$ and gets $L'_1 := g'_1(L_1, L_2, c, sk_1), L'_2 := g'_2(L_1, L_2, c, sk_2)$ from the challenger.
- **Decryption Access Patterns:** The challenger also sends the access pattern $(S^1, S^2) \xleftarrow{\text{Access}} Decrypt^{sk_1 \| sk_2}(c)$, to $\mathcal{A}$. S^i is a set of indices s^i_j of sk_i for $i \in \{1, 2\}$ and $j \in [n]$, where $|sk_1| = |sk_2| = n$. Also, $|S^i| = t$, where t is the number of locations of sk_1 and sk_2 required to be accessed to decrypt any ciphertext.
- **Output:** The adversary $\mathcal{A}$ outputs a bit $b' \in \{0,1\}$. We say that $\mathcal{A}$ wins the game if $b' = b$.

For any adversary $\mathcal{A}$, the advantage of $\mathcal{A}$ in the above game is defined as $\mathbf{Adv}^{\text{SS-BRM-PKE-CPA}}_{\mathcal{E},\mathcal{A}}(\lambda, \ell) \stackrel{\text{def}}{=} |\Pr[\mathcal{A} \text{ wins}] - \frac{1}{2}|$. It should be noted that the decryption access patterns indicating which parts of secret key were accessed during the decryption must be provided to the adversary only *after* the leakage information, otherwise the adversary can simply ask for the leakage on the secret key positions "relevant" to the decryption of the challenge ciphertext.

Chosen Ciphertext Attack (CCA) security for SS-BRM-PKE can be defined as the natural analogue of the above SS-BRM-PKE-CPA security experiment above. We refer reader to full version of the paper [27] for the formal definition and the construction. Given a SS-BRM-PKE-CPA scheme, a SS-BRM-PKE-CCA scheme can be constructed via the double encryption paradigm (cf. [9,60,64]).

2.3 Additional Preliminaries

In this section we present definitions which are being used in the constructions.

Definition 8 (Entropy). *The min-entropy of a random variable X is defined as $H_\infty(X) = -\log(\max_x \Pr[X = x])$. The conditional min-entropy of a random variable X, conditioned on the experiment $\mathcal{E}$ is $\tilde{H}_\infty(X|\mathcal{E}) = -\log(\max_{\mathcal{A}} \Pr[\mathcal{A}^{\mathcal{E}(\cdot)}() = X])$. In the special case that $\mathcal{E}$ is a non-interactive experiment which simply outputs a random variable Z, it is written as $\tilde{H}_\infty(X|Z)$.*

Definition 9 (Seed-Dependent Condenser [33]**).** *An efficient function* $\mathsf{Cond} : \{0,1\}^n \times \{0,1\}^d \to \{0,1\}^m$ *is a seed-dependent* $([H_\infty \geq k] \to_\varepsilon [H_\infty \geq k'], t)$-*condenser if for all probabilistic adversaries $\mathcal{A}$ of size at most t who take a random seed $S \leftarrow \{0,1\}^d$ and output (using more coins) a sample $X \leftarrow \mathcal{A}(S)$ of entropy $H_\infty(X|S) \geq k$, the joint distribution $(S, \mathsf{Cond}(X; S))$ is ε-close to some (S, R), where $H_\infty(R|S) \geq k'$.*

We present the collision resistant hash function and Merkle Tree which are being used to prevent mauling attacks.

Definition 10 (Collision-Resistant Hash Function Family [33]**).** *A family of hash functions $\mathcal{H} := \{h : \{0,1\}^* \to \{0,1\}^m\}$ is (t,δ)-collision-resistant if for any (non-uniform) attacker $\mathcal{B}$ of size at most t,*

$$\Pr[H(X_1) = H(X_2) \wedge X_1 \neq X_2] \leq \delta \text{ where } H \leftarrow \mathcal{H} \text{ and } (X_1, X_2) \leftarrow \mathcal{B}(H).$$

Theorem 2 (Theorem 4.1 [33]**).** *Fix any $\beta > 0$. If $\mathcal{H}$ is a $(2t, 2^{\beta-1}/2^m)$-collision-resistant hash function family, then $\mathsf{Cond}(X; H) \stackrel{def}{=} H(x)$ for $H \leftarrow \mathcal{H}$ is a seed-dependent $(([H_\infty \geq m - \beta + 1] \to [H_\infty \geq m - \beta + \log \varepsilon]), t)$-condenser.*

Definition 11 (Merkle Tree). *Let $h : \mathcal{X} \times \mathcal{X} \to \mathcal{X}$ be a hash function that maps two blocks of messages to one.[3] A Merkle Tree $\mathsf{Tree}_h(M)$ takes as input a message $M = (m_1, m_2, \ldots, m_n) \in \mathcal{X}^n$. Then it applies the hash on each pair (m_{2i-1}, m_{2i}), resulting in $n/2$ blocks. Then again, it partitions the blocks into pairs and applies the hash on the pairs, which results in $n/4$ blocks. This is repeated $\log n$ times, resulting a binary tree with hash values, until one block remains. We call this value the root of Merkle Tree denoted $\mathsf{Root}_h(M)$, and the internal nodes (including the root) as $\mathsf{Tree}_h(M)$. Here M can be viewed as leaves.*

Theorem 3. *Assuming h is a collision resistant hash function. Then for any message $M = (m_1, m_2, \ldots, m_n) \in \mathcal{X}^n$, any polynomial time adversary $\mathcal{A}$, $\Pr\left[(m'_i, p_i) \leftarrow \mathcal{A}(M, h) : m'_i \neq m_i, p_i \text{ is a consistent path with } \mathsf{Root}_h(M)\right] \leq \mathsf{negl}(\lambda)$.*

Moreover, given a path p_i passing through the leaf m_i; and a new value m'_i, there is an algorithm that computes $\mathsf{Root}_h(M')$ in time $\mathsf{poly}(\log n, \lambda)$, where $M' = (m_1, \ldots, m_{i-1}, m'_i, m_{i+1}, \ldots, m_n)$.

---

[3] Here we assume $|\mathcal{X}|$ is greater than the security parameter.

In the following we present simulation-sound extractable NIZK proof for which an efficient construction can be found in [47].

Definition 12 (NIZK Proof System). *Let R be an efficiently computable binary relation. For pairs $(x, w) \in R$ we call x the statement and w the witness. Let L be the language consisting of statements in R. A proof system for a relation R consists of a crs generation algorithm (CRSGEN), prover (P) and verifier (V), which satisfy completeness and soundness properties as follows.*

Definition 13 (Completeness). *For all $x \in L$ and all the witnesses w*

$$\Pr\left[V(crs, x, \pi \leftarrow P(crs, x, w)) = 1\right] \geq 1 - negl(\lambda)$$

Definition 14 (Computational Zero-Knowledge). *We call (CRSGEN, P, V) an NIZK proof for relation R if there exists a polynomial time simulator $\mathcal{S} = (\mathcal{S}_1, \mathcal{S}_2)$ such that for all non-uniform polynomial time adversaries $\mathcal{A}$ we have*

$$\Pr\left[crs \leftarrow \mathsf{CRSGEN}(1^\lambda) : \mathcal{A}^{\mathsf{P}(crs,\cdots)}(crs) = 1\right]$$
$$\overset{c}{\approx}$$
$$\Pr\left[(crs, \tau) \leftarrow \mathcal{S}_1(1^\lambda) : \mathcal{A}^{\mathcal{S}(crs,\tau,\cdots)}(crs) = 1\right]$$

where $\mathcal{S}(crs, \tau, x, w) = \mathcal{S}_2(crs, \tau, x)$ for $(x, w) \in R$ and both oracles output failure if $(x, w) \notin R$.

Definition 15 (Simulation-Sound Extractability [47]). *Consider an NIZK proof of knowledge (CRSGEN, P, V, $\mathcal{S}_1, \mathcal{S}_2, E_1, E_2$). Let SE_1 be an algorithm that outputs (crs, τ, ξ) such that it is identical to $\mathcal{S}_1$ when restricted to the first two parts (crs, τ). We say the NIZK proof is simulation sound if for all non-uniform polynomial time adversaries we have*

$$\Pr[(crs, \tau, \xi) \leftarrow SE_1(1^\lambda); (x, \pi) \leftarrow \mathcal{A}^{\mathcal{S}_2(crs,\tau,\cdot)}(crs, \xi); w \leftarrow E_2(crs, \xi, x, \pi) :$$
$$(x, \pi) \notin Q \text{ and } (x, w) \notin R \text{ and } V(crs, x, \pi) = 1] \approx 0 \tag{1}$$

where Q is the list of simulation queries and responses (x_i, π_i).

Definition 16 (Probabilistically Checkable Proofs [14]). *For functions $r, q : \mathbb{N} \rightarrow \mathbb{N}$ we say that a probabilistic oracle machine V is a (r, q)-PCP verifier if, on input a binary string x of length n and given oracle access to a binary string π, V runs in time $2^{O(r(n))}$, tosses $r(n)$ coins, makes $q(n)$ queries to π, and outputs either 1 ("accept") or 0 ("reject"). A language L belongs in the class $PCP_s[r(n), q(n)]$ if there exists a (r, q)-PCP verifier V_L such that the following holds:*

1. *Completeness: If $x \in L$ then there exists π such that $\Pr_R[V_L^\pi(x; R) = 1] = 1$.*
2. *Soundness: If $x \notin L$ then for every π it holds that $\Pr_R[V_L^\pi(x; R) = 1] < 1/2$.*

Theorem 4 (PCP Theorem). *$NP = PCP[O(log\ n), O(1)]$.*

To achieve negligible soundness, we can run the verifier polylogarithmic number of times in parallel, which results in polylogarithmic number of verifier queries to the proof, π. In [14], they give constructions of PCPs with the above properties, which also allow for knowledge extraction. I.e., assuming $\Pr_R[V_L^\pi(x; R) = 1] \geq 1/2$, there is an efficient extractor which, given π, can extract a witness w for the statement $x \in L$.

3   Achieving Full One-Time Tamper and Leakage Resilience (OT-TLR)

We next present our construction to achieve full resilience against one time leakage and tampering attacks. The relevant definitions can be found in Subsect. 2.3. As a preliminary step, we present a construction for achieving resilience against one time leakage and partial tampering attacks and we refer to full version of the paper [27] for the details of the construction.

Construction $\Pi = (\text{ENC}, \text{DEC}, \text{UPDATE})$. Let $\mathcal{E} = (\text{KeyGen}, \text{Encrypt}, \text{Decrypt})$ be a CCA-secure SS-BRM-PKE scheme, $\mathcal{V} = (\text{Gen}, \text{Sign}, \text{Verify})$ be a signature scheme in the BRM and H is a family of collision resistance hash functions and Π_{NIZK}, Π_{PCP} which are NIZK and PCP proof systems, respectively. Then we consider the following coding scheme:

Preprocessing. $crs \leftarrow \text{CRSGEN}(1^\lambda)$ and $h \leftarrow H$ are sampled and $CRS := (crs, h)$ is published. Note that the size of CRS depends on security parameter, but not on the size of the database nor on the leakage parameter ℓ. Note that CRS is implicit input to all algorithms.

$\text{ENC}(D)$: On input database $D = (D_1, D_2, \ldots, D_n) \in \Sigma^n$:

- Choose $(\text{pk}, \text{sk}_\varepsilon^1, \text{sk}_\varepsilon^2) \leftarrow \mathcal{E}.\text{KeyGen}(1^\lambda, 1^\ell)$, where $\text{sk}_\varepsilon^1 \in \hat{\Sigma}^{n_1'}$, $\text{sk}_\varepsilon^2 \in \hat{\Sigma}^{n_2'}$, and define $\text{sk}_\varepsilon := (\text{sk}_\varepsilon^1 || \text{sk}_\varepsilon^2)$, $(\text{vk}, \text{sk}_\sigma) \leftarrow \mathcal{V}.\text{Gen}(1^\lambda)$.
- Set $\tilde{D}_0 := 0$.
- Compute $\tilde{D}_i \leftarrow \mathcal{E}.\text{Encrypt}^{\text{pk}}(D_i)$ for $i \in [n]$. Let $\tilde{D} := \tilde{D}_0, \ldots, \tilde{D}_n$. Set[4] $T_{\tilde{D}} := \text{Tree}_h(\tilde{D})$, $\sigma := \mathcal{V}.\text{Sign}^{\text{sk}_\sigma}(R_{\tilde{D}})$, where $R_{\tilde{D}} := \text{Root}_h(T_{\tilde{D}})$.
- Construct the hash tree for secret keys $\text{sk}_\varepsilon^1, \text{sk}_\sigma, T_{\text{sk}^1} = \text{Tree}_h(\text{sk}_\varepsilon^1, \text{sk}_\sigma)$ and $R_{\text{sk}^1} := \text{Root}_h(T_{\text{sk}^1})$. Repeat the same procedure for secret key sk_ε^2 and compute $T_{\text{sk}^2} = \text{Tree}_h(\text{sk}_\varepsilon^2)$ and $R_{\text{sk}^2} := \text{Root}_h(T_{\text{sk}^2})$.
- For the statement $x_{NIZK} = (\text{pk}, \text{vk})||$ "I know pre-images of hashes $R_{\text{sk}^1}, R_{\text{sk}^2}$" and witness $w = (\text{sk}_\varepsilon || \text{sk}_\sigma)$ construct the proof $\pi_{NIZK} \leftarrow \Pi_{NIZK}.\text{P}(crs, x_{NIZK}, w)$.
- For the statement $x_{PCP} = $ "I know an accepting NIZK proof for the statement x_{NIZK}", construct a proof $\pi_{PCP} \leftarrow \Pi_{PCP}.\text{P}(crs, x_{PCP}, \pi_{NIZK})$.

---

[4] We additionally pad the tree T with dummy leaves consisting of uniform random values to ensure that the relative leakage on the second split state, C_2 is at least $\frac{1}{6}$.

- Output codeword $C := (C_1, C_2, C_3) \in \hat{\Sigma}^{n_1} \times \hat{\Sigma}^{n_2} \times \hat{\Sigma}^{n_3}$, where

$$C_1 := (\mathsf{sk}_\varepsilon^1, \mathsf{sk}_\sigma, T_{\mathsf{sk}^1}, R_{\mathsf{sk}^1}) \quad C_2 := (\mathsf{sk}_\varepsilon^2, T_{\mathsf{sk}^2}, R_{\mathsf{sk}^2})$$
$$C_3 := (\mathsf{pk}, \mathsf{vk}, \tilde{D}, T_{\tilde{D}}, R_{\tilde{D}}, \sigma, \pi_{PCP})$$

$\mathsf{DEC}^C(i)$: On input $i \in [n]$:

- Parse $C := (\mathsf{sk}_\varepsilon^1, \mathsf{sk}_\sigma, T_{\mathsf{sk}^1}, R_{\mathsf{sk}^1}, \mathsf{sk}_\varepsilon^2, T_{\mathsf{sk}^2}, R_{\mathsf{sk}^2}, \mathsf{pk}, \mathsf{vk}, \tilde{D}, T_{\tilde{D}}, R_{\tilde{D}}, \sigma, \pi_{PCP})$.
- Check whether $\tilde{D}_0 := 0$. If not, output $\perp$ and terminate.
- Read path p_i in $T_{\tilde{D}}$, corresponding to leaf i and use p_i to recompute $\hat{R} = \mathsf{Root}_h(p_i)$.
- Check that $\hat{R} := R_{\tilde{D}}$. If not, output $\perp$ and terminate.
- Check that $\mathcal{V}.\mathsf{Verify}^{\mathsf{vk}}(R_{\tilde{D}}, \sigma) = 1$. If not, output $\perp$ and terminate.
- Run $\Pi_{PCP}.\mathsf{V}(crs, x_{PCP}, \pi_{PCP})$ if outputs 0, output $\perp$ and terminate.
- For each accessed location of $\mathsf{sk}_\varepsilon^1$ and $\mathsf{sk}_\varepsilon^2$, read the paths in T_{sk^1} and T_{sk^2}, respectively. Compute $\hat{R}_{\mathsf{sk}^1} = \mathsf{Root}_h(T_{\mathsf{sk}^1})$, $\hat{R}_{\mathsf{sk}^2} = \mathsf{Root}_h(T_{\mathsf{sk}^2})$ and verify that $\hat{R}_{\mathsf{sk}^1} = R_{\mathsf{sk}^1}$ and $\hat{R}_{\mathsf{sk}^2} = R_{\mathsf{sk}^2}$ for each of them. If any of the verification failed, output $\perp$ and terminate.
- Output $D_i := \mathcal{E}.\mathsf{Decrypt}^{\mathsf{sk}_\varepsilon^1 || \mathsf{sk}_\varepsilon^2}(\tilde{D}_i)$.

$\mathsf{UPDATE}^C(i, v)$: On inputs an index $i \in [n]$, and a value $v \in \Sigma$:

- Run $\mathsf{DEC}^C(i)$. If it outputs $\perp$, set $\tilde{D}_0 := 1$, write back to memory and terminate.
- Parse $C := (\mathsf{sk}_\varepsilon^1, \mathsf{sk}_\sigma, T_{\mathsf{sk}^1}, R_{\mathsf{sk}^1}, \mathsf{sk}_\varepsilon^2, T_{\mathsf{sk}^2}, R_{\mathsf{sk}^2}, \mathsf{pk}, \mathsf{vk}, \tilde{D}, T_{\tilde{D}}, R_{\tilde{D}}, \sigma, \pi_{PCP})$.
- Set $\tilde{D}_i' \leftarrow \mathcal{E}.\mathsf{Encrypt}^{\mathsf{pk}}(v)$. Let $\tilde{D}' := \tilde{D}_0, \ldots \tilde{D}_{i-1}, \tilde{D}_i', \tilde{D}_{i+1}, \ldots, \tilde{D}_n$.
- Read path p_i in $T_{\tilde{D}}$, corresponding to leaf i and use $(p_i, \tilde{D}_i')$ to compute a new path p_i' (that replaces $\tilde{D}_i$ by $\tilde{D}_i'$). Set $R_{\tilde{D}}' = \mathsf{Root}_h(p_i')$. Let $T_{\tilde{D}}'$ denote the updated tree.
- Compute $\sigma' := \mathcal{V}.\mathsf{Sign}^{\mathsf{sk}_\sigma}(R_{\tilde{D}}')$.
- For each accessed location of sk_σ read the paths in T_{sk^1}. Compute $\hat{R}_{\mathsf{sk}^1} = \mathsf{Root}_h(T_{\mathsf{sk}^1})$ and verify that $\hat{R}_{\mathsf{sk}^1} = R_{\mathsf{sk}^1}$ for each of them. If any of the verification failed, output $\perp$ and terminate.
- Write back $(\tilde{D}_i', T_{\tilde{D}}', p_i', R_{\tilde{D}}', \sigma')$ yielding updated codeword $C' := (C_1', C_2', C_3')$ where

$$C_1' := (\mathsf{sk}_\varepsilon^1, \mathsf{sk}_\sigma, T_{\mathsf{sk}^1}, R_{\mathsf{sk}^1}) \quad C_2' := (\mathsf{sk}_\varepsilon^2, T_{\mathsf{sk}^2}, R_{\mathsf{sk}^2})$$
$$C_3' := (\mathsf{pk}, \mathsf{vk}, \tilde{D}', T_{\tilde{D}'}', R_{\tilde{D}'}', \sigma', \pi_{PCP}).$$

Locality of the construction. DEC and UPDATE must read the entire CRS, whose size depends only on security parameter λ and not on the size of the data. In addition, using the SS-BRM-PKE scheme, refer to full version [27] for construction, (along with sub-exponentially hard PRG), and the PCP of [14], DEC and UPDATE must make polylog(λ) number of random accesses to C.

Remark 2. Note that although computing the PCP proof π_{PCP} is expensive, it is only done a single time, during ENC, but remains static during UPDATE.

Theorem 5. *For security parameter $\lambda \in \mathbb{N}$, leakage parameter $\ell := \ell(\lambda)$, alphabet Σ such that $\log |\Sigma| \in \Omega(\lambda)$, and database size $n := n(\lambda)$: Assume $\mathcal{E} = (\mathsf{KeyGen}, \mathsf{Encrypt}, \mathsf{Decrypt})$ is a CCA-secure SS-BRM PKE scheme with leakage parameter $2\ell + \lambda$ and relative leakage $\alpha < 1$, $\mathcal{V} = (\mathsf{Gen}, \mathsf{Sign}, \mathsf{Verify})$ is a signature scheme in the BRM with leakage parameter $2\ell + \lambda$ and relative leakage $\alpha < 1$, H is a family of collision resistant hash functions with sub-exponential security, and Π_{NIZK}, Π_{PCP} are NIZK with simulation-sound extractability and PCP proof systems, respectively. Then Π is a one-time tamper and leakage resilient locally decodable and updatable code taking messages in Σ^n to codewords in $\hat{\Sigma}^{n_1} \times \hat{\Sigma}^{n_2} \times \hat{\Sigma}^{n_3}$, which is secure against tampering class*

$$\bar{\mathcal{F}} \overset{\text{def}}{=} \left\{ \begin{array}{l} f : \hat{\Sigma}^{n_1} \times \hat{\Sigma}^{n_2} \times \hat{\Sigma}^{n_3} \to \hat{\Sigma}^{n_1} \times \hat{\Sigma}^{n_2} \times \hat{\Sigma}^{n_3} \text{ and } |f| \leq \text{poly}(\lambda), \text{ s. t.:} \\ f = (f_1, f_2, f_3), \ f_1 : \hat{\Sigma}^{n_1} \to \hat{\Sigma}^{n_1}, \ f_2 : \hat{\Sigma}^{n_2} \to \hat{\Sigma}^{n_2}, \ f_3 : \hat{\Sigma}^{n_3} \to \hat{\Sigma}^{n_3}. \end{array} \right\},$$

and is leakage resilient against the class

$$\bar{\mathcal{G}} \overset{\text{def}}{=} \left\{ \begin{array}{l} g : \hat{\Sigma}^{n_1} \times \hat{\Sigma}^{n_2} \times \hat{\Sigma}^{n_3} \to \{0,1\}^\ell \times \{0,1\}^\ell \times \{0,1\}^{\frac{n_3 \cdot \log |\hat{\Sigma}|}{6}} \\ \text{and } |g| \leq \text{poly}(\lambda), \ s.t.: \\ g = (g_1, g_2, g_3), \ g_1 : \hat{\Sigma}^{n_1} \to \{0,1\}^\ell, \ g_2 : \hat{\Sigma}^{n_2} \to \{0,1\}^\ell, \\ g_3 : \hat{\Sigma}^{n_3} \to \{0,1\}^{\frac{n_3 \cdot \log |\hat{\Sigma}|}{6}}. \end{array} \right\}.$$

Moreover, Π has relative leakage $\frac{\alpha}{8} - o(1)$.

Proof. To prove the theorem, for any efficient adversary $\mathcal{A}$, we must construct a simulator $\mathcal{S}$, such that for any initial database $D \in \Sigma^n$ and any efficient updater $\mathcal{U}$, the experiment of one time attack $\mathbf{TamperLeak}_{\mathcal{A},\mathcal{U},D}$ is indistinguishable from the ideal experiment $\mathbf{Ideal}_{\mathcal{S},\mathcal{U},D}$.

The simulator $\mathcal{S}$ first samples random coins for the updater $\mathcal{U}$, so its output just depends on its input given the random coins. Then $\mathcal{S}$ works as follows:

- Initially $\mathcal{S}$ samples $(\mathsf{pk}, \mathsf{sk}_\varepsilon^1, \mathsf{sk}_\varepsilon^2) \leftarrow \mathcal{E}.\mathsf{KeyGen}(1^\lambda, 1^\ell)$, $(\mathsf{vk}, \mathsf{sk}_\sigma) \leftarrow \mathcal{V}.\mathsf{Gen}(1^\lambda)$, $crs \leftarrow \mathsf{CRSGEN}(1^\lambda)$ and $h \leftarrow H$, sets $\tilde{D}_0 = 0$ and generates n encryptions of 0, i.e., $\tilde{D}_1, \tilde{D}_2, \ldots, \tilde{D}_n$ where $\tilde{D}_i \leftarrow \mathcal{E}.\mathsf{Encrypt}^{\mathsf{pk}}(0)$ for $i \in [n]$. Let $\tilde{D}^{(1)} := \tilde{D}_0, \tilde{D}_1, \ldots, \tilde{D}_n$. $\mathcal{S}$ computes $T_{\tilde{D}}^{(1)} := \mathsf{Tree}_h(\tilde{D}^{(1)})$. Let $\sigma^{(1)} = \mathcal{V}.\mathsf{Sign}^{\mathsf{sk}_\sigma}(R_{\tilde{D}}^{(1)})$, where $R_{\tilde{D}}^{(1)}$ is the root of the tree $T_{\tilde{D}}^{(1)}$. $\mathcal{S}$ computes $T_{\mathsf{sk}^i} := \mathsf{Tree}_h(\mathsf{sk}^i)$ for $i \in \{1, 2\}$, R_{sk^i} denotes the root of the tree T_{sk^i}. $\mathcal{S}$ keeps global variables flag, Leaked, Tampered $= 0$.
- At each round j, let $C^{(j)} := (C_1^{(j)}, C_2^{(j)}, C_3^{(j)})$, where

$$C_1^{(j)} := (\mathsf{sk}_\varepsilon^1, \mathsf{sk}_\sigma, T_{\mathsf{sk}^1}, R_{\mathsf{sk}^1}) \quad C_2^{(j)} := (\mathsf{sk}_\varepsilon^2, T_{\mathsf{sk}^2}, R_{\mathsf{sk}^2})$$
$$C_3^{(j)} := (\mathsf{pk}, \mathsf{vk}, \tilde{D}^{(j)}, T_{\tilde{D}}^{(j)}, R_{\tilde{D}}^{(j)}, \sigma^{(j)}, \pi_{PCP}),$$

denote the current simulated codeword stored by $\mathcal{S}$ and let $w^{(j)}$ denote the simulator's output in the previous round. In the first round, $w_i^{(0)} :=$ same for all $i \in [n]$. In each round, $\mathcal{S}$ does the following:

Simulating Update:
- If flag $= 0, \mathcal{S}$ does the following: Receives an index $i^{(j)} \in [n]$ from the updater. Runs $\mathsf{UPDATE}^{C^{(j)}}(i^{(j)}, 0)$. Let $C^{(j+1)}$ be the resulting codeword after the update.
- If flag $= 1, \mathcal{S}$ does the following: Computes $(i^{(j)}, v) \leftarrow \mathcal{U}(\boldsymbol{w}^{(j)})$ on his own, and runs $\mathsf{UPDATE}^{C^{(j)}}(i^{(j)}, v)$. Let $C^{(j+1)}$ be the resulting codeword after the update.

Simulating the Round's Output:
- $\mathcal{S}$ sets $(\tilde{D}_0, \tilde{D}_1, \ldots, \tilde{D}_n) := \tilde{D}^{(j+1)}$.
- $\mathcal{S}$ emulates the adversary $\mathcal{A}$ and receives $g_1, g_2, g_3 \in \bar{\mathcal{G}}$ and $f_1, f_2, f_3 \in \bar{\mathcal{F}}$.
- If Leaked is 0, then $\mathcal{S}$ computes $\ell_1 := g_1(\mathsf{sk}_\varepsilon^1, \mathsf{sk}_\sigma, T_{\mathsf{sk}^1}, R_{\mathsf{sk}^1}), \ell_2 := g_2(\mathsf{sk}_\varepsilon^2, T_{\mathsf{sk}^2}, R_{\mathsf{sk}^2}), \ell_3 := g_3(\mathsf{pk}, \mathsf{vk}, \tilde{D}^{(j+1)}, T_{\tilde{D}}^{(j+1)}, R_{\tilde{D}}^{(j+1)}, \sigma^{(j+1)}, \pi_{PCP})$ sets $\ell := (\ell_1, \ell_2, \ell_3)$ and sets Leaked to 1.
- If Leaked $= 1$ and Tampered $= 0, \mathcal{S}$ computes $C' = (C_1', C_2', C_3')$ where

$$C_1' := (\mathsf{sk}_\varepsilon^{'1}, \mathsf{sk}_\sigma', T_{\mathsf{sk}^1}', R_{\mathsf{sk}^1}') := f_1(C_1) \quad C_2' := (\mathsf{sk}_\varepsilon^{'2}, T_{\mathsf{sk}^2}', R_{\mathsf{sk}^2}') := f_2(C_2)$$
$$C_3' := (\mathsf{pk}', \mathsf{vk}', \tilde{D}', T_{\tilde{D}'}', R_{\tilde{D}'}', \sigma', \pi_{PCP}') := f_3(C_3).$$

and sets Tampered to 1.
- If flag $= 0, \mathcal{S}$ does the following:
  - $\mathcal{S}$ sets $\mathcal{I}^{(j+1)} = \{u : \forall u \in [n] \text{ s.t. } \tilde{D}_u' \neq \tilde{D}_u \vee \mathsf{DEC}^{C'}(u) = \bot\}$, i.e. the indices where $\tilde{D}'$ is not equal to $\tilde{D}$ or where decode evaluates to $\bot$. $\mathcal{S}$ sets $\mathcal{I}^{(j+1)} = [n]$ if $x_{NIZK}' \neq x_{NIZK}$. If $\mathcal{I}^{(j+1)} = [n], \mathcal{S}$ sets flag $:= 1$. If $\mathcal{I}^{(j+1)} \neq [n], \mathcal{S}$ outputs $\{\ell, \boldsymbol{w}^{(j+1)}\}$, where $\boldsymbol{w}^{(j+1)}[i] = \bot$ for $i \in \mathcal{I}^{(j+1)}$ and $\boldsymbol{w}^{(j+1)}[i] = same$ for $i \notin \mathcal{I}^{(j+1)}$.
- If flag $= 1, \mathcal{S}$ simulates the real experiment faithfully: For $i \in [n], \mathcal{S}$ sets $\boldsymbol{w}^{(j+1)}[i] := \mathsf{DEC}^{(C')}(i)$, i.e. running the real decoding algorithm. Then $\mathcal{S}$ outputs $\{\ell, \boldsymbol{w}^{(j+1)}\}$.

To show $\mathbf{TamperLeak}_{\mathcal{A}, \mathcal{U}, D} \approx \mathbf{Ideal}_{\mathcal{S}, \mathcal{U}, D}$, we consider several hybrids.

Hybrid H_0: This is exactly the experiment $\mathbf{Ideal}_{\mathcal{S}, \mathcal{U}, D}$.

Hybrid H_1: Change π_{PCP} to a simulated proof, using ZK property of the underlying NIZK.

Claim 3.1. $H_0 \overset{c}{\approx} H_1$.

Event EV_3: $x_{NIZK} \neq x_{NIZK}'$, the verifier accepts, but the extractor fails to extract the witness from π_{PCP}.

The following claim is due to the simulation-sound extractability property of the proof system.

Claim 3.2. EV_3 occurs with negligible probability in hybrid H_1.

Hybrid H_2: We use the knowledge extractor of the PCP and NIZK to extract $sk'_\varepsilon, sk'_\sigma$. Everything in the decoding algorithm remains the same up to the final bullet in which the decryption is done by using sk'_ε, instead of using the contents of memory. Everything in the update algorithm also remains the same up to second to last bullet, where signing will now be done with sk'_σ, instead of using the contents of memory.

The following claim is due to collision resistance of h.

Claim 3.3. $H_1 \overset{c}{\approx} H_2$.

Hybrid H_3: The simulator does not encrypt all 0's (i.e. $\mathcal{E}.\mathsf{Encrypt}^{pk}(0)$); instead, it encrypts the real messages.

Claim 3.4. $H_2 \overset{c}{\approx} H_3$.

Proof. Assume there exists an efficient adversary $\mathcal{A}$ distinguishing hybrids H_2 and H_3 with non-negligible advantage. We construct an efficient adversary $\mathcal{A}'$ breaking the SS-BRM-PKE-CCA security of the encryption scheme $\mathcal{E}$. $\mathcal{A}'$ participates externally in the security game for the SS-BRM PKE scheme (See Subsect. 2.2 for definition) while internally instantiating $\mathcal{A}$. We next describe $\mathcal{A}'$:

- $\mathcal{A}'$ receives pk from **Key Generation** of its external challenger.
- $\mathcal{A}'$ samples $(\mathsf{vk}, \mathsf{sk}_\sigma) \leftarrow \mathcal{V}.\mathsf{Gen}(1^\lambda), h \leftarrow H, (crs', \tau, \xi) \leftarrow SE_1(1^\lambda)$. $\mathcal{A}'$ sets $CRS := (crs', h)$.
- Let $D_1, \ldots, D_n$ denote the initial contents of the database. $\mathcal{A}'$ runs the updater (with fixed coins, as described above) to obtain all the updates $D'_1, \ldots, D'_p$ in advance (where $p := p(\lambda)$ for polynomial $p(\cdot)$ denotes the runtime of the Updater). $\mathcal{A}'$ submits vectors of messages $\boldsymbol{D}_0, \boldsymbol{D}_1$, of dimension $n + p$, as **Message Commitment**. Where $\boldsymbol{D}_0$ is a vector of all 0's and $\boldsymbol{D}_1$ corresponds to the messages as described above.
- $\mathcal{A}'$ instantiates $\mathcal{A}$ on input CRS and waits to receive leakage query (g_1, g_2, g_3) from $\mathcal{A}$.
- Upon receiving leakage query (g_1, g_2, g_3), $\mathcal{A}'$ submits the following **Pre-challenge** split-state leakage query to its challenger:

$$G_1(\mathsf{sk}^1_\varepsilon) := (\mathsf{Root}_h(\mathsf{Tree}_h(\mathsf{sk}^1_\varepsilon, \mathsf{sk}_\sigma)), g_1(\mathsf{sk}^1_\varepsilon, \mathsf{sk}_\sigma, T_{\mathsf{sk}^1}, R_{\mathsf{sk}^1}))$$
$$G_2(\mathsf{sk}^2_\varepsilon) := (\mathsf{Root}_h(\mathsf{Tree}_h(\mathsf{sk}^2_\varepsilon)), g_2(\mathsf{sk}^2_\varepsilon, T_{\mathsf{sk}^2}, R_{\mathsf{sk}^2})),$$

where $R_{\mathsf{sk}^1} := \mathsf{Root}_h(\mathsf{Tree}_h(\mathsf{sk}^1_\varepsilon, \mathsf{sk}_\sigma))$ and $R_{\mathsf{sk}^2} := \mathsf{Root}_h(\mathsf{Tree}_h(\mathsf{sk}^2_\varepsilon))$.
- $\mathcal{A}'$ receives in return the output of its leakage queries $(R_{\mathsf{sk}^1}||\ell_1, R_{\mathsf{sk}^2}||\ell_2)$ as well as challenge ciphertexts $\tilde{D}_i, i \in [n]$ and $\tilde{D}'_j, j \in [p]$. Let $\tilde{D}^{(1)} := (\tilde{D}_1, \ldots, \tilde{D}_n, \tilde{D}'_1, \ldots, \tilde{D}'_p)$. $\mathcal{A}'$ computes $T^{(1)}_{\tilde{D}} := \mathsf{Tree}_h(\tilde{D}^{(1)})$ and computes $\sigma^{(1)} = \mathcal{V}.\mathsf{Sign}^{\mathsf{sk}_\sigma}(R^{(1)}_{\tilde{D}})$, where $R^{(1)}_{\tilde{D}} := \mathsf{Root}_h(\mathsf{Tree}_h(\tilde{D}^{(1)}))$. $\mathcal{A}'$ keeps global variables flag, Leaked, Tampered $= 0$.

- $\mathcal{A}'$ uses the simulated proof $\pi'_{NIZK} \leftarrow S_2(crs', \tau, x_{NIZK} = (R_{sk^1}, R_{sk^2}))$ to construct the simulated PCP proof π'_{PCP}. Note that $\mathcal{A}'$ now knows the entire contents of the third partition of the codeword, $C_3 := (\mathsf{pk}, \mathsf{vk}, \tilde{D}^{(1)}, T_{\tilde{D}}^{(1)}, R_{\tilde{D}'}^{(1)}, \sigma^{(1)}, \pi'_{PCP})$. Also note that we assume the proof π'_{PCP} contains the statement x'_{PCP} (and thus also x'_{NIZK}) to be proven, which includes the hash values R_{sk^1}, R_{sk^2}.
- $\mathcal{A}'$ rewinds $\mathcal{A}$ back to the beginning and instantiates $\mathcal{A}$.
- At each round j, let

$$C_3^{(j)} := (\mathsf{pk}, \mathsf{vk}, \tilde{D}^{(j)}, T_{\tilde{D}}^{(j)}, R_{\tilde{D}}^{(j)}, \sigma^{(j)}, \pi'_{PCP})$$

denote the third partition of the current simulated codeword stored by $\mathcal{A}'$. We maintain the invariant that $\mathcal{A}'$ knows the entire contents of $C_3^{(j)}$, for $j \in [p]$. Let $w^{(j)}$ denote the simulator's output in the previous round. In the first round, $w_i^{(0)} := \mathsf{same}$ for all $i \in [n]$. In each round, $\mathcal{A}'$ does the following:

Simulating Update:
  - If flag $= 0, \mathcal{A}'$ does the following: Computes the next index $i^{(j)} \in [n]$ generated by the updater. Runs $\overline{\mathsf{UPDATE}}^{C^{(j)}}(i^{(j)}, \bot, \tilde{D}'_j)$. Let $C^{(j+1)}$ be the resulting codeword after the update.
  - If flag $= 1, \mathcal{A}'$ does the following: Computes $(i^{(j)}, v) \leftarrow \mathcal{U}(w^{(j)})$ on his own, and runs $\overline{\mathsf{UPDATE}}^{C^{(j)}}(i^{(j)}, v, \bot)$. Let $C^{(j+1)}$ be the resulting codeword after the update.

Simulating the Round's Output:
  - $\mathcal{A}'$ sets $(\tilde{D}_0, \tilde{D}_1, \ldots, \tilde{D}_n) := \tilde{D}^{(j+1)}, T_{\tilde{D}} := T_{\tilde{D}}^{(j+1)}$, and $R_{\tilde{D}} := R_{\tilde{D}}^{(j+1)}$ and $\sigma = \sigma^{(j+1)}$.
  - $\mathcal{A}'$ emulates the adversary $\mathcal{A}$ and receives $g_1, g_2, g_3 \in \bar{\mathcal{G}}, f_1, f_2, f_3 \in \bar{\mathcal{F}}$.
  - If Leaked is 0, then $\mathcal{A}'$ computes $\ell_3 := g_3(C_3^{(j+1)})$ (recall ℓ_1, ℓ_2 were received previously), returns $\ell := (\ell_1, \ell_2, \ell_3)$ to $\mathcal{A}$ and sets Leaked to 1.
  - If Leaked is 1 and Tampered is 0, then $\mathcal{A}'$ computes $C_3' := f_3(C_3^{(j+1)})$, and sets Tampered to 1. $\mathcal{A}'$ submits the following **Post-challenge** split-state leakage query to its challenger: $F_1(\mathsf{sk}_\varepsilon^1) := f_1'(\mathsf{sk}_\varepsilon^1, \mathsf{sk}_\sigma, R_{\mathsf{sk}^1}^{(j+1)})$ and $F_2(\mathsf{sk}_\varepsilon^2) := f_2'(\mathsf{sk}_\varepsilon^2, R_{\mathsf{sk}^2}^{(j+1)})$, where f_1' computes $C_1' := f_1(C_1^{(j+1)})$ and then outputs a vector $\boldsymbol{\eta_1} \in \{0,1\}^{n_1'}$ such that for all $i \in [n_1'], \boldsymbol{\eta_1}[i] = 1$ if the path p_i in the Merkle tree in C_1' is consistent with the root contained in π'_{PCP} and 0 otherwise. Similarly, f_2' computes $C_2' := f_2(C_2^{(j+1)})$ and then outputs a vector $\boldsymbol{\eta_2} \in \{0,1\}^{n_2'}$ such that for all $i \in [n_2'], \boldsymbol{\eta_2}[i] = 1$ if the path p_i in the Merkle tree in C_2' is consistent with the root contained in π'_{PCP} and 0 otherwise.
  - $\mathcal{A}'$ additionally receives the **Decryption Access Patterns** for the challenge ciphertexts, i.e. , $(S_i^1, S_i^2) \xleftarrow{Access} \mathcal{E}.\mathsf{Decrypt}^{\mathsf{sk}_\varepsilon^1 || \mathsf{sk}_\varepsilon^2}(\tilde{D}_i), i \in [n]$ and $(S_j^1, S_j^2) \xleftarrow{Access} \mathcal{E}.\mathsf{Decrypt}^{\mathsf{sk}_\varepsilon^1 || \mathsf{sk}_\varepsilon^2}(\tilde{D}'_j), j \in [p]$.
  - If flag $= 0, \mathcal{A}'$ does the following:

- $\mathcal{A}'$ sets $\mathcal{I}^{(j+1)} = \{u : \forall u \in [n]$ s.t. $\tilde{D}'_u \neq \tilde{D}_u \vee \overline{\mathsf{DEC}}^{C'}(u) = \bot\}$, i.e. the indices where $\tilde{D}'$ is not equal to $\tilde{D}$ or where decode evaluates to $\bot$. $\mathcal{A}'$ checks π'_{PCP} and sets $\mathcal{I}^{(j+1)} = [n]$ if $x'_{NIZK} \neq x_{NIZK}$. If $\mathcal{I}^{(j+1)} = [n], \mathcal{A}'$ sets flag $:= 1$. If $\mathcal{I}^{(j+1)} \neq [n], \mathcal{S}$ outputs $\{\ell, \boldsymbol{w}^{(j+1)}\}$, where $\boldsymbol{w}^{(j+1)}[i] = \bot$ for $i \in \mathcal{I}^{(j+1)}$ and $\boldsymbol{w}^{(j)}[i] = same$ for $i \notin \mathcal{I}^{(j+1)}$.
  - If flag $= 1, \mathcal{A}'$ sets $\boldsymbol{w}^{(j+1)}[i] := \overline{\mathsf{DEC}}^{(C')}(i)$, for $i \in [n]$, and outputs $\{\ell, \boldsymbol{w}^{(j+1)}\}$.
- Once p rounds have completed, $\mathcal{A}'$ outputs whatever $\mathcal{A}$ does and terminates.

$\overline{\mathsf{DEC}}, \overline{\mathsf{UPDATE}}$ are defined as follows.

- $\overline{\mathsf{DEC}}^C(i)$: On input $i \in [n]$ in round $j \in [p]$:
  - Parse $C_3 := (\mathsf{pk}', \mathsf{vk}', \tilde{D}, T_{\tilde{D}}, R_{\tilde{D}}, \sigma, \pi'_{PCP})$.
  - Check whether $\tilde{D}_0 := 0$. If not, output $\bot$ and terminate.
  - Read path p_i in $T_{\tilde{D}}$, corresponding to leaf i and use p_i to recompute $\hat{R} = \mathsf{Root}_h(p_i)$.
  - Check that $\hat{R} := R_{\tilde{D}}$. If not, output $\bot$ and terminate.
  - Check that $\mathcal{V}.\mathsf{Verify}^{\mathsf{vk}'}(R_{\tilde{D}}, \sigma) = 1$. If not, output $\bot$ and terminate.
  - Run $V_{PCP}(crs', \pi'_{PCP})$ if outputs 0, output $\bot$ and terminate.
  - Let $(\mathcal{S}^1_j, \mathcal{S}^2_j)$ be decryption access patterns; $\forall s^1 \in \mathcal{S}^1_j$ and $\forall s^2 \in \mathcal{S}^2_j$, if $\boldsymbol{\eta}_1[s^1] = 1$ and $\boldsymbol{\eta}_2[s^2] = 1$ then continue. Else, output $\bot$ and terminate.
  - If $x'_{NIZK} \neq x_{NIZK}$ output $D_i := \mathcal{E}.\mathsf{Decrypt}^{\mathsf{sk}'_\varepsilon}(\tilde{D}_i)$, where $\mathsf{sk}'_\varepsilon \leftarrow \Pi_{NIZK}.E_2(crs', \xi, \pi_{NIZK})$ is the secret key extracted from the proof π'_{PCP}. E_2 is the witness extractor similar to Definition 15. Else, compute $D_i := \mathcal{E}.\mathsf{Decrypt}^{\mathsf{sk}_\varepsilon}(\tilde{D}_i)$, by querying the decryption oracle for the CCA secure SS-BRM-PKE with the original secret key.
- $\overline{\mathsf{UPDATE}}^C(i, v, \tilde{D}'_j)$: On inputs an index $i \in [n]$, a value $v \in \Sigma$ and a ciphertext $\tilde{D}'_j \in \widehat{\Sigma}$ in round $j \in [p]$:
  - Run $\overline{\mathsf{DEC}}^C(i)$. If it outputs $\bot$, set $\tilde{D}_0 := 1$, write back to memory and terminate.
  - Parse $C_3 := (\mathsf{pk}', \mathsf{vk}', \tilde{D}, T_{\tilde{D}}, R_{\tilde{D}}, \sigma, \pi'_{PCP})$.
  - If $v = \bot$. Let $\tilde{D}' := \tilde{D}_0, \ldots, \tilde{D}_{i-1}, \tilde{D}'_j, \tilde{D}_{i+1}, \ldots, \tilde{D}_n$. Read path p_i in $T_{\tilde{D}}$, corresponding to leaf i and use $(p_i, \tilde{D}'_j)$ to compute a new path p'_i (that replaces $\tilde{D}_i$ by $\tilde{D}'_j$). Set $R_{\tilde{D}'} = \mathsf{Root}_h(p'_i)$. Let $T_{\tilde{D}'}$ denote the updated tree.
  - If $v \neq \bot$, set $\tilde{D}''_i \leftarrow \mathcal{E}.\mathsf{Encrypt}^{\mathsf{pk}'}(v)$. Otherwise, set $\tilde{D}''_i := \tilde{D}'_j$. Let $\tilde{D}' := \tilde{D}_0, \ldots, \tilde{D}_{i-1}, \tilde{D}''_i, \tilde{D}_{i+1}, \ldots, \tilde{D}_n$. Read path p_i in $T_{\tilde{D}}$, corresponding to leaf i and use $(p_i, \tilde{D}''_i))$ to compute a new path p'_i (that replaces $\tilde{D}_i$ by $\tilde{D}''_i$). Set $R_{\tilde{D}'} = \mathsf{Root}_h(p'_i)$. Let $T_{\tilde{D}'}$ denote the updated tree.
  - Let $S^\sigma_j \xleftarrow{Access} \mathcal{V}.\mathsf{Sign}^{\mathsf{sk}_\sigma}(R_{\tilde{D}'})$; $\forall s \in S^\sigma_j$, if $\boldsymbol{\eta}_1[s] = 1$ then continue. Else, output $\bot$ and terminate.
  - If $x'_{NIZK} \neq x_{NIZK}$ Compute $\sigma' := \mathcal{V}.\mathsf{Sign}^{\mathsf{sk}'_\sigma}(R'_{\tilde{D}})$, where $\mathsf{sk}'_\sigma \leftarrow E_2(crs, \xi, \pi_{NIZK})$ is the secret key extracted from the proof π'_{PCP}. E_2 is the witness extractor similar to Definition 15. Otherwise, compute $\sigma' := \mathcal{V}.\mathsf{Sign}^{\mathsf{sk}_\sigma}(R'_{\tilde{D}})$, where sk_σ is the original secret key.

– Write back $(\tilde{D}'_i, p'_i, R_{\tilde{D}'}, \sigma')$ yielding updated codeword

$$C'_3 := (\mathsf{pk}', \mathsf{vk}', h, \tilde{D}', T_{\tilde{D}'}, R_{\tilde{D}'}, \sigma', \pi'_{PCP}).$$

If $\tilde{D}_i, i \in [n]$ and $\tilde{D}'_j, j \in [p]$ are encryptions of all 0's then the view of $\mathcal{A}$ is identical to its view in Hybrid H_2. Alternatively, if $\tilde{D}_i, i \in [n]$ and $\tilde{D}'_j, j \in [p]$ are encryptions of the honest data values, then the view of $\mathcal{A}$ is identical to its view in Hybrid H_3. Thus, if $\mathcal{A}$ distinguishes with non-negligible advantage, then $\mathcal{A}'$ distinguishes encryptions of all 0's from encryptions of correct data with non-negligible advantage, breaking the CCA security of the encryption scheme and resulting in contradiction.

Hybrid H_4: In the case that pk, vk are changed and $flag = 1$, go back to using $\mathsf{sk}^1_\varepsilon$ and $\mathsf{sk}^2_\varepsilon$ for decryption.

The following claim is due to collision resistance of h.

Claim 3.5. $H_3 \overset{c}{\approx} H_4$.

Hybrid H_5: Go back to using the real crs and real proof π_{PCP}.

The following claim is due to the zero knowledge property of the proof system.

Claim 3.6. $H_4 \overset{c}{\approx} H_5$.

Hybrid H_6: This is exactly the experiment $\mathbf{TamperLeak}_{\mathcal{A}, \mathcal{U}, \mathcal{D}}$.

Claim 3.7. $H_5 \overset{c}{\approx} H_6$.

Proof. The only difference between H_5 and real experiment is the case where

$$\mathsf{flag} = 0, \tilde{D}'_u \neq \tilde{D}_u \text{ and } \mathsf{DEC}^{C'}(u) \neq \bot,$$

($\mathcal{S}$ would output $\bot$ at position u whereas real experiment would output $\mathsf{DEC}^{C'}(u) \neq \bot$) which can only happen if events EV_1 or EV_2 occur (see Fig. 1 for their definition).

We next claim that both events occur with negligible probability, thus showing that Hybrids H_5 and H_6 differ with negligible probability.

Event EV_1:	**Event EV_2:**
– $\mathsf{pk}' \|\| \mathsf{vk}' = \mathsf{pk} \|\| \mathsf{vk}$. (otherwise $\mathsf{flag} = 1$)	– $\mathsf{pk}' \|\| \mathsf{vk}' = \mathsf{pk} \|\| \mathsf{vk}$. (otherwise $\mathsf{flag} = 1$)
– $\mathcal{I}^{(j+1)} \neq [n]$. (otherwise $\mathsf{flag} = 1$)	– $\mathcal{I}^{(j+1)} \neq [n]$. (otherwise $\mathsf{flag} = 1$)
– $R' \neq R^{(j+1)}$.	– $R' = R^{(j+1)}$.
– $\mathsf{Verify}(\mathsf{vk}, R', \sigma') = 1$.	– For some $i \in \mathcal{I}^{(j+1)}$, we have that for $\tilde{D}'_i$ and corresponding path p'_i, $R'_{\tilde{D}} = \mathsf{Root}_h(p'_i)$.

Fig. 1. Events EV_1 and EV_2.

Claim 3.8. EV_1 and EV_2 occur with negligible probability in H_5.

We omit the proof of the above claim since it is nearly identical to the corresponding claims in the proof of the construction for partial one-time tamper and leakage resilience and we refer reader to the full version of the paper [27] for that proof.

This completes the proof of Theorem 5.

References

1. Aggarwal, D., Agrawal, S., Gupta, D., Maji, H.K., Pandey, O., Prabhakaran, M.: Optimal computational split-state non-malleable codes. In: Kushilevitz and Malkin [59], pp. 393–417
2. Aggarwal, D., Dodis, Y., Kazana, T., Obremski, M.: Non-malleable reductions and applications. In: Servedio, R.A., Rubinfeld, R. (eds.) 47th ACM STOC, pp. 459–468. ACM Press, June 2015
3. Aggarwal, D., Dodis, Y., Lovett, S.: Non-malleable codes from additive combinatorics. In: Shmoys, D.B. (ed.) 46th ACM STOC, pp. 774–783. ACM Press, May/June 2014
4. Aggarwal, D., Dziembowski, S., Kazana, T., Obremski, M.: Leakage-resilient non-malleable codes. In: Dodis and Nielsen [32], pp. 398–426
5. Aggarwal, D., Kazana, T., Obremski, M.: Inception makes non-malleable codes stronger. Cryptology ePrint Archive, Report 2015/1013 (2015). http://eprint.iacr.org/2015/1013
6. Agrawal, S., Gupta, D., Maji, H.K., Pandey, O., Prabhakaran, M.: Explicit non-malleable codes against bit-wise tampering and permutations. In: Gennaro, R., Robshaw, M. (eds.) CRYPTO 2015, Part I. LNCS, vol. 9215, pp. 538–557. Springer, Heidelberg (2015). https://doi.org/10.1007/978-3-662-47989-6_26
7. Agrawal, S., Gupta, D., Maji, H.K., Pandey, O., Prabhakaran, M.: A rate-optimizing compiler for non-malleable codes against bit-wise tampering and permutations. In: Dodis and Nielsen [32], pp. 375–397
8. Akavia, A., Goldwasser, S., Vaikuntanathan, V.: Simultaneous hardcore bits and cryptography against memory attacks. In: Reingold, O. (ed.) TCC 2009. LNCS, vol. 5444, pp. 474–495. Springer, Heidelberg (2009). https://doi.org/10.1007/978-3-642-00457-5_28
9. Alwen, J., Dodis, Y., Naor, M., Segev, G., Walfish, S., Wichs, D.: Public-key encryption in the bounded-retrieval model. In: Gilbert, H. (ed.) EUROCRYPT 2010. LNCS, vol. 6110, pp. 113–134. Springer, Heidelberg (2010). https://doi.org/10.1007/978-3-642-13190-5_6
10. Alwen, J., Dodis, Y., Wichs, D.: Leakage-resilient public-key cryptography in the bounded-retrieval model. In: Halevi [48], pp. 36–54
11. Alwen, J., Dodis, Y., Wichs, D.: Survey: leakage resilience and the bounded retrieval model. In: Kurosawa, K. (ed.) ICITS 2009. LNCS, vol. 5973, pp. 1–18. Springer, Heidelberg (2010). https://doi.org/10.1007/978-3-642-14496-7_1
12. Ball, M., Dachman-Soled, D., Kulkarni, M., Malkin, T.: Non-malleable codes for bounded depth, bounded fan-in circuits. In: Fischlin, M., Coron, J.-S. (eds.) EURO-CRYPT 2016, Part II. LNCS, vol. 9666, pp. 881–908. Springer, Heidelberg (2016). https://doi.org/10.1007/978-3-662-49896-5_31

13. Ball, M., Dachman-Soled, D., Kulkarni, M., Malkin, T.: Non-malleable codes from average-case hardness: AC0, decision trees, and streaming space-bounded tampering. Cryptology ePrint Archive, Report 2017/1061 (2017). http://eprint.iacr.org/2017/1061

14. Ben-Sasson, E., Chiesa, A., Genkin, D., Tromer, E.: On the concrete efficiency of probabilistically-checkable proofs. In: Boneh, D., Roughgarden, T., Feigenbaum, J. (eds.) 45th ACM STOC, pp. 585–594. ACM Press, June 2013

15. Cash, D., Ding, Y.Z., Dodis, Y., Lee, W., Lipton, R., Walfish, S.: Intrusion-resilient key exchange in the bounded retrieval model. In: Vadhan, S.P. (ed.) TCC 2007. LNCS, vol. 4392, pp. 479–498. Springer, Heidelberg (2007). https://doi.org/10.1007/978-3-540-70936-7_26

16. Chandran, N., Goyal, V., Mukherjee, P., Pandey, O., Upadhyay, J.: Block-wise non-malleable codes. Cryptology ePrint Archive, Report 2015/129 (2015). http://eprint.iacr.org/2015/129

17. Chandran, N., Kanukurthi, B., Ostrovsky, R.: Locally updatable and locally decodable codes. In: Lindell [61], pp. 489–514

18. Chandran, N., Kanukurthi, B., Raghuraman, S.: Information-theoretic local non-malleable codes and their applications. In: Kushilevitz and Malkin [59], pp. 367–392

19. Chattopadhyay, E., Li, X.: Non-malleable codes and extractors for small-depth circuits, and affine functions. In: Hatami, H., McKenzie, P., King, V. (eds.) 49th ACM STOC, pp. 1171–1184. ACM Press, June 2017

20. Chattopadhyay, E., Zuckerman, D.: Non-malleable codes against constant split-state tampering. In: 55th FOCS, pp. 306–315. IEEE Computer Society Press, October 2014

21. Chattopadhyay, E., Zuckerman, D.: Explicit two-source extractors and resilient functions. In: Wichs and Mansour [69], pp. 670–683

22. Cheraghchi, M., Guruswami, V.: Capacity of non-malleable codes. In: Naor, M. (ed.) ITCS 2014, pp. 155–168. ACM, January 2014

23. Cheraghchi, M., Guruswami, V.: Non-malleable coding against bit-wise and split-state tampering. In: Lindell [61], pp. 440–464

24. Choi, S.G., Kiayias, A., Malkin, T.: BiTR: built-in tamper resilience. In: Lee, D.H., Wang, X. (eds.) ASIACRYPT 2011. LNCS, vol. 7073, pp. 740–758. Springer, Heidelberg (2011). https://doi.org/10.1007/978-3-642-25385-0_40

25. Coretti, S., Dodis, Y., Tackmann, B., Venturi, D.: Non-malleable encryption: simpler, shorter, stronger. In: Kushilevitz, E., Malkin, T. (eds.) TCC 2016-A, Part I. LNCS, vol. 9562, pp. 306–335. Springer, Heidelberg (2016). https://doi.org/10.1007/978-3-662-49096-9_13

26. Coretti, S., Maurer, U., Tackmann, B., Venturi, D.: From single-bit to multi-bit public-key encryption via non-malleable codes. In: Dodis and Nielsen [32], pp. 532–560

27. Dachman-Soled, D., Kulkarni, M., Shahverdi, A.: Locally decodable and updatable non-malleable codes in the bounded retrieval model. Cryptology ePrint Archive, Report 2017/303 (2017). https://eprint.iacr.org/2017/303

28. Dachman-Soled, D., Kulkarni, M., Shahverdi, A.: Tight upper and lower bounds for leakage-resilient, locally decodable and updatable non-malleable codes. In: Fehr, S. (ed.) PKC 2017, Part I. LNCS, vol. 10174, pp. 310–332. Springer, Heidelberg (2017). https://doi.org/10.1007/978-3-662-54365-8_13

29. Dachman-Soled, D., Liu, F.H., Shi, E., Zhou, H.S.: Locally decodable and updatable non-malleable codes and their applications. In: Dodis and Nielsen [32], pp. 427–450

30. Di Crescenzo, G., Lipton, R.J., Walfish, S.: Perfectly secure password protocols in the bounded retrieval model. In: Halevi and Rabin [49], pp. 225–244
31. Dodis, Y., Kalai, Y.T., Lovett, S.: On cryptography with auxiliary input. In: Mitzenmacher, M. (ed.) 41st ACM STOC, pp. 621–630. ACM Press, May/June 2009
32. Dodis, Y., Nielsen, J.B. (eds.): TCC 2015, Part I. LNCS, vol. 9014. Springer, Heidelberg (2015). https://doi.org/10.1007/978-3-662-46494-6
33. Dodis, Y., Ristenpart, T., Vadhan, S.: Randomness condensers for efficiently samplable, seed-dependent sources. In: Cramer, R. (ed.) TCC 2012. LNCS, vol. 7194, pp. 618–635. Springer, Heidelberg (2012). https://doi.org/10.1007/978-3-642-28914-9_35
34. Dolev, D., Dwork, C., Naor, M.: Nonmalleable cryptography. SIAM J. Comput. **30**(2), 391–437 (2000)
35. Dziembowski, S.: Intrusion-resilience via the bounded-storage model. In: Halevi and Rabin [49], pp. 207–224
36. Dziembowski, S., Kazana, T., Obremski, M.: Non-malleable codes from two-source extractors. In: Canetti, R., Garay, J.A. (eds.) CRYPTO 2013, Part II. LNCS, vol. 8043, pp. 239–257. Springer, Heidelberg (2013). https://doi.org/10.1007/978-3-642-40084-1_14
37. Dziembowski, S., Kazana, T., Wichs, D.: Key-evolution schemes resilient to space-bounded leakage. In: Rogaway [68], pp. 335–353
38. Dziembowski, S., Pietrzak, K.: Intrusion-resilient secret sharing. In: 48th FOCS, pp. 227–237. IEEE Computer Society Press, October 2007
39. Dziembowski, S., Pietrzak, K., Wichs, D.: Non-malleable codes. In: Yao, A.C.C. (ed.) ICS 2010, pp. 434–452. Tsinghua University Press, January 2010
40. Faonio, A., Nielsen, J.B., Venturi, D.: Fully leakage-resilient signatures revisited. Theor. Comput. Sci. **660**(C), 23–56 (2017). https://doi.org/10.1016/j.tcs.2016.11.016
41. Faust, S., Hostáková, K., Mukherjee, P., Venturi, D.: Non-malleable codes for space-bounded tampering. In: Katz, J., Shacham, H. (eds.) CRYPTO 2017, Part II. LNCS, vol. 10402, pp. 95–126. Springer, Cham (2017). https://doi.org/10.1007/978-3-319-63715-0_4
42. Faust, S., Mukherjee, P., Nielsen, J.B., Venturi, D.: Continuous non-malleable codes. In: Lindell [61], pp. 465–488
43. Faust, S., Mukherjee, P., Nielsen, J.B., Venturi, D.: A tamper and leakage resilient von Neumann architecture. In: Katz, J. (ed.) PKC 2015. LNCS, vol. 9020, pp. 579–603. Springer, Heidelberg (2015). https://doi.org/10.1007/978-3-662-46447-2_26
44. Faust, S., Mukherjee, P., Venturi, D., Wichs, D.: Efficient non-malleable codes and key-derivation for poly-size tampering circuits. In: Nguyen, P.Q., Oswald, E. (eds.) EUROCRYPT 2014. LNCS, vol. 8441, pp. 111–128. Springer, Heidelberg (2014). https://doi.org/10.1007/978-3-642-55220-5_7
45. Gennaro, R., Lysyanskaya, A., Malkin, T., Micali, S., Rabin, T.: Algorithmic tamper-proof (ATP) security: theoretical foundations for security against hardware tampering. In: Naor, M. (ed.) TCC 2004. LNCS, vol. 2951, pp. 258–277. Springer, Heidelberg (2004). https://doi.org/10.1007/978-3-540-24638-1_15
46. Goyal, V., Pandey, O., Richelson, S.: Textbook non-malleable commitments. In: Wichs and Mansour [69], pp. 1128–1141
47. Groth, J.: Simulation-sound NIZK proofs for a practical language and constant size group signatures. In: Lai, X., Chen, K. (eds.) ASIACRYPT 2006. LNCS, vol. 4284, pp. 444–459. Springer, Heidelberg (2006). https://doi.org/10.1007/11935230_29

48. Halevi, S. (ed.): CRYPTO 2009. LNCS, vol. 5677. Springer, Heidelberg (2009). https://doi.org/10.1007/978-3-642-03356-8
49. Halevi, S., Rabin, T. (eds.): TCC 2006. LNCS, vol. 3876. Springer, Heidelberg (2006). https://doi.org/10.1007/11681878
50. Ishai, Y., Prabhakaran, M., Sahai, A., Wagner, D.: Private circuits II: keeping secrets in tamperable circuits. In: Vaudenay, S. (ed.) EUROCRYPT 2006. LNCS, vol. 4004, pp. 308–327. Springer, Heidelberg (2006). https://doi.org/10.1007/11761679_19
51. Jafargholi, Z., Wichs, D.: Tamper detection and continuous non-malleable codes. In: Dodis and Nielsen [32], pp. 451–480
52. Kalai, Y.T., Kanukurthi, B., Sahai, A.: Cryptography with tamperable and leaky memory. In: Rogaway [68], pp. 373–390
53. Kanukurthi, B., Obbattu, S.L.B., Sekar, S.: Four-state non-malleable codes with explicit constant rate. In: Kalai, Y., Reyzin, L. (eds.) TCC 2017, Part II. LNCS, vol. 10678, pp. 344–375. Springer, Cham (2017). https://doi.org/10.1007/978-3-319-70503-3_11
54. Katz, J., Trevisan, L.: On the efficiency of local decoding procedures for error-correcting codes. In: 32nd ACM STOC, pp. 80–86. ACM Press, May 2000
55. Katz, J., Vaikuntanathan, V.: Signature schemes with bounded leakage resilience. In: Matsui, M. (ed.) ASIACRYPT 2009. LNCS, vol. 5912, pp. 703–720. Springer, Heidelberg (2009). https://doi.org/10.1007/978-3-642-10366-7_41
56. Kiayias, A., Liu, F.H., Tselekounis, Y.: Practical non-malleable codes from l-more extractable hash functions. In: Weippl, E.R., Katzenbeisser, S., Kruegel, C., Myers, A.C., Halevi, S. (eds.) ACM CCS 16, pp. 1317–1328. ACM Press, October 2016
57. Kocher, P.C.: Timing attacks on implementations of Diffie-Hellman, RSA, DSS, and other systems. In: Koblitz, N. (ed.) CRYPTO 1996. LNCS, vol. 1109, pp. 104–113. Springer, Heidelberg (1996). https://doi.org/10.1007/3-540-68697-5_9
58. Kocher, P., Jaffe, J., Jun, B.: Differential power analysis. In: Wiener, M. (ed.) CRYPTO 1999. LNCS, vol. 1666, pp. 388–397. Springer, Heidelberg (1999). https://doi.org/10.1007/3-540-48405-1_25
59. Kushilevitz, E., Malkin, T. (eds.): TCC 2016-A, Part II. LNCS, vol. 9563. Springer, Heidelberg (2016). https://doi.org/10.1007/978-3-662-49099-0
60. Lindell, Y.: A simpler construction of CCA2-secure public-key encryption under general assumptions. In: Biham, E. (ed.) EUROCRYPT 2003. LNCS, vol. 2656, pp. 241–254. Springer, Heidelberg (2003). https://doi.org/10.1007/3-540-39200-9_15
61. Lindell, Y. (ed.): TCC 2014. LNCS, vol. 8349. Springer, Heidelberg (2014). https://doi.org/10.1007/978-3-642-54242-8
62. Liu, F.-H., Lysyanskaya, A.: Tamper and leakage resilience in the split-state model. In: Safavi-Naini, R., Canetti, R. (eds.) CRYPTO 2012. LNCS, vol. 7417, pp. 517–532. Springer, Heidelberg (2012). https://doi.org/10.1007/978-3-642-32009-5_30
63. Naor, M., Segev, G.: Public-key cryptosystems resilient to key leakage. In: Halevi [48], pp. 18–35
64. Naor, M., Yung, M.: Public-key cryptosystems provably secure against chosen ciphertext attacks. In: 22nd ACM STOC, pp. 427–437. ACM Press, May 1990
65. Nielsen, J.B., Venturi, D., Zottarel, A.: Leakage-resilient signatures with graceful degradation. In: Krawczyk, H. (ed.) PKC 2014. LNCS, vol. 8383, pp. 362–379. Springer, Heidelberg (2014). https://doi.org/10.1007/978-3-642-54631-0_21
66. Pietrzak, K.: A leakage-resilient mode of operation. In: Joux, A. (ed.) EUROCRYPT 2009. LNCS, vol. 5479, pp. 462–482. Springer, Heidelberg (2009). https://doi.org/10.1007/978-3-642-01001-9_27

67. Regev, O.: On lattices, learning with errors, random linear codes, and cryptography. In: Gabow, H.N., Fagin, R. (eds.) 37th ACM STOC, pp. 84–93. ACM Press, May 2005
68. Rogaway, P. (ed.): CRYPTO 2011. LNCS, vol. 6841. Springer, Heidelberg (2011). https://doi.org/10.1007/978-3-642-22792-9
69. Wichs, D., Mansour, Y. (eds.): 48th ACM STOC. ACM Press, June 2016

Non-malleability vs. CCA-Security:
The Case of Commitments

Brandon Broadnax[(✉)], Valerie Fetzer, Jörn Müller-Quade, and Andy Rupp

Karlsruhe Institute of Technology, Karlsruhe, Germany
{brandon.broadnax,valerie.fetzer,joern.mueller-quade,andy.rupp}@kit.edu

Abstract. In this work, we settle the relations among a variety of security notions related to non-malleability and CCA-security that have been proposed for commitment schemes in the literature. Interestingly, all our separations follow from two generic transformations. Given two appropriate security notions X and Y from the class of security notions we compare, these transformations take a commitment scheme that fulfills notion X and output a commitment scheme that still fulfills notion X but not notion Y.

Using these transformations, we are able to show that some of the known relations for public-key encryption do not carry over to commitments. In particular, we show that, surprisingly, parallel non-malleability and parallel CCA-security are not equivalent for commitment schemes. This stands in contrast to the situation for public-key encryption where these two notions are equivalent as shown by Bellare et al. at CRYPTO '99.

1 Introduction

A commitment scheme is a two-party protocol that enables one party, called the sender, to commit himself to a value, while keeping it hidden from others and to later reveal that value to the other party, called the receiver. Commitment schemes belong to the most important building blocks of cryptography and have many applications including coin flipping protocols, signature schemes and zero-knowledge proofs.

Non-malleability (first introduced in [15]) is an important security notion for commitment schemes that is, like its counterpart for encryption schemes, concerned with defending against man-in-the-middle attacks. Informally, a commitment scheme is called (stand-alone) *non-malleable* if it is impossible for a man-in-the-middle adversary that receives a commitment to a value v to "successfully" commit to a related value $\tilde{v}$.

B. Broadnax, J. Müller-Quade and A. Rupp—The author is supported by the German Federal Ministry of Education and Research within the framework of the project "Sicherheit vernetzter Infrastrukturen (SVI)" in the Competence Center for Applied Security Technology (KASTEL).

V. Fetzer and A. Rupp—The author is supported by DFG grant RU 1664/3-1.

M. Abdalla and R. Dahab (Eds.): PKC 2018, LNCS 10770, pp. 312–337, 2018.
https://doi.org/10.1007/978-3-319-76581-5_11

Several variants of non-malleability have been defined in the literature. For *parallel non-malleability* [16] the adversary receives multiple commitments in parallel and commits to multiple values in parallel. For *concurrent non-malleability* [26] the adversary receives and sends multiple commitments in an arbitrary schedule determined by the adversary.

There are many works on non-malleable commitment schemes in the literature, e.g., [11,13,16,18,19,22,27,31]. Non-malleable commitment schemes have numerous applications in the field of multi-party computation. For instance, parallel non-malleable commitment schemes have been used for constructing round-efficient (six round) MPC protocols [16], concurrently non-malleable commitment schemes have been used as a building block for black-box MPC protocols [31] and (stand-alone) non-malleable commitment schemes have been used for concurrently composable protocols [27].

Another security notion related to non-malleability is *CCA-security* [25]. A commitment scheme is called *CCA-secure* if it remains hiding even if the adversary has access to an oracle that "breaks" polynomially many commitments. There exist several relaxed variants of CCA-security. For *parallel CCA-security* [24] the adversary can ask the oracle a single query that consists of polynomially many commitments sent to the oracle in parallel. For *one-one CCA-security* [23] the adversary can ask the oracle a single query that consists of exactly one commitment.

CCA-secure commitment schemes are a central building block for concurrently secure multi-party computation in the *plain model*, i.e., without trusted setup apart from authenticated channels. CCA-secure commitment schemes were introduced by [9] in the context of "angel-based security". Angel-based security, first proposed by [30], relaxes the security notion of the universal composability framework (UC) [6] in order to circumvent the broad impossibility results of the latter. In the angel-based security framework, concurrently secure multi-party computation in the plain model can be achieved for (almost) every cryptographic task [9,10,23–25]. This stands in contrast to the UC framework where many important functionalities such as commitments or zero-knowledge cannot be realized in the plain model (see, e.g., [7,8]). Moreover, parallel CCA-secure commitment schemes [5,23] and one-one CCA-secure commitment schemes [23,24] were used as building blocks for several recent round-efficient concurrently secure general multi-party computation protocols in the plain model.

Considering this great variety of useful security notions, it is a natural question to ask how these notions are related. Surprisingly, only a few relations have been analyzed so far (cf. Fig. 1). Most works focus either on security notions related to CCA-security *or* on security notions related to non-malleability. In this work we focus on the relations *between* the two concepts and provide a more complete relation diagram. Motivated by public-key encryption, we also define and analyze the hierarchy of *q-bounded CCA-security* [14], where the adversary can adaptively ask the oracle at most q queries for a fixed natural number q.

Related Work. This work is in the vein of a series of papers establishing relations between different variants of security definitions for public-key encryption and commitments such as [1–4,12,14,29]. For instance, Bellare et al. [1] prove relations among non-malleability-based and indistinguishability-based notions of security for public-key encryption. In particular, they show that IND-CCA2-security and NM-CCA2-security are equivalent. Bellare and Sahai [3] show that the indistinguishability-based definition of non-malleable encryption is equivalent to the simulation-based definition. Moreover, they show that non-malleability is equivalent to indistinguishability for public-key encryption under a "parallel chosen ciphertext attack". Bellare et al. [2] show that standard security for commitment schemes does not imply selective opening security. Böhl et al. [4] analyze the relations between indistinguishability-based and simulation-based definitions of selective opening security for public-key encryption.

For the class of security notions for commitment schemes that are considered in this work, only a few relations are resolved, however. Pandey et al. [28] show that CCA-security implies concurrent non-malleability. In [13] Ciampi et al. show that the non-malleable commitment scheme from a preliminary version of [20] is not concurrently non-malleable. Lin et al. [26] construct a commitment scheme that separates non-malleability and parallel non-malleability. The remaining relations are, to the best of our knowledge, unsettled.

Our Contribution. We settle the relations among a variety of security notions related to non-malleability and CCA-security that have been proposed for commitment schemes in the literature (see Fig. 1).[1]

Our results show, in particular, that some of the known results from previous works that dealt with public-key encryption do not carry over to the case of commitment schemes. In particular, the result of Bellare and Sahai [3], who showed that parallel non-malleability and parallel CCA-security are equivalent for public-key encryption schemes, does not hold for commitment schemes, in general. These two notions are only equivalent for non-interactive commitment schemes (see Appendix A).

Interestingly, we are able to obtain all of our separation results using two generic transformations. Given two appropriate security notions X and Y from the class of security notions we compare in this work, these transformations take a commitment scheme that fulfills notion X and output a commitment scheme that still fulfills notion X but not notion Y. Both transformations are fully black-box and require no additional computational assumptions.

The first transformation is used for separations where Y is a CCA-related security notion. The key idea of this transformation is to expand a commitment scheme that fulfills a security notion X by a "puzzle phase" where the sender sends a specific computationally hard puzzle to the receiver. If the receiver answers with a correct solution, then the sender "gives up" and sends his input

---

[1] Note that we always use *statistically binding* commitment schemes in this work, since we want the committed values in the experiments for CCA-security and non-malleability (as well as their variants) to be uniquely defined (with overwhelming probability). We note that using *strong computationally binding* commitment schemes would also work.

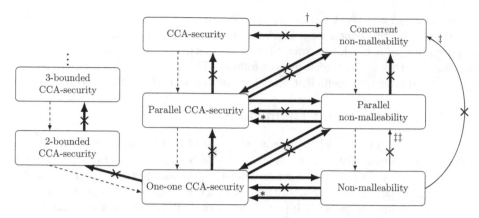

* only for non-interactive commitment schemes

Fig. 1. The relations between several security notions for commitment schemes. The dotted arrows indicate trivial implications. The thin solid arrows indicate relations proved in the literature (see [28] for † and [13] for ‡) or separating commitment schemes from the literature (such as the scheme $\langle \tilde{C}, \tilde{R} \rangle$ from [26] for ‡‡). The thick arrows indicate our results.

to the receiver who can then trivially win in the security game in this case. If the puzzle is tailored appropriately, then the expanded commitment scheme still fulfills notion X but fails to fulfill notion Y. Intuitively, this separation holds because an adversary in the Y-security game has access to an oracle that "breaks" the puzzle but an adversary in the X-security game does not.

The second transformation is used for separations where Y is a variant of non-malleability. This transformation expands a given commitment scheme by adding a "share phase" in which the sender commits to two random shares of his input in a specific order. This is done in such a way that a man-in-the-middle adversary is able to forward these commitments to the receiver in his experiment. After the commit phase is over, these shares will be opened by the implicit oracle in the experiment and given to the distinguisher, who can then reconstruct the committed value.

On Black-Box Separations. We note that the separations proven in this work differ from *black-box separations*. Separating a security notion X from a security notion Y by a black-box separation means that one cannot construct a scheme satisfying X from a scheme satisfying Y in a *black-box manner*.

Black-box separations are stronger than our separations. However, we note that one cannot achieve black-box separations between the security notions described in this work. This is because, given a (statistically binding) commitment scheme satisfying any of the security notions considered in this work, one can construct a commitment scheme satisfying any other security notion in this work in a black-box way. This can be shown as follows: First, each of the notions described in this work implies the standard hiding property for commitment schemes. Furthermore, given a commitment scheme that is binding and hiding, one can construct a one-way function in a black-box way [21]. Moreover, [23] showed how to construct a CCA-secure commitment scheme from any one-way function in a black-box way. Since CCA-security implies any other notion described in this work, the statement follows. This transformation is, of course, highly redundant and inefficient and therefore only of theoretical interest.

2   Preliminaries and Definitions

For any $x \in \{0,1\}^*$, we let $|x|$ denote the size of x. If S is a set, then $s \xleftarrow{\$} S$ denotes the operation of picking an element s of S uniformly at random. We use the term PPT as abbreviation for probabilistic polynomial time (in the security parameter) in the context of algorithms or machines. We write $\mathcal{A}(x)$ to indicate that $\mathcal{A}$ is an algorithm with input x, we write $\mathcal{A}^{\mathcal{O}}(x)$ to indicate that $\mathcal{A}$ is an algorithm with input x and black-box access to the oracle $\mathcal{O}$ and we write $y \leftarrow \mathcal{A}(x)$ to denote the output y of $\mathcal{A}$ with input x.

The term *negligible* is used for denoting functions that are (asymptotically) smaller than one over any polynomial. More precisely, a function $f(\cdot)$ from non-negative integers to reals is called *negligible* if for every constant $c > 0$ and all sufficiently large k, it holds that $|f(k)| < k^{-c}$.

Commitment Schemes. A commitment scheme is a two-phase two-party protocol in which one party, the sender, commits himself in the first phase (the commit phase) to a value while keeping it secret from the other party, the receiver. In the second phase (the reveal phase) the sender reveals the value he committed to. At the end of this phase the receiver outputs this value. In addition to the requirement that both sender and receiver run in polynomial time, we require that a commitment scheme fulfills the following two properties:

- *Hiding*: The commit phase yields no knowledge of the value to the receiver. This also applies to cheating receivers.
- *Binding*: Given the transcript of the interaction in the first phase, there exists at most one value that the receiver can accept as the correct opening in the reveal phase. This also applies to cheating senders.

For a formal definition see [17]. In this work we focus on statistically binding and computationally hiding (string) commitment schemes, i.e., the binding property holds against unbounded adversaries, while the hiding property only holds against computationally bounded (non-uniform) adversaries. This is because committed values are then uniquely defined with overwhelming probability.

In a tag-based commitment scheme both parties get a bit string called tag as additional input. We will denote by $\mathsf{Com}_{tag}(v)$ a (possibly interactive) commitment to the value $v \in \{0,1\}^k$ under the tag $tag \in \{0,1\}^k$ using the commitment scheme Com.[2] In the following, we only consider tag-based commitment schemes

---

[2] Note that if we later use a formulation like "the sender sends $\mathsf{Com}_{tag}(v)$ to the receiver", we do not necessarily assume that the commitment scheme is non-interactive and hence consists of only one message. We rather use this formulation as an abbreviation for "the sender commits to v under the tag tag to the receiver using the commitment scheme Com".

because the definitions of security notions considered here require tag-based commitment schemes.

CCA-Secure Commitment Schemes. Roughly speaking, a tag-based commitment scheme Com is said to be CCA-secure [25], if the value committed to using a tag tag remains hidden even if the receiver has access to an oracle that "breaks" polynomially many commitments using a different tag $tag' \neq tag$ for him. In this work we consider committed value oracles (oracles that return the committed value) only, but not decommitment oracles (oracles that return the full decommitment information).

The CCA-oracle $\mathcal{O}_{cca}$ for Com acts as follows in an interaction with an adversary $\mathcal{A}$: It participates with $\mathcal{A}$ in polynomially many sessions of the commit phase of Com as an honest receiver (the adversary determines the tag he wants to use at the start of each session). At the end of each session, if the session is valid, the oracle returns the unique value v committed to in the interaction; otherwise, it returns $\perp$. Note that if a session has multiple valid committed values, the CCA-oracle also returns $\perp$. The statistical binding property guarantees that this happens with only negligible probability.

Let $\mathsf{Exp}^{cca}_{\mathsf{Com},\mathcal{A}}(k)$ denote the output of the following probabilistic experiment: Let $\mathcal{O}_{cca}$ be the CCA-oracle for Com. The adversary has access to $\mathcal{O}_{cca}$ during the entire course of the experiment. On input $1^k, z$, the adversary $\mathcal{A}^{\mathcal{O}_{cca}}$ picks a tag tag and two strings v_0 and v_1 with $|v_0| = |v_1|$ and sends this triple to the experiment. The experiment randomly selects a bit $b \overset{\$}{\leftarrow} \{0,1\}$ and then commits to v_b using the tag tag to $\mathcal{A}^{\mathcal{O}_{cca}}$. Finally, $\mathcal{A}^{\mathcal{O}_{cca}}$ sends a bit b' to the experiment, which outputs 1 if $b = b'$ and 0 otherwise. The output of the experiment is replaced by $\perp$ if during the execution the adversary queries the oracle on a commitment that uses the challenge tag tag.

Definition 1 (CCA-secure commitment scheme). *Let Com be a tag-based commitment scheme and $\mathcal{O}_{cca}$ be the CCA-oracle for Com. We say that Com is CCA-secure, if for every* PPT*-adversary $\mathcal{A}$ and all $z \in \{0,1\}^*$ the advantage*

$$\mathsf{Adv}^{cca}_{\mathsf{Com},\mathcal{A}(z)}(k) := \Pr[\,\mathsf{Exp}^{cca}_{\mathsf{Com},\mathcal{A}(z)}(k) = 1\,] - \frac{1}{2}$$

is a negligible function.

Parallel CCA-Secure Commitment Schemes. Parallel CCA-secure commitment schemes are for example defined by Kiyoshima [23]. The parallel CCA-oracle $\mathcal{O}_{pcca}$ is defined like the CCA-oracle, except that the adversary is restricted to a parallel query, i.e., the adversary can only send a single query that may contain multiple commitments sent in parallel. Let $\mathsf{Exp}^{pcca}_{\mathsf{Com},\mathcal{A}}(k)$ define the output of the security game for parallel CCA-security (PCCA). The formal definition is then analogous to the definition of CCA-security.

One-One CCA-Secure Commitment Schemes. One-one CCA-secure commitment schemes are for example defined by Kiyoshima [23]. The one-one CCA-oracle $\mathcal{O}_{1cca}$ is defined like the CCA-oracle, except that the adversary is restricted to a single query consisting of exactly one commitment. Let $\mathsf{Exp}^{\mathsf{1cca}}_{\mathsf{Com},\mathcal{A}}(k)$ define the output of the security game for one-one CCA-security (1CCA). The formal definition is then analogous to the definition of CCA-security.

q-Bounded CCA-Secure Commitment Schemes. The q-bounded CCA-oracle $\mathcal{O}_{q\mathsf{cca}}$ is defined like the CCA-oracle, except that the adversary is restricted to $q \in \mathbb{N}$ queries where each query consists of exactly one commitment. Let $\mathsf{Exp}^{q\mathsf{cca}}_{\mathsf{Com},\mathcal{A}}(k)$ define the output of the security game for q-bounded CCA-security (qCCA). The formal definition is then analogous to the definition of CCA-security. Note that by definition 1-bounded CCA-security equals one-one CCA-security.

Non-malleable Commitment Schemes. We now specify a definition of non-malleable commitment schemes that is essentially a game-based variant of the definition by Goyal et al. [20]. It is easy to see that the two definitions are equivalent. Using a game-based variant of [20] makes it easier to compare this notion with CCA-security.

Let $\mathsf{Exp}^{\mathsf{nm}}_{\mathsf{Com},\mathcal{A},\mathcal{D}}(k)$ denote the output of the following probabilistic experiment: On input $1^k, z$, the adversary $\mathcal{A}$ picks a tag tag and two strings v_0 and v_1 with $|v_0| = |v_1|$, sends this triple to the sender S and gets back the challenge commitment $\mathsf{Com}_{tag}(v_b)$, where b is a random bit chosen by the sender. The adversary then sends a commitment $\mathsf{Com}_{\widetilde{tag}}(\tilde{v}_b)$ to the receiver R. If $\widetilde{tag} = tag$, $\tilde{v}_b$ is set to $\bot$. At the end of this interaction the adversary outputs his view $view_\mathcal{A}$ and the receiver outputs the value $\tilde{v}_b$. Note that the experiment plays the role of the sender and the receiver in the interaction. Also note that the receiver has implicit access to a super-polynomial-time oracle $\mathcal{O}$ that breaks the received commitment for him and that the adversary's view contains the randomness of the adversary and a transcript of all messages sent and received by the adversary. After the interaction has finished, the distinguisher $\mathcal{D}$ gets z, the view $view_\mathcal{A}$ of the adversary and the value $\tilde{v}_b$ as input and outputs a bit b'. The experiment outputs 1 if $b = b'$ and 0 otherwise.

Definition 2 (Non-malleable commitment scheme). *A commitment scheme* Com *is* non-malleable *if for every* PPT *man-in-the-middle adversary* $\mathcal{A}$, *for every* PPT *distinguisher* $\mathcal{D}$ *and all* $z \in \{0,1\}^*$ *the advantage*

$$\mathsf{Adv}^{\mathsf{nm}}_{\mathsf{Com},\mathcal{A}(z),\mathcal{D}}(k) := \Pr[\,\mathsf{Exp}^{\mathsf{nm}}_{\mathsf{Com},\mathcal{A}(z),\mathcal{D}}(k) = 1\,] - \frac{1}{2}$$

is a negligible function.

Concurrent Non-malleable Commitment Schemes. Tag-based concurrent non-malleable commitment schemes are examined by Lin et al. [26]. Here, man-in-the-middle adversaries are participating in left and right interactions in which $m = poly(k)$ commitments take place (where $k \in \mathbb{N}$ is the security parameter).

In the concurrent setting, the adversary $\mathcal{A}$ is simultaneously participating in m left and right interactions. He sends a triple of sequences $(\boldsymbol{tag}, \boldsymbol{v}^0, \boldsymbol{v}^1)$ with $\boldsymbol{tag} = (tag_1, \ldots, tag_m)$, $\boldsymbol{v}^0 = (v_1^0, \ldots, v_m^0)$ and $\boldsymbol{v}^1 = (v_1^1, \ldots, v_m^1)$ to the sender and receives commitments to values $v_1^b, \ldots, v_m^b$ with tags $tag_1, \ldots, tag_m$ from the sender S and commits to values $\tilde{v}_1^b, \ldots, \tilde{v}_m^b$ with tags $\widetilde{tag}_1, \ldots, \widetilde{tag}_m$ to the receiver R. For any i such that $\widetilde{tag}_i = tag_j$ for some j, set $\tilde{v}_i^b = \perp$. Let $\mathsf{Exp}_{\mathsf{Com}, \mathcal{A}, \mathcal{D}}^{\mathsf{cnm}}(k)$ define the output of the security game for concurrent non-malleability (CNM). The formal definition is then analogous to the definition of non-malleability.

Parallel Non-malleable Commitment Schemes. A relaxed notion of concurrent non-malleability is parallel non-malleability [16]. Here, like for concurrent non-malleability, the adversary receives m commitments from the sender and sends m commitments to the receiver. However, for parallel non-malleability the commitments are always sent in parallel. Again, any commitment in the right interaction that uses a tag that is also present in the left interaction is considered invalid. Let $\mathsf{Exp}_{\mathsf{Com}, \mathcal{A}, \mathcal{D}}^{\mathsf{pnm}}(k)$ define the output of the security game for parallel non-malleability (PNM). The formal definition is then analogous to the definition of non-malleability.

$\mathcal{O}$-One-Way Commitment Schemes. Informally speaking, a tag-based commitment scheme Com with message space $\{0,1\}^k$ and tag space $\{0,1\}^k$ is said to be $\mathcal{O}$-one-way, if no PPT-adversary can break a commitment to a random value, even with access to the oracle $\mathcal{O}$. The property can be formally defined with a security game. Let $\mathsf{Exp}_{\mathsf{Com}, \mathcal{A}, \mathcal{O}}^{\mathsf{ow}}(k)$ denote the output of the following probabilistic experiment: The experiment generates a random value v and a random tag tag, i.e., $v \xleftarrow{\$} \{0,1\}^k$, $tag \xleftarrow{\$} \{0,1\}^k$. It then sends the commitment $\mathsf{Com}_{tag}(v)$ as challenge to the PPT-adversary $\mathcal{A}^{\mathcal{O}}$. On input 1^k, z, the adversary now tries to break the commitment and sends at some time his solution v' back to the experiment which outputs 1 if $v = v'$ and 0 otherwise. Note that during the entire course of the game the adversary has access to the oracle $\mathcal{O}$. The output of the experiment is replaced by $\perp$ if during the execution the adversary queries the oracle on a commitment that uses the challenge tag tag.

Definition 3 ($\mathcal{O}$-one-way commitment scheme). *Let* Com *be a tag-based commitment scheme and $\mathcal{O}$ be a specific oracle for it. We say that* Com *is $\mathcal{O}$-one-way, if for every* PPT-*adversary $\mathcal{A}$ and all $z \in \{0,1\}^*$ the advantage*

$$\mathsf{Adv}_{\mathsf{Com}, \mathcal{A}(z), \mathcal{O}}^{\mathsf{ow}}(k) := \Pr[\mathsf{Exp}_{\mathsf{Com}, \mathcal{A}(z), \mathcal{O}}^{\mathsf{ow}}(k) = 1]$$

is a negligible function.

This definition can be instantiated with various oracles. For example, $\mathcal{O}_{\mathsf{cca}}$-one-wayness describes a security notion where the one-way adversary has access to the CCA-oracle for the commitment scheme in question. Note that CCA-security implies $\mathcal{O}_{\mathsf{cca}}$-one-wayness. Similarly, parallel CCA-security implies $\mathcal{O}_{\mathsf{pcca}}$-one-wayness, one-one CCA-security implies $\mathcal{O}_{\mathsf{1cca}}$-one-wayness and q-bounded CCA-security implies $\mathcal{O}_{\mathsf{qcca}}$-one-wayness. Also note that non-malleability (and its stronger variants) implies ε-one-wayness for the empty oracle ε. Note that the empty oracle just returns $\perp$ for each query.

Extractable Commitment Schemes. Finally, we define extractable commitment schemes:

Definition 4 (Extractable commitment scheme). *Let* Com *be a statistically binding commitment scheme. Then,* Com *is* extractable *if there exists a* PPT *oracle machine E (the "extractor") such that for any* PPT *sender* S^*, E^{S^*} *outputs a pair (τ, σ) such that*

- *τ is identically distributed to the view of* S^* *at the end of interacting with an honest receiver* R *in the commit phase.*
- *the probability that τ is accepting and $\sigma \neq \perp$ is negligible.*
- *if $\sigma \neq \perp$, then it is statistically impossible to decommit τ to any value other than σ.*

3   The First Transformation: Puzzle-Solution Approach

In this section, we describe the first transformation in this work. We call this approach the *puzzle-solution approach* because the general idea is to expand a commitment scheme by a puzzle phase that is executed at the beginning. Let X and Y be security notions for commitment schemes for which one wants to show that X does not imply Y. For the first transformation, Y will always be a CCA-related security notion. Let $\mathcal{O}_X$ be the oracle an adversary can use in the security game for the notion X. Let analogously $\mathcal{O}_Y$ be the oracle an adversary can use in the security game for the notion Y (note that these oracles can be the "empty oracle"). Let Com be a (possibly interactive) commitment scheme that fulfills X. We will sometimes call Com the base commitment scheme.

3.1   The Construction

Using Com, one can then define the separating commitment scheme, which we will denote by Com$'$. We define Com$'$ as output of a transformation PComGen that gets a base commitment scheme, a number $l \in \mathbb{N}$ and a string sch $\in \{seq, par\}$ as input, i.e., Com$' \leftarrow$ PComGen(Com, l, sch).

In the commitment scheme Com$'$ the sender S, who wants to commit to a value v given a tag tag, first sends a puzzle to the receiver R and, depending on whether R solves the puzzle or not, sends v either as plaintext or commits to v using the base commitment scheme Com. The puzzle consists of l commitments to random messages (using Com) that are either sent in parallel (if sch $= par$) or sequentially (if sch $= seq$) to R. More specifically, the sender randomly generates l tags of length k and l values also of length k, i.e., $(tag_p^1, \ldots, tag_p^l) \xleftarrow{\$} (\{0,1\}^k)^l$, $(w_1, \ldots, w_l) \xleftarrow{\$} (\{0,1\}^k)^l$.

If sch $= par$, the sender commits in *parallel* to $(w_1, \ldots, w_l)$ under the tags $(tag_p^1, \ldots, tag_p^l)$ to the receiver. The receiver then answers with a possible solution to the puzzle by simply guessing, i.e., sending random $(w_1', \ldots, w_l')$. The sender then checks if for all $i \in \{1, \ldots, l\}$ it holds that $w_i = w_i'$. If this is the case, S sends v as plaintext to the receiver. If it does not hold, S commits to v using the tag tag and the commitment scheme Com to R.

If sch $= seq$, the sender *sequentially* commits to $(w_1, \ldots, w_l)$ under the tags $(tag_p^1, \ldots, tag_p^l)$ to the receiver. More specifically, he first commits to w_1 using the tag tag_p^1 and the commitment scheme Com and waits for the possible solution. The receiver R then sends a random value w_1' to S. If the solution is incorrect, then S commits to v using the tag tag and the base commitment scheme Com to R. Otherwise, he continues the puzzle phase by sending the second puzzle commitment, i.e., $\mathsf{Com}_{tag_p^2}(w_2)$, to R and again waits for the possible solution. The receiver R then sends another random value w_2' to S. If the solution is incorrect, then S commits to v using the tag tag and the commitment scheme Com. Otherwise, he continues by sending the third puzzle commitment and so forth. If R has correctly solved all l puzzle commitments, S sends v as plaintext to the receiver.

Remark 1. When designing the separating commitment scheme, l and sch should be carefully picked. The puzzle should be selected in such a way that it can be solved with $\mathcal{O}_Y$ but not with $\mathcal{O}_X$.

3.2 The Proof Strategy

To prove that X does not imply Y, one shows that the constructed commitment scheme Com' still fulfills X if the base commitment scheme Com fulfills X, but not Y.

Show that Com' is not Y-secure. For that purpose, one constructs an adversary $\mathcal{A}$, who breaks the Y-security of Com'. The strategy for $\mathcal{A}$ is to let $\mathcal{O}_Y$ solve the puzzle for him. He then gets the challenge value as plaintext and can thus trivially win in the security game for Y.

The probability that $\mathcal{A}$ wins the game is overwhelming because the only possibilities how $\mathcal{A}$ can lose are: (1) the oracle solves the puzzle it gets before the query, (2) a session with the oracle has multiple valid committed values and $\mathcal{O}_Y$ thus returns $\bot$, (3) during the execution the adversary queries the oracle on a commitment that uses the challenge tag (which happens if a puzzle commitment uses the challenge tag). Since one can show that each possibility occurs only with negligible probability, the overall winning probability of $\mathcal{A}$ is overwhelming.

Show that Com' is X-secure (under the assumption that Com is X-secure). Let $\mathcal{A}$ be an adversary on Com' in the security game for X, who wins the game with non-negligible advantage. Depending whether or not $\mathcal{A}$ solves at least one puzzle[3] in the security game for X, one has to distinguish two cases. For each case one builds an adversary who breaks the X-security of the commitment scheme Com.

Case 1: $\mathcal{A}$ solves at least one puzzle. In this case, one constructs an adversary $\mathcal{B}_1$ on the $\mathcal{O}_X$-one-wayness of Com. Recall that X-security implies $\mathcal{O}_X$-one-wayness for our cases. We denote by n the number of challenge commitments

---

[3] Note that for example in the concurrent non-malleability security game multiple puzzles (with $l = 1$ for each puzzle) are sent (one for each session).

$\mathcal{A}$ awaits. Since each of the n corresponding puzzles contains l commitments, $\mathcal{A}$ expects in total $m = l \cdot n$ puzzle commitments. The strategy of $\mathcal{B}_1$ is then first to randomly generate $m - 1$ puzzle values and tags and to randomly select a $j \in \{1, \ldots, m\}$. After $\mathcal{B}_1$ has received the challenge $\mathsf{Com}_{tag}(v)$ from the experiment, he starts to send $\mathcal{A}$ the puzzle(s). For all puzzle commitments except the jth he uses the honestly generated values and tags. As j^{th} puzzle commitment he uses the challenge. After $\mathcal{A}$ has sent the solution to the jth puzzle commitment (aka the challenge), $\mathcal{B}_1$ terminates the simulation of $\mathcal{A}$ and sends $\mathcal{A}$'s solution to the jth puzzle commitment as his own solution to the experiment.

If $\mathcal{A}$ asks his oracle $\mathcal{O}_X$ during the game, $\mathcal{B}_1$ sends random answers in the puzzle phase (to simulate the oracle) and forwards the actual oracle query to his own $\mathcal{O}_X$. There is a chance that $\mathcal{B}_1$'s experiment returns $\perp$ at the end of the experiment. This happens if one of $\mathcal{A}$'s oracle queries contains a tag that equals $\mathcal{B}_1$'s challenge tag. This case may occur with non-negligible probability because the challenge tags of $\mathcal{A}$ and $\mathcal{B}_1$ are not necessarily identical. Fortunately, the opposite event also occurs with non-negligible probability.

The adversary $\mathcal{B}_1$ thus wins his game if $\mathcal{A}$ solves the puzzle commitment that is the challenge and $\mathcal{A}$'s oracle queries do not involve the challenge tag.

Case 2: $\mathcal{A}$ solves none of the puzzles. In this case one builds an adversary $\mathcal{B}_2$ on the X-security of Com. The strategy of $\mathcal{B}_2$ is to send random puzzle(s) to $\mathcal{A}$, who fails to solve them (by assumption). After the puzzle phase, $\mathcal{B}_2$ forwards his own challenge to $\mathcal{A}$. The adversary $\mathcal{B}_2$ also forwards $\mathcal{A}$'s solution as his own solution to the experiment.

If $\mathcal{A}$ asks his oracle $\mathcal{O}_X$ during the game, $\mathcal{B}_2$ sends random answers in the puzzle phase (to simulate the oracle) and forwards the actual oracle query to his own $\mathcal{O}_X$. Here, the challenge tags of $\mathcal{A}$ and $\mathcal{B}_2$ are always identical (because $\mathcal{B}_2$ forwards it to his experiment), so the possibility of $\mathcal{B}_2$'s experiment outputting $\perp$ is not a problem in this case.

The adversary $\mathcal{B}_2$ thus wins his game if $\mathcal{A}$ wins his own game and solves no puzzle.

4 A Concrete Example of the Puzzle Solution Approach: Concurrent Non-malleability Does Not Imply CCA-Security

In this section, we apply the puzzle-solution approach to separate the notion of CCA-security from the notion of concurrent non-malleability.[4] To this end, we define Com' as $\mathsf{Com}' \leftarrow \mathsf{PComGen}(\mathsf{Com}, 1, seq)$ where Com is a statistically binding, concurrent non-malleable commitment scheme. The puzzle hence consists of just one commitment (thus the scheduling does not matter in this case). We follow the proof strategy described in Sect. 3.

---

[4] While the separation of CCA-security from concurrent non-malleability is not very surprising, we have nonetheless chosen to give a full proof for this separation. This is because this proof is one of the easier applications of our puzzle-solution approach and therefore (hopefully) a good example for the reader.

Theorem 1 (CNM $\not\Rightarrow$ CCA). *If* Com *is a statistically binding, concurrent non-malleable commitment scheme, then* Com$'$ $\leftarrow$ PComGen(Com, 1, seq) *is also statistically binding and concurrent non-malleable but not CCA-secure.*

Proof. The statistical binding property of Com$'$ follows readily from the statistical binding property of the underlying commitment scheme Com. In the following, we prove that Com$'$ is concurrent non-malleable but not CCA-secure.[5]

Claim 1: Com$'$ is not CCA-secure. We show that we can build a CCA-adversary $\mathcal{A}$, such that $\mathcal{A}$ wins the CCA-security game for the commitment scheme Com$'$ with non-negligible advantage.

The CCA-adversary $\mathcal{A}$ acts as depicted in Fig. 2. His strategy is to let the oracle solve the puzzle he got from the experiment and to hence get the challenge as plaintext. There are three possibilities how $\mathcal{A}$ can lose the game:

- The oracle solves the puzzle, i.e., $y = w_p^*$.
- The puzzle tag equals the challenge tag, i.e., $tag = tag_p$ (in that case the experiment returns $\bot$ as result instead of a bit).
- The query sent to the oracle has more than one valid opening (in that case the oracle returns $w_p' = \bot$).

The first possibility occurs with probability $1/2^k$ because the oracle uniformly selects a solution. The second possibility also occurs with probability $1/2^k$ because the puzzle tag is uniformly selected. The third possibility occurs with negligible probability, which we denote by $\mathsf{negl}_1(k)$, because Com is by assumption statistically binding. Thus, $\mathcal{A}$'s advantage is non-negligible:

$$\mathsf{Adv}^{\mathsf{cca}}_{\mathsf{Com}',\mathcal{A}}(k) = \Pr[\mathsf{Exp}^{\mathsf{cca}}_{\mathsf{Com}',\mathcal{A}}(k) = 1] - \frac{1}{2}$$

$$\geq 1 - \frac{1}{2^k} - \frac{1}{2^k} - \mathsf{negl}_1(k) - \frac{1}{2}$$

$$= \frac{1}{2} - \frac{1}{2^{k-1}} - \mathsf{negl}_1(k)$$

Claim 2: Com$'$ is concurrent non-malleable. Let us assume Com$'$ is not concurrent non-malleable. Then we show that Com is also not concurrent non-malleable. Consider an adversary $\mathcal{A}$ and distinguisher $\mathcal{D}_{\mathcal{A}}$ such that $\mathcal{A}$ wins in the concurrent non-malleability security game for the commitment scheme Com$'$ with advantage $\mathsf{Adv}^{\mathsf{cnm}}_{\mathsf{Com}',\mathcal{A},\mathcal{D}_{\mathcal{A}}}(k)$. Let $m = poly(k)$, where k is the security parameter, be the number of concurrent commitment sessions initiated by the sender in the concurrent non-malleability security game for Com$'$. Then we can split up $\mathcal{A}$'s advantage into

$$\mathsf{Adv}^{\mathsf{cnm}}_{\mathsf{Com}',\mathcal{A},\mathcal{D}_{\mathcal{A}}}(k) = \Pr[\mathsf{Exp}^{\mathsf{cnm}}_{\mathsf{Com}',\mathcal{A},\mathcal{D}_{\mathcal{A}}}(k) = 1 \wedge \exists i : \mathcal{A} \text{ solves puzzle } i]$$

$$+ \Pr[\mathsf{Exp}^{\mathsf{cnm}}_{\mathsf{Com}',\mathcal{A},\mathcal{D}_{\mathcal{A}}}(k) = 1 \wedge \nexists i : \mathcal{A} \text{ solves puzzle } i] - \frac{1}{2} \quad (1)$$

---

[5] For ease of notation, we omit the (non-uniform) input z of the adversary and distinguisher. The proof can be easily adapted to include this input.

$\mathsf{Exp}_{\mathsf{cca}}$ $\qquad\qquad\qquad\qquad$ $\mathcal{A}$ $\qquad\qquad\qquad\qquad$ $\mathcal{O}_{\mathsf{cca}}$

$$tag \xleftarrow{\$} \{0,1\}^k$$
$$(v_0,v_1) \xleftarrow{\$} \left(\{0,1\}^k\right)^2$$

$\xleftarrow{\quad (tag,v_0,v_1) \quad}$

$$b \xleftarrow{\$} \{0,1\}$$
$$tag_p \xleftarrow{\$} \{0,1\}^k$$
$$w_p \xleftarrow{\$} \{0,1\}^k$$

$\xrightarrow{\quad \mathsf{Com}_{tag_p}(w_p) \quad}$

$$tag_p^* \xleftarrow{\$} \{0,1\}^k$$
$$w_p^* \xleftarrow{\$} \{0,1\}^k$$

$\xrightarrow{\quad \mathsf{Com}_{tag_p^*}(w_p^*) \quad}$
$\xleftarrow{\quad y \quad}$ $\quad y \xleftarrow{\$} \{0,1\}^k$

If $y = w_p^*$, give up
Else, continue

$\xrightarrow{\quad \mathsf{Com}_{tag_p}(w_p) \quad}$
$\xleftarrow{\quad w_p' \quad}$

$\xleftarrow{\quad w_p' \quad}$

If $w_p' = w_p$, send v_b
Else, send $\mathsf{Com}_{tag}(v_b)$

$\xrightarrow{\quad =: x \quad}$
$\quad v_b \ / \ \mathsf{Com}_{tag}(v_b)$

If $x \notin \{v_0,v_1\}$, give up
Else, continue

$$b' := \begin{cases} 1 & \text{, if } x \text{ equals } v_1 \\ 0 & \text{, otherwise} \end{cases}$$

$\xleftarrow{\quad b' \quad}$

$\downarrow$

$\bot$, if $tag_p = tag_p^*$
1, if $b = b'$
0, otherwise

Fig. 2. Graphical depiction of the behavior of the adversary $\mathcal{A}$ in the CCA-security game for the commitment scheme Com'. Note that $w_p' \in \{w_p, \bot\}$ is either the unique committed value w_p or, if the commitment has more than one valid opening, $\bot$.

Hence, in the following it suffices to consider that $\mathcal{A}$ wins and

– Case 1: $\mathcal{A}$ solves at least one of the m puzzles.
– Case 2: $\mathcal{A}$ solves none of the m puzzles.

Case 1: $\mathcal{A}$ solves at least one of the m puzzles. Using $\mathcal{A}$ we construct an adversary $\mathcal{B}_1$ against the ε-one-wayness (for the empty oracle ε) of the commitment scheme Com. The adversary $\mathcal{B}_1$ acts as depicted in Fig. 3 in the ε-one-way security game for the commitment scheme Com. His strategy is to mimic the experiment for $\mathcal{A}$ in the concurrent non-malleability security game and to replace a random puzzle commitment with the challenge he got from his own experiment. Note that depending on the behavior of $\mathcal{A}$, it may at some time happen that $\mathcal{A}$ sends a puzzle to who he believes is the receiver, but is actually $\mathcal{B}_1$. If $\mathcal{B}_1$ receives such a puzzle $\mathsf{Com}_{\widetilde{tag}_p^i}(\tilde{w}_i)$ from $\mathcal{A}$, he acts as an honest receiver and sends a random

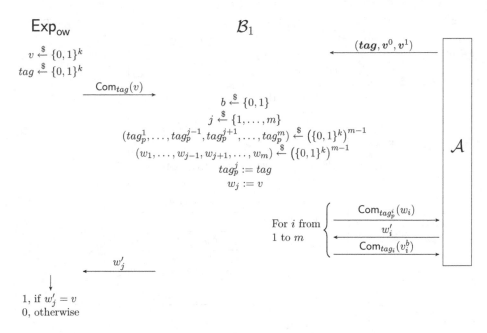

Fig. 3. Graphical depiction of the behavior of the adversary $\mathcal{B}_1$ in the ε-one-way security game for the commitment scheme Com. Note that $\boldsymbol{tag} = (tag_1, \ldots, tag_m)$, $\boldsymbol{v}^0 = (v_1^0, \ldots, v_m^0)$ and $\boldsymbol{v}^1 = (v_1^1, \ldots, v_m^1)$.

solution $\tilde{w}_i'$ back. The time of $\mathcal{A}$'s interaction with the "receiver" or the contents of the puzzle do not matter in this case, therefore this interaction is omitted in Fig. 3.

By construction, $\mathcal{B}_1$ wins the game if v equals w_j', which happens if $\mathcal{A}$ correctly solves the jth puzzle. Thus, the advantage of $\mathcal{B}_1$ is as follows:

$$
\begin{aligned}
\mathsf{Adv}^{\mathsf{ow}}_{\mathsf{Com},\mathcal{B}_1,\varepsilon}(k) &= \Pr[\mathsf{Exp}^{\mathsf{ow}}_{\mathsf{Com},\mathcal{B}_1,\varepsilon}(k) = 1] \\
&\geq \Pr[\mathsf{Exp}^{\mathsf{ow}}_{\mathsf{Com},\mathcal{B}_1,\varepsilon}(k) = 1 \mid \exists i : \mathcal{A} \text{ solves puzzle } i] \\
&\quad \cdot \Pr[\exists i : \mathcal{A} \text{ solves puzzle } i] \\
&\geq \frac{1}{m} \cdot \Pr[\exists i : \mathcal{A} \text{ solves puzzle } i] \\
&\geq \frac{1}{m} \cdot \Pr[\mathsf{Exp}^{\mathsf{cnm}}_{\mathsf{Com}',\mathcal{A},\mathcal{D}_\mathcal{A}}(k) = 1 \wedge \exists i : \mathcal{A} \text{ solves puzzle } i]
\end{aligned}
\tag{2}
$$

Case 2: $\mathcal{A}$ solves none of the m puzzles. Using $\mathcal{A}$, we construct an adversary $\mathcal{B}_2$ against the concurrent non-malleability property of the commitment scheme Com. For each $i \in \{1, \ldots, m\}$, $\mathcal{B}_2$ sends an honestly generated puzzle to $\mathcal{A}$ (thereby simulating the sender), who fails to solve it, and then forwards the ith commitment he gets from the sender to $\mathcal{A}$. When $\mathcal{A}$ interacts with his receiver, who is simulated by $\mathcal{B}_2$, $\mathcal{B}_2$ answers randomly in the puzzle phases (to simulate an honest receiver) and forwards the commitments from $\mathcal{A}$ to his own receiver (cf. Fig. 4).

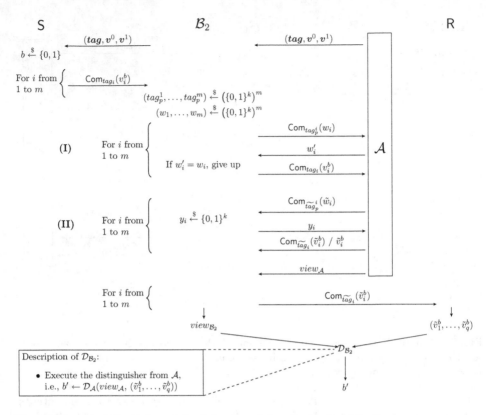

Fig. 4. Graphical depiction of the behavior of the adversary $\mathcal{B}_2$ in the concurrent non-malleability security game for the commitment scheme Com. At **(I)** $\mathcal{A}$'s interaction with the "sender" is depicted and at **(II)** $\mathcal{A}$'s interaction with the "receiver". Note that $\boldsymbol{tag} = (tag_1, \ldots, tag_m)$, $\boldsymbol{v}^0 = (v_1^0, \ldots, v_m^0)$ and $\boldsymbol{v}^1 = (v_1^1, \ldots, v_m^1)$. Note that $\mathsf{Com}_{\widetilde{tag}_i}(\tilde{v}_i^b)/\tilde{v}_i^b$ denotes that, depending on whether $\mathcal{B}_2$ correctly guessed the solution y_i or not, the ith result value is sent as a commitment or as a plaintext value. In the (negligible) case that $\mathcal{B}_2$ correctly solves a puzzle and gets a value $\tilde{v}_i$ as plaintext, he himself commits to this value before sending the commitment to the receiver. Also note that $view_{\mathcal{B}_2}$ contains $view_{\mathcal{A}}$.

The advantage of $\mathcal{B}_2$ in this case is as follows:

$$\mathsf{Adv}_{\mathsf{Com},\mathcal{B}_2,\mathcal{D}_{\mathcal{B}_2}}^{\mathsf{cnm}}(k) = \Pr[\mathsf{Exp}_{\mathsf{Com},\mathcal{B}_2,\mathcal{D}_{\mathcal{B}_2}}^{\mathsf{cnm}}(k) = 1] - \frac{1}{2}$$

$$\geq \Pr[\mathsf{Exp}_{\mathsf{Com},\mathcal{B}_2,\mathcal{D}_{\mathcal{B}_2}}^{\mathsf{cnm}}(k) = 1 \mid \nexists i : \mathcal{A} \text{ solves puzzle } i]$$

$$\cdot \Pr[\nexists i : \mathcal{A} \text{ solves puzzle } i] - \frac{1}{2}$$

$$= \Pr[\mathsf{Exp}_{\mathsf{Com}',\mathcal{A},\mathcal{D}_{\mathcal{A}}}^{\mathsf{cnm}}(k) = 1 \mid \nexists i : \mathcal{A} \text{ solves puzzle } i] \tag{3}$$

$$\cdot \Pr[\nexists i : \mathcal{A} \text{ solves puzzle } i] - \frac{1}{2}$$

$$= \Pr[\mathsf{Exp}_{\mathsf{Com}',\mathcal{A},\mathcal{D}_{\mathcal{A}}}^{\mathsf{cnm}}(k) = 1 \wedge \nexists i : \mathcal{A} \text{ solves puzzle } i] - \frac{1}{2}$$

Putting things together. Putting Eqs. 2 and 3 back into Eq. 1, we get the following:

$$\mathsf{Adv}^{\mathsf{cnm}}_{\mathsf{Com}',\mathcal{A},\mathcal{D}_\mathcal{A}}(k) = \Pr[\mathsf{Exp}^{\mathsf{cnm}}_{\mathsf{Com}',\mathcal{A},\mathcal{D}_\mathcal{A}}(k) = 1 \wedge \exists i : \mathcal{A} \text{ solves puzzle } i]$$

$$+ \Pr[\mathsf{Exp}^{\mathsf{cnm}}_{\mathsf{Com}',\mathcal{A},\mathcal{D}_\mathcal{A}}(k) = 1 \wedge \nexists i : \mathcal{A} \text{ solves puzzle } i] - \frac{1}{2}$$

$$\leq m \cdot \mathsf{Adv}^{\mathsf{ow}}_{\mathsf{Com},\mathcal{B}_1,\varepsilon}(k) + \mathsf{Adv}^{\mathsf{cnm}}_{\mathsf{Com},\mathcal{B}_2,\mathcal{D}_{\mathcal{B}_2}}(k) + \frac{1}{2} - \frac{1}{2}$$

$$= m \cdot \mathsf{Adv}^{\mathsf{ow}}_{\mathsf{Com},\mathcal{B}_1,\varepsilon}(k) + \mathsf{Adv}^{\mathsf{cnm}}_{\mathsf{Com},\mathcal{B}_2,\mathcal{D}_{\mathcal{B}_2}}(k)$$

Since Com is by assumption concurrent non-malleable, it holds that $\mathsf{Adv}^{\mathsf{ow}}_{\mathsf{Com},\mathcal{B}_1,\varepsilon}(k)$ and $\mathsf{Adv}^{\mathsf{cnm}}_{\mathsf{Com},\mathcal{B}_2,\mathcal{D}_{\mathcal{B}_2}}(k)$ are negligible. Thus, $\mathsf{Adv}^{\mathsf{cnm}}_{\mathsf{Com}',\mathcal{A},\mathcal{D}_\mathcal{A}}(k)$ is also negligible, which concludes the proof of the theorem.   □

5   More Instantiations of the Puzzle-Solution Approach

In this section, we show how more separation results can be obtained by appropriate instantiations of the puzzle-solution approach. Therefore, we illustrate how the puzzle-solution approach from Sect. 3 should be instantiated to show the respective result.

Using the same puzzle and very similar arguments as in the proof of Theorem 1, one can prove that parallel non-malleability does not imply parallel CCA-security, that non-malleability does not imply one-one CCA-security, that concurrent non-malleability does not imply parallel CCA-security and that parallel non-malleability does not imply one-one CCA-security.

Theorem 2 (PNM $\not\Rightarrow$ PCCA). *If* Com *is a statistically binding, parallel non-malleable commitment scheme, then* Com' $\leftarrow$ PComGen(Com, 1, seq) *is also statistically binding and parallel non-malleable but not parallel CCA-secure.*

Theorem 3 (NM $\not\Rightarrow$ 1CCA). *If* Com *is a statistically binding, non-malleable commitment scheme, then* Com' $\leftarrow$ PComGen(Com, 1, seq) *is also statistically binding and non-malleable but not one-one CCA-secure.*

Theorem 4 (CNM $\not\Rightarrow$ PCCA). *If* Com *is a statistically binding, concurrent non-malleable commitment scheme, then* Com' $\leftarrow$ PComGen(Com, 1, seq) *is also statistically binding and concurrent non-malleable but not parallel CCA-secure.*

Theorem 5 (PNM $\not\Rightarrow$ 1CCA). *If* Com *is a statistically binding, parallel non-malleable commitment scheme, then* Com' $\leftarrow$ PComGen(Com, 1, seq) *is also statistically binding and parallel non-malleable but not one-one CCA-secure.*

We can prove additional separations using other puzzles.

Theorem 6 (1CCA $\not\Rightarrow$ PCCA). *If* Com *is a statistically binding, one-one CCA-secure commitment scheme, then* Com' $\leftarrow$ PComGen(Com, 2, par) *is also statistically binding and one-one CCA-secure but not parallel CCA-secure.*

Proof Idea. The puzzle consists of two parallel commitments. It is thus solvable with a parallel CCA-oracle but not with a one-one CCA-oracle. The probability that in the reduction of the first case of the second claim the oracle query can be answered is at least $1/2 - 1/2^k$ (with k the tag length).   □

Theorem 7 (PCCA $\not\Rightarrow$ CCA). *If* Com *is a statistically binding, parallel CCA-secure commitment scheme, then* Com' $\leftarrow$ PComGen(Com, 2, seq) *is also statistically binding and parallel CCA-secure but not CCA-secure.*

Proof Idea. The puzzle consists of two sequentially sent commitments. It is thus solvable with a CCA-oracle but not with a parallel CCA-oracle. The probability that in the reduction of the first case of the second claim the oracle query can be answered is at least $1/2 - m/2^k$ (with m the number of commitments in the oracle query and k the tag length).   □

Theorem 8 (qCCA $\not\Rightarrow$ ($q+1$)CCA). *Let $q \geq 1$ be a positive integer. If* Com *is a statistically binding, q-bounded CCA-secure commitment scheme, then* Com' $\leftarrow$ PComGen(Com, $q+1$, seq) *is also statistically binding and q-bounded CCA-secure but not ($q+1$)-bounded CCA-secure.*

Proof Idea. The puzzle consists of $q+1$ sequentially sent commitments. It is thus solvable with a ($q+1$)-bounded CCA-oracle but not with a q-bounded CCA-oracle. The probability that in the reduction of the first case of the second claim the oracle query can be answered is at least $1/q+1 - 1/2^k$ (with k the tag length).   □

6   The Second Transformation: Sharing Approach

In this section, we settle the remaining separations. Up to now we have been able to prove our separations using the puzzle-solution approach. However, in order to prove the remaining separations, we cannot use the puzzle-solution approach anymore. This is because we need to construct commitment schemes that do not fulfill a certain *variant of non-malleability* for the remaining separations. We can therefore no longer insert a puzzle into a given commitment scheme since an adversary (i.e., a man-in-the-middle) in a non-malleability-related experiment does not have a committed value oracle at his disposal that can be used to solve the puzzle.

We therefore deviate from the puzzle-solution approach in the following way: Instead of sending a puzzle, i.e., commitments to random strings, we let the sender commit to *shares* of the message to be committed to using two different random tags. This way, the man-in-the-middle will be able to forward the commitments to the shares to the receiver in his experiment. After the commit phase is over, these shares will then be opened by the implicit oracle in the experiment. The distinguisher will then be able to reconstruct the message and win in the experiment.

Using the above approach, we first show that parallel CCA-security does not imply concurrent non-malleability. To this end, consider the following scheme Com', given a commitment scheme Com:

On input $v \in \{0,1\}^k$, $tag \in \{0,1\}^k$, the sender generates message shares $s_0, s_1 \in \{0,1\}^k$ such that $s_0 \oplus s_1 = v$. He then sends $\mathsf{Com}_{tag_0}(s_0)$ and $\mathsf{Com}_{tag_1}(s_1)$ to the receiver in a *sequential* order using random tags $tag_0, tag_1 \in \{0,1\}^k$. Afterwards, the sender sends $\mathsf{Com}_{tag}(v)$ to the receiver. The unveil phase is the same as in Com (notice that the shares are never unveiled).

First note that, in general, the above construction Com' does not yield a separation between concurrent non-malleability and parallel CCA-security, even if Com is parallel CCA-secure. This is because Com' may fulfill *neither* of these two security notions. For instance, assuming Com is *non-interactive*, an adversary against the parallel CCA-security of Com' can simply forward the two commitments to the shares to his oracle and thereby easily win in his experiment.

In order to obtain a separation, we therefore additionally assume that Com is *extractable*. Note that if a statistically binding, parallel CCA-secure commitment scheme exists, then there also exists a statistically binding, parallel CCA-secure commitment scheme that is additionally extractable. This is because one-way functions can be constructed from commitment schemes [21] (in a black-box way) and [23] showed how to construct an extractable CCA-secure commitment scheme from one-way functions (in a black-box way).

For the proof of the separation between concurrent non-malleability and parallel CCA-security, we use the following experiment as an auxiliary tool:

Definition 5 (RepeatPCCA). *RepeatPCCA is like the ordinary parallel CCA-security game except that the adversary can "reset" the experiment at any given moment.*

More specifically, the adversary (on input 1^k, z) first chooses two strings (v_0, v_1) such that $|v_0| = |v_1|$ and a challenge tag tag and sends (v_0, v_1, tag) to the experiment. The experiment then chooses a random bit $b \leftarrow \{0,1\}$ and commits to v_b using the tag tag. The adversary can then send **reset** *to the experiment or a bit b'. If the adversary sends* **reset***, then he can send new strings (v_0', v_1') and a new challenge tag to the experiment. The experiment then commits to v_b' using the new challenge tag (note that the challenge bit b remains the same.) The adversary may reset the experiment polynomially many times. If the adversary sends a bit b', then the experiment outputs 1 if $b = b'$ and 0 otherwise. Throughout the experiment, the adversary may send a single parallel query to $\mathcal{O}_{\mathsf{pcca}}$ on tags that are different from the current challenge tag. If the adversary sends* **reset** *but hasn't finished his query yet, then his query is invalidated, i.e., the oracle ignores all further messages.*

Denote by $\mathsf{Exp}^{\mathsf{rpcca}}_{\mathsf{Com},\mathcal{A}}(k)$ the output of the above experiment. We say that a tag-based commitment scheme Com is RepeatPCCA-secure if for every PPT-adversary $\mathcal{A}$ and all $z \in \{0,1\}^*$ the advantage

$$\mathsf{Adv}^{\mathsf{rpcca}}_{\mathsf{Com},\mathcal{A}(z)}(k) := \Pr[\,\mathsf{Exp}^{\mathsf{rpcca}}_{\mathsf{Com},\mathcal{A}(z)}(k) = 1\,] - \frac{1}{2}$$

is a negligible function.

We have the following lemma:

Lemma 1. *If a commitment scheme is parallel CCA-secure and extractable, then it is also RepeatPCCA-secure.*

Proof Idea. The proof is by reduction to parallel CCA-security. The reduction $\mathcal{B}$ can answer the oracle query of the adversary $\mathcal{A}$ against the RepeatPCCA-security in the following way: If $\mathcal{A}$ sends his query during $\mathcal{B}$'s challenge phase, then $\mathcal{B}$ forwards the query to his own parallel CCA-oracle. If $\mathcal{A}$ sends his query before or after $\mathcal{B}$'s challenge phase, then $\mathcal{B}$ uses the extractability property. □

We are now ready to prove the following theorem:

Theorem 9 (PCCA $\not\Rightarrow$ CNM). *If there exists a statistically binding, parallel CCA-secure commitment scheme, then there also exists a statistically binding and parallel CCA-secure commitment scheme that is not concurrent non-malleable.*

Proof. Let Com$'$ be as above with a statistically binding, parallel CCA-secure and extractable commitment scheme Com as its base commitment scheme (as noted above, such a Com exists if a statistically binding, parallel CCA-secure commitment scheme exists).

The statistical binding property of Com$'$ follows readily from the statistical binding property of the underlying commitment scheme Com. In the following, we prove that Com$'$ is parallel CCA-secure but not concurrent non-malleable.[6]

Claim 1: Com$'$ is not concurrent non-malleable. A man-in-the-middle adversary in the concurrent non-malleability game first sends $((v_1^0, \ldots, v_m^0),$ $(v_1^1, \ldots, v_m^1), (tag_1, \ldots, tag_m))$ to the sender, who randomly selects a bit b. The sender then commits for each $i \in \{1, \ldots, m\}$ to the shares $s_{i_0}^b$ and $s_{i_1}^b$ using random tags and to v_i^b using tag tag_i to the adversary (with $s_{i_0}^b \oplus s_{i_1}^b = v_i^b$). Let $h := \lfloor \frac{m}{2} \rfloor$. For each $j \in \{1, \ldots, h\}$ the adversary forwards the commitments to $s_{j_0}^b$ and $s_{j_1}^b$ to the sender (as shares for these commitments he just uses commitments to 0^k).[7] If m is odd, he chooses 0^k as his last message to commit to (he also uses commitments to 0^k as shares). The distinguisher is then given $(s_{1_0}^b, s_{1_1}^b, \ldots, s_{h_0}^b, s_{h_1}^b)$ as input (and possibly 0^k) and can thus reconstruct $(v_1^b, \ldots, v_h^b)$, which suffices to deduce the correct b if the challenge messages are chosen appropriately.

Claim 2: Com$'$ is parallel CCA-secure. Let $\mathcal{A}$ be a PPT-adversary against the parallel CCA-security of Com$'$. Consider the following hybrids for the commitment scheme Com$'$: H_0 is the ordinary parallel CCA-security game, H_1 is

---

[6] For ease of notation, we again omit the (non-uniform) input z of the adversary and distinguisher. The proof can be easily adapted to include this input.

[7] Note that the receiver in Com$'$ does not "examine" the commitments to the shares. This would, of course, not work anyway. Since we assume that the commitment scheme Com is hiding, it is impossible for the receiver to learn the values of the shares by any efficient procedure.

like H_0 except that the sender now commits to two random and *independently distributed* strings s_0, t (that therefore do not fulfill $s_0 \oplus t = v$ in general) and finally H_2 that is like H_1 except that the sender commits to 0^k instead of (his input) v.

Let out_i be the output of the hybrid H_i.

Sub-Claim 1: $|\Pr[out_0 = 1] - \Pr[out_1 = 1]| \leq \mathsf{negl}(k)$. Consider the following adversary $\mathcal{B}$ against Com in the RepeatPCCA game: The adversary $\mathcal{B}$ simulates the experiment H_0 for $\mathcal{A}$. $(*)$ After $\mathcal{A}$ has sent (v_0, v_1, tag), $\mathcal{B}$ chooses a random bit $b \leftarrow \{0, 1\}$ and generates shares s_0, s_1 such that $s_0 \oplus s_1 = v_b$ and a random string $t \in \{0, 1\}^k$. The adversary $\mathcal{B}$ then sends (s_1, t, tag_1), where tag_1 is a random tag of length k, to his experiment. Afterwards, $\mathcal{B}$ randomly selects one of the two (sequentially ordered) commit sessions to the shares of v_b in the commit phase of Com' and inserts his challenge C^* into the selected session and $\mathsf{Com}_{tag_0}(s_0)$ into the other session (for a randomly chosen tag $tag_0 \in \{0, 1\}^k$). If the adversary $\mathcal{A}$ starts his (parallel) oracle query *during the challenge phase of $\mathcal{B}$* (i.e., during the session in which $\mathcal{B}$ has inserted his challenge C^*), then $\mathcal{B}$ resets his experiment and repeats the aforementioned strategy (i.e., jumps back to $(*)$).

Otherwise, $\mathcal{B}$ answers $\mathcal{A}$'s oracle query in the following way:

Case 1: If $\mathcal{A}$ starts his query *before* $\mathcal{B}$'s challenge phase has begun *and* $\mathcal{A}$'s query does not use $\mathcal{B}$'s challenge tag tag_1, then $\mathcal{B}$ forwards $\mathcal{A}$'s query to his own parallel CCA-oracle (if $\mathcal{A}$'s query uses $\mathcal{B}$'s challenge tag, then $\mathcal{B}$ aborts).

Case 2: If $\mathcal{A}$ starts his query *after* $\mathcal{B}$'s challenge phase is over, then $\mathcal{B}$ answers the query by extracting $\mathcal{A}$.[8]

Afterwards, $\mathcal{B}$ continues simulating the experiment H_0 for $\mathcal{A}$. After the simulated experiment is over, $\mathcal{B}$ outputs what the simulated experiment outputs. The adversary $\mathcal{B}$ repeats the experiment at most $k - 1$ times (and aborts if the kth iteration leads to another reset).

Denote by **BadQuery** the event that the adversary $\mathcal{A}$ queries the parallel CCA-oracle during the challenge phase of $\mathcal{B}$ in *all* iterations.

Let $j \in \{1, 2\}$ be the session into which $\mathcal{B}$ has chosen to insert his challenge C^*. Since $\mathcal{B}$ chooses j *randomly* in each iteration and $\mathcal{A}$'s view is *independent* of j in each iteration, it holds that $\Pr[\mathbf{BadQuery}] \leq 1/2^k$.

Denote by **GuessTag** the event that $\mathcal{A}$ queries his parallel CCA-oracle *before* the challenge C^* has started *using $\mathcal{B}$'s challenge tag tag_1* in one of the iterations.

---

[8] Note that, in general, $\mathcal{B}$ cannot use his own oracle in case 2. This is because, in this case, $\mathcal{A}$ queries his parallel CCA-oracle after $\mathcal{B}$'s challenge phase is over. Hence, $\mathcal{A}$ knows the challenge tag tag_1 and may query his parallel CCA-oracle using tag_1. Therefore, $\mathcal{B}$ cannot simply forward $\mathcal{A}$'s query to his own parallel CCA-oracle since $\mathcal{A}$'s query may contain $\mathcal{B}$'s challenge tag. Furthermore, $\mathcal{B}$ cannot use the extractability property in case 1 since the messages of $\mathcal{A}$'s oracle query and the messages of $\mathcal{B}$'s challenge phase may *overlap* in this case. Hence, $\mathcal{B}$ cannot extract $\mathcal{A}$ since this may require "rewinding" the experiment of $\mathcal{B}$ to a specific point in $\mathcal{B}$'s challenge phase.

Since the challenge tag tag_1 is chosen randomly (from the set of strings of length k) and $\mathcal{A}$'s view is independent of tag_1 before the challenge phase C^* begins, it holds that $\Pr[\textbf{GuessTag}] \leq k \cdot i / 2^k$, where $i = poly(k)$ is the number of commitments in the parallel oracle query.

Now it holds that *conditioned on* **BadQuery** and **GuessTag** both *not* occurring, the output of $\mathcal{B}$ is either identically distributed to the output of H_0 (this holds if $C^* = \mathsf{Com}_{tag_1}(s_1)$) or identically distributed to the output of H_1 (this holds if $C^* = \mathsf{Com}_{tag_1}(t)$).

Let $E = \textbf{BadQuery} \vee \textbf{GuessTag}$ and let $\mathrm{Output}_{b^*}(\mathcal{B})$ denote the output of $\mathcal{B}$ in the RepeatPCCA-experiment if the challenge bit b^* was chosen by the RepeatPCCA-experiment. Then we have the following:

$$
\begin{aligned}
|\Pr[out_0 = 1] - \Pr[out_1 = 1]| &\leq \Pr[E] + |\Pr[out_0 = 1 | \neg E] - \Pr[out_1 = 1 | \neg E]| \\
&= \Pr[E] + |\Pr[\mathrm{Output}_0(\mathcal{B}) = 1 | \neg E] \\
&\quad - \Pr[\mathrm{Output}_1(\mathcal{B}) = 1 | \neg E]| \\
&\leq \frac{k \cdot i + 1}{2^k} + \mathsf{negl}(k) \\
&= \mathsf{negl}'(k)
\end{aligned}
$$

Note that $|\Pr[\mathrm{Output}_0(\mathcal{B}) = 1 | \neg E] - \Pr[\mathrm{Output}_1(\mathcal{B}) = 1 | \neg E]| \leq \mathsf{negl}(k)$ holds because Com is RepeatPCCA-secure by Lemma 1 and $\Pr[\neg E] = 1 - k \cdot i + 1/2^k$ is overwhelming in k (see Appendix B).

Sub-Claim 2: $|\Pr[out_1 = 1] - \Pr[out_2 = 1]| \leq \mathsf{negl}(k)$. This follows from a standard reduction argument to the parallel CCA-security of Com. Consider an adversary $\mathcal{B}'$ against the parallel CCA-security of Com. The adversary $\mathcal{B}'$ simulates the experiment H_1 for $\mathcal{A}$. After $\mathcal{A}$ has sent (v_0, v_1, tag), $\mathcal{B}'$ chooses a random bit $b \leftarrow \{0, 1\}$ and sends $(v_b, 0^k, tag)$ to his experiment. Afterwards, $\mathcal{B}'$ forwards his challenge C^* to $\mathcal{A}$ as $\mathcal{A}$'s challenge. If $\mathcal{A}$ queries his oracle, then $\mathcal{B}'$ forwards this query to his own oracle. After the simulated experiment is over, $\mathcal{B}'$ outputs what the simulated experiment outputs. It holds that the output of $\mathcal{B}'$ is identically distributed to the output of H_1 if $C^* = \mathsf{Com}_{tag}(v_b)$ and identically distributed to the output of H_2 if $C^* = \mathsf{Com}_{tag}(0^k)$. Sub-Claim 2 now follows from the parallel CCA-security of Com.

Sub-Claim 3: $\Pr[out_2 = 1] = 1/2$. This follows from the fact that the view of $\mathcal{A}$ in the hybrid H_2 is independent of the challenge bit.

In conclusion, $|\Pr[out_0 = 1] - 1/2| \leq \mathsf{negl}(k)$. Hence, Com' is parallel CCA-secure. $\qquad\square$

Using the transformation implied by [21, 23] described earlier and Theorem 9, we also get the following separation:

Theorem 10 (PNM $\not\Rightarrow$ CNM). *If there exists a statistically binding, parallel non-malleable commitment scheme, then there also exists a statistically binding and parallel non-malleable commitment scheme that is not concurrent non-malleable.*

Using similar arguments as in the proof of Theorem 9, one can also show that one-one CCA-security does not imply parallel non-malleability.

Theorem 11 (1CCA $\nRightarrow$ PNM). *If there exists a statistically binding, one-one CCA-secure commitment scheme, then there also exists a statistically binding and one-one CCA-secure commitment scheme that is not parallel non-malleable.*

Proof Idea. This separation follows by adapting the techniques used for the separation in Theorem 9. In the commitment scheme Com' the sender commits to the shares s_0 and s_1 *in parallel* instead of sequentially. The experiment Repeat1CCA is like RepeatPCCA except that the adversary may now query $\mathcal{O}_{1cca}$ instead of $\mathcal{O}_{pcca}$. □

Remark 2. We remark that all results, except for Theorems 3, 5 and 8, carry over to *bit* commitment schemes. This can be shown by similar arguments as in the proofs of Theorems 1 and 9. The main difference for the proofs using the puzzle-solution approach is that the puzzle consists of k parallel (bit) commitments. The main difference for the proofs using the sharing approach is that the sender generates $2k$ shares. We do not know if Theorems 3, 5 or 8 carry over to bit commitment schemes because those theorems cannot be proven using the above modification of the puzzle-solution approach. This is because the number of queries that can be sent to the oracle in these cases is bounded by a constant. Hence, the oracle cannot be used to solve a puzzle consisting of k parallel bit commitments.

Remark 3. We note that the (known) separation between (stand-alone) non-malleability and parallel non-malleability can also be proven using the sharing approach. This follows from the transformation implied by [21,23] and Theorem 11.

Remark 4. Note that if one-way functions exist, all base commitment schemes required for this work exist. In all results one can use, e.g., the commitment scheme from [9] that is based on one-way functions as base commitment scheme Com. This scheme is CCA-secure and therefore fulfills all other desired security notions.

A   The Implication Results

Here we prove all our implication results (cf. Fig. 1). The results in themselves are not surprising, but are included for the sake of completeness. To this end, we adapt proof techniques from Bellare and Sahai [3]. They show that for public-key encryption schemes the notions of parallel CCA-security and parallel non-malleability are equivalent. We show that for *non-interactive* commitment schemes this is also the case. However, for *interactive* commitment schemes the situation is different, as we have constructed in Sect. 5 a commitment scheme that separates the two notions.

Theorem 12 (PCCA ⇒ PNM). *Let* Com *be a parallel CCA-secure commitment scheme. Then* Com *is also parallel non-malleable.*

Proof Idea. By taking the strategy from Bellare and Sahai (cf. proof of Theorem 5.3 in [3]) and adapting the proof to commitment schemes, the proof of this theorem is straightforward. The general strategy for the parallel CCA-adversary is to forward his challenge to the parallel non-malleability adversary and use his parallel CCA-oracle to decommit the messages the parallel non-malleability adversary sends to the receiver. □

Note that this proof holds for general commitment schemes, regardless of whether they are interactive or non-interactive. With a very similar proof one can show that one-one CCA-security implies non-malleability.

Theorem 13 (1CCA ⇒ (NM). *Let* Com *be a one-one CCA-secure commitment scheme. Then* Com *is also non-malleable.*

In contrast to public-key encryption schemes, the theorem that parallel non-malleability implies parallel CCA-security only holds for non-interactive commitment schemes.

Theorem 14 (PNM $\overset{\text{n.-i.}}{\Longrightarrow}$ PCCA). *Let* Com *be a non-interactive, parallel non-malleable commitment scheme. Then* Com *is also parallel CCA-secure.*

Proof Idea. We again adapt the strategy from Bellare and Sahai (cf. proof of Theorem 5.2 in [3]). The general strategy for the parallel non-malleability adversary is to forward his challenge to the parallel CCA-adversary and to forward the oracle query of the parallel CCA-adversary to the receiver. Then the distinguisher gets what is effectively the oracle answer as input (via the implicit committed value oracle of the experiment) and can continue the simulation of the parallel CCA-adversary until he outputs his solution. □

With essentially the same proof one can show that non-malleability implies one-one CCA-security for non-interactive commitment schemes.

Theorem 15 (NM $\overset{\text{n.-i.}}{\Longrightarrow}$ 1CCA). *Let* Com *be a non-interactive, non-malleable commitment scheme. Then* Com *is also one-one CCA-secure.*

B   A Technical Detail

The statement $|\Pr[\text{Output}_0(\mathcal{B}) = 1|\neg E] - \Pr[\text{Output}_1(\mathcal{B}) = 1|\neg E]| \leq \mathsf{negl}(k)$ holds (cf. proof of Sub-Claim 1 in Theorem 9).

Proof

$$|\Pr[\text{Output}_0(\mathcal{B}) = 1] - \Pr[\text{Output}_1(\mathcal{B}) = 1]| =$$
$$|\Pr[\neg E] \cdot (\Pr[\text{Output}_0(\mathcal{B}) = 1|\neg E] - \Pr[\text{Output}_1(\mathcal{B}) = 1|\neg E])$$
$$+ \Pr[E] \cdot (\Pr[\text{Output}_0(\mathcal{B}) = 1|E] - \Pr[\text{Output}_1(\mathcal{B}) = 1|E])|$$
$$\geq \Pr[\neg E] \cdot |\Pr[\text{Output}_0(\mathcal{B}) = 1|\neg E] - \Pr[\text{Output}_1(\mathcal{B}) = 1|\neg E]|$$
$$- \Pr[E] \cdot |\Pr[\text{Output}_0(\mathcal{B}) = 1|E] - \Pr[\text{Output}_1(\mathcal{B}) = 1|E]|$$
(because $|x + y| \geq |x| - |y|$)
$$\geq \Pr[\neg E] \cdot |\Pr[\text{Output}_0(\mathcal{B}) = 1|\neg E] - \Pr[\text{Output}_1(\mathcal{B}) = 1|\neg E]| - \Pr[E] \cdot 1$$
(because $|\Pr[\text{Output}_0(\mathcal{B}) = 1|E] - \Pr[\text{Output}_1(\mathcal{B}) = 1|E]| \leq 1$)
$$\geq \frac{1}{2} \cdot |\Pr[\text{Output}_0(\mathcal{B}) = 1|\neg E] - \Pr[\text{Output}_1(\mathcal{B}) = 1|\neg E]| - \Pr[E] \cdot 1$$

(This holds for sufficiently large k because $\Pr[\neg E]$ is overwhelming.
Note that $1/2$ is arbitrary, any constant $0 < c < 1$ works.)

Since $|\Pr[\text{Output}_0(\mathcal{B}) = 1] - \Pr[\text{Output}_1(\mathcal{B}) = 1]|$ and $\Pr[E]$ are negligible, $|\Pr[\text{Output}_0(\mathcal{B}) = 1|\neg E] - \Pr[\text{Output}_1(\mathcal{B}) = 1|\neg E]|$ must also be negligible.   □

References

1. Bellare, M., Desai, A., Pointcheval, D., Rogaway, P.: Relations among notions of security for public-key encryption schemes. In: Krawczyk, H. (ed.) CRYPTO 1998. LNCS, vol. 1462, pp. 26–45. Springer, Heidelberg (1998). https://doi.org/10.1007/BFb0055718
2. Bellare, M., Dowsley, R., Waters, B., Yilek, S.: Standard security does not imply security against selective-opening. In: Pointcheval, D., Johansson, T. (eds.) EUROCRYPT 2012. LNCS, vol. 7237, pp. 645–662. Springer, Heidelberg (2012). https://doi.org/10.1007/978-3-642-29011-4_38
3. Bellare, M., Sahai, A.: Non-malleable encryption: equivalence between two notions, and an indistinguishability-based characterization. In: Wiener, M. (ed.) CRYPTO 1999. LNCS, vol. 1666, pp. 519–536. Springer, Heidelberg (1999). https://doi.org/10.1007/3-540-48405-1_33
4. Böhl, F., Hofheinz, D., Kraschewski, D.: On definitions of selective opening security. In: Fischlin, M., Buchmann, J., Manulis, M. (eds.) PKC 2012. LNCS, vol. 7293, pp. 522–539. Springer, Heidelberg (2012). https://doi.org/10.1007/978-3-642-30057-8_31
5. Broadnax, B., Döttling, N., Hartung, G., Müller-Quade, J., Nagel, M.: Concurrently composable security with shielded super-polynomial simulators. In: Coron, J.-S., Nielsen, J.B. (eds.) EUROCRYPT 2017, Part I. LNCS, vol. 10210, pp. 351–381. Springer, Cham (2017). https://doi.org/10.1007/978-3-319-56620-7_13
6. Canetti, R.: Universally composable security: a new paradigm for cryptographic protocols. In: Proceedings of the 42th Annual IEEE Symposium on Foundations of Computer Science, FOCS 2001, pp. 136–145. IEEE (2001)
7. Canetti, R., Fischlin, M.: Universally composable commitments. In: Kilian, J. (ed.) CRYPTO 2001. LNCS, vol. 2139, pp. 19–40. Springer, Heidelberg (2001). https://doi.org/10.1007/3-540-44647-8_2

8. Canetti, R., Kushilevitz, E., Lindell, Y.: On the limitations of universally composable two-party computation without set-up assumptions. In: Biham, E. (ed.) EUROCRYPT 2003. LNCS, vol. 2656, pp. 68–86. Springer, Heidelberg (2003). https://doi.org/10.1007/3-540-39200-9_5
9. Canetti, R., Lin, H., Pass, R.: Adaptive hardness and composable security in the plain model from standard assumptions. In: Proceedings of the 51st Annual IEEE Symposium on Foundations of Computer Science, FOCS 2010, pp. 541–550. IEEE (2010)
10. Canetti, R., Lin, H., Pass, R.: From unprovability to environmentally friendly protocols. In: Proceedings of the 54th Annual IEEE Symposium on Foundations of Computer Science, FOCS 2013, pp. 70–79. IEEE (2013)
11. Cao, Z., Visconti, I., Zhang, Z.: Constant-round concurrent non-malleable statistically binding commitments and decommitments. In: Nguyen, P.Q., Pointcheval, D. (eds.) PKC 2010. LNCS, vol. 6056, pp. 193–208. Springer, Heidelberg (2010). https://doi.org/10.1007/978-3-642-13013-7_12
12. Choi, S.G., Dachman-Soled, D., Malkin, T., Wee, H.: A black-box construction of non-malleable encryption from semantically secure encryption. J. Cryptol. **31**, 1–30 (2017)
13. Ciampi, M., Ostrovsky, R., Siniscalchi, L., Visconti, I.: Concurrent non-malleable commitments (and more) in 3 rounds. In: Robshaw, M., Katz, J. (eds.) CRYPTO 2016. LNCS, vol. 9816, pp. 270–299. Springer, Heidelberg (2016). https://doi.org/10.1007/978-3-662-53015-3_10
14. Cramer, R., Hanaoka, G., Hofheinz, D., Imai, H., Kiltz, E., Pass, R., Shelat, A., Vaikuntanathan, V.: Bounded CCA2-secure encryption. In: Kurosawa, K. (ed.) ASIACRYPT 2007. LNCS, vol. 4833, pp. 502–518. Springer, Heidelberg (2007). https://doi.org/10.1007/978-3-540-76900-2_31
15. Dolev, D., Dwork, C., Naor, M.: Non-malleable cryptography. In: Proceedings of the Twenty-Third Annual ACM Symposium on Theory of Computing, STOC 1991, pp. 542–552. ACM (1991)
16. Garg, S., Mukherjee, P., Pandey, O., Polychroniadou, A.: The exact round complexity of secure computation. In: Fischlin, M., Coron, J.-S. (eds.) EUROCRYPT 2016, Part II. LNCS, vol. 9666, pp. 448–476. Springer, Heidelberg (2016). https://doi.org/10.1007/978-3-662-49896-5_16
17. Goldreich, O.: Foundations of Cryptography: Basic Tools, vol. 1. Cambridge University Press, Cambridge (2001)
18. Goldreich, O., Lindell, Y.: Session-key generation using human passwords only. In: Kilian, J. (ed.) CRYPTO 2001. LNCS, vol. 2139, pp. 408–432. Springer, Heidelberg (2001). https://doi.org/10.1007/3-540-44647-8_24
19. Goyal, V.: Constant round non-malleable protocols using one way functions. In: Proceedings of the Forty-Third Annual ACM Symposium on Theory of Computing, STOC 2011, pp. 695–704. ACM (2011)
20. Goyal, V., Pandey, O., Richelson, S.: Textbook non-malleable commitments. In: Proceedings of the 48th Annual ACM SIGACT Symposium on Theory of Computing, STOC 2016, pp. 1128–1141. ACM (2016)
21. Impagliazzo, R., Luby, M.: One-way functions are essential for complexity based cryptography. In: Proceedings of the 30th Annual Symposium on Foundations of Computer Science, FOCS 1989, pp. 230–235. IEEE (1989)
22. Katz, J., Ostrovsky, R., Smith, A.: Round efficiency of multi-party computation with a dishonest majority. In: Biham, E. (ed.) EUROCRYPT 2003. LNCS, vol. 2656, pp. 578–595. Springer, Heidelberg (2003). https://doi.org/10.1007/3-540-39200-9_36

23. Kiyoshima, S.: Round-efficient black-box construction of composable multi-party computation. In: Garay, J.A., Gennaro, R. (eds.) CRYPTO 2014. LNCS, vol. 8617, pp. 351–368. Springer, Heidelberg (2014). https://doi.org/10.1007/978-3-662-44381-1_20
24. Kiyoshima, S., Manabe, Y., Okamoto, T.: Constant-round black-box construction of composable multi-party computation protocol. In: Lindell, Y. (ed.) TCC 2014. LNCS, vol. 8349, pp. 343–367. Springer, Heidelberg (2014). https://doi.org/10.1007/978-3-642-54242-8_15
25. Lin, H., Pass, R.: Black-box constructions of composable protocols without set-up. In: Safavi-Naini, R., Canetti, R. (eds.) CRYPTO 2012. LNCS, vol. 7417, pp. 461–478. Springer, Heidelberg (2012). https://doi.org/10.1007/978-3-642-32009-5_27
26. Lin, H., Pass, R., Venkitasubramaniam, M.: Concurrent non-malleable commitments from any one-way function. In: Canetti, R. (ed.) TCC 2008. LNCS, vol. 4948, pp. 571–588. Springer, Heidelberg (2008). https://doi.org/10.1007/978-3-540-78524-8_31
27. Lin, H., Pass, R., Venkitasubramaniam, M.: A unified framework for concurrent security: universal composability from stand-alone non-malleability. In: Proceedings of the 41st annual ACM symposium on Theory of computing, STOC 2009, pp. 179–188. ACM (2009)
28. Pandey, O., Pass, R., Vaikuntanathan, V.: Adaptive one-way functions and applications. In: Wagner, D. (ed.) CRYPTO 2008. LNCS, vol. 5157, pp. 57–74. Springer, Heidelberg (2008). https://doi.org/10.1007/978-3-540-85174-5_4
29. Pass, R., Shelat, A., Vaikuntanathan, V.: Construction of a non-malleable encryption scheme from any semantically secure one. In: Dwork, C. (ed.) CRYPTO 2006. LNCS, vol. 4117, pp. 271–289. Springer, Heidelberg (2006). https://doi.org/10.1007/11818175_16
30. Prabhakaran, M., Sahai, A.: New notions of security: achieving universal composability without trusted setup. In: Proceedings of the 36th Annual ACM Symposium on Theory of Computing, STOC 2004, pp. 242–251. ACM (2004)
31. Wee, H.: Black-box, round-efficient secure computation via non-malleability amplification. In: Proceedings of the 51st Annual IEEE Symposium on Foundations of Computer Science, FOCS 2010, pp. 531–540. IEEE (2010)

Obfuscation-Based Cryptographic Constructions

Interactively Secure Groups
from Obfuscation

Thomas Agrikola$^{(\boxtimes)}$ and Dennis Hofheinz

Karlsruhe Institute of Technology, Karlsruhe, Germany
{Thomas.Agrikola,Dennis.Hofheinz}@kit.edu

Abstract. We construct a mathematical group in which an interactive variant of the very general Uber assumption holds. Our construction uses probabilistic indistinguishability obfuscation, fully homomorphic encryption, and a pairing-friendly group in which a mild and standard computational assumption holds. While our construction is not practical, it constitutes a feasibility result that shows that under a strong but generic, and a mild assumption, groups *exist* in which very general computational assumptions hold. We believe that this grants additional credibility to the Uber assumption.

Keywords: Indistinguishability obfuscation · Uber assumption

1   Introduction

Cyclic groups in cryptography. Cyclic groups (such as subgroups of the multiplicative group of a finite field, or certain elliptic curves) are a popular mathematical building block in cryptography. Countless cryptographic constructions are formulated in a cyclic group setting. Usually these constructions are accompanied by a security reduction that transforms any adversarial algorithm that breaks the scheme into an algorithm that solves a computational problem in that group. Among the more popular computational problems are the (computational or decisional) Diffie-Hellman problem [25], or the discrete logarithm problem.

The currently known security reductions of several relevant cryptographic schemes require somewhat more exotic computational assumptions, however. For instance, the security of the Digital Signature Algorithm is only proven in a generic model of computation [14] (see also [15]). Moreover, the semi-adaptive (i.e., IND-CCA1) security of the ElGamal encryption scheme requires a "one-more type" assumption [33]. The currently most efficient structure-preserving signature schemes require complex interactive assumptions [1,2]. Finally, some proofs (e.g., [6,23,24,31]) even require "knowledge assumptions" that essentially state that the only way to generate new group elements is as linear combinations of given group elements (with extractable coefficients).

T. Agrikola—Supported by ERC Project PREP-CRYPTO 724307.

D. Hofheinz—Supported by ERC Project PREP-CRYPTO 724307, and by DFG grants HO 4534/4-1 and HO 4534/2-2.

© International Association for Cryptologic Research 2018
M. Abdalla and R. Dahab (Eds.): PKC 2018, LNCS 10770, pp. 341–370, 2018.
https://doi.org/10.1007/978-3-319-76581-5_12

While more exotic assumptions can thus be very helpful for constructing cryptographic schemes, their use also has a downside: reductions to more exotic (and less investigated) assumptions tend to lower our confidence in the corresponding scheme. (See [12,32] for two very different views on this matter).

The Uber-assumption family. An example of a somewhat exotic but very general and strong class of computational assumptions in a cyclic group setting is the "Uber" assumption family ([10], see also [12]). Essentially, this assumption states that no efficient adversary $\mathcal{A}$ can win the following guessing game significantly better than with probability $1/2$. The game is formulated in a group $\mathcal{G} = \langle g \rangle$ of order q, and is parameterized over polynomials $P_1, \ldots, P_l, P^* \in \mathbb{Z}_q[X_1, \ldots, X_m]$. Initially, the game chooses secret exponents $s_1, \ldots, s_m \in \mathbb{Z}_q$ uniformly, and hands $\mathcal{A}$ the group elements $g^{P_i(s_1,\ldots,s_m)}$, and a challenge element $Z \in \mathcal{G}$ with either $Z = g^{P^*(s_1,\ldots,s_m)}$ or independently random Z. Given these elements, $\mathcal{A}$ has to guess if Z is random or not.[1]

Depending on the number m of variables, and the concrete polynomials P_i and P^*, the Uber assumption generalizes many popular existing assumptions, such as the Decisional Diffie-Hellman assumption, the k-Linear family of assumptions, and so-called "q-type assumptions". However, it is a priori not at all clear how plausible such general assumptions are. In fact, there are indications that, e.g., q-type assumptions are indeed easier to break than, say, the discrete log assumption [21].

Fortunately, a number of cryptographic constructions that rely on q-type assumptions can be transported into composite-order groups, with the advantage that now their security holds under a simpler, subgroup indistinguishability assumption [19,20]. However, this change of groups will not work for every cryptographic construction, and currently we only know how to perform this technique for a subclass of q-type assumptions.

Our contribution. In this work, we shed new light on the plausibility of Uber-style assumptions. Concretely, we construct a group in which an interactive variant of Uber-style assumptions (in which the adversary may choose the P_i and P^* adaptively) holds. We believe that this lends additional credibility to the Uber assumption itself, and also strengthens plausibility results obtained from the Uber assumption (see [12] for an overview).

Our construction assumes subexponentially secure indistinguishability obfuscation (iO, a very strong but generic assumption), a perfectly correct additively homomorphic encryption scheme for addition modulo a given prime, and a pairing-friendly group in which a standard assumption (SXDH, the symmetric external Diffie-Hellman assumption) holds. We stress that we consider our result as a feasibility result. Indeed, due to the use of indistinguishability obfuscation, our construction is far from practical. Still, our result shows that even interactive generalizations of the Uber assumption family are no less plausible than

---

[1] Owing to the original application, the Uber assumption family was formulated in [10] in a setting with a pairing-friendly group, with a final challenge in the target group.

indistinguishability obfuscation (plus a standard assumption in cyclic groups and additively homomorphic encryption).

Before describing our results in more detail, we remark that the group we construct actually has non-unique element encodings (much like in a "graded encoding scheme" [26], only without any notion of multilinear map). It is hence possible to compare and operate with group elements, but it is not directly possible to use, e.g., the encoding of group elements to hide an encrypted message. (In particular, it is not immediately possible to implement, say, the ElGamal encryption scheme with our group as there is no obvious way to decrypt ciphertexts. Signature schemes, however, do not require unique encodings of group elements and can hence be implemented using our group.) Furthermore, due to technical reasons our construction requires the maximum degree of the adversarially chosen polynomials to be bounded a priori.

Related work. Pass et al. [36] introduce semantically secure multilinear (and graded) encoding schemes (of groups). A semantically secure encoding scheme guarantees security of a class of algebraic decisional assumptions. On a high level, the security property requires that encodings are computationally indistinguishable whenever there is no way to distinguish the corresponding elements using only generic operations. The generic multilinear encoding model implies semantic security of a multilinear encoding scheme. Furthermore, Pass et al. show that many existing iO candidates [5,13,27] that are proven secure in the generic multilinear encoding model can also be proven secure assuming semantically secure encoding schemes. Hence, this result relaxes the necessary assumptions to prove the security of certain iO constructions. Bitansky et al. [8] slightly strengthen the security property of encoding schemes formulated in [36]. Assuming the resulting security property allows to prove that existing obfuscation candidates [5] provide virtual grey-box security[2].

In [4] Albrecht et al. construct a group scheme providing a multilinear map from iO. This result complements earlier results that construct iO from multilinear maps [27,38]. The notion of encoding schemes used in [4] is a direct adaption of the "cryptographic" multilinear group setting from [11]. In contrast to [8,36], the encoding scheme of Albrecht et al. provides an extraction algorithm producing a unique string for all encodings that are equal with respect to the equality relation of the scheme. Furthermore, [4] requires a publicly available sampling algorithm that produces encodings for given exponents. Hence, the encoding scheme of [4] grants adversaries slightly more power.

In this paper we use a similar notion of encoding schemes as in [4]. Furthermore, [8,36] define the security property for encoding schemes implicitly. We, in contrast, consider a concrete strong interactive hardness assumption that holds in our encoding scheme.

---

[2] An obfuscator $\mathcal{O}$ satisfies virtual grey-box security for a class of circuits $\mathcal{C}$ if for any circuit $C \in \mathcal{C}$, a PPT adversary given $\mathcal{O}(C)$ can not compute significally more about C than a simulator given unbounded computational resources and polynomially many queries to the circuit C.

Technical approach. The assumption we consider is defined similarly to the Uber assumption above, only with an interactive and adaptive choice of arbitrary (multivariate) polynomials P_i, P^* over $\mathbb{Z}_q$, where q is the order of the group. That is, there is a secret point $s := (s_1, \ldots, s_m) \in \mathbb{Z}_q^m$, and $\mathcal{A}$ may freely and adaptively choose the P_i and P^* during the course of the security game. To avoid trivialities, we require that P^* does not lie in the linear span of the polynomials P_i. We call this assumption the *Interactive Uber assumption*. For convenience only, we will describe our approach assuming only univariate polynomials in the Interactive Uber assumption. However, we will see that similar techniques yield security even for multivariate polynomials.

Our starting point is a recent work by Albrecht et al. [4], which constructs a group with a multilinear map from (probabilistic) iO, an additively homomorphic encryption scheme, a dual mode NIZK proof system, and a group $\mathcal{G}$ in which (a variant of) the Strong Diffie-Hellman assumption [9] holds. For our purposes, we are not interested in obtaining a multilinear map, however, and we would also like to avoid relying on a strong (i.e., q-type) assumption to begin with. Moreover, [4] only proves relatively mild computational assumptions in the constructed group.

In a nutshell, a group element in the construction of [4] has the form

$$(g^z, C = \text{ENC}(z), \pi), \tag{1}$$

where $z \in \mathbb{Z}$ is the discrete logarithm of that group element, $g \in \mathcal{G}$ is a generator of the used existing group $\mathcal{G}$, ENC is the encryption algorithm of an additively homomorphic encryption scheme, and π is a non-interactive zero-knowledge proof of consistency. Concretely, π proves that C encrypts the discrete logarithm z of g^z, *or* that C encrypts a polynomial f with $f(w) = z$, for a fixed value w committed to in the public parameters.

In their security analysis, Albrecht et al. [4] crucially use a "switching lemma" that states that different encodings $(g^z, \text{ENC}(z), \pi)$ and $(g^{f(w)}, \text{ENC}(f), \pi')$ are computationally indistinguishable whenever $f(w) = z$. This allows to switch to, and argue about encodings with higher-degree f. Note, however, that any such encoding must also carry a valid $g^z = g^{f(w)}$. Hence, changing the values $z = f(w)$ in such encodings with higher-degree f (as is often required to prove security) would seem to already necessitate Uber-style assumptions. Indeed, Albrecht et al. require a variant of the Strong Diffie-Hellman assumption, a q-type assumption.

Group elements in our group. To avoid making Uber-style assumptions in the first place, we simply omit the initial g^z value in encodings of group elements, and modify the consistency proof from Eq. (1). That is, group elements in our group are of the form

$$(C = \text{ENC}(z), \pi), \tag{2}$$

where ENC is the encryption algorithm of an additively homomorphic encryption scheme, and π is a proof of knowledge of some (potentially constant) polynomial f' with $f'(w) = z$ or $f'(w) = f(w)$ (in case C encrypts a polynomial f). The value w is some point in $\mathbb{Z}_q$ that is fixed, but hidden, in the public parameters of our group, where q is the group order. The proof of knowledge is realized through an additional encryption C' that contains the polynomial f'. Hence, group elements are actually of the form

$$(C = \text{Enc}(z),\ C' = \text{Enc}(f'),\ \pi). \tag{3}$$

In a nutshell, such an encoding implicitly represents the group element $g^{f(w)} = g^{f'(w)}$, where f and f' are the polynomials defined by C and C' respectively. For clarity, we sometimes omit the component C' in this overview.

More precisely, C and C' contain representation vectors $\vec{f}$ and $\vec{f'}$ of the polynomials f and f' with respect to a basis $\{a_1, \ldots, a_d\}$ of $\mathbb{Z}_q^d$. That is, given a vector $\vec{f}$ that is encrypted in C, the coefficients of the corresponding polynomial f are defined as follows

$$(a_1 \mid \ldots \mid a_d)^{-1} \cdot \vec{f} \tag{4}$$

using the homomorphic mapping between polynomials over $\mathbb{Z}_q$ and vectors in $\mathbb{Z}_q^d$. This basis is not public, but committed to in the public parameters. The reason for using a hidden basis is that we need to deal with adaptive queries. We postpone the details to a subsequent paragraph. In this overview, however, we will pretend the ciphertexts C and C' contain mere polynomials.

Intuitively, the crux of the matter for the proof of security will be to remove the dependency on the point w. This changes the group structure to be isomorphic to $\mathbb{Z}_q^d$ which makes it possible to argue with linear algebra.

A public sampling algorithm allows to produce arbitrary encodings of group elements. Given an exponent z, the sampling algorithm produces the ciphertexts C and C' using the constant polynomials $f := f' := z$ and produces the consistency proof accordingly. We remark that our group allows for re-randomization of encodings assuming some natural additional properties of the homomorphic encryption scheme.

The group operation is performed in a similar way to [4]. Namely, suppose we want to add two encodings $(\text{Enc}(f_1), \pi_1)$ and $(\text{Enc}(f_2), \pi_2)$. The resulting $(\text{Enc}(f_3), \pi_3)$ should satisfy $f_3 = f_1 + f_2$ as abstract polynomials. Hence, $\text{Enc}(f_3)$ can be computed homomorphically from $\text{Enc}(f_1)$ and $\text{Enc}(f_2)$. To compute the proof π_3, however, we require an obfuscated circuit C_{Add} that extracts f_1, f_2, and generates a fresh proof using the knowledge of $f_3 = f_1 + f_2$ as witness. Thus, the implementation of C_{Add} needs to know both decryption keys for C and C'. (The details are somewhat technical and similar to [4], so we omit them in this overview.) We prove that it is possible to implement a circuit C_{Add}'' that has almost the same functionality as C_{Add} but produces a simulated proof of consistency that is identically distributed to a real one. Hence, the implementation of C_{Add}'' does not need to know the decryption keys. Therefore, exploiting the security of the used obfuscator, we are able to unnoticeably replace the obfuscation of C_{Add} with an obfuscation of C_{Add}''.

We note that our modification to omit the entry g^z from the encodings in Eq. (1) makes it nontrivial to decide whether two given encodings represent the same group element, or, equivalently, to decide whether a given encoding represents the identity element of the group. Recall that an encoding $(C = \text{ENC}(f), \pi)$ represents the group element $g^{f(w)}$. (This operation is trivial in the setting of Albrecht et al., since their encodings carry a value $g^z = g^{f(w)}$.) Thus, our construction needs to provide a public algorithm that tests whether a given encoding $(C = \text{ENC}(f), \pi)$ represents the identity element of the group, i.e. that tests whether $f(w) = 0$.

At this point two problems arise. First, this public algorithm must be able to obtain at least one of the polynomials that are encrypted in C and C' respectively. Second, the value w must not be explicitly known during the proof of security as our strategy is to remove the dependency on w. We solve both problems by using an *obfuscated* circuit C_{Zero} for testing whether a given encoding represents the identity element. More precisely, given an encoding $(C = \text{ENC}(f), \pi)$, C_{Zero} decrypts C (using one fixed decryption key) to obtain the polynomial f. In order to avoid the necessity to explicitly know the value w, C_{Zero} factors the univariate polynomial f (in $\mathbb{Z}_q[X]$), and obtains the small set $\{x_1, \ldots, x_n\}$ of all zeros of f.[3] As mentioned above, the value w is fixed but hidden inside the public parameters. Particularly, we store the value w in form of a point function obfuscation (i.e., in form of a publicly evaluable function $\text{po}: \mathbb{Z}_q \to \{0, 1\}$ with $\text{po}(x) = 1 \Leftrightarrow x = w$, such that it is hard to determine the value w given only the function description po). The zero testing circuit C_{Zero} treats an encoding as the identity element if f is the zero polynomial or $w \in \{x_1, \ldots, x_n\}$.

Observe that this implementation of C_{Zero} only requires one decryption key allowing to apply the Naor-Yung strategy [35]. Furthermore, C_{Zero} does not need to know the value w in the clear. Hence, using an obfuscation of this implementation of C_{Zero} avoids both problems described above.

Switching of encodings. Similarly to Albrecht et al. [4] we prove a "switching lemma" that states that encodings $(C_1 = \text{ENC}(f_1), \pi_1)$ and $(C_2 = \text{ENC}(f_2), \pi_2)$ are computationally indistinguishable whenever $f_1(w) = f_2(w)$. In other words, encodings of the same group element are computationally indistinguishable. To prove this lemma, we exploit the security of the used double-encryption in a similar way as in the IND-CCA proof of Naor and Yung [35]. Particularly, when using an obfuscation of the circuit C''_{Add}, it is not necessary to know both decryption keys to produce public parameters for the group. We recall that the circuit C_{Zero} only knows the decryption key to decrypt the first component of encodings. Furthermore, it is possible to produce a consistency proof without knowing the content of the ciphertexts C and C' by simply simulating it in the same way C''_{Add} does. Therefore, we can reduce to the IND-CPA security of the encryption scheme. In order to apply the same argument for the first component of encodings, we need the circuit C_{Zero} to forget about the first decryption key. We accomplish that by replacing the obfuscation of C_{Zero} with an obfuscation of the circuit $\overline{C}_{\text{Zero}}$ that uses only the second decryption key instead of the first one.

---

[3] We note that there are probabilistic polynomial time algorithms that factor univariate polynomials over finite fields, for instance the Cantor-Zassenhaus algorithm [18].

This is possible due to the security of the obfuscator and the soundness of the proof system. Then, we can use the same argument as above to reduce to the IND-CPA security of the encryption scheme.

Obtaining the *Interactive Uber assumption* in our group. We recall that the Interactive Uber assumption (in one variable) generates one secret point $s \in \mathbb{Z}_q$ uniformly at random at which all queried polynomials are evaluated. To show that the Interactive Uber assumption holds in our group, we first set up that secret point s as $c \cdot w$ for some independent random c from $\mathbb{Z}_q^\times$, where w is the secret value of our group introduced above. Hence, a polynomial P that is evaluated at $s = c \cdot w$ can be interpreted as a (different) polynomial in w. Particularly, given a polynomial $P(X)$, the polynomial $\overline{P}(X) := P(c \cdot X)$ satisfies the equation $P(s) = \overline{P}(w)$. Thus, an encoding that contains the polynomial $\overline{P}(X)$ determines the exponent of the represented group element to equal $\overline{P}(w) = P(c \cdot w) = P(s)$. This observation paves the way for using higher-degree polynomials $\overline{P}(X)$ to produce encodings for oracle answers and the challenge. As the resulting group elements (i.e. the corresponding exponents) remain the same, the "switching lemma" described above justifies that this modification is unnoticeable. Furthermore, by a similar argument as above, we simulate the proofs of consistency π for every produced encoding, in particular for the encodings that are produced by the addition circuit.[4] As the consistency proof can now be produced independently of the basis $\{a_1, \dots, a_d\}$, we are able to unnoticeably "erase" this basis from the commitment in the public parameters.

Our goal now is to alter the structure of the group in the following sense. By definition, our group is isomorphic to the additive group $\mathbb{Z}_q$. We aim to alter that structure such that our group is isomorphic to the additive group of polynomials in $\mathbb{Z}_q[X]$ (of bounded degree). Particularly, we alter the equality relation that is defined on the set of encodings such that two encodings are considered equal only if the thereby defined polynomials are equal as abstract polynomials. For that purpose, we remove the dependency on the point w by altering the point function obfuscation po such that it maps all inputs to 0. Therefore, the zero testing circuit C_{Zero} only treats an encoding that contains the zero polynomial as an encoding of the identity element of the group. As the value w is never used explicitly in the game (as all the proofs of consistency are simulated), this modification is unnoticeable due to the security property of the point function obfuscation po. This is a crucial step paving the way for employing arguments from linear algebra to enable randomization.

The final step requires to randomize the challenge encoding such that there is no detectable difference between a real challenge and a randomly sampled one. First, we recall that encodings do not encrypt polynomials in the plain. The encodings contain the representation of polynomials with respect to some basis $\{a_1, \dots, a_d\}$. That is, given a polynomial $P(X)$, the encoding corresponding to $g^{P(s)}$ encrypts the vectors

---

[4] More precisely, we again use an obfuscation of C''_{Add} instead of an obfuscation of C_{Add} as described above.

$$\vec{f} = \vec{f'} = (a_1 \mid \ldots \mid a_d) \cdot \underbrace{P(c \cdot X)}_{=\overline{P}(X)}, \tag{5}$$

where $P(c \cdot X)$ is interpreted as a vector of coefficients in the natural way. Therefore, the only information about the matrix $(a_1 \mid \ldots \mid a_d)$ is given by matrix vector products. To avoid trivialities, the challenge polynomial P^* can be assumed not to lie in the span of the queries $P_1, \ldots, P_l$, which is why $P^*(c \cdot X)$ does not lie in the span of $P_1(c \cdot X), \ldots, P_l(c \cdot X)$. Hence, we may resort to an information-theoretic argument. More precisely, an adversary that is able to adaptively ask for matrix vector products, information-theoretically learns nothing about matrix vector products that are linearly independent of its queries. Therefore, the polynomial that is contained in the real challenge encoding information-theoretically looks like a randomly sampled polynomial (with bounded degree) given that the matrix $(a_1 \mid \ldots \mid a_d)$ is uniformly distributed.

Obtaining the *multivariate* Interactive Uber assumption. The main difficulty that arises from generalizing our results to the multivariate Interactive Uber assumption is that we do not have a polynomial-time algorithm that computes all zeros of a multivariate polynomial. Hence, the zero testing circuit C_{Zero} needs to know the point $\boldsymbol{\omega} := (\omega_1, \ldots, \omega_m) \in \mathbb{Z}_q^m$ in the clear to explicitly evaluate the polynomial f that is defined by a given encoding. Our previous proof strategy, however, crucially relies on removing the dependency on w such that C_{Zero} only treats encodings containing the zero polynomial as encodings of the identity element. This is equivalent to altering the group structure such that it is isomorphic to the additive group of polynomials over $\mathbb{Z}_q$ (of bounded degree).

Although the zero testing circuit C_{Zero} knows $\boldsymbol{\omega}$ in the clear, it is nevertheless possible to pursue a similar strategy. Our solution is to gradually alter C_{Zero} such that it "forgets" the components ω_i of $\boldsymbol{\omega}$ one by one. Particularly, we define intermediate circuits $C_{\mathsf{Zero}}^{(i)}$ that test if the polynomial

$$F_i^{(f)}(X_1, \ldots, X_i) := f(X_1, \ldots, X_i, \omega_{i+1}, \ldots, \omega_m) \tag{6}$$

equals the zero polynomial in $\mathbb{Z}_q[X_1, \ldots, X_i]$. Observe that the original circuit C_{Zero} tests whether $F_0^{(f)} \equiv 0$. Our goal is to unnoticeably establish $C_{\mathsf{Zero}}^{(m)}$ as zero testing circuit, as it realizes the stricter equality relation we aim for.

In order to unnoticeably replace an obfuscation of $C_{\mathsf{Zero}}^{(i)}$ with an obfuscation of $C_{\mathsf{Zero}}^{(i+1)}$, we first alter the implementation of $C_{\mathsf{Zero}}^{(i)}$ such that it performs the test whether $F_i^{(f)}$ is the zero polynomial by evaluating it at a randomly sampled point $\boldsymbol{r} \in \mathbb{Z}_q^i$. Applying the Schwartz-Zippel lemma upper bounds the statistical distance of the output distributions of the two circuits enabling to reduce this step to the security of the obfuscator.

Furthermore, the condition that $F_i^{(f)}(\boldsymbol{r}) = F_{i+1}^{(f)}(\boldsymbol{r}, \omega_{i+1}) = 0$ is equivalent to the condition that the univariate polynomial $F_{i+1}^{(f)}(\boldsymbol{r}, X_{i+1})$ is zero at the point ω_{i+1}. This can be implemented in a similar manner as in the univariate case using a point function obfuscation of ω_{i+1}. In addition, this circuit contains a conceptional logical or statement testing whether the polynomial $F_{i+1}^{(f)}(r, X_{i+1})$ equals the zero polynomial. Using a similar argument as above we are able to alter the point function obfuscation for ω_{i+1} to a point function obfuscation that never triggers.

Hence, our zero testing circuit effectively only tests whether $F_{i+1}^{(f)}(r, X_{i+1})$ equals the zero polynomial in $\mathbb{Z}_q[X_{i+1}]$. Applying the Schwartz-Zippel lemma again, we are able to unnoticeably alter the implementation of the zero testing circuit such that it tests whether $F_{i+1}^{(f)}$ equals the zero polynomial in $X_1, \ldots, X_{i+1}$ concluding the argument.

Roadmap. After fixing notation and recalling some basic definitions in Sect. 2, we present our main group construction in Sect. 3. Our main theorem, Theorem 1, states the validity of (our variant of) the Interactive Uber assumption relative to the group construction from Sect. 3. For the detailed proofs we refer the reader to the full version [3].

2   Preliminaries

2.1   Notation

For $n \in \mathbb{N}$, let 1^n denote the string consisting of n times the digit 1. For a probabilistic algorithm A, let $y \leftarrow A(x)$ denote that y is the output of A on input x. The randomness which A uses during the computation can be made explicit by $y \leftarrow A(x; r)$, where r denotes the randomness. Let λ denote the security parameter. We assume that the security parameter is implicitly given to all algorithms as 1^λ.

Let $\mathcal{G}$ be a group and let h be a fixed generator of $\mathcal{G}$. Then, $[n]$ denotes the group element h^n.

Let $n \in \mathbb{N}$ be a number, let $\mathbb{K}$ be a field, and let $\mathbb{K}^n$ denote the vector space of n-tuples of elements of $\mathbb{K}$. Further, for any $i \in \{1, \ldots, n\}$, let $e_i \in \mathbb{K}^n$ be the vector such that the i-th entry of e_i equals 1 and any remaining entry equals 0. Then, the set $\{e_1, e_2, \ldots, e_n\}$ denotes the *standard basis* of $\mathbb{K}^n$. Let $b_1, \ldots,$ $b_i \in \mathbb{K}^n$, then $\langle b_1, \ldots, b_i \rangle \subseteq \mathbb{K}^n$ denotes the span of those vectors.

2.2   Assumptions

Let $(\mathcal{G}_\lambda)_{\lambda \in \mathbb{N}}$ be a family of finite cyclic groups. If it is clear from the context, we write $\mathcal{G}$ instead of $\mathcal{G}_\lambda$. We assume that the order $q := |*|\mathcal{G}$ of the group is known and *prime*. Let $\mathsf{Gens}_{\mathcal{G}}$ be the set of generators of $\mathcal{G}$. We assume that we can efficiently sample elements uniformly at random from $\mathsf{Gens}_{\mathcal{G}}$.

A very basic and well-established cryptographic assumption is the decisional Diffie-Hellman (DDH) assumption. The DDH assumption states that the distributions $([x], [y], [x \cdot y])$ and $([x], [y], [z])$ are computationally indistinguishable for $x, y, z \leftarrow \mathbb{Z}_q$.

Definition 1 (Decisional Diffie-Hellman (DDH) assumption). *For any PPT adversary $\mathcal{A}$, the advantage $Adv_{\mathcal{G},\mathcal{A}}^{ddh}(\lambda)$ is negligible in λ, where*

$$Adv_{\mathcal{G},\mathcal{A}}^{ddh}(\lambda) := \Pr\left[\mathcal{A}(1^\lambda, [x], [y], [x \cdot y]) = 1 | x, y \leftarrow \mathbb{Z}_q\right]$$
$$- \Pr\left[\mathcal{A}(1^\lambda, [x], [y], [z]) = 1 | x, y, z \leftarrow \mathbb{Z}_q\right]$$

and q is the order of the group $\mathcal{G}$.

Let $(\mathcal{G}_1, \mathcal{G}_2, e)$ be finite cyclic groups of prime order $|*|\mathcal{G}_1 = |*|\mathcal{G}_2$ and let $e \colon \mathcal{G}_1 \times \mathcal{G}_2 \to \mathcal{G}_T$ be a pairing (i.e. a non-degenerate and bilinear map). The groups $\mathcal{G}_1, \mathcal{G}_2, \mathcal{G}_T$, as well as the pairing e depend on the security parameter. For greater clarity, we omit this dependency in this setting.

A natural extension of the DDH assumption to the bilinear setting is the symmetric external Diffie-Hellman (SXDH) assumption. The SXDH assumption states that the DDH assumption holds in both groups $\mathcal{G}_1$ and $\mathcal{G}_2$.

2.3 Point Obfuscation

In our construction we employ a cryptographic primitive that is called *point obfuscation* [16,37]. A point obfuscation serves the purpose to hide a certain point, but to enable a test whether a given value is hidden inside. Equivalently, this notion can be seen as an "obfuscation" of a point-function that evaluates to 1 at exactly this given point and to 0 everywhere else. We require that it is infeasible to distinguish a point obfuscation that triggers at a randomly sampled point from a point obfuscation that never triggers. This security requirement is rather weak compared to similar notions [7].

Definition 2 (Point obfuscation). *A* point obfuscation *for message space $\mathcal{M}_\lambda$ is a PPT algorithm* POBF.

POBF$(1^\lambda, x) \to po$ *On input a message $x \in \mathcal{M}_\lambda \cup \{\bot\}$, POBF produces a description of the point function*

$$po \colon \mathcal{M}_\lambda \to \{0, 1\}, y \mapsto \begin{cases} 1 & \text{if } y = x \\ 0 & \text{otherwise} \end{cases}.$$

We require the following two properties to hold:

Correctness: *For any x, $y \in \mathcal{M}_\lambda$ and any $po \leftarrow$ POBF$(1^\lambda, x)$, $po(y) \mapsto 1$ if and only if $x = y$.*

Soundness: *For any PPT adversary $\mathcal{A}$, the advantage $Adv_{\text{POBF},\mathcal{A}}^{po}(\lambda)$ is negligible in λ, where*

$$Adv_{\text{POBF},\mathcal{A}}^{po}(\lambda) := \Pr\left[\mathcal{A}(1^\lambda, po) = 1 | po \leftarrow \text{POBF}(1^\lambda, x), x \leftarrow \mathcal{M}_\lambda\right]$$
$$- \Pr\left[\mathcal{A}(1^\lambda, po) = 1 | po \leftarrow \text{POBF}(1^\lambda, \bot)\right].$$

An adaption of a construction proposed in [16] yields a point obfuscation POBF with message space $\mathbb{Z}_p$ based on the DDH assumption. Furthermore, a point obfuscation with message space $\mathbb{Z}_p$ can be used to construct a point obfuscation for message space $\mathbb{Z}_q$, where q is a prime such that $\frac{p}{q}$ is negligible in λ. For further details, we refer the reader to the full version [3].

Remark 1. According to a reviewer of TCC 2017, a point obfuscation with message space $\{0,1\}^{\mathsf{poly}(\lambda)}$ can be constructed from an injective one-way function F together with a corresponding hardcore bit B.

Given a string x, the tuple $(F(x), B(x))$ is the obfuscation of x. The tuple $(F(y), 1 - B(y))$ is an obfuscation of $\perp$, where y is a random element from the message space.

2.4   Subset Membership Problems

The notion of subset membership problems was introduced in [22]. Informally, a hard subset membership problem specifies a set, such that it is intractable to decide whether a value is inside this set or not. Let $\mathcal{L} = (\mathcal{L}_\lambda)_{\lambda \in \mathbb{N}}$ be a family of families of languages $L \subseteq \mathcal{X}_\lambda$ in a universe $\mathcal{X}_\lambda = \mathcal{X}$. Further, let $\mathcal{R}$ be an efficiently computable witness relation, such that $x \in L$ if and only if there exists a witness $w \in \{0,1\}^{\mathsf{poly}(|x|)}$ with $\mathcal{R}(x, w) = 1$, where poly is a fixed polynomial. We assume that we are able to efficiently and uniformly sample elements from L together with a corresponding witness, and that we are able to efficiently and uniformly sample elements from $\mathcal{X} \setminus L$.

Definition 3 (Hard subset membership problem). *The* subset membership problem *(SMP)* $L \subseteq \mathcal{X}$ *is* hard, *if for any PPT adversary $\mathcal{A}$, the advantage*

$$Adv_{\mathcal{L},\mathcal{A}}^{smp}(\lambda) := \Pr\left[\mathcal{A}(1^\lambda, x) = 1 | x \leftarrow L\right] - \Pr\left[\mathcal{A}(1^\lambda, x) = 1 | x \leftarrow \mathcal{X} \setminus L\right]$$

is negligible in λ.

For our construction we need a family $\mathcal{L} = (\mathcal{L}_\lambda)_{\lambda \in \mathbb{N}}$ such that for any $L \in \mathcal{L}_\lambda$ and any $x \in L$, there exists exactly one witness $r \in \{0,1\}^*$ with $\mathcal{R}(x, w) = 1$.

Let $\mathcal{G} = \{\mathcal{G}_\lambda\}$ be a family of finite cyclic groups of prime order such that the DDH assumption holds. A possible instantiation of a hard SMP meeting our requirements is the Diffie-Hellman language $\mathcal{L}^{\mathrm{dh}} := (\mathcal{L}_\lambda^{\mathrm{dh}})_{\lambda \in \mathbb{N}}$. For any $\lambda \in \mathbb{N}$, $\mathcal{L}_\lambda^{\mathrm{dh}} := \{L_{g,h} \mid g, h \in \mathsf{Gens}_{\mathcal{G}}\}$, $\mathcal{X}_\lambda = \mathsf{Gens}_{\mathcal{G}} \times \mathsf{Gens}_{\mathcal{G}}$, and $L_{g,h} := \{(g^r, h^r) \mid r \in \mathbb{Z}_q\}$, where $q = |*|\mathcal{G}_k|$. The SMP $L_{g,h} \subseteq \mathcal{X}$ is hard for randomly chosen generators $g, h \leftarrow \mathsf{Gens}_{\mathcal{G}}$. Given $(g^r, h^r) \in L_{g,h}$, the corresponding unique witness is $r \in \mathbb{Z}_q$.

2.5   Non-interactive Commitments

Non-interactive commitment schemes are a commonly used cryptographic primitive [29]. They enable to commit to a chosen value without revealing this value. Additionally, once committed to a value, this value cannot be changed. In contrast to the notion of point obfuscations, a commitment scheme prevents to test whether a particular value is hidden inside a commitment.

Definition 4 (Perfectly binding non-interactive commitment scheme (syntax and security)). *A perfectly binding non-interactive commitment scheme for message space $\mathcal{M}_\lambda$ is a triple of PPT algorithms* COM = (COMSETUP, COMMIT, OPEN).

COMSETUP$(1^\lambda) \to ck$ *On input the unary encoded security parameter, the algorithm* COMSETUP *outputs a commitment key ck.*
COMMIT$_{ck}(m) \to (com, op)$ *On input the commitment key ck and a message $m \in \mathcal{M}_\lambda$,* COMMIT *outputs a tuple (com, op).*
OPEN$_{ck}(com, op) \to \tilde{m}$ *On input the commitment key ck and a commitment-opening pair (com, op),* OPEN *outputs the committed message m if op is a valid opening for com. Otherwise,* OPEN *outputs $\perp$.*

We require COM *to be* perfectly correct, perfectly binding, *and* computationally hiding.

Correctness COM *is correct if for any $\lambda \in \mathbb{N}$, any $ck \leftarrow$ COMSETUP(1^λ), and any $m \in \mathcal{M}_\lambda$,* OPEN$_{ck}($COMMIT$_{ck}(m)) = m$.
Perfectly binding COM *is perfectly binding if it is not possible to find a commitment that has valid openings for more than one message, i.e. for any (possibly unbounded) adversary $\mathcal{A}$, $Adv_{COM,\mathcal{A}}^{binding}(\lambda) = 0$, where*

$$Adv_{COM,\mathcal{A}}^{binding}(\lambda) := \Pr\left[Exp_{COM,\mathcal{A}}^{binding}(\lambda) = 1\right].$$

Computationally hiding COM *is computationally hiding if commitments for different messages are computationally indistinguishable, i.e. for any PPT adversary $\mathcal{A}$, $Adv_{\mathcal{A}}^{hiding}(\lambda)$ is negligible, where*

$$Adv_{COM,\mathcal{A}}^{hiding}(\lambda) := \Pr\left[Exp_{COM,\mathcal{A}}^{hiding}(\lambda) = 1\right] - \frac{1}{2}.$$

The games $Exp_{COM,\mathcal{A}}^{binding}(\lambda)$ and $Exp_{COM,\mathcal{A}}^{hiding}(\lambda)$ are defined in Fig. 1.

Such a commitment scheme can be obtained from a group in which the DDH assumption holds.

EXPERIMENT $Exp_{COM,\mathcal{A}}^{binding}(\lambda)$

$ck \leftarrow$ COMSETUP(1^λ)
$(c, o_1, o_2) \leftarrow \mathcal{A}(1^\lambda, ck)$
$m_1 \leftarrow$ OPEN$_{ck}(c, o_1)$, $m_2 \leftarrow$ OPEN$_{ck}(c, o_2)$
if $m_1 \neq \perp \wedge m_2 \neq \perp \wedge m_1 \neq m_2$ then
    return 1
return 0

EXPERIMENT $Exp_{COM,\mathcal{A}}^{hiding}(\lambda)$

$ck \leftarrow$ COMSETUP(1^λ)
$(m_0, m_1, st) \leftarrow \mathcal{A}(1^\lambda, ck, \mathsf{find})$
$b \leftarrow \{0,1\}$, $(c, o) \leftarrow$ COMMIT$_{ck}(m_b)$
$b' \leftarrow \mathcal{A}(1^\lambda, c, st, \mathsf{attack})$
if $b = b'$ then return 1
return 0

Fig. 1. The description of the Binding game $Exp_{COM,\mathcal{A}}^{binding}(\lambda)$ (left) and the Hiding game $Exp_{COM,\mathcal{A}}^{hiding}(\lambda)$ (right).

2.6   Dual Mode NIWI Proof System

The notion of dual mode NIWI proof systems abstracts from the NIWI proof system proposed in [30]. A similar abstraction was used in [4].

Definition 5 (Dual mode NIWI proof system (syntax and security)).
A dual mode non-interactive witness-indistinguishable (NIWI) proof system for a relation $\mathcal{R}$ is a tuple of PPT algorithms $\Pi = (Setup_\Pi, K, S, Prove, Verify, Extract)$.

$Setup_\Pi(1^\lambda) \rightarrow (gpk, gsk)$ *On input the unary encoded security parameter, $Setup_\Pi$ outputs a group key gpk and, additionally, may output some related information gsk. The relation $\mathcal{R}$ is an efficiently computable ternary relation consisting of triplets of the form (gpk, x, w) and defines a group-dependent language L. The language L consists of the statements x, such that there exists a witness w with $(gpk, x, w) \in \mathcal{R}$.*

$K(gpk, gsk) \rightarrow (crs, td_{ext})$ *On input the group keys gpk and gsk, K outputs a binding common reference string (CRS) crs and a corresponding extraction trapdoor td_{ext}.*

$S(gpk, gsk) \rightarrow (crs, \perp)$ *On input the group keys gpk and gsk, S outputs a hiding CRS crs.*

$Prove(gpk, crs, x, w) \rightarrow \pi$ *On input the public group key gpk, the CRS crs, a statement x, and a corresponding witness w, Prove produces a proof π.*

$Verify(gpk, crs, x, \pi) \rightarrow \{0, 1\}$ *On input the public group key gpk, the CRS crs, a statement x, and a proof π, Verify outputs 1 if the proof is valid and 0 if the proof is rejected.*

$Extract(td_{ext}, x, \pi) \rightarrow w$ *On input the extraction trapdoor td_{ext}, a statement x, and a proof π, Extract outputs a witness w.*

We require Π to meet the following requirements:

CRS indistinguishability. *Common reference strings generated via $K(gpk, gsk)$ and $S(gpk, gsk)$ are computationally indistinguishable, i.e.*

$$Adv_{\Pi,\mathcal{A}}^{crs}(\lambda) := \Pr\left[Exp_{\Pi,\mathcal{A}}^{crs}(\lambda) = 1\right] - \frac{1}{2}$$

is negligible in λ, where $Exp_{\Pi,\mathcal{A}}^{crs}(\lambda)$ is defined as in Fig. 2.

Perfect completeness under K and S. *For any $\lambda \in \mathbb{N}$, any $(gpk, gsk) \leftarrow Setup_\Pi(1^\lambda)$, any CRS $(crs, \cdot) \leftarrow K(gpk, gsk)$, any (x, w) such that $(gpk, x, w) \in \mathcal{R}$, and any $\pi \leftarrow Prove(gpk, crs, x, w)$, $Verify(gpk, crs, x, \pi) \rightarrow 1$. The same holds for any $(crs, \cdot) \leftarrow S(gpk, gsk)$.*

Perfect soundness under K. *For any $\lambda \in \mathbb{N}$, any $(gpk, gsk) \leftarrow Setup_\Pi(1^\lambda)$, any $(crs, \cdot) \leftarrow K(gpk, gsk)$, any statement x such that there exists no witness w with $(gpk, x, w) \in \mathcal{R}$, and any $\pi \in \{0, 1\}^*$, $Verify(gpk, crs, x, \pi) \rightarrow 0$.*

Perfect extractability under K. *For any $\lambda \in \mathbb{N}$, any key pair $(gpk, gsk) \leftarrow Setup_\Pi(1^\lambda)$, any $(crs, td_{ext}) \leftarrow K(gpk, gsk)$, any (x, π) such that $Verify(gpk, crs, x, \pi) \rightarrow 1$, and for any $w \leftarrow Extract(td_{ext}, x, \pi)$, w is a satisfying witness for the statement x, i.e. $(gpk, x, w) \in \mathcal{R}$.*

$$\text{EXPERIMENT } Exp_{\Pi,\mathcal{A}}^{\text{crs}}(\lambda)$$

$(gpk, gsk) \leftarrow \mathsf{Setup}_{\Pi}(1^\lambda)$

$(crs_0, \cdot) \leftarrow \mathsf{K}(gpk, gsk), (crs_1, \cdot) \leftarrow \mathsf{S}(gpk, gsk)$

$b \leftarrow \{0,1\}, b' \leftarrow \mathcal{A}(1^\lambda, gpk, crs_b)$

if $b' = b$ **then return** 1

return 0

Fig. 2. The description of the CRS inistinguishability game $Exp_{\Pi,\mathcal{A}}^{\text{crs}}(\lambda)$.

Perfect witness-indistinguishability under S. *For any* $\lambda \in \mathbb{N}$, *any* $(gpk, gsk) \leftarrow Setup_{\Pi}(1^\lambda)$, *any* $(crs, \cdot) \leftarrow S(gpk, gsk)$, *any* (x, w_0) *and* (x, w_1) *with* (gpk, x, w_0), $(gpk, x, w_1) \in \mathcal{R}$, *the output of* $\mathsf{Prove}(gpk, crs, x, w_0)$ *and the output of* $\mathsf{Prove}(gpk, crs, x, w_1)$ *are identically distributed.*

An exemplary dual mode NIWI proof system satisfying computational CRS indistinguishability, perfect completeness, perfect soundness, perfect extractability, and perfect witness-indistinguishability is the proof system proposed by Groth and Sahai in [30]. The soundness, in particular the indistinguishability of common reference strings, of this construction can for instance be based on the SXDH assumption. The Groth-Sahai proof system allows perfect extractability for group elements, however, does not provide a natural way to extract scalars. Nevertheless, perfect extractability can be achieved by using the proof system for the bit representation of the particular scalars [34].

2.7 Probabilistic Indistinguishability Obfuscation

The notion of probabilistic circuit obfuscation was proposed in [17]. Informally, probabilistic circuit obfuscation enables to conceal the implementation of probabilistic circuits while preserving their functionality. Let $\mathcal{C} = (\mathcal{C}_\lambda)_{\lambda \in \mathbb{N}}$ be a family of sets $\mathcal{C}_\lambda$ of probabilistic circuits. The set $\mathcal{C}_\lambda$ contains circuits of polynomial size in λ. A *circuit sampler* for $\mathcal{C}$ is defined as a set of (efficiently samplable) distributions $S = (S_\lambda)_{\lambda \in \mathbb{N}}$, where S_λ is a distribution over triplets (C_0, C_1, z) with $C_0, C_1 \in \mathcal{C}_\lambda$ such that C_0 and C_1 take inputs of the same length and $z \in \{0,1\}^{\mathsf{poly}(\lambda)}$.

Definition 6 (Probabilistic indistinguishability obfuscation for a class of samplers $\mathcal{S}$, [4,17]). *A probabilistic indistinguishability obfuscator (pIO) for a class of samplers S over the probabilistic circuit family $\mathcal{C} = (\mathcal{C}_\lambda)_{\lambda \in \mathbb{N}}$ is a uniform PPT algorithm $pi\mathcal{O}$, such that the following properties hold:*

Correctness. *On input the unary encoded security parameter 1^λ and a circuit $C \in \mathcal{C}_\lambda$, $pi\mathcal{O}$ outputs a deterministic circuit Λ of polynomial size in $|*|C$ and λ. For any $\lambda \in \mathbb{N}$, any $C \in \mathcal{C}_\lambda$, any $\Lambda \leftarrow pi\mathcal{O}(1^\lambda, C)$, and any inputs $m \in \{0,1\}^*$ (of matching length), there exists a randomness r, such that $C(m; r) = \Lambda(m)$.*

Experiment $Exp^{\text{pio-c}}_{C,z,\mathcal{D}}(\lambda)$	Experiment $Exp^{\text{pio-ind}}_{pi\mathcal{O},S,\mathcal{A}}(\lambda)$	Experiment $Exp^{\text{sel-ind}}_{S,\mathcal{A}}(\lambda)$
$C_0 := C$	$(C_0, C_1, z) \leftarrow S_\lambda$	$(x, st) \leftarrow \mathcal{A}_1(1^\lambda)$
$C_1 := pi\mathcal{O}(1^\lambda, C)$	$b \leftarrow \{0,1\}$	$(C_0, C_1, z) \leftarrow S_\lambda,\ b \leftarrow \{0,1\}$
$b \leftarrow \{0,1\}$	$\Lambda \leftarrow pi\mathcal{O}(1^\lambda, C_b)$	$y \leftarrow C_b(x; r) /\!\!/$ for fresh randomness r
$b' \leftarrow \mathcal{A}^{C_b(\cdot)}(1^\lambda, C, z)$	$b' \leftarrow \mathcal{A}(1^\lambda, C_0, C_1, \Lambda, z)$	$b' \leftarrow \mathcal{A}_2(1^\lambda, C_0, C_1, z, y, st)$
if $b' = b$ then return 1	if $b' = b$ then return 1	if $b' = b$ then return 1
return 0	return 0	return 0

Fig. 3. The descriptions of the games $Exp^{\text{pio-c}}_{C,z,\mathcal{D}}(\lambda)$ (left), $Exp^{\text{pio-ind}}_{pi\mathcal{O},S,\mathcal{A}}(\lambda)$ (middle), and $Exp^{\text{sel-ind}}_{S,\mathcal{A}}(\lambda)$ (right). In $Exp^{\text{pio-c}}_{C,z,\mathcal{D}}(\lambda)$, $\mathcal{D}$ has oracle access to either a probabilistic circuit C_0 using fresh randomness for every oracle query or to a deterministic circuit C_1. $\mathcal{D}$ can make an unbounded number of oracle queries with the restriction that no input is queried twice.

Furthermore, for every non-uniform PPT distinguisher $\mathcal{D}$, every $\lambda \in \mathbb{N}$, every $C \in \mathcal{C}_\lambda$, and every auxiliary input $z \in \{0,1\}^{poly(\lambda)}$, the advantage

$$Adv^{\text{pio-c}}_{C,z,\mathcal{D}}(\lambda) := \Pr\left[Exp^{\text{pio-c}}_{C,z,\mathcal{D}}(\lambda) = 1\right] - \frac{1}{2}$$

is negligible in λ, where $Exp^{\text{pio-c}}_{C,z,\mathcal{D}}(\lambda)$ is defined as in Fig. 3.

Security with respect to S. *For any circuit sampler $S = \{S_\lambda\}_{\lambda \in \mathbb{N}}$, for any non-uniform PPT adversary $\mathcal{A}$, the advantage*

$$Adv^{\text{pio-ind}}_{pi\mathcal{O},S,\mathcal{A}}(\lambda) := \Pr\left[Exp^{\text{pio-ind}}_{pi\mathcal{O},S,\mathcal{A}}(\lambda) = 1\right] - \frac{1}{2}$$

is negligible in λ, where $Exp^{\text{pio-ind}}_{pi\mathcal{O},S,\mathcal{A}}(\lambda)$ is defined as in Fig. 3.

We remark that the construction proposed in [17] also satisfies our definition of correctness.

Let $X \colon \mathbb{N} \to \mathbb{N}$ be a function. For our purposes we use a class of circuit samplers, such that the sampled circuits are functionally equivalent for all inputs outside of a set $\mathcal{X}$, and the outputs of the circuits are indistinguishable for inputs inside of this set $\mathcal{X}$. The set $\mathcal{X}$ is a subset of the circuits' domain of cardinality at most $X(\lambda)$. Two circuits C_0 and C_1 are functionally equivalent if for any input x of matching length and any randomness r, $C_0(x; r) = C_1(x; r)$.

Definition 7 (X-Ind sampler, [4,17]). *Let $X \colon \mathbb{N} \to \mathbb{N}$ be a function with $X(\lambda) \leq 2^\lambda$, for all $\lambda \in \mathbb{N}$. The class $\mathcal{S}^{X-ind}$ of X-Ind samplers for a circuit family $\mathcal{C}$ contains all circuit samplers S for $\mathcal{C}$ satisfying, that for any $\lambda \in \mathbb{N}$, there exists a set $\mathcal{X} = \mathcal{X}_\lambda \subseteq \{0,1\}^*$ with $|*|\mathcal{X} \leq X(\lambda)$, such that the following two properties hold:*

X-differing inputs. *For any (possibly unbounded) deterministic adversary $\mathcal{A}$, the advantage*

$$Adv_{S,\mathcal{A}}^{eq\$}(\lambda) := \Pr \left[C_0(x;r) \neq C_1(x;r) \wedge x \notin \mathcal{X} \,\middle|\, \begin{matrix} (C_0, C_1, z) \leftarrow S_\lambda, \\ (x, r) \leftarrow \mathcal{A}(C_0, C_1, z) \end{matrix} \right]$$

is negligible in λ.

X-indistinguishability. *For any non-uniform PPT distinguisher $\mathcal{A} = (\mathcal{A}_1, \mathcal{A}_2)$, the advantage*

$$X(\lambda) \cdot Adv_{S,\mathcal{A}}^{sel\text{-}ind}(\lambda) := X(\lambda) \cdot \left(\Pr \left[Exp_{S,\mathcal{A}}^{sel\text{-}ind}(\lambda) = 1 \right] - \frac{1}{2} \right)$$

is negligible in λ, where $Exp_{S,\mathcal{A}}^{sel\text{-}ind}(\lambda)$ is defined as in Fig. 3.

For our construction we use an obfuscator for the class $\mathcal{S}^{X\text{-}ind}$.

According to Theorem 2 in the proceedings of [17], a pIO which is secure with respect to $\mathcal{S}^{X\text{-}ind}$ for a circuit family $\mathcal{C}$ that only contains circuits of size at most λ can be obtained from sub-exponentially secure indistinguishability obfuscation (IO) for deterministic circuits in conjunction with sub-exponentially secure puncturable PRF. The construction given in [17] satisfies this security requirement even if the circuit family $\mathcal{C} = \{\mathcal{C}_\lambda\}_{\lambda \in \mathbb{N}}$ contains circuits with polynomial size in λ as long as the input length of those circuits is at most λ.

2.8 Fully Homomorphic Encryption Scheme

Let $\mathcal{C} = (\mathcal{C}_\lambda)_{\lambda \in \mathbb{N}}$ be a family of sets of polynomial sized circuits of arity $a(\lambda)$, i.e. the set $\mathcal{C}_\lambda$ contains circuits of polynomial size in λ. We assume that for any $\lambda \in \mathbb{N}$ the circuits in $\mathcal{C}_\lambda$ share the common input domain $(\{0,1\}^{\mathsf{poly}(\lambda)})^{a(\lambda)}$ for a fixed polynomial $\mathsf{poly}(\lambda)$. A homomorphic encryption scheme enables evaluation of circuits on encrypted data. The first fully homomorphic encryption scheme was proposed in [28]. In this paper, we abide by the notation used in [4].

Definition 8 (Homomorphic public-key encryption (HPKE) scheme (syntax and security)). *A homomorphic public-key encryption scheme with message space $\mathcal{M} \subseteq \{0,1\}^*$ for a deterministic circuit family $\mathcal{C} = (\mathcal{C}_\lambda)_{\lambda \in \mathbb{N}}$ of arity $a(\lambda)$ and input domain $(\{0,1\}^{\mathsf{poly}(\lambda)})^{a(\lambda)}$ is a tuple of PPT algorithms $\mathrm{HPKE} = (\mathrm{GEN}, \mathrm{ENC}, \mathrm{DEC}, \mathrm{EVAL})$.*

$\mathrm{GEN}(1^\lambda) \to (pk, sk)$ *On input the unary encoded security parameter 1^λ, GEN outputs a public key pk and a secret key sk.*

$\mathrm{ENC}(pk, m) \to c$ *On input the public key pk and a message $m \in \mathcal{M}$, ENC outputs a ciphertext $c \in \{0,1\}^{\mathsf{poly}(\lambda)}$ for message m.*

$\mathrm{DEC}(sk, c) \to m$ *On input the secret key sk and a ciphertext $c \in \{0,1\}^{\mathsf{poly}(\lambda)}$, DEC outputs the corresponding message $m \in \mathcal{M}$ (or $\bot$, if the ciphertext is not valid).*

EXPERIMENT $Exp_{\text{HPKE},\mathcal{A}}^{\text{ind-cpa}}(\lambda)$

$(pk, sk) \leftarrow \text{GEN}(1^\lambda),\ (m_0, m_1, st) \leftarrow \mathcal{A}(1^\lambda, pk, \text{find})$

$b \leftarrow \{0, 1\},\ c \leftarrow \text{ENC}(pk, m_b)$

$b' \leftarrow \mathcal{A}(1^\lambda, c, st, \text{attack})$

if $b' = b$ then return 1

return 0

Fig. 4. The description of the IND-CPA game $Exp_{\text{HPKE},\mathcal{A}}^{\text{ind-cpa}}(\lambda)$.

$\text{EVAL}(pk, C, c_1, \ldots, c_{a(\lambda)}) \to c$ *On input the public key pk, a deterministic circuit $C \in \mathcal{C}_\lambda$, and ciphertexts $(c_1, \ldots, c_{a(\lambda)}) \in (\{0, 1\}^{poly(\lambda)})^{a(\lambda)}$, EVAL outputs a ciphertext $c \in \{0, 1\}^{poly(\lambda)}$.*

We require HPKE to meet the following requirements:

Perfect correctness. *The triple (GEN, ENC, DEC) is perfectly correct as a PKE scheme, i.e. for any $\lambda \in \mathbb{N}$, any $(pk, sk) \leftarrow \text{GEN}(1^\lambda)$, any $m \in \mathcal{M}$, and any $c \leftarrow \text{ENC}(pk, m)$, $\text{DEC}(sk, c) = m$. Furthermore, the evaluation algorithm EVAL is perfectly correct in the sense that for any $\lambda \in \mathbb{N}$, any $(pk, sk) \leftarrow \text{GEN}(1^\lambda)$, any $m_1, \ldots, m_{a(\lambda)} \in \mathcal{M}$, any $c_i \leftarrow \text{ENC}(pk, m_i)$, any $C \in \mathcal{C}_\lambda$, and any $c \leftarrow \text{EVAL}(pk, C, c_1, \ldots, c_{a(\lambda)})$, $\text{DEC}(sk, c) = C(m_1, \ldots, m_{a(\lambda)})$.*

Compactness. *The size of the output of EVAL is polynomial in λ and independent of the size of the circuit C.*

Security. *For any legitimate PPT adversary $\mathcal{A}$, the advantage*

$$Adv_{\text{HPKE},\mathcal{A}}^{ind\text{-}cpa}(\lambda) := Exp_{\text{HPKE},\mathcal{A}}^{ind\text{-}cpa}(\lambda) - \frac{1}{2}$$

is negligible in λ, where $Exp_{\text{HPKE},\mathcal{A}}^{ind\text{-}cpa}$ is defined as in Fig. 4. An adversary $\mathcal{A}$ is legitimate if it outputs two messages m_0, m_1 of identical length.

Without loss of generality, we assume that the secret key is the randomness that was used during the key generation. This enables to test whether key pairs are valid.

3 Construction

3.1 Group Scheme

A group scheme is an abstraction from the properties of groups formalized via a tuple of PPT algorithms. For our purposes, we further abstract this notion to suit groups where group elements do not necessarily have unique encodings. We adapt the notion described in [4] which in turn generalizes the notion introduced in [11]. As demonstrated in [4], such group schemes benefit from the fact that group elements can be represented with many different encodings. This allows to add auxiliary information inside encodings of group elements in order to add more structure to the group. In our case, however, we exploit that group schemes with non-unique encodings can be used to conceal the structure of the group.

Definition 9 (Group scheme with non-unique encodings). *A group scheme with non-unique encodings Γ is a tuple of PPT algorithms $\Gamma = (\text{SETUP}, \text{VAL}, \text{SAM}, \text{ADD}, \text{EQUAL})$.*

$\text{SETUP}(1^\lambda) \rightarrow pp$ *On input the unary encoded security parameter 1^λ, SETUP outputs public parameters pp. In particular, pp contains the group order q. We assume that pp is given implicitly to the following algorithms.*

We assume that any encoding is represented as a bit string. In order to decide, whether a given bit string is a valid encoding of a group element, Γ provides a validation algorithm VAL. We refer to bit strings causing VAL to output 1 as (valid) encodings of group elements.

$\text{VAL}(h) \rightarrow \{0, 1\}$ *On input a bit string $h \in \{0, 1\}^*$, VAL outputs 1 if h is a valid encoding with respect to pp, otherwise VAL outputs 0.*

In general, it is not sufficient to compare encodings as bit strings in order to decide whether they represent the same group element. Hence, a group scheme needs to define an algorithm that provides this functionality. This algorithm is called EQUAL. We require EQUAL to realize an equivalence relation on the set of valid encodings. For any valid encoding $h \in \{0, 1\}^*$, let $\mathcal{G}(h)$ denote the equivalence class of this encoding. In other words, $\mathcal{G}(h)$ contains all encodings that correspond to the same group element as the encoding h. For any valid encoding h, we require that $|\{a \in \{0, 1\}^* \mid \text{VAL}(a) = 1\}/\mathcal{G}(h)| = q$ is the order of the group. We refer to the equivalence classes in $\{a \in \{0, 1\}^* \mid \text{VAL}(a) = 1\}/\mathcal{G}(h)$ as group elements.

$\text{EQUAL}(a, b) \rightarrow \{0, 1, \bot\}$ *On input two valid encodings a and b, EQUAL outputs 1 if a and b represent the same group element, otherwise EQUAL outputs 0. If either a or b is invalid, EQUAL outputs $\bot$.*

In order to perform the group operation on two given encodings, we define an addition algorithm ADD.

$\text{ADD}(a, b)$ *On input two valid encodings a and b, ADD outputs an encoding corresponding to the group element that results from the addition of the group elements represented by a and b. If either a or b is invalid, ADD outputs $\bot$.*

The sampling algorithm SAM enables to produce an encoding of a group element and only uses information that is part of the public parameters pp. Let h be a bit string produced via $\text{SAM}(1)$.

For any $z \in \mathbb{N}$, let $[z]$ denote the group element corresponding to the equivalence class $\mathcal{G}(h^z)$, where the group operation is performed using ADD. We require the distribution of $\text{SAM}(z)$ to be computationally indistinguishable from uniform distribution over $[z]$.

SAM(z) → a *On input an exponent* $z \in \mathbb{N}$, SAM *outputs an encoding a from the equivalence class* $\mathcal{G}(h^z)$.

Given the order q of the group, it is sufficient to provide an addition algorithm to enable inversion of group elements. To invert a given group element, we use the square-and-multiply approach to add the given encoding $q - 1$ times to itself. Further, it suffices to define an algorithm ZERO that tests whether a given encoding corresponds to the identity element of the group instead of an algorithm EQUAL as above. To implement the algorithm EQUAL on input two encodings a and b, we invert b, add the result to a and test whether the result corresponds to the identity element using ZERO.

According to [4], a group scheme with non-unique encodings, in addition to the algorithms defined above, provides an extraction algorithm. The extraction algorithm, given a valid encoding, produces a bit string such that all encodings that represent the same group element lead to the same bit string. However, we omit this algorithm, as our construction does not provide one. It remains an open problem to extend our construction with an extraction algorithm such that the validity of the (m, n)-Interactive Uber assumption (see Definition 10) can still be proven.

3.2   Interactive Uber Assumption

The Uber assumption is a very strong cryptographic assumption in bilinear groups first proposed in [10] and refined in [12]. It provides a natural framework that enables to assess the plausibility of cryptographic assumptions in bilinear groups.

In contrast to the original definition, we consider adaptive attacks (in which an adversary may ask adaptively for more information about the game secrets and choose his challenge).

Definition 10 ((m, n)-Interactive Uber assumption for group schemes).
Let $m = m(\lambda)$ and $n = n(\lambda)$ such that $d := \binom{n+m}{m}$ is a polynomial [5] in λ, and let Γ be a group scheme. The (m, n)-Interactive Uber assumption holds for Γ if for any legitimate PPT adversary $\mathcal{A}$, the advantage $Adv_{\Gamma,\mathcal{A}}^{uber}(\lambda)$ is negligible in λ, where

$$Adv_{\Gamma,\mathcal{A}}^{uber}(\lambda) := \Pr\left[Exp_{\Gamma,\mathcal{A}}^{uber}(\lambda) = 1\right] - \frac{1}{2}.$$

The game $Exp_{\Gamma,\mathcal{A}}^{uber}(\lambda)$ is described in Fig. 5. An adversary $\mathcal{A}$ is legitimate, if and only if it always guarantees $P^*(\mathbf{X}) \notin \langle 1, P_1(\mathbf{X}), \ldots, P_l(\mathbf{X})\rangle$ and for any $P(\mathbf{X}) \in \{P^*(\mathbf{X}), P_1(\mathbf{X}), \ldots, P_l(\mathbf{X})\}$, $\deg(P(\mathbf{X})) \leq n$ in $Exp_{\Gamma,\mathcal{A}}^{uber}(\lambda)$, where $\{P_1(\mathbf{X}), \ldots, P_l(\mathbf{X})\}$ are the polynomials that $\mathcal{A}$ requests from its oracle $\mathcal{O}$.

For technical reasons, we need the maximum total degree n of the polynomials appearing in $Exp_{\Gamma,\mathcal{A}}^{uber}(\lambda)$ and the number of unknowns m to be bounded a priori.

---

[5] If the parameters m and n both grow at most logarithmically in λ or one of them grows polynomially in λ while the other one is a constant, the binomial coefficient $d = \binom{n+m}{m}$ grows polynomially in λ.

$$\begin{array}{ll}
\text{EXPERIMENT } Exp^{uber}_{\Gamma,\mathcal{A}}(\lambda) & \text{ORACLE } \mathcal{O}(P(\boldsymbol{X})) \\
\hline
pp \leftarrow \text{SETUP}(1^\lambda),\ \boldsymbol{s} \leftarrow (\mathbb{Z}_q)^m & \textbf{return } \text{SAM}(P(\boldsymbol{s})) \\
(P^*(\boldsymbol{X}), st) \leftarrow \mathcal{A}^{\mathcal{O}(\cdot)}(1^\lambda, pp, \text{find}) & \\
b \leftarrow \{0,1\},\ r \leftarrow \mathbb{Z}_q & \\
z_0 \leftarrow \text{SAM}(P^*(\boldsymbol{s})),\ z_1 \leftarrow \text{SAM}(r) & \\
b' \leftarrow \mathcal{A}^{\mathcal{O}(\cdot)}(1^\lambda, z_b, st, \text{attack}) & \\
\textbf{if } b = b' \textbf{ then return } 1 & \\
\textbf{return } 0 &
\end{array}$$

Fig. 5. The description of the (m,n)-Interactive Uber game $Exp^{uber}_{\Gamma,\mathcal{A}}(\lambda)$. The oracle $\mathcal{O}$ on input a polynomial $P(\boldsymbol{X})$, returns an encoding of the group element $[P(\boldsymbol{s})]$. We refer to $P^*(\boldsymbol{X})$ as "challenge polynomial" and to z_b as "challenge encoding". Further, we call the polynomials that $\mathcal{A}$ requests from the oracle $\mathcal{O}$ "query polynomials".

3.3 Our Construction

Inspired by the construction in [4], an encoding of a group element includes two ciphertexts each encrypting a vector determining an m-variate polynomial over $\mathbb{Z}_q$ of maximum total degree n with respect to some randomly sampled basis $\{a_1, \ldots, a_d\}$. That basis is hidden inside the public parameters of the group scheme via a perfectly binding commitment. An encoding corresponds to the group element whose discrete logarithm equals the evaluation of the thus determined polynomial at a random point $\boldsymbol{\omega} \in \mathbb{Z}_q^m$. That random point $\boldsymbol{\omega}$ is fixed in the public parameters via a point obfuscation po.

For our construction we employ the following building blocks: (i) a dual mode NIWI proof system Π, (ii) a homomorphic encryption scheme HPKE with message space $\mathcal{M} = \mathbb{Z}_q^d$ for a family of circuits of arity $a(\lambda) = 2$ adding two tuples in $\mathbb{Z}_q^d$ component-by-component modulo q, (iii) a point obfuscation POBF for message space $\mathcal{M}_k = \mathbb{Z}_q$, (iv) a family $\mathcal{TD} = (\mathcal{TD}_\lambda)_{\lambda \in \mathbb{N}}$ of families $\mathcal{TD}_\lambda$ of languages TD in a universe $\mathcal{X} = \mathcal{X}_\lambda$ with unique witnesses for $y \in \text{TD}$ such that the subset membership problem $\text{TD} \subseteq \mathcal{X}$ is hard, (v) a perfectly binding non-interactive commitment scheme COM for message space $\mathbb{Z}_q^{d \times d}$, and (vi) a general purpose X-Ind pIO $pi\mathcal{O}$ (i.e. a pIO that is secure with respect to $\mathcal{S}^{X\text{-ind}}$ for a circuit family that only contains circuits with input length at most l, where l is the security parameter used for $pi\mathcal{O}$). Let $n = n(\lambda)$ and let $m = m(\lambda)$ such that $\binom{n+m}{m}$ is a polynomial in λ. The group scheme we construct depends on n and m. We emphasize this fact by calling it $\Gamma_{m,n} := (\text{SETUP}, \text{VAL}, \text{SAM}, \text{ADD}, \text{EQUAL})$. As mentioned above, we provide an algorithm that tests if a given encoding is an encoding of the identity group element, instead of implementing EQUAL.

In Fig. 6 we describe the algorithm SETUP of our construction. The number q is a prime number that is greater than $2^{p(\lambda)}$ and will serve as the order of our group scheme. We require p to be a polynomial such that $p(\lambda) \geq poly(\lambda)$, where $poly$ is used to scale the security parameter of $pi\mathcal{O}$. We emphasize that our construction allows to arbitrarily choose the group order q as long as q is greater than $2^{p(\lambda)}$ and prime. Therefore, q can be understood as an input of

Algorithm Setup(1^λ)

$(gpk, gsk) \leftarrow \mathsf{Setup}_\Pi(1^\lambda)$

$(pk, sk) \leftarrow \mathrm{Gen}(1^\lambda),\ (pk', sk') \leftarrow \mathrm{Gen}(1^\lambda)$

$\omega \leftarrow (\mathbb{Z}_q)^m,\ \mathsf{po}_i \leftarrow \mathrm{POBF}(1^\lambda, \omega_i)$ for $1 \leq i \leq m$, $\mathsf{po} := (\mathsf{po}_1, \ldots, \mathsf{po}_m)$

$\mathrm{TD} \leftarrow \mathcal{TD}_\lambda,\ y \leftarrow \mathcal{X} \setminus \mathrm{TD}$

$A \leftarrow \{B \in \mathrm{GL}_d(\mathbb{Z}_q) \mid B \cdot e_1 = e_1\}$

$ck \leftarrow \mathrm{ComSetup}(1^\lambda),\ (com, op) \leftarrow \mathrm{Commit}_{ck}(A)$

$(crs, td_{\mathrm{ext}}) \leftarrow \mathsf{K}(gpk, gsk)$

$\Lambda_{\mathrm{add}} \leftarrow pi\mathcal{O}(1^{poly(\lambda)}, C_{\mathrm{Add}}),\ \Lambda_{\mathrm{zero}} \leftarrow pi\mathcal{O}(1^{poly(\lambda)}, C_{\mathrm{Zero}}^{(0)})$

return $pp := (q, gpk, crs, y, \mathrm{TD}, pk, pk', \Lambda_{\mathrm{add}}, \Lambda_{\mathrm{zero}}, \mathsf{po}, ck, com)$

Fig. 6. The implementation of the Setup algorithm producing public parameters pp.

the algorithm Setup. For the sake of simplicity, we do not write q as input and assume that Setup generates a suitable group order.

We remark that the circuits C_{Add} and $C_{\mathrm{Zero}}^{(0)}$ that appear in the algorithm Setup implement the addition of two group elements and a test for the identity element respectively. For a description of these circuits we refer the reader to Fig. 7. The polynomial $poly(\lambda) \geq \lambda$ that is used to scale the security parameter for the obfuscator $pi\mathcal{O}$ upper bounds the input length of these circuits C_{Add} and $C_{\mathrm{Zero}}^{(0)}$. All versions of addition circuits and all versions zero testing circuits that appear during the proofs are padded to the same length respectively. We emphasize that it is necessary to scale the used security parameter as the pIO $pi\mathcal{O}$ we rely on is secure with respect to $\mathcal{S}^{X\text{-ind}}$ for a circuit family that only contains circuits with input length at most λ', where λ' denotes the security parameter that is used to invoke $pi\mathcal{O}$.

Encodings of Group Elements. Encodings of group elements are of the form $h = (C, C', \pi)$. The first two entries C and C' are ciphertexts encrypting vectors $\vec{f} \in \mathbb{Z}_q^d$ and $\vec{f'} \in \mathbb{Z}_q^d$ respectively under the public keys pk and pk' respectively, where d is the dimension of the $\mathbb{Z}_q$ vector space of m-variate polynomials over $\mathbb{Z}_q$ with total degree at most n, i.e. $d = \binom{n+m}{m}$. We require the dimension d of the vector space to grow at most polynomially in λ. The last entry π is the so-called consistency proof. We refer to the vectors $\vec{f}$ and $\vec{f'}$ as *representation vectors* of the group element and to the tuple $(\vec{f}, \vec{f'})$ as *representation* of the group element. Let $\alpha = (\alpha_1, \ldots, \alpha_m) \in \mathbb{N}^m$ denote tuples with $\sum_{i=1}^m \alpha_i \leq n$ and let

$$\varphi_{\mathrm{pol}}\colon \mathbb{Z}_q^d \to \mathbb{Z}_q[\boldsymbol{X}], (\ldots, v_\alpha, \ldots)^T \mapsto \sum_\alpha v_\alpha \cdot X_1^{\alpha_1} \cdots X_m^{\alpha_m}$$

be the vector space homomorphism mapping the standard basis of $\mathbb{Z}_q^d$ to a natural basis of the vector space of m-variate polynomials of degree at most n. For well-definedness we use the lexicographical order on the tuples $(\alpha_1, \ldots, \alpha_m) \in \mathbb{N}^m$, particularly, the first vector of the standard basis of $\mathbb{Z}_q^d$ is mapped to the constant polynomial 1. The image of φ_{pol} is $\mathrm{Im}(\varphi_{pol}) = \{p \in \mathbb{Z}_q[\boldsymbol{X}] \mid \deg(p) \leq n\}$ and the kernel is $\ker(\varphi_{pol}) = \{0\}$. Hence, φ_{pol} is an isomorphism between the vector spaces $\mathbb{Z}_q^d$ and $\mathrm{Im}(\varphi_{pol})$.

We recall that $\mathrm{SETUP}(1^\lambda)$ samples the matrix A uniformly at random from $\mathrm{GL}_d(\mathbb{Z}_q)$ such that the first column equals e_1. Hence, the matrix A^{-1} exists and has the form $A^{-1} = (a_1 \mid a_2 \mid \ldots \mid a_d)$ such that $a_1 = e_1$. The columns $a_1, \ldots, a_d \in \mathbb{Z}_q^d$ form a basis of the vector space $\mathbb{Z}_q^d$.

The coefficients of the representation vectors $\overrightarrow{f} = (f_1, \ldots, f_d)^T$ and $\overrightarrow{f'} = (f_1', \ldots, f_d')^T$ of a group element define the polynomials $f(\boldsymbol{X})$, $f'(\boldsymbol{X}) \in \mathrm{Im}(\varphi_{pol})$ via

$$f(\boldsymbol{X}) := \sum_{i=1}^{d} f_i \cdot \varphi_{pol}(a_i) \qquad f'(\boldsymbol{X}) := \sum_{i=1}^{d} f_i' \cdot \varphi_{pol}(a_i)$$

$$= \varphi_{pol}\left(A^{-1} \cdot \overrightarrow{f}\right) \qquad\qquad = \varphi_{pol}\left(A^{-1} \cdot \overrightarrow{f'}\right)$$

In other words, the representation vectors $\overrightarrow{f}$ and $\overrightarrow{f'}$ are the representations of the abstract polynomials $f(\boldsymbol{X})$ and $f'(\boldsymbol{X})$ respective to the basis $\{\varphi_{pol}(a_1) = \varphi_{pol}(e_1), \varphi_{pol}(a_2), \ldots, \varphi_{pol}(a_d)\}$. Intuitively, a valid encoding that contains the representation vector $\overrightarrow{f} \in \mathbb{Z}_q^d$ corresponds to the group element $[f(\omega)]$, where ω is the value that is fixed in the public parameters of the group scheme via po. The same holds for the representation vector $\overrightarrow{f'}$ resulting in a redundant encoding. This approach is similar to the Naor-Yung paradigm [35].

We call the representation $(\overrightarrow{f}, \overrightarrow{f'})$ *consistent* if both representation vectors correspond to the same group element, i.e. the evaluation of the corresponding polynomials $f(\boldsymbol{X})$ and $f'(\boldsymbol{X})$ at ω are equal. Otherwise, we call such a representation *inconsistent*. If the representation $(\overrightarrow{f}, \overrightarrow{f'})$ is consistent, we call this representation *constant* if the corresponding polynomials $f(\boldsymbol{X})$ and $f'(\boldsymbol{X})$ are constant (i.e. are of total degree at most 0). If a consistent representation is not constant we call this representation *non-constant*. The purpose of the so-called consistency proof is to ensure consistency of encodings, i.e. to ensure that the corresponding representation is consistent. Further, we use the terms constant, non-constant, consistent, and inconsistent to characterize encodings if the associated representation has the respective properties.

Consistency Proof and Validation Algorithm. The above mentioned *consistency proof* ensures that the representations, that are encrypted inside of encodings, are consistent. In other words, the consistency proof ensures that both representation vectors $\overrightarrow{f}$ and $\overrightarrow{f'}$ used for an encoding lead to the same group element. We realize this by using the dual mode NIWI proof system Π to produce the consistency proof π for a relation $\mathcal{R}$. The relation $\mathcal{R}$ is a disjunction of three main statements $\mathcal{R} = \mathcal{R}_1 \vee \mathcal{R}_2 \vee \mathcal{R}_3$:

The relation $\mathcal{R}_1$ is satisfied for representations that are constant and consistent. We formalize this via relation $\mathcal{R}_{1.a}$:

$$\mathcal{R}_{1.a} := \left[\vec{f} = \vec{f'} \wedge \deg\left(\varphi_{\text{pol}}(\vec{f})\right) \leq 0\right]$$

We recall the convention that the degree of the zero polynomial is defined to be $-\infty$. For technical reasons, we need to make sure that the knowledge of the secret decryption keys (sk, sk') and the knowledge of the used encryption randomness are both sufficient as witnesses. Thus, additionally to $\mathcal{R}_{1.a}$ we define the two relations $\mathcal{R}_b$ and $\mathcal{R}_c$. The relations $\mathcal{R}_b$ and $\mathcal{R}_c$ connect the ciphertexts C, C' of the encoding with the corresponding representation vectors $\vec{f}$, $\vec{f'}$ appearing in relation $\mathcal{R}_{1.a}$.

$$\mathcal{R}_b := \left[\quad C = \text{ENC}(pk, \vec{f}; R) \wedge C' = \text{ENC}(pk', \vec{f'}; R') \quad\right]$$

$$\mathcal{R}_c := \left[\begin{array}{c} (pk, sk) = \text{GEN}(sk) \wedge \vec{f} = \text{DEC}(sk, C) \wedge \\ (pk', sk') = \text{GEN}(sk') \wedge \vec{f'} = \text{DEC}(sk', C') \end{array}\right]$$

At this point we make use of the assumption that a secret decryption key equals the randomness that was used to produce the corresponding public encryption key. The relation $\mathcal{R}_1$ is defined as follows:

$$\mathcal{R}_1 := \mathcal{R}_{1.a} \wedge (\mathcal{R}_b \vee \mathcal{R}_c). \tag{7}$$

Given a consistent and constant representation $(\vec{f}, \vec{f'})$ and resulting ciphertexts C and C', there are two possible witnesses to produce the consistency proof for the relation $\mathcal{R}_1$: using the secret decryption keys $(sk, sk', \vec{f}, \vec{f'})$ and using the encryption randomness $((\vec{f}, R), (\vec{f'}, R'))$.

The relation $\mathcal{R}_2$ is satisfied for representations that are consistent. Again, we formalize this via a relation $\mathcal{R}_{2.a}$:

$$\mathcal{R}_{2.a} := \left[\begin{array}{ll} \varphi_{\text{pol}}\left(A^{-1} \cdot \vec{f}\right)(\omega) & = \varphi_{\text{pol}}\left(A^{-1} \cdot \vec{f'}\right)(\omega) \wedge \\ \forall i \in \{1, \ldots, m\}: \text{po}_i(\omega_i) = 1 & \wedge \\ \text{OPEN}_{ck}(com, op) & = A \wedge A \neq \bot \end{array}\right]$$

The relation $\mathcal{R}_2$ is defined as follows:

$$\mathcal{R}_2 := \mathcal{R}_{2.a} \wedge (\mathcal{R}_b \vee \mathcal{R}_c). \tag{8}$$

Given a consistent representation $(\vec{f}, \vec{f'})$ and resulting ciphertexts C and C', there are two possible witnesses to produce the consistency proof for the relation $\mathcal{R}_2$: using the secret decryption keys $(sk, sk', \vec{f}, \vec{f'}, \omega, op)$ and using the encryption randomness $((\vec{f}, R), (\vec{f'}, R'), \omega, op)$. To be precise, the matrix A

also is part of these witnesses. However, as we can assume that A is a part of op, we omit this fact in our notation.

The relation $\mathcal{R}_3$ introduces a trapdoor enabling production of consistency proofs for inconsistent encodings.

$$\mathcal{R}_3 := [y \in \mathrm{TD}]. \tag{9}$$

This relation only depends on the instance (TD, y) of the subset membership problem $\mathrm{TD} \subseteq \mathcal{X}$ defined in the public parameters. We recall that if $y \in \mathrm{TD}$, there exists a unique witness w_y satisfying the witness relation for the SMP. Hence, the witness for the relation $\mathcal{R}_3$ is (w_y). Given public parameters pp that are generated via $\mathrm{SETUP}(1^\lambda)$, y is not in TD. Therefore, there exists no trapdoor if pp is generated honestly.

Let rp denote the parts of the public parameters that are necessary to produce consistency proofs, i.e. $rp := (q, pk, pk', \mathsf{po}, ck, com, \mathrm{TD}, y)$. To be precise, the corresponding language L has the following form:

$$L := \{x = \underbrace{(q, pk, pk', \mathsf{po}, ck, com, \mathrm{TD}, y}_{=rp}, C, C') \mid \exists w : (x, w) \in \mathcal{R}\}$$

$$= L_1 \cup L_2 \cup L_3,$$

where $L_i := \{x = (rp, C, C') \mid \exists w : (x, w) \in \mathcal{R}_i\}$. For the sake of clarity, we henceforth omit the parameters rp and treat the tuple (C, C') as the statement.

The validation algorithm VAL, on input a bit string $h \in \{0, 1\}^*$, parses h into (C, C', π) and executes $\mathsf{Verify}(gpk, crs, x, \pi)$ of the underlying NIWI proof system Π for the relation $\mathcal{R}$.

Addition and Zero Algorithm. The implementations of the algorithms ADD and ZERO need to know secret information that is associated with the public parameters, for instance the secret decryption keys. Therefore, we implement these algorithms as probabilistic circuits and "hard-code" the necessary secret parameters inside. The security requirement of the employed obfuscator $pi\mathcal{O}$ enables to conceal the implementation of these circuits and, hence, conceals the secret parameters that are hard-coded. The PPT algorithms ADD and ZERO simply execute the respective obfuscated circuit Λ_{add} and Λ_{zero}.

In Fig. 7 we present the implementation of the circuit C_{Add} and the implementation of the circuit $C_{\mathrm{Zero}}^{(0)}$. We remark that C_{Zero} only uses the representation vector $\vec{f}$ and ignores the representation vector $\vec{f'}$. This enables to exploit the Naor-Yung like double encryption.

The addition circuit C_{Add} is similar to the one constructed in [4]. The difference is limited to the fact that in our case C_{Add} differentiates between three instead of two different possibilities to produce the new consistency proof. The encodings of group elements in the construction of [4] are of the form (h, C, C', π), where C and C' are some ciphertexts and π is a corresponding consistency proof. The value h is the group element in an underlying group that

CIRCUIT $C_{\mathsf{Add}}[gpk, rp, sk, sk', \omega, op, td_{\mathsf{ext}}](a, b)$ CIRCUIT $C_{\mathsf{Zero}}^{(0)}[q, sk, \omega, A](a)$

if $\neg\mathrm{VAL}(a) \vee \neg\mathrm{VAL}(b)$ **then return** $\bot$

parse $a =: (C^{(a)}, C'^{(a)}, \pi^{(a)})$

parse $b =: (C^{(b)}, C'^{(b)}, \pi^{(b)})$

$C^{(c)} := \mathrm{EVAL}(pk, \oplus, C^{(a)}, C^{(b)})$

$C'^{(c)} := \mathrm{EVAL}(pk', \oplus, C'^{(a)}, C'^{(b)})$

$\vec{f}^{(a)} := \mathrm{DEC}(sk, C^{(a)}), \vec{f'}^{(a)} := \mathrm{DEC}(sk', C'^{(a)})$

$\vec{f}^{(b)} := \mathrm{DEC}(sk, C^{(b)}), \vec{f'}^{(b)} := \mathrm{DEC}(sk', C'^{(b)})$

$\vec{f}^{(c)} := \oplus(\vec{f}^{(a)}, \vec{f}^{(b)}), \vec{f'}^{(c)} := \oplus(\vec{f'}^{(a)}, \vec{f'}^{(b)})$

if $(C^{(a)}, C'^{(a)}), (C^{(b)}, C'^{(b)}) \in L_1$ **then**

    $\pi^{(c)} \leftarrow \mathsf{Prove}(gpk, crs, (C^{(c)}, C'^{(c)}), (sk, sk', \vec{f}^{(c)}, \vec{f'}^{(c)}))$

elseif $(C^{(a)}, C'^{(a)}), (C^{(b)}, C'^{(b)}) \in L_2$ **then**

    $\pi^{(c)} \leftarrow \mathsf{Prove}(gpk, crs, (C^{(c)}, C'^{(c)}), (sk, sk', \vec{f}^{(c)}, \vec{f'}^{(c)}, \omega, op))$

else

    let $\alpha \in \{a, b\} : (C^{(\alpha)}, C'^{(\alpha)}) \notin L_1 \cup L_2$

    $w_y \leftarrow \mathsf{Extract}(td_{\mathsf{ext}}, (C^{(\alpha)}, C'^{(\alpha)}), \pi^{(\alpha)})$

    $\pi^{(c)} \leftarrow \mathsf{Prove}(gpk, crs, (C^{(c)}, C'^{(c)}), (w_y))$

return $c := (C^{(c)}, C'^{(c)}, \pi^{(c)})$

CIRCUIT $C_{\mathsf{Zero}}^{(0)}[q, sk, \omega, A](a)$

if $\neg\mathrm{VAL}(a)$ **then**

    return $\bot$

parse $a =: (C, C', \pi)$

$\vec{f} \leftarrow \mathrm{DEC}(sk, C)$

$f(X) := \varphi_{\mathsf{pol}}(A^{-1} \cdot \vec{f})$

if $f(\omega) = 0$ **then**

    return 1

return 0

Fig. 7. Circuit C_{Add} (left) for addition of two group elements, and circuit $C_{\mathsf{Zero}}^{(0)}$ (right) for testing whether a given encoding is an encoding of the identity element. Additionally to the publicly available parameters gpk and rp, C_{Add} has the secret decryption keys sk, sk', the values ω, the opening op, and the extraction trapdoor td_{ext} hard-coded. The circuit $C_{\mathsf{Zero}}^{(0)}$ knows the publicly available parameter q and additionally has the secret parameters sk, ω, and A hard-coded. The circuit $\oplus$ realizes addition in $\mathbb{Z}_q^d$.

is represented by the encoding. As h uniquely identifies the represented group element, the equality test simply compares these values of the given encodings. In our case, however, the encodings do not contain a similar entry. Therefore, the implementation of the equality test, or rather the zero test, needs to decrypt the ciphertext C in order to be able to make a statement about the represented group element.

Sampling Algorithm. The sampling algorithm SAM, on input an exponent $z \in \mathbb{N}$, uses the representation $(\vec{f}, \vec{f'}) := ((z, 0, \ldots, 0)^T, (z, 0, \ldots, 0)^T)$ to produce an encoding of the requested group element. The consistency proof is produced for relation $\mathcal{R}_1$ using the witness $((\vec{f}, R), (\vec{f'}, R'))$, where R and R' are the randomnesses that are used to encrypt $\vec{f}$ and $\vec{f'}$ respectively. If the sampling algorithm does not receive any input, it samples the exponent z from $\{0, \ldots, q-1\}$ uniformly at random and proceeds as above. Due to the IND-CPA security of HPKE, the distribution of the output of SAM(z) is computationally indistinguishable from uniform distribution over the equivalence class $\mathcal{G}(\text{SAM}(z))$.

We remark that our group scheme allows for re-randomization of encodings. To re-randomize a given encoding, we sample an encoding of the identity element and use the addition algorithm to add it to the encoding to be randomized. We require the employed homomorphic encryption scheme to satisfy an additional natural property. Namely, we require that ciphertexts can be re-randomized by homomorphically adding a fresh ciphertext of 0. This property is also known as circuit privacy.

3.4 Main Theorem

Theorem 1. *Let $\Gamma_{m,n}$ be the group scheme constructed in Sect. 3.3. Further, let $pi\mathcal{O}$ be a probabilistic indistinguishability obfuscator with respect to $\mathcal{S}^{X\text{-}ind}$ for a circuit family containing circuits with input length at most $poly(\lambda)$, let $\mathcal{TD} = (\mathcal{TD}_\lambda)_{\lambda \in \mathbb{N}}$ be a family of families $\mathcal{TD}_\lambda = \{TD\}$ of languages $TD \subseteq \mathcal{X}_\lambda$ such that the subset membership problem is hard, let Π be a dual mode NIWI proof system, let HPKE be an IND-CPA secure HPKE scheme, let COM be a perfectly binding non-interactive commitment scheme, and let POBF be a point obfuscation. Then, the (m, n)-Interactive Uber assumption (cf. Definition 10) holds for $\Gamma_{m,n}$.*

In Table 1 we give an overview on the proof of Theorem 1. Informally, the "Switching lemma" states that encodings containing different representations of the same group element are hard to distinguish. The distribution $\widetilde{pp}$ denotes the distribution of public parameters that are sampled according to SETUP with the difference that y is sampled from within the trapdoor language TD. The distribution $\widehat{pp}$ denotes the same distribution as $\widetilde{pp}$ with the difference that the CRS is sampled in hiding mode and Λ_{add} is computed for an addition circuit that simulates consistency proofs and, hence, does not need to know the matrix A or the value ω. On a high level, the "Swap lemma" states that these two distributions of public parameters are computationally indistinguishable.

The distribution $\overline{pp}^{(i)}$ (for $i \in \{0, \ldots, m\}$) denotes the same distribution as $\widehat{pp}$ with the difference that Λ_{zero} is an obfuscation of a zero testing circuit that tests whether the polynomial $f(X_1, \ldots, X_i, \omega_{i+1}, \ldots, \omega_m)$ equals the zero polynomial. Furthermore, the point obfuscations in $\widehat{pp}$ obfuscate $\bot$ whereas the point obfuscations in $\overline{pp}^{(i)}$ obfuscate the values $\omega_{i+1}, \ldots, \omega_m$. The distribution pp is the same as $\overline{pp}^{(m)}$ with the difference that Λ_{zero} is produced for a zero testing circuit that simply tests whether the representation vector $\vec{f}$ equals zero in $\mathbb{Z}_q^d$ and, hence, does not need to know the matrix A and ω anymore.

The "Randomization lemma" basically states that the images of a certain subspace under a randomly sampled vector space isomorphism do not leak any information on the behavior of that isomorphism on pre-images that do not lie in that span.

For the formal definitions and the full proofs we refer the reader to the full version [3].

Table 1. An overview on the steps of the proof of 1. The ⟨boxes⟩ emphasize changes compared to the previous game. Let W_i denote the witness that is used to prove relation $\mathcal{R}_i$ for $i \in \{1, 2, 3\}$. The witnesses W_1 and W_2 contain the used encryption randomness. Further, for a polynomial $P(\boldsymbol{X})$, let $R_P := A \cdot \varphi_{\mathrm{pol}}^{-1}(P(\boldsymbol{c} \circ \boldsymbol{X}))$, and for a vector $v^* \in \mathbb{Z}_q^d$, let $\overline{R}_{v^*} := \varphi_{\mathrm{pol}}\left(A^{-1} \cdot v^*\right)(\boldsymbol{\omega}) \cdot e_1$.

	Publ. param.	Secret s	Representations for queries P / challenge P^*		Witness for π	Remark
Game$_0$	pp	$s \leftarrow \mathbb{Z}_q^m$	$P(s) \cdot e_1$	$P^*(s) \cdot e_1$	W_1	the real Uber game
Game$_1$	pp	$\boxed{\begin{array}{l} s := \boldsymbol{c} \circ \boldsymbol{\omega} \\ \boldsymbol{c} \leftarrow \left(\mathbb{Z}_q^\times\right)^m \end{array}}$	$P(s) \cdot e_1$	$P^*(s) \cdot e_1$	W_1	negl. statistical distance
Game$_2$	pp	$\begin{array}{l} s := \boldsymbol{c} \circ \boldsymbol{\omega} \\ \boldsymbol{c} \leftarrow \left(\mathbb{Z}_q^\times\right)^m \end{array}$	$\boxed{R_P}$	$\boxed{R_{P^*}}$	W_1, W_2	Switching lemma (see [3])
Game$_3$	$\boxed{\widetilde{pp}}$	$\begin{array}{l} s := \boldsymbol{c} \circ \boldsymbol{\omega} \\ \boldsymbol{c} \leftarrow \left(\mathbb{Z}_q^\times\right)^m \end{array}$	R_P	R_{P^*}	W_1, W_2	SMP TD $\subseteq \mathcal{X}$
Game$_4$	$\boxed{\widehat{pp}}$	$\begin{array}{l} s := \boldsymbol{c} \circ \boldsymbol{\omega} \\ \boldsymbol{c} \leftarrow \left(\mathbb{Z}_q^\times\right)^m \end{array}$	R_P	R_{P^*}	W_1, W_2	Swap lemma (see [3])
Game$_5$	$\widehat{pp}$	$\begin{array}{l} s := \boldsymbol{c} \circ \boldsymbol{\omega} \\ \boldsymbol{c} \leftarrow \left(\mathbb{Z}_q^\times\right)^m \end{array}$	R_P	R_{P^*}	$\boxed{W_3}$	perfect WI of Π
Game$_6$	$\boxed{\overline{pp}^{(0)}}$	$\begin{array}{l} s := \boldsymbol{c} \circ \boldsymbol{\omega} \\ \boldsymbol{c} \leftarrow \left(\mathbb{Z}_q^\times\right)^m \end{array}$	R_P	R_{P^*}	W_3	hiding property of COM
Game$_7$	$\boxed{\overline{pp}^{(m)}}$	$\begin{array}{l} s := \boldsymbol{c} \circ \boldsymbol{\omega} \\ \boldsymbol{c} \leftarrow \left(\mathbb{Z}_q^\times\right)^m \end{array}$	R_P	R_{P^*}	W_3	see [3]
Game$_8$	$\boxed{pp}$	$\begin{array}{l} s := \boldsymbol{c} \circ \boldsymbol{\omega} \\ \boldsymbol{c} \leftarrow \left(\mathbb{Z}_q^\times\right)^m \end{array}$	R_P	R_{P^*}	W_3	security of $pi\mathcal{O}$
Game$_9$	pp	$\begin{array}{l} s := \boldsymbol{c} \circ \boldsymbol{\omega} \\ \boldsymbol{c} \leftarrow \left(\mathbb{Z}_q^\times\right)^m \end{array}$	R_P	$\boxed{v^* \leftarrow \mathbb{Z}_q^d}$	W_3	Rand. lemma (see [3])
Game$_{10}$	$\boxed{\overline{pp}^{(m)}}$	$\begin{array}{l} s := \boldsymbol{c} \circ \boldsymbol{\omega} \\ \boldsymbol{c} \leftarrow \left(\mathbb{Z}_q^\times\right)^m \end{array}$	R_P	$v^* \leftarrow \mathbb{Z}_q^d$	W_3	security of $pi\mathcal{O}$
Game$_{11}$	$\boxed{\overline{pp}^{(0)}}$	$\begin{array}{l} s := \boldsymbol{c} \circ \boldsymbol{\omega} \\ \boldsymbol{c} \leftarrow \left(\mathbb{Z}_q^\times\right)^m \end{array}$	R_P	$v^* \leftarrow \mathbb{Z}_q^d$	W_3	see [3]
Game$_{12}$	$\boxed{\widehat{pp}}$	$\begin{array}{l} s := \boldsymbol{c} \circ \boldsymbol{\omega} \\ \boldsymbol{c} \leftarrow \left(\mathbb{Z}_q^\times\right)^m \end{array}$	R_P	$v^* \leftarrow \mathbb{Z}_q^d$	W_3	hiding property of COM
Game$_{13}$	$\widehat{pp}$	$\begin{array}{l} s := \boldsymbol{c} \circ \boldsymbol{\omega} \\ \boldsymbol{c} \leftarrow \left(\mathbb{Z}_q^\times\right)^m \end{array}$	R_P	$v^* \leftarrow \mathbb{Z}_q^d$	$\boxed{W_1, W_2}$	perfect WI of Π
Game$_{14}$	$\boxed{\widetilde{pp}}$	$\begin{array}{l} s := \boldsymbol{c} \circ \boldsymbol{\omega} \\ \boldsymbol{c} \leftarrow \left(\mathbb{Z}_q^\times\right)^m \end{array}$	R_P	$v^* \leftarrow \mathbb{Z}_q^d$	W_1, W_2	Swap lemma (see [3])
Game$_{15}$	$\boxed{pp}$	$\begin{array}{l} s := \boldsymbol{c} \circ \boldsymbol{\omega} \\ \boldsymbol{c} \leftarrow \left(\mathbb{Z}_q^\times\right)^m \end{array}$	R_P	$v^* \leftarrow \mathbb{Z}_q^d$	W_1, W_2	SMP TD $\subseteq \mathcal{X}$
Game$_{16}$	pp	$\begin{array}{l} s := \boldsymbol{c} \circ \boldsymbol{\omega} \\ \boldsymbol{c} \leftarrow \left(\mathbb{Z}_q^\times\right)^m \end{array}$	$\boxed{P(s) \cdot e_1}$	$\boxed{\begin{array}{l} \overline{R}_{v^*}, \\ v^* \leftarrow \mathbb{Z}_q^d \end{array}}$	W_1	Switching lemma (see [3])
Game$_{17}$	pp	$\boxed{s \leftarrow \mathbb{Z}_q^m}$	$P(s) \cdot e_1$	$\begin{array}{l} \overline{R}_{v^*}, \\ v^* \leftarrow \mathbb{Z}_q^d \end{array}$	W_1	negl. statistical distance
Game$_{18}$	pp	$s \leftarrow \mathbb{Z}_q^m$	$P(s) \cdot e_1$	$\boxed{\begin{array}{l} r \cdot e_1, \\ r \leftarrow \mathbb{Z}_q \end{array}}$	W_1	identically distributed

Acknowledgements. We would like to thank Antonio Faonio, Pooya Farshim, and Jesper Buus Nielsen for many interesting discussions. We would also like to thank the reviewers for many helpful comments.

References

1. Abe, M., Groth, J., Haralambiev, K., Ohkubo, M.: Optimal structure-preserving signatures in asymmetric bilinear groups. In: Rogaway, P. (ed.) CRYPTO 2011. LNCS, vol. 6841, pp. 649–666. Springer, Heidelberg (2011). https://doi.org/10.1007/978-3-642-22792-9_37

2. Abe, M., Groth, J., Ohkubo, M., Tibouchi, M.: Unified, minimal and selectively randomizable structure-preserving signatures. In: Lindell, Y. (ed.) TCC 2014. LNCS, vol. 8349, pp. 688–712. Springer, Heidelberg (2014). https://doi.org/10.1007/978-3-642-54242-8_29

3. Agrikola, T., Hofheinz, D.: Interactively secure groups from obfuscation. Cryptology ePrint Archive, report 2018/010. https://eprint.iacr.org/2018/010 (2018)

4. Albrecht, M.R., Farshim, P., Hofheinz, D., Larraia, E., Paterson, K.G.: Multilinear maps from obfuscation. In: Kushilevitz, E., Malkin, T. (eds.) TCC 2016. LNCS, vol. 9562, pp. 446–473. Springer, Heidelberg (2016). https://doi.org/10.1007/978-3-662-49096-9_19

5. Barak, B., Garg, S., Kalai, Y.T., Paneth, O., Sahai, A.: Protecting obfuscation against algebraic attacks. In: Nguyen, P.Q., Oswald, E. (eds.) EUROCRYPT 2014. LNCS, vol. 8441, pp. 221–238. Springer, Heidelberg (2014). https://doi.org/10.1007/978-3-642-55220-5_13

6. Bellare, M., Palacio, A.: The knowledge-of-exponent assumptions and 3-round zero-knowledge protocols. In: Franklin, M. (ed.) CRYPTO 2004. LNCS, vol. 3152, pp. 273–289. Springer, Heidelberg (2004). https://doi.org/10.1007/978-3-540-28628-8_17

7. Bellare, M., Stepanovs, I.: Point-function obfuscation: a framework and generic constructions. In: Kushilevitz, E., Malkin, T. (eds.) TCC 2016. LNCS, vol. 9563, pp. 565–594. Springer, Heidelberg (2016). https://doi.org/10.1007/978-3-662-49099-0_21

8. Bitansky, N., Canetti, R., Kalai, Y.T., Paneth, O.: On virtual grey box obfuscation for general circuits. In: Garay, J.A., Gennaro, R. (eds.) CRYPTO 2014. LNCS, vol. 8617, pp. 108–125. Springer, Heidelberg (2014). https://doi.org/10.1007/978-3-662-44381-1_7

9. Boneh, D., Boyen, X.: Efficient selective-id secure identity-based encryption without random oracles. In: Cachin, C., Camenisch, J.L. (eds.) EUROCRYPT 2004. LNCS, vol. 3027, pp. 223–238. Springer, Heidelberg (2004). https://doi.org/10.1007/978-3-540-24676-3_14

10. Boneh, D., Boyen, X., Goh, E.-J.: Hierarchical identity based encryption with constant size ciphertext. In: Cramer, R. (ed.) EUROCRYPT 2005. LNCS, vol. 3494, pp. 440–456. Springer, Heidelberg (2005). https://doi.org/10.1007/11426639_26

11. Boneh, D., Silverberg, A.: Applications of multilinear forms to cryptography. Contemp. Math. **324**(1), 71–90 (2003)

12. Boyen, X.: The uber-assumption family. In: Galbraith, S.D., Paterson, K.G. (eds.) Pairing 2008. LNCS, vol. 5209, pp. 39–56. Springer, Heidelberg (2008). https://doi.org/10.1007/978-3-540-85538-5_3

13. Brakerski, Z., Rothblum, G.N.: Virtual black-box obfuscation for all circuits via generic graded encoding. In: Lindell, Y. (ed.) TCC 2014. LNCS, vol. 8349, pp. 1–25. Springer, Heidelberg (2014). https://doi.org/10.1007/978-3-642-54242-8_1

14. Brown, D.R.L.: Generic Groups, Collision Resistance, and ECDSA. Des. Codes Cryptograph. **35**(1), 119–152 (2005)

15. Brown, D.R.L.: Toy factoring by Newton's method. IACR ePrint Archive, report 2008/149 (2008). http://eprint.iacr.org/2008/149

16. Canetti, R.: Towards realizing random oracles: Hash functions that hide all partial information. In: Kaliski, B.S. (ed.) CRYPTO 1997. LNCS, vol. 1294, pp. 455–469. Springer, Heidelberg (1997). https://doi.org/10.1007/BFb0052255

17. Canetti, R., Lin, H., Tessaro, S., Vaikuntanathan, V.: Obfuscation of probabilistic circuits and applications. In: Dodis, Y., Nielsen, J.B. (eds.) TCC 2015. LNCS, vol. 9015, pp. 468–497. Springer, Heidelberg (2015). https://doi.org/10.1007/978-3-662-46497-7_19

18. Cantor, D.G., Zassenhaus, H.: A new algorithm for factoring polynomials over finite fields. Math. Comput. **36**, 587–592 (1981)

19. Chase, M., Maller, M., Meiklejohn, S.: Déjà Q all over again: tighter and broader reductions of q-type assumptions. In: Cheon, J.H., Takagi, T. (eds.) ASIACRYPT 2016. LNCS, vol. 10032, pp. 655–681. Springer, Heidelberg (2016). https://doi.org/10.1007/978-3-662-53890-6_22

20. Chase, M., Meiklejohn, S.: Déjà Q: using dual systems to revisit q-type assumptions. In: Nguyen, P.Q., Oswald, E. (eds.) EUROCRYPT 2014. LNCS, vol. 8441, pp. 622–639. Springer, Heidelberg (2014). https://doi.org/10.1007/978-3-642-55220-5_34

21. Cheon, J.H.: Security analysis of the strong Diffie-Hellman problem. In: Vaudenay, S. (ed.) EUROCRYPT 2006. LNCS, vol. 4004, pp. 1–11. Springer, Heidelberg (2006). https://doi.org/10.1007/11761679_1

22. Cramer, R., Shoup, V.: Universal hash proofs and a paradigm for adaptive chosen ciphertext secure public-key encryption. In: Knudsen, L.R. (ed.) EUROCRYPT 2002. LNCS, vol. 2332, pp. 45–64. Springer, Heidelberg (2002). https://doi.org/10.1007/3-540-46035-7_4

23. Damgård, I.: Towards practical public key systems secure against chosen ciphertext attacks. In: Feigenbaum, J. (ed.) CRYPTO 1991. LNCS, vol. 576, pp. 445–456. Springer, Heidelberg (1992). https://doi.org/10.1007/3-540-46766-1_36

24. Danezis, G., Fournet, C., Groth, J., Kohlweiss, M.: Square span programs with applications to succinct NIZK arguments. In: Sarkar, P., Iwata, T. (eds.) ASIACRYPT 2014. LNCS, vol. 8873, pp. 532–550. Springer, Heidelberg (2014). https://doi.org/10.1007/978-3-662-45611-8_28

25. Diffie, W., Hellman, M.E.: New directions in cryptography. IEEE Trans. Inf. Theory **22**(6), 644–654 (1976)

26. Garg, S., Gentry, C., Halevi, S.: Candidate multilinear maps from ideal lattices. In: Johansson, T., Nguyen, P.Q. (eds.) EUROCRYPT 2013. LNCS, vol. 7881, pp. 1–17. Springer, Heidelberg (2013). https://doi.org/10.1007/978-3-642-38348-9_1

27. Garg, S., Gentry, C., Halevi, S., Raykova, M., Sahai, A., Waters, B.: Candidate indistinguishability obfuscation and functional encryption for all circuits. In: Proceedings of FOCS 2013. IEEE Computer Society, pp. 40–49 (2013)

28. Gentry, C.: A fully homomorphic encryption scheme. Ph.D thesis. Stanford University (2009)

29. Goldreich, O.: Foundations of Cryptography: Basic Tools. Cambridge University Press, Cambridge (2001)

30. Groth, J., Sahai, A.: Efficient non-interactive proof systems for bilinear groups. In: Smart, N. (ed.) EUROCRYPT 2008. LNCS, vol. 4965, pp. 415–432. Springer, Heidelberg (2008). https://doi.org/10.1007/978-3-540-78967-3_24
31. Hada, S., Tanaka, T.: On the existence of 3-round zero-knowledge protocols. In: Krawczyk, H. (ed.) CRYPTO 1998. LNCS, vol. 1462, pp. 408–423. Springer, Heidelberg (1998). https://doi.org/10.1007/BFb0055744
32. Koblitz, N., Menezes, A.: The brave new world of bodacious assumptions in cryptography. Not. AMS **57**, 357–365 (2010)
33. Lipmaa, H.: On the CCA1-security of Elgamal and Damgård's Elgamal. In: Lai, X., Yung, M., Lin, D. (eds.) Inscrypt 2010. LNCS, vol. 6584, pp. 18–35. Springer, Heidelberg (2011). https://doi.org/10.1007/978-3-642-21518-6_2
34. Meiklejohn, S.: An extension of the Groth-Sahai proof system. Ph.D thesis. Brown University (2009)
35. Naor, M., Yung, M.: Public-key cryptosystems provably secure against chosen ciphertext attacks. In: Proceedings of the Twenty-Second Annual ACM Symposium on Theory of Computing, pp. 427–437. ACM (1990)
36. Pass, R., Seth, K., Telang, S.: Indistinguishability obfuscation from semantically-secure multilinear encodings. In: Garay, J.A., Gennaro, R. (eds.) CRYPTO 2014. LNCS, vol. 8616, pp. 500–517. Springer, Heidelberg (2014). https://doi.org/10.1007/978-3-662-44371-2_28
37. Wee, H.: On obfuscating point functions. In: Proceedings of the Thirty-seventh Annual ACM Symposium on Theory of Computing, pp. 523–532. ACM (2005)
38. Zimmerman, J.: How to obfuscate programs directly. In: Oswald, E., Fischlin, M. (eds.) EUROCRYPT 2015. LNCS, vol. 9057, pp. 439–467. Springer, Heidelberg (2015). https://doi.org/10.1007/978-3-662-46803-6_15

Graded Encoding Schemes
from Obfuscation

Pooya Farshim[1,2], Julia Hesse[1,2,3], Dennis Hofheinz[3(✉)], and Enrique Larraia[4]

[1] DIENS, École normale supérieure, CNRS, PSL Research University, Paris, France
[2] Inria, Rocquencourt, France
[3] Karlsruhe Institute of Technology, Karlsruhe, Germany
dennis.hofheinz@kit.edu
[4] Royal Holloway, University of London, London, UK

Abstract. We construct a graded encoding scheme (GES), an approximate form of graded multilinear maps. Our construction relies on indistinguishability obfuscation, and a pairing-friendly group in which (a suitable variant of) the strong Diffie–Hellman assumption holds. As a result of this abstract approach, our GES has a number of advantages over previous constructions. Most importantly:

- We can *prove* that the multilinear decisional Diffie–Hellman (MDDH) assumption holds in our setting, assuming the used ingredients are secure (in a well-defined and standard sense). Hence, our GES does not succumb to so-called "zeroizing" attacks if the underlying ingredients are secure.
- Encodings in our GES do not carry any noise. Thus, unlike previous GES constructions, there is no upper bound on the number of operations one can perform with our encodings. Hence, our GES essentially realizes what Garg et al. (EUROCRYPT 2013) call the "dream version" of a GES.

Technically, our scheme extends a previous, non-graded approximate multilinear map scheme due to Albrecht et al. (TCC 2016-A). To introduce a graded structure, we develop a new view of encodings at different levels as polynomials of different degrees.

Keywords: Multilinear maps · Graded encoding schemes
Indistinguishability obfuscation

1 Introduction

THE GGH CANDIDATE MULTILINEAR MAP. In 2013, Garg, Gentry, and Halevi (GGH) [22] proposed the first plausible construction of an (approximate) multilinear map (MLM). In a nutshell, an MLM is a map $e : \mathbb{G}^\kappa \longrightarrow \mathbb{G}_T$ (for groups $\mathbb{G}$ and $\mathbb{G}_T$) that is linear in each input. Of course, we are most interested in the case of "cryptographically interesting" groups $\mathbb{G}$ (in which, e.g., computing discrete logarithms is infeasible), non-trivial maps e (with non-trivial kernel),

© International Association for Cryptologic Research 2018
M. Abdalla and R. Dahab (Eds.): PKC 2018, LNCS 10770, pp. 371–400, 2018.
https://doi.org/10.1007/978-3-319-76581-5_13

and preferably large values of κ. The surprising cryptographic consequences of such "cryptographically interesting" MLMs were already investigated in 2003 by Boneh and Silverberg [6], but an actual construction of an MLM remained elusive until the candidate construction of GGH.

Unfortunately, GGH only presented an "approximate" MLM in the following sense:

- Instead of group elements, their e inputs (and outputs) are *encodings*. An encoding is a non-unique representation of a group element, and there is no guarantee about which particular encoding the group operation (or e) outputs. However, every encoding allows to derive a "canonical form" that uniquely determines the encoded group element. (This canonical form allows no further operations, though.)
- Each encoding carries a "noise level" that increases with each operation. If the noise level grows beyond a certain threshold, no further operations are possible.

However, the GGH MLM also has an important *graded* property that allows to evaluate e partially, in a sense we will detail later. In particular this graded structure has made the GGH MLM tremendously useful: notable applications of *graded* MLMs include indistinguishability obfuscation [23], witness encryption [25], attribute-based encryption for general circuits [24], and constrained pseudorandom functions for general circuits [7]. Furthermore, graded MLMs enable a very powerful class of programmable hash functions [32], which in turn allows to implement random oracles in certain "algebraic" applications [20,33].

After GGH's MLM construction, several other (graded and approximate) MLM constructions have been proposed [15,16,28,34]. However, *all* of these constructions (including the original GGH scheme) succumb to cryptanalytic attacks [12–14,37]. In particular, currently there is no obvious way to instantiate schemes relying on multilinear maps, e.g., the schemes from [7,20,24,25,33].[1]

GRADED MLMs. There is one (approximate) MLM construction of Albrecht, Farshim, Hofheinz, Larraia, and Paterson (AFHLP) [2] that does not fall victim to any of the mentioned cryptanalytic attacks on MLMs. However, this construction does not offer a *graded* MLM, and thus cannot be used to bootstrap, e.g., witness encryption. Graded MLMs are algebraic tools that can enable other algebraic tools such as multilinear Groth-Sahai proofs, or multilinear programmable hash functions. It is thus still an interesting open problem whether graded MLMs exist, and whether the results of [23] can be augmented to even show equivalence to indistinguishability obfuscation.

OUR CONTRIBUTION. In this work, we construct graded, approximate MLMs that do not succumb to any of the known attacks. Technically, we extend the non-graded MLM construction from AFHLP [2] to a graded MLM. We prove

---

[1] We note, however, that the cryptographic *tasks* that the constructions from [7,25] aim to achieve can be directly achieved with indistinguishability obfuscation [1,23,42].

that the multilinear decisional Diffie–Hellman (MDDH) assumption [22] holds relative to our MLM, provided that the used ingredients are secure.

Interestingly, our MLM has two technical features that previous graded approximate MLMs do not have:

1. Our encodings do not carry any noise (although they are not unique). In particular, there is no limit on the number of operations that one can perform with our encodings.
2. The canonical forms derived from encodings allow further group operations (but no further pairings).

Our new MLM (when implemented with the indistinguishability obfuscator from [23,26]) currently forms the only plausible graded MLM, and thus the only plausible way to implement a number of MLM-based constructions [7,20,24,25,33].

Furthermore, our construction is generic and modular. In particular, we reduce the quest to develop a secure (graded) MLM to the quest for a secure indistinguishability obfuscator. This seems natural (and is standard in most areas of cryptography), but given the history of previous MLM candidates (which were based on complex algebraic or combinatorial assumptions), this is not an "understood feature" at all for MLMs.

In fact, taken together with recent constructions of indistinguishability obfuscation (iO) from multilinear maps (e.g., [3,23,35,36]), our result shows a (somewhat loose) equivalence of indistinguishability obfuscation (iO) and (graded and approximate) MLMs, in the presence of a pairing-friendly group. This equivalence is loose in the following sense. First, the assumptions on both ends of the equivalence do not match: some of these works (e.g., [23]) construct iO from MLMs which support very strong computational assumptions (much stronger than MDDH) or require asymmetric multilinear maps. On the other hand, we use iO to construct *symmetric* MLMs in which we can (at this point) only prove comparatively mild (though still useful) computational assumptions (such as MDDH). Still, there seems no inherent barrier to proving stronger computational assumptions for our construction, or to adapt our construction to asymmetric pairings, and we leave open to tighten this equivalence. Second, going through our equivalence suffers subexponential security loss. Namely, we require *probabilistic* indistinguishability obfuscation, which can be constructed from iO [11], but currently only through a sub-exponential reduction.

However, we note that such an equivalence would not be highly surprising given recent results on constructing iO from MLMs [3,35]. These works only require "one-shot" (but asymmetric) MLMs, and not even *graded* encodings as we construct them.

RELATED WORK. Our work is closely related to [2], since the non-graded MLM there serves as a starting point for our graded MLM. We will summarize their construction in Sect. 4 and give an informal overview below.

Recently, Paneth and Sahai [39] have shown a near-equivalence of a suitable abstraction of MLMs with iO. Their result requires no computational assumptions at all, but also does not consider MLMs in our sense. In particular, they construct an abstraction of a MLM that only admits restricted access to encodings similar to the one in [23]. Beyond the group operation and the multilinear map, efficient procedures for, e.g., uniform sampling, comparison or rerandomization of encodings, are not part of this abstraction. Conversely, our notion of a MLM, like the ones from [2,22], contains descriptions of efficient procedures for these tasks.

It would be interesting to see how the restricted MLMs of [39] can be used to instantiate the constructions from [5,8,20,33] directly, i.e., without making the detour via iO. However, since iO alone is not even known to imply one-way functions (see [29] for a discussion), this will require additional assumptions.

Pass et al. [40] give a security definition of graded MLMs that requires that whenever encodings are generically equivalent (that is, cannot be distinguished with generic operations alone), they should be computationally indistinguishable as encodings. They show that this MLMs which satisfy this strong assumption imply indistinguishability obfuscation. It is not clear, however, how to construct such strongly secure MLMs (without resorting to idealized models such as the generic group model).

1.1   The (Non-graded) Approximate Multilinear Map of AFHLP

ENCODINGS. Since our own construction is an extension of the (non-graded) approximate MLM of [2], we first recall their work. Simplifying slightly, AFHLP encode a group element g^z (from a cyclic group $\mathbb{G}$ of order p) as

$$h \; = \; (g^z, c = \mathbf{Enc}((\alpha, \beta), pk), \pi),$$

where

- c is a homomorphic encryption (under some public key pk) of exponents $\alpha, \beta \in \mathbb{Z}_p$,
- π is a non-interactive zero-knowledge proof that these exponents represent z in the sense that $g^z = g^\alpha u^\beta$ for a publicly known group element u. (Hence, if we write $u = g^\omega$, we have $z = \alpha + \beta \cdot \omega$.)

Hence, AFHLP simply enhance the group element $g^z \in \mathbb{G}$ by an encrypted representation of its discrete logarithm z (and a suitable consistency proof). This added information will be instrumental in computing a multilinear map on many encodings. Note that since c and π will not be uniquely determined, there are many possible encodings of a $\mathbb{G}$-element g^z.

ADDITION. Encodings in the AFHLP construction can be added with an (obfuscated) public circuit **Add**. This circuit takes as input two encodings $h_1 = (g^{z_1}, c_1, \pi_1)$ and $h_2 = (g^{z_2}, c_2, \pi_2)$, and computes the new encoding $h_1 + h_2 = (g^z, c, \pi)$ as follows:

1. $g^z = g^{z_1+z_2}$ is computed using the group operation in $\mathbb{G}$;
2. c is computed homomorphically from c_1 and c_2 (adding the encrypted exponent vectors (α_i, β_i));

3. the consistency proof π is computed using the decryption key sk as a witness to show that the resulting c indeed contains a valid representation of $z = z_1 + z_2$.

Here, only the computation of π requires secret information (namely, the decryption key sk). This secret information allows to derive a valid representation (α, β) of g^z. The most delicate part of the security proof from [2] is to argue that the obfuscated circuit knowing sk does not help in solving (a multilinear variant of) the decisional Diffie–Hellman problem.

THE MULTILINEAR MAP. The AFHLP encodings can also be multiplied with an (obfuscated) public circuit **Mult**; this takes as input κ encodings $h_1, \ldots, h_\kappa$ with $h_i = (g^{z_i}, c_i, \pi_i)$, and outputs a single group element $g^{\prod_{i=1}^{\kappa} z_i}$. (Hence, elements from the target group $\mathbb{G}_T$ are trivially and uniquely encoded as $\mathbb{G}$-elements.) To compute $g^{\prod z_i}$ from the h_i, **Mult** first checks the validity of all proofs π_i, and then uses the decryption key sk to retrieve representations (α_i, β_i). If all π_i are verifying proofs, we may assume that $z_i = \alpha_i + \beta_i \cdot \omega$ (for $u = g^\omega$), so we can write

$$g^{\prod_{i=1}^{\kappa} z_i} = \prod_{i=0}^{\kappa} (g^{\omega^i})^{\gamma_i} \quad \text{for} \quad (\gamma_0, \ldots, \gamma_\kappa) = (\alpha_1, \beta_1) * \cdots * (\alpha_\kappa, \beta_\kappa), \quad (1)$$

where "$*$" denotes the convolution product of vectors.[2] The values g^{ω^i} (for $i \leq \kappa$) are hardwired into **Mult**, so **Mult** can compute $g^{\prod z_i}$ through (1). Note that this way, **Mult** can compute a κ-linear map on encodings, but not a $(\kappa + 1)$-linear map. This observation is the key to showing that the MDDH assumption holds in this setting. (Indeed, the MDDH assumption states that given $\kappa + 1$ encodings $h_1, \ldots, h_{\kappa+1}$ as above, it is hard to distinguish $g^{\prod_{i=1}^{\kappa+1} z_i}$ from random.)

1.2   Our New Graded Encoding Scheme

Before proceeding any further, we briefly recall the notions of a graded multilinear map and a graded encoding scheme.

GRADED MAPS. In a *graded* multilinear map setting, we have groups $\mathbb{G}_1, \ldots, \mathbb{G}_\kappa$, and (efficiently computable) bilinear maps $e_{i,j} : \mathbb{G}_i \times \mathbb{G}_j \longrightarrow \mathbb{G}_{i+j}$ for $i + j \leq \kappa$. Hence, the $e_{i,j}$ also allow the evaluation of a multilinear map $e : \mathbb{G}_1^\kappa \longrightarrow \mathbb{G}_\kappa$ iteratively, e.g., through

$$e(g_1, \ldots, g_\kappa) := e_{1,\kappa-1}(g_1, e_{1,\kappa-2}(g_2, \cdots, e_{1,1}(g_{\kappa-1}, g_\kappa) \cdots)).$$

However, the $e_{i,j}$ also allow "partial" evaluation of e, which is the key to entirely new applications such as those in [7,23–25].

---

[2] Recall that the multiplication of polynomials can be implemented through the convolution product on the respective coefficient vectors. In particular, we have $\sum_{i=0}^{\kappa} \gamma_i X^i = \prod_{i=1}^{\kappa} (\alpha_i + \beta_i X)$.

Unfortunately, we do not currently know how to implement such a "clean" graded multilinear map. Instead, all known graded MLM constructions work on encodings (i.e., non-unique representations of group elements). Such a construction is usually called a graded encoding scheme (GES). Following the GES notation, we will henceforth also call an encoding of a $\mathbb{G}_\ell$-element a *level-ℓ encoding*.

In the following, we will describe the main ideas for our GES.

ENCODINGS IN OUR SCHEME. In our GES, we generalize the linear representation of exponents in AFHLP to polynomials of higher degree. Additionally, we divide encodings into levels by restricting the maximum degree of the representing polynomial in each level. More formally, level-ℓ encodings take the form

$$h = (g^z, c = \mathbf{Enc}(P, pk), \pi, \ell),$$

where

- $g^z \in \mathbb{G}$ for a cyclic group $\mathbb{G}$ (that does not depend on ℓ) of prime order p,
- $P \in \mathbb{Z}_p[X]$ is a polynomial of degree up to ℓ, represented by its coefficient vector from $\mathbb{Z}_p^{\ell+1}$,
- c is the encryption (under a fully homomorphic encryption scheme) of P,
- π is a non-interactive zero-knowledge proof of the equality $g^z = g^{P(\omega)}$, where ω is defined through public values $u_0, \ldots, u_\kappa \in \mathbb{G}$ with $u_i = g^{\omega^i}$. (Hence, $g^z = g^{P(\omega)}$ is equivalent to $g^z = \prod_i u_i^{\gamma_i}$ for $P(X) = \sum_i \gamma_i X^i$.)

The encodings of AFHLP can be viewed as level-1 encodings in our scheme (with linear polynomials P).

ADDING ENCODINGS. Encodings can be added using a public (obfuscated) circuit $\mathbf{Add}$ that proceeds similarly to the AFHLP scheme. In particular, $\mathbf{Add}$ adds the g^z and c parts of the input encodings homomorphically, and derives a consistency proof π with the decryption key sk as witness.

MULTIPLYING ENCODINGS. The pairings $e_{i,j} : \mathbb{G}_i \times \mathbb{G}_j \longrightarrow \mathbb{G}_{i+j}$ are implemented over our encodings by (obfuscated) circuits $\mathbf{Mult}_{i,j}$. Circuit $\mathbf{Mult}_{i,j}$ takes as input two encodings $h_1 = (g^{z_1}, c_1, \pi_1, i)$ and $h_2 = (g^{z_2}, c_2, \pi_2, j)$ at levels i and j, respectively. The output of $\mathbf{Mult}_{i,j}$ is a level-$(i+j)$ encoding $h = (g^z, c, \pi, i+j)$, computed as follows:[3]

- g^z is computed as $g^z = g^{(P_1 \cdot P_2)(\omega)}$, where the polynomials P_1 and P_2 are extracted from c_1 and c_2 with sk, then multiplied to form $P := P_1 \cdot P_2 \in \mathbb{Z}_p[X]$, and finally used to compute

$$g^{(P_1 \cdot P_2)(\omega)} = g^{P(\omega)} = \prod_{\ell=0}^{i+j} u_\ell^{\gamma_\ell} \quad \text{for} \quad P(X) = \sum_{\ell=0}^{i+j} \gamma_\ell X^\ell.$$

(Since the u_ℓ are public, this value can be computed as long as $i + j \leq \kappa$.)

---

[3] Since $\mathbf{Mult}_{i,j}$ can be used to multiply two encodings at level i as long as $2i \leq \kappa$, our GES can be viewed as *symmetric*. We note that we do not deal with the construction of generalized GES (see [22, Appendix A] for a definition).

- c is computed homomorphically from c_1 and c_2, as an encryption of the polynomial $P_1 \cdot P_2$.
- The consistency proof π (showing that indeed $g^z = g^{P(\omega)}$ for the polynomial P encrypted in c) is computed with the decryption key sk as witness.

The key insight needed to show that the MDDH assumption holds for our GES is the same as in AFHLP's non-graded, approximate MLM. Namely, observe that any $\mathbf{Mult}_{i,j}$ can only multiply encodings if $i + j \leq \kappa$. To compute the first component g^z of any "higher-level" encoding, knowledge of g^{ω^ℓ} for $\ell > i + j$ seems to be required. Under the SDDH assumption in $\mathbb{G}$, such g^{ω^ℓ} look random, even when given $u_0, \ldots, u_\kappa$. Of course, to turn this observation into a full proof, more work is required.

NEGLECTED DETAILS. For a useful GES, it should be possible to generate encodings with "known discrete logarithm"; that is, we would like to be able to generate encodings for an externally given (or at least known) $z \in \mathbb{Z}_p$. For this reason, the standard way to generate encodings (at any level) is to set up P as a *constant* polynomial of the form $P(X) = z \in \mathbb{Z}_p$. (That is, we "reserve space" in c for polynomials P of degree ℓ in level-ℓ encodings, but, by default, use only constant polynomials.) For this type of encoding with "low-degree P," however, our security argument above does not apply. Rather, it requires that the degree of P increases at higher levels.

Hence, the central technical piece in our MDDH security proof will be a "switching theorem" that allows to replace a low-degree P in an encoding with an *equivalent* high-degree P' (that satisfies $P'(\omega) = P(\omega)$). The proof of this switching theorem is delicate, since it must work in a setting with (obfuscated) algorithms that use the decryption key sk. (Note that free access to sk would allow the retrieval of the used polynomial P from an encoding, and hence would prevent such a switching of polynomials.)

To this end, we will use *double encryptions* c (instead of the single encryption $c = \mathbf{Enc}(P, pk)$ described above), along with a Naor–Yung-style consistency proof in π. However, this consistency proof does not show equality of encryptions, but *equivalence* of encrypted representations P, P' in the sense of $P(\omega) = P'(\omega)$. This allows to switch representations without invalidating the consistency of the double encryption. As a result, the full consistency language used for π is considerably more complicated than the one sketched before. Additionally, the proof of our switching theorem requires a special and explicit "simulation trapdoor" and Groth–Sahai-style dual-mode proof systems.

We note that similar complications arose already in AFHLP's proof, and required similar measures. The main technical difference in our setting is that our multiplication circuits $\mathbf{Mult}_{i,j}$ output *encodings* (and not just group elements as in the multilinear map of AFHLP). Hence, our $\mathbf{Mult}_{i,j}$ circuits also need to construct consistency proofs π, which requires additional secrets (as witnesses) in the description of $\mathbf{Mult}_{i,j}$ and which entails additional steps in our switching theorem. (We give more details on the technical differences with AFHLP in the main body. However, we note that, in addition to providing a *graded* encoding scheme, we also provide simplified and tighter proofs.

Fortunately, the indistinguishability obfuscator from [23] requires only a relatively weak MLM variant and hence is not affected by the above-mentioned cryptanalyses.[4]

ASSUMPTIONS. In summary, our construction uses a cyclic group in which the SDDH assumption holds, a probabilistic indistinguishability obfuscation scheme [11], a perfectly correct fully homomorphic encryption (FHE), a dual-mode non-interactive zero-knowledge proof systems, and a language with hard membership. All of these assumptions are implied by pairing-friendly SDDH groups (equipped with an asymmetric pairing) and sub-exponentially secure indistinguishability obfuscation (see [31]). We stress that plausible candidates for both ingredients exist (e.g., by combining [22,23] to an indistinguishability obfuscator candidate).

ROAD MAP. We first recall some preliminaries in Sect. 2 and the GES definition in Sect. 3. Section 4 recalls the AFHLP construction. We are then ready to present our GES construction in Sect. 5, and establish our central technical tool (the "switching theorem") in Sect. 6. We prove the hardness of MDDH in Sect. 7. In the appendices, we give a technical overview of AFHLP and the full proofs of the theorems from the main body of the paper.

2   Preliminaries

NOTATION. We denote the security parameter by $\lambda \in \mathbb{N}$ and assume that it is implicitly given to all algorithms in the unary representation 1^λ. By an algorithm we mean a stateless Turing machine. Algorithms are randomized unless stated otherwise, and PPT as usual stands for "probabilistic polynomial-time." In this paper, by a PPT algorithm we mean an algorithm that runs in polynomial time in the security parameter (rather than the total length of its inputs). Given a randomized algorithm $\mathcal{A}$ we denote the action of running $\mathcal{A}$ on input(s) $(1^\lambda, x_1, \ldots)$ with uniform random coins r and assigning the output(s) to $(y_1, \ldots)$ by $(y_1, \ldots) \leftarrow_\$ \mathcal{A}(1^\lambda, x_1, \ldots; r)$. For a finite set X, we denote its cardinality by $|X|$ and the action of sampling a uniformly random element x from X by $x \leftarrow_\$ X$. We write $[k] := \{1, \ldots, k\}$. Vectors are written in boldface $\mathbf{x}$, and slightly abusing notation, running algorithms on vectors of elements indicates component-wise operation. Throughout the paper $\perp$ denotes a special error symbol, and $\mathrm{poly}(\cdot)$ stands for a fixed (but unspecified) polynomial. A real-valued function $\mathrm{negl}(\lambda)$ is negligible if $\mathrm{negl}(\lambda) \in \mathcal{O}(\lambda^{-\omega(1)})$. We denote the set of all negligible functions by NEGL. We use bracket notation for elements in $\mathbb{G}$, i.e., writing $[z]$ and $[z']$ for two elements g^z and $g^{z'}$ in $\mathbb{G}$ and $[z] + [z']$ for their product $g^z g^{z'}$.

CIRCUITS. A polynomial-sized deterministic circuit family $\mathcal{C} := \{\mathcal{C}_\lambda\}_{\lambda \in \mathbb{N}}$ is a sequence of sets $\mathcal{C}_\lambda$ of $\mathrm{poly}(\lambda)$-sized deterministic circuits (for a fixed polynomial $\mathrm{poly}(\lambda)$). We assume that for all $\lambda \in \mathbb{N}$ all circuits $C \in \mathcal{C}_\lambda$ share a common

---

[4] A recent attack on MLMs (see [37]) tackles even the weak MLM security requirements the indistinguishability obfuscator from [23] has. However, the construction of [23] (resp., its MLM building block) can be suitably enhanced to thwart this attack [26].

input domain $(\{0,1\}^\lambda)^{a(\lambda)}$, where $a(\lambda)$ is the arity of the circuit family, and an output co-domain $\{0,1\}^\lambda$. A randomized circuit family is defined similarly except that the circuits also take random coins $r \in \{0,1\}^{\mathrm{rl}(\lambda)}$, for a polynomial $\mathrm{rl}(\lambda)$ specifying the length of necessary random coins. To make the coins used by a circuit explicit (e.g., to view a randomized circuit as a deterministic one) we write $C(x; r)$.

2.1 Homomorphic Public-Key Encryption

SYNTAX. A homomorphic public-key encryption (PKE) scheme for a deterministic circuit family $\mathcal{C} = \{\mathcal{C}_\lambda\}_{\lambda \in \mathbb{N}}$ of arity at most $a(\lambda)$ is a tuple of PPT algorithms $\Pi := (\mathbf{Gen}, \mathbf{Enc}, \mathbf{Dec}, \mathbf{Eval})$ such that $(\mathbf{Gen}, \mathbf{Enc}, \mathbf{Dec})$ is a conventional public-key encryption scheme with message space $\{0,1\}^\lambda$ and $\mathbf{Eval}$ is a *deterministic* algorithm that on input a public key pk a circuit $C \in \mathcal{C}_\lambda$ and ciphertexts $c_1, \ldots, c_n$ with $n \leq a(\lambda)$ outputs a ciphertext c. Without loss of generality, we assume that secret keys of a homomorphic PKE scheme are the random coins used in key generation. This will allow us to check key pairs for validity.

CORRECTNESS AND COMPACTNESS. For the scheme $\Pi := (\mathbf{Gen}, \mathbf{Enc}, \mathbf{Dec})$, we require *perfect* correctness as a PKE scheme; that is, for any $\lambda \in \mathbb{N}$, any $m \in \{0,1\}^\lambda$, any $(sk, pk) \leftarrow_\$ \mathbf{Gen}(1^\lambda)$, and any $c \leftarrow_\$ \mathbf{Enc}(m, pk)$ we have that $\mathbf{Dec}(c, sk) = m$. We also require the FHE scheme to be fully compact in the following sense. For any $\lambda \in \mathbb{N}$, any $m_1, \ldots, m_n \in \{0,1\}^\lambda$ with $n \leq a(\lambda)$, any $C \in \mathcal{C}_\lambda$, any $(sk, pk) \leftarrow_\$ \mathbf{Gen}(1^\lambda)$ and any $c_i \leftarrow_\$ \mathbf{Enc}(m_i, pk)$ we have that $\mathbf{Eval}(pk, C, c_1, \ldots, c_n)$ is in the range of $\mathbf{Enc}(C(m_1, \ldots, m_n), pk)$.

A *fully* homomorphic encryption (FHE) scheme is a homomorphic PKE that correctly and compactly supports any circuit family containing polynomial-sized circuits of polynomial arity (for any a priori fixed polynomial bounds on the size and arity). In our constructions, full correctness and compactness are used to ensure that the outputs of the addition and multiplications circuits can be iteratively operated on. This in particular means that our GES is "noise-free" in the sense that its correctness is not affected by the number of operations operated on encodings.

A perfectly correct FHE scheme can be constructed from probabilistic indistinguishability obfuscation (and a re-randomizable public-key encryption scheme such as ElGamal), see [11]. (We note that the FHE scheme from [11] only enjoys perfect correctness when the obfuscator and encryption scheme are also perfectly correct.)

SECURITY. The IND-CPA security of a homomorphic PKE scheme is defined identically to a standard PKE scheme without reference to the $\mathbf{Dec}$ and $\mathbf{Eval}$ algorithms. Formally, we require that for any legitimate PPT adversary $\mathcal{A} := (\mathcal{A}_1, \mathcal{A}_2)$,

$$\mathbf{Adv}_{\Pi,\mathcal{A}}^{\mathrm{ind\text{-}cpa}}(\lambda) := 2 \cdot \Pr\left[\mathrm{IND\text{-}CPA}_{\Pi}^{\mathcal{A}}(\lambda)\right] - 1 \in \mathrm{NEGL},$$

where game $\mathrm{IND\text{-}CPA}_{\Pi}^{\mathcal{A}}(\lambda)$ is shown in Fig. 1 (left). Adversary $\mathcal{A}$ is legitimate if it outputs two messages of equal lengths.

IND-CPA$_{\Pi}^{\mathcal{A}}(\lambda)$:	IND$_{\mathbf{Obf}}^{\mathcal{A}}(\lambda)$:	Sel-IND$_{\mathcal{A}}^{\mathcal{D}}(\lambda)$:
$(sk, pk) \leftarrow_{\$} \mathbf{Gen}(1^{\lambda})$	$(C_0, C_1, st) \leftarrow_{\$} \mathcal{A}_1(1^{\lambda})$	$(x, z) \leftarrow_{\$} \mathcal{D}_1(1^{\lambda})$
$(m_1, m_1, st) \leftarrow_{\$} \mathcal{A}_1(pk)$	$b \leftarrow_{\$} \{0, 1\}$	$(C_0, C_1, st) \leftarrow_{\$} \mathcal{A}_1(1^{\lambda})$
$b \leftarrow_{\$} \{0, 1\}$	$\overline{C} \leftarrow_{\$} \mathbf{Obf}(1^{\lambda}, C_b)$	$b \leftarrow_{\$} \{0, 1\}; r \leftarrow_{\$} \{0, 1\}^{\mathrm{rl}(\lambda)}$
$c \leftarrow_{\$} \mathbf{Enc}(m, pk)$	$b' \leftarrow_{\$} \mathcal{A}_2(\overline{C}, st)$	$y \leftarrow C_b(x; r)$
$b' \leftarrow_{\$} \mathcal{A}_2(c, st)$	Return $(b = b')$	$b' \leftarrow_{\$} \mathcal{D}_2(y, C_0, C_1, st, z)$
Return $(b = b')$		Return $(b = b')$

Fig. 1. Left: IND-CPA security of a (homomorphic) PKE scheme. Middle: Indistinguishability security of an obfuscator. We require $\mathcal{A}_1$ to output two circuits of equal sizes. Right: Static-input (a.k.a. selective) X-IND property of $\mathcal{A} := (\mathcal{A}_1, \mathcal{A}_2)$.

2.2 Obfuscators

SYNTAX AND CORRECTNESS. A PPT algorithm $\mathbf{Obf}$ is called an *obfuscator* for a (deterministic or randomized) circuit class $\mathcal{C} = \{\mathcal{C}_{\lambda}\}_{\lambda \in \mathbb{N}}$ if $\mathbf{Obf}$ on input the security parameter 1^{λ} and the description of a (deterministic or randomized) circuit $C \in \mathcal{C}_{\lambda}$ of arity $a(\lambda)$ outputs a *deterministic* circuit $\overline{C}$. For deterministic circuits, we require $\mathbf{Obf}$ to be perfectly correct in the sense the circuits C and $\overline{C}$ are functionally equivalent; that is, that for all $\lambda \in \mathbb{N}$, all $C \in \mathcal{C}_{\lambda}$, all $\overline{C} \leftarrow_{\$} \mathbf{Obf}(1^{\lambda}, C)$, and all $m_i \in \{0, 1\}^{\lambda}$ for $i \in [a(\lambda)]$ we have that $C(m_1, \ldots, m_{a(\lambda)}) = \overline{C}(m_1, \ldots, m_{a(\lambda)})$. For randomized circuits, the authors of [11] define correctness via computational indistinguishability of the outputs of C and $\overline{C}$. For our constructions we do *not* rely on this property and instead require that C and $\overline{C}$ are functionally equivalent up to a change in randomness; that is, for all $\lambda \in \mathbb{N}$, all $C \in \mathcal{C}_{\lambda}$, all $\overline{C} \leftarrow_{\$} \mathbf{Obf}(1^{\lambda}, C)$ and all $m_i \in \{0, 1\}^{\lambda}$ for $i \in [a(\lambda)]$ there is an r such that $\overline{C}(m_1, \ldots, m_{a(\lambda)}) = C(m_1, \ldots, m_{a(\lambda)}; r)$. We note that the construction from [11] is correct in this sense as it relies on a correct indistinguishability obfuscator and a PRF to internally generate the required random coins.

SECURITY. The security of an obfuscator $\mathbf{Obf}$ requires that for any legitimate PPT adversary $\mathcal{A} := (\mathcal{A}_1, \mathcal{A}_2)$

$$\mathbf{Adv}_{\mathbf{Obf}, \mathcal{A}}^{\mathrm{ind}}(\lambda) := 2 \cdot \Pr\left[\mathrm{IND}_{\mathbf{Obf}}^{\mathcal{A}}(\lambda)\right] - 1 \in \mathrm{NEGL},$$

where game IND is shown in Fig. 1 (middle). Depending on the adopted notion of legitimacy, different security notions for the obfuscator emerge; we consider the following one.

X-IND SAMPLERS [11]. Roughly speaking, the first phase of $\mathcal{A} := (\mathcal{A}_1, \mathcal{A}_2)$ is an X-IND sampler if there is a set $\mathcal{X}$ of size at most X such that the circuits output by $\mathcal{A}$ are functionally equivalent outside $\mathcal{X}$, and furthermore within $\mathcal{X}$ the outputs of the circuits are computationally indistinguishable. Formally, let $X(\cdot)$ be a function such that $X(\lambda) \leq 2^{\lambda}$ for all $\lambda \in \mathbb{N}$. We call $\mathcal{A} := (\mathcal{A}_1, \mathcal{A}_2)$ an X-IND *sampler* if there are sets $\mathcal{X}_{\lambda}$ of size at most $X(\lambda)$ such that the following two conditions hold: (1) For all (even unbounded) $\mathcal{D}$ the advantage function below is negligible.

$$\mathbf{Adv}^{\mathrm{eq}}_{\mathcal{A},\mathcal{D}}(\lambda) := \Pr\left[(\mathrm{C}_0,\mathrm{C}_1,st) \leftarrow_{\$} \mathcal{A}_1(1^\lambda); (x,r) \leftarrow_{\$} \mathcal{D}(\mathrm{C}_0,\mathrm{C}_1,st) : \right.$$
$$\left. \mathrm{C}_0(x;r) \neq \mathrm{C}_1(x;r) \wedge x \notin \mathcal{X}_\lambda\right]$$

(2) For all non-uniform PPT distinguishers $\mathcal{D} := (\mathcal{D}_1,\mathcal{D}_2)$ it holds that

$$X(\lambda) \cdot \mathbf{Adv}^{\mathrm{sel\text{-}ind}}_{\mathcal{A},\mathcal{D}}(\lambda) := X(\lambda) \cdot \left(2\Pr\left[\mathrm{Sel\text{-}IND}^{\mathcal{D}}_{\mathcal{A}}(\lambda)\right] - 1\right) \in \mathrm{NEGL},$$

where game $\mathrm{Sel\text{-}IND}^{\mathcal{D}}_{\mathcal{A}}(\lambda)$ is shown in Fig. 1 (right). This game is named "static-input-IND" in [11]. and has a selective (or static) flavor since $\mathcal{D}_1$ chooses a differing-input x *before* it gets to see the challenge circuits. We call an obfuscator meeting this level of security a *probabilistic indistinguishability obfuscator* [11] and use **PIO** instead of **Obf** to emphasize this.

REMARK. We note that samplers that output two (possibly randomized) circuits $(\mathrm{C}_0,\mathrm{C}_1)$ for which the output distributions of $\mathrm{C}_0(x)$ and $\mathrm{C}_1(x)$ are identical on any input x, are Sel-IND-secure for any function $X(\lambda)$. The circuits samplers that we will use in our security proofs enjoy this property.

2.3 Dual-Mode NIZK Proof Systems

In our constructions we will be relying on special types of "dual-mode" non-interactive zero-knowledge (NIZK) proof systems. These systems have two common reference string (CRS) generation algorithms that produce indistinguishable CRSs in the "binding" and "hiding" modes. They are also perfectly complete in both modes, perfectly sound and extractable in the binding mode, and perfectly witness indistinguishable (WI) and perfectly zero knowledge (ZK) in the hiding mode. The standard prototype for such schemes are the pairing-based Groth–Sahai proofs [30], and using a generic NP reduction to the satisfiability of quadratic equations we can obtain a suitable proof system for any NP language.[5] We formalize the syntax and security of such proof systems next.

SYNTAX. A (group) setup algorithm $\mathbf{G}$ is a PPT Turing machine that on input 1^λ outputs gpk. A ternary relation $\mathbf{R}(gpk,x,w)$ is a deterministic algorithm that outputs 1 for true or 0 for false. A dual-mode extractable non-interactive zero-knowledge (NIZK) proof system Σ *for setup* $\mathbf{G}$ *and relation* $\mathbf{R}$ consists of six algorithms as follows. (1) $\mathbf{BCRS}(gpk)$ on input gpk in the support of $\mathbf{G}$ outputs a (binding) CRS crs and an extraction trapdoor td_e; (2) $\mathbf{HCRS}(gpk)$ on input gpk in the support of $\mathbf{G}$ outputs a (hiding) CRS crs and a simulation

---

[5] We note that extraction in Groth–Sahai proofs does not recover a witness for all types of statements. (Instead, for some types of statements, only g^{w_i} for a witness variable $w_i \in \mathbb{Z}_p$ can be recovered.) Here, however, we will only be interested in witnesses $w = (w_1,\ldots,w_n) \in \{0,1\}^n$ that are bit strings, in which case extraction always recovers w. (Extraction will recover g^{w_i} for all i, and thus all w_i too.).

trapdoor td_{zk}; (3) **Prove**(gpk, crs, x, w) on input gpk a first coordinate in the support of **G**, a CRS crs, an instance x, and a witness w, outputs a proof π; (4) **Verify**(gpk, crs, x, π) on input gpk, crs, an instance x, and a proof π, outputs 1 for accept or 0 for reject; (5) **WExt**(td_e, x, π) on input an extraction trapdoor td_e, an instance x, and a proof π, outputs a witness w; and (6) **Sim**(td_{zk}, x) on input the simulation trapdoor td_{zk} and an instance x, outputs a simulated proof π.

We require the extractable dual-mode NIZK Σ for $(\mathbf{G}, \mathbf{R})$ to meet the following requirements.

CRS INDISTINGUISHABILITY. For $gpk \leftarrow_\$ \mathbf{G}(1^\lambda)$, the two CRSs generated with **BCRS**(gpk) and **HCRS**(gpk) are computationally indistinguishable. Formally, we require the advantage of any PPT adversary $\mathcal{A}$ defined below to be negligible.

$$\mathbf{Adv}^{crs}_{\Sigma,\mathcal{A}}(\lambda) := 2 \cdot \Pr\left[b \leftarrow_\$ \{0,1\}; gpk \leftarrow_\$ \mathbf{G}(1^\lambda); (crs_0, td_e) \leftarrow_\$ \mathbf{BCRS}(gpk);\right.$$
$$\left.(crs_1, td_{zk}) \leftarrow_\$ \mathbf{HCRS}(gpk); b' \leftarrow_\$ \mathcal{A}(gpk, crs_b) : b = b'\right] - 1$$

PERFECT COMPLETENESS. For any $\lambda \in \mathbb{N}$, any $gpk \leftarrow_\$ \mathbf{G}(1^\lambda)$, any $(crs, td_e) \leftarrow_\$ \mathbf{BCRS}(gpk)$, any (x, w) where it holds that $\mathbf{R}(gpk, x, w) = 1$, and any $\pi \leftarrow_\$ \mathbf{Prove}(gpk, crs, x, w)$, it holds that $\mathbf{Verify}(gpk, crs, x, \pi) = 1$. We require this property to also hold for any choice of hiding CRS.

PERFECT SOUNDNESS UNDER **BCRS**. For any $\lambda \in \mathbb{N}$, any $gpk \leftarrow_\$ \mathbf{G}(1^\lambda)$, any CRS $(crs, td_e) \leftarrow_\$ \mathbf{BCRS}(gpk)$, any x where it holds that $\mathbf{R}(gpk, x, w) = 0$ for all $w \in \{0,1\}^*$, and any $\pi \in \{0,1\}^*$ we have that $\mathbf{Verify}(gpk, crs, x, \pi) = 0$.

PERFECT EXTRACTION UNDER **BCRS**. For any $\lambda \in \mathbb{N}$, any $gpk \leftarrow_\$ \mathbf{G}(1^\lambda)$, any CRS $(crs, td_e) \leftarrow_\$ \mathbf{BCRS}(gpk)$, any (x, π) with $\mathbf{Verify}(gpk, crs, x, \pi) = 1$, and any $w \leftarrow_\$ \mathbf{WExt}(td_e, x, \pi)$ we have that $\mathbf{R}(gpk, x, w) = 1$.

PERFECT WITNESS INDISTINGUISHABILITY UNDER **HCRS**. For any $\lambda \in \mathbb{N}$, any $gpk \leftarrow_\$ \mathbf{G}(1^\lambda)$, any $(crs, td_{zk}) \leftarrow_\$ \mathbf{HCRS}(gpk)$, and any (x, w_b) such that $\mathbf{R}(gpk, x, w_b) = 1$ for $b \in \{0,1\}$, the two distributions $\pi_b \leftarrow_\$ \mathbf{Prove}(gpk, crs, x, w_b)$ are identical.

PERFECT ZERO KNOWLEDGE UNDER **HCRS**. For any $\lambda \in \mathbb{N}$, any $gpk \leftarrow_\$ \mathbf{G}(1^\lambda)$, any $(crs, td_{zk}) \leftarrow_\$ \mathbf{HCRS}(gpk)$, and any (x, w) such that $\mathbf{R}(gpk, x, w) = 1$, the two distributions $\pi_0 \leftarrow_\$ \mathbf{Prove}(gpk, crs, x, w)$ and $\pi_1 \leftarrow_\$ \mathbf{Sim}(td_{zk}, x)$ are identical.

2.4   Languages with Hard Membership

In our proofs of security we also rely on languages for which the membership problem is hard and whose yes-instances have unique witnesses. Formally, such a language family is defined as a tuple of four algorithms $\Lambda := (\mathbf{Gen_L}, \mathbf{YesSam_L}, \mathbf{NoSam_L}, \mathbf{R_L})$ as follows. (1) $\mathbf{Gen_L}(1^\lambda)$ is randomized and on input the security parameter outputs a language key lk; (2) $\mathbf{YesSam_L}(lk)$ is randomized and on input the language key lk outputs a yes-instance y; (3) $\mathbf{NoSam_L}(lk)$ is

randomized and on input the language key lk outputs a no-instance y; and
(4) $\mathbf{R_L}(lk, y, w)$ is deterministic and on input lk, an instance y and a witness w
outputs 1 for true or 0 for false.

We require $\mathbf{R_L}$ to satisfy the following correctness requirements. For all $\lambda \in$
$\mathbb{N}$, all $lk \leftarrow_\$ \mathbf{Gen_L}(1^\lambda)$ and all $y \leftarrow_\$ \mathbf{YesSam_L}(lk)$ there is a $w \in \{0,1\}^*$ such
that $\mathbf{R_L}(lk, y, w) = 1$. For a given lk, we denote the set of yes-instance by $\mathcal{L}_{lk}$. For
all $\lambda \in \mathbb{N}$, all $lk \leftarrow_\$ \mathbf{Gen_L}(1^\lambda)$ and all $y \leftarrow_\$ \mathbf{NoSam_L}(lk)$ there is no $w \in \{0,1\}^*$
such that $\mathbf{R_L}(lk, y, w) = 1$. We also require $\mathbf{R_L}$ to have unique witnesses: for
all $\lambda \in \mathbb{N}$, all $lk \leftarrow_\$ \mathbf{Gen_L}(1^\lambda)$, all $y \leftarrow_\$ \mathbf{YesSam_L}(lk)$ and all $w, w' \in \{0,1\}^*$ if
$\mathbf{R_L}(lk, y, w) = \mathbf{R_L}(lk, y, w') = 1$ then $w = w'$.

Finally, the language is required to have a hard membership problem in the
sense that for any PPT adversary $\mathcal{A}$

$$\mathbf{Adv}_{\Lambda, \mathcal{A}}^{\mathrm{mem}}(\lambda) := 2 \cdot \Pr\left[b \leftarrow_\$ \{0,1\}; lk \leftarrow_\$ \mathbf{Gen_L}(1^\lambda); y_0 \leftarrow_\$ \mathbf{NoSam_L}(lk);\right.$$
$$\left. y_1 \leftarrow_\$ \mathbf{YesSam_L}(lk); b' \leftarrow_\$ \mathcal{A}(lk, y_b) : b = b'\right] - 1 \in \mathrm{NEGL}.$$

Such languages can be instantiated using the DDH problem as follows. Algorithm $\mathbf{Gen_L}(1^\lambda)$ outputs the description of a prime-order group $(\mathbb{G}, g, p, 1)$ as
lk. Algorithm $\mathbf{YesSam_L}(lk)$ samples a Diffie–Hellman tuple (g^a, g^b, g^{ab}), and
$\mathbf{NoSam_L}(lk)$ outputs a non-Diffie–Hellman tuple (g^a, g^b, g^c) for a random $c \neq ab$
(mod p) when $b = 0$. Relation $\mathbf{R_L}$ on instance (g_1, g_2, g_3) and witness $w = a$
checks if $g_1 = g^a$ and $g_3 = g_2^a$. The hardness of membership for this language
family follows from the DDH assumption.

3   Graded Encoding Schemes

We start by recalling (a slight variant of) the definition of graded encoding
systems from Garg, Gentry and Halevi (GGH) [22].

κ-GRADED ENCODING SYSTEM. Let R be a (non-trivial) commutative ring and
$S := \{S_i^{(a)} \subset \{0,1\}^* : a \in R, 0 \leq i \leq \kappa\}$ a system of sets. Then (R, S) is called
a κ-graded encoding system if the following conditions are met.

1. For each level $i \in \{0, \ldots, \kappa\}$ and for any $a_1, a_2 \in R$ with $a_1 \neq a_2$ we have
   that $S_i^{(a_1)} \cap S_i^{(a_2)} = \emptyset$.
2. For each level $i \in \{0, \ldots, \kappa\}$, the set $\{S_i^{(a)} : a \in R\}$ is equipped with a
   binary operation "+" and a unary operation "−" such that for all $a_1, a_2 \in R$
   and every $u_1 \in S_i^{(a_1)}, u_2 \in S_i^{(a_2)}$ it holds that

   $$u_1 + u_2 \in S_i^{(a_1+a_2)} \quad \text{and} \quad -u_1 \in S_i^{(-a_1)}.$$

   Here $a_1 + a_2$ and $-a_1$ denote addition and negation is R.
3. For each two levels $i, j \in \{0, \ldots, \kappa\}$ with $i + j \leq \kappa$, there is a binary operation
   "×" such that for all $a_1, a_2 \in R$ and every $u_1 \in S_i^{(a_1)}, u_2 \in S_j^{(a_2)}$ it holds
   that

   $$u_1 \times u_2 \in S_{i+j}^{(a_1 \cdot a_2)}.$$

   Here $a_1 \cdot a_2$ denotes multiplication in R.

The difference to the GGH definition is that we do not require the operations "+" and "×" to be associative or commutative. (Indeed, our upcoming construction does not satisfy these properties.) We are not aware of any applications that require the associativity or commutativity of *encodings*. However, we stress that the operations "+" and "×" must respect the ring operations from R. For instance, while we may have $(u_1 + u_2) + u_3 \neq u_1 + (u_2 + u_3)$ for some $u_i \in S_j^{(a_i)}$, both the left-hand and the right-hand sides lie in $S_j^{(a_1 + a_2 + a_3)}$.

Throughout the paper, we refer to an element $a \in R$ as an *exponent* and a bit string $u \in S_i^{(a)}$ as an *encoding* of a. Further, we write $S_i := \bigcup_{a \in R} S_i^{(a)}$ for the set of all level-i encodings.

We now define graded encoding *schemes* by introducing explicit algorithms for manipulating encodings of a graded encoding system.

κ-GRADED ENCODING SCHEME. Let (R, S) be a κ-graded encoding system. A *graded encoding scheme (GES)*

$$\Gamma = (\mathbf{Setup}, \mathbf{Eq}, \mathbf{Add}, \mathbf{Mult}, \mathbf{Sam}, \mathbf{Ext})$$

associated to (R, S) consists of the following PPT algorithms.

Setup$(1^\lambda, 1^\kappa)$: On input the security parameter 1^λ and the (multi)linearity 1^κ, it outputs parameters of Γ (which are assumed to be provided to all other algorithms). We note that this algorithm runs in time $\text{poly}(\lambda)$ as long as κ is polynomial in λ.

Eq$_i(h_1, h_2)$: For $i \in \{0, \ldots, \kappa\}$ and two encodings $h_1 \in S_i^{(a)}$ and $h_2 \in S_i^{(b)}$, this deterministic algorithm outputs 1 if and only if $a = b$ in R.

Add$_i(h_1, h_2)$: This deterministic algorithm performs the "+" operation of (R, S) in level i. For $i \in \{0, \ldots, \kappa\}$ and encodings $h_1 \in S_i^{(a_1)}$ and $h_2 \in S_i^{(a_2)}$ this algorithm outputs an encoding in $h \in S_i^{(a_1 + a_2)}$.

Mult$_{i,j}(h_1, h_2)$: This deterministic algorithm performs the "×" operation of (R, S). For $i, j \in \{0, \ldots, \kappa\}$ with $i + j \leq \kappa$ and encodings $h_1 \in S_i^{(a_1)}$ and $h_2 \in S_j^{(a_2)}$ this algorithm outputs an encoding in $S_{i+j}^{(a_1 \cdot a_2)}$.

Sam$_i(a)$: For $i \in \{0, \ldots, \kappa\}$ and $a \in R$, this probabilistic algorithm samples an encoding from $S_i^{(a)}$.

Ext$_i(h)$: For $i \in \{0, \ldots, \kappa\}$ and input $h \in S_i$, this deterministic algorithm outputs a bit string. Algorithm **Ext**$_i$ is required to respect membership in $S_i^{(a)}$, i.e., it outputs identical strings for any two encodings $h_1, h_2 \in S_i^{(a)}$.

Our definition of a GES essentially implements the "dream version" of GESs [22], but differs in two aspects:

- GGH do not permit sampling for specific values $a \in R$. (Instead, GGH provide an algorithm to sample a random a along with its encoding.)
- GGH's zero-testing algorithm is substituted with an equality test (through **Eq**$_i$) above. Our equality test must only work for *consistent* encodings from some $S_i^{(a)}$ and $S_i^{(b)}$. In contrast, the dream version of GGH requires that the set $S_i^{(0)}$ is efficiently recognizable.

4   Approximate Multilinear Maps

We recall the approximate multilinear maps due to AFHLP [2]. The authors construct both symmetric and asymmetric multilinear maps. Their symmetric construction can be seen as a starting point for our GES.

4.1   Syntax

We start with the syntax of multilinear group (MLG) schemes [2]. Informally, a κ-MLG scheme is a restricted form of a graded encoding scheme where encodings belong to levels 0, 1 and κ only and the **Mult** algorithm takes κ encodings at level 1 and outputs an encoding at level κ. We formalize MLG schemes in terms of a GES.

SYMMETRIC MLG SCHEMES. A symmetric κ-linear group scheme is a κ-graded encoding scheme associated to (R, S), where (R, S) is defined similarly to a κ-graded encoding system except that $S := \{S_i^{(a)} \subset \{0,1\}^* : a \in R, i \in \{0,1,\kappa\}\}$ and the "$\times$" operation is redefined as a κ-ary map that for any $a_1, \ldots, a_\kappa \in R$ and any $u_1 \in S_1^{(a_1)}, \ldots, u_\kappa \in S_1^{(a_\kappa)}$ satisfies

$$u_1 \times \cdots \times u_\kappa \in S_\kappa^{(a_1 \cdots a_\kappa)}.$$

The associated **Mult** algorithm on inputs $h_i \in S_1^{(a_i)}$ for $i \in [\kappa]$ outputs an encoding in $S_\kappa^{(a_1 \cdots a_\kappa)}$. Algorithms **Eq**, **Add**, **Sam** and **Ext** are defined analogously and restricted to $i \in \{0,1,\kappa\}$ only.

4.2   Overview of AFHLP

In a nutshell, [2] works with redundant encodings of elements h of the base group $\mathbb{G}$ of the form $h = g^{x_0}(g^\omega)^{x_1}$ where g^ω comes from an SDDH instance. Vector $\mathbf{x} = (x_0, x_1)$ *represents* element h. The set S_1 consists of all strings of the form (h, c_1, c_2, π) where $h \in \mathbb{G}$, ciphertext c_1 is a homomorphic encryption under public key pk_1 of a vector $\mathbf{x}$ representing h, ciphertext c_2 is a homomorphic encryption under a second public key pk_2 of another vector $\mathbf{y}$ also representing h, and π is a NIZK proof showing consistency of the two vectors $\mathbf{x}$ and $\mathbf{y}$. Here consistency means that the plaintexts vectors $\mathbf{x}$ and $\mathbf{y}$ underlying c_1 and c_2 encode the same group element h. Note that each element of the base group $\mathbb{G}$ is multiply represented in S_1, but that equality of elements in S_1 is easy to test (via checking the equality of first components).

   Addition of two elements in S_1 is carried out by an obfuscation of a circuit $C_{\text{Add}}[sk_1, sk_2]$, which has the two secret keys hardwired in. The circuit checks the respective proofs, adds the group elements in $\mathbb{G}$ and uses the additive homomorphic property of the encryption scheme to combine ciphertexts. It then uses witness (sk_1, sk_2) to generate a NIZK proof showing equality of encodings. Note that the new encoding is as compact as the two input encodings.

The multilinear map on inputs $(h_i, c_{i,1}, c_{i,2}, \pi_i)$ for $1 \leq i \leq \kappa$ is computed using an obfuscation of a circuit $C_{\mathrm{Map}}[sk_1, \omega]$, which has sk_1 and ω hardwired in. The circuit recovers the exponents of h_i in the form $(x_{i,1} + \omega \cdot x_{i,2})$ from $c_{i,1}$ via the decryption algorithm $\mathbf{Dec}(\cdot, sk_1)$. It then uses these to compute the group element $g^{\prod_i (x_{i,1} + \omega \cdot x_{i,2})}$, which is defined to be the output of $\mathbf{Mult}$. (The target set S_κ is therefore $\mathbb{G}$, the base group.) The κ-linearity of $\mathbf{Mult}$ follows immediately from the form of the exponent. See the full version [19] for technical details.

In the original paper, this construction is generalized to the asymmetric setting via representations of the form $g^{\langle \mathbf{x}, \boldsymbol{\omega} \rangle}$ with $\mathbf{x}, \boldsymbol{\omega} \in \mathbb{Z}_N^\ell$ for $\ell \in \{2,3\}$ (where $\langle \mathbf{x}, \boldsymbol{\omega} \rangle$ denotes inner products modulo the base-group order). The special case $\boldsymbol{\omega} := (1, \omega)$ then gives an MLG scheme where MDDH is shown to be hard. We refer the reader to the original work [2] for the details.

5 The GES Construction

We now present our construction of a graded encoding scheme Γ according to the syntax introduced in Sect. 3. We will use the following ingredients in our construction. A similar set of building blocks were used in [2].

1. A group setup algorithm $\mathbf{Setup}_{\mathbb{G}}(1^\lambda)$ that samples (the description of) a group $\mathbb{G}$, along with a random generator g of $\mathbb{G}$ and the group order p and the identity element 1.[6] We implicitly assume efficient algorithms for checking group membership, performing the group operation, inversion, and randomly sampling group elements. We further assume a unique binary representation for every group element and a randomness extractor for this group.
2. A general-purpose probabilistic indistinguishability obfuscator $\mathbf{PIO}$ that we assume is secure against X-IND samplers.
3. A perfectly correct and IND-CPA-secure fully homomorphic PKE scheme Π with plaintext space $\mathbb{Z}_p^{\kappa+1}$.
4. An extractable dual-mode NIZK proof system Σ.
5. A language family Λ with hard membership problem and unique witnesses.

Given the above components, with formal syntax and security as defined in Sect. 2, our graded encoding scheme Γ consists of the algorithms detailed in the sections that follow. (See the introduction for an intuition.)

5.1 Setup

The $\mathbf{Setup}$ algorithm of Γ gets as input 1^λ and 1^κ. It samples parameters $pp_{\mathbb{G}} \leftarrow_\$ \mathbf{Setup}_{\mathbb{G}}(1^\lambda)$ with $pp_{\mathbb{G}} := (\mathbb{G}, g, p, 1)$, generates two encryption key pairs $(pk_j, sk_j) \leftarrow_\$ \mathbf{Gen}(1^\lambda)$ for $j = 1, 2$, and an element $\omega \leftarrow_\$ \in \mathbb{Z}_p$. We will refer to $\mathbb{G}$ as the *base group*. It sets

$$[\boldsymbol{\omega}] := ([\omega], \ldots, [\omega^\kappa]),$$

---

[6] It is conceivable that our security proofs also hold for non-prime p up to statistical defect terms related to randomization of elements modulo a composite number.

a vector of κ elements in the base group $\mathbb{G}$, with κ the number of desired levels It then samples $lk \leftarrow_{\$} \mathbf{Gen_L}(1^\lambda)$, and sets

$$gpk := (pp_\mathbb{G}, pk_1, pk_2, [\boldsymbol{\omega}], lk).$$

We define $\mathbf{G}(1^\lambda)$ to be the randomized algorithm that runs the above steps and outputs gpk. This algorithm will be used to define the NIZK proof system.

The **Setup** algorithm continues by generating a *binding* CRS (crs', td_e) $\leftarrow_{\$} \mathbf{BCRS}(gpk)$, and also a *no-instance* of $\mathcal{L}_{lk}$ via $y \leftarrow_{\$} \mathbf{NoSam_L}(lk)$. It sets $crs := (crs', y)$. (The relation $\mathbf{R}$ that the NIZK should support will be defined shortly in Sect. 5.2.)

Finally, it constructs two obfuscated circuits $\overline{C}_{\text{Mult}}$ and $\overline{C}_{\text{Add}}$ of circuits C_{Mult} and C_{Add}, which will be described in Sects. 5.3 and 5.4, respectively. **Setup** also selects a seed hk for a randomness extractor and outputs the scheme parameters

$$pp := (gpk, crs, hk, \overline{C}_{\text{Add}}, \overline{C}_{\text{Mult}}).$$

5.2   Encodings and Equality

LEVEL-0 ENCODINGS. We treat algorithms for level-0 encodings separately in our construction as they behave somewhat differently to those from the other levels. For instance, when multiplied by other encodings, they do not result in an increase in encoding levels. The canonical choice for level-0 encodings is the ring $\mathbb{Z}_p$, which we adopt in this paper. These encodings, therefore, come with natural algorithms for generation, manipulation and testing of elements. Algorithm **Mult** when applied to inputs one of which is at level 0 corresponds to multiplication with the element in the zeroth level. The latter can in turn be implemented with a shift-and-add algorithm that employs the encoding addition **Add** of Sect. 5.3. We omit explicit mention of operations for level-0 encodings to ease notation and focus on the more interesting cases at levels 1 and above.[7]

LEVEL-κ ENCODINGS. We set $S_\kappa := \mathbb{G}$ in our scheme and use the algorithms associated with $\mathbb{G}$ for generation, equality testing, and addition of encodings at level κ. Once again, we omit these operations from the addition circuit for clarity. The multiplication circuit can only be called on a level-κ together with a level-0 encoding, which we have already excluded. However, we still have to deal with outputs at level κ in **Mult**.

OTHER LEVELS. For $0 < \ell < \kappa$ and $z \in \mathbb{Z}_p$, the encodings in $S_\ell^{(z)}$ consist of all tuples of the form

$$h := ([z], c_1, c_2, \pi, \ell),$$

---

[7] We mention that previous GESs used more complex level-0 encodings, and since their encodings were *noisy*, they allowed only a limited number of operations on each encoding. Hence, implementing **Mult** on level-0 inputs via shift-and-add could be too costly in their settings.

where c_1, c_2 are two ciphertexts in the range of $\mathbf{Enc}(\cdot, pk_1)$ and $\mathbf{Enc}(\cdot, pk_2)$, respectively,[8] and π is a verifying NIZK proof under crs' that:

(1) either c_1 and c_2 contain polynomials P_1 and P_2 of degree at most ℓ, such that $P_1(\omega) = P_2(\omega) = z$,
(2) or $y \in \mathcal{L}_{lk}$ (or both).

More formally, π must be a verifying proof that $(gpk, ([z], c_1, c_2, \ell))$ satisfies one relation $\mathbf{R}_1$ or $\mathbf{R}_2$ as follows.

Relation $\mathbf{R}_1$ on input gpk, an encoding $([z], c_1, c_2, \ell)$, and a witness $(P_1, P_2, r_1, r_2, sk_1, sk_2)$ accepts iff all of the following hold:

- $[z] \in \mathbb{G}$;
- both P_1 and P_2 are polynomials over $\mathbb{Z}_p$ of degree $\leq \ell$ (given by their coefficient vectors);
- both P_1 and P_2 represent z in the sense that $[z] = [P_1(\omega)]$ and $[z] = [P_2(\omega)]$;
- both c_i are encryptions of (or decrypt to) P_i in the following sense:

$$\text{for both } i \in \{1, 2\} \ : \ c_i = \mathbf{Enc}(P_i, pk_i; r_i)$$

$$\vee$$

$$\text{for both } i \in \{1, 2\} \ : \ (pk_i, sk_i) = \mathbf{Gen}(sk_i) \wedge P_i = \mathbf{Dec}(c_i, sk_i).$$

Note that there are two types of witnesses that can be used in proof generation for $\mathbf{R}_1$, namely (P_1, P_2, r_1, r_2) and (sk_1, sk_2).

Let $\mathbf{R_L}$ be the relation for the trapdoor language Λ. Relation $\mathbf{R}_2$, given gpk, an encoding, and a witness w_y, accepts iff $\mathbf{R_L}(lk, y, w_y)$ accepts. (Note that the output of $\mathbf{R}_2$ is independent of input encodings.) Hence, intuitively, $\mathbf{R}_2$ provides an explicit trapdoor to simulate consistency proofs (in case $y \in \mathcal{L}_{lk}$).

We define $\mathbf{R} := \mathbf{R}_1 \vee \mathbf{R}_2$ and assume that Σ is a proof system with respect to $(\mathbf{G}, \mathbf{R})$ with $\mathbf{G}$ as defined in Sect. 5.1.

VALID AND CONSISTENT ENCODINGS. The following convention will be useful in the context of valid of encodings and the correctness of out scheme. We call an encoding h *valid* if the proof π verifies correctly under crs'. We write $\mathbf{Val}_\ell(h)$ iff h is valid and the level implicit in h matches ℓ. We call h *consistent* (with respect to gpk) if h is in the language defined by the first three conditions of relation $\mathbf{R}_1$ as well as the *first* clause of the disjunction above. (In particular, the corresponding ciphertexts c_i are possible outputs of $\mathbf{Enc}(P_i, pk_i)$; this implies that these ciphertexts behave as expected under the homomorphic evaluation algorithm $\mathbf{Eval}$.) Note that consistency implies validity but the converse is not necessarily the case and hence a valid encoding may not lie in any S_ℓ. For example this would be the case if an "anomalous" ciphertext *decrypts* correctly to a valid representation, but does not lie in the range of $\mathbf{Enc}$. Furthermore, validity can be publicly and efficiently checked, while this is *not* necessarily the

---

[8] This "honest-ciphertext-generation" condition is necessary for the (bi)linearity of our addition and multiplication algorithms. Unfortunately, this also prevents the sets $S_\ell^{(z)}$ from being efficiently recognizable.

case for consistency. We note, however, that if the encryption scheme does not allow for anomalous ciphertexts, our GES would also have efficiently recognizable encodings. We leave the construction of such FHE schemes as an open problem.

ALGORITHM **Eq**. The equality algorithm $\mathbf{Eq}_\ell$ returns 1 iff the first components of the inputs match. The correctness of this algorithm follows from the fact that the base group $\mathbb{G}$ has unique representations. (Recall from GES syntax that $\mathbf{Eq}_\ell$ is only required to work with respect to consistent encodings.)

POLYNOMIAL REPRESENTATIONS. A significant conceptual difference with the work of AFHLP is that we represent exponents in $\mathbb{Z}_p$ with polynomials instead of vectors. This generalization enables natural notion of levels corresponding to the degrees of the representing polynomials. We observe that a level-ℓ encoding h is not a *valid* level-ℓ' encoding if $\ell' \neq \ell$ as the perfectly sound proof π included in h depends on the instance and in particular on the level.

5.3   Addition

We now provide a procedure for adding two level-ℓ encodings $h = ([z], c_1, c_2, \pi, \ell)$ and $h' = ([z'], c_1', c_2', \pi', \ell)$ in S_ℓ. Conceptually, our addition circuit operates similarly to that of AFHLP. The main difference is that encodings contain polynomials and the levels. We exploit the structure of the base group as well as the homomorphic properties of the encryption scheme to "add together" the first and second components of the inputs. We then use (sk_1, sk_2) as a witness to generate a proof π'' that the new tuple is well formed. For technical reasons we check both the validity of h and h' (by checking π and π') and their consistency (using (sk_1, sk_2)).

Figure 2 details the operation of the addition circuit C_{Add}. A **PIO** of this circuit will be made public via the parameters pp. We emphasize that step 5,

---

CIRCUIT $C_{\mathrm{Add}}[gpk, crs, sk_1, sk_2, td_e](\ell, h, h')$:   // for $1 \leq \ell \leq \kappa - 1$
1. if $\neg(\mathbf{Val}_\ell(h) \wedge \mathbf{Val}_\ell(h'))$ then return $\bot$
2. parse $([z], c_1, c_2, \pi, \ell) \leftarrow h$ and $([z'], c_1', c_2', \pi', \ell) \leftarrow h'$
3. $[z''] \leftarrow [z] + [z']$; $c_1'' \leftarrow c_1 + c_1'$; $c_2'' \leftarrow c_2 + c_2'$
4. $P_1 \leftarrow \mathbf{Dec}(c_1, sk_1)$; $P_2 \leftarrow \mathbf{Dec}(c_2, sk_2)$
   $P_1' \leftarrow \mathbf{Dec}(c_1', sk_1)$; $P_2' \leftarrow \mathbf{Dec}(c_2', sk_2)$
5. if $[z] \neq [P_1(\omega)] \vee [z] \neq [P_2(\omega)] \vee [z'] \neq [P_1'(\omega)] \vee [z'] \neq [P_2'(\omega)]$ then
   5.1. $w_y' \leftarrow_\$ \mathbf{WExt}(td_e, ([z], c_1, c_2), \pi)$
   5.2. if $\neg\mathbf{R}_2(gpk, ([z], c_1, c_2, \ell), w_y')$ then return $\bot$
   5.3. $\pi'' \leftarrow_\$ \mathbf{Prove}(gpk, crs, ([z''], c_1'', c_2''), w_y')$
6. else $\pi'' \leftarrow_\$ \mathbf{Prove}(gpk, crs, ([z''], c_1'', c_2''), (sk_1, sk_2))$
7. return $([z''], c_1'', c_2'', \pi'', \ell)$

Fig. 2. The probabilistic circuit used to add encodings for levels $1 \leq \ell \leq \kappa - 1$. The checks at 5 are never passed in an honest execution of the protocol. We emphasize that the test in step 5 is implemented using the values $[\omega^i]$. The random coins needed for randomized operations are internally generated after obfuscating with **PIO**.

that is, the explicit consistency check, is never reached under a binding crs' (due to the perfect soundness of the proof system), but they may be reached with a hiding crs' later in the security analysis. Let us expand on this.

In the analysis, we need to specify how C_{Add} behaves if it encounters valid inputs (in the sense the proofs pass NIZK verification), but nevertheless are inconsistent in the sense that at least one of encodings does not decrypt to a valid representation. Let us call such inputs *bad*.

With the knowledge of secret keys, such bad inputs can be recognized, and the natural choice would be to define C_{Add} to abort when this is the case. With this choice, however, we run into the following problem. During the security proof we will set the addition circuit to answer all valid inputs (including bad ones) with simulated proofs. On the other hand, the original addition circuit rejects such inputs. (Furthermore, it cannot even simulate proofs for wrong statements, and hence cannot answer bad inputs with valid-looking proofs.)

On a high level, we would like to modify how C_{Add} reacts on bad inputs so that it uses a NIZK simulation trapdoor on bad inputs. The difficulty with this strategy is that no such simulation trapdoor exists when the NIZK CRS is binding. Hence, we create our own NIZK trapdoor through an extra "OR branch" in the proved statement (akin to the Feige–Lapidot–Shamir transform). This gives us a little more flexibility in defining and using that trapdoor.

More specifically, recall that our CRS is of the form $crs = (crs', y)$ where crs' is a binding CRS for the dual-mode NIZK proof system, and y is a no-instance of $\mathcal{L}_{lk}$. However our actual means to fake proofs will be to switch y to a yes-instance and use a witness w_y to produce proofs. Specifically, in the security proof, we will eventually let C_{Add} use a simulation trapdoor w_y (instead of a simulation trapdoor for the NIZK). The benefit of this is that C_{Add} will know an extraction trapdoor td'_e (that of course only exists if the CRS crs' is in the binding mode) which it can use to extract a witness from a given proof π. Thus, whenever C_{Add} encounters a bad input, it can extract a witness w'_y, which *must* at that point be a simulation trapdoor w_y. This simulation trapdoor w_y can then immediately be used to produce a fake proof π'' even upon bad inputs. In other words, C_{Add} knows no simulation trapdoor a priori, but it can extract one from any simulated proof for a false statement.

The $\mathbf{Add}_\ell$ algorithm simply runs the obfuscated circuit on the input encodings and ℓ. The correctness of this algorithm follows from that of Π, the completeness of Σ and the correctness, in our sense, of the (probabilistic) obfuscator $\mathbf{PIO}$. Note that FHE correctness is only guaranteed to hold with respect to ciphertexts that are in the range of encryption or evaluation (and not necessarily for anomalous ones that decrypt correctly). This, in particular, means that we cannot enlarge the set of encodings to contain all valid ones (as opposed to just consistent ones) to get efficient decidability of encoding sets as correctness can no longer be established. (See also remark on validity on page 18.) Note that full compactness ensures that the ciphertexts output by $\mathbf{Add}_\ell$ are in the range of encryption, and hence they can be further operated on with $\mathbf{Eval}$.

5.4 Multiplication

Given two encodings $h = ([z], c_1, c_2, \pi, \ell)$ and $h' = ([z'], c_1', c_2', \pi', \ell')$ at levels ℓ and ℓ' respectively, the multiplication algorithms operates analogously to addition as follows. The corresponding circuit C_{Mult} has both decryption keys and now also $\omega \in \mathbb{Z}_p$ hardwired in. After validity checks and decrypting the input ciphertexts, it performs the multiplication of the polynomials encrypted under c_i and c_i' homomorphically using a convolution operation on the coefficient vectors. However, it cannot obviously compute the element $[zz']$ in the base group $\mathbb{G}$. Suppose c_1 and c_1' encrypt polynomials P and P' of degrees at most ℓ and ℓ' respectively and such that $[z] = [P(\omega)]$ and $[z'] = [P'(\omega)]$. The multiplication circuit uses the explicit knowledge of ω and polynomials P and P' to compute $[zz'] = [(P * P')(\omega)]$.[9] Circuit C_{Mult} is shown in Fig. 3. Note that similarly to addition, step 6 performs explicit checks of consistency of encodings that will only be used in the analysis under a hiding crs'.

The correctness of these maps follows from the correctness of Π and **PIO**, and the completeness of Σ.

ENABLING GRADED MULTIPLICATION. The main difference between our circuit C_{Mult} and that of [2] is that here we need to output auxiliary information (c_1, c_2, π) for multiplied encodings at output levels below κ. This information allows the multiplication algorithm to operate in a graded fashion as any output encoding by C_{Mult} can be fed back into C_{Mult} as long as it lies at a level

---

CIRCUIT $C_{\mathrm{Mult}}[gpk, crs, \omega, sk_1, sk_2, td_e](\ell, \ell', h, h')$:   // for $1 \le \ell, \ell' \le \kappa - 1$

1. if $\neg(\mathbf{Val}_\ell(h) \wedge \mathbf{Val}_{\ell'}(h')) \vee \ell + \ell' > \kappa$ then return $\perp$
2. parse $([z], c_1, c_2, \pi, \ell) \leftarrow h$ and $([z'], c_1', c_2', \pi', \ell') \leftarrow h'$
3. $c_1'' \leftarrow c_1 * c_1'$; $c_2'' \leftarrow c_2 * c_2'$
4. $P_1 \leftarrow \mathbf{Dec}(c_1, sk_1)$; $P_2 \leftarrow \mathbf{Dec}(c_2, sk_2)$
   $P_1' \leftarrow \mathbf{Dec}(c_1', sk_1)$; $P_2' \leftarrow \mathbf{Dec}(c_2', sk_2)$
5. $z'' \leftarrow (P_1 * P_1')(\omega)$
6. if $[z] \neq [P_1(\omega)] \vee [z] \neq [P_2(\omega)] \vee [z'] \neq [P_1'(\omega)] \vee [z'] \neq [P_2'(\omega)]$ then
   6.1. $w_y' \leftarrow_{\$} \mathbf{WExt}(td_e, ([z], c_1, c_2), \pi)$
   6.2. if $\neg \mathbf{R}_2(gpk, ([z], c_1, c_2), w_y')$ then return $\perp$
   6.3. $\pi'' \leftarrow_{\$} \mathbf{Prove}(gpk, crs, ([z''], c_1'', c_2''), w_y')$
7. else $\pi'' \leftarrow_{\$} \mathbf{Prove}(gpk, crs, ([z''], c_1'', c_2''), (sk_1, sk_2))$
8. If $(\ell + \ell' = \kappa)$ then return $[z'']$ else return $([z''], c_1'', c_2'', \pi'', \ell + \ell')$

Fig. 3. Circuit used for multiplying encodings for levels $1 \le \ell, \ell' \le \kappa - 1$. Step 6 is never reached in an honest execution of the protocol with a binding crs. The random coins needed for randomized operations are internally generated after obfuscating with **PIO**.

---

[9] Observe that with the explicit knowledge of $P * P'$ and the powers $([\omega^i])_{1 \le i \le \kappa}$ it is also possible to compute $[zz']$ as long as $P * P'$ is of degree $\le \kappa$; this will be exploited in the security analysis in Sect. 7.

$\ell < \kappa$.[10] In order to enable C_{Mult} to generate this auxiliary information, we use an encryption scheme that is also homomorphic with respect to multiplication in the plaintext ring. In contrast, AFHLP only rely on an additively homomorphic encryption scheme.

5.5   Sampling

Given polynomials P_1 and P_2 of degree at most ℓ and satisfying $P_1(\omega) = P_2(\omega) = z$ we can generate an encoding from $S_\ell^{(z)}$ by computing

$$
\begin{aligned}
h \leftarrow \big([z], c_1 = \mathbf{Enc}(P_1, pk_1; r_1), c_2 = \mathbf{Enc}(P_2, pk_2; r_2), \\
\pi = \mathbf{Prove}(gpk, crs, ([z]_i, c_1, c_2, \ell), (P_1, P_2, r_1, r_2); r), \ell\big).
\end{aligned} \tag{2}
$$

Hence, our sampling algorithm $\mathbf{Sam}_\ell(z)$ sets $P_1(X) = P_2(X) = z \in \mathbb{Z}_p$ and computes an encoding through (2). We call these the *canonical* encodings of z, independently of ℓ. We note that this procedure is that in [2] adapted to the generalized notion of polynomial representations.

5.6   Extraction

Since at each level ℓ the first component $[z]$ is unique for each set $S_\ell^{(z)}$, we may extract a uniform string from $h = ([z], c_1, c_2, \pi, \ell)$ for a uniform z by applying a randomness extractor seeded with hk to $[z]$.

6   Indistinguishability of Encodings

We show that a key property used by AFHLP in the analysis of their multilinear map [2, Theorem 5.3] is also exhibited by our graded scheme. Roughly speaking, this property states that for any given level ℓ, any two valid encodings of the same $\mathbb{Z}_p$-element are computationally indistinguishable. This claim is formalized via the κ-Switch game shown in Fig. 4. Note that in this game, we allow the adversary to not only choose the representation polynomials, but also let him see part of the private information not available through the public parameters, namely the exponent ω.

Theorem 1 (Encoding switch). *Let* Γ *be the GES constructed in Sect. 5 with respect to an* X-*IND-secure probabilistic obfuscator* **PIO**, *an IND-CPA-secure encryption scheme* Π, *a dual-mode NIZK proof system* Σ, *and a language family* Λ. *Then, encodings of the same ring element* $z \in \mathbb{Z}_p$ *are indistinguishable at all levels. More precisely, for any legitimate* PPT *adversary* $\mathcal{A}$ *there are* PPT *adversaries* $\mathcal{B}_1, \mathcal{B}_2, \mathcal{B}_3$ *and* $\mathcal{B}_4$ *of essentially the same complexity as* $\mathcal{A}$ *such that for all* $\lambda \in \mathbb{N}$

$$\mathbf{Adv}_{\Gamma,\mathcal{A}}^{\kappa\text{-switch}}(\lambda) \leq 3 \cdot \big(\mathbf{Adv}_{\Lambda,\mathcal{B}_1}^{mem}(\lambda) + 6 \cdot \mathbf{Adv}_{\mathbf{PIO},\mathcal{B}_2}^{ind}(\lambda) + \mathbf{Adv}_{\Sigma,\mathcal{B}_3}^{crs}(\lambda)\big) + 2 \cdot \mathbf{Adv}_{\Pi,\mathcal{B}_4}^{ind\text{-}cpa}(\lambda).$$

---

[10] Recall that encodings at level κ can only be multiplied with level-0 encodings, i.e., with elements in $\mathbb{Z}_p$.

$\kappa\text{-Switch}_\Gamma^A(\lambda)$:

$(pp; \omega) \leftarrow_\$ \mathbf{Setup}(1^\lambda, 1^\kappa)$ // ω generated within **Setup**

$((P_{0,1}, P_{0,2}), (P_{1,1}, P_{1,2}), \ell, st) \leftarrow_\$ A_1(pp, \omega)$

$b \leftarrow_\$ \{0,1\}; \ r_1, r_2 \leftarrow_\$ \{0,1\}^{\mathrm{rl}(\lambda)}$

$c_1 \leftarrow \mathbf{Enc}(P_{b,1}, pk_1; r_1); \ c_2 \leftarrow \mathbf{Enc}(P_{b,2}, pk_2; r_2)$

$\pi \leftarrow_\$ \mathbf{Prove}(gpk, crs, ([P_{b,1}(\omega)], c_1, c_2, \ell), (P_{b,1}, P_{b,2}, r_1, r_2))$

$h_b \leftarrow ([P_{b,1}(\omega)], c_1, c_2, \pi, \ell)$

$b' \leftarrow_\$ A_2(h_b, st)$

Return $(b = b')$

Fig. 4. Game formalizing the indistinguishability of encodings. (This game is specific to our construction Γ from Sect. 5.) An adversary is legitimate if it outputs polynomials such that $P_{0,1}(\omega) = P_{0,2}(\omega) = P_{1,1}(\omega) = P_{1,2}(\omega)$ of degree at most ℓ. We note that A gets explicit access to secret exponent ω generated at setup. Here $\mathrm{rl}(\lambda)$ is a polynomial indicating the length of the random coins used by the encryption algorithm.

The proof of this result follows largely that in [2] and we include it in the full version [19] of this paper. The main difference is that we have to deal with obfuscations of the new multiplication circuit.

Proof (Outline). We proceed via a sequence of 5 games, starting with κ-Switch and ending in a game where the challenge encoding is independent of the bit b. Figure 5 shows the steps used in the proof of the theorem. We use helper Lemma 1 for changing the addition and multiplication circuits to "forget" (one or both) the secret keys and the extraction trapdoor. We now justify each of these steps in more detail below. See the full version [19] of this paper for a full proof.

Gm.	crs'	y	C_{Add} knows	C_{Mult} knows	c_1 enc.	c_2 enc.	**Remark**
0	bind.	$\notin \mathcal{L}_{lk}$	sk_1, sk_2, td_e	sk_1, sk_2, td_e	$P_{b,1}$	$P_{b,2}$	
1	hid.	$\in \mathcal{L}_{lk}$	w_y	$\underline{sk_1}, w_y$	$P_{b,1}$	$P_{b,2}$	Lemma 1 ($i = 1$)
2	hid.	$\in \mathcal{L}_{lk}$	w_y	$\underline{sk_1}, w_y$	$P_{b,1}$	$P_{1,2}$	IND-CPA wrt. pk_2
3	bind.	$\notin \mathcal{L}_{lk}$	sk_1, sk_2, td_e	$\underline{sk_1}, sk_2, td_e$	$P_{b,1}$	$P_{1,2}$	Lemma 1 (reverse, $i = 1$)
4	hid.	$\in \mathcal{L}_{lk}$	w_y	$\underline{sk_2}, w_y$	$P_{b,1}$	$P_{1,2}$	Lemma 1 ($i = 2$)
5	hid.	$\in \mathcal{L}_{lk}$	w_y	$\underline{sk_2}, w_y$	$P_{1,1}$	$P_{1,2}$	IND-CPA wrt. pk_1
							Encoding indep. of b

Fig. 5. Outline of the proof steps of Theorem 1. The underlined secret key in the "C_{Mult} knows" column indicates the key that is used in decryption to construct $[z'']$. For instance, in Game$_0$, key sk_1 is used to obtain P_1 and P_1', which are then used to compute $[z''] = [(P_1 * P_1')(\omega)]$ within C_{Mult}.

Game_0: This is the κ-Switch game with a binding crs' and $y \notin \mathcal{L}_{lk}$. The addition and multiplication circuits are defined in Figs. 2 and 3, respectively.

Game_1: We change the public parameters so that they include a *hiding* crs', a yes instance y via $\textbf{YesSam}_\textbf{L}(lk)$ and obfuscations of circuits $\widehat{C}_{\text{Add}}$ and $\widehat{C}_{\text{Mult}}^{(1)}$ (see Fig. 6). Thus, the second circuit uses sk_1 to decrypt the first ciphertexts given as inputs. Observe that these circuits use the witness w_y to $y \in \mathcal{L}_{lk}$ to produce the output proofs π'', and therefore the *simultaneous* knowledge of decryption keys sk_1, sk_2 is no longer needed. The difference with the previous game can be bounded by our helper Lemma 1 with $i = 1$, where we rely on PIO security, CRS indistinguishability, and the membership problem.

Game_2: This game generates the second challenge ciphertext c_2 by encrypting polynomial $P_{1,2}$ *even when* $b = 0$. We bound this transition via the IND-CPA security of Π with respect to pk_2. The reduction will choose a first decryption key sk_1 and a witness w_y so as to be able to construct $\widehat{C}_{\text{Mult}}^{(1)}$. It will also generate a NIZK simulation trapdoor td_{zk} (recall the CRS is in the hiding mode) to construct simulated proofs π for the (inconsistent) challenge encoding h_b. Note that the perfect ZK property guarantees that these proofs are identically distributed to the real ones in Game_1.

Game_3: The public parameters are changed back to include a binding crs', a no-instance $y \notin \mathcal{L}_{lk}$ and a (PIO) obfuscation of the original circuits $C_{\text{Add}}, C_{\text{Mult}}$ with both decryption keys hardwired. The difference with the previous game is bounded again via Lemma 1 (in the reverse direction and with $i = 1$).

Game_4: This transitions is defined analogously to that introduced in Game_1 except that this time we invoke Lemma 1 with $i = 2$ and switch to circuits $\widehat{C}_{\text{Add}}$ and $\widehat{C}_{\text{Mult}}^{(2)}$. Observe that knowledge of sk_1 is no longer needed.

Game_5: This transitions is defined analogously to that introduced in Game_2. The only difference is that this game generates the *first* challenge ciphertext c_1 by encrypting $P_{1,1}$ even when $b = 0$.

Finally, note that the challenge encoding in Game_5 is independent of the random bit b and the advantage of any (even unbounded) adversary $\mathcal{A}$ is 0.

In the proof of Theorem 1, we need the next Lemma for changing the addition and multiplication circuits to "forget" (one or both) the secret keys and the extraction trapdoor. The proof can be found in the full version [19] of this paper.

Lemma 1 (Forgetting secret keys). *Let Γ be the GES from Sect. 5 with respect to an X-IND-secure probabilistic obfuscator* **PIO**, *an IND-CPA-secure encryption scheme Π, a dual-mode NIZK proof system Σ, and a language family Λ. For $i = 1, 2$, consider the modified parameter generation algorithm* $\textbf{Setup}^{(i)}$ *that samples a yes-instance $y \in \mathcal{L}_{lk}$ and outputs obfuscations of the circuits $\widehat{C}_{\text{Add}}$ and $\widehat{C}_{\text{Mult}}^{(i)}$ shown in Fig. 6. Let*

$$\textbf{Adv}_{\Gamma, i, \mathcal{A}}^{\kappa\text{-forget}}(\lambda) := 2 \cdot \Pr \left[pp_0 \leftarrow_{\!\$} \textbf{Setup}(1^\lambda, 1^\kappa);\ pp_1 \leftarrow_{\!\$} \textbf{Setup}^{(i)}(1^\lambda, 1^\kappa);\right.$$
$$\left. b \leftarrow_{\!\$} \{0, 1\}; b' \leftarrow_{\!\$} \mathcal{A}(pp_b)\ :\ b = b' \right] - 1.$$

CIRCUIT $\widehat{\mathrm{C}}_{\mathrm{Add}}[gpk, crs, w_y](\ell, h, h')$:

1. if $\neg(\mathbf{Val}_\ell(h) \wedge \mathbf{Val}_\ell(h'))$ then return $\bot$
2. parse $([z], c_1, c_2, \pi, \ell) \leftarrow h$, and $([z'], c_1', c_2', \pi', \ell) \leftarrow h'$
3. $[z''] \leftarrow [z] + [z']$; $c_1'' \leftarrow c_1 + c_1'$; $c_2'' \leftarrow c_2 + c_2'$
4.   // omitted: depends on sk_1 and sk_2
5. $\pi'' \leftarrow_\$ \mathbf{Prove}(gpk, crs, ([z''], c_1'', c_2'', \ell), w_y)$
6.   // omitted: depends on sk_1 and sk_2
7. return $([z''], c_1'', c_2'', \pi'', \ell)$

CIRCUIT $\widehat{\mathrm{C}}_{\mathrm{Mult}}^{(i)}[gpk, crs, \omega, sk_i, w_y](\ell, \ell', h, h')$:

1. if $\neg(\mathbf{Val}_\ell(h) \wedge \mathbf{Val}_{\ell'}(h')) \vee \ell + \ell' > \kappa$ then return $\bot$
2. parse $([z], c_1, c_2, \pi, \ell) \leftarrow h$ and $([z'], c_1', c_2', \pi', \ell') \leftarrow h'$
3. $c_1'' \leftarrow c_1 \cdot c_1'$; $c_2'' \leftarrow c_2 \cdot c_2'$
4. $P_i \leftarrow \mathbf{Dec}(c_i, sk_i)$; $P_i' \leftarrow \mathbf{Dec}(c_i', sk_i)$ // depends on sk_i only
5. $z'' \leftarrow (P_i * P_i')(\omega)$
6. $\pi'' \leftarrow_\$ \mathbf{Prove}(gpk, crs, ([z''], c_1'', c_2'', \ell + \ell'), w_y)$
7.   // omitted: depends on sk_1 and sk_2
8. If $(\ell + \ell' = \kappa)$ then return $[z'']$ else return $([z''], c_1'', c_2'', \pi'', \ell + \ell')$

Fig. 6. Top: Circuit $\widehat{\mathrm{C}}_{\mathrm{Add}}$ where witness w_y to $y \in \mathcal{L}_{lk}$ is used to produce π''. Note that the secret keys (sk_1, sk_2) or the extraction trapdoor td_e are no longer used by this circuit. Bottom: Circuits $\widehat{\mathrm{C}}_{\mathrm{Mult}}^{(i)}$ were only one key sk_i is used to decrypt P_i and P_i' and witness w_y to $y \in \mathcal{L}_{lk}$ is used to produce π''. The secret key sk_{3-i} and the extraction trapdoor td_e are not used by this circuit.

Then, for any $i \in \{1, 2\}$ and any PPT adversary $\mathcal{A}$ there are PPT adversaries $\mathcal{B}_1, \mathcal{B}_2$ and $\mathcal{B}_3$ of essentially the same complexity as $\mathcal{A}$ such that for all $\lambda \in \mathbb{N}$

$$\mathbf{Adv}_{\Gamma, i, \mathcal{A}}^{\kappa\text{-forget}}(\lambda) \le \mathbf{Adv}_{\Lambda, \mathcal{B}_1}^{\mathrm{mem}}(\lambda) + 6 \cdot \mathbf{Adv}_{\mathrm{PIO}, \mathcal{B}_2}^{\mathrm{ind}}(\lambda) + \mathbf{Adv}_{\Sigma, \mathcal{B}_3}^{\mathrm{crs}}(\lambda).$$

7 Hardness of MDDH

We are now ready to show that MDDH is hard for our GES. We improve [2] by providing a simpler and tighter proof of security. One corollary of our result is that there are no "zeroizing" attacks on our scheme as such attacks immediately lead to the break of MDDH [12,13,22]. We start by providing formal definition of MDDH as well as the strong DDH problem whose hardness we assume in our analyses.

THE q-SDDH PROBLEM [4,43]. For $q \in \mathbb{N}$ we say that the q-SDDH problem is hard for a group $\mathbb{G}$ if

$$\mathbf{Adv}_{\mathbb{G}, \mathcal{A}}^{q\text{-sddh}}(\lambda) := 2 \cdot \Pr\left[q\text{-SDDH}_{\mathbb{G}}^{\mathcal{A}}(\lambda)\right] - 1 \in \mathrm{NEGL},$$

where game q-SDDH$_{\mathbb{G}}^{\mathcal{A}}(\lambda)$ is shown in Fig. 7 (left). We note that this assumption can only hold in *asymmetric* pairing-friendly groups. (With such asymmetric pairings, we could then implement, e.g., the dual-mode NIZK proof system

$q\text{-SDDH}_{\mathbb{G}}^{\mathcal{A}}(\lambda)$	$\kappa\text{-MDDH}_{\Gamma}^{\mathcal{A}}(\lambda)$
$pp_{\mathbb{G}} \leftarrow_{\$} \textbf{Setup}_{\mathbb{G}}(1^{\lambda})$	$pp \leftarrow_{\$} \textbf{Setup}(1^{\lambda}, 1^{\kappa})$
$b \leftarrow_{\$} \{0,1\}$	$b \leftarrow_{\$} \{0,1\}$
$\omega, \tau_0 \leftarrow_{\$} \mathbb{Z}_p$	$a_1, \ldots, a_{\kappa+1}, z \leftarrow_{\$} \mathbb{Z}_p$
$\tau_1 \leftarrow \omega^{q+1} \pmod{p}$	$h_i \leftarrow_{\$} \textbf{Sam}_1(a_i)$
$b' \leftarrow_{\$} \mathcal{A}(pp_{\mathbb{G}}, \{[\omega^i]\}_{i=1}^{q}, [\tau_b])$	$h_0^* \leftarrow_{\$} \textbf{Sam}_{\kappa}(z)$
Return $(b = b')$	$h_1^* \leftarrow \textbf{Mult}(h_1, \ldots, h_{\kappa})^{a_{\kappa+1}}$
	$b' \leftarrow_{\$} \mathcal{A}(pp, \{h_i\}_{i=1}^{\kappa+1}, h_b^*)$
	Return $(b = b')$

Fig. 7. Left: The SDDH problem. Here $p = p(\lambda)$ denotes the group order implicit in pp. Right: The MDDH problem. The sampler algorithms output canonical encodings. The κ-ary algorithm **Mult** is defined by applying the 2-ary algorithm **Mult** of the scheme iteratively to inputs.

from [30].) It is not too difficult to show via re-randomization of the group generator that hardness of q-SDDH implies that of $(q-1)$-SDDH. We use this fact to simplify our theorem statement below.

THE κ-MDDH PROBLEM [6,22]. For $\kappa \in \mathbb{N}$ we say that the κ-MDDH problem is hard for a GES Γ if

$$\textbf{Adv}_{\Gamma,\mathcal{A}}^{\kappa\text{-mddh}}(\lambda) := 2 \cdot \Pr\left[\kappa\text{-MDDH}_{\Gamma}^{\mathcal{A}}(\lambda)\right] - 1 \in \text{NEGL},$$

where game κ-MDDH$_{\Gamma}^{\mathcal{A}}(\lambda)$ is shown in Fig. 7 (middle).

THE $(\kappa, m, n, r_0, r_1, l)$-RANK PROBLEM [18]. For $\kappa, m, n, r_0, r_1 \in \mathbb{N}$ and a level function $l : [m] \times [n] \longrightarrow [\kappa]$, we say that the $(\kappa, m, n, r_0, r_1, l)$-RANK problem is hard for a GES Γ if

$$\textbf{Adv}_{\Gamma,\mathcal{A}}^{(\kappa,m,n,r_0,r_1,l)\text{-rank}}(\lambda) := 2 \cdot \Pr\left[(\kappa, m, n, r_0, r_1, l)\text{-RANK}_{\Gamma}^{\mathcal{A}}(\lambda)\right] - 1 \in \text{NEGL},$$

where game $(\kappa, m, n, r_0, r_1, l)$-RANK$_{\Gamma}^{\mathcal{A}}(\lambda)$ is shown in Fig. 7 (right).

7.1   Hardness of MDDH

Recall that the GES of Sect. 5 represents an element $z \in \mathbb{Z}_p$ at level ℓ with polynomials P_1 and P_2 of degree at most ℓ such that $P_j(\omega) = z$.

Theorem 1 (κ-SDDH $\Longrightarrow$ κ-MDDH). *Let Γ be the GES constructed in Sect. 5 with respect to a base group $\mathbb{G}$ and an X-IND-secure probabilistic obfuscator* **PIO**.

Then, assuming the κ-SDDH assumption (see Fig. 7) holds in $\mathbb{G}$, and using our switching lemma, the κ-MDDH assumption holds in Γ.

More specifically, for any $\kappa \in \mathbb{N}$ and any PPT adversary $\mathcal{A}$ there are PPT adversaries $\mathcal{B}_1$, $\mathcal{B}_2$ and $\mathcal{B}_3$ of essentially the same complexity as $\mathcal{A}$ such that for all $\lambda \in \mathbb{N}$

$$\textbf{Adv}_{\Gamma,\mathcal{A}}^{\kappa\text{-mddh}}(\lambda) \le (\kappa + 1) \cdot \textbf{Adv}_{\Gamma,\mathcal{B}_1}^{\kappa\text{-switch}}(\lambda) + \textbf{Adv}_{\textbf{PIO},\mathcal{B}_2}^{\text{ind}}(\lambda) + \textbf{Adv}_{\mathbb{G},\mathcal{B}_3}^{\kappa\text{-sddh}}(\lambda).$$

Proof (Outline). We provide a simpler proof compared to that of [2, Theorem 6.2] at the expense of relying on the slightly stronger κ-SDDH (instead of the $(\kappa - 1)$-SDDH) problem. At a high level, our reduction has two steps: (1) Switch *all* encodings from polynomials of degree 0 to those of degree 1; and (2) Randomize the κ-MDDH challenge using the κ-SDDH instance. The key difference with the proof of [2, Theorem 6.2] is that we no longer need to carry out a two-step process to randomize the exponent of the MDDH challenge. In particular, we do not change the implementation of the multiplication circuit according to a κ-SDDH challenge. We outline the proof along a sequence of $\kappa + 5$ games here and leave the full details to the full version [19].

Game$_0$: This is the κ-MDDH problem (Fig. 7, middle). We use $P_{i,1}$ and $P_{i,2}$ to denote the canonical degree-zero representation polynomials of a_i as generated by the sampler $\mathbf{Sam}_1(a_i)$.

Game$_1$–Game$_{\kappa+1}$: In these games we gradually switch the polynomials representations for level-1 encodings h_i for $1 \le i \le \kappa + 1$ so that they take the form

$$P_{i,1}(X) = P_{i,2}(X) = X + a_i - \omega.$$

These polynomials are still valid and their degrees are *exactly* 1. Hence when multiplied together, the resulting polynomial will be of degree $s(\kappa+1)$. Each of these hops can be bounded via the κ-Switch game via Theorem 1.

Game$_{\kappa+2}$: This game only introduces a conceptual change: a_i for $1 \le i \le \kappa + 1$ are generated as $a_i + \omega$. The distributions of these values are still uniform and the exponent of the MDDH challenge when $b = 1$ is now

$$z_1 = \prod_{i=1}^{\kappa+1}(a_i + \omega),$$

which is a polynomial in ω of degree κ.

Game$_{\kappa+3}$: In this game we replace C_{Mult} with C^*_{Mult}, a circuit that uses the implicit values $[\omega^i]$ for $0 \le i \le \kappa$ in steps 5 and 6. (Note that $[P(\omega)]$ can be computed using $[\omega^i]$ when the coefficients of P are explicitly known.) This change does not affect the functionality of the multiplication circuit and hence we can bound this hope via PIO security. As a result, the explicit knowledge ω is no longer needed to generate the multiplication circuit.

Game$_{\kappa+4}$: In this game, we replace $[\omega^\kappa]$ with a random value $[\sigma]$ in challenge preparation. (Note that level-κ encodings correspond to the base group.) We can bound this hop via the κ-SDDH game.

In the final game the challenge exponent (when $b = 1$) is fully randomized. This means that the challenge is independent of b in Game$_{\kappa+4}$, which concludes the proof.

7.2 Downgrading Attacks

It might appear that our GES could be subject to a "downgrading" attack as follow. Start with any consistent encoding h at level ℓ whose representation polynomial is of degree 0. Then "maul" h into an encoding at a lower level $\ell' < \ell$ by simply changing ℓ to ℓ' in h. Then use this malleability to attack, say, MDDH where challenge encodings are canonical and of degree 0 (see Sect. 5.5).

What is crucial and prevents this downgrade attack is the proof system. The consistency proof π proves that the encrypted values correspond to a polynomial P of degree up to ℓ such that $P(\omega) = z$. Note that this statement *depends on* ℓ. Hence, a proof for a level-2 encoding cannot be "reused" for a level-1 encoding, as in the attack: a single proof will not necessarily pass against two different statements even if they both have the same witness. In order to downgrade, the proof would have to be changed.

Indeed, suppose that one had a method for changing a proof π_2 of a level-2 encoding to a proof π_1 of the level-1 encoding (that is derived by simply omitting encrypted coefficients, as in a downgrading attack). Consider what happens if one start with equivalent level-2 encoding (in the sense of our switching lemma) with degree-2 polynomials P. Then, the statement that π_1 proves becomes false, so any such attack would contradict the soundness of the proof system.

Acknowledgments. We thank the anonymous reviewers for their helpful comments, and Kenny Paterson and Geoffroy Couteau for useful discussions. Pooya Farshim was supported in part by grant ANR-14-CE28-0003 (Project EnBid). Dennis Hofheinz was supported by ERC grant 724307, and by DFG grants HO 4534/2-2 and HO 4534/4-1. Enrique Larraia was supported by EPSRC grant EP/L018543/1.

References

1. Abusalah, H., Fuchsbauer, G., Pietrzak, K.: Constrained PRFs for unbounded inputs. In: Sako, K. (ed.) CT-RSA 2016. LNCS, vol. 9610, pp. 413–428. Springer, Cham (2016). https://doi.org/10.1007/978-3-319-29485-8_24
2. Albrecht, M.R., Farshim, P., Hofheinz, D., Larraia, E., Paterson, K.G.: Multilinear maps from obfuscation. In: Kushilevitz, E., Malkin, T. (eds.) TCC 2016. LNCS, vol. 9562, pp. 446–473. Springer, Heidelberg (2016). https://doi.org/10.1007/978-3-662-49096-9_19
3. Ananth, P., Sahai, A.: Projective arithmetic functional encryption and indistinguishability obfuscation from degree-5 multilinear maps. In: Coron, J.-S., Nielsen, J.B. (eds.) EUROCRYPT 2017. LNCS, vol. 10210, pp. 152–181. Springer, Cham (2017). https://doi.org/10.1007/978-3-319-56620-7_6
4. Boneh, D., Boyen, X.: Short signatures without random oracles. In: Cachin, C., Camenisch, J.L. (eds.) EUROCRYPT 2004. LNCS, vol. 3027, pp. 56–73. Springer, Heidelberg (2004). https://doi.org/10.1007/978-3-540-24676-3_4
5. Boneh, D., Lewi, K., Raykova, M., Sahai, A., Zhandry, M., Zimmerman, J.: Semantically secure order-revealing encryption: multi-input functional encryption without obfuscation. In: Oswald and Fischlin (eds.) [38], pp. 563–594
6. Boneh, D., Silverberg, A.: Applications of multilinear forms to cryptography. Contemp. Math. **324**, 71–90 (2003)
7. Boneh, D., Waters, B.: Constrained pseudorandom functions and their applications. In: Sako, K., Sarkar, P. (eds.) ASIACRYPT 2013. LNCS, vol. 8270, pp. 280–300. Springer, Heidelberg (2013). https://doi.org/10.1007/978-3-642-42045-0_15

8. Boneh, D., Waters, B., Zhandry, M.: Low overhead broadcast encryption from multilinear maps. In: Garay and Gennaro [21], pp. 206–223

9. Canetti, R., Garay, J.A. (eds.): CRYPTO 2013, Part I. LNCS, vol. 8042. Springer, Heidelberg (2013). https://doi.org/10.1007/978-3-642-40041-4

10. Canetti, R., Garay, J.A. (eds.): CRYPTO 2013, Part II. LNCS, vol. 8043. Springer, Heidelberg (2013). https://doi.org/10.1007/978-3-642-40084-1

11. Canetti, R., Lin, H., Tessaro, S., Vaikuntanathan, V.: Obfuscation of probabilistic circuits and applications. In: Dodis and Nielsen [17], pp. 468–497

12. Cheon, J.H., Han, K., Lee, C., Ryu, H., Stehlé, D.: Cryptanalysis of the multilinear map over the integers. In: Oswald, E., Fischlin, M. (eds.) EUROCRYPT 2015, Part I. LNCS, vol. 9056, pp. 3–12. Springer, Heidelberg (2015). https://doi.org/10.1007/978-3-662-46800-5_1

13. Coron, J.-S., Gentry, C., Halevi, S., Lepoint, T., Maji, H.K., Miles, E., Raykova, M., Sahai, A., Tibouchi, M.: Zeroizing without low-level zeroes: new MMAP attacks and their limitations. In: Gennaro and Robshaw [27], pp. 247–266

14. Coron, J.-S., Lee, M.S., Lepoint, T., Tibouchi, M.: Cryptanalysis of GGH15 multilinear maps. In: Robshaw and Katz [41], pp. 607–628

15. Coron, J.-S., Lepoint, T., Tibouchi, M.: Practical multilinear maps over the integers. In: Canetti and Garay [9], pp. 476–493

16. Coron, J.-S., Lepoint, T., Tibouchi, M.: New multilinear maps over the integers. In: Gennaro and Robshaw [27], pp. 267–286

17. Dodis, Y., Nielsen, J.B. (eds.): TCC 2015, Part II. LNCS, vol. 9015. Springer, Heidelberg (2015). https://doi.org/10.1007/978-3-662-46497-7

18. Escala, A., Herold, G., Kiltz, E., Ràfols, C., Villar, J.: An algebraic framework for Diffie-Hellman assumptions. In: Canetti and Garay [10], pp. 129–147

19. Farshim, P., Hesse, J., Hofheinz, D., Larraia, E.: Graded encoding schemes from indistinguishability obfuscation. Cryptology ePrint Archive, Report 2018/011 (2015)

20. Freire, E.S.V., Hofheinz, D., Paterson, K.G., Striecks, C.: Programmable hash functions in the multilinear setting. In: Canetti and Garay [9], pp. 513–530

21. Garay, J.A., Gennaro, R. (eds.): CRYPTO 2014, Part I. LNCS, vol. 8616. Springer, Heidelberg (2014). https://doi.org/10.1007/978-3-662-44371-2

22. Garg, S., Gentry, C., Halevi, S.: Candidate multilinear maps from ideal lattices. In: Johansson, T., Nguyen, P.Q. (eds.) EUROCRYPT 2013. LNCS, vol. 7881, pp. 1–17. Springer, Heidelberg (2013). https://doi.org/10.1007/978-3-642-38348-9_1

23. Garg, S., Gentry, C., Halevi, S., Raykova, M., Sahai, A., Waters, B.: Candidate indistinguishability obfuscation and functional encryption for all circuits. In: 54th FOCS, pp. 40–49. IEEE Computer Society Press, October 2013

24. Garg, S., Gentry, C., Halevi, S., Sahai, A., Waters, B.: Attribute-based encryption for circuits from multilinear maps. In: Canetti and Garay [10], pp. 479–499

25. Garg, S., Gentry, C., Sahai, A., Waters, B.: Witness encryption and its applications. In: Boneh, D., Roughgarden, T., Feigenbaum, J. (eds.) 45th ACM STOC, pp. 467–476. ACM Press, June 2013

26. Garg, S., Mukherjee, P., Srinivasan, A.: Obfuscation without the vulnerabilities of multilinear maps. Cryptology ePrint Archive, Report 2016/390 (2016)

27. Gennaro, R., Robshaw, M. (eds.): CRYPTO 2015, Part I. LNCS, vol. 9215. Springer, Heidelberg (2015). https://doi.org/10.1007/978-3-662-47989-6

28. Gentry, C., Gorbunov, S., Halevi, S.: Graph-induced multilinear maps from lattices. In: Dodis and Nielsen [17], pp. 498–527

29. Goldwasser, S., Rothblum, G.N.: On best-possible obfuscation. In: Vadhan, S.P. (ed.) TCC 2007. LNCS, vol. 4392, pp. 194–213. Springer, Heidelberg (2007). https://doi.org/10.1007/978-3-540-70936-7_11

30. Groth, J., Sahai, A.: Efficient non-interactive proof systems for bilinear groups. In: Smart, N. (ed.) EUROCRYPT 2008. LNCS, vol. 4965, pp. 415–432. Springer, Heidelberg (2008). https://doi.org/10.1007/978-3-540-78967-3_24

31. Groth, J., Sahai, A.: Efficient noninteractive proof systems for bilinear groups. SIAM J. Comput. **41**(5), 1193–1232 (2012)

32. Hofheinz, D., Kiltz, E.: Programmable hash functions and their applications. In: Wagner, D. (ed.) CRYPTO 2008. LNCS, vol. 5157, pp. 21–38. Springer, Heidelberg (2008). https://doi.org/10.1007/978-3-540-85174-5_2

33. Hohenberger, S., Sahai, A., Waters, B.: Full domain hash from (leveled) multilinear maps and identity-based aggregate signatures. In: Canetti and Garay [9], pp. 494–512

34. Langlois, A., Stehlé, D., Steinfeld, R.: GGHLite: more efficient multilinear maps from ideal lattices. In: Nguyen, P.Q., Oswald, E. (eds.) EUROCRYPT 2014. LNCS, vol. 8441, pp. 239–256. Springer, Heidelberg (2014). https://doi.org/10.1007/978-3-642-55220-5_14

35. Lin, H.: Indistinguishability obfuscation from DDH on 5-linear maps and locality-5 PRGs. Cryptology ePrint Archive, Report 2016/1096 (2016)

36. Lin, H., Tessaro, S.: Indistinguishability obfuscation from bilinear maps and block-wise local PRGs. Cryptology ePrint Archive, Report 2017/250 (2017)

37. Miles, E., Sahai, A., Zhandry, M.: Annihilation attacks for multilinear maps: cryptanalysis of indistinguishability obfuscation over GGH13. In: Robshaw and Katz [41], pp. 629–658

38. Oswald, E., Fischlin, M. (eds.): EUROCRYPT 2015, Part II. LNCS, vol. 9057. Springer, Heidelberg (2015). https://doi.org/10.1007/978-3-662-46803-6

39. Paneth, O., Sahai, A.: On the equivalence of obfuscation and multilinear maps. Cryptology ePrint Archive, Report 2015/791 (2015)

40. Pass, R., Seth, K., Telang, S.: Indistinguishability obfuscation from semantically-secure multilinear encodings. In: Garay and Gennaro [21], pp. 500–517

41. Robshaw, M., Katz, J. (eds.): CRYPTO 2016, Part II. LNCS, vol. 9815. Springer, Heidelberg (2016). https://doi.org/10.1007/978-3-662-53008-5

42. Sahai, A., Waters, B.: How to use indistinguishability obfuscation: deniable encryption, and more. In: Shmoys, D.B. (eds.) 46th ACM STOC, pp. 475–484. ACM Press, May/June 2014

43. Zhang, F., Safavi-Naini, R., Susilo, W.: An efficient signature scheme from bilinear pairings and its applications. In: Bao, F., Deng, R., Zhou, J. (eds.) PKC 2004. LNCS, vol. 2947, pp. 277–290. Springer, Heidelberg (2004). https://doi.org/10.1007/978-3-540-24632-9_20

Protocols

Hashing Solutions Instead of Generating Problems: On the Interactive Certification of RSA Moduli

Benedikt Auerbach[1] and Bertram Poettering[2(✉)]

[1] Ruhr University Bochum, Bochum, Germany
benedikt.auerbach@rub.de
[2] Royal Holloway, University of London, London, UK
bertram.poettering@rhul.ac.uk

Abstract. Certain RSA-based protocols, for instance in the domain of group signatures, require a prover to convince a verifier that a set of RSA parameters is well-structured (e.g., that the modulus is the product of two distinct primes and that the exponent is co-prime to the group order). Various corresponding proof systems have been proposed in the past, with different levels of generality, efficiency, and interactivity.

This paper proposes two new proof systems for a wide set of properties that RSA and related moduli might have. The protocols are particularly efficient: The necessary computations are simple, the communication is restricted to only one round, and the exchanged messages are short. While the first protocol is based on prior work (improving on it by reducing the number of message passes from four to two), the second protocol is novel. Both protocols require a random oracle.

1 Introduction

A common property of cryptographic primitives in the domain of public-key cryptography (PKC) is that there is, in most cases, a natural distinction between a secret-key holder (SKH) and a public-key holder (PKH). For instance, in the digital signature (DS) context the SKH is the signer, and in public-key encryption (PKE) the SKH is the receiver; the verifier and the sender, respectively, are PKHs. The security properties of such schemes are typically focused on protecting primarily the SKH: In the signature context, unforgeability means that the signer cannot be impersonated by an adversary, and security notions for PKE require that messages encrypted to the receiver remain confidential. Thus, naturally, the SKH has a vital interest in its keys being properly generated, i.e., in a way covered by the security model, while this is only of secondary importance to the PKH.

In some PKC applications, however, also parties not holding the secret key might require assurance about that the key material has been generated in a

The full version of this article can be found in the IACR eprint archive as article 2018/013.

proper way. Typical examples arise in multi-party settings where the SKH manages a set of mutually distrusting parties who require protection from each other. For instance, in group signature schemes there is a group manager that issues certificates to registered parties, allowing them to sign messages on behalf of the whole group. While the resulting signatures should in principle be anonymous (cannot be linked to the particular signer), to prevent misuse there is often a traceability feature that allows the group manager to revoke the anonymity of a signer by creating a publicly-verifiable non-interactive proof that testifies that an indicated signer created a particular signature. If such a tracing option exists, the group manager should however not be able to falsely accuse a member of having signed some document. Many group signature schemes have been proposed in the past, but some of them (e.g., [1]) provably provide the latter property only if the group manager's keys are properly formed.[1] Other settings where trust in the secret keys generated by other parties is required include e-cash [13], cryptographic accumulators [9], undeniable signatures [18], double-authentication preventing signatures [2,27].

If a cryptographic scheme is solely based on the discrete logarithm problem (DLP) in a prime-order group, checking that keys of the type $X = g^x$ are well-formed is a trivial job (because *all* keys are well-formed). In the RSA setting the situation is more subtle: Given parameters (N, e), before assuming the security of the system the PKH might want to be convinced that the following questions can be answered affirmatively: (1) does N have precisely two prime divisors, (2) is N square-free, (3) is e coprime to $\varphi(N)$, i.e., is the mapping $m \mapsto m^e \bmod N$ a bijection (rather than lossy). Further, in some settings it might be necessary to know (4) whether $N = pq$ is a safe-prime modulus, i.e., whether $(p-1)/2$ and $(q-1)/2$ are primes by themselves. In settings specifically based on the hardness of factoring an additional question might be (5) whether squaring is a bijection on $\mathbf{QR}(N)$, more specifically (6) whether N is a Blum integer, and even more specifically (7) whether N is a Rabin–Williams integer.[2]

What are known approaches for convincing participants of the validity of predicates like the ones listed above? In some research papers corresponding arguments are just missing [1], or they are side-stepped by explicitly assuming honesty of key generation in the model [2]. Other papers refer to works like [10] that propose non-interactive proof systems for convincing verifiers of the validity of such relations. Concretely, [10] provides a NIZK framework for showing that an RSA number is the product of two safe primes. While powerful, the NIZK technique turns out to be practically not usable: The argument is over the intermediate results of four Miller–Rabin tests, a large number of range tests,

---

[1] Concretely, the protocol from [1] is presented in the safe-prime-RSA setting where $N = pq$ with $p = 2p' + 1, q = 2q' + 1$ such that p, q, p', q' are all primes. Some of the security properties of [1] hold in respect to the CDH problem in $\mathbb{Z}_N^*$. If $N = pq$ and thus $\mathbb{Z}_N^* = \mathbb{Z}_p^* \times \mathbb{Z}_q^*$ as it should, CDH is arguably hard. However, if the group manager announces a malformed N that is made up of a large number of (small) prime factors, solving CDH becomes easy.

[2] An RSA modulus $N = pq$ is a Blum integer if $p \equiv q \equiv 3 \pmod 4$, and it is a Rabin–Williams integer if $p \equiv 3 \pmod 8$ and $q \equiv 7 \pmod 8$.

etc., making the resulting proof string prohibitively long. Another approach is to pick prime numbers, moduli, and exponents in a certain way such that showing specific properties becomes feasible with number-theoretic techniques. Working with restricted parameter classes might however remove standard conformance and render implementations less efficient; for instance, the authors of [23] develop tools for showing that the mapping $m \mapsto m^e$ is a permutation, but these tools work only for fairly large values of e.

A third approach is tightly connected with the number-theoretic structures that motivate the requirements for the conditions listed above. (It is less general than the NIZK approach of [10] but usually does not require picking parameters in a specific way.) For instance, if an application of RSA requires that e be coprime to $\varphi(N)$ then this is for a specific reason, namely that information shall not be lost (but remain recoverable) when raising it to the power of e. Thus, instead of abstractly checking the $e \mid \varphi(N)$ relation, a corresponding check could be centered precisely around the information-loss property of the exponentiation operation. Our results are based on this strategy. Our techniques are inspired by, and improving on, prior work that we describe in detail in the following.

1.1   Interactive Zero-Knowledge Testing of Certain Relations

We reproduce results of Gennaro et al. [19]. As a running example, consider the question of whether $e \mid \varphi(N)$ holds, where N is an RSA modulus and e a small prime exponent. The relation holds if and only if the mapping $x \mapsto x^e \bmod N$ is bijective, characterized by all $y \in \mathbb{Z}_N^*$ having an eth root. This motivates an (interactive) protocol in which a prover convinces a verifier of relation $e \mid \varphi(N)$ by first letting the verifier pick a random value $y \in \mathbb{Z}_N^*$ and send it to the prover, then letting the prover (who knows the factorization of N) compute the eth root $x \in \mathbb{Z}_N^*$ of y and return it to the verifier, and finally letting the verifier accept if and only if $x^e = y \bmod N$. Prover and verifier may run multiple repetitions of this protocol, each time with a fresh challenge y. If the prover is able to return a valid response for each challenge, then the verifier is eventually convinced of the $e \mid \varphi(N)$ claim. Indeed, if $e \nmid \varphi(N)$, then only about one of e elements of $\mathbb{Z}_N^*$ have an eth root, so the protocol would detect this with high probability and a cheating prover would be caught.

Note that if the protocol would be deployed in precisely the way we described it, it would be of limited use. The reason is that it is not zero-knowledge; in particular, the prover would effectively implement an 'eth root oracle' for values y arbitrarily picked by the verifier, and this would likely harm the security of most applications. The proposal of [19] considers fixing this by making sure that challenges y are picked in a sufficiently random way. Concretely, the full protocol [19, Sect. 4.1] involves four message passes as follows: (1) the verifier picks $y_1 \in \mathbb{Z}_N^*$ and sends a commitment to this value to the prover, (2) the prover picks $y_2 \in \mathbb{Z}_N^*$ and sends this value to the verifier, (3) the verifier opens the commitment; both parties now compute $y \leftarrow y_1 y_2$, (4) the prover computes the eth root of y and sends it to the verifier. Unfortunately, the security analysis of [19] does not cover the full protocol; rather it restricts attention to only the last prover-to-verifier message and shows that it is zero-knowledge under the assumption that value y "can be thought as provided by a trusted third party" [19, Sect. 2.3]. We stress that a proof for the full four-message protocol is not immediate: Proving it zero-knowledge seems to require assuming an extractability property of the commitment scheme (so that the simulator can find 'the right' y_2 value), and the increased interactiveness calls for a fresh analysis in a concurrent communication setting anyway (if the protocol shall be of practical relevance). Neither of these issues is mentioned, let alone resolved, in [19].

1.2 Our Results

We construct practical protocols for convincing a verifier that certain relevant number-theoretic properties hold for RSA parameters. This includes statements on the number of prime factors of the modulus, its square-freeness, etc. Concretely, we propose two generic protocol frameworks that can be instantiated to become proof systems for many different relations: The first framework is based on [19] and effectively compresses the first three messages of the full protocols into a single one by, intuitively speaking, using a random oracle to implement the mentioned trusted third party. Precisely, continuing our running example, we let the verifier only specify a random seed r and let both parties derive value y as per $y \leftarrow H(r)$ via a random oracle. The random oracle model turns out to be strong enough to make the full protocol sound and zero-knowledge. Because of the reduced number of message passes, concurrency is not an issue.

The second framework is similar in spirit but uses the random oracle in a different and novel way. Here, the challenge y can be freely picked by the verifier (no specific distribution is required), the prover again computes the eth root x of it, but instead of sharing x with the verifier it only discloses the hash $H(x)$ of it. Note that, unless the verifier knows value x anyway, if H behaves like a random oracle then the hash value does not leak anything.

We highlight that the second protocol has two important advantages over the first: (1) The first protocol requires a random oracle that maps into the 'problem space' (here: challenge space $\mathbb{Z}_N^*$). However, for some number-theoretic tests, e.g., whether N is a Blum integer, the problem space we (and [19]) work with is $\mathbf{QR}(N)$, i.e., the set of quadratic residues modulo N, and for such spaces it is unclear how to construct a random oracle mapping into them. Note that, in contrast, the second protocol does not require hashing into any particular set. (2) Some number-theoretic relations allow for an easier check when the second framework is used. For instance, identifying Blum integers involves the prover computing the four square roots that quadratic residues always have. In the first protocol framework, returning all four square roots is prohibitive as this would immediately allow for factorizing N. In the second framework, however, hash values of all square roots can be returned without doing harm to security.

Please consider Sect. 5 for the full list of number-theoretic properties for which we provide a proof system.

1.3   Related Work

We note that techniques similar to ours appear implicitly or explicitly in a couple of prior works. For instance, the validation of RSA parameters is a common challenge in password-based key agreement; in particular, adversaries might announce specially crafted parameters (N, e) that would lead to partial password exposure. The work of Zhu et al. [34] addresses this, but without a formal analysis, by pursuing approaches that are similar to our second protocol instantiated with one particular number-theoretic relation. The work of [28] provides a security analysis of [34]. (It seems, however, that the analysis is incomplete: The output length of the hash function does not appear in the theorem statement, but for short output lengths the statement is obviously wrong.) We conclude by noting that both [28,34], and also a sequence of follow-up works in the domain of password-based key agreement, employ variants of our two protocols in an ad-hoc fashion, and not at the generic level and for the large number of number-theoretic problems as we do.

A higher level of abstraction, also in the domain of password-based key agreement, can be found in the work of Catalano et al. [11]. Their work considers exclusively our first approach. Further, while considering soundness and zero-knowledge definitions for language problems, their constructions are not on that level but directly targeting specific number-theoretic problems.

Considering proof systems not relying on random oracles, basically any desired property of an RSA modulus can be proven by employing general zero-knowledge proof systems for NP languages [8, 20, 21]. However, these protocols are usually less efficient than proof systems designed to establish a particular property. Thus a vast amount of papers provides systems of the latter type. Targeted properties include that an RSA modulus N has factors of approximately equal size [6, 12, 16, 17, 24] or is the product of two safe primes [10]. The approach of having the prover provide solutions to number-theoretic problems is taken in several proof systems. Concretely, there are protocols of this type proving that N is square-free [7,19], has at most two prime factors [5, 19, 25, 29], satisfies a weakened definition of Blum integer [5, 29], is the product of two almost strong primes [19]. A shortcoming common to the protocols deciding whether N has at most two prime factors is that they either have a two-sided error or have to impose additional restrictions on N, the first leading to an increased number of repetitions of the protocol in order to achieve security, the latter to artificially restricted choices of N.

Bellare and Yung [3] show that any trapdoor permutation can be certified, i.e., they provide a protocol to prove that a function is invertible on an overwhelming fraction of its range. Kakvi et al. [23] show that given an RSA modulus N and an exponent e such that $e \geq N^{1/4}$ Coppersmith's method can be used to efficiently determine whether the RSA function $x \mapsto x^e$ defines a permutation on $\mathbb{Z}_N^*$. However, their result does not apply to exponents of size smaller than $N^{1/4}$. A proof for RSA key generation with verifiable randomness is given in [22].

The protocol makes use of the protocols of [7, 29] as subroutines and relies on a trusted third party. Benhamouda et al. [4] provide a protocol proving in the random oracle model that at least two of the factors of a number N were generated using a particular prime number generator. However, in order to achieve security the construction requires N to be the product of many factors, which usually is prohibitive in the RSA setting.

We note that a topic in cryptography somewhat connected to our work is the fraudulent creation of parameters. More specifically, the works in [30–33] consider Kleptography, i.e., the creation of asymmetric key pairs by an adversary-modified generation algorithm such that, using a trapdoor, the adversary can recover the secret key from the public key. Preventing such attacks is not the goal of our work, and our protocols will indeed not succeed in catching properly performed Kleptography.

By nothing-up-my-sleeves (NUMS) parameter generation one subsumes techniques to propose parameters for cryptosystems in an explainable and publicly reproducible way. For instance, the internal constants of the hash functions of the SHA family are derived from the digits of the square and cube roots of small prime numbers, making the existence of trapdoors (e.g., for finding collisions) rather unlikely. While we do not advise against NUMS techniques, we note that using them restricts freedom in parameter generation and thus might break standard conformance and lead to less efficient systems. Moreover, and more relevantly in the context of our work, NUMS techniques typically apply to DL-based cryptosystems and not to RSA-based ones.

1.4   Organization

The overall focus of this work is on providing practical methods for proving certain properties of RSA-like parameter sets. Our interactive proof systems, however, follow novel design principles that promise finding application also outside of the number-theoretic domain. We thus approach our goal in a layered fashion, by first exposing our proof protocols such that they work for abstract formulations of problems and corresponding solutions, and then showing how these formalizations can be instantiated with the number-theoretic relations we are interested in.

More concretely, the structure of this article is as follows: In Sect. 2 we fix notation and recall some general results from number theory. In Sect. 3 we formulate a variant of the is-word-in-language problem and connect it to problems and solutions in some domain; we further introduce the concept of a challenge-response protocol for proving solutions of the word problem. In Sect. 4 we study two such protocols: Hash-then-Solve, which is inspired by the work of [19], and Solve-then-Hash, which is novel. Finally, in Sect. 5 we show how RSA-related properties can be expressed as instances of our general framework so that they become accessible by our proof systems.

2 Preliminaries

We fix notation and recall basic facts from number theory.

2.1 Notation

Parts of this article involve the specification of program code. In such code we use assignment operator '←' when the assigned value results from a constant expression (including from the output of a deterministic algorithm), and we write '←$_s$' when the value is either sampled uniformly at random from a finite set or is the output of a randomized algorithm. In a security experiment, the event that some algorithm A outputs the value v is denoted with $A \Rightarrow v$. In particular, $\Pr[A \Rightarrow 1]$ denotes the probability, taken over the coins of A, that A outputs value 1. We use bracket notation to denote associative arrays (a data structure that implements a 'dictionary'). For instance, for an associative array A the instruction $A[7] \leftarrow 3$ assigns value 3 to memory position 7, and the expression $A[2] = 5$ tests whether the value at position 2 is equal to 5. Associative arrays can be indexed with elements from arbitrary sets. When assigning lists to each other, with '_' we mark "don't-care" positions. For instance, $(a, \_) \leftarrow (9, 4)$ is equivalent to $a \leftarrow 9$ (value 4 is discarded). We use the ternary operator known from the C programming language: If C is a Boolean condition and e_1, e_2 are arbitrary expressions, the expression "C ? e_1 : e_2" evaluates to e_1 if C holds, and to e_2 if C does not hold. We further use Iverson brackets to convert Booleans to numerical values. That is, writing "$[C]$" is equivalent to writing "C ? 1 : 0". If A is a randomized algorithm we write $[A(x)]$ for the set of outputs it produces with non-zero probability if invoked on input x. If u, v are (row) vectors of values, $u \| v$ denotes their concatenation, i.e., the vector whose first elements are those of u, followed by those of v. We use symbol $\uplus$ to indicate when the union of two sets is a disjoint union.

2.2 Number Theory

We write $\mathbb{N} = \{1, 2, 3, \ldots\}$ and $\mathbb{P} \subseteq \mathbb{N}$ for the set of natural numbers and prime numbers, respectively. For every natural number $N \in \mathbb{N}$ we denote the set of prime divisors of N with $\mathbb{P}(N)$. Thus, for any $N \in \mathbb{N}$ there exists a unique family $(\nu_p)_{p \in \mathbb{P}(N)}$ of multiplicities $\nu_p \in \mathbb{N}$ such that

$$N = \prod_{p \in \mathbb{P}(N)} p^{\nu_p}.$$

We denote with $\mathrm{odd}(N)$ the 'odd part' of N, i.e., what remains of N after all factors 2 are removed; formally, $\mathrm{odd}(N) = \prod_{p \in \mathbb{P}(N), p \neq 2} p^{\nu_p}$.

Consider $N \in \mathbb{N}$ and the ring $\mathbb{Z}_N = \mathbb{Z}/N\mathbb{Z}$. The multiplicative group $\mathbb{Z}_N^*$ of $\mathbb{Z}_N$ has order $\varphi(N) = \prod_{p \in \mathbb{P}(N)} (p-1) p^{\nu_p - 1}$, where φ is Euler's totient function. By the Chinese Remainder Theorem (CRT) there exists a ring isomorphism

$$\psi \colon \mathbb{Z}_N \overset{\sim}{\longrightarrow} \underset{p \in \mathbb{P}(N)}{\times} \mathbb{Z}_{p^{\nu_p}}.$$

For $N, e \in \mathbb{N}$ consider the exponentiation mapping $x \mapsto x^e \bmod N$. This mapping is 1-to-1 on $\mathbb{Z}_N^*$ iff $\gcd(e, \varphi(N)) = 1$. The general statement, that holds for all N, e, is that the exponentiation mapping is L-to-1 for

$$L = \prod_{p \in \mathbb{P}(N)} \gcd(e, \varphi(p^{\nu_p})). \tag{1}$$

We write $\mathbf{QR}(N)$ for the (group of) quadratic residues (i.e., squares) modulo N.

3   Challenge-Response Protocols for Word Problems

We define notions of languages, statements, witnesses, and a couple of algorithms that operate on such objects. We then introduce the notion of a challenge-response protocol for the word problem in such a setting.

3.1   Associating Problems with the Words of a Language

STATEMENTS, CANDIDATES, WITNESSES. Let Σ be an alphabet and let $\mathcal{L} \subseteq \mathcal{U} \subseteq \Sigma^*$ be languages. We assume that deciding membership in $\mathcal{U}$ is efficient, while for $\mathcal{L}$ this might not be the case. Each element $x \in \Sigma^*$ is referred to as a *statement*. A statement x is a *candidate* if $x \in \mathcal{U}$. A statement x is *valid* if $x \in \mathcal{L}$; otherwise, it is *invalid*. (Thus, in general there coexist valid and invalid candidates.) For all candidates x we assume a (possibly empty) set of witnesses $\mathcal{W}_x$ such that valid candidates are characterized by having a witness: $\forall x \in \mathcal{U} \colon |\mathcal{W}_x| \geq 1 \iff x \in \mathcal{L}$.

RELATING PROBLEMS WITH CANDIDATES. For all candidates $x \in \mathcal{U}$ let $\mathcal{P}_x$ be a problem space and $\mathcal{S}_x$ a solution space, where we require that deciding membership in $\mathcal{P}_x$ is efficient. Let $\mathcal{R}el_x \subseteq \mathcal{P}_x \times \mathcal{S}_x$ be a relation that (abstractly) matches problems with solutions. For any problem $P \in \mathcal{P}_x$ we write $\mathcal{S}ol_x(P) := \{S \mid (P, S) \in \mathcal{R}el_x\} \subseteq \mathcal{S}_x$ for the set of its solutions. Not necessarily all problems are solvable, so we partition the problem space as $\mathcal{P}_x = \mathcal{P}_x^+ \uplus \mathcal{P}_x^-$ such that precisely the elements of $\mathcal{P}_x^+$ have solutions: $P \in \mathcal{P}_x^+ \iff |\mathcal{S}ol_x(P)| \geq 1$ and, equivalently, $P \in \mathcal{P}_x^- \iff \mathcal{S}ol_x(P) = \emptyset$. We extend relation $\mathcal{R}el_x$ to $\mathcal{R}el_x^* := \mathcal{R}el_x \cup (\mathcal{P}_x^- \times \{\bot\})$ by marking problems without solution with the special value $\bot$, and we extend notion $\mathcal{S}ol_x$ to $\mathcal{S}ol_x^*$ such that for all $P \in \mathcal{P}_x^-$ we have $\mathcal{S}ol_x^*(P) = \{\bot\}$. We require that every candidate has at least one problem-solution pair: $\forall x \in \mathcal{U} \colon |\mathcal{R}el_x| \geq 1$.

We assume four efficient algorithms, Verify, Sample, Sample*, and Solve, that operate on these sets. Deterministic algorithm Verify implements for all candidates the indicator function of $\mathcal{R}el$, i.e., decides whether a problem and a solution are matching. More precisely, Verify takes a candidate $x \in \mathcal{U}$, a problem $P \in \mathcal{P}_x$, and a potential solution $S \in \mathcal{S}_x$ for P, and outputs a bit that indicates whether (P, S) is contained in $\mathcal{R}el_x$ or not. Formally, $\forall x \in \mathcal{U}, (P, S) \in \mathcal{P}_x \times \mathcal{S}_x \colon \mathrm{Verify}(x, P, S) = 1 \iff (P, S) \in \mathcal{R}el_x$. Algorithm Sample is randomized, takes a candidate $x \in \mathcal{U}$, and outputs a (matching) problem-solution pair $(P, S) \in \mathcal{R}el_x$. Algorithm Sample* is randomized, takes a candidate $x \in \mathcal{U}$, and outputs a pair $(P, S) \in \mathcal{R}el_x^*$ (note that $S = \perp$ if $P \in \mathcal{P}_x^-$). Finally, deterministic algorithm Solve takes a (valid) statement $x \in \mathcal{L}$, a witness $w \in \mathcal{W}_x$ for it, and a problem $P \in \mathcal{P}_x$, and outputs the subset of $\mathcal{S}_x$ that contains *all* solutions of P. (If no solution exists, Solve outputs the empty set.) Formally, $\forall x \in \mathcal{L}, w \in \mathcal{W}_x, P \in \mathcal{P}_x \colon \mathrm{Solve}(x, w, P) = \mathcal{S}ol_x(P)$.

If we write $\mathcal{P} = \bigcup \mathcal{P}_x$, $\mathcal{S} = \bigcup \mathcal{S}_x$, $\mathcal{R}el = \bigcup \mathcal{R}el_x$, $\mathcal{R}el^* = \bigcup \mathcal{R}el_x^*$, $\mathcal{W} = \bigcup \mathcal{W}_x$, where the unions are over all $x \in \mathcal{U}$, a shortcut notation for the syntax of the four algorithms is

$$
\begin{array}{rclcl}
\mathcal{U} \times \mathcal{P} \times \mathcal{S} & \rightarrow & \text{Verify} & \rightarrow & \{0, 1\} \\
\mathcal{U} & \rightarrow & \text{Sample} & \rightarrow_{\$} & \mathcal{R}el \\
\mathcal{U} & \rightarrow & \text{Sample}^* & \rightarrow_{\$} & \mathcal{R}el^* \\
\mathcal{L} \times \mathcal{W} \times \mathcal{P} & \rightarrow & \text{Solve} & \rightarrow & \text{Powerset}(\mathcal{S})
\end{array}
$$

NUMBER OF SOLUTIONS, SPECTRUM, SOLVABLE-PROBLEM DENSITY. Note that different problems $P \in \mathcal{P}^+$ have, in general, different numbers of solutions. For any set $\mathcal{M} \subseteq \mathcal{U}$ of candidates, the *spectrum* $\#\mathcal{M}$ collects the cardinalities of the solution sets of all solvable problems associated with the candidates listed in $\mathcal{M}$. Formally,

$$
\#\mathcal{M} := \{ |\mathcal{S}ol_x(P)| : x \in \mathcal{M}, P \in \mathcal{P}_x^+ \}.
$$

Consequently, $\max \#\mathcal{L}$ is the largest number of solutions that solvable problems associated with valid candidates might have, and $\min \#(\mathcal{U} \setminus \mathcal{L})$ is the smallest number of solutions of solvable problems associated with invalid candidates. Further, for a set $\mathcal{M} \subseteq \mathcal{U}$ the *solvable-problem density distribution* $\Delta \mathcal{M}$, defined as

$$
\Delta \mathcal{M} := \{ |\mathcal{P}_x^+|/|\mathcal{P}_x| : x \in \mathcal{M} \},
$$

indicates the fractions of problems that are solvable (among the set of all problems), for all candidates in $\mathcal{M}$. Most relevant in this article are the derived quantities $\min \Delta \mathcal{L}$ and $\max \Delta(\mathcal{U} \setminus \mathcal{L})$.

UNIFORMITY NOTIONS FOR SAMPLING ALGORITHMS. For the two sampling algorithms defined above we introduce individual measures of quality. For Sample we say it is *problem-uniform* (on invalid candidates) if for all $x \in \mathcal{U} \setminus \mathcal{L}$ the problem output by $\mathrm{Sample}(x)$ is uniformly distributed in $\mathcal{P}_x^+$. Formally, for all $x \in \mathcal{U} \setminus \mathcal{L}, P' \in \mathcal{P}_x^+$ we require that

$$
\Pr[(P, \_) \leftarrow_{\$} \mathrm{Sample}(x) : P = P'] = 1/|\mathcal{P}_x^+|.
$$

Further we say that Sample is *solution-uniform* (on invalid candidates) if for all $x \in \mathcal{U} \setminus \mathcal{L}$ and each pair (P, S) output by $\mathrm{Sample}(x)$, solution S is uniformly distributed among all solutions for P. Formally, we require that for all $x \in \mathcal{U} \setminus \mathcal{L}, (P', S') \in [\mathrm{Sample}(x)]$ we have

$$
\Pr[(P, S) \leftarrow_{\$} \mathrm{Sample}(x) : S = S' \mid P = P'] = 1/|\mathcal{S}ol_x(P')|.
$$

For Sample* we say it is *problem-uniform* (on valid candidates) if for all $x \in \mathcal{L}$ the problem output by Sample*(x) is uniformly distributed in $\mathcal{P}_x$. Formally, for all $x \in \mathcal{L}, P' \in \mathcal{P}_x$ we require that

$$\Pr[(P,\_) \leftarrow_\$ \text{Sample}^*(x) : P = P'] = 1/|\mathcal{P}_x|.$$

Further we say that Sample* is *solution-uniform* (on valid candidates) if for all $x \in \mathcal{L}$ and each pair (P, S) output by Sample*(x), the solution S is uniformly distributed among all solutions of P (if a solution exists at all, i.e., if $S \neq \perp$). Formally, we require that for all $x \in \mathcal{L}, (P', S') \in [\text{Sample}^*(x)]$ we have

$$\Pr[(P, S) \leftarrow_\$ \text{Sample}^*(x) : S = S' \mid P = P'] = 1/|\mathcal{Sol}_x^*(P')|.$$

3.2   Challenge-Response Protocols

In the context of Sect. 3.1, a *challenge-response protocol* (CRP) for $(\mathcal{L}, \mathcal{U})$ specifies a (verifier) state space $\mathcal{St}$, a challenge space $\mathcal{Ch}$, a response space $\mathcal{Rsp}$, and efficient algorithms V_1, P, V_2 such that $V = (V_1, V_2)$ implements a stateful verifier and P implements a (stateless) prover. In more detail, algorithm V_1 is randomized, takes a candidate $x \in \mathcal{U}$, and returns a pair (st, c), where $st \in \mathcal{St}$ is a state and $c \in \mathcal{Ch}$ a challenge. Prover P, on input of a valid statement $x \in \mathcal{L}$, a corresponding witness $w \in \mathcal{W}_x$, and a challenge $c \in \mathcal{Ch}$, returns a response $r \in \mathcal{Rsp}$. Finally, deterministic algorithm V_2, on input a state $st \in \mathcal{St}$ and a response $r \in \mathcal{Rsp}$, outputs a bit that indicates acceptance (1) or rejection (0). An overview of the algorithms' syntax is as follows.

$$
\begin{array}{ccccc}
\mathcal{U} & \rightarrow & V_1 & \rightarrow_\$ & \mathcal{St} \times \mathcal{Ch} \\
\mathcal{L} \times \mathcal{W} \times \mathcal{Ch} & \rightarrow & P & \rightarrow_\$ & \mathcal{Rsp} \\
\mathcal{St} \times \mathcal{Rsp} & \rightarrow & V_2 & \rightarrow & \{0,1\}
\end{array}
$$

We define the following correctness and security properties for CRPs.

Correctness. Intuitively, a challenge-response protocol is correct if honest provers convince honest verifiers of the validity of valid statements. Formally, we say a CRP is δ-*correct* if for all valid candidates $x \in \mathcal{L}$ and corresponding witnesses $w \in \mathcal{W}_x$ we have

$$\Pr\left[(st, c) \leftarrow_\$ V_1(x); r \leftarrow_\$ P(x, w, c) : V_2(st, r) \Rightarrow 1\right] \geq \delta.$$

If the CRP is 1-correct we also say it is perfectly correct.

Soundness. Intuitively, a challenge-response protocol is sound if (dishonest) provers cannot convince honest verifiers of the validity of invalid statements. Formally, a CRP is ε-*sound* if for all invalid candidates $x \in \mathcal{U} \setminus \mathcal{L}$ and all (potentially unbounded) algorithms P* we have

$$\Pr\left[(st, c) \leftarrow_\$ V_1(x); r \leftarrow_\$ P^*(x, c) : V_2(st, r) \Rightarrow 0\right] \geq \varepsilon.$$

If the CRP is 1-sound we also say it is perfectly sound. To quantity $1 - \varepsilon$ we also refer to as the soundness error.

Zero-knowledge. Intuitively, a challenge-response protocol is (perfectly) zero-knowledge if (dishonest) verifiers do not learn anything from interacting with (honest) provers, beyond the fact that the statement is valid. Formally, a CRP is *(perfectly) zero-knowledge* if there exists a simulator S such that for all (potentially unbounded) distinguishers D, all valid candidates $x \in \mathcal{L}$, and all corresponding witnesses $w \in \mathcal{W}_x$, we have

$$|\Pr[\mathrm{D}^{\mathrm{P}(x,w,\cdot)} \Rightarrow 1] - \Pr[\mathrm{D}^{\mathrm{S}(x,\cdot)} \Rightarrow 1]| = 0.$$

Here, with $\mathrm{P}(x,w,\cdot)$ and $\mathrm{S}(x,\cdot)$ we denote oracles that invoke the prover algorithm P on input x,w,c and the simulator S on input x,c, respectively, where challenge c is in both cases provided by distinguisher D on a call-by-call basis.

In Sect. 4 we study two frameworks for constructing challenge-response protocols of the described type. The analyses of the corresponding protocols will be in the random oracle model, meaning that the algorithms $\mathrm{V}_1, \mathrm{P}, \mathrm{V}_2$ have access to an oracle H implementing a function drawn uniformly from the set of all functions between some fixed domain and range. Also the above correctness and security definitions need corresponding adaptation by (1) extending the probability spaces to also include the random choice of H, and (2) giving all involved algorithms, i.e., $\mathrm{V}_1, \mathrm{P}, \mathrm{V}_2, \mathrm{P}^*, \mathrm{D}$, oracle access to H. In the zero-knowledge definition, simulator S simulates both P and H.

4   Constructing Challenge-Response Protocols

In Sect. 3 we linked the word decision problem of a language to challenge-response protocols (CRP). Concretely, if $\mathcal{L} \subseteq \mathcal{U}$ are languages, a corresponding CRP would allow a prover to convince a verifier that a given candidate statement is in $\mathcal{L}$ rather than in $\mathcal{U} \setminus \mathcal{L}$. In the current section we study two such protocols, both requiring a random oracle. The first protocol, **Hash-then-Solve**, is inspired by prior work but significantly improves on it, while the second protocol, **Solve-then-Hash**, is novel. The bounds on correctness and security of the two protocols are, in general, incomparable. In the following paragraphs we give a high-level overview of their working principles.

Let $x \in \mathcal{U}$ be a (valid or invalid) candidate statement. In the protocol of Sect. 4.1 a random oracle H is used to generate problem instances for x as per $P \leftarrow \mathrm{H}(r)$, where r is a random seed picked by the verifier. If P has a solution S, the prover recovers it and shares it with the verifier who accepts iff the solution is valid. (If P has multiple solutions, the prover picks one of them at random.) Note that solving problems is in general possible also for invalid candidates, but the idea behind this protocol is that it allows for telling apart elements of $\mathcal{L}$ and $\mathcal{U} \setminus \mathcal{L}$ if the fraction of solvable problems among the set of all problems associated with valid candidates is strictly bigger than the fraction of solvable problems among all problems associated with invalid candidates, i.e., if $\min \Delta\mathcal{L} > \max \Delta(\mathcal{U} \setminus \mathcal{L})$. (As we show in Sect. 5, this is the case for some interesting number-theoretic decision problems.)

We now turn to the protocol of Sect. 4.2. Here, the random oracle is not used to generate problems as above. Rather, the random oracle is used to hash solutions into bit strings. Concretely, the verifier randomly samples a problem P with corresponding solution S. It then sends P to the prover who derives the set of all solutions for it; this set obviously includes S. The prover hashes all these solutions and sends the set of resulting hash values to the verifier. The latter accepts if the hash value of S is contained in this set. Note that finding the set of all solutions for problems is in general possible also for invalid candidates, but the protocol allows for telling apart valid from invalid candidates if (solvable) problems associated with valid candidates have strictly less solutions than problems associated with invalid candidates, i.e., if $\max \#\mathcal{L} < \min \#(\mathcal{U} \setminus \mathcal{L})$. Indeed, if the verifier does not accept more hash values than the maximum number of solutions for valid statements, a cheating prover will make the verifier accept only with a limited probability, while in the valid case the verifier will always accept. (We again refer to Sect. 5 for number-theoretic problems that have the required property.)

Let us quickly compare the two approaches. In principle, whether they are applicable crucially depends on languages $\mathcal{L}, \mathcal{U}$ and the associated problem and solution spaces. Note that the random oracles are used in very different ways: in the first protocol to ensure a fair sampling of a problem such that no solution is known a priori (to neither party), and in the second protocol to hide those solutions from the verifier that the latter does not know anyway. That the random oracle in the first protocol has to map into the problem space might represent a severe technical challenge as for some relevant problem spaces it seems unfeasible to find a construction for such a random oracle.[3] In such cases the second protocol might be applicable.

4.1   A GMR-Inspired Protocol: Hash-then-Solve

A general protocol framework for showing that certain properties hold for a candidate RSA modulus (that it is square-free, Blum, etc.) was proposed by Gennaro, Micali, and Rabin in [19]. Recall from the discussion in the introduction that the full version of their protocol has a total of four message passes and involves both number-theoretic computations and the use of a commitment scheme. In this section we study a variant of this protocol where the commitment scheme is implemented via a random oracle. The benefit is that the protocol becomes more compact and less interactive. Concretely, the number of message passes decreases from four to two.

Let $\mathcal{L} \subseteq \mathcal{U} \subseteq \Sigma^*$ be as in Sect. 3.1, and let $l \in \mathbb{N}$ be a security parameter. Let $(H_x)_{x \in \mathcal{U}}$ be a family of hash functions (in the security reduction: random oracles) such that for each $x \in \mathcal{U}$ we have a mapping $H_x : \{0, 1\}^l \to \mathcal{P}_x$. Consider the challenge-response protocol with algorithms V_1, P, V_2 as specified in Fig. 1. The idea of the protocol is that the verifier picks a random seed r which it

---

[3] For instance if the problem space is the set of quadratic residues modulo some composite integer.

communicates to the prover and from which both parties deterministically derive a problem as per $P \leftarrow H_x(r)$. The prover, using its witness, computes the set $\mathbf{S}$ of all solutions of P, denotes one of them with S, and sends S to the verifier. (If P has no solution, the prover sends $\perp$.) The verifier accepts (meaning: concludes that $x \in \mathcal{L}$) iff $S \neq \perp$ and S is indeed a solution for P. Importantly, while the prover selects the solution S within set $\mathbf{S}$ in a deterministic way (so that for each seed r and thus problem P it consistently exposes the same solution even if queried multiple times), from the point of view of the verifier the solution S is picked uniformly at random from the set of all solutions of P. This behavior is implemented by letting the prover make its selection based on an additional random oracle that is made private to the prover by including the witness w in each query. Theorem 1 assesses the correctness and security of the protocol.

Protocol Hash-then-Solve

Verifier (on input $x \in \mathcal{U}$)	**Prover** (on input $x \in \mathcal{L}, w \in \mathcal{W}_x$)
00 $r \leftarrow_\$ \{0,1\}^l$	
01 Send r $\longrightarrow$	06 Receive r
	07 $P \leftarrow H_x(r)$
	08 $\mathbf{S} \leftarrow \text{Solve}(x, w, P)$
	09 $S \leftarrow (\mathbf{S} \neq \emptyset)$? $\$_P(\mathbf{S})$: $\perp$
02 Receive S $\longleftarrow$	10 Send S
03 If $S = \perp$: Return 0	
04 $P \leftarrow H_x(r)$	
05 Return Verify(x, P, S)	

Fig. 1. Hash-then-Solve: Random-oracle based version of the GMR protocol from [19]. Specifications of the three CRP algorithms can be readily extracted from the code: algorithm V_1 is in lines 00–01, algorithm V_2 is in lines 02–05, and algorithm P is in lines 06–10. The expression of the form $S \leftarrow \$_P(\mathbf{S})$ in line 09 is an abbreviation for $S \leftarrow \text{RO}(x, w, P, \mathbf{S})$, where $\text{RO}: \{0,1\}^* \to \mathbf{S}$ is a (private) random oracle.

Theorem 1. *The Hash-then-Solve protocol defined in Fig. 1 is δ-correct and ε-sound and perfectly zero-knowledge, where*

$$\delta = \min \Delta(\mathcal{L}) \qquad and \qquad \varepsilon = 1 - \max \Delta(\mathcal{U} \setminus \mathcal{L}),$$

if hash functions $(H_x)_{x \in \mathcal{U}}$ are modeled as random oracles. For this result we assume that the Sample* *algorithm is both problem-uniform and solution-uniform.*

Proof. Correctness. Let $x \in \mathcal{L}$ and $w \in \mathcal{W}_x$. Since H_x is modeled as a random oracle, problem P assigned in line 07 is uniformly distributed in $\mathcal{P}_x$. Set $\mathbf{S}$ from line 08 is empty if $P \in \mathcal{P}_x^-$ and contains elements if $P \in \mathcal{P}_x^+$. The probability that the prover outputs a solution, and that the verifier accepts it in line 05, is thus precisely $|\mathcal{P}_x^+|/|\mathcal{P}_x|$. A lower bound for this value is $\delta = \min \Delta(\mathcal{L})$.

Soundness. Let $x \in \mathcal{U} \setminus \mathcal{L}$. A necessary condition for the verifier to accept in line 05 is that there exists a solution to problem $P = \mathrm{H}_x(r)$, i.e., that $P \in \mathcal{P}_x^+$. Since H_x is modeled as a random oracle, P is uniformly distributed in $\mathcal{P}_x$. The probability of P having a solution is thus $|\mathcal{P}_x^+|/|\mathcal{P}_x|$. This value is at most $\max \Delta(\mathcal{U} \setminus \mathcal{L})$. Thus $\varepsilon = 1 - \max \Delta(\mathcal{U} \setminus \mathcal{L})$ is a lower bound for the probability of the verifier not accepting in a protocol run.

Zero-knowledge. We show that the protocol is zero-knowledge by specifying and analyzing a simulator S. Its code is in Fig. 2. The prover oracle $\mathrm{P}(x, w, \cdot)$ and the random oracle $\mathrm{H}_x(\cdot)$ are simulated by algorithms $\mathrm{P}_{\mathrm{sim}}$ and $\mathrm{H}_{\mathrm{sim}}$, respectively. Associative array $\mathbf{R}$ reflects the input-output map of the random oracle and is initialized such that all inputs map to special value $\perp$. If $\mathrm{H}_{\mathrm{sim}}$ is queried on a seed r, a fresh problem-solution pair is sampled using the Sample* algorithm, the pair is registered in $\mathbf{R}$, and the problem part is returned to the caller. Note that by the assumed problem-uniformity of Sample*(x) this is an admissible implementation of a random oracle that maps to set $\mathcal{P}_x$.

The task of the $\mathrm{P}_{\mathrm{sim}}$ algorithm is to return, for any seed r, a uniformly picked solution for the problem $P = \mathrm{H}_x(r)$; if no solution exists, the oracle shall return $\perp$. This is achieved by returning the solution part of the problem-solution pair that was sampled using Sample* when processing the random oracle query $\mathrm{H}_x(r)$. Note that this argument uses both the solution uniformity of Sample* and the fact that the P algorithm from Fig. 1 is deterministic and in particular always outputs the same solution if a seed is queried multiple times to a $\mathrm{P}(x, w, \cdot)$ prover. $\square$

Oracle $\mathrm{P}_{\mathrm{sim}}(r)$	**Oracle $\mathrm{H}_{\mathrm{sim}}(r)$**
00 If $\mathbf{R}[r] = \perp$:	06 If $\mathbf{R}[r] = \perp$:
01 $(P, S) \leftarrow_\$ \text{Sample*}(x)$	07 $(P, S) \leftarrow_\$ \text{Sample*}(x)$
02 $\mathbf{R}[r] \leftarrow (P, S)$	08 $\mathbf{R}[r] \leftarrow (P, S)$
03 $(P, S) \leftarrow \mathbf{R}[r]$	09 $(P, S) \leftarrow \mathbf{R}[r]$
04 If $S = \perp$: Return $\perp$	10 Return P
05 Return S	

Fig. 2. Simulator S. Associative array $\mathbf{R}$ is initialized as per $\mathbf{R}[\cdot] \leftarrow \perp$, i.e., such that all values initially map to $\perp$. Note that lines 00–02 become redundant if one requires (w.l.o.g.) that $\mathrm{H}_{\mathrm{sim}}(r)$ is always queried before $\mathrm{P}_{\mathrm{sim}}(r)$.

4.2   Our New Protocol: Solve-then-Hash

We propose a new challenge-response protocol for the word decision problem in languages. Like the one from Sect. 4.1 it uses a random oracle, but it does so in a quite different way: The random oracle is not used for generating problems, but for hashing solutions. The advantage is that constructing a random oracle that maps into a problem space might be difficult (for certain problem spaces), while hashing solutions to bit strings is always easy.

Let $\mathcal{L} \subseteq \mathcal{U} \subseteq \Sigma^*$ be as in Sect. 3.1. Let $\mathcal{H}$ be a finite set and H: $\{0,1\}^* \to \mathcal{H}$ a hash function (in the security reduction: a random oracle). The idea of the protocol is that the verifier samples a problem-solution pair (P, S) and communicates the problem to the prover, the latter then, using its witness, computes the sets $\mathbf{S}$ of all solutions of P and $\mathbf{h}$ of hash values of these solutions, and returns set $\mathbf{h}$ to the verifier, and the verifier finally checks whether the hash value h of S is contained in this set. An important detail is that the prover uses pseudorandom bit-strings to pad the returned set of hash values to constant-size: If $k = \max \#\mathcal{L}$ is the maximum number of solutions of problems associated with valid candidates, then the prover exclusively outputs sets $\mathbf{h}$ of this cardinality. The algorithms of the corresponding challenge-response protocol are specified in Fig. 3. (Note that when transmitting $\mathbf{h}$ from the prover to the verifier an encoding has to be chosen that hides the order in which elements were added to $\mathbf{h}$.) The analysis of our protocol is in Theorem 2. The main technical challenge of the proof is that it has to deal with collisions of the random oracle (two or more solutions might hash to the same string).

Protocol Solve-then-Hash

Verifier (on input $x \in \mathcal{U}$)		**Prover** (on input $x \in \mathcal{L}, w \in \mathcal{W}_x$)
00 $(P, S) \leftarrow_\$ \text{Sample}(x)$		
01 $h \leftarrow \text{H}(P, S)$		
02 Send P	$\longrightarrow$	06 Receive P (abort if $P \notin \mathcal{P}_x$)
		07 $\mathbf{S} \leftarrow \text{Solve}(x, w, P)$
		08 $\{S_1, \ldots, S_t\} \leftarrow \mathbf{S}$
		09 $h_1, \ldots, h_t \leftarrow \text{H}(P, S_1), \ldots, \text{H}(P, S_t)$
		10 $h_{t+1}, \ldots, h_k \leftarrow \$_P^{t+1}(\mathcal{H}), \ldots, \$_P^k(\mathcal{H})$
		11 $\mathbf{h} \leftarrow \{h_1, \ldots, h_k\}$
03 Receive $\mathbf{h}$	$\longleftarrow$	12 Send $\mathbf{h}$ (hiding the order of elements)
04 Require $|\mathbf{h}| \leq k$		
05 Return $[h \in \mathbf{h}]$		

Fig. 3. Solve-then-Hash: Our new challenge-response protocol. We assume $k = \max \#\mathcal{L}$. Specifications of the three CRP algorithms can be readily extracted from the code: algorithm V_1 is in lines 00–02, algorithm V_2 is in lines 03–05, and algorithm P is in lines 06–12. In line 08, the cardinality of set $\mathbf{S}$ is denoted with t. Expressions of the form $h \leftarrow \$_v^u(\mathcal{H})$ in line 10 are abbreviations for $h \leftarrow \text{RO}(x, w, u, v)$, where RO: $\{0,1\}^* \to \mathcal{H}$ is a (private) random oracle.

Theorem 2. Let $k = \max \#\mathcal{L}$, $m = \min \#(\mathcal{U} \setminus \mathcal{L})$, and $M = \max \#(\mathcal{U} \setminus \mathcal{L})$, such that $k \leq m \leq M$. Then the Solve-then-Hash protocol defined in Fig. 3 is perfectly correct and ε-sound and perfectly zero-knowledge, where

$$\varepsilon = 1 - \left(k/m + k/|\mathcal{H}| + (\min(M, q))^2/|\mathcal{H}| \right) \approx 1 - k/m,$$

if H is modeled as a random oracle and q is the maximum number of random oracle queries posed by any (dishonest) prover P*. For this result we assume that the Sample algorithm is both problem-uniform and solution-uniform.

Proof. Correctness. Let $x \in \mathcal{L}$ and $w \in \mathcal{W}_x$. Then for (P, S) from line 00 we have $S \in \mathbf{S}$ in line 07. Further, as $x \in \mathcal{L}$ we have $t \leq k = \max \#\mathcal{L}$ in line 08 and thus $|\mathbf{h}| \leq k$ in line 04 and $h \in \mathbf{h}$ in line 05. Thus V_2 accepts with probability 1.

Soundness. Let $x \in \mathcal{U} \setminus \mathcal{L}$ be an invalid candidate and P^* a (malicious) prover. Let *Win* denote the event that P^* succeeds in finding a response $\mathbf{h}$ such that verifier V_2 accepts, i.e. the event $\{(h, P) \leftarrow_\$ V_1(x); \mathbf{h} \leftarrow_\$ P^*(x, P) : V_2(h, \mathbf{h}) \Rightarrow 1\}$. Recall that $Sol_x(P)$ denotes the set of solutions of problem P, and let $S_1, \ldots, S_l \in Sol_x(P)$ denote the solutions to the problem on which P^* queries random oracle H, i.e., the elements such that P^* queries for $H(P, S_i)$ with $i \in \{1, \ldots, l\}$. We define $Col = \{\exists i \neq j : H(P, S_i) = H(P, S_j)\}$ as the event that the hash values of at least two of the queried solutions collide. We have

$$\Pr[Win] = \Pr[Win \mid Col] \Pr[Col] + \Pr[Win \mid \neg Col] \Pr[\neg Col]$$
$$\leq \Pr[Col] + \Pr[Win \mid \neg Col].$$

We conclude that $\Pr[Win] < k/m + k/|\mathcal{H}| + (\min(M, q))^2/|\mathcal{H}|$ by showing that

$$\text{(a) } \Pr[Col] < (\min(M, q))^2/|\mathcal{H}|$$

and

$$\text{(b) } \Pr[Win \mid \neg Col] \leq k/m + k/|\mathcal{H}|.$$

For claim (a), note that $x \in \mathcal{U} \setminus \mathcal{L}$ implies that the set $\mathcal{Rel}_x(P)$ of solutions of problem P has at most $\max \#(\mathcal{U} \setminus \mathcal{L}) = M$ elements. P^* makes at most q queries to H. Hence $l \leq \min(M, q)$. We obtain

$$\Pr[Col] = \Pr[\exists i \neq j : H(P, S_i) = H(P, S_j)]$$
$$\leq l^2 \Pr[H(P, S_1) = H(P, S_2)] \leq \min(M, q)^2/|\mathcal{H}|,$$

where the last two inequalities hold since H is modeled as a random oracle.

We conclude the proof by showing claim (b). Recall that S is the solution sampled alongside problem P. Since algorithm Sample is solution-uniform, S is distributed uniformly in $Sol_x(P)$, which implies that $H(P, S)$ is uniformly distributed in $\{H(P, S') : S' \in Sol_x(P)\}$. Note that $|Sol_x(P)| \geq m = \min \#(\mathcal{U} \setminus \mathcal{L})$ and that —conditioned on $\neg Col$— all values $H(P, S')$ that P^* knows are distinct. Conditioned on the events $S \in \{S_1, \ldots, S_l\}$ and $\neg Col$, prover P^* guesses $H(P, S)$ with probability at most $1/l$. If, on the other hand, $S \notin \{S_1, \ldots, S_l\}$, then $H(P, S)$ is uniformly distributed from P^*'s point of view. Hence its best chance of guessing it is $1/|\mathcal{H}|$. Note that $\Pr[S \in \{S_1, \ldots, S_l\}] \leq l/m$. Summing up —conditioned on $\neg Col$— P^*'s chance of correctly guessing $H(P, S)$ is bounded by $l/m \cdot 1/l + 1/|\mathcal{H}| = 1/m + 1/|\mathcal{H}|$. Event *Win* according to line 04 cannot occur if $\mathbf{h}$ contains more than k elements, so we obtain $\Pr[Win \mid \neg Col] \leq k/m + k/|\mathcal{H}|$.

Zero-knowledge. We show that the protocol is zero-knowledge by specifying and analyzing a simulator S. Its code is in Fig. 4. The prover oracle $P(x, w, \cdot)$ and the random oracle $H(\cdot, \cdot)$ are simulated by algorithms P_{sim} and H_{sim}, respectively. For oracle H we assume w.l.o.g. that it is not queried twice on the same input.

Initialization	Oracle $H_{sim}(P, S)$
00 For all $P \in \mathcal{P}_x$:	05 If $\text{Verify}(x, P, S) = 0$:
01 $\quad \mathbf{R}_U[P] \leftarrow \varepsilon$	06 $\quad h \leftarrow_\$ \mathcal{H}$; Return h
02 $\quad \mathbf{R}_F[P] \leftarrow \$^1_P(\mathcal{H}), \ldots, \$^k_P(\mathcal{H})$	07 $h_1, \ldots, h_{t-1} \| h_t, \ldots, h_k \leftarrow \mathbf{R}_U[P] \| \mathbf{R}_F[P]$
	08 $\mathbf{R}_U[P] \| \mathbf{R}_F[P] \leftarrow h_1, \ldots, h_t \| h_{t+1}, \ldots, h_k$
Oracle $P_{sim}(P)$	09 Return h_t
03 $\mathbf{h} \leftarrow \mathbf{R}_U[P] \| \mathbf{R}_F[P]$	
04 Return $\mathbf{h}$ (hiding the order of elements)	

Fig. 4. Simulator S for the protocol of Fig. 3. We require (w.l.o.g.) that $H_{sim}(\cdot)$ is queried at most once on each input. Expressions of the form $h \leftarrow \$^u_v(\mathcal{H})$ in line 02 are abbreviations for $h \leftarrow \text{RO}(u, v)$, where $\text{RO}: \{0, 1\}^* \to \mathcal{H}$ is a (private) random oracle. In line 07, the lengths of vectors $\mathbf{R}_U[P]$ and $\mathbf{R}_F[P]$ are $t - 1$ and $k - t + 1$, respectively. In line 08, the new lengths of vectors $\mathbf{R}_U[P]$ and $\mathbf{R}_F[P]$ are t and $k - t$, respectively.

Core components of our simulator are the associative arrays $\mathbf{R}_U[\cdot]$ and $\mathbf{R}_F[\cdot]$ that associate problems with used and fresh random hash values, respectively. The simulator starts with initializing for each problem a vector of k-many fresh hash values.[4] Oracle H_{sim} on input a problem-solution pair (P, S) checks whether S is a solution to P. If not, a random hash value is returned. Otherwise the vector of (fresh) hash values $\mathbf{R}_F[P]$ associated to P is retrieved. The first element of this vector is taken as the response of the random oracle query; however, before the response is output, the element is appended to the vector of (used) hash values $\mathbf{R}_U[P]$ associated to P. Note this procedure will never fail (i.e., never a value has to be taken from $\mathbf{R}_F[P]$ after the list is emptied) since there are at most $k = \max \#\mathcal{L}$ solutions to P. Queries to P_{sim} on input P are responded with the set $\mathbf{h}$ of all elements contained in $\mathbf{R}_F[P]$ and $\mathbf{R}_U[P]$, which by definition of H_{sim} stays unchanged throughout the simulation. Since these elements are initialized as random hash values, responses to queries to P_{sim} have the correct distribution. Furthermore, for every $S \in \mathcal{S}ol_x(P)$ we have that $H_{sim}(P, S)$ is contained in $P_{sim}(P)$. Summing up, the output of P_{sim} and H_{sim} is correctly distributed and simulator S provides distinguisher D with a perfect simulation of $P(x, w, \cdot)$. $\qquad \square$

4.3 Generalizing the Analysis of the Solve-then-Hash Protocol

We generalize the statement of Theorem 2, making it applicable to a broader class of languages. Recall that our protocol from Sect. 4.2 decides membership in a language $\mathcal{L} \subseteq \mathcal{U}$ if for every (invalid) candidate $x \in \mathcal{U} \setminus \mathcal{L}$ and every solvable problem $P \in \mathcal{P}_x^+$ the number $|\mathcal{S}ol_x(P)|$ of solutions to P exceeds the maximum number $\max \#\mathcal{L}$ of solutions to problems associated with valid candidates. We next relax this condition by showing that for soundness it already suffices if the

---

[4] Of course it is inefficient to assign to each $P \in \mathcal{P}_x$ a vector of values ahead of time. However, our code can easily be implemented in an equivalent form that uses lazy sampling.

expected value of $|Sol_x(P)|$ (over randomly sampled $P \in \mathcal{P}_x^+$) exceeds $\max \#\mathcal{L}$. In order to do so, we associate to $\mathcal{L}$ and $\mathcal{U}$ the function $\varepsilon_{\mathcal{L},\mathcal{U}} \colon [0,1] \to \mathbb{R}^+$ such that

$$\varepsilon_{\mathcal{L},\mathcal{U}}(\gamma) := \min\{\varepsilon' \mid \forall x \in \mathcal{U} \setminus \mathcal{L} \colon \Pr[P \leftarrow_\$ \mathcal{P}_x^+ : \max \#(\mathcal{L})/|Sol_x(P)| \le \varepsilon'] \ge \gamma\},$$

i.e., the function that associates to each probability value $\gamma \in [0,1]$ the smallest factor ε' such that for every invalid x a uniformly sampled problem with probability of at least γ has at least $\max \#(\mathcal{L})/\varepsilon'$ solutions.

In Theorem 3 we give a correspondingly refined soundness analysis of the Solve-then-Hash protocol. Note that, as the protocol itself did not change, the correctness and zero-knowledge properties do not require a new analysis. Note further that $\varepsilon_{\mathcal{L},\mathcal{U}}(1) = \max \#(\mathcal{L})/\min \#(\mathcal{U} \setminus \mathcal{L})$, and that thus the soundness analysis of Theorem 2 is just the special case of Theorem 3 where $\gamma = 1$.

Theorem 3. *Let* $k = \max \#\mathcal{L}$ *and* $M = \max \#(\mathcal{U} \setminus \mathcal{L})$ *such that* $k \le M$. *Then for every* $\gamma \in [0,1]$ *the Solve-then-Hash protocol defined in Fig. 3 is perfectly correct and* ε-*sound and perfectly zero-knowledge, where*

$$\varepsilon = 1 - \big(\varepsilon_{\mathcal{L},\mathcal{U}}(\gamma) + (1 - \gamma)/(1 - c) + k/|\mathcal{H}| + c\big) \approx \gamma - \varepsilon_{\mathcal{L},\mathcal{U}}(\gamma),$$

if H *is modeled as a random oracle,* q *is the maximum number of random oracle queries posed by any (dishonest) prover* P* *and* $c = (\min(M,q))^2/|\mathcal{H}|$. *For this result we assume that the* Sample *algorithm is both problem-uniform and solution-uniform.*

Proof. The correctness and zero-knowledge property of the protocol were already shown in the proof of Theorem 2. We thus show the bound on the soundness error. Fix $\gamma \in [0,1]$ and let $\varepsilon_{\mathcal{L},\mathcal{U}} = \varepsilon_{\mathcal{L},\mathcal{U}}(\gamma)$. Let $x \in \mathcal{U} \setminus \mathcal{L}$ be an invalid candidate and P* a (malicious) prover. Let Win denote the event that P* succeeds in finding a response $\mathbf{h}$ such that verifier V_2 accepts, i.e. the event $\{(h, P) \leftarrow_\$ V_1(x); \mathbf{h} \leftarrow_\$ P^*(x, P) : V_2(h, \mathbf{h}) \Rightarrow 1\}$. Recall that $Sol_x(P)$ denotes the set of solutions of problem P, and let $S_1, \ldots, S_l \in Sol_x(P)$ denote the solutions to the problem on which P* queries random oracle H, i.e., the elements such that P* queries for $H(P, S_i)$ with $i \in \{1, \ldots, l\}$. We define $Col = \{\exists i \neq j : H(P, S_i) = H(P, S_j)\}$ as the event that the hash values of at least two of the queried solutions collide. We have

$$\Pr[Win] = \Pr[Win \mid Col]\Pr[Col] + \Pr[Win \mid \neg Col]\Pr[\neg Col]$$
$$\le \Pr[Col] + \Pr[Win \mid \neg Col].$$

We conclude that $\Pr[Win] < \varepsilon_{\mathcal{L},\mathcal{U}} + (1 - \gamma)/(1 - c) + k/|\mathcal{H}| + c$ by showing that

$$\text{(a) } \Pr[Col] < (\min(M,q))^2/|\mathcal{H}| = c$$

and

$$\text{(b) } \Pr[Win \mid \neg Col] \le \varepsilon_{\mathcal{L},\mathcal{U}} + (1 - \gamma)/(1 - c) + k/|\mathcal{H}|.$$

Claim (a) follows as in the proof of Theorem 2. In order to prove (b) we denote by PG the event that the problem P given as input to P^* by the verifier is "good" in the sense of having many solutions, i.e. the event $\{\max \#(\mathcal{L})/|\mathcal{S}ol_x(P)| \leq \varepsilon_{\mathcal{L},\mathcal{U}}\}$. We have

$$\Pr[\mathit{Win} \mid \neg\mathit{Col}] = \Pr[\mathit{Win} \mid \neg\mathit{Col} \wedge PG]\Pr[PG \mid \neg\mathit{Col}]$$
$$+ \Pr[\mathit{Win} \mid \neg\mathit{Col} \wedge \neg PG]\Pr[\neg PG \mid \neg\mathit{Col}]$$
$$\leq \Pr[\mathit{Win} \mid \neg\mathit{Col} \wedge PG] + \Pr[\neg PG \mid \neg\mathit{Col}]$$
$$\leq \Pr[\mathit{Win} \mid \neg\mathit{Col} \wedge PG] + \Pr[\neg PG]/\Pr[\neg\mathit{Col}].$$

As stated above, we have $\Pr[\neg\mathit{Col}] \geq 1-c$. Further, by problem-uniformity, P is distributed uniformly on $\mathcal{P}_x^+$ and by the definition of $\varepsilon_{\mathcal{L},\mathcal{U}}$ we have $\Pr[\neg PG] \leq 1 - \gamma$. Hence $\Pr[\neg PG]/\Pr[\neg\mathit{Col}] \leq (1 - \gamma)/(1 - c)$ and it remains to show that $\Pr[\mathit{Win} \mid \neg\mathit{Col} \wedge PG] \leq \varepsilon_{\mathcal{L},\mathcal{U}} + k/|\mathcal{H}|$. Since S is sampled with (solution-uniform) Sample, it is distributed uniformly on $\mathcal{S}ol_x(P)$, which implies that $\mathrm{H}(P, S)$ is uniformly distributed on $\{\mathrm{H}(P, S') : S' \in \mathcal{S}ol_x(P)\}$. Recall that $k = \max \#\mathcal{L}$. If event PG occurs then $|\mathcal{S}ol_x(P)| \geq k/\varepsilon_{\mathcal{L},\mathcal{U}}$. Further —conditioned on $\neg\mathit{Col}$— all values $\mathrm{H}(P, S')$ that P^* knows are distinct. Conditioned on the events $S \in \{S_1, \dots, S_l\}$, PG and $\neg\mathit{Col}$ prover P^* guesses $\mathrm{H}(P, S)$ with probability at most $1/l$. If, on the other hand, $S \notin \{S_1, \dots, S_l\}$, then from P^*'s point of view $\mathrm{H}(P, S)$ is uniformly distributed on $\mathcal{H}$. Hence in this case its best chance of guessing it is $1/|\mathcal{H}|$. Note that $\Pr[S \in \{S_1, \dots, S_l\} \mid \neg\mathit{Col} \wedge PG] \leq l \cdot \varepsilon_{\mathcal{L},\mathcal{U}}/k$. Summing up —conditioned on $\neg\mathit{Col}$ and PG— prover P^*'s chance of correctly guessing $\mathrm{H}(P, S)$ is bounded by $l\varepsilon_{\mathcal{L},\mathcal{U}}/k \cdot 1/l + 1/|\mathcal{H}| = \varepsilon_{\mathcal{L},\mathcal{U}}/k + 1/|\mathcal{H}|$. Event Win according to line 04 cannot occur if $\mathbf{h}$ contains more than k elements, so we obtain $\Pr[\mathit{Win} \mid \neg\mathit{Col}] \leq \varepsilon_{\mathcal{L},\mathcal{U}} + k/|\mathcal{H}|$. $\qquad\square$

5   Challenge-Response Protocols in the Domain of Number-Theory

We provide several protocols to prove number theoretic properties of a number $N \in \mathbb{N}$, the corresponding witness being the factorization of N. More formally, we consider the universe

$$\mathcal{L}_{\mathrm{odd}} = \{N \in \mathbb{N} : \nu_2 = 0; |\mathbb{P}(N)| \geq 2\}$$

of odd numbers, which have at least two prime factors. Note that $\mathcal{L}_{\mathrm{odd}}$ can be efficiently decided. We associate problem and solution spaces as defined in Sect. 3.1 to several languages $\mathcal{L} \subseteq \mathcal{L}_{\mathrm{odd}}$, hence obtaining membership checking protocols via Theorems 1 and 2. In most cases the problem and solution space associated to a statement $N \in \mathcal{L}_{\mathrm{odd}}$ are defined as $\mathbb{Z}_N^*$, while the defining relation $\mathcal{R}el_N$ for problem b and solution a is of the type $b \equiv a^e \bmod N$, where the exponent e is chosen according to the number theoretic property of N we want to prove. Equation (1) of Sect. 2.2 serves as a primary tool to deduce bounds on $\max \#(\mathcal{L})$ and $\min \#(\mathcal{L}_{\mathrm{odd}} \setminus \mathcal{L})$. Defining $\mathcal{R}el_N$ in the described way enables us to to sample from it as follows. Algorithm Sample first chooses a solution a uniformly from $\mathcal{S}_N = \mathbb{Z}_N^*$. Then the corresponding problem b is set to a^e. In this way a is uniformly distributed on $Sol_N(b)$ and the proposed algorithm samples *solution-uniformly* (for both valid and invalid candidates) as required for the Solve-then-Hash protocol of Sect. 4.2.

For some of the considered languages the map $a \mapsto a^e$ defines a permutation on $\mathbb{Z}_N^*$ for every valid statement $N \in \mathcal{L}$. In this case every problem is solvable, we hence have $\mathcal{P}_N^+ = \mathcal{P}_N$, and the described sampling algorithm also fulfills the property of *problem-uniformity* and can be used in the Hash-then-Solve protocol of Sect. 4.1. For other of the considered languages the space $\mathcal{P}_N^+$ of solvable problems is a proper subset of $\mathcal{P}_N$ and it seems not feasible to construct an algorithm with the desired properties. In this cases only the Solve-then-Hash protocol can be used to decide the language.

CONSIDERED LANGUAGES. We provide a toolbox of protocols checking arguably the most important properties required of RSA-type moduli. An overview of our results is given in Table 1. Combining several of the protocols gives a method to check for properties required of typical applications. For example the property that the RSA map $a \mapsto a^e \bmod N$ defined by numbers (N, e) is "good" can be checked by showing that N has exactly two prime factors and is square free and that e indeed defines a permutation on $\mathbb{Z}_N^*$. If an application requires a feature more specific than the ones we treat, then likely corresponding problem and solution spaces and a corresponding relation can be found. As a starting point we consider the languages

$$\mathcal{L}_{\mathrm{sf}} := \{N \in \mathcal{L}_{\mathrm{odd}} : \gcd(N, \varphi(N)) = 1\}$$
$$\mathcal{L}_{\mathrm{ppp}} := \{N \in \mathcal{L}_{\mathrm{odd}} : |\mathbb{P}(N)| = 2\}$$

of square free numbers and prime power products, i.e. numbers having exactly two prime factors. For both languages the corresponding relation was implicitly

Table 1. Protocols for properties of RSA moduli. Assume $k = \max \#\mathcal{L}$ and $m = \min \#(\mathcal{U} \setminus \mathcal{L})$. Columns seven and eight indicate whether the Hash-then-Solve (HtS) or Solve-then-Hash (StH) protocol can be used to decide $\mathcal{L}$. $\mathcal{L}_{\mathrm{pp}}$ and $\mathcal{L}_{\mathrm{rsa}}$ are intersections of other decidable languages and can be decided by running the corresponding protocols in parallel.

$\mathcal{L}$	$\mathcal{U}$	$\mathcal{P}_N$	$\mathcal{S}_N$	$\mathcal{R}el_N$	k/m	HtS	StH	Sections
$\mathcal{L}_{\mathrm{sf}}$	$\mathcal{L}_{\mathrm{odd}}$	$\mathbb{Z}_N^*$	$\mathbb{Z}_N^*$	(a^n, a)	$1/3$	✓	✓	5.1
$\mathcal{L}_{\mathrm{ppp}}$	$\mathcal{L}_{\mathrm{odd}}$	$\mathbb{Z}_N^*$	$\mathbb{Z}_N^*$	(a^2, a)	$1/2$		✓	5.2
$\mathcal{L}_{\mathrm{per}}$	$\mathcal{L}_{\mathrm{odd}}$	$\mathbb{Z}_N^*$	$\mathbb{Z}_N^*$	(a^e, a)	$1/2$	✓	✓	5.3
$\mathcal{L}_{\mathrm{pp}}$	$\mathcal{L}_{\mathrm{odd}}$	$(\mathbb{Z}_N^*)^2$	$(\mathbb{Z}_N^*)^2$		$1/2$		✓	5.4
$\mathcal{L}_{\mathrm{rsa}}$	$\mathcal{L}_{\mathrm{odd}}$	$(\mathbb{Z}_N^*)^3$	$(\mathbb{Z}_N^*)^3$		$1/2$		✓	5.4
$\mathcal{L}_{\mathrm{blum}}$	$\mathcal{L}_{\mathrm{pp}}$	$\mathbb{Z}_N^*$	$\mathbb{Z}_N^*$	(a^4, a)	$1/2$		✓	5.5
$\mathcal{L}_{\mathrm{pai}}$	$\mathcal{L}_{\mathrm{pp}}$	$\mathbb{Z}_{n^2}^*$	$\mathbb{Z}_n \times \mathbb{Z}_N^*$	$(f_{(n,g)}(a), a)$	$1/2$	✓	✓	5.6

given in [19]. Note that by definition of $\varphi(N)$ condition $(\gcd(\varphi(N), N) = 1)$ implies that $\nu_p = 1$ for every $p \in \mathbb{P}(N)$ and hence indeed the number is square free. Due to the choice of the relation it additionally implies that $p \nmid (q - 1)$ for every $p, q \in \mathbb{P}(N)$. Intersecting both languages yields the language

$$\mathcal{L}_{\mathrm{pp}} := \{pq \in \mathcal{L}_{\mathrm{odd}} : p, q \in \mathbb{P}, p \neq q, p \nmid (q-1), q \nmid (p-1)\}$$

of prime products. Each N in this language is the product of two distinct primes, a minimal requirement on RSA moduli. We further give relations for the languages

$$\mathcal{L}_{\mathrm{per}} := \{(N, e) \in \mathcal{L}_{\mathrm{odd}} \times \mathbb{N} : a \mapsto a^e \text{ defines a permutation}\}$$
$$\mathcal{L}_{\mathrm{rsa}} := \{(N, e) \in \mathcal{L}_{\mathrm{pp}} \times \mathbb{N} : a \mapsto a^e \text{ defines a permutation}\}$$

of pairs (N, e) such that exponentiation with e defines a permutation on $\mathbb{Z}_N^*$ and N being a prime product such that e defines a permutation on $\mathbb{Z}_N^*$. The relations were implicitly used in [11,34]. Building on the protocol for $\mathcal{L}_{\mathrm{pp}}$ we consider the language

$$\mathcal{L}_{\mathrm{blum}} := \{pq \in \mathcal{L}_{\mathrm{pp}} : p \equiv q \equiv 3 \bmod 4\}$$

of Blum integers, i.e. prime products with both primes being equal to 3 modulo 4. We give problem and solution spaces and a corresponding relation, which up to our knowledge has not been used so far, such that $\mathcal{L}_{\mathrm{blum}}$ can be decided in universe $\mathcal{L}_{\mathrm{pp}}$. Finally, we show that it can be efficiently decided whether the trapdoor function corresponding to Paillier's encryption scheme, which corresponds to pairs (N, g) consisting of a prime product N and an element g of $\mathbb{Z}_{N^2}^*$, indeed defines a bijection. A protocol for this property has up to our knowledge not been given so far. Note that given (N, g) it is assumed to be hard to decide whether the corresponding map is bijective, since it has been shown to be a lossy trapdoor function under the decisional quadratic residuosity assumption [15].

5.1   Deciding $\mathcal{L}_{\mathrm{sf}}$

Consider the language

$$\mathcal{L}_{\mathrm{sf}} := \{N \in \mathcal{L}_{\mathrm{odd}} : \gcd(N, \varphi(N)) = 1\}$$

of square free integers, i.e. of odd numbers such that for every $p, q \in \mathbb{P}(N)$ we have $\nu_p = 1$ and $p \nmid q - 1$. We show that $\mathcal{L}_{\mathrm{sf}}$ can be decided in universe $\mathcal{L}_{\mathrm{odd}}$. For a statement $N \in \mathcal{L}_{\mathrm{odd}}$ let the corresponding witness be its factorization. We define the corresponding problem and solution spaces and the defining relation as

$$\mathcal{P}_N = \mathbb{Z}_N^*$$
$$\mathcal{S}_N = \mathbb{Z}_N^*$$
$$\mathcal{R}el_N = \{(b, a) \in (\mathbb{Z}_N^*)^2 : b \equiv a^N \bmod N\}.$$

Rel_N is defined via the map $\mathbb{Z}_N^* \to \mathbb{Z}_N^*$; $a \mapsto a^N$. By Eq. (1) of Sect. 2.2 this map is a bijection exactly if $N \in \mathcal{L}_{sf}$, i.e. if $\gcd(N, \varphi(N)) = 1$, and, since N is odd, at least 3-to-1 if $N \in \mathcal{L}_{odd} \setminus \mathcal{L}_{sf}$. Hence $\max \#(\mathcal{L}_{sf}) = 1$ and $\min \#(\mathcal{L}_{odd} \setminus \mathcal{L}_{sf}) = 3$.

We now describe the corresponding algorithms. Algorithms Sample samples from Rel_N by choosing $a \leftarrow_s \mathbb{Z}_N^*$, setting $b \leftarrow a^N$ and returning the problem-solution pair (b, a). As discussed above, since the solution a is sampled at random and the corresponding problem b is derived from it afterwards, a is uniformly distributed on $Sol_N(b)$ and Sample is solution-uniform. Verify on input (b, a) checks whether $b \equiv a^n \bmod n$ and responds accordingly. Note that Nth roots modulo N can be efficiently computed given the factorization of N. Hence it is possible to construct the problem solving algorithm Solve and by Theorem 2 language $\mathcal{L}_{sf}$ can be decided using the Solve-then-Hash protocol.

For every valid statement $N \in \mathcal{L}_{sf}$ the map $\mathbb{Z}_N^* \to \mathbb{Z}_N^*$; $a \mapsto a^N$ defining the relation Rel_N is a bijection. Hence in this case every problem $b \in \mathcal{P}_N$ is solvable. Further the problems sampled by Sample are uniformly distributed on $\mathcal{P}_N$ and solutions are uniformly distributed on the corresponding solution set $Sol_N(b)$. Thus Sample is both problem-uniform and solution-uniform, and therefore fulfills the requirements, which are necessary to be used as sampling algorithm Sample* in the Hash-then-Solve protocol of Sect. 4.1.

5.2 Deciding $\mathcal{L}_{ppp}$

Consider the language

$$\mathcal{L}_{ppp} := \{N \in \mathcal{L}_{odd} : |\mathbb{P}(N)| = 2\}$$

of prime power products, i.e. of odd numbers that have exactly two prime factors. We show that $\mathcal{L}_{ppp}$ can be decided in universe $\mathcal{L}_{odd}$. For a statement $N \in \mathcal{L}_{odd}$ let the corresponding witness be its factorization. We define the corresponding problem and solution spaces and the defining relation as

$$\mathcal{P}_N = \mathbb{Z}_N^*$$
$$\mathcal{S}_N = \mathbb{Z}_N^*$$
$$Rel_N = \{(b, a) \in (\mathbb{Z}_N^*)^2 : b \equiv a^2 \bmod N\}.$$

Rel_N is defined via the map $\mathbb{Z}_N^* \to \mathbb{Z}_N^*$; $a \mapsto a^2$. Since N is odd we obtain by Eq. (1) of Sect. 2.2 that this map is 4-to-1 if $N \in \mathcal{L}_{ppp}$, i.e. if N has at most 2 distinct prime factors, and at least 8-to-1 if $N \in \mathcal{L}_{odd} \setminus \mathcal{L}_{ppp}$. Hence $\max \#(\mathcal{L}_{ppp}) = 4$ and $\min \#(\mathcal{L}_{odd} \setminus \mathcal{L}_{ppp}) = 8$.

We now describe the corresponding algorithms. Algorithm Sample samples from Rel_N by choosing $a \leftarrow_s \mathbb{Z}_N^*$, setting $b \leftarrow a^2$ and returning the problem-solution pair (b, a). Note that Sample is solution-uniform. Verify on input (b, a) checks whether $b \equiv a^2 \bmod N$ and responds accordingly. Note that square roots modulo N can be efficiently computed given the factorization of N. Hence it is possible to construct the problem solving algorithm Solve and by Theorem 2 language $\mathcal{L}_{ppp}$ can be decided using the Solve-then-Hash protocol.

Let $N \in \mathcal{L}_{\text{ppp}}$ be a valid statement. The set $\mathcal{P}_N^+$ of solvable problems is the set $\mathbf{QR}(N)$ of quadratic residues modulo N. Hence a sampling algorithm Sample* compatible with the Hash-then-Solve protocol of Sect. 4.1 would require that (a) the sampled problems are uniformly distributed in $\mathbb{Z}_N^*$ and (b) if a sampled problem is solvable then it is accompanied by a solution. While both sampling uniformly from $\mathbb{Z}_N^*$ or sampling uniformly from $(b, a) \in Rel_N \subseteq \mathbf{QR}(N) \times \mathbb{Z}_N^*$ is easy, it is unclear how to construct an algorithm with the required properties that does not need access to the factorization of N. The authors of [19] overcome this problem by imposing additional requirements on N. They give a protocol able to verify that $pq = N \in \mathcal{L}_{\text{ppp}}$ such that $p, q \not\equiv 1 \bmod 8$ and $p \not\equiv q \bmod 8$. For this restricted language exactly one element of the set $\{+b, -b, +2b, -2b\}$ has a square root for every $b \in \mathbb{Z}_N^*$. Changing the relation to pairs (b, a), such that a is the root of one of those elements one then defines Sample* to sample (b, a) with algorithm Sample from above and then output (cb, a), where $c \leftarrow_\$ \{+1, -1, +2, -2\}$.

5.3   Deciding $\mathcal{L}_{\text{per}}$

Consider the language

$$\mathcal{L}_{\text{per}} := \{(N, e) \in \mathcal{L}_{\text{odd}} \times \mathbb{N} : a \mapsto a^e \text{ defines a permutation}\}$$

of pairs (N, e) such that the map $a \mapsto a^e$ defines a permutation. We show that $\mathcal{L}_{\text{per}}$ can be decided in universe $\mathcal{L}_{\text{odd}}$. For a statement $N \in \mathcal{L}_{\text{odd}}$ let the corresponding witness be its factorization. We define the corresponding problem and solution spaces and the defining relation as

$$\mathcal{P}_N = \mathbb{Z}_N^*$$
$$\mathcal{S}_N = \mathbb{Z}_N^*$$
$$Rel_N = \{(b, a) \in (\mathbb{Z}_N^*)^2 : b \equiv a^e \bmod N\}.$$

Rel_N is defined via the map $\mathbb{Z}_N^* \to \mathbb{Z}_N^*; a \mapsto a^e$. Since this map is a homomorphism, it is at least 2-to-1 if it is not bijective. Hence $\max \#(\mathcal{L}_{\text{sf}}) = 1$ and $\min \#(\mathcal{L}_{\text{odd}} \setminus \mathcal{L}_{\text{sf}}) = 2$.

We now describe the corresponding algorithms. Algorithm Sample samples from Rel_N by choosing $a \leftarrow_\$ \mathbb{Z}_N^*$, setting $b \leftarrow a^e$ and returning the problem-solution pair (b, a). Note that Sample is both problem-uniform and solution-uniform. Verify on input (b, a) checks whether $b \equiv a^e \bmod N$ and responds accordingly. Note that eth roots modulo N can be efficiently computed given the factorization of N. Hence it is possible to construct the problem solving algorithm Solve and by Theorem 2 language $\mathcal{L}_{\text{per}}$ can be decided using the Solve-then-Hash protocol.

Further, for every valid statement $N \in \mathcal{L}_{\text{per}}$ the map $\mathbb{Z}_N^* \to \mathbb{Z}_N^*; a \mapsto a^e$ defining the relation Rel_N is a bijection. Hence in this case every problem $b \in \mathcal{P}_N$ is solvable. Further the problems sampled by Sample are uniformly distributed on $\mathcal{P}_N$ and solutions are uniformly distributed on the corresponding solution set $Sol_N(b)$. Thus Sample is both problem-uniform and solution-uniform, and therefore fulfills the requirements, which are necessary to be used as sampling algorithm Sample* in the Hash-then-Solve protocol of Sect. 4.1.

5.4   Deciding $\mathcal{L}_{pp}$ and $\mathcal{L}_{rsa}$

Consider the languages

$$\mathcal{L}_{pp} := \{pq \in \mathcal{L}_{odd} : p, q \in \mathbb{P}, p \neq q, p \nmid (q-1), q \nmid (p-1)\}$$

of prime products, i.e. square-free numbers having exactly two prime factors, and

$$\mathcal{L}_{rsa} := \{(N, e) \in \mathcal{L}_{pp} \times \mathbb{N} : a \mapsto a^e \text{ defines a permutation}\}$$

of pairs (N, e) such that N is a prime product and the RSA map $\mathbb{Z}_N^* \to \mathbb{Z}_N^*; a \mapsto a^e$ defines a permutation. We have $\mathcal{L}_{pp} = \mathcal{L}_{ppp} \cap \mathcal{L}_{sf}$ and $\mathcal{L}_{rsa} = \mathcal{L}_{per} \cap \mathcal{L}_{ppp} \cap \mathcal{L}_{sf}$. The protocols deciding $\mathcal{L}_{sf}$, $\mathcal{L}_{ppp}$ and $\mathcal{L}_{per}$ are all defined with respect to the same universe $\mathcal{L}_{odd}$. By running them in parallel we hence obtain protocols deciding $\mathcal{L}_{pp}$ or $\mathcal{L}_{rsa}$ respectively with respect to $\mathcal{L}_{odd}$.

5.5   Deciding $\mathcal{L}_{blum}$

Consider the language

$$\mathcal{L}_{blum} := \{pq \in \mathcal{L}_{pp} : p \equiv q \equiv 3 \bmod 4\}$$

of Blum integers. We show that $\mathcal{L}_{blum}$ can be decided in universe $\mathcal{L}_{pp}$. For a statement $N \in \mathcal{L}_{pp}$ let the corresponding witness be its factorization. We define the corresponding problem and solution spaces and the defining relation as

$$\mathcal{P}_N = \mathbb{Z}_N^*$$
$$\mathcal{S}_N = \mathbb{Z}_N^*$$
$$\mathcal{Rel}_N = \{(b, a) \in (\mathbb{Z}_N^*)^2 : b \equiv a^4 \bmod N\}.$$

Since all statements are elements of $\mathcal{L}_{pp}$ and hence have two odd prime factors, every square in $\mathbb{Z}_N^*$ has four square roots. Further, if N a is Blum integer then each element of $\mathbf{QR}(N)$ has exactly one root that is again a square. This implies that every problem of $\mathcal{P}^+ = \{b \in \mathbb{Z}_N^* : b \equiv a^4 \text{ for some } a \in \mathbb{Z}_N^*\}$ has four corresponding solutions, i.e. $\max \#(\mathcal{L}_{sf}) = 2$. If on the other hand $N \in \mathcal{L}_{pp} \setminus \mathcal{L}_{blum}$, then every element of the form $b = a^4$ has at least two square roots, which are elements of $\mathbf{QR}(N)$. Hence in this case we obtain $\min \#(\mathcal{L}_{pp} \setminus \mathcal{L}_{blum}) = 8$.

We now describe the corresponding algorithms. Algorithm Sample samples from $\mathcal{Rel}_N$ by choosing $a \leftarrow_{\$} \mathbb{Z}_N^*$, setting $b \leftarrow a^4$ and returning the problem-solution pair (b, a). Note that Sample is solution-uniform. Verify on input (b, a) checks whether $b \equiv a^4 \bmod N$ and responds accordingly. Note that 4th roots modulo N can be efficiently computed given the factorization of N. Hence it is possible to construct the problem solving algorithm Solve and by Theorem 2 language $\mathcal{L}_{\mathrm{blum}}$ can be decided using the Solve-then-Hash protocol.

Let $N \in \mathcal{L}_{\mathrm{blum}}$ be a valid statement. Since for Blum integers squaring is a permutation on $\mathbf{QR}(N)$, the space of solvable problems is given by $\mathbf{QR}(N)$. Hence as in the case of the relation for language $\mathcal{L}_{\mathrm{ppp}}$ it seems unfeasible to construct an alternative sampling algorithm Sample* that admits the use of the Hash-then-Solve protocol of Sect. 4.1.

5.6   Deciding $\mathcal{L}_{\mathrm{pai}}$

Let $N \in \mathcal{L}_{\mathrm{pp}}$ and $g \in \mathbb{Z}_{N^2}^*$ such that N divides the order of the group generated by g. In this case the following function associated to N and g, which is used in Paillier's encryption scheme [26], defines a bijection that can be efficiently inverted given the factorization of N.

$$
f_{n,g} \colon \begin{cases} \mathbb{Z}_N \times \mathbb{Z}_N^* & \to \mathbb{Z}_{N^2}^* \\ (a_1, a_2) & \mapsto g^{a_1} \, a_2^N \bmod N^2 \end{cases}
$$

In this section we show that our protocols can be used to check in universe $\mathcal{L}_{\mathrm{pp}}$, whether a public key (N, g) for the Paillier encryption scheme indeed defines a bijection. Hence consider the language

$$
\mathcal{L}_{\mathrm{pai}} := \{(N, g) \in \mathcal{L}_{\mathrm{pp}} \times \mathbb{N} : g \in \mathbb{Z}_{N^2}^*, f_{N,g} \text{ is permutation}\}.
$$

Note that the condition $g \in \mathbb{Z}_{N^2}^*$ can be efficiently checked. For a statement $N \in \mathcal{L}_{\mathrm{pp}}$ let the corresponding witness be its factorization. We define the corresponding problem and solution spaces and the defining relation as

$$
\begin{aligned}
\mathcal{P}_N &= \mathbb{Z}_{N^2}^* \\
\mathcal{S}_N &= \mathbb{Z}_N \times \mathbb{Z}_N^* \\
\mathcal{Rel}_N &= \{(b, a) \in \mathcal{P}_{(N,g)} \times \mathcal{S}_{(N,g)} : b \equiv f_{N,g}(a) \bmod N\}.
\end{aligned}
$$

$\mathcal{Rel}_N$ is defined via map $f_{(N,g)}$, which is a homomorphism. Hence if it is not bijective it is at least 2-to-1 and we obtain $\max \#(\mathcal{L}_{\mathrm{sf}}) = 1$ and $\min \#(\mathcal{L}_{\mathrm{odd}} \setminus \mathcal{L}_{\mathrm{sf}}) = 2$.

We now describe the corresponding algorithms. Algorithm Sample samples from $\mathcal{Rel}_N$ by choosing $a \leftarrow_s \mathbb{Z}_N \times \mathbb{Z}_N^*$, setting $b \leftarrow f_{(N,g)}(a)$ and returning the problem-solution pair (b, a). Note that Sample is both problem-uniform and solution-uniform. Verify on input (b, a) checks whether $b \equiv f_{(N,g)}(a)$ and responds accordingly. Map $f_{(N,g)}$ can be efficiently inverted given the factorization of N. Hence it is possible to construct the problem solving algorithm Solve and by Theorem 2 language $\mathcal{L}_{\mathrm{pai}}$ can be decided using the Solve-then-Hash protocol.

For every valid statement $N \in \mathcal{L}_{\mathrm{pai}}$ the map $f_{(N,g)}$ defining the relation $\mathcal{Rel}_N$ is a bijection. Hence in this case every problem $b \in \mathcal{P}_N$ is solvable. Further the problems sampled by Sample are uniformly distributed on $\mathcal{P}_N$ and solutions are uniformly distributed on the corresponding solution set $Sol_N(b)$. Thus Sample is both problem-uniform and solution-uniform, and therefore fulfills the requirements, which are necessary to be used as sampling algorithm Sample* in the Hash-then-Solve protocol of Sect. 4.1.

The constructions can be easily adapted to handle the generalized version of the trapdoor function from [14], which uses domain $\mathbb{Z}_{N^s} \times \mathbb{Z}_N^*$ and range $\mathbb{Z}_{N^{s+1}}^*$ for some $s \in \mathbb{N}$.

Acknowledgments. We are grateful to the anonymous reviewers for their valuable comments. Benedikt Auerbach was supported by the NRW Research Training Group SecHuman. Bertram Poettering conducted part of the research at Ruhr University Bochum, supported by ERC Project ERCC (FP7/615074).

References

1. Ateniese, G., Camenisch, J., Joye, M., Tsudik, G.: A practical and provably secure coalition-resistant group signature scheme. In: Bellare, M. (ed.) CRYPTO 2000. LNCS, vol. 1880, pp. 255–270. Springer, Heidelberg (2000). https://doi.org/10.1007/3-540-44598-6_16

2. Bellare, M., Poettering, B., Stebila, D.: Deterring certificate subversion: efficient double-authentication-preventing signatures. In: Fehr, S. (ed.) PKC 2017. LNCS, vol. 10175, pp. 121–151. Springer, Heidelberg (2017). https://doi.org/10.1007/978-3-662-54388-7_5

3. Bellare, M., Yung, M.: Certifying permutations: noninteractive zero-knowledge based on any trapdoor permutation. J. Cryptol. **9**(3), 149–166 (1996)

4. Benhamouda, F., Ferradi, H., Géraud, R., Naccache, D.: Non-interactive provably secure attestations for arbitrary RSA prime generation algorithms. In: Foley, S.N., Gollmann, D., Snekkenes, E. (eds.) ESORICS 2017. LNCS, vol. 10492, pp. 206–223. Springer, Cham (2017). https://doi.org/10.1007/978-3-319-66402-6_13

5. Berger, R., Kannan, S., Peralta, R.: A framework for the study of cryptographic protocols. In: Williams, H.C. (ed.) CRYPTO 1985. LNCS, vol. 218, pp. 87–103. Springer, Heidelberg (1986). https://doi.org/10.1007/3-540-39799-X_9

6. Boudot, F.: Efficient proofs that a committed number lies in an interval. In: Preneel, B. (ed.) EUROCRYPT 2000. LNCS, vol. 1807, pp. 431–444. Springer, Heidelberg (2000). https://doi.org/10.1007/3-540-45539-6_31

7. Boyar, J., Friedl, K., Lund, C.: Practical zero-knowledge proofs: giving hints and using deficiencies. In: Quisquater, J.-J., Vandewalle, J. (eds.) EUROCRYPT 1989. LNCS, vol. 434, pp. 155–172. Springer, Heidelberg (1990). https://doi.org/10.1007/3-540-46885-4_18

8. Brassard, G., Crépeau, C.: Non-transitive transfer of confidence: a perfect zero-knowledge interactive protocol for SAT and beyond. In: 27th FOCS, pp. 188–195. IEEE Computer Society Press, Toronto, 27–29 October 1986

9. Camenisch, J., Lysyanskaya, A.: Dynamic accumulators and application to efficient revocation of anonymous credentials. In: Yung, M. (ed.) CRYPTO 2002. LNCS, vol. 2442, pp. 61–76. Springer, Heidelberg (2002). https://doi.org/10.1007/3-540-45708-9_5

10. Camenisch, J., Michels, M.: Proving in zero-knowledge that a number is the product of two safe primes. In: Stern, J. (ed.) EUROCRYPT 1999. LNCS, vol. 1592, pp. 107–122. Springer, Heidelberg (1999). https://doi.org/10.1007/3-540-48910-X_8

11. Catalano, D., Pointcheval, D., Pornin, T.: IPAKE: isomorphisms for password-based authenticated key exchange. In: Franklin, M. (ed.) CRYPTO 2004. LNCS, vol. 3152, pp. 477–493. Springer, Heidelberg (2004). https://doi.org/10.1007/978-3-540-28628-8_29

12. Chan, A., Frankel, Y., Tsiounis, Y.: Easy come - easy go divisible cash. In: Nyberg, K. (ed.) EUROCRYPT 1998. LNCS, vol. 1403, pp. 561–575. Springer, Heidelberg (1998). https://doi.org/10.1007/BFb0054154

13. Chaum, D., Fiat, A., Naor, M.: Untraceable electronic cash. In: Goldwasser, S. (ed.) CRYPTO 1988. LNCS, vol. 403, pp. 319–327. Springer, New York (1990). https://doi.org/10.1007/0-387-34799-2_25

14. Damgård, I., Jurik, M.: A generalisation, a simplification and some applications of Paillier's probabilistic public-key system. In: Kim, K. (ed.) PKC 2001. LNCS, vol. 1992, pp. 119–136. Springer, Heidelberg (2001). https://doi.org/10.1007/3-540-44586-2_9

15. Freeman, D.M., Goldreich, O., Kiltz, E., Rosen, A., Segev, G.: More constructions of lossy and correlation-secure trapdoor functions. J. Cryptol. **26**(1), 39–74 (2013)

16. Fujisaki, E., Okamoto, T.: Statistical zero knowledge protocols to prove modular polynomial relations. In: Kaliski, B.S. (ed.) CRYPTO 1997. LNCS, vol. 1294, pp. 16–30. Springer, Heidelberg (1997). https://doi.org/10.1007/BFb0052225

17. Fujisaki, E., Okamoto, T.: A practical and provably secure scheme for publicly verifiable secret sharing and its applications. In: Nyberg, K. (ed.) EUROCRYPT 1998. LNCS, vol. 1403, pp. 32–46. Springer, Heidelberg (1998). https://doi.org/10.1007/BFb0054115

18. Gennaro, R., Krawczyk, H., Rabin, T.: RSA-based undeniable signatures. In: Kaliski, B.S. (ed.) CRYPTO 1997. LNCS, vol. 1294, pp. 132–149. Springer, Heidelberg (1997). https://doi.org/10.1007/BFb0052232

19. Gennaro, R., Micciancio, D., Rabin, T.: An efficient non-interactive statistical zero-knowledge proof system for quasi-safe prime products. In: ACM CCS 1998, pp. 67–72. ACM Press, San Francisco, 2–5 November 1998

20. Goldreich, O., Micali, S., Wigderson, A.: Proofs that yield nothing but their validity or all languages in NP have zero-knowledge proof systems. J. ACM **38**(3), 691–729 (1991)

21. Groth, J., Ostrovsky, R., Sahai, A.: Perfect non-interactive zero knowledge for NP. In: Vaudenay, S. (ed.) EUROCRYPT 2006. LNCS, vol. 4004, pp. 339–358. Springer, Heidelberg (2006). https://doi.org/10.1007/11761679_21

22. Juels, A., Guajardo, J.: RSA key generation with verifiable randomness. In: Naccache, D., Paillier, P. (eds.) PKC 2002. LNCS, vol. 2274, pp. 357–374. Springer, Heidelberg (2002). https://doi.org/10.1007/3-540-45664-3_26

23. Kakvi, S.A., Kiltz, E., May, A.: Certifying RSA. In: Wang, X., Sako, K. (eds.) ASIACRYPT 2012. LNCS, vol. 7658, pp. 404–414. Springer, Heidelberg (2012). https://doi.org/10.1007/978-3-642-34961-4_25

24. Mao, W.: Verifiable partial sharing of integer factors. In: Tavares, S., Meijer, H. (eds.) SAC 1998. LNCS, vol. 1556, pp. 94–105. Springer, Heidelberg (1999). https://doi.org/10.1007/3-540-48892-8_8

25. Micali, S.: Fair public-key cryptosystems. In: Brickell, E.F. (ed.) CRYPTO 1992. LNCS, vol. 740, pp. 113–138. Springer, Heidelberg (1993). https://doi.org/10.1007/3-540-48071-4_9

26. Paillier, P.: Public-key cryptosystems based on composite degree residuosity classes. In: Stern, J. (ed.) EUROCRYPT 1999. LNCS, vol. 1592, pp. 223–238. Springer, Heidelberg (1999). https://doi.org/10.1007/3-540-48910-X_16

27. Poettering, B., Stebila, D.: Double-authentication-preventing signatures. Int. J. Inf. Sec. **16**(1), 1–22 (2017)
28. Shin, S., Kobara, K., Imai, H.: RSA-based password-authenticated key exchange, revisited. IEICE Trans. Inf. Syst. **91**(5), 1424–1438 (2008)
29. van de Graaf, J., Peralta, R.: A simple and secure way to show the validity of your public key. In: Pomerance, C. (ed.) CRYPTO 1987. LNCS, vol. 293, pp. 128–134. Springer, Heidelberg (1988). https://doi.org/10.1007/3-540-48184-2_9
30. Young, A., Yung, M.: The dark side of "Black-Box" cryptography or: should we trust Capstone? In: Koblitz, N. (ed.) CRYPTO 1996. LNCS, vol. 1109, pp. 89–103. Springer, Heidelberg (1996). https://doi.org/10.1007/3-540-68697-5_8
31. Young, A., Yung, M.: Kleptography: using cryptography against cryptography. In: Fumy, W. (ed.) EUROCRYPT 1997. LNCS, vol. 1233, pp. 62–74. Springer, Heidelberg (1997). https://doi.org/10.1007/3-540-69053-0_6
32. Young, A., Yung, M.: The prevalence of kleptographic attacks on discrete-log based cryptosystems. In: Kaliski, B.S. (ed.) CRYPTO 1997. LNCS, vol. 1294, pp. 264–276. Springer, Heidelberg (1997). https://doi.org/10.1007/BFb0052241
33. Young, A., Yung, M.: A space efficient backdoor in RSA and its applications. In: Preneel, B., Tavares, S. (eds.) SAC 2005. LNCS, vol. 3897, pp. 128–143. Springer, Heidelberg (2006). https://doi.org/10.1007/11693383_9
34. Zhu, F., Wong, D.S., Chan, A.H., Ye, R.: Password authenticated key exchange based on RSA for imbalanced wireless networks. In: Chan, A.H., Gligor, V. (eds.) ISC 2002. LNCS, vol. 2433, pp. 150–161. Springer, Heidelberg (2002). https://doi.org/10.1007/3-540-45811-5_11

Two-Factor Authentication
with End-to-End Password Security

Stanislaw Jarecki[1(✉)], Hugo Krawczyk[2], Maliheh Shirvanian[3],
and Nitesh Saxena[3]

[1] University of California Irvine, Irvine, USA
sjarecki@uci.edu
[2] IBM Research, Yorktown Heights, USA
hugo@ee.technion.ac.il
[3] University of Alabama, Birmingham, USA
{maliheh,saxena}@uab.edu

Abstract. We present a secure two-factor authentication (TFA) scheme based on the possession by the user of a password and a crypto-capable device. Security is "end-to-end" in the sense that the attacker can attack all parts of the system, including all communication links and any subset of parties (servers, devices, client terminals), can learn users' passwords, and perform active and passive attacks, online and offline. In all cases the scheme provides the highest attainable security bounds given the set of compromised components. Our solution builds a TFA scheme using any Device-Enhanced PAKE, defined by Jarecki et al., and any Short Authenticated String (SAS) Message Authentication, defined by Vaudenay. We show an efficient instantiation the modular, generic construction we give is not PAKE-agnostic because it doesn't even use PAKE, but the instantiation of this scheme which instantiates DE-PAKE with PTR+PAKE is PAKE-agnostic as you say of this modular construction which utilizes any password-based client-server authentication method, with or without reliance on public-key infrastructure. The security of the proposed scheme is proven in a formal model that we formulate as an extension of the traditional PAKE model.

We also report on a prototype implementation of our schemes, including TLS-based and PKI-free variants, as well as several instantiations of the SAS mechanism, all demonstrating the practicality of our approach.

1 Introduction

Passwords provide the dominant mechanism for electronic authentication, protecting a plethora of sensitive information. However, passwords are vulnerable to both *online* and *offline* attacks. A network adversary can test password guesses in online interactions with the server while an attacker who compromises the authentication data stored by the server (i.e., a database of salted password hashes) can mount an *offline dictionary attack* by testing each user's authentication information against a dictionary of likely password choices. Offline dictionary attacks are a major threat, routinely experienced by commercial vendors,

© International Association for Cryptologic Research 2018
M. Abdalla and R. Dahab (Eds.): PKC 2018, LNCS 10770, pp. 431–461, 2018.
https://doi.org/10.1007/978-3-319-76581-5_15

and they lead to the compromise of *billions* of user accounts [6,7,12,15,17,20]. Moreover, because users often re-use their passwords across multiple services, compromising one service typically also compromises user accounts at other services.

Two-factor password authentication (TFA), where user U authenticates to server S by "proving possession" of an auxiliary personal device D (e.g. a smartphone or a USB token) in addition to knowing her password, forms a common defense against *online* password attacks as well as a second line of defense in case of password leakage. A TFA scheme which uses a device that is not directly connected to U's client terminal C typically works as follows: D displays a short one-time secret PIN, either received from S (e.g. using an SMS message) or computed by D based on a key shared with S, and the user manually types the PIN into client C in addition to her password. Examples of systems that are based on such one-time PINs include SMS-based PINs, TOTP [10], HOTP [14], Google Authenticator [4], FIDO U2F [2], and schemes in the literature such as [47].

Vulnerabilities of traditional TFA schemes. Existing TFA schemes, both PIN-based and those that do not rely on PINs, e.g. [1,8], combine password authentication and 2nd-factor authentication as separate authentication mechanisms leading to several limitations. Chief among these is that such TFA solutions remain vulnerable to *offline dictionary attacks* upon server compromise in the same way as non-TFA password authentication schemes (i.e. via exposure of users' salted hashes), thus perpetuating the main source of password leakage. Moreover, existing TFA's have several vulnerabilities against *online* attacks: (1) The read-and-copy PIN-transfer is subject to a variety of *eavesdropping attacks*, including SMS hijacking[1], shoulder-surfing, PIN recording, client-side or device-side attacks via keyloggers or screen scrapers, e.g. [43], and PIN *phishing* [16]. (2) The read-and-copy PIN-transfer allows only *limited PIN entropy* and while, say, a 6-digit PIN is hard to guess, PIN guessing can be used in a large-scale online attack against accounts whose passwords the attacker already collected, e.g. [12,15,17,20]. For example, if the attacker obtains password information for a large set of accounts, PINs are 6-digit long, and the attacker can try 10 PIN guesses per account, one expects a successful impersonation per 100,000 users. (3) Current PIN-based TFAs perform *sequential authentication* using the password and the PIN, i.e. C sends the password to S (over TLS), S confirms whether pwd is correct, and only then C sends to S the PIN retrieved from D. This enables online password attacks without requiring PIN guessing or interaction with a device, thus voiding the effects of PIN on password-guessing or password-confirmation online attacks.

Our Contributions. In this paper we aim to address the vulnerabilities of the currently deployed TFA schemes by (1) introducing a precise security model for TFA schemes capturing well-defined *maximally-attainable* security bounds, (2)

---

[1] E.g., SIM card swap attacks [18] and SMS re-direction where PINs are diverted to the attacker's phone exploiting SS7 vulnerabilities [21]. The latter led to NIST's recent decision to deprecate SMS PINs as a TFA mechanism [19].

exhibiting a practical TFA scheme which we prove to achieve the strong security guaranteed by our formal model, and (3) prototyping several methods for validating user's possession of the secondary authentication factor. We expand on each of these aspects next.

TFA Security Model with End-to-End Security. We introduce a *Two-Factor Authenticated Key Exchange (TFA-KE)* model in which a user authenticates to server S by (1) entering a password into client terminal C and (2) proving possession of a personal device D which forms the second authenticator factor. In the TFA-KE model, possession of D is proved by the user confirming in the device equality of a t-bit *checksum* displayed by D with a *checksum* displayed by C. Following [50] (see below), this implements a t-bit C-to-D *user-authenticated channel*, which confirms that the same person is in control of client C and device D. This channel authentication requirement is weaker than the *private* channel required by current PIN-based TFAs and, as we show, it allows TFA schemes to be both more secure *and* easier to use.

The TFA-KE model, that we define as an extension of the standard Password-Authenticated Key Exchange (PAKE) [24] and the Device-Enhanced PAKE (DE-PAKE) [37] models, captures what we call *end-to-end security* by allowing the adversary to *control all communication channels and compromise any protocol party*. For each subset of compromised parties, the model specifies *best-possible security bounds*, leaving inevitable (but costly) exhaustive online guessing attacks as the only feasible attack option. In particular, in the common case that D and S are uncorrupted, the only feasible attack is an active *simultaneous online* attack against *both* S and D that also requires guessing the password *and* the t-bit checksum. Compromising server S allows the attacker to impersonate S, but does not help in impersonating the user to S, and in particular does not enable an offline-dictionary attack against the user's password. Compromising device D makes the authentication effectively password-only, hence offering best possible bounds in the PAKE model (in particular, the offline dictionary attack is possible only if D and S are both compromised). Finally, compromising client C leaks the password, but even then impersonating the user to the server requires an active attack on D. We prove our protocols in this strong security model.

Practical TFA with End-to-End Security. Our main result is a TFA scheme, GenTFA that achieves end-to-end security as formalized in our TFA-KE model and is based on two general tools. The first is a Device-Enhanced Password Authenticated Key Exchange (DE-PAKE) scheme as introduced by Jarecki et al. [37]. Such a scheme assumes the availability of a user's auxiliary device, as in our setting, and utilizes the device to protect against offline dictionary attacks in case of server compromise. However, DE-PAKE schemes provide no protection in case that the client machine C is compromised and, moreover, security completely breaks down if the user's password is leaked. Thus, our approach for achieving TFA-KE security is to start with a DE-PAKE scheme and armor it against client compromise (and password leakage) using our second tool, namely, a SAS-MA (Short-Authentication-String Message Authentication) as defined by Vaudenay [50]. In our application, a SAS-MA scheme utilizes a t-bit

user-authenticated channel, called a *SAS channel*, to authenticate data sent from
C to D. More specifically, the SAS channel is implemented by having the user
verify and confirm the equality of two t-bit strings, called *checksums*, displayed
by both C and D. It follows from [50] that if the displayed checksums coincide
then the information received by D from C is correct except for a 2^{-t} probability
of authentication error. We then show how to combine a DE-PAKE scheme with
such a SAS channel to obtain a scheme, GenTFA, for which we can prove TFA-
KE security, hence provably avoiding the shortcomings of PIN-based schemes.
Moreover, the use of the SAS channel relaxes the required user's actions from a
read-and-copy action in traditional schemes to a simpler compare-and-confirm
which also serves as a proof of physical possession of the device by the user (see
more below).

We show a concrete *practical* instantiation of our general scheme GenTFA,
named OpTFA, that inherits from GenTFA its TFA-KE security. Protocol OpTFA
is modular with respect to the (asymmetric) password protocol run between
client and server, thus it can utilize protocols that assume PKI as the traditional
password-over-TLS, or those that do not require any form of secure channels, as
in the (PKI-free) asymmetric PAKE schemes [25,32]. In the PKI case, OpTFA
can run over TLS, offering a ready replacement of current TFA schemes in the
PKI setting. In the PKI-free case one gets the advantages of the TFA-KE setting
without relying on PKI, thus obtaining a strict strengthening of (password-only)
PAKE security [24,44] as defined by the TFA-KE model.

The cost of OpTFA is two communication rounds between D and C, with
4 exponentiations by C and 3 by D, plus the cost of a password authentication
protocol between C and S. In the PKI setting the latter is the cost of establishing
a server-authenticated TLS channel, while in the PKI-free case one can use an
asymmetric PAKE (e.g., [27,36]) with cost (some of it computable offline) of 3
exponentiations for C, 2 for S, and one multi-exponentiation for each.

Implementation and SAS Channel Designs. We prototyped protocol
OpTFA, in both the PKI and PKI-free versions, with the client implemented as a
Chrome browser extension, the device as an Android app, and D-C communication implemented using Google Cloud Messaging. We also designed and implemented several instantiations of the human-assisted C-to-D SAS channel required
by our TFA-KE solution and model. Recall that a SAS channel replaces the
user's *read-and-copy* action of a PIN-based TFA with the *compare-and-confirm*
action used to validate the checksums displayed by C and D. The security of a
SAS-model TFA-KE depends on the checksum entropy t, called the *SAS channel capacity*, hence the two important characteristics of a physical design of a
SAS channel are its capacity t and the ease of the compare-and-confirm action
required of the user. In Sect. 6 we show several SAS designs that present different
options in terms of channel capacity and user-friendliness.

Our base-line implementation of a SAS channel encodes 20-bit checksums as
6-digit decimal PINs, which the user compares when displayed by C and D (no
copying involved). However, we also propose two novel and higher-capacity SAS
channels. In the first design, the device D is assumed to have a camera and the

checksum calculated by the client is encoded as a QR code and displayed by C. The user prompts D to capture this QR code which D decodes and compares against its own computed checksum. The second design is based on an audio channel implemented using a human speech transcription software. If device D is a smartphone then the user can read out an alphanumeric checksum displayed by C into D's microphone[2], and D decodes the audio using the transcriber tool and compares it to its checksum.

Related Works. We discuss related works in greater detail in Sect. 7. The main observations are: First, multiple methods have been proposed in the crypto literature for strengthening password authentication against offline dictionary attacks in case of server compromise by introducing an additional party in the protocol (e.g., *password-hardened* or *device-enhanced* authentication [23,27,31,37] and Threshold-PAKE or 2-PAKE, e.g. [28,40,44]), but these schemes offer no security against an active attacker in case of password leakage or client compromise, hence they are not TFAs. Second, many TFA schemes offer alternatives to PIN-based TFAs, but *none of them offer protection against offline attacks upon server compromise* except for the scheme of [47] (see Sect. 7). Moreover, if these schemes consider D as an independent entity (rather than a local component of client C) then they either have on-line security vulnerabilities or they require a pre-set secure full-bandwidth C-D channel. In our case, we do with just a SAS channel that as we show in Sect. 6 has several practical implementations. Third, we are not aware of any attempt to model security of TFA schemes where D and C are not co-located, nor do we know any PKI-free TFA schemes proposed for this setting.

Road-Map. In Sect. 2 we present TFA-KE security model. In Sect. 3 we describe our protocol building blocks. In Sect. 4 we present a practical TFA-KE protocol OpTFA, and we provide informal rationale for its design choices. In Sect. 5 we show a more general TFA-KE protocol GenTFA, of which OpTFA is an instance, together with its formal security proof. In Sect. 6 we report on the implementation and testing of protocol OpTFA, and we describe several SAS channel designs. In Sect. 7 we include more detailed direlated works.

2   TFA-KE Security

We introduce the *Two-Factor Authenticated Key Exchange (TFA-KE)* security model that defines the assumed environment and participants in our protocols as well as the attacker's capabilities and the model's security guarantees. Our starting point is the *Device-Enhanced PAKE (DE-PAKE)* model, introduced in [37], which extends the well-known two-party *Password-Authenticated Key Exchange (PAKE)* model [24] to a multi-party setting that includes users U, communicating from client machines C, servers S to which users log in, and auxiliary *devices* D, e.g. a smartphone. A DE-PAKE scheme has the security

---

[2] Note that thanks to the full resistance of our TFA-KE schemes to eavesdropping, overhearing the spoken checksum is of no use for the attacker.

properties of a two-server PAKE (2-PAKE) [28,40] where D plays the role of the 2nd server. Namely, a compromise of either S or D (but not both) essentially does not help the attacker, and in particular leaks no information about the user's password. However, whereas 2-PAKE might be insecure in case of a compromise of *both* S and D, in a DE-PAKE the adversary who compromises S and D must stage an offline dictionary attack to learn anything about the password.

The TFA-KE model considers the same set of parties as in the DE-PAKE model (which we recall in Appendix A) and all the same adversarial capabilities, including controlling all communication links, the ability to mount online active attacks, offline dictionary attacks, and to compromise devices and servers. However, the DE-PAKE model does not consider client corruption or password leakage. Indeed, in case of password leakage an active adversary can authenticate to S by impersonating the legitimate user in a single DE-PAKE session with D and S. Since a TFA scheme is supposed to protect against the client corruption and password leakage attacks, our TFA-KE model enhances the DE-PAKE model by adding these capabilities to the adversary while preserving all the other strict security requirements of DE-PAKE. In general, DE-PAKE requirements were such that the only allowable attacks on the system, under a given set of corrupted parties, are the unavoidable exhaustive online guessing attacks for that setting; the same holds for TFA-KE but with additional best resilience to client compromise and password leakage.

Note, however, that if C, D, S communicate only over insecure links then an attacker who learns the user's password will always be able to authenticate to S as in the case of DE-PAKE, by impersonating the user to D and S. Consequently, to allow device D to become a true *second factor* and maintain security in case the password leaks, one has to assume some form of authentication in the C to D communication which would allow the user to validate that D communicates with the user's own client terminal C and not with the attacker who performs a man-in-the-middle attack and impersonates this user to D.

To that end our TFA-KE model augments the communication model by an authentication abstraction on the client-to-device channel, but it does so without requiring the client to store any long-term keys (other than the user's password). Namely, we assume a uni-directional C-to-D "Short Authenticated String" (SAS) channel, introduced by Vaudenay [50], which allows C to communicate t bits to D that cannot be changed by the attacker. The t-bit C-to-D SAS channel abstraction comes down to a requirement that the user compares a t-bit *checksum* displayed by both C and D, and approves (or denies) their equality by choosing the corresponding option on device D.

As is standard, we quantify security by attacker's resources that include the computation time and the number of instances of each protocol party the adversary interacts with. We denote these as q_D, q_S, q_C, q'_C, where the first two count the number of active sessions between the attacker and D and S, resp., while q_C (resp. q'_C) counts the number of sessions where the attacker poses to C as S (resp. as D). Security is further quantified by the password entropy d (we assume the password is chosen from a dictionary of size 2^d known to the attacker), and parameter t, which is called the SAS channel *capacity*. As we explain in Sect. 3, a C-to-D SAS channel allows for establishing a D-authenticated secure channel between D and C, except for the 2^{-t} probability of error [50], which explains 2^{-t} factors in the TFA-KE security bounds stated below.

TFA Security Definition. We consider a communication model of open channels plus the t-bit SAS-channel between C and D, and a man-in-the-middle adversary that interacts with q_D, q_S, q_C, q'_C sessions of D, S, C, as described above. The adversary can also corrupt any party, S, D, or C, learning its stored secrets and the internal state as that party executes its protocol, which in the case of C implies learning the user's password. All other adversarial capabilities as well as the test session experiment defining the adversary's goal are as in DE-PAKE (and PAKE) models – see Appendix A. In particular, the adversary's advantage is, as in DE-PAKE and PAKE, an advantage in distinguishing between a random string and a key computed by S or C on a test session.

The security requirements set by Definition 1 below are the *strictest* one can hope for given the communication and party corruption model. That is, wherever we require the attacker's advantage to be no more than a given bound with a set of corrupted parties, then there is an (unavoidable) attack - in the form of exhaustive guessing attack - that achieves this bound under the given compromised parties. Importantly, and *in contrast to typical two-factor authentication solutions*, the TFA-KE model requires that the second authentication factor D not only provides security in case of client and/or password compromise, but that *it also strengthens online and offline security (by 2^t factors) even when the password has not been learned by the attacker.*

Definition 1. *A TFA-KE protocol* TFA *is* (T, ϵ)-*secure if for any password dictionary* Dict *of size* 2^d, *any* t-*bit SAS channel, and any attacker* A *bounded by time* T, A*'s advantage* $\mathsf{Adv}_A^{\mathsf{TFA}}$ *in distinguishing the tested session key from random is bounded as follows, for* q_S, q_C, q'_C, q_D *as defined above:*

1. *If* S, D, *and* C *are all uncorrupted:*

$$\mathsf{Adv}_A^{\mathsf{TFA}} \leq \min\{q_C + q_S/2^t, q'_C + q_D/2^t\}/2^d + \epsilon$$

2. *If only* D *is corrupted:* $\mathsf{Adv}_A^{\mathsf{TFA}} \leq (q_C + q_S)/2^d + \epsilon$
3. *If only* S *is corrupted:* $\mathsf{Adv}_A^{\mathsf{TFA}} \leq (q'_C + q_D/2^t)/2^d + \epsilon$
4. *If only* C *is corrupted (or the user's password leaks by any other means):* $\mathsf{Adv}_A^{\mathsf{TFA}} \leq \min(q_S, q_D)/2^t + \epsilon$
5. *If both* D *and* S *are corrupted (but not* C*), and* $\bar{q}_S$ *and* $\bar{q}_D$ *count* A*'s offline operations performed based on resp.* S*'s and* D*'s state:* $\mathsf{Adv}_A^{\mathsf{TFA}} \leq \min\{\bar{q}_S, \bar{q}_D\}/2^d$

Explaining the bounds. The security of the TFA scheme relative to the DE-PAKE model can be seen by comparing the above bounds to those in Definition 2 in Appendix A. Here we explain the meaning of some of these bounds. In the default case of no corruptions, the adversary's probability of attack is at most $\min(q_C+q_S/2^t, q_C'+q_D/2^t)/2^d$ improving on DE-PAKE bound $\min(q_C+q_S, q_C'+q_D)/2^d$ and on the PAKE bound $(q_C+q_S)/2^d$. For simplicity, assume that $q_C = q_C' = 0$ (e.g., in the PKI setting where C talks to S over TLS and the communication from D to C is authenticated), in which case the bound reduces to $\min(q_S, q_D)/2^{t+d}$. The interpretation of this bound, and similarly for the other bounds in this model, is that in order to have a probability $q/2^{t+d}$ to impersonate the user, the attacker needs to run q online sessions with S *and also* q online sessions with D. (In each such session the attacker can test one password out of a dictionary of 2^d passwords, and can do so successfully only if its communication with D is accepted over the SAS channel, which happens with probability 2^{-t}.) This is the optimal security bound in the TFA-KE setting since an adversary who guesses both the user's password and the t-bit SAS-channel checksum can successfully authenticate as the user to the server.

In case of client corruption (and password leakage), the adversary's probability of impersonating the user to the server is at most $\min(q_S, q_D)/2^t$, which is the best possible bound when the attacker holds the user's password. In case of device corruption, the adversary's advantage is at most $(q_C+q_S)/2^d$, which matches the optimal PAKE probability, namely, when a device is not available. Finally, upon server corruption, the adversary's probability of success in impersonating the user to any uncorrupted server session is (assuming $q_C' = 0$ for simplicity) at most $q_D/2^{t+d}$. In other words, learning server's private information necessarily allows the adversary to authenticate as the server to the client, but it does not help to impersonate as the client to the server. In contrast, widely deployed PIN-based TFA schemes that transmit passwords and PINs over a TLS channel are subject to an offline dictionary attack in this case.

Extension: The Case of C and S Corruption. Note that when C and D are corrupted, there is no security to be offered because the attacker has possession of all authenticator factors, the password and the auxiliary device. However, in the case that both C and S are corrupted one can hope that the attacker could not authenticate to sessions in S that the attacker does not actively control. Indeed, the above model can be extended to include this case with a bound of $q_D/2^t$. Our protocols as described in Figs. 3 and 4 do not achieve this bound, but it can be easily achieved for example by the following small modification (refer to the figures): S is initialized with a public key of D and before sending the value zid to D (via C), S encrypts it under D's public key.

3   Building Blocks

We recall several of the building blocks used in our TFA-KE protocol.

SAS-MA Scheme of Vaudenay [50]. The Short Authentication String Message Authentication (SAS-MA) scheme allows the transmission of a message from a sender to a receiver so that the receiver can check the integrity of the received message. A SAS-MA scheme considers two communication channels. One that allows the transmission of messages of arbitrary length and is controlled by an active man-in-the-middle, and another that allows sending up to t bits that cannot be changed by the attacker (neither channel is assumed to provide secrecy). We refer to these as the *open channel* and the *SAS channel*, respectively, and call the parameter t the *SAS channel capacity*. A SAS-MA scheme is called *secure* if the probability that the receiver accepts a message modified by a (computationally bounded) attacker on the open channel is no more than 2^{-t} (plus a negligible fraction). In Fig. 1 we show a secure SAS-MA implementation of [50] for a sender C and a receiver D. The SAS channel is abstracted as a comparison of two t-bit strings checksum$_C$ and checksum$_D$ computed by sender and receiver, respectively. As shown in [50], the probability that an active man-in-the-middle attacker between D and C succeeds in changing message M$_C$ while D and C compute the same checksum is at most 2^{-t}. Note that this level of security is achieved without any keying material (secret or public) pre-shared between the parties. Also, importantly, there is no requirement for checksums to be secret. (In Sect. 5 we present a formal SAS-MA security definition.)

Thus, the SAS-MA protocol reduces integrity verification of a received message M$_C$ to verifying the equality of two strings (checksums) assumed to be transmitted "out-of-band", namely, away from adversarial control. In our application, the checksums will be values displayed by device D and client C whose equality the user verifies and confirms via a physical action, e.g. a click, a QR snapshot, or an audio read-out (see Sect. 6). In the TFA-KE application this user-confirmation of checksum equality serves as evidence for the physical control of the terminal C and device D by the same user, and a confirmation of user's possession of the 2nd authentication factor implemented as device D.

Input: Sender C holds message M$_C$; Receiver D holds M$_C'$.

Output: Receiver D accepts if M$_C$ = M$_C'$ and rejects otherwise.

Assumptions: C-to-D SAS channel with capacity t; security parameter κ; hash function H_{com} onto $\{0,1\}^\kappa$.

SAS-MA Protocol:
1. C sends Com $= H_{com}(M_C, R_C, d)$ to D for random R_C, d s.t. $|R_C| = t$ and $|d| = \kappa$;
2. D sends to C a random string R_D of length t;
3. C sends (R_C, d) to D and enters checksum$_C = R_C \oplus R_D$ into C-to-D SAS channel;
4. D sets checksum$_D = R_C \oplus R_D$ and it accepts if and only if Com $= H_{com}(M_C', R_C, d)$ *and* checksum$_C$ received on the SAS channel equals checksum$_D$.

Fig. 1. SAS Message Authentication (SAS-MA) [50]

SAS-SMT. One can use a SAS-MA mechanism from C to D to bootstrap a *confidential channel* from D to C. The transformation is standard: To send a message m securely from D to C (in our application m is a one-time key and D's PTR response, see below), C picks a CCA-secure public key encryption key pair (sk, pk) (e.g., pair (x, g^x)) for an encryption scheme (KG, Enc, Dec), sends pk to D, and then C and D execute the SAS-MA protocol on $M_C = $ pk. If D accepts, it sends m encrypted under pk to C, who decrypts it using sk. The security of SAS-MA and the public-key encryption imply that an attacker can intercept m (or modify it to some related message) only by supplying its own key pk′ instead of C's key, and causing D to accept in the SAS-MA authentication of pk′ which by SAS-MA security can happen with probability at most 2^{-t}. The resulting protocol has 4 messages, and the cost of a plain Diffie-Hellman exchange if implemented using ECIES [22] encryption. We refer to this scheme as SAS-SMT (SMT for "secure message transmission").

aPAKE. Informally, an aPAKE (for asymmetric or augmented PAKE) is a password protocol secure against server compromise [25,32], namely, one where the server stores a one-way function of the user's password so that an attacker who breaks into the server can only learn information on the password through an exhaustive offline dictionary attack. While the aPAKE terminology is typically used in the context of password-only protocols that do not rely on public keys, we extend it here (following [37]) to the standard PKI-based password-over-TLS protocol. This enables the use of our techniques in the context of TLS, a major benefit of our TFA schemes. Note that this standard protocol, while secure against server compromise is not strictly an aPAKE as it allows an attacker to learn plaintext passwords (decrypted by TLS) for users that authenticate while the attacker is in control of the server. As shown in [37], dealing with this property requires a tweak in the DE-PAKE protocol (C needs to authenticate the value b sent by D in the PTR protocol described below - see also Sect. 6).

DE-PAKE. A Device-Enhanced PAKE (DE-PAKE) [37] is an extension of the asymmetric PAKE model by an auxiliary device, which strengthens aPAKE protocols by eliminating offline dictionary attacks upon server compromise. We discuss DE-PAKE in more detail in Sect. 2 and recall its formal model in Appendix A. We use DE-PAKE protocols as a main module in our general construction of TFA-KE, and our practical instantiation of this construction, protocol OpTFA, uses the DE-PAKE scheme of [37] which combines an asymmetric aPAKE with a password hardening procedure PTR described next.

Password-to-Random Scheme PTR. A PTR is a password hardening procedure that allows client C to translate with the help of device D (which stores a key k) a user's *master password* pwd into independent pseudorandom passwords (denoted rwd) for each user account. The PTR instantiation from [37] is based on the Ford-Kaliski's Blind Hashed Diffie-Hellman technique [31]: Let G be a group of prime order q, let H' and H be hash functions which map onto, respectively, elements of G and κ-bit strings, where κ is a security parameter. Define $F_k(x) = H(x, (H'(x))^k)$, where the key k is chosen at random in $\mathbb{Z}_q$. In PTR this function is computed jointly between C and D where D inputs key k and C inputs $x = $ pwd as the argument, and the output, denoted rwd $= F_k($pwd$)$, is learned by C only. The protocol is simple: C sends $a = (H'($pwd$))^r$ for r random in $\mathbb{Z}_q$, D responds with $b = a^k$, and C computes rwd $= H(x, b^{1/r})$. Under the One-More (Gap) Diffie-Hellman (OM-DH) assumption in the Random Oracle

Model (ROM), this scheme realizes a universally composable oblivious PRF (OPRF) [36], which in particular implies that $x = $ pwd is hidden from all observers and function $F_k(\cdot)$ remains pseudorandom on all inputs which are not queried to D.

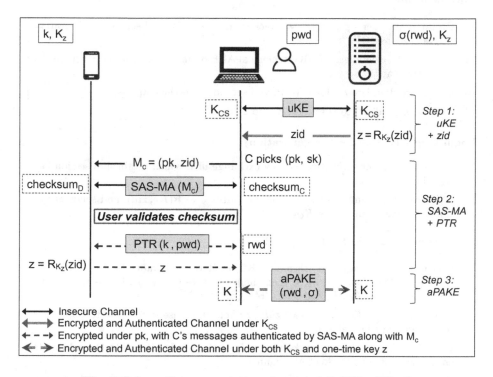

Fig. 2. Schematic representation of protocol OpTFA of Fig. 3

4   OpTFA: A Practical Secure TFA-KE Protocol

In Sect. 5 we present and prove a general design, GenTFA, of a TFA-KE protocol based on two generic components, namely, a SAS-MA and DE-PAKE protocols. But first, in this section, we show a practical instantiation of GenTFA using the specific building blocks presented in Sect. 3, namely, the SAS-MA scheme from Fig. 1 and the DE-PAKE scheme from [37] (that uses the DH-based PTR scheme described in that section composed with any asymmetric PAKE). This concrete instantiation serves as the basis of our implementation work (Sect. 6) and helps explaining the rationale of our general construction. OpTFA is presented in Fig. 3. A schematic representation is shown in Fig. 2.

Enhanced TFA via SAS. Before going into the specifics of OpTFA, we describe a *general technique* for designing TFA schemes using a SAS channel. In traditional TFA schemes, a PIN is displayed to the user who copies it into a login screen to prove access to that PIN. As discussed in the introduction, this mechanism suffers of significant weaknesses mainly due to the low entropy of PINs (and

Components: In addition to the SAS-MA, PTR and aPAKE tools introduced in Sec. 3, OpTFA uses an unauthenticated KE (uKE) protocol, a PRF R, a CCA-secure public key encryption scheme (KG, Enc, Dec), and a MAC function.

Initialization:

1. On input the user's password pwd, pick random k in $\mathbb{Z}_q$ and set rwd $= F_k(\text{pwd}) = H(\text{pwd}, (H'(\text{pwd}))^k)$;

2. Initialize the asymmetric PAKE scheme aPAKE on input rwd and let σ denote the user's state at the server.

3. Choose random key K_z for PRF R, and set zidSet to the empty set;

4. Give (k, K_z, zidSet) to D and (σ, K_z) to S.

Login step I (C-S uKE + *zid* generation):

1. S and C run a (unauthenticated) key exchange uKE which establishes session key K_{CS} between them;

2. S generates random κ-bit nonce zid, computes $z \leftarrow \text{R}(K_z, zid)$, and sends zid to C authenticated under key K_{CS}.

Login step II (C-D SAS-MA + PTR):

1. C generates PKE key pair $(\text{sk}, \text{pk}) \leftarrow \text{KG}$, t-bit random value R_C, κ-bit random value d, and random r in $\mathbb{Z}_q$. C then computes $a \leftarrow H'(\text{pwd})^r$, $\text{M}_C \leftarrow (\text{pk}, zid, a)$, Com $\leftarrow H_{\text{com}}(\text{M}_C, R_C, d)$, and sends (M_C, Com) to D;

2. D on $((\text{pk}, zid, a), \text{Com})$, aborts if $zid \in \text{zidSet}$, otherwise it adds zid to zidSet and sends random t-bit value R_D to C.

3. C receives R_D, computes $\text{checksum}_C \leftarrow R_C \oplus R_D$, sends (R_C, d) to D, and inputs checksum_C into the C-to-D SAS channel.

4. D computes $\text{checksum}_D \leftarrow R_C \oplus R_D$ and upon receiving checksum_C on the C-to-D SAS channel, it checks if $\text{checksum}_C = \text{checksum}_D$ and Com $= H_{\text{com}}(\text{M}_C, R_C, d)$ and aborts if not. Otherwise D computes $b \leftarrow a^k$ and $z \leftarrow \text{R}(K_z, zid)$, and sends $e_D \leftarrow \text{Enc}(\text{pk}, (z, b))$ to C.

5. C computes $(z, b) \leftarrow \text{Dec}(\text{sk}, e_D)$ and rwd $\leftarrow H(\text{pwd}, b^{1/r})$ $[= F_k(\text{pwd})]$, and aborts if Dec outputs $\perp$.

Login step III (C-S aPAKE over Authenticated Link):

1. C and S run protocol aPAKE on resp. inputs rwd and σ with all aPAKE messages authenticated by keys z and K_{CS} (each key is used to compute a MAC on each aPAKE message).

    Each party aborts and sets local output to $\perp$ if any of the MAC verifications fails.

2. The final output of C and S equals their outputs in the aPAKE instance: either a session key K or a rejection sign $\perp$.

Fig. 3. OpTFA: efficient TFA-KE protocol with optimal security bounds

inconvenience of copying them). We suggest automating the transmission of the PIN over a *confidential channel* from device D to client C. To implement such channel, we use the SAS-SMT scheme from Sect. 3 where security boils down to having D and C display t-bit strings (checksums) that the user checks for equality. In this way, low-entropy PINs can be replaced with full-entropy values (we refer to them as *one-time keys (OTK)*) that are immune to eavesdropping and bound active attacks to a success probability of 2^{-t}. These active attacks are impractical even for $t = 20$ (more a denial-of-service than an impersonation threat) and with larger t's as illustrated in Sect. 6 they are just infeasible. Note that this approach works with any form of generation of OTK's, e.g., time-based mechanisms, challenge-response between device and server, etc.

4.1   OpTFA Explained

Protocol OpTFA (Fig. 3) requires several mechanisms that are necessary to obtain the strong security bounds of the TFA-KE model. To provide rationale for the need of these mechanisms we show how the protocol is built bottom-up to deliver the required security properties. We stress that while the design is involved the resultant protocol is efficient and practical. The presentation and discussion of security properties here is informal but the intuition can be formalized as we do via the TFA-KE model (Sect. 2), the generic protocol GenTFA in next section and the proof of Theorem 1.

In general terms, OpTFA can be seen as a DE-PAKE protocol using the PTR scheme from Sect. 3 and enhanced with fresh OTKs transmitted from D to C via the above SAS-SMT mechanism. The OTK is generated by the device and server for each session and then included in the aPAKE interaction between C and S. We note that OpTFA treats aPAKE generically, so any such scheme can be used. In particular, we start by illustrating how OpTFA works with the standard password-over-TLS aPAKE, and then generalize to the use of any aPAKE, including PKI-free ones.

• OpTFA 0.0. This is standard password-over-TLS where the user's password is transmitted from C to S under the protection of TLS.

• OpTFA 0.1. We enhance password-over-TLS with the OTK-over-SAS mechanism described above. First, C transmits the user's password to S over TLS and if the password verifies at S, S sends a nonce zid to C who relays it to D. On the basis of zid (which also acts as session identifier in our analysis), D computes a OTK $z = \mathsf{R}_{K_z}(zid)$ where R is a PRF and K_z a key shared between D and S. D transmits z to C over the SAS-SMT channel and C relays it to S over TLS. The user is authenticated only if the received value z is the same as the one computed by S.

This scheme offers defense in case of password leakage. With a full-entropy OTK it ensures security against eavesdroppers on the D-C link and limits the advantage of an active attacker to a probability of 2^{-t} for SAS checksums of length t. However, the scheme is open to online password attacks (as in current commonly deployed schemes) because the attacker can try online guesses without having to deal with the transmission of OTK z. In addition, it offers no security against offline dictionary attacks upon server compromise.

- **OpTFA 0.2.** We change OpTFA 0.1 so that the user's password pwd is only transmitted to S at the end of the protocol together with the OTK z (it is important that if z does not verify as the correct OTK, that the server does not reveal if pwd is correct or not). This change protects the protocol against online guessing attacks and reduces the probability of the successful testing of a candidate password to $2^{-(d+t)}$ rather than 2^{-d} in version 0.1.

- **OpTFA 0.3.** We add defense against offline dictionary attacks upon server compromise by resorting to the DE-PAKE construction of [37] and, in particular, to the password-to-random hardening procedure PTR from Sect. 3. For this, we now assume that the user has a master password pwd that PTR converts into randomized passwords rwd for each user account. By registering rwd with server S and using PTR for the conversion, DE-PAKE security ensures that offline dictionary attacks are infeasible even if the server is compromised (case (3) in Definition 1). Note that the PTR procedure runs between D and C following the establishment of the SAS-SMT channel.

- **OpTFA 0.4.** We change the run of PTR between D and C so that the value a computed by C as part of PTR is transmitted over the SAS-authenticated channel from C to D. Without this authentication the strict bound of case (3) in Definition 1 (simplified for $q_C' = 0$), namely, $\mathsf{Adv}_A^{\mathsf{TFA}} \leq q_D/2^{d+t} + \epsilon$ upon server compromise, would not be met. Indeed, when the attacker compromises server S, it learns the key K_z used to compute the OTK z so the defense provided by OTK is lost. So, how can we still ensure the 2^t denominator in the above bound expression? The answer is that by authenticating the PTR value a under SAS-MA, the attacker is forced to run (expected) 2^t sessions to be able to inject its own value a over that channel. Such injection is necessary for testing a password guess even when K_z is known. When considering a password dictionary of size 2^d this ensures the denominator 2^{d+t} in the security bound.

- **OpTFA 0.5.** We add the following mechanism to OpTFA: Upon initialization of an authentication session (for a given user), C and S run an *unauthenticated* (a.k.a. anonymous) key exchange uKE (e.g., a plain Diffie-Hellman protocol) to establish a shared key K_{CS} that they use as a MAC key applied to all subsequent OpTFA messages. To see the need for uKE assume it is omitted. For simplicity, consider the case where attacker A knows the user's password. In this case, all A needs for impersonating the user is to learn one value of z which it can attempt by acting as a man-in-the-middle on the C-D channel. After q_D such attempts, A has probability of $q_D/2^t$ to learn z which together with the user's password allows A to authenticate to S. In contrast, the bound required by Definition 1 in this case is the stricter $\min\{q_S, q_D\}/2^t$. This requires that for *each* attempt at learning z in the C-D channel, not only A needs to try to break SAS-MA authentication but it also needs to establish a new session with S. For this we resort to the uKE channel. It ensures that a response z to a value zid sent by S over a uKE session will only be accepted by S if this response comes back on the *same* uKE session (i.e., authenticated with the same keys used by S to send the challenge zid). It means that both zid and z are exchanged with the same party. If zid was sent to the legitimate user then the attacker, even if it learns the corresponding z, cannot use it to authenticate back to S. We note that uKE is also needed in the case that the attacker does not know the password. Without it, the success probability for this case is about a factor $2^d/q_S$ higher than acceptable by Definition 1.

Note. When all communication between C and S goes over TLS, there is no need to establish a dedicated uKE channel; TLS serves as such.

• OpTFA 0.6. We stipulate that D never responds twice to the same zid value (for this, D keeps a stash of recently seen zid's; older values become useless to the attacker once they time out at the server). Without this mechanism the attacker gets multiple attempts at learning z for a single challenge zid. However, this would violate bound (1) (for the case $q_C = q'_C = 0$) $\min\{q_S, q_D\}/2^{d+t}$ which requires that each guess attempt at z be bound to the establishment of a new session of the attacker with S.

• OpTFA 0.7. Finally, we generalize OpTFA so that the password protocol run as the last stage of OpTFA (after PTR generates rwd) can be implemented with *any* asymmetric aPAKE protocol, with or without assuming PKI, using the server-specific user's password rwd. As shown in [37], running any aPAKE protocol on a password rwd produced by PTR results in a DE-PAKE scheme, a property that we use in an essential way in our analysis.

We need one last mechanism for C to prove knowledge of z to S, namely, we specify that both C and S use z as a MAC key to authenticate the messages sent by protocol aPAKE (this is in addition to the authentication of these messages with key K_{CS}). Without this, an attack is possible where in case that OpTFA fails the attacker learns if the reason for it was an aPAKE failure or a wrong z. This allows the attacker to mount an online attack on the password without the attacker having to learn the OTK. (When the aPAKE is password-over-TLS the above MAC mechanism is not needed, the same authentication effect is achieved by encrypting rwd and z under the same CCA-secure ciphertext [33].)

• OpTFA. Version 0.7 constitutes the full specification of the OpTFA protocol, described in Fig. 3, with generic aPAKE.

Performance: The number of exponentiations in OpTFA is reported in the introduction; implementation and performance information is presented in Sect. 6.

OpTFA Security. Security of OpTFA follows from that of protocol GenTFA because OpTFA is its instantiation. See Theorem 1 in Sect. 5 and Corollary 1.

5   The Generic GenTFA Protocol

In Fig. 4 we show protocol GenTFA which is a generalization of protocol OpTFA shown in Fig. 3 in Sect. 4. Protocol GenTFA is a compiler which converts *any* secure DE-PAKE and SAS-MA schemes into a secure TFA-KE. It uses the same uKE and CCA-PKE tools as protocol OpTFA, but it also generalizes two other mechanisms used in OpTFA as, resp. a generic symmetric *Key Encapsulation Mechanism* (KEM) scheme and an *Authenticated Channel* (AC) scheme.

A Key Encapsulation Mechanism, denoted (KemE, KemD) (see e.g. [48]), allows for encrypting a random session key given a (long-term) symmetric key K_z, i.e., if $(zid, z) \leftarrow \mathsf{KemE}(K_z)$ then $z \leftarrow \mathsf{KemD}(K_z, zid)$. A KEM is secure if key z corresponding to $zid \notin \{zid_1, ..., zid_q\}$ is pseudorandom even given the keys z_i corresponding to all zid_i's. In protocol OpTFA of Fig. 3, KEM is implemented using PRF R: zid is a random κ-bit string and $z = R(K_z, zid)$. We also generalize the usage of the MAC function in OpTFA as an Authenticated Channel, defined by a pair ACSend, ACRec, which implements bi-directional authenticated communication between two parties sharing a symmetric key K [29,34]. Algorithm ACSend takes inputs key K and message m and outputs m with authentication tag computed with key K, while the receiver procedure, $\mathsf{ACRec}(K, \cdot)$, outputs either a message or the rejection symbol $\perp$. We assume that the AC scheme is stateful and provides authenticity and protection against replay.

The security of GenTFA is stated in the following theorem:

Theorem 1. *Assuming security of the building blocks DE-PAKE, SAS, uKE, PKE, KEM, and AC, protocol* GenTFA *is a* (T, ϵ)-*secure TFA-KE scheme for* ϵ *upper bounded by*

$$\epsilon^{\mathsf{DEPAKE}} + n \cdot (\epsilon^{\mathsf{SAS}} + \epsilon^{\mathsf{uKE}} + \epsilon^{\mathsf{PKE}} + \epsilon^{\mathsf{KEM}} + 6\epsilon^{\mathsf{AC}}) + n^2/2^\kappa$$

for $n = q_{HbC} + \max(q_S, q_D, q_C, q'_C)$ *where* q_{HbC} *denotes the number of* GenTFA *protocol sessions in which the adversary is only eavesdropping, and each quantity of the form* ϵ^{P} *is a bound on the advantage of an attacker that works in time* $\approx T$ *against the protocol building block* P.

As a corollary we obtain a proof of TFA-KE security for protocol OpTFA from Fig. 3 which uses specific secure instantiations of GenTFA components. The corollary follows by applying the result of Vaudenay [50], which implies in particular that the SAS-MA scheme used in OpTFA is secure in ROM, and the result of [37], which implies that the DE-PAKE used in OpTFA is secure under the OM-DH assumption if the underlying aPAKE is a secure asymmetric PAKE.

We note that protocol OpTFA optimizes GenTFA instantiated with the DE-PAKE of [37] by piggybacking the C-D round of communication in that protocol, $a = H'(\mathsf{pwd})^r$ and $b = a^k$, onto resp. C's message $\mathsf{M_C}$ and the plaintext in D's ciphertext e_D. The security proof extends to this round-optimized case because SAS-MA authentication of $\mathsf{M_C}$ and CCA-security of PKE bind DE-PAKE messages a, b to this session just as the $\mathsf{ACSend}(K_{CD}, \cdot)$ mechanism does in (non-optimized) protocol GenTFA.

Corollary 1. *Assuming that aPAKE is a secure asymmetric PAKE, uKE is secure Key Exchange, (KG, Enc, Dec) is a CCA-secure PKE, R is a secure PRF, and MAC is a secure message authentication code, protocol OpTFA is a secure TFA-KE scheme under the OM-DH assumption in ROM.*

Initialization: Given the user's password pwd, we initialize the DE-PAKE scheme on pwd. Let k and σ be the resulting user-specific states stored at resp. D and S. Let K_z be a random KEM key. Let zidSet be an empty set. D is initialized with (k, K_z, zidSet) and S is initialized with (σ, K_z).

Login step I (C-S KE + KEM generation):

1. S and C create shared key K_{CS} using a (non-authenticated) key exchange uKE.
2. S generates $(zid, z) \leftarrow \text{KemE}(K_z)$, sets $e_S \leftarrow \text{ACSend}(K_{CS}, zid)$, and sends e_S to C, who computes $zid \leftarrow \text{ACRec}(K_{CS}, e_S)$, or aborts if decryption fails.

Login step II (C-D SAS-MA + KEM decryption):

1. C generates a PKE key pair $(\text{sk}, \text{pk}) \leftarrow \text{KG}$, sends $M_C = (\text{pk}, zid)$ to D, and C and D run SAS-MA to authenticate M_C using the t-bit C-to-D SAS channel.
2. D aborts if $zid \in \text{zidSet}$ or if the SAS scheme fails. Otherwise, D adds zid to zidSet, computes $z \leftarrow \text{KemD}(K_z, zid)$, picks a random MAC key K_{CD}, computes $e_D \leftarrow \text{Enc}(\text{pk}, (z, K_{CD}))$ and sends e_D to C.
3. C computes $(z, K_{CD}) \leftarrow \text{Dec}(\text{sk}, e_D)$ (aborts if $\perp$).

Login step III (DE-PAKE over Authenticated Links):

C, D, and S run DE-PAKE on resp. inputs pwd, k, and σ, modified as follows:

(a) All communication between D and S is routed through C.

(b) Communication between C and D goes over a channel authenticated by key K_{CD}, i.e. it is sent via $\text{ACSend}(K_{CD}, \cdot)$ and received via $\text{ACRec}(K_{CD}, \cdot)$, Either party aborts if its ACRec ever outputs $\perp$.

(c) Communication between C and S goes over a channel authenticated by key z and then the result of that is sent over a channel authenticated by key K_{CS}, i.e. it is sent via $\text{ACSend}(K_{CS}, \text{ACSend}(z, \cdot))$ and received via $\text{ACRec}(K_{CS}, \text{ACRec}(z, \cdot))$. Each party aborts and sets local output to $\perp$ if its ACRec instance ever outputs $\perp$.

The final outputs of C and S are their respective outputs in this DE-PAKE instance, either session key K or a rejection $\perp$.

Fig. 4. Generic TFA-KE scheme: protocol GenTFA

Security definition of SAS authentication. For the purpose of the proof below we state the security property assumed of a SAS-MA scheme which was informally described in Sect. 3. While [50] defines the security of SAS-MA using a game-based formulation, here we do it via the following (universally composable) functionality $F_{\text{SAS}[t]}$: On input a message $[\text{SAS.SEND}, sid, P', m]$ from an honest party P, functionality $F_{\text{SAS}[t]}$ sends $[\text{SAS.SEND}, sid, P, P', m]$ to A, and then, if A's response is $[\text{SAS.CONNECT}, sid]$, then $F_{\text{SAS}[t]}$ sends $[\text{SAS.SEND}, sid, P, m]$ to P', if A's response is $[\text{SAS.ABORT}, sid]$, then $F_{\text{SAS}[t]}$ sends $[\text{SAS.SEND}, sid, P, \perp]$ to P', and if A's response is $[\text{SAS.ATTACK}, sid, m']$ then $F_{\text{SAS}[t]}$ throws a coin ρ

which comes out 1 with probability 2^{-t} and 0 with probability $1 - 2^{-t}$, and if $\rho = 1$ then $\mathsf{F}_{\mathsf{SAS}[t]}$ sends succ to A and [SAS.SEND, sid, P, m'] to P', and if $\rho = 0$ then $\mathsf{F}_{\mathsf{SAS}[t]}$ sends fail to A and [SAS.SEND, $sid, P, \perp$] to P'.

In our main instantiation of the generic protocol GenTFA of Fig. 4, i.e. in protocol OpTFA of Fig. 3, we instantiate SAS-MA with the scheme of [50], but even though the original security argument given for it in [50] used the game-based security notion, it is straightforward to adopt this argument to see that this scheme securely realizes the above (universally composable) functionality.

Proof of Theorem 1. Let A be an adversary limited by time T playing the TFA-KE security game, which we will denote G_0, instantiated with the TFA-KE scheme GenTFA. Let the security advantage defined in Definition 1 for adversary A satisfy $\mathsf{Adv}_\mathsf{A}^\mathsf{TFA} = \epsilon$. Let Π_i^S, Π_j^C, Π_l^D refer to respectively the i-th, j-th, and l-th instances of S, C, and D entities which A starts up. Let t be the SAS channel capacity, κ the security parameter, q_S, q_D, q_C, q_C' the limits on the numbers of rogue sessions of S, D, C when communicating with S, and C when communicating with D, and let q_{HbC} be the number of GenTFA protocol sessions in which A plays only a passive eavesdropper role except that we allow A to abort any of these protocol executions at any step. Let $n_S = q_S + q_{HbC}$, $n_D = q_D + q_{HbC}$, $n_C = q_C + q_C' + q_{HbC}$, and note that these are the ranges of indexes i, j, l for instances Π_i^S, Π_j^C, and Π_l^D. We will use $[n]$ to denote range $\{1, ..., n\}$.

The security proof goes by cases depending on the type of corrupt queries A makes. In all cases the proof starts from the security-experiment game G_0 and proceeds via a series of game changes, $\mathsf{G}_1, \mathsf{G}_2$, etc., until a modified game G_i allows us to reduce an attack on the DE-PAKE with the same corruption pattern (except in the case of corrupt client C) to the attack on G_i. In the case of the corrupt client the argument is different because it does not rely on the underlying DE-PAKE (note that DE-PAKE does not provide any security properties in the case of client corruption). In some game changes we will consider a modified adversary algorithm, for example an algorithm constructed from the original adversary A interacting with a simulator of some higher-level procedure, e.g. the SAS−MA simulator. Wlog, we use A_i for an adversary algorithm in game G_i.

We will use p_i to denote the probability that A_i interacting with game G_i outputs b' s.t. $b' = b$ where b is the bit chosen by the game on the test session. Recall that when A makes the test session query test(P, i), for $P \in \{\mathsf{S}, \mathsf{C}\}$, then, assuming that instance Π_i^P produced a session key sk, game G_0 outputs that session key if $b = 1$ or produces a random string of equal size if $b = 0$ (and if session Π_i^P did not produce the key then G_0 outputs $\perp$ regardless of bit b). Note that by assumption $\mathsf{Adv}_\mathsf{A}^\mathsf{TFA} = \epsilon$ we have that $p_0 = 1/2 + 1/2 \cdot \mathsf{Adv}_\mathsf{A}^\mathsf{TFA} = 1/2 + \epsilon/2$.

Case 1: No party is compromised. This is the case when A makes no corrupt queries, i.e. it's the default "network adversary" case. For lack of space we describe below only the game changes in the proof, and we state what we claim about the effects of that game change and what assumption we use. The full details of the proof are included in the full version of the paper [38].

Game G_1 : Let Z be a random function which maps onto κ-bit strings. If (zid_i, z_i) dentes the KEM (ciphertext,key) pair generated by Π_i^S then in G_1 we set

$z_i = Z(zid_i)$ instead of using KemE, and we abort if there is ever a collision in z_i values. Security of KEM implies that $p_1 \leq p_0 + \epsilon^{\mathsf{KEM}}(n_S) + n_S^2/2^\kappa$.

Game G_2 : Here we replace the SAS-MA procedure with the simulator $\mathsf{SIM}_{\mathsf{SAS}}$ implied by the UC security of the SAS-MA scheme of [50]. In other words, whenever Π_j^C and Π_l^D execute the SAS$-$MA sub-protocol, we replace this execution with a simulator $\mathsf{SIM}_{\mathsf{SAS}}$ interacting with A and the ideal SAS$-$MA functionality $\mathsf{F}_{\mathsf{SAS}[t]}$. For example, Π_j^C, instead of sending $\mathsf{M}_\mathsf{C} = (\mathsf{pk}, zid)$ to A_1 and starting a SAS$-$MA instance to authenticate M_C to D, will send $[\mathsf{SAS.SEND}, sid, \Pi_l^\mathsf{D}, \mathsf{M}_\mathsf{C}]$ to $\mathsf{F}_{\mathsf{SAS}[t]}$, which triggers $\mathsf{SIM}_{\mathsf{SAS}}$ to start simulating to A the SAS$-$MA protocol on input M_C between Π_j^C and Π_l^D. The rules of $\mathsf{F}_{\mathsf{SAS}[t]}$ imply that $\mathcal{A}$ can make this connection either succeed, abort, or, if it attacks it then Π_l^D will abort with probability $1 - 2^{-t}$, but with probability 2^{-t} it will accept $\mathcal{A}$'s message M_C^* instead of M_C. Security of SAS$-$MA implies that $p_2 \leq p_1 + \min(n_C, n_D) \cdot \epsilon^{\mathsf{SAS}}$.

Game G_3 : Here we re-name entities involved in game G_2. Note that adversary A_2 interacts with G_2 which internally runs algorithms $\mathsf{SIM}_{\mathsf{SAS}}$ and $\mathsf{F}_{\mathsf{SAS}[t]}$, and that $\mathsf{SIM}_{\mathsf{SAS}}$ interacts only with $\mathsf{F}_{\mathsf{SAS}[t]}$ on one end and A_2 on the other. We can therefore draw the boundaries between the adversarial algorithm and the security game slightly differently, by considering an adversary A_3 which executes the steps of A_2 and $\mathsf{SIM}_{\mathsf{SAS}}$, and a security game G_3 which executes the rest of game G_2, including the operation of functionality $\mathsf{F}_{\mathsf{SAS}[t]}$. In other words, G_3 interacts with A_3 using the $\mathsf{F}_{\mathsf{SAS}[t]}$ interface to $\mathsf{SIM}_{\mathsf{SAS}}$, i.e. G_3 sends to A_3 messages of the type $[\mathsf{SAS.SEND}, sid, \Pi_j^\mathsf{C}, \Pi_l^\mathsf{D}, \mathsf{M}_\mathsf{C}]$, and A_3's response must be one of $[\mathsf{SAS.CONNECT}, sid]$, $[\mathsf{SAS.ABORT}, sid]$, and $[\mathsf{SAS.ATTACK}, sid, \mathsf{M}_\mathsf{C}^*]$. Since we are only re-drawing the boundaries between the adversarial algorithm and the security game, we have that $p_3 = p_2$.

Game G_4 : Here we change game G_3 s.t. if A sends $[\mathsf{SAS.CONNECT}, sid]$ to let the SAS-MA instance go through between Π_j^C and Π_l^D with M_C containing Π_j^C's key pk, then we replace the ciphertext e_D subsequently sent by Π_l^D by encrypting a constant string instead of $\mathsf{Enc}(\mathsf{pk}, (z, K_{CD}))$, and if A passes this e_D to Π_j^C then it decrypts it as (z, K_{CD}) generated by Π_l^D. In other words, we replace the encryption under SAS-authenticated key pk by a "magic" delivery of the encrypted plaintext. The CCA security of PKE implies that $p_4 \leq p_3 + \min(n_C, n_D) \cdot \epsilon^{\mathsf{PKE}}$.

Game G_5 : Here we abort if, assuming that key pk and ciphertext e_D were exchanged between Π_j^C and Π_l^D correctly, any party accepts wrong messages in the subsequent DE-PAKE execution authenticated by K_{CD} created by Π_l^D. The authentic channel security implies that $p_5 \leq p_4 + \min(n_C, n_D) \cdot \epsilon^{\mathsf{AC}}$.

Game G_6 : We perform some necessary cleaning-up, and abort if the SAS-MA instance between Π_j^C and Π_l^D) sent M_C correctly, but adversary did not deliver Π_l^D's response e_D back to Π_j^C and yet Π_l^D did not abort in subsequent DE-PAKE. Since this way Π_j^C has no information about key K_{CD} we get $p_6 \leq p_5 + q_D \cdot \epsilon^{\mathsf{AC}}$.

Game G_7 : We replace the keys created by uKE for every Π_i^S-Π_j^C session in step I.1 *on which* A *was only an eavesdropper*, with random keys. Security of uKE implies that $p_7 \leq p_6 + \min(n_C, n_S) \cdot \epsilon^{uKE}$.

At this point the game has the following properties: If A is passive on the C-S key exchange in step I then A is forced to be passive on the C-S link in the DE-PAKE in step III. Also, if A does not attack the SAS−MA and delivers D's response to C then A is forced to be passive on the C-D link in the DE-PAKE in step III (and if A does not deliver D's respt to C then this D instance will abort too). The remaining cases are either (1) active attacks on the key exchange in step I or (2) when A attacks the SAS−MA sub-protocol and gets D to accept $M_{C*} \neq M_C$ or (3) A sends $e_D^* \neq e_D$ to C. In handling these cases the crucial issue is what A does with the *zid* created by S. Consider any S instance Π_i^S in which the adversary interferes with the key exchange protocol in step I.1. Without loss of generality assume that the adversary learns key K_{CS} output by Π_i^S in this step. Note that D keeps a variable zidSet in which it stores all *zid* values it ever receives, and that D aborts if it sees any *zid* more than once. Therefore each game execution defines a 1-1 function $L : [n_S] \rightarrow [n_D] \cup \{\bot\}$ s.t. if $L(i) \neq \bot$ then $L(i)$ is the unique index in $[n_D]$ s.t. $\Pi_{L(i)}^D$ receives $M_C = (pk, zid_i)$ in step II.1 for some pk, and $L(i) = \bot$ if and only if no D session receives zid_i. If $L(i) \neq \bot$ then we consider two cases: First, if $M_C = (pk, zid_i)$ which contains zid_i originates with some session Π_j^C, and second if $M_C = (pk, zid_i)$ is created by the adversary.

Game G_9 : Let Π_i^S and Π_j^C be rogue sessions s.t. A sends zid_i to Π_j^C in step I.2, but then stop Π_j^C from getting the corresponding z_i by either attacking SAS-MA or misdelivering D's response e_D. In that case neither Π_j^C nor A have any information about z_i, and therefore Π_i^S should reject. Namely, if in G_9 we set Π_i^S's output to $\bot$ in such cases then $p_9 \leq p_8 + q_S \cdot \epsilon^{AC}$.

Game G_{10} : Let Π_i^S and Π_j^C be rogue sessions and A send zid_i to Π_j^C as above, but now consider the case that A lets Π_j^C learn z_i but A does not learn z_i itself, i.e. A lets SAS-MA and e_D go through. In this case we will abort if in DE-PAKE communication in Step III between Π_i^S and Π_j^C either party accepts a message not sent by the other party. Since A has no information about z_i the authenticated channel security implies that $p_{10} \leq p_9 + \min(q_C, q_S) \cdot \epsilon^{AC}$.

Note that at this point if A interferes with the KE in step I.1 with session Π_i^S, sends zid_i to some Π_j^C and does not send it to some Π_l^D by sending [SAS.ATTACK, sid, (pk^*, zid_i)] for any l then A is forced to be a passive eavesdropper on the DE-PAKE protocol in step III. Note that this holds when $L(i) = l$ s.t. the game issues [SAS.SEND, sid, Π_j^C, Π_l^D, (pk, zid_i)] for some pk, i.e. if some Π_l^D receives value zid_i, it receives it as part of a message M_C sent by some Π_j^C.

Game G_{11} : Finally consider the case when A itself sends zid_i to D, i.e. when $L(i) = l$ s.t. A sends [SAS.ATTACK, sid, $M_C^* = (pk^*, zid_i)$] in response to [SAS.SEND, sid, Π_j^C, Π_l^D, M_C], but the $F_{SAS[t]}$ coin-toss comes out $\rho_l = 0$, i.e. A fails in this SAS-MA attack. In that case we can let Π_i^S abort in step III because if $\rho_l = 0$ then A has no information about $z_i = Z(zid_i)$, hence $p_{11} \leq p_{10} + q_S \cdot \epsilon^{AC}$.

After these game changes, we finally make a reduction from an attack on underlying DE-PAKE to an attack on TFA-KE. Namely, we construct A^* which achieves advantage $\mathsf{Adv}_{A^*}^{\mathsf{DEPAKE}} = 2 \cdot (p_{11} - 1/2)$ against DE-PAKE, and makes q_S^*, q_D^*, q_C, q_C rogue queries respectively to S, D, to C on its connection to S, and to C on its connection with D, where $q_S^* = q_D^* = q^*$ where q^* is a random variable equal to the sum of $q = \min(q_S, q_D)$ coin tosses which come out 1 with probability 2^{-t} and 0 with probability $1 - 2^{-t}$. Recall that $\mathsf{Adv}_A^{\mathsf{TFA}} = 2 \cdot (p_0 - 1/2)$ and that by the game changes above we have that $|p_{11} - p_0|$ is a negligible quantity, and hence $\mathsf{Adv}_{A^*}^{\mathsf{DEPAKE}}$ is negligibly close to $\mathsf{Adv}_A^{\mathsf{TFA}}$.

The reduction goes through because after the above game-changes A can either essentially let a DE-PAKE instance go through undisturbed, or it can attempt to actively attack the underlying DE-PAKE instance either via a rogue C session or via rogue sessions with device S and server D. However, each rogue D session is bound to a unique rogue S session, because of the uKE and (zid, z) mechanism, and for each such D, S session $pair$, the probability that an active attack is not aborted is only 2^{-t}. This implies that the (q_S, q_D, q_C) parameters characterizing the TFA-KE attacker A scale-down to $(q_S/2^t, q_D/2^t, q_C)$ parameters for the resulting DE-PAKE attacker A^*, which leads to the claimed security bounds by the security of DE-PAKE. The details of construction for A^* and the above argument are included in the full version of this paper [38].

Case 2: Party corruptions. In the full version of the paper [38] we include the cases of client corruption and of device and/or server corruption, showing that our scheme achieves all the bounds from Definition 1. Here we just comment on how these bounds are derived. For the case of device corruption, the value z is learned by the attacker hence it is equivalent to setting $t = 0$. Also, rogue queries to D are free for the attacker hence q_D is virtually unbounded (can think of it as "infinity"). Setting these values in the bound of Case 1, one obtains the claimed bound $(q_C + q_S)/2^d$ for the case of device corruption. Similarly, in case of server corruption one sets q_S to "infinity". In addition, and in spite of the attacker learning z in this case, one obtains a bound involving 2^{-t} thanks to the fact that we run the PTR protocol over the SAS channel, hence reducing the probability of the attacker successfully testing a candidate password pwd' by 2^{-t}. In the case of client compromise where the attacker learns the user's password pwd, we set $d = 0$ (a dictionary of size 1) and set $q_C = q_C' = 0$ since C is corrupted and the attacker cannot choose a test session at C. Finally, when both D and S (but not C) are corrupted one gets the same security as plain DE-PAKE, namely, requiring a full offline dictionary attack to recover pwd.

6   System Development and Testing

Here we report on an experimental prototype of protocol OpTFA from Fig. 3 on page 12 and present novel designs for the SAS channel implementation. We experiment with OpTFA using two different instantiations of the password protocol between C and S. One is PKI-based that runs OpTFA over a server-authenticated TLS connection; in particular, it uses this connection in lieu of the

Table 1. Average execution time of OpTFA and its components (10,000 iterations)

Protocol	Purpose	Parties	Average Time in ms (std. dev.)
SAS (excluding user's checksum validation)	Authenticate C-D Channel	C and D	128.59 (0.48)
PTR	Reconstruct rwd	C and D	160.46 (3.71)
PKI-free PAKE	PAKE	C and S	182.27 (3.67)
PKI PAKE (TLS)	C-S link encryption	C and S	32.54 (1.38)
Overall in PKI-free model		C, D and S	**410.77 ms**
Overall in PKI model		C, D and S	**263.27 ms**

uKE in step I and implements step III by simply transmitting the concatenation of password rwd and the value z under the TLS authenticated encryption. The second protocol we experimented with is a PKI-free asymmetric PAKE borrowed from [27,36]. Roughly, it runs the same PTR protocol as described in Sect. 3 but this time between C and S. C's input is rwd and the result $F_k(\mathsf{rwd})$ serves as a user's private key for the execution of an authenticated key-exchange between C and S. We implement the latter with HMQV [41] (as an optimization, the DH exchange used to implement uKE in step I of OpTFA is "reused" in HMQV).

In Table 1 we provide execution times for the various protocol components, including times for the TLS-based protocol and the PKI-free one with some elements borrowed from the implementation work from [37]. We build on the following platform. The webserver S is a Virtual Machine running Debian 8.0 with 2 Intel Xeon 3.20 GHz and 3.87 GB of memory. Client terminal C is a Mac-Book Air with 1.3 GHz Intel Core i5 and 4 GB of memory. Device D is a Samsung Galaxy S5 smartphone running Android 6.0.1. C and D are connected to the same WiFi network with the speed of 100 Mbps and S has Internet connection speed of 1 Gbps. The server side code is implemented in HTML5, PHP and JavaScipt. On the client terminal, the protocol is implemented in JavaScript as an extension for the Chrome browser and the smartphone app in Java for Android phones.

All DH-based operations (PTR, key exchange and SAS-SMT encryption) use elliptic curve NIST P-256, and hashing and PRF use HMAC-SHA256. Hashing into the curve is implemented with simple iterated hashing till an abscissa x on the curve is found (it will be replaced with a secure mechanism such as [26]).

Communication between C and S uses a regular internet connection between the browser C and web server S. Communication between C and D (except for checksum comparison) goes over the internet using a bidirectional Google Cloud Messaging (GCM) [5], in which D acts as the GCM server and C acts as the GCM client. GCM involves a registration phase during which GCM client (here C) registers with the GCM generated client ID to the GCM server (here D), to assure that D only responds to the registered clients. In case that the PAKE protocol in OpTFA is implemented with password-over-TLS, [37] specifies the need for D to authenticate the PTR value b sent to C (see Sect. 3). In this case, during the GCM registration we install at C a signature public key of D.

6.1   Checksum Validation Design

An essential component in our approach and solutions (in particular in protocol OpTFA) is the use of a SAS channel implemented via the user-assisted equality verification of checksums displayed by both C and D (denoted hereafter as checksum$_C$ and checksum$_D$, resp.). Here we discuss different implementations of such user-assisted verification which we have designed and experimented with.

Manual Checksum Validation. In the simplest approach, the user compares the checksums displayed on D and C and taps the Confirm button on D in case the two match [49]. Although, this type of code comparison has recently been deployed in TFA systems, e.g., [8], it carries the danger of neglectful users pressing the confirm button without comparing the checksum strings. Another common solution for checksum validation is "Copy-Confirm" [49] where the user types the checksum displayed on C into D, and only if this matches D's checksum does D proceeds with the protocol. We implemented this scheme using a 6 digit number. We stress that in spite of the similarity between this mechanism and PIN copying in traditional TFA schemes, there is an essential security difference: Stealing the PIN in traditional schemes suffices to authenticate instead of the user (for an attacker that holds the user's password) while stealing the checksum value entered by the user in OpTFA is worthless to the attacker (the checksum is a validation code, not the OTK value needed for authentication).

The above methods using human visual examination and/or copying limit the SAS channel capacity (typically to 4–6 digits) and may degrade usability [46]. As an alternative we consider the following designs (however one may fallback to the manual schemes when the more secure schemes below cannot be used, e.g., missing camera or noisy environments).

QR Code Checksum Validation. In this checksum validation model, we encode the full, 256-bit checksum computed in protocol OpTFA into a hexstring and show it as a 230×230 pixel QR Code on the web-page. We used ZXing library to encode the QR code and display it on the web page and read and decode it D. To send the checksum to D, the user opens the app on D and captures the QR code. D decodes the QR code and compares checksums, and proceeds with the protocol if the match happens. In this setting, the user does not need to enter the checksum but only needs to hold her phone and capture a picture of the browser's screen. With the larger checksum ($t = 256$) active attacks on SAS-SMT turn infeasible and the expressions 2^{-t} in Definition 1) negligible.

Voice-based Checksum Validation. We implement a voice-based checksum validation approach that assumes a microphone-equipped device (typically a smartphone) where the user speaks a numerical checksum displayed by the client into the device. The device D receives this audio, recognizes and transcribes it using a speech recognition tool, and then compares the result with the checksum computed by D itself. The client side uses a Chrome extension as in the manual checksum validation case while on the device we developed a transcriber application using Android.Speech API. The user clicks on a "Speak" button added to the app and speaks out loud the displayed number (6-digit in our implementation). The transcriber application in D recognizes the speech and convert it to text that is then compared to D's checksum. To further improve the usability of this approach one can incorporate a text-to-speech tool that would speak the checksum automatically (i.e., replacing the user). The transcription approach would perhaps be easy for the users to employ compared to the QR-based approach, but would only be suitable if the user is in an environment that is non-noisy and allows her to speak out-loud. We note that the QR-code and audio-based approaches do not require a browser plugin or add-on and can be deployed on any browser with HTML5 support.

Performance Evaluation. As preliminary information, we report on 30 checksum validation iterations performed by one experimenter. The time taken by manual checksum validation was 8.50 s on average (standard deviation 2.84 s). The time taken by QR-Coded validation was 4.87 s on average for capturing the code (standard deviation 1.32s) and 0.02 s on average for decoding the code (standard deviation 0.00s). The time taken by audio-based validation was 4.08 s on average for speaking the checksum (standard deviation 0.34 s) and 1.18 s on average for transcribing the spoken checksum (standard deviation 0.42 s). The average time for these tasks may vary between different users. The time taken by the device to perform the checksum comparison is negligible. Our preliminary testing of these two channels shows virtually-0 error rate.

7   Discussion of Related Work

Device-enhanced password-authentication with security against offline dictionary attacks (ODA). There are several proposals in cryptographic literature for password authentication schemes that utilize an auxiliary computing component to protect against ODA in case of server compromise. This was a context of the *Password Hardening* proposal of Ford-Kaliski [31], which was generalized as *Hidden Credential Retrieval* by Boyen [27], and then formalized as *(Cloud) Single Password Authentication* (SPA) by Acar et al. [23] and as a *Device-Enhanced PAKE* (DE-PAKE) by Jarecki et al. [37]. These schemes are functionally similar to a TFA scheme if the role of the auxiliary component is played by the user's device D, but they are insecure in case of password leakage e.g. via client compromise.[3] The threat of an ODA attack on compromise of an

---

[3] We note that [23] also show a *Mobile Device* SPA, which provides client-compromise resistance, but it requires the user to type the password onto the device D, and to copy a high-entropy key from D to C, thus increasing manually transmitted data even in comparison to traditional TFAs. By contrast, OpTFA dispenses entirely with manual transmission of information to and from D.

authentication server also motivated the notion of *Threshold* Password Authenticated Key Exchange (T-PAKE) [44], i.e. a PAKE in which the password-holding server is replaced by n servers so that a corruption of up to $t < n$ of them leaks no information about the password. In addition to general T-PAKE's, several solutions were also given for the specific case of $n = 2$ servers tolerating $t = 1$ corruption, known as *2-PAKE* [28,40], and every 2-PAKE, with the user's device D playing the role of the second server, is a password authentication scheme that protects against ODA in case of server compromise. However, as in the case of [23,27,31,37], if a password is leaked then 2-PAKE offers no security against an active attacker who engages with a single 2-PAKE session.

TFA with ODA security. Shirvanian et al. [47] proposed a TFA scheme which extends the security of traditional PIN-based TFAs against ODA in case of server compromise. However, OpTFA offers several advantages compared to [47]: First, [47] relies on PKI (the client sends the password and the one-time key, OTK, to the PKI-authenticated server) while OpTFA has both a PKI-model and a PKI-free instantiation. Second, [47] assumes full security of the t-bit D-C channel for OTK transmission while we reduce this assumption to a t-bit *authenticated* channel between C and D. Consequently, we improve user experience by replacing the *read-and-copy* action with simpler and easier *compare-and-confirm*. On the other hand, [47] can use *only* the t-bit secure D-C link while OpTFA requires transmission of full-entropy values between D and C.

TFA with the 2nd factor as a *local* cryptographic component. Some Two-Factor Authentication schemes consider a scenario where the 2nd factor is a device D capable of storing cryptographic keys and performing cryptographic algorithms, but unlike in our model, D is connected directly to client C, i.e. it effectively communicates with C over secure links. (However, security must hold assuming the adversary can stage a lunch-time attack on device D, so D cannot simply hand off its private keys to C.) The primary example is a USB stick, like YubiKey [13], implementing e.g. the FIDO U2F authentication protocol [2,42]. A generalized version of this problem, including biometric authentication, was formalized by Pointcheval and Zimmer as *Multi-Factor Authentication* [45], but the difference between that model and our TFA-KE notion is that we consider device D which has *no pre-set secure channel with client* C. Moreover, to the best of our knowledge, all existing MFA/TFA schemes even in the secure-channel D-C model are still insecure against ODA on server compromise, except for the aforementioned TFA of Shirvanian et al. [47].

Alternatives to PIN-based TFA with remote auxiliary device. Many TFA schemes improve on PIN-based TFAs by either reducing user involvement, by not requiring the user to copy a PIN from D to C, or by improving on its online security, but *none of them protect against ODA in case of server compromise*, and their usability and online security properties also have downsides.

PhoneAuth [30] and Authy [11] replace PINs with S-to-D challenge-response communication channeled by C, but they require a pre-paired Bluetooth connection to secure the C-D channel. A full-bandwidth secure C-D channel reduces the three-party TFA notion to a two-party setting, where device D is a local component of client C, but requiring an establishment of such secure connection between a browser C and a cell phone D makes a TFA scheme harder to use. TFA schemes like SlickLogin (acquired by Google) [3], Sound-Login [9], and Sound-Proof [39] in essence attempt to implement such secure C-to-D channel using physical security assumptions on physical media e.g. near-ultrasounds [3], audible sounds [9], or ambient sounds detecting proximity of D to C [39], but they are subject to eavesdropping attacks and co-located attackers.

Several TFA proposals, including Google Prompt [8] and Duo [1], follow a *one-click* approach to minimize user's involvement if D is a data-connected device like a smartphone. In [1,8] S communicates directly over data-network to D, which prompts the user to approve (or deny) an authentication session, where the approve action prompts D to respond in an entity authentication protocol with S, e.g. following the U2F standard [2]. This takes even less user's involvement than the compare-and-confirm action of our TFA-KE, but it does not establish a strong binding between the C-S login session and the D-S interaction. E.g., if the adversary knows the user's password, and hence the TFA security depends entirely on D-S interaction, a man-in-the-middle adversary who detects C's attempt to establish a session with S, and succeeds in establishing a session with S before C does, will authenticate as that user to S because the honest user's approval on D's prompt will result in S authenticating the adversarial session.

A   PAKE and DE-PAKE Security Models

We recall the *Device-Enhanced PAKE (DE-PAKE)* security model of [37], which forms a basis of our TFA model, and which extends the the Password Authentication Key Exchange (PAKE) model [24] to the case where the user controls an auxiliary device which constitutes the user's second authentication token in addition to the password. We refer to the full version [38] for a more detailed and modular presentation of DE-PAKE as an extension of the PAKE model.

Protocol participants. There are three types of protocol participants in DE-PAKE, client C, server S, and device D. We assume that client C is controlled by a *user* U. The role of D can be played by any data-connected entity, including a hand-held device owned by user U or an auxiliary web service which has an account for U. (The definition in [37] identifies C with U, but in the TFA context U and C are separate entities, and U is assumed to operate both client C and device D.) We assume that C interacts with a unique server S and device D, but server S interacts with multiple users. For notational convenience we take a simplifying assumption that in a DE-PAKE protocol both D and S interact only with client C, and not with each other directly.

Protocol execution. A DE-PAKE protocol has two phases: initialization and key exchange. In the initialization phase user U chooses a random password pwd from a given dictionary Dict and interacts with its associated server S and device D. Initialization produces state $\sigma_S(U)$ for server S, which S stores in an account associated with user U, and state σ_D for device D, while client C has no permanent storage except for public parameters. *Initialization is assumed to* *be executed securely, e.g., over secure channels.* In the key exchange phase, user types her password pwd into the client C, and the three parties, C on input pwd, D on input σ_D, and S on input $\sigma_S(U)$, interact over insecure (adversary-controlled) channels. Parties C and S terminate by outputing a session key or a rejection symbol, while D has no local output. All parties may execute the protocol multiple times in a concurrent fashion. Protocol execution by any party defines a protocol *instance*, also referred to as a protocol *session*, denoted respectively Π_i^C, Π_i^D, or Π_i^S, where integer pointer i serves to differentiates between multiple protocol instances executed by a given party. Each protocol session by C and S is associated with a *peer identity* pid, a *session identifier* sid which we equate with the transcript of exchanges with its peer observed by this instance, and a *session key* sk. The output of C or S protocol instance consists of the above three variables, which can be set to $\perp$ if the party aborts the session (e.g., when authentication fails, a misformed message is received, etc.). When a session Π_i^C or Π_i^S outputs sk $\neq\perp$ we say that it *accepts*.

Security. To define security we consider a probabilistic attacker A which schedules all actions in the protocol and controls all communication channels with full ability to transport, modify, inject, delay or drop messages. In addition, the attacker knows (or even chooses) the dictionaries used by users. The model defines the following queries or activations through which the adversary interacts with, and learns information from, the protocol's participants.

send(P, i, P', M): Delivers message M to instance Π_i^P purportedly coming from P'. In response to a send query the instance takes the actions specified by the protocol and outputs a message given to A. When a session accepts, a message indicating acceptance is given to A. A send message with a new value i (possibly with null M) creates a new instance at P with pid P' (if $P \neq D$).

reveal(P, i): If instance Π_i^P for $P \in \{C, S\}$ has accepted, outputs its session key sk; otherwise outputs $\perp$.

corrupt(P): Outputs all data held by party $P \in \{D, S\}$. The state includes σ_D if $P = D$ and $\sigma_S(U)$ if $P = S$, but it also includes all temporary session information. Adversary A gains full control of P, and we say that P is *corrupted*.

compromise(S, U): Outputs state $\sigma_S(U)$ of S. We say that S is U-*compromised*.

test(P, i): If instance Π_i^P has accepted, for $P \in \{C, S\}$, this query causes Π_i^P to flip a random bit b. If $b = 1$ the instance's session key sk is output and if $b = 0$ a string drawn uniformly from the space of session keys is output. A test query may be asked at any time during the execution of the protocol, but may only be asked once. We will refer to the party P against which a test query was issued and to its peer as the *target parties*.

The following notion taken from [35] is used in the security definition below to ensure that legitimate messages exchanged between honest parties do not help the attacker in online password guessing attempts (only adversarially-generated messages count towards such online attacks). It has similar motivation as the execute query in [24], but the latter fails to capture the ability of the attacker to delay and interleave messages from different sessions.

Rogue **send** *queries:* We say that a $\mathsf{send}(P, i, P', M)$ query is *rogue* if it was not generated and/or delivered according to the specification of the protocol, i.e. message M has been changed or injected by the attacker, or the delivery order differs from what is stipulated by the protocol (delaying message delivery or interleaving messages from different sessions is not considered a rogue operation as long as internal session ordering is preserved). We also consider as rogue any $\mathsf{send}(P, i, P', M)$ query where P is uncorrupted and P' is corrupted. We call messages delivered through rogue send queries *rogue activations* by A, and we call session which receives rogue mesages *rogue session*. We denote the number of rogue sessions of D as q_D, of S as q_S, the number of rogue sessions of C where rogue send queries come with the server as the sender as q_C, and those where rogue send queries come with the device as the sender as q'_C.

Matching sessions. Session instances Π_i^P and $\Pi_j^{P'}$ for $\{P, P'\} = \{\mathsf{C}, \mathsf{S}\}$ are said to be *matching* if both have the same session identifier sid (i.e., their transcripts match), the first has $\mathsf{pid} = P'$, the second has $\mathsf{pid} = P$, and both have accepted.

Fresh sessions. Session Π_i^C with $\mathsf{pid} = \mathsf{S}$ is called *fresh* if none of the queries $\mathsf{corrupt}(\mathsf{C})$, $\mathsf{corrupt}(\mathsf{S})$, $\mathsf{compromise}(\mathsf{S}, U)$, $\mathsf{reveal}(\mathsf{C}, i)$ or $\mathsf{reveal}(\mathsf{S}, i')$ were issued, where $\Pi_{i'}^\mathsf{S}$ is an instance whose session matches Π_i^C. Session Π_i^S with $\mathsf{pid} = \mathsf{C}$ is called *fresh* if none of the queries $\mathsf{corrupt}(\mathsf{C})$, $\mathsf{reveal}(\mathsf{S}, i)$ or $\mathsf{reveal}(\mathsf{C}, i')$ were issued, where $\Pi_{i'}^\mathsf{C}$ is an instance whose session matches Π_i^S. Note that Π_i^S can be fresh even after if query $\mathsf{compromise}(\mathsf{S}, U)$ or $\mathsf{corrupt}(\mathsf{S})$ are issued, as long as adversary has no access to local information of session Π_i^S.

Correctness. If the adversary forwards all protocol messages then matching sessions between uncorrupted peers output the same session key.

Let DEPAKE be a DE-PAKE protocol and A be an attacker with the above capabilities running against DEPAKE. Assume that A issues a single **test** query against some C or S session and ends its run by outputing bit b'. We say that A *wins* if $b' = b$ where b is the bit chosen by the **test** session. We define the *advantage* of A *against* DEPAKE as $\mathsf{Adv}_\mathsf{A}^{\mathsf{DEPAKE}} = 2 \cdot Pr\,[\mathsf{A} \text{ wins against DEPAKE}] - 1$.

Definition 2. *A DE-PAKE protocol is called* $(q_S, q_C, q'_C, q_D, T, \epsilon)$-*secure if it is correct, and for any password dictionary* Dict *of size* 2^d *and any attacker that runs in time* T, *the following properties hold:*

1. *If* S *and* D *are uncorrupted, the following bound holds:*

$$\mathsf{Adv}_\mathsf{A}^{\mathsf{DEPAKE}} \leq \frac{\min\{q_C + q_S, q'_C + q_D\}}{2^d} + \epsilon. \tag{1}$$

2. *If* D *is corrupted then* $\mathsf{Adv}_\mathsf{A}^{\mathsf{DEPAKE}} \leq (q_C + q_S)/2^d + \epsilon$.
3. *If* S *is corrupted then* $\mathsf{Adv}_\mathsf{A}^{\mathsf{DEPAKE}} \leq (q'_C + q_D)/2^d + \epsilon$.
4. *When both* D *and* S *are corrupted, expression (1) holds but* q_D *and* q_S *are replaced by the number of offline operations performed based on* D's *and* S's *state, respectively.*

Strong KCI Resistance: Discussion. DE-PAKE is intended to provide stronger notion of security in case of server compromise than PAKE. In PAKE the adversary can authenticate to S in case of U-compromise through an offline dictionary attack, but in DE-PAKE this is prohibited. To formalize this requirement we follow the treatment of KCI resistance from [41] and we strengthen the attacker capabilities through a more liberal notion of fresh sessions at a server S. This is why all sessions considered *fresh* in the PAKE model are also considered fresh in the DE-PAKE model, but in addition, in the DE-PAKE model a session Π_i^S at server S with peer U is considered fresh *even if queries* corrupt(S) *or* compromise(S, U) *were issued* as long as all other requirements for freshness are satisfied and *the attacker* A *does not have access to the temporary state information created by session* Π_i^S. This relaxation of the notion of freshness captures the case where the attacker A might have corrupted S and gained access to S's secrets (including long-term ones), yet A is not actively controlling S during the generation of session Π_i^S. In this case we would still want to prevent A from authenticating as U to S on that session. Definition 2 (item 2) ensures that this is the case for DE-PAKE secure protocols even when *unbounded* offline attacks against S are allowed.

References

1. Duo Security Two-Factor Authentication. https://goo.gl/wT3ur9
2. FIDO Universal 2nd Factor. https://www.yubico.com/
3. Google acquires slicklogin, the sound-based password alternative. https://goo.gl/V9J8rv
4. Google Authenticator Android app. https://goo.gl/Q4LU7k
5. Google Cloud Messaging. https://goo.gl/EFvXt9
6. LinkedIn Confirms Account Passwords Hacked. http://goo.gl/UBWuY0
7. RSA breach leaks data for hacking securid tokens. http://goo.gl/tcEoS
8. Sign in faster with 2-Step Verification phone prompts. https://goo.gl/3vjngW
9. Sound Login Two Factor Authentication. https://goo.gl/LJFkvT
10. TOTP: Time-Based One-Time Password Algorithm. https://goo.gl/9Ba5hv
11. Two-factor authentication - authy. https://www.authy.com/
12. Yahoo Says 1 Billion User Accounts Were Hacked. https://goo.gl/q4WZi9
13. YubiKeys: Your key to two-factor authentication. https://goo.gl/LLACvP
14. RFC 4226 HOTP: An HMAC-based One-Time Password Algorithm (2005). https://goo.gl/wxHBvT
15. Russian Hackers Amass Over a Billion Internet Passwords (2014). https://goo.gl/KCrFjS
16. London Calling: Two-Factor Authentication Phishing From Iran (2015). https://goo.gl/w6RD67
17. Hack Brief: Yahoo Breach Hits Half a Billion Users (2016). https://goo.gl/nz4uJG
18. SIM swap fraud: The multi-million pound security issue that UK banks won't talk about (2016). http://www.ibtimes.co.uk/sim-swap-fraud-multi-million-pound-security-issue-that-uk-banks-wont-talk-about-1553035
19. SMS Deprecated (2016). https://github.com/usnistgov/800-63-3/issues/168
20. Over 560 Million Passwords Discovered in Anonymous Online Database (2017). https://goo.gl/upDqzt

21. Real-World SS7 Attack - Hackers Are Stealing Money From Bank Accounts (2017). https://thehackernews.com/2017/05/ss7-vulnerability-bank-hacking.html
22. Abdalla, M., Bellare, M., Rogaway, P.: The oracle Diffie-Hellman assumptions and an analysis of DHIES. In: Naccache, D. (ed.) CT-RSA 2001. LNCS, vol. 2020, pp. 143–158. Springer, Heidelberg (2001). https://doi.org/10.1007/3-540-45353-9_12
23. Acar, T., Belenkiy, M., Küpçü, A.: Single password authentication. Comput. Netw. **57**(13), 2597–2614 (2013)
24. Bellare, M., Pointcheval, D., Rogaway, P.: Authenticated key exchange secure against dictionary attacks. In: Advances in Cryptology - Eurocrypt (2000)
25. Bellovin, S.M., Merritt, M.: Augmented encrypted key exchange: a password-based protocol secure against dictionary attacks and password file compromise. In: ACM Conference on Computer and Communications Security (1993)
26. Bernstein, D.J., Hamburg, M., Krasnova, A., Lange, T.: Elligator: elliptic-curve points indistinguishable from uniform random strings (2013)
27. Boyen, X.: Hidden credential retrieval from a reusable password. In: Proceedings of ASIACCS (2009)
28. Brainard, J., Juels, A., Kaliski, B., Szydlo, M.: A new two-server approach for authentication with short secrets. In: 12th USENIX Security Symposium (2003)
29. Canetti, R., Krawczyk, H.: Analysis of key-exchange protocols and their use for building secure channels. In: International Conference on the Theory and Applications of Cryptographic Techniques, pp. 453–474 (2001)
30. Czeskis, A., Dietz, M., Kohno, T., Wallach, D., Balfanz, D.: Strengthening user authentication through opportunistic cryptographic identity assertions. In: Proceedings of ACM Conference on Computer and Communications Security (2012)
31. Ford, W., Kaliski, Jr, B.S.: Server-assisted generation of a strong secret from a password. In: WETICE, pp. 176–180 (2000)
32. Gentry, C., MacKenzie, P., Ramzan, Z.: A method for making password-based key exchange resilient to server compromise. In: Advances in Cryptology (2006)
33. Halevi, S., Krawczyk, H.: Public-key cryptography and password protocols. ACM Trans. Inf. Syst. Secur. **2**(3), 230–268 (1999)
34. Jager, T., Kohlar, F., Schäge, S., Schwenk, J.: On the security of TLS-DHE in the standard model. In: Safavi-Naini, R., Canetti, R. (eds.) CRYPTO 2012. LNCS, vol. 7417, pp. 273–293. Springer, Heidelberg (2012). https://doi.org/10.1007/978-3-642-32009-5_17
35. Jarecki, S., Kiayias, A., Krawczyk, H.: Round-optimal password-protected secret sharing and T-PAKE in the password-only model. In: Sarkar, P., Iwata, T. (eds.) ASIACRYPT 2014. LNCS, vol. 8874, pp. 233–253. Springer, Heidelberg (2014). https://doi.org/10.1007/978-3-662-45608-8_13
36. Jarecki, S., Kiayias, A., Krawczyk, H., Xu, J.: Highly efficient and composable password-protected secret sharing. In: 1st IEEE European Symposium on Security and Privacy (EuroS&P) (2015)
37. Jarecki, S., Krawczyk, H., Shirvanian, M., Saxena, N.: Device-enhanced password protocols with optimal online-offline protection. In: ASIACCS 2016 (2016). http://eprint.iacr.org/2015/1099
38. Jarecki, S., Krawczyk, H., Shirvanian, M., Saxena, N.: Two-factor authentication with end-to-end password security. IACR Cryptology ePrint Archive: Report 2018/033, January 2018. http://eprint.iacr.org/2018/033
39. Karapanos, N., Marforio, C., Soriente, C., Capkun, S.: Sound-proof: usable two-factor authentication based on ambient sound. In: 24th USENIX Security Symposium (USENIX Security 15) (2015)

40. Katz, J., MacKenzie, P.D., Taban, G., Gligor, V.D.: Two-server password-only authenticated key exchange. In: ACNS, pp. 1–16 (2005)
41. Krawczyk, H.: HMQV: a high-performance secure Diffie-Hellman protocol. In: Annual International Cryptology Conference, pp. 546–566 (2005)
42. Lang, J., Czeskis, A., Balfanz, D., Schilder, M., Srinivas, S.: Security keys: practical cryptographic second factors for the modern web. In: Grossklags, J., Preneel, B. (eds.) FC 2016. LNCS, vol. 9603, pp. 422–440. Springer, Heidelberg (2017). https://doi.org/10.1007/978-3-662-54970-4_25
43. Lin, C.-C., Li, H., Zhou, X.-Y., Wang, X.: Screenmilker: how to milk your android screen for secrets. In: Network & Distributed System Security Symposium (2014)
44. MacKenzie, P., Shrimpton, T., Jakobsson, M.: Threshold password-authenticated key exchange. In: Yung, M. (ed.) CRYPTO 2002. LNCS, vol. 2442, pp. 385–400. Springer, Heidelberg (2002). https://doi.org/10.1007/3-540-45708-9_25
45. Pointcheval, D., Zimmer, S.: Multi-factor authenticated key exchange. In: Bellovin, S.M., Gennaro, R., Keromytis, A., Yung, M. (eds.) ACNS 2008. LNCS, vol. 5037, pp. 277–295. Springer, Heidelberg (2008). https://doi.org/10.1007/978-3-540-68914-0_17
46. Saxena, N., Ekberg, J.-E., Kostiainen, K., Asokan, N.: Secure device pairing based on a visual channel. In: IEEE Symposium on Security and Privacy (2006)
47. Shirvanian, M., Jarecki, S., Saxena, N., Nathan, N.: Two-factor authentication resilient to server compromise using mix-bandwidth devices. In: Network & Distributed System Security Symposium (2014)
48. Shoup, V.: ISO 18033–2: an emerging standard for public-key encryption. Final Committee Draft, December 2004
49. Uzun, E., Karvonen, K., Asokan, N.: Usability analysis of secure pairing methods. In: Dietrich, S., Dhamija, R. (eds.) FC 2007. LNCS, vol. 4886, pp. 307–324. Springer, Heidelberg (2007). https://doi.org/10.1007/978-3-540-77366-5_29
50. Vaudenay, S.: Secure communications over insecure channels based on short authenticated strings. In: Shoup, V. (ed.) CRYPTO 2005. LNCS, vol. 3621, pp. 309–326. Springer, Heidelberg (2005). https://doi.org/10.1007/11535218_19

Blockchain

Bootstrapping the Blockchain, with Applications to Consensus and Fast PKI Setup

Juan A. Garay[3], Aggelos Kiayias[1(✉)], Nikos Leonardos[2], and Giorgos Panagiotakos[1(✉)]

[1] School of Informatics, University of Edinburgh, Edinburgh, UK
akiayias@inf.ed.ac.uk, giorgos.pan@ed.ac.uk
[2] Department of Informatics and Telecommunications, University of Athens, Athens, Greece
nikos.leonardos@gmail.com
[3] Department of Computer Science and Engineering, Texas A&M University, College Station, USA
garay@cse.tamu.edu

Abstract. The Bitcoin backbone protocol (Eurocrypt 2015) extracts basic properties of Bitcoin's underlying *blockchain* data structure, such as "common prefix" and "chain quality," and shows how fundamental applications including consensus and a robust public transaction ledger can be built on top of them. The underlying assumptions are "proofs of work" (POWs), adversarial hashing power strictly less than $1/2$ *and* no adversarial pre-computation—or, alternatively, the existence of an unpredictable "genesis" block.

In this paper we first show how to remove the latter assumption, presenting a "bootstrapped" Bitcoin-like blockchain protocol relying on POWs that builds genesis blocks "from scratch" in the presence of adversarial pre-computation. Importantly, the round complexity of the genesis block generation process is *independent* of the number of participants.

Next, we consider applications of our construction, including a PKI generation protocol and a consensus protocol without trusted setup assuming an honest majority (in terms of computational power). Previous results in the same setting (unauthenticated parties, no trusted setup, POWs) required a round complexity linear in the number of participants.

1 Introduction

As the first decentralized cryptocurrency, Bitcoin [33] has ignited much excitement, not only for its novel realization of a central bank-free financial instrument, but also as an alternative approach to classical distributed computing problems,

A. Kiayias—Research partly supported by ERC project CODAMODA, No. 259152, and Horizon 2020 project PANORAMIX, No. 653497.

M. Abdalla and R. Dahab (Eds.): PKC 2018, LNCS 10770, pp. 465–495, 2018.
https://doi.org/10.1007/978-3-319-76581-5_16

such as reaching agreement distributedly in the presence of misbehaving parties. Formally capturing such reach has been the intent of several recent works, notably [21], where the core of the Bitcoin protocol, called the Bitcoin *backbone*, is extracted and analyzed. The analysis includes the formulation of fundamental properties of its underlying *blockchain* data structure, which parties ("miners") maintain and try to extend by generating "proofs of work" (POW, aka "cryptographic puzzle" [3,16,24,37])[1], called *common prefix* and *chain quality*. It is then shown in [21] how applications such as consensus (aka Byzantine agreement) [31,36] and a robust public transaction ledger (i.e., Bitcoin) can be built "on top" of such properties, assuming that the hashing power of an adversary controlling a fraction of the parties is strictly less than $1/2$.

Importantly, those properties hold assuming that all parties—honest and adversarial—"wake up" and start computing at the same time, or, alternatively, that they compute on a common random string only made available at the exact time when the protocol execution is to begin (see further discussion under related work below). Indeed, the coinbase parameter in Bitcoin's "genesis" block, hardcoded into the software, contains text from *The Times* 03/Jan/2009 issue [5], arguably unpredictable.

While satisfactory in some cases, such a trusted setup/behavioral assumption might be unrealistic in other POW-based systems where details may have been released a lot earlier than the actual time when the system starts to run. A case in point is Ethereum, which was discussed for over a year before the system officially kicked off. That's from a practical point of view. At a foundational level, one would in addition like to understand what kind of cryptographic primitives can be realized without any trusted setup assumption and based on POWs, and whether that is in particular the case for the Bitcoin backbone functionality and its enabling properties mentioned above.

The former question was recently considered by Andrychowicz and Dziembowski [1], who, building on previous suggestions by Aspnes *et al.* [2] of using POWs as an identity-assignment tool and constructions by Fitzi *et al.* [12,19] showing how to morph "graded" consistency into global consistency, showed how to create a consistent PKI using POWs and no other trusted setup, which can then be used to run secure computation protocols (e.g., [23,38]) and realize any cryptographic functionality assuming an honest majority among parties. While this in principle addresses the foundational concerns, it leaves open the questions of doing it in *scalable* way—i.e., with round complexity independent of the number of parties, and in the context of blockchain protocols in particular, designing one that is *provably* secure without a trusted setup.

Our contributions. In this paper we answer the above questions. First, we present a Bitcoin-like protocol that neither assumes a simultaneous start nor the existence of an unpredictable genesis block, and has round complexity

---

[1] In Bitcoin, solving a proof of work essentially amounts to brute-forcing a hash inequality based on SHA-256.

essentially independent of the number of participants[2]. Effectively, the protocol, starting "from scratch," enables the coexistence of multiple genesis blocks with blockchains stemming from them, eventually enabling the players to converge to a single blockchain. This takes place despite the adversary being allowed (polynomial in the security parameter) pre-computation time. We work in the same model as [21] and we assume a 1/2 bound on adversarial hashing power. We call this protocol the *bootstrapped* (Bitcoin) backbone protocol. A pictorial overview of the protocol's phases, preceded by a period of potential precomputation by the corrupt players, is given in Fig. 1.

Fig. 1. Timeline and phases of the bootstrapped Bitcoin backbone protocol.

Second, we present applications of our bootstrapped construction, starting with its original one: a distributed ledger, i.e., a public and permanent summary of all transactions that honest parties can agree on as well as add their own, despite the potentially disruptive behavior of parties harnessing less than 1/2 of the hashing power. This entails proving that the ledger's required security properties (Persistence and Liveness—cf. [21]) hold in a genesis block-less setting.

Next, we consider the problem of setting up a PKI in our unauthenticated network setting *from scratch*. As mentioned above, the idea of using POWs as an identity-assignment tool was put forth by Aspnes *et al.* [2]. Here we build on this idea as well as on the "2-for-1 POWs" technique from [21] to use our bootstrapped protocol to assign identities to parties. The assignment relation will possibly assign more than one identity to the same party, while guaranteeing that the majority of them is assigned to honest parties. Such an identity infrastructure/"pseudonymous PKI" has numerous applications, including the bootstrapping of a proof-of-stake protocol [28,30], and the election of honest-majority "subcommittees," which would enable the application of traditional Byzantine fault-tolerant techniques for ledger creation and maintenance (cf. [7]) to permissionless (as opposed to permissioned) networks.

Finally, applying the 2-for-1 POWs technique we can also solve the consensus (aka Byzantine agreement) problem [31,36] probabilistically and from scratch, even if the adversary has almost the same hashing power as the honest parties[3],

---

[2] "Essentially" because even though there will be a dependency of the round complexity of the setup phase on the probability of computing POWs, which in turn depends on the number of parties, this dependency can be made small enough so as to be considered a constant. See Remark 3.

[3] Thus marking a contrast with the $\frac{2}{3}$ lower bound for consensus on the number of honest parties in the traditional network setting with no setup [6].

and with round complexity independent of the number of parties. Indeed, all our protocols have round complexity linear in the security parameter, and enjoy simultaneous termination. We conclude with an additional modification to the protocol that reduces (by a factor of n) the protocol's communication costs.

Related work. Nakamoto [32] proposed Bitcoin, the first decentralized currency system based on POWs while relaxing the anonymity property of a digital currency to mere pseudonymity. This work was followed by a multitude of other related proposals including Litecoin, Primecoin [29], and Zerocash [4], and further analysis improvements (e.g., [17,18]), to mention a few.

As mentioned above, we work in a model that generalizes the model put forth by Garay et al. [21], who abstracted out and formalized the core of the Bitcoin protocol—the Bitcoin *backbone*. As presented in [21], however, the protocol considers as valid any chain that extends the empty chain, which is not going to work in our model. Indeed, if the adversary is allowed polynomial-time pre-computation, he can prepare a very long, private chain; then, by revealing blocks of this chain at the rate that honest players compute new blocks, he can break security. As also mentioned above, to overcome this problem one can assume that at the time honest parties start the computation, they have access to a fresh common random string (a "genesis" block). Then, if we consider as valid only the chains that extend this block, all results proved in [21] follow, since the probability that the adversary can use blocks mined before honest players "woke up" is negligible in the security parameter. In this paper we show how to establish such genesis block directly, and in a number of rounds essentially independent of the number of participants.

To our knowledge, the idea of using POWs to distributedly agree on something (specifically, a PKI) in an unauthenticated setting with no trusted setup was first put forth by Aspnes et al. [2], who suggested to use them as an identity-assignment tool as a way to combat *Sybil* attacks [14], and in such a way that the number of identities assigned to the honest and adversarial parties can be made proportional to their aggregate computational power, respectively. For example, by assuming that the adversary's computational power is less than 50%, one of the algorithms in [2] results in a number of adversarial identities less than half of that obtained by the honest parties. By running this procedure in a pre-processing stage, it is then suggested in [2] that a standard authenticated broadcast protocol (specifically, the one by Dolev and Strong [13]) could be run. Such protocols, however, would require that the PKI be *consistent*, details of which are not laid out in [2].

They are in [1], where Andrychowicz and Dziembowski address the more general goal of secure computation in this setting based on POWs, as mentioned earlier; the POWs are used to build a "graded" PKI, where keys have "ranks." The graded PKI is an instance of a "graded agreement," or "partial consistency" problem [12,19,20], where honest parties do not disagree "by much," according to some metric. In [19], Fitzi calls this the *b-set-neighboring* problem ("proxcast" in [12]), with b the number of possible "grades," and shows how to achieve global consistency by running the *b*-set-neighboring protocol multiple times. In [1], the fact is used that an unreliable broadcast is available among honest parties to achieve the same—global consistency on a PKI, where the number of identities each party gets is proportional to its hashing power, as suggested in [2].

The protocol in [1], however, suffers from a total running time that depends on the number of parties, because of two factors: (1) the way in which it uses POWs, and (2) the use of the Dolev-Strong authenticated broadcast protocol (run multiple times in parallel based on the graded PKI), which takes a linear number of rounds. Regarding (1), and in more detail, in order to assign exactly one key per party, a low variance POW scheme is used. This implies that the time needed by an honest party to mine a POW is going to be proportional to the ratio of the adversarial hashing power to the hashing power of the weakest honest party. Otherwise, the "rushing" adversary would be able to compute more identities in the additional time she has due to the latency of the communication infrastructure.[4] Regarding (2), we note that potentially an expected-constant-round protocol could be used instead of Dolev-Strong, although the parallel composition of n instances would require more involved techniques [11].

Furthermore, having a PKI allows parties to generate an unpredictable beacon (in the random oracle model), which is then suggested in [1] as a genesis block-generation method for a new cryptocurrency. Yet, no formal treatment of the security of the resulting blockchain protocol is presented, and—as already mentioned—the round complexity of the suggested genesis block generation procedure is linear in the number of participants, both in contrast to our work.

As in [1], Katz et al. [26] also consider achieving pseudonymous broadcast and secure computation from POWs ("cryptographic puzzles") and the existence of digital signatures without prior PKI setup, but under the assumption of an existing unpredictable beacon. Finally, Pass et al. [35] consider a partially synchronous model of communication where parties are not guaranteed to receive messages at the end of each round but rather after a specified delay Δ (cf. [15]), and show that the backbone protocol can be proven secure in this setting. In principle, our results about the bootstrapped backbone protocol can be extended to their setting as shown in [22].

Organization of the paper. The rest of the paper is organized as follows. In Sect. 2 we describe the network and adversarial model, introduce some basic blockchain notation, and enumerate the various security properties. In Sect. 3 we present the bootstrapped Bitcoin backbone protocol and its analysis. Applications are presented in Sect. 4: a robust public transaction ledger, and PKI generation and consensus without trusted setup and with round complexity independent of the number of parties. Due to space limitations, some of the proofs and further details are presented in the full version of the paper.

---

[4] On the flip side, the benefit of the approach in [1] is that when all honest parties have the *same* hashing power, a PKI that maps each party to exactly one identity and preserves an honest majority on the keys can be achieved. However, in today's environments where even small devices (e.g., mobile phones, smart watches) have powerful CPUs with different clock frequencies, this assumption is arguably weak.

2   Model and Definitions

We describe our protocols in a model that extends the synchronous communication network model presented in [21] for the analysis of the Bitcoin backbone protocol (which in turn is based on Canetti's formulation of "real world" execution for multi-party cryptographic protocols [8,9]). As in [21], the protocol execution proceeds in rounds with inputs provided by an environment program denoted by $\mathcal{Z}$ to parties that execute the protocol.

Next we provide a high level overview of the model, focusing on the differences that are intrinsic to our setting where the adversary has a precomputation advantage. The adversarial model in the network is actively malicious following the standard cryptographic approach. The adversary is *rushing*, meaning that in any given round it gets to see all honest players's messages before deciding its strategy. Message delivery is provided by a "diffusion" mechanism that is guaranteed to deliver all messages, without however preserving their order and allowing the adversary to arbitrarily inject its own messages. Importantly, the honest parties are not guaranteed to have the same view of the messages delivered in each round, except for the fact that all honest messages from the previous round are delivered. Furthermore, the adversary is allowed to change the source information on every message (i.e., communication is not authenticated). In the protocol description, we will use DIFFUSE as the message transmission command to capture the "send-to-all" functionality that is available in our setting.[5] Note that, as in [21], an adversarial sender may abuse DIFFUSE and attempt to confuse honest parties by sending and delivering inconsistent messages to them.

In contrast to [21], where all parties (the honest ones and the ones controlled by the adversary), are activated for the first time in the execution of the protocol in the same round[6], in our model the environment will choose the round at which all the honest parties will become active; the corrupted parties, on the other hand, are activated in the first round. Once honest parties become active they will remain active until the end of the execution. In each round, after the honest parties become active, the environment activates each one by providing input to the party and receives the party's output when it terminates. When activated, parties are able to read their input tape INPUT() and communication tape RECEIVE(), perform some computation that will be suitably restricted (see below) and issue a DIFFUSE message that is guaranteed to be delivered to all parties at the beginning of the next round.

In more detail, we model the execution in the following manner. We employ the parameterized system of ITM's from [9] (2013 version) that is comprised of an initial ITM $\mathcal{Z}$, called the environment, and C, a control function that is specified below. We remark that our control function C is suitably restricted compared to that of [9,10] to take into account restrictions in the order of execution that are relevant to our setting.

---

[5] In [21] the command name BROADCAST is used for this functionality, which we sometimes also will use informally.

[6] After their first-time activation, the environment keeps activating parties in every round (cf. [8]).

The execution is defined with respect to a protocol Π, a set of parties $P_1, \ldots, P_n$ and an adversary $\mathcal{A}$. The adversary is allowed to corrupt parties adaptively up to a number of $t < n$. The protocol Π has access to two resources or "ideal functionalities," the random oracle, and the diffusion channel. Initially, the environment may pass input to either the adversary $\mathcal{A}$ or spawn an instance running the protocol Π which will be restricted to be assigned to the lexicographically smallest honest party (such restrictions are imposed by the control function [9]). After a party P_i is activated, the environment is restricted to activate the lexicographically next honest party, except in the case when no such party is left, in which case the next program to be activated is the adversary $\mathcal{A}$; subsequently, the round-robin execution order between the honest parties will be repeated.

Whenever a party is activated the control function allows for q queries to be made to the random oracle while in the case of an activation of $\mathcal{A}$ a number of $t \cdot q$ queries are allowed where t is the number of corrupted parties. Honest parties are also allowed to annotate their queries to the random oracle for verification purposes, in which case an unlimited amount of queries is permitted (that still counts towards the overall running time of the system execution). Note that the adversary is not permitted to take advantage of this feature of the execution. With foresight, this asymmetry will be necessary, since otherwise it would be trivial for the adversary to break the properties of our protocols by simply "jamming" the incoming communication tape of the honest parties with messages whose verification would deplete their access quota to the random oracle per activation. Furthermore, for each party a single invocation to the diffusion channel is permitted. The diffusion channel maintains the list of messages diffused by each party, and permits the adversary $\mathcal{A}$ to perform a "fetch" operation so that it obtains the messages that were sent. When the adversary $\mathcal{A}$ is activated, the adversary will interact with the diffusion channel, preparing the messages to be delivered to the parties and performing a fetch operation. This write and fetch mode of operation with the communication channel enables the channel to enforce synchrony among the parties running the protocol (cf. [25]).

The term $\{\text{VIEW}_{\Pi,\mathcal{A},\mathcal{Z}}^{P}(\kappa, z)\}_{\kappa \in \mathbb{N}, z \in \{0,1\}^*}$ denotes the random variable ensemble describing the view of party P after the completion of an execution with environment $\mathcal{Z}$, running protocol Π, and adversary $\mathcal{A}$, on auxiliary input $z \in \{0,1\}^*$. We often drop the parameters κ and z and simply refer to the ensemble by $\text{VIEW}_{\Pi,\mathcal{A},\mathcal{Z}}^{P}$ if the meaning is clear from the context. Following the resource-bounded computation model of [9], it holds that the total length of the execution is bounded by a polynomial in the security parameter κ and the length of the auxiliary string $|z|$, provided that the environment is *locally bounded* by a polynomial (cf. Proposition 3 in [9]). Note that the above execution model captures adversarial precomputation since it permits the environment to activate the adversary an arbitrary number of times (bounded by a polynomial in the security parameter κ of course) before the round-robin execution of the honest parties commences.

We note that the above modeling obviates the need for a strict upper bound on the number of messages that may be transmitted by the adversary in each activation (as imposed by [1]). In our setting, honest parties, at the discretion of the environment, will be given sufficient time to process all the messages delivered via the diffusion channel including all messages that are injected by the adversary.

The concatenation of the view of all parties ever activated in the execution, say, $P_1, \ldots, P_n$, is denoted by $\mathrm{VIEW}_{\Pi,\mathcal{A},\mathcal{Z}}$. As in [21], we are interested in protocols Π that do not make explicit use of the number of parties n or their identities. Further, note that because of the unauthenticated nature of the communication model the parties may never be certain about the number of participants in a protocol execution.

In our correctness and security statements we will be concerned with *properties* of protocols Π running in the above setting (as opposed to simulation-based notions of security). Such properties will be defined as predicates over the random variable $\mathrm{VIEW}_{\Pi,\mathcal{A},\mathcal{Z}}(\kappa, q, z)$ by quantifying over all locally polynomial-bounded adversaries $\mathcal{A}$ and environments $\mathcal{Z}$ (in the sense of [9]). Note that all our protocols will only satisfy properties with a small probability of error in κ as well as in a parameter k that is selected from $\{1, \ldots, \kappa\}$. (Note that, in practice, one may choose k to be much smaller than κ, e.g., $k = 6$).

2.1 Blockchain Notation

Next, we introduce some basic blockchain notation, following [21]. A *block* is any triple of the form $B = \langle s, x, ctr \rangle$ where $s \in \{0,1\}^\kappa, x \in \{0,1\}^*, ctr \in \mathbb{N}$ are such that satisfy predicate $\mathsf{validblock}_q^D(B)$ defined as

$$(H(ctr, G(s,x)) < D) \wedge (ctr \leq q),$$

where H, G are cryptographic hash functions (e.g., SHA-256) modelled as random oracles. The parameter $D \in \mathbb{N}$ is also called the block's *difficulty level*. The parameter $q \in \mathbb{N}$ is a bound that in the Bitcoin implementation determines the size of the register ctr; in our treatment we allow this to be arbitrary, and use it to denote the maximum allowed number of hash queries in a round. We do this for convenience and our analysis applies in a straightforward manner to the case that ctr is restricted to the range $0 \leq ctr < 2^{32}$ and q is independent of ctr.

A *blockchain*, or simply a *chain* is a sequence of *blocks*. The rightmost block is the *head* of the chain, denoted $\mathrm{head}(\mathcal{C})$. Note that the empty string ε is also a chain; by convention we set $\mathrm{head}(\varepsilon) = \varepsilon$. A chain $\mathcal{C}$ with $\mathrm{head}(\mathcal{C}) = \langle s', x', ctr' \rangle$ can be extended to a longer chain by appending a valid block $B = \langle s, x, ctr \rangle$ that satisfies $s = H(ctr', G(s', x'))$. In case $\mathcal{C} = \varepsilon$, by convention any valid block of the form $\langle s, x, ctr \rangle$ may extend it. In either case we have an extended chain $\mathcal{C}_{\mathsf{new}} = \mathcal{C}B$ that satisfies $\mathrm{head}(\mathcal{C}_{\mathsf{new}}) = B$. Consider a chain $\mathcal{C}$ of length m and any nonnegative integer k. We denote by $\mathcal{C}^{\lceil k}$ the chain resulting from the "pruning" of the k rightmost blocks. Note that for $k \geq \mathrm{len}(\mathcal{C})$, $\mathcal{C}^{\lceil k} = \varepsilon$. If $\mathcal{C}_1$ is a prefix of $\mathcal{C}_2$ we write $\mathcal{C}_1 \preceq \mathcal{C}_2$.

2.2   Basic Security Properties of the Blockchain

We are going to show that the blockchain data structure built by our protocol satisfies a number of basic properties, as formulated in [21,27]. At a high level, the first property, called *common prefix*, has to do with the existence, as well as persistence in time, of a common prefix of blocks among the chains of honest players [21]. Here we will consider a stronger variant of the property, presented in [27,34], which allows for the black-box proof of application-level properties (such as the *persistence* of transactions entered in a public transaction ledger built on top of the Bitcoin backbone—cf. Sect. 4).

Definition 1 ((Strong) Common Prefix Property). *The* strong common prefix property Q_{cp} *with parameter $k \in \mathbb{N}$ states that the chains C_1, C_2 reported by two, not necessarily distinct honest parties P_1, P_2, at rounds r_1, r_2, with $r_1 \leq r_2$, satisfy $C_1^{\lceil k} \preceq C_2$.*

The next property relates to the proportion of honest blocks in any portion of some honest player's chain.

Definition 2 (Chain Quality Property). *The* chain quality property Q_{cq} *with parameters $\mu \in \mathbb{R}$ and $k, k_0 \in \mathbb{N}$ states that for any honest party P with chain C in* $\text{VIEW}_{\Pi, \mathcal{A}, \mathcal{Z}}(\kappa, z)$, *it holds that for any k consecutive blocks of C, excluding the first k_0 blocks, the ratio of adversarial blocks is at most μ.*

Further, in the derivations in [21] an important lemma was established relating to the rate at which the chains of honest players were increasing as the Bitcoin backbone protocol was run. This was explicitly considered in [27] as a property under the name *chain growth*. Similarly to the variant of the common prefix property above, this property along with chain quality were shown sufficient for the black-box proof of application-level properties (in this case, transaction ledger *liveness*; see Sect. 4).

Definition 3 (Chain Growth Property). *The* chain growth property Q_{cg} *with parameters $\tau \in \mathcal{R}$ (the "chain speed" coefficient) and $s, r_0 \in \mathbb{N}$ states that for any round $r > r_0$, where honest party P has chain C_1 at round r and chain C_2 at round $r + s$ in* $\text{VIEW}_{\Pi, \mathcal{A}, \mathcal{Z}}(\kappa, z)$, *it holds that $|C_2| - |C_1| \geq \tau \cdot s$.*

3   The Bootstrapped Backbone Protocol

We begin this section by presenting the "bootstrapped" Bitcoin backbone protocol, followed by its security analysis. In a nutshell, the protocol is a generalization of the protocol in [21], which is enhanced in two ways: (1) an initial challenge-exchange phase, in which parties contribute random values, towards the establishment of an unpredictable genesis block, despite the precomputation efforts of corrupt players, and (2) a ranking process and chain-validation predicate that, in addition to its basic function (checking the validity of a chain's content), enables the identification of "fresh" candidate genesis blocks. The ranking process yields a graded list of genesis blocks and is inspired by the "key ranking" protocol in [1], where it is used to produce a "graded" PKI, as mentioned in Sect. 1.

Before describing the bootstrapped backbone protocol in detail, we highlight its unique features.

- *No trusted setup and individual genesis block mining.* Parties start without any prior coordination and enter an initial challenge-exchange phase, where they will exchange random values that will be used to construct "freshness" proofs for candidate genesis blocks. The parties will run the initial challenge-exchange phase for a small number of rounds, and subsequently will try to mine their own genesis blocks individually. Once they mine or accept a genesis block from the network they will engage in mining further blocks and exchanging blockchains as in Bitcoin's blockchain protocol. On occasion they might switch to a chain with a different genesis block. Nevertheless, as we will show, quite soon they will stabilize in a common prefix and a single genesis block.
- *Freshness of genesis block impacts chains' total weight.* Chains rooted at a genesis block will incorporate its weight in their total valuation. Genesis blocks can be quite "heavy" compared to regular blocks and their total valuation will depend on how fresh they are. Their weight in general might be as much as a linear number of regular blocks in the security parameter. Furthermore, each regular block in a chain accounts for 3 units in terms of the total weight of the chain, something that, as we show, will be crucial to account for differences in terms of weight that are assigned to the same genesis block by different parties running the protocol (cf. Remark 1).
- *Personalized chain selection rule.* Given the co-existence of multiple genesis blocks, a ranking process is incorporated into the chain selection rule that, in addition to its basic function (checking the validity of a chain's content) and picking the longest chain, it now also takes into account the freshness degree of a genesis block from the perspective of each player running the protocol. The ranking process effectively yields a graded list of genesis blocks and is inspired by the "key ranking" protocol in [1], where it is used to produce a "graded" PKI (see further discussion below). The weight value for each genesis block will be thus proportional to its *perceived* "freshness" by each party running the protocol (the fresher the block the higher its weight). It follows that honest players use different chain selection procedures since each predicate is "keyed" with the random coins that were contributed by each player in the challenge-exchange phase (and thus guaranteed to be fresh from the player's perspective). This has the side effect that the same genesis block might be weighed differently by different parties. Despite these differences, we show that eventually all parties accept the same chains as valid and hence will unify their chain selection rule in the course of the protocol.
- *Robustness is achieved after an initial period of protocol stabilization.* All our modifications integrate seamlessly with the Bitcoin backbone protocol [21], and we are able to show that our blockchain protocol is a robust transaction ledger, in the sense of satisfying the properties of persistence and liveness.

Nevertheless, contrary to [21], the properties are satisfied only after an initial period of rounds where persistence is uncertain and liveness might be slower; this is the period where the parties still stabilize the genesis block and they might be more susceptible to attacks. Despite this, a ledger built on top of our blockchain will be available immediately after the challenges exchange phase. Furthermore, once the stabilization period is over the robust transaction ledger behavior is guaranteed with overwhelming probability (in the length of the security parameter).

3.1 Protocol Description

The bootstrapped Bitcoin backbone protocol is executed by an arbitrary number of parties over an unauthenticated network (cf. Sect. 2). For concreteness, we assume that the number of parties running the protocol is n; however, parties need not be aware of this number when they execute the protocol. Communication over the network is achieved by utilizing a send-to-all DIFFUSE functionality that is available to all parties (and may be abused by the adversary in the sense of delivering different messages to different parties). After an initial ("challenge") phase, each party is to maintain a data structure called a "blockchain," as defined above. Each party's chain may be different, but, as we will prove, under certain well-defined conditions, the chains of honest parties will share a large common prefix.

The protocol description intentionally avoids specifying the type of values that parties try to insert in the chain, the type of chain validation they perform (beyond checking for its structural properties with respect to the hash functions $G(\cdot), H(\cdot)$), and the way they interpret the chain. In the protocol description, these actions are abstracted by the external functions $V(\cdot), I(\cdot), R(\cdot)$ which are specified by the application that runs "on top" of the backbone protocol.

The protocol is specified as Algorithm 1. At a high level, the protocol first executes a challenge-exchange phase for $l+1$ rounds (l will be determined later), followed by the basic backbone functions, i.e., mining and broadcasting blocks; a crucial difference here with respect to the original backbone protocol is that the chain validation process must also verify candidate genesis blocks, which in turn requires updating the validation function as the protocol proceeds. (This, however, only happens in the next l rounds after the challenge phase.) The protocol's supporting algorithms are specified next.

The challenge-exchange phase. In order to generate an unpredictable genesis block, players first execute a "challenge-exchange" phase, where they broadcast, for a given number of rounds ($l + 1$), randomly generated challenges that depend on the challenges received in the previous rounds. The property that is assured is that an honest player's k-round challenge, $1 \leq k \leq l$, depends on the $(k-1)$-round challenges of all honest players. This dependence is made explicit through the random oracle. The code of the challenge-exchange phase is shown in Algorithm 2.

Algorithm 1. The *bootstrapped backbone* protocol, parameterized by the *input contribution function* $I(\cdot)$, the *chain reading function* $R(\cdot)$, and parameter l.

```
 1: C ← ε
 2: st ← ε
 3: round ← 1                                          ▷ Global variable round
 4: Gen ← ∅                                      ▷ Set of candidate genesis blocks
 5: Rank ← ⟨ε⟩
 6: (c, A, c) ← exchangeChallenges(1^κ)
 7: while TRUE do
 8:     k ← round − l − 2
 9:     M_Gen ← {(⟨s', x', ctr'⟩, ⟨A'_{l+1}, ..., A'_{l+1−k}⟩)} from RECEIVE()
10:     M_Chain ← chains C' found in RECEIVE()
11:     (Gen, Rank) ← updateValidate(c, A, M_Gen, Gen, Rank)
12:     C̃ ← maxvalid(C, M_Chain, Gen, Rank)
13:     ⟨st, x⟩ ← I(st, C̃, round, INPUT(), RECEIVE())
14:     C_new ← pow(x, C̃, c)
15:     if C ≠ C_new then
16:         if C = ε then                        ▷ New genesis block has been produced
17:             DIFFUSE( (C_new, ⟨A_{l+1}, ..., A_{l+1−(k+1)}⟩) )
18:         C ← C_new
19:         DIFFUSE(C)
20:     round ← round + 1
21:     if INPUT() contains READ then
22:         write R(x_C) to OUTPUT()
```

Validation predicate update. In the original backbone protocol [21], the chain validation function (called validate—see below) performs a validation of the structural properties of a given chain $\mathcal{C}$, and remains unchanged throughout the protocol. In our case, however, where there is no initial fresh common random string, the function plays the additional role of checking for valid genesis blocks, and players have to update their validation predicate as the protocol advances (for the first l rounds after the challenge phase).

Indeed, using the challenges distributed in the challenge-exchange phase of the protocol, players are able to identify fresh candidate genesis blocks that have been shared during that phase and are accompanied by a valid proof. In addition, the valid genesis blocks are ranked with a negative dependence on the round they were received. In order to help other players to also identify the same genesis blocks, players broadcast the valid genesis blocks they have accepted together with the additional information needed by the other players for verification. The validation predicate update function is shown in Algorithm 3. Recall that *Gen* is the set of candidate genesis blocks.

Chain validation. A chain is considered valid if in addition to the checks performed by the basic backbone protocol regarding the chain's structural

Algorithm 2. The *challenge-exchange* function. Note that variable *round* is global, and originally set to 1.

```
1: function exchangeChallenges(1^κ)
2:     c_1 ←^R {0,1}^κ
3:     DIFFUSE(c_1)
4:     round ← round + 1
5:     while round ≤ l + 1 do
6:         A_round ← κ-bit messages found in RECEIVE()
7:         r_round ←^R {0,1}^κ
8:         A_round ← A_round||r_round
9:         c_round ← H(A_round)                                    ▷ Compute challenge
10:        DIFFUSE(c_round)
11:        round ← round + 1
12:    return (⟨c_1,...c_l⟩, ⟨A_2,...A_{l+1}⟩, c_{l+1})
```

Algorithm 3. The *validation predicate update* function.

```
1: function updateValidate(c, A, M_{Gen}, Gen, Rank)
2:     k ← round − l − 2
3:     if k ≥ l then
4:         return Gen, Rank                                       ▷ No updates after round 2l + 2
5:     for each (⟨s', x', ctr'⟩, ⟨A'_{l+1},...,A'_{l+1−k}⟩) in M_{Gen} do
6:         if validblock_q^D(⟨s, x, ctr⟩) ∧ ⟨s, x, ctr⟩ ∉ Gen then
7:             flag ← (H(A'_{l+1}) = s) ∧ (c_{l−k} ∈ A'_{l+1−k})
8:             for i = l + 1 − k to l do
9:                 if H(A'_i) ∉ A'_{i+1} then
10:                    flag ← FALSE
11:            if flag = TRUE then
12:                Gen ← Gen ∪ ⟨s, x, ctr⟩
13:                Rank[⟨s, x, ctr⟩] ← l − k
14:                DIFFUSE(⟨s, x, ctr⟩, ⟨A'_{l+1},...,A'_{l+1−k}, A_{l−k}⟩)     ▷ Augment A'
       sequence with own A value.
15:    return Gen, Rank
```

properties, its genesis block is in the *Gen* list, which is updated by the updateValidate function (Algorithm 3). The chain validation function is shown in Algorithm 4.

Chain selection. The objective of the next algorithm in Algorithm 1, called maxvalid, is to find the "best possible" chain. The accepted genesis blocks have different *weights* depending on when a player received them. It is possible that the same genesis block is received by honest players in two different rounds (as we show later, those rounds have to be consecutive). In order to take into account the "slack" introduced by the different views honest players may have regarding the same block, as well as the different weights different blocks may have, we let the *weight of a chain* C be equal to the *weight of its genesis block plus three times its length minus one*. The chain selection function is shown in Algorithm 5.

Algorithm 4. The *chain validation predicate*, parameterized by q, D, the hash functions $G(\cdot), H(\cdot)$, and the *content validation predicate* $V(\cdot)$. The input is C.

1: **function** validate(C, *Gen*)
2:     $b \leftarrow V(\mathbf{x}_C) \wedge (C \neq \varepsilon) \wedge (\text{tail}(C) \in Gen)$
3:     **if** $b =$ True **then**
4:         $\langle s, x, ctr \rangle \leftarrow \text{head}(C)$
5:         $s' \leftarrow H(ctr, G(s, x))$
6:         **repeat**
7:             $\langle s, x, ctr \rangle \leftarrow \text{head}(C)$
8:             **if** validblock$_q^D(\langle s, x, ctr \rangle) \wedge (H(ctr, G(s, x)) = s')$ **then**
9:                 $(s', C) \leftarrow (s, C^{\lceil 1})$ ▷ Retain hash value and remove the head from C
10:            **else**
11:                $b \leftarrow$ False
12:        **until** $(C = \varepsilon) \vee (b =$ False)
13:    **return** b

Algorithm 5. The function that finds the "best" chain. The input is a set of chains and the list of genesis blocks.

1: **function** maxvalid($C_1, \ldots, C_k$, *Gen*)
2:     $temp \leftarrow \varepsilon$
3:     $maxweight \leftarrow 0$
4:     **for** $i = 1$ to k **do**
5:         **if** validate(C_i, Gen) **then**
6:             $weight \leftarrow Rank(\text{tail}(C_i)) + 3(|C_i| - 1)$
7:             **if** $maxweight < weight$ **then**
8:                 $maxweight \leftarrow weight$
9:                 $temp \leftarrow C_i$
10:    **return** $temp$

The proof-of-work function. Finally, we need to modify the proof-of-work function in [21], so that when a genesis block is mined, the challenge computed in the last round of the challenge-exchange phase will be included in the block. This, in addition to the proof of genesis information sent in the backbone protocol, is required so that other honest players accept this block as valid and rank it accordingly. The code is presented in Algorithm 6.

Algorithm 6. The *proof of work* function, parameterized by q, D and hash functions $H(\cdot), G(\cdot)$. The input is $(x, \mathcal{C}, c)$.

```
 1: function pow(x, C, c)
 2:     if C = ε then
 3:         s ← c                                          ▷ c is required to prove freshness
 4:     else
 5:         ⟨s′, x′, ctr′⟩ ← head(C)
 6:         s ← H(ctr′, G(s′, x′))
 7:     ctr ← 1
 8:     B ← ε
 9:     h ← G(s, x)
10:     while (ctr ≤ q) do
11:         if (H(ctr, h) < D) then                        ▷ Proof of work found
12:             B ← ⟨s, x, ctr⟩
13:             break
14:         ctr ← ctr + 1
15:     return CB                                          ▷ Extend chain
```

Figure 2 presents the overall structure (phases and corresponding rounds) of the bootstrapped backbone protocol. Next, we turn to its analysis.

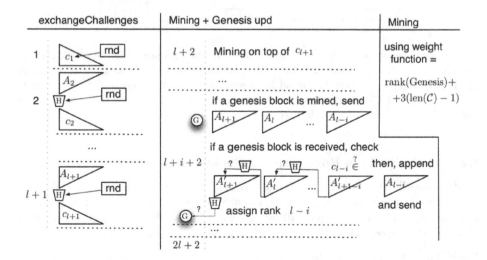

Fig. 2. The different phases of the bootstrapped backbone protocol.

Remark 1. To understand some of our design choices we briefly give some examples of simpler protocols that don't work. For the first example, assume that we only have one round of challenge exchange i.e. l equal to 1. With some non-negligible probability, the adversary can send one block to half of the honest players and another block to the other half. By splitting the honest players in two groups such that no one in the first group will choose the chain of the second and vice versa, agreement becomes impossible. Moreover, l must be large enough so that at least one honest party computes a genesis block with overwhelming probability. Otherwise the adversary can choose to remain silent and no genesis block will be mined with non-negligible probability.

For the second example assume that blocks weigh less than 3 units, as in the original protocol. Also, assume that somehow the problem of the first example was avoided and honest parties only adopted chains with genesis blocks that everyone had in their genesis block list. In this case, uniquely successful rounds would not imply agreement on a single chain (see Fig. 3), as the adversary would have been able to take advantage of the different views that honest players have regarding the weight of genesis blocks. However, if we set the block weight to 3, this event becomes impossible and makes the analysis a lot easier.

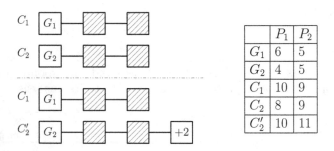

Fig. 3. An example where blocks weigh 2 units. In the table the weights of the respective chains are depicted. Initially player P_1 has adopted chain C_1 and player P_2 chain C_2. Then a uniquely successful round happens and C_2 is extended to C_2'. Notice that, P_1 will not adopt C_2' since it has the same weight as C_1. If the new block weighted 3 units, all players would have adopted chain C_2'.

3.2 Analysis of the Bootstrapped Backbone Protocol

First, some additional definitions that will become handy in the analysis. We saw in the previous section that genesis blocks are assigned weights, and, further, that a single genesis block may have different weights for different parties depending on when they received it. We extend this notion to chains of blocks.

Definition 4. *Let $w_P(B)$ be the weight that P assigned to genesis block B. We define the weight of a chain C with genesis block B (with respect to party P) to be:*

$$w_P(C) = w_P(B) + 3(|C| - 1).$$

If block B was not received by P until round $2l+1$, or if $C = \epsilon$, then $w_P(C) = -1$.

In [21], all parties assign the same weight to the same chain, i.e., the length of the chain; thus, for all parties P_i, P_j we have that $w_{P_i}(C) = w_{P_j}(C)$. In contrast, in our case the genesis block of each chain may have different weight for different parties, akin to some bounded amount of "noise" that is party-dependent being added to the chain weights. We are going to show that if the amount of noise is at most 1, then by letting each new block weigh 3 units our protocol satisfies the chain growth, common prefix and chain quality properties.

Definition 5. *Regarding chains and their weight:*

- *Define $h_C = \max_P\{w_P(C)\}$ and $\ell_C = \min_P\{w_P(C)\}$.*
- *Let $C(B)$ denote the truncation of chain C after its block B.*
- *For a block B of a chain C, define $h_C(B) = h_{C(B)}$ and similarly for $\ell_C(B)$. (Sometimes we will abuse notation and write $\ell(B)$ instead of $\ell_C(B)$. As long as no collision happens $\ell(B)$ is well defined. The same holds for $h(B)$.)*
- *For chains C_1 and C_2, define $C_1 \cap C_2$ to be the chain formed by their common prefix.*

The following are important concepts introduced in [21], which we are also going to use in our analysis:

Definition 6. *A round is called:*

- successful *if at least one honest party computes a solution;*
- uniquely successful *if exactly one honest party computes a solution.*

Definition 7. *In an execution blocks are called:*

- honest, *if mined by an honest party,*
- adversarial, *if mined by the adversary, and*
- u.s. blocks, *if mined in a uniquely successful round by an honest player.*

Recall that our model is "flat" in terms of computational power in the sense that all honest parties are assumed to have the same computational power while the adversary has computational power proportional to the number of players that it controls. The total number of parties is n and the adversary is assumed to control up to t of them (honest parties do not know any of these parameters). Obtaining a new block is achieved by finding a hash value that is smaller than the difficulty parameter D. Thus, the success probability that a single hash query produces a solution is $p = \frac{D}{2^\kappa}$, where κ is the length of the hash. The total hashing power of the honest players is $\alpha = pq(n-t)$, the hashing power of the adversary is $\beta = pqt$, and the total hashing power is $f = \alpha + \beta$. Moreover, in [21], a lower bound on the probability that a round is uniquely successful was established; denoted by γ and equal to $\alpha - \alpha^2$. Notice that γ is also a bound for the probability of a round being just successful.

For each round j, we define the Boolean random variables X_j and Y_j as follows. Let $X_j = 1$ iff j was a *successful round*, i.e., at least one honest party computed a POW at round j, and let $Y_j = 1$ iff j was a *uniquely successful round*, i.e., exactly one honest party computed a POW at round j. With respect to a set of rounds S, let $Z(S)$ denote the number of POWs obtained by the adversary during the rounds in S (i.e., in $qt|S|$ queries). Also, let $X(S) = \sum_{j \in S} X_j$ and define $Y(S)$ similarly. Note that $\gamma|S| \leq \mathbb{E}[Y(S)] \leq \mathbb{E}[X(S)] \leq \alpha|S|$ and $\mathbb{E}[Z(S)] = \beta|S|$.

Lemma 1. *If $|S| = k$ and $\gamma \geq (1 + \delta)\beta$ for some $\delta \in (0, 1)$, then*

$$\Pr[Y(S) > (1 + \frac{5\delta}{9})Z(S)] > 1 - e^{-\Omega(\delta^2 k)}.$$

Proof. By the Chernoff bound we have that:

$$\Pr[Y(S) \leq (1 - \frac{\delta}{8})\mathbb{E}[Y(S)]] \leq e^{-\frac{\delta^2 \gamma k}{128}} \text{ and } Pr[Z(S) \geq (1 - \frac{\delta}{9})\mathbb{E}[Z(S)] \leq e^{-\frac{\delta^2 \beta k}{243}}.$$

Suppose none of the above events happens. Then, from the union bound, we get that with probability $1 - e^{-(2\min(\frac{\beta}{243}, \frac{\gamma}{128})\delta^2 k - \ln(2))}$ it holds that

$$Y(S) > (1 - \frac{\delta}{8})\gamma k \geq (1 - \frac{\delta}{8})(1 + \delta)\beta k \geq (1 + \frac{5\delta}{9})(1 + \frac{\delta}{9})\beta k > (1 + \frac{5\delta}{9})Z(S).$$

$\square$

Remark 2. For ease of exposition, in our analysis we will assume that there are no collisions; that is, for any two different queries to the random oracle, always a different response is returned. This would generally be a problem since for example it would break independence of X_i, X_j, for $i \neq j$, and we would not be able to apply the Chernoff bound in the previous lemma. However, since the probability of a collision happening, as well as all other events we consider, is at most $e^{-\Omega(\kappa)}$, we can always use the union bound to include the event of no collision occurring to our other assumptions. In addition, we assume that no two queries to the oracle are the same, as formalized by the Input Entropy condition in [21].

Properties of the genesis block generation process. We now establish a number of properties of the genesis block generation process.

Lemma 2 (Graded Consistency). *If any honest party P_i accepts genesis block B with rank $w_{P_i}(B) > 1$, then all honest parties accept B with rank at least $w_{P_i}(B) - 1$.*

Proof. Let $w_{P_i}(B) = k > 1$. Since P_i accepted B with rank k at some round r, he must have received a message of the form $(B, E_{l+1}, \ldots, E_{k+1})$, where

- B is a valid block that contains $H(E_{l+1})$;
- E_{k+1} contains c_k and for $k + 2 < j \leq l + 1$, E_j contains $H(E_{j-1})$; and
- c_k is the challenge computed by P_i at round k.

Since $k > 0$, according to Algorithm 3, P_i is going to broadcast $(B, E_{l+1}, \ldots,$
$E_{k+1}, A_k)$, where $H(A_k) = c_k$ is contained in E_{k+1} and A_k contains all the
messages received by P_i at round k. All honest-party challenges of round $k - 1$
were received in this round; therefore, all honest parties have accepted or will
accept block B by the next round and the lemma follows.   □

Lemma 3 (Validity). *Genesis blocks computed by honest parties before round*
$2l + 2$, *will be accepted by all honest parties in the next round.*

Proof. Suppose honest party P_i mined genesis block B at round m. According to
Algorithm 1, B contains the challenge he has computed at the last round of the
challenge-exchange phase. In addition, when the party broadcasts it, it includes
the message sets $A_{l+1}, \ldots, A_r$, where A_j contains the messages received by P_i
at round j and $r = 2l + 2 - m$. Since P_i is honest, the following hold:

- B is a valid block that contains $H(A_{l+1})$;
- for $r + 1 < j \leq l + 1$, A_j contains $H(A_{j-1})$;
- if c_r is the challenge sent by some honest party at round r, then c_r is contained
  in A_{r+1}; and
- all honest parties are going to receive the message.

Thus, all honest parties are going to accept B at round $m + 1$ and the lemma
follows.   □

Lemma 4 (Freshness). *Let $r \leq l + 2$. Every block computed before round r*
cannot be part of some chain with genesis block B, where $w_P(B) \geq r - 1$ for
some honest party P, with overwhelming probability in the security parameter κ.

Weak chain growth. We now turn our attention to the weight of chains and
prove a *weak* chain-growth property. In the original Bitcoin backbone protocol [21], it was proved that chains grow at least at the rate of successful rounds,
independently of the adversary's behavior. Here, at least initially, the chains of
honest parties grow in a "weak" manner, in the sense that the adversary is able
to slow down this growth by using his own blocks. Later on, we will show that
after some specific round our protocol also achieves optimal chain growth.

Lemma 5. *Let round r such that $l + 2 \leq r < 2l + 2$, and suppose that at round*
r an honest party, say, P_1 has a chain $\mathcal{C}$ such that $w_{P_1}(\mathcal{C}) = d$. Then, by round
s, where $r \leq s < 2l + 2$, every honest party P will have received a chain $\mathcal{C}'$ of
weight at least $w_P(\mathcal{C}') = d - 2 + 3 \sum_{i=r}^{s-1} Y_i - \sum_{i=r}^{s-1} Z_i$.

Proof (Sketch). Note that every time a uniquely successful round happens, the
minimum weight over all parties' chains will increase by 2. Moreover, if the
adversary has not diffused any block in the same round the minimum weight
increases by 3. By applying this result iteratively, the lemma follows. We refer
the reader to the full version of the paper for the full proof.   □

Universal chain validity. A novelty of our construction is that the same genesis block may have different weight for different parties. Unfortunately, it could be the case that due to the adversary's influence, a genesis block is valid for one party but invalid for another. This could lead to disagreement, in the sense that some honest parties may adopt a chain that others don't because it is not valid for them. We will show that with overwhelming probability such an event cannot occur for our protocol; as such, chain validity is a "universal" property; if some honest party accepts a chain $\mathcal{C}$ as valid, then $\mathcal{C}$ will also be valid for all other parties.

Notice, that in order to prove the following lemma we need l to be greater than a value that depends on $1/\gamma$, i.e. the expected time it takes for honest parties to mine a block, and the security parameter κ (see also Remark 1). Intuitively l should be large enough so that (i) honest parties mine at least one block at this time interval, and (ii) any adversarial chain that is based on a genesis block broadcast at the end of the bootstraping phase will never be adopted by honest parties (because such genesis block will have too small weight in comparison).

Lemma 6. *Suppose that for some* $\delta \in (0,1), 3(1+\delta)f < 1, l > \frac{(1-\delta)k/\gamma+3}{1-3(1+\delta)f}$, *and* $\gamma \geq (1+\delta)\beta$, *and that at round* r *an honest party* P *has chain* $\mathcal{C}$. *Then* $\mathcal{C}$ *will also be valid for all other parties from this round on with probability* $1 - e^{-\Omega(\delta^2 k)}$.

The complete version of the weak chain growth lemma follows from the argument we've made above.

Corollary 1. *Suppose that for some* $\delta \in (0,1)$, $3(1+\delta)f < 1$, $l > \frac{(1-\delta)k/\gamma+3}{1-3(1+\delta)f}$, *and* $\gamma \geq (1+\delta)\beta$. *Let round* r *such that* $r \geq l+2$, *and suppose that at round* r *an honest party, say,* P_1 *has a chain* $\mathcal{C}$ *such that* $w_{P_1}(\mathcal{C}) = d$. *Then, by round* s, *where* $r \leq s$, *every honest party* P *will have received a chain* $\mathcal{C}'$ *of weight at least* $w_P(\mathcal{C}') = d - 2 + 3\sum_{i=r}^{s-1} Y_i - \sum_{i=r}^{s-1} Z_i$ *with probability at most* $1 - e^{-\Omega(\delta^2 k)}$.

Remark 3. Note further that the dependency of γ on n does not undermine the scalability of the round complexity of our protocol. This claim is argued on the basis that the difficulty level D can be set proportional to $1/n$, so that γ can be treated as a constant and then l is in essence independent of n (note that both parameters would be polynomials in κ).

A bound on adversarially precomputed blocks. The honest parties begin mining right after the challenge-exchange phase. Note that it does not help the adversary to precompute blocks before the challenge-exchange phase, except for the small probability of the event that some of his blocks happen to extend future blocks. We have shown that the adversary cannot create a private chain that honest parties will adopt if he starts mining at the first round of the challenge-exchange phase. It is though possible to start mining *after* the first round in order to gain some advantage over the honest parties. The following lemma provides a bound on the number of blocks mined during the challenge-exchange phase with sufficient weight so that they can be later used by the adversary.

Lemma 7 (Precomputed blocks). *Assume* $3(1+\delta)f < 1$ *and* $l > \frac{(1-\delta)k/\gamma+3}{1-3(1+\delta)f}$, *for some* $\delta \in (0,1)$. *Let* R *be the set that contains any adversarial block* B *mined before round* $l + 2$, *where* $h(B) > l - 1 - (1 - \delta)\delta^2 k$. *Then* $\Pr[\|R\| > \frac{5\delta}{9}k\beta] \le e^{-\Omega(\delta^4 k)}$.

Proof (Sketch). We first show that the adversary cannot take advantage of blocks which belong to chains whose genesis block was computed early on in the challenge exchange phase. Hence, with overwhelming probability she can only use blocks computed near the end of the challenge exchange phase; remember that the weight of a genesis block is small if it is mined early in the challenge exchange phase. By applying appropriate Chernoff bounds the result follows. We refer the reader to the full version of the paper for the full proof. □

We are now ready to prove the security properties listed in Sect. 2.2.

Common Prefix. Every time a uniquely successful round happens all honest players converge to one chain, unless the adversary broadcasts some new block. This turns out to be a very important fact and a consequence of it is described in the next lemma.

Lemma 8. *Suppose block* B *in chain* $\mathcal{C}$ *is a u.s. block and consider a chain* $\mathcal{C}'$ *such that* $B \notin \mathcal{C}'$. *If* $\ell_{\mathcal{C}'} \ge \ell_{\mathcal{C}}(B) - 1$ *then there exists a unique adversarial block* B' *such that* $\ell_{\mathcal{C}'}(B') \in [\ell_{\mathcal{C}}(B) - 1, \ell_{\mathcal{C}}(B) + 1]$. *Moreover, if* B *is not a genesis block, then* B' *will also not be a genesis block.*

Proof. Assume block B was mined at some round r. If B is not a genesis block, then for any honest block B'' mined before round r it should hold that $\ell(B'') \le \ell(B) - 2$. Otherwise, at round r no honest party would choose the parent of B to mine new blocks. If B is a genesis block, then no other honest party has mined a block in some previous round. On the other hand, for any honest block B'' mined after round r it must hold that $\ell(B'') \ge \ell(B) - 1 + 3 = \ell(B) + 2$, since honest parties will only extend chains of length at least $\ell(B) - 1$ after this round. Thus, if a block with weight in the given interval exists, it must be adversarial.

For the sake of contradiction, suppose B is not a genesis block while B' is a genesis block and let B'' be the parent of B. Then $h_{\mathcal{C}}(B'') < \ell_{\mathcal{C}'}(B')$ since $h_{\mathcal{C}}(B'') \le \ell_{\mathcal{C}}(B) - 2$. This implies than every honest party received B' before block B''. But then, no honest party would mine on the parent of B, because he would have lower weight than B', which leads to a contradiction. Hence, the lemma follows. □

We use Lemma 8 in order to show that the existence of a fork implies that the adversary has mined blocks proportional in number to the time the fork started.

Theorem 1. *Assume* $3(1+\delta)f < 1$, $l > \frac{(1-\delta)k/\gamma+3}{1-3(1+\delta)f}$, $\gamma \ge (1+\delta)\beta$, *for some real* $\delta \in (0,1)$. *Let* S *be the set of the chains of the honest parties from round* $2l + 2$ *and onwards of the bootstrapped backbone protocol. Then the probability that* S *does not satisfy the strong common-prefix property with parameter* k *is at most* $e^{-\Omega(\delta^4 k)}$.

Proof (Sketch). We are going to use Lemma 8 to match u.s. blocks to adversarial ones. Function ℓ will help us show that the matched blocks are distinct; every pair of matched blocks is very close with respect to the ℓ function, while pairs of u.s. blocks can be very far under specific conditions. Initially, we construct such a matching whenever we have a fork between two chains $\mathcal{C}_1$, $\mathcal{C}_2$, either by matching adversarial blocks alternatively to each of the chains or by matching consecutive u.s. blocks on the same chain to consecutive adversarial blocks in the other chain.

Using this result, we prove that if a "deep" enough fork exists, the adversary must have mined more blocks than his hashing power allows, which leads to a contradiction. In more detail, the initial fork implies the existence of some honestly mined block B that is part of the common prefix of the two chains. Starting from B we construct a matching of all u.s. blocks mined after it, by picking "deeper" and "deeper" forks and repeatedly applying the matching procedure. Using the upper bound on precomputed blocks established in Lemma 7, we can show that the adversary is able to mine a sufficient number of blocks only with negligible probability. Hence, the theorem follows. □

Chain Growth. We proved that after round $2l + 1$ the strong common-prefix property is satisfied. This implies that all players share a common genesis block after this round. The next lemma shows that this is sufficient in order to get chain growth at the same level as in the original Backbone protocol.

Lemma 9. *Suppose that at round r an honest party P_1 has a chain $\mathcal{C}$ of weight $w_{P_1}(\mathcal{C}) = d$ and all honest parties after round $r - 1$ adopt chains that share the same genesis block B. Then, by round $s \geq r$, every honest party P will have received a chain $\mathcal{C}'$ of weight at least $w_P(\mathcal{C}') = d - 1 + 3\sum_{i=r}^{s-1} X_i$.*

Proof. Since all parties adopt chains with the same genesis block after round $r - 1$, and P_1 has adopted a chain $\mathcal{C}$ of weight d, there are two cases: either (1) $\ell_{\mathcal{C}} = d - 1$ and any chain that honest parties adopt after round $r - 1$ has a weight that is congruent to d or $d - 1$ modulo 3, or (2) $\ell_{\mathcal{C}} = d$ and the weight is congruent to d or $d + 1$ modulo 3. This observation is implied from the fact that each extra block adds 3 units of weight to the chain and B can only have two different weights under the views of honest parties.

It is sufficient to study only one of the two cases so w.l.o.g. suppose that the weight of the chains is congruent to d or $d - 1$ modulo 3. The proof is by induction on $s - r \geq 0$. For the basis ($s = r$), observe that if at round r P_1 has a chain $\mathcal{C}$ of weight $w_{P_1}(\mathcal{C}) = d$, then he broadcast $\mathcal{C}$ at an earlier round (than r). It follows that every honest party P will receive $\mathcal{C}$ by round r and $w_P(\mathcal{C}) \geq d - 1$.

For the inductive step, note that by the inductive hypothesis every honest party P has received a chain $\mathcal{C}'$ of weight at least $w_P(\mathcal{C}') = d' = d - 1 + 3\sum_{i=r}^{s-2} X_i$ by round $s - 1$. When $X_{s-1} = 0$ the statement follows directly, so assume $X_{s-1} = 1$. Observe that every honest party queried the oracle with a chain of weight at least d' at round $s - 1$. It follows that every honest party P successful at round $s - 1$ broadcast a chain $\mathcal{C}'$ of weight at least $w_P(\mathcal{C}') = d' + 3$. For every other party P' it holds that $w_{P'}(\mathcal{C}') \geq d' + 2 \geq d - 1 + 3\sum_{i=r}^{s-1} X_i - 1$. However, no chain that an honest party adopts can have length $d' + 2$, because $d' + 2$ is congruent to $d - 2$ modulo 3. Thus all honest parties adopt chains that have length at least $d' + 3$ and the lemma follows. $\qquad\square$

It can be easily shown that Lemma 9 implies the chain growth property after round $2l + 1$.

Theorem 2. *Assume* $3(1+\delta)f < 1$, $l > \frac{(1-\delta)k/\gamma+3}{1-3(1+\delta)f}$, $\gamma \geq (1+\delta)\beta$, *for some real* $\delta \in (0,1)$. *The bootstrapped Bitcoin protocol satisfies the chain growth property for* $r_0 = 2l+2$ *with speed coefficient* $(1-\delta)\gamma$ *and probability at least* $1 - e^{-\Omega(\delta^4 s)}$.

Chain Quality. We first observe a consequence of Theorem 1.

Lemma 10. *Assume* $3(1+\delta)f < 1$, $l > \frac{(1-\delta)k/\gamma+3}{1-3(1+\delta)f}$, $\gamma \geq (1+\delta)\beta$, *for some real* $\delta \in (0,1)$. *From round* $2l+2$ *and onwards of the bootstrapped backbone protocol, the probability that the adversary has a chain which is more than* k *blocks longer than the chain of some honest party is at most* $e^{-\Omega(\delta^4 k)}$.

Proof. Given any execution and an adversary that at a round r has a chain $\mathcal{C}$ which is k blocks longer than the chain $\mathcal{C}'$ of an honest party P, we can define an adversary such that at round $r+1$ the common-prefix property does not hold for parameter k. The adversary simply sends $\mathcal{C}$ to $P' \neq P$ at round r. $\qquad\square$

Theorem 3. *Assume* $3(1+\delta)f < 1$, $l > \frac{(1-\delta)k/\gamma+3}{1-3(1+\delta)f}$, $\gamma \geq (1+\delta)\beta$, *for some real* $\delta \in (0,1/2)$. *Suppose* $\mathcal{C}$ *belongs to an honest party and consider any* k *consecutive blocks of* $\mathcal{C}$ *computed after round* $2l+2$ *of the bootstrapped backbone protocol. The probability that the adversary has contributed more than* $(1+\frac{\delta}{2})\frac{\beta}{\gamma} \cdot k \leq (1-\frac{\delta}{3})k$ *of these blocks is less than* $e^{-\Omega(\delta^5 k)}$.

Corollary 2. *Assume* $3(1+\delta)f < 1$, $l > \frac{(1-\delta)k/\gamma+3}{1-3(1+\delta)f}$, $\gamma \geq (1+\delta)\beta$, *for some real* $\delta \in (0,1/2)$. *The bootstrapped Bitcoin protocol satisfies the chain-quality property with parameters* $\mu = (1+\frac{\delta}{2})\frac{\beta}{\gamma}$, $k_0 = 2f(1+\delta)(l+1)$, *and* k, *with probability at least* $1 - e^{\Omega(\delta^5 k)}$.

Proof. Note that the next two events occur with probability at least $1 - e^{\Omega(\delta^2 l)}$, for any $\delta \in (0,1)$. The honest parties in the first $l+1$ rounds have computed at most $\alpha(1+\delta)(l+1)$ blocks. The adversary, who might have been mining also during the challenges phase, has computed at most $2\beta(1+\delta)(l+1)$. The statement then follows from Theorem 3, since $\alpha(1+\delta)(l+1) + 2\beta(1+\delta)(l+1) < 2f(1+\delta)(l+1)$. $\qquad\square$

4   Applications of the Bootstrapped Backbone Protocol

In this section we present applications of our construction, starting with its primary/original one: a distributed ledger, i.e., a public and permanent summary of all transactions that honest parties can agree on as well as add their own, despite the potentially disruptive behavior of parties harnessing less than $1/2$ of the hashing power. This entails proving that the ledger's required security properties (Persistence and Liveness—cf. [21]) hold in a genesis block-less setting.

Next, we consider the problem of setting up a PKI in our unauthenticated network setting *from scratch*, i.e., without any trusted setup. As mentioned in Sect. 1, the idea of using POWs as an identity-assignment tool was put forth by Aspnes *et al.* [2]. Here we build on this idea as well as on the "2-for-1 POWs" technique from [21] to use our bootstrapped protocol to assign identities to parties. The assignment relation will possibly assign more than one identities to the same party, while guaranteeing that the majority of them is assigned to honest parties.

Finally, applying the 2-for-1 POWs technique we can also solve the consensus (aka Byzantine agreement) problem [31,36] without any trusted setup, even if the adversary has almost the same hashing power as the honest parties, and in a number of rounds independent of the number of parties. Indeed, all our protocols have round complexity linear in the security parameter, and enjoy simultaneous termination.

Compared to other works, most notably [1], our approach is different in the order in which it sets up a "bulletin board" and assigns identities to parties. We choose to first establish the former—i.e., the ledger—and then assign the identities; in contrast, in [1] identities are established first in a graded manner, and then using that infrastructure the parties can implement a broadcast channel.

We now turn to the applications in detail.

Robust public transaction ledger. A *public transaction ledger* is defined with respect to a set of valid ledgers $\mathcal{L}$ and a set of valid transactions $\mathcal{T}$, each one possessing an efficient membership test. A ledger $\mathbf{x} \in \mathcal{L}$ is a vector of sequences of transactions tx $\in \mathcal{T}$. Each transaction tx may be associated with one or more *accounts*. Ledgers correspond to chains in the backbone protocol. In the protocol execution there also exists an oracle Txgen that generates valid transactions. Note, that it is possible for the adversary to create two transactions that are conflicting; valid ledgers must not contain conflicting transaction. We will assume that the oracle is unambiguous, i.e., that the adversary cannot create transactions that come in 'conflict' with the transactions generated by the oracle. A transaction is called *neutral* if there does not exist any transactions that comes in conflict with it.

In order to turn the backbone protocol into a protocol realizing a public transaction ledger suitable definitions were given for functions $V(\cdot), R(\cdot), I(\cdot)$ in [21]. Namely, $V(\langle x_1, \ldots, x_m \rangle)$ is true if its input is a valid ledger. Function $R(\mathcal{C})$ returns the contents of the chain if they constitute a valid ledger, otherwise it is undefined. Finally, $I(st, \mathcal{C}, round, \text{INPUT}(), \text{RECEIVE}())$ returns the largest subsequence of transactions in the input and receive tapes that constitute a valid ledger, with respect to the contents of the chain the party already has, together with a randomly generated neutral transaction. We denote the instantiation of our protocol with these functions by $\Pi_{\mathsf{PL}}^{\mathsf{Boot}}$. For more details we refer to [21].

Definition 8. *A protocol* Π *implements a* robust public transaction ledger *in the q-bounded synchronous setting without trusted setup if there is a round* r_0 *so that the following two properties are satisfied:*

- Persistence: *Parameterized by* $k \in \mathbb{N}$ *(the "depth" parameter), if in a certain round after* r_0 *an honest player reports a ledger that contains a transaction* tx *in a block more than* k *blocks away from the end of the ledger, then* tx *will always be reported in the same position in the ledger by any honest player from this round on.*
- Liveness: *Parameterized by* $u, k \in \mathbb{N}$ *(the "wait time" and "depth" parameters, resp.), provided that a transaction either (i) issued by* Txgen, *or (ii) is neutral, is given as input to all honest players continuously for* u *consecutive rounds after round* r_0, *then there exists an honest party who will report this transaction at a block more than* k *blocks from the end of the ledger.*

Chain quality, chain growth and the strong common prefix property were shown in [27] to be sufficient to implement such a ledger[7] in a black-box manner. Our protocol satisfies all these properties after a specific condition is met. Chain quality holds after the $2f(1 + \delta)(l + 1)$ block in the chain of any player, as Corollary 2 dictates, and common prefix and chain growth hold after round $2l+2$, according to Theorem 1. Finally, due to chain growth, after at most $(2(1+\delta)(1 - \delta)f/\gamma + 2)(l + 1) \leq 14(l + 1)$ rounds all necessary conditions will have been met with overwhelming probability.

Lemma 11 (Persistence). *Assume* $3(1+\delta)f < 1$, $l > \frac{(1-\delta)k/\gamma+3}{1-3(1+\delta)f}$, $\gamma \geq (1+\delta)\beta$, *for some real* $\delta \in (0, 1/2)$. *Then for all* $k \in \mathbb{N}$ *protocol* $\Pi_{\mathsf{PL}}^{\mathsf{Boot}}$ *satisfies Persistence after round* $2l + 2$ *with probability* $1 - e^{-\Omega(\delta^5 k)}$, *where* k *is the depth parameter.*

Lemma 12 (Liveness). *Assume* $3(1 + \delta)f < 1$, $l > \frac{(1-\delta)k/\gamma+3}{1-3(1+\delta)f}$, $\gamma \geq (1 + \delta)\beta$, *for some real* $\delta \in (0, 1/2)$. *Further, assume oracle* Txgen *is unambiguous. Then for all* $k \in \mathbb{N}$ *protocol* $\Pi_{\mathsf{PL}}^{\mathsf{Boot}}$ *satisfies Liveness after round* $14(l+1)$ *with wait time* $u = \frac{3}{(1-\delta)\gamma} \cdot \max(k, \frac{1}{1-(1+\frac{\delta}{2})\frac{\beta}{\gamma}})$ *rounds and depth parameter* k *with probability at least* $1 - e^{-\Omega(\delta^5 k)}$.

Corollary 3. *Assume* $3(1 + \delta)f < 1$, $l > \frac{(1-\delta)k/\gamma+3}{1-3(1+\delta)f}$, $\gamma \geq (1 + \delta)\beta$, *for some real* $\delta \in (0, 1/2)$. *Then protocol* $\Pi_{\mathsf{PL}}^{\mathsf{Boot}}$ *implements a robust transaction ledger with parameter* $r_0 = 14(l + 1)$.

Fast PKI setup. Next, we use the ledger to generate an honest majority PKI from scratch in a number of rounds that is linear in the security parameter. The first idea that we are going to use is that of a *2-for-1 POW* described in [21]. At a high level, the technique allows to do combined mining for two POW schemes in the price of one. In more detail, we can add additional information in the queries to the random oracle, and if the response to the query is less than some value

---

[7] A similar definitional approach was pursued in [34].

T_1, then we consider it a valid POW of type 1; if it is greater than some value T_2 we consider it as a valid POW of type 2. T_1 and T_2 should be appropriately chosen so that the events of success in either of these POWs are independent. The second POW is used to "mine" transactions, in the same way blocks are mined. This guarantees that the *number of transactions* is proportional to the hashing power of each player. By having parties broadcast their transactions on one hand, and making sure that at least one honest block that contains these transactions is in the chain of all honest parties due to liveness on the other hand, the protocol in [21] manages to achieve consensus assuming an honest-majority hashing power.

In our case, transactions will contain the public keys, and in this way we will obtain an honest-majority PKI. However, in contrast with [21], we cannot let parties start mining transactions from the beginning of the execution, since the adversary would have some additional precomputation time. Instead, we are going to wait for the public ledger to be established, and then use some of the blocks added by honest parties to guarantee that all transactions where mined recently enough. In more detail, any POW will be represented by a triple $\langle w, ctr, label \rangle$. The verification procedure for "block level" POWs ("block POWs" for short) will be of the form

$$H(ctr, \langle G(w), label \rangle) < T_1,$$

while the verification procedure for the "transaction level" POWs will be of the form

$$[H(ctr, \langle label, G(w) \rangle)]^R < T_2,$$

where $[a]^R$ denotes the reverse of the bitstring a. In w we are going to encode the information needed for each application. For example, in block POWs, w will contain the transactions related to this block as well as the hash of the previous block. Note that by making one hash query of the form $H(ctr, \langle G(w_0), G(w_1) \rangle)$ and only two comparisons, we will be mining POWs of both types at the same time. Moreover, if $\lceil \log(T_1) \rceil + \lceil \log(T_2) \rceil$ is less than κ, where κ is the size of the hash's output, then the events of succeeding in any of the two POWs are independent, since they depend on different bits of the hash which are sampled independently and uniformly at random by the random oracle.

Next, we describe our protocol $\Pi_{\mathsf{PL}}^{\mathsf{PKI}}$ for an honest party P. L_1, L_2 are constants such that $L_1 < L_2$.

- *Initialization.* P runs $\Pi_{\mathsf{PL}}^{\mathsf{Boot}}$, as described so far, until she receives a chain of length at least L_1. We choose L_1 so that it is guaranteed that all security properties hold, and about k new blocks have been inserted in the common-prefix of the chains of all honest players.
- *2-for-1 mining.* Let $\mathcal{C}$ be P's chain at the end of the initialization phase. From now on, she is going to do 2-for-1 POW mining, and include in her transaction POWs (i) the hash of the $(L_1 - k)$-th block of $\mathcal{C}$, and (ii) a randomly generated public key for which she has stored the corresponding secret key. Obviously, a new key must be generated every time she starts mining a new transaction.

Whenever P mines a new transaction, she diffuses it to the network, and whenever she receives one, she includes it in the transactions of the block she is mining.

The first time P receives a chain of length greater or equal to L_2, she runs the Key extraction procedure (below). The phase ends at round $\frac{L_2}{(1-\delta)\gamma}$, where P runs the Termination procedure.

- *Key extraction.* P extracts and stores a set of keys from her current chain according to the following rules: If chain $\mathcal{C}'$ is her chain at this round, she stores any public key which belongs to a transaction that (i) is in the first $L_2 - k$ blocks of $\mathcal{C}'$, and (ii) the hash of the block contained in the transaction matches the hash of the $(L_1 - k)$-th block in her chain.
- *Termination.* P outputs the keys from the key extraction phase and terminates.

Next, we prove that a consistent PKI with an honest majority is generated at the end of the execution of protocol $\Pi_{\mathsf{PL}}^{\mathsf{PKI}}$. Two properties are guaranteed: (1) honest parties output the same set of keys and (2) more than half of these keys have been generated by them. For the rest of this section let α_2, β_2, f_2 be the corresponding values of α, β, f for the difficulty level T_2, e.g. $f_2 = nq\frac{T_2}{2^\kappa}$. The full proof of the following theorem is provided in the full version of the paper.

Theorem 4. *Assume $3(1 + \delta)f < 1$, $l > \frac{(1-\delta)k/\gamma+3}{1-3(1+\delta)f}$, $\gamma \geq (1 + \delta)\beta$, for some real $\delta \in (0, 1/2)$ and $\lceil \log(T_1) \rceil + \lceil \log(T_2) \rceil \leq \kappa$. Then, for parameters $L_1 = 14(l + 1)(1 + \delta)f + 2k$ and $L_2 = L_1 + 2k \cdot (1 + \frac{10}{\delta})\frac{(1+\delta)f}{(1-\delta)\gamma}$ the following hold for protocol $\Pi_{\mathsf{PL}}^{\mathsf{PKI}}$ with probability $1 - e^{-\Omega(\delta^5 k)}$:*

- *All honest players output the same set of public keys, the size of which is*

$$k\frac{\alpha_2}{\gamma}\frac{20}{\delta} \leq N \leq 60k\frac{f_2}{\gamma}(1 + \frac{10}{\delta});$$

- *the majority of the keys are generated by honest parties; and*
- *$\Pi_{\mathsf{PL}}^{\mathsf{PKI}}$ has round complexity linear in κ.*

Proof (Sketch). First, note that the adversary can start precomputing transactions at most $2k/\gamma$ rounds before the honest parties. Otherwise, she will be unable to predict the hash of their chain as dictated by our protocol, since by the chain quality property the chain of each honest player will contain an honest block near the tail of the chain. Moreover, again by the chain quality and common prefix properties, the adversary will stop mining transactions at most $2k/\gamma$ rounds after the honest parties. After this round, she will be unable to insert her transactions deep enough in the chain for the honest parties to take them into account. Finally, by choosing an appropriate value for δ, we are sure that the number of keys mined by the honest parties is greater than the number of keys mined by the adversary. $\square$

Remark 4. To better understand Π_{PL}^{PKI} we compute different parameters of the system for the Bitcoin network parameters. Assume that $f = 2\%, \alpha = 1.33\%, \gamma = 1.31\%, \beta = 0.6\%, k = 10$, and $\delta = 0.25$. The choice of f approximately corresponds to a rate of one block per 10 min with a round duration of about 12 s; the adversary's hashing power is half of that of the honest parties. Then, $l \approx 623$, which corresponds in terms of rounds to about 2 h. Moreover, if we set f_2 to be equal to f/k we have that $80 < N < 600$. We note that the parameters of Bitcoin are quite conservative and that's why our runtime suffers. In principle, by carefully analyzing and re-engineering our protocol we can get tighter bounds; many of the design decisions we got here, were made to aid the readability of our work.

Remark 5. The probability that some honest party succeeds in mining at least one transaction is:

$$\Pr[\geq 1 \text{ key}] = 1 - \Pr[0 \text{ keys}] = 1 - (1 - \frac{T_2}{2^\kappa})^{q \frac{20k}{(1-\delta)\gamma\delta}} \geq 1 - e^{-\frac{T_2}{2^\kappa} \cdot q \frac{20k}{(1-\delta)\gamma\delta}}.$$

Hence, by setting $T_2 > \frac{\ln(\frac{1}{\epsilon})2^\kappa(1-\delta)\gamma\delta}{q \cdot 20k}$, each party will obtain at least one key with probability at least $1 - \epsilon$, for any $\epsilon \in (0, 1)$. Note here that T_2 and κ must be carefully chosen to retain the independence of the 2 POWs. In case this is not possible, the *2-for-1* mining phase may be extended.

Consensus and other applications. Next, we describe how Π_{PL}^{PKI} can be used in other contexts. First, a direct application of our protocol is in the context of *proof of stake* protocols. In this type of protocols, blocks are mined by randomly selecting stake holders with probability proportional to their stake. A typical requirement for bootstrapping such protocols (e.g. [28,30]), is that in the initial state of the economy the majority of the coins is controlled by honest parties. By assigning one coin to each public key produced by our protocol, we can efficiently and securely bootstrap a proof of stake protocol.

A more general application of Π_{PL}^{PKI} is in solving consensus (aka Byzantine agreement) [31,36], with no trusted setup, and in a number of rounds independent of the number of parties. If parties submit transactions containing their input instead of public keys, it follows that by taking the majority of their output they are going to achieve Byzantine agreement. That is, everyone will agree on the same value (the Agreement property), and if all honest parties have the same input v, they are all going to output v (Validity).

Finally, our protocol for the establishment of an honest-majority PKI enables the application of traditional Byzantine fault-tolerant techniques for ledger creation and maintenance based on "subcommittees" as opposed to mining (cf. [7]) to permissionless networks. Instead of having arbitrary membership authorities, these committees can be elected using our protocol with the guarantee of an honest majority. Note that by changing the difficulty of the transaction-level POW we can force the number of parties in the committee to be in a specific predefined interval.

Reducing the communication cost. While the round complexity of our protocol is independent of the number of parties, this does not hold for its communication cost, measured by the number of transmitted messages. The reason is that in the challenge-exchange phase, all parties have to diffuse their random challenges, thus increasing the communication cost of the protocol by an $O(n)$ factor. We can redesign the challenge-exchange phase so that the number of *different* messages diffused by honest parties is independent of their number, and only depends on the security parameter and the precomputation time available to the adversary.[8] We do this in the following way: instead of having all parties sent a random challenge in order to be sure that the genesis blocks that are later mined are fresh, we demand that each random challenge be accompanied by a POW. This way, all honest parties will be sure that at least one honest challenge is generated with high probability every $O(\kappa)$ rounds. Moreover, honest parties will only diffuse random challenges that are tied to a POW. Thus, the total number of different messages sent will be upper-bounded by the number of POWs that the adversary and the honest parties combined have generated. Also, again different honest parties will have received the same block with at most one round difference. By combining the above ideas, we can again create a graded-agreement-type procedure for the genesis blocks and in the same way achieve consensus. We defer further details to the full version of the paper.

References

1. Andrychowicz, M., Dziembowski, S.: PoW-based distributed cryptography with no trusted setup. In: Gennaro, R., Robshaw, M. (eds.) CRYPTO 2015. LNCS, vol. 9216, pp. 379–399. Springer, Heidelberg (2015). https://doi.org/10.1007/978-3-662-48000-7_19
2. Aspnes, J., Jackson, C., Krishnamurthy, A.: Exposing computationally-challenged Byzantine impostors. Technical report YALEU/DCS/TR-1332 (2005)
3. Back, A.: Hashcash (1997). http://www.cypherspace.org/hashcash
4. Ben-Sasson, E., Chiesa, A., Garman, C., Green, M., Miers, I., Tromer, E., Virza, M.: Zerocash: decentralized anonymous payments from Bitcoin. IACR Cryptology ePrint Archive 2014:349 (2014)
5. Bitcoinwiki: Genesis block. https://en.bitcoin.it/wiki/Genesis_block
6. Borderding, M.: Levels of authentication in distributed agreement. In: 10th International Workshop on Distributed Algorithms, WDAG 1996 (1996)
7. Cachin, C.: Architecture of the hyperledger blockchain fabric. In: Workshop on Distributed Cryptocurrencies and Consensus Ledgers (2016)
8. Canetti, R.: Security and composition of multiparty cryptographic protocols. J. Cryptol. **13**(1), 143–202 (2000)
9. Canetti, R.: Universally composable security: a new paradigm for cryptographic protocols. IACR Cryptology ePrint Archive 2000:67 (2000)
10. Canetti, R.: Universally composable security: a new paradigm for cryptographic protocols. In: FOCS 2001, pp. 136–145. IEEE Computer Society (2001)

---

[8] Note, that each diffusion requires sending the same message at least $O(n)$ times.

11. Cohen, R., Coretti, S., Garay, J., Zikas, V.: Probabilistic termination and composability of cryptographic protocols. In: Robshaw, M., Katz, J. (eds.) CRYPTO 2016. LNCS, vol. 9816, pp. 240–269. Springer, Heidelberg (2016). https://doi.org/10.1007/978-3-662-53015-3_9
12. Considine, J., Fitzi, M., Franklin, M.K., Levin, L.A., Maurer, U.M., Metcalf, D.: Byzantine agreement given partial broadcast. J. Cryptol. 18(3), 191–217 (2005)
13. Dolev, D., Strong, H.R.: Authenticated algorithms for byzantine agreement. SIAM J. Comput. 12(4), 656–666 (1983)
14. Douceur, J.R.: The sybil attack. In: Druschel, P., Kaashoek, F., Rowstron, A. (eds.) IPTPS 2002. LNCS, vol. 2429, pp. 251–260. Springer, Heidelberg (2002). https://doi.org/10.1007/3-540-45748-8_24
15. Dwork, C., Lynch, N.A., Stockmeyer, L.J.: Consensus in the presence of partial synchrony. J. ACM 35(2), 288–323 (1988)
16. Dwork, C., Naor, M.: Pricing via processing or combatting junk mail. In: Brickell, E.F. (ed.) CRYPTO 1992. LNCS, vol. 740, pp. 139–147. Springer, Heidelberg (1993). https://doi.org/10.1007/3-540-48071-4_10
17. Eyal, I., Gencer, A.E., Sirer, E.G., van Renesse, R.: Bitcoin-NG: a scalable blockchain protocol. CoRR, abs/1510.02037 (2015)
18. Eyal, I., Sirer, E.G.: Majority is not enough: Bitcoin mining is vulnerable. In: Christin, N., Safavi-Naini, R. (eds.) FC 2014. LNCS, vol. 8437, pp. 436–454. Springer, Heidelberg (2014). https://doi.org/10.1007/978-3-662-45472-5_28
19. Fitzi, M.: Generalized communication and security models in Byzantine agreement. Ph.D. thesis, ETH Zurich, Zürich, Switzerland (2003)
20. Garay, J.A., Katz, J., Koo, C., Ostrovsky, R.: Round complexity of authenticated broadcast with a dishonest majority. In: FOCS 2007, pp. 658–668 (2007)
21. Garay, J., Kiayias, A., Leonardos, N.: The Bitcoin backbone protocol: analysis and applications. In: Oswald, E., Fischlin, M. (eds.) EUROCRYPT 2015. LNCS, vol. 9057, pp. 281–310. Springer, Heidelberg (2015). https://doi.org/10.1007/978-3-662-46803-6_10
22. Garay, J.A., Kiayias, A., Leonardos, N., Panagiotakos, G.: Bootstrapping the blockchain-directly. IACR Cryptology ePrint Archive 2016:991 (2016)
23. Goldreich, O., Micali, S., Wigderson, A.: How to play any mental game or a completeness theorem for protocols with honest majority. In: STOC. ACM (1987)
24. Juels, A., Brainard, J.G.: Client puzzles: a cryptographic countermeasure against connection depletion attacks. In: NDSS. The Internet Society (1999)
25. Katz, J., Maurer, U., Tackmann, B., Zikas, V.: Universally composable synchronous computation. IACR Cryptology ePrint Archive 2011:310 (2011)
26. Katz, J., Miller, A., Shi, E.: Pseudonymous secure computation from time-lock puzzles. IACR Cryptology ePrint Archive 2014:857 (2014)
27. Kiayias, A., Panagiotakos, G.: Speed-security tradeoffs in blockchain protocols. Technical report, IACR, Cryptology ePrint Archive (2015)
28. Kiayias, A., Russell, A., David, B., Oliynykov, R.: Ouroboros: a provably secure proof-of-stake blockchain protocol. In: Katz, J., Shacham, H. (eds.) CRYPTO 2017. LNCS, vol. 10401, pp. 357–388. Springer, Cham (2017). https://doi.org/10.1007/978-3-319-63688-7_12
29. King, S.: Primecoin: cryptocurrency with prime number proof-of-work, July 2013. http://primecoin.io/bin/primecoin-paper.pdf
30. King, S., Nadal, S.: PPcoin: peer-to-peer crypto-currency with proof-of-stake. Self-published paper, 19 August 2012
31. Lamport, L., Shostak, R.E., Pease, M.C.: The Byzantine generals problem. ACM Trans. Program. Lang. Syst. 4(3), 382–401 (1982)

32. Nakamoto, S.: Bitcoin: a peer-to-peer electronic cash system (2008). http://bitcoin.org/bitcoin.pdf
33. Nakamoto, S.: Bitcoin open source implementation of P2P currency, February 2009. http://p2pfoundation.ning.com/forum/topics/bitcoin-open-source
34. Pass, R., Seeman, L., Shelat, A.: Analysis of the blockchain protocol in asynchronous networks. Cryptology ePrint Archive, Report 2016/454 (2016)
35. Pass, R., Seeman, L., Shelat, A.: Analysis of the blockchain protocol in asynchronous networks. In: Coron, J.-S., Nielsen, J.B. (eds.) EUROCRYPT 2017. LNCS, vol. 10211, pp. 643–673. Springer, Cham (2017). https://doi.org/10.1007/978-3-319-56614-6_22
36. Pease, M.C., Shostak, R.E., Lamport, L.: Reaching agreement in the presence of faults. J. ACM **27**(2), 228–234 (1980)
37. Rivest, R.L., Shamir, A., Wagner, D.A.: Time-lock puzzles and timed-release crypto. Technical report, Cambridge, MA, USA (1996)
38. Yao, A.C.: Protocols for secure computations (extended abstract). In: FOCS, pp. 160–164. IEEE (1982)

Zero-Knowledge

Efficient Adaptively Secure
Zero-Knowledge from Garbled Circuits

Chaya Ganesh[1], Yashvanth Kondi[2(✉)], Arpita Patra[3], and Pratik Sarkar[3]

[1] Department of Computer Science, Aarhus University, Aarhus, Denmark
ganesh@cs.nyu.edu
[2] Northeastern University, Boston, USA
ykondi@ccs.neu.edu
[3] Indian Institute of Science, Bengaluru, India
{arpita,pratiks}@iisc.ac.in

Abstract. Zero-knowledge (ZK) protocols are undoubtedly among the central primitives in cryptography, lending their power to numerous applications such as secure computation, voting, auctions, and anonymous credentials to name a few. The study of efficient ZK protocols for non-algebraic statements has seen rapid progress in recent times, relying on secure computation techniques. The primary contribution of this work lies in constructing efficient UC-secure constant round ZK protocols from garbled circuits that are secure against *adaptive* corruptions, with communication linear in the size of the statement. We begin by showing that the practically efficient ZK protocol of Jawurek et al. (CCS 2013) is adaptively secure when the underlying oblivious transfer (OT) satisfies a mild adaptive security guarantee. We gain adaptive security with little to no overhead over the static case. A conditional verification technique is then used to obtain a three-round adaptively secure zero-knowledge argument in the non-programmable random oracle model (NPROM). Our three-round protocol yields a proof size that is shorter than the known UC-secure practically-efficient schemes in the short-CRS model with the right choice of security parameters.

We draw motivation from state-of-the-art non-interactive secure computation protocols and leveraging specifics of ZK functionality show a two-round protocol that achieves static security. It is a proof, while most known efficient ZK protocols and our three round protocol are only arguments.

1 Introduction

Zero-knowledge (ZK) proofs introduced in [36] provide a powerful tool in designing a variety of cryptographic protocols. Since then, they have been an important building block in various applications. Zero-knowledge proofs allow a prover to convince a verifier about the validity of a statement, while giving no information beyond the truth of the statement. Informally, an honest prover should always convince a verifier about a true statement (completeness). Moreover, a malicious

© International Association for Cryptologic Research 2018
M. Abdalla and R. Dahab (Eds.): PKC 2018, LNCS 10770, pp. 499–529, 2018.
https://doi.org/10.1007/978-3-319-76581-5_17

verifier learns nothing beyond the validity of the statement (zero-knowledge) and a malicious prover cannot convince a verifier of a false statement (soundness). In addition to soundness, a ZK protocol in which the prover's witness can be extracted by a simulator offers *proof of knowledge.*

It is known that every language in NP has a zero-knowledge proof system [34]. Despite this, proving generic statements is inefficient in practice, and there are few techniques that allow efficient proofs. These techniques almost always apply to a restricted set of languages, with a series of works [13,39,40,68] on proving algebraic relationships like knowledge of roots, discrete logarithms etc.

Kilian's zero-knowledge argument [50] achieves sub-linear communication, but relies on PCP and is of theoretical interest. Groth [37] gave the first constant-size non-interactive ZK proofs. Since then, many constructions of SNARKs (Succinct non-interactive arguments of knowledge) have been presented [26,28,38,60], and have been implemented as well [23,64]. Though SNARKs have short proofs and allow efficient verification, they have shortcomings in prover efficiency. The prover performs public-key operations proportional to the size of the circuit representing the statement. In addition, they rely on a large trusted parameter; for example, a long common reference string (CRS).

Around the same time that ZK was introduced, Yao introduced secure two-party computation (2PC) and garbled circuits (GC) [69]. The problem of general multi-party computation (MPC) [10,33,70] considers a set of parties holding private inputs with the task of computing a joint function while preserving certain desired security properties. An interesting line of recent works [3,12,21,31,42,43,45,48] establishes connections between MPC and ZK, and use the techniques of 2PC and MPC for truly efficient ZK protocols. The two main streams of works connecting MPC with efficient ZK protocols rely on "MPC-in-the-head" approach [45,46] and garbled circuit based approach [48], as elaborated below.

1.1 Efficient ZK Protocols

Ishai et al. [45,46] show how to use an MPC protocol to obtain a ZK proof for an NP relation in the commitment-hybrid model. This approach, called "MPC-in-the-head", provides a powerful tool to obtain black-box constructions for generic statements without relying on expensive Karp reductions. Recently, this technique spurred progress in constructing practical ZK protocols [20,31] resulting in efficient ZK arguments tailored for Boolean circuits, known as 'ZKBoo' and 'ZKBoo++' respectively. They study variants of the "MPC-in-the-head" framework, plug in different MPC protocols, and provide concrete estimates of soundness. In yet another recent attempt, [3] proposes 'Ligero', a 4 round interactive ZK argument with sub-linear (in the circuit size) proof-size relying on interactive PCPs and plugging in a refined MPC of [25] in the "MPC-in-the-head" approach. Specifically, they achieve a proof size of $\mathcal{O}(\lambda\sqrt{|C|}\log|C|)$. The construction uses Reed Solomon Codes from coding theory techniques. The marked improvement in the proof size is obtained by careful tweaking of the protocol parameters. The prover and verifier time is $\mathcal{O}(|C|\log|C|)$ symmetric key operations, and without any public key operations. The protocol does not require any setup and the security is proven in the stand-alone setting. The constructions of [3,20,31] can be made non-interactive using the Fiat-Shamir heuristic in the programmable RO model.

Jawurek et al. [48] construct a UC-secure ZK protocol (referred to as ZKGC henceforth) using garbled circuits as the primary building block. The communication required for their protocol is linear in the size of the circuit implementing the NP relation, and is also concretely efficient as it achieves malicious security with only one garbled circuit. However, the protocol is inherently interactive. ZKGC is essentially a version of Yao's original constant-round 2PC protocol where the GC constructor has no input; this yields full malicious security at little overhead over the semi-honest case as Yao's protocol in this case is already secure against a malicious evaluator. The protocol uses oblivious transfer (OT). The use of OT in ZK protocols dates back to [51]. Notably, Zero-knowledge, when viewed as a special case of 2PC, allows for a relaxation in the properties required of the underlying GCs, as noted in [48]. This led to the introduction of the notion of *privacy-free* garbling schemes [27], which are optimized for the ZK setting of [48]. A privacy-free garbling scheme only achieves authenticity, and leverages privacy-freeness in order to save on communication and computation costs of garbling. Privacy-free GCs are further studied by Zahur et al. [71], who construct a privacy-free scheme using the HalfGates approach. Their privacy-free scheme makes use of FreeXOR [53] to garble and evaluate XOR gates at no cost, and produces only one ciphertext when garbling an AND gate (along with two calls to a hash function H). Their construction comprises the current state-of-the-art in privacy-free garbling for circuits. When formulaic circuits are of concern, [54] shows how to do privacy-free garbling with *zero* ciphertext and with information-theoretic security.

The interactive schemes based on garbled circuits allow for the flexibility of how the keys for the underlying GCs are constructed and how the garbled input (i.e. witness) is encoded. This leads to interesting applications making non-blackbox use of ZKGC [21,52]. For instance, Kolesnikov et al. [52] introduce a new primitive called "attribute selective encryption" as a method of input encoding in ZKGC in order to construct attribute-based key-exchange. This allows a client to prove to a server that it holds a certificate corresponding to its attributes issued by a trusted authority, and that these attributes satisfy a policy constructed by the server. Note that only proving knowledge of attributes satisfying a given policy is insufficient in this setting. Another point of comparison is that the PROM assumption required by non-interactive 'MPC-in-the-head' based ZK protocols can be used to construct highly efficient adaptively secure garbled circuits [8] allowing ZKGC and our protocol to be cast in the online-offline paradigm, with all circuit-dependent communication moved to a preprocessing stage.

Lastly, we note that all of the above protocols deal with *static* adversaries, where the adversary is allowed to choose the party it wishes to corrupt only at the outset of the protocol. In this work, we are interested in building efficient concurrently composable ZK protocols that can tolerate adaptive adversaries [6,15]. In the following section, we summarize the literature on practical ZK protocols for non-algebraic statements, and zero-knowledge protocols secure against adaptive adversaries.

1.2   Adaptively Secure Zero-Knowledge

An adaptive adversary may dynamically decide which party to corrupt as the protocol progresses. Its choice of corruptions may be adapted according to the specific information it sees, possibly even corrupting both the parties. Tolerating an adaptive adversary in a ZK protocol in the UC setting requires a straight-line simulator that can generate a transcript on behalf of the prover without knowledge of the witness, and later be able to "explain" the transcript for any given witness (i.e. concoct valid-looking corresponding local randomness). In [6], the authors show that the zero-knowledge proof system of GMW [35] is not secure against adaptive adversaries or else the polynomial hierarchy collapses, and proceed to build ZK arguments. This work is further advanced in [18] where UC-secure ZK arguments are presented relying on adaptive commitments schemes. In [59], it is shown that adaptive ZK proofs exist for all of NP assuming only one-way functions. They present constructions of adaptively secure ZK proofs from adaptive instance dependent commitment schemes.

Adaptive ZK via Adaptive MPC. The recent work of Cannetti et al. [19] shows how to construct constant-round two party computation using garbled circuits in the standard model. They solve the problem of equivocating a garbled circuit in order to explain the view of a constructor who has already sent a GC in Yao's protocol by means of a *functionally equivocal* encryption scheme. However this comes at the cost of a GC whose size is quadratic in the size of the circuit that is garbled. Previous adaptively secure constant round secure computation protocols have relied on obfuscation [16,22,24].

Adaptive ZK from MPC-in-the-Head Approach. We note that the "MPC-in-the-head" approach is likely to generate adaptively secure ZK protocols by relying on adaptive commitments and possibly adaptively secure MPC. An adaptive commitment scheme is used to commit to the views of the virtual parties. The adaptive commitment schemes from standard assumptions [41,42] may be taxing in terms of both communication and round efficiency. Alternatively, the commitments used in IKOS-style protocols can be implemented in the programmable random oracle model, allowing the simulator to equivocate committed views, which yields adaptive security in a straightforward manner. Another related method is via non-committing encryption (NCE), an approach that has in other circumstances allowed circumvention of known lower bounds in the plain model. For instance, the adaptively secure garbling scheme of [8] uses a programmable RO to achieve NCE, which results in the circumvention of a lower bound in the online communication complexity of adaptively secure garbling schemes shown by Applebaum et al. [5].

Adaptive ZK via 2PC-in-the-Head [42]. The work of [42] uses the "MPC-in-the-head" technique [46] to construct adaptive ZK proofs. Their use of interactive hashing [62] to construct instance dependent commitments to equivocate committed views requires a non-constant number of rounds. The overall round complexity of their adaptive ZK protocol is $\mathcal{O}(\mu \log \mu)$, where μ is the soundness parameter. The proof size is $\mathcal{O}(\mu |\mathbf{C}| \mathsf{poly}(\lambda))$ and the $\mathsf{poly}(\lambda)$ factor is $\Omega(\lambda)$. While their scheme can be made constant round by plugging in the appropriate instance-dependent commitment scheme, it comes at the cost of proofs that are quadratic in the size of the circuit implementing the NP relation.

In this work, we explore the possibility of building protocols that lie at the intersection of all of these desirable qualities. Specifically we address the following question:

> Can we construct constant-round UC-secure ZK protocols that are secure against adaptive corruptions, with proof size linear in the size of the circuit that implements the NP relation?

1.3   Our Contributions

Inspired by the recent progress in the domain of garbling schemes as primitives and interesting applications of garbled circuit (GC) based ZK protocols, we revisit ZK protocols from GCs. Recent works including [21,52] make non-blackbox use of the GC-based ZK protocols of [48], exploiting particularly the way the keys for the underlying GCs are constructed and the method by which the garbled input (i.e. witness) is encoded. Such applications will directly benefit from any improvement in the domain of garbled circuit based ZK protocols. Our contributions are listed below.

Efficient Constant-Round Adaptively Secure ZK Protocols. While security against static adversaries provides a convenient stepping-stone for designing protocols against strong malicious attacks, a general real-life scenario certainly calls for adaptive security where the adversary can use its resources in a gradual fashion, making dynamic corruption decisions as the protocol progresses. Our first contribution is to show that the ZK protocol of [48] can be proven to be adaptively secure in the UC setting if the underlying oblivious transfer (OT) primitive satisfies a mild adaptive security guarantee. Namely, we require that the receiver's communication can be equivocated to any input of the receiver. Such an OT is referred to as receiver equivocal OT (**RE-OT**). We show that the framework of [65] itself, in one of its incarnation, provides **RE-OT**. Specifically, the mode of [65] that offers statistical security for the receiver also offers the flavor of adaptive security that we demand from **RE-OT**. The main observation instrumental in crafting the adaptive proof of security for ZKGC is that the constructor of GC has no input. Therefore, the primary challenge of explaining the randomness of the GC construction in post-execution corruption case is bypassed.

Next, we focus on reducing the exact round complexity of ZKGC style protocols. We propose a three-round protocol. Since neither zero-knowledge proofs nor arguments can be achieved in less than four rounds without additional assumptions [32], we devise our protocols in the CRS model where the CRS is short unlike those used in SNARKs. Starting with ZKGC, our three-round protocol cuts down two rounds in [48] using the idea of conditional opening [12] of a secret information that enables garbled circuit verification. That is, the key to GC verification can be unlocked only when the prover possesses a valid witness. Though fairly simple, implementing this idea makes the security proof of the resulting protocol challenging and subtle due to a circularity issue. Loosely speaking, when the prover does not hold a valid witness, the authenticity of GC should translate to the security of the key and at the same time, the security of the key should translate to the authenticity of the GC. We handle this issue by implementing the conditional disclosure via encryption in the Random Oracle Model (ROM). While the ZKGC protocol requires at least 5 rounds in its most round-efficient instantiation, we improve the complexity to three at *no* additional cost of communication (in fact with slight improvement), and little change in computation (one hash invocation versus a commitment in [48]). We show this protocol to be adaptively secure too, when plugged in with **RE-OTs**.

In terms of concrete proof size (communication), our three-round protocol yields a better result than ZKBoo [31] (and even it's more efficient successor ZKB++ [20]) both in its interactive and non-interactive form with the right choice of the security parameters. We assume that circuit C computes the statement to be proven. While our three-round ZK needs a communication of $\lambda|C|$ bits (ignoring the circuit-independent parts), [31] needs at least $3.41\lambda|C|$ to achieve the same ($\frac{1}{2^\lambda}$) soundness. In the table below, we compare our protocol asymptotically with the existing efficient constructions. Let 'PKE' and 'SKE' denote the number of public key and respectively secret key operations. We note that **RE-OT** can be efficiently constructed assuming DDH assumption, with no overhead over the regular OT in the framework of [65] (Table 1).

Table 1. Comparison among zero knowledge protocols

Protocols	Proof size	Prover runtime	Verifier runtime	Rounds	Assumptions	Security
ZKGC [48]	$\mathcal{O}(\lambda \cdot |C|)$	$\mathcal{O}(|C|)$ SKE + $\mathcal{O}(n)$ PKE	$\mathcal{O}(|C|)$ SKE + $\mathcal{O}(n)$ PKE	5	Standard (OWF) +OT	Static (UC)
ZKBoo [31]	$\mathcal{O}(\lambda \cdot |C|)$	$\mathcal{O}(\lambda|C|)$ SKE	$\mathcal{O}(\lambda|C|)$ SKE	1	PROM	Adaptive
ZKB++ [20]	$\mathcal{O}(\lambda \cdot |C|)$	$\mathcal{O}(\lambda|C|)$ SKE	$\mathcal{O}(\lambda|C|)$ SKE	1	PROM	Adaptive
Ligero (Arithmetic)	$\mathcal{O}(\lambda^{1.5}\sqrt{|C|})$	$\mathcal{O}(|C|\log|C|)$ SKE	$\mathcal{O}(|C|\log|C|)$ SKE	1	PROM	Adaptive
Ligero (Boolean)	$\mathcal{O}(\lambda\sqrt{|C|}\log|C|)$	$\mathcal{O}(|C|\log|C|)$ SKE	$\mathcal{O}(|C|\log|C|)$ SKE	1	PROM	Adaptive
[42]	$\mathcal{O}(\mu|C|\mathrm{poly}(\lambda))$	$\mathcal{O}(\mu|C|\mathrm{poly}(\lambda))$ SKE	$\mathcal{O}(\mu|C|\mathrm{poly}(\lambda))$ SKE	$\mathcal{O}(\mu\log\mu)$	Standard (OWP)	Adaptive
ZKGC (**This paper**)	$\mathcal{O}(\lambda \cdot |C|)$	$\mathcal{O}(|C|)$ SKE + $\mathcal{O}(n)$ PKE	$\mathcal{O}(|C|)$ SKE + $\mathcal{O}(n)$ PKE	5	Standard (OWF) + RE-OT (DDH)	Adaptive (UC)
This paper	$\mathcal{O}(\lambda \cdot |C|)$	$\mathcal{O}(|C|)$ SKE + $\mathcal{O}(n)$ PKE	$\mathcal{O}(|C|)$ SKE + $\mathcal{O}(n)$ PKE	3	ROM + RE-OT (DDH)	Adaptive (UC)

2-Round Zero-Knowledge Proofs. We next investigate the possibility of building efficient GC based ZK protocols with fewer than three rounds of interaction. In the spirit similar to that of [42], our two round protocol borrows techniques from non-interactive two-party computation (2PC) literature [1,44,61] except for the following: We do not need the gadgets for input consistency checks of the prover, and input recovery mechanisms in case of inconsistent outputs [56,57,61,67]. Our protocol is a proof, while most known efficient ZK protocols and our three round protocol are only arguments. The two round ZK may be cast as a sigma protocol and by applying the Fiat-Shamir transform, one may obtain NIZK arguments in the random oracle model. Finally, we observe that for the 2-round and NIZK argument we do not rely on the authenticity property of the garbling scheme. However, more efficient garbled circuit constructions by giving up on authenticity is precluded by the result of [4]. While the result of [4] needs to encode a different circuit (the underlying circuit augmented with a MAC computation) to achieve authenticity using a private scheme, we show a similar result while encoding the *same* underlying circuit. Both results essentially show that any garbling scheme that satisfies privacy also has authenticity.

1.4   Organization

We begin by briefly discussing definitions and constructions required for this work in Sect. 2. In Sect. 3 we show that the ZK protocol of [48] is adaptively secure. Section 4 presents our three-round ZK protocol from conditional disclosure. Section 5 discusses our 2-round ZK. We include our result on authenticity-free garbling in the full version.

2   Preliminaries

Notation. We denote probabilistic polynomial time by PPT. Let λ be the security parameter. $[n]$ and $[m,n]$ for $n > m$ denote the sets $\{1,\ldots,n\}$ and $\{m, m+1,\ldots,n\}$ respectively. $|t|$ denote the number of bits in a string t. We use $||$ to denote concatenation of bit strings, and write $x \xleftarrow{R} \mathcal{X}$ to mean sampling a value x uniformly from the set $\mathcal{X}$. A function $f(\cdot)$ is said to be negligible if $\forall c \in \mathbb{N}$, there exists $n_0 \in \mathbb{N}$ such that $\forall n \geq n_0, f(n) < n^{-c}$. Let S be an infinite set and $X = \{X_s\}_{s \in S}, Y = \{Y_s\}_{s \in S}$ be distribution ensembles. We say X and Y are computationally indistinguishable, if for any PPT distinguisher $\mathcal{D}$ and all sufficiently large $s \in S$, we have $|\Pr[\mathcal{D}(X_s) = 1] - \Pr[\mathcal{D}(Y_s) = 1]| < 1/p(|s|)$ for every polynomial $p(\cdot)$. In the following, we review few building blocks. The ZK and Oblivious Transfer (OT) functionality are recalled in Appendix B.

2.1   Garbled Circuits

The work of Bellare et al. [9] formalizes *Garbling Schemes* as a primitive for modular use in cryptographic protocols, by defining several notions of security, including *obliviousness*, *privacy* and *authenticity*, of which we are interested in the latter two. Informally, privacy aims to protect the privacy of encoded inputs, while authenticity captures the unforgeability of the output of a garbled circuit evaluation. Majority of the schemes in the literature, including the classical scheme of Yao [70], satisfy the two aforementioned properties. Using the language of [9] for circuits; the circuit itself is a directed acyclic graph, where each gate g is indexed by its outgoing wire, and its left and right incoming wires $A(g)$ and $B(g)$ are numbered such that $g > B(g) > A(g)$. Also, a circuit output wire can not be an input wire to any gate. We denote the number of input wires, gates and output wires using n, q and m respectively in a circuit C.

At a high-level, a garbling scheme consists of the following algorithms: Gb takes a circuit as input and outputs a garbled circuit, encoding information, and decoding information. En takes an input x and encoding information and outputs a garbled input $\mathbf{X}$. Ev takes a garbled circuit and garbled input $\mathbf{X}$ and outputs a garbled output $\mathbf{Y}$. De takes a garbled output $\mathbf{Y}$ and decoding information and outputs a plain circuit-output (or an error, $\perp$). Finally, we use an additional verification algorithm in the garbling scheme that output 1 or 0 based certain validity checks performed on a triple $(C, \mathbf{C}, e)$. Formally, a *garbling scheme* is defined by a tuple of functions Garble $= (\mathsf{Gb}, \mathsf{En}, \mathsf{Ev}, \mathsf{De}, \mathsf{Ve})$, described as follows:

- *Garble* algorithm $\mathsf{Gb}\left(1^\lambda, C\right)$: A randomized algorithm which takes as input the security parameter and a circuit $C : \{0,1\}^n \to \{0,1\}^m$ and outputs a tuple of strings $(\mathbf{C}, e, d)$, where $\mathbf{C}$ is the garbled circuit, e denotes the input-wire labels, and d denotes the decoding information.
- *Encode* algorithm $\mathsf{En}\left(x, e\right)$: a deterministic algorithm that outputs the garbled input $\mathbf{X}$ corresponding to input x.
- *Evaluation* algorithm $\mathsf{Ev}\left(\mathbf{C}, \mathbf{X}\right)$: A deterministic algorithm which evaluates garbled circuit $\mathbf{C}$ on garbled input $\mathbf{X}$, and outputs a garbled output $\mathbf{Y}$.
- *Decode* algorithm $\mathsf{De}\left(\mathbf{Y}, d\right)$: A deterministic algorithm that outputs the plain-text output corresponding to $\mathbf{Y}$ or $\perp$ signifying an error if the garbled output $\mathbf{Y}$ is invalid.
- *Verify* algorithm $\mathsf{Ve}\left(C, \mathbf{C}, e\right)$: A deterministic algorithm which takes as input a circuit $C : \{0,1\}^n \mapsto \{0,1\}^m$, a garbled circuit (possibly malicious) $\mathbf{C}$, encoding information e, and outputs 1 when $\mathbf{C}$ is a valid garbling of C, and 0 otherwise.

A garbling scheme may satisfy several properties such as *correctness, privacy, authenticity and notions of verifiability*. The definitions for correctness, privacy and authenticity are standard: correctness enforces that a correctly garbled circuit, when evaluated, outputs the correct output of the underlying circuit; privacy aims to protect the privacy of encoded inputs; authenticity enforces that the evaluator can only learn the output label that corresponds to the value of the function. We use two notions of verifiability. One of the notions enforces that the garbling of a circuit indeed implements the specified plaintext circuit C. This notion of verification is used in our two-round protocol, NIZK and also in the Yao-based 2PC protocols using cut-and-choose (where the check circuits are verified according to this notion) [56,57,61,67]. The other notion of verifiability introduced in [48] enforces that the garbled output corresponding to a given clear output can be extracted for a verified tuple $(C, \mathbf{C}, e)$. This is used in our three round protocol. For the sake of completeness, we give the definitions of these properties in Appendix A.

We are interested in a class of garbling schemes referred to as *projective* in [9]. When garbling a circuit $C : \{0, 1\}^n \mapsto \{0, 1\}^m$, a projective garbling scheme produces encoding information of the form $e = \left(k_i^0, k_i^1\right)_{i \in [n]}$, and the encoded input $\mathbf{X}$ corresponding to $x = (x_i)_{i \in [n]}$ can be interpreted as $\mathbf{X} = \mathsf{En}(x, e) = \left(k_i^{x_i}\right)_{i \in [n]}$.

2.2   Hash Function and Random Oracle Model

We use a hash function $H : \{0, 1\}^* \to \{0, 1\}^{\mathsf{poly}(\lambda)}$ which we model as a random oracle. Namely, we prove the security of our protocol assuming that H implements a functionality $\mathcal{F}_{\mathrm{RAND}}$ which for different inputs x, returns uniform random output values from the range of $H(x)$. In the proof, we rely on observability of H i.e. the reduction can observe the queries made to the H by the distinguisher of certain two views. Note that the simulator does not observe queries to the random oracle.

3   Adaptive Security of [JKO13]

In this section, we show that the garbled circuit based ZKGC protocol is adaptively secure when instantiated with an OT that satisfies a special property of Receiver Equivocality. We formalize the notion of Receiver Equivocal Oblivious Transfer which is an OT primitive with mild adaptive security guarantees. Essentially, we require that the view of a receiver be reconstructable in the case of a post-execution corruption. A similar notion was introduced in [7]. We show that the OT framework of [65] is already receiver equivocal when it is instantiated with statistical security against a corrupt sender ("decryption mode"). We then show that when the zero-knowledge protocol of [48] is instantiated with **RE-OT**, it achieves *adaptive security* without any additional effort. Below, we formulate **RE-OT**, recall the construction of [48], describe the adaptive proof of security of [48] and conclude with an instantiation of **RE-OT**.

Definition of RE-OT. An oblivious transfer protocol is said to be receiver equivocal if it is possible to produce the receiver's message in the protocol *without committing to a choice bit*. For this to be meaningful, we also require that it be possible to efficiently generate the local randomness which when combined with either choice bit would make an honest receiver output the same message. This is formalized by requiring the existence of a simulator $\mathcal{S}^{\mathsf{RE}}$ which can perform this task, in Definition 3.1.

Definition 3.1 (RE-OT). *Let $\Pi_{\mathsf{OT}} = (\Pi_{\mathsf{OT}}^S, \Pi_{\mathsf{OT}}^R)$ be a 2-round OT protocol securely implementing the $\mathcal{F}_{\mathsf{OT}}$ functionality in the CRS model where S and R run their respective algorithms as specified by $\Pi_{\mathsf{OT}}^S(\mathsf{crs}, a_0, a_1, m^R; r^S)$ and $\Pi_{\mathsf{OT}}^R(\mathsf{crs}, \sigma; r^R)$ respectively. Here, a_0, a_1 are the sender's inputs, σ is the receiver's choice bit, r^S, r^R are the sender's and receiver's respective local randomness, and m^R is the receiver's message. Let (crs, t) be the output of the setup functionality for an* *instance of the protocol, where* crs *is the string that both parties have access to, and* t *is the corresponding trapdoor which is accessible only to the simulator* $\mathcal{S}$. *Then* Π_{OT} *is an* **RE-OT** *if there exists an algorithm* $\mathcal{S}^{\mathsf{RE}}$ (crs, t) *which outputs* $\left(m^R, r_0^R, r_1^R\right)$ *such that* $m^R = \Pi_{\mathsf{OT}}^R(\mathsf{crs}, 0; r_0^R) = \Pi_{\mathsf{OT}}^R(\mathsf{crs}, 1; r_1^R)$, *and* $r_0^R, r_1^R \overset{s}{\approx} r^R$.

On the use of a CRS. We note here that there is nothing inherent in receiver equivocation that demands a CRS to implement **RE-OT**. As we are interested in achieving UC-security, we take the liberty of assuming that the protocol realizing **RE-OT** will make use of a CRS. However, this does not preclude the existence of **RE-OT** in the standalone model without a CRS, or even a UC-secure **RE-OT** in the Global Random Oracle hybrid model [17] alone.

3.1 Recap of [JKO13]

We recall the ZKGC protocol below in the $(\mathcal{F}_{\mathsf{COT}}, \mathcal{F}_{\mathsf{COM}})$ hybrid model. The functionalities are presented in Appendix B (Fig. 1).

Π_{ZKGC}

- **Oracles and Cryptographic Primitives:** A *correct, authentic, verifiable* garbling scheme Garble = (Gb, En, De, Ev, (Ve₁, Ve₂)) (according to Appendix A). A committing OT oracle $\mathcal{F}_{\mathsf{COT}}$.
- **Common Inputs of P and V:** A security parameter λ, relation R realized by circuit C, statement z.
- **Input of P:** A witness x of size $n = \mathsf{poly}(\lambda)$ such that $R(z, x) = 1$.
- **Input of V:** Nothing.

Witness input phase: For all $i \in [n]$, P sends (choose, id, x_i) to $\mathcal{F}_{\mathsf{COT}}$.

GC Construction and wire label transfer phase: V garbles the circuit, $\left(\mathbf{C}, \left(K_i^0, K_i^1\right)_{i \in [n]}, Z\right) \leftarrow \mathsf{Gb}\left(1^\kappa, C\right)^a$. On receiving messages (chosen, id) for $i \in [n]$ from $\mathcal{F}_{\mathsf{COT}}$, V sends (transfer, id, K_i^0, K_i^1) as input to $\mathcal{F}_{\mathsf{COT}}$ for all $i \in [n]$.

GC Evaluation and output commitment phase: P receives (transferred, $id, K_i^{x_i}$) for $i \in [n]$ from $\mathcal{F}_{\mathsf{COT}}$, and parses $X = K_1^{x_1} \cdots K_i^{x_i} \cdots K_n^{x_n}$. P obtains $Z' = \mathsf{Ev}(C, X)$ and sends (commit, id, Z') to $\mathcal{F}_{\mathsf{COM}}$.

GC verification and conditional output disclosure phase: On receiving (committed, $id, |Z'|$) from $\mathcal{F}_{\mathsf{COM}}$, V sends the message (open-all, id) to $\mathcal{F}_{\mathsf{COT}}$. On receiving (transfer, id, K_i^0, K_i^1) for all $i \in [n]$ from $\mathcal{F}_{\mathsf{COT}}$, P verifies if the garbled circuit C which sent by the verifier earlier was correctly constructed.

  i if $\mathsf{Ve}\left(\mathbf{C}, f, \left\{K_i^0, K_i^1\right\}_{i \in [n']}\right) \neq 1$, P aborts.

  ii else P sends (reveal, id) to $\mathcal{F}_{\mathsf{COM}}$.

Final verification phase: On receiving the message (reveal, id, Z') from $\mathcal{F}_{\mathsf{COM}}$, V outputs accept if $Z = Z'$.

---

^{a} Instead of returning d, Gb is tweaked to return the 1-key on the output wire.

Fig. 1. Zero-knowledge from garbled circuits [48]

3.2   Proof of Adaptive Security for [JKO13] from RE-OT

In this section we show that instantiating the ZKGC protocol with **RE-OT** satisfying Definition 3.1 yields a UC-secure protocol realizing $\mathcal{F}_{\mathsf{ZK}}^R$ (see Fig. 10) tolerating adaptive adversaries.

Recalling Static Proof of Security. The simulator for a corrupt P plays the role of an honest verifier V. It constructs and communicates a correct garbled circuit, extracts the witness acting on behalf of $\mathcal{F}_{\mathsf{COT}}$ functionality, and accepts the proof only if the extracted witness is a valid one. On the other hand the real verifier accepts when the opening of the commitment is the correct output wire key Z. In $\mathcal{F}_{\mathsf{COM}}$-hybrid model, we can show that a malicious prover who is able make a real verifier output 'accept' (but not the simulator) can be used to break authenticity of the underlying garbling scheme. We can use such a malicious prover P* to construct an adversary $\mathcal{A}$ for the authenticity game of [9] as follows:

1. $\mathcal{A}$ receives the invalid witness x^* from P* on behalf of $\mathcal{F}_{\mathsf{COT}}$ and forwards it to the authenticity challenger.
2. $\mathcal{A}$ receives $\mathbf{C}, X$ from the authenticity challenger and forwards it to P*
3. $\mathcal{A}$ receives forged key Z' from P* on behalf of $\mathcal{F}_{\mathsf{COM}}$ and submits it to the authenticity challenger.

Clearly, the event that $\mathcal{A}$ successfully forges an output for the given $\mathbf{C}, X$ is equivalent to the event that P* convinces a verifier to output 'accept' without a valid witness. By authenticity of the garbling scheme, this event occurs with negligible probability.

The simulator for a corrupt V receives the encoding information from V on behalf of the $\mathcal{F}_{\mathsf{COT}}$ functionality and extracts the output 1-key Z using received garbled circuit and encoding information. It then sends Z to the verifier only after receiving the correct encoding information from V in the open-all phase. Otherwise, it sends $\bot$ to V. Security in this case follows from the verifiability (that allows extraction of the output key from encoding information) of the underlying garbling scheme.

Adaptive Proof of Security. The bottleneck faced in simulating garbled circuit based protocols for post-execution corruptions usually lies in "explaining" the randomness of the GC constructor once her input is known. In the case of two-party computation, equivocating the view of the garbled circuit constructor requires heavy machinery such as in Canetti et al. [19]. However in the ZKGC protocol verifier V is the GC constructor and *has no input*. The simulator can therefore run the code of honest V, which includes being an honest sender in the OT protocol (this is also why our OT need not achieve full-fledged adaptive security). On the prover's side, receiver equivocality of the OT allows a simulator to equivocate an adaptively corrupted prover's view of the OT protocol, as per the witness once known. We make the observation that *every step of* P *following the OT is independent of the witness*. Specifically, once the output key

Z has been obtained by evaluating the GC sent by V, P does not use the witness again. Note that the simulator does not need the witness to obtain Z; the ZKGC simulator invokes the Π_{OT} simulator in order to extract all inputs of V and obtain all keys of the GC. Once the simulator obtains Z, the code of honest P can be run to complete the simulation. The implication of this for simulation of a post-execution corruption of P is that no additional work needs to be done besides equivocating the view of P in the OT. We now give a formal proof for all the cases:

- **Simulation for V.** The verifier, until it is corrupted, can be simulated following the static simulator for the corrupt P, irrespective of when P is corrupted. As recalled above, the simulation can be carried out by running the code of honest verifier (constructing a correct garbled circuit, participating in the **RE-OT**s with the correct encoding information and sending the correctly constructed garbled circuit). Upon corruption, the simulator can explain to the corrupt V the communication by means of the randomness used in its honest execution of V's code. The indistinguishability follows from the proof in the static corrupt prover case.

- **Simulation for P.** If the prover is corrupted at the outset, then there is nothing to simulate. So we consider the worst scenario of post-execution corruption. If the verifier is also not corrupt during the construction of the garbled circuit, then simulator acts on behalf of both the honest parties and runs the code of honest verifier. In the $\mathcal{F}_{COM}$-hybrid model, the simulator, without having access to the actual witness, runs $(m^R, r_0^R, r_1^R) \leftarrow \mathcal{S}^{RE}(\text{crs}, t)$ to generate the transcript that needs to be communicated on behalf of P in **RE-OT** instances. The rest of the simulation is straight-forward irrespective of whether the verifier is corrupt or not. In the final step, the simulator may have to communicate Z which it picked itself while simulating V in this case. When P is corrupt in the end, its input x_i to the ith **RE-OT** instance can be explained as per any input using the randomness $r_{x_i}^R$ returned by $\mathcal{S}^{RE}$ of the **RE-OT**s. On the other hand, if V was corrupt before the garbled circuit construction phase, then the simulator gets Z via unlocking the GC using encoding information extracted from the corrupt V's communication. The rest remains the same as the previous case.

  Security in the former case follows via receiver equivocality of **RE-OT**. In the latter, it follows additionally from verifiability that ensures the encoding information leads to the correct Z with high probability.

3.3   Instantiation of RE-OT

The OT framework of [65] is already receiver equivocal as per Definition 3.1 when instantiated in "decryption mode". The protocol can be constructed efficiently under the Decisional Diffie Hellman, Quadratic Residuosity, or Learning With Errors hardness assumptions. For simplicity, in this paper we recall the instantiation of Π_{PVW} and describe $\mathcal{S}_{PVW}^{RE}$ under the DDH hardness assumption alone (Fig. 2).

$$\Pi_{\mathsf{PVW}}$$

The parties have access to a common reference string $\mathsf{crs} = (g_0, h_0, g_1, h_1) \in \mathbb{G}^4$. The trapdoor available to the simulator is t such that $g_0^t = g_1$ and $h_0^t = h_1$. Operations are over group $\mathbb{G}$ of prime order q, generated by g.

$\Pi_{\mathsf{PVW}}^{\mathsf{R}} (\mathsf{crs}, \sigma)$:

- Sample $\alpha \in \mathbb{Z}_q$ uniformly at random.
- Compute $g = (g_\sigma)^\alpha$, $h = (h_\sigma)^\alpha$
- Send (g, h)

$\Pi_{\mathsf{PVW}}^{\mathsf{S}} (\mathsf{crs}, a_0, a_1, m^{\mathsf{R}})$:

- Sample random elements r_0, s_0, r_1, s_1 from $\mathbb{Z}_q$.
- Compute $u_0 = g_0^{r_0} h_0^{s_0}$, $v_0 = g^{r_0} h^{s_0}$, $u_1 = g_1^{r_1} h_1^{s_1}$, $v_1 = g^{r_1} h^{s_1}$.
- Send $(u_0, w_0 = v_0 a_0)$, $(u_1, w_1 = v_1 a_1)$

R can retreive the chosen message as $a_\sigma = w_\sigma \cdot (u_\sigma)^{-\alpha}$

$\mathcal{S}^{\mathsf{RE}}(\mathsf{crs}, t)$:

- Sample $r \in \mathbb{Z}_q$ and compute $m^{\mathsf{R}} = (g_0^r, h_0^r)$.
- Compute local randomness for both possible receiver inputs as $r_0^{\mathsf{R}} = r$ and $r_1^{\mathsf{R}} = r \cdot t^{-1}$.
- Output $(m^{\mathsf{R}}, r_0^{\mathsf{R}}, r_1^{\mathsf{R}})$

Fig. 2. RE-OT assuming DDH: as per [65]

Theorem 3.2. *The protocol Π_{PVW} in Fig. 2 is a **RE-OT**, assuming that DDH is hard for $\mathbb{G}$.*

Proof. The protocol Π_{PVW} in Fig. 2 is proven to realize the $\mathcal{F}_{\mathsf{OT}}$ functionality in the UC model by Peikert et al. [65]. It is easy to see how $\mathcal{S}_{\mathsf{PVW}}^{\mathsf{RE}}$ allows for receiver equivocation as per Definition 3.1:

- The randomness r_σ^{R} provided is interpreted as R's secret exponent α.
- Recall that the message m^{R} is (g^r, h_0^r), and candidate randomness output by $\mathcal{S}_{\mathsf{PVW}}^{\mathsf{RE}}$ is $r_0^{\mathsf{R}} = r$, and $r_1^{\mathsf{R}} = r_0^{\mathsf{R}} \cdot t^{-1} = r \cdot t^{-1}$.
- Correctness of message m^{R} can be seen as follows:

  1. $\Pi_{\mathsf{PVW}} \left(\mathsf{crs}, 0; r_0^{\mathsf{R}} \right)$ will output $\left(g_0^{r_0^{\mathsf{R}}}, h_0^{r_0^{\mathsf{R}}} \right) = (g_0^r, h_0^r) = m^{\mathsf{R}}$

  2. $\Pi_{\mathsf{PVW}} \left(\mathsf{crs}, 1; r_1^{\mathsf{R}} \right)$ will output $\left(g_1^{r_1^{\mathsf{R}}}, h_1^{r_1^{\mathsf{R}}} \right) = \left(g_1^{(r \cdot t^{-1})}, h_1^{(r \cdot t^{-1})} \right)$

     Recall that the trapdoor t relates g_0 to g_1 as $g_0^t = g_1$ and similarly $h_0^t = h_1$.

     Therefore we have that $\left(g_1^{(r \cdot t^{-1})}, h_1^{(r \cdot t^{-1})} \right) = (g_0^r, h_0^r) = m^{\mathsf{R}}$.

- Finally, $r_0^{\mathsf{R}}, r_1^{\mathsf{R}} = r, r \cdot (t^{-1})$ are clearly uniformly random, as r is sampled uniformly at random.

$\square$

Also note that **RE-OT** is strictly weaker than OT with security against adaptive corruptions; any protocol satisfying the latter notion will necessarily be receiver-equivocal in order for the receiver's view to be fully simulatable in the event of a post-execution corruption.

4   Zero Knowledge in Three Rounds

In this section, we present a *3-round ZK protocol* against a malicious verifier requiring just one GC in the non-programmable random oracle model, with *no increase in communication complexity*. Our protocol achieves this by a technique for non-interactive GC verification which allows us to remove the commitment and OT-open-all phases from ZKGC. Our approach is reminiscent of the technique of *conditional disclosure of secrets* (CDS) [30]. CDS has since been generalized [47], and used in several works, including in applications to improve round complexity of protocols [2,11]. We show that the protocol is adaptively secure when the underlying OTs are receiver equivocal.

4.1   High-Level Idea

The high round cost of ZKGC makes it undesirable for many applications. However its usage of only one GC for an actively secure protocol is an attractive feature, prompting us to examine whether we can improve on the number of rounds required to realize ZK with only one GC. We now describe our intuition behind the protocol, beginning with informal observations about the number of rounds in ZKGC. Assuming the ZKGC paradigm to be broadly characterized by a protocol where the verifier V constructs a GC which is then evaluated by prover P, we make the following (informal) observations:

- As V constructs the GC, P's witness bits must be encoded as garbled input and delivered by means of an OT. The most efficient UC-secure OT in the literature [65] requires 2 rounds to instantiate.
- Assuming the underlying GC to be statically secure in the terminology of Bellare et al. [8], the GC can at best be sent to P along with the final message of the OT (if not after the OT).
- P must communicate some information as a 'response' to V's GC 'challenge'; for instance the garbled output obtained as a result of evaluating the GC with her witness. This must necessarily be after she receives the GC, adding at least one more round after the OT.

In summary, it appears that the ZKGC paradigm requires at least 2 rounds for the OT, plus the GC transmission, and one round following that. Therefore, a 3-round ZK protocol appears to be optimal in the ZKGC paradigm, informally suggesting the optimality of our protocol. In the following, we make several observations that are instrumental to our protocol.

Conditional Verification of Garbled Circuits. We begin by making the following observation about the original ZKGC protocol: even a prover who does not have a witness is given the chance to first commit to her garbled output and verify that the GC she received was correctly generated. Verification of the GC is a process that takes two additional rounds of interaction in their protocol. We ask, can we use conditional disclosure of secrets to reduce the number of rounds: *"can we provide some additional information with a GC that will allow an evaluator to non-interactively verify that the GC was correctly constructed only when it possess a valid witness?"* We answer this question in the affirmative, at least for the ZKGC setting. An idea somewhat similar in spirit was proposed in [12] to construct a three-round 'weak' ZK protocol from a garbling scheme and point-obfuscation. That is, knowing the witness gives the prover access to a secret via a garbled circuit handed over by the verifier. The secret, then, can be used to unlock the seed that opens the garbled circuit and enables verifying the correct construction of the GC. Technique-wise, we depart from the work of [12] as follows. The secret is encoded in the circuit output in [12] and hence, privacy of the garbling circuit is one of the properties they rely on to achieve soundness. On the contrary, the secret, in our case is the output key corresponding to bit 1 and hence, soundness is achieved via authenticity. Qualitatively, their protocol is not a full-fledged ZK, is in the plain model, has a non-black-box simulator and relies on strong assumptions such as obfuscation. Our ZK protocol is proven UC-secure with a black-box simulator and relies on standard assumptions, albeit assuming a CRS setup.

Interestingly, the intuition behind the ability of [48] to achieve full black-box simulation was that the relaxation in round complexity rendered the four-round barrier in the plain model [32] inapplicable. However, our result demonstrates that the trusted setup required to implement a full black-box simulatable two-round OT is sufficient to construct a three round zero-knowledge argument using the concretely efficient [48] technique and a non-programmable random oracle.

Our intuition is implemented as follows: Given that $\left(\mathbf{C}, \left\{(k_j^0, k_j^1)\right\}_{j \in [n]}, (k^0, k^1)\right) \leftarrow \mathsf{Gb}\left(1^\lambda, C\right)$ and an honest P has obtained encoded input $\mathbf{X} = \left(k_j^{x_j}\right)_{j \in [n]}$ for a witness $x = (x_1 \ldots, x_n)$, she can compute $k^1 = \mathsf{Ev}(\mathbf{C}, \mathbf{X})$. Now that P has evaluated the GC, we wish to enable her to 'open' the GC and verify that it was constructed correctly. To do this, we provide her with a ciphertext encrypting some useful information. Concretely, the ciphertext $T = H(k^1) \oplus r^\mathsf{S}$, where H is a random oracle and r^S contains the randomness used by the sender in the OT instances. Once P gets this randomness, she can unlock $\left\{k_j^0, k_j^1\right\}_{j \in [n]}$ and can verify if the circuit has been constructed correctly. In the following, we formalize the property needed from the OT protocol, namely that the randomness of the sender reveals the inputs of the sender.

Sender-Extractability of OT. Let $\Pi_{\mathsf{OT}} = (\Pi_{\mathsf{OT}}^\mathsf{S}, \Pi_{\mathsf{OT}}^\mathsf{R})$ be a 2-round OT protocol securely implementing the $\mathcal{F}_{\mathsf{OT}}$ functionality in the CRS model where S and R run their respective algorithm as specified by $\Pi_{\mathsf{OT}}^\mathsf{S}$ and $\Pi_{\mathsf{OT}}^\mathsf{R}$ respectively. Let crs be the string that both parties have access to. We denote the first message of the protocol sent by the receiver R by $m^\mathsf{R} = \Pi_{\mathsf{OT}}^\mathsf{R}(\mathsf{crs}, \sigma; r^\mathsf{R})$ where σ is R's choice bit and r^R his randomness. Let the input of the sender S be a_0, a_1; we denote the second message of the OT protocol, sent by S, by $m^{\mathsf{S}} = \Pi_{\mathsf{OT}}^{\mathsf{S}}(\mathsf{crs}, a_0, a_1, m^{\mathsf{R}}; r^{\mathsf{S}})$. The receiver can now compute the chosen message, $x_\sigma = \Pi_{\mathsf{OT}}^{\mathsf{R}}(\mathsf{crs}, \sigma, m_{\mathsf{S}}; r^{\mathsf{R}})$. We assume that Π_{OT} has the following sender-extractable property: revealing the randomness of the sender, allows the receiver to reconstruct the sender's messages correctly with high probability. That is, there exists a public efficiently computable function, Ext such that $\mathsf{Ext}(\mathsf{crs}, \mathcal{T}_{\mathsf{OT}}(a_0, a_1, \sigma), r^{\mathsf{S}})$ outputs (a_0, a_1) where $\mathcal{T}_{\mathsf{OT}}(a_0, a_1, \sigma)$ refers to the transcript of Π_{OT} with sender's input as a_0, a_1 and receiver's input as σ. Namely, $\mathcal{T}_{\mathsf{OT}}(a_0, a_1, \sigma) = (m^{\mathsf{R}}, m^{\mathsf{S}})$ where m^{R} and m^{S} are as defined above.

Definition 4.1. *A protocol Π_{OT} is a secure sender-extractable OT protocol if*

- *it securely implements $\mathcal{F}_{\mathsf{OT}}$ in the presence of malicious adversaries, and*
- $\forall\, a_0, a_1, \sigma$, *such that* $|a_0|, |a_1| \leq poly\,(\lambda)$, $\sigma \in \{0, 1\}$, $\exists$ *a PPT algorithm* Ext *such that the following probability is negligible in λ.*

$$\Pr\left((a_0', a_1') \neq (a_0, a_1) : \mathsf{Ext}(\mathsf{crs}, \mathcal{T}_{\mathsf{OT}}(a_0, a_1, \sigma), r^{\mathsf{S}}) = (a_0', a_1')\right).$$

We note that the protocol of [65] is UC-secure in the CRS model, is 2-rounds, and satisfies the sender-extractability property of Definition 4.1. We use such a protocol in our construction.

4.2   Our Construction

At a high-level, our construction proceeds as follows. The verifier constructs a garbled circuit of the circuit C implementing the relation. The prover obtains the wire keys corresponding to his witness via an OT protocol. Now, the verifier sends the garbled circuit to the prover, and, in addition, a ciphertext. This ciphertext allows the prover to open and verify the garbled circuit, but only if he possesses a valid witness. The complete description of our protocol Π_{ZK3} is presented in Fig. 3. We now prove security of Π_{ZK3} in Universal Composability (UC) framework. As we do not rely on programming the Random Oracle, we can also adapt our proof in the UC setting to use a Global Random Oracle [17].

Theorem 4.2. *Let* Garble *be a correct, authentic, verifiable garbling scheme, Π_{OT} be an sender-extractable OT protocol, and H be an extractable random oracle. The protocol Π_{ZK3} in Fig. 3 securely implements $\mathcal{F}_{\mathsf{ZK}}^R$ in the presence of malicious adversaries.*

Proof. To prove the security of our protocol, we describe two simulators. The simulator $\mathcal{S}_{\mathsf{P}}$ simulates the view of a corrupt prover and appears in Fig. 4. The simulator $\mathcal{S}_{\mathsf{V}}$ simulates the view of a corrupt verifier and is presented in Fig. 5.

Security against a Corrupt Prover $\mathsf{P}^\star$. We now prove that $\mathrm{IDEAL}_{\mathcal{F}_{\mathsf{ZK}}^R, \mathcal{S}_{\mathsf{P}}, \mathcal{Z}} \overset{c}{\approx} \mathrm{REAL}_{\Pi_{\mathsf{ZK3}}, \mathcal{A}, \mathcal{Z}}$ when $\mathcal{A}$ corrupts P. We begin by noting that the simulated and the real worlds are identical when P uses a valid witness x. The view of a malicious $\mathsf{P}^\star$ who does not possess a valid witness x is proven to be computationally close to the simulation through an intermediate hybrid HYB_1. The hybrid HYB_1 is

---

Π_{ZK3}

- **Oracles and Cryptographic Primitives:** A *correct, authentic, verifiable* garbling scheme Garble = $(\text{Gb}, \text{En}, \text{De}, \text{Ev}, (\text{Ve}_1, \text{Ve}_2))$ (according to Appendix A). A sender-extractable 2-round OT Π_{OT} with the common reference string crs. A hash function $H : \{0,1\}^* \rightarrow \{0,1\}^{\text{poly}(\lambda)}$ which we model as a random oracle.
- **Common Inputs of P and V:** A security parameter λ, relation R realized by circuit C, statement z, common reference string crs for Π_{OT}.
- **Input of P:** A witness x of size $n = \text{poly}(\lambda)$ such that $R(z, x) = 1$.
- **Input of V:** Nothing.

OT First Message Phase: P plays the role of the receiver R in n instances of Π_{OT} and provides his witness bit x_j as input to the jth instance of Π_{OT}. Specifically, it:

    ○ chooses $r_j^R \xleftarrow{R} \{0,1\}^\lambda$, and computes $m_j^R = \Pi_{\text{OT}}^R(\text{crs}, x_j; r_j^R), \forall j \in [n]$ as the first message in the jth instance of Π_{OT}

    ○ sends $\{m_j^R\}_{j \in [n]}$ to V.

GC Construction and OT Second Message Phase: V constructs a garbled circuit **C** for C as $(\mathbf{C}, \{k_j^0, k_j^1\}_{j \in [n]}, (k^0, k^1)) \leftarrow \text{Gb}(1^\lambda, C)$. V now provides the wire labels for the input wires of **C** by playing the role of the sender S in n instances of Π_{OT}. Specifically, it

    ○ samples randomness $r_j^S \xleftarrow{R} \{0,1\}^\lambda$, $\forall j \in [n]$ and parses $r^S = r_1^S || \cdots || r_n^S$

    ○ computes $m_j^S = \Pi_{\text{OT}}^S(\text{crs}, k_j^0, k_j^1, m_j^R; r_j^S), \forall j \in [n]$ and $T = H(k^1) \oplus r^S$ and

    ○ sends $(\mathbf{C}, \{m_j^S\}_{j \in [n]}, T)$ to P.

P computes the wire-keys corresponding to his input: $k_j^{x_j} = \Pi_{\text{OT}}^R(\text{crs}, m_j^R, m_j^S, r_j^R), \forall j \in [n]$.

GC Evaluation, Verification and Output Disclosure Phase: P evaluates **C** and obtains the garbled output. He then recovers the randomness used by the sender (namely, V) using the output-wire key he obtained. By the sender-extractability of Π_{OT}, P recovers the input-wire labels which are the OT inputs of V. P can now verify that the garbled circuit was correctly constructed using the recovered wire keys. Specifically, it:

    ○ executes $\mathbf{Y} = \text{Ev}(\mathbf{C}, \{k_j^{x_j}\}_{j \in [n]})$

    ○ recovers $r^S = H(\mathbf{Y}) \oplus T$, and parses $r^S = r_1^S || \cdots || r_n^S$

    ○ aborts if $\exists j$ such that $\text{Ext}(\text{crs}, m_j^R, m_j^S, r_j^S) = \bot$ and extracts $(k_j^0, k_j^1) = \text{Ext}(\text{crs}, m_j^R, m_j^S, r_j^S), \forall j \in [n]$ otherwise

    ○ aborts if $\text{Ve}_2(C, \mathbf{C}, \{k_j^0, k_j^1\}_{j \in [n]}) = 0$ and sends $\mathbf{Y}$ to V otherwise.

Output Phase: If $\mathbf{Y} = k^1$, then V outputs **accept**, else he outputs **reject**.

Fig. 3. 3-round GC based zero knowledge protocol

constructed identically to $\text{IDEAL}_{\mathcal{F}_{\text{ZK}}^R, \mathcal{S}_{\text{P}}, \mathcal{Z}}$ with the exception of the criterion to output **accept**. In HYB$_1$, the verifier accepts if P* outputs the correct k^1 (as in the REAL view) regardless of the witness used. We begin our analysis by noting that unless a P* queries the correct k^1 to the random oracle H, the string T appears completely random. Therefore, given that a P* attempting to distinguish between the REAL view and the view generated by HYB$_1$, we branch our analysis into the following cases:

Simulator $\mathcal{S}_P$

The simulator plays the role of the honest V and simulates each step of the protocol Π_{ZK3} as follows. The communication of the $\mathcal{Z}$ with the adversary $\mathcal{A}$ who corrupts P is handled as follows: Every input value received by the simulator from $\mathcal{Z}$ is written on $\mathcal{A}$'s input tape. Likewise, every output value written by $\mathcal{A}$ on its output tape is copied to the simulator's output tape (to be read by the environment $\mathcal{Z}$).

OT First Message Phase: $\mathcal{S}_P$ invokes the simulator of Π_{OT} for corrupt receiver and extracts P's input bit to the jth instance of Π_{OT}, namely the jth witness bit x_j.

GC Construction and OT Second Message Phase: $\mathcal{S}_P$ emulates an honest V if the extracted witness x is valid i.e. $R(z, x) = 1$. Otherwise, $\mathcal{S}_P$ does the following:

   - It constructs a garbled circuit **C** for C as $(\mathbf{C}, \{(k_j^0, k_j^1)\}_{j \in [n]}, (k^0, k^1)) \leftarrow \mathsf{Gb}(1^\lambda, C)$.
   - It samples r^S uniformly at random and parses it as $r^S = r_1^S || \cdots || r_n^S$,
   - It computes $m_j^S = \Pi_{\mathsf{OT}}^S(\mathsf{crs}, k_j^{x_j}, 0^\lambda, m_j^R; r_j^S), \forall j \in [n]$ and samples T uniformly at random and
   - It sends $(\mathbf{C}, \{m_j^S\}_{j \in [n]}, T)$ to $P^\star$.

GC Evaluation, Verification and Output Disclosure Phase: $\mathcal{S}_P$ does nothing in this step.

Output Phase: $\mathcal{S}_P$ sends x to $\mathcal{F}_{\mathsf{ZK}}^R$ on behalf of $P^\star$ if $R(z, x) = 1$. Otherwise, it sends $\bot$.

Fig. 4. Simulator $\mathcal{S}_P$

– **$P^\star$ does not output the correct k^1 in either world.** Here we assume that a $P^\star$ also does not query the correct k^1 to the random oracle H to be able to unlock ciphertext T. If the prover does indeed query the correct k^1 to H with non-negligible probability, we move on to the next case. A $P^\star$ who is successful in distinguishing $\mathrm{REAL}_{\Pi_{\mathsf{ZK3}}, \mathcal{A}, \mathcal{Z}}$ from HYB_1 in this case can be used to break OT sender security. The reduction computes a garbled circuit **C** and sends the input keys to the OT challenger (by means of the environment for the OTs) as the sender's input. The reduction then extracts the input x of $P^\star$ and forwards to the OT challenger as the choice bits of the receiver. The response of OT challenger who computes the sender's message either by invoking a real sender i.e. as $m_j^S = \Pi_{\mathsf{OT}}^S(\mathsf{crs}, k_j^0, k_j^1, m_j^R; r_j^S), \forall j \in [n]$ or by invoking a simulator i.e. as $m_j^S = \Pi_{\mathsf{OT}}^S(\mathsf{crs}, k_j^{x_j}, 0^\lambda, m_j^R; r_j^S), \forall j \in [n]$ is sent to the reduction who further forwards the message to $P^\star$ along with **C** and a random T. In case the OT challenger invokes a simulator the view of $P^\star$ is identical to HYB_1, whereas when the OT challenger uses a real execution of Π_{OT} the view of $P^\star$ is identical to REAL (T is random given that the correct k^1 is never queried to H). Therefore, the probability of distinguishing between the REAL and HYB_1 view translates to the probability of distinguishing between the real and the simulated view of the OT protocols for the case when the receiver is corrupt.

- $\mathsf{P}^\star$ **outputs the correct** k^1 **in** $\mathrm{real}_{\Pi_{\mathsf{ZK3}},\mathcal{A},\mathcal{Z}}$ **with significantly higher probability than in** hyb_1. This case is similar to the previous case in that $\mathsf{P}^\star$ can be used to break sender security of the OT by computing $\mathbf{C}$ locally in the reduction. If $\mathsf{P}^\star$ outputs a correct k^1, the reduction is interacting with Π_{OT} whereas if not, the challenger must have invoked the simulator for Π_{OT}. The advantage of this reduction is the difference in probabilities with which $\mathsf{P}^\star$ forges k^1 successfully in the REAL and HYB1 worlds.
- $\mathsf{P}^\star$ **outputs the correct** k^1 **in both worlds with almost the same probability.** The corrupt $\mathsf{P}^\star$ can be used directly to break authenticity of the garbling scheme. Clearly the OT message corresponding to inactive input keys are not used by the corrupt P; the ability to output the correct k^1 must be derivative of the ability to forge a key for the garbled circuit alone. It is therefore straightforward to use $\mathsf{P}^\star$ to forge k^1 for a given garbled circuit $\mathbf{C}$, as its view can be generated as per HYB1, which does not require the inactive garbled circuit keys to compute the OT messages.

Note that in Cases 2 and 3, we consider a $\mathsf{P}^\star$ who outputs k^1 to be equivalent to a $\mathsf{P}^\star$ who queries the random oracle on k^1 to unlock T in its effort to distinguish REAL from HYB1. Instead of receiving k^1 directly from $\mathsf{P}^\star$, our reductions will observe its query to the random oracle.

Finally $\mathrm{IDEAL}_{\mathcal{F}_{\mathsf{ZK}}^R,\mathcal{S}_\mathsf{P},\mathcal{Z}}$ deviates from HYB1 only in its criteria to output accept. Only a corrupt P who is able to output k^1 will be able to distinguish HYB1 from $\mathrm{IDEAL}_{\mathcal{F}_{\mathsf{ZK}}^R,\mathcal{S}_\mathsf{P},\mathcal{Z}}$. Such a P can be used directly to forge an output key for a given $\mathbf{C}$ with the same probability (which by authenticity of the garbling scheme, must be negligible).

Security against a Corrupt Verifier $\mathsf{V}^\star$. We now argue that $\mathrm{IDEAL}_{\mathcal{F}_{\mathsf{ZK}}^R,\mathcal{S}_\mathsf{V},\mathcal{Z}} \overset{c}{\approx}$ REAL$_{\Pi_{\mathsf{ZK3}},\mathcal{A},\mathcal{Z}}$ when $\mathcal{A}$ corrupts V. The above two views of $\mathsf{V}^\star$ are shown to be indistinguishable via a series of intermediate hybrids.

- HYB0: Same as REAL$_{\Pi_{\mathsf{ZK3}},\mathcal{A},\mathcal{Z}}$.
- HYB1: Same as HYB0, except that **OT First Message phase** is emulated by invoking the simulator of Π_{OT} for corrupt receiver.
- HYB2: Same as HYB1, except that k^1 is computed in the following way instead of running $\mathsf{Ev}(\mathbf{C},\mathbf{X})$. The simulator of Π_{OT} for corrupt receiver is used to extract (k_j^0, k_j^1) for $j \in [n]$. Then $\mathsf{Ve}_2(C, \mathbf{C}, \{k_j^0, k_j^1\}_{j \in [n]})$ is run. If the output is 0, the prover aborts. Otherwise $\mathsf{Ve}_1(\mathbf{C}, e, 1)$ is run to extract k^1 and the prover runs the rest of the protocol using k^1.
- HYB3: Same as HYB2, except that the following check for abort in **GC Evaluation, Verification and Output Disclosure Phase** is removed: On computing $r_1^\mathsf{S} || \cdots || r_n^\mathsf{S} = r^\mathsf{S} = T \oplus H(k^1)$, the prover aborts if any call to the extractor Ext of the sender's input to OT returns $\perp$.

Clearly, HYB3 $= \mathrm{IDEAL}_{\mathcal{F}_{\mathsf{ZK}}^R,\mathcal{S}_\mathsf{V},\mathcal{Z}}$. Our proof will conclude, as we show that every two consecutive hybrids are computationally indistinguishable.

Simulator $\mathcal{S}_\mathsf{V}$

The simulator plays the role of the honest P and simulates each step of the protocol Π_{ZK3} as follows. The communication of the $\mathcal{Z}$ with the adversary $\mathcal{A}$ who corrupts V is handled as follows: Every input value received by the simulator from $\mathcal{Z}$ is written on $\mathcal{A}$'s input tape. Likewise, every output value written by $\mathcal{A}$ on its output tape is copied to the simulator's output tape (to be read by the environment $\mathcal{Z}$).

OT First Message Phase: $\mathcal{S}_\mathsf{V}$ invokes the simulator of Π_{OT} for corrupt receiver to simulate the first OT message.

GC Construction and OT Second Message Phase: $\mathcal{S}_\mathsf{V}$ uses the OT simulator to extract V's inputs to the jth instance of Π_{OT}, namely (k_j^0, k_j^1).

GC Evaluation, Verification and Output Disclosure Phase: On receiving the garbled circuit C and T from V, $\mathcal{S}_\mathsf{V}$ runs $\mathsf{Ve}_2(C, \mathbf{C}, \{k_j^0, k_j^1\}_{j\in[n]})$. It aborts if the output of Ve_2 is 0. Else, it sends k^1 to V where $k^1 \leftarrow \mathsf{Ve}_1(\mathbf{C}, e, 1)$.

Output Phase: It does nothing in this step.

Fig. 5. Simulator $\mathcal{S}_\mathsf{V}$

$\mathrm{HYB}_0 \overset{c}{\approx} \mathrm{HYB}_1$: The difference between these hybrids lies in the way OT first message is generated. In HYB_0, the message is generated by a real receiver that possesses the choice bits x, whereas in HYB_1, the simulator for Π_{OT} for the corrupt receiver generates the message. The indistinguishability follows via reduction to the sender security of n instances of OT.

$\mathrm{HYB}_1 \overset{c}{\approx} \mathrm{HYB}_2$: The difference between these hybrids lies in the way k^1 is computed. In HYB_1, k^1 is computed as a real prover does. On the other hand, k^1 is extracted using Ve_1 and the encoding information extracted from the OTs in HYB_2. By the verifiability property (Verifiability I in Appendix A) of the garbling scheme, the view of $\mathsf{V}^\star$ in HYB_2 and HYB_1 are indistinguishable.

$\mathrm{HYB}_2 \overset{c}{\approx} \mathrm{HYB}_3$: The difference between these hybrids lies in the conditions checked by P for abort in **GC Evaluation, Verification and Output Disclosure Phase**. In the former, the protocol is aborted when one of the invocations to Ext returns messages different from corresponding input labels which does not happen in the latter as the check is removed. By the sender extractability of the OT protocol (Definition 4.1), the hybrids are indistinguishable except with negligible probability. □

4.3 Making Π_{ZK3} Adaptively Secure

The challenge in achieving adaptive security for Π_{ZK3} is essentially the same as ZKGC; once the GC output key Z has been retrieved, all of P's steps are independent of the witness.

Simulation for P. Consider the worst case scenario of post-execution corruption. The simulator runs $(m^\mathsf{R}, r_0^\mathsf{R}, r_1^\mathsf{R}) \leftarrow \mathcal{S}^{\mathsf{RE}}(\mathsf{crs}, t)$ to generate the first message of P, and obtains the GC output key Z either by extracting the encoding information from V's response (if V is corrupt) or using the key it picked itself when simulating V. The rest of the simulation is straightforward, as the code of honest P can be run from this point. In case the adversary chooses to corrupt P, the simulator hands over the randomness $r_{x_i}^R$ for each OT instance encoding witness bit x_i.

Simulation for V. As V has no input, the simulator proceeds by running the code of the honest verifier, with the only difference being that it accepts a proof by checking whether P has input a valid witness in the OT. A malicious P can distinguish between the real protocol and the simulation only by forging Z, for which there is no advantage afforded by adaptive corruptions; a dishonest P who is successful in this setting can be used to break authenticity of the garbling scheme just as in the static case.

5   Zero Knowledge in Two Rounds

As discussed in Sect. 4, it seems unlikely that we can do better than three rounds to obtain a zero-knowledge from only one garbled circuit. Therefore, we explore whether we can save on the number of rounds when constructing ZK protocols by allowing multiple garbled circuits. In this section, we adopt a 'cut-and-choose' approach in order to construct a GC-based ZK protocol that requires *only* two rounds.

Our protocol is similar in spirit to the protocol of [42], who extend the technique of "MPC-in-the-head" [45]. The "MPC-in-the-head" is a technique introduced by Ishai et al. that allows a generic transformation of an MPC protocol into a zero-knowledge proof. In [42], the authors extend this idea, and give a generic transformation from a secure two-party computation protocol to a ZK proof.

The protocol is essentially a special case of general cut-and-choose. Since the verifier has no input, we do not have to handle selective failure where the evaluator's abort could leak a bit of his input, or ensure input consistency of the garbler, again, since the circuit is evaluated on an input entirely known to the garbler. While in [42], the protocol is seen as "2PC-in-the-head", we cast our protocol as cut-and-choose, and apply a standard transformation based on OT. Loosely speaking, choosing to reveal P_1's view in "2PC-in-the-head" in [42] is equivalent to choosing a circuit to be a check circuit in our protocol; and choosing to reveal P_2's view corresponds to a circuit being an evaluation circuit. Taking this view, we get a zero-knowledge argument whereas the "2PC-in-the-head" of [42] gives a zero-knowledge proof. We note that we do not need to enforce output recovery when two evaluated circuits result in different outputs. The output recovery mechanism that is used in general 2PC protocols [1,56–58,61] relies on authenticity property of the underlying garbling scheme. Our protocol can be compiled into a NIZK using standard techniques and transformations.

Next, we note that we can upgrade our argument to a proof following the idea of [42]; we augment our two-round argument with statistically binding commitments to the input GC keys from P. The inputs of P to the OT consist of the openings of all commitments (for a check circuit) as one message, and only the committed keys required to evaluate the GC on the garbled witness as the other message. Notably, the efficient ZK protocols such as those from garbled circuits [48] (including our 3 round construction presented in the previous section), ZKBoo [31], SNARKs and SNARGs are arguments. Our transformation requires public key operations proportional to the witness size alone whereas the best way we can think of for transforming ZKBoo to a proof involves public key operations proportional to the circuit size. For instance, running a 3-out-of-2 OT where the prover feeds three views that it creates 'in the head' as the input of the OT sender and the verifier chooses two indices picked uniformly at random indicating the two views to be opened for verification.

Once more, we consider the scenario where a prover P would like to prove to a verifier V that she knows a witness x for instance z such that $C(x) = 1$, where C is the circuit implementing the relation $R(z, x)$.

5.1   Our Construction

Informally, P garbles C to produce μ independent garbled circuits, and sends them to V, where μ is a statistical security parameter. Meanwhile, V samples a challenge string $c \xleftarrow{R} \{0, 1\}^{\mu}$. The positions at which bit string c is 0 will indicate which circuits V would like to verify (check circuits), whereas the positions at which c is 1 indicate which circuits V would like to evaluate (evaluation circuits). If all the check circuits are valid, and all the evaluation circuits decode to the correct output, V believes that P indeed has a witness x for the instance z. P would have to correctly guess V's entire challenge string in order to cheat and avoid detection.

Intuitively, P constructs μ independent garbled circuits of C, and for each instance acts as a sender in the OT protocol with messages corresponding to verification and evaluation information, respectively of the garbled circuit C, while sending the garbled circuit and decoding information directly to V (with the final message of the OT). V acts as the receiver in the OT protocol with choice bit c_i in the ith OT instance. She receives the first message to check or the second message to evaluate a given circuit, as per her challenge. When instantiated with the UC-secure OT in the framework of [65], our protocol requires only 2 rounds. Our 2-round ZK protocol Π_{ZK2} is described in Fig. 6. We include a proof that the protocol is UC-secure in the $\mathcal{F}_{\text{OT}}$-hybrid model in the full version.

The zero knowledge protocol Π_{ZK2} is not a zero knowledge proof. It is only an argument. We may obtain a proof using the idea of [42], resulting in a 2-round zero-knowledge proof.

5.2   Our Construction for ZK Proof

The zero knowledge protocol Π_{ZK2} is not a zero knowledge proof. It is only an argument. We may obtain a proof using the idea of [42], resulting in a 2-round zero-knowledge proof. We outline the approach below for completeness, and give

---

Π_{ZK2}

- **Oracles and Cryptographic Primitives:** A *correct, private, verifiable* (according to Definition A.4) garbling scheme Garble = (Gb, En, De, Ev, Ve). The ideal OT functionality $\mathcal{F}_{OT}$.
- **Common Inputs of P and V:** A security parameter λ, soundness parameter μ, relation R realized by circuit C, statement z.
- **Input of P:** A witness x of size $n = \text{poly}(\lambda)$ such that $R(z, x) = 1$.
- **Input of V:** Nothing.

OT First Message Phase: For all $i \in [\mu]$, V samples challenge bit $c_i \xleftarrow{R} \{0, 1\}$ and sends $(\text{rec}, \text{sid}, c_i)$ to $\mathcal{F}_{OT}$.

OT Second Message and Circuit Communication Phase: For all $i \in [\mu]$, P
  - constructs an independent garbling of C; $(\mathbf{C}_i, e_i, d_i) \leftarrow \text{Gb}(1^\lambda, C)$
  - encodes the witness as $\mathbf{X}_i = \text{En}(x, e_i)$
  - sends $(\text{sen}, \text{sid}, e_i, \mathbf{X}_i)$ to $\mathcal{F}_{OT}$ and $(\mathbf{C}_i, d_i)$ to V.

Circuit Checking, Evaluation and Output Phase: This is a local computation phase run by V. For all $i \in [\mu]$, V does the following:
  - If $c_i = 0$, then it receives $(\text{sent}, \text{sid}, e_i)$ from $\mathcal{F}_{OT}$. If $\text{Ve}(C, \mathbf{C}_i, e_i) = 0$, then it outputs **reject** and halt.
  - Else if $c_i = 1$, then it receives $(\text{sent}, \text{sid}, \mathbf{X}_i)$ from $\mathcal{F}_{OT}$. If $\text{De}(\text{Ev}(\mathbf{C}_i, \mathbf{X}_i), d_i) \neq 1$ then it outputs **reject** and halt.
  - If it has not halted, it outputs **accept**.

Fig. 6. 2-round zero-knowledge protocol.

the complete protocol in the full version. For a legitimately constructed garbled circuit $\mathbf{C}$ implementing an unsatisfiable circuit (implying there is no witness for the statement), an unbounded P* can find a set of keys, completely unrelated to the legitimate encoding information e, (say, by breaking the security of the underlying cryptographic primitive used in the garbled circuit) which evaluates $\mathbf{C}$ to the legitimate key corresponding to one. For instance, by breaking the collision-resistance of the hash function used to garble the gates. With such a circuit, the verification will always pass when legitimate encoding information is passed on. On the other hand, the other set of keys will allow to evaluate to 1 despite the fact that C is unsatisfiable. P* can thus convince V of a false statement. To prevent P from cheating we ensure that the wire labels that it provides for evaluation correspond to the valid encoding information e. This is done by asking P to commit to the encoding information in a randomly permuted order. Formally, for circuit i and input wire j, P must prepare and send the following commitments where e_{ij} denotes the encoding information corresponding to jth input wire of the ith circuit:

$$(\mathcal{B}_{ij}^0, \mathcal{B}_{ij}^1) = (\text{Com}(\text{En}(b_{ij}, e_{ij})), \text{Com}(\text{En}(1 - b_{ij}, e_{ij}))), \text{ for } b_{ij} \xleftarrow{R} \{0, 1\}$$

The commitment Com is statistically binding and computationally hiding commitment scheme ensuring the binding property against an unbounded powerful P*. An ElGamal based commitment scheme suffices for our requirement. V checks if the commitments $(\mathcal{B}_{ij}^0, \mathcal{B}_{ij}^1)$ opens to legitimate encoding information if the ith circuit is a check circuit. On the other hand, if the ith circuit is an evaluation circuit, then it verifies that every received input wire label is consistent with one of the given commitments. The commitments used as above makes sure that V evaluates the evaluation circuits on the legitimate wire labels consistent with e. The cut-and-choose guarantees that correct circuits are used for evaluation.

A   Properties of Garbling Schemes

Definition A.1 *(Correctness).* *A garbling scheme* Garble *is* **correct** *if for all input lengths* $n \leq \mathsf{poly}(\lambda)$, *circuits* $C : \{0, 1\}^n \to \{0, 1\}^m$ *and inputs* $x \in \{0, 1\}^n$, *the following probability is negligible in* λ:

$$\Pr\left(\mathsf{De}(\mathsf{Ev}(\mathbf{C}, \mathsf{En}(e, x)), d) \neq C(x) : (\mathbf{C}, e, d) \leftarrow \mathsf{Gb}(1^\lambda, C)\right).$$

Definition A.2 *(Privacy).* *A garbling scheme* Garble *is* **private** *if for all input lengths* $n \leq \mathsf{poly}(\lambda)$, *circuits* $C : \{0, 1\}^n \to \{0, 1\}^m$, *there exists a* PPT *simulator* $\mathcal{S}$ *such that for all inputs* $x \in \{0, 1\}^n$, *for all probabilistic polynomial-time adversaries* $\mathcal{A}$, *the following two distributions are computationally indistinguishable:*

- $\mathrm{REAL}(C, x)$: *run* $(\mathbf{C}, e, d) \leftarrow \mathsf{Gb}(1^\lambda, C)$, *and output* $(\mathbf{C}, \mathsf{En}(x, e), d)$.
- $\mathrm{IDEAL}_{\mathcal{S}}(C, C(x))$: *output* $(\mathbf{C}', \mathbf{X}, d') \leftarrow \mathcal{S}(1^\lambda, C, C(x))$

Definition A.3 *(Authenticity).* *A garbling scheme* Garble *is* **authentic** *if for all input lengths* $n \leq \mathsf{poly}(\lambda)$, *circuits* $C : \{0, 1\}^n \to \{0, 1\}^m$, *inputs* $x \in \{0, 1\}^n$, *and all probabilistic polynomial-time adversaries* $\mathcal{A}$, *the following probability is negligible in* λ:

$$\Pr\left(\begin{array}{c}\widehat{\mathbf{Y}} \neq \mathsf{Ev}(\mathbf{C}, \mathbf{X}) \\ \wedge \mathsf{De}(\widehat{\mathbf{Y}}, d) \neq \bot\end{array} : \begin{array}{c}\mathbf{X} = \mathsf{En}(x, e), \ (\mathbf{C}, e, d) \leftarrow \mathsf{Gb}(1^\lambda, C) \\ \widehat{\mathbf{Y}} \leftarrow \mathcal{A}(C, x, \mathbf{C}, \mathbf{X})\end{array}\right).$$

Definition A.4 *(Verifiability I).* *A garbling scheme* Garble *is* **verifiable** *if for all input lengths* $n \leq \mathsf{poly}(\lambda)$, *circuits* $C : \{0, 1\}^n \to \{0, 1\}^m$, *inputs* $x \in \{0, 1\}^n$, *and* PPT *adversaries* $\mathcal{A}$, *the following probability is negligible in* λ:

$$\Pr\left(\mathsf{De}\left(\mathsf{Ev}(\mathbf{C}, \mathsf{En}(x, e)), d\right) \neq C(x) : \begin{array}{c}(\mathbf{C}, e, d) \leftarrow \mathcal{A}(1^\lambda, C) \\ \mathsf{Ve}\left(C, \mathbf{C}, e, d\right) = 1\end{array}\right)$$

For completeness, we also require the following property of a verifiable garbling scheme:

$$\forall (\mathbf{C}, e, d) \leftarrow \mathsf{Gb}\left(1^\lambda, C\right), \ \mathsf{Ve}\left(C, \mathbf{C}, e, d\right) = 1$$

B   Functionalities

Oblivious Transfer. Oblivious transfer (OT) [49,63,66] is a protocol between a sender (S) and a receiver (R). In a 1-out-of-2 OT, the sender holds two inputs $a_0, a_1 \in \{0,1\}^k$ and the receiver holds a choice bit σ. At the end of the protocol, the receiver obtains a_σ. The sender learns nothing about the choice bit, and the receiver learns nothing about the sender's other input. The ideal OT functionality is recalled below in Fig. 7.

Committed OT and Commitment Functionalities. The $\mathcal{F}_{\mathsf{COT}}$ and $\mathcal{F}_{\mathsf{COM}}$ functionalities are provided in Figs. 8 and 9 respectively. The $\mathcal{F}_{\mathsf{COT}}$ functionality can be securely realised in the framework of [65] with an augmentation for the **Open-all** property, as discussed in [48]. The $\mathcal{F}_{\mathsf{COM}}$ functionality can be securely and efficiently realised as well [55].

$\mathcal{F}_{\mathsf{OT}}$

Choose: On input $(\mathbf{rec}, \mathrm{sid}, b)$ from R, with $\sigma \in \{0,1\}$, if no messages of the form $(\mathbf{rec}, \mathrm{sid}, \sigma)$ is present in memory, store $(\mathbf{rec}, \mathrm{sid}, \sigma)$ and send $(\mathbf{rec}, \mathrm{sid})$ to S.

Transfer: On input $(\mathbf{sen}, \mathrm{sid}, a_0, a_1)$ from S, with $a_0, a_1 \in \{0,1\}^k$, if no messages of the form $(\mathbf{sen}, \mathrm{sid}, a_0, a_1)$ is present in memory and a message of the form $(\mathbf{rec}, \mathrm{sid}, \sigma)$ is stored, send $(\mathbf{sent}, \mathrm{sid}, a_\sigma)$ to R.

Fig. 7. The ideal functionality $\mathcal{F}_{\mathsf{OT}}$ for oblivious transfer

Zero Knowledge. A Zero-knowledge (ZK) proof allows a prover to convince a verifier of the validity of a statement, without revealing any other information beyond that. Let R be an NP relation, and $\mathcal{L}$ be the associated language. $\mathcal{L} = \{z \mid \exists x : R(z,x) = 1\}$. A zero-knowledge proof for $\mathcal{L}$ lets the prover convince a verifier that $z \in \mathcal{L}$ for a common input z. A proof of knowledge captures not only the truth of a statement $z \in \mathcal{L}$, but also that the prover "possesses" a witness x to this fact. A proof of knowledge for a relation $R(\cdot, \cdot)$ is an interactive protocol where a prover P convinces a verifier V that P knows a x such that $R(z,x) = 1$, where z is a common input to P and V. The prover can always successfully convince the verifier if indeed P knows such a x. Conversely, if P can convince the verifier with high probability, then he "knows" such a x, that is, such a x can be efficiently computed given z and the code of P. When the soundness holds only for a PPT prover, it is called an *argument*. As in [48], we define the ideal functionality for zero-knowledge $\mathcal{F}_{\mathsf{ZK}}^R$ in the framework of [14] in order to capture all the properties that we require, in Fig. 10.

This is the ideal functionality for Committing Oblivious Transfer, borrowed from [48]. A Sender S provides two messages, of which a Receiver R chooses to receive one. S doesn't know which message R chose, and R has no information about the message it didn't choose. Upon receiving a signal from S, the functionality reveals both messages to R.

$$\mathcal{F}_{\mathsf{COT}}$$

1. **Choose:** Receive ($\mathtt{choose}, id, b$) from R, where $b \in \{0,1\}$. If no message of the form ($\mathtt{choose}, id, \cdot$) exists in memory, store ($\mathtt{choose}, id, b$) and send ($\mathtt{chosen}, id$) to S.
2. **Transfer:** Receive ($\mathtt{transfer}, id, tid, m_0, m_1$) from S, where $m_0, m_1 \in \{0,1\}^\kappa$. If no message of the form ($\mathtt{transfer}, id, tid, \cdot, \cdot$) exists in memory, and a message of the form ($\mathtt{choose}, id, b$) exists in memory, then send ($\mathtt{transferred}, id, tid, m_b$) to R.
3. **Open-all:** Receive ($\mathtt{open\text{-}all}$) from the S. Send all messages of the form ($\mathtt{transfer}, id, tid, m_0, m_1$) to R.

Fig. 8. The ideal committing OT functionality

The ideal commitment functionality, borrowed from [48]. A Sender S commits to a message m, which she later reveals to the receiver R. S is 'bound' to only the message that she committed, while the message is hidden from R until S opens her commitment.

$$\mathcal{F}_{\mathsf{COM}}$$

1. **Commit:** Receive ($\mathtt{commit}, id, m$) from the sender, where $m \in \{0,1\}^*$. If no such message already exists in memory, then store ($\mathtt{commit}, id, m$) and send ($\mathtt{committed}, id, |m|$) to R.
2. **Reveal:** Receive ($\mathtt{reveal}, id$) from S, send ($\mathtt{reveal}, id, m$) to R if corresponding ($\mathtt{commit}, id, m$) exists in memory.

Fig. 9. The ideal commitment functionality

$$\mathcal{F}_{\mathsf{ZK}}^R$$

1. Receive ($\mathtt{prove}, \mathrm{sid}, z, x$) from P and ($\mathtt{verify}, \mathrm{sid}, z'$) from V
2. **if** $z = z'$ and $R(z, x) = 1$ **then** output ($\mathtt{verified}, \mathrm{sid}, z$) to V

Fig. 10. The zero-knowledge functionality

References

1. Afshar, A., Mohassel, P., Pinkas, B., Riva, B.: Non-interactive secure computation based on cut-and-choose. In: Nguyen, P.Q., Oswald, E. (eds.) EUROCRYPT 2014. LNCS, vol. 8441, pp. 387–404. Springer, Heidelberg (2014). https://doi.org/10. 1007/978-3-642-55220-5_22
2. Aiello, B., Ishai, Y., Reingold, O.: Priced oblivious transfer: how to sell digital goods. In: Pfitzmann, B. (ed.) EUROCRYPT 2001. LNCS, vol. 2045, pp. 119–135. Springer, Heidelberg (2001). https://doi.org/10.1007/3-540-44987-6_8
3. Ames, S., Hazay, C., Ishai, Y., Venkitasubramaniam, M.: Ligero: lightweight sublinear arguments without a trusted setup. In: CCS 2017, pp. 2087–2104 (2017)
4. Applebaum, B., Ishai, Y., Kushilevitz, E.: From secrecy to soundness: efficient verification via secure computation. In: Abramsky, S., Gavoille, C., Kirchner, C., Meyer auf der Heide, F., Spirakis, P.G. (eds.) ICALP 2010, Part I. LNCS, vol. 6198, pp. 152–163. Springer, Heidelberg (2010). https://doi.org/10.1007/978-3-642-14165-2_14
5. Applebaum, B., Ishai, Y., Kushilevitz, E., Waters, B.: Encoding functions with constant online rate, or how to compress garbled circuit keys. SIAM J. Comput. **44**(2), 433–466 (2015)
6. Beaver, D.: Adaptive zero knowledge and computational equivocation (extended abstract). In: STOC 1996, pp. 629–638 (1996)
7. Beaver, D.: Equivocable oblivious transfer. In: Maurer, U. (ed.) EUROCRYPT 1996. LNCS, vol. 1070, pp. 119–130. Springer, Heidelberg (1996). https://doi.org/10.1007/3-540-68339-9_11
8. Bellare, M., Hoang, V.T., Rogaway, P.: Adaptively secure garbling with applications to one-time programs and secure outsourcing. In: Wang, X., Sako, K. (eds.) ASIACRYPT 2012. LNCS, vol. 7658, pp. 134–153. Springer, Heidelberg (2012). https://doi.org/10.1007/978-3-642-34961-4_10
9. Bellare, M., Hoang, V.T., Rogaway, P.: Foundations of garbled circuits. In: CCS 2012, pp. 784–796 (2012)
10. Ben-Or, M., Goldwasser, S., Wigderson, A.: Completeness theorems for non-cryptographic fault-tolerant distributed computation. In: STOC 1988, pp. 1–10 (1988)
11. Benhamouda, F., Couteau, G., Pointcheval, D., Wee, H.: Implicit zero-knowledge arguments and applications to the malicious setting. In: Gennaro and Robshaw [29], pp. 107–129
12. Bitansky, N., Paneth, O.: Point obfuscation and 3-round zero-knowledge. In: Cramer, R. (ed.) TCC 2012. LNCS, vol. 7194, pp. 190–208. Springer, Heidelberg (2012). https://doi.org/10.1007/978-3-642-28914-9_11
13. Camenisch, J., Michels, M.: Proving in zero-knowledge that a number is the product of two safe primes. In: Stern, J. (ed.) EUROCRYPT 1999. LNCS, vol. 1592, pp. 107–122. Springer, Heidelberg (1999). https://doi.org/10.1007/3-540-48910-X_8
14. Canetti, R.: Universally composable security: a new paradigm for cryptographic protocols. In: 42nd FOCS, pp. 136–145. IEEE Computer Society Press, October 2001
15. Canetti, R., Feige, U., Goldreich, O., Naor, M.: Adaptively secure multi-party computation. In: STOC 1996, pp. 639–648 (1996)
16. Canetti, R., Goldwasser, S., Poburinnaya, O.: Adaptively secure two-party computation from indistinguishability obfuscation. In: Dodis, Y., Nielsen, J.B. (eds.) TCC 2015. LNCS, vol. 9015, pp. 557–585. Springer, Heidelberg (2015). https://doi.org/10.1007/978-3-662-46497-7_22

17. Canetti, R., Jain, A., Scafuro, A.: Practical UC security with a global random oracle. In: Ahn, G.-J., Yung, M., Li, N. (eds.) ACM CCS 2014, pp. 597–608. ACM Press, November 2014
18. Canetti, R., Lindell, Y., Ostrovsky, R., Sahai, A.: Universally composable two-party and multi-party secure computation. In: STOC 2002, pp. 494–503 (2002)
19. Canetti, R., Poburinnaya, O., Venkitasubramaniam, M.: Equivocating yao: constant-round adaptively secure multiparty computation in the plain model. In: STOC 2017, pp. 497–509 (2017)
20. Chase, M., Derler, D., Goldfeder, S., Orlandi, C., Ramacher, S., Rechberger, C., Slamanig, D., Zaverucha, G.: Post-quantum zero-knowledge and signatures from symmetric-key primitives. In: CCS 2017, pp. 1825–1842 (2017)
21. Chase, M., Ganesh, C., Mohassel, P.: Efficient zero-knowledge proof of algebraic and non-algebraic statements with applications to privacy preserving credentials. In: Robshaw, M., Katz, J. (eds.) CRYPTO 2016, Part III. LNCS, vol. 9816, pp. 499–530. Springer, Heidelberg (2016). https://doi.org/10.1007/978-3-662-53015-3_18
22. Cohen, R., Peikert, C.: On adaptively secure multiparty computation with a short CRS. In: SCN 2015, pp. 129–146 (2016)
23. Costello, C., Fournet, C., Howell, J., Kohlweiss, M., Kreuter, B., Naehrig, M., Parno, B., Zahur, S.: Geppetto: versatile verifiable computation. In: 2015 IEEE Symposium on Security and Privacy, pp. 253–270. IEEE Computer Society Press, May 2015
24. Dachman-Soled, D., Katz, J., Rao, V.: Adaptively secure, universally composable, multiparty computation in constant rounds. In: Dodis, Y., Nielsen, J.B. (eds.) TCC 2015. LNCS, vol. 9015, pp. 586–613. Springer, Heidelberg (2015). https://doi.org/10.1007/978-3-662-46497-7_23
25. Damgrard, I., Ishai, Y.: Scalable secure multiparty computation. In: Dwork, C. (ed.) CRYPTO 2006. LNCS, vol. 4117, pp. 501–520. Springer, Heidelberg (2006). https://doi.org/10.1007/11818175_30
26. Danezis, G., Fournet, C., Groth, J., Kohlweiss, M.: Square span programs with applications to succinct NIZK arguments. In: Sarkar, P., Iwata, T. (eds.) ASIACRYPT 2014, Part I. LNCS, vol. 8873, pp. 532–550. Springer, Heidelberg (2014). https://doi.org/10.1007/978-3-662-45611-8_28
27. Frederiksen, T.K., Nielsen, J.B., Orlandi, C.: Privacy-free garbled circuits with applications to efficient zero-knowledge. In: Oswald, E., Fischlin, M. (eds.) EUROCRYPT 2015. LNCS, vol. 9057, pp. 191–219. Springer, Heidelberg (2015). https://doi.org/10.1007/978-3-662-46803-6_7
28. Gennaro, R., Gentry, C., Parno, B., Raykova, M.: Quadratic span programs and succinct NIZKs without PCPs. In: Johansson, T., Nguyen, P.Q. (eds.) EUROCRYPT 2013. LNCS, vol. 7881, pp. 626–645. Springer, Heidelberg (2013). https://doi.org/10.1007/978-3-642-38348-9_37
29. Gennaro, R., Robshaw, M. (eds.): CRYPTO 2015, Part II. LNCS, vol. 9216. Springer, Heidelberg (2015). https://doi.org/10.1007/978-3-662-48000-7
30. Gertner, Y., Ishai, Y., Kushilevitz, E., Malkin, T.: Protecting data privacy in private information retrieval schemes. In: 30th ACM STOC, pp. 151–160. ACM Press, May 1998
31. Giacomelli, I., Madsen, J., Orlandi, C.: ZKBoo: faster zero-knowledge for Boolean circuits. In: USENIX Security Symposium 2016 (2016)
32. Goldreich, O., Krawczyk, H.: On the composition of zero-knowledge proof systems. SIAM J. Comput. 25(1), 169–192 (1996)

33. Goldreich, O., Micali, S., Wigderson, A.: How to play any mental game or a completeness theorem for protocols with honest majority. In: Aho, A., (ed.) 19th ACM STOC, pp. 218–229. ACM Press, May 1987

34. Goldreich, O., Micali, S., Wigderson, A.: How to prove all NP statements in zero-knowledge and a methodology of cryptographic protocol design (extended abstract). In: Odlyzko, A.M. (ed.) CRYPTO 1986. LNCS, vol. 263, pp. 171–185. Springer, Heidelberg (1987). https://doi.org/10.1007/3-540-47721-7_11

35. Goldreich, O., Micali, S., Wigderson, A.: Proofs that yield nothing but their validity or all languages in NP have zero-knowledge proof systems. J. ACM **38**(3), 691–729 (1991)

36. Goldwasser, S., Micali, S., Rackoff, C.: The knowledge complexity of interactive proof-systems (extended abstract). In: STOC 1985, pp. 291–304 (1985)

37. Groth, J.: Short non-interactive zero-knowledge proofs. In: Abe, M. (ed.) ASIACRYPT 2010. LNCS, vol. 6477, pp. 341–358. Springer, Heidelberg (2010). https://doi.org/10.1007/978-3-642-17373-8_20

38. Groth, J.: On the size of pairing-based non-interactive arguments. In: Fischlin, M., Coron, J.-S. (eds.) EUROCRYPT 2016, Part II. LNCS, vol. 9666, pp. 305–326. Springer, Heidelberg (2016). https://doi.org/10.1007/978-3-662-49896-5_11

39. Groth, J., Sahai, A.: Efficient non-interactive proof systems for bilinear groups. In: Smart, N. (ed.) EUROCRYPT 2008. LNCS, vol. 4965, pp. 415–432. Springer, Heidelberg (2008). https://doi.org/10.1007/978-3-540-78967-3_24

40. Guillou, L.C., Quisquater, J.-J.: A practical zero-knowledge protocol fitted to security microprocessor minimizing both transmission and memory. In: Barstow, D., Brauer, W., Brinch Hansen, P., Gries, D., Luckham, D., Moler, C., Pnueli, A., Seegmüller, G., Stoer, J., Wirth, N., Günther, C.G. (eds.) EUROCRYPT 1988. LNCS, vol. 330, pp. 123–128. Springer, Heidelberg (1988). https://doi.org/10.1007/3-540-45961-8_11

41. Hazay, C., Polychroniadou, A., Venkitasubramaniam, M.: Constant round adaptively secure protocols in the tamper-proof hardware model. In: PKC 2017, pp. 428–460 (2017)

42. Hazay, C., Venkitasubramaniam, M.: On the power of secure two-party computation. In: Robshaw, M., Katz, J. (eds.) CRYPTO 2016, Part II. LNCS, vol. 9815, pp. 397–429. Springer, Heidelberg (2016). https://doi.org/10.1007/978-3-662-53008-5_14

43. Hu, Z., Mohassel, P., Rosulek, M.: Efficient zero-knowledge proofs of non-algebraic statements with sublinear amortized cost. In: Gennaro and Robshaw [29], pp. 150–169

44. Ishai, Y., Kushilevitz, E., Ostrovsky, R., Prabhakaran, M., Sahai, A.: Efficient non-interactive secure computation. In: Paterson, K.G. (ed.) EUROCRYPT 2011. LNCS, vol. 6632, pp. 406–425. Springer, Heidelberg (2011). https://doi.org/10.1007/978-3-642-20465-4_23

45. Ishai, Y., Kushilevitz, E., Ostrovsky, R., Sahai, A.: Zero-knowledge from secure multiparty computation. In: Johnson, D.S., Feige, U. (eds.) 39th ACM STOC, pp. 21–30. ACM Press, June 2007

46. Ishai, Y., Kushilevitz, E., Ostrovsky, R., Sahai, A.: Zero-knowledge proofs from secure multiparty computation. SIAM J. Comput. **39**(3), 1121–1152 (2009)

47. Ishai, Y., Wee, H.: Partial garbling schemes and their applications. In: Esparza, J., Fraigniaud, P., Husfeldt, T., Koutsoupias, E. (eds.) ICALP 2014, Part I. LNCS, vol. 8572, pp. 650–662. Springer, Heidelberg (2014). https://doi.org/10.1007/978-3-662-43948-7_54

48. Jawurek, M., Kerschbaum, F., Orlandi, C.: Zero-knowledge using garbled circuits: how to prove non-algebraic statements efficiently. In: CCS 2013, pp. 955–966 (2013)
49. Kilian, J.: Founding cryptography on oblivious transfer. In: STOC 1988, pp. 20–31 (1988)
50. Kilian, J.: A note on efficient zero-knowledge proofs and arguments (extended abstract). In: 24th ACM STOC, pp. 723–732. ACM Press, May 1992
51. Kilian, J., Micali, S., Ostrovsky, R.: Minimum resource zero-knowledge proofs (extended abstract). In: FOCS 1989, pp. 474–479 (1989)
52. Kolesnikov, V., Krawczyk, H., Lindell, Y., Malozemoff, A.J., Rabin, T.: Attribute-based key exchange with general policies. In: CCS 2016, pp. 1451–1463 (2016)
53. Kolesnikov, V., Schneider, T.: Improved garbled circuit: free XOR gates and applications. In: Aceto, L., Damgrard, I., Goldberg, L.A., Halldórsson, M.M., Ingólfsdóttir, A., Walukiewicz, I. (eds.) ICALP 2008, Part II. LNCS, vol. 5126, pp. 486–498. Springer, Heidelberg (2008). https://doi.org/10.1007/978-3-540-70583-3_40
54. Kondi, Y., Patra, A.: Privacy-free garbled circuits for formulas: size zero and information-theoretic. In: Katz, J., Shacham, H. (eds.) CRYPTO 2017. LNCS, vol. 10401, pp. 188–222. Springer, Cham (2017). https://doi.org/10.1007/978-3-319-63688-7_7
55. Lindell, Y.: Highly-efficient universally-composable commitments based on the DDH assumption. In: Paterson, K.G. (ed.) EUROCRYPT 2011. LNCS, vol. 6632, pp. 446–466. Springer, Heidelberg (2011). https://doi.org/10.1007/978-3-642-20465-4_25
56. Lindell, Y.: Fast cut-and-choose based protocols for malicious and covert adversaries. In: Canetti, R., Garay, J.A. (eds.) CRYPTO 2013, Part II. LNCS, vol. 8043, pp. 1–17. Springer, Heidelberg (2013). https://doi.org/10.1007/978-3-642-40084-1_1
57. Lindell, Y., Riva, B.: Cut-and-choose yao-based secure computation in the online/offline and batch settings. In: Garay, J.A., Gennaro, R. (eds.) CRYPTO 2014, Part II. LNCS, vol. 8617, pp. 476–494. Springer, Heidelberg (2014). https://doi.org/10.1007/978-3-662-44381-1_27
58. Lindell, Y., Riva, B.: Blazing fast 2PC in the offline/online setting with security for malicious adversaries. In: Ray, I., Li, N., Kruegel, C. (eds.) ACM CCS 2015, pp. 579–590. ACM Press, October 2015
59. Lindell, Y., Zarosim, H.: Adaptive zero-knowledge proofs and adaptively secure oblivious transfer. J. Cryptol. 24(4), 761–799 (2011)
60. Lipmaa, H.: Succinct non-interactive zero knowledge arguments from span programs and linear error-correcting codes. In: Sako, K., Sarkar, P. (eds.) ASIACRYPT 2013, Part I. LNCS, vol. 8269, pp. 41–60. Springer, Heidelberg (2013). https://doi.org/10.1007/978-3-642-42033-7_3
61. Mohassel, P., Rosulek, M.: Non-interactive secure 2PC in the offline/online and batch settings. In: Coron, J.-S., Nielsen, J.B. (eds.) EUROCRYPT 2017. LNCS, vol. 10212, pp. 425–455. Springer, Cham (2017). https://doi.org/10.1007/978-3-319-56617-7_15
62. Naor, M., Ostrovsky, R., Venkatesan, R., Yung, M.: Perfect zero-knowledge arguments for NP using any one-way permutation. J. Cryptol. 11(2), 87–108 (1998)
63. Naor, M., Pinkas, B.: Computationally secure oblivious transfer. J. Cryptol. 18(1), 1–35 (2005)
64. Parno, B., Howell, J., Gentry, C., Raykova, M.: Pinocchio: nearly practical verifiable computation. In: 2013 IEEE Symposium on Security and Privacy, pp. 238–252. IEEE Computer Society Press, May 2013

65. Peikert, C., Vaikuntanathan, V., Waters, B.: A framework for efficient and composable oblivious transfer. In: Wagner, D. (ed.) CRYPTO 2008. LNCS, vol. 5157, pp. 554–571. Springer, Heidelberg (2008). https://doi.org/10.1007/978-3-540-85174-5_31

66. Rabin, M.O.: How to exchange secrets with oblivious transfer. Cryptology ePrint Archive, Report 2005/187 (2005). http://eprint.iacr.org/2005/187

67. Rindal, P., Rosulek, M.: Faster malicious 2-party secure computation with online/offline dual execution. In: USENIX Security 2016, pp. 297–314 (2016)

68. Schnorr, C.P.: Efficient identification and signatures for smart cards. In: Brassard, G. (ed.) CRYPTO 1989. LNCS, vol. 435, pp. 239–252. Springer, New York (1990). https://doi.org/10.1007/0-387-34805-0_22

69. Yao, A.C.-C.: Protocols for secure computations (extended abstract). In: 23rd FOCS, pp. 160–164. IEEE Computer Society Press, November 1982

70. Yao, A.C.-C.: How to generate and exchange secrets (extended abstract). In: 27th FOCS, pp. 162–167. IEEE Computer Society Press, October 1986

71. Zahur, S., Rosulek, M., Evans, D.: Two halves make a whole. In: Oswald, E., Fischlin, M. (eds.) EUROCRYPT 2015. LNCS, vol. 9057, pp. 220–250. Springer, Heidelberg (2015). https://doi.org/10.1007/978-3-662-46803-6_8

Compact Zero-Knowledge Proofs of Small Hamming Weight

Ivan Damgård[1], Ji Luo[2], Sabine Oechsner[1], Peter Scholl[1($\boxtimes$)], and Mark Simkin[1]

[1] Aarhus University, Aarhus, Denmark
{ivan,oechsner,peter.scholl,simkin}@cs.au.dk
[2] Tsinghua University, Beijing, China
j-luo14@mails.tsinghua.edu.cn

Abstract. We introduce a new technique that allows to give a zero-knowledge proof that a committed vector has Hamming weight bounded by a given constant. The proof has unconditional soundness and is very compact: It has size independent of the length of the committed string, and for large fields, it has size corresponding to a constant number of commitments. We show five applications of the technique that play on a common theme, namely that our proof allows us to get malicious security at small overhead compared to semi-honest security: (1) actively secure k-out-of-n OT from black-box use of 1-out-of-2 OT, (2) separable accountable ring signatures, (3) more efficient preprocessing for the TinyTable secure two-party computation protocol, (4) mixing with public verifiability, and (5) PIR with security against a malicious client.

1 Introduction

Commitments and zero-knowledge proofs are extremely important universal tools that protocol designers use to upgrade semi-honestly secure protocols to maliciously secure constructions. This follows the well known paradigm of proving you "did the right thing", without revealing any secret data. For this to be interesting, we want of course that the size of the proofs is small, in order to have small communication overhead for getting malicious security.

Generic techniques using NP reductions will of course always work, but are extremely inefficient. If proof size is the only goal to optimise for, then Succinct Non-Interactive Arguments (SNARGs) give a much better option that works in general, but it is very costly to construct a proof, though verification can sometimes be fast [5]. Moreover, soundness is only computational and requires non-falsifiable assumptions that are regarded as controversial by some. A different general approach was introduced in [23] (based on [28]), the ZKBoo protocol, which is computationally much more efficient than SNARGs and based on standard assumptions, but the proof size is much larger.

Thus a natural question is: Can we, at least for special types of statements, have both the prover and the verifier be very efficient, have unconditional soundness based on standard assumptions, and still have the size of the proof be

© International Association for Cryptologic Research 2018
M. Abdalla and R. Dahab (Eds.): PKC 2018, LNCS 10770, pp. 530–560, 2018.
https://doi.org/10.1007/978-3-319-76581-5_18

much smaller than that of the statement? Where, of course, we would like that the statements we can prove are useful to get malicious security in meaningful applications.

More specifically, we consider an arbitrary linearly homomorphic commitment scheme that allows committing to elements in a finite field $\mathbb{F}$ (we show several examples later), and the following scenario: A prover has committed to a string $x \in \mathbb{F}^n$, using n commitments, and claims that the Hamming weight of x is at most d. Such a statement can be proved with unconditional soundness, using the techniques based on Σ-protocols from [16], but the size of the proof would be dominated by the cost of sending a number of commitments that is linear in n.

Related Work. Efficiently proving properties of one or a small number of committed values from a public list $c_1, \ldots, c_n$ (of committed or public values) has been considered in several works. Brands et al. [9] propose a zero-knowledge protocol for proving non-membership in a list with squareroot complexity in the size of the list. Groth [25] gives zero-knowledge arguments for algebraic statements about matrices from a list of committed matrices with sublinear communication complexity. Bayer and Groth [3] give logarithmic size zero-knowledge arguments of list membership. Groth and Kohlweiss [26] present a logarithmic size zero-knowledge proof for a list of commitments where at least one commitments opens to 0. This result was improved with respect to practical efficiency by Bootle et al. [7].

Our contributions. We present a protocol that allows the prover to show in ZK with unconditional soundness that at most d out of n commitments do not contain 0, or alternatively, that the Hamming weight of the message vector of the commitments is at most d. The communication complexity is dominated by sending $O\left(\frac{kd}{\log |\mathbb{F}|}\right)$ commitments for an error probability of $2^{-\Omega(k)}$. Thus, if the size of $\mathbb{F}$ is exponential in the security parameter, we only need a constant number of commitments, and the communication overhead is always independent of n. Since the complexity grows linearly in d, our construction is more interesting for small values of d compared to n, and particularly constant d. In addition, the protocol is public-coin hence can be made non-interactive in the random oracle model using the Fiat-Shamir paradigm [21].

We show several applications of this type of proof: Our first application is to efficient secure computation with active security. We obtain an actively secure d-out-of-n oblivious transfer (OT) protocol which makes only black-box use of 1-out-of-2 OT and hence allows the use of efficient OT extension techniques, avoiding costly public-key operations [27]. The only previously known black-box constructions (without relying on public-key assumptions like DDH or pairings) are not actively secure [34], or only realise a weaker form of approximate d-out-of-n OT [39]. Our protocol has a communication complexity of $O(nk + k^2 d)$ bits, and we show how to reduce this to $O(nk)$ in an amortized setting using recent advances in homomorphic commitments based on OT and error-correcting codes [13]. This gives constant overhead when the sender's strings are of length $\Omega(k)$, for arbitrary d.[1]

Second, we construct a separable accountable ring signature scheme. A ring signature scheme allows to generate signatures proving that someone in a given set of parties signed the message without revealing the identity of the signer. Accountability means that the signer can dynamically choose a trusted party who will be able to compute her (the signer's) identity from the signature, whereas no one else can. Separability means that members of the set are not required to use the same type of key or signature algorithm, but can rather use different types keys like El Gamal and RSA keys. In our case, the only requirement we impose on the public key of each participant is that there exists a Σ-protocol for showing knowledge of the corresponding secret key. Note that accountable ring signatures imply group signatures where the trusted party is chosen and fixed at key generation time. We first construct a separable ring signature using the standard OR-proof technique from [16], and then add accountability using our compact proofs. Compared to doing the OR-proof only, the involved overhead is very small: it is additive and independent of the number of parties.

Third, we also show how to apply our compact proof to generate preprocessing data for the TinyTable secure computation protocol [18]. This can give a concrete reduction in communication complexity of around a factor of two, compared with previous approaches [30], depending on the sizes of the lookup table gates used in the circuit.

Fourth, we show how to upgrade the "shuffle in public" paradigm by Adida and Wikström [1] so that the publicly verifiable proof that the shuffle is correctly formed has size $O(n)$ (where n is the number of ciphertexts to be shuffled). More precisely, [1] shows how to make a quite efficient use-once obfuscation of a shuffle operation that can then be applied later to applying a secret permutation to a set of ciphertexts. We also show a special purpose MPC protocol that a set of parties can use to efficiently generate both the obfuscation and the proof.

Finally, we show how to upgrade a standard single-server PIR protocol to be secure against a malicious client with overhead a factor $o(1)$. This protocol can be based on any additively homomorphic encryption scheme.

2   Preliminaries

2.1   Definition of Commitment Schemes

We will consider two types of linearly homomorphic commitment schemes that allow us to commit to elements in a finite field $\mathbb{F}$.

Type 1 commitments. This type of commitment scheme consists of two algorithms KeyGen and Commit. We assume for now that $\mathbb{F}$ is a prime field of order q for some prime q, and will consider extension fields later in Sect. 3.1.

---

[1] One could also obtain constant overhead with generic secure two-party computation techniques [29], but this would be prohibitively expensive.

KeyGen is run by a prover P and takes as input 1^k, where k is the security parameter, and outputs a public key pk that is sent to the verifier V. We assume that the verifier can convince himself that pk is valid, i.e., it is a possible output from KeyGen. This can be a direct check or via an interactive protocol, but we will not be concerned with the details of this.

Commit is run by P and takes as input $x \in \mathbb{F}$ and randomness $r \in H$, and outputs a commitment $\mathsf{Commit}_{\mathrm{pk}}(x, r) \in G$ (to the verifier), where G, H are finite groups. To open a commitment c, P sends x, r to V who checks that $c = \mathsf{Commit}_{\mathrm{pk}}(x, r)$ and accepts or rejects accordingly.

We assume the commitment scheme is:

Perfectly binding. For any valid public key pk, x is uniquely determined from $\mathsf{Commit}_{\mathrm{pk}}(x, r)$.

Computationally hiding. Consider the following experiment: Run $\mathsf{KeyGen}(1^k)$ to get pk, give it to a probabilistic polynomial time adversary A who chooses two elements $x_0, x_1 \in \mathbb{F}$ and gets $\mathsf{Commit}_{\mathrm{pk}}(x_b, r)$ where b is either 0 or 1. A outputs a guess bit b'. For all such A, we require its advantage

$$|\Pr[b' = 1 \mid b = 0] - \Pr[b' = 1 \mid b = 1]|$$

to be negligible in k.

Homomorphic. We write the group operations in G and H additively and note that since $\mathbb{F}$ is a prime field, we can think of $u \in \mathbb{F}$ as an integer and hence, e.g., $ur \in H$ is well defined. We then require Commit to be a homomorphism in the sense that

$$u\mathsf{Commit}_{\mathrm{pk}}(x, r) + v\mathsf{Commit}_{\mathrm{pk}}(y, s) = \mathsf{Commit}_{\mathrm{pk}}(ux + vy, ur + vs)$$

for all $x, y, u, v \in \mathbb{F}$ and $r, s \in H$.

q-invertible. Note that, since q is the order of $\mathbb{F}$, qc is a commitment to 0 for any commitment c (by the homomorphic property). In addition, we require that qc can be "explained" as a commitment to 0, even given only c. More precisely, there exists a polynomial time computable function $f_0 : G \mapsto H$ such that for any commitment $c \in G$, we have $qc = \mathsf{Commit}(0, f_0(c))$.

The q-inversion property was defined (with minor differences) in [15]. Note that if H is a vector space over $\mathbb{F}$, then the property is trivially satisfied, we can set $f_0(c) = 0$.

Type 2 commitments. This type of scheme is defined by an algorithm Verify and an ideal functionality $\mathsf{F}_{\mathrm{Com}}$, which we assume is available to prover P and verifier V. The parties initially agree on the field $\mathbb{F}$ and a statistical security parameter k, both are sent to $\mathsf{F}_{\mathrm{Com}}$ once and for all. $\mathsf{F}_{\mathrm{Com}}$ then sends a global, private verification key, sk, to V. To commit to a field element x, P sends x to $\mathsf{F}_{\mathrm{Com}}$ which then returns a bit string $\boldsymbol{m}_x$ to P and also sends a string $\boldsymbol{k}_x$ to V. To open, P sends $x, \boldsymbol{m}_x$ to V. Then V runs $\mathsf{Verify}_{\mathrm{sk}}(x, \boldsymbol{m}_x, \boldsymbol{k}_x)$ which returns accept or reject.

Intuitively, one can think of m_x as a MAC on x and k_x as a key that V uses to check the MAC. We assume the commitment scheme is:

Statistically binding. If, when opening a commitment to x, the prover sends x', m'_x and $x' \neq x$, then V accepts with negligible probability.

Perfectly hiding. For each commitment created by $\mathsf{F_{Com}}$ to some x, the distribution of k_x is independent of x (and of any other value sent to $\mathsf{F_{Com}}$).

Homomorphic. The strings m_x, k_x created for a commitment come from finite-dimensional vector spaces G, H over $\mathbb{F}$, respectively. Furthermore, for any two commitments (x, m_x, k_x) and (y, m_y, k_y) and all $u, v \in \mathbb{F}$, we have that $(ux + vy, um_x + vm_y, uk_x + vk_y)$ is a valid commitment to $ux + vy$, i.e., it can be opened to $ux + vy$ and not to any other value.

Notation. In the following, we will use $\langle x \rangle$ as a shorthand for either type of commitment, so we suppress for simplicity public key and randomness from the notation. Likewise, we will use $\langle x \rangle + \langle y \rangle = \langle x + y \rangle$ and $c\langle x \rangle = \langle cx \rangle$ for a public value $c \in \mathbb{F}$ as a shorthand for applications of the homomorphic properties as defined above.

2.2   Example Commitment Schemes

Type 1 schemes. An example of a Type 1 commitment scheme is based on El Gamal encryption with the message in the exponent. More concretely, we let KeyGen choose p, q to be primes where q divides $p - 1$ and is k bits long. KeyGen also chooses random elements $g, h \in \mathbb{Z}_p^*$ of order q. We then set $\mathbb{F} = G = \mathbb{Z}_q$, $H = \{(g^r, g^x h^r) : x, r \in \mathbb{Z}\}$, $\mathrm{pk} = (p, q, g, h)$ and $\mathsf{Commit}_{\mathrm{pk}}(x, r) = (g^r, g^x h^r)$. This is well known to be hiding under the DDH assumption. Note that if a party knows the corresponding El Gamal secret key, he cannot decrypt a committed message since it is in the exponent, but he can decide if a committed value is 0 or not. We may of course do something completely similar in an elliptic curve group of order q. More generally, a commitment scheme with the right properties follows from the existence of q-one way functions as introduced in [15], which implies also constructions based on the quadratic residuosity assumption (for $\mathbb{F} = \mathbb{Z}_2$) and generalizations thereof.

Another example can be derived from Paillier encryption [37]. Here the plaintext space is $\mathbb{Z}_N$ for an RSA modulus N, which is not a field but nevertheless compatible with our main construction. See Appendix A for detailed discussion.

It seems tempting to use a somewhat homomorphic encryption scheme based on (Ring-)LWE as basis for our commitments, simply by letting a commitment to x be an encryption of x. But this does not quite fit in our model. The reason is that in this case, the randomness should not be chosen uniformly but must be small enough to avoid overflow, which, should it happen, would invalidate binding. This means the prover must convince the verifier that a commitment is well-formed. Moreover, the above Σ-protocols must be modified to work for this example and there is a limit to the number of homomorphic operations we can support. Modulo this, however, it is possible to make our main protocol work in this case as well.

Type 2 schemes. We construct Type 2 commitment schemes from UC commitments based on oblivious transfer, which can be used to implement a form of the $\mathsf{F_{Com}}$ functionality. A simple example of $\mathsf{F_{Com}}$ is based on information-theoretic MACs: On initialisation, $\mathsf{F_{Com}}$ samples and sends a random field element $\mathrm{sk} := \alpha \in \mathbb{F}$ to the verifier, V. To commit to a message $x \in \mathbb{F}$ from P, $\mathsf{F_{Com}}$ samples $\beta \in \mathbb{F}$, computes $\gamma = x \cdot \alpha + \beta$ to P, before sending $\boldsymbol{m}_x = \gamma$ to P and $\boldsymbol{k}_x = \beta$ to V. The verification algorithm simply checks that $\gamma = x \cdot \alpha + \beta$. This is unconditionally hiding and statistically binding if $|\mathbb{F}| = 2^{\Omega(k)}$, since forging an opening requires guessing the secret α. Realising this $\mathsf{F_{Com}}$ functionality can be done using 1-out-of-2 correlated oblivious transfer to commit to bits [35], and repeating this k times allows committing to arbitrary field elements when $|\mathbb{F}| \le 2^k$ (similarly to [32]). We provide more details in Sect. 4.1.

Another approach is to use recent, more efficient constructions of UC homomorphic commitment schemes [13, 22], which have message space $\mathbb{F}^\ell$ for $\ell = \Omega(k)$. This has the advantage that arbitrary field elements can be committed to with $o(1)$ overhead, using only 1-out-of-2 oblivious transfer and error-correcting codes. However, because the message space is now a vector space and not a finite field, this can only be applied to our zero-knowledge proof and applications in a batch setting, where many proofs are carried out in parallel. In Appendix B, we show how to instantiate $\mathsf{F_{Com}}$ in this way, and give a simpler presentation of the commitment scheme of [13] in terms of code-based information-theoretic MACs.

2.3   Auxiliary Protocols

Proof of Commitment to 0. The homomorphic property of both types of commitments implies, as is well known, that P can efficiently convince V that a commitment c contains the value 0:[2]

1. P sends $a = \langle 0 \rangle$ (using fresh randomness) to V.
2. V sends a random challenge $e \in \mathbb{F}$ to P.
3. P opens $d = a + ec$ and V checks that d was correctly opened to reveal 0.

It is easy to see that this is a Σ-protocol, i.e., it is complete, honest verifier zero-knowledge, and special sound in the sense that if any P^* can send a and answer correctly to two different challenges e, e', he must know how to open c to reveal 0. To see this for Type 1 commitments, note that we have randomness values s, s' such that $\mathsf{Commit}(0, s) = a + ec$ and $\mathsf{Commit}(0, s') = a + e'c$ which implies $\mathsf{Commit}(0, s - s') = (e - e')c$. Multiplying by $y = (e - e')^{-1}$ on both sides, we obtain $\mathsf{Commit}(0, y(s - s')) = c + tqc$ for some integer t. By the q-inversion property we can rewrite this as $\mathsf{Commit}(0, y(s - s') - tf_0(c)) = c$ as desired. The proof for Type 2 commitment is trivial and is left to the reader.

---

[2] This can be useful if revealing the randomness used for c might leak side information, so that we do not want to simply open c.

Proof of Multiplication. Another well-known Σ-protocol proves, for commitments $c_x = \langle x \rangle, c_y = \langle y \rangle, c_z = \langle z \rangle$, that $z = xy$:

1. P sends V two commitments $a = \langle \alpha \rangle$ and $b = \langle \alpha y \rangle$ for some random α.
2. V sends a random challenge $e \in \mathbb{F}$ to P.
3. P opens $ec_x + a$, that is, he reveals $w = ex + \alpha$. He also opens $wc_y - ec_z - b$ to reveal 0.
4. V checks that both openings are valid and that the second opening indeed reveals 0.

3 Construction of Compact Proofs of Small Hamming Weight

In this section, we assume that the size of the field $\mathbb{F}$ in the commitments is exponential in the security parameter and hence also (much) larger than n. We will explain how to get rid of this assumption in Sect. 3.1.

We consider a prover who has committed to a vector of field elements $x = (x_1, \ldots, x_n)$ and that wants to claim that the Hamming weight of x is at most d. The idea of the protocol is the following: We first choose distinct elements $a_1, \ldots, a_n \in \mathbb{F}$, and think of a_i as the "index" of the i'th position in the committed string. The way these indices are chosen is fixed in advance, i.e., part of the protocol specification, so that both parties can compute them on their own. In particular, for a field whose characteristic is no less than n, a_i can be simply chosen as i. Now, if the Hamming weight of x is at most d, there exists a monic polynomial of degree at most d whose zeros cover the set of indices a_i where $x_i \neq 0$. The prover is thus asked to prove the existence of such a polynomial $f(x)$ by committing to its coefficients, and then convince the verifier that $\sum_{i=1}^{n} f(a_i)x_i = 0$.

However, this approach fails if used naïvely: The above equation can be easily satisfied for an adversarially chosen $f(x)$, whose zeros might not even intersect with $\{a_i\}$, since the prover knows the x_i's when he chooses $f(x)$. Therefore, to ensure soundness, the committed vector x must be randomised appropriately after the polynomial has been fixed. Multiplying each x_i by independent random values chosen by the verifier will work but requires too much communication. It is possible to resolve this by replacing independent random values with a series of values generated by a secure PRG. The drawback of this method is that it makes the soundness only computational. Below, we propose another idea that uses less randomness while still giving us unconditional soundness.

Protocol Π_{HW}: The public input is the committed vector, $\langle x_1 \rangle, \ldots, \langle x_n \rangle$.

1. The prover commits to d field elements $f_0, \ldots, f_{d-1} \in \mathbb{F}$;
2. The verifier sends a random challenge $\beta \in \mathbb{F}$;
3. Both parties compute $\langle y_i \rangle = \beta^{i-1} \langle x_i \rangle$ for $i = 1, \ldots, n$ and

$$\langle z_j \rangle = \sum_{i=1}^{n} a_i^j \langle y_i \rangle \text{ for } j = 0, \ldots, d;$$

4. The prover commits to d field elements $g_0, \ldots, g_{d-1} \in \mathbb{F}$;
5. Both parties compute

$$\langle v \rangle = \langle z_d \rangle + \sum_{j=0}^{d-1} \langle g_j \rangle;$$

6. The prover proves that $g_j = f_j z_j$ for $j = 0, \ldots, d-1$ and that $v = 0$, using the subprotocols described in the preliminaries.

The theorem below makes the informal statement that Protocol Π_{HW} is complete, sound and zero-knowledge with respect to the statement that the Hamming weight of the committed vector is at most d. For Type 1 commitments this more formally means that it is a zero-knowledge proof system for the language consisting of commitments to a vector of Hamming weight at most d. We cannot use exactly the same formalization for Type 2 commitments since here both the prover and the verifier hold private information and there is no "public" commitment. Instead, we define soundness to mean that if the vector defined by the values sent to $\mathsf{F}_{\mathsf{Com}}$ has Hamming weight greater then d, then the verifier accepts with negligible probability. Completeness means, as usual, that if prover and verifier are honest, then the verifier accepts. Likewise, zero-knowledge means, as usual, that the verifier's view of the protocol with an honest prover can be simulated with (perfectly) indistinguishable distribution. In the proof below, we first give the proof for Type 1 commitments and then state the (minor) changes needed for Type 2.

Theorem 1. *Protocol Π_{HW} is complete, sound and zero-knowledge, with respect to the statement that the Hamming weight of the committed vector $\boldsymbol{x}$ does not exceed d.*

Proof. We prove the protocol satisfies the completeness, soundness and zero-knowledge properties. We define the following two polynomials

$$f(x) = x^d + \sum_{j=0}^{d-1} f_j x^j, \quad F(x) = \sum_{i=0}^{n-1} f(a_{i+1}) x_{i+1} x^i,$$

which will be used in the proof.

Completeness. If the Hamming weight of $\boldsymbol{x}$ does not exceed d, or equivalently, there exists d indices $a_{i_1}, \ldots, a_{i_d}$ s.t. $x_i = 0$ for all $i \notin S = \{i_1, \ldots, i_d\}$, the prover should determine the values to commit to by

$$f(x) = \prod_{j=1}^{d} (x - a_{i_j}), \quad g_j = f_j z_j,$$

and behave as the protocol requires. Computing v, we find

$$
v = z_d + \sum_{j=0}^{d-1} g_j = \sum_{i=1}^{n} a_i^d \beta^{i-1} x_i + \sum_{j=0}^{d-1} \sum_{i=1}^{n} f_j a_i^j \beta^{i-1} x_i
$$

$$
= \sum_{i=1}^{n} \left(a_i^d + \sum_{j=0}^{d-1} f_j a_i^j \right) \beta^{i-1} x_i = \sum_{i=1}^{n} f(a_i) \beta^{i-1} x_i
$$

$$
= \sum_{i \in S} f(a_i) \beta^{i-1} x_i + \sum_{i \notin S} f(a_i) \beta^{i-1} x_i
$$

$$
= \sum_{i \in S} 0 \cdot \beta^{i-1} x_i + \sum_{i \notin S} f(a_i) \beta^{i-1} \cdot 0 = 0,
$$

and the verifier will always accept.

Soundness. Note that $v = F(\beta)$ if $g_j = f_j z_j$ for $j = 0, \ldots, d-1$. Since the degree of $f(x)$ is (exactly) d, it has at most d zeros. If there are at least $d+1$ non-zero x_i's, $F(x)$ cannot be the zero polynomial. Now that $0 \leq \deg F(x) < n$, the probability that a random field element is a zero of $F(x)$ is at most $\frac{n-1}{|\mathbb{F}|}$. For the proof to be accepted, either one of the proofs produced by the subprotocols (to prove $g_j = f_j z_j$, $v = 0$) is false and accepted (each of which occurs with probability at most $|\mathbb{F}|^{-1}$), or β happens to be a zero of $F(x)$. Hence, by union bound and by our assumption on the size of $\mathbb{F}$, the verifier will reject with probability $1 - 2^{-\Omega(k)}$.

For Type 2 commitments, the only additional event that could make the verifier accept is that the prover manages to open any of the commitments in an incorrect way. But by assumption on Type 2 commitments, this occurs with exponentially small probability.

Zero-knowledge. We define a machine T that takes two oracles $\mathcal{O}_f, \mathcal{O}_g$, each of which provides d field elements. The machine T:

1. Starts an instance of the verifier;
2. Reads d field elements from $\mathcal{O}_f$ as $f_0, \ldots, f_{d-1}$;
3. Outputs $\langle f_j \rangle$ (committed with fresh randomness);
4. Reads β from the verifier;
5. Computes $\langle y_i \rangle$ and $\langle z_j \rangle$ as described in the protocol;
6. Reads d field elements from $\mathcal{O}_g$ as $g_0, \ldots, g_{d-1}$;
7. Outputs $\langle g_j \rangle$ (committed with fresh randomness);
8. Computes $\langle v \rangle$ as described in the protocol;
9. Runs the simulators for "proving" $g_j = f_j z_j$ and $v = 0$, and outputs the transcripts.

We will use some special oracles: $\mathcal{O}_f^{\text{real}}$ provides f_j's the honest prover uses; $\mathcal{O}_f^{\text{forged}}$ provides forged f_j's, just zeros, for instance. $\mathcal{O}_g^{\text{real}}$ and $\mathcal{O}_g^{\text{forged}}$ are defined similarly.

The simulator is defined as T taking $\mathcal{O}_f^{\text{forged}}, \mathcal{O}_g^{\text{forged}}$. We employ a standard hybrid argument to show that the simulator works. Consider the following distributions:

- D_1: the transcript created by the honest prover and the verifier;
- D_2: the transcript created by the honest prover and the verifier, but with simulated transcripts for the subprotocols; or equivalently, the transcript produced by T taking $\mathcal{O}_f^{\text{real}}, \mathcal{O}_g^{\text{real}}$;
- D_3: the transcript created by T taking $\mathcal{O}_f^{\text{real}}, \mathcal{O}_g^{\text{forged}}$;
- D_4: the transcript created by T taking $\mathcal{O}_f^{\text{forged}}, \mathcal{O}_g^{\text{forged}}$, or equivalently, that produced by the simulator.

Since the subprotocols are (honest-verifier) zero-knowledge, D_1 and D_2 are indistinguishable. The difference between D_2 and D_3 is whether g_j's contain real or forged values, and D_3 and D_4, f_j's. Since the commitment scheme is hiding, D_2, D_3 and D_3, D_4 are pairs of indistinguishable distributions, which follows from the definition of hiding by a standard computational reduction.

Formally, let D be an effective distinguisher telling D_2 from D_3, we build the following adversary that tries to break the hiding property:

1. The adversary makes a commitment to x and uses it as the public input; note that since the adversary knows x, it is capable of implementing $\mathcal{O}_t^{\text{real}}$ ($t = f, g$);
2. The adversary creates an oracle $\mathcal{O}_g^{\text{challenge}}$, which:
   (a) Runs $\mathcal{O}_g^{\text{real}}$ to produce g_j^{real}'s;
   (b) Runs $\mathcal{O}_g^{\text{forged}}$ to produce g_j^{forged}'s;
   (c) Sends the two batches to the challenger, and outputs whatever the challenger outputs;
3. The adversary runs T with $\mathcal{O}_f^{\text{real}}, \mathcal{O}_g^{\text{challenge}}$ to obtain a transcript;
4. It sends the transcript to D;
5. If D says the transcript is from D_2, the adversary concludes that the commitments the call to $\mathcal{O}_g^{\text{challenge}}$ received from the challenger are those of g_j^{real}'s; otherwise, those of g_j^{forged}'s.

D sees D_2 [resp. D_3] if $\mathcal{O}_g^{\text{challenge}}$ (the adversary) was given the commitments of g_j^{real}'s [resp. g_j^{forged}'s]. Therefore, the adversary has the same advantage against the hiding property as D has against D_2 and D_3. Moreover, the adversary is also effective. Since the commitment scheme is hiding, the adversary must have negligible advantage and so must D. A similar construction proves that D_3 and D_4 are also indistinguishable.

For Type 2 commitments, the argument becomes simpler: We define the oracles to output only what the verifier sees when a Type 2 commitment is created. Further, as these commitments are perfectly hiding, the forged and the real oracles now output exactly the same distribution, so we immediately get perfect zero-knowledge.

3.1   Field Extension

The basic protocol we just described does not work for small fields: we may not be able to choose n distinct values a_i, and even if we can, the field size may be too small to guarantee a small enough soundness error. In addition, we assumed the field was prime when defining Type 1 commitments.

We can solve both problems by going to an extension field $\mathbb{K}$, which we choose as a degree t extension of $\mathbb{F}$, so that $|\mathbb{K}|$ is exponential in the security parameter k. One possible value for t is $\left\lceil \frac{k}{\log |\mathbb{F}|} \right\rceil$.

Going from $\mathbb{F}$ to its extension $\mathbb{K}$ also requires enlarging G, H. For Type 2 commitments where these are vector spaces, this can be done using the tensor product, i.e., use $G' = G \otimes \mathbb{K}$ and $H' = H \otimes \mathbb{K}$, and induce the commitment schemes accordingly. Type 1 commitments can be extended in a similar manner. The following is a concrete explanation for extending Type 1 commitments. It also applies to Type 2 commitments, which is exactly the computational way of doing tensor products.

We have to fix a basis of $\mathbb{K}$ over $\mathbb{F}$ in advance. The new sets of randomness and commitments are $G' = G^t, H' = H^t$, in which additions are induced naturally. For all $b \in \mathbb{K}$ and $r = (r_1, \ldots, r_t)^{\mathrm{T}} \in G'$, we first find the matrix M_b of endomorphism $x \mapsto bx$ of $\mathbb{K}$ under the fixed basis, and define

$$ br = M_b \begin{pmatrix} r_1 \\ \vdots \\ r_t \end{pmatrix}, $$

where the multiplication on the right-hand side is formal and regarding elements in $\mathbb{F}$ as integers. Scalar multiplication in H' is defined similarly. For the induction of commitment algorithm, one simply commits to $a \in \mathbb{K}$ with randomness $r \in U'$ by committing coordinatewise. That is, let the coordinates of a under the fixed basis be $(a_1, \ldots, a_t)^{\mathrm{T}}$, we define

$$ \mathsf{Commit}_{\mathrm{pk}}(a, r) = (\mathsf{Commit}_{\mathrm{pk}}(a_1, r_1), \ldots, \mathsf{Commit}_{\mathrm{pk}}(a_t, r_t))^{\mathrm{T}}. $$

The newly defined $\mathsf{Commit}_{\mathrm{pk}}$ is binding, hiding and additively homomorphic thanks to the commitment scheme of $\mathbb{F}$. Moreover, it is trivial to verify that the commitment scheme is capable of performing scalar multiplication, or precisely $b\mathsf{Commit}_{\mathrm{pk}}(a, r) = \mathsf{Commit}_{\mathrm{pk}}(ba, br)$ for all $a, b \in \mathbb{K}, r \in G'$, thus linearly homomorphic. For the q-inversion property, for all $c = (c_1, \ldots, c_t)^{\mathrm{T}}$, after a series of additions and multiplication by clear-text field elements, the resulting commitment is $d = Mc$ for some integer matrix M. Note well that modulo operation cannot be performed on M in between the operations. However, should d always contain 0, it must be the case that entries of M are multiples of $|\mathbb{F}|$, therefore, by the q-inversion property of the scheme in $\mathbb{F}$, along with its (additively) homomorphic property, we obtain a similar property that allows us to "explain" commitments that should always contain 0 as 0.

If the basis starts with 1 (the field identity), when we are given the input commitments over $\mathbb{F}$ $\langle x_1 \rangle, \ldots, \langle x_n \rangle$ for $x_i \in \mathbb{F}$, we can easily modify these to commitments over $\mathbb{K}$ by appending $t - 1$ default commitments to 0 to each $\langle x_i \rangle$ (the randomness input used for these commitments should be deterministic so that no communication overhead is incurred). We can then execute the main protocol exactly as described using $\mathbb{K}$ instead of $\mathbb{F}$ as the base field.

By moving to $\mathbb{K}$, we now get soundness error $2^{-\Omega(k)}$, and the complexity in terms of number of commitments over $\mathbb{F}$ sent is indeed $O\left(\frac{kd}{\log |\mathbb{F}|}\right)$ as promised in the introduction.

4 Applications

4.1 Actively Secure d-out-of-n Oblivious Transfer

In a d-out-of-n OT protocol, a sender has n messages, and a receiver wishes to learn exactly d of these, without revealing to the sender which messages were chosen. We consider the *non-adaptive* setting, where the receiver's d selections are chosen all at once, and refer to this functionality as $\binom{n}{d}$-OT_k, where the sender's messages are strings of length k (the security parameter).

Naor and Pinkas [34] showed how to construct $\binom{n}{d}$-OT in a black-box manner from $O(d \log n)$ instances of $\binom{2}{1}$-OT, however, their protocol is only secure in a half-simulation paradigm, and is vulnerable to selective failure attacks against a corrupt sender [12]. Another construction by Shankar et al. [41] uses only $O(n)$ 1-out-of-2 OTs, and an elegant mechanism based on secret-sharing to prevent the receiver from learning more than d messages. However, this is also not fully secure against a corrupt sender. The only known actively secure protocols are based on specific assumptions like DDH or pairings [12,24] and require $\Omega(n)$ public-key operations. These are inherently less efficient than constructions based on $\binom{2}{1}$-OT as they cannot make use of efficient OT extension techniques, which reduce the number of public key operations needed for OT to $O(k)$ (independent of the total number of OTs) [27].

We show how to use the proof of Hamming weight from Sect. 3 to construct an actively secure protocol for $\binom{n}{d}$-OT_k, which makes only black-box use of $\binom{2}{1}$-OT_k and symmetric primitives. The communication cost of the basic protocol is $O(kn+k^2d)$, or can be reduced to an amortized cost of $O(kn)$ in a batch setting, which is optimal up to a constant factor.

The Commitment Scheme. Our construction uses a specific form of Type 2 homomorphic commitment scheme defined by the functionality $\mathsf{F}_{\mathrm{Com}}$ below. Note that this is identical to the aBit functionality from [35] (optimized in [36]), only here we use it as a commitment scheme instead of for two-party computation. $\mathsf{F}_{\mathrm{Com}}$ can be efficiently implemented using black-box access to k oblivious transfers in a setup phase and a pseudorandom generator.

Functionality $\mathsf{F}_{\mathsf{Com}}$

On initialisation with the security parameter k, the functionality samples a random field element $\alpha \in \mathbb{F}_{2^k}$ and sends it to P_R.
On receiving a message $x \in \mathbb{F}_{2^k}$ from P_S:

1. Sample $\beta \in \mathbb{F}_{2^k}$ at random.
2. Send β to P_R and $\gamma := \alpha \cdot x + \beta$ to P_S.

To commit to a message x, the sender P_S sends x to $\mathsf{F}_{\mathsf{Com}}$. The verification algorithm for the receiver, P_R, takes as input a message x_i and the verification information $(\gamma_i, \alpha, \beta_i)$, then simply checks that $\gamma_i = \alpha \cdot x_i + \beta_i$.

The scheme is perfectly hiding, since the verifier's data α, β_i is uniformly random and independent of the sender's messages. The scheme is statistically binding, because opening to $x_i' \neq x_i$ requires coming up with $\gamma_i' = \alpha \cdot x_i' + \beta_i$, hence $\gamma_i' - \gamma_i = \alpha \cdot (x_i' - x_i)$, but this requires guessing α so happens with probability at most 2^{-k}. The scheme is also *linearly homomorphic* over $\mathbb{F}_{2^k}$, since if $f : \mathbb{F}_{2^k}^n \rightarrow \mathbb{F}_{2^k}$ is a linear map, then

$$f(\alpha \cdot x_1 + \beta_1, \ldots, \alpha \cdot x_n + \beta_n) = \alpha \cdot f(x_1, \ldots, x_n) + f(\beta_1, \ldots, \beta_n),$$

so applying f to the commitment and opening information results in a valid commitment to $f(x_1, \ldots, x_n)$.

The functionality $\mathsf{F}_{\mathsf{Com}}$ can be implemented using 1-out-of-2 string-OT, as shown in previous works for messages in $\{0, 1\}$. To commit to a bit $x \in \{0, 1\}$, the parties perform an OT where P_A is the sender with inputs $(\beta, \beta + \alpha)$, for randomly sampled $\alpha, \beta \in \mathbb{F}_{2^k}$, and P_B inputs the choice bit x. P_B receives $\gamma = \beta + x \cdot \alpha$, as required. To obtain active security, a consistency check is needed to ensure that the correct inputs are provided to the OTs. This can be done with only a small, constant overhead [36] using techniques based on OT extension [31,35].

We can extend the above to commit to arbitrary field elements instead of just bits using the homomorphic property, as follows. To commit to the field element $x \in \mathbb{F}_{2^k}$, first write x as $\sum_{i=1}^{k} x_i \cdot X^{k-1}$, for $x_i \in \mathbb{F}_2$, where the vector $(1, X, \ldots, X^{k-1})$ defines a basis of $\mathbb{F}_{2^k}$ over $\mathbb{F}_2$. Then, P_B commits to the individual bits x_i, obtaining commitments $\langle x_i \rangle$, and both parties then compute the commitment $\langle x \rangle = \sum_{i=1}^{k} \langle x_i \rangle \cdot X^{i-1}$.

Efficiency. Using the protocol from [36] (based on [35]), after a setup phase consisting of $O(k)$ OTs, the cost of committing to a bit is that of sending $O(k)$ bits, plus some computation with a PRG. To commit to an arbitrary field element we require k bit commitments, which gives a communication cost of $O(k^2)$.

d-out-of-n OT Protocol. We now show how to realise $\binom{n}{d}$-OT_k using this commitment scheme, and applying the zero-knowledge proof of Hamming weight from Sect. 3. The idea is for the OT receiver to commit to a selection vector $(x_1, \ldots, x_n) \in \{0, 1\}^n$ defining its d choices, and prove that at most d of these are non-zero. Then, we use a hash function to convert the commitments to the x_i's into 1-out-of-2 OTs, where the second message in each OT is one of the sender's inputs. The zero-knowledge proof ensures that the receiver learns at most d of these inputs.

We use the definition of a *correlation robust* hash function $H : \mathbb{F}_{2^k} \to \{0,1\}^k$, which satisfies the following security property:

Definition 1 [27]. *Let $n = \mathsf{poly}(k)$ and $t_1, \ldots, t_n, \alpha$ be uniformly sampled from $\{0,1\}^k$. Then, H is* correlation robust *if the distribution*

$$(t_1, \ldots, t_n, H(t_1 \oplus \alpha), \ldots, H(t_n \oplus \alpha))$$

is computationally indistinguishable from the uniform distribution on $2nk$ bits.

Protocol: The receiver, P_R, has d choices $c_1, \ldots, c_d \in [n]$. The sender, P_S, inputs strings $y_1, \ldots, y_n \in \{0,1\}^k$.

1. P_R defines $\boldsymbol{x} = (x_1, \ldots, x_n) \in \{0,1\}^n$ to be the weight-d selection vector defined by P_R's choices.
2. The parties initialise $\mathsf{F}_{\mathsf{Com}}$, where P_S acts as receiver and obtains $\alpha \in \mathbb{F}_{2^k}$.
3. P_R commits to x_i using $\mathsf{F}_{\mathsf{Com}}$, for $i = 1, \ldots, n$, and receives γ_i. P_S receives the commitments β_i.
4. P_R proves that $w_H(\boldsymbol{x}) \leq d$ using Π_{HW}.
5. P_S sends to P_R the values

$$z_i = H(\beta_i + \alpha) \oplus y_i$$

6. P_R outputs $y_i = z_i \oplus H(\gamma_i)$, for the values where $x_i = 1$.

Theorem 2. *If H satisfies the correlation robustness property then the protocol above securely realises the $\binom{n}{d}$-OT functionality in the $\mathsf{F}_{\mathsf{Com}}$-hybrid model.*

Proof. We first consider the simpler case of a corrupt sender, P_S^*. The simulator, $\mathcal{S}$, sends random field elements α, β_i to simulate the outputs of $\mathsf{F}_{\mathsf{Com}}$ to P_S^*. $\mathcal{S}$ then runs the zero-knowledge simulator from Π_{HW}. Next, $\mathcal{S}$ receives the values z_i from P_S^* and recovers $y_i = z_i \oplus H(\beta_i + \alpha)$, for $i = 1, \ldots, n$. Finally, $\mathcal{S}$ sends the sender's inputs $y_1, \ldots, y_n$ to the $\binom{n}{d}$-OT functionality. It is easy to see that the simulation is identically distributed to the view of P_S^* in the real protocol, because the α, β_i values are sampled identically to the real protocol, and the zero-knowledge simulator for Π_{HW} is perfect when used with Type 2 commitments.

When the receiver, P_R^*, is corrupted, the simulator $\mathcal{S}$ proceeds as follows. First, $\mathcal{S}$ receives the bits $x_1, \ldots, x_n$ as the receiver's input to $\mathsf{F}_{\mathsf{Com}}$, and sends back random field elements $\gamma_1, \ldots, \gamma_n$. $\mathcal{S}$ simulates the verifier's messages in Π_{HW} with uniformly random values, and aborts if the proof fails. If the proof succeeds, then by the soundness property of Π_{HW} it holds that $w_H(\boldsymbol{x}) \leq d$, so $\mathcal{S}$ extracts d choices $c_1, \ldots, c_d \in \{1, \ldots, n\}$ from the non-zero entries of $\boldsymbol{x}$ (if $w_H(\boldsymbol{x}) < d$ then $\mathcal{S}$ chooses arbitrary indices for the last $d - w_H(\boldsymbol{x})$ choices). $\mathcal{S}$ sends $c_1, \ldots, c_d$ to $\binom{n}{d}$-OT, and receives back the strings $y_{c_1}, \ldots, y_{c_d}$. In the final step, for the indices i where $x_i = 1$, $\mathcal{S}$ sends $z_i = H(\gamma_i) \oplus y_i$, and for all i where $x_i = 0$, $\mathcal{S}$ samples z_i uniformly from $\{0, 1\}^k$.

Up until the final step, the simulation for a corrupt receiver is perfect, because the γ_i values are identically distributed to those output by $\mathsf{F_{Com}}$, and Π_{HW} (and its subprotocols) are public-coin, so the verifier's messages are uniformly random. Regarding the z_i values, first note that whenever $x_i = 1$, P_R^* obtains the correct output y_i in both the real and simulated executions. When $x_i = 0$, the z_i's sent in the protocol are computationally indistinguishable from the simulated random values, by the correlation robustness property. More formally, suppose there exists an environment $\mathcal{Z}$ and an adversary $\mathcal{A}$, who corrupts the receiver, such that $\mathcal{Z}$ distinguishes the real and ideal executions. We construct a distinguisher D for the correlation robust function, as follows:

- D receives a correlation robustness challenge $(t_1, \ldots, t_n, u_1, \ldots, u_n)$.
- D invokes $\mathcal{Z}$ with the corrupt receiver, $\mathcal{A}$, starting a simulated execution of the d-out-of-n OT protocol. D receives the sender's inputs $y_1, \ldots, y_n$, chosen by $\mathcal{Z}$.
- Instead of sampling γ_i at random, D sends $t_1, \ldots, t_n$ to simulate these values sent to $\mathcal{A}$.
- For the indices i where $x_i = 0$, D lets $z_i = u_i \oplus y_i$. The rest of the execution is simulated the same way as $\mathcal{S}$.
- After the execution, D outputs the same as $\mathcal{Z}$.

Note that if the $u_1, \ldots, u_n$ values from the challenge are uniformly random, then the view of $\mathcal{Z}$ is identical to the view in the previous simulation. On the other hand, if $u_1, \ldots, u_n$ are computed as $H(t_i \oplus \alpha)$, for some random $\alpha \in \{0, 1\}^k$, then $z_i = u_i \oplus y_i$ (where $x_i = 0$) is distributed the same as in the real protocol, so the view of $\mathcal{Z}$ is identical to the real execution. Therefore, D breaks the correlation robustness property of H with exactly the same probability that $\mathcal{Z}$ distinguishes the real and ideal executions.

Efficiency. The main cost of the protocol is the initial n calls to $\mathsf{F_{Com}}$ to commit to the x_i bits, followed by running the proof Π_{HW}, which requires committing to $O(d)$ additional field elements. Since committing to a bit costs $O(k)$ bits of communication, and a field element $O(k^2)$, we get an overall communication complexity of $O(nk + k^2d)$.

Reducing Communication with Amortization. In a batch setting, where two parties wish to perform multiple, parallel instances of $\binom{n}{d}$-OT_k, for the same values of d and n, we can reduce the amortized communication cost to $O(nk)$, which is optimal up to a constant factor. Instead of using the commitment scheme $\mathsf{F_{Com}}$, we make use of recent advances homomorphic commitments based on OT and error-correcting codes [13, 22]. These allow to commit to a vector of ℓ field elements with $o(1)$ communication overhead, for $\ell = \Omega(k)$. When performing many parallel executions of our protocol, this means steps 1–4 can be done with only $O(nk)$ amortized communication, instead of $O(nk + k^2d)$. However, now we have a problem in the final step where the sender hashes the commitments to transfer its inputs, because this is not compatible with the schemes of [13,22]. To get around this, the receiver will also commit to $x_1, \ldots, x_n$ using $\mathsf{F}_{\mathrm{Com}}$, and then prove that the two sets of commitments contain the same values. This can be shown by opening a (masked) random linear combination of the $\mathsf{F}_{\mathrm{Com}}$ commitments, then opening the same linear combination with the code-based commitments and checking that these give the same value. We give more details on this protocol and how to instantiate a Type 2 commitment scheme with code-based commitments in Appendix B.

4.2   Separable Accountable Ring Signatures

Ring signatures [40] enable a member of a group to leak information on behalf of the group without compromising its own identity. More precisely, ring signatures allow a signer to dynamically choose a group of potential signers and then sign a message on behalf of this group. A verifier can verify that the signature was indeed created by one of the group members, but cannot learn who the signer is. In [42], Xu and Yung introduce the notion of accountable ring signatures, where, in addition to a regular ring signature scheme, the signer can dynamically pick a trusted entity, called the opener, and, in addition to signing anonymously on behalf of the group, prove that this entity can revoke the signers anonymity. Accountable ring signatures imply traditional group signatures [7].

Since the members of a ring signatures are chosen dynamically, realistically speaking we can not always assume that all members use the same signing algorithm or even have the same type of public keys. Ideally, we would like to have a ring signature scheme, where we can sign on behalf of a group even if all members use different signing algorithms and different types of keys. This issue of *separability* has been first considered in the context of identity escrow [33] and later also in the context of group signatures [10,11]. Here, to the best of our knowledge, we provide the first construction of accountable ring signatures that achieves such separability. The only assumption we make on the public keys of the group members is that there exists a Σ-protocol for proving knowledge of the corresponding secret key.

Assume there are n parties $P_1, \ldots, P_n$, each holding a key pair $(\mathrm{pk}_i, \mathrm{sk}_i)$. Furthermore, assume that for each key pair, there is a Σ-protocol Σ_i to prove knowledge of the secret key sk_i corresponding to pk_i. Using an OR-proof [16] over all Σ_i, it is straightforward to prove knowledge of one of the secret keys while not revealing its own identity. Combining such an OR-proof with the Fiat-Shamir heuristic, we immediately get a separable ring signature scheme. To construct a separable accountable ring signature scheme, we additionally need to ensure that the designated opener, who has the key pair $(\mathrm{pk}_{\mathrm{op}}, \mathrm{td}_{\mathrm{op}})$, can extract the signer's identity from the Σ-protocol's transcript. Our main idea here is to "encode" the signer's identity into the protocol's challenge values and then use our compact proofs to prove that this has been done correctly. More concretely, recall that when an honest prover P_j does the OR-proof, there will be a Σ-protocol instance executed for each of the n parties. These will all be simulated executions, except the j'th one. Now, we will interpret all challenges $e_1, \ldots, e_n$ in the Σ-protocols as commitments, and exploit the fact that P_j can choose all the simulated challenges as he likes, only e_j will be random. We can therefore instruct P_j to pick e_i where $i \neq j$ to be homomorphic commitments to 0. This means that $e_1, \ldots, e_n$, when seen as commitments, will represent a vector of Hamming weight at most 1, so P_j will prove this fact using our compact proof.

Assume we are using computationally hiding, perfectly binding, commitments. A (polynomial time) verifier cannot distinguish commitments to random bit strings from commitments to 0. Therefore, by the properties of Σ-protocols, the verifier cannot distinguish a simulated from a real transcript. The opener, who possesses a trapdoor $\mathrm{td_{op}}$, can break the hiding property of the commitment scheme. That is, the opener can use $\mathrm{td_{op}}$ to check whether a commitment contains a specific message, e.g. 0, or not. This is the case if, for example, the commitment scheme is actually a public-key encryption scheme. To identify a signer, the opener can open all challenge commitments and find the commitment to a non-zero value.

We will now describe our separable accountable ring signature scheme in the form of a group identification scheme with revocable anonymity. Combining this identification scheme with Fiat-Shamir then gives us our desired signature scheme. For a full formal definition of accountable ring signatures we refer the reader to [7].

Group identification scheme with revocable anonymity: Let Encode be a bijective function that maps elements from the commitment's message, randomness, and commitment space to bit strings. Let Decode be the inverse of Encode. Let P_j be the prover and $\{P_1, \ldots, P_n\}$ the group. Let $(\mathrm{pk_{op}}, \mathrm{td_{op}})$ be the opener's key pair for a perfectly binding, computationally hiding commitment scheme, where $\mathrm{td_{op}}$ can be used to break the hiding property of a commitment.

Membership protocol

1. For $i \neq j$, the prover chooses uniformly random values r_i, computes $c_i = \mathrm{Commit_{pk_{op}}}(0, r_i)$, and encodes it as $e_i = \mathrm{Encode}(c_i)$. Next, for each e_i, the prover uses the simulator Σ_i to obtain transcripts (a_i, e_i, z_i). Finally, the prover chooses a random a_j according to Σ_j and sends $(a_1, \ldots, a_n)$ to the verifier.
2. The verifier chooses a random $x \neq 0$ and r and sends the challenge $e = \mathrm{Encode}(x, r)$ to the prover.
3. The prover computes $(x, r) = \mathrm{Decode}(e)$, picks commitment c_j such that $\sum_{i=1}^{n} c_i = \mathrm{Commit_{pk_{op}}}(x, r)$, and computes proof π for $w_H((c_1, \ldots, c_n)) \leq 1$ using Π_{HW}. Knowing a_j and $e_j = \mathrm{Encode}(c_j)$, the prover computes z_j honestly according to Σ_j. It sends $(c_1, \ldots, c_n)$, $(z_1, \ldots, z_n)$, and π to the verifier.
4. The verifier checks the validity of π, it checks that $\sum_{i=1}^{n} c_i = \mathrm{Commit_{pk_{op}}}(x, r)$, and finally it checks that for $1 \leq i \leq n$ each transcript (a_i, e_i, z_i) is an accepting transcript for Σ_i.

Anonymity Revocation. Given the transcript $\{(a_i, e_i, z_i)\}_{1 \leq i \leq n}$ of an invocation of the membership protocol described above, the opener can, for each i, compute $c_i = \mathsf{Decode}(e_i)$ and using his trapdoor $\mathsf{td_{op}}$ it can reveal which commitment c_j is to a value not equal 0.

There are two things to note at this point. First, since the commitment scheme is *perfectly* binding, even an computationally unbounded opener can not open any of the commitments to any value other than the actually committed one. Secondly, the opener only needs to be able to distinguish commitments to 0 from commitments to any other value. In particular, this is a weaker requirement that recovering the exact committed message.

Security: In the following we provide an informal description of the security properties of accountable ring signatures. We sketch why our construction is secure according to these properties. The formal security definitions can be found in [7].

Full Unforgeability. From a high-level perspective, this property encompasses two security requirements. First, a corrupted opener cannot falsely accuse any member of a group of creating a signature. Second, no coalition of corrupted members in a ring can create an signature on behalf of an honest member.

Proof (sketch). Let $\sigma = (a_1, \ldots, a_n, e_1, \ldots, e_n, z_1, \ldots, z_n)$ be a valid signature created the adversary. Due to the (special) soundness of Π_{HW} we know that at most one commitment from $e_1, \ldots, e_n$ is not a commitment to 0. Let i be the index of the commitment that is not equal to 0 and j be the index of an honest member. Assume the opener accuses P_j of being the signer and consider the two following cases: If $i \neq j$, then the commitment c_j is a commitment to 0 and thus a malicious opener, who successfully accuses P_j would immediately contradict the binding property of the commitment scheme. In the case of $i = j$, the adversary successfully signed on behalf of an honest member P_j, which would contradict the (special) soundness of Σ_j.

Anonymity. This property ensures that nobody but the opener can reveal the identity of the ring member that created a signature. The anonymity property has to hold even when the secret keys of all members are revealed.

Proof (sketch). This property directly follows from the hiding property of the commitment scheme and the witness indistinguishability of the OR-proof construction.

Traceability. This property guarantees that the opener can always identify the signer and that the opener can provide a publicly verifiable proof thereof.

Proof (sketch). Let $\sigma = (a_1, \ldots, a_n, e_1, \ldots, e_n, z_1, \ldots, z_n)$ be a valid signature created by the adversary. Consider the following cases. If $\mathsf{HW}(c_1, \ldots, c_n) > 1$, then the adversary can be used to break the soundness property of Π_{HW}. In the case of $\mathsf{HW}(c_1, \ldots, c_n) = 1$, let i be the index of the commitment not equal to 0 and let P_j be the member that is accused by the opener. In this case either P_j was indeed the signer or we can use the adversary to break the soundness of Σ_j.

Tracing Soundness. This soundness property ensures that even if all members in a group and the opener are fully corrupt, the opener can still not accuse two different members of the ring.

Proof (sketch). This directly follows from the soundness of Π_{HW}.

4.3   More Efficient Preprocessing for the TinyTable Protocol

TinyTable [18] is a secure two-party computation protocol based on a 'gate scrambling' technique. It evaluates a circuit by expressing every non-linear gate with its truth table, and using a scrambled version of this table to perform the secure computation. This leads to a protocol in the preprocessing model with a very efficient online phase, where each non-linear gate requires just one message to be sent from each party, and linear gates can be evaluated without interaction. For small tables such as two-input AND gates, [18] showed to efficiently implement the preprocessing phase based on TinyOT [35], but for larger tables (such as representations of the S-boxes in 3-DES or AES) this approach does not scale well. Keller et al. [30] recently presented a more efficient approach to creating the masked tables using multiplication triples over a finite field of characteristic two. For the case of secure computation of AES, this gives a preprocessing phase that is almost as efficient as the best 2-party computation protocols based on garbled circuits, but with the benefits of the high throughput available in the TinyTable online phase.

We show how to further reduce the cost of the preprocessing phase, by combining our compact proof of Hamming weight with secret-shared finite field multiplications. Our approach requires just one multiplication triple per lookup table, whereas the previous method [30] needs at least $\log_2 N - 1$ triples for a table of size N (albeit over a smaller field). Our method concretely reduces the amount of communication needed for the preprocessing by around a factor of two, for lookup tables of size 32–64.

TinyTable Background. TinyTable uses linearly homomorphic, information-theoretic MACs to authenticate secret-shared data between the two parties.[3] The MACs are identical to our commitments produced by $\mathsf{F_{Com}}$ in Sect. 4.1: the MACs on a shared value $x = x_1 + x_2$ are of the form $\gamma_{x_1} = x_1 \cdot \alpha_2 + \beta_{x_1}$ and $\gamma_{x_2} = x_2 \cdot \alpha_1 + \beta_{x_2}$, where P_A holds $(x_1, \gamma_{x_1}, \beta_{x_1}, \alpha_1)$ and P_B holds $(x_2, \gamma_{x_2}, \beta_{x_2}, \alpha_2)$. We use the notation $\langle x_1 \rangle_A$ and $\langle x_2 \rangle_B$ to denote these committed values held by P_A and P_B.

The goal of the preprocessing phase is to produce, for a public lookup table $T = (T[0], \ldots, T[n-1])$, the values:

$$\left(\langle s_i \rangle_i, \langle v_0^i \rangle_i, \ldots, \langle v_{n-1}^i \rangle_i \right)_{i \in \{A,B\}}$$

---

[3] TinyTable can also be extended to the multi-party setting [30], but here we focus on the two-party case.

where v_j^A, v_j^B are random shares that sum to $T[j \oplus s_A \oplus s_B]$, and s_A, s_B are random strings of length $\ell = \log_2 n$.

In [30], it was shown that it is enough for the parties to produce these values for the simple table where $T[0] = 1$ and $T[j] = 0$ for all $j > 0$. In other words, if the above shares satisfy $v_s^A + v_s^B = 1$ (where $s = s_A \oplus s_B$ is represented as an integer in $\{0, \ldots, n-1\}$), and $v_j^A + v_j^B = 0$ for all $j \neq s$, the parties can locally convert these shares into a scrambled table for *any* lookup table T of size n.

Preprocessing Protocol. We now show how to compute the above preprocessing data, using the Type 2 commitment scheme from Sect. 4.1 based on $\mathsf{F_{Com}}$, and our proof of Hamming weight.

Additional Tools. Our protocol also requires the parties to be able to bit decompose committed values, and multiply secret-shared, committed values. Bit decomposition of a committed value $\langle x \rangle$, for $x \in \mathbb{F}_{2^k}$, can be done by first committing to the bits $\langle x_1 \rangle, \ldots, \langle x_k \rangle$, then opening $\langle x \rangle + \sum_i \langle x_i \rangle X^{i-1}$ and checking that this equals zero.

To produce a secret-sharing of the product of two committed values, where each value is held by a different party, we use a multiplication triple and Beaver's technique [4]. The current, most efficient methods of generating multiplication triples are based on oblivious transfer with the MASCOT [32] or Tiny-OLE [19] protocols. Note that these protocols create information-theoretic MACs on shares of the triples, but these MACs have the same form as the commitments produced by $\mathsf{F_{Com}}$, so we can use them for our purpose.

With these building blocks, our protocol for preprocessing a masked lookup table of size n is as follows. We assume that $\mathsf{F_{Com}}$ operates over the field $\mathbb{F}_{2^{2n}}$ and fix $(1, X, \ldots, X^{2n-1})$ as a basis over $\mathbb{F}_2$ of this field.

Protocol Π_{Prep}:

1. P_A samples a random, weight-one vector $(a_1, \ldots, a_n) \in \mathbb{F}_2^n$, and P_B samples $(b_1, \ldots, b_n)$ in the same way.
2. Both parties commit to the components of their vectors using $\mathsf{F_{Com}}$, obtaining $\langle a_1 \rangle_A, \ldots, \langle a_n \rangle_A$ and $\langle b_1 \rangle_B, \ldots, \langle b_n \rangle_B$.
3. Compute $\sum_{i=1}^n \langle a_i \rangle_A$ and $\sum_i \langle b_i \rangle_B$ and check that these both open to 1.
4. Run Π_{HW} twice to prove that $w_H(\boldsymbol{a}) \leq 1$ and $w_H(\boldsymbol{b}) \leq 1$.
5. Let $\langle a \rangle_A = \sum_{i=1}^n \langle a_i \rangle_A \cdot X^{i-1}$ and $\langle b \rangle_B = \sum_{i=1}^n \langle b_i \rangle_B \cdot X^{i-1}$.
6. Using a random multiplication triple over $\mathbb{F}_{2^{2n}}$, compute commitments $\langle c^A \rangle_A$ and $\langle c^B \rangle_B$, such that $c^A + c^B = a \cdot b$.
7. For $j \in \{A, B\}$, bit decompose $\langle c^j \rangle_j$ to obtain $\langle c_1^j \rangle_j, \ldots, \langle c_{2n}^j \rangle_j$.
8. For $j \in \{A, B\}$, P_j outputs $(\langle c_1^j \rangle_j + \langle c_{n+1}^j \rangle_j, \ldots, \langle c_n^j \rangle_j + \langle c_{2n}^j \rangle_j)$.

Correctness and security. First note that the check that $\sum_i a_i = \sum_i b_i = 1$ rules out these vectors being all zero, therefore after Π_{HW} we know that they must have weight one. This means we can write the corresponding field elements as $a = X^r$ and $b = X^s$, where r and s represent the position of the one in each party's random vector. Viewing these as elements of the larger field $\mathbb{F}_{2^{2n}}$, the product computed in step 6 then satisfies $c = X^{r+s}$, and has freshly random shares and MACs from the multiplication triple. The bit decomposition and computation in steps 7–8 then ensure that the output contains a one in position $r + s \pmod{n}$, and is zero elsewhere, as required.

Comparison with Other Approaches. The main cost in our protocol is that of generating one multiplication triple over $\mathbb{F}_{2^{2n}}$. In contrast, the protocol of [30] requires at least $\log_2 n - 1$ triples over a smaller field (depending on the table size, n). For example, if working over $\mathbb{F}_{2^{40}}$, [30] needs 4 triples for a table of size 32, but this increases to 7 triples when $n = 128$ and 11 when $n = 256$. We compare the communication complexity of our protocol with [30] in Table 1. The cost describes the total communication needed to generate enough triples for one masked table of size n, when using either the MASCOT [32] or TinyOLE [19] protocols for triple generation. For small tables of sizes 32–64, our protocol reduces the communication cost by around a factor of 2 compared with previous work. The reduction in communication seems more significant with TinyOLE, since MASCOT scales as $O(n^2)$ if n is the bit-length of the field, whereas TinyOLE is $O(n)$.

Table 1. Communication complexity, in kbits, of our protocol and the previous protocol when instantiated using MASCOT or TinyOLE to generate triples.

Protocol	$n = 32$	64	128	256	
[30]	279.0	348.8	488.3	767.4	} MASCOT
Ours	139.3	360.4	917.8	2612	
[30]	225.0	281.3	393.8	618.8	} TinyOLE
Ours	90.0	180.0	360.0	720.0	

4.4   Shuffling in Public

Suppose that n parties wish to run a protocol in which each party inputs a message and the output is a (secret) permutation of the messages. This is called a *shuffle*. Of course, this shuffle could be executed by a trusted party. In absence of a trusted party, a *mixnet* [14] can be used. A mixnet consists of a number of servers and takes n ciphertexts as input. Each server permutes the ciphertexts, re-encrypts them, and hands them to the next server. If at least one server is honest, then the resulting permutation is unknown to an adversary. In addition, each server provides a *proof of correct shuffle* (e.g. [2,20]). Hence, each server needs to verify the correctness of all previous shuffles before applying its own, and only consider the correct shuffles.

In [1], Adida and Wikström presented a new approach to this problem: They show how to construct an obfuscated program for shuffling a set of n ciphertexts.

The obfuscated program P_π depends on a permutation π on n elements, but π should remain computationally hidden even given P_π. Obfuscating the shuffle has the advantage that it can be precomputed. Hence the parties only need to publish their encrypted messages and then compute the shuffle locally, while correctness of the shuffle can be verified in advance. Furthermore, the protocols enjoy public verifiability, i.e. the obfuscated program can be published together with a correctness proof that can be publicly verified.

The idea is that one takes ciphertexts $c_1, \ldots, c_n$ as input, generated in some appropriate cryptosystem, and processes them using P_π locally. If the shuffle is a re-encryption shuffle, then the output will be a re-encryption of the permuted messages to ciphertexts $c_1', \ldots, c_n'$. If we let $m_1, \ldots, m_n$ and $m_1', \ldots, m_n'$ denote the corresponding plaintexts, then the guarantee is that $m_i' = m_{\pi(i)}$ for $i = 1, \ldots, n$. The result can then be used for further computation. To obtain the messages, the parties can e.g. execute a distributed decryption protocol. In case of a decryption shuffle, the shuffle outputs the permuted messages directly.

The program constructed in [1] represents the shuffle as a permutation matrix. The obfuscated program has hence size roughly $O(n^2)$ ciphertexts and the correctness proof, using standard techniques as suggested by the authors, is of the same size. The program can only be used once, but on the other hand it is reasonably efficient and can be based on cryptosystems with only rather weak homomorphic properties. The authors propose three construction: The first one is a generic obfuscator for any somewhat homomorphic encryption (SHE) scheme allowing one multiplication and many additions. Such a scheme exists e.g. based on lattices (e.g. [8]) and pairings, e.g. the Boneh, Goh and Nissim cryptosystem [6]. However, the obfuscated program consists of double encryptions and hence distributed decryption with active security is expensive. The other two constructions avoid this problem by focussing on specific encryption schemes: the BGN cryptosystem for a decryption shuffle and Paillier encryption [37] (with some twists) for a re-encryption shuffle. Of course, one could also use fully homomorphic encryption, represent the permutation using only $O(n)$ ciphertexts and compute the permutations "inside" the encryption, but this would be completely impractical with current state of the art.

Another protocol for shuffling in public was proposed by Parampalli et al. [38]. The protocol computes an obfuscated re-encryption shuffle based on the Damgård-Jurik cryptosystem [17]. By using a permutation network to represent the shuffle, they could reduce the size of the obfuscated shuffle to $O(n \log n)$. The public proof of correctness has size $O(n \log n)$ using standard techniques. Due to the use of permutation networks, however, the resulting distribution over permutations may be biased, depending on the network that was used.

In the following, we will show how our techniques can be used to reduce the size of the public proof for the [1] BGN decryption shuffle to $O(n)$. Furthermore, we sketch an MPC protocol that outputs an obfuscated decryption shuffle together with a correctness proof.

Revisiting the BGN decryption shuffle. The obfuscated program P_π as constructed in [1] uses a public key pk for an SHE scheme as mentioned above and consists of a matrix of ciphertexts $P_\pi = \{E_{\mathrm{pk}}(\Pi_{i,j})\}_{i,j=1\ldots n}$, where $\{\Pi_{i,j}\}_{i,j=1,\ldots,n}$ is the permutation matrix corresponding to π. It is now clear that one can apply π to a set of ciphertexts by multiplying the vector of input ciphertexts by the matrix P_π.

An obvious question from a practical point of view is of course who produces P_π in the first place, and how do we know it is correctly formed? In [1], it is suggested that P_π is produced by some secure multiparty protocol and that this protocol would also produce a zero-knowledge proof that anyone can verify that P_π is correctly formed. For this, they used existing techniques for proving correctness of shuffles, basically doing such a proof for each row (column) of the matrix. This means that the proof would typically have size $O(n^2)$. Using our techniques we can improve this to $O(n)$ as we now explain:

First, we can observe that the BGN cryptosystem can be seen as an unconditionally binding and homomorphic commitment scheme based on which our protocol can run. The proof then consists of two parts: First, show that in each column and each row, the sum of all entries is 1. This can be done by computing the product of ciphertexts across each column and row of P_π and prove using standard methods that each such product contains 1. Second, we use our protocol to show that the weight of each row is at most 1. Combined with the first step, we obtain now that each column and each row has weight exactly 1. These proofs can be made non-interactive using Fiat-Shamir paradigm and will clearly imply that the matrix underlying P_π is indeed a permutation matrix.

Finally, we sketch how to generate the obfuscated program and proof of correctness in a multiparty protocol. The BGN cryptosystem uses a group of order $N = q_1 q_2$ where q_1, q_2 are primes. Therefore it is convenient to use an MPC protocol based on linear secret sharing modulo N. This will mean that given a secret-shared representation of a message m, which we will denote $[m]$, it is easy using standard methods to securely generate an encryption $E_{\mathrm{pk}}(m)$ where pk is the BGN public key. It is therefore sufficient to generate secret shared values corresponding to a permutation matrix $[\Pi_{i,j}]$. This can be done, for instance, if each party (verifiably) secret shares his own permutation matrix, and then we multiply these using standard matrix multiplication. Generating the proof of correctness is standard for the most part, by simply emulating the prover's algorithm. Whenever the original prover would output a commitment, we will have a secret-shared representation of the same value, which we can convert to a BGN encryption (commitment) as we go. One slightly non-standard detail is that given the i'th row $\{[\Pi_{i,j}]\}_{j=1,\ldots,n}$, we want to show it has weight at most 1 and for this we need a secret shared representation of the (unique) index j_0 where $\Pi_{i,j_0} = 1$. But this we can get easily by forming the row $[1], [2], \ldots, [n]$ and computing the inner product with the row $\{[\Pi_{i,j}]\}_{j=1,\ldots,n}$.

4.5 PIR for Malicious Users

Consider a very simple folklore PIR protocol based on additively homomorphic encryption, e.g. Paillier, where a user wishes to retrieve single elements. Assume that the database holds elements $d_1, \ldots, d_n$. To retrieve a data element j from the database, the user could send ciphertexts $c_1, \ldots, c_n$ to the database of which at most one contains a non-zero message, namely j. The database can then compute a new ciphertext $d = \sum_{i=1}^{n} c_i d_i$ corresponding to the selected element and return d to the user. Finally, the user can decrypt d to obtain the selected element d_j.

It is easy to see that this protocol has passive security. To achieve security against a malicious user, one can add our protocol (interactive or non-interactive) to prove that the user's first message to the database is well-formed.

Note that using fully homomorphic encryption, one can get an incomparable solution where the client sends only a single ciphertext containing the index of the entry he wants (j). The server can now compute, "inside the encryption", a ciphertext that contains d_j and send it back to the client. This requires much less communication but cannot be implemented based on only additively homomorphic encryption, and has a very large computational overhead compared to the more standard solution (note that in any solution the server must touch all entries in the database, or the scheme is not secure).

Acknowledgements. This work has been supported by the European Research Council (ERC) under the European Unions's Horizon 2020 research and innovation programme under grant agreement No. 669255 (MPCPRO); the European Union's Horizon 2020 research and innovation programme under grant agreement No. 731583 (SODA); and the Danish Independent Research Council under Grant-ID DFF–6108-00169 (FoCC).

A   Considerations for Paillier Construction

In Paillier construction [37] where the clear text space $\mathbb{Z}_N$ is not a field, some properties we employ in the construction might not hold. On a field, a polynomial of degree d has at most d zeros, while on a general ring, this is not true. For the special case $\mathbb{Z}_N$ where $N = pq$ is the product of two distinct primes p, q, we resort to the factorisation assumption.

Factorisation Assumption. Let $N = pq$ where p, q are distinct, uniformly random primes of length $\Omega(k)$. For all probabilistic polynomial time adversary A, $\Pr[A(N) = p \text{ or } A(N) = q]$ is negligible in k.

It is well known that if RSA is secure, the above assumption holds. We need two tweaks in the proof for the soundness of Π_{HW} instantiated with Paillier commitment schemes.

Malicious $f(x)$. In the protocol the prover selects a monic polynomial $f(x)$ of degree d. We say such a polynomial is malicious if it has at least $d + 1$ distinct zeros on the index set $\{a_i\}$. The factorisaton of N can be reduced to finding a malicious polynomial, therefore, the probability that a cheating prover succeeds committing to a malicious $f(x)$ is negligible.

Proof (sketch). Observe that monic linear polynomials cannot be malicious. Let $f(x)$ be malicious, of degree $d > 1$ and $x_0, \ldots, x_d$ its $d + 1$ known, distinct roots. By division with remainder, we have $f(x) = (x - x_0)g(x)$ for some monic polynomial $g(x)$ of degree $d - 1$. Consider $\gcd(N, x_j - x_0)$ $(j = 1, \ldots, d)$, if one of them is not 1, it must be p or q, giving the factorisation of N. Otherwise, $x_j - x_0$ $(j = 1, \ldots, d)$ are invertible in $\mathbb{Z}_N$. Substituting $x_1, \ldots, x_d$ into the equation of division, we conclude that $g(x)$ is malicious, of degree $d - 1$ and $x_1, \ldots, x_d$ are its d distinct zeros. We then continue this process with $g(x)$. However, the process must stop before reaching linear polynomials by the observation, finding either p or q.

Weak $F(x)$. The protocol verifies $f(a_i)x_i = 0$ with a "checksum" polynomial $F(x)$ whose coefficients are $f(a_i)x_i$, where we exploit the property that $F(x)$ has at most n zeros if $F(x) \neq 0$. In $\mathbb{Z}_N$, $F(x)$ of degree n could have at most $\max\{pn, qn\}$ distinct roots. This bound still guarantees asymptotic soundness, but is a great sacrifice of the concrete soundness error. By assuming the hardness of factorisation, we can prove a better bound. We define a polynomial $F(x)$ on $\mathbb{Z}_N$ of degree n to be weak, if it has more than n^2 distinct zeros. We shall show that with negligible probability, the $F(x)$ used in the protocol is weak.

Proof. By Chinese Remainder Theorem, $\mathbb{Z}_N = \mathbb{Z}_p \times \mathbb{Z}_q$. For $x_0 \in \mathbb{Z}_N$, write $x_0 = (y_0, z_0)$ by this decomposition, where $y_0 \in \mathbb{Z}_p, z_0 \in \mathbb{Z}_q$. We can naturally regard $F(x)$ as polynomial $F_p(x)$ on $\mathbb{Z}_p$ or $F_q(x)$ in $\mathbb{Z}_q$ by keeping only the relevant component (coefficients modulo the corresponding prime). It is trivial to verify that $F(x_0) = (F_p(y_0), F_q(z_0))$ and that $F(x_0) = 0$ is equivalent to $F_p(y_0) = 0$ and $F_q(z_0) = 0$. If neither $F_p(x)$ nor $F_q(x)$ is the zero polynomial, both of them have at most n distinct roots. In such case, $F(x)$ has at most n^2 roots as the set of roots of $F(x)$ is exactly the Cartesian product of the sets of roots of $F_p(x)$ and $F_q(x)$. Otherwise, suppose $F_p(x)$ is the zero polynomial, the coefficients of $F(x)$ are multiples of p, while at least one of them is not a multiple of N. Computing the greatest common divisor of the coefficients of $F(x)$ gives p, factorising N. Similar argument applies to the case $F_q(x)$ is zero. Note that the prover is able to find the coefficients of $F(x)$ himself, therefore the $F(x)$ used in the protocol is weak with negligible probability.

Combining the two tweaks ensures the soundness of the instantiation of Π_{HW} with Paillier commitment schemes. Complete and zero-knowledge properties follow by the general proof presented in the text.

It is also noticeable that the method for extension does not work with $\mathbb{Z}_N$. Therefore, N must be large enough for the construction to be sound, which is, after all, true for practical scenarios.

B   Details on Code-Based Homomorphic Commitments

In this section we provide more details on instantiating our protocols using recent, UC-secure homomorphic commitment schemes, and using this to reduce the cost of batch d-out-of-n OT.

B.1   The Type 2 Commitment Scheme

We now show how to instantiate Type 2 commitments with efficient, rate-1 homomorphic commitment schemes based on 1-out-of-2 OT and error-correcting codes. The commitment functionality, F^*_{Com}, is given below. We first show how this gives a Type 2 commitment scheme where the message space is $\mathbb{F}^\ell$ instead of $\mathbb{F}$, and then discuss how existing homomorphic commitment schemes [13, 22] can be used to realise this functionality.

Functionality F^*_{Com}

Parameters: $\mathbb{F}$, a finite field; ℓ, the message length; C, an $[m, \ell, s]$ linear code over $\mathbb{F}$, where s is the security parameter.
On initialisation with the public parameters, the functionality samples a random $\alpha = (\alpha_1, \ldots, \alpha_m) \in \{0, 1\}^m$ and sends it to P_A.
On receiving a message $x \in \mathbb{F}^\ell$ from P_B:

1. Sample $\beta \in \mathbb{F}^m$ at random.
2. Send β to P_A and $\gamma := \alpha * C(x) + \beta$ to P_B, where $*$ denotes component-wise product.

Leakage: If P_B is corrupt, the adversary may send any number of key queries of the form $(\mathbf{guess}, i, b_i)$. If $b_i = \alpha_i$ then send $(\mathbf{success})$ to the adversary, otherwise send $(\mathbf{abort})$ to all parties and terminate.

To verify a commitment to x with the opening information (α, β, γ), P_A checks that $\gamma = \alpha * C(x) + \beta$.

Clearly, the scheme is unconditionally hiding as with F_{Com}. To see the statistical binding property, notice that to forge an opening of a commitment to x, P_B must come up with $x' \neq x$ and $\gamma' \in \mathbb{F}^m$ such that $\gamma' = \alpha * C(x') + \beta$. We then define $\delta := \gamma - \gamma' = \alpha * C(x - x')$, by linearity of the code. Since $x \neq x'$ and C has minimum distance s, the Hamming weight of $C(x - x')$ is at least s, so coming up with such a δ requires guessing at least s bits of α, with probability $\leq 2^{-s}$. Note that including the key queries in F^*_{Com} does not change the overall success probability, since for each query a single bit of α can be guessed only with probability $1/2$, and the functionality aborts if any query fails.

This functionality can be realised from the commitment phase of [22] or [13]. To see this, recall that after the commitment phase in these protocols, the sender holds a committed message $x \in \mathbb{F}^\ell_2$, and a random additive sharing of $C(x)$, where C is a linear $[m, \ell, s]$ error-correcting code. Meanwhile, for each component of $C(x)$, the receiver holds exactly one of the two shares. That is, the sender has two vectors $y_0, y_1 \in \mathbb{F}^m$ such that $y_0 + y_1 = C(x)$, whereas the receiver holds a random secret vector $(r_1, \ldots, r_n) \in \{0, 1\}^m$, which is fixed once for all the commitments. For the commitment to $\boldsymbol{x}$, the receiver knows a vector $\boldsymbol{z}$ satisfying $\boldsymbol{z}[i] = \boldsymbol{y}_{r_i}[i]$, from the 1-out-of-2 OT setup phase. Notice that:

$$\boldsymbol{z}[i] = \boldsymbol{y}_{r_i}[i] = (\boldsymbol{y}_0 \cdot (1 + r_i) + \boldsymbol{y}_1 \cdot r_i)[i]$$
$$= (\boldsymbol{y}_0 + r_i \cdot (\boldsymbol{y}_0 + \boldsymbol{y}_1))[i]$$
$$= (\boldsymbol{y}_0 + r_i \cdot C(\boldsymbol{x}))[i]$$

This is clearly the same form as the commitments produced by $\mathsf{F}_{\mathrm{Com}}^*$, since we have $\boldsymbol{z} = \boldsymbol{y}_0 + \boldsymbol{r} * C(\boldsymbol{x})$.

Note that $\mathsf{F}_{\mathrm{Com}}^*$ also allows a corrupt sender to attempt to guess the bits of $\boldsymbol{r}$, but aborts if any guess fails. This is needed because the consistency check in [13], used to ensure the sender inputs correct codewords, may leak a few of these bits to a cheating sender. This can be seen from the proof of Lemma 8, where the exact set of bits of $\boldsymbol{r}$ which the sender attempts to guess is defined. That proof can be applied directly to show that the commitment phase of Protocol Π_{HCOM} from [13] can be used to securely realise $\mathsf{F}_{\mathrm{Com}}^*$. Finally, we remark that although the protocol in [13] is defined over the field $\mathbb{F}_2$, it can be used to commit to vectors over any finite field with a suitable error-correcting code, and the communication complexity is still $O(m)$ field elements per commitment.

B.2   Switching Between Schemes

As we will see in the application to d-out-of-n OT in the batch setting (described in the full version of this paper), it can be useful to use the most efficient, rate-1 homomorphic commitments for the most expensive part of a protocol, before switching to another homomorphic commitment scheme that is more suited to the application. This can be done by committing to the messages with both schemes and then proving that both sets of commitments contain the same messages. With the Type 2 schemes $\mathsf{F}_{\mathrm{Com}}$ and $\mathsf{F}_{\mathrm{Com}}^*$, this proof works as follows (and the same technique can be adapted for any scheme).

Protocol Π_{EQ}: The input is two sets of committed vectors $\langle \boldsymbol{x}_1 \rangle^*, \ldots, \langle \boldsymbol{x}_n \rangle^*$ and $\{\langle y_1^i \rangle, \ldots, \langle y_n^i \rangle\}_{i=1}^{\ell}$, where $\langle \cdot \rangle^*$ denotes a commitment to an element of $\mathbb{F}^{\ell}$ with $\mathsf{F}_{\mathrm{Com}}^*$ and $\langle \cdot \rangle$ a commitment using $\mathsf{F}_{\mathrm{Com}}$ over $\mathbb{F}$. We prove that $\boldsymbol{x}_j[i] = y_j^i$ for all i, j.

1. The proves samples at random and commits to $\boldsymbol{r} = (r_1, \ldots, r_{\ell}) \in \mathbb{F}^{\ell}$ with both schemes, obtaining commitments $\langle \boldsymbol{r} \rangle^*, \langle r_1 \rangle, \ldots, \langle r_{\ell} \rangle$.
2. The verifier sends a random challenge $s \in \mathbb{F}$.
3. The prover opens $\langle \boldsymbol{a} \rangle^* = \sum_{j=1}^{n} \langle \boldsymbol{x}_j \rangle^* \cdot s^j + \langle \boldsymbol{r} \rangle^*$. Write $\boldsymbol{a} = (a_1, \ldots, a_{\ell})$.
4. The prover opens $\langle b_i \rangle = \sum_{j=1}^{n} \langle y_j^i \rangle \cdot s^j + \langle r_i \rangle$, for $i = 1, \ldots \ell$.
5. The verifier checks that $a_i = b_i$ for all i.

Completeness is evident, and zero-knowledge holds because the values r_i are uniformly random and used to mask the opened values as one-time pads. To argue soundness, note that if the proof succeeds then we have $a_i = b_i$, and so

$\sum_{j=1}^{n}(x_j[i] - y_j^i) \cdot s^j = 0$. However, if the committed inputs were not the same then there is at least one pair i, j such that $x_j[i] \neq y_j^i$. This means that the probability of success is at most $n/|\mathbb{F}|$, since it corresponds to the degree n polynomial with coefficients $(x_j[i] - y_j^i)_j$ having a root at s.

Finally, we remark that the communication cost of the protocol is independent of n, since it is $O(k^2\ell)$ bits, dominated by committing to the elements $r_1, \ldots, r_\ell$ (assuming $|\mathbb{F}| = 2^k$).

References

1. Adida, B., Wikström, D.: How to shuffle in public. In: Vadhan, S.P. (ed.) TCC 2007. LNCS, vol. 4392, pp. 555–574. Springer, Heidelberg (2007). https://doi.org/10.1007/978-3-540-70936-7_30

2. Bayer, S., Groth, J.: Efficient zero-knowledge argument for correctness of a shuffle. In: Pointcheval, D., Johansson, T. (eds.) EUROCRYPT 2012. LNCS, vol. 7237, pp. 263–280. Springer, Heidelberg (2012). https://doi.org/10.1007/978-3-642-29011-4_17

3. Bayer, S., Groth, J.: Zero-knowledge argument for polynomial evaluation with application to blacklists. In: Johansson, T., Nguyen, P.Q. (eds.) EUROCRYPT 2013. LNCS, vol. 7881, pp. 646–663. Springer, Heidelberg (2013). https://doi.org/10.1007/978-3-642-38348-9_38

4. Beaver, D.: Efficient multiparty protocols using circuit randomization. In: Feigenbaum, J. (ed.) CRYPTO 1991. LNCS, vol. 576, pp. 420–432. Springer, Heidelberg (1992). https://doi.org/10.1007/3-540-46766-1_34

5. Ben-Sasson, E., Chiesa, A., Genkin, D., Tromer, E., Virza, M.: SNARKs for C: verifying program executions succinctly and in zero knowledge. In: Canetti, R., Garay, J.A. (eds.) CRYPTO 2013. LNCS, vol. 8043, pp. 90–108. Springer, Heidelberg (2013). https://doi.org/10.1007/978-3-642-40084-1_6

6. Boneh, D., Goh, E.-J., Nissim, K.: Evaluating 2-DNF formulas on ciphertexts. In: Kilian, J. (ed.) TCC 2005. LNCS, vol. 3378, pp. 325–341. Springer, Heidelberg (2005). https://doi.org/10.1007/978-3-540-30576-7_18

7. Bootle, J., Cerulli, A., Chaidos, P., Ghadafi, E., Groth, J., Petit, C.: Short accountable ring signatures based on DDH. In: Pernul, G., Ryan, P.Y.A., Weippl, E. (eds.) ESORICS 2015. LNCS, vol. 9326, pp. 243–265. Springer, Cham (2015). https://doi.org/10.1007/978-3-319-24174-6_13

8. Brakerski, Z., Vaikuntanathan, V.: Fully homomorphic encryption from ring-LWE and security for key dependent messages. In: Rogaway, P. (ed.) CRYPTO 2011. LNCS, vol. 6841, pp. 505–524. Springer, Heidelberg (2011). https://doi.org/10.1007/978-3-642-22792-9_29

9. Brands, S., Demuynck, L., De Decker, B.: A practical system for globally revoking the unlinkable pseudonyms of unknown users. In: Pieprzyk, J., Ghodosi, H., Dawson, E. (eds.) ACISP 2007. LNCS, vol. 4586, pp. 400–415. Springer, Heidelberg (2007). https://doi.org/10.1007/978-3-540-73458-1_29

10. Camenisch, J., Damgård, I.: Verifiable encryption, group encryption, and their applications to separable group signatures and signature sharing schemes. In: Okamoto, T. (ed.) ASIACRYPT 2000. LNCS, vol. 1976, pp. 331–345. Springer, Heidelberg (2000). https://doi.org/10.1007/3-540-44448-3_25

11. Camenisch, J., Michels, M.: Separability and efficiency for generic group signature schemes. In: Wiener, M. (ed.) CRYPTO 1999. LNCS, vol. 1666, pp. 413–430. Springer, Heidelberg (1999). https://doi.org/10.1007/3-540-48405-1_27

12. Camenisch, J., Neven, G., Shelat, A.: Simulatable adaptive oblivious transfer. In: Naor, M. (ed.) EUROCRYPT 2007. LNCS, vol. 4515, pp. 573–590. Springer, Heidelberg (2007). https://doi.org/10.1007/978-3-540-72540-4_33

13. Cascudo, I., Damgård, I., David, B., Döttling, N., Nielsen, J.B.: Rate-1, linear time and additively homomorphic UC commitments. In: Robshaw, M., Katz, J. (eds.) CRYPTO 2016. LNCS, vol. 9816, pp. 179–207. Springer, Heidelberg (2016). https://doi.org/10.1007/978-3-662-53015-3_7

14. Chaum, D.: Untraceable electronic mail, return addresses, and digital pseudonyms. Commun. ACM **24**(2), 84–88 (1981). http://doi.acm.org/10.1145/358549.358563

15. Cramer, R., Damgård, I.: Zero-knowledge proofs for finite field arithmetic, or: can zero-knowledge be for free? In: Krawczyk, H. (ed.) CRYPTO 1998. LNCS, vol. 1462, pp. 424–441. Springer, Heidelberg (1998). https://doi.org/10.1007/BFb0055745

16. Cramer, R., Damgård, I., Schoenmakers, B.: Proofs of partial knowledge and simplified design of witness hiding protocols. In: Desmedt, Y.G. (ed.) CRYPTO 1994. LNCS, vol. 839, pp. 174–187. Springer, Heidelberg (1994). https://doi.org/10.1007/3-540-48658-5_19

17. Damgård, I., Jurik, M.: A generalisation, a simplification and some applications of Paillier's probabilistic public-key system. In: Kim, K. (ed.) PKC 2001. LNCS, vol. 1992, pp. 119–136. Springer, Heidelberg (2001). https://doi.org/10.1007/3-540-44586-2_9

18. Damgård, I., Nielsen, J.B., Nielsen, M., Ranellucci, S.: The tinytable protocol for 2-party secure computation, or: gate-scrambling revisited. In: Katz, J., Shacham, H. (eds.) CRYPTO 2017. LNCS, vol. 10401, pp. 167–187. Springer, Cham (2017). https://doi.org/10.1007/978-3-319-63688-7_6

19. Döttling, N., Ghosh, S., Nielsen, J.B., Nilges, T., Trifiletti, R.: TinyOLE: efficient actively secure two-party computation from oblivious linear function evaluation. In: ACM Conference on Computer and Communications Security, CCS 2017 (2017)

20. Fauzi, P., Lipmaa, H., Zając, M.: A shuffle argument secure in the generic model. In: Cheon, J.H., Takagi, T. (eds.) ASIACRYPT 2016. LNCS, vol. 10032, pp. 841–872. Springer, Heidelberg (2016). https://doi.org/10.1007/978-3-662-53890-6_28

21. Fiat, A., Shamir, A.: How to prove yourself: practical solutions to identification and signature problems. In: Odlyzko, A.M. (ed.) CRYPTO 1986. LNCS, vol. 263, pp. 186–194. Springer, Heidelberg (1987). https://doi.org/10.1007/3-540-47721-7_12

22. Frederiksen, T.K., Jakobsen, T.P., Nielsen, J.B., Trifiletti, R.: On the complexity of additively homomorphic UC commitments. In: Kushilevitz, E., Malkin, T. (eds.) TCC 2016. LNCS, vol. 9562, pp. 542–565. Springer, Heidelberg (2016). https://doi.org/10.1007/978-3-662-49096-9_23

23. Giacomelli, I., Madsen, J., Orlandi, C.: ZKBoo: faster zero-knowledge for Boolean circuits. In: USENIX Security Symposium, pp. 1069–1083. USENIX Association (2016)

24. Green, M., Hohenberger, S.: Universally composable adaptive oblivious transfer. In: Pieprzyk, J. (ed.) ASIACRYPT 2008. LNCS, vol. 5350, pp. 179–197. Springer, Heidelberg (2008). https://doi.org/10.1007/978-3-540-89255-7_12

25. Groth, J.: Linear algebra with sub-linear zero-knowledge arguments. In: Halevi, S. (ed.) CRYPTO 2009. LNCS, vol. 5677, pp. 192–208. Springer, Heidelberg (2009). https://doi.org/10.1007/978-3-642-03356-8_12

26. Groth, J., Kohlweiss, M.: One-out-of-many proofs: or how to leak a secret and spend a coin. In: Oswald, E., Fischlin, M. (eds.) EUROCRYPT 2015. LNCS, vol. 9057, pp. 253–280. Springer, Heidelberg (2015). https://doi.org/10.1007/978-3-662-46803-6_9

27. Ishai, Y., Kilian, J., Nissim, K., Petrank, E.: Extending oblivious transfers efficiently. In: Boneh, D. (ed.) CRYPTO 2003. LNCS, vol. 2729, pp. 145–161. Springer, Heidelberg (2003). https://doi.org/10.1007/978-3-540-45146-4_9

28. Ishai, Y., Kushilevitz, E., Ostrovsky, R., Sahai, A.: Zero-knowledge from secure multiparty computation. In: Johnson, D.S., Feige, U. (eds.) 39th ACM STOC, pp. 21–30. ACM Press, June 2007

29. Ishai, Y., Prabhakaran, M., Sahai, A.: Founding cryptography on oblivious transfer – efficiently. In: Wagner, D. (ed.) CRYPTO 2008. LNCS, vol. 5157, pp. 572–591. Springer, Heidelberg (2008). https://doi.org/10.1007/978-3-540-85174-5_32

30. Keller, M., Orsini, E., Rotaru, D., Scholl, P., Soria-Vazquez, E., Vivek, S.: Faster secure multi-party computation of AES and DES using lookup tables. In: Gollmann, D., Miyaji, A., Kikuchi, H. (eds.) ACNS 2017. LNCS, vol. 10355, pp. 229–249. Springer, Cham (2017). https://doi.org/10.1007/978-3-319-61204-1_12

31. Keller, M., Orsini, E., Scholl, P.: Actively secure OT extension with optimal overhead. In: Gennaro, R., Robshaw, M. (eds.) CRYPTO 2015. LNCS, vol. 9215, pp. 724–741. Springer, Heidelberg (2015). https://doi.org/10.1007/978-3-662-47989-6_35

32. Keller, M., Orsini, E., Scholl, P.: MASCOT: faster malicious arithmetic secure computation with oblivious transfer. In: Proceedings of the 2016 ACM SIGSAC Conference on Computer and Communications Security, Vienna, Austria, 24–28 October 2016, pp. 830–842 (2016)

33. Kilian, J., Petrank, E.: Identity escrow. In: Krawczyk, H. (ed.) CRYPTO 1998. LNCS, vol. 1462, pp. 169–185. Springer, Heidelberg (1998). https://doi.org/10.1007/BFb0055727

34. Naor, M., Pinkas, B.: Computationally secure oblivious transfer. J. Cryptol. **18**(1), 1–35 (2005)

35. Nielsen, J.B., Nordholt, P.S., Orlandi, C., Burra, S.S.: A new approach to practical active-secure two-party computation. In: Safavi-Naini, R., Canetti, R. (eds.) CRYPTO 2012. LNCS, vol. 7417, pp. 681–700. Springer, Heidelberg (2012). https://doi.org/10.1007/978-3-642-32009-5_40

36. Nielsen, J.B., Schneider, T., Trifiletti, R.: Constant round maliciously secure 2PC with function-independent preprocessing using LEGO. In: 24th NDSS Symposium. The Internet Society (2017). http://eprint.iacr.org/2016/1069

37. Paillier, P.: Public-key cryptosystems based on composite degree residuosity classes. In: Stern, J. (ed.) EUROCRYPT 1999. LNCS, vol. 1592, pp. 223–238. Springer, Heidelberg (1999). https://doi.org/10.1007/3-540-48910-X_16

38. Parampalli, U., Ramchen, K., Teague, V.: Efficiently shuffling in public. In: Fischlin, M., Buchmann, J., Manulis, M. (eds.) PKC 2012. LNCS, vol. 7293, pp. 431–448. Springer, Heidelberg (2012). https://doi.org/10.1007/978-3-642-30057-8_26

39. Rindal, P., Rosulek, M.: Improved private set intersection against malicious adversaries. In: Coron, J.-S., Nielsen, J.B. (eds.) EUROCRYPT 2017. LNCS, vol. 10210, pp. 235–259. Springer, Cham (2017). https://doi.org/10.1007/978-3-319-56620-7_9

40. Rivest, R.L., Shamir, A., Tauman, Y.: How to leak a secret. In: Boyd, C. (ed.) ASIACRYPT 2001. LNCS, vol. 2248, pp. 552–565. Springer, Heidelberg (2001). https://doi.org/10.1007/3-540-45682-1_32

41. Shankar, B., Srinathan, K., Rangan, C.P.: Alternative protocols for generalized oblivious transfer. In: Rao, S., Chatterjee, M., Jayanti, P., Murthy, C.S.R., Saha, S.K. (eds.) ICDCN 2008. LNCS, vol. 4904, pp. 304–309. Springer, Heidelberg (2007). https://doi.org/10.1007/978-3-540-77444-0_31
42. Xu, S., Yung, M.: Accountable ring signatures: a smart card approach. In: Quisquater, J.J., Paradinas, P., Deswarte, Y., El Kalam, A.A. (eds.) Smart Card Research and Advanced Applications VI. IFIPAICT, vol. 153, pp. 271–286. Springer, Boston (2004). https://doi.org/10.1007/1-4020-8147-2_18

Efficient Batch Zero-Knowledge
Arguments for Low Degree Polynomials

Jonathan Bootle$^{(\boxtimes)}$ and Jens Groth

University College London, London, UK
jonathan.bootle.14@ucl.ac.uk

Abstract. Bootle et al. (EUROCRYPT 2016) construct an extremely efficient zero-knowledge argument for arithmetic circuit satisfiability in the discrete logarithm setting. However, the argument does not treat relations involving commitments, and furthermore, for simple polynomial relations, the complex machinery employed is unnecessary.

In this work, we give a framework for expressing simple relations between commitments and field elements, and present a zero-knowledge argument which, by contrast with Bootle et al., is constant-round and uses fewer group operations, in the case where the polynomials in the relation have low degree. Our method also directly yields a batch protocol, which allows many copies of the same relation to be proved and verified in a single argument more efficiently with only a square-root communication overhead in the number of copies.

We instantiate our protocol with concrete polynomial relations to construct zero-knowledge arguments for membership proofs, polynomial evaluation proofs, and range proofs. Our work can be seen as a unified explanation of the underlying ideas of these protocols. In the instantiations of membership proofs and polynomial evaluation proofs, we also achieve better efficiency than the state of the art.

Keywords: Sigma-protocol · Zero-knowledge argument
Batch-verification · Discrete logarithm assumption

1 Introduction

Zero-knowledge proofs and arguments allow a prover to convince a verifier that a particular statement is true, without revealing anything beyond that fact. More formally, the statement is an element u from an NP-language $\mathcal{L}$, and the prover convinces the verifier that there exists a witness w to the fact that $u \in \mathcal{L}$. They are useful both in theory and in practice, as they can be used to construct signature schemes, encryption schemes, anonymous credentials, and multi-party computation schemes with strong security guarantees.

The research leading to these results has received funding from the European Research Council under the European Union's Seventh Framework Programme (FP/2007-2013) / ERC Grant Agreement n. 307937.

M. Abdalla and R. Dahab (Eds.): PKC 2018, LNCS 10770, pp. 561–588, 2018.
https://doi.org/10.1007/978-3-319-76581-5_19

Zero-knowledge arguments are computationally sound, meaning that cheating the verifier to accept when $u \notin \mathcal{L}$ reduces to breaking a computational intractability assumption. In this paper, we focus on the discrete logarithm assumption. There are many examples of zero-knowledge arguments based on the discrete logarithm assumption, for both general, NP-complete languages such as arithmetic circuit satisfiability [7], and for simpler languages such as range and membership arguments, shuffle arguments, and discrete logarithm relations.

While very efficient, arguments for general statements often make use of generic reductions and complex machinery, and fail to be as efficient as arguments specialised for a particular language.

1.1 Contributions

In this paper, we aim to bridge the gap between general and simple languages. We do this in three ways.

Framework for Low Degree Relations. We provide a framework to describe the types of languages commonly encountered. Protocols such as the 1-out-of-N membership argument of [28], and the polynomial evaluation argument of [2] prove membership in languages where the witnesses are zeroes of low-degree polynomial relations. In other words, the statement is an arithmetic circuit of low degree, and part of the witness is a satisfying assignment for the circuit. We give a general relation which allows us to recover specific protocols by instantiating with concrete polynomial relations. By separating the task of developing more efficient ways to perform the zero knowledge proof, and the task of designing better relations to describe a given language, we can explain the logic behind past optimisations of membership proofs in [6,28], and produce new optimisations for membership proofs and polynomial evaluation proofs.

Common Construction Techniques. We unify the approaches used in [2,6,28] to construct zero-knowledge proofs for membership and polynomial evaluation, which can all be viewed as employing the same construction method. The constructions of zero-knowledge arguments for low degree polynomial relations in these works proceed by masking an input variable u as $f_u = ux + u_b$, using a random challenge x and a random blinder u_b. During the proof, the polynomial or circuit from the statement is computed with f_u in place of u, so that the original relation appears in the leading x coefficient. The communication and computational complexity of the resulting arguments is determined by the degree of the polynomial relation and the number of inputs. By contrast, the complexity of general arithmetic circuit protocols is determined by the number of gates. In the case of [7], the authors embed a polynomial evaluation argument for a polynomial of degree N into a low degree polynomial with $\log N$ inputs and degree $\log N$, obtaining a protocol with $O(\log N)$ communication using 3 moves, and requiring $O(\log N)$ exponentiations in a suitably chosen cryptographic group. On the other hand, a polynomial of degree N requires N multiplication gates to evaluate in general, so the best arithmetic circuit protocol [7] can only achieve

$O(\log N)$ communication in $O(\log N)$ moves, and uses $O(N)$ group exponentiations. In particular, since the cost of computing group exponentiations is much higher than that of computing finite-field multiplications in the discrete logarithm setting, computing $O(\log N)$ group exponentiations rather than $O(N)$ leads to a significant performance advantage when considering implementation on constrained devices.

Bayer [1] gives two efficient batch proofs for multiplication and polynomial evaluation, which achieve a square-root communication overhead in the number of proofs to be batched. The key to achieving square-root overhead in [1] is to use Lagrange interpolation to embed many instances of the same relation into a single field element. This technique can be applied more generally to produce efficient batch proofs for the low-degree relations described above. Furthermore, by combining this with the polynomial commitment subprotocol in Sect. 3, we improve the communication cost of the batched proof from $\sqrt{t}c$ to $\sqrt{tc}$, where c is the communication cost of the original non-batched proof, and t is a large number representing the number of proofs to be batched together.

Efficient Protocols for Applications. We exhibit a general protocol in our framework, and give an efficient batch protocol for proving and verifying t instances of the same relation simultaneously. We then show how to recover protocols of previous works with some optimisation. More specifically, we give new 1-out-of-N membership arguments and polynomial evaluation arguments. Our new instantiations simultaneously decrease communication costs and reduce prover and verifier computation, while retaining the conceptual clarity and simple 3-move structure of the originals. As an example, we obtain the most communication efficient Σ-protocols for membership or non-membership of a committed value in a public list, in the discrete logarithm setting. We also include an argument for range proofs, which captures the folklore method for performing range proofs and demonstrates the expressivity of our general relation. Our arguments all possess the following desirable properties:

- Perfect completeness and perfect special honest verifier zero-knowledge.
- Computational soundness based on the discrete logarithm assumption.
- Simple 3-move public coin structure.
- Common reference strings are formed from random group elements. They require no special structure.
- Prover and verifier both have efficient computation.

The discrete logarithm assumption is well-known, well-examined, and widely used in cryptography. Our protocols rely on the discrete logarithm assumption in groups with prime order p. The assumption is believed to hold in suitable subgroups of elliptic-curve groups. The best algorithms for finding discrete logarithms in such elliptic curve groups are still generic algorithms with complexity $\Omega(\sqrt{p})$. For these groups we therefore enjoy lower parameter sizes than protocols based on RSA groups that are subject to sub-exponential attacks.

The discrete logarithm assumption is also believed to hold in well-chosen multiplicative sub-groups of finite fields. Finite fields of prime order should have moduli of $\frac{\lambda^3}{\text{polylog}\lambda}$ bits in order to achieve λ bits of security against the best known attacks. This makes protocols communicating large numbers of group elements highly impractical in this setting. As an improvement on previous works, in the case where $t = 1$ and we have a single relation, our protocols can be tuned so that they only require a constant number of group elements, resulting in much better efficiency when instantiated in finite fields of prime order, since the $\frac{\lambda^3}{\text{polylog}\lambda}$ communication cost can then appear as a constant additive factor rather than a multiplicative one.

As a building block in our arguments, we also present an adaptation of the polynomial commitment sub-protocol appearing in [7], which allows the prover to commit to a polynomial so that the verifier can learn an evaluation of the polynomial in a secure manner.

1.2 Efficiency

Table 1 compares the efficiency of our protocol with other works. One notable place where we improve communication efficiency over previous proofs is in our membership and polynomial evaluation proofs, which use a constant number of group elements, but have better communication efficiency regardless of whether the proofs are instantiated in elliptic curve groups or multiplicative subgroups of finite fields. Another is the polynomial evaluation argument with $O(\frac{\log N}{\log \log N})$ communication costs, which is an asymptotic improvement over the previous state-of-the-art, $O(\log N)$. Finally, our batch polynomial evaluation argument improves on [1] by putting the $\log N$ cost inside a square root.

1.3 Related Work

Zero Knowledge and Batching. There has been much work constructing efficient zero-knowledge arguments. For general statements, Kilian [34] gave the first zero-knowledge argument for circuit-satisfiability with poly-logarithmic communication complexity, but with high computational complexity. Bootle et al. [7] construct arguments with logarithmic communication complexity and linear computation costs based on the discrete logarithm assumption. Recent progress [8] yields zero-knowledge arguments with constant overhead for the prover, and square-root communication costs, though the large constants involved in the construction prevent it from being practical. For more specialised languages, such as range proofs, membership arguments, and polynomial evaluation arguments, there are numerous constructions [2,28], including some extremely simple Σ-protocols.

Camenisch and Stadler [15] provide a well-known symbolic notation for describing statements for zero-knowledge arguments of knowledge, and constructing protocols more easily from simple building blocks. By contrast, our general relation aims to describe languages defined by low degree polynomials and produce protocols for this case.

The idea of embedding many statements into a single polynomial using Lagrange interpolation polynomials in a challenge x originates in the quadratic arithmetic programs of Gennaro et al. [26]. It was used in the context of interactive zero-knowledge arguments by Bayer [1]. The technique was originally applied

Table 1. Efficiency Comparisons. N is the instance-size, t is the number of batched instances, $\mathbb{G}$ means the number of group elements transmitted, $\mathbb{Z}_p$ means the number of field elements transmitted, $(\mathbb{G}, exp)$ means the number of group exponentiations and $(\mathbb{Z}_p, \times)$ means the number of field multiplications. In the membership proofs, N is the number of items in the list that we wish to prove membership for. In the polynomial evaluation proofs, N is the degree of the polynomial. In the range proofs, N is the width of the range that we consider.

Protocol	Reference	Communication		Prover computation		Verifier computation	
		$\mathbb{G}$	$\mathbb{Z}_p$	$(\mathbb{G}, exp)$	$(\mathbb{Z}_p, \times)$	$(\mathbb{G}, exp)$	$(\mathbb{Z}_p, \times)$
Membership proof	[7]	$4\log N + 8$	$2\log N + 7$	$12N$	$O(N)$	$4N$	$O(N)$
Membership proof [a]	[28]	$4\log N$	$3\log N + 1$	$O(\log N)$	$O(N\log N)$	$O(\log N)$	$O(N)$
Membership proof [b]	[6]	$\log N + 12$	$\frac{3}{2}\log N + 6$	$O(\log N)$	$O(N\log N)$	$O(\log N)$	$O(N)$
Membership proof	This work, Sect. 5.1	7	$4\log N + 4$	$O(\frac{\log N}{\log\log N})$	$O(N\log N)$	$O(\frac{\log N}{\log\log N})$	$O(N)$
Membership proof	This work, Sect. 5.1	$2.7\sqrt{\log N}+5$	$1.9\log N + 2.7\sqrt{\log N}+4$	$O(\frac{\log N}{\log\log N})$	$O(N\log N)$	$O(\frac{\log N}{\log\log N})$	$O(N)$
Batch membership proof	This work, Sect. 5.1	$4.1\sqrt{t}\log N$	$4.1\sqrt{t}\log N$	$O(tN\log tN)$	$O(tN\log tN)$	$O(\sqrt{t}\log tN)$	$O(tN)$
Polynomial evaluation	[7]	$4\log N + 8$	$2\log N + 7$	$12N$	$O(N)$	$4N$	$O(N)$
Polynomial evaluation	[2]	$4\log N + 2$	$3\log N + 3$	$O(\log N)$	$O(N\log N)$	$O(\log N)$	$O(N)$
Polynomial evaluation	This work, Sect. 5.2	7	$3\log N + 4$	$O(\frac{\log N}{\log\log N})$	$O(N\log N)$	$O(\frac{\log N}{\log\log N})$	$O(N)$
Polynomial evaluation	This work, Sect. 5.2	$O(\frac{\log N}{\log\log N})$	$O(\frac{\log N}{\log\log N})$	$O(\frac{\log N}{\log\log N})$	$O(N\log N)$	$O(\frac{\log N}{\log\log N})$	$O(N)$
Batch polynomial evaluation	[1]	$O(\sqrt{t}\log N)$	$O(\sqrt{t}\log N)$	$O(t\log N)$	$O(tN\log N)$	$O(\sqrt{t}\log N)$	$O(tN)$
Batch polynomial evaluation	This work, Sect. 5.2	$2.8\sqrt{t}\log N$	$2.8\sqrt{t}\log N$	$O(tN\log tN)$	$O(tN\log tN)$	$O(\sqrt{t}\log tN)$	$O(tN)$
Range proof	This work, Sect. 5.3	7	$3\log N + 4$	$O(\log N)$	$O(\log N)$	$O(\log N)$	$O(\log N)$
Range proof	This work, Sect. 5.3	$O(\frac{\log N}{\log\log N})$	$O(\frac{\log N}{\log\log N})$	$O(\log N)$	$O(\log N)$	$O(\log N)$	$O(\log N)$
Batch range proof	This work, Sect. 5.3	$2.8\sqrt{t}\log N$	$2.8\sqrt{t}\log N$	$O(t\log N)$	$O(t\log N)$	$O(t\log N)$	$O(t\log N)$

[a] We compare against the efficiency when [28] is instantiated using Pedersen commitments, and the prover and verifier know the openings of the list of commitments.

[b] We compare against the efficiency when [6] is instantiated using Pedersen commitments rather than Elgamal ciphertexts.

to construct a Hadamard product argument and batched polynomial evaluation argument. We show here that the same technique can be applied to our general relation. Earlier work by Gennaro et al. [25] batches Schnorr proofs using simple powers of x.

Other batch arguments in the literature use methods from [3] and multiply different instances of the proof by small exponents before compressing the proofs together. This approach may be used to trade soundness for efficiency. Our batching process proves and verifies the logical AND of many statements simultaneously. There are also batch proofs for OR statements [44], and k-out-of-N batch proofs [29]. Finally, Henry and Goldberg [29] define a notion of conciseness to characterise batch proofs.

Polynomial Commitments. Our polynomial commitment protocol is a key part of our zero-knowledge argument, and builds on the polynomial commitment protocol presented in [7]. Polynomial commitments were first introduced by Kate et al. [33], who give a construction using bilinear maps. The original construction has also been extended to the multivariate case [41,46]. Libert et al. [37] also gave a construction relying on much simpler pairing-based assumptions. Our polynomial commitment protocol gives square-root communication complexity based on the discrete logarithm assumption.

Applications. In a membership argument [10,11], a prover demonstrates that a secret committed value λ is an element of a list $\mathcal{L} = \{\lambda_0, \ldots, \lambda_{N-1}\}$, without revealing any other information about λ.

In a polynomial evaluation argument [10,23], a prover demonstrates that a secret committed value v is the evaluation of a public polynomial $h(U)$ at another secret committed value u.

In a range proof [9,38], a prover demonstrates that a secret committed value a is an element of the interval $[A; B]$.

One approach to constructing protocols for these applications is to design an arithmetic circuit which captures the desired conditions on the witness, and then apply existing zero-knowledge protocols for proving satisfiability in general circuits. There are currently several efficient arguments in the discrete logarithm setting. The methods of Cramer et al. [18] lead to arguments with communication complexity linear in the size of the circuit. The best interactive zero-knowledge protocol based on the discrete logarithm assumption for arithmetic circuits [7] yields a logarithmic communication complexity, but requires a non-constant number of rounds.

There are existing protocols for all three applications in the discrete logarithm setting that do not rely on general Circuit Satisfiability protocols. Cramer et al. [19] give techniques for composing sigma-protocols, producing proofs for AND composition, OR composition, and 1-out-of-many statements using sigma protocols for the individual statements. These techniques can be applied in a straightforward manner to produce sigma-protocols with linear communication complexity for the mentioned applications.

The goals of membership arguments are related to those of zero-knowledge sets [39]. Membership arguments allow a prover to commit to a secret value and show that it lies in a public set, without leaking information on the value. On the other hand, zero-knowledge sets allow the prover to commit to a secret set, and handle membership and non-membership queries in a verifiable manner, without leaking information on the set.

Herranz constructs attribute-based signatures [30] using what is essentially a set membership argument for multiple values. Like this work, the argument relies only on the discrete logarithm assumption, but the communication complexity is much higher; linear in the size of the set. Camenisch and Chaabouni [12] also provide set membership proofs with logarithmic communication complexity, and Fauzi et al. [22] construct constant size arguments for more complex relations between committed sets. The latter two works both rely on pairing-based assumptions.

Range arguments can be seen as a special case of membership arguments, where $\mathcal{L}$ is simply a list of consecutive integers. Many are based on the strong RSA assumption, and use Lagrange's Four-Square Theorem. Couteau et al. show that this assumption can be replaced by an RSA-variant which is much closer to the standard RSA assumption [17]. Examples are [27,38]. The work [16] gives an argument with sub-logarithmic communication complexity in the size of the list, which is comparable to the efficiency we achieve, and also relies on the hardness of the discrete logarithm problem, but uses pairings for verification.

Membership arguments also generalise arguments that a committed value lies in a linear subspace such as [31,32,35], which all make use of pairings. Peng [43] achieves a square-root complexity. Some existing protocols [2,28] even achieve logarithmic communication complexity. Our single-value membership proof is an extension of the latter works where we reduce the number of commitments from logarithmic to constant.

Cryptographic accumulators, [4,13,14,40], can also be used to give membership proofs. The members of a set are absorbed into a constant-size accumulated value. Witnesses for set-membership can then be generated and verified using the accumulated value. Efficient instantiations of accumulators exist and often rely on the Strong RSA assumption or pairing-based assumptions. An RSA modulus has to be $\frac{\lambda^3}{\text{polylog}\lambda}$ bits to provide security against factorisation using the General Number Field Sieve. Security of pairing-based schemes with constant embedding degree scale similarly due to sub-exponential algorithms for attacking the discrete logarithm problem in the target group. Furthermore, such schemes require a trusted setup. By contrast, we only require random group elements of size $O(\lambda)$ bits for security against discrete logarithm attacks in elliptic curve groups.

Some of the schemes can be adapted to give zero-knowledge arguments for non-membership, from a variety of settings. For example, [2,43] also give non-membership arguments in the discrete logarithm setting. Accumulators that support non-membership arguments have been constructed, based on both pairing assumptions ([21]) and the strong RSA assumption ([36]).

1.4   Outline

Section 2 contains preliminary definitions needed to understand our protocols. Section 3 gives an adaptation of the polynomial commitment scheme used in [5]. Section 4 gives a general batched witness relation and efficient batched argument. Finally, Sect. 5 gives concrete choices of parameters to obtain zero knowledge arguments for several useful languages.

2   Preliminaries

Write $y = A(x; r)$ when the algorithm A outputs y on input x with randomness r. We write $y \leftarrow A(x)$ to mean selecting r at random and setting $y = A(x; r)$. We write $y \leftarrow S$ for sampling y uniformly at random from a set S. We define $[n]$ to be the set of integers $1, \ldots, n$.

Let $\lambda \in \mathbb{N}$ be a security parameter, usually provided to the algorithms in unary form 1^λ. We say that $f : \mathbb{N} \mapsto [0, 1]$, is negligible if for every positive polynomial p, we have $f(\lambda) \leq \frac{1}{p(\lambda)}$ for $\lambda \gg 0$. We write $f(\lambda) \approx g(\lambda)$ if $|f(\lambda) - g(\lambda)|$ is negligible. We say that f is overwhelming if $f(\lambda) \approx 1$.

2.1   Assumptions

The results in this paper rely on the Discrete Logarithm Assumption. Let $\mathcal{G}$ be a probabilistic polynomial time algorithm that takes input 1^λ and outputs $gk = (\mathbb{G}, p, g)$. Here, $\mathbb{G}$ is a cyclic group of order p, which has efficient polynomial time algorithms for deciding membership and for computing group operations and inverses. The prime p has λ bits. The group is generated by the element g.

Definition 1 (Discrete Logarithm Assumption). *The discrete logarithm assumption holds relative to $\mathcal{G}$ if for all probabilistic polynomial time algorithms $\mathcal{A}$*

$$\Pr\left[gk = (\mathbb{G}, p, g) \leftarrow \mathcal{G}(1^\lambda); x \leftarrow \mathbb{Z}_p : x \leftarrow \mathcal{A}(gk, g^x)\right] \approx 0$$

2.2   Homomorphic Commitment Schemes

A commitment scheme allows a sender to commit to a secret value. Later on, the sender may open the commitment and reveal the value to another party, who can check that the value matches what was committed to. Commitment schemes should be hiding so that information about the secret value is not revealed prematurely, and binding so that the sender cannot reveal a different value to the one committed.

A non-interactive commitment scheme consists of two probabilistic polynomial time algorithms (Gen, Com). The first algorithm creates a commitment key $ck \leftarrow \text{Gen}(1^\lambda)$. The key specifies a message space $\mathcal{M}_{ck}$, a commitment space $\mathcal{C}_{ck}$ and a randomiser space $\mathcal{R}_{ck}$. The sender commits to $m \in \mathcal{M}_{ck}$ by selecting $r \leftarrow \mathcal{R}_{ck}$ and computing the commitment $c = \text{Com}_{ck}(m; r) \in \mathcal{C}_{ck}$.

Definition 2 (Hiding). *A commitment scheme* (Gen, Com) *is (computationally) hiding if for all probabilistic polynomial time stateful algorithms $\mathcal{A}$*

$$\Pr\left[ck \leftarrow \text{Gen}(1^\lambda); (m_0, m_1) \leftarrow \mathcal{A}(ck); b \leftarrow \{0, 1\}; c \leftarrow \text{Com}_{ck}(m_b) : \mathcal{A}(c) = b\right] \approx \frac{1}{2}$$

If we have equality above then we say that the commitment scheme is perfectly hiding.

Definition 3 (Binding). *A commitment scheme is (computationally) binding if for all probabilistic polynomial time adversaries $\mathcal{A}$*

$$\Pr\left[\begin{array}{l} ck \leftarrow \text{Gen}(1^\lambda); (m_0, r_1, m_1, r_1) \leftarrow \mathcal{A}(ck) : \\[2mm] m_0 \neq m_1 \wedge \text{Com}_{ck}(m_0; r_0) = \text{Com}_{ck}(m_1; r_1) \end{array}\right] \approx 0$$

If we have equality above then we say that the commitment scheme is perfectly binding.

Suppose further that $(\mathcal{M}_{ck}, +)$, $(\mathcal{R}_{ck}, +)$ and $(\mathcal{C}_{ck}, \cdot)$ are groups.

Definition 4 (Homomorphic Commitment Scheme). *We call the commitment scheme homomorphic if for all $\lambda \in \mathbb{N}$ and for all $ck \leftarrow \text{Gen}(1^\lambda)$ the commitment function* $\text{Com} : \mathcal{M}_{ck} \times \mathcal{R}_{ck} \to \mathcal{C}_{ck}$ *is a group-homomorphism, i.e., for all $m, m' \in \mathcal{M}_{ck}$ and all $r, r' \in \mathcal{R}_{ck}$*

$$\text{Com}_{ck}(m + m'; r + r') = \text{Com}_{ck}(m; r) \cdot \text{Com}_{ck}(m'; r')$$

Pedersen Commitments. Our zero-knowledge arguments can be instantiated with any homomorphic, perfectly hiding and computationally binding commitment scheme. For concreteness, we will focus on the Pedersen commitment scheme [42] to multiple values. The generator outputs a description of a group of prime order p and a set of random group elements $ck = (p, \mathbb{G}, g_1, \ldots, g_n, h)$. The message space is $\mathbb{Z}_p^n$, the randomness space is $\mathbb{Z}_p$ and the commitment space is $\mathbb{G}$. To commit to a vector $\boldsymbol{m} = (m_1, \ldots, m_n)$ pick $r \leftarrow \mathbb{Z}_p$ and return the commitment $c = \text{Com}_{ck}(\boldsymbol{m}; r) = h^r \prod_{i=1}^n g_i^{m_i}$. The Pedersen commitment scheme is homomorphic, perfectly hiding and computationally binding under the discrete logarithm assumption.

Throughout the paper, we make use of commitments for vectors of different sizes. We can use the same commitment key for this and just append the vectors with enough zeros to get length n.

2.3 Σ-Protocols

A Σ-protocol is a 3-move public-coin interactive protocol that enables a prover to convince a verifier that a particular statement is true. First, the prover sends an initial message to the verifier. The verifier sends back a randomly selected challenge. The prover responds to the challenge. Finally, the verifier decides whether or not to accept the proof based on the conversation.

We assume a probabilistic polynomial time algorithm $\mathcal{G}$ that generates a common reference string crs known to all parties. In this paper crs consists of the key for a homomorphic commitment scheme. For Pedersen commitments, this is just a list of random group elements.

Let R be a polynomial-time decidable relation. We call w a witness for statement u if $(crs, u, w) \in R$. A Σ-protocol for R is a collection of stateful probabilistic polynomial time algorithms $(\mathcal{G}, \mathcal{P}, \mathcal{V})$. The algorithm $\mathcal{G}$ provides a common reference string (which in our paper will be a commitment key as described above). Algorithms $\mathcal{P}, \mathcal{V}$ function as shown in Fig. 1. The challenge space $\mathcal{X}$ is implicitly given by the common reference string. Intuitively, $\mathcal{V}$ outputs 1 if accepting the proof and 0 if rejecting.

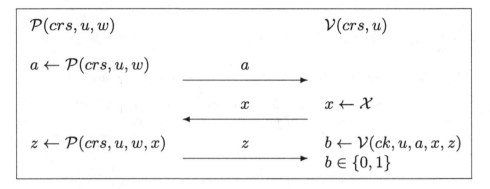

Fig. 1. A general Σ-protocol

Algorithms $(\mathcal{G}, \mathcal{P}, \mathcal{V})$ are a Σ-protocol if they satisfy completeness, special soundness, and special honest verifier zero-knowledge:

Definition 5 (Perfect Completeness). $(\mathcal{G}, \mathcal{P}, \mathcal{V})$ *is perfectly complete if for all probabilistic polynomial time algorithms* $\mathcal{A}$, *we have*

$$\Pr\left[\begin{array}{c} crs \leftarrow \mathcal{G}(1^\lambda); (u, w) \leftarrow \mathcal{A}(crs); a \leftarrow \mathcal{P}(crs, u, w); x \leftarrow \mathcal{X}; z \leftarrow \mathcal{P}(x): \\ (crs, u, w) \notin Ror\mathcal{V}(crs, u, a, x, z) = 1 \end{array}\right] = 1$$

Definition 6 (n-Special Soundness). $(\mathcal{G}, \mathcal{P}, \mathcal{V})$ *is n-special sound if there exists a probabilistic polynomial time algorithm* χ *that uses n accepting transcripts with the same initial message a and distinct challenges to compute the witness. For all probabilistic polynomial time algorithms* $\mathcal{A}$

$$\Pr\left[\begin{array}{c} crs \leftarrow \mathcal{G}(1^\lambda); (u, a, x_1, z_1, \ldots, x_n, z_n) \leftarrow \mathcal{A}(crs); \\ w \leftarrow \chi(u, a, x_1, z_1, \ldots, x_n, z_n): \\ (crs, u, w) \in Ror\exists i \in [n] such that\mathcal{V}(crs, u, a, x_i, z_i) \neq 1 \end{array}\right] \approx 1,$$

where the adversary outputs distinct $x_1, \ldots, x_n$.

If the above holds with equality, then we say that $(\mathcal{G}, \mathcal{P}, \mathcal{V})$ *has perfect n-special soundness.*

Definition 7 (Special Honest Verifier Zero Knowledge (SHVZK)). *We say that $(\mathcal{G}, \mathcal{P}, \mathcal{V})$ has SHVZK if there exists a probabilistic polynomial time simulator $\mathcal{S}$ such that for all interactive probabilistic polynomial time algorithms $\mathcal{A}$*

$$\Pr\left[crs \leftarrow \mathcal{G}(1^\lambda); (u, w, x) \leftarrow \mathcal{A}(crs); a \leftarrow \mathcal{P}(crs, u, w); z \leftarrow \mathcal{P}(x) : \mathcal{A}(crs, a, z) = 1\right]$$
$$\approx \Pr\left[crs \leftarrow \mathcal{G}(1^\lambda); (u, w, x) \leftarrow \mathcal{A}(crs); (a, z) \leftarrow \mathcal{S}(crs, u, x) : \mathcal{A}(crs, a, z) = 1\right]$$

If the above holds with equality, then we say that $(\mathcal{G}, \mathcal{P}, \mathcal{V})$ has perfect SHVZK.

Full Zero-Knowledge. In real life applications special honest verifier zero-knowledge may not suffice since a malicious verifier may give non-random challenges. However, it is easy to convert an SHVZK argument into a full zero-knowledge argument secure against *arbitrary* verifiers in the common reference string model using standard techniques. The conversion can be very efficient and only costs a small additive overhead. Details of conversion methods can be found in [20, 24, 27].

2.4 Relations

In this section, we describe the relations for our zero-knowledge proofs. The prover's witness is a secret vector a satisfying some conditions, and an opening to a commitment C which is computed from a.

This type of relation could be modelled using a relation with a polynomial P to impose conditions on a, and another polynomial Q to compute the opening to C. The value r is the randomness used to make the commitment.

$$\mathbf{P}(a) = 0, \quad C = \mathrm{Com}(\mathbf{Q}(a); r)$$

For example, $a = (a_0, a_1, a_2)$ could be a secret vector of bits, imposed by $P(a) = a \circ (1 - a)$, and $Q(a) = a_0 + 2a_1 + 4a_2$ could compute the integer represented by the bits.

We also incorporate a public vector b, which can be seen as a 'tweak' and allows modification of the statement. For example, setting $Q(a, b) = a \cdot b$, we can recover the range proof above by using $b = (1, 2, 4)$. We can also get relations about other knapsacks by using a different value of b.

More formally, let $\mathbf{P}(\mathrm{a}, \mathrm{b}), \mathbf{Q}(\mathrm{a}, \mathrm{b})$ be length ℓ_P, ℓ_Q vectors of polynomials of degrees d_P, d_Q respectively. Let C be a commitment. Let $\mathbf{b} \in \mathbb{Z}_p^{\ell_b}$ be a public vector of field elements. The prover gives a zero-knowledge argument of knowledge of $\mathrm{a} \in \mathbb{Z}_p^{\ell_a}$ and $r \in \mathbb{Z}_p$ such that

$$\mathbf{P}(\mathrm{a}, \mathrm{b}) = 0, \quad C = \mathrm{Com}(\mathbf{Q}(\mathrm{a}, \mathrm{b}); r)$$

We give more general batched proofs which can handle t instances at once. Let $C_1, \ldots, C_m$ be commitments. Let $t = mn$. Let $\mathbf{b}_{1,1}, \ldots, \mathbf{b}_{m,n} \in \mathbb{Z}_p^{\ell_b}$ be public vectors of field elements. The $\mathbf{b}_{i,j}$ values allow a single instance to capture some variation in the statement. The batched argument is an argument of knowledge of values $\{\mathbf{a}_{i,j}\}_{i,j=1}^{m,n}$ and $\{r_i\}_{i=1}^{m}$, such that $\mathbf{P}(\mathbf{a}_{i,j}, \mathbf{b}_{i,j}) = \mathbf{0}$ for $i \in [m], j \in [n]$, and the prover knows commitment openings

$$
\begin{aligned}
C_1 &= \mathrm{Com}(\mathbf{Q}(\mathbf{a}_{1,1}, \mathbf{b}_{1,1}), \quad \mathbf{Q}(\mathbf{a}_{1,2}, \mathbf{b}_{1,2}), \quad \ldots, \mathbf{Q}(\mathbf{a}_{1,n}, \mathbf{b}_{1,n}); \quad r_1) \\
C_2 &= \mathrm{Com}(\mathbf{Q}(\mathbf{a}_{2,1}, \mathbf{b}_{2,1}), \quad \mathbf{Q}(\mathbf{a}_{2,2}, \mathbf{b}_{2,2}), \quad \ldots, \mathbf{Q}(\mathbf{a}_{2,n}, \mathbf{b}_{2,n}); \quad r_2)
\end{aligned}
$$

$$
\vdots
$$

$$
C_m = \mathrm{Com}(\mathbf{Q}(\mathbf{a}_{m,1}, \mathbf{b}_{m,1}), \mathbf{Q}(\mathbf{a}_{m,2}, \mathbf{b}_{m,2}), \ldots, \mathbf{Q}(\mathbf{a}_{m,n}, \mathbf{b}_{m,n}); r_m)
$$

When $m = n = 1$, we have $t = 1$ and recover the relation for a zero-knowledge argument of knowledge for a single instance.

The idea is that $\mathbf{Q}$ allows the prover to prove things about parts of the witness that were included as commitments in the statement for the zero-knowledge proof. Then $\mathbf{P}$ deals with parts of the witness that were not included as commitments in the statement. Therefore, by choosing $\mathbf{P}$ and $\mathbf{Q}$ appropriately, we can easily deal with applications where the evaluation of a polynomial is known, and applications where it is in committed form.

We can easily generalise to the case where multiple polynomials $\mathbf{Q}_1(\mathbf{a}, \mathbf{b}), \ldots, \mathbf{Q}_k(\mathbf{a}, \mathbf{b})$ are given in separate commitments.

2.5   Lagrange Polynomials

Let $z_1, \ldots, z_m$ be distinct points in some field. The Lagrange polynomials $l_1(X), \ldots, l_m(X)$ are the unique polynomials of degree $m - 1$ such that $l_i(z_j) = \delta_{i,j}$, where $\delta_{i,j}$ is the Kronecker-delta. In cryptography, Lagrange polynomials have been used for secret-sharing [45].

For $j \in [m]$, $l_j(X)$ can be computed as

$$
\ell_j(X) := \prod_{\substack{0 \le m \le k \\ m \ne j}} \frac{X - z_m}{z_j - z_m} = \frac{(X - z_0)}{(z_j - z_0)} \cdots \frac{(X - z_{j-1})}{(z_j - z_{j-1})} \frac{(X - z_{j+1})}{(z_j - z_{j+1})} \cdots \frac{(X - z_k)}{(z_j - z_k)}
$$

3   Polynomial Commitment Schemes

We present a protocol which allows a prover to commit to a polynomial in the discrete-logarithm setting, using a homomorphic commitment scheme. The prover may then later reveal to the verifier an evaluation of the polynomial in a specific point x chosen by the verifier and prove the evaluation is correct. Bootle et al. [7] dealt with a similar problem for Laurent polynomials with constant term zero, whose coefficients were single field elements. We use the same techniques and generalise to the case of vector coefficients. We treat only positive powers and ignore the condition on the constant term since this suffices for our needs. However, the case of Laurent polynomials is straightforward and similar to [7].

3.1   Definition

A polynomial commitment scheme $(\mathrm{Gen}, \mathrm{PolyCommit}, \mathrm{PolyEval}, \mathrm{PolyVerify})$ enables a prover to commit to a secret vector of polynomials $\mathbf{h}(X) \in \mathbb{Z}_p^l[X]$

of some known degree N. Later on the prover may choose to evaluate the committed polynomial in a point $x \in \mathbb{Z}_p$ and send an opening to the verifier.

$\text{Gen}(1^\lambda) \rightarrow ck$: Gen is a probabilistic polynomial time algorithm that returns a commitment key ck. The commitment key specifies among other things a prime p of size $|p| = \lambda$.

$\text{PolyCommit}(ck, \mathbf{h}(X)) \rightarrow (\mathsf{msg}_1, \mathsf{st})$: PolyCommit is a probabilistic polynomial time algorithm that given a commitment key ck and a vector of degree N polynomials returns a commitment message msg_1 and a state st.

$\text{PolyEval}(\mathsf{st}, x) \rightarrow \mathsf{msg}_2$: PolyEval is a deterministic polynomial time algorithm that given a state and a point $x \in \mathbb{Z}_p$ returns an evaluation message msg_2.

$\text{PolyVerify}(ck, \mathsf{msg}_1, \mathsf{msg}_2, x) \rightarrow \bar{\mathbf{h}}$: PolyVerify is a deterministic polynomial time algorithm that given a commitment key, a commitment message, an evaluation message and a point $x \in \mathbb{Z}_p$ returns $\perp$ if it rejects the input, or a purported evaluation of the committed vector of polynomials in x.

A polynomial commitment scheme should be complete, $(m + 1)$-special sound and special honest verifier zero-knowledge as defined below.

The definition of completeness simply guarantees that if PolyCommit and PolyVerify are carried out honestly, then PolyVerify will return the correct polynomial evaluation $\mathbf{h}(x)$.

Definition 8 (Perfect Completeness)
(Gen, PolyCommit, PolyEval, PolyVerify) has perfect completeness if for all $\lambda \in \mathbb{N}$, for all $ck \leftarrow \text{Gen}(1^\lambda)$, and all $\mathbf{h}(X) \in \mathbb{Z}_p^l[X]$ of degree N, and all $x \in \mathbb{Z}_p$

$$\Pr \left[\begin{array}{l} (\mathsf{msg}_1, \mathsf{st}) \leftarrow \text{PolyCommit}(ck, \mathbf{h}(X)) \\ \mathsf{msg}_2 \leftarrow \text{PolyEval}(\mathsf{st}, x) \\ \bar{\mathbf{h}} \leftarrow \text{PolyVerify}(ck, \mathsf{msg}_1, \mathsf{msg}_2, x) \end{array} : \bar{\mathbf{h}} = \mathbf{h}(x) \right] = 1.$$

The definition of $(m + 1)$-Special Soundness guarantees that given $m + 1$ accepting evaluations for different evaluation points, but from the same polynomial commitment message msg_1, then it is possible to extract a polynomial $\mathbf{h}(X)$ that is consistent with the evaluations produced. Furthermore, any other accepting evaluations for the same commitment will also be evaluations of $\mathbf{h}(X)$.

Definition 9 (Computational $(m + 1)$-Special Soundness)
(Gen, PolyCommit, PolyEval, PolyVerify) is $(m+1)$-special sound if there exists a probabilistic polynomial time algorithm χ that uses $m+1$ accepting transcripts with the same commitment message msg_1 to compute the committed polynomial $\mathbf{h}(X)$. For all probabilistic polynomial time adversaries $\mathcal{A}$ and all $L \geq m$

$$\Pr \left[\begin{array}{l} ck \leftarrow \text{Gen}(1^\lambda) \\ (\mathsf{msg}_1, x^{(0)}, \mathsf{msg}_2^{(0)}, \ldots, x^{(L)}, \mathsf{msg}_2^{(L)}) \leftarrow \mathcal{A}(ck) \\ \mathbf{h}(X) \leftarrow \chi(ck, \mathsf{msg}_1, x^{(0)}, \mathsf{msg}_2^{(0)}, \ldots, x^{(m)}, \mathsf{msg}_2^{(m)}) \\ \bar{\mathbf{h}}_i \leftarrow \text{PolyVerify}(ck, \mathsf{msg}_1, \mathsf{msg}_2^{(i)}, x^{(i)}) \end{array} : \begin{array}{l} \textit{There is a } \bar{\mathbf{h}}_i = \perp \\ \textit{or all } \bar{\mathbf{h}}_i = \mathbf{h}(x^{(i)}) \end{array} \right] \approx 1,$$

where the adversary outputs distinct points $x^{(0)}, \ldots, x^{(L)} \in \mathbb{Z}_p$ and the extractor returns a degree N vector of polynomials.

Perfect special honest verifier zero-knowledge means that given any evaluation point x and an evaluation $\mathbf{h}(x)$, it is possible to simulate $\mathsf{msg}_1, \mathsf{msg}_2$ that are distributed exactly as in a real execution of the protocol, in a way that is consistent with the evaluation $\mathbf{h}(x)$.

Definition 10 (Perfect Special Honest Verifier Zero Knowledge)
(Gen, PolyCommit, PolyEval, PolyVerify) *has* perfect special honest verifier zero knowledge *(SHVZK) if there exists a probabilistic polynomial time simulator $\mathcal{S}$ such that for all stateful probabilistic polynomial time adversaries $\mathcal{A}$*

$$\Pr\left[\begin{array}{l} ck \leftarrow \mathrm{Gen}(1^\lambda); (\mathbf{h}(X), x) \leftarrow \mathcal{A}(ck) \\ (\mathsf{msg}_1, \mathsf{st}) \leftarrow \mathrm{PolyCommit}(ck, \mathbf{h}(X)) \; : \; \mathcal{A}(\mathsf{msg}_1, \mathsf{msg}_2) = 1 \\ \mathsf{msg}_2 \leftarrow \mathrm{PolyEval}(\mathsf{st}, x) \end{array}\right]$$

$$= \Pr\left[\begin{array}{l} ck \leftarrow \mathrm{Gen}(1^\lambda); (\mathbf{h}(X), x) \leftarrow \mathcal{A}(ck) \\ (\mathsf{msg}_1, \mathsf{msg}_2) \leftarrow \mathcal{S}(ck, x, \mathbf{h}(x)) \end{array} \; : \; \mathcal{A}(\mathsf{msg}_1, \mathsf{msg}_2) = 1\right]$$

3.2 Construction

In the following, we will build a polynomial commitment scheme on top of a perfectly-hiding, homomorphic commitment scheme (Gen, Com) to vectors in $\mathbb{Z}_p^{nl}$. Let us first give some intuition about how the construction will work.

Let $\mathbf{h}(X) = \sum_{i=0}^{N} \mathbf{h}_i X^i$ be a polynomial of degree $N = (n+1)m - 1$ with coefficients that are row-vectors in $\mathbb{Z}_p^l$. Define an $m \times (n+1)l$ matrix

$$\begin{pmatrix} \mathbf{h}_{0,0} & \mathbf{h}_{0,1} & \cdots & \mathbf{h}_{0,n} \\ \mathbf{h}_{1,0} & \mathbf{h}_{1,1} & \cdots & \mathbf{h}_{1,n} \\ \vdots & \vdots & \ddots & \\ \mathbf{h}_{m-1,0} & \mathbf{h}_{m-1,1} & \cdots & \mathbf{h}_{m-1,n} \end{pmatrix} = \begin{pmatrix} \mathbf{h}_0 & \mathbf{h}_m & \cdots & \mathbf{h}_{nm} \\ \mathbf{h}_1 & \mathbf{h}_{m+1} & \cdots & \mathbf{h}_{nm+1} \\ \vdots & \vdots & \ddots & \\ \mathbf{h}_{m-1} & \mathbf{h}_{2m-1} & \cdots & \mathbf{h}_N \end{pmatrix}$$

With this matrix we have $\mathbf{h}(X) = \sum_{j=0}^{n} (\sum_{i=0}^{m-1} \mathbf{h}_{i,j} X^i) X^{mj}$. In the polynomial commitment scheme, the prover commits to each row of the matrix with commitments $\{H_i\}_{i=0}^{m-1}$. After receiving a point x from the verifier, the prover computes for each column $\bar{\mathbf{h}}_j = \sum_{i=0}^{m} \mathbf{h}_{i,j} x^i$ and sends them to the verifier as part of openings of the commitment $\prod_{i=0}^{m-1} H_i^{x^i}$. The verifier can use the homomorphic property of the commitments to check that the $\bar{\mathbf{h}}_j$ values are correctly formed and compute $\mathbf{h}(x) = \sum_{j=0}^{n} \bar{\mathbf{h}}_j x^{jm}$.

While the main idea we have sketched above gives the verifier assurance that the committed polynomial has been correctly evaluated, the prover may not be happy. The problem is that the solution gives away information about the coefficients of $\mathbf{h}(X)$. We will therefore introduce some random blinding vectors to ensure no information is leaked about the committed coefficients except the evaluation of the polynomial. We will also adjust the protocol to handle an arbitrary polynomial degree $N = mn + d$ for $0 \leq d < m$ by shifting the first column of the matrix.

We pick random blinders $\mathbf{b}_1, \ldots, \mathbf{b}_n \leftarrow \mathbb{Z}_p^l$ and define an $(m+1) \times (n+1)l$ matrix $\{\mathbf{h}_{i,j}\}_{i=0,j=0}^{m,n}$ as follows:

$$
\begin{pmatrix}
\mathbf{h}_0 & \mathbf{b}_1 & \cdots \mathbf{b}_{n-1} & \mathbf{b}_n \\
\mathbf{h}_1 & \mathbf{h}_{d+1} & \cdots \mathbf{h}_{(n-2)m+d+1} & \mathbf{h}_{(n-1)m+d+1} \\
 & & & \vdots \\
\mathbf{h}_d - \mathbf{b}_1 & \vdots & \ddots & \mathbf{h}_{nm} \\
0 & & & \mathbf{h}_{nm+1} \\
\vdots & & & \vdots \\
0 & \mathbf{h}_{m+d-1} & \cdots \mathbf{h}_{(n-2)m+d-1} & \mathbf{h}_{N-1} \\
0 & \mathbf{h}_{m+d} - \mathbf{b}_2 & \cdots \mathbf{h}_{(n-2)m+d} - \mathbf{b}_n & \mathbf{h}_N
\end{pmatrix}
$$

We can therefore rewrite the polynomial as

$$
\mathbf{h}(X) = \sum_{i=0}^{m} \mathbf{h}_{i,0} X^i + \sum_{j=1}^{n} \left(\sum_{i=0}^{m} \mathbf{h}_{i,j} X^i \right) X^{(j-1)m+d}.
$$

In the polynomial commitment scheme, the prover commits to each row of the matrix with commitments $\{H_i\}_{i=0}^m$. After receiving a point x from the verifier, the prover computes for each column $\bar{\mathbf{h}}_j = \sum_{i=0}^{m} \mathbf{h}_{i,j} x^i$ and sends them to the verifier as part of an opening of the commitment $\prod_{i=0}^m H_i^{x^i}$. The verifier can use the opening to check that the $\bar{\mathbf{h}}_j$ values are correct and compute $\mathbf{h}(x) = \bar{\mathbf{h}}_0 + \sum_{j=1}^{n} \bar{\mathbf{h}}_j x^{(j-1)m+d}$. We describe the full polynomial commitment scheme below.

Common Input: ck

PolyCommit$(ck, \mathbf{h}(X)) \rightarrow (\mathsf{msg}_1, \mathsf{st})$: The prover randomly selects $\mathbf{b}_1, \ldots,$ $\mathbf{b}_n \leftarrow \mathbb{Z}_p^l$ and arranges them into a matrix with entries $\{\mathbf{h}_{i,j}\}_{i=0,j=0}^{m,n}$ as follows:

$$
\begin{pmatrix}
\mathbf{h}_0 & \mathbf{b}_1 & \cdots \mathbf{b}_{n-1} & \mathbf{b}_n \\
\mathbf{h}_1 & \mathbf{h}_{d+1} & \cdots \mathbf{h}_{(n-2)m+d+1} & \mathbf{h}_{(n-1)m+d+1} \\
 & & & \vdots \\
\mathbf{h}_d - \mathbf{b}_1 & \vdots & \ddots & \mathbf{b}_n \\
0 & & & \mathbf{h}_{nm+1} \\
\vdots & & & \vdots \\
0 & \mathbf{h}_{m+d-1} & \cdots \mathbf{h}_{(n-2)m+d-1} & \mathbf{h}_{N-1} \\
0 & \mathbf{h}_{m+d} - \mathbf{b}_2 & \cdots \mathbf{h}_{(n-2)m+d} - \mathbf{b}_n & \mathbf{h}_N
\end{pmatrix}
$$

For $0 \le i \le m$, the prover randomly selects $r_i \leftarrow \mathbb{Z}_p$ and computes a commitment H_i to the ith row of the matrix using randomness r_i.

$$
\mathsf{msg}_1 = \left(\{H_i\}_{i=0}^m \right), \qquad \mathsf{st} = \left(\mathbf{h}(X), \{\mathbf{b}_j\}_{j=1}^n, \{r_i\}_{i=0}^m \right)
$$

The prover sends msg_1 to the verifier.

PolyEval(st, x): $\to$ (msg$_2$): For $0 \le j \le n$, the prover computes

$$\bar{\mathbf{h}}_j = \sum_{i=0}^{m} \mathbf{h}_{i,j} x^{i+1}.$$

The prover also computes $\bar{r} = \sum_{i=0}^{m} r_i x^i$.
Set $\mathsf{msg}_2 = \left(\{\bar{\mathbf{h}}_j\}_{j=0}^{n}, \bar{r} \right)$.
The prover sends msg_2 to the verifier.
PolyVerify(ck, msg_1, msg_2, x): $\to$ (cmt): The verifier checks whether

$$\mathsf{com}(\bar{\mathbf{h}}_0, \dots, \bar{\mathbf{h}}_n; \bar{r}) = \prod_{i=0}^{m} H_i^{x^i}.$$

Return $\bot$ if this fails.
After accepting the commitment opening, the verifier returns

$$\bar{\mathbf{h}} = \sum_{i=0}^{m} \mathbf{h}_{i,0} x^i + \sum_{j=1}^{n} \left(\sum_{i=0}^{m} \mathbf{h}_{i,j} x^i \right) x^{(j-1)m+d}.$$

Lemma 1. *The polynomial commitment protocol given above has perfect completeness, computational $(m+1)$-special-soundness, and perfect special honest verifier zero-knowledge.*

Proof. By inspection, it follows that when the prover is honest, the verifier always recovers $\bar{\mathbf{h}} = \mathbf{h}(x)$.

Given x and $\mathbf{h}(x)$, we describe an efficient simulator to prove special honest verifier zero knowledge. The simulator first picks random $\bar{\mathbf{h}}_1, \dots, \bar{\mathbf{h}}_n \leftarrow \mathbb{Z}_p^l$ and then computes $\bar{\mathbf{h}}_0 = \mathbf{h}(x) - \sum_{j=1}^{n} \bar{\mathbf{h}}_j x^{(j-1)m+d}$. In other words, the $\mathbf{h}_j$ are chosen uniformly at random, conditional on giving the correct evaluation $\mathbf{h}(x)$. The simulator also picks at random $\bar{r} \in \mathbb{Z}_p$ and $r_1, \dots, r_m \leftarrow \mathbb{Z}_p$ and sets $H_i = \mathsf{Com}_{ck}(\mathbf{0}; r_i)$. Finally, it computes $H_0 = \mathsf{Com}_{ck}(\bar{\mathbf{h}}_0, \dots, \bar{\mathbf{h}}_n; \bar{r}) \prod_{i=1}^{m} H_i^{-x^i}$.

This is a perfect SHVZK simulation. First, because the commitment scheme is perfectly hiding, the commitments $H_1, \dots, H_m$ are identically distributed in real proofs and simulated proofs. The values $\bar{\mathbf{h}}_1, \dots, \bar{\mathbf{h}}_n$ and $\bar{r}$ are also independently and uniformly at random in real proofs due to the choices of $\mathbf{b}_1, \dots, \mathbf{b}_n$ and r_0, just as in the simulated proofs. Finally, given these random values both real and simulated proofs, the matching H_0 and $\bar{\mathbf{h}}_0$ are uniquely determined. This means we have identical distributions of real and simulated proofs which are consistent with the evaluation $\mathbf{h}(x)$.

Finally, we prove $(m+1)$-special soundness. Suppose that we are given msg_1 and $x^{(0)}, \dots, x^{(m)}$, $\mathsf{msg}_2^{(0)}, \dots, \mathsf{msg}_2^{(m)}$ which are all accepting, and where the $x^{(i)}$ are distinct. Consider the Vandermonde matrix:

$$\begin{pmatrix} 1 & 1 & \cdots & 1 \\ x^{(0)} & x^{(1)} & \cdots & x^{(m)} \\ \vdots & \vdots & \ddots & \vdots \\ \left(x^{(0)}\right)^m & \left(x^{(1)}\right)^m & \cdots & \left(x^{(m)}\right)^m \end{pmatrix}$$

This matrix is invertible, meaning that for any $0 \leq k \leq m$, we can take linear combinations of the columns to obtain $(0, \ldots, 0, 1, 0, \ldots, 0)^T$, where the kth entry is 1. We may take the same linear combinations of the verification equation $\text{com}(\bar{\mathbf{h}}_0, \ldots, \bar{\mathbf{h}}_n; \bar{r}) = \prod_{i=0}^{m} H_i^{x^i}$ in order to find openings to each H_k. We now have that $H_0, \ldots, H_m$ are commitments to known row vectors $(\mathbf{h}_{i,0}, \ldots, \mathbf{h}_{i,n})$ with known randomness r_i. We define the extracted vector of polynomials to be $\mathbf{h}(X) = \sum_{i=0}^{m} \mathbf{h}_{i,0} X^i + \sum_{j=1}^{n} \left(\sum_{i=0}^{m} \mathbf{h}_{i,j} X^i \right) X^{(j-1)m+d}$, which is a vector of degree N polynomials.

By the binding property of the commitment scheme, for each accepting transcript, we have

$$\bar{\mathbf{h}}_k = \sum_{i=0}^{m} \mathbf{h}_{i,0}(x^{(k)})^i + \sum_{j=1}^{n} \left(\sum_{i=0}^{m} \mathbf{h}_{i,j}(x^{(k)})^i \right) (x^{(k)})^{(j-1)m+d}.$$

Therefore, all openings are consistent with the extracted polynomial $\mathbf{h}(X)$.   □

Communication. The prover must send $m+1$ group elements and $l(n+1)+1$ field elements to the verifier.

Computation. Prover computation is dominated by $m + 1$ multi-exponentiations of width $l(n + 1) + 1$ costing approximately $\frac{lmn}{\log ln} + \frac{l}{\log l}$ exponentiations. Verifier computation is dominated by a multi-exponentiation of width $l(n + 1) + m + 1$ costing approximately $\frac{ln+m}{\log(ln+m)}$ exponentiations.

4   Batch Protocol for Low Degree Relations

We give an argument of knowledge of values $\{\mathbf{a}_{i,j}\}_{i \in [m], j \in [n]}$ and $\{r_i\}_{i \in [m]}$, such that $\mathbf{P}(\mathbf{a}_{i,j}, \mathbf{b}_{i,j}) = \mathbf{0}$ for $i \in [m], j \in [n]$, and the prover knows commitment openings

$$
\begin{aligned}
C_1 &= \text{com}(\mathbf{Q}(\mathbf{a}_{1,1}, \mathbf{b}_{1,1}), \quad \mathbf{Q}(\mathbf{a}_{1,2}, \mathbf{b}_{1,2}), \quad \ldots, \mathbf{Q}(\mathbf{a}_{1,n}, \mathbf{b}_{1,n}); \quad r_1) \\
C_2 &= \text{com}(\mathbf{Q}(\mathbf{a}_{2,1}, \mathbf{b}_{2,1}), \quad \mathbf{Q}(\mathbf{a}_{2,2}, \mathbf{b}_{2,2}), \quad \ldots, \mathbf{Q}(\mathbf{a}_{2,n}, \mathbf{b}_{2,n}); \quad r_2) \\
&\vdots \\
C_m &= \text{com}(\mathbf{Q}(\mathbf{a}_{m,1}, \mathbf{b}_{m,1}), \mathbf{Q}(\mathbf{a}_{m,2}, \mathbf{b}_{m,2}), \ldots, \mathbf{Q}(\mathbf{a}_{m,n}, \mathbf{b}_{m,n}); r_m)
\end{aligned}
$$

The protocol we design will be more efficient than repeating $t = mn$ instances of the basic protocol in parallel, as the communication depends on $\sqrt{t}$ rather than t.

In the following we will refer to the parameters $\ell_a, \ell_b, \ell_P, d_P, \ell_Q, d_Q$ such that $\mathbf{a}_{i,j} \in \mathbb{Z}_p^{\ell_a}$, $\mathbf{b}_{i,j} \in \mathbb{Z}_p^{\ell_b}$, $\mathbf{P}$ is a vector of ℓ_P $(\ell_a + \ell_b)$-variate polynomials of total degree d_P, and $\mathbf{Q}$ is a vector of ℓ_Q $(\ell_a + \ell_b)$-variate polynomials of total degree d_Q.

4.1   Intuition Behind Protocol

The protocol embeds multiple instances of the same polynomial equality into a single polynomial by using Lagrange interpolation polynomials, inspired by [1,26]. To recover a single instance, simply evaluate the polynomial in one of the interpolation points.

More concretely, let $z_1, \ldots, z_m$ be distinct points in $\mathbb{Z}_p$, and let $l_1(X), \ldots, l_m(X)$ be their associated Lagrange polynomials such that $l_i(z_j) = \delta_{i,j}$. Let $l_0(X) = \prod_{i=1}^{m}(X - z_i)$. The prover produces the following commitments.

$$
\begin{aligned}
A_0 &= \mathrm{com}(\mathbf{a}_{0,1}, \ \mathbf{a}_{0,2}, \ \ldots, \mathbf{a}_{0,n} \ ; r_0 \ ) \\
A_1 &= \mathrm{com}(\mathbf{a}_{1,1}, \ \mathbf{a}_{1,2}, \ \ldots, \mathbf{a}_{1,n} \ ; r_1 \ ) \\
A_2 &= \mathrm{com}(\mathbf{a}_{2,1}, \ \mathbf{a}_{2,2}, \ \ldots, \mathbf{a}_{2,n} \ ; r_2 \ ) \\
&\ \vdots \\
A_m &= \mathrm{com}(\mathbf{a}_{m,1}, \mathbf{a}_{m,2}, \ \ldots, \mathbf{a}_{m,n} \ ; r_m \ )
\end{aligned}
$$

Here, the values $\mathbf{a}_{0,1}, \ldots, \mathbf{a}_{0,n} \in \mathbb{Z}_p^{l_a}$, where the value of the first index is 0, are blinding values chosen uniformly at random. These are completely unrelated to the values of the witness, which are $\mathbf{a}_{1,1}, \ldots, \mathbf{a}_{m,n}$, where the first index has a value strictly greater than 0. After receiving a random challenge x from the verifier, the prover sends $\bar{\mathbf{a}}_j = \sum_{i=0}^{m} \mathbf{a}_{i,j} l_i(x)$ to the verifier for each $j \in [n]$.

The verifier now checks the received $\bar{\mathbf{a}}_j$ against the commitments A_i. This proves knowledge of the $\mathbf{a}$ values. It remains to demonstrate that $\mathbf{a}_{i,j}, \mathbf{b}_{i,j}$ satisfy the polynomial relations in the statement. Let $\bar{\mathbf{b}}_j = \sum_{i=1}^{m} \mathbf{b}_{ij} l_i(x)$. The verifier evaluates $\mathbf{P}, \mathbf{Q}$ using $\bar{\mathbf{a}}_j$ and $\bar{\mathbf{b}}_j$ for each j. By definition of $\bar{\mathbf{a}}_j$ and $\bar{\mathbf{b}}_j$, when evaluating at an interpolation point z_i, we obtain the single evaluation of the original polynomial, $\mathbf{P}(\mathbf{a}_{i,j}, \mathbf{b}_{i,j})$. This implies, for example, that $\mathbf{P}(\bar{\mathbf{a}}_j, \bar{\mathbf{b}}_j) \equiv \mathbf{0}$ mod $l_0(x)$, or in other words, that $\mathbf{P}(\bar{\mathbf{a}}_j, \bar{\mathbf{b}}_j)$ is a multiple of $l_0(X)$ for each j. The prover must commit to the coefficients of $\mathbf{P}(\bar{\mathbf{a}}_j, \bar{\mathbf{b}}_j)/l_0(x)$ in advance (as a polynomial in x), and uses the polynomial commitment scheme to achieve this for every j simultaneously.

Finally, the prover needs to convince the verifier that the commitments C_i contain commitments to $\mathbf{Q}(\mathbf{a}_{i,j}, \mathbf{b}_{i,j})$. This is done in a similar way to the $\mathbf{P}$ polynomial, except here we build up polynomial equalities over committed values. The full protocol can be found below.

Common Reference String: $crs = (ck, z_1, \ldots, z_m)$ where $ck \leftarrow \mathrm{Gen}(1^\lambda)$ and $z_1, \ldots, z_m$ are distinct points in $\mathbb{Z}_p$ defining Lagrange polynomials $l_1(X), \ldots, l_m(X)$ such that $l_i(z_j) = \delta_{i,j}$ and defining $l_0(X) = \prod_{j=1}^{m}(X - z_j)$.
Statement: $\{C_i\}_{i \in [m]}, \{\mathbf{b}_{i,j}\}_{i \in [m], j \in [n]}, \mathbf{P}, \mathbf{Q}$ polynomials.
Prover's Witness: $\{\mathbf{a}_{i,j}\}_{i \in [m], j \in [n]}, \{r_i\}_{i \in [m]}$ such that

$$
\mathbf{P}(\mathbf{a}_{i,j}, \mathbf{b}_{i,j}) = \mathbf{0} \text{ for } i \in [m], j \in [n]
$$

$$
C_i = \mathrm{com}(\mathbf{Q}(\mathbf{a}_{i,1}, \mathbf{b}_{i,1}), \mathbf{Q}(\mathbf{a}_{i,2}, \mathbf{b}_{i,2}), \ldots, \mathbf{Q}(\mathbf{a}_{i,n}, \mathbf{b}_{i,n}); r_i) \text{ for } i \in [m]
$$

$\mathbf{P} \rightarrow \mathbf{V}$: Pick $r_0, s_0, \ldots, s_m \leftarrow \mathbb{Z}_p$ and $\mathbf{a}_{0,1}, \ldots, \mathbf{a}_{0,n} \leftarrow \mathbb{Z}_p^{\ell_a}$ and $\mathbf{c}_1, \ldots, \mathbf{c}_n \leftarrow \mathbb{Z}_p^{\ell_Q}$. Compute

$$C_0 = \mathrm{Com}_{ck}(\mathbf{c}_1, \ldots, \mathbf{c}_n; r_0) \quad \text{and} \quad A_i = \mathrm{Com}_{ck}(\mathbf{a}_{i,1}, \ldots, \mathbf{a}_{i,n}; s_i) \text{ for } i \in \{0\} \cup [m].$$

Define

$$\bar{\mathbf{a}}_j(X) = \sum_{i=0}^m \mathbf{a}_{i,j} l_i(X) \quad \bar{\mathbf{b}}_j(X) = \sum_{i=1}^m \mathbf{b}_{i,j} l_i(X)$$

$$\mathbf{P}_j^*(X) = \frac{\mathbf{P}\left(\bar{\mathbf{a}}_j(X), \bar{\mathbf{b}}_j(X)\right)}{l_0(X)} \quad \mathbf{Q}_j^*(X) = \mathbf{c}_j + \frac{\sum_{i=1}^m \mathbf{Q}(\mathbf{a}_{i,j}, \mathbf{b}_{i,j}) l_i(X) - \mathbf{Q}\left(\bar{\mathbf{a}}_j(X), \bar{\mathbf{b}}_j(X)\right)}{l_0(X)}$$

Run $\mathrm{PolyCommit}(ck, \{\mathbf{P}_j^*(X)\}_{j \in [n]}) \rightarrow (\mathsf{msg}_{P,1}, \mathsf{st}_P)$.
Run $\mathrm{PolyCommit}(ck, \{\mathbf{Q}_j^*(X)\}_{j \in [n]}) \rightarrow (\mathsf{msg}_{Q,1}, \mathsf{st}_Q)$.
The prover sends $\{A_i\}_{i \in [m]}$ and $\mathsf{msg}_{P,1}, \mathsf{msg}_{Q,1}$ to the verifier.
$\mathbf{P} \leftarrow \mathbf{V}$: Send the challenge $x \leftarrow \mathbb{Z}_p \setminus \{z_1, \ldots, z_m\}$ to the prover.
$\mathbf{P} \rightarrow \mathbf{V}$: Run

$$\mathrm{PolyEval}(\mathsf{st}_P, x) \rightarrow \mathsf{msg}_{P,2} \qquad \mathrm{PolyEval}(\mathsf{st}_Q, x) \rightarrow \mathsf{msg}_{Q,2}.$$

Compute

$$\bar{\mathbf{a}}_j = \bar{\mathbf{a}}_j(x) \qquad \bar{r} = \sum_{i=0}^m r_i l_i(x) \qquad \bar{s} = \sum_{i=0}^m s_i l_i(x).$$

The prover sends $\{\bar{\mathbf{a}}_j\}_{j \in [n]}, \bar{r}, \bar{s}, \mathsf{msg}_{P,2}, \mathsf{msg}_{Q,2}$ to the verifier.
$\mathbf{V}$: Run

$$\mathrm{PolyVerify}(ck, \mathsf{msg}_{P,1}, \mathsf{msg}_{P,2}, x) \rightarrow \bar{\mathbf{p}} = (\bar{\mathbf{p}}_1, \ldots, \bar{\mathbf{p}}_n)$$

and

$$\mathrm{PolyVerify}(ck, \mathsf{msg}_{Q,1}, \mathsf{msg}_{Q,2}, x) \rightarrow \bar{\mathbf{q}} = (\bar{\mathbf{q}}_1, \ldots, \bar{\mathbf{q}}_n).$$

Return 0 if $\bar{\mathbf{p}} = \perp$ or $\bar{\mathbf{q}} = \perp$.
Check

$$\mathrm{Com}_{ck}(\bar{\mathbf{a}}_1, \ldots, \bar{\mathbf{a}}_n; \bar{s}) = \prod_{i=0}^m A_i^{l_i(x)}.$$

Compute $\bar{\mathbf{b}}_j = \bar{\mathbf{b}}_j(x)$ and check for all $j \in [n]$ that

$$\mathbf{P}(\bar{\mathbf{a}}_j, \bar{\mathbf{b}}_j) = \bar{\mathbf{p}}_j l_0(x).$$

Check that

$$\mathrm{Com}_{ck}(\{\bar{\mathbf{q}}_j l_0(x) + \mathbf{Q}(\bar{\mathbf{a}}_j, \bar{\mathbf{b}}_j)\}_{j \in [n]}; \bar{r}) = \prod_{i=0}^m C_i^{l_i(x)}.$$

If all checks are satisfied, then the verifier outputs 1, and otherwise 0.

Lemma 2. *The batch protocol has perfect completeness, m_s-special-soundness, and perfect special honest verifier zero-knowledge, where $m_s = (m \max(d_P, d_Q) + 1)$.*

Proof. Perfect completeness of the protocol follows by perfect completeness of the PolyCommit sub-protocol, and by careful inspection.

For perfect special honest verifier zero knowledge, we provide an efficient simulator for the protocol. The simulator selects $z_1, \ldots, z_m$ as the prover. She then selects $\bar{\mathbf{a}}_j \leftarrow \mathbb{Z}_p^{\ell_a}$, $\bar{r}, \bar{s} \leftarrow \mathbb{Z}_p$, $\bar{\mathbf{q}}_j \leftarrow \mathbb{Z}_p^{\ell_Q}$, and $A_1, \ldots, A_m$ as uniformly random commitments to 0. All these values are distributed exactly as in a real protocol, where they are also uniformly random.

She then simulates the polynomial commitment and evaluation messages $\mathsf{msg}_{P,1}, \mathsf{msg}_{P,2}, \mathsf{msg}_{Q,1}, \mathsf{msg}_{Q,2}$ using the evaluation point x and evaluations $\bar{p}$ and $\bar{q}$, which are determined by the values already simulated. By the perfect SHVZK of the polynomial commitment scheme, the simulated values have identical distribution to the real proofs. Furthermore, since the polynomial commitment simulator takes the polynomial evaluation as input, the simulated polynomial commitments are consistent with the rest of the simulated values in the outer protocol.

In both the real and simulated protocols, the verification equations now determine the values of A_0 and C_0 uniquely, and the simulator can easily compute the correct values by rearranging the equations. The entire simulated proof therefore has the same distribution as a real proof.

Finally, we prove special soundness. Suppose that we have $m_s = (m \max (d_P, d_Q) + 1)$ accepting transcripts for the same first message, and distinct challenges x.

Pick any $m + 1$ of the challenges, and note that the matrix

$$M = \begin{pmatrix} l_0(x^{(1)}) & l_1(x^{(1)}) & \cdots & l_m(x^{(1)}) \\ l_0(x^{(2)}) & l_1(x^{(2)}) & \cdots & l_m(x^{(2)}) \\ \vdots & \vdots & \ddots & \vdots \\ l_0(x^{(m+1)}) & l_1(x^{(m+1)}) & \cdots & l_m(x^{(m+1)}) \end{pmatrix}$$

is invertible. This follows from linear independence of the polynomials $l_0(X), \ldots, l_m(X)$. If the determinant was zero, there would be a non-trivial linear dependence between the columns of the matrix. This would give a non-trival dependence relation between the polynomials.

Therefore, for each i, it is possible to take a linear combination of the rows to produce $(0, \ldots, 0, 1, 0, \ldots, 0)$, where the 1 is at the ith entry. By taking the same linear combinations of the left and right hand sides of the verification equation $\mathsf{Com}_{ck}(\bar{\mathbf{a}}_1, \ldots, \bar{\mathbf{a}}_n; \bar{s}) = \prod_{i=0}^{m} A_i^{l_i(x)}$ for $m + 1$ different transcripts, we can for each $i \in \{0\} \cup [m]$ extract an opening $\{\mathbf{a}_{i,j}\}_{j \in [n]}$ and s_i of A_i. By the binding property of the commitment scheme, we now have in each transcript that $\bar{\mathbf{a}}_j$ is correctly formed as a polynomial determined by the openings of the A_i evaluated in x.

By the special soundness of the polynomial commitment protocols, we extract polynomials $\mathbf{P}_j^*(X)$ of degree $(d_P - 1)m$, and $\mathbf{Q}_j^*(X)$ of degree $(d_Q - 1)m$ such that in each transcript, $\bar{\mathbf{p}}_j = \mathbf{P}_j^*(x)$ and $\bar{\mathbf{q}} = \mathbf{Q}_j^*(x)$ for the challenge x appearing in that transcript.

Consider the verification equations $\mathbf{P}(\bar{\mathbf{a}}_j, \bar{\mathbf{b}}_j) = \bar{\mathbf{p}}_j l_0(x)$. By the binding property of the commitment scheme, we have that $\mathbf{P}(\bar{\mathbf{a}}_j(x), \bar{\mathbf{b}}_j(x)) = \mathbf{P}_j^*(x) l_0(x)$ holds for m_s different challenges x. Since m_s is larger than the degree of the polynomial this implies that we have an equality of polynomials. By evaluating the polynomial expression at a particular interpolation point z_i, and parsing the resulting vector correctly, we see that $\mathbf{P}(\mathbf{a}_{i,j}, \mathbf{b}_{i,j}) = \mathbf{P}_j^*(z_i) l_0(z_i) = \mathbf{0}$ for each i, j.

We can in a similar manner to the extraction of the A_i extract openings of all C_i to values $\mathbf{c}_{i,1}, \ldots, \mathbf{c}_{i,n}$. The last verification equation tells us that for each $j \in [n]$

$$\bar{\mathbf{q}}_j l_0(x) + \mathbf{Q}(\bar{\mathbf{a}}_j, \bar{\mathbf{b}}_j) = \sum_{i=0}^{m} c_{i,j} l_i(x).$$

Since m_s is larger than the degree of the polynomials this implies that we have an equality of polynomials. By plugging in the evaluation points z_i, we get $\mathbf{Q}(\mathbf{a}_{i,j}, \mathbf{b}_{i,j}) = c_{i,j}$ for each $i \in [m], j \in [n]$. $\qquad\square$

Communication. Let k_1, k_2 be the dimensions of the matrix used in the Poly-Commit subprotocol when committing to $\mathbf{P}^*$, and similarly, let t_1, t_2 be the dimensions of the matrix in the subprotocol for committing to $\mathbf{Q}^*$. The total communication cost of the protocol is $m + k_1 + t_1 + 4$ group elements and $\ell_a n + \ell_P n(k_2 + 1) + \ell_Q n(t_2 + 1) + 4$ field elements.

Single Proof Case. When $t = mn = 1$ and the prover is proving a single relation, we may choose parameters so that the protocol only uses a constant number of group elements. Set $k_1 = t_1 = 1$, $k_2 = d_P - 1$, $t_2 = d_Q - 1$. Then the protocol has communication costs of 7 group elements plus $\ell_a + \ell_P d_P + \ell_Q d_Q + 4$ field elements. This minimises communication in the case where the protocol is instantiated over a multiplicative subgroup of a finite field, where group elements are much bigger than field elements.

In the case where the protocol is instantiated using an elliptic curve group, group elements and field elements have roughly the same size. Then, we can minimise the total communication costs by choosing $k_2 = \left\lceil \sqrt{\frac{d_P}{\ell_P}} \right\rceil$, $k_1 \approx \frac{d_P}{k_2}$. Set $t_2 = \left\lceil \sqrt{\frac{d_Q}{\ell_Q}} \right\rceil$, $t_1 \approx \frac{d_Q}{t_2}$. Then the protocol has costs $\sqrt{\ell_P d_P} + \sqrt{\ell_Q d_Q} + 5$ group elements and $\ell_a + \sqrt{\ell_P d_P} + \sqrt{\ell_Q d_Q} + 4$ field elements.

Batch Proof Case. When t is large, we choose parameters so that the communication costs are proportional to $\sqrt{t}$ rather than t. Set $k_2 = \left\lceil \sqrt{\frac{d_P m}{\ell_P n}} \right\rceil$, $k_1 \approx \frac{d_P m}{k_2}$. Set $t_2 = \left\lceil \sqrt{\frac{d_Q m}{\ell_Q n}} \right\rceil$, $t_1 \approx \frac{d_Q m}{t_2}$. Finally, set $m \approx \sqrt{\ell_a t}, n \approx \frac{t}{m}$. Then the protocol has communication costs of roughly $\sqrt{\ell_a t} + \sqrt{d_P \ell_P t} + \sqrt{d_Q \ell_Q t}$ group elements and $\sqrt{\ell_a t} + \sqrt{d_P \ell_P t} + \sqrt{d_Q \ell_Q t}$ field elements.

Computation. The prover's computational costs are dominated by

$$O\left(\frac{\ell_a t}{\log \ell_a n} + \frac{\ell_Q n}{\log \ell_Q n} + \frac{\ell_P d_P t}{\log \ell_P n k_2} + \frac{\ell_P d_P t}{\log \ell_P n t_2}\right)$$

exponentiations. Over $\mathbb{Z}_p$, the prover must perform

$$O((\ell_a + \ell_b + \ell_P)t d_P \log m d_P + (\ell_a + \ell_b + \ell_Q)t d_Q \log m d_Q) + t d_P \mathsf{Eval}_P + t d_Q \mathsf{Eval}_Q$$

multiplications. Here, Eval_P is the cost of evaluating P once, and similarly for Q. The vectors of polynomials $\mathbf{P}^*(X), \mathbf{Q}^*(X)$ are computed using FFT techniques.

The verifier's computational costs are dominated by

$$O\left(\frac{m + \ell_a n}{\log(m + \ell_a n)} + \frac{m + \ell_Q n}{\log(m + \ell_Q n)} + \frac{k_1 + \ell_P n k_2}{\log(k_1 + \ell_P n k_2)} + \frac{t_1 + \ell_Q n t_2}{\log(t_1 + \ell_Q n t_2)}\right)$$

exponentiations. Over $\mathbb{Z}_p$, the verifier must perform

$$O((\ell_P + \ell_Q)n) + n\mathsf{Eval}_P + n\mathsf{Eval}_Q$$

multiplications.

5   Applications

In this section, we specify concrete choices of relations for $\mathbf{P}, \mathbf{Q}$, which give rise to zero-knowledge arguments for several useful applications.

5.1   Membership Argument with Public List

In membership arguments [10,11], the prover wishes to convince the verifier that a commitment contains one of the values in a given list $\mathcal{L} = (\lambda_0, \ldots, \lambda_{N-1})$. Groth and Kohlweiss [28] give an efficient membership argument, which with minor tweaks fits into our framework. For simplicity, we will in the following assume N is a power of 2.

Statement: $(c, \lambda_0, \ldots, \lambda_{N-1})$
Witness: ℓ, r such that $c = \mathsf{Com}_{ck}(\lambda_\ell; r)$
Polynomial Encoding: Let $m = \log_2 N$ and let $(l_0, \ldots, l_{m-1})$ be the binary expansion of l, satisfying $l_j(1 - l_j) = 0$ for $0 \le j \le m - 1$. Define $l_{j,1} := l_j$ and $l_{j,0} = 1 - l_j$. We have that

$$\sum_{i=0}^{N-1} \lambda_i \prod_{j=0}^{m-1} l_{j,i_j} = \lambda_l$$

where we write the binary expansion of i as $(i_0, \ldots, i_{m-1})$.
Parameter Choice: Writing $\circ$ for the entry-wise product of two vectors
  – $\ell_a = \log_2 N, \ell_b = N, \ell_P = \log_2 N, d_P = 2, \ell_Q = 1, d_Q = \log_2 N$

- $\mathbf{a} = (l_0, \ldots, l_{m-1})$
- $\mathbf{b} = (\lambda_0, \ldots, \lambda_{N-1})$
- $\mathbf{P}(\mathbf{a}, \mathbf{b}) = \mathbf{a} \circ (1 - \mathbf{a})$
- $Q(\mathbf{a}, \mathbf{b}) = \sum_{i=0}^{N-1} \lambda_i \prod_{j=0}^{m-1} l_{j,i_j}$

An alternative construction was given in [6] that optimises the membership argument by using an n-ary representation of l. This alternative construction is captured by our framework as follows, this time assuming for simplicity that N is a power of n, using different polynomials $\mathbf{P}$ and $\mathbf{Q}$.

Polynomial Encoding: Let $m = \log_n N$ and let $(l_0, \ldots, l_{m-1})$ be the n-ary expansion of l. Let δ_{rs} be the Kronecker delta symbol, which is equal to 1 if $r = s$ and 0 otherwise. Consider the bit-string $(\delta_{l_0,0}, \delta_{l_0,1}, \ldots, \delta_{l_{m-1},n-1})$, each element satisfying $\delta_{i,j}(1 - \delta_{i,j}) = 0$, and with $\sum_{i=0}^{n-1} \delta_{l_j,i} = 1$ for each j. As described in [6], we have that

$$\sum_{i=0}^{N-1} \lambda_i \prod_{j=0}^{m-1} \delta_{j,i_j} = \lambda_l$$

where i_j the jth n-ary digit of i.

Parameter Choice:
- $\ell_a = n \log_n N$, $\ell_b = N$, $\ell_P = n \log_n N$, $d_P = 2$, $\ell_Q = 1$, $d_Q = \log_n N$
- $\mathbf{a} = (\delta_{l_0,1}, \ldots, \delta_{l_{m-1},n-1})$, not including $\delta_{j,0}$ for any j.
- $\mathbf{b} = (\lambda_0, \ldots, \lambda_{N-1})$.
- $\delta_{l_j,0} = 1 - \sum_{i=1}^{n-1} \delta_{l_j,i}$ for each j.
- $\mathbf{v} = (\delta_{l_0,0}, \ldots, \delta_{l_{m-1},n-1})$, with the $\delta_{j,0}$ included.
- $\mathbf{P}(\mathbf{a}, \mathbf{b}) = \mathbf{v} \circ (1 - \mathbf{v})$
- $Q(\mathbf{a}, \mathbf{b}) = \sum_{i=0}^{N-1} \lambda_i \prod_{j=0}^{m-1} \delta_{j,i_j} = \lambda_l$

When $t = 1$ and we are aiming for a constant number of group elements, the simple binary version of the argument gives the lowest communication costs. Otherwise, in the cases where t is large, or where $t = 1$ and we aim to minimise the total number of elements communicated, setting $n = 3$ gives the lowest communication costs. The protocol efficiency is reported in Table 1.

5.2 Polynomial Evaluation Argument

In a polynomial evaluation argument [10,23], we have a polynomial of degree N and commitments to a point and its purported evaluation in that point. The prover wants to convince the verifier that the committed evaluation of the polynomial is correct.

The most efficient discrete logarithm based polynomial evaluation argument was given by Bayer and Groth [2]. We will now use our framework of polynomial relations to capture their protocol.

Statement: $(c_u, c_v, h(X))$, where $h(X)$ is a polynomial of degree N.
Witness: u, η, v, ν such that $c_u = \mathrm{Com}_{ck}(u; \eta)$, $c_v = \mathrm{Com}_{ck}(v; \nu)$, and $h(u) = v$.

Polynomial Encoding: Set $u_i = u^{2^i}$ for $0 \leq i \leq \log_2 N - 1$, so that $u_i = u_{i-1}^2$ for each i. If $h(X) = \sum_{i=0}^{N-1} h_i X^i$, then we can write $h(u) = \sum_{i=0}^{N-1} h_i \prod_{j=0}^{\log_2 N - 1} u_j^{i_j}$.

Parameter Choice:
- $\ell_a = \log_2 N$, $\ell_b = N$, $\ell_P = \log_2 N - 1$, $d_P = 2$, $\ell_Q = 1$, $d_Q = \log_2 N$
- $\mathbf{a} = (u_0, \ldots, u_{\log N - 1})$
- $\mathbf{b} = (h_0, \ldots, h_{N-1})$
- $\mathbf{P}(\mathbf{a}, \mathbf{b}) = (u_1 - u_0^2, \ldots, u_{\log N - 1} - u_{\log N - 2}^2)$
- $\mathbf{Q}(\mathbf{a}, \mathbf{b}) = \sum_{i=0}^{N-1} h_i \prod_{j=0}^{\log N - 1} u_j^{i_j}$

With alternative choices of the matrices $\mathbf{P}, \mathbf{Q}$, we can improve the communication costs of their argument by switching to an n-ary encoding of the powers in the polynomial.

Polynomial Encoding: Set $u_i = u^{n^i}$ for $0 \leq i \leq \log_n N - 1$, so that $u_i = u_{i-1}^n$ for each i. If $h(X) = \sum_{i=0}^{N-1} h_i X^i$, then we can write $h(u) = \sum_{i=0}^{N-1} h_i \prod_{j=0}^{\log_n N - 1} u_j^{i_j}$, where this time, i_j is the jth digit of the $n$ary representation of i. This gives rise to the efficiencies listed in Table 1.

Parameter Choice:
- $\ell_a = \log_n N$, $\ell_b = N$, $\ell_P = \log_n N$, $d_P = n$, $\ell_Q = 1$, $d_Q = \log_n N$
- $\mathbf{a} = (u_0, \ldots, u_{\log_n N - 1})$
- $\mathbf{b} = (h_0, \ldots, h_{N-1})$
- $\mathbf{P}(\mathbf{a}, \mathbf{b}) = (u_1 - u_0^n, \ldots, u_{\log_n N - 1} - u_{\log_n N - 2}^n)$
- $\mathbf{Q}(\mathbf{a}, \mathbf{b}) = \sum_{i=0}^{N-1} h_i \prod_{j=0}^{\log_n N - 1} u_j^{i_j}$

When $t = 1$ and we are aiming for a constant number of group elements, setting $n = 4$ gives the lowest communication costs. When $t = 1$ and we aim to minimise the total number of elements communicated, we set $n = \frac{\log_2 N}{\log_2 \log_2 N}$. Otherwise, in the cases where t is large, setting $n = 6$ gives the lowest communication costs. The protocol efficiency is reported in Table 1.

We note that [1] gives a batch argument for polynomial evaluation based on similar ideas. However, ours is more communication efficient.

Remark. The relations above arise from choices of a small set of powers of u which generate all powers from u to u^{N-1}. This is the same as choosing an additive basis for $[N - 1]$. For certain parameter choices, we have found modest benefits to using more complex bases, such as generalised Zeckendorf bases, but these give only slight improvements, so are omitted for simplicity.

5.3 Range Proof

In range proofs [9,38], we have a commitment and a range $[A; B]$. The prover wants to convince the verifier that the committed value inside the commitment falls in the given range. A common strategy for constructing a range proof is to write the committed value in binary, prove all the bits are indeed 0 or 1, and that their weighted sum yields a number within the range. We now describe this type of range proof in our framework of polynomial relations, where we for simplicity focus on intervals $[0, N]$ with $N = 2^m - 1$.

Statement: (N, c)

Witness: a, r such that $c = \text{Com}_{ck}(a; r), a \in [0, N]$.

Polynomial Encoding: Let $a_0, \ldots, a_{m-1}$ be the binary representation of a, so that $a_i(1 - a_i) = 0$ for $0 \leq i \leq m - 1$. Then $a = \sum_{i=0}^{m-1} a_i 2^i$.

Parameter Choice:

- $\ell_a = m, \ell_b = m, \ell_P = m, d_P = 2, \ell_Q = 1, d_Q = m + 1$
- $\mathbf{a} = (a_0, \ldots, a_{m-1})$
- $\mathbf{b} = (2^0, 2^1, \ldots, 2^{m-1})$
- $\mathbf{P}(\mathbf{a}, \mathbf{b}) = \mathbf{a} \circ (1 - \mathbf{a})$
- $\mathbf{Q}(\mathbf{a}, \mathbf{b}) = \sum_{i=0}^{m-1} a_i 2^i$

With an alternative choice of $\mathbf{P}, \mathbf{Q}$, following [16], it is possible to improve the communication costs of the argument by using an n-ary base. This gives rise to the efficiencies listed in Table 1.

Polynomial Encoding: Let $N = n^m - 1$. Let $a_0, \ldots, a_{m-1}$ be the n-ary representation of a, so that $\prod_{k=0}^{n-1}(a_i - k) = 0$ for $0 \leq i \leq m - 1$. Then $a = \sum_{i=0}^{m-1} a_i n^i$.

Parameter Choice:

- $\ell_a = m, \ell_b = m, \ell_P = m, d_P = n, \ell_Q = 1, d_Q = 1$
- $\mathbf{a} = (a_0, \ldots, a_{m-1})$
- $\mathbf{b} = (1, n, \ldots, n^{m-1})$
- $\mathbf{P}(\mathbf{a}, \mathbf{b}) = \mathbf{a} \circ (\mathbf{a} - 1) \circ \ldots (\mathbf{a} - n + 1)$
- $\mathbf{Q}(\mathbf{a}, \mathbf{b}) = \sum_{i=0}^{m-1} a_i n^i$

When $t = 1$ and we are aiming for a constant number of group elements, setting $n = 4$ gives the lowest communication costs. When $t = 1$ and we aim to minimise the total number of elements communicated, we set $n = \frac{\log_2 N}{\log_2 \log_2 N}$. Otherwise, in the cases where t is large, setting $n = 6$ gives the lowest communication costs. The protocol efficiency is reported in Table 1.

6   Conclusion

We have provided zero-knowledge arguments for simple polynomial relations, relying solely on the discrete logarithm assumption. When we only have one instance of the argument, $t = 1$, the single value membership arguments and polynomial evaluation arguments compiled within our framework improve on the state of the art both asymptotically and for practical parameters. When there are many instances, $t > 1$, we have a batch argument for polynomial relations, which is significantly more efficient than the naïve solution of repeating single instance arguments many times.

References

1. Bayer, S.: Practical zero-knowledge protocols based on the discrete logarithm assumption. Ph.D. thesis, University College London (2014)
2. Bayer, S., Groth, J.: Zero-knowledge argument for polynomial evaluation with application to blacklists. In: Johansson, T., Nguyen, P.Q. (eds.) EUROCRYPT 2013. LNCS, vol. 7881, pp. 646–663. Springer, Heidelberg (2013). https://doi.org/10.1007/978-3-642-38348-9_38
3. Bellare, M., Garay, J.A., Rabin, T.: Batch verification with applications to cryptography and checking. In: EUROCRYPT, pp. 236–250 (1998)
4. Benaloh, J., de Mare, M.: One-way accumulators: a decentralized alternative to digital signatures. In: Helleseth, T. (ed.) EUROCRYPT 1993. LNCS, vol. 765, pp. 274–285. Springer, Heidelberg (1994). https://doi.org/10.1007/3-540-48285-7_24
5. Bootle, J., Cerulli, A., Chaidos, P., Ghadafi, E., Groth, J.: Foundations of fully dynamic group signatures. In: Manulis, M., Sadeghi, A.R., Schneider, S. (eds.) ACNS 2016. LNCS, vol. 9696, pp. 117–136. Springer, Cham (2016). https://doi.org/10.1007/978-3-319-39555-5_7
6. Bootle, J., Cerulli, A., Chaidos, P., Ghadafi, E., Groth, J., Petit, C.: Short accountable ring signatures based on DDH. In: Pernul, G., Ryan, P.Y.A., Weippl, E. (eds.) ESORICS 2015. LNCS, vol. 9326, pp. 243–265. Springer, Cham (2015). https://doi.org/10.1007/978-3-319-24174-6_13
7. Bootle, J., Cerulli, A., Chaidos, P., Groth, J., Petit, C.: Efficient zero-knowledge arguments for arithmetic circuits in the discrete log setting. In: Fischlin, M., Coron, J.-S. (eds.) EUROCRYPT 2016. LNCS, vol. 9666, pp. 327–357. Springer, Heidelberg (2016). https://doi.org/10.1007/978-3-662-49896-5_12
8. Bootle, J., Cerulli, A., Ghadafi, E., Groth, J., Hajiabadi, M., Jakobsen, S.K.: Linear-time zero-knowledge proofs for arithmetic circuit satisfiability. Cryptology ePrint Archive, Report 2017/872 (2017). http://eprint.iacr.org/2017/872
9. Boudot, F.: Efficient proofs that a committed number lies in an interval. In: Preneel, B. (ed.) EUROCRYPT 2000. LNCS, vol. 1807, pp. 431–444. Springer, Heidelberg (2000). https://doi.org/10.1007/3-540-45539-6_31
10. Brands, S., Demuynck, L., De Decker, B.: A practical system for globally revoking the unlinkable pseudonyms of unknown users. In: Pieprzyk, J., Ghodosi, H., Dawson, E. (eds.) ACISP 2007. LNCS, vol. 4586, pp. 400–415. Springer, Heidelberg (2007). https://doi.org/10.1007/978-3-540-73458-1_29
11. Bresson, E., Stern, J.: Efficient revocation in group signatures. In: Kim, K. (ed.) PKC 2001. LNCS, vol. 1992, pp. 190–206. Springer, Heidelberg (2001). https://doi.org/10.1007/3-540-44586-2_15
12. Camenisch, J., Chaabouni, R., Shelat, A.: Efficient protocols for set membership and range proofs. In: Pieprzyk, J. (ed.) ASIACRYPT 2008. LNCS, vol. 5350, pp. 234–252. Springer, Heidelberg (2008). https://doi.org/10.1007/978-3-540-89255-7_15
13. Camenisch, J., Kohlweiss, M., Soriente, C.: An accumulator based on bilinear maps and efficient revocation for anonymous credentials. In: Jarecki, S., Tsudik, G. (eds.) PKC 2009. LNCS, vol. 5443, pp. 481–500. Springer, Heidelberg (2009). https://doi.org/10.1007/978-3-642-00468-1_27
14. Camenisch, J., Lysyanskaya, A.: Dynamic accumulators and application to efficient revocation of anonymous credentials. In: Yung, M. (ed.) CRYPTO 2002. LNCS, vol. 2442, pp. 61–76. Springer, Heidelberg (2002). https://doi.org/10.1007/3-540-45708-9_5

15. Camenisch, J., Stadler, M.: Proof systems for general statements about discrete logarithms. Technical report 260. ETH Zurich (1997)
16. Chaabouni, R., Lipmaa, H., Shelat, A.: Additive combinatorics and discrete logarithm based range protocols. In: Steinfeld, R., Hawkes, P. (eds.) ACISP 2010. LNCS, vol. 6168, pp. 336–351. Springer, Heidelberg (2010). https://doi.org/10.1007/978-3-642-14081-5_21
17. Couteau, G., Peters, T., Pointcheval, D.: Removing the strong RSA assumption from arguments over the integers. In: Coron, J.-S., Nielsen, J.B. (eds.) EUROCRYPT 2017. LNCS, vol. 10211, pp. 321–350. Springer, Cham (2017). https://doi.org/10.1007/978-3-319-56614-6_11
18. Cramer, R., Damgård, I.: Zero-knowledge proofs for finite field arithmetic, or: can zero-knowledge be for free? In: Krawczyk, H. (ed.) CRYPTO 1998. LNCS, vol. 1462, pp. 424–441. Springer, Heidelberg (1998). https://doi.org/10.1007/BFb0055745
19. Cramer, R., Damgård, I., Schoenmakers, B.: Proofs of partial knowledge and simplified design of witness hiding protocols. In: Desmedt, Y.G. (ed.) CRYPTO 1994. LNCS, vol. 839, pp. 174–187. Springer, Heidelberg (1994). https://doi.org/10.1007/3-540-48658-5_19
20. Damgård, I.: Efficient concurrent zero-knowledge in the auxiliary string model. In: Preneel, B. (ed.) EUROCRYPT 2000. LNCS, vol. 1807, pp. 418–430. Springer, Heidelberg (2000). https://doi.org/10.1007/3-540-45539-6_30
21. Damgård, I., Triandopoulos, N.: Supporting non-membership proofs with bilinear-map accumulators. IACR ePrint archive report 538 (2008)
22. Fauzi, P., Lipmaa, H., Zhang, B.: Efficient non-interactive zero knowledge arguments for set operations. In: Christin, N., Safavi-Naini, R. (eds.) FC 2014. LNCS, vol. 8437, pp. 216–233. Springer, Heidelberg (2014). https://doi.org/10.1007/978-3-662-45472-5_14
23. Fujisaki, E., Okamoto, T.: Statistical zero knowledge protocols to prove modular polynomial relations. In: Kaliski, B.S. (ed.) CRYPTO 1997. LNCS, vol. 1294, pp. 16–30. Springer, Heidelberg (1997). https://doi.org/10.1007/BFb0052225
24. Garay, J.A., MacKenzie, P., Yang, K.: Strengthening zero-knowledge protocols using signatures. In: Biham, E. (ed.) EUROCRYPT 2003. LNCS, vol. 2656, pp. 177–194. Springer, Heidelberg (2003). https://doi.org/10.1007/3-540-39200-9_11
25. Gennaro, R., Leigh, D., Sundaram, R., Yerazunis, W.: Batching schnorr identification scheme with applications to privacy-preserving authorization and low-bandwidth communication devices. In: Lee, P.J. (ed.) ASIACRYPT 2004. LNCS, vol. 3329, pp. 276–292. Springer, Heidelberg (2004). https://doi.org/10.1007/978-3-540-30539-2_20
26. Gennaro, R., Gentry, C., Parno, B., Raykova, M.: Quadratic span programs and succinct NIZKs without PCPs. In: Johansson, T., Nguyen, P.Q. (eds.) EUROCRYPT 2013. LNCS, vol. 7881, pp. 626–645. Springer, Heidelberg (2013). https://doi.org/10.1007/978-3-642-38348-9_37
27. Groth, J.: Honest verifier zero-knowledge arguments applied. Ph.D. thesis, Aarhus University (2004)
28. Groth, J., Kohlweiss, M.: One-out-of-many proofs: or how to leak a secret and spend a coin. In: Oswald, E., Fischlin, M. (eds.) EUROCRYPT 2015. LNCS, vol. 9057, pp. 253–280. Springer, Heidelberg (2015). https://doi.org/10.1007/978-3-662-46803-6_9
29. Henry, R., Goldberg, I.: Batch proofs of partial knowledge. In: Jacobson, M., Locasto, M., Mohassel, P., Safavi-Naini, R. (eds.) ACNS 2013. LNCS, vol. 7954, pp. 502–517. Springer, Heidelberg (2013). https://doi.org/10.1007/978-3-642-38980-1_32

30. Herranz, J.: Attribute-based versions of schnorr and elgamal. Appl. Algebra Eng. Commun. Comput. **27**(1), 17–57 (2016)
31. Jutla, C.S., Roy, A.: Shorter quasi-adaptive NIZK proofs for linear subspaces. In: Sako, K., Sarkar, P. (eds.) ASIACRYPT 2013. LNCS, vol. 8269, pp. 1–20. Springer, Heidelberg (2013). https://doi.org/10.1007/978-3-642-42033-7_1
32. Jutla, C.S., Roy, A.: Switching lemma for bilinear tests and constant-size NIZK proofs for linear subspaces. In: Garay, J.A., Gennaro, R. (eds.) CRYPTO 2014. LNCS, vol. 8617, pp. 295–312. Springer, Heidelberg (2014). https://doi.org/10.1007/978-3-662-44381-1_17
33. Kate, A., Zaverucha, G.M., Goldberg, I.: Constant-size commitments to polynomials and their applications. In: Abe, M. (ed.) ASIACRYPT 2010. LNCS, vol. 6477, pp. 177–194. Springer, Heidelberg (2010). https://doi.org/10.1007/978-3-642-17373-8_11
34. Kilian, J.: A note on efficient zero-knowledge proofs and arguments. In: STOC, pp. 723–732 (1992)
35. Kiltz, E., Wee, H.: Quasi-adaptive NIZK for linear subspaces revisited. In: Oswald, E., Fischlin, M. (eds.) EUROCRYPT 2015. LNCS, vol. 9057, pp. 101–128. Springer, Heidelberg (2015). https://doi.org/10.1007/978-3-662-46803-6_4
36. Li, J., Li, N., Xue, R.: Universal accumulators with efficient nonmembership proofs. In: Katz, J., Yung, M. (eds.) ACNS 2007. LNCS, vol. 4521, pp. 253–269. Springer, Heidelberg (2007). https://doi.org/10.1007/978-3-540-72738-5_17
37. Libert, B., Ramanna, S.C., Yung, M.: Functional commitment schemes: from polynomial commitments to pairing-based accumulators from simple assumptions. In: 43rd International Colloquium on Automata, Languages, and Programming, ICALP 2016, 11–15 July 2016, Rome, Italy, pp. 30:1–30:14 (2016)
38. Lipmaa, H.: On diophantine complexity and statistical zero-knowledge arguments. In: Laih, C.-S. (ed.) ASIACRYPT 2003. LNCS, vol. 2894, pp. 398–415. Springer, Heidelberg (2003). https://doi.org/10.1007/978-3-540-40061-5_26
39. Micali, S., Rabin, M.O., Kilian, J.: Zero-knowledge sets. In: FOCS, pp. 80–91 (2003)
40. Nguyen, L.: Accumulators from Bilinear pairings and applications. In: Menezes, A. (ed.) CT-RSA 2005. LNCS, vol. 3376, pp. 275–292. Springer, Heidelberg (2005). https://doi.org/10.1007/978-3-540-30574-3_19
41. Papamanthou, C., Shi, E., Tamassia, R.: Signatures of correct computation. In: Sahai, A. (ed.) TCC 2013. LNCS, vol. 7785, pp. 222–242. Springer, Heidelberg (2013). https://doi.org/10.1007/978-3-642-36594-2_13
42. Pedersen, T.P.: Non-interactive and information-theoretic secure verifiable secret sharing. In: Feigenbaum, J. (ed.) CRYPTO 1991. LNCS, vol. 576, pp. 129–140. Springer, Heidelberg (1992). https://doi.org/10.1007/3-540-46766-1_9
43. Peng, K.: A General, flexible and efficient proof of inclusion and exclusion. In: Chen, L., Yung, M., Zhu, L. (eds.) INTRUST 2011. LNCS, vol. 7222, pp. 168–183. Springer, Heidelberg (2012). https://doi.org/10.1007/978-3-642-32298-3_12
44. Peng, K., Bao, F.: Batch ZK proof and verification of OR logic. In: Yung, M., Liu, P., Lin, D. (eds.) Inscrypt 2008. LNCS, vol. 5487, pp. 141–156. Springer, Heidelberg (2009). https://doi.org/10.1007/978-3-642-01440-6_13
45. Shamir, A.: How to share a secret. Commun. ACM **22**(11), 612–613 (1979)
46. Zhang, Y., Genkin, D., Katz, J., Papadopoulos, D., Papamanthou, C.: vSQL: verifying arbitrary SQL queries over dynamic outsourced databases. In: 2017 IEEE Symposium on Security and Privacy, SP 2017, San Jose, CA, USA, 22–26 May 2017, pp. 863–880 (2017)

On the Security of Classic Protocols
for Unique Witness Relations

Yi Deng[1,2], Xuyang Song[1,2], Jingyue Yu[1,2], and Yu Chen[1,2(⊠)]

[1] State Key Laboratory of Information Security,
Institute of Information Engineering, Chinese Academy of Sciences, Beijing, China
[2] School of Cyber Security, University of Chinese Academy of Sciences,
Beijing, China

Abstract. We revisit the problem of whether the known classic constant-round public-coin argument/proof systems are witness hiding for languages/distributions with unique witnesses. Though strong black-box *impossibility* results are known, we provide some less unexpected *positive* results on the witness hiding security of these classic protocols:

- We give sufficient conditions on a hard distribution over *unique* witness NP relation for which all witness indistinguishable protocols (including all public-coin ones, such as ZAPs, Blum protocol and GMW protocol) are indeed witness hiding. We also show a wide range of cryptographic problems with unique witnesses satisfy these conditions, and thus admit constant-round public-coin witness hiding proof system.
- For the classic Schnorr protocol (for which the distribution of statements being proven seems not to satisfy the above sufficient conditions), we develop an embedding technique and extend the result of Bellare and Palacio to base the witness hiding property of the Schnorr protocol in the standalone setting on a *relaxed* version of one-more like discrete logarithm (DL) assumption, which essentially assumes there does not exist *instance compression* scheme for the DL problem, and show that breaking this assumption would lead to some surprising consequences, such as zero knowledge protocols for the AND-DL language with extremely efficient communication and highly non-trivial hash combiner for hash functions based on the DL problem. Similar results hold for the Guillou-Quisquater protocol.

1 Introduction

Witness hiding proof system, introduced by Feige and Shamir [12], is a relaxed yet natural notion of zero knowledge proof [15]. Instead of requiring an efficient simulation for the view of the verifier as in zero knowledge proof, witness hiding property only requires that, roughly speaking, the interaction with honest prover does not help the verifier compute any new witness for the statement being proven that he did not know before. One immediate application of such a security notion is identification: Witness hiding proof allows a prover to prove his identity

© International Association for Cryptologic Research 2018
M. Abdalla and R. Dahab (Eds.): PKC 2018, LNCS 10770, pp. 589–615, 2018.
https://doi.org/10.1007/978-3-319-76581-5_20

without leaking the associated secret key, and this security notion is sufficient for preventing impersonation attack from malicious verifiers.

The witness hiding property of some practical protocols, which are usually not zero knowledge, is often proved via another beautiful and widely applicable notion of witness indistinguishability introduced in the same paper of [12]. A witness indistinguishable proof guarantees that if the statement has two independent witnesses, then the malicious verifier cannot tell which witness is being used by the prover in an execution of the protocol. The idea underlying the security proof of witness hiding via witness indistinguishability is as follows. Suppose that for a hard language, each instance has two witnesses and it is infeasible for an efficient algorithm, given one witness as input, to compute the other one, then the witness indistinguishable protocol is actually witness hiding with respect to such instances. This is because we can take one witness as input to play the role of honest prover and then use the verifier's ability of breaking witness hiding to either break witness indistinguishability of this protocol or obtain a new witness. Therefore, the parallelized version of 3-round public-coin classic protocols of [3,14] are witness hiding with respect to such languages.

What happens if the hard language consists of instances that have exactly one witness? This problem has turned out to be quite subtle. The Guillou-Quisquater [17] and the Schnorr [28] identification protocols are perhaps the best-known efficient protocols for unique witness relations, but their security has long remained open. On the positive side, Shoup [29] presented positive result that the Schnorr identification protocol is secure in the generic group model, and Bellare and Palacio [2] showed that the security of the Guillou-Quisquater and Schnorr identification protocols can be based on the so-called one-more RSA and one-more discrete logarithm assumptions, respectively [1,2]. These security proofs of course imply that the Schnorr and the Guillou-Quisquater identification protocols are witness hiding in the standalone setting where there is only a single execution of the protocol. However, the underlying assumptions/models are quite strong and non-standard.

Indeed, there is an obstacle in the way of basing constant-round public-coin protocols for unique witness relations on standard assumptions. As mentioned before, the basic approach to prove witness hiding of a protocol is to find an efficient way to exploit the power of the malicious verifier to break some hardness assumptions. For the instance that has exactly one witness, however, to exploit the power of the malicious verifier requires the reduction itself to know the unique witness to the statement being proven in the first place (by the soundness property of the protocol), which usually does not lead to a desired contradiction even if the malicious verifier does have the ability to break witness hiding of the protocol.

Haitner et al. [18] gave the first proof that constant-round public-coin witness hiding protocols for unique witness relations cannot be based on standard assumptions via some restricted types of black-box reductions. Pass [24] showed that if we further require witness hiding to hold under sequential repetition, then we can significantly strengthen the impossibility result of [18]. Some similar impossibility results on the problem whether we can base the aforementioned one-more discrete logarithm assumption on standard hardness assumption were also given in [24, 30]. We would like to point out that these impossibility results may have some impact on other important problems. For example, in [23] Pass showed a deep connection between the problem of whether the classic constant-round public-coin proofs are witness hiding for all NP languages and the longstanding problem whether we can base one-way functions on NP-complete problem.

1.1   Our Contribution

Our main contribution reflects an optimistic point of view on the witness hiding security of the classic public-coin proof systems.

We observe that all previously known impossibility results [18, 24] on the witness hiding of public-coin protocols make an *implicit* restriction (which has not been mentioned explicitly in the statements of their main results) on the black-box reduction: For a distribution $(\mathcal{X}, \mathcal{W})$ on an *unique* witness relation, for the proof of lower bound to go through, the (black-box) reduction R is restricted to invoke the adversarial verifier V^* *only* on instances in $\mathcal{X}$.[1]

This leaves a problem of whether one can get around these impossibility results by removing the above restriction on the black-box reduction. We provide a positive answer to this problem. Specifically, we develop an input-distribution-switching technique and prove that, for any hard language L, if a distribution $(\mathcal{X}, \mathcal{W})$ on a *unique* witness relation R_L has an indistinguishable counterpart distribution over some *multiple* witnesses relation, then any witness indistinguishable protocols (including ZAPs and all known 3-round public-coin protocols, such as Blum protocol and GMW protocol) are indeed witness hiding for the unique witness distribution $(\mathcal{X}, \mathcal{W})$. We also show a wide range of cryptographic problems with unique witnesses satisfy the "if condition" of this result, and thus admit constant-round public-coin witness hiding proof system. This is the *first* positive result on the witness-hiding property of the classic protocols for unique witness relations.

For the classic Schnorr protocol (for which the distribution of statements being proven seems not to satisfy the above sufficient conditions), we develop an embedding technique and extend the result of [2] to base the witness hiding property of the standalone Schnorr (and Guillou-Quisquater) protocol based on a relaxed version of one-more like DL (RSA, respectively) assumption. To see the plausibility of our still-non-standard assumption, we follow the framework of [19] and introduce the notion of *tailored instance compression*, which captures the

---

[1] This restriction can be seen from the last paragraph "on the role of unique witness", page 7 of the full version (see http://www.cs.cornell.edu/~rafael/papers/schnorr.pdf) of [24]: "...(in the reduction) If the statement x has a unique witness w, we can ensure that the extracted witness will be identical to the witness that the oracle A (which is V^* in our setting) would have returned..".

essence of the known one-more like assumptions, and more importantly, provides new insight into the hardness of one-more DL/RSA problems and allows us to reveal some surprising consequences of breaking our version of the one-more like assumptions, including zero knowledge proofs with extremely low communication complexity for the AND-DL and AND-RSA languages and non-trivial hash combiner for hash functions based on DL problem.

We summarize our results in the Table 1.

Table 1. Our results for languages with unique witnesses compared to previous work. Here we refer to the impossibility results of further basing instance incompressibility/one-more assumptions on standard hard problems as "BB negative results/evidences", and refer to the surprising consequences of breaking these assumptions as "positive results/evidences" in favor of these assumptions. As we observe, the impossibility results of [18, 24] make an *implicit* restriction on the black-box reduction.

	Security of Schnorr/GQ	Instance incompressibility/one-more assumptions	WH of PC protocols for unique witness R
BB negative results/evidences	[24]	[24, 30]	[18, 24]
Positive results/ evidences	[2] This work (with relaxed assum.)	This work	This work

1.2   Techniques

INPUT-DISTRIBUTION-SWITCHING TECHNIQUE: JUMPING OUT OF THE BOX. As mentioned before, the previously known impossibility results hold only with respect to *restricted* reduction. We introduce an *input-distribution-switching* technique to get around these impossibility results for general unique witness NP relations.

Suppose that, for a hard language L_1 with *unique* witness relation R_{L_1}, and a distribution ensemble $(\mathcal{X}^1, \mathcal{W}^1)$ over R_{L_1}, there exists a coupled distribution ensemble $(\mathcal{X}^2, \mathcal{W}^2)$ over relation R_{L_2} of a language L_2 with *two or more* witnesses that is indistinguishable from $(\mathcal{X}^1, \mathcal{W}^1)$. What can we say about the security of the classic public-coin protocols for $(\mathcal{X}^1, \mathcal{W}^1)$? At least we know that such protocols are witness indistinguishable for $(\mathcal{X}^2, \mathcal{W}^2)$.

A very vague intuition behind this positive result is that, for the same malicious verifier V^*, if we invoke V^* on both instances in $\mathcal{X}^1$ and $\mathcal{X}^2$, it should have the same behavior in these two settings since these instances are indistinguishable. This vague idea leads us to introduce the *input-distribution-switching technique*, which enables us to prove that if the ensembles $(\mathcal{X}^1, \mathcal{W}^1)$ and $(\mathcal{X}^2, \mathcal{W}^2)$ further satisfy the following properties:

- Given a sample x from $\mathcal{X}^1$, it is hard to find the unique witness for x;
- For every x in the support of $\mathcal{X}^2$, witnesses in $R_{L_2}(x)$ are uniformly distributed.

Then the classic constant-round public-coin protocols are actually witness hiding for $(\mathcal{X}^1, \mathcal{W}^1)$.

The proof of this result is a reduction of witness hiding for $(\mathcal{X}^1, \mathcal{W}^1)$ to witness indistinguishability for $(\mathcal{X}^2, \mathcal{W}^2)$, which is more complicated than one might imagine. See Sect. 3 for the detailed proof.

The idea of considering different types of distributions $\mathcal{X}^1$ and $\mathcal{X}^2$ on the common input already appeared in Goldreich's definition of strong witness indistinguishability [13], but there they do not require indistinguishability of $(\mathcal{X}^1, \mathcal{W}^1)$ and $(\mathcal{X}^2, \mathcal{W}^2)$ since such requirement on the witness distributions $\mathcal{W}^1$ and $\mathcal{W}^2$ would trivialize the definition of witness indistinguishability.

In our setting, the indistinguishability requirement on witness distributions $\mathcal{W}^1$ and $\mathcal{W}^2$ is helpful in achieving significant positive results on witness hiding protocols that bypass some previously known limitations. We give several examples of such distribution ensembles $(\mathcal{X}^1, \mathcal{W}^1)$ based on standard assumptions such as DDH, the existence of lossy trapdoor functions [25] and mixed commitments [9,16], and applying the above result we show the classic protocols of [3,11,14,16] are actually witness hiding under sequential repetition for a wide range of useful cryptographic problems with unique witnesses.

EMBEDDING TECHNIQUE AND THE INSTANCE COMPRESSION PROBLEM. Before proceeding to our embedding reduction, we recall the Schnorr protocol and Bellare and Palacio's security proof for it [2]. Let $\mathbb{G}$ be a group of prime order q generated by g, the prover P wants to convince the verifier V of knowledge of the discrete logarithm (unique witness) $w \in \mathbb{Z}_q$ of an element $y = g^w \in \mathbb{G}$. To do so, P first sends a random element $a = g^r \in \mathbb{G}$ to V, and upon receiving the V's challenge $c \in \mathbb{Z}_q$, it answers with a value $z \in \mathbb{Z}_q$. V accepts the proof if and only if $g^z = a \cdot y^c$. Note that, if V finally outputs the witness $w \in \mathbb{Z}_q$ at the end of interaction, then we can build an algorithm R solving two random discrete logarithm instances y and a at the same time if R is allowed to make one query to the discrete logarithm solver oracle $\mathcal{O}_{\text{dlog}}$: R have y serve as the common input and a as the first prover message, after receiving V's challenge c, R queries $\mathcal{O}_{\text{dlog}}$ on $a \cdot y^c$ and forwards the response z from the oracle to the verifier; when V outputs w, R can solve the linear equation $z = r + cw \bmod q$ and obtain r. This useful observation was also exploited by Bellare and Palacio [2] to prove the security of the Schnorr protocol as an identification scheme under the hardness of one-more discrete logarithm problem.

We now show how to conduct embedding reduction R that leads to better security proof based on a relaxed version of the one-more DL assumption.

Suppose we are given a set of discrete logarithm instances $(y_1, y_2, \ldots, y_\ell)$ to solve. For simplicity, we assume $\ell = 2^l$ for some integer l. The first part of R is a *compressing* process. R partitions them into $\ell/2$ pairs, for each pair of instances, one serving as the common input and the other serving as the first prover message in a session, and invokes $\ell/2$ incarnations of the verifier in parallel. After collecting $\ell/2$ challenges from the $\ell/2$ invocations of the verifier, R has to solve $\ell/2$ new instances in order to answer each verifier. At this point, rather than querying $\mathcal{O}_{\text{dlog}}$ on these new instances, R pauses all these interactions and partitions the new $\ell/2$ instances into $\ell/4$ pairs, and then repeats the above step and invokes $\ell/4$ incarnations of the verifier in parallel, and will get $\ell/8$ new instances to solve. Continuing to repeat this, by viewing each partial interaction with a verifier as a node we get a tree in which each node takes in two instances and outputs one instance. Finally, R reaches the root and has only one instance to solve.

The second part of R is an *unfolding* process. R queries $\mathcal{O}_{\mathrm{dlog}}$ on the root instance, then by using the verifier's power of breaking witness hiding as above, R is able to solve the two instances flowing into this node. Note that, the two instances R just solved will help it solve the four instances that flow into the two nodes at the level above the root (without making queries to oracle anymore), and repeating this process R will solve all these ℓ instances $(y_1, y_2, \ldots, y_\ell)$. Observe that in the entire embedding reduction, R makes only a single query (at the root of the tree) to $\mathcal{O}_{\mathrm{dlog}}$ and solves all ℓ DL instances. This process is exemplified in Fig. 2.

The actual embedding reduction needs to make each invocation of the verifier independent by using the random self-reducibility of the discrete logarithm problem. As we will see, the quantity ℓ can be an arbitrarily large integer, or any polynomial when the verifier's success probability is close to 1. Thus, assuming that it is infeasible for a PPT oracle algorithm to solve ℓ discrete logarithm instances at the same time when restricted to making a *single* query to the discrete logarithm solver oracle, the standalone Schnorr protocol is witness hiding. Similar results can also be obtained for the Guillou-Quisquater's protocol and some other Σ-protocols for group homomorphisms.

Our reduction R leads to the following *tailored instance compression* problem for DL: Construct a triplet of efficient algorithms $(\mathsf{Z}, \mathsf{C}, \mathsf{U})$ such that: On input ℓ instances $(y_1, \ldots, y_\ell)$ of DL, the compression algorithm Z outputs a single DL instance y; on input $(y_1, \ldots, y_\ell)$ together with their corresponding witnesses $(w_1, \ldots, w_\ell)$, the witness compression algorithm C[2] outputs a witness w to the instance $y \leftarrow \mathsf{Z}(y_1, \ldots, y_\ell)$; given the witness w to y, the unfolding algorithm U outputs all witnesses $(w_1, \ldots, w_\ell)$ to these ℓ instances.

Note that if there exists a successful malicious verifier V, then our reduction R together with V can be used to construct a good instance compression scheme for DL problem. Thus, our result on Schnorr protocol can be rephrased as follows: If the tailored instance compression scheme for DL does not exist, then Schnorr protocol is secure.

What if instance compression schemes exist for DL and RSA? We observe that the existence of instance compression scheme for DL/RSA with strong parameters has somewhat surprising consequences.

The first consequence is that, assuming the existence of good instance compression scheme for DL, then for any polynomial ℓ, the AND-DL statement $\{(y_1, y_2, \ldots, y_\ell, g, \mathbb{G}) : \exists w_1, w_2, \ldots, w_\ell, \text{ s.t. } \wedge_{i=1}^{\ell} g^{w_i} = y_i\}$ admits a zero knowledge proof with extremely efficient communication of size $O(1)$ group elements.

---

[2] It is easy to see that we can construct the witness compression algorithm C by making simple adaptation to the compressing part of our embedding reduction.

The existence of tailored instance compression scheme for RSA yields a similar consequence.

The second consequence is a construction of non-trivial hash combiner for hash functions based on DL problem. Recall that given a group $\mathbb{G}$, its generator g and a random element $y \in \mathbb{G}$, we have a hash function $H_{(g,y)} : (m_0, m_1) \to g^{m_0} y^{m_1}$ that is collision-resistant. The hash combiner for DL-based hash functions is of particular interest in the scenario where a set of mutually untrusting parties, given a group $\mathbb{G}$ and g, want to set up a single collision-resistant hash function trusted by every one.

Several previous papers [6,26,27] defined *universal* hash combiners (that works for arbitrary hash functions), and showed non-trivial fully black-box combiners do not exist. Note that the above hash combiner needs to take the common parameters of the group and its generator, and works only for DL-based hash functions. However, it is still inconceivable that the above hash combiner with large ℓ exists in the real world.

We view these strong consequences as positive evidences for the security of Schnorr and Guillou-Quisquater protocols.

1.3   Comparison with a Concurrent Work

In a very recent concurrent work [20], Jain et al. develop a new exciting simulation strategy and construct 2/3-round witness hiding protocol based on some standard number theoretic assumptions for *all* unique witness NP-relations. Our Input-distribution-switching technique gives only witness hiding for *some* cryptographic unique witness relations, however, it applies to existing classic protocols, which are much more efficient and require weaker assumptions[3] than the constructions of [20]. Furthermore, these classic protocols are all public-coin, and such a property usually makes them more versetile and applicable.

2   Preliminaries

Due to space limitations, we refer readers to [13,21] for formal definitions of basic notions and primitives. Here we give only definitions of witness indistinguishable and witness hiding protocols.

Interactive Proofs. An *interactive proof system* $\langle P, V \rangle$ [15] for a language L is a pair of interactive Turing machines in which the prover P wishes to convince the verifier V of some statement $x \in L$. We denote by $\langle P, V \rangle(x)$ the output of V at the end of interaction on common input x, and without loss of generality, we have the verifier V outputs 1 (resp. 0) if V accepts (resp. rejects).

Definition 1 (Interactive Proofs). *A pair of interactive Turing machines $\langle P, V \rangle$ is called an interactive proof system for language L if V is a PPT machine and the following conditions hold:*

---

[3] Note that the 3-round Blum protocol and GMW protocol can be constructed from one way permutations.

- *Completeness: For every $x \in L$, $\Pr[\langle P, V \rangle(x) = 1] = 1$.*
- *Soundness: For every $x \notin L$, and every (unbounded) prover P^*, there exists a negligible function $\mu(n)$ (where $|x| = n$) such that*

$$\Pr[\langle P^*, V \rangle(x) = 1] < \mu(n).$$

An interactive *argument* [4] is an interactive proof except that for which soundness is only required to hold against PPT cheating provers. We often use "protocol" to refer to both proof system and argument system.

Witness Indistinguishability. Witness indistinguishable proof system guarantees that if the statement has two independent witnesses, then the malicious verifier cannot tell which witness is being used by the prover in an execution of the protocol.

Definition 2 (Witness Indistinguishability). *Let L be an NP language defined by R_L. We say that $\langle P, V \rangle$ is witness indistinguishable for relation R_L if for every PPT V^* and every sequence $\{(x, w, w')\}_{x \in L}$, where $(x, w), (x, w') \in R_L$, the following two probability ensembles are computationally indistinguishable:*

$$\{\langle P(w), V^* \rangle(x)\}_{x \in L} \overset{c}{\approx} \{\langle P(w'), V^* \rangle(x)\}_{x \in L}.$$

Witness Hiding. Loosely speaking, witness hiding of a protocol [12] refers to the following property: for an input $x \in L$ that is being proven, if a verifier can extract a witness in $R_L(x)$ after interacting with the prover, then he could have done so without such an interaction. This notion is formally defined with respect to a distribution ensemble over inputs as follows.

Definition 3 (Distribution of Hard Instances). *Let L be an NP language defined by R_L. Let $\mathcal{X} = \{X_n\}_{n \in \mathbb{N}}$ be a distribution ensemble. We say that $\mathcal{X}$ is hard for R_L if for every PPT machine M*

$$\Pr[M(X_n) \in R_L(X_n)] < \mu(n).$$

Definition 4 (Witness Hiding (under Sequential Repetition)). *Let L be an NP language defined by R_L, $(\mathcal{X}, \mathcal{W}) = \{(X_n, W_n)\}_{n \in \mathbb{N}}$ be a distribution over R_L. We say $\langle P, V \rangle$ is witness hiding for $(\mathcal{X}, \mathcal{W})$ if for every PPT machine V^**

$$\Pr[\langle P(W_n), V^* \rangle(X_n) \in R_L(X_n)] < \mu(n).$$

We say that $\langle P, V \rangle$ is witness hiding under sequential repetition if it is witness hiding for $(\mathcal{X}, \mathcal{W})$ under any polynomially number of sequential repetitions.

Remark 1. According to our definition of witness hiding, it is easy to verify that if there is witness hiding protocol for $(\mathcal{X}, \mathcal{W})$, then the distribution ensemble $\mathcal{X} = \{X_n\}_{n \in \mathbb{N}}$ on instances must be hard.

3   Witness Hiding Protocols for Hard Distributions with Unique Witnesses

In this section we prove a general theorem on witness hiding of constant-round public-coin proofs systems for unique witness relations and present its applications to several cryptographic problems.

3.1   A General Theorem

Let L_1 and L_2 be NP languages (possibly the same), R_{L_1} and R_{L_2} be their corresponding witness relations. Let $(\mathcal{X}^1, \mathcal{W}^1) = \{(X_n^1, W_n^1)\}_{n \in \mathbb{N}}$ be a distribution ensemble over R_{L_1} with *unique* witnesses, and $(\mathcal{X}^2, \mathcal{W}^2) = \{(X_n^2, W_n^2)\}_{n \in \mathbb{N}}$ be a distribution ensemble over R_{L_2} with *multiple* witnesses.

Theorem 1. *If the above distribution ensembles satisfy the following conditions:*

1. $(\mathcal{X}^1, \mathcal{W}^1)$ *and* $(\mathcal{X}^2, \mathcal{W}^2)$ *are computationally indistinguishable.*
2. *For every PPT machine M, there is negligible function $\mu(n)$, such that*

$$\Pr\left[(x, w) \leftarrow (X_n^2, W_n^2); w' \leftarrow M(x, w) : w' \in R_L(x) \wedge w \neq w'\right] < \mu(n).$$

3. *For every n and x in X_n^2, witnesses in $R_{L_2}(x)$ are uniformly distributed.[4]*

Then, any witness indistinguishable proof systems (including the parallelized version of 3-round public-coin proofs of [3,14] and ZAPs of [11,16]) are witness hiding (under sequential repetition) for $(\mathcal{X}^1, \mathcal{W}^1)$.

Proof. Let $\langle P, V \rangle$ be an arbitrary witness indistinguishable proof system. In the following, we present our proof only for the standalone case. Note that the same proof works also for these protocols under sequential repetition.

Suppose, towards a contradiction, that there are infinitely many n, a polynomial p, and a PPT verifier V^* such that

$$\Pr\left[\langle P(W_n^1), V^* \rangle (X_n^1) \in R_{L_1}(X_n^1)\right] > \frac{1}{p(n)}. \tag{1}$$

Let $\mathbb{S}$ be the set of such n's. Fix an $n \in \mathbb{S}$ and consider the following two experiments:

EXP^b ($b \in \{1, 2\}$): Sample $(x, w) \leftarrow (X_n^b, W_n^b)$, play the role of honest prover $P(x, w)$ and interact with $V^*(x)$. When V^* terminates, output what V^* outputs.

Denote by WIN^b that EXP^b outputs a witness for x. By the indistinguishability of $(\mathcal{X}^1, \mathcal{W}^1)$ and $(\mathcal{X}^2, \mathcal{W}^2)$, we have the following claim (we shall turn to detailed proof shortly) for some negligible function $\mu(n)$:

---

[4] This condition can be significantly relaxed, but we stick to it for simplifying presentation.

Claim 1. The probabililiy $\Pr[\mathrm{WIN}^2]$ is negligibly close to $\frac{1}{p(n)}$, i.e.,

$$\Pr\left[\mathrm{WIN}^2\right] = \Pr\left[\langle P(W_n^2), V^*\rangle(X_n^2) \in R_{L_2}(X_n^2)\right] > \frac{1}{p(n)} - \mu(n). \tag{2}$$

It follows from the second property of (X_n^2, W_n^2) that

$$\Pr\left[(x, w) \leftarrow (X_n^2, W_n^2) : \langle P(w), V^*\rangle(x) = w' \in R_{L_2}(x) \wedge w' \neq w\right] < \mu(n). \tag{3}$$

Now by (2) and (3), we have

$$\Pr\left[(x, w) \leftarrow (X_n^2, W_n^2) : \langle P(w), V^*\rangle(x) = w' \wedge w' = w\right] > \frac{1}{p(n)} - \mu(n). \tag{4}$$

which can be rewritten as

$$\Pr\left[(x, w) \leftarrow (X_n^2, W_n^2) : \langle P(w), V^*\rangle(x) = w' \wedge w' = w\right]$$
$$= \sum_w \sum_x \Pr\left[\langle P(w), V^*\rangle(x) = w' \wedge w' = w\right] \Pr\left[w \leftarrow W_n^2 | x\right] \Pr\left[x \leftarrow X_n^2\right]$$
$$> \frac{1}{p(n)} - \mu(n).$$

Theorem 1 follows from the following two claims.

Claim 2. There exists x in the support of X_n^2 satisfying the following two conditions:

$$- \sum_w \Pr\left[\langle P(w), V^*\rangle(x) = w' \wedge w' = w\right] \Pr\left[w \leftarrow W_n^2 | x\right] > \frac{1}{2p(n)} - \mu(n).$$

$$- \sum_w \Pr\left[\langle P(w), V^*\rangle(x) = w' \in R_{L_2}(x) \wedge w' \neq w\right] \Pr\left[w \leftarrow W_n^2 | x\right] < \mu(n).$$

Claim 3. There exists x in the support of X_n^2, $w_1, w_2 \in R_{L_2}(x)$ such that

$$\left|\Pr\left[\langle P(w_1), V^*\rangle(x) = w_1\right] - \Pr\left[\langle P(w_2), V^*\rangle(x) = w_1\right]\right| > \frac{1}{\mathsf{poly}(n)}.$$

Note that Claim 3 holds for each $n \in \mathbb{S}$, and thus we conclude that V^* breaks the witness indistinguishability of $\langle P, V\rangle$ on a sequence $\{(x, w_1, w_2)\}_{x \in X_n^2, n \in \mathbb{S}}$, which contradicts the fact that $\langle P, V\rangle$ is witness indistinguishable for *multiple witnesses relation*. This proves Theorem 1. □

We now give the detailed proofs of the above three claims.

*Proof (of **Claim 1**).* Let $p_1(n) = \frac{1}{p(n)}$ (as in (1)), and

$$p_2(n) = \Pr\left[\mathrm{WIN}^2\right] = \Pr\left[\langle P(W_n^2), V^*\rangle(X_n^2) \in R_{L_2}(X_n^2)\right].$$

Suppose toward a contradiction that $p_1 - p_2 > 1/\mathsf{poly}(n)$. (w.l.o.g., and we assume $p_1 > p_2$.) Consider the following D for distinguishing (X_n^1, W_n^1) and

(X_n^2, W_n^2): Given a sample (x, w) from (X_n^b, W_n^b) (for unknown b), D plays the role of honest prover $P(x, w)$ and interact with $V^*(x)$. When V^* terminates, output 1 if the output of V^* is in $R_{L_1}(x)$[5] and 0 otherwise.

Observe that,

$$
\begin{aligned}
&\Pr[D(X_n^1, W_n^1) = 1] - \Pr[D(X_n^2, W_n^2) = 1] \\
&= \Pr[\langle P(W_n^1), V^* \rangle (X_n^1) \in R_{L_1}(X_n^1)] - \Pr[\langle P(W_n^2), V^* \rangle (X_n^2) \in R_{L_1}(X_n^2)] \\
&= p_1 - \Pr[\langle P(W_n^2), V^* \rangle (X_n^2) \in R_{L_1}(X_n^2) \wedge \langle P(W_n^2), V^* \rangle (X_n^2) \in R_{L_2}(X_n^2)] \\
&\quad - \Pr[\langle P(W_n^2), V^* \rangle (X_n^2) \in R_{L_1}(X_n^2) \wedge \langle P(W_n^2), V^* \rangle (X_n^2) \notin R_{L_2}(X_n^2)] \\
&> p_1 - p_2 - \Pr[\langle P(W_n^2), V^* \rangle (X_n^2) \in R_{L_1}(X_n^2) \wedge \langle P(W_n^2), V^* \rangle (X_n^2) \notin R_{L_2}(X_n^2)].
\end{aligned}
$$

Now if the last term

$$
p_3(n) = \Pr[\langle P(W_n^2), V^* \rangle (X_n^2) \in R_{L_1}(X_n^2) \wedge \langle P(W_n^2), V^* \rangle (X_n^2) \notin R_{L_2}(X_n^2)]
$$

is negligible, we conclude that D distinguishes (X_n^1, W_n^1) and (X_n^2, W_n^2), contradicting our assumption. Now we show $p_3(n)$ is negligible. For simplicity, denote by $optV^*(x)$ the output of V^* after interaction with the prover, and we have

$$
\begin{aligned}
p_4(n) &= \Pr[\langle P(W_n^1), V^* \rangle (X_n^1) \in R_{L_1}(X_n^1) \wedge \langle P(W_n^1), V^* \rangle (X_n^1) \notin R_{L_2}(X_n^1)] \\
&= \Pr[(x, w) \leftarrow (X_n^1, W_n^1) : optV^*(x) \in R_{L_1}(x) \wedge optV^*(x) \notin R_{L_2}(x)] \\
&\leq \Pr[(x, w) \leftarrow (X_n^1, W_n^1) : w \in R_{L_1}(x) \wedge w \notin R_{L_2}(x)].
\end{aligned}
$$

The last equation follows from the uniqueness of $R_{L_1}(x)$ (that is, the valid witness output by V^* in $R_{L_1}(x)$ must be w). Observe that p_4 must be negligible since otherwise R_{L_2} will serve as a distinguisher that can distinguish (X_n^1, W_n^1) and (X_n^2, W_n^2).

It follows that p_3 is negligible either, since otherwise we will have that $|p_3 - p_4|$ is non-negligible, and this leads to the following distinguisher D': Act in the same way as D, except that D' output 1 if the output of V^* is in $R_{L_1}(x)$ but not in $R_{L_2}(x)$. It is easy to verify that D' can distinguish (X_n^1, W_n^1) and (X_n^2, W_n^2) with non-negligible probability. □

We now turn to the proof of Claim 2.

*Proof (of **Claim 2**).* We define the following two random events conditioned on a given fixed pair (x, w):

- $\text{EVENT}_{eq}|_{(x,w)}$: $\langle P(w), V^* \rangle (x) = w' \wedge w' = w$;
- $\text{EVENT}_{neq}|_{(x,w)}$: $\langle P(w), V^* \rangle (x) = w' \in R_{L_2}(x) \wedge w' \neq w$,

---

[5] Note that here we always use R_{L_1} as the tester.

where both events take over the randomnesses used by P and V^*. Define the following two sets:

- $\mathbb{H}$: $\{x : \sum_w \Pr\left[\text{EVENT}_{eq}|_{(x,w)}\right] \Pr\left[w \leftarrow W_n^2|x\right] > \frac{1}{2p(n)} - \mu(n)\}$.
- $\mathbb{K}$: $\{x : \sum_w \Pr\left[\text{EVENT}_{neq}|_{(x,w)}\right] \Pr\left[w \leftarrow W_n^2|x\right] < \mu(n)\}$.

Observe that

$$\frac{1}{p(n)} - \mu(n) < \Pr\left[(x,w) \leftarrow (X_n^2, W_n^2) : \langle P(w), V^* \rangle(x) = w' \wedge w' = w\right]$$

$$= \sum_w \sum_{x \in \mathbb{H}} \Pr\left[\text{EVENT}_{eq}|_{(x,w)}\right] \Pr\left[w \leftarrow W_n^2|x\right] \Pr\left[x \leftarrow X_n^2\right]$$

$$+ \sum_w \sum_{x \notin \mathbb{H}} \Pr\left[\text{EVENT}_{eq}|_{(x,w)}\right] \Pr\left[w \leftarrow W_n^2|x\right] \Pr\left[x \leftarrow X_n^2\right]$$

$$= \sum_w \Pr\left[\text{EVENT}_{eq}|_{(x,w)}\right] \Pr\left[w \leftarrow W_n^2|x \in \mathbb{H}\right] \Pr\left[x \leftarrow X_n^2 : x \in \mathbb{H}\right]$$

$$+ \sum_w \Pr\left[\text{EVENT}_{eq}|_{(x,w)}\right] \Pr\left[w \leftarrow W_n^2|x \notin \mathbb{H}\right] \Pr\left[x \leftarrow X_n^2 : x \notin \mathbb{H}\right],$$

which, by the definitions of EVENT_{eq} and set $\mathbb{H}$, leads to

$$\Pr\left[x \leftarrow X_n^2 : x \in \mathbb{H}\right] > \frac{1}{2p(n)} - \mu(n). \tag{5}$$

Similarly, by (3), we have

$$\mu(n) > \Pr\left[(x,w) \leftarrow (X_n^2, W_n^2) : \langle P(w), V^* \rangle(x) = w' \in R_{L_2}(x) \wedge w' \neq w\right]$$

$$= \sum_w \sum_{x \in \mathbb{K}} \Pr\left[\text{EVENT}_{neq}|_{(x,w)}\right] \Pr\left[w \leftarrow W_n^2|x\right] \Pr\left[x \leftarrow X_n^2\right]$$

$$+ \sum_w \sum_{x \notin \mathbb{K}} \Pr\left[\text{EVENT}_{neq}|_{(x,w)}\right] \Pr\left[w \leftarrow W_n^2|x\right] \Pr\left[x \leftarrow X_n^2\right]$$

$$= \sum_w \Pr\left[\text{EVENT}_{neq}|_{(x,w)}\right] \Pr\left[w \leftarrow W_n^2|x \in \mathbb{K}\right] \Pr\left[x \leftarrow X_n^2 : x \in \mathbb{K}\right]$$

$$+ \sum_w \Pr\left[\text{EVENT}_{neq}|_{(x,w)}\right] \Pr\left[w \leftarrow W_n^2|x \notin \mathbb{K}\right] \Pr\left[x \leftarrow X_n^2 : x \notin \mathbb{K}\right],$$

which, by the definitions of EVENT_{neq} and set $\mathbb{K}$, leads to

$$\Pr\left[x \leftarrow X_n^2 : x \in \mathbb{K}\right] > 1 - \mu'(n) \tag{6}$$

for some negligible function $\mu'(n)$.

Thus, by (5) and (6), we conclude

$$\Pr\left[x \leftarrow X_n^2 : x \in \mathbb{H} \cap \mathbb{K}\right] > \frac{1}{2p(n)} - \mu(n) - \mu'(n),$$

which means there exist at least one x in the support of X_n^2 that satisfies both conditions of Claim 2, as desired. $\qquad\square$

The proof of Claim 3 is based on Claim 2.

*Proof (of **Claim 3**).* Fix a x in the support of X_n^2 that satisfies the two conditions of Claim 1. Note that W_n^2 is uniformly distributed on $R_{L_2}(x)$, and by the first condition of Claim 2, we have a $w_1 \in R_{L_2}(x)$ such that

$$\Pr\left[\langle P(w_1), V^* \rangle (x) = w_1\right] > \frac{1}{2p(n)} - \mu(n).$$

By the second condition of Claim 2, we can obtain another witness $w_2 \in R_{L_2}(x)$, $w_2 \neq w_1$, such that

$$\Pr\left[\langle P(w_2), V^* \rangle (x) = w_1\right] < \mu(n),$$

since otherwise, we would have

$$\sum_w \Pr\left[\langle P(w), V^* \rangle (x) = w' \in R_{L_2}(x) \land w' \neq w\right] \Pr\left[w \leftarrow W_n^2 | x\right]$$

$$\geq \sum_{w_2(\neq w_1)} \Pr\left[\langle P(w_2), V^* \rangle (x) = w_1\right] \Pr\left[w_2 \leftarrow W_n^2 | x : w_2 \neq w_1\right]$$

$$= \sum_{w_2(\neq w_1)} \Pr\left[\langle P(w_2), V^* \rangle (x) = w_1\right] \frac{|R_{L_2}(x)| - 1}{|R_{L_2}(x)|}$$

$$> \frac{1}{\mathsf{poly}(n)} \cdot \frac{|R_{L_2}(x)| - 1}{|R_{L_2}(x)|},$$

which breaks the second condition of Claim 2[6]. Thus we obtain a desired tuple (x, w_1, w_2), completing the proof of Claim 3.   □

3.2   Examples of Distributions on Unique Witness Relations

In this subsection, we present several examples of distributions $(\mathcal{X}^1, \mathcal{W}^1)$ on hard unique witness relations that have coupled distributions (satisfing the "if conditions" of Theorem 1), including distributions over OR-DDH tuples with unique witnesses, the images of lossy trapdoor functions and commitments with unique openings. Thus, for these distributions on unique witness relations, the classic constant-round public-coin proof systems, such as parallelized version of classic 3-round public-coin proofs of [3,14] and ZAPs of [11,16], are witness hiding.

Example 1: OR-DDH Tuples with Unique Witnesses. The first example is for distribution $(\mathcal{X}^1, \mathcal{W}^1)$ on hard instances with unique witnesses based on DDH assumption.

---

[6] Note that $|R_{L_2}(x)| > 1$.

DDH assumption: Let Gen be a randomized algorithm that on security parameter n outputs $(\mathbb{G}, g, q)$, where $\mathbb{G}$ is a cyclic group of order q with generator g. Then for a randomly chosen triplet (a, b, c), for every PPT algorithm $\mathcal{A}$, there exists a negligible function $\mu(n)$ such that

$$|\Pr[\mathcal{A}((\mathbb{G}, g, q), g^a, g^b, g^{ab}) = 1] - \Pr[\mathcal{A}((\mathbb{G}, g, q), g^a, g^b, g^c) = 1]| < \mu(n).$$

Now, we consider the following two distribution ensembles $(\mathcal{X}^1, \mathcal{W}^1) = \{(X_n^1, W_n^1)\}_{n \in \mathbb{N}}$ and $(\mathcal{X}^2, \mathcal{W}^2) = \{(X_n^2, W_n^2)\}_{n \in \mathbb{N}}$ based on the DDH assumption:

- $(X_n^1, W_n^1) = \{((\mathbb{G}, g, q), x, w) : (\mathbb{G}, g, q) \leftarrow \mathsf{Gen}(1^n),$ the instance x is an OR-DDH tuples $(g^{a_1}, g^{a_2}, g^{a_1 a_2})$ or (g^{b_1}, g^{b_2}, g^c) (where $c \neq b_1 b_2$) with the unique witness $w = (a_1, a_2, a_1 a_2)\}$;
- $(X_n^2, W_n^2) = \{((\mathbb{G}, g, q), x, w) : (\mathbb{G}, g, q) \leftarrow \mathsf{Gen}(1^n),$ the instance x is an OR-DDH tuples $(g^{a_1}, g^{a_2}, g^{a_1 a_2})$ or $(g^{b_1}, g^{b_2}, g^{b_1 b_2})$ with multiple witnesses $w_0 = (a_1, a_2, a_1 a_2)$, $w_1 = (b_1, b_2, b_1 b_2)\}$.

Based on Theorem 1, we have that all the witness hiding protocols for $(\mathcal{X}^2, \mathcal{W}^2)$ above are also witness hiding for $(\mathcal{X}^1, \mathcal{W}^1)$ above, under the DDH assumption.

Example 2: Lossy Trapdoor Functions. We now present another example of distribution ensembles $(\mathcal{X}^1, \mathcal{W}^1)$ based on lossy trapdoor functions.

Recall the definition of lossy trapdoor functions [25]. Let n be the security parameter (representing the input length of the function) and $\ell(n)$ be the lossiness of the collection.

Definition 5. *A collection of (m, k)-lossy trapdoor functions is given by a tuple of PPT algorithms $(\mathsf{Gen}, \mathsf{F}, \mathsf{F}^{-1})$. It satisfies the following property:*

- *Easy to sample an injective function with trapdoor: $\mathsf{Gen}_{inj}(\cdot) := \mathsf{Gen}(\cdot, 1)$ outputs (s, t) where s is the description of an injective function f_s and t is its trapdoor, $\mathsf{F}(s, \cdot)$ computes the function $f_s(\cdot)$ over the domain $\{0, 1\}^n$, and $\mathsf{F}(t, \cdot)$ computes the function $f_s^{-1}(\cdot)$. If a value y is not in the image of f_s, then $\mathsf{F}(t, y)$ is unspecified.*
- *Easy to sample a lossy function: $\mathsf{Gen}_{lossy}(\cdot) := \mathsf{Gen}(\cdot, 0)$ outputs $(s, \perp)$ where s is the description of function f_s, and $\mathsf{F}(s, \cdot)$ computes the function $f_s(\cdot)$ over the domain $\{0, 1\}^m$ whose image has size at most 2^{m-k}.*
- *Hard to distinguish injective and lossy: the first outputs of Gen_{inj} and Gen_{lossy} are computationally indistinguishable.*

Now we consider the following two distribution ensembles $(\mathcal{X}^1, \mathcal{W}^1) = \{(X_n^1, W_n^1)\}_{n \in \mathbb{N}}$ and $(\mathcal{X}^2, \mathcal{W}^2) = \{(X_n^2, W_n^2)\}_{n \in \mathbb{N}}$ based on lossy trapdoor function:

- $(X_n^1, W_n^1) := \{((s, y), w) : s \leftarrow \mathsf{Gen}_{inj}(1^n); w \leftarrow \{0, 1\}^n; f_s(w) = y\}$.
- $(X_n^2, W_n^2) := \{((s, y), w) : s \leftarrow \mathsf{Gen}_{lossy}(1^n); w \leftarrow \{0, 1\}^n; f_s(w) = y\}$.

Note that the description of a lossy function is indistinguishable from that of an injective function, thus the distribution (X_n^2, W_n^2) over the description of lossy function together with its input-output pair is also indistinguishable from the distribution (X_n^1, W_n^1) over injective function together with its input-output pair, since otherwise if we have a PPT D' that can distinguish (X_n^1, W_n^1) from (X_n^2, W_n^2), we will have a PPT D that can tell apart lossy functions from injective ones: When being given a description of a function f, D samples input w and computes $y = f(w)$ and then invokes D' on (f, y, w) and outputs what D' outputs.

It is also easy to verify (using the fact that there is only a single w such that $f(w) = y$ for a fixed injective function f and y.)that the second condition of Theorem 1 holds. When sampling w in the domain of a lossy function f uniformly, then for a fixed output y, those pre-images of y are uniformly distributed over $\{w : f(w) = y\}$. Hence, the above two distributions satisfy the third condition of Theorem 1.

Thus, it follows from Theorem 1 that all the witness hiding protocols for $(\mathcal{X}^2, \mathcal{W}^2)$ above are also witness hiding for $(\mathcal{X}^1, \mathcal{W}^1)$ above, under the existence of lossy trapdoor functions.

Example 3: Commitments with Unique Openings. Our third example of distribution ensembles $(\mathcal{X}^1, \mathcal{W}^1)$ is based on mixed commitments [9,16].

A mixed commitment scheme is basically a commitment scheme that has two different flavors of key generation algorithms. In the binding mode, Gen_1 generates a perfectly binding commitment key, in which case a valid commitment uniquely defines one possible message. In the hiding mode, Gen_2 generates a perfectly hiding commitment key, in which case the commitment reveals no information whatsoever about the message. Moreover, two kinds of keys are computationally indistinguishable.

Now, we consider the following two distribution ensembles $(\mathcal{X}^1, \mathcal{W}^1) = \{(X_n^1, W_n^1)\}_{n \in \mathbb{N}}$ and $(\mathcal{X}^2, \mathcal{W}^2) = \{(X_n^2, W_n^2)\}_{n \in \mathbb{N}}$ based on the mixed commitments:

- $(X_n^1, W_n^1) = \{((x, pk), (m, r)) : pk \leftarrow \mathsf{Gen}_1(1^n); m \xleftarrow{\text{R}} M; r \xleftarrow{\text{R}} R; x \leftarrow \mathsf{Com}_{pk}(m; r)\}$.
- $(X_n^2, W_n^2) = \{((x, pk), (m, r)) : pk \leftarrow \mathsf{Gen}_2(1^n); m \xleftarrow{\text{R}} M; r \xleftarrow{\text{R}} R; x \leftarrow \mathsf{Com}_{pk}(m; r)\}$.

Assuming the existence of mixed commitments, we can use the reasoning similar to the case of lossy functions and conclude that all the witness hiding protocols for $(\mathcal{X}^2, \mathcal{W}^2)$ above are also witness hiding for $(\mathcal{X}^1, \mathcal{W}^1)$ above.

4 Embedding Reduction: The Security of Schnorr and Guillou-Quisquater Protocols and Instance Compression

In this section, we develop an embedding reduction technique to base the witness hiding security[7] of Schnorr protocol on non-existence of tailored instance compression scheme for discrete logarithm.

Similar results can also be obtained for the Guillou-Quisquater's protocol and some other Σ-protocols for group homomorphisms. Note that, given a successful adversary V^*, our technique yields a tailored instance compression scheme with parameters much stronger than the ones in [2], and thus strengthens the results of [2].

The formal study of instance compression was initiated by Harnik and Naor [19]. We tailor their definition for our purpose. Roughly speaking, a tailored instance compression scheme for a (search) NP problem can compress a long instance(s) into a shorter instance, and given the solution to the shorter instance, we can solve all the original instance(s). It should be noted that the impossibility results of [10] with respect to NP-complete languages also hold for our tailored definition.

Definition 6 (Tailored Instance Compression for Search Problem). *Let L be an NP language and R_L its NP relation, and $\mathcal{X} = \{X_n\}_{n \in \mathbb{N}}$ be a distribution ensemble over L. A $(\ell(\cdot), \varepsilon(\cdot))$-tailored instance compression scheme for R_L consists of three PPT algorithms $(\mathsf{Z}, \mathsf{C}, \mathsf{U})$, such that for sufficiently large n:*

- *$(x, st) \leftarrow \mathsf{Z}(x_1, \cdots, x_\ell)$: On input $x_i \in L$ for $i \in [\ell]$, the PPT instances compression algorithm Z outputs a single $x \in L$ and the state st.*
- *$w \leftarrow \mathsf{C}((x_1, w_1), \cdots, (x_\ell, w_\ell))$: On input $(x_i, w_i) \in R_L$ for $i \in [\ell]$, the PPT witness compression algorithm C outputs a valid witness w to the instance x generated by $\mathsf{Z}(x_1, \cdots, x_\ell)$.*
- *$(w_1, \cdots, w_\ell) \leftarrow \mathsf{U}(x, w, st)$: On input $x \in L$, st, together with the corresponding witness $w \in R_L(x)$, the PPT unfolding algorithm U outputs the witnesses $w_i \in R_L(x_i)$ for all $i \in [\ell]$.*
- *For all $w \in R_L(x)$, the following holds:*

$$\Pr\left[\begin{array}{l} (x_1, \ldots, x_\ell) \leftarrow X_n^\ell; \\ (x, st) \leftarrow \mathsf{Z}(x_1, \ldots, x_\ell); \\ (w_1, \ldots, w_\ell) \leftarrow \mathsf{U}(x, w, st); \end{array} : \wedge_{i=1}^\ell w_i \in R_L(x_i)\right] > \varepsilon(n)$$

Remark 2. Our definition is stronger than the one of [19] in several respects. In the Definition 2.25 of [19], the retrieving algorithm (that corresponds to our witness compression algorithm) does not take witnesses to $(x_1, \ldots, x_\ell)$ as input, and thus is not required to be efficient; the unfolding algorithm above is also not required in [19], but that is the key for our applications of instance compression scheme (if exists).

---

[7] Note that witness hiding implies the security of identification protocol.

Observe that the one-more like assumptions can be rephrased in the framework of instance compression. For example, the one-more DL assumption is equivalent to assume non-existence of (ℓ, ε)-tailored instance compression scheme for DL with weaker requirements: (1) The witness compression algorithm is not required; (2) The instance compression algorithm is allowed to output $\ell - 1$ instances (which leads to much weak compression ratio) and the unfolding algorithm needs to take $\ell - 1$ witnesses correspondingly.

4.1   The Security of Schnorr Protocol

Let $\mathbb{G}$ be a cyclic group of order q with the generator g, where q is a prime such that $q \mid p - 1$, p is a prime $2^{n-1} \le p \le 2^n$. Given a common input x, the Schnorr protocol allows the prover P to convince the verifier V of knowledge of the unique discrete logarithm w of x (i.e., $x = g^w$). Formal description of this protocol can be found in Fig. 1.

Given $(g, \mathbb{G})$, we define the NP relation $R_{(g,\mathbb{G})} := \{(x, w) : x = g^w\}$. We show that a successful adversarial verifier will lead to a non-trivial tailored instance compression scheme for discrete logarithm (DL) instances.

Theorem 2. *If there exists a PPT algorithm V^* that breaks witness hiding of Schnorr protocol with probability p (i.e. V^* after interaction with the prover P outputs a valid discrete logarithm w of x with probability greater than p), then there exists $(\ell, p^{\ell-1})$-tailored instance compression scheme for DL instances in $\mathbb{G}$ for any ℓ.*

Remark 3. It should be noted that for a negligible probability ε, the (ℓ, ε)-tailored instance compression scheme (if exists) is barely applicable. For achieving meaningful compression scheme from V^*, we should set ℓ to be (arbitrary) constant when p is an inverse polynomial; if p is negligibly close to 1, then ℓ can be set to be (arbitrary) polynomial. Note also that the technique of [2] gives us only $\ell = 2$.

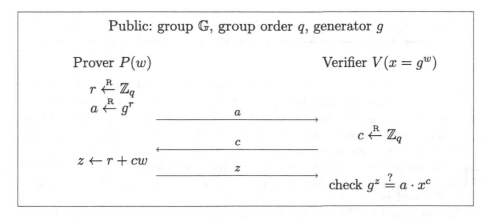

Fig. 1. Schnorr identification scheme

D^{V^*}

input : instances $x_1, x_2 \in \mathbb{G}$, random tape R_V

1: Run V^* with random tape R_V on instance x_1;
2: Send x_2 as the first prover message to V^*;

   output: output: If V^* answers with a challenge $c \in \mathbb{Z}_q$, output $x = x_1^c x_2$; else
        output $\perp$.

B^{V^*}

input : $z \in \mathbb{Z}_q$, $x_1, x_2 \in \mathbb{G}$, random tape R_V

1: Execute the Schnorr protocol with V^* in exactly the same way as $D(x_1, x_2, R_V)$
    until receiving the challenge c from V^*;
2: Send z, which is supposed to be such that $g^z = x_1^c x_2$, to V^*;

   output: If V^* outputs the witness w satisfying $x_1 = g^w$, output $z_1 = w$ and
        $z_2 = z - cw$; else output $\perp$.

The compression algorithm Z^{V^*}

input : $(x_1, x_2, \cdots, x_\ell)$

1: $st \leftarrow \{x_1, \cdots, x_\ell\}$;
2: set $x_j^0 = x_j$, for $j = 1, 2, \cdots, \ell$;
3: **for** $i \leftarrow 0$ **to** $l - 1$ **do**
4:      **for** $j \leftarrow 1$ **to** 2^{l-i-1} **do**
5:          $x_{2j-1}^i \leftarrow x_{2j-1}^i \cdot g^{r_{2j-1}^i}$, $x_{2j}^i \leftarrow x_{2j}^i \cdot g^{r_{2j}^i}$, where $r_{2j-1}^i, r_{2j}^i \xleftarrow{\text{R}} \mathbb{Z}_q$;
6:          $R_{V_j^i} \xleftarrow{\text{R}} \{0,1\}^{poly(n)}$, where $poly(n)$ denotes the length of the random
          tape $R_{V_j^i}$;
7:          $x_j^{i+1} \leftarrow D^{V^*}(x_{2j-1}^i, x_{2j}^i, R_{V_j^i})$ (if D outputs $\perp$, return $\perp$);
8:          Add $(x_j^{i+1}, r_{2j-1}^i, r_{2j}^i, R_{V_j^i})$ to st;
9:      **end**
10: **end**

11: set $x \leftarrow x_1^l$;
12: Return x, st;

We first construct two efficient subroutines D and B for our embedding reduction. On input two instances (x_1, x_2), the algorithm D interacts with V^* (where x_1 serves as the common input, and x_2 serves as the first prover message) until the challenge c from V^* is received, and outputs a new instance $x_1^c x_2$; on input discrete logarithm z of $x_1^c x_2$, the algorithm B interacts with V^* until the output of V^* is received, and outputs two discrete logarithms of the two instances (x_1, x_2). Formal descriptions of D and B can be found in Algorithm D^{V^*} and B^{V^*}.

As illustrated in Fig. 2, our embedding black-box reduction naturally corresponds to a pair of efficient algorithms, a compression algorithm Z and an

---

The unfolding algorithm U^{V^*}

---

input : $x \in \mathbb{G}$, $w \in \mathbb{Z}_q$, st

1: set $x_1^l \leftarrow x$, $z_1^l \leftarrow w$;
2: **for** $i = l - 1$ **to** 0 **do**
3:      **for** $j = 1$ **to** 2^{l-i-1} **do**
4:          Retrieve $x_{2j-1}^i, x_{2j}^i, r_{2j-1}^i, r_{2j}^i$ and Rv_j^i from st;
5:          $(z_{2j-1}^i, z_{2j}^i) \leftarrow B^{V^*}(z_j^{i+1}, x_{2j-1}^i, x_{2j}^i, Rv_j^i)$ (if B outputs $\perp$, return $\perp$);
6:          $z_{2j-1}^i \leftarrow z_{2j-1}^i - r_{2j-1}^i$, $z_{2j}^i \leftarrow z_{2j}^i - r_{2j}^i$;
7:      **end**
8: **end**

output: $(w_1, w_2, \cdots, w_\ell) = (z_1^0, z_2^0, \cdots, z_\ell^0)$

---

unfolding algorithm U. In the first phase, the compression algorithm Z, taking as input discrete logarithm instances $(x_1, \ldots, x_\ell)$, invokes D recursively to generate new instance, each time D transforms two new instances into a new single one. Z outputs the final single instance $x = x_1^3$ and the corresponding st consisting of all instances input to D and the random tape of Z.

On input a witness $w = z_1^3$ to $x = x_1^3$, the unfolding algorithm U invokes B recursively, by feeding B with a discrete logarithm of an instance, to solve two instances. Finally, U will solve all instances $(x_1, x_2, ..., x_\ell)$.

For our analysis to go through, given two instances x_1, x_2, the compression algorithm Z has to choose two random strings r_1, r_2 and a fresh random tape for V^*, and then runs D on input $(x_1 g^{r_1}, x_2 g^{r_2})$. Z will store all these randomnesses in st. The formal descriptions of Z and U can be found in Algorithm D^{V^*} and B^{V^*} respectively. Without loss of generality, we assume that $\ell = 2^l$ for some integer l.

Proof (of Theorem 1). From Fig. 2, we see the symmetry that, on input two instances (x_{2j-1}^i, x_{2j}^i), $D^{V^*}(x_{2j-1}^i, x_{2j}^i, Rv_j^i)$ generates a new instance x_j^{i+1}; whereas, on input a discrete logarithm z_j^{i+1} of x_j^{i+1}, $B^{V^*}(z_j^{i+1}, x_{2j-1}^i, x_{2j}^i, Rv_j^i)$ produces the two discrete logarithms (z_{2j-1}^i, z_{2j}^i) of the two instances (x_{2j-1}^i, x_{2j}^i) that are inputs to D.

We say an algorithm wins if it does not output "$\perp$". Note that all these invocations of D are independent, and that, for every i, j, the V^* success probability p is the probability that both $D^{V^*}(x_{2j-1}^i, x_{2j}^i, Rv_j^i)$ and $B^{V^*}(z_j^{i+1}, x_{2j-1}, x_{2j}, Rv_j^i)$ win, that is,

$$\Pr[D^{V^*}(x_{2j-1}^i, x_{2j}^i, Rv_j^i) \text{ wins} \wedge B^{V^*}(z_j^{i+1}, x_{2j-1}, x_{2j}, Rv_j^i) \text{ wins}] = p.$$

Observe that in the entire reduction there are exactly $(\ell - 1)$ pairs of invocations of D^{V^*} and B^{V^*}, thus we have the probability

$$\Pr\left[\begin{array}{l} \Pr[(x, st) \leftarrow Z^{V^*}(x_1, x_2, \cdots, x_\ell); \\ (w_1, w_2, \cdots, w_\ell) \leftarrow U^{V^*}(x, st, w) \end{array} : \wedge_{i=1}^\ell x_i = g^{w_i} \right] = p^{\ell-1}$$

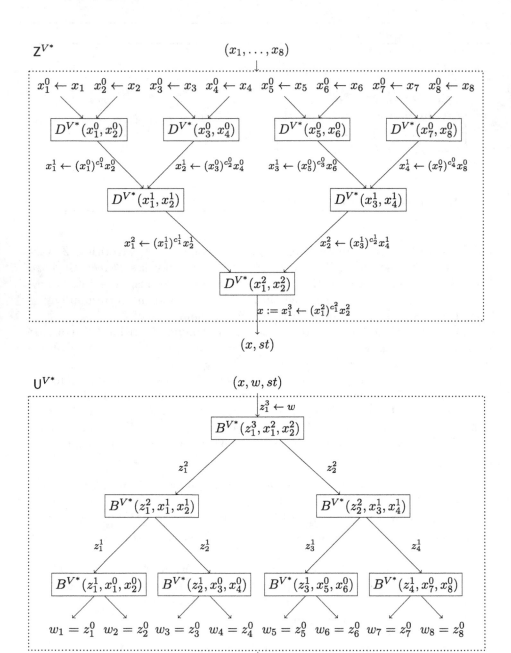

Fig. 2. Simplified reduction for $\ell = 8$. We assume that V^* is deterministic and with probability 1 it breaks witness hiding of Schnorr protocol.

Note that when given as input all the witnesses $(w_1, \cdots, w_\ell)$ of the target instances $(x_1, \cdots, x_\ell)$ to Z, Z is able to compute the witness to every instance output by D. Thus by making a straightforward adaptation of Z we get a PPT witness compression algorithm C as desired. This completes the proof.   □

4.2 Security of the Guillou-Quisquater Protocol

In this section we state a similar result on Guillou-Quisquater identification protocol [17]. The reduction is essentially the same as the one for Schnorr protocol, and here we omit it.

The Guillou-Quisquater Protocol. Let $N = pq$ be an RSA modulus (i.e. p and q are large distinct primes for security parameter n) and $e < \phi(N)$ be an odd prime satisfying $\gcd(d, \phi(N)) = 1$ and $ed \equiv 1 \mod \phi(N)$. The Guillou-Quisquater protocol proceeds as follows (See Fig. 3). The prover P wants to convince the verifier V of the unique e-th root w modulo N of a given number x. First, P chooses $r \in \mathbb{Z}_N^*$ at random and sends $a = r^e \mod N$ to the verifier V. Upon receiving the verifier's challenge c, P responses with $z = r \cdot w^c$. V accepts if and only if $z^e = a \cdot x^c$.

Given (e, N), we define the NP relation $R_{e,N} := \{(x, w) : x = w^e \mod N\}$. Similar to the Schnorr protocol, we have the following theorem.

Theorem 3. *If there exists a PPT algorithm V^* that breaks witness hiding of Guillou-Quisquater protocol with probability p (i.e. V^* after interaction outputs the witness w with probability greater than p), then there exists $(\ell, p^{\ell-1})$-tailored instance compression scheme for RSA instances in $\mathbb{Z}_N^*$ for any ℓ.*

Remark 4. We also note that our reduction can also apply to Σ−protocols for group homomorphisms [7,22].

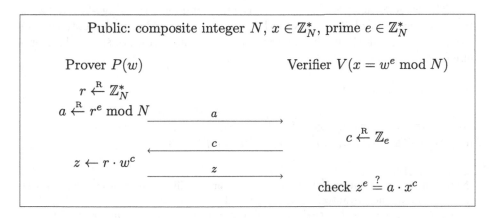

Fig. 3. GQ identification scheme

5   Some Consequences of Existence of Good Tailored Instance Compression Schemes for DL and RSA

In this section, we show some strong consequences of the existence of good tailored instance compression schemes for DL and RSA problems. To simplify our presentation, we consider only $(poly(n), 1 - negl(n))$-tailored instance compression schemes, where $poly(n)$ denotes an arbitrary polynomial in security parameter n. Such an instance compression scheme can be constructed from the efficient adversary that can break the witness hiding of Schnorr/Guillou-Quisquater protocol with probability negligibly close to 1. We also stress that, as showed in [24], even for such an adversary, no black-box reduction can turn it into an algorithm that breaks some standard assumptions and reach a contradiction.

5.1   Extremely Communication-Efficient Zero Knowledge Protocols for AND-DL and AND-RSA

Suppose that there is a $(poly(n), 1 - negl(n))$-tailored instance compression scheme (Z, C, U) for DL. In this subsection we further assume that the compression algorithm Z is deterministic without loss of generality: Since almost all possible random tapes for Z are good in the sense that on every such random tape Z will output an instance, together with some state information, for which the unfolding algorithm will succeed, we can publish a good random tape and let each party execute Z on the same random tape when needed[8].

The immediate consequence of such a tailored instance compression scheme is that, for an arbitrary polynomial ℓ, the AND-DL statement, $\{(x_1, x_2, \ldots, x_\ell, g, \mathbb{G}) : \exists w_1, w_2 \ldots, w_\ell, s.t. \wedge_{i=1}^\ell g^{w_i} = x_i\}$, has a proof of size $|w_i|$, since we can have both the prover and the verifier run Z on $(x_1, x_2, \ldots, x_\ell)$ and obtain a single instance x of the same size of x_i, and then the prover send the w (such that $g^w = x$) to the verifier, which accepts if $g^w = x$ and all w_i, obtained from the unfolding algorithm U, satisfy $g^{w_i} = x_i$.

With this succinct proof for the AND-DL statement, the Feige-Shamir zero knowledge protocol of [12] for AND-DL statements can be implemented in an extremely communication-efficient way (with communication of size $O(1)$ group elements).

PROTOCOL FEIGE-SHAMIR

Common input: $x_1, x_2, \ldots, x_\ell \in \mathbb{G}$.
The prover P's input: $w_1, w_2, \ldots, w_\ell, s.t. \wedge_{i=1}^\ell g^{w_i} = x_i$.

---

[8] Note that in the last item in Definition 6, the probability takes over the randomness of drawing all the instantces $(x_1, \ldots, x_\ell)$ and the randomnesses of Z and U. Thus, when $\epsilon(\cdot)$ is set to be $1 - negl(\cdot)$, by a simple counting argument, we will have a single random tape of Z (and U) that works for all but negligible fraction of inputs of ℓ-tuple $(x_1, \ldots, x_\ell)$.

First phase: The verifier chooses $w_0', w_1' \xleftarrow{\text{R}} \mathbb{Z}_q$ independently and at random, computes $x_0' = g^{w_0'}$ and $x_1' = g^{w_1'}$, and then executes the 3-round Σ_{OR} protocol (OR-composition of the Schnorr protocol [8]), in which V plays the role of the prover, to prove the knowledge of the witness to the statement $(x_0' \vee x_1')$;

Second phase: Both the prover and the verifier run Z on $(x_1, x_2, \ldots, x_\ell)$ and obtain a new instance $x \in \mathbb{G}$, and then the prover runs the witness compression algorithm C on $w_1, w_2, \ldots, w_\ell$ to obtain w such that $g^w = x$, and proves to the verifier the knowledge of the witness to the statement $(x \vee x_0' \vee x_1')$ using Σ_{OR} protocol of [8].

This leads to the following proposition.

Proposition 1. *If there exists a* $(\mathsf{poly}(n), 1-\mathsf{negl}(n))$*-tailored instance compression scheme for AND-DL, then for an arbitrary polynomial $\ell(n)$, the AND-DL statement,* $\{(x_1, x_2, \ldots, x_\ell, g, \mathbb{G}) : \exists w_1, w_2, \ldots, w_\ell, \text{ s.t. } \wedge_{i=1}^{\ell} g^{w_i} = x_i\}$, *has a zero knowledge protocol with communication complexity of $O(1)$ group elements.*

5.2 Special Hash Combiner

The second consequence is a construction of non-trivial hash combiner for hash functions based on the DL problem, which would help a set of ℓ mutually untrusting parties set up a single trusted collision-resistant hash function from a given group.

Consider the cyclic group $\mathbb{G}$ mentioned in Sect. 4.1. Let $x = g^w$ for some w. $h^x : \mathbb{Z}_q^2 \to \mathbb{G}$ is *collision resistant hash functions* (CRHFs) based on DL problem defined as follows:

$$h^x(m_0, m_1) = g^{m_0} x^{m_1}.$$

Clearly, finding a collision for h^x is equivalent to solving the discrete logarithm problem $w = \log_g x$.

Definition 7 (Hash Combiner for CRHFs Based on DL Problem). *A non-uniform PPT Turing machine* $\mathsf{H} : \mathcal{R} \times \mathbb{Z}_q^2 \to \{0, 1\}^v$ *is said to be a randomized (k, ℓ)-combiner for CRHFs based on DL, if it satisfies the following conditions:*

- *For any given ℓ elements of $\mathbb{G}$ (i.e. $x_1, \cdots, x_\ell$), for every $r \in \mathcal{R}$, $\mathsf{H}^{x_1, x_2, \cdots, x_\ell}(r, \cdot, \cdot)$ is a collision resistant hash function, if at least k components x_i can be used to construct collision resistant hash functions $h^{x_i}(\cdot, \cdot)$.*
- *For every PPT adversary $\mathcal{B}$ breaking the collision resistent hash combiner $\mathsf{H}^{x_1, x_2, \cdots, x_\ell}(r, \cdot, \cdot)$, there exists a PPT reduction R, s.t. $R^{\mathcal{B}}$ can find collisions for at least $\ell - k + 1$ hash functions h^{x_i}, $i \in [\ell]$, with overwhelming probability.*

Now we will show that the combiner for CRHFs based on the DL problem can be constructed by the compression algorithm for DL instances. The previous papers [6,26,27] showed that there doesn't exist "fully"[9] black-box combiners whose output length is significantly smaller than what can be achieved by trivially concatenating the output of any $\ell - k + 1$ of the components. We can construct a special non-black-box $(1, \ell)$-combiner for CRHFs based on DL problem whose output length is significantly smaller using the instances compression algorithm mentioned in Corollary 2, under the discrete logarithm assumption.

Proposition 2. *Suppose there exists a* $(\text{poly}(n), 1 - \text{negl}(n))$-*tailored instance compression algorithm for any given* $\ell (= \text{poly}(n))$ *DL instances* $x_1, x_2, \ldots, x_\ell$ *in* $\mathbb{G}$. *Then there exists a randomized* $(1, \ell)$-*combiner* $\mathsf{H}^{x_1, x_2, \ldots, x_\ell}$ *for CRHFs based on DL problem, with the same output length* v *as the regular discrete logarithm hash functions* h^{x_i}.

Proof. Assume that there exists $(\text{poly}(n), 1 - \text{negl}(n))$-tailored instance compression algorithms for DL. That is, for any polynomial ℓ, there exists a pair of PPT algorithms (Z, U), for $w = \log_g x$, such that

$$\Pr\left[\begin{array}{l} (x, st) \leftarrow \mathsf{Z}(x_1, \ldots, x_\ell); \\ (w_1, \ldots, w_\ell) \leftarrow \mathsf{U}(x, w, st) \end{array} : \wedge_{i=1}^{\ell} w_i = \log_g x_i \right] > 1 - \text{negl}(n).$$

The combiner has the following form:

$$\mathsf{H}^{(x_1, x_2, \cdots, x_\ell)}(r, m_0, m_1) = h^x(m_0, m_1) = g^{m_0} x^{m_1}.$$

where $x \leftarrow \mathsf{Z}(x_1, x_2, \cdots, x_\ell)$, and r is the same random tape as the compression algorithm Z used.

Note that a pair of collisions for h^y will give the discrete logarithm of x, which in turn can be used (by applying U) to solve all DL instances $x_1, \ldots, x_\ell$, and therefore we can find a pair of collisions for each hash function h^{x_i} efficiently. Thus this combiner is a $(1, \ell)$-combiner for CRHFs based on DL problem as defined in Definition 7.   □

Application of Special Hash Combiner: How to Set up a Global Hash. Suppose in a multi-party setting, a given number of participants, $P_1, \cdots, P_\ell$, each P_i has its own hash function h^{x_i} with the same common parameter $\mathbb{G}, g$, and want to set up a *single* hash function trusted by all of them. The need for a global hash function was also addressed in [5]. While we can't simple choose some participant's hash function as the global hash function for obvious reasons. we can use our special hash combiner to solve this puzzle: Each participant runs the instance compression algorithm Z on these $(x_1, \cdots, x_l)$ locally and generates a single common $x \in \mathbb{G}$, and then they set $H_{(g,x)} : (m_0, m_1) \rightarrow g^{m_0} x^{m_1}$ to be the global hash function. This function is collision-resistant free since every collision would lead to a solution to the instance x', which will enable the unfolding algorithm U to find all discrete logarithms of these random x_i's, and thus if there is one x_i generated at random by an honest party, no PPT algorithm can find a collision for $H_{(g,x)}$.

---

[9] Fully black box combiners mean both constructions and security proofs are black-box.

6 Open Problems

Our results also leave several interesting problems. The first one is to pinpoint the necessary and sufficient conditions on the hard distribution that admits constant-round public-coin witness hiding protocol. It is known that instance compression scheme is impossible with respect to NP-complete languages, and that the DL and RSA problems are unlikely to be NP-complete. We wonder if tailored instance compression schemes (with moderate parameters) exist for DL/RSA. It is shown that both positive and negative answers to this problem will have interesting consequences.

Acknowledgments. All authors are supported by the National Natural Science Foundation of China (Grant No. 61379141, No. 61772521), Key Research Program of Frontier Sciences, CAS (Grant No. QYZDB-SSW-SYS035), and the Open Project Program of the State Key Laboratory of Cryptology. The fourth author is also supported in by the National Key Research and Development Plan (Grant No. 2016YFB0800403), the National Natural Science Foundation of China (Grant No. 61772522) and Youth Innovation Promotion Association CAS.

References

1. Bellare, M., Namprempre, C., Pointcheval, D., Semanko, M.: The one-more-RSA-inversion problems and the security of Chaum's blind signature scheme. J. Cryptol. **16**(3), 185–215 (2003)
2. Bellare, M., Palacio, A.: GQ and schnorr identification schemes: proofs of security against impersonation under active and concurrent attacks. In: Yung, M. (ed.) CRYPTO 2002. LNCS, vol. 2442, pp. 162–177. Springer, Heidelberg (2002). https://doi.org/10.1007/3-540-45708-9_11
3. Blum, M.: How to prove a theorem so no one else can claim it. In: ICM, pp. 1444–1451 (1986)
4. Brassard, G., Chaum, D., Crépeau, C.: Minimum disclosure proofs of knowledge. J. Comput. Syst. Sci. **37**(2), 156–189 (1988)
5. Canetti, R., Lin, H., Paneth, O.: Public-coin concurrent zero-knowledge in the global hash model. In: Sahai, A. (ed.) TCC 2013. LNCS, vol. 7785, pp. 80–99. Springer, Heidelberg (2013). https://doi.org/10.1007/978-3-642-36594-2_5
6. Canetti, R., Rivest, R., Sudan, M., Trevisan, L., Vadhan, S., Wee, H.: Amplifying collision resistance: a complexity-theoretic treatment. In: Menezes, A. (ed.) CRYPTO 2007. LNCS, vol. 4622, pp. 264–283. Springer, Heidelberg (2007). https://doi.org/10.1007/978-3-540-74143-5_15
7. Catalano, D., Fiore, D., Gennaro, R., Vamvourellis, K.: Algebraic (trapdoor) one-way functions and their applications. In: Sahai, A. (ed.) TCC 2013. LNCS, vol. 7785, pp. 680–699. Springer, Heidelberg (2013). https://doi.org/10.1007/978-3-642-36594-2_38
8. Cramer, R., Damgård, I., Schoenmakers, B.: Proofs of partial knowledge and simplified design of witness hiding protocols. In: Desmedt, Y.G. (ed.) CRYPTO 1994. LNCS, vol. 839, pp. 174–187. Springer, Heidelberg (1994). https://doi.org/10.1007/3-540-48658-5_19

9. Damgård, I., Nielsen, J.B.: Perfect hiding and perfect binding universally composable commitment schemes with constant expansion factor. In: Yung, M. (ed.) CRYPTO 2002. LNCS, vol. 2442, pp. 581–596. Springer, Heidelberg (2002). https://doi.org/10.1007/3-540-45708-9_37

10. Drucker, A.: New limits to classical and quantum instance compression. SIAM J. Comput. **44**(5), 1443–1479 (2015)

11. Dwork, C., Naor, M.: Zaps and their applications. In: FOCS, pp. 283–293. IEEE (2000)

12. Feige, U., Shamir, A.: Witness indistinguishable and witness hiding protocols. In: STOC, pp. 416–426 (1990)

13. Goldreich, O.: The Foundations of Cryptography. Basic Techniques, vol. 1. Cambridge University Press, Cambridge (2001)

14. Goldreich, O., Micali, S., Wigderson, A.: Proofs that yield nothing but their validity or all languages in NP have zero-knowledge proof systems. J. ACM **38**(3), 690–728 (1991)

15. Goldwasser, S., Micali, S., Rackoff, C.: The knowledge complexity of interactive proof systems. SIAM J. Comput. **18**(1), 186–208 (1989)

16. Groth, J., Ostrovsky, R., Sahai, A.: New techniques for noninteractive zero-knowledge. J. ACM **59**(3), 11:1–11:35 (2012)

17. Guillou, L.C., Quisquater, J.-J.: A practical zero-knowledge protocol fitted to security microprocessor minimizing both transmission and memory. In: Barstow, D., et al. (eds.) EUROCRYPT 1988. LNCS, vol. 330, pp. 123–128. Springer, Heidelberg (1988). https://doi.org/10.1007/3-540-45961-8_11

18. Haitner, I., Rosen, A., Shaltiel, R.: On the (im)possibility of arthur-merlin witness hiding protocols. In: Reingold, O. (ed.) TCC 2009. LNCS, vol. 5444, pp. 220–237. Springer, Heidelberg (2009). https://doi.org/10.1007/978-3-642-00457-5_14

19. Harnik, D., Naor, M.: On the compressibility of NP instances and cryptographic applications. SIAM J. Comput. **39**(5), 1667–1713 (2010)

20. Jain, A., Kalai, Y.T., Khurana, D., Rothblum, R.: Distinguisher-dependent simulation in two rounds and its applications. In: Katz, J., Shacham, H. (eds.) CRYPTO 2017. LNCS, vol. 10402, pp. 158–189. Springer, Cham (2017). https://doi.org/10.1007/978-3-319-63715-0_6

21. Katz, J., Lindell, Y.: Introduction to Modern Cryptography. Chapman and Hall/CRC Press, London/Boca Raton (2007)

22. Maurer, U.: Zero-knowledge proofs of knowledge for group homomorphisms. Des. Codes Crypt. **77**(2–3), 663–676 (2015)

23. Pass, R.: Parallel repetition of zero-knowledge proofs and the possibility of basing cryptography on NP-hardness. In: IEEE CCC, pp. 96–110. IEEE (2006)

24. Pass, R.: Limits of provable security from standard assumptions. In: STOC, pp. 109–118. ACM (2011)

25. Peikert, C., Waters, B.: Lossy trapdoor functions and their applications. In: STOC, pp. 187–196. ACM (2008)

26. Pietrzak, K.: Non-trivial black-box combiners for collision-resistant hash-functions don't exist. In: Naor, M. (ed.) EUROCRYPT 2007. LNCS, vol. 4515, pp. 23–33. Springer, Heidelberg (2007). https://doi.org/10.1007/978-3-540-72540-4_2

27. Pietrzak, K.: Compression from collisions, or why CRHF combiners have a long output. In: Wagner, D. (ed.) CRYPTO 2008. LNCS, vol. 5157, pp. 413–432. Springer, Heidelberg (2008). https://doi.org/10.1007/978-3-540-85174-5_23

28. Schnorr, C.P.: Efficient identification and signatures for smart cards. In: Quisquater, J.-J., Vandewalle, J. (eds.) EUROCRYPT 1989. LNCS, vol. 434, pp. 688–689. Springer, Heidelberg (1990). https://doi.org/10.1007/3-540-46885-4_68

29. Shoup, V.: Lower bounds for discrete logarithms and related problems. In: Fumy, W. (ed.) EUROCRYPT 1997. LNCS, vol. 1233, pp. 256–266. Springer, Heidelberg (1997). https://doi.org/10.1007/3-540-69053-0_18

30. Zhang, J., Zhang, Z., Chen, Y., Guo, Y., Zhang, Z.: Black-box separations for one-more (static) CDH and its generalization. In: Sarkar, P., Iwata, T. (eds.) ASIACRYPT 2014. LNCS, vol. 8874, pp. 366–385. Springer, Heidelberg (2014). https://doi.org/10.1007/978-3-662-45608-8_20

Lattices

New (and Old) Proof Systems
for Lattice Problems

Navid Alamati[1(✉)], Chris Peikert[1], and Noah Stephens-Davidowitz[2]

[1] University of Michigan, Ann Arbor, USA
alamati@umich.edu
[2] Princeton University, Princeton, USA

Abstract. We continue the study of *statistical zero-knowledge* (SZK) proofs, both interactive and noninteractive, for computational problems on point lattices. We are particularly interested in the problem GapSPP of approximating the ε-*smoothing parameter* (for some $\varepsilon < 1/2$) of an n-dimensional lattice. The smoothing parameter is a key quantity in the study of lattices, and GapSPP has been emerging as a core problem in lattice-based cryptography, e.g., in worst-case to average-case reductions. We show that GapSPP admits SZK proofs for *remarkably low* approximation factors, improving on prior work by up to roughly $\sqrt{n}$. Specifically:

- There is a *noninteractive* SZK proof for $O(\log(n)\sqrt{\log(1/\varepsilon)})$-approximate GapSPP. Moreover, for any negligible ε and a larger approximation factor $\widetilde{O}(\sqrt{n \log(1/\varepsilon)})$, there is such a proof with an *efficient prover*.
- There is an (interactive) SZK proof with an efficient prover for $O(\log n + \sqrt{\log(1/\varepsilon)/\log n})$-approximate coGapSPP. We show this by proving that $O(\log n)$-approximate GapSPP is in coNP.

In addition, we give an (interactive) SZK proof with an efficient prover for approximating the lattice *covering radius* to within an $O(\sqrt{n})$ factor, improving upon the prior best factor of $\omega(\sqrt{n \log n})$.

1 Introduction

Informally, a *proof system* [5,26] is a protocol that allows a (possibly unbounded and malicious) prover to convince a skeptical verifier of the truth of some statement. A proof system is *zero knowledge* if the verifier "learns nothing more"

C. Peikert—This material is based upon work supported by the National Science Foundation under CAREER Award CCF-1054495 and CNS-1606362, the Alfred P. Sloan Foundation, and by a Google Research Award. The views expressed are those of the authors and do not necessarily reflect the official policy or position of the National Science Foundation, the Sloan Foundation, or Google.

N. Stephens-Davidowitz—Supported by the National Science Foundation (NSF) under Grant No. CCF-1320188, and the Defense Advanced Research Projects Agency (DARPA) and Army Research Office (ARO) under Contract No. W911NF-15-C-0236. Part of this work was done while visiting the second author at the University of Michigan.

© International Association for Cryptologic Research 2018
M. Abdalla and R. Dahab (Eds.): PKC 2018, LNCS 10770, pp. 619–643, 2018.
https://doi.org/10.1007/978-3-319-76581-5_21

from the interaction, other than the statement's veracity. The system is said to be *statistical* zero knowledge if the revealed information is negligible, even to an unbounded verifier; the class of problems having such proof systems is called SZK. Since their introduction, proof systems and zero-knowledge have found innumerable applications in cryptography and complexity theory. As a few examples, they have been used in constructions of secure multiparty computation [22], digital signatures [9], actively secure public-key encryption [39], and "ZAPs" [19]. And if a problem has an SZK (or even coAM) proof, it is not NP-hard unless the polynomial-time hierarchy collapses [11], so interactive proofs have been used as evidence against NP-hardness; see, e.g., [21,23,26,28].

A proof system is *noninteractive* [10,25] if it consists of just one message from the prover, assuming both it and the verifier have access to a truly random string. Noninteractive statistical zero-knowledge (NISZK) proof systems are especially powerful cryptographic primitives: they have minimal message complexity; they are concurrently and even "universally" composable [15]; and their security holds against unbounded malicious provers *and* verifiers, without any computational assumptions. However, we do not understand the class NISZK of problems that have noninteractive statistical zero-knowledge proof systems nearly as well as SZK. In particular, while NISZK is known to have complete problems, it is not known whether it is closed under complement or disjunction [25], unlike SZK [43,48].

Lattices and proofs. An n-dimensional lattice is a (full-rank) discrete additive subgroup of $\mathbb{R}^n$, and consists of all integer linear combinations of some linearly independent vectors $\mathbf{B} = \{\mathbf{b}_1, \ldots, \mathbf{b}_n\}$, called a *basis* of the lattice. Lattices have been extensively studied in computer science, and lend themselves to many natural computational problems. Perhaps the most well-known of these are the *Shortest Vector Problem* (SVP), which is to find a shortest nonzero vector in a given lattice, and the *Closest Vector Problem* (CVP), which is to find a lattice point that is closest to a given vector in $\mathbb{R}^n$. Algorithms for these problems and their approximation versions have many applications in computer science; see, e.g., [17,30,31,33,34,41,42]. In addition, many cryptographic primitives, ranging from public-key encryption and signatures to fully homomorphic encryption, are known to be secure assuming the (worst-case) hardness of certain lattice problems (see, e.g., [12,14,20,37,44,46]).

Due to the importance of lattices in cryptography, proof systems and zero-knowledge protocols for lattice problems have received a good deal of attention. Early on, Goldreich and Goldwasser [21] showed that for $\gamma = O(\sqrt{n/\log n})$, the γ-approximate Shortest and Closest Vector Problems, respectively denoted γ-GapSVP and γ-GapCVP, have SZK proof systems; this was later improved to coNP for $\gamma = O(\sqrt{n})$ factors [3].[1] Subsequently, Micciancio and Vadhan [38] gave

---

[1] As described, the proofs from [21] are statistical zero knowledge against only *honest* verifiers, but any such proof can unconditionally be transformed to one that is statistical zero knowledge against *malicious* verifiers [24]. We therefore ignore the distinction for the remainder of the paper.

different SZK proofs for the same problems, where the provers are *efficient* when given appropriate witnesses; this is obviously an important property if the proof systems are to be used by real entities as components of other protocols. Peikert and Vaikuntanathan [45] gave the first *noninteractive* statistical zero-knowledge proof systems for certain lattice problems, showing that, for example, $O(\sqrt{n})$-coGapSVP has an NISZK proof. The proof systems from [45] also have efficient provers, although for larger $\widetilde{O}(n)$ approximation factors.

Gaussians and the smoothing parameter. *Gaussian measures* have become an increasingly important tool in the study of lattices. For $s > 0$, the Gaussian measure of parameter (or width) s on $\mathbb{R}^n$ is defined as $\rho_s(\mathbf{x}) = \exp(-\pi\|\mathbf{x}\|^2/s^2)$; for a lattice $\mathcal{L} \subset \mathbb{R}^n$, the Gaussian measure of the lattice is then

$$\rho_s(\mathcal{L}) := \sum_{\mathbf{v} \in \mathcal{L}} \rho_s(\mathbf{v}).$$

Gaussian measures on lattices have innumerable applications, including in worst-case to average-case reductions for lattice problems [37,46], the construction of cryptographic primitives [20], the design of algorithms for SVP and CVP [1,2], and the study of the geometry of lattices [7,8,18,47].

In all of the above applications, a key quantity is the lattice *smoothing parameter* [37]. Informally, for a parameter $\varepsilon > 0$ and a lattice $\mathcal{L}$, the smoothing parameter $\eta_\varepsilon(\mathcal{L})$ is the minimal Gaussian parameter that "smooths out" the discrete structure of $\mathcal{L}$, up to error ε. Formally, for $\varepsilon > 0$ we define

$$\eta_\varepsilon(\mathcal{L}) := \min\{s > 0 \; : \; \rho_{1/s}(\mathcal{L}^*) \leq 1 + \varepsilon\},$$

where $\mathcal{L}^* := \{\mathbf{w} \in \mathbb{R}^n \; : \; \forall \mathbf{y} \in \mathcal{L}, \; \langle \mathbf{w}, \mathbf{y} \rangle \in \mathbb{Z}\}$ is the dual lattice of $\mathcal{L}$. All of the computational applications from the previous paragraph rely in some way on the "smoothness" of the Gaussian with parameter $s \geq \eta_\varepsilon(\mathcal{L})$ where $2^{-n} \ll \varepsilon < 1/2.$[2] For example, several of the proof systems from [45] start with deterministic reductions to an intermediate problem, which asks whether a lattice is "smooth" or well-separated.

The GapSPP problem. Given the prominence of the smoothing parameter in the theory of lattices, it is natural to ask about the complexity of computing it. Chung *et al.* [16] formally defined the problem γ-GapSPP$_\varepsilon$ of approximating the smoothing parameter $\eta_\varepsilon(\mathcal{L})$ to within a factor of $\gamma \geq 1$ and gave upper bounds on its complexity in the form of proof systems for *remarkably low* values of γ. For example, they showed that γ-GapSPP$_\varepsilon \in$ SZK for $\gamma = O(1 + \sqrt{\log(1/\varepsilon)/\log n})$. This in fact subsumes the prior result that $O(\sqrt{n/\log n})$-GapSVP $\in$ SZK of [21],

---

[2] For $\varepsilon = 2^{-\Omega(n)}$ the smoothing parameter is determined (up to a constant factor) by the dual minimum distance, so it is much less interesting to consider as a separate quantity. The upper bound of $1/2$ could be replaced by any constant less than one. For $\varepsilon \geq 1$, $\eta_\varepsilon(\mathcal{L})$ is still formally defined, but its interpretation in terms of the "smoothness" of the corresponding Gaussian measure over $\mathcal{L}$ is much less clear.

via known relationships between the minimum distance and the smoothing parameter.

Chung *et al.* also showed a worst-case to average-case (quantum) reduction from $\widetilde{O}(\sqrt{n}/\alpha)$-GapSPP to a very important average-case problem in lattice-based cryptography, Regev's Learning With Errors (LWE), which asks us to decode from a random "q-ary" lattice under error proportional to α [46]. Again, this subsumes the prior best reduction for GapSVP due to Regev. Most recently, Dadush and Regev [18] showed a similar worst-case to average-case reduction from GapSPP to the Short Integer Solution problem [4, 37], another widely used average-case problem in lattice-based cryptography.

In hindsight, the proof systems and reductions of [21, 37, 46] can most naturally be viewed as applying to GapSPP all along. This suggests that GapSPP may be a better problem than GapSVP on which to base the security of lattice-based cryptography. However, both [16, 18] left open several questions and asked for a better understanding of the complexity of GapSPP. In particular, while interactive proof systems for this problem seem to be relatively well understood, nothing nontrivial was previously known about *noninteractive* proof systems (whether zero knowledge or not) for this problem.

1.1   Our Results

In this work we give new proof systems for lattice problems, and extend the reach of prior proof systems to new problems. Our new results, and how they compare to the previous state of the art, are as follows.

Our first main result is a NISZK proof system for γ-GapSPP$_\varepsilon$ with $\gamma = O(\log(n)\sqrt{\log(1/\varepsilon)})$. This improves, by a $\Theta(\sqrt{n}/\log n)$ factor, upon the previous best approximation factor of $\gamma = O(\sqrt{n\log(1/\varepsilon)})$, which follows from [45].

Theorem 1. *For any $\varepsilon \in (0, 1/2)$, $O(\log(n)\sqrt{\log(1/\varepsilon)})$-GapSPP$_\varepsilon \in$ NISZK.*

In fact, we demonstrate two different proof systems to establish this theorem (see Sect. 3). The first is identical to a proof system from [45], but with a very different analysis that relies on a recent geometric theorem of [47]. However, this proof system only works for negligible $\varepsilon < n^{-\omega(1)}$, so we also show an alternative that works for any $\varepsilon \in (0, 1/2)$ via reduction to the NISZK-complete *Entropy Approximation* problem [25].

The prover in the proof system from [45] can be made efficient at the expense of a factor of $O(\sqrt{n\log n})$ in the approximation factor. From this we obtain the following.

Theorem 2. *For any negligible $0 < \varepsilon < n^{-\omega(1)}$, there is a NISZK proof system with an* efficient prover *for $O(\sqrt{n\log^3(n)\log(1/\varepsilon)})$-GapSPP$_\varepsilon$.*

Next, we show that $O(\log n)$-GapSPP$_\varepsilon \in$ coNP for any $\varepsilon \in (0, 1)$. This improves, again by up to a $\Theta(\sqrt{n}/\log n)$ factor, the previous best known result of $O(1 + \sqrt{n/\log(1/\varepsilon)})$-GapSPP$_\varepsilon \in$ coNP, which follows from [7].

Theorem 3. *For any* $\varepsilon \in (0, 1/2)$, $O(\log n)$-$\mathsf{GapSPP}_\varepsilon \in \mathsf{coNP}$.

From this, together with the SZK protocol of [16] and the result of Nguyen and Vadhan [40] that any problem in $\mathsf{SZK} \cap \mathsf{NP}$ has an SZK proof system with an efficient prover, we obtain the following corollary. (The proof systems in [16] do not have efficient provers.)

Corollary 1. *For any* $\varepsilon \in (0, 1/2)$, *there is an* SZK *proof system with an effi-cient prover for* $O(\log n + \sqrt{\log(1/\varepsilon)/\log n})$-$\mathsf{coGapSPP}_\varepsilon$.

Finally, we observe that $O(\sqrt{n})$-$\mathsf{GapCRP} \in \mathsf{SZK}$, where GapCRP is the prob-lem of approximating the *covering radius*, i.e., the maximum possible distance from a given lattice. For comparison, the previous best approximation factor was from [45], who showed that γ-$\mathsf{GapCRP} \in \mathsf{NISZK} \subseteq \mathsf{SZK}$ for any $\gamma = \omega(\sqrt{n \log n})$. We obtain this result via a straightforward reduction to $O(1)$-$\mathsf{GapSPP}_\varepsilon$ for con-stant $\varepsilon < 1/2$, which, to recall, is in SZK [16]. Furthermore, since Guruswami et al. showed that $O(\sqrt{n})$-$\mathsf{GapCRP} \in \mathsf{NP} \cap \mathsf{coNP}$ [27], it follows that the protocol can be made efficient.

Theorem 4. *We have* $O(\sqrt{n})$-$\mathsf{GapCRP} \in \mathsf{SZK}$. *Furthermore,* $O(\sqrt{n})$-GapCRP *and* $O(\sqrt{n})$-$\mathsf{coGapCRP}$ *each have an* SZK *proof system with an efficient prover.*

1.2 Techniques

Sparse projections. Our main technical tool will be *sparse lattice projections*. In particular, we use the *determinant* of a lattice, defined as $\det(\mathcal{L}) := |\det(\mathbf{B})|$ for any basis $\mathbf{B}$ of $\mathcal{L}$, as our measure of sparsity.[3] It is an immediate consequence of the Poisson Summation Formula (Lemma 3) that $\det(\mathcal{L})^{1/n} \leq 2\eta_{1/2}(\mathcal{L})$. Notice that this inequality formalizes the intuitive notion that "a lattice cannot be smooth and sparse simultaneously."

Dadush and Regev made the simple observation that the same statement is true when we consider *projections* of the lattice [18]. I.e., for any projection π such that $\pi(\mathcal{L})$ is still a lattice, we have $\det(\pi(\mathcal{L}))^{1/\mathrm{rank}(\pi(\mathcal{L}))} \leq 2\eta_{1/2}(\mathcal{L})$, where $\mathrm{rank}(\pi(\mathcal{L}))$ is the dimension of the span of $\pi(\mathcal{L})$. (Indeed, this fact is immediate from the above together with the identity $(\pi(\mathcal{L}))^* = \mathcal{L}^* \cap \mathrm{span}(\pi(\mathcal{L}))$.) Therefore, if we define

$$\eta_{\det}(\mathcal{L}) := \max_\pi \det(\pi(\mathcal{L}))^{1/\mathrm{rank}(\pi(\mathcal{L}))},$$

where the maximum is taken over all projections π such that $\pi(\mathcal{L})$ is a lattice, then we have

$$\eta_{\det}(\mathcal{L}) \leq 2\eta_{1/2}(\mathcal{L}). \tag{1}$$

Dadush and Regev conjectured that Eq. (1) is tight up to a factor of $\mathrm{polylog}(n)$. I.e., up to polylog factors, a lattice is not smooth if and only if it has a sparse

---

[3] This is indeed a measure of sparsity because $1/\det(\mathcal{L})$ is the average number of lattice points inside a random shift of any unit-volume body, or equivalently, the limit as r goes to infinity of the number of lattice points per unit volume in a ball of radius r.

projection. Regev and Stephens-Davidowitz proved this conjecture [47], and the resulting theorem, presented below, will be our main technical tool.

Theorem 5 ([47]). *For any lattice $\mathcal{L} \subset \mathbb{R}^n$,*

$$\eta_{1/2}(\mathcal{L}) \le 10(\log n + 2)\eta_{det}(\mathcal{L}).$$

I.e., if $\eta_{1/2}(\mathcal{L}) \ge 10(\log n + 2)$, then there exists a lattice projection π such that $det(\pi(\mathcal{L})) \ge 1$.

coNP proof system. Notice that Theorem 5 (together with Eq. (1)) immediately implies that $O(\log n)$-GapSPP$_\varepsilon$ is in coNP for $\varepsilon = 1/2$. Indeed, a projection π such that $det(\pi(\mathcal{L}))^{1/\text{rank}(\pi(\mathcal{L}))} \ge \eta_{1/2}(\mathcal{L})/O(\log n)$ can be used as a witness of "non-smoothness." Theorem 5 shows that such a witness always exists, and Eq. (1) shows that no such witness exists with $det(\pi(\mathcal{L}))^{1/\text{rank}(\pi(\mathcal{L}))} > 2\eta_{1/2}(\mathcal{L})$. In order to extend this result to all $\varepsilon \in (0,1)$, we use basic results about how $\eta_\varepsilon(\mathcal{L})$ varies with ε (See Sect. 4.).

NISZK proof systems. We give two different NISZK proof systems for $O(\log(n)\sqrt{\log(1/\varepsilon)})$-GapSPP$_\varepsilon$, both of which rely on Theorem 5.

Our first proof system (shown in Fig. 1, Sect. 3.1) uses many vectors $\mathbf{t}_1, \ldots, \mathbf{t}_m$ sampled uniformly at random from a fundamental region of the lattice $\mathcal{L}$ as the common random string. The prover samples short vectors $\mathbf{e}_i$ (for $i = 1, \ldots, m$) from the *discrete Gaussian* distributions over the lattice cosets $\mathbf{e}_i + \mathcal{L}$. The verifier accepts if and only if the matrix $\mathbf{E} = \sum \mathbf{e}_i \mathbf{e}_i^T$ has small enough spectral norm. (I.e., the verifier accepts if the $\mathbf{e}_i$ are "short in all directions.") In fact, Peikert and Vaikuntanathan used the exact same proof system for the different lattice problem $O(\sqrt{n})$-coGapSVP, and their proofs of correctness and zero knowledge also apply to our setting. However, the proof of soundness is quite different: we show that, if the lattice has a sparse projection π, then $\text{dist}(\pi(\mathbf{t}_i), \pi(\mathcal{L}))$ will tend to be fairly large. It follows that $\sum \|\pi(\mathbf{e}_i)\|^2 = \text{Tr}\left(\sum \pi(\mathbf{e}_i)\pi(\mathbf{e}_i)^T\right)$ will be fairly large with high probability, and therefore $\sum \mathbf{e}_i \mathbf{e}_i^T$ must have large spectral norm.

Our second proof system follows from a reduction to the Entropy Approximation problem, which asks to estimate the entropy of the output distribution of a circuit on random input. Goldreich et al. [25] showed that Entropy Approximation is NISZK-complete, so that a problem is in NISZK if and only if it can be (Karp-)reduced to approximating the entropy of a circuit. If $\eta_\varepsilon(\mathcal{L})$ is small, then we know that a continuous Gaussian modulo the lattice will be very close to the uniform distribution, and so (a suitable discretization of) this distribution will have high entropy. On the other hand, if $\eta_\varepsilon(\mathcal{L})$ is large, then Theorem 5 says that most of the measure of a continuous Gaussian modulo the lattice lies in a low-volume subset of $\mathbb{R}^n/\mathcal{L}$, and so (a discretization of) this distribution must have low entropy.

This second proof system works for a wider range of ε. In particular, the first proof system is only statistical zero knowledge when ε is negligible in the input size, whereas the second proof system works for any $\varepsilon \in (0, 1/2)$.

1.3   Organization

The remainder of the paper is organized as follows.

- In Sect. 2 we recall the necessary background on lattices, proof systems, and probability.
- In Sect. 3 we give two different NISZK proof systems for $O(\log(n)\sqrt{\log(1/\varepsilon)})$-GapSPP$_\varepsilon$.
- In Sect. 4 we give a coNP proof system for $O(\log n)$-GapSPP$_\varepsilon$.
- In Sect. 5 we show that $O(\sqrt{n})$-GapCRP $\in$ SZK, via a simple reduction to $O(1)$-GapSPP$_{1/4}$.

2   Preliminaries

2.1   Notation

For any positive integer d, $[d]$ denotes the set $\{1, \ldots, d\}$. We use bold lower-case letters to denote vectors. We write matrices in capital letters. The ith component (column) of a vector $\mathbf{x}$ (matrix $\mathbf{X}$) is written as $\mathbf{x}_i$ ($\mathbf{X}_i$). The function log denotes the natural logarithm unless otherwise specified. For $\mathbf{x} \in \mathbb{R}^n$, $\|\mathbf{x}\| := \sqrt{x_1^2 + x_2^2 + \cdots + x_n^2}$ is the Euclidean norm. For a matrix $\mathbf{A} \in \mathbb{R}^{n \times m}$, $\|\mathbf{A}\| := \max_{\|\mathbf{x}\|=1} \|\mathbf{A}\mathbf{x}\|$ is the operator norm.

We write rB_2^n for the n-dimensional Euclidean ball of radius r. A set $S \subseteq \mathbb{R}^n$ is said to be *symmetric* if $-S = S$. The distance from a point $\mathbf{x} \in \mathbb{R}^n$ to a set $S \subseteq \mathbb{R}^n$ is defined to be $\text{dist}(\mathbf{x}, S) = \inf_{\mathbf{s} \in S} \text{dist}(\mathbf{x}, \mathbf{s})$. We write $S^\perp$ to denote the subspace of vectors orthogonal to S. For a set $S \subseteq \mathbb{R}^n$ and a point $\mathbf{x} \in \mathbb{R}^n$, $\pi_S(\mathbf{x})$ denotes the orthogonal projection of $\mathbf{x}$ onto span(S). For sets $A, B \subseteq \mathbb{R}^n$, we denote their Minkowski sum by $A + B = \{\mathbf{a} + \mathbf{b} : \mathbf{a} \in A, \mathbf{b} \in B\}$. We extend a function f to a countable set in the natural way by defining $f(A) := \sum_{a \in A} f(a)$.

Throughout the paper, we write C for an arbitrary universal constant $C > 0$, whose value might change from one use to the next.

2.2   Lattices

Here we provide some backgrounds on lattices. An n-dimensional *lattice* $\mathcal{L} \subset \mathbb{R}^n$ of rank d is the set of integer linear combinations of d linearly independent vectors $\mathbf{B} := (\mathbf{b}_1, \ldots, \mathbf{b}_d)$,

$$\mathcal{L} = \mathcal{L}(\mathbf{B}) = \Big\{ \mathbf{B}\mathbf{z} = \sum_{i \in [d]} z_i \cdot \mathbf{b}_i : \mathbf{z} \in \mathbb{Z}^d \Big\}.$$

We usually work with *full-rank* lattices, where $d = n$. A *sublattice* $\mathcal{L}' \subseteq \mathcal{L}$ is an additive subgroup of $\mathcal{L}$. The *dual lattice* of $\mathcal{L}$, denoted by $\mathcal{L}^*$, is defined as the set

$$\mathcal{L}^* = \Big\{ \mathbf{y} \in \mathbb{R}^n : \forall \mathbf{v} \in \mathcal{L}, \langle \mathbf{v}, \mathbf{y} \rangle \in \mathbb{Z} \Big\}$$

of all integer vectors having integer inner products with all vectors in $\mathcal{L}$. It is easy to check that $(\mathcal{L}^*)^* = \mathcal{L}$ and that, if $\mathbf{B}$ is a basis for $\mathcal{L}$, then $\mathbf{B}^* = \mathbf{B}(\mathbf{B}^T\mathbf{B})^{-1}$ is a basis for $\mathcal{L}^*$. The *fundamental parallelepiped* of a lattice $\mathcal{L}$ with respect to basis $\mathbf{B}$ is the set

$$\mathcal{P}(\mathbf{B}) = \Big\{ \sum_{i\in[d]} c_i \mathbf{b}_i : 0 \le c_i < 1 \Big\}.$$

It is easy to see that $\mathcal{P}(\mathbf{B})$ is a *fundamental domain* of $\mathcal{L}$. I.e., it tiles $\mathbb{R}^n$ with respect to $\mathcal{L}$. For any lattice $\mathcal{L}(\mathbf{B})$ and point $\mathbf{x} \in \mathbb{R}^n$, there exists a unique point $\mathbf{y} \in \mathcal{P}(\mathbf{B})$ such that $\mathbf{y} - \mathbf{x} \in \mathcal{L}(\mathbf{B})$. We denote this vector by $\mathbf{y} = \mathbf{x} \bmod \mathbf{B}$. Notice that $\mathbf{y}$ can be computed in polynomial time given $\mathbf{B}$ and $\mathbf{x}$. We sometimes write $\mathbf{x} \bmod \mathcal{L}$ when the specific fundamental domain is not important, and we write $\mathbb{R}^n/\mathcal{L}$ for an arbitrary fundamental domain.

The *determinant* of a lattice $\mathcal{L}$, is defined to be $\det(\mathcal{L}) = \sqrt{\det(\mathbf{B}^T\mathbf{B})}$. It is easy to verify that the determinant does not depend on the choice of basis and that $\det(\mathcal{L})$ is the volume of any fundamental domain of $\mathcal{L}$.

The *minimum distance* of a lattice $\mathcal{L}$, is the length of the shortest non-zero lattice vector,

$$\lambda_1(\mathcal{L}) := \min_{\mathbf{y}\in\mathcal{L}\setminus\{\mathbf{0}\}} \|\mathbf{y}\|.$$

Similarly, we define

$$\lambda_n(\mathcal{L}) := \min \max_i \|\mathbf{y}_i\|,$$

where the minimum is taken over linearly independent lattice vectors $\mathbf{y}_1, \dots, \mathbf{y}_n \in \mathcal{L}$. The *covering radius* of a lattice $\mathcal{L}$ is

$$\mu(\mathcal{L}) := \max_{\mathbf{t}\in\mathbb{R}^n} \operatorname{dist}(\mathbf{t}, \mathcal{L}).$$

The *Voronoi cell* of a lattice $\mathcal{L}$ is the set

$$\mathcal{V}(\mathcal{L}) := \{\mathbf{x} \in \mathbb{R}^n : \|\mathbf{t}\| \le \|\mathbf{y} - \mathbf{t}\|, \forall \mathbf{y} \in \mathcal{L}\setminus\{\mathbf{0}\}\}$$

of vectors in $\mathbb{R}^n$ that are closer to $\mathbf{0}$ than any other point of $\mathcal{L}$. It is easy to check that $\mathcal{V}(\mathcal{L})$ is a symmetric polytope and that it tiles $\mathbb{R}^n$ with respect to $\mathcal{L}$. The following claim is an immediate consequence of the fact that an n-dimensional unit ball has volume at most $(2\pi e/n)^{n/2}$.

Claim. For any lattice $\mathcal{L} \subset \mathbb{R}^n$,

$$\mu(\mathcal{L}) \ge \sqrt{n/(2\pi e)} \cdot \det(\mathcal{L})^{1/n}.$$

Lemma 1. *For any lattice $\mathcal{L} \subset \mathbb{R}^n$ and $r \ge 0$,*

$$|\mathcal{L} \cap r B_2^n| \le (5/\sqrt{n})^n \cdot \frac{(r + \mu(\mathcal{L}))^n}{\det(\mathcal{L})}.$$

Proof. For each vector $\mathbf{y} \in \mathcal{L} \cap rB_2^n$, notice that $\mathcal{V}(\mathcal{L}) + \mathbf{y} \subseteq (r + \mu(\mathcal{L}))B_2^n$. And, for distinct vectors $\mathbf{y}, \mathbf{y}' \in \mathcal{L}$, $\mathcal{V}(\mathcal{L}) + \mathbf{y}$ and $\mathcal{V}(\mathcal{L}) + \mathbf{y}'$ are disjoint (up to a set of measure zero). Therefore,

$$\mathrm{vol}((r + \mu(\mathcal{L}))B_2^n) \geq \mathrm{vol}\Big(\bigcup_{\mathbf{y} \in \mathcal{L} \cap rB_2^n} \mathcal{V}(\mathcal{L}) + \mathbf{y} \Big) = |\mathcal{L} \cap rB_2^n| \mathrm{vol}(\mathcal{V}(\mathcal{L})) = |\mathcal{L} \cap rB_2^n| \cdot \det(\mathcal{L}).$$

The result follows by recalling that for any $r' > 0$, $\mathrm{vol}(r'B_2^n) \leq (5r'/\sqrt{n})^n$.

Lemma 2 ([27]). *For any lattice $\mathcal{L} \subset \mathbb{R}^n$,*

$$\mathop{\mathbb{E}}_{\mathbf{t} \sim \mathbb{R}^n/\mathcal{L}} [dist(\mathbf{t}, \mathcal{L})^2] \geq \mu(\mathcal{L})^2/4,$$

where $\mathbf{t} \in \mathbb{R}^n/\mathcal{L}$ is sampled uniformly at random.

Proof. Let $\mathbf{v} \in \mathbb{R}^n$ such that $\mathrm{dist}(\mathbf{v}, \mathcal{L}) = \mu(\mathcal{L})$. Notice that $\mathbf{v} - \mathbf{t} \bmod \mathcal{L}$ is uniformly distributed. And, by the triangle inequality, $\mathrm{dist}(\mathbf{v} - \mathbf{t}, \mathcal{L}) + \mathrm{dist}(\mathbf{t}, \mathcal{L}) \geq \mathrm{dist}(\mathbf{v}, \mathcal{L}) = \mu(\mathcal{L})$. So,

$$\mathop{\mathbb{E}}_{\mathbf{t} \sim \mathbb{R}^n/\mathcal{L}} [\mathrm{dist}(\mathbf{t}, \mathcal{L})] = \frac{1}{2} \cdot \mathop{\mathbb{E}}_{\mathbf{t} \sim \mathbb{R}^n/\mathcal{L}} [\mathrm{dist}(\mathbf{v} - \mathbf{t}, \mathcal{L}) + \mathrm{dist}(\mathbf{t}, \mathcal{L})] \geq \mu(\mathcal{L})/2.$$

The result then follows by Markov's inequality.

A *lattice projection* for a lattice $\mathcal{L} \subset \mathbb{R}^n$ is an orthogonal projection $\pi : \mathbb{R}^n \to \mathbb{R}^n$ defined by $\pi(\mathbf{x}) := \pi_{S^\perp}(\mathbf{x})$ for lattice vectors $S \subset \mathcal{L}$.

Claim. For any $\mathcal{L} \subset \mathbb{R}^n$ and any lattice projection π, $\pi(\mathcal{L})$ is a lattice. Furthermore, if $\mathbf{t} \in \mathbb{R}^n/\mathcal{L}$ is sampled uniformly at random, then $\pi(\mathbf{t})$ is uniform mod $\pi(\mathcal{L})$.

Proof. The first statement follows from the well known fact that, if $W = \mathrm{span}S$ for some set of lattice vectors $S \subset \mathcal{L}$, then there exists a basis $\mathbf{B} := (\mathbf{b}_1, \ldots, \mathbf{b}_n)$ of $\mathcal{L}$ such that $\mathrm{span}(\mathbf{b}_1, \ldots, \mathbf{b}_k) = W$, where $k := \dim W$. (See, e.g., [35].) From this, it follows immediately that $\pi(\mathbf{b}_{k+1}), \ldots \pi(\mathbf{b}_n)$ are linearly independent and $\pi(\mathcal{L})$ is the lattice spanned by these vectors, where $\pi := \pi_{S^\perp}$.

The second statement follows from the following similarly well known fact. Let $\widetilde{\mathbf{b}}_i := \pi_{\{\mathbf{b}_1, \ldots, \mathbf{b}_{i-1}\}^\perp}(\mathbf{b}_i)$ be the Gram-Schmidt vectors of the basis $\mathbf{B}$ described above. Then, the hyperrectangle

$$\widetilde{R} := \Big\{ \sum_i a_i \widetilde{\mathbf{b}}_i \ : \ -1/2 < a_i \leq 1/2 \Big\}$$

is a fundamental domain of the lattice. (See, e.g., [6].) I.e., for each $\mathbf{t} \in \mathbb{R}^n/\mathcal{L}$, there is a unique representative $\widetilde{\mathbf{t}} \in \widetilde{R}$ with $\widetilde{\mathbf{t}} \equiv \mathbf{t} \bmod \mathcal{L}$. The result then follows by noting that, if $\widetilde{\mathbf{t}} \in \widetilde{R}$ is chosen uniformly at random, then clearly $\pi(\widetilde{\mathbf{t}}) \in \pi(\widetilde{R})$ is uniform in $\pi(\widetilde{R})$, which is a fundamental region of $\pi(\mathcal{L})$.

2.3   Gaussian Measure

Here we review some useful background on Gaussians over lattices. For a positive parameter $s > 0$ and vector $\mathbf{x} \in \mathbb{R}^n$, we define the Gaussian mass of $\mathbf{x}$ as $\rho_s(\mathbf{x}) = e^{-\pi \|\mathbf{x}\|^2 / s^2}$. For a measurable set $A \subseteq \mathbb{R}^n$, we define $\gamma_s(A) = s^{-n} \int_A \rho_s(\mathbf{x}) \, d\mathbf{x}$. It is easy to see that $\gamma_s(\mathbb{R}^n) = 1$ and hence γ_s is a probability measure. We define the *discrete Gaussian distribution* over a countable set A as

$$D_{A,s}(\mathbf{x}) = \frac{\rho_s(\mathbf{x})}{\rho_s(A)}, \forall \mathbf{x} \in A.$$

In all cases, the parameter s is taken to be one when omitted. The following lemma is the Poisson Summation Formula for the Gaussian mass of a lattice.

Lemma 3. *For any (full-rank) lattice $\mathcal{L}$ and $s > 0$,*

$$\rho_s(\mathcal{L}) = \frac{1}{\det(\mathcal{L})} \cdot \rho_{1/s}(\mathcal{L}^*).$$

We will also need Banaszczyk's celebrated lemma [7, Lemma 1.5].

Lemma 4 ([7]). *For any lattice $\mathcal{L} \subset \mathbb{R}^n$, shift vector $\mathbf{t} \in \mathbb{R}^n$, and $r \geq 1/\sqrt{2\pi}$,*

$$\rho((\mathcal{L} + \mathbf{t}) \setminus \sqrt{n} B_2^n) \leq \left(\sqrt{2\pi e r^2} e^{-\pi r^2}\right)^n \cdot \rho(\mathcal{L}).$$

Micciancio and Regev introduced a lattice parameter called the smoothing parameter. For an n-dimensional lattice $\mathcal{L}$ and $\varepsilon > 0$, the *smoothing parameter* $\eta_\varepsilon(\mathcal{L})$ is defined as the smallest s such that $\rho_{1/s}(\mathcal{L}^*) \leq 1 + \varepsilon$. The motivation for defining smoothing parameter comes from the following two facts [37].

Claim. For any lattice $\mathcal{L} \subset \mathbb{R}^n$, shift vector $\mathbf{t} \in \mathbb{R}^n$, $\varepsilon \in (0, 1)$, and parameter $s \geq \eta_\varepsilon(\mathcal{L})$,

$$\frac{1 - \varepsilon}{1 + \varepsilon} \cdot \rho_s(\mathcal{L}) \leq \rho_s(\mathcal{L} - \mathbf{t}) \leq \rho_s(\mathcal{L}).$$

Lemma 5. *For any lattice $\mathcal{L}, \mathbf{c} \in \mathbb{R}^n$ and $s \geq \eta_\varepsilon(\mathcal{L})$,*

$$\Delta((D_s \bmod \mathbf{B}), U(\mathbb{R}^n / \mathcal{L})) \leq \varepsilon/2,$$

where D_s is the continuous Gaussian distribution with parameter s and $U(\mathbb{R}^n/\mathcal{L})$ denotes the uniform distribution over $\mathbb{R}^n/\mathcal{L}$.

We use the following epsilon-decreasing tool which has been introduced in [16].

Lemma 6 ([16], Lemma 2.4). *For any lattice $\mathcal{L} \subset \mathbb{R}^n$ and any $0 < \varepsilon' \leq \varepsilon < 1$,*

$$\eta_{\varepsilon'}(\mathcal{L}) \leq \sqrt{\log(1/\varepsilon')/\log(1/\varepsilon)} \cdot \eta_\varepsilon(\mathcal{L}).$$

Proof. We may assume without loss of generality that $\eta_\varepsilon(\mathcal{L}) = 1$. Notice that this implies that $\lambda_1(\mathcal{L}^*) \geq \sqrt{\log(1/\varepsilon)/\pi}$. Then, for any $s \geq 1$,

$$\rho_{1/s}(\mathcal{L}^* \backslash \{\mathbf{0}\}) = \sum \exp(-\pi(s^2 - 1)\|\mathbf{w}\|^2) \cdot \rho(\mathbf{w}) \leq \exp(-\pi(s^2 - 1)\lambda_1(\mathcal{L})^2)\rho(\mathcal{L}^* \backslash \{\mathbf{0}\}) \leq \varepsilon^{s^2}.$$

Setting $s := \sqrt{\log(1/\varepsilon')/\log(1/\varepsilon)}$ gives the result.

Lemma 7. *For any lattice $\mathcal{L} \subset \mathbb{Q}^n$ with basis $\mathbf{B}$ whose bit length is β and any $\varepsilon \in (0, 1/2)$, we have $\eta_\varepsilon(\mathcal{L}(\mathbf{B})) \leq 2^{\mathrm{poly}(\beta)}\sqrt{\log(1/\varepsilon)}$, and $\lambda_n(\mathcal{L}) \leq 2\mu(\mathcal{L}) \leq 2^{\mathrm{poly}(\beta)}$.*

2.4 Sampling from the Discrete Gaussian

For any $\mathbf{B} = (\mathbf{b}_1, \dots, \mathbf{b}_n) \in \mathbb{R}^{n \times n}$, let

$$\|\widetilde{\mathbf{B}}\| := \max_i \|\pi_{\{\mathbf{b}_1, \dots, \mathbf{b}_{i-1}\}^\perp}(\mathbf{b}_i)\|,$$

i.e., $\|\widetilde{\mathbf{B}}\|$ is the length of the longest Gram-Schmidt vector of $\mathbf{B}$.

We recall the following result from a sequence of works due to Klein [32]; Gentry et al. [20]; and Brakerski et al. [13].

Theorem 6. *There is an efficient algorithm that takes as input a basis $\mathbf{B} \in \mathbb{Q}^{n \times n}$ and any parameter $s \geq \|\widetilde{\mathbf{B}}\|\sqrt{\log n}$ and outputs a sample from $D_{\mathcal{L},s}$, where $\mathcal{L} \subset \mathbb{R}^n$ is the lattice generated by $\mathbf{B}$.*

Corollary 2. *There is an efficient algorithm that takes as input a (basis for a) lattice $\mathcal{L} \subset \mathbb{Q}^n$ and parameter $s \geq 2^n \eta_\varepsilon(\mathcal{L})$ and outputs a sample from $D_{\mathcal{L},s}$.*

Proof. Combine the above with the celebrated LLL algorithm [33], which in particular allows us to find a basis for $\mathcal{L}$ with $\|\widetilde{\mathbf{B}}\| \leq 2^{n/2}\eta_\varepsilon(\mathcal{L})$.

We also need the following result, which is implicit in [7]. See, e.g., [18] for a proof.

Lemma 8. *For any lattice $\mathcal{L} \subset \mathbb{R}^n$ and $\varepsilon \in (0, 1/2)$,*

$$\lambda_n(\mathcal{L}) \leq 2\mu(\mathcal{L}) \leq \sqrt{n} \cdot \eta_\varepsilon(\mathcal{L}).$$

In particular, there exists a basis $\mathbf{B}$ of $\mathcal{L}$ with $\|\widetilde{\mathbf{B}}\| \leq \lambda_n(\mathcal{L}) \leq \sqrt{n} \cdot \eta_{1/2}(\mathcal{L})$.

Corollary 3. *For any lattice $\mathcal{L} \subset \mathbb{Q}^n$ with basis $\mathbf{B}$, there exists preprocessing P whose size is polynomial in the bit length of $\mathbf{B}$ and an efficient algorithm that, on input P and $s \geq \sqrt{n \log n} \cdot \eta_{1/2}(\mathcal{L})$ outputs a sample from $D_{\mathcal{L},s}$.*

Proof. By Lemma 8, there exists a basis $\mathbf{B}'$ with $\|\widetilde{\mathbf{B}'}\| \leq \sqrt{n} \cdot \eta_{1/2}(\mathcal{L})$. By Lemma 7, the bit length of $\mathbf{B}'$ is polynomial in the bit length of $\mathbf{B}$. We use this as our preprocessing P. The result then follows by Theorem 6.

2.5   Computational Problems

Here we define two promise problems that will be considered in this paper.

Definition 1 (Covering Radius Problem). *For any approximation factor* $\gamma = \gamma(n) \geq 1$, *an instance of* γ-GapCRP *is a (basis for a) lattice* $\mathcal{L} \subset \mathbb{Q}^n$. *It is a YES instance if* $\mu(\mathcal{L}) \leq 1$ *and a NO instance if* $\mu(\mathcal{L}) > \gamma$.

Definition 2 (Smoothing Parameter Problem). *For any approximation factor* $\gamma = \gamma(n) \geq 1$ *and* $\varepsilon = \varepsilon(n) > 0$, *an instance of* γ-GapSPP$_\varepsilon$ *is a (basis for a) lattice* $\mathcal{L} \subset \mathbb{Q}^n$. *It is a YES instance if* $\eta_\varepsilon(\mathcal{L}) \leq 1$ *and a NO instance if* $\eta_\varepsilon(\mathcal{L}) > \gamma$.

We will need the following result from [16].

Theorem 7. *For any* $\varepsilon \in (0, 1/2)$, γ-GapSPP$_\varepsilon$ *is in* SZK *for* $\gamma = O(1 + \sqrt{\log(1/\varepsilon)/\log(n)})$.[4]

2.6   Noninteractive Proof Systems

Definition 3 (Noninteractive Proof System). *A pair* (P, V) *is a noninteractive proof system for a promise problem* $\Pi = (\Pi^{YES}, \Pi^{NO})$ *if P is a (possibly unbounded) algorithm and V is a polynomial-time algorithm such that*

- Completeness: *for every* $x \in \Pi_n^{YES}$, $\Pr[V(x, r, P(x, r)) \, accepts] \geq 1 - \varepsilon$; *and*
- Soundness: *for every* $x \in \Pi_n^{NO}$, $\Pr[\exists \, \pi \, : \, V(x, r, \pi) \, accepts] \leq \varepsilon$,

where n is the input length, $\varepsilon = \varepsilon(n) \leq negl(n)$, *and the probabilities are taken over r, which is sampled uniformly at random from* $\{0, 1\}^{\mathrm{poly}(n)}$.

   A noninteractive proof system (P, V) *for a promise problem* $\Pi = (\Pi^{YES}, \Pi^{NO})$ *is* statistical zero knowledge *if there exists a probabilistic polynomial-time algorithm S (called a* simulator*) such that for all* $x \in \Pi^{YES}$, *the statistical distance between* $S(x)$ *and* $(r, P(x, r))$ *is negligible in n. The class of promise problems having noninteractive statistical zero-knowledge proof systems is denoted* NISZK.

2.7   Probability

The *entropy* of a random variable X over a countable set S is given by

$$H(X) := \sum_{a \in S} \Pr[X = a] \cdot \log_2(1/\Pr[X = a]).$$

We will also need the Chernoff-Hoeffding bound [29].

---

[4] In [16], this result is proven only for $\varepsilon < 1/3$. However, it is immediate from, e.g., Lemma 6 that the result can be extended to any $\varepsilon < 1/2$.

Lemma 9 (Chernoff-Hoeffding bound). *Let $X_1, \ldots, X_m \in [0,1]$ be independent and identically distributed random variables with $\overline{X} := \mathbb{E}[X_i]$. Then, for any $s > 0$,*

$$\Pr\left[m\overline{X} - \sum X_i \geq s \right] \leq \exp(-s^2/(2m)).$$

Finally, we will need a minor variant of the above inequality.

Lemma 10. *Let $X_1, \ldots, X_m \in \mathbb{R}$ be independent (but not necessarily identically distributed) random variables. Suppose that there exists an $\alpha \geq 0$ and $s > 0$ such that for any $r > 0$,*

$$\Pr[|X_i| \geq r] \leq \alpha \exp(-r^2/s^2).$$

Then, for any $r > 0$,

$$\Pr\left[\sum X_i^2 \geq r \right] \leq (1+\alpha)^m \exp(-r/(2s^2)).$$

Proof. For any index i, we have

$$\mathbb{E}[\exp(X_i^2/(2s^2))] = 1 + \frac{1}{s^2} \cdot \int_0^\infty r \exp(r^2/(2s^2)) \Pr[|X_i| \geq r] \, dr$$

$$\leq 1 + \frac{\alpha}{s^2} \cdot \int_0^\infty r \exp(-r^2/(2s^2)) \, dr$$

$$= 1 + \alpha.$$

Since the X_i are independent, it follows that

$$\mathbb{E}\left[\exp\left(\sum X_i^2/(2s^2) \right) \right] = \mathbb{E}\left[\prod_i \exp(X_i^2/(2s^2)) \right] \leq (1+\alpha)^m.$$

The result then follows by Markov's inequality. $\qquad\blacksquare$

3 Two **NISZK** Proofs for **GapSPP**

Recall the definition

$$\eta_{\det}(\mathcal{L}) := \max_\pi \det(\pi(\mathcal{L}))^{1/\text{rank}(\pi(\mathcal{L}))}.$$

We will also need the following definition from [18],

$$C_\eta(n) := \sup_{\mathcal{L}} \frac{\eta_{1/2}(\mathcal{L})}{\eta_{\det}(\mathcal{L})},$$

where the supremum is taken over all lattices $\mathcal{L} \subset \mathbb{R}^n$. In this notation, Theorem 5 is equivalent to the inequality

$$C_\eta(n) \leq 10(\log n + 2).$$

We note that the true value of $C_\eta(n)$ is still not known. (In particular, the best lower bound is $C_\eta(n) \geq \sqrt{\log(n)/\pi} + o(1)$, which follows from the fact that $\eta_{1/2}(\mathbb{Z}^n) = \sqrt{\log(n)/\pi} + o(1)$.) We therefore state our results in terms of $C_\eta(n)$.

3.1   An Explicit Proof System

We first consider the NISZK proof system for $\sqrt{n}$-coGapSVP due to [45], shown in Fig. 1. We show that this is actually also a NISZK proof system for $O(\sqrt{\log(1/\varepsilon)} \cdot \log n)$-GapSPP$_\varepsilon$ for negligible ε. (In Sect. 3.2, we show a different proof system that works for all $\varepsilon \in (0, 1/2)$, also with an approximation factor of $O(\log(n)\sqrt{\log(1/\varepsilon)})$.)

Theorem 8. *For any $\varepsilon \leq negl(n)$, γ-GapSPP$_\varepsilon$ is in NISZK for*

$$\gamma := O(C_\eta(n)\sqrt{\log(1/\varepsilon)}) \leq O(\log(n)\sqrt{\log(1/\varepsilon)})$$

via the proof system shown in Fig. 1.

We will prove in turn that the proof system is statistical zero knowledge, complete, and sound. In fact, the proofs of statistical zero knowledge and completeness are nearly identical to the corresponding proofs in [45].

To prove the zero-knowledge property of the proof system, we consider the simulator that behaves as follows. Let $\mathbf{e}_1, \ldots, \mathbf{e}_m \in \mathbb{R}^m$ be sampled independently from the continuous Gaussian centered at $\mathbf{0}$. Let $\mathbf{t}_1, \ldots, \mathbf{t}_m \in \mathcal{P}(\mathbf{B})$ such that $\mathbf{e}_i \equiv \mathbf{t}_i \bmod \mathcal{L}$. The simulator then outputs $\mathbf{t}_1, \ldots, \mathbf{t}_m$ as the random input and $\mathbf{e}_1, \ldots, \mathbf{e}_m$ as the proof.

Lemma 11 (Statistical zero knowledge). *For any $\varepsilon \in (0, 1)$ and lattice $\mathcal{L} \subset \mathbb{Q}^n$ with $\eta_\varepsilon(\mathcal{L}) \leq 1$, the output of the simulator described above is within statistical distance εm of honestly generated random input and an honestly generated proof as in Fig. 1. In particular, the proof system in Fig. 1 is statistical zero knowledge for negligible ε.*

Proof. Notice that, conditioned on the random input $\mathbf{t}_i$, the distribution of $\mathbf{e}_i$ is exactly $D_{\mathcal{L}+\mathbf{t}_i, s}$. So, we only need to show that the random input $\mathbf{t}_1, \ldots, \mathbf{t}_m \in \mathcal{P}(\mathbf{B})$ chosen by the simulator is within statistical distance εm of uniform. Indeed, this follows from Lemma 5 and the union bound.

NISZK proof system for GapSPP.

Common Input: A basis $\mathbf{B}$ for a lattice $\mathcal{L} \subset \mathbb{Q}^n$.
Random Input : m vectors $\mathbf{t}_1, \ldots, \mathbf{t}_m \in \mathcal{P}(\mathbf{B})$, sampled uniformly at random.
Prover P: Sample m vectors $\mathbf{e}_1, \ldots, \mathbf{e}_m \in \mathbb{R}^n$ independently from $D_{\mathcal{L}+\mathbf{t}_i}$, and output them as the proof.
Verifier V: Accept if and only if $\mathbf{e}_i \equiv \mathbf{t}_i \bmod \mathcal{L}$ for all i *and* $\| \sum \mathbf{e}_i \mathbf{e}_i^T \| \leq 3m$.

Fig. 1. The non-interactive zero-knowledge proof system for GapSPP, where $m := 100n$.

The proof of completeness is a bit tedious and nearly identical to proofs of similar statements in [3, 18, 45]. We include a proof in Appendix A.

Lemma 12 (Completeness). *For any lattice $\mathcal{L} \subset \mathbb{Q}^n$ with $\eta_{1/2}(\mathcal{L}) \leq 1$, the proof given in Fig. 1 will be accepted except with negligible probability. I.e., the proof system is complete.*

Soundness. We now show the soundness of the proof system shown in Fig. 1, using Theorem 5. We note that [18] contains an implicit proof of a very similar result in a different context. (Dadush and Regev conjectured a form of Theorem 5 and showed a number of implications [18]. In particular, they showed that with non-negligible probability over a *single* uniformly random shift $\mathbf{t} \in \mathbb{R}^n/\mathcal{L}$, there is no list of vectors $\mathbf{e}_1, \ldots, \mathbf{e}_m \in \mathcal{L} + \mathbf{t}$ with small covariance.)

Theorem 9. *For any lattice $\mathcal{L} \subset \mathbb{R}^n$ with basis $\mathbf{B}$ satisfying $\eta_{1/2}(\mathcal{L}) \geq 100 C_\eta(n)$ (and in particular any lattice with $\eta_{1/2}(\mathcal{L}) \geq 1000(\log(n) + 2))$, if $\mathbf{t}_1, \ldots, \mathbf{t}_m$ are sampled uniformly from $\mathbb{R}^n/\mathcal{L}$, then the probability that there exists any proof $\mathbf{e}_1, \ldots, \mathbf{e}_m$ with $\mathbf{e}_i \equiv \mathbf{t} \bmod \mathcal{L}$ and*

$$\left\| \sum \mathbf{e}_i \mathbf{e}_i^T \right\| \leq 3m$$

is at most $\exp(-\Omega(m^2))$.

Proof. By the definition of $C_\eta(n)$ there is a lattice projection π such that $\det(\pi(\mathcal{L})) \geq 100^k$, where $k := \text{rank}(\pi(\mathcal{L}))$. For any $\mathbf{e}_1, \ldots, \mathbf{e}_m$ with $\mathbf{e}_i \equiv \mathbf{t}_i \bmod \mathcal{L}$, we have

$$\left\| \sum \mathbf{e}_i \mathbf{e}_i^T \right\| \geq \left\| \sum \pi(\mathbf{e}_i) \pi(\mathbf{e}_i)^T \right\|$$
$$\geq \frac{1}{k} \text{Tr} \left(\sum \pi(\mathbf{e}_i) \pi(\mathbf{e}_i)^T \right)$$
$$= \frac{1}{k} \sum \|\pi(\mathbf{e}_i)\|^2$$
$$\geq \frac{1}{k} \sum \text{dist}(\pi(\mathbf{t}_i), \pi(\mathcal{L}))^2,$$

where the first inequality on the spectral norms follows from the fact that $\langle \mathbf{u}, \pi(\mathbf{e}_i) \rangle = \langle \pi(\mathbf{u}), \pi(\mathbf{e}_i) \rangle$ and $\|\pi(\mathbf{u})\| \leq \|\mathbf{u}\|$; the second inequality follows from the fact that the spectral norm is the largest eigenvalue and the trace is the sum of the k eigenvalues; and the equality is by definition of trace.

Now by Sect. 2.2, $\pi(\mathbf{t}_i)$ is uniformly distributed mod $\pi(\mathcal{L})$, and therefore by Lemma 2,

$$\mathbb{E}[\text{dist}(\pi(\mathbf{t}_i), \pi(\mathcal{L}))^2] \geq \mu(\pi(\mathcal{L}))^2/4.$$

Furthermore, since the $\mathbf{t}_i$ are independent and identically distributed with $\text{dist}(\pi(\mathbf{t}_i), \pi(\mathcal{L})) \leq \mu(\pi(\mathcal{L}))$, we can apply the Chernoff-Hoeffding bound (Lemma 9) to get

$$\Pr \left[\sum \text{dist}(\pi(\mathbf{t}_i), \pi(\mathcal{L}))^2 \leq m\mu(\pi(\mathcal{L}))^2/5 \right] \leq \exp(-Cm^2).$$

The result follows by noting that $\mu(\pi(\mathcal{L}))^2/(5k) \geq 3$ by Sect. 2.2, together with the fact that $\det(\pi(\mathcal{L})) \geq 100^k$.

Corollary 4 (Soundness). *For any $\varepsilon \in (0, 1/2)$ and lattice $\mathcal{L} \subset \mathbb{R}^n$ with basis* **B** *satisfying $n \geq 2$ and $\eta_\varepsilon(\mathcal{L}) \geq 100 C_\eta(n)\sqrt{\log(1/\varepsilon)}$ (and in particular any lattice with $\eta_\varepsilon(\mathcal{L}) \geq 1000(\log(n) + 2)\sqrt{\log(1/\varepsilon)}$), if $\mathbf{t}_1, \ldots, \mathbf{t}_m$ are sampled uniformly from $\mathcal{P}(\mathbf{B})$, then the probability that there exists a proof $\mathbf{e}_1, \ldots, \mathbf{e}_m$ with $\mathbf{e}_i \equiv \mathbf{t} \bmod \mathcal{L}$ and*

$$\left\| \sum \mathbf{e}_i \mathbf{e}_i^T \right\| \leq 3m$$

is at most $\exp(-\Omega(m^2))$. In other words, the proof system in Fig. 1 is $\exp(-\Omega(m^2))$-statistically sound.

Proof. By Lemma 6, we have $\eta_{1/2} \geq 100 C_\eta(n)$, and the result follows from Theorem 9. ∎

Making the prover efficient. Finally, following [45] we observe that the prover in the proof system shown in Fig. 1 can be made efficient if we relax the approximation factor. In particular, if $\eta_\varepsilon(\mathcal{L}) \leq 1/\sqrt{n \log n}$, then by Corollary 3, there is in fact an efficient prover. Theorem 2 then follows immediately from the above analysis.

3.2   A Proof via Entropy Approximation

We recall from Goldreich et al. [25] the Entropy Approximation problem, which asks us to approximate the entropy of the distribution obtained by calling some input circuit $\mathcal{C}$ on the uniform distribution over its input space. In particular, we recall that [25] proved that this problem is NISZK-complete. (Formally, we only need the fact that Entropy Approximation is in NISZK.)

Definition 4. *An instance of the Entropy Approximation problem is a circuit $\mathcal{C}$ and an integer k. It is a YES instance if $H(\mathcal{C}(U)) > k + 1$ and a NO instance if $H(\mathcal{C}(U)) < k - 1$, where U is the uniform distribution on the input space of $\mathcal{C}$.*

Theorem 10 ([25]). *Entropy Approximation is NISZK-complete.*

In the rest of this section, we show a Karp reduction from $O(\log(n)\sqrt{\log(1/\varepsilon)})$-GapSPP$_\varepsilon$ to Entropy Approximation. I.e., we give an efficient algorithm that takes as input a basis for a lattice $\mathcal{L}$ and outputs a circuit $\mathcal{C}_\mathcal{L}$ such that (1) if $\eta_\varepsilon(\mathcal{L}) \leq 1$, then $H(\mathcal{C}_\mathcal{L}(U))$ is large; but (2) if $\eta_\varepsilon(\mathcal{L}) \geq C \log(n)\sqrt{\log(1/\varepsilon)}$, then $H(\mathcal{C}_\mathcal{L}(U))$ is small.

Intuitively, we want to use a circuit that samples from the *continuous* Gaussian with parameter one modulo the lattice $\mathcal{L}$. Then, by Lemma 4, if $\eta_\varepsilon(\mathcal{L}) \leq 1$, the resulting distribution will be nearly uniform over $\mathbb{R}^n/\mathcal{L}$. On the other hand, we know that, with high probability, the continuous Gaussian lies in a set of volume roughly one. And, by definition, if $\eta_\varepsilon(\mathcal{L}) \geq \Omega(C_\eta(n)\sqrt{\log(1/\varepsilon)})$, then there exists a projection π such that, say, $\mathrm{vol}(\pi(\mathbb{R}^n/\mathcal{L})) = \det(\pi(\mathcal{L})) \geq 100$.

Therefore, the projected Gaussian lies in a small fraction of $\pi(\mathbb{R}^n/\mathcal{L})$ with high probability.

To make this precise, we must discretize $\mathbb{R}^n/\mathcal{L}$ appropriately to, say, $(\mathcal{L}/q)/\mathcal{L}$ for some large integer $q > 1$ and sample from a discretized version of the continuous Gaussian. Naturally, we choose $D_{\mathcal{L}/q}$. The following theorem shows that $D_{\mathcal{L}/q} \bmod \mathcal{L}$ lies in a small subset of $(\mathcal{L}/q)/\mathcal{L}$ when $\eta_{1/2}(\mathcal{L})$ is large.

Theorem 11. *For any lattice $\mathcal{L} \subset \mathbb{R}^n$ with sufficiently large n and integer $q \geq 2^n(\eta_{2-n}(\mathcal{L}) + \mu(\mathcal{L}))$, if $\eta_{1/2}(\mathcal{L}) \geq 1000 C_n(n)$ (and in particular if $\eta_{1/2}(\mathcal{L}) \geq 10^4(\log(n)+2)$), then there is a subset $S \subset (\mathcal{L}/q)/\mathcal{L}$ with $|S| \leq q^n/200$ such that*

$$\Pr_{\mathbf{X} \sim D_{\mathcal{L}/q} \bmod \mathcal{L}}[\mathbf{X} \in S] \geq \frac{9}{10}.$$

Proof. It is easy to see that $D_{\mathcal{L}/q}$ is statistically close to the distribution obtained by sampling from a *continuous* Gaussian with parameter one and rounding to the closest vector in $\mathcal{L}/q$. (One must simply recall from Lemma 4 that nearly all of the mass of $D_{\mathcal{L}/q}$ lies in a ball of radius $\sqrt{n}$ and notice that for such short points, shifts of size $\mu(\mathcal{L}/q) < 2^{-n}$ have little effect on the Gaussian mass.) It therefore suffices to show that the above probability is at least $19/20$ when $\mathbf{X}$ is sampled from this new distribution. We write $\mathsf{CVP}(\mathbf{t})$ for the closest vector in $\mathcal{L}/q$ to $\mathbf{t}$.

By assumption, there is a lattice projection π onto a k-dimensional subspace such that $\det(\pi(\mathcal{L})) \geq 1000^k$. Notice that $\|\pi(\mathsf{CVP}(\mathbf{t}))\| \leq \|\pi(\mathbf{t})\| + \mu(\mathcal{L})/q \leq \|\mathbf{t}\| + 2^{-n}$ for any $\mathbf{t} \in \mathbb{R}^n$. In particular, if $\mathbf{X}$ is sampled from a continuous Gaussian with parameter one,

$$\Pr\left[\|\pi(\mathsf{CVP}(\mathbf{X}))\| \geq \sqrt{k}\right] \leq \Pr\left[\|\pi(\mathbf{X})\| \geq \sqrt{k} - 2^{-n}\right] \leq \frac{1}{20},$$

where we have applied Lemma 10. But, by Lemma 1, there are at most $(q/200)^k$ points $\mathbf{y} \in (\pi(\mathcal{L})/q)/\pi(\mathcal{L})) \cap \sqrt{k}B_2^k$. Therefore, there are at most $q^n/200^k \leq q^n/200$ points $\mathbf{y} \in (\mathcal{L}/q)/\mathcal{L}$ with $19/20$ of the mass, as needed.

Corollary 5. *For any lattice $\mathcal{L} \subset \mathbb{R}^n$ with $n \geq 2$, $\varepsilon \in (0, 1/2)$, and integer $q \geq 2$, let $\mathbf{X} \sim D_{\mathcal{L}/q} \bmod \mathcal{L}$. Then,*

1. *if $\eta_\varepsilon(\mathcal{L}) \leq 1$, then $H(\mathbf{X}) > n\log_2 q - 2$; but*
2. *if $\eta_\varepsilon(\mathcal{L}) \geq 1000 C_n(n) \cdot \sqrt{\log(1/\varepsilon)}$ (and in particular if $\eta_\varepsilon(\mathcal{L}) \geq 10^4 \log(n)\sqrt{\log(1/\varepsilon)}$ and $q \geq 2^n(\eta_{2-n}(\mathcal{L}) + \mu(\mathcal{L}))$), then $H(\mathbf{X}) < n\log_2 q - 6$.*

Proof. Suppose that $\eta_\varepsilon(\mathcal{L}) \leq 1$. Then, by Lemma 4, for any $\mathbf{y} \in (\mathcal{L}/q)/\mathcal{L}$,

$$\Pr_{\mathbf{X} \sim D_{\mathcal{L}/q} \bmod \mathcal{L}}[\mathbf{X} = \mathbf{y}] = \frac{\rho(\mathcal{L} + \mathbf{y})}{\rho(\mathcal{L}/q)} \leq \frac{1+\varepsilon}{1-\varepsilon} \cdot \frac{1}{q^n}.$$

It follows that

$$H(D_{\mathcal{L}/q} \bmod \mathcal{L}) \geq n\log_2 q + \log_2(1 - \varepsilon) - \log_2(1 + \varepsilon) > n\log_2 q - 2,$$

as needed.

Suppose, on the other hand, that $\eta_\varepsilon(\mathcal{L}) \geq 1000 C_\eta(n) \cdot \sqrt{\log(1/\varepsilon)}$ and $q \geq 2^n(\eta_{2^{-n}}(\mathcal{L}) + \mu(\mathcal{L}))$. By Lemma 6, $\eta_{1/2}(\mathcal{L}) \geq 1000 C_\eta(n)$, so that by Theorem 11, there is a set S of size $|S| = q^n/200$ with at least $9/10$ of the mass of $D_{\mathcal{L}/q} \bmod \mathcal{L}$. Therefore,

$$H(D_{\mathcal{L}/q} \bmod \mathcal{L}) \leq \frac{9}{10} \cdot \log_2 |S| + \frac{1}{10} \cdot n \log_2 q < n \log_2 q - 6,$$

as needed.

Corollary 5 shows that, in order to reduce $O(\log(n)\sqrt{\log(1/\varepsilon)})$-GapSPP$_\varepsilon$ to Entropy Approximation, it suffices to construct a circuit that samples from $D_{\mathcal{L}/q} \bmod \mathcal{L}$. The main result of this section follows immediately from Corollary 2.

Theorem 12. *There is an efficient Karp reduction from γ-GapSPP$_\varepsilon$ to Entropy Approximation for*

$$\gamma := O(C_\eta(n)\sqrt{\log(1/\varepsilon)}) \leq O(\log(n)\sqrt{\log(1/\varepsilon)}).$$

and any $\varepsilon \in (0, 1/2)$. I.e., γ-GapSPP$_\varepsilon$ is in NISZK.

Proof. The reduction behaves as follows on input $\mathcal{L} \subset \mathbb{Q}^n$. By Lemma 7, we can find an integer $q \geq 2$ with polynomial bit length that satisfies $q \geq 2^n(\eta_{2^{-n}}(\mathcal{L}) + \mu(\mathcal{L}))$. The reduction constructs the circuit $\mathcal{C}_{\mathcal{L}/q}$ from Corollary 2 and outputs the modified circuit $\mathcal{C}_{(\mathcal{L}/q)/\mathcal{L}}$ that takes the output from $\mathcal{C}_{\mathcal{L}/q}$ and reduces it modulo $\mathcal{L}$. It then outputs the Entropy Approximation instance $(\mathcal{C}_{(\mathcal{L}/q)/\mathcal{L}}, k := n \log_2 q - 4)$.

The running time is clear. Suppose that $\eta_\varepsilon(\mathcal{L}) \leq 1$. Then, by Corollary 5,

$$H(D_{\mathcal{L}/q} \bmod \mathcal{L}) > n \log_2 q - 2.$$

Since the output of $\mathcal{C}_{(\mathcal{L}/q)/\mathcal{L}}$ is statistically close to $D_{\mathcal{L}/q} \bmod \mathcal{L}$, it follows that $H(\mathcal{C}_{(\mathcal{L}/q)/\mathcal{L}}(U)) > n \log_2 q - 3$, as needed.

If, on the other hand, $\eta_\varepsilon(\mathcal{L}) \geq \Omega(C_\eta(n) \cdot \sqrt{\log(1/\varepsilon)})$, then by Corollary 5,

$$H(D_{\mathcal{L}/q} \bmod \mathcal{L}) < n \log_2 q - 6.$$

Since the output of $\mathcal{C}_{(\mathcal{L}/q)/\mathcal{L}}$ is statistically close to $D_{\mathcal{L}/q} \bmod \mathcal{L}$, it follows that $H(\mathcal{C}_{(\mathcal{L}/q)/\mathcal{L}}(U)) < n \log_2 q - 5$.

4   A coNP Proof for $O(\log n)$-GapSPP

We will need the following result from [47], which extends Theorem 5 to smaller ε by noting that $\rho_{1/s}(\mathcal{L}^* \backslash \{0\})$ decays at least as quickly as $\rho_{1/s}(\lambda_1(\mathcal{L}^*))$.

Theorem 13. *For any lattice $\mathcal{L} \subset \mathbb{R}^n$ and any $\varepsilon \in (0, 1/2)$,*

$$\eta_\varepsilon(\mathcal{L})^2 \leq C_\eta(n)^2 \eta_{det}(\mathcal{L})^2 + \frac{\log(1/\varepsilon)}{\pi \lambda_1(\mathcal{L}^*)^2} \leq 100(\log n + 2)^2 \eta_{det}(\mathcal{L})^2 + \frac{\log(1/\varepsilon)}{\pi \lambda_1(\mathcal{L}^*)^2}.$$

Proof. We may assume without loss of generality that $\eta_{\det}(\mathcal{L}) = 1$. Then, by definition, $\rho_{1/C_\eta(n)}(\mathcal{L}^* \backslash \{\mathbf{0}\}) \leq 1/2$. Therefore, for any $s \geq C_\eta(n)$,

$$
\begin{aligned}
\rho_{1/s}(\mathcal{L}^*) &= 1 + \sum_{\mathbf{w} \in \mathcal{L}^* \backslash \{\mathbf{0}\}} \exp(-\pi(s^2 - C_\eta(n)^2)\|\mathbf{w}\|^2)\rho_{1/C_\eta(n)}(\mathbf{w}) \\
&\leq 1 + \sum_{\mathbf{w} \in \mathcal{L}^* \backslash \{\mathbf{0}\}} \exp(-\pi(s^2 - C_\eta(n)^2)\lambda_1(\mathcal{L}^*)^2)\rho_{1/C_\eta(n)}(\mathbf{w}) \\
&\leq 1 + \exp(-\pi(s^2 - C_\eta(n)^2)\lambda_1(\mathcal{L}^*)^2)/2,
\end{aligned}
$$

and the result follows.

Next, we prove an easy lower bound with a similar form (by taking the average of two trivial lower bounds).

Lemma 13. *For any lattice $\mathcal{L} \subset \mathbb{R}^n$ and any $\varepsilon \in (0, 1/2)$,*

$$
\eta_\varepsilon(\mathcal{L})^2 \geq \eta_{det}(\mathcal{L})^2/8 + \frac{\log(2/\varepsilon)}{2\pi\lambda_1(\mathcal{L}^*)^2}.
$$

Proof. First, note that $\rho_{1/s}(\mathcal{L}^* \backslash \{\mathbf{0}\}) \geq 2\rho_{1/s}(\lambda_1(\mathcal{L}^*))$. Rearranging, we see that

$$
\eta_\varepsilon(\mathcal{L})^2 \geq \frac{\log(2/\varepsilon)}{\pi\lambda_1(\mathcal{L}^*)^2}.
$$

On the other hand, recall that for any lattice projection π onto a subspace W, $\det(\mathcal{L}^* \cap W) = 1/\det(\pi(\mathcal{L}))$. I.e., $\eta_{\det}(\mathcal{L}) = \max_{\mathcal{L}' \subseteq \mathcal{L}^*} \det(\mathcal{L}')^{-1/\operatorname{rank}(\mathcal{L}')}$. So, suppose $s \leq \eta_{\det}(\mathcal{L})/2$. Then, by Lemma 3,

$$
\rho_{1/s}(\mathcal{L}^*) = \max_{\mathcal{L}' \subseteq \mathcal{L}^*} \rho_{1/s}(\mathcal{L}') \geq \max_{\mathcal{L}' \subseteq \mathcal{L}^*} s^{-\operatorname{rank}(\mathcal{L}')}/\det(\mathcal{L}') \geq 2.
$$

So, $\eta_\varepsilon(\mathcal{L})^2 \geq \eta_1(\mathcal{L})^2 \geq \eta_{\det}(\mathcal{L})^2/4$. The result follows by taking the average of the two bounds.

The main theorem of this section now follows immediately.

Theorem 14. *For any $\varepsilon \in (0, 1/2)$, γ-GapSPP$_\varepsilon$ is in coNP for $\gamma = O(C_\eta(n)) \leq O(\log n)$.*

Proof. Let $\gamma := 2\sqrt{2}C_\eta(n)$. On input a lattice $\mathcal{L} \subset \mathbb{R}^n$, the prover simply sends a lattice projection π with $\det(\pi(\mathcal{L}))^{1/\operatorname{rank}(\pi(\mathcal{L}))} = \eta_{\det}(\mathcal{L})$ and a vector $\mathbf{w} \in \mathcal{L}^*$ with $\|\mathbf{w}\| = \lambda_1(\mathcal{L}^*)$. The verifier checks that π is indeed a lattice projection and that $\mathbf{w} \in \mathcal{L}^* \backslash \{\mathbf{0}\}$. It then answers NO if and only if

$$
\gamma^2 \det(\pi(\mathcal{L}))^{2/\operatorname{rank}(\pi(\mathcal{L}))}/8 + \frac{\log(1/\varepsilon)}{\pi\|\mathbf{w}\|^2} > \gamma^2. \tag{2}
$$

To prove completeness, suppose that $\eta_\varepsilon(\mathcal{L}) > \gamma$. Then, by Theorem 13,

$$
\gamma^2 \eta_{\det}(\mathcal{L})^2/8 + \frac{\log(1/\varepsilon)}{\pi\lambda_1(\mathcal{L}^*)^2} \geq \eta_\varepsilon(\mathcal{L})^2 > \gamma^2.
$$

I.e., there exists a valid proof, as needed.

To prove soundness, suppose that $\eta_\varepsilon(\mathcal{L}) \leq 1$. Then, by Lemma 13,

$$\eta_{\det}(\mathcal{L})^2/8 + \frac{\log(1/\varepsilon)}{2\pi\lambda_1(\mathcal{L}^*)^2} \leq \eta_\varepsilon(\mathcal{L})^2 \leq 1.$$

Therefore,

$$\gamma^2\eta_{\det}(\mathcal{L})^2/8 + \frac{\log(1/\varepsilon)}{\pi\lambda_1(\mathcal{L}^*)^2} \leq \frac{\gamma^2\eta_{\det}(\mathcal{L})^2/8 + \frac{\log(1/\varepsilon)}{\pi\lambda_1(\mathcal{L}^*)^2}}{\eta_{\det}(\mathcal{L})^2/8 + \frac{\log(1/\varepsilon)}{2\pi\lambda_1(\mathcal{L}^*)^2}}$$
$$\leq \max\{\gamma^2, 2\}$$
$$\leq \gamma^2.$$

In other words, Eq. (2) cannot hold for any pair $\mathbf{w} \in \mathcal{L}^*\backslash\{\mathbf{0}\}$ and lattice projection π. I.e., the verifier will always answer YES, as needed.

Finally, we derive the following corollary.

Corollary 6. *For any $\varepsilon \in (0, 1/2)$, γ-coGapSPP$_\varepsilon$ has an SZK proof system with an efficient prover for*

$$\gamma := O(C_\eta(n) + \sqrt{\log(1/\varepsilon)/\log n}) \leq O(\log n + \sqrt{\log(1/\varepsilon)/\log n}).$$

Proof. By Theorem 7, γ-GapSPP$_\varepsilon$ is in SZK. Since SZK is closed under complements [43,48], γ-coGapSPP$_\varepsilon$ is in SZK as well. By Theorem 14, γ-coGapSPP$_\varepsilon$ is in NP. The result then follows by the fact that any language in SZK ∩ NP has an SZK proof system with an efficient prover [40]. ∎

5 An SZK Proof for $O(\sqrt{n})$-GapCRP

In this section we prove that $O(\sqrt{n})$-GapCRP is in SZK, which improves the previous known result by a $\omega(\sqrt{\log n})$ factor [45]. First we need the following result from [16].

Lemma 14. *For any lattice $\mathcal{L}$ and parameter $s > 0$,*

$$\rho_s(\mathcal{L}) \cdot \gamma_s(\mathcal{V}(\mathcal{L})) \leq 1.$$

Here we prove an upper bound on the smoothing parameter of a lattice in terms of its covering radius. This bound is implicit in [18].

Lemma 15. *For any lattice $\mathcal{L} \subset \mathbb{R}^n$ and $\varepsilon > 0$, we have*

$$\eta_\varepsilon(\mathcal{L}) \leq \sqrt{\frac{\pi}{\log(1+\varepsilon)}} \cdot \mu(\mathcal{L}).$$

In particular, $\eta_\varepsilon(\mathcal{L}) \leq O(\mu(\mathcal{L}))$ for any $\varepsilon \geq \Omega(1)$.

Proof

$$\rho_{1/s}(\mathcal{L}^*) = s^{-n} \cdot \det(\mathcal{L}) \cdot \rho_s(\mathcal{L}) \qquad \text{(Lemma 3)}$$

$$\leq \frac{s^{-n} \cdot \det(\mathcal{L})}{\gamma_s(\mathcal{V}(\mathcal{L}))} \qquad \text{(Lemma 14)}$$

$$\leq \frac{s^{-n} \cdot \det(\mathcal{L})}{\int_{\mathcal{V}(\mathcal{L})} s^{-n} \cdot \exp(-\pi \mathbf{x}^2/s^2)\, d\mathbf{x}}$$

$$\leq \frac{\det(\mathcal{L})}{\int_{\mathcal{V}(\mathcal{L})} \exp(-\pi \mu(\mathcal{L})^2/s^2)\, d\mathbf{x}}$$

$$\leq \exp(\pi \mu(\mathcal{L})^2/s^2),$$

where we used the fact that $\|\mathbf{x}\| \leq \mu(\mathcal{L})$ for any $\mathbf{x} \in \mathcal{V}(\mathcal{L})$. By setting $s = \sqrt{\frac{\pi}{\log(1+\varepsilon)}} \cdot \mu(\mathcal{L})$ we have the desired result.

Theorem 15. *The problem $O(\sqrt{n})$-GapCRP has an SZK proof system with an efficient prover, as does $O(\sqrt{n})$-coGapCRP.*

Proof. Fix some some constant $\varepsilon \in (0, 1/2)$. By Lemmas 8 and 15, we know that there exist C_1 and C_2 such that

$$C_1 \eta_\varepsilon(\mathcal{L}) \leq \mu(\mathcal{L}) \leq C_2 \sqrt{n} \cdot \eta_\varepsilon(\mathcal{L}),$$

and hence there is a simple reduction from $O(\sqrt{n})$-GapCRP to $O(1)$-GapSPP$_\varepsilon$. It follows from Theorem 7 that $O(\sqrt{n})$-GapCRP is in SZK. To see that the prover can be made efficient, we recall from [27] that $O(\sqrt{n})$-GapCRP is in NP $\cap$ coNP. The result then follows by the fact that any language in SZK $\cap$ NP has an SZK proof system with an efficient prover [40].

A   Proof of Lemma 12

Definition 5. *For any $\delta > 0$, $S \subseteq \mathbb{R}^n$, we say that $A \subseteq S$ is a δ-net of S if for each $\mathbf{v} \in S$, there is some $\mathbf{u} \in A$ such that $\|\mathbf{u} - \mathbf{v}\| \leq \delta$.*

Lemma 16. *For any $\delta > 0$, there exists a δ-net of the unit sphere in $\mathbb{R}^n$ with at most $(1 + 2/\delta)^n$ points.*

Proof. Let N be maximal such that N points can be placed on the unit sphere in such a way that no pair of points is within distance δ of each other. Clearly, there exists a δ-net of size N.

So, it suffices to show that any collection of vectors A in the unit sphere with $|A| > (1 + 2/\delta)^n$ must contain two points within distance δ of each other. Let

$$\mathcal{B} := \bigcup_{\mathbf{u} \in A} ((\delta/2)B_2^n + \mathbf{u})$$

be the union of balls of radius $\delta/2$ centered at each point in A. Notice that $\mathcal{B} \subseteq (1 + \delta/2)B_2^n$. If all of these balls were disjoint, then we would have

$$\mathrm{vol}(\mathcal{B}_2^n) = |A| \cdot (\delta/2)^n \mathrm{vol}(B_2^n) > \mathrm{vol}((1 + \delta/2)B_2^n),$$

a contradiction. Therefore, two such balls must overlap. I.e., there must be two points within distance δ of each other, as needed.

We will need the following result from [49, Lemma 5.4].

Lemma 17. *For a symmetric matrix $M \in \mathbb{R}^{n \times n}$ and a δ-net of the unit sphere A with $\delta \in (0, 1/2)$,*

$$\|M\| \leq \frac{1}{1 - 2\delta} \cdot \max_{\mathbf{v} \in A} |\langle M\mathbf{v}, \mathbf{v} \rangle|.$$

We will also need the following result from [36, Lemma 2.8], which shows that the discrete Gaussian distribution is subgaussian.

Lemma 18. *For any lattice $\mathcal{L} \subset \mathbb{R}^n$ with $\eta_{1/2}(\mathcal{L}) \leq 1$, shift vector $\mathbf{t} \in \mathbb{R}^n$, unit vector $\mathbf{v} \in \mathbb{R}^n$, and any $r > 0$,*

$$\Pr_{\mathbf{X} \sim D_{\mathcal{L} - \mathbf{t}}}[|\langle \mathbf{v}, \mathbf{X} \rangle| \geq r] \leq 10 \exp(-\pi r^2).$$

Proof (Proof of Lemma 12). Let $\{\mathbf{v}_1, \dots, \mathbf{v}_N\}$ be a $(1/10)$-net of the unit sphere with $N \leq 25^n$, as guaranteed by Lemma 16. By Lemma 18, we have that for any $\mathbf{e}_i$ in the proof, any $\mathbf{v}_j$, and any $r \geq 0$, $\Pr[|\langle \mathbf{v}_j, \mathbf{e}_i \rangle| \geq r] \leq 10 \exp(-\pi r^2)$. Therefore, by Lemma 10

$$\Pr\left[\sum_i \langle \mathbf{v}_j, \mathbf{e}_i \rangle^2 \geq r\right] \leq 2^m e^{-\pi r/2}.$$

Applying the union bound, we have

$$\Pr\left[\exists j, \sum_i \langle \mathbf{v}_j, \mathbf{e}_i \rangle^2 \geq r\right] \leq N 2^m e^{-\pi r/2}.$$

Taking $r := 2m$, we see that this probability is negligible. Applying Lemma 17 shows that

$$\left\|\sum_i \mathbf{e}_i \mathbf{e}_i^T\right\| \leq 2m \cdot \frac{5}{4} < 3m,$$

except with negligible probability, as needed.

References

1. Aggarwal, D., Dadush, D., Regev, O., Stephens-Davidowitz, N.: Solving the shortest vector problem in 2^n time using discrete Gaussian sampling. In: STOC, pp. 733–742 (2015)
2. Aggarwal, D., Dadush, D., Stephens-Davidowitz, N.: Solving the closest vector problem in 2^n time - the discrete Gaussian strikes again! In: FOCS, pp. 563–582 (2015)

3. Aharonov, D., Regev, O.: Lattice problems in NP ∩ coNP. J. ACM **52**(5), 749–765 (2005). Preliminary version in FOCS 2004
4. Ajtai, M.: Generating hard instances of lattice problems. Quaderni di Matematica **13**, 1–32 (2004). Preliminary version in STOC 1996
5. Babai, L.: Trading group theory for randomness. In: STOC, pp. 421–429 (1985)
6. Babai, L.: On Lovász' lattice reduction and the nearest lattice point problem. Combinatorica **6**(1), 1–13 (1986). Preliminary version in STACS 1985
7. Banaszczyk, W.: New bounds in some transference theorems in the geometry of numbers. Math. Ann. **296**(4), 625–635 (1993)
8. Banaszczyk, W.: Inequalites for convex bodies and polar reciprocal lattices in $\mathbb{R}^n$. Discrete Comput. Geom. **13**, 217–231 (1995)
9. Bellare, M., Goldwasser, S.: New paradigms for digital signatures and message authentication based on non-interactive zero knowledge proofs. In: Brassard, G. (ed.) CRYPTO 1989. LNCS, vol. 435, pp. 194–211. Springer, New York (1990). https://doi.org/10.1007/0-387-34805-0_19
10. Blum, M., De Santis, A., Micali, S., Persiano, G.: Noninteractive zero-knowledge. SIAM J. Comput. **20**(6), 1084–1118 (1991). Preliminary version in STOC 1988
11. Boppana, R.B., Håstad, J., Zachos, S.: Does co-NP have short interactive proofs? Inf. Process. Lett. **25**(2), 127–132 (1987)
12. Brakerski, Z., Gentry, C., Vaikuntanathan, V.: (Leveled) fully homomorphic encryption without bootstrapping. TOCT **6**(3), 13 (2014). Preliminary version in ITCS 2012
13. Brakerski, Z., Langlois, A., Peikert, C., Regev, O., Stehlé, D.: Classical hardness of learning with errors. In: STOC, pp. 575–584 (2013)
14. Brakerski, Z., Vaikuntanathan, V.: Efficient fully homomorphic encryption from (standard) LWE. SIAM J. Comput. **43**(2), 831–871 (2014). Preliminary version in FOCS 2011
15. Canetti, R.: Universally composable security: a new paradigm for cryptographic protocols. In: FOCS, pp. 136–145 (2001)
16. Chung, K.-M., Dadush, D., Liu, F.-H., Peikert, C.: On the lattice smoothing parameter problem. In: IEEE Conference on Computational Complexity, pp. 230–241 (2013)
17. Dadush, D., Peikert, C., Vempala, S.: Enumerative lattice algorithms in any norm via M-ellipsoid coverings. In: FOCS, pp. 580–589 (2011)
18. Dadush, D., Regev, O.: Towards strong reverse Minkowski-type inequalities for lattices. In: FOCS, pp. 447–456 (2016)
19. Dwork, C., Naor, M.: Zaps and their applications. SIAM J. Comput. **36**(6), 1513–1543 (2007)
20. Gentry, C., Peikert, C., Vaikuntanathan, V.: Trapdoors for hard lattices and new cryptographic constructions. In: STOC, pp. 197–206 (2008)
21. Goldreich, O., Goldwasser, S.: On the limits of nonapproximability of lattice problems. J. Comput. Syst. Sci. **60**(3), 540–563 (2000). Preliminary version in STOC 1998
22. Goldreich, O., Micali, S., Wigderson, A.: How to play any mental game or a completeness theorem for protocols with honest majority. In: STOC, pp. 218–229 (1987)
23. Goldreich, O., Micali, S., Wigderson, A.: Proofs that yield nothing but their validity for all languages in NP have zero-knowledge proof systems. J. ACM **38**(3), 691–729 (1991)
24. Goldreich, O., Sahai, A., Vadhan, S.P.: Honest-verifier statistical zero-knowledge equals general statistical zero-knowledge. In: STOC, pp. 399–408 (1998)

25. Goldreich, O., Sahai, A., Vadhan, S.: Can statistical zero knowledge be made non-interactive? or on the relationship of SZK and *NISZK*. In: Wiener, M. (ed.) CRYPTO 1999. LNCS, vol. 1666, pp. 467–484. Springer, Heidelberg (1999). https://doi.org/10.1007/3-540-48405-1_30

26. Goldwasser, S., Micali, S., Rackoff, C.: The knowledge complexity of interactive proof systems. SIAM J. Comput. **18**(1), 186–208 (1989). Preliminary version in STOC 1985

27. Guruswami, V., Micciancio, D., Regev, O.: The complexity of the covering radius problem. Comput. Complex. **14**(2), 90–121 (2005). Preliminary version in CCC 2004

28. Haviv, I., Regev, O.: On the lattice isomorphism problem. In: SODA, pp. 391–404 (2014)

29. Hoeffding, W.: Probability inequalities for sums of bounded random variables. J. Am. Stat. Assoc. **58**, 13–30 (1963)

30. Joux, A., Stern, J.: Lattice reduction: a toolbox for the cryptanalyst. J. Cryptology **11**(3), 161–185 (1998)

31. Kannan, R.: Improved algorithms for integer programming and related lattice problems. In: STOC, pp. 193–206 (1983)

32. Klein, P.N.: Finding the closest lattice vector when it's unusually close. In: SODA, pp. 937–941 (2000)

33. Lenstra, A.K., Lenstra Jr., H.W., Lovász, L.: Factoring polynomials with rational coefficients. Math. Ann. **261**(4), 515–534 (1982)

34. Lenstra, H.W.: Integer programming with a fixed number of variables. Math. Oper. Res. **8**(4), 538–548 (1983)

35. Micciancio, D., Goldwasser, S.: Complexity of Lattice Problems: A Cryptographic Perspective. The Kluwer International Series in Engineering and Computer Science, vol. 671. Kluwer Academic Publishers, Boston (2002)

36. Micciancio, D., Peikert, C.: Trapdoors for lattices: simpler, tighter, faster, smaller. In: Pointcheval, D., Johansson, T. (eds.) EUROCRYPT 2012. LNCS, vol. 7237, pp. 700–718. Springer, Heidelberg (2012). https://doi.org/10.1007/978-3-642-29011-4_41

37. Micciancio, D., Regev, O.: Worst-case to average-case reductions based on Gaussian measures. SIAM J. Comput. **37**(1), 267–302 (2007). Preliminary version in FOCS 2004

38. Micciancio, D., Vadhan, S.P.: Statistical zero-knowledge proofs with efficient provers: lattice problems and more. In: Boneh, D. (ed.) CRYPTO 2003. LNCS, vol. 2729, pp. 282–298. Springer, Heidelberg (2003). https://doi.org/10.1007/978-3-540-45146-4_17

39. Naor, M., Yung, M.: Public-key cryptosystems provably secure against chosen ciphertext attacks. In: STOC, pp. 427–437 (1990)

40. Nguyen, M.-H., Vadhan, S.P.: Zero knowledge with efficient provers. In: STOC, pp. 287–295 (2006)

41. Nguyen, P.Q., Stern, J.: The two faces of lattices in cryptology. In: Silverman, J.H. (ed.) CaLC 2001. LNCS, vol. 2146, pp. 146–180. Springer, Heidelberg (2001). https://doi.org/10.1007/3-540-44670-2_12

42. Odlyzko, A.M.: The rise and fall of knapsack cryptosystems. In: Pomerance, C. (ed.) Cryptology and Computational Number Theory, Proceedings of Symposia in Applied Mathematics, vol. 42, pp. 75–88 (1990)

43. Okamoto, T.: On relationships between statistical zero-knowledge proofs. J. Comput. Syst. Sci. **60**(1), 47–108 (2000). Preliminary version in STOC 1996

44. Peikert, C.: Public-key cryptosystems from the worst-case shortest vector problem. In: STOC, pp. 333–342 (2009)
45. Peikert, C., Vaikuntanathan, V.: Noninteractive statistical zero-knowledge proofs for lattice problems. In: Wagner, D. (ed.) CRYPTO 2008. LNCS, vol. 5157, pp. 536–553. Springer, Heidelberg (2008). https://doi.org/10.1007/978-3-540-85174-5_30
46. Regev, O.: On lattices, learning with errors, random linear codes, and cryptography. J. ACM 56(6), 1–40 (2009). Preliminary version in STOC 2005
47. Regev, O., Stephens-Davidowitz, N.: A reverse Minkowski theorem. In: STOC, pp. 941–953 (2017)
48. Sahai, A., Vadhan, S.P.: A complete problem for statistical zero knowledge. J. ACM 50(2), 196–249 (2003). Preliminary version in FOCS 1997
49. Vershynin, R.: Introduction to the non-asymptotic analysis of random matrices, pp. 210–268. Cambridge University Press (2012). http://www-personal.umich.edu/~romanv/papers/non-asymptotic-rmt-plain.pdf

Hash Proof Systems over Lattices Revisited

Fabrice Benhamouda[1](✉), Olivier Blazy[2], Léo Ducas[3], and Willy Quach[4]

[1] IBM Research, New York, USA
fabrice.benhamouda@normalesup.org
[2] XLim, Université de Limoges, Limoges, France
olivier.blazy@unilim.fr
[3] CWI, Amsterdam, The Netherlands
leo.ducas@cwi.nl
[4] Northeastern University, Boston, USA
willy.quach@ens-lyon.fr

Abstract. Hash Proof Systems or Smooth Projective Hash Functions (SPHFs) are a form of implicit arguments introduced by Cramer and Shoup at Eurocrypt'02. They have found many applications since then, in particular for authenticated key exchange or honest-verifier zero-knowledge proofs. While they are relatively well understood in group settings, they seem painful to construct directly in the lattice setting.

Only one construction of an SPHF over lattices has been proposed in the standard model, by Katz and Vaikuntanathan at Asiacrypt'09. But this construction has an important drawback: it only works for an ad-hoc language of ciphertexts. Concretely, the corresponding decryption procedure needs to be tweaked, now requiring q many trapdoor inversion attempts, where q is the modulus of the underlying Learning With Errors (LWE) problem.

Using harmonic analysis, we explain the source of this limitation, and propose a way around it. We show how to construct SPHFs for standard languages of LWE ciphertexts, and explicit our construction over a tag-IND-CCA2 encryption scheme à la Micciancio-Peikert (Eurocrypt'12). We then improve our construction and our analysis in the case where the tag is known in advance or fixed (in the latter case, the scheme is only IND-CPA) with a super-polynomial modulus, to get a stronger type of SPHF, which was never achieved before for any language over lattices.

Finally, we conclude with applications of these SPHFs: password-based authenticated key exchange, honest-verifier zero-knowledge proofs, and a relaxed version of witness encryption.

Keywords: Hash Proof Systems · SPHF · Lattices
Learning with Errors · Harmonic analysis

O. Blazy—This work has been supported by the French ANR project ID-FIX (ANR-16-CE39-0004).
L. Ducas—This work has been supported by a Veni Grant from NWO.
W. Quach—Research supported in part by NSF grants CNS-1314722, CNS-1413964. This work was partly realized during an internship program at CWI.

M. Abdalla and R. Dahab (Eds.): PKC 2018, LNCS 10770, pp. 644–674, 2018.
https://doi.org/10.1007/978-3-319-76581-5_22

1 Introduction

Harmonic analysis is a powerful tool in geometry of numbers, especially in combination with Gaussian measure, which has lead to important progress on transference theory [3]. Those tools also played a crucial role for the foundation of lattice-based cryptography, being at the heart of proofs of worst-case hardness for lattice problems, such as the Short Integer Solution problem (SIS) and the Learning with Errors (LWE) problem [14,28,29]. Later, security proofs relied on a few convenient lemmas in a black-box manner, and for most applications this was sufficient: lattice-based cryptography quickly caught up with pairing-based cryptography, for example with the constructions of (Hierarchical) Identity Based Encryption's [9,14,27] and beyond [8,15,16].

There nevertheless remains one primitive for which lattice-based cryptography is still far behind: Hash Proof Systems or Smooth Projective Hash Functions (SPHFs) [11]. Beyond the original Chosen-Ciphertext secure encryption scheme of Cramer and Shoup [10], SPHFs give rise to generalized classes of Authenticated Key Exchange (Password-based, Language-based, ...) [2,4,13, 23]. They also have been used in Oblivious Transfer [18,21], One-Time Relatively-Sound Non-Interactive Zero-Knowledge Arguments [20], and Zero-Knowledge Arguments [5].

An SPHF can be seen as an implicit (designated-verifier) zero-knowledge proof for a language. The most useful languages for SPHFs are the languages of ciphertexts of a given plaintext M.

To our knowledge, there is only one construction of SPHF for a lattice-based encryption scheme in the standard model, given by Katz and Vaikuntanathan [22]. There is also a subsequent work by Zhang and Yu who propose an interesting new lattice-based SPHF in [30]. But the language of the SPHF relies on simulation-sound non-interactive zero-knowledge proofs which we do not know how to construct just under lattice-based assumptions without random oracle.

Unfortunately, the only standard-model lattice-based SPHF construction in [22] has a main drawback: the language of the SPHF is not simply defined as the set of valid standard LWE ciphertexts. Naturally, the set of valid ciphertexts of 0 should correspond to the set of ciphertexts close to the lattice defined by the public key. Instead, their language includes all the ciphertexts c such that at least one integer multiple is close to the public lattice. This makes the decryption procedure very costly (about q trapdoor inversions), and forbids the use of super-polynomial modulus q. This limitation is a serious obstacle to the construction of a stronger type of SPHF introduced in [23], namely *word-independent* SPHF for which the *projection key* (which can be seen as the public key of the SPHF) does not depend on the ciphertext c (a.k.a., word in the SPHF terminology).[1]

This strongly contrasts with SPHFs in a group-based setting, which can handle classical ElGamal or Cramer-Shoup encryption schemes—for example

---

[1] Word-independent SPHFs are also called KV-SPHF in [5], in reference to [23].

[11,13]—without any modification of the decryption procedure. This is a technical hassle to carry when building on top of such an SPHF.

We therefore view as an important question to determine whether this caveat is inherent to lattice-based SPHFs, or if it can be overcome. We shall find an answer by re-introducing some harmonic analysis.

Contributions. Our main contribution consists in constructing SPHFs for standard lattice-based encryption schemes. We provide general theorems to ease the proofs of correctness and security (a.k.a., *smoothness* or *universality*) of SPHFs over standard lattice-based encryption schemes. We detail two particular instantiations: one over an IND-CCA2 encryption scheme à la Micciancio-Peikert [27], and one over an IND-CPA restriction of the same scheme. While the second instantiation is over a simpler language, it is a word-independent SPHF. To our knowledge, this is the first word-independent SPHF over any lattice-based language. We remark that while Zhang and Yu construct an interesting *approximate* word-independent SPHF over a lattice-based language in [30], its correctness is only approximate contrary to our SPHF; and its language also relies on simulation-sound non-interactive zero-knowledge proofs, which we do not know how to construct just from lattice assumptions in the standard model.

As with many zero-knowledge-type primitives in the lattice setting [24,25] and as with the SPHFs of [22] and of [30], there is a gap between the correctness property and the smoothness property. Concretely, smoothness holds for ciphertexts which do not decrypt to a given message, while correctness holds only for honestly generated ciphertexts. However, contrary to [22], we use a standard encryption scheme and do not need to tweak the decryption procedure nor the language. We thus avoid the main caveat of the latter paper.

Applications. Having built these new SPHFs, we can now proceed with several applications showing that the gap between smoothness (or universality) and correctness is not an issue in most cases. We start by proposing an efficient password-authenticated key exchange (PAKE) scheme in three flows. We do so by plugging our first SPHF in the framework from [22]. Following the GK-PAKE construction from [1] which is an improvement of the Groce-Katz framework [17,19], we also obtain a PAKE in two flows over lattices in the standard model. Finally, using our word-independent SPHF together with simulation-sound non-interactive zero-knowledge proofs (SS-NIZK), by following [23], we obtain a one-round PAKE.

Compared to the recent work of Zhang and Yu [30], which proposes the first two-round lattice-based PAKE assuming in addition SS-NIZK, our two-round PAKE does not require SS-NIZK. While there exist very efficient SS-NIZKs in the random oracle model for the languages considered by Zhang and Yu, constructing SS-NIZK in the standard model under a lattice-based assumption remains an important open problem. Our two-round PAKE is thus the first two-round PAKE solely based on lattice assumptions in the standard model. In addition, our one-round PAKE assuming LWE and SS-NIZK is the first one-round PAKE in this setting and closes an open problem of [30].

In addition to PAKE, we also show how to construct honest-verifier zero-knowledge proofs for any NP language from lattice-based SPHF. We conclude by showing a relaxed version of witness encryption for some lattice-based languages. Witness encryption is a very recent primitive introduced in [12] which enables a user to encrypt a message to a given word of some NP language. The message can be decrypted using a witness for the word.

Technical Overview. Let us now give a technical overview of our main contribution, namely the constructions of new lattice-based SPHFs. We focus on the language of dual-Regev ciphertexts c of 0: $c = As + e \in \mathbb{Z}_q^m$, where $A \in \mathbb{Z}_q^{m \times n}$ is a public matrix, while $s \in \mathbb{Z}_q^n$ and $e \in \mathbb{Z}_q^m$ correspond to the randomness of the ciphertext. The vector e is supposed to be small, i.e., c is close to the q-ary lattice Λ generated by A.

Intuitively, an SPHF allows a prover knowing s and e to prove to a verifier that c is indeed a ciphertext of 0. The naive and natural construction works as follows.[2] The verifier generates a *small* random vector $\mathsf{hk} = h \in \mathbb{Z}_q^m$ called a *hashing key*. It then "hashes" the ciphertext into a *hash value* $\mathsf{H} = R(\langle h, c \rangle) \in \{0, 1\}$, where R is a *rounding function* from $\mathbb{Z}_q$ to $\{0, 1\}$ to be chosen later. The verifier also derives from $\mathsf{hk} = h$, a *projection key* $\mathsf{hp} = p = A^t h \in \mathbb{Z}_q^n$ that it sends to the prover. The prover can then compute the *projected hash value* $\mathsf{pH} = R(\langle p, s \rangle)$ from the projection key p and the randomness of the ciphertext s and e. It can send this projected hash value to the verifier which will accept the proof, if pH matches its hash value H.

We remark that if indeed $c = As + e$ with e small enough (recall that h is small as well):

$$\langle h, c \rangle = h^t As + h^t e \approx h^t As = \langle p, s \rangle.$$

Hence, if R is carefully chosen, we can ensure that with high probability (e.g., at least $3/4$), $\mathsf{H} = \mathsf{pH}$, and the verifier will accept the prover's "proof." This property is called *approximate correctness*. An SPHF also needs to satisfy a security property to be useful, called *smoothness* or *universality*, which ensures that if c is far from the q-ary lattice Λ generated by A (in particular if it is an encryption of 1), then given the projection key p (and A and c), the prover cannot guess the hash value H with probability more than $1/2 + \mathrm{negl}(n)$. In [22], Katz and Vaikuntanathan argued universality for ciphertexts c, for which every multiple of c is far from the lattice Λ. To be useful in their PAKE application, the decryption procedure of the encryption scheme therefore needs to be tweaked to try to decrypt not only the ciphertext itself but also all its multiples. In particular, their construction cannot work with super-polynomial moduli.

The question we wish to answer is whether universality holds without this tweak. In other words, is the condition that jc is far from Λ for all $j \neq 0$ truly

---

[2] Actually, what we construct in this overview are bit-PHF and not SPHF, i.e., the hash value defined later is just a bit and the security property is universality instead of smoothness. Classical SPHFs can be derived from these bit-PHFs. See Fig. 2 and Sect. 2.3.

necessary or is it is an artifact of the proof? To approach this question, let us discuss two case studies.

Two case studies. Let us first take a look at the special case where q is even, and where c is a perfect encryption of 1: $c = As + (0, \ldots, 0, q/2)^t$ for some $s \in \mathbb{Z}_q^n$. We observe that

$$\langle h, c \rangle = \langle p, s \rangle + (h_m \bmod 2) \cdot q/2,$$

where h_m is the last coordinate of h. In particular, the distribution of $\langle h, c \rangle$, when h is drawn from a discrete Gaussian (over $\mathbb{Z}^m$), conditioned on A, c and $A^t h = p$, is concentrated on merely 2 values out of q and is therefore far from uniform.

Yet, assuming the discrete Gaussian has large enough parameter (more precisely, twice as large as the smoothing parameter of $\mathbb{Z}$), we note that h_m is close to uniform modulo 2. In that case we observe that while $\langle h, c \rangle$ is not itself uniform, the rounding $R(\langle h, c \rangle)$ is close to uniform when choosing the typical rounding function $R : x \in \mathbb{Z}_q \mapsto \lfloor 2x/q \rceil \bmod 2$, regardless of the value of $\langle p, s \rangle$. So it seems that the rounding function does not only help in ensuring approximate correctness, but it can also improve universality of the scheme as well!

Unfortunately, we cannot always expect universality from this trick. Now assume that q is divisible by 3, and set $c = As + (0, \ldots, 0, q/3)^t$. This time,

$$\langle h, c \rangle = \langle p, s \rangle + (h_m \bmod 3) \cdot q/3$$

is (almost) uniformly distributed over three values, separated by $q/3$. In particular $R(\langle h, c \rangle)$ will take one value with probability (roughly) $1/3$, and the other value with probability (roughly) $2/3$. Despite imperfect universality, this still guarantees some entropy in $\mathsf{Hash}(h, A, c)$ knowing A, c, and p.

Harmonic analysis. The core of our work consists in using harmonic analysis to better understand the caveat of [22], namely that universality is only proven when all the multiples of the ciphertext are far from the lattice. For that, we extend the rounding function R to a q-periodic signal $\mathbb{R} \to \mathbb{R}$.

We proceed to a general analysis (Theorem 3.1), which shows that universality holds for ciphertexts c such that its multiples jc are far away from the lattice Λ, for all non-zero integers j corresponding to non-zero real harmonics of the rounding signal R.

This unravels the causes of the caveat in [22]: the weight of the j-th harmonic of the naive rounding function $R : x \in \mathbb{Z}_q \mapsto \lfloor 2x/q \rceil \bmod 2$ (seen as a q-periodic signal, as in Fig. 1a) is as large as $\Theta(1/j)$ for odd integers j.

First solution (Universality, Approximate Correctness, Sect. 3). Having identified the source of the caveat, it becomes clear how to repair it: the rounding should be *randomized*, with a weight signal for which only the first harmonic is non-zero (in addition to the average), namely with a *pure cosine* weight:

$$\Pr[R(x) = 1] := \frac{1}{2} + \frac{1}{2}\cos\left(\frac{2\pi x}{q}\right).$$

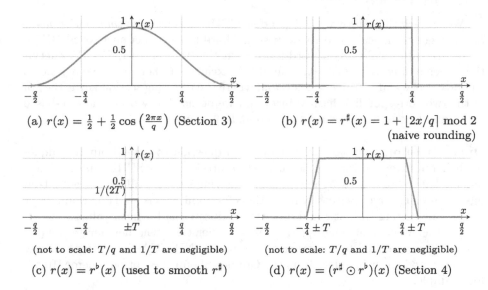

(a) $r(x) = \frac{1}{2} + \frac{1}{2}\cos\left(\frac{2\pi x}{q}\right)$ (Section 3)

(b) $r(x) = r^{\#}(x) = 1 + \lfloor 2x/q \rceil \bmod 2$
(naive rounding)

(not to scale: T/q and $1/T$ are negligible)

(c) $r(x) = r^{b}(x)$ (used to smooth $r^{\#}$)

(not to scale: T/q and $1/T$ are negligible)

(d) $r(x) = (r^{\#} \odot r^{b})(x)$ (Section 4)

Fig. 1. Probability that the rounding functions $R(x)$ of Sects. 3 and 4 output 1

This choice ensures universality as soon as just $1 \cdot c = c$ is far from the lattice Λ (Corollary 3.2 and Theorem 3.4).

This solution nevertheless only provides approximate correctness (correctness holds with probability $3/4 + o(1)$, see Lemma 3.3), which is also problematic for some applications. This can be solved using correctness amplification via error-correcting codes, but at the price of preventing the resulting SPHF to be word-independent.

Second solution (Imperfect Universality, Statistical Correctness, Sect. 4). In our second instantiation, we therefore proceed to construct an almost-square rounding function (see Fig. 1d, $\odot$ denotes the convolution operator), which offers statistical correctness[3] and imperfect universality (namely the probability that a prover knowing only $\mathsf{hp} = \boldsymbol{p}$ can guess the hash value H is at most $1/3 + o(1)$, as proved in Theorem 4.5). This instantiation requires a more subtle analysis, taking account of *destructive interferences*.

We can then amplify universality to get statistical universality (i.e., the above probability of guessing is at most $1/2 + \mathsf{negl}(n)$ as in our first solution) while keeping a statistical correctness. Contrary to the correctness amplification, this transformation preserves the independence of the projection key from the ciphertext. In particular, if the ciphertexts are from an IND-CPA scheme such as dual-Regev, then we get the first word-independent SPHF over a lattice-based language.

---

[3] More precisely, the probability of error is $\mathsf{poly}(n, \sigma)/q$, which is $\mathsf{negl}(n)$ for superpolynomial approximation factors q/σ.

We remark that our word-independent SPHF uses a *super-polynomial modulus* q, to get statistical correctness. It seems hard to construct such an SPHF for a polynomial modulus, as a word-independent SPHF for an IND-CPA encryption scheme directly yields a one-round key exchange (where each party sends a ciphertext of 0 and a projection key, and where the resulting session key is the xor of the two corresponding hash values) and we do not know of any lattice-based one-round key exchange using a polynomial modulus.

Open Question. We see as the main open question to extend our techniques to their full extent in the ring-setting. More precisely, our SPHF only produces one-bit hashes, and is easily extended to the ring-setting still asking with 1-bit hash values. This requires costly repetitions for applications, and one would hope that a ring setting variant could directly produce $\Theta(n)$-bit hash values.

Another important open question is to understand whether our techniques can further be refined to construct lattice-based IND-CCA encryption schemes without trapdoor, using ideas from the Cramer-Shoup encryption scheme [10,11] for example.

Road Map. We start by some preliminaries on lattices and SPHFs in Sect. 2. In particular, we define several variants of lattice-based (approximate) SPHFs (in particular universal bit-PHFs) and formally show various transformations which were only implicit in [22]. We also define the IND-CCA2 encryption scheme "à la Micciancio-Peikert" we will be using. In Sect. 3, we then show step-by-step how to construct an SPHF for IND-CCA2 ciphertexts à la Micciancio-Peikert and how to avoid the caveat of the construction of [22]. In Sect. 4, we construct a word-independent SPHF for ciphertexts under an IND-CPA scheme à la Micciancio-Peikert, when the modulus is super-polynomial. In Sect. 5, we conclude by exhibiting several applications.

Figure 2 summarizes our results and the paper road map. All the notions in this figure are formally defined in Sect. 2.

2   Preliminaries

2.1   Notations

The security parameter is denoted n. The notation $\mathrm{negl}(n)$ denotes any function f such that $f(n) = n^{-\omega(1)}$. For a probabilistic algorithm alg(inputs), we may explicit the randomness it uses with the notation alg(inputs; coins), otherwise the random coins are implicitly fresh.

Column vectors will be denoted by bold lower-case letters, e.g., $\boldsymbol{x}$, and matrices will be denoted by bold upper-case letters, e.g., $\boldsymbol{A}$. If $\boldsymbol{x}$ is vector and $\boldsymbol{A}$ is a matrix, $\boldsymbol{x}^t$ and $\boldsymbol{A}^t$ will denote their transpose. We use $[\boldsymbol{A}|\boldsymbol{B}]$ for the horizontal concatenation of matrices, and $[\boldsymbol{A}\,;\,\boldsymbol{B}] = [\boldsymbol{A}^t|\boldsymbol{B}^t]^t$ for the vertical concatenation. For $\boldsymbol{x} \in \mathbb{R}^m$, $\|\boldsymbol{x}\|$ will denote the canonical euclidean norm of $\boldsymbol{x}$. We will use $\mathcal{B}$ to denote the euclidean ball of radius 1, where, unless specifically

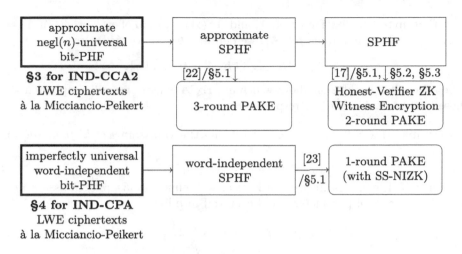

Fig. 2. Summary of results

stated otherwise, the ball is m-dimensional. If $\boldsymbol{x}, \boldsymbol{y} \in \mathbb{R}^m$, $\langle \boldsymbol{x}, \boldsymbol{y} \rangle$ will denote their canonical inner product, and $d(\boldsymbol{x}, \boldsymbol{y}) = \|\boldsymbol{x} - \boldsymbol{y}\|$ their distance. If $E \subset \mathbb{R}^m$ is countable and discrete, we will denote $d(\boldsymbol{x}, E) = \min_{\boldsymbol{y} \in E} d(\boldsymbol{x}, \boldsymbol{y})$. For a function $f \colon E \to \mathbb{C}$ or $f \colon E \to \mathbb{R}, f(E)$ will denote the sum $\sum_{x \in E} f(x)$. For $a, b \in \mathbb{R}$, $[a, b] = \{x \in \mathbb{R} \mid a \leq x \leq b\}$ will denote the closed real interval with endpoints a and b, $\lfloor a \rfloor, \lceil a \rceil$, and $\lfloor a \rceil$ will respectively denote the largest integer smaller than a, the smallest integer greater than a, and the closest integer to a (the largest one if there are two). The xor of two bit strings $a, b \in \{0, 1\}^k$ is denoted by $a \oplus b$. The cardinal of a finite set S is denoted $|S|$.

The modulus $q \in \mathbb{Z}$ will be taken as an odd prime, for simplicity.

2.2   Lattices and Gaussians

Lattices. An m-dimensional *lattice* Λ is a discrete subgroup of $\mathbb{R}^m$. Equivalently, Λ is a lattice if it can be written $\Lambda = \{\boldsymbol{B}\boldsymbol{s} \mid \boldsymbol{s} \in \mathbb{Z}^n\}$ where $n \leq m$, for some $\boldsymbol{B} \in \mathbb{R}^{m \times n}$, where the columns of $\boldsymbol{B}$ are linearly independent. In that case, $\boldsymbol{B}$ is called a *basis* of Λ. Then, we define the *determinant* of Λ as $\det(\Lambda) = \sqrt{\det(\boldsymbol{B}^t \boldsymbol{B})}$, which does not depend on the choice of the basis $\boldsymbol{B}$.

We define the *dual lattice* of Λ as

$$\Lambda^* = \{\boldsymbol{x} \in \mathrm{Span}_{\mathbb{R}}(\Lambda) \mid \forall \boldsymbol{y} \in \Lambda, \langle \boldsymbol{x}, \boldsymbol{y} \rangle \in \mathbb{Z}\}.$$

Recall the identity $(\Lambda^*)^* = \Lambda$. Given $\boldsymbol{A} \in \mathbb{Z}_q^{m \times n}$ where $m \geq n$, and modulus $q \geq 2$, we define the following q-ary lattices:

$$\Lambda(\boldsymbol{A}) = \{\boldsymbol{A}\boldsymbol{s} \mid \boldsymbol{s} \in \mathbb{Z}_q^n\} + q\mathbb{Z}^m, \quad \Lambda^{\perp}(\boldsymbol{A}) = \{\boldsymbol{h} \in \mathbb{Z}^m \mid \boldsymbol{h}^t \boldsymbol{A} = \boldsymbol{0}^t \bmod q\}.$$

Note that up to a scaling factor, $\Lambda(\boldsymbol{A})$ and $\Lambda^{\perp}(\boldsymbol{A})$ are dual of each other: $\Lambda(\boldsymbol{A}) = q \cdot \Lambda^{\perp}(\boldsymbol{A})^*$. For a syndrome $\boldsymbol{p} \in \mathbb{Z}_q^n$, we define the coset of $\Lambda^{\perp}(\boldsymbol{A})$:

$$\Lambda_{\boldsymbol{p}}^{\perp}(\boldsymbol{A}) = \{\boldsymbol{h} \in \mathbb{Z}^m \mid \boldsymbol{h}^t \boldsymbol{A} = \boldsymbol{p}^t \bmod q\}.$$

When there is no confusion about which matrix $\boldsymbol{A}$ is used, we will simply denote these lattices $\Lambda, \Lambda^{\perp}$, and $\Lambda_{\boldsymbol{p}}^{\perp}$ respectively.

Gaussians. If $s > 0$ and $\boldsymbol{c} \in \mathbb{R}^m$, we define the *Gaussian weight function* on $\mathbb{R}^m$ as

$$\rho_{s,\boldsymbol{c}} \colon \boldsymbol{x} \mapsto \exp(-\pi \|\boldsymbol{x} - \boldsymbol{c}\|^2 / s^2).$$

Similarly, if Λ is an m-dimensional lattice, we define the *discrete Gaussian distribution* over Λ, of parameter s and centered in $\boldsymbol{c}$ by:

$$\forall \boldsymbol{x} \in \Lambda, \; D_{\Lambda,s,\boldsymbol{c}}(\boldsymbol{x}) = \frac{\rho_{s,\boldsymbol{c}}(x)}{\rho_{s,\boldsymbol{c}}(\Lambda)}.$$

When $\boldsymbol{c} = \boldsymbol{0}$, we will simply write ρ_s and $D_{\Lambda,s}$. We recall the tail-bound of Banaszczyk for discrete Gaussians:

Lemma 2.1 ([3, Lemma 1.5], **as stated in** [28, Lemma 2.10]). *For any $c > 1/\sqrt{2\pi}, m$-dimensional lattice Λ and any vector $\boldsymbol{v} \in \mathbb{R}^m$:*

$$\rho_s(\Lambda \setminus sc\sqrt{m}\mathcal{B}) \leq C^m \rho_s(\Lambda), \qquad \rho_s((\Lambda + \boldsymbol{v}) \setminus sc\sqrt{m}\mathcal{B}) \leq 2C^m \rho_s(\Lambda).$$

where $C = c\sqrt{2\pi e} \cdot e^{-\pi c^2} < 1$.

An important quantity associated to a lattice is its *smoothing parameter*, introduced by Micciancio and Regev [28]:

Definition 2.2 (Smoothing parameter [28]). *For $\epsilon > 0$, the smoothing parameter of a lattice Λ, denoted $\eta_{\epsilon}(\Lambda)$, is the smallest $s > 0$ such that $\rho_{1/s}(\Lambda^* \setminus \{0\}) \leq \epsilon$.*

The following lemma states that if the parameter of the discrete Gaussian is above the smoothing parameter of the lattice, then the Gaussian weight of the cosets of Λ are essentially the same:

Lemma 2.3 [29, Claim 3.8]. *For any lattice $\Lambda \subset \mathbb{R}^m, \boldsymbol{c} \in \mathbb{R}^m$, and $s \geq \eta_{\epsilon}(\Lambda)$:*

$$(1 - \epsilon)s^m \det(\Lambda^*) \leq \rho_s(\Lambda + \boldsymbol{c}) \leq (1 + \epsilon)s^m \det(\Lambda^*).$$

The smoothing parameter of the dual of a random q-ary lattice can be controlled using the following:

Lemma 2.4 (Corollary of [27, Lemma 2.4]). *Fix parameters n, q a prime, and $m \geq \Theta(n \log q)$. Let $\epsilon \geq 2^{-O(n)}$ and $s > 2\eta_{\epsilon}(\mathbb{Z}^m)$. Fix $0 < \delta \leq 1$. Then, for $\boldsymbol{A}$ uniformly random in $\mathbb{Z}_q^{m \times n}$, we have $s \geq \eta_{2\epsilon/\delta}(\Lambda^{\perp}(\boldsymbol{A}))$ except with probability at most δ over the choice of $\boldsymbol{A}$.*

To instantiate the above, we recall the smoothing parameter of $\mathbb{Z}^m$.

Lemma 2.5 (Corollary of [28, Lemma 3.3]). *For all integer $m \geq 1, \epsilon \in (0, 1/2)$, the smoothing parameter of $\mathbb{Z}^m$ satisfies $\eta_{\epsilon}(\mathbb{Z}^m) \leq C\sqrt{\log(m/\epsilon)}$ for some universal constant $C > 0$.*

Harmonic analysis. Let us recall the exponential basis of periodic functions and their vectorial analogues:

$$e_x : y \mapsto \exp(2i\pi xy), \qquad e_x : y \mapsto \exp(2i\pi \langle x, y \rangle).$$

The Fourier transform of $f : \mathbb{R}^m \to \mathbb{C}$ is defined by:

$$\hat{f}(\xi) = \int_{\mathbb{R}^m} f(x) e^{-2i\pi \langle x, \xi \rangle} dx.$$

The Fourier transform of the Gaussian weight function ρ_s is $\hat{\rho}_s = s^m \rho_{1/s}$. Recall the time-shift-phase-shift identity: if $g(x) = f(x) e_z(x)$ for some $z \in \mathbb{R}^m$, then $\hat{g}(\xi) = \hat{f}(\xi - z)$. Similarly, if $g(x) = f(x + t)$ for some $t \in \mathbb{R}^m$, then $\hat{g}(\xi) = \hat{f}(\xi) e_t(\xi)$. For two functions $f, g : \mathbb{R}^m \to \mathbb{C}$, we will denote by $f \odot g$ their convolution product:

$$f \odot g(x) = \int_{\mathbb{R}^m} f(y) g(x - y) dy.$$

The Fourier transform turns convolutions into pointwise products, and conversely:

$$\widehat{f \odot g}(\xi) = \hat{f}(\xi) \cdot \hat{g}(\xi), \qquad \widehat{f \cdot g}(\xi) = \hat{f}(\xi) \odot \hat{g}(\xi).$$

Finally, let us recall the Poisson summation formula:

Lemma 2.6 (Poisson summation formula). *For any lattice Λ and $f : \mathbb{R}^m \to \mathbb{C}$, we have $f(\Lambda) = \det(\Lambda^*) \hat{f}(\Lambda^*)$.*

Learning with Errors

Definition 2.7 (Learning with Errors (LWE)). *Let $q \geq 2$, and χ be a distribution over $\mathbb{Z}$. The Learning with Errors problem $\mathrm{LWE}_{\chi,q}$ consists in, given polynomially many samples, distinguishing the two following distributions:*

- *$(a, \langle a, s \rangle + e)$, where a is uniform in $\mathbb{Z}_q^n$, $e \leftarrow \chi$, and $s \in \mathbb{Z}_q^n$ is a fixed secret chosen uniformly,*
- *(a, b), where a is uniform in $\mathbb{Z}_q^n$, and b is uniform in $\mathbb{Z}_q$.*

In [29], Regev showed that for $\chi = D_{\mathbb{Z},\sigma}$, for any $\sigma \geq 2\sqrt{n}$, and q such that $q/\sigma = \mathrm{poly}(n)$, $\mathrm{LWE}_{\chi,q}$ is at least as hard as solving worst-case SIVP for polynomial approximation factors.

Trapdoor for LWE. Throughout this paper, we will use the trapdoors introduced in [27] to build our public matrix A. Define $g_A(s, e) = As + e$, let $G^t = I_n \otimes g^t$, where $g^t = [1, 2, \ldots, 2^k]$ and $k = \lceil \log q \rceil - 1$, and let $H \in \mathbb{Z}_q^{n \times n}$ be invertible.

Lemma 2.8 [27, Theorems 5.1 and 5.4]. *There exist two PPT algorithms* TrapGen *and* $g_{(\cdot)}^{-1}$ *with the following properties assuming $q \geq 2$ and $m \geq \Theta(n \log q)$:*

- TrapGen($1^n, 1^m, q$) *outputs* $(\boldsymbol{T}, \boldsymbol{A}_0)$, *where the distribution of the matrix* $\boldsymbol{A}_0$ *is at negligible statistical distance from uniform in* $\mathbb{Z}_q^{m \times n}$, *and such that* $\boldsymbol{T}\boldsymbol{A}_0 = \boldsymbol{0}$, *where* $s_1(\boldsymbol{T}) \le O(\sqrt{m})$ *and where* $s_1(\boldsymbol{T})$ *is the operator norm of* $\boldsymbol{T}$, *which is defined as* $\max_{\boldsymbol{x} \neq 0} \|\boldsymbol{T}\boldsymbol{x}\|/\|\boldsymbol{x}\|$.[4]
- *Let* $(\boldsymbol{T}, \boldsymbol{A}_0) \leftarrow$ TrapGen($1^n, 1^m, q$). *Let* $\boldsymbol{A}_H = \boldsymbol{A}_0 + [\boldsymbol{0}\,;\,\boldsymbol{GH}]$ *for some invertible matrix* $\boldsymbol{H}$ *called a* tag. *Then, we have* $\boldsymbol{T}\boldsymbol{A}_H = \boldsymbol{GH}$. *Furthermore, if* $\boldsymbol{x} \in \mathbb{Z}_q^m$ *can be written as* $\boldsymbol{A}_H \boldsymbol{s} + \boldsymbol{e}$ *where* $\|\boldsymbol{e}\| \le B' := q/\Theta(\sqrt{m})$, *then* $g_{\boldsymbol{A}_H}^{-1}(\boldsymbol{T}, \boldsymbol{x}, \boldsymbol{H})$ *outputs* $(\boldsymbol{s}, \boldsymbol{e})$.

More precisely, to sample $(\boldsymbol{T}, \boldsymbol{A}_0)$ with TrapGen, we sample a uniform $\bar{\boldsymbol{A}} \in \mathbb{Z}_q^{\bar{m} \times n}$ where $\bar{m} = m - nk = \Theta(n \log q)$, and some $\boldsymbol{R} \leftarrow \mathcal{D}^{nk \times \bar{m}}$, where the distribution $\mathcal{D}^{nk \times \bar{m}}$ assigns probability $1/2$ to 0, and $1/4$ to ± 1. We output $\boldsymbol{T} = [-\boldsymbol{R} \,|\, \boldsymbol{I}_{nk}]$ along with $\boldsymbol{A}_0 = [\bar{\boldsymbol{A}}\,;\,\boldsymbol{R}\bar{\boldsymbol{A}}]$. Then, given a tag $\boldsymbol{H}$, we have: $\boldsymbol{T}(\boldsymbol{A}_0 + [\boldsymbol{0}\,;\,\boldsymbol{GH}]) = \boldsymbol{GH}$.

Tag-IND-CCA2 LWE Encryption à la Micciancio-Peikert. For our applications, we will need a (labelled) encryption scheme that is IND-CCA2. This can be built generically and efficiently from a tag-IND-CCA2 encryption scheme. The formal definitions and the latter transformation are recalled in the full version [6]. Below, we describe a simplified variant of the scheme of [27, Sect. 6.3].

For this scheme, we assume q to be an odd prime. We set an encoding function for messages $\mathsf{Encode}(\mu \in \{0,1\}) = \mu \cdot (0, \ldots 0, \lceil q/2 \rceil)^t$. Note that $2 \cdot \mathsf{Encode}(\mu) = (0, \ldots, 0, \mu)^t \bmod q$.

Let $\mathcal{R}$ be a ring with a subset $\mathcal{U} \subset \mathcal{R}^{\times}$ of invertible elements, of size 2^n, and with the *unit differences* property: if $u_1 \neq u_2 \in \mathcal{U}$, then $u_1 - u_2$ is invertible in $\mathcal{R}$. Let h be an injective ring homomorphism from $\mathcal{R}$ to $\mathbb{Z}_q^{n \times n}$ (see [27, Sects. 6.1 and 6.3] for an explicit construction). Note that if $u_1 \neq u_2 \in \mathcal{U}$, then $h(u_1 - u_2)$ is invertible, and thus an appropriate tag $\boldsymbol{H} = h(u_1 - u_2)$ for the trapdoor.

Let $(\boldsymbol{T}, \boldsymbol{A}_0) \leftarrow$ TrapGen($1^n, 1^m, q$). The public encryption key is $\mathsf{ek} = \boldsymbol{A}_0$, and the secret decryption key is $\mathsf{dk} = \boldsymbol{T}$.

- $\mathsf{Encrypt}(\mathsf{ek} = \boldsymbol{A}_0,\ u \in \mathcal{U},\ \mu \in \{0,1\})$ encrypts the message μ under the public key ek and for the tag u, as follows: Let $\boldsymbol{A}_u = \boldsymbol{A}_0 + [\boldsymbol{0}\,;\,\boldsymbol{G}h(u)]$. Pick $\boldsymbol{s} \in \mathbb{Z}_q^n$, $\boldsymbol{e} \leftarrow D_{\mathbb{Z},t}^m$ where $t = \sigma\sqrt{m} \cdot \omega(\sqrt{\log n})$. Restart if $\|\boldsymbol{e}\| > B$, where $B := 2t\sqrt{m}$.[5] Output the ciphertext:

$$c = \boldsymbol{A}_u \boldsymbol{s} + \boldsymbol{e} + \mathsf{Encode}(\mu) \bmod q.$$

---

[4] The bound on $s_1(\boldsymbol{T})$ holds except with probability at most 2^{-n} in the original construction, but for convenience we assume the algorithm restarts if it does not hold.

[5] This happens only with exponentially small probability $2^{-\Theta(n)}$ by Lemma 2.1.

- Decrypt(dk $= T$, $u \in \mathcal{U}$, $c \in \mathbb{Z}_q^m$) decrypts the ciphertext c for the tag u using the decryption key dk as follows: Output[6]

$$\begin{cases} \mu & \text{if } g_{A_u}^{-1}(T, 2c, h(u)) = 2e + (0, \dots, 0, \mu) \text{ where } e \in \mathbb{Z}^m \text{ and } \|e\| \leq B', \\ \perp & \text{otherwise.} \end{cases}$$

Since $\lceil q/2 \rceil$ is the inverse of 2 mod q, we have:

$$\mu' := \text{Decrypt}(T, u, c) \neq \perp \quad \Longleftrightarrow \quad d(c - \text{Encode}(\mu'), \Lambda(A_u)) < B'.$$

Suppose that $m \geq \Theta(n \log q)$. Note that $d(\text{Encode}(1), \Lambda(A_u)) > B'$ simultaneously for all u with overwhelming probability over the randomness of TrapGen (using a union bound, as in [14, Lemma 5.3] for instance). Then, by Lemma 2.8, the scheme is correct as long as $B \leq B'$, or equivalently $\sigma m^{3/2} \cdot \omega(\sqrt{\log n}) \leq q$.

Theorem 2.9. *Assume $m \geq \Theta(n \log q)$. The above scheme is tag-IND-CCA2 assuming the hardness of the $LWE_{\chi,q}$ problem for $\chi = D_{\mathbb{Z},\sigma}$.*

The precise definition for tag-IND-CCA2 and the proof of the above theorem are provided in the full version [6].

Remark 2.10. If a constant tag u is hardcoded in Encrypt and Decrypt, then the resulting encryption scheme is just an IND-CPA scheme using trapdoors from [27].

Lemma 2.11. *Assume $m \geq \Theta(n \log q)$. With A_0 sampled as above, except with probability 2^{-n}, it holds that for all $u \in \mathcal{U}, \eta_{2^{-n}}(\Lambda^{\perp}(A_u)) \leq C\sqrt{n}$ for some universal constant C.*

Proof. Note that A_0 is (about) uniform under the randomness of TrapGen, and so is A_u for a fixed $u \in \mathcal{U}$. Apply Lemmas 2.4 and 2.5 with $\epsilon = 8^{-n}/2$ and $\delta = 4^{-n}$ to A_u, ensuring that $\eta_{2^{-n}}(\Lambda^{\perp}(A_u)) \leq C\sqrt{n}$ except with probability δ. Conclude by the union bound over the 2^n elements $u \in \mathcal{U}$. $\quad\square$

2.3 Approximate Smooth Projective Hash Functions

We consider approximate smooth projective hash functions (approximate SPHFs) defined in [22].

Languages. We consider a family of languages $(\mathscr{L}_{\text{lpar,ltrap}})_{\text{lpar,ltrap}}$ indexed by some *parameter* lpar and some *trapdoor* ltrap, together with a family of NP languages $(\widetilde{\mathscr{L}}_{\text{lpar}})_{\text{lpar}}$ indexed by some parameter lpar, with witness relation $\widetilde{\mathscr{R}}_{\text{lpar}}$, such that:

$$\widetilde{\mathscr{L}}_{\text{lpar}} = \{x \in \mathcal{X}_{\text{lpar}} \mid \exists w, \ \widetilde{\mathscr{R}}_{\text{lpar}}(x, w) = 1\} \subseteq \mathscr{L}_{\text{lpar,ltrap}} \subseteq \mathcal{X}_{\text{lpar}},$$

---

[6] Note that the inversion algorithm $g_{(\cdot)}^{-1}$ can succeed even if $\|e\| > B'$, depending on the randomness of the trapdoor. It is crucial to reject decryption nevertheless when $\|e\| > B'$ to ensure CCA2 security. We also recall that $B' := q/\Theta(\sqrt{m})$.

where $(\mathcal{X}_{\mathsf{lpar}})_{\mathsf{lpar}}$ is a family of sets. The trapdoor ltrap and the parameter lpar are generated by a polynomial-time algorithm Setup.lpar which takes as input a unary representation of the security parameter n. We suppose that membership in $\mathcal{X}_{\mathsf{lpar}}$ and $\widetilde{\mathcal{R}}_{\mathsf{lpar}}$ can be checked in polynomial time given lpar and that membership in $\mathcal{L}_{\mathsf{lpar},\mathsf{ltrap}}$ can be checked in polynomial time given lpar and ltrap. The parameters lpar and ltrap are often omitted when they are clear from context.

We are mostly interested in languages of ciphertexts.

Example 2.12 (Languages of Ciphertexts). Let (KeyGen, Encrypt, Decrypt) be a labeled encryption scheme. We define the following languages (Setup.lpar = KeyGen and (ltrap, lpar) = (dk, ek)):

$$\widetilde{\mathcal{L}} = \{(\mathsf{label}, C, M) \mid \exists \rho, \; C = \mathsf{Encrypt}(\mathsf{ek}, \mathsf{label}, M; \rho)\},$$
$$\mathcal{L} = \{(\mathsf{label}, C, M) \mid \mathsf{Decrypt}(\mathsf{dk}, \mathsf{label}, C) = M\},$$

where the witness relation $\widetilde{\mathcal{R}}$ is implicitly defined as: $\widetilde{\mathcal{R}}((\mathsf{label}, C, M), \rho) = 1$ if and only if $C = \mathsf{Encrypt}(\mathsf{ek}, \mathsf{label}, M; \rho)$.

Approximate SPHFs. Let us now define approximate SPHFs following [22].

Definition 2.13. *Let* $(\widetilde{\mathcal{L}}_{\mathsf{lpar}} \subseteq \mathcal{L}_{\mathsf{lpar},\mathsf{ltrap}} \subseteq \mathcal{X}_{\mathsf{lpar}})_{\mathsf{lpar},\mathsf{ltrap}}$ *be languages defined as above. An approximate smooth projective hash function (SPHF) for these languages is defined by four probabilistic polynomial-time algorithms:*

- HashKG(lpar) *generates a hashing key* hk *for the language parameter* lpar;
- ProjKG(hk, lpar, x) *derives a projection key* hp *from the hashing key* hk, *the language parameter* lpar, *and the word* x;
- Hash(hk, lpar, x) *outputs a hash value* H $\in \{0,1\}^{\nu}$ *(for some positive integer* $\nu = \Omega(n)$*) from the hashing key* hk, *for the word* $x \in \mathcal{X}_{\mathsf{lpar}}$ *and the language parameter* lpar;
- ProjHash(hp, lpar, x, w) *outputs a projected hash value* pH $\in \{0,1\}^{\nu}$ *from the projection key* hp, *and the witness* w, *for the word* $x \in \widetilde{\mathcal{L}}_{\mathsf{lpar}}$ *(i.e.,* $\widetilde{\mathcal{R}}_{\mathsf{lpar}}(x, w) = 1$*) and the language parameter* lpar;

which satisfy the following properties:

- **Approximate correctness.** *For any* $n \in \mathbb{N}$, *if* (ltrap, lpar) $\leftarrow$ Setup.lpar(1^n), *with overwhelming probability over the randomness of* Setup.lpar, *for any* $x \in \widetilde{\mathcal{L}}_{\mathsf{lpar},\mathsf{ltrap}}$ *(and associated witness* w*), the value* H *output by* Hash(hk, lpar, x) *is approximately determined by* ProjKG(hk, lpar, x) *relative to the Hamming metric. More precisely, writing* $\mathsf{HW}(a,b)$ *the Hamming distance between two strings* $a, b \in \{0,1\}^{\nu}$, *the SPHF is* ϵ-correct, *if:*

$$\Pr_{\mathsf{hk}} \left[\mathsf{HW}(\mathsf{Hash}(\mathsf{hk}, \mathsf{lpar}, x), \mathsf{ProjHash}(\mathsf{hp}, \mathsf{lpar}, x, w)) > \epsilon \cdot \nu \right] = \mathsf{negl}(n),$$

where the probability is taken over the choice of hk $\leftarrow$ HashKG(lpar) *and the random coins of* Hash *and* ProjHash.[7]

---

[7] Contrary to previously known SPHFs, some of our SPHFs have randomized algorithms Hash and ProjHash.

– **Smoothness.** *For any $n \in \mathbb{N}$, if $(\mathsf{ltrap}, \mathsf{lpar}) \leftarrow \mathsf{Setup.lpar}(1^n)$, with overwhelming probability over the randomness of $\mathsf{Setup.lpar}$, for all $\chi \in \mathcal{X} \setminus \mathscr{L}_{\mathsf{lpar}}$ the following distributions have statistical distance negligible in n:*

$$\left\{ (\mathsf{lpar}, \chi, \mathsf{hp}, \mathsf{H}) \; \middle| \; \begin{array}{l} \mathsf{hk} \leftarrow \mathsf{HashKG}(\mathsf{lpar}), \; \mathsf{H} \leftarrow \mathsf{Hash}(\mathsf{hk}, \mathsf{lpar}, \chi), \\ \mathsf{hp} = \mathsf{ProjKG}(\mathsf{hk}, \mathsf{lpar}, \chi) \end{array} \right\},$$

$$\left\{ (\mathsf{lpar}, \chi, \mathsf{hp}, \mathsf{H}) \; \middle| \; \begin{array}{l} \mathsf{hk} \leftarrow \mathsf{HashKG}(\mathsf{lpar}), \; \mathsf{H} \leftarrow \{0,1\}^\nu, \\ \mathsf{hp} = \mathsf{ProjKG}(\mathsf{hk}, \mathsf{lpar}, \chi) \end{array} \right\}.$$

Finally, an approximate SPHF is called an SPHF if it is 0-correct. In that case, we also say that the SPHF is *statistically correct*.

Approximate Word-Independent SPHFs. For some applications, in particular the one-round PAKE from [23], a stronger notion of SPHF is required, where the projection key hp does not depend on the word χ and the smoothness holds even if the word is chosen adaptively after seeing the projection key. We call such SPHFs approximate word-independent SPHFs and we formally define them in the full version [6].

Approximate Universal Bit-PHFs. Instead of directly building (approximate) (word-independent) SPHF, we actually build what we call (approximate) (word-independent) universal bit-PHF.

Definition 2.14. *An approximate universal bit projective hash function (bit-PHF) is defined as in Definition 2.13 except that the hash values are bits ($\nu = 1$), and that approximate correctness and smoothness are replaced by the following properties:*

– **Approximate correctness.** *The bit-PHF is ϵ-correct if for any $n \in \mathbb{N}$, if $(\mathsf{ltrap}, \mathsf{lpar}) \leftarrow \mathsf{Setup.lpar}(1^n)$, with overwhelming probability over the randomness of $\mathsf{Setup.lpar}$, for any $\chi \in \widetilde{\mathscr{L}}_{\mathsf{lpar}, \mathsf{ltrap}}$:*

$$\Pr_{\mathsf{hk}} \left[\mathsf{Hash}(\mathsf{hk}, \mathsf{lpar}, \chi) = \mathsf{ProjHash}(\mathsf{hp}, \mathsf{lpar}, \chi, w) \right] \geq 1 - \epsilon,$$

where the probability is taken over the choice of $\mathsf{hk} \leftarrow \mathsf{HashKG}(\mathsf{lpar})$ and the random coins of Hash and $\mathsf{ProjHash}$.

– **Universality.**[8] *The bit-PHF is ϵ-universal if, for any $n \in \mathbb{N}$, if $(\mathsf{ltrap}, \mathsf{lpar}) \leftarrow \mathsf{Setup.lpar}(1^n)$, with overwhelming probability over the randomness of $\mathsf{Setup.lpar}$, for any word $\chi \in \mathcal{X} \setminus \mathscr{L}_{\mathsf{lpar}}$, any projection key hp:*

$$\left| 2 \cdot \Pr_{\mathsf{hk}} \left[\mathsf{Hash}(\mathsf{hk}, \mathsf{lpar}, \chi) = 1 \mid \mathsf{hp} = \mathsf{ProjKG}(\mathsf{hk}, \mathsf{lpar}, \chi) \right] - 1 \right| \leq \epsilon,$$

where the probability is taken over the choice of $\mathsf{hk} \leftarrow \mathsf{HashKG}(\mathsf{lpar})$ and the random coins of Hash. The bit-PHF is said to be statistically universal *if it is $\mathsf{negl}(n)$-universal. Otherwise, the bit-PHF is said to be* imperfectly universal.

---

[8] Our definition of universality is equivalent to the one of Cramer and Shoup in [11], up to the use of language parameters.

An approximate bit-PHF is called a bit-PHF if it is negl(n)-correct. In that case, the bit-PHF is said to be *statistically correct*. Furthermore, an (approximate) bit-PHF is called an (approximate) (word-independent) bit-PHF, if hp does not depend on the word χ.

From Bit-PHFs to SPHFs. In the full version [6], we show how to generically convert an approximate ϵ-correct negl(n)-universal bit-PHF into an approximate ($\epsilon + \epsilon'$)-correct SPHF (for any positive constant ϵ') and then into an SPHF. This is used in our first construction in Sect. 3. These transformations were implicit in [22]. We should point out that even if the original bit-PHF was word-independent, the resulting (approximate) SPHF would still not be word-independent: its projection key depends on the word χ. If there was way to avoid this restriction, we actually would get the first one-round key exchange based on LWE with polynomial modulus.

In the full version [6], we also show how to generically convert an ϵ-universal *word-independent* bit-PHF into a *word-independent* SPHF, by amplifying the smoothness or universality property (assuming $1 - \epsilon \geq 1/\operatorname{poly}(n)$). We should point out that the original word-independent bit-PHF is supposed to be statistically correct, contrary to the previous transformation where it could just be approximately correct.

We recall that the above transformations were summarized in Fig. 2 together with our results.

3   SPHF for IND-CCA2 Ciphertexts

As we have shown in Sect. 2.3, there exists a generic transformation from approximate bit-PHF to a regular approximate SPHF or even classical SPHF. So, in this section, we are going to focus on building such an approximate bit-PHF. For the sake of simplicity, in this section we often call such an approximate bit-PHF simply a bit-PHF.

3.1   Languages and Natural Bit-PHF

Languages. We want to construct an (approximate) bit-PHF for the language of ciphertexts (Example 2.12) for our IND-CCA2 LWE encryption à la Micciancio-Peikert described in Sect. 2.2. More generally our approach works with typical trapdoored LWE encryption schemes [9,14].

We first remark that it is sufficient to construct a bit-PHF for the tag-IND-CCA2 version, i.e., for the following languages:

$$\widetilde{\mathscr{L}} = \{(u, \boldsymbol{c}, \mu) \mid \exists \boldsymbol{s}, \boldsymbol{e}, \ \boldsymbol{c} \leftarrow \mathsf{Encrypt}(\boldsymbol{A}_0, u, \mu; \boldsymbol{s}, \boldsymbol{e})\}$$
$$\subseteq \{(u, \boldsymbol{c}, \mu) \mid d(\boldsymbol{c} - \mathsf{Encode}(\mu), \ \varLambda(\boldsymbol{A}_u)) \leq B\},$$
$$\mathscr{L} = \{(u, \boldsymbol{c}, \mu) \mid \mathsf{Decrypt}(\boldsymbol{T}, u, \boldsymbol{c}) = \mu\}$$
$$= \{(u, \boldsymbol{c}, \mu) \mid d(\boldsymbol{c} - \mathsf{Encode}(\mu), \ \varLambda(\boldsymbol{A}_u)) \leq B'\},$$

where $u \in \mathcal{U}, c \in \mathbb{Z}_q^m, \mu \in \{0, 1\}$, $(\mathsf{ltrap}, \mathsf{lpar}) = (T, A_0) \leftarrow \mathsf{TrapGen}(1^n, 1^m, q) =$ $\mathsf{Setup.lpar}(1^n)$, and where $\mathsf{Encrypt}, \mathsf{Decrypt}, B$, and B' are defined in Sect. 2.2. Indeed, the signature parts, used to transform the tag-IND-CCA2 encryption scheme into a labeled IND-CCA2 encryption scheme (see the full version [6]), can be publicly checked by anyone, therefore one can generically adapt the bit-PHF by overriding Hash to a fresh uniform random value when the signature is invalid.

We can now fix the tag $u \in \mathcal{U}$ for the rest of this section, and will simply denote A for A_u and Λ for $\Lambda(A_u)$. Also, note that $(u, c, 1) \in \widetilde{\mathscr{L}}$ (resp. $\mathscr{L}$) is equivalent to $(u, c - \mathsf{Encode}(1), 0) \in \widetilde{\mathscr{L}}$ (resp $\mathscr{L}$). Therefore we can focus only on the languages of ciphertexts of 0 for a fixed tag u, and we restrict our languages to

$$\widetilde{\mathscr{L}} = \{c \in \mathbb{Z}_q^m \mid \exists s, e, \ c \leftarrow \mathsf{Encrypt}(A_0, 0, u; s, e)\} \subseteq \{c \in \mathbb{Z}_q^m \mid d(c, \Lambda) \leq B\},$$
$$\mathscr{L} = \{c \in \mathbb{Z}_q^m \mid \mathsf{Decrypt}(T, c, u) = 0\} \qquad = \{c \in \mathbb{Z}_q^m \mid d(c, \Lambda) \leq B'\},$$

for the rest of this section.

Natural Bit-PHF. A natural approach to define an approximate bit-PHF is the following:

- $\mathsf{HashKG}(A)$ outputs $\mathsf{hk} = h \leftarrow D_{\mathbb{Z}, s}^m$;
- $\mathsf{ProjKG}(h, A)$ outputs $\mathsf{hp} = p = A^t h$;
- $\mathsf{Hash}(h, A, c)$ outputs $\mathsf{H} = R(\langle h, c \rangle)$;
- $\mathsf{ProjHash}(p, A, c, (s, e))$ outputs $\mathsf{pH} = R(\langle p, s \rangle)$;

where R is a *rounding* function to be chosen later and $s > 0$ is a parameter to be chosen later too.

3.2 Universality

Naive Approach. For now let us just assume $R : \mathbb{Z}_q \to \mathbb{Z}_2$ to be the usual rounding function $R(x) = \lfloor 2x/q \rceil \bmod 2$, as in [22]. We have:

$$\langle h, c \rangle = h^t(As + e) = \langle p, s \rangle + \langle h, e \rangle \approx \langle p, s \rangle,$$

which guarantees correctness whenever $c \in \widetilde{\mathscr{L}}$. Indeed $\langle h, c \rangle$ is almost uniform for large enough parameter s, therefore $R(\langle h, c \rangle) = R(\langle p, s \rangle)$ will hold except with probability $\approx 2|\langle h, e \rangle|/q$.

For universality, we need to prove that $\mathsf{Hash}(h, A, c) = \langle h, c \rangle$ is uniform given the knowledge of A, p and c, when $c \notin \mathscr{L}$. Unfortunately, this seems to require a stronger assumption than $c \notin \mathscr{L}$, more precisely, that $j \cdot c \notin \mathscr{L}$ for all $j \in \mathbb{Z}_q^*$: this is the key lemma [14, Lemma 5.3] (from [22, Lemma 2]).

The caveat is that it is necessary not only for c to be far from Λ, but also for all its non-zero multiples modulo q: the language is extended to $\mathscr{L}' = \{c \mid \exists j \in \mathbb{Z}_q^*, jc \in \mathscr{L}\}$. Algorithmically, the price to pay is that the decryption function must be changed, and that the usual LWE decryption now must be attempted for each multiple jc of c to ensure universality for words outside $\mathscr{L}'$. This makes the new decryption very inefficient since q is typically quite a large $\text{poly}(n)$. This change of language is also a technical hassle for constructing protocols above the bit-PHF (or the resulting SPHF).

Note that the key lemma ensures uniformity of $\langle h, c \rangle$, while we only need the uniformity of $R(\langle h, c \rangle)$. We show in the technical overview of the introduction that this condition is truly necessary and is not an artifact of the proof, at least for $j = 3$ by considering $c = As + (0, \ldots, 0, q/3)^t$ (with q assumed to be divisible by 3 for the sake of simplicity).

But what should happen in more general cases?

Harmonic Analysis. Let us fix $p \in \mathbb{Z}_q^n$ and $c \in \mathbb{Z}_q^m$. For the rest of the section, we restrict the rounding function R to have binary values $\{0, 1\}$, yet this function may be probabilistic.

We want to study the conditional probability $P = \Pr[R(\langle h, c \rangle) = 1 \mid h^t A = p^t]$, where the probability is taken over the randomness of R and the distribution of h (conditioned on $h^t A = p^t$); we want P to be not too far from $1/2$ when $c \notin \mathscr{L}$. For $x \in \mathbb{Z}$, denote by $r(x)$ the probability that $R(x \bmod q) = 1$. Because $r : \mathbb{Z} \to [0, 1]$ is q-periodic, it can be interpolated over the reals by a function of the form:

$$r = \sum_{j \in \mathbb{Z}_q} \hat{r}_j \cdot e_{j/q},$$

where the complex values $\hat{r}_j \in \mathbb{C}$ are the Fourier coefficients of $r : \mathbb{Z} \to [0, 1]$. Note that as we are only interested in the restriction of r on $\mathbb{Z}$ (which is q-periodic), we only need q harmonics to fully describe r. Also note that $r(x) \in [0, 1]$ for all $x \in \mathbb{Z}_q$, so that $|\hat{r}_j| \leq 1$ for all j.

We rewrite:

$$P = \sum_{h \in \Lambda_p^\perp} \frac{\rho_s(h)}{\rho_s(\Lambda_p^\perp)} \cdot r(\langle h, c \rangle) = \frac{1}{\rho_s(\Lambda_p^\perp)} \sum_{j \in \mathbb{Z}_q} \hat{r}_j \sum_{h \in \Lambda^\perp} (\rho_s \cdot e_{jc/q})(h + h_0),$$

where h_0 is any vector of the coset $\Lambda_p^\perp$. We will now apply the Poisson Summation Formula (Lemma 2.6): $f(\Lambda^\perp) = \det((\Lambda^\perp)^*)\hat{f}((\Lambda^\perp)^*) = \det(\frac{1}{q}\Lambda)\hat{f}(\frac{1}{q}\Lambda)$. Set $f(h) = (\rho_s \cdot e_{jc/q})(h + h_0)$. We have:

$$\hat{f} = \widehat{\rho_s \cdot e_v} \cdot e_{h_0} = s^m \rho_{1/s, v} \cdot e_{h_0}.$$

We proceed:

$$P = \frac{\det((\Lambda^\perp)^*)s^m}{\rho_s(\Lambda_p^\perp)} \sum_{j \in \mathbb{Z}_q} \hat{r}_j \cdot (\rho_{1/s, jc/q} \cdot e_{h_0})\left(\frac{1}{q}\Lambda\right)$$

$$P = \frac{\det((\Lambda^\perp)^*)s^m}{\rho_s(\Lambda_p^\perp)} \sum_{j \in \mathbb{Z}_q} \hat{r}_j \cdot \sum_{y \in \Lambda}(\rho_{q/s, jc} \cdot e_{h_0/q})(y).$$

Assuming $s \geq \eta_\epsilon(\Lambda^\perp)$ for some negligible ϵ ensures that $\frac{\det((\Lambda^\perp)^*)s^m}{\rho_s(\Lambda_p^\perp)} = 1 + O(\epsilon)$ by Lemma 2.3. We shall split the sum into three parts:

- $j = 0, \boldsymbol{y} = \boldsymbol{0}$, contributing exactly $\hat{r}_0$ (where $\hat{r}_0 = \frac{1}{q}\sum_{x \in \mathbb{Z}_q} r(x) \in [0, 1]$),
- $j = 0, \boldsymbol{y} \neq \boldsymbol{0}$, contributing at most $|\hat{r}_0|\rho_{q/s}(\Lambda \setminus \{\boldsymbol{0}\})$ in absolute value,
- $j \neq 0$, contributing at most $|\hat{r}_j|\rho_{q/s}(\Lambda - j\boldsymbol{c})$ in absolute value for each j.

We can now bound P:

$$\left|\frac{P}{1 - O(\epsilon)} - \hat{r}_0\right| \leq |\hat{r}_0|\rho_{q/s}(\Lambda \setminus \{\boldsymbol{0}\}) + \sum_{j \in \mathbb{Z}_q \setminus \{0\}} |\hat{r}_j|\rho_{q/s}(\Lambda - j\boldsymbol{c}).$$

We now want to bound the right-hand side using Lemma 2.1, with $c = 1$ for simplicity. Fix $j \in \mathbb{Z}_q \setminus \{0\}$, and let $\alpha = q\sqrt{m}/s$. If $\alpha < d(j\boldsymbol{c}, \Lambda)$, then $(\Lambda - j\boldsymbol{c}) \setminus \alpha\mathcal{B} = (\Lambda - j\boldsymbol{c})$. Also, note that $\rho_{q/s}(\Lambda) = \rho_{1/s}(\frac{1}{q}\Lambda) = \rho_{1/s}((\Lambda^\perp)^*)$. So, as long as $s \geq \eta_\epsilon(\Lambda^\perp)$ for some negligible ϵ (which we already assumed earlier), it holds that $\rho_{q/s}(\Lambda) \leq 1 + \epsilon$ by definition of $\eta_\epsilon(\Lambda^\perp)$. Under those conditions, $\rho_{q/s}(\Lambda - j\boldsymbol{c}) = \rho_{q/s}((\Lambda - j\boldsymbol{c}) \setminus \alpha\mathcal{B}) \leq 2C^m \rho_{q/s}(\Lambda) \leq 2C^m(1 + \epsilon)$ is negligible. Using Lemma 2.1, we deduce the following:

Theorem 3.1. *Fix $\boldsymbol{A} \in \mathbb{Z}_q^{m \times n}, \boldsymbol{c} \in \mathbb{Z}_q^m$, and $\boldsymbol{p} \in \mathbb{Z}_q^n$, where m is polynomial in n. Fix a probabilistic rounding function $R : \mathbb{Z}_q \to \{0, 1\}$ such that for all $x \in \mathbb{Z}_q$,*

$$\Pr[R(x) = 1] = r(x) = \sum_{j \in J} \hat{r}_j e_{j/q}(x),$$

where $J \subseteq \mathbb{Z}_q$ and $\hat{r}_j \in \mathbb{C}$. Let $s \geq \eta_\epsilon(\Lambda^\perp(\boldsymbol{A}))$ for some $\epsilon = \mathrm{negl}(n)$. Assume furthermore that

$$\forall j \in J \setminus \{0\}, \quad s \cdot d(j\boldsymbol{c}, \Lambda(\boldsymbol{A})) > q\sqrt{m}.$$

Denote $P(\boldsymbol{c}) = \Pr[R(\langle \boldsymbol{h}, \boldsymbol{c} \rangle) = 1 \mid \boldsymbol{h}^t \boldsymbol{A} = \boldsymbol{p}^t]$, where the probability is taken over the randomness of R, and the distribution of $\boldsymbol{h} \leftarrow D_{\mathbb{Z},s}^m$, conditioned on $\boldsymbol{h}^t \boldsymbol{A} = \boldsymbol{p}^t$. Then:

$$|P(\boldsymbol{c}) - \hat{r}_0| \leq (2 + O(\epsilon)) |J| C^m + O(\epsilon) \quad \text{where} \quad C = \sqrt{2\pi e} \cdot e^{-\pi} < 1.$$

Setting up the Rounding Function. If one wishes to avoid having to attempt decryption of many multiples of the ciphertext $\boldsymbol{c}$, one should choose a probabilistic rounding function with a small number of harmonics.

In particular, the typical deterministic rounding function $R(x) = \lfloor 2x/q \rceil \bmod 2$—the so-called square-signal—and has harmonic coefficients $\hat{r}_j$ decreasing as $\Theta(1/j)$ in absolute value (for odd $j \in \{\lceil -q/2 \rceil, \ldots, \lfloor q/2 \rfloor\}$). With such a rounding function, one would still need to attempt trapdoor inversion for $q/2$ many multiples of $\boldsymbol{c}$, as it was already the case in [22].

On the contrary, one may easily avoid costly harmonics by setting the rounding function so that $2r(x) = 1 + \cos(2\pi x/q)$, which has Fourier coefficients

$\hat{r}_0 = 1/2, \hat{r}_1 = \hat{r}_{-1} = 1/4$, and $\hat{r}_j = 0$ for any other j.[9] More precisely, we have the following corollary by remarking that when $c \notin \mathcal{L}$ and $\alpha = q\sqrt{m}/s < B'$, we have $d(c, \Lambda) \geq B'$ and $(\Lambda - c) \setminus (\alpha \mathcal{B}) = (\Lambda - c)$.

Corollary 3.2. *Let* $A \in \mathbb{Z}_q^{m \times n}$ *with* $m = \Theta(n \log q)$, *and fix* $p \in \mathbb{Z}_q^n$. *Let* $B' = q/\Theta(\sqrt{m})$, *and* $\mathcal{L} = \{c \in \mathbb{Z}_q^m \mid d(c, \Lambda(A)) \leq B'\}$. *Suppose that* R *satisfies:*

$$\Pr[R(x) = 1] = r(x) = \frac{1}{2} + \frac{1}{2} \cos\left(\frac{2\pi x}{q}\right), \tag{1}$$

and let $s \geq \eta_\epsilon(\Lambda^\perp(A))$ *for some* $\epsilon = \mathrm{negl}(n)$. *Suppose also that:* $s > \frac{q\sqrt{m}}{B'}$.

Denote again $P(c) = \Pr[R(\langle h, c \rangle) = 1 \mid h^t A = p^t]$, *where the probability is taken over the randomness of* R, *and the distribution of* $h \leftarrow D_{\mathbb{Z},s}^m$, *conditioned on* $h^t A = p^t$. *Then, for all* $c \notin \mathcal{L}$:

$$|2P(c) - 1| \leq 2(6 + O(\epsilon)) C^m + O(\epsilon) \leq \mathrm{negl}(n),$$

where $C = \sqrt{2\pi e} \cdot e^{-\pi} < 1$.

3.3   Approximate Correctness

Let us check that the scheme above achieves approximate correctness, that is, for all $c \in \widetilde{\mathcal{L}}$, $\mathsf{Hash}(h, A, c) = \mathsf{ProjHash}(p, A, c, (s, e))$ with probability substantially greater than $1/2$. Using our rounding function R, this means that we want $R(\langle h, c \rangle)$ and $R(\langle p, s \rangle)$ to output the same bit with some probability Q substantially greater than $1/2$, where the two applications of R use independent coins.

Recall that $r(x)$ is the probability that the rounding function R outputs 1 on input x, and that for $c \in \widetilde{\mathcal{L}}$, we can write $\langle h, c \rangle = \langle p, s \rangle + \langle h, e \rangle$, where $c = As + e$. We argue that as long as $\langle h, e \rangle$ is small with respect to q, then our scheme achieves approximate correctness:

Lemma 3.3. *Fix* $A \in \mathbb{Z}_q^{m \times n}$ *and* $c = As + e \in \widetilde{\mathcal{L}}$, *where* m *and* q *are polynomial in* n, *and where* $\|e\| \leq B = 2t\sqrt{m}$. *Let* $s \geq \eta_\epsilon(\Lambda^\perp(A))$ *for some* $\epsilon = \mathrm{negl}(n)$. *Assume that* R *is the cosine rounding function (Eq. (1)). Let* Q *be the probability that* $R(\langle A^t h, s \rangle; \mathsf{coins}_1)$ *and* $R(\langle h, c \rangle; \mathsf{coins}_2)$ *output the same bit, over the randomness of* $h \leftarrow D_{\mathbb{Z},s}^m$, *and the randomness of the two independent coins* coins_1 *and* coins_2 *used by* R. *If* $tsm = o(q)$, *then* $Q = 3/4 + o(1)$.

Proof. As $s \geq \eta_\epsilon(\Lambda^\perp)$ for $\epsilon = \mathrm{negl}(n)$, the distribution of $h^t A$, when $h \leftarrow D_{\mathbb{Z},s}^m$, is at negligible statistical distance from uniform.

Therefore, Q is negligibly close to $\Pr[R(x; \mathsf{coins}_1) = R(x + \langle h, e \rangle; \mathsf{coins}_2)]$ where the probability is taken over uniform $x \in \mathbb{Z}_q$, $h \leftarrow D_{\mathbb{Z},s}^m$, and the randomness of the two independent coins coins_1 and coins_2 used by R.

---

[9] Of course, one could also obtain perfect universality by setting a constant rounding function $r(x) = 1/2$, and even avoid the first harmonic, but there is no way to reach correctness even with amplification in that case.

Then:

$$Q = \frac{1}{q} \sum_{x \in \mathbb{Z}_q} (r(x)r(x + \langle h, e \rangle) + (1 - r(x))(1 - r(x + \langle h, e \rangle))) + \mathrm{negl}(n)$$

$$= \frac{1}{2} + \frac{1}{q} \sum_{x \in \mathbb{Z}_q} \frac{1}{2} \cos\left(2\pi \frac{x}{q}\right) \cos\left(2\pi \frac{x + \langle h, e \rangle}{q}\right) + \mathrm{negl}(n).$$

As $tsm = o(q)$, we have $\langle h, e \rangle = o(q)$ with overwhelming probability. As cos is a Lipschitz continuous function, we can approximate the sum by an integral: $Q = \frac{1}{2} + \frac{1}{2} \int_0^1 \cos^2(2\pi x) dx + o(1) = \frac{3}{4} + o(1)$. $\qquad\square$

3.4   Wrap-Up

Consider the bit-PHF described in Sect. 3.1 instantiating R with the cosine rounding function (Eq. (1)), together with the encryption scheme of Sect. 2.2. Let us now show that all the parameters can be instantiated to satisfy security and correctness of the encryption scheme, simultaneously with statistical universality and approximate correctness of the bit-PHF.

IND-CCA2. To base the security of the scheme described in Sect. 2.2 on $\mathrm{LWE}_{\chi,q}$ for $\chi = D_{\mathbb{Z},\sigma}$ and $\sigma = 2\sqrt{n}$,[10] we apply Theorem 2.9 with $m = \Theta(n \log q)$ and $t = \sqrt{mn} \cdot \omega(\sqrt{\log n})$.

Decryption Correctness. For the encryption scheme to be correct, we want $B < B'$, recalling that $B := 2t\sqrt{m}$ and $B' := q/\Theta(\sqrt{m})$.

Universality. In Corollary 3.2, we used the hypothesis $s \geq \eta_\epsilon(\Lambda^\perp(A_u))$ for some negligible ϵ. Assuming $s \geq \Theta(\sqrt{n})$, one can apply Lemma 2.11, to ensure the above hypothesis for $\epsilon = 2^{-n}$ simultaneously for all $u \in \mathcal{U}$ except with probability 2^{-n} over the randomness of TrapGen.

Still in Corollary 3.2, we also needed $s > q\sqrt{m}/B'$, where $B' = q/\Theta(\sqrt{m})$. This holds for $s = \Theta(m)$.

Approximate correctness. For Lemma 3.3, we assumed that $tsm = o(q)$. Equivalently, it is sufficient that $sm^{3/2}n^{1/2}\omega(\sqrt{\log n}) = o(q)$.

Summary. Therefore, all the desired conditions can be satisfied with $q = \tilde{\Theta}(n^3)$, $m = \tilde{\Theta}(n)$, $s = \tilde{\Theta}(n)$, and $t = \tilde{\Theta}(n)$. We have proved the following:

Theorem 3.4. *Set parameters $q = \tilde{\Theta}(n^3), m = \tilde{\Theta}(n), s = \tilde{\Theta}(n), t = \tilde{\Theta}(n)$. Define a probabilistic rounding function $R : \mathbb{Z}_q \rightarrow \{0, 1\}$ such that $\Pr[R(x) = 1] = 1/2 + \cos(2\pi x/q)/2$. Then, (i) the encryption scheme of Sect. 2.2 is correct and tag-IND-CCA2 under the hardness of $LWE_{\chi,q}$ for $\chi = D_{\mathbb{Z},2\sqrt{n}}$; and (ii) the bit-PHF described in Sect. 3.1 achieves statistical universality and $(1/4 - o(1))$-correctness.*

---

[10] This is the smallest parameter σ for which $\mathrm{LWE}_{\chi,q}$ is known reduce to a worst-case problem. One may of course choose to use a different width for the LWE error, and derive different appropriate parameters.

4   Word-Independent SPHF for IND-CPA Ciphertexts

4.1   Overview

In the previous section, we built a bit-PHF with negl(n)-universality but approximate correctness. Even though correctness can be amplified, the transformation inherently makes the new projection key depend on the word we want to hash, even if that was not the case for the initial bit-PHF.

We now build a bit-PHF with statistical correctness and K-universality for some universal constant $K < 1$ (but using a super-polynomial LWE modulus q). The main benefit of such a construction is that amplifying universality can be done regardless of the word we want to hash, that is, the projection key will not depend on the word. When the tag u of the ciphertext c is known in advance or is constant (in which case, the encryption scheme is only IND-CPA instead of IND-CCA2), we therefore get a word-independent bit-PHF which can be transformed into a word-independent SPHF. This is the first word-independent SPHF for any lattice-based language.

We use the same natural approach as described in Sect. 3.1. The only differences with the construction in the previous section are the probabilistic rounding function we use, and the parameters necessary to argue correctness and universality. Recall that in the last section, we used a rounding function with only low order harmonics to get negl(n)-universality.

The starting point is the observation that, for the naive square rounding introduced in the previous section, the correctness is statistical, but clearly not negl(n)-universal, depending on which word c is hashed (as seen in the two case studies in the technical overview in the introduction, where $j \cdot c$ is close to Λ for some $j \in \mathbb{Z}_q^*$). However, the distribution of $R(\langle h, c \rangle)$ conditioned on $h^t A$ might still have enough entropy to give us K-universality, for some constant $K < 1$. In other words, we can hope that $|2 \cdot \Pr[R(\langle h, c \rangle) = 1 \mid p] - 1| \leq K$ for all $c \in \mathbb{Z}_q^m$.

Let $R^\sharp$ be a rounding function defined by: $R^\sharp(x) = 1 + \lfloor 2x/q \rceil \bmod 2$, that is:

$$\forall x \in [-q/2, q/2], \quad R^\sharp(x) = \begin{cases} 1 & \text{if } x \in [-q/4, q/4), \\ 0 & \text{otherwise.} \end{cases}$$

Using this rounding function gives good correctness: when $s \geq \eta_\epsilon(\Lambda^\perp)$, $\langle h, c \rangle$ is statistically close to uniform in $[-q/2, q/2]$, and therefore $R^\sharp(\langle h, c \rangle)$ is a uniform bit up to some statistical distance $O(\epsilon + 1/q)$ (due to the fact that q is odd). So for super-polynomial q, we get *statistical correctness* using $R^\sharp$ as rounding function, as long as $\langle h, e \rangle$ is sufficiently small with respect to q.

For *universality*, we express the probability distribution defined by $R^\sharp$, seen as a q-periodic function over $\mathbb{R}$, as a Fourier series:

$$\forall x \in [-q/2, q/2], \quad r^\sharp(x) := \Pr[R^\sharp(x) = 1] = \sum_{j \in \mathbb{Z}} \hat{r}_j^\sharp \cdot e_{j/q}(x),$$

where $\hat{r}_j^\sharp$ are the Fourier coefficients of the q-periodic function $r^\sharp \colon \mathbb{R} \to \mathbb{R}$.

However, one can show that $|\hat{r}_j^\sharp| = \Theta(1/j)$ (for odd integers j). Therefore, it is not clear how to show universality with a similar analysis as in Sect. 3.2: the total contribution of harmonics j such that $j \cdot c$ is close to Λ could potentially be arbitrarily large!

To solve this issue, we consider a new rounding function R, which has the same probability distribution as $R^\sharp$ but on a negligible fraction of integer points (so that statistical correctness is preserved), and such that its Fourier coefficients of high enough order have small enough amplitude.

Then, we use the observation that the set of integers j such that $j \cdot c$ is in Λ is an ideal of $\mathbb{Z}$, which is proper if c itself is not in Λ. More generally, the set of *small* integers $j \in \mathbb{Z}$ such that $j \cdot c$ is *close* to Λ is contained in an ideal of $\mathbb{Z}$; furthermore, if c is far from Λ, then the smallest such ideal is a proper ideal of $\mathbb{Z}$. This will allow us to discard all harmonics whose order is not in this ideal. As we will show, the remaining harmonics necessarily have destructive interferences, which allows us to establish K-universality for some constant $K < 1$.

The roadmap follows. First, in Sect. 4.2, we smooth the discontinuities of the probability distribution of the square rounding function $r^\sharp$ so that the Fourier coefficients of high order have small magnitude, but such that we keep statistical correctness. Then to prove universality, in Sect. 4.3, we show that for c far from Λ, the set of small $j \in \mathbb{Z}$ such that $j \cdot c$ is close to Λ is contained in a proper ideal of $\mathbb{Z}$. Finally, in Sect. 4.4 we show that the distribution of $R(\langle h, c \rangle)$ conditioned on $h^t A$ has some bounded min entropy.

4.2   Smoothing the Discontinuities: A New Rounding Function

In the following, unless specified otherwise, we will see $\mathbb{Z}_q$ as embedded in $\{\lceil -q/2 \rceil, \ldots, \lfloor q/2 \rfloor\}$, and the canonical period we use for q-periodic functions will be $[-q/2, q/2]$. Recall that $r^\sharp$ satisfies:

$$\forall x \in [-q/2, q/2], \quad r^\sharp(x) = \begin{cases} 1 & \text{if } |x| \in [-q/4, q/4), \\ 0 & \text{otherwise.} \end{cases}$$

In particular, $r^\sharp$ has two discontinuities on $q/4$ and on $-q/4$. To smooth those discontinuities, we consider the convolution product of the square signal $r^\sharp$ with a rectangular signal of appropriate width T such that $T/q = \text{negl}(n)$. More precisely, consider the q-periodic function $r^\flat$ defined on $[-q/2, q/2]$ by:

$$\forall x \in [-q/2, q/2], \quad r^\flat(x) = \begin{cases} \frac{1}{2T} & \text{if } |x| \leq T, \\ 0 & \text{otherwise.} \end{cases}$$

We define a new rounding function R such that for all $x \in \mathbb{R}$ (see Fig. 1):

$$\Pr[R(x) = 1] := r(x) := (r^\sharp \odot r^\flat)(x) := \int_{-q/2}^{q/2} r^\sharp(u) \cdot r^\flat(x - u) \, du,$$

where, in this context, $\odot$ corresponds to the convolution of q-periodic functions.

Intuitively, this corresponds to replace the discontinuities on $r^\sharp(\pm q/4)$ by a linear slope ranging from $\pm q/4 - T$ to $\pm q/4 + T$ (see Fig. 1). Therefore, over $[-q/2, q/2]$, the functions r and $r^\sharp$ only differ on at most $4\lceil T \rceil$ integer points (the points on the slope). Recall that if $s \geq \eta_\epsilon(\Lambda^\perp)$ for some negligible ϵ, then $\langle h, c \rangle$ is statistically close to uniform in $\{\lceil -q/2 \rceil, \ldots, \lfloor q/2 \rfloor\}$. Therefore, if $\langle h, e \rangle / q$ and T/q are negligible, then:

$$\Pr[R(\langle h, c \rangle) \neq R(\langle p, s \rangle)] \leq \mathrm{negl}(n),$$

and we get statistical correctness using such a rounding function.

Lemma 4.1 (Correctness). *Suppose that $s \geq \eta_\epsilon(\Lambda^\perp)$ for some $\epsilon = \mathrm{negl}(n)$, $tsm/q = \mathrm{negl}(n)$, and $T/q = \mathrm{negl}(n)$. Assume that R satisfies: $\Pr[R(x) = 1] = r(x) = (r^\sharp \odot r^\flat)(x)$. Then the approximate bit-PHF defined in Sect. 3.1 achieves statistical correctness.*

Furthermore, r is q-periodic, and can therefore be expressed as a Fourier series:

$$\forall x \in [-q/2, q/2], \quad r(x) = \sum_{j \in \mathbb{Z}} \hat{r}_j e_{j/q}(x),$$

with Fourier coefficients $\hat{r}_j$. As $r = r^\sharp \odot r^\flat$, we have $\hat{r}_j = q \cdot \hat{r}_j^\sharp \cdot \hat{r}_j^\flat$ for $j \in \mathbb{Z}$, where $\hat{r}_j^\sharp$ and $\hat{r}_j^\flat$ are the Fourier coefficients of the q-periodic functions $r^\sharp$ and $r^\flat$ respectively. Thus, $\hat{r}_0 = 1/2$, and for $j \in \mathbb{Z} \setminus \{0\}$, the jth harmonic of r is:

$$\hat{r}_j = \frac{q}{2\pi^2 T j^2} \cdot \sin(\pi j/2) \cdot \sin(2\pi T j/q) \leq \frac{q}{19 T j^2}. \tag{2}$$

4.3   Inclusion of Contributing Harmonics in a Proper Ideal

In the following, we focus on showing that even though we do not have $\mathrm{negl}(n)$-universality using this new rounding function, we still have some K-universality for some constant $K < 1$ (that we can amplify).

We start by a simple useful lemma:

Lemma 4.2. *Let $N = kq/T$ for some k. Then $\sum_{j \in \mathbb{Z}, |j| > N} |\hat{r}_j| \leq 1/k$.*

Proof. It follows from Eq. (2) and the fact that for all $N > 2$: $\sum_{k=N}^{+\infty} \frac{1}{k^2} \leq \sum_{k=N}^{+\infty} \left(\frac{1}{k-1} - \frac{1}{k}\right) = \frac{1}{N-1}$. $\square$

Suppose now that $d(c, \Lambda) \geq B'$. Consider the set of $j \in \mathbb{Z}$ such that $d(j \cdot c, \Lambda) \leq \delta$ for some appropriately chosen δ. Let $P = P(c) = \Pr[R(\langle h, c \rangle) = 1 \mid h^t A = p^t]$, for our new rounding function R. For any $h_0 \in \Lambda_p^\perp$, we can show similarly to Sect. 3.2, that:

$$P = \frac{\det((\Lambda^\perp)^*) s^m}{\rho_s(\Lambda_p^\perp)} \sum_{j \in \mathbb{Z}} \hat{r}_j \sum_{y \in \Lambda} (\rho_{q/s, jc} \cdot e_{h_0/q})(y), \tag{3}$$

where $\frac{\det((\Lambda^{\perp})^{*})s^{m}}{\rho_{s}(\Lambda_{p}^{\perp})} = (1 + O(\epsilon))$ as long as $s \geq \eta_{\epsilon}(\Lambda^{\perp})$. Note that $\sum_{|j| \geq N} |\hat{r}_{j}|$ can be made arbitrarily small for appropriate N, by Lemma 4.2. Thus only the terms of the sum corresponding to $|j| \leq N$ will have a substantial contribution to the sum above (recall that $\rho_{q/s}(\Lambda - jc) \leq 1 + \epsilon$ for all c, for appropriate parameters). Therefore we only consider those small j such that $|j| < N$ for some appropriately chosen N (with respect to q). Furthermore, for large enough δ, the terms corresponding to indices j such that $d(j \cdot c, \Lambda) > \delta$ also have a negligible contribution to the sum by Lemma 2.1. For appropriate parameters N and δ to be instantiated later, let:

$$J = \{j \in \mathbb{Z} \mid |j| < N \wedge d(j \cdot c, \Lambda) \leq \delta\}. \tag{4}$$

As a subset of $\mathbb{Z}$, J is contained in the ideal $j_{0}\mathbb{Z}$ of $\mathbb{Z}$, where $j_{0} = \gcd(J)$. Let us show that it is a proper ideal of $\mathbb{Z}$, i.e., $j_{0} \neq 1$. To do so, we rely on the existence of small Bézout coefficients.

Lemma 4.3 (Corollary of [26, Theorem 9]). *Let $a_{1}, \ldots, a_{k} \in \mathbb{Z}$, and let $g = \gcd(a_{1}, \ldots, a_{k})$. Then there exists $u_{1}, \ldots, u_{k} \in \mathbb{Z}$ such that the following conditions hold:*

$$\sum_{i=1}^{k} u_{i}a_{i} = g, \qquad \sum_{i=1}^{k} |u_{i}| \leq \frac{k}{2} \max |a_{i}|.$$

We can now prove that J is a proper ideal of $\mathbb{Z}$:

Lemma 4.4. *Suppose that $\delta N^{2} < B'$. Then, for $c \in \mathbb{Z}_{q}^{m}$ such that $d(c, \Lambda) > B'$, the set $J = \{j \in \mathbb{Z} \mid |j| < N \wedge d(j \cdot c, \Lambda) \leq \delta\}$ is contained in a proper ideal of $\mathbb{Z}$.*

Proof. Let $j_{0} = \gcd(J)$. By definition, $J \subseteq j_{0}\mathbb{Z}$. Suppose by contradiction that $j_{0} = 1$. By Lemma 4.3, there exists a set of integers $\{u_{j}, j \in J\}$ such that $\sum_{j \in J} u_{j} \cdot j = 1$ and then $\sum_{j \in J} u_{j} \cdot (j \cdot c) = c$. But by definition of $J, d(j \cdot c, \Lambda) \leq \delta$ for all $j \in J$, and therefore:

$$d(c, \Lambda) \leq \delta \cdot \sum_{j \in J} |u_{j}| \leq \frac{\delta \cdot |J|}{2} \max_{j \in J} |j| \leq \delta N^{2} < B',$$

which is absurd as we assumed $d(c, \Lambda) > B'$. □

4.4 Imperfect Universality from Destructive Interferences

We now want to quantify how biased $R(\langle h, c \rangle)$ conditioned on $h^{t}A$ can be when c is far from Λ. We start from Eq. (3):

$$P = \frac{\det((\Lambda^{\perp})^{*})s^{m}}{\rho_{s}(\Lambda_{p}^{\perp})} \sum_{j \in \mathbb{Z}} \hat{r}_{j} \sum_{y \in \Lambda} (\rho_{q/s, jc} \cdot e_{h_{0}/q})(y),$$

where $\frac{\det((\Lambda^{\perp})^{*})s^{m}}{\rho_{s}(\Lambda_{p}^{\perp})} = 1 + O(\epsilon)$ as long as $s \geq \eta_{\epsilon}(\Lambda^{\perp})$.

We split the sum into three parts $P = P_1 + P_2 + P_3$:

P_1. $|j| > N \wedge j \notin j_0\mathbb{Z}$: those indices have a negligible contribution to the sum by Lemma 4.2.

P_2. $|j| \leq N \wedge j \notin j_0\mathbb{Z}$: those indices contribute negligibly since $\rho_{q/s}(\Lambda - j\boldsymbol{c})$ is small as $j\boldsymbol{c}$ is far from Λ (by definition of δ and $J \subset j_0\mathbb{Z}$).

P_3. $j \in j_0\mathbb{Z}$: the contributing terms. Unlike the previous ones we won't use absolute bounds for each term, and must consider destructive interferences.

It remains to study P_3, for which a similar computation as in Sect. 3.2 gives:

$$P_3 = \frac{\det((\Lambda^\perp)^*)s^m}{\rho_s(\Lambda_p^\perp)} \sum_{j \in j_0\mathbb{Z}} \hat{r}_j \sum_{\boldsymbol{y} \in \Lambda} (\rho_{q/s,j\boldsymbol{c}} \cdot e_{h_0/q})(\boldsymbol{y})$$

$$= \sum_{\boldsymbol{h} \in \Lambda_p^\perp} \frac{\rho_s(\boldsymbol{h})}{\rho_s(\Lambda_p^\perp)} \sum_{j \in j_0\mathbb{Z}} \hat{r}_j e_{j/q}(\langle \boldsymbol{h}, \boldsymbol{c} \rangle).$$

If we were to have $j_0 = 1$ (i.e. $j_0\mathbb{Z} = \mathbb{Z}$), we could compute the inner sum simply by inverse Fourier transform, evaluating r at $x = \langle \boldsymbol{h}, \boldsymbol{c} \rangle$. Instead, we note that selecting only the harmonics in $j_0\mathbb{Z}$, corresponds in the temporal domain to averaging the function r over all its temporal shifts by multiples of q/j_0. More formally, recall the identity:

$$\sum_{k=0}^{j_0-1} e_{j/j_0}(k) = \begin{cases} j_0 & \text{if } j \in j_0\mathbb{Z} \\ 0 & \text{otherwise.} \end{cases}$$

We may now rewrite:

$$\sum_{j \in j_0\mathbb{Z}} \hat{r}_j e_{j/q}(x) = \frac{1}{j_0} \sum_{j \in \mathbb{Z}} \hat{r}_j e_{j/q}(x) \sum_{k=0}^{j_0-1} e_{j/j_0}(k) = \frac{1}{j_0} \sum_{k=0}^{j_0-1} r(x + k\frac{q}{j_0}),$$

Note that $\frac{1}{j_0} \sum_{k=0}^{j_0-1} r^\sharp(x + k\frac{q}{j_0})$ is not too far away from $1/2$: if j_0 is even, this is exactly $1/2$ (for all x), and if $j_0 = 2k+1$, this is either k/j_0 or $(k+1)/j_0$ (depending on x), which is at distance $1/(2j_0) \leq 1/6$ from $1/2$ (recall that $j_0 > 1$ by Lemma 4.4). Furthermore, we have:

$$\forall x \in [-q/2, q/2], \ r(x) = \frac{1}{2T} \int_{-T}^{T} r^\sharp(x + u) du,$$

which gives, for all $x \in [-q/2, q/2]$:

$$\left| \frac{1}{j_0} \sum_{k=0}^{j_0-1} r(x + k\frac{q}{j_0}) - \frac{1}{2} \right| \leq \frac{1}{2T} \int_{-T}^{T} \left| \frac{1}{j_0} \sum_{k=0}^{j_0-1} r^\sharp(x + u + k\frac{q}{j_0}) - \frac{1}{2} \right| du \leq 1/6.$$

Therefore, P_3 is also not too far from $1/2$ as a convex combination of values not too far from $1/2$. More precisely we have $|P_3 - 1/2| \leq 1/6$.

Putting everything together, we can quantify the distance from P to $1/2$:

Theorem 4.5 (Universality). *Let $A \in \mathbb{Z}_q^{m \times n}$ with $m = \Theta(n \log q)$, and fix $p \in \mathbb{Z}_q^n$. Let $B' = q/\Theta(\sqrt{m})$, and $\mathscr{L} = \{c \in \mathbb{Z}_q^m \mid d(c, \Lambda(A)) \leq B'\}$. Let R be as defined in Sect. 4.2 and let $s \geq \eta_\epsilon(\Lambda^\perp(A))$ for some $\epsilon = \mathrm{negl}(n)$. Suppose also that parameters T, N, δ, and k satisfy $\delta > \frac{q\sqrt{m}}{s}, N = \frac{kq}{T}$, and $\delta N^2 < B'$.*

Denote again $P(c) = \Pr[R(\langle h, c \rangle) = 1 \mid h^t A = p^t]$, where the probability is taken over the randomness of R, and the distribution of $h \leftarrow D_{\mathbb{Z},s}^m$, conditioned on $h^t A = p^t$. Then, for all $c \notin \mathscr{L}$:

$$|P(c) - 1/2| \leq \frac{1}{6} + (1 + O(\epsilon))\left(\frac{1}{k} + 4NC^m\right),$$

where $C = \sqrt{2\pi e} \cdot e^{-\pi} < 1$.

Remark 4.6. Informally, this theorem states that the second case study of the technical overview of the introduction is essentially the worst case.

Proof. Writing $P = P_1 + P_2 + P_3$ as above, we showed that $|P_3 - 1/2| \leq 1/6$. Moreover, as $s \geq \eta_\epsilon(\Lambda^\perp(A))$, we have:

$$\frac{\det((\Lambda^\perp)^*)s^m}{\rho_s(\Lambda_p^\perp)} = 1 + O(\epsilon),$$

and, for any $j \in \mathbb{Z}$ and c, we also have:

$$\left|\sum_{y \in \Lambda}(\rho_{q/s,jc} \cdot e_{h_0/q})(y)\right| \leq \rho_{q/s}(\Lambda - jc) \leq 1 + \epsilon.$$

Therefore, by Lemma 4.2, and as $\epsilon = \mathrm{negl}(n)$, we have:

$$|P_1| \leq (1 + O(\epsilon))(1 + \epsilon)\sum_{|j| > N}|\hat{r}_j| \leq \frac{1 + O(\epsilon)}{k}.$$

Furthermore, as $\delta > \frac{q\sqrt{m}}{s}$, and $|\hat{r}_j| \leq 1$ for all j, Lemma 2.1 gives us that $|P_2| \leq 4NC^m(1 + O(\epsilon))$, which concludes the proof. $\square$

4.5   Wrap-Up

Let us now show that all the parameters can be instantiated to get approximate smoothness and correctness for the SPHF, using a rounding function R defined by $\Pr[R(x) = 1] = r^\sharp \odot r^\flat(x)$.

IND-CPA. To apply Theorem 2.9 with Remark 2.10, we can use the fact that $m = \Theta(n \log q)$ and $t = \sqrt{mn} \cdot \omega(\sqrt{\log n})$.

Decryption Correctness. For the encryption scheme to be correct, we want $B < B'$, with $B = 2t\sqrt{m}$ and $B' = q/\Theta(\sqrt{m})$.

Correctness. For correctness of the bit-PHF, we need a super-polynomial modulus q, and require T/q to be negligible. Furthermore, we need tsm/q to be negligible, so that $\langle h, e \rangle$ can only take a negligible fraction of values in $\mathbb{Z}_q$. Also, we need $s \geq \eta_\epsilon(\Lambda^\perp(A_u))$, which is satisfied with high probability by Lemma 2.11 for $\epsilon = 2^{-n}$ as long as $s \geq \Theta(\sqrt{n})$.

Bounding the amplitude of high frequencies. The parameter N which upper bounds the elements of J must be taken so that $\sum_{|j| \geq N} |\hat{r}_j|$ is small. By Lemma 4.2, by taking $N = kq/T$, this sum is $\leq 1/k$.

Threshold distance to Λ defining J. The parameter δ, which denotes how close $j \cdot c$ is close to Λ for $j \in J$ (Eq. (4)) has to be chosen so that $N \cdot \rho_{q/s}(\Lambda - v)$ must be small whenever $d(v, \Lambda) \geq \delta$. As in the analysis for the cosine rounding function, setting $\delta = q\sqrt{m}/s$ implies that $\rho_{q/s}(\Lambda - v) \leq 2C^m(1 + O(\epsilon))$ by Lemma 2.1.

Showing that $j_0 \neq 1$. We also required $\delta N^2 < B'$ to conclude that J was included in a proper ideal of $\mathbb{Z}$. As we have $\delta N^2 = \Theta\left(\frac{q^3 k \sqrt{m}}{s T^2}\right)$, this holds as long as $s \geq \Omega(\frac{mk^2 q^2}{T^2})$.

Putting everything together, we get the following theorem:

Theorem 4.7. *Suppose $q = O(2^n)$ is superpolynomial in n, $m = \Theta(n \log q)$. Set parameters: (i) T such that T/q and q/T^2 are both negligible in n (using $T = q^{2/3}$ for instance), (ii) $k = \Theta(n)$, and (iii) $s \geq \Theta(\sqrt{n})$ such that $s/q = \mathsf{negl}(n)$ and $s = \Omega(\frac{mk^2 q^2}{T^2})$, which exists by construction of T. Define a probabilistic rounding function $R : \mathbb{Z}_q \to \{0, 1\}$ such that $\Pr[R(x) = 1] = r^\sharp \odot r^b(x)$. Then the bit-PHF described in Sect. 3.1 achieves $(1/3 + o(1))$-universality and statistical correctness.*

Proof. The theorem follows from the discussion above and Theorem 4.5 using: (i) $N = kq/T$ (in which case NC^m is negligible in n), and (ii) $\delta = \frac{q\sqrt{m}}{s}$.   □

5   Applications

In this section, we present several applications of our new construction. It underlines the importance of revisiting this primitive.

5.1   Password-Authenticated Key Exchange

3-Round PAKE. Gennaro and Lindell proposed in [13] a generic framework for building 3-round PAKE protocols based on an IND-CCA2 encryption scheme and an associated SPHF. Later in [22], Katz and Vaikuntanathan refined it to be compatible with approximate SPHF over a CCA2-secure encryption scheme.

We can instantiate the construction in [22] using the encryption scheme à la Micciancio-Peikert in Sect. 2.2 together with an approximate SPHF generically derived from the approximate bit-PHF constructed in Sect. 3. This allows us to achieve a PAKE protocol in three flows, with a polynomial modulus.

Moving to a 2-Round PAKE. An interesting optimization in cryptography is to reduce the number of rounds, so that each user only has to speak once. Is it possible to achieve a PAKE, where each user sends simply one flow?

In [1], the authors revisited the Groce-Katz framework [17]. Their construction (called GK-PAKE) uses a pseudo-random generator, an IND-CPA encryption scheme, with a simple regular SPHF on one hand, and an IND-PCA (Indistinguishable against Plaintext-Checkable Attacks) encryption on the other.

Every IND-CCA2 encryption being also IND-PCA, we can trivially meet the requirements and achieve the expected 2-rounds efficiency, using our SPHF from Sect. 3.[11] Contrary to the construction of Zhang and Yu [30], we do not need a simulation-sound non-interactive proof (SS-NIZK), which we do not know how to construct from lattice assumptions in the standard model.

Achieving a 1-Round PAKE. Actually, if we allow ourselves to use SS-NIZK, we can construct a 1-round PAKE by combining our word-independent SPHF with the ideas in [23], which solves an open problem in [30]. Concretely, we use the first instantiation of [23], except that the ElGamal encryption scheme and its associated SPHF are replaced by our IND-CPA LWE-based encryption scheme à la Micciancio-Peikert and the word-independent SPHF is the one from Sect. 4. The SS-NIZK can be a simple variant of the one in [30]. Details are provided in the full version [6].

5.2 Honest-Verifier Zero-Knowledge

Following the methodology from [7], using our SPHF in Sect. 3, we can construct honest-verifier zero-knowledge proofs for any NP language of the form $\mathscr{L} = \{\ddot{x} \mid \exists \ddot{w}, \ddot{\mathscr{R}}(\ddot{x}, \ddot{w})\}$ where $\ddot{\mathscr{R}}$ is a polynomial-size circuit. At a very high level, the prover simply encrypts each wire of the circuit using an IND-CPA encryption scheme[12] and then shows the correct evaluation at each gate, using SPHFs.

For the sake of simplicity, we suppose that all gates of the circuit $\ddot{\mathscr{R}}$ are NAND gates. We just need to construct an SPHF for the languages $\widetilde{\mathscr{L}} \subseteq \mathscr{L}$ of ciphertexts C_1, C_2, C_3 encrypting values (b_1, b_2, b_3) so that $b_3 = \mathrm{NAND}(b_1, b_2)$, such that $\widetilde{\mathscr{L}}$ is the set of encryptions of b_i that fits the NAND gate evaluation, while $\mathscr{L}$ is the set of ciphertexts whose decryptions fit the gate evaluation. We can do that by combining our SPHFs using the classical techniques described in [2]. Details are provided in the full version [6].

5.3 Witness Encryption

Witness encryption [12] allows to encrypt a message, with respect to a particular word χ and a language $\mathscr{L}$, instead of using a classical public key. If the word

---

[11] In this application, as in our 3-round PAKE from [22], the gap between correctness and smoothness is not an issue: the proof of the resulting 2-round PAKE works exactly as in [1].

[12] We actually will use our IND-CCA2 encryption scheme à la Micciancio-Peikert.

is in the language, then a user knowing a witness for the word can decrypt the ciphertext, otherwise the ciphertext hides the message.

An SPHF can be used to construct such a primitive as follows: To encrypt a message M with respect to a word χ and a language $\mathscr{L}$, use an SPHF for $\mathscr{L}$ to generate a hashing key hk, a projection key hp, and a hash value H, and output the *ciphertext* $C = (\mathsf{hp}, \mathsf{H} \oplus M)$. To decrypt such a ciphertext, simply use the witness w associated with the word χ together with the projection key hp to compute the projected hash value and recover M. Details are available in the full version [6].

Acknowledgments. We would like to sincerely thank Zvika Brakerski for many useful and interesting discussions.

References

1. Abdalla, M., Benhamouda, F., Pointcheval, D.: Public-key encryption indistinguishable under plaintext-checkable attacks. In: Katz, J. (ed.) PKC 2015. LNCS, vol. 9020, pp. 332–352. Springer, Heidelberg (2015). https://doi.org/10.1007/978-3-662-46447-2_15
2. Abdalla, M., Chevalier, C., Pointcheval, D.: Smooth projective hashing for conditionally extractable commitments. In: Halevi, S. (ed.) CRYPTO 2009. LNCS, vol. 5677, pp. 671–689. Springer, Heidelberg (2009). https://doi.org/10.1007/978-3-642-03356-8_39
3. Banaszczyk, W.: New bounds in some transference theorems in the geometry of numbers. Math. Ann. **296**(1), 625–635 (1993)
4. Ben Hamouda, F., Blazy, O., Chevalier, C., Pointcheval, D., Vergnaud, D.: Efficient UC-secure authenticated key-exchange for algebraic languages. In: Kurosawa, K., Hanaoka, G. (eds.) PKC 2013. LNCS, vol. 7778, pp. 272–291. Springer, Heidelberg (2013). https://doi.org/10.1007/978-3-642-36362-7_18
5. Benhamouda, F., Blazy, O., Chevalier, C., Pointcheval, D., Vergnaud, D.: New techniques for SPHFs and efficient one-round PAKE protocols. In: Canetti, R., Garay, J.A. (eds.) CRYPTO 2013, Part I. LNCS, vol. 8042, pp. 449–475. Springer, Heidelberg (2013). https://doi.org/10.1007/978-3-642-40041-4_25
6. Benhamouda, F., Blazy, O., Ducas, L., Quach, W.: Hash proof systems over lattices revisited. Cryptology ePrint Archive, Report 2017/997 (2017). http://eprint.iacr.org/2017/997
7. Benhamouda, F., Couteau, G., Pointcheval, D., Wee, H.: Implicit zero-knowledge arguments and applications to the malicious setting. In: Gennaro, R., Robshaw, M. (eds.) CRYPTO 2015, Part II. LNCS, vol. 9216, pp. 107–129. Springer, Heidelberg (2015). https://doi.org/10.1007/978-3-662-48000-7_6
8. Boyen, X.: Attribute-based functional encryption on lattices. In: Sahai, A. (ed.) TCC 2013. LNCS, vol. 7785, pp. 122–142. Springer, Heidelberg (2013). https://doi.org/10.1007/978-3-642-36594-2_8
9. Cash, D., Hofheinz, D., Kiltz, E., Peikert, C.: Bonsai trees, or how to delegate a lattice basis. In: Gilbert, H. (ed.) EUROCRYPT 2010. LNCS, vol. 6110, pp. 523–552. Springer, Heidelberg (2010). https://doi.org/10.1007/978-3-642-13190-5_27
10. Cramer, R., Shoup, V.: A practical public key cryptosystem provably secure against adaptive chosen ciphertext attack. In: Krawczyk, H. (ed.) CRYPTO 1998. LNCS, vol. 1462, pp. 13–25. Springer, Heidelberg (1998). https://doi.org/10.1007/BFb0055717

11. Cramer, R., Shoup, V.: Universal hash proofs and a paradigm for adaptive chosen ciphertext secure public-key encryption. In: Knudsen, L.R. (ed.) EUROCRYPT 2002. LNCS, vol. 2332, pp. 45–64. Springer, Heidelberg (2002). https://doi.org/10.1007/3-540-46035-7_4

12. Garg, S., Gentry, C., Sahai, A., Waters, B.: Witness encryption and its applications. In: Boneh, D., Roughgarden, T., Feigenbaum, J. (eds.) 45th ACM STOC, pp. 467–476. ACM Press, June 2013

13. Gennaro, R., Lindell, Y.: A framework for password-based authenticated key exchange. ACM Trans. Inf. Syst. Secur. 9(2), 181–234 (2006)

14. Gentry, C., Peikert, C., Vaikuntanathan, V.: Trapdoors for hard lattices and new cryptographic constructions. In: Ladner, R.E., Dwork, C. (eds.) 40th ACM STOC, pp. 197–206. ACM Press, May 2008

15. Gorbunov, S., Vaikuntanathan, V., Wee, H.: Attribute-based encryption for circuits. In: Boneh, D., Roughgarden, T., Feigenbaum, J. (eds.) 45th ACM STOC, pp. 545–554. ACM Press, June 2013

16. Gorbunov, S., Vaikuntanathan, V., Wee, H.: Predicate encryption for circuits from LWE. In: Gennaro, R., Robshaw, M. (eds.) CRYPTO 2015, Part II. LNCS, vol. 9216, pp. 503–523. Springer, Heidelberg (2015). https://doi.org/10.1007/978-3-662-48000-7_25

17. Groce, A., Katz, J.: A new framework for efficient password-based authenticated key exchange. In: Al-Shaer, E., Keromytis, A.D., Shmatikov, V. (eds.) ACM CCS 10, pp. 516–525. ACM Press, October 2010

18. Halevi, S., Kalai, Y.T.: Smooth projective hashing and two-message oblivious transfer. J. Cryptol. 25(1), 158–193 (2012)

19. Jiang, S., Gong, G.: Password based key exchange with mutual authentication. In: Handschuh, H., Hasan, M.A. (eds.) SAC 2004. LNCS, vol. 3357, pp. 267–279. Springer, Heidelberg (2004). https://doi.org/10.1007/978-3-540-30564-4_19

20. Jutla, C., Roy, A.: Relatively-sound NIZKs and password-based key-exchange. In: Fischlin, M., Buchmann, J., Manulis, M. (eds.) PKC 2012. LNCS, vol. 7293, pp. 485–503. Springer, Heidelberg (2012). https://doi.org/10.1007/978-3-642-30057-8_29

21. Kalai, Y.T.: Smooth projective hashing and two-message oblivious transfer. In: Cramer, R. (ed.) EUROCRYPT 2005. LNCS, vol. 3494, pp. 78–95. Springer, Heidelberg (2005). https://doi.org/10.1007/11426639_5

22. Katz, J., Vaikuntanathan, V.: Smooth projective hashing and password-based authenticated key exchange from lattices. In: Matsui, M. (ed.) ASIACRYPT 2009. LNCS, vol. 5912, pp. 636–652. Springer, Heidelberg (2009). https://doi.org/10.1007/978-3-642-10366-7_37

23. Katz, J., Vaikuntanathan, V.: Round-optimal password-based authenticated key exchange. In: Ishai, Y. (ed.) TCC 2011. LNCS, vol. 6597, pp. 293–310. Springer, Heidelberg (2011). https://doi.org/10.1007/978-3-642-19571-6_18

24. Lyubashevsky, V.: Lattice-based identification schemes secure under active attacks. In: Cramer, R. (ed.) PKC 2008. LNCS, vol. 4939, pp. 162–179. Springer, Heidelberg (2008). https://doi.org/10.1007/978-3-540-78440-1_10

25. Lyubashevsky, V.: Fiat-Shamir with aborts: applications to lattice and factoring-based signatures. In: Matsui, M. (ed.) ASIACRYPT 2009. LNCS, vol. 5912, pp. 598–616. Springer, Heidelberg (2009). https://doi.org/10.1007/978-3-642-10366-7_35

26. Majewski, B.S., Havas, G.: The complexity of greatest common divisor computations. In: Adleman, L.M., Huang, M.-D. (eds.) ANTS 1994. LNCS, vol. 877, pp. 184–193. Springer, Heidelberg (1994). https://doi.org/10.1007/3-540-58691-1_56

27. Micciancio, D., Peikert, C.: Trapdoors for lattices: simpler, tighter, faster, smaller. In: Pointcheval, D., Johansson, T. (eds.) EUROCRYPT 2012. LNCS, vol. 7237, pp. 700–718. Springer, Heidelberg (2012). https://doi.org/10.1007/978-3-642-29011-4_41

28. Micciancio, D., Regev, O.: Worst-case to average-case reductions based on Gaussian measures. In: 45th FOCS, pp. 372–381. IEEE Computer Society Press, October 2004

29. Regev, O.: On lattices, learning with errors, random linear codes, and cryptography. In: Gabow, H.N., Fagin, R. (eds.) 37th ACM STOC, pp. 84–93. ACM Press, May 2005

30. Zhang, J., Yu, Y.: Two-round PAKE from approximate SPH and instantiations from lattices. In: Takagi, T., Peyrin, T. (eds.) ASIACRYPT 2017, Part III. LNCS, vol. 10626, pp. 37–67. Springer, Cham (2017). https://doi.org/10.1007/978-3-319-70700-6_2

Privately Constraining and Programming PRFs, the LWE Way

Chris Peikert$^{(\boxtimes)}$ and Sina Shiehian

Computer Science and Engineering, University of Michigan, Ann Arbor, USA
cpeikert@umich.edu

Abstract. *Constrained* pseudorandom functions allow for delegating "constrained" secret keys that let one compute the function at certain authorized inputs—as specified by a constraining predicate—while keeping the function value at unauthorized inputs pseudorandom. In the *constraint-hiding* variant, the constrained key hides the predicate. On top of this, *programmable* variants allow the delegator to explicitly set the output values yielded by the delegated key for a particular set of unauthorized inputs.

Recent years have seen rapid progress on applications and constructions of these objects for progressively richer constraint classes, resulting most recently in constraint-hiding constrained PRFs for *arbitrary* polynomial-time constraints from Learning With Errors (LWE) [Brakerski, Tsabary, Vaikuntanathan, and Wee, TCC'17], and privately programmable PRFs from indistinguishability obfuscation (iO) [Boneh, Lewi, and Wu, PKC'17].

In this work we give a unified approach for constructing both of the above kinds of PRFs from LWE with subexponential $\exp(n^\varepsilon)$ approximation factors. Our constructions follow straightforwardly from a new notion we call a *shift-hiding shiftable function*, which allows for deriving a key for the *sum* of the original function and any desired hidden shift function. In particular, we obtain the first privately programmable PRFs from non-iO assumptions.

1 Introduction

Since the introduction of pseudorandom functions (PRFs) more than thirty years ago by Goldreich et al. [19], many variants of this fundamental primitive have been proposed. For example, *constrained* PRFs (also known as *delegatable* or *functional* PRFs) [9,11,22] allow issuing "constrained" keys which can be used to evaluate the PRF on an "authorized" subset of the domain, while preserving the pseudorandomness of the PRF values on the remaining unauthorized inputs.

Assuming the existence of one-way functions, constrained PRFs were first constructed for the class of *prefix-fixing* constraints, i.e., the constrained

C. Peikert—This material is based upon work supported by the National Science Foundation under CAREER Award CCF-1054495 and CNS-1606362. The views expressed are those of the authors and do not necessarily reflect the off or position of the National Science Foundation or the Sloan Foundation.

M. Abdalla and R. Dahab (Eds.): PKC 2018, LNCS 10770, pp. 675–701, 2018.
https://doi.org/10.1007/978-3-319-76581-5_23

key allows evaluating the PRF on inputs which start with a specified bit string [9,11,22]. Subsequently, by building on a sequence of works [2,3,7] that gave PRFs from the Learning With Errors (LWE) problem [28], Brakerski and Vaikuntanathan [14] constructed constrained PRFs where the set of authorized inputs can be specified by an *arbitrary* polynomial-time predicate, although for a weaker security notion that allows the attacker to obtain only a single constrained key and function value.

In the original notion of constrained PRF, the constrained key may reveal the constraint itself. Boneh et al. [8] proposed a stronger variant in which the constraint is hidden, calling them *privately constrained PRFs*—also known as *constraint-hiding constrained PRFs* (CHC-PRFs)—and gave several compelling applications, like searchable symmetric encryption, watermarking PRFs, and function secret sharing [10]. They also constructed CHC-PRFs for arbitrary polynomial-time constraining functions under the strong assumption that indistinguishability obfuscation (iO) exists [4,17]. Soon after, CHC-PRFs for various constraint classes were constructed from more standard LWE assumptions:

- Boneh et al. [6] constructed them for the class of point-function constraints (i.e., all but one input is authorized).
- Thorough a different approach, Canetti and Chen [15] constructed them for constraints in NC^1, i.e., polynomial-size formulas.
- Most recently, Brakerski et al. [13] improved on the construction from [6] to support arbitrary polynomial-size constraints.

All these constructions have a somewhat weaker security guarantee compared to the iO-based construction of [8], namely, the adversary gets just one constrained key (but an unbounded number of function values), whereas in [8] it can get unboundedly many constrained keys. Indeed, this restriction reflects a fundamental barrier: CHC-PRFs that are secure for even two constrained keys (for arbitrary constraining functions) imply iO [15].

Boneh *et al.* [8] also defined and constructed what they call *privately programmable PRFs* (PP-PRFs), which are CHC-PRFs for the class of point functions along with an additional programmability property: when deriving a constrained key, one can specify the outputs the key yields at the unauthorized points. They showed how to use PP-PRFs to build *watermarking* PRFs, a notion defined in [16]. While the PP-PRF and resulting watermarking PRF from [8] were based on indistinguishability obfuscation, Kim and Wu [23] later constructed watermarking PRFs from LWE, but via a different route that does not require PP-PRFs. To date, it has remained an open question whether PP-PRFs exist based on more standard (non-iO) assumptions.

1.1 Our Results

Our main contribution is a unified approach for constructing both constraint-hiding constrained PRFs for arbitrary polynomial-time constraints, and privately programmable PRFs, from LWE with subexponential $\exp(n^\varepsilon)$ approximation factors (i.e., inverse error rates), for any constant $\varepsilon > 0$. Both objects follow straightforwardly from a single LWE-based construction that we call a *shift-hiding shiftable function* (SHSF). Essentially, an SHSF allows for deriving a "shifted" key for a desired shift function, which remains hidden. The shifted key allows one to evaluate the *sum* of the original function and the shift function. We construct CHC-PRFs and PP-PRFs very simply by using an appropriate shift function, which is zero at authorized inputs, and either pseudorandom or programmed at unauthorized inputs.

CHC-PRFs. In comparison with [13], while we achieve the same ultimate result of CHC-PRFs for arbitrary constraints (with essentially the same efficiency metrics), our construction is more modular and arguably a good deal simpler.[1] Specifically, our SHSF construction uses just a few well-worn techniques from the literature on LWE-based fully homomorphic and attribute-based cryptography [5,18,20,21], and we get a CHC-PRF by invoking our SHSF with an *arbitrary* PRF as the shift function. By contrast, the construction from [13] melds the FHE/ABE techniques with a specific LWE-based PRF [2], and involves a handful of ad-hoc techniques to deal with various technical complications that arise.

PP-PRFs. Our approach also yields the first privately programmable PRFs from LWE, or indeed, any non-iO assumption. In fact, our PP-PRF allows for programming any polynomial number of inputs. Previously, the only potential approach for constructing PP-PRFs without iO [23] was from CHC-PRFs having certain extra properties (which constructions prior to our work did not possess), and was limited to programming only a logarithmic number of inputs.

1.2 Techniques

As mentioned above, the main ingredient in our constructions is what we call a *shift-hiding shiftable function* (SHSF). We briefly describe its properties. We have a keyed function $\mathsf{Eval} : \mathcal{K} \times \mathcal{X} \to \mathcal{Y}$, where $\mathcal{Y}$ is some finite additive group, and an algorithm $\mathsf{Shift}(\cdot, \cdot)$ to derive *shifted keys*. Given a secret key $msk \in \mathcal{K}$ and a function $H : \mathcal{X} \to \mathcal{Y}$, we can derive a shifted key $sk_H \leftarrow \mathsf{Shift}(msk, H)$. This key has the following two main properties:

- sk_H hides the shifting function H, and
- given sk_H we can compute an *approximation* of $\mathsf{Eval}(msk, \cdot) + H(\cdot)$ at any input, i.e., there exists a "shifted evaluation" algorithm SEval such that for every $x \in \mathcal{X}$,

$$\mathsf{SEval}(sk_H, x) \approx \mathsf{Eval}(msk, x) + H(x). \tag{1}$$

We emphasize that the SHSF itself does not have any pseudorandomness property; this will come from "rounding" the function in our PRF constructions, described next.

---

[1] Our construction was actually developed independently of [13], though not concurrently; we were unaware of its earlier non-public versions.

CHC-PRFs and PP-PRFs. We first briefly outline how we use SHSFs to construct CHC-PRFs and PP-PRFs. To construct a CHC-PRF we instantiate the SHSF with range $\mathcal{Y} = \mathbb{Z}_q^m$ for an appropriately chosen q. The CHC-PRF key is just a SHSF master key msk.

- To evaluate on an input $x \in \mathcal{X}$ using msk we output $\lfloor \mathsf{Eval}(msk, x) \rceil_p$, where $\lfloor \cdot \rceil_p$ denotes (coordinate-wise) "rounding" from $\mathbb{Z}_q$ to $\mathbb{Z}_p$ for some appropriate $p \ll q$.
- To generate a constrained key for a constraint circuit $C : \mathcal{X} \to \{0,1\}$, we sample a key k for an ordinary PRF F, define the shift function $H_{C,k}(x) := C(x) \cdot F_k(x)$, and output the shifted key

$$sk_C \leftarrow \mathsf{Shift}(msk, H_{C,k}).$$

Since Shift hides the circuit $H_{C,k}$, it follows that sk_C hides C.
- To evaluate on an input x using the constrained key sk_C, we output $\lfloor \mathsf{SEval}(sk_C, x) \rceil_p$.

Observe that for authorized inputs x (where $C(x) = 0$), we have $H_{C,k}(x) = 0$, so $\mathsf{SEval}(sk_C, x) \approx \mathsf{Eval}(msk, x)$ and therefore their rounded counterparts are equal with high probability. (This relies on the additional property that $\mathsf{Eval}(msk, x)$ is not to close to a "rounding border.") For unauthorized points x (where $C(x) = 1$), to see that the CHC-PRF output is pseudorandom given sk_C, notice that by Eq. (1), the output is (with high probability)

$$\lfloor \mathsf{Eval}(msk, x) \rceil_p = \lfloor \mathsf{SEval}(sk_C, x) - H(x) \rceil_p. \tag{2}$$

Because F is a pseudorandom function, $H(x) = F_k(x)$ completely "randomizes" the right-hand side above.

Turning now to PP-PRFs, for simplicity consider the case where we want to program the constrained key at a single input x^* (generalizing to polynomially many inputs is straightforward). A first idea is to use the same algorithms as in the above CHC-PRF, except that to program a key to output y at input x^* we define the shift function

$$H_{x^*,y}(x) = \begin{cases} y' - \mathsf{Eval}(msk, x^*) & \text{if } x = x^*, \\ 0 & \text{otherwise,} \end{cases} \tag{3}$$

where $y' \in \mathbb{Z}_q^m$ is chosen uniformly conditioned on $\lfloor y' \rceil_p = y$. As before, the programmed key is just the shifted key $sk_{x^*,y} \leftarrow \mathsf{Shift}(msk, H_{x^*,y})$. By Eq. (1), evaluating on the unauthorized input x^* using $sk_{x^*,y}$ indeed yields $\lfloor y' \rceil_p = y$. However, it is unclear whether the true (non-programmed) value of the function at the unauthorized input $x = x^*$ is pseudorandom given $sk_{x^*,y}$: in particular, because y is chosen by the adversary, $y' \in \mathbb{Z}_q^m$ may not be uniformly random.

To address this issue, we observe that the above construction satisfies a weaker pseudorandomness guarantee: if the adversary does not specify y but instead y is uniformly random, then by Eq. (2) the PP-PRF is pseudorandom at x^*. This observation leads us to our actual PP-PRF construction: we instantiate two of the above "weak" PP-PRFs with keys msk_1 and msk_2. To generate a programmed key for input x^* and output y, we first generate random additive shares y_1, y_2 such that $y = y_1 + y_2$, and output the programmed key $sk_{x^*,y} := (sk_{x^*,y_1}, sk_{x^*,y_2})$ where $sk_{x^*,y_i} \leftarrow \mathsf{Shift}(msk_i, H_{x^*,y_i})$ for $i = 1, 2$. Each evaluation algorithm (ordinary and programmed) is then defined simply as the sum of the corresponding evaluation algorithm from the "weak" construction using the two component keys. Because both programmed keys are generated for random target outputs y_i, we can prove pseudorandomness of the real function value.

Constructing SHSFs. We now give an overview of our construction of shift-hiding shifted functions. For simplicity, suppose the range of the functions is $\mathcal{Y} = \mathbb{Z}_q$; extending this to $\mathbb{Z}_q^m$ (as in our actual constructions) is straightforward. As in [6,23] our main tools are the "gadget-matrix homomorphisms" developed in the literature on fully homomorphic and attribute-based cryptography [5,18,20,21].

At a high level, our SHSF works as follows. The master secret key is just an LWE secret $\mathbf{s}$ whose first coordinate is 1. A shifted key for a shift function $H \colon \mathcal{X} \to \mathbb{Z}_q$ consists of LWE vectors (using secret $\mathbf{s}$) relative to some public matrices that have been "shifted" by multiples of the gadget matrix $\mathbf{G}$ [24]; more specifically, the multiples are the bits of FHE ciphertexts encrypting H, and the $\mathbb{Z}_q$-entries of the FHE secret key sk. To compute the shifted function on an input x, we do the following:

1. Using the gadget homomorphisms for boolean gates [5,18] on the LWE vectors corresponding to the FHE encryption of H, we compute LWE vectors relative to some publicly computable matrices, shifted by multiples of $\mathbf{G}$ corresponding to the bits of an FHE ciphertext encrypting $H(x)$.
2. Then, using the gadget homomorphisms for hidden linear functions [20] with the LWE vectors corresponding to the FHE secret key, we compute LWE vectors relative to some publicly computable matrix $\mathbf{B}_x$, but shifted by $(H(x) + e)\mathbf{G}$ where $H(x) + e \approx H(x) \in \mathbb{Z}_q$ is the "noisy plaintext" arising as the inner product of the FHE ciphertext and secret key. Taking just the first column, we therefore have an LWE sample relative to some vector $\mathbf{b}_x + (H(x) + e)\mathbf{u}_1$, where $\mathbf{u}_1$ is the first standard basis (column) vector.
3. Finally, because the first coordinate of the LWE secret $\mathbf{s}$ is 1, the above LWE sample is simply $\langle \mathbf{s}, \mathbf{b}_x \rangle + H(x) + e \approx \langle \mathbf{s}, \mathbf{b}_x \rangle + H(x) \in \mathbb{Z}_q$.

With the above in mind, we then define the (unshifted) function itself on an input x to simply compute $\mathbf{b}_x$ from the public parameters as above, and output $\langle \mathbf{s}, \mathbf{b}_x \rangle$. This yields Eq. (1).

2   Preliminaries

We denote row vectors by lower-case bold letters, e.g., $\mathbf{a}$. We denote matrices by upper-case bold letters, e.g., $\mathbf{A}$. The Kronecker product $\mathbf{A} \otimes \mathbf{B}$ of two matrices (or vectors) $\mathbf{A}$ and $\mathbf{B}$ is obtained by replacing each entry $a_{i,j}$ of $\mathbf{A}$ with the block $a_{i,j}\mathbf{B}$. The Kronecker product obeys the *mixed-product* property: $(\mathbf{A} \otimes \mathbf{B})(\mathbf{C} \otimes \mathbf{D}) = (\mathbf{AC}) \otimes (\mathbf{BD})$ for any matrices $\mathbf{A}, \mathbf{B}, \mathbf{C}, \mathbf{D}$ with compatible dimensions.

2.1   Gadgets and Homomorphisms

Here we recall "gadgets" [24] over $\mathbb{Z}_q$ and several of their homomorphic properties, some of which were implicit in [18], and which were developed and exploited further in [5,20,21].

For an integer modulus q, the gadget (or powers-of-two) vector over $\mathbb{Z}_q$ is defined as

$$\mathbf{g} = (1, 2, 4, \ldots, 2^{\lceil \lg q \rceil - 1}) \in \mathbb{Z}_q^{\lceil \lg q \rceil}. \tag{4}$$

For every $u \in \mathbb{Z}_q$, there is an (efficiently computable) binary vector $\mathbf{x} \in \{0, 1\}^{\lceil \lg q \rceil}$ such that $\langle \mathbf{g}, \mathbf{x} \rangle = \mathbf{g} \cdot \mathbf{x}^t = u \pmod{q}$. Phrased differently,

$$(\mathbf{x} \otimes \mathbf{g}) \cdot \mathbf{r}^t = \mathbf{u} \pmod{q} \tag{5}$$

for a certain binary $\mathbf{r} \in \{0, 1\}^{\lceil \lg q \rceil^2}$, namely, the one that selects all the products of the corresponding entries of $\mathbf{x}$ and $\mathbf{g}$.

The gadget matrix is defined as

$$\mathbf{G}_n = \mathbf{I}_n \otimes \mathbf{g} \in \mathbb{Z}_q^{n \times m},$$

where $m = n\lceil \lg q \rceil$. We often drop the subscript n when it is clear from context. We use algorithms BoolEval and LinEval, which have the following properties.

- BoolEval$(C, x, \mathbf{A})$, given a boolean circuit $C \colon \{0, 1\}^\ell \to \{0, 1\}^k$ of depth d, an $x \in \{0, 1\}^\ell$, and some $\mathbf{A} \in \mathbb{Z}_q^{n \times (\ell+1)m}$, outputs an integral matrix $\mathbf{R}_{C,x} \in \mathbb{Z}^{(\ell+1)m \times km}$ with $m^{O(d)}$-bounded entries for which

  $$(\mathbf{A} + (1, x) \otimes \mathbf{G}) \cdot \mathbf{R}_{C,x} = \mathbf{A}_C + C(x) \otimes \mathbf{G}, \tag{6}$$

  where $\mathbf{A}_C \in \mathbb{Z}_q^{n \times m}$ depends only on $\mathbf{A}$ and C (and not on x).[2]

- LinEval$(\mathbf{x}, \mathbf{C})$, given an $\mathbf{x} \in \{0, 1\}^\ell$ and a matrix $\mathbf{C} \in \mathbb{Z}_q^{n \times \ell m}$, outputs an integral matrix $\mathbf{R}_\mathbf{x} \in \mathbb{Z}^{2\ell m \times m}$ with $\mathrm{poly}(m, \ell)$-bounded entries such that, for all $\mathbf{A}, \mathbf{C} \in \mathbb{Z}_q^{n \times \ell m}$ and $\mathbf{k} \in \mathbb{Z}_q^\ell$,

  $$[\mathbf{A} + \mathbf{x} \otimes \mathbf{G} \mid \mathbf{C} + \mathbf{k} \otimes \mathbf{G}] \cdot \mathbf{R}_x = \mathbf{B} + \langle \mathbf{x}, \mathbf{k} \rangle \cdot \mathbf{G}, \tag{7}$$

  where $\mathbf{B} \in \mathbb{Z}_q^{n \times m}$ depends only on $\mathbf{A}$ and $\mathbf{C}$ (and not on $\mathbf{x}$ or $\mathbf{k}$).[3]

  More generally, for $\mathbf{x} \in \{0, 1\}^{k\ell}$ by applying the above to the ℓ-bit chunks of $\mathbf{x}$, in Eq. (7) we replace $\langle \mathbf{x}, \mathbf{k} \rangle \cdot \mathbf{G} = (\mathbf{x} \cdot \mathbf{k}^t) \cdot \mathbf{G}$ with $(\mathbf{x} \cdot (\mathbf{I}_k \otimes \mathbf{k}^t)) \otimes \mathbf{G}$, and now $\mathbf{R}_\mathbf{x} \in \mathbb{Z}^{(k+1)\ell m \times km}$, $\mathbf{A} \in \mathbb{Z}_q^{n \times k\ell m}$, and $\mathbf{B} \in \mathbb{Z}_q^{n \times km}$.

---

[2] This property is obtained by composing homomorphic addition and multiplication of $\mathbf{G}$-multiples; the extra 1 attached to x is needed to support NOT gates.

[3] We stress that LinEval does not need to know $\mathbf{k}$, which we view as representing a secret linear function that is hidden by $\mathbf{C}$.

2.2 Fully Homomorphic Encryption

We use the GSW (leveled) fully homomorphic encryption scheme [18] (KG, Enc, Eval), whose relevant properties for our needs are summarized as follows (we use only a symmetric-key version, which is sufficient for our purposes):

- KG($1^\lambda, q$), given a security parameter λ and a requested modulus q, outputs a secret key $\mathbf{k} \in \mathbb{Z}_q^\tau$ (for some $\tau = \text{poly}(\lambda, \log q)$).
- Enc($\mathbf{k}, m$), given a secret key $\mathbf{k}$ and a message $m \in \{0, 1\}$, outputs a ciphertext ct, which is a binary string.
- Eval($C, ct_1, \ldots, ct_\ell$), given a boolean circuit $C \colon \{0, 1\}^\ell \to \{0, 1\}$ and ciphertexts $ct_1, ct_2, \ldots, ct_\ell$, outputs a ciphertext $ct \in \{0, 1\}^{\tau\lceil \lg q \rceil}$.

Notice that in the above definition there is no explicit decryption algorithm. Instead we express the essential "noisy" linear relation between the result of homomorphic evaluation and the secret key: for any $\mathbf{k} \leftarrow \text{KG}(1^\lambda, q)$, any boolean circuit $C \colon \{0, 1\}^\ell \to \{0, 1\}$ of depth at most d, any messages $m_j \in \{0, 1\}$ and ciphertexts $ct_j \leftarrow \text{Enc}(\mathbf{k}, m_j)$ for $j = 1, \ldots, \ell$, we have

$$\text{Eval}(C, ct_1, \ldots, ct_\ell) \cdot (\mathbf{I}_{\lceil \lg q \rceil} \otimes \mathbf{k}^t) = C(m_1, \ldots, m_\ell) \otimes \mathbf{g} + \mathbf{e}(\bmod\ q) \quad (8)$$

for some integral error vector $\mathbf{e} \in [-B, B]^{\lceil \lg q \rceil}$, where $B = \lambda^{O(d)}$. In other words, multiplying (the τ-bit chunks of) the result of homomorphic evaluation with the secret key yields a "noisy" version of a robust encoding of the result (where the encoding is via the powers of two). While the robust encoding allows the noise to be removed, we will not need to do so explicitly.

More generally, if the circuit C has k-bit output, then Eval outputs a ciphertext in $\{0, 1\}^{\tau k \lceil \lg q \rceil}$ and Eq. (8) holds with $\mathbf{I}_{\lceil \lg q \rceil}$ replaced by $\mathbf{I}_{k \lceil \lg q \rceil}$.

2.3 Learning with Errors

For a positive integer dimension n and modulus q, and an error distribution χ over $\mathbb{Z}$, the LWE distribution and decision problem are defined as follows. For an $\mathbf{s} \in \mathbb{Z}^n$, the LWE distribution $A_{\mathbf{s}, \chi}$ is sampled by choosing a uniformly random $\mathbf{a} \leftarrow \mathbb{Z}_q^n$ and an error term $e \leftarrow \chi$, and outputting $(\mathbf{a}, b = \langle \mathbf{s}, \mathbf{a} \rangle + e) \in \mathbb{Z}_q^{n+1}$.

Definition 1. *The decision-LWE$_{n,q,\chi}$ problem is to distinguish, with nonnegligible advantage, between any desired (but polynomially bounded) number of independent samples drawn from $A_{\mathbf{s},\chi}$ for a single $\mathbf{s} \leftarrow \mathbb{Z}_q^n$, and the same number of uniformly random and independent samples over $\mathbb{Z}_q^{n+1}$.*

In this work we use a form of LWE where the first coordinate of the secret vector $\mathbf{s}$ is 1, i.e. $\mathbf{s} = (1, \bar{\mathbf{s}})$ where $\bar{\mathbf{s}} \leftarrow \mathbb{Z}_q^{n-1}$. It is easy to see that this is equivalent to LWE with an $(n-1)$-dimensional secret: the transformation mapping $(\mathbf{a}, b) \in \mathbb{Z}_q^{n-1} \times \mathbb{Z}_q$ to $((r, \mathbf{a}), b + r)$ for a uniformly random $r \in \mathbb{Z}_q$ (chosen freshly for each sample) maps samples from $A_{\bar{\mathbf{s}},\chi}$ to samples from $A_{\mathbf{s},\chi}$, and maps uniform samples to uniform samples.

A standard instantiation of LWE is to let χ be a *discrete Gaussian* distribution (over $\mathbb{Z}$) with parameter $r = 2\sqrt{n}$. A sample drawn from this distribution has magnitude bounded by, say, $r\sqrt{n} = \Theta(n)$ except with probability at most 2^{-n}. For this parameterization, it is known that LWE is at least as hard as *quantumly* approximating certain "short vector" problems on n-dimensional lattices, in the worst case, to within $\tilde{O}(q\sqrt{n})$ factors [27,28]. Classical reductions are also known for different parameterizations [12,26].

2.4 One Dimensional Rounded Short Integer Solution

As in [6,14,23] we make use of a special "one-dimensional, rounded" variant of the short integer solution problem (SIS). For the parameters we will use, this problem is actually no easier to solve than LWE is, but it is convenient to define it separately.

Definition 2 (1D-R-SIS [6,14]). *Let $p \in \mathbb{N}$ and let $p_1 < p_2 < \cdots < p_k$ be pairwise coprime and coprime with p. Let $q = p \cdot \prod_{i=1}^{k} p_i$. Then for positive numbers $m \in \mathbb{N}$ and B, the 1D-R-SIS$_{m,p,q,B}$ problem is as follows: given a uniformly random vector $\mathbf{v} \leftarrow \mathbb{Z}_q^m$, find $\mathbf{z} \in \mathbb{Z}^m$ such that $\|\mathbf{z}\| \leq B$ and*

$$\langle \mathbf{v}, \mathbf{z} \rangle \in \frac{q}{p}(\mathbb{Z} + \tfrac{1}{2}) + [-B, B]. \tag{9}$$

For sufficiently large $p_1 \geq B \cdot \mathrm{poly}(k, \log q)$, solving 1D-R-SIS is at least as hard as approximating certain "short vector" problems on k-dimensional lattices, in the worst case, to within certain $B \cdot \mathrm{poly}(k)$ factors [1,6,14,25].

3 Shift-Hiding Shiftable Functions

Here we present our construction of what we call *shift-hiding shiftable functions* (SHSFs), which we use in our subsequent constructions of CHC-PRFs and PP-PRFs. Because there are several parameters and we need some specific algebraic properties, we do not give an abstract definition of SHSF, but instead just give a construction (Sect. 3.2) and show the requisite properties (Sect. 3.3).

3.1 Notation

Let $\mathsf{GSW} = (\mathsf{KG}, \mathsf{Enc}, \mathsf{Eval})$ denote the GSW fully homomorphic encryption scheme (Sect. 2.2), where the secret key is in $\mathbb{Z}_q^\tau$ for some $\tau = \tau(\lambda)$. Recall that homomorphic evaluation of a function with k output bits produces a $\tau k \lceil \lg q \rceil$-bit ciphertext.

Our construction represents shift functions $H: \{0,1\}^\ell \to \mathbb{Z}_q^m$ by (bounded-size) boolean circuits. Specifically, we let $H': \{0,1\}^\ell \to \{0,1\}^k$ for $k = m\lceil \lg q \rceil$ be a boolean circuit where $H'(x)$ is the binary decomposition of $H(x)$, so that, following Eq. (5),

$$(H'(x) \otimes \mathbf{g}) \cdot (\mathbf{I}_m \otimes \mathbf{r}^t) = H(x) \in \mathbb{Z}_q^m. \tag{10}$$

Let $U(H', x) = H'(x)$ denote a universal circuit for boolean circuits $H' \colon \{0,1\}^\ell \to \{0,1\}^k$ of size σ, and let $U_x(\cdot) = U(\cdot, x)$. Its homomorphic analogue is as follows: letting $\overline{z}$ be the total length of fresh GSW ciphertexts encrypting a circuit of size σ, for any $x \in \{0,1\}^\ell$ define

$$\overline{U}_x \colon \{0,1\}^{\overline{z}} \to \{0,1\}^{\tau k \lceil \lg q \rceil} \tag{11}$$

$$\overline{U}_x(ct) = \mathsf{GSW.Eval}(U_x, ct). \tag{12}$$

Observe that $\overline{U}_x$ can be implemented as a boolean circuit of size (and hence depth) $\mathrm{poly}(\lambda, \sigma)$.

3.2 Construction

Here we give the tuple of algorithms $(\mathsf{Setup}, \mathsf{KeyGen}, \mathsf{Eval}, \mathsf{Shift}, \mathsf{SEval}, \mathcal{S})$ that make up our SHSF. For security parameter λ and constraint circuit size σ the algorithms are parameterized by some $n = \mathrm{poly}(\lambda, \sigma)$ and $q = 2^{\mathrm{poly}(\lambda,\sigma)}$, with $m = n\lceil \lg q \rceil = \mathrm{poly}(\lambda, \sigma)$; we instantiate these more precisely in Sect. 3.4 below.

Construction 1. Let $\mathcal{X} = \{0,1\}^\ell$ and $\mathcal{Y} = \mathbb{Z}_q^m$. Define:

- $\mathsf{Setup}(1^\lambda, 1^\sigma)$: Sample uniformly random and independent matrices $\mathbf{A} \in \mathbb{Z}_q^{n \times (\overline{z}+1)m}$ and $\mathbf{C} \in \mathbb{Z}_q^{n \times \tau m}$, and output $pp = (\mathbf{A}, \mathbf{C})$.
  (The n-by-m chunks of $\mathbf{A}$ will correspond to the $\overline{z}$ bits of a GSW encryption of the shift function; similarly, the chunks of $\mathbf{C}$ will correspond to the GSW secret key in $\mathbb{Z}_q^\tau$.)
- $\mathsf{KeyGen}(pp)$: Sample $\mathbf{s}' \leftarrow \mathbb{Z}_q^{n-1}$ and set $\mathbf{s} = (1, \mathbf{s}')$. Output the master secret key $msk = \mathbf{s}$.
- $\mathsf{Eval}(pp, msk, x \in \{0,1\}^\ell)$: compute

$$\mathbf{R}_0 = \mathsf{BoolEval}(\overline{U}_x, 0^{\overline{z}}, \mathbf{A}) \in \mathbb{Z}^{(\overline{z}+1)m \times \tau k \lceil \lg q \rceil m} \tag{13}$$

and let

$$\mathbf{A}_x = (\mathbf{A} + (1, 0^{\overline{z}}) \otimes \mathbf{G}) \cdot \mathbf{R}_0 - \overline{U}_x(0^{\overline{z}}) \otimes \mathbf{G} \in \mathbb{Z}_q^{n \times \tau k \lceil \lg q \rceil m}. \tag{14}$$

(Observe that by Eq. (6), $\mathbf{A}_x = \mathbf{A}_C$ for the circuit $C = \overline{U}_x$, and does not depend on the "dummy" ciphertext $0^{\overline{z}}$, which stands in for a GSW encryption of a shift function.)
Next, compute

$$\mathbf{R}_0' = \mathsf{LinEval}(\overline{U}_x(0^{\overline{z}}), \mathbf{C}) \in \mathbb{Z}^{\tau(k \lceil \lg q \rceil + 1)m \times k \lceil \lg q \rceil m} \tag{15}$$

and let

$$\mathbf{B}_x = [\mathbf{A}_x + \overline{U}_x(0^{\overline{z}}) \otimes \mathbf{G} \mid \mathbf{C}] \cdot \mathbf{R}_0' \in \mathbb{Z}_q^{n \times k \lceil \lg q \rceil m}. \tag{16}$$

(Observe that this corresponds to taking $\mathbf{k} = \mathbf{0}$ in Eq. (7), so $\mathbf{B}_x$ does not depend on the "dummy" ciphertext $0^{\bar{z}}$; it depends only on $\mathbf{A}_x$, hence $\mathbf{A}$ and x, and $\mathbf{C}$.)

Finally, output

$$\mathbf{s} \cdot \mathbf{B}_x \cdot (\mathbf{I}_m \otimes \mathbf{r}^t \otimes \mathbf{u}_1^t) \in \mathbb{Z}_q^m, \tag{17}$$

where $\mathbf{r} \in \{0, 1\}^{\lceil \lg q \rceil^2}$ is as in Eq. (10) and $\mathbf{u}_1 \in \mathbb{Z}^m$ is the first standard basis vector.

- Shift(pp, msk, H): for a shift function $H \colon \{0, 1\}^\ell \to \mathbb{Z}_q^m$ whose binary decomposition $H' \colon \{0, 1\}^\ell \to \{0, 1\}^k$ can be implemented by a circuit of size σ, sample a GSW encryption key $\mathbf{k} \leftarrow \mathsf{GSW.KG}(1^\lambda, q)$, then encrypt H' bit-by-bit under this key to obtain a ciphertext $ct \leftarrow \mathsf{GSW.Enc}_\mathbf{k}(H')$. Next, let

$$\mathbf{a} = \mathbf{s}(\mathbf{A} + (1, ct) \otimes \mathbf{G}) + \mathbf{e} \tag{18}$$
$$\mathbf{c} = \mathbf{s}(\mathbf{C} + \mathbf{k} \otimes \mathbf{G}) + \mathbf{e}' \tag{19}$$

where $\mathbf{e}$ and $\mathbf{e}'$ are error vectors whose entries are sampled independently from χ. Output

$$sk_H = (ct, \mathbf{a}, \mathbf{c}). \tag{20}$$

(Recall that $\mathbf{A}' = \mathbf{A} + (1, ct) \otimes \mathbf{G}$ and $\mathbf{C}' = \mathbf{C} + \mathbf{k} \otimes \mathbf{G}$ support homomorphic operations on ct and $\mathbf{k}$ via right-multiplication by short matrices, using the gadget homomorphisms. Shifted evaluation, defined next, performs such right-multiplications on $\mathbf{a} \approx \mathbf{s}\mathbf{A}', \mathbf{c} \approx \mathbf{s}\mathbf{C}'$.)

- SEval(pp, sk_H, x): On input $sk_H = (ct, \mathbf{a}, \mathbf{c})$ and $x \in \{0, 1\}^\ell$, compute

$$\mathbf{R}_{ct} = \mathsf{BoolEval}(\overline{U}_x, ct, \mathbf{A}) \tag{21}$$
$$\mathbf{a}_x = \mathbf{a} \cdot \mathbf{R}_{ct}. \tag{22}$$

(By Eq. (6), we have $\mathbf{a}_x \approx \mathbf{s}(\mathbf{A}_x + \overline{U}_x(ct) \otimes \mathbf{G})$, where recall that $\overline{U}_x(ct)$ is a GSW encryption of $H'(x)$, computed homomorphically.)

Next, compute

$$\mathbf{R}'_{ct} = \mathsf{LinEval}(\overline{U}_x(ct), \mathbf{C}) \tag{23}$$
$$\mathbf{b}_x = [\mathbf{a}_x \mid \mathbf{c}] \cdot \mathbf{R}'_{ct}. \tag{24}$$

(By Eqs. (7) for LinEval and (8) for GSW decryption, we have $\mathbf{b}_x \approx \mathbf{s}(\mathbf{B}_x + \mathbf{h}' \otimes \mathbf{G})$, where $\mathbf{h}'$ is a noisy version of the robust encoding $H'(x) \otimes \mathbf{g}$.)

Finally, output

$$\mathbf{b}_x \cdot (\mathbf{I}_m \otimes \mathbf{r}^t \otimes \mathbf{u}_1^t) \in \mathbb{Z}_q^m, \tag{25}$$

where $\mathbf{r}, \mathbf{u}_1$ are as in Eval above.

(Here the $\mathbf{I}_m \otimes \mathbf{r}^t$ term reconstructs a noisy version of $H(x) \in \mathbb{Z}_q^m$ from $\mathbf{h}'$ as in Eq. (10), and the $\mathbf{u}_1^t \in \mathbb{Z}^m$ term selects the first column of $\mathbf{G}$, whose inner product with $\mathbf{s}$ is 1.)

- $\mathcal{S}(1^\lambda, 1^\sigma)$: Sample a GSW secret key $\mathbf{k} \leftarrow \mathsf{GSW.KG}(1^\lambda, q)$ and compute (by encrypting bit-by-bit) $ct \leftarrow \mathsf{GSW.Enc}_\mathbf{k}(C)$, where C is some arbitrary size-σ boolean circuit. Sample uniformly random and independent $\mathbf{A} \leftarrow \mathbb{Z}_q^{n \times (\bar{z}+1)m}, \mathbf{a} \leftarrow \mathbb{Z}_q^{(\bar{z}+1)m}, \mathbf{C} \leftarrow \mathbb{Z}_q^{n \times \tau m}, \mathbf{c} \leftarrow \mathbb{Z}_q^{\tau m}$. Output $pp = (\mathbf{A}, \mathbf{C})$ and $sk = (ct, \mathbf{a}, \mathbf{c})$.

3.3 Properties

Here we prove the three main properties of our SHSF that we will use in subsequent sections.

Lemma 1 (Shift Hiding). *Assuming the hardness of $LWE_{n-1,q,\chi}$ and CPA security of the GSW encryption scheme, for any PPT $\mathcal{A}$ and any $\sigma = \sigma(\lambda) = \mathrm{poly}(\lambda)$,*

$$\{\mathsf{RealKey}_{\mathcal{A}}(1^\lambda, 1^\sigma)\}_{\lambda \in \mathbb{N}} \stackrel{c}{\approx} \{\mathsf{IdealKey}_{\mathcal{A}}(1^\lambda, 1^\sigma)\}_{\lambda \in \mathbb{N}}, \tag{26}$$

where $\mathsf{RealKey}$ and $\mathsf{IdealKey}$ are the respective views of $\mathcal{A}$ in the experiments defined in Fig. 1.

Proof. Let $\mathcal{A}$ be any polynomial-time adversary. To show that Eq. (26) holds we define a sequence of hybrid experiments and show that they are indistinguishable.

Hybrid H_0: This is the experiment $\mathsf{RealKey}$.

Hybrid H_1: This is the same as H_0, except that we modify how the $\mathbf{A}$ and $\mathbf{C}$ are constructed as follows: after we generate ct and $\mathbf{k}$ we choose uniformly random $\mathbf{A}'$ and $\mathbf{C}'$ and set

$$\mathbf{A} = \mathbf{A}' - (1, ct) \otimes \mathbf{G} \tag{27}$$
$$\mathbf{C} = \mathbf{C}' - \mathbf{k} \otimes \mathbf{G}. \tag{28}$$

Hybrid H_2: This is the same as H_1, except that we sample the $\mathbf{a}_i$ and $\mathbf{c}_j$ uniformly at random from $\mathbb{Z}_q^m$.

Hybrid H_3: This is the same as H_2, except that we again directly choose $\mathbf{A}, \mathbf{C}$ uniformly at random (without choosing $\mathbf{A}', \mathbf{C}'$).

Hybrid H_4: This is the same as H_2, except that ct encrypts the (arbitrary) size-σ circuit C (as in $\mathcal{S}$) instead of H', i.e., we set $ct \leftarrow \mathsf{GSW.Enc}_{\mathbf{k}'}(C)$. Observe that this is exactly the experiment $\mathsf{IdealKey}$.

Claim 1. H_0 and H_1 are identical.

Proof. This is because $\mathbf{A}'$ and $\mathbf{C}'$ are uniformly random and independent of ct and $\mathbf{k}$.

procedure $\mathsf{RealKey}_{\mathcal{A}}(1^\lambda, 1^\rho)$
   $H \leftarrow \mathcal{A}(1^\lambda, 1^\sigma)$
   $pp \leftarrow \mathsf{Setup}(1^\lambda, 1^\rho)$
   $msk \leftarrow \mathsf{KeyGen}(pp)$
   $sk \leftarrow \mathsf{Shift}(pp, msk, H)$
   $(pp, sk) \to \mathcal{A}$

(a) The real shifted key generation experiment

procedure $\mathsf{IdealKey}_{\mathcal{A}}(1^\lambda, 1^\sigma)$
   $H \leftarrow \mathcal{A}(1^\lambda, 1^\sigma)$
   $(pp, sk) \leftarrow \mathcal{S}(1^\lambda, 1^\sigma)$
   $(pp, sk) \to \mathcal{A}$

(b) The random key generation experiment

Fig. 1. The real and random shifted key generation experiments.

Claim 2. Assuming the hardness of $\mathsf{LWE}_{n-1,q,\chi}$, we have $H_1 \overset{c}{\approx} H_2$.

Proof. We use any adversary $\mathcal{A}$ that attempts to distinguish H_1 from H_2 to build an adversary $\mathcal{A}'$ that solves $\mathsf{LWE}_{n-1,q,\chi}$ with the same advantage. First, $\mathcal{A}'$ receives samples $(\mathbf{A}', \mathbf{a}) \in \mathbb{Z}_q^{n \times (\bar{z}+1)m} \times \mathbb{Z}_q^{(\bar{z}+1)m}$ and $(\mathbf{C}', \mathbf{c}) \in \mathbb{Z}_q^{n \times \tau m} \times \mathbb{Z}_q^{\tau m}$, then proceeds exactly as in H_1 to interact with $\mathcal{A}$, and outputs what $\mathcal{A}$ outputs. If the samples are LWE samples from $A_{\mathbf{s},\chi}$ where $\mathbf{s} = (1, \mathbf{s}')$ for $\mathbf{s}' \leftarrow \mathbb{Z}_q^{n-1}$, then

$$\mathbf{a} = \mathbf{s} \cdot \mathbf{A}' + \mathbf{e} = \mathbf{s}(\mathbf{A} + (1, ct) \otimes \mathbf{G}) + \mathbf{e}$$
$$\mathbf{c} = \mathbf{s} \cdot \mathbf{C}' + \mathbf{e}' = \mathbf{s}(\mathbf{C} + \mathbf{k} \otimes \mathbf{G}) + \mathbf{e}'$$

for error vectors $\mathbf{e}, \mathbf{e}'$ whose entries are drawn from χ, therefore $\mathcal{A}$'s view is identical to its view in H_1. If the samples are uniformly random, then $\mathcal{A}$'s view is identical to its view in H_2. This proves the claim.

Claim 3. H_2 and H_3 are identical.

Proof. This is because $\mathbf{A}', \mathbf{C}'$ are uniformly random and independent of ct and $\mathbf{k}$.

Claim 4. If GSW is CPA-secure then $H_3 \overset{c}{\approx} H_4$.

Proof. This follows immediately from the fact that the GSW secret key $\mathbf{k} \leftarrow \mathsf{GSW.KG}(1^\lambda, q)$ is used only to encrypt H (yielding ct) or the arbitrary circuit C, respectively, in H_3 and H_4.

This completes the proof of Lemma 1.

Lemma 2 (Border Avoiding). *For any PPT $\mathcal{A}$, $i \in [m]$, $\lambda \in \mathbb{N}$ and $\sigma = \mathrm{poly}(\lambda)$, assuming the hardness of $\mathsf{1D\text{-}R\text{-}SIS}_{(\bar{z}+\tau+1)m,p,q,B}$ for some large enough $B = m^{\mathrm{poly}(\lambda,\sigma)} = \lambda^{\mathrm{poly}(\lambda)}$, we have*

$$\Pr_{\substack{(pp,sk) \leftarrow \mathcal{S}(1^\lambda, 1^\sigma) \\ x \leftarrow \mathcal{A}(pp,sk)}} \left[\mathsf{Eval}(pp, sk, x)_i \in \tfrac{q}{p}(\mathbb{Z} + \tfrac{1}{2}) + [-B, +B] \right] \leq \mathrm{negl}(\lambda). \tag{29}$$

Proof. We show how to use an adversary which finds an $x \in \mathcal{X}$ such that

$$\mathsf{SEval}(pp, sk, x)_i \in \tfrac{q}{p}(\mathbb{Z} + \tfrac{1}{2}) + [-B, +B] \tag{30}$$

for some $i \in [m]$ to solve 1D-R-SIS.

Given a (uniformly random) $\mathsf{1D\text{-}R\text{-}SIS}_{(\bar{z}+\tau+1)m,p,q,B}$ challenge $\mathbf{v} = (\mathbf{a}, \mathbf{c}) \in \mathbb{Z}_q^{(\bar{z}+1)m} \times \mathbb{Z}_q^{\tau m}$, we put $\mathbf{a}, \mathbf{c}$ in the sk given to $\mathcal{A}$, and generate pp in the same way as in the $\mathcal{S}$ algorithm. Let x be a query output by $\mathcal{A}$, and consider the response

$$\mathbf{y}_x = \mathsf{SEval}(pp, (ct, \mathbf{a}, \mathbf{c}), x) \tag{31}$$
$$= \mathbf{b}_x \cdot \mathbf{U} \tag{32}$$
$$= [\mathbf{a} \mid \mathbf{c}] \underbrace{\begin{bmatrix} \mathbf{R}_{ct} \\ & \mathbf{I}_{\tau m} \end{bmatrix} \cdot \mathbf{R}'_{ct} \cdot \mathbf{U}}_{\mathbf{T}}, \tag{33}$$

where $\mathbf{R}_{ct}, \mathbf{R}'_{ct}$ are $m^{\mathrm{poly}(\lambda,\sigma)}$-bounded matrices as computed by SEval, and $\mathbf{U}$ is a binary matrix. Now if Eq. (30) holds for some $i \in [m]$, then $(\mathbf{y}_x)_i \in \frac{q}{p}(\mathbb{Z} + \frac{1}{2}) + [-B, B]$, which means that the ith column of $\mathbf{T}$ is a valid 1D-R-SIS$_{(\overline{z}+\tau+1)m,p,q,B}$ solution to the challenge $\mathbf{v} = (\mathbf{a}, \mathbf{c})$, as desired.

Lemma 3 (Approximate Shift Correctness). *For any shift function $H\colon \{0,1\}^\ell \to \mathbb{Z}_q^m$ whose binary decomposition $H'\colon \{0,1\}^\ell \to \{0,1\}^k$ can be represented by a boolean circuit of size σ, and any $x \in \{0,1\}^\ell$, $pp \leftarrow \mathsf{Setup}(1^\lambda, 1^\rho)$, $msk \leftarrow \mathsf{KeyGen}(pp)$ and $sk_H \leftarrow \mathsf{Shift}(pp, msk, H)$, we have*

$$\mathsf{SEval}(pp, sk_H, x) \approx \mathsf{Eval}(pp, msk, x) + H(x) \tag{34}$$

where the approximation hides some $\lambda^{\mathrm{poly}(\lambda)}$-bounded error vector.

Proof. Let $\mathbf{a}, \mathbf{a}_x, \mathbf{b}_x, \mathbf{c}, \mathbf{A}_x$ and $\mathbf{B}_x$ be as defined in algorithms SEval, Eval and Shift. First, observe that by definition of $\mathbf{a} \approx \mathbf{s}(\mathbf{A} + (1, ct) \otimes \mathbf{G})$, $\mathbf{a}_x = \mathbf{a} \cdot \mathbf{R}_{ct}$, and Eq. (6), we have

$$\mathbf{a}_x \approx \mathbf{s}(\mathbf{A} + (1, ct) \otimes \mathbf{G}) \cdot \mathbf{R}_{ct} \tag{35}$$
$$= \mathbf{s}(\mathbf{A}_x + \overline{U}_x(ct) \otimes \mathbf{G}), \tag{36}$$

where the approximation hides an error vector with entries bounded by $m^{\mathrm{poly}(\lambda,\sigma)} = \lambda^{\mathrm{poly}(\lambda)}$. Similarly, by definition of $\mathbf{b}_x$, the generalized Eq. (7), and the generalized Eq. (8) we have

$$\mathbf{b}_x = [\mathbf{a}_x \mid \mathbf{c}] \cdot \mathbf{R}'_{ct} \tag{37}$$
$$\approx \mathbf{s}[\mathbf{A}_x + \overline{U}_x(ct) \otimes \mathbf{G} \mid \mathbf{C} + \mathbf{k} \otimes \mathbf{G}] \cdot \mathbf{R}'_{ct} \tag{38}$$
$$= \mathbf{s}(\mathbf{B}_x + (\overline{U}_x(ct) \cdot (\mathbf{I}_{k\lceil \lg q \rceil} \otimes \mathbf{k}^t)) \otimes \mathbf{G}) \tag{39}$$
$$= \mathbf{s}(\mathbf{B}_x + (H'(x) \otimes \mathbf{g} + \mathbf{e}_x) \otimes \mathbf{G}) \tag{40}$$

where the approximation hides some $\lambda^{\mathrm{poly}(\lambda)}$-bounded error, and $\mathbf{e}_x$ is also $\lambda^{\mathrm{poly}(\lambda)}$-bounded. Therefore, by Eq. (10), the mixed-product property, and because $\mathbf{G} \cdot \mathbf{u}_1^t = \mathbf{u}_1^t \in \mathbb{Z}_q^n$, and the first coordinate of $\mathbf{s}$ is 1, the output of $\mathsf{SEval}(pp, sk_H, x)$ is

$$\mathbf{b}_x \cdot (\mathbf{I}_m \otimes \mathbf{r}^t \otimes \mathbf{u}_1^t) \approx \mathbf{s}\mathbf{B}_x \cdot (\mathbf{I}_m \otimes \mathbf{r}^t \otimes \mathbf{u}_1^t) + \mathbf{s}((H'(x) \otimes \mathbf{g} + \mathbf{e}_x) \otimes \mathbf{G})$$
$$\cdot (\mathbf{I}_m \otimes \mathbf{r}^t \otimes \mathbf{u}_1^t) \tag{41}$$
$$= \mathsf{Eval}(pp, msk, x) + \mathbf{s}((H(x) + \mathbf{e}_x(\mathbf{I}_m \otimes \mathbf{r}^t)) \otimes \mathbf{u}_1^t) \tag{42}$$
$$= \mathsf{Eval}(pp, msk, x) + H(x) + \mathbf{e}_x(\mathbf{I}_m \otimes \mathbf{r}^t) \tag{43}$$
$$\approx \mathsf{Eval}(pp, msk, x) + H(x), \tag{44}$$

where again the approximations hide $\lambda^{\mathrm{poly}(\lambda)}$-bounded error vectors, as claimed.

The following is an immediate consequence of Lemma 3.

Corollary 1. *Fix the same notation as in Lemma 3. If for all $i \in [m]$ we have*

$$(\mathsf{SEval}(pp, sk, x) - H(x))_i \notin \tfrac{q}{p}(\mathbb{Z} + \tfrac{1}{2}) + [-B, +B], \tag{45}$$

then

$$\lfloor \mathsf{SEval}(pp, sk, x) - H(x) \rceil_p = \lfloor \mathsf{Eval}(pp, msk, x) \rceil_p. \tag{46}$$

3.4   Parameter Instantiation

We now instantiate the LWE parameters n, q and the 1D-R-SIS parameter k to correspond with subexponential $\exp(n^{\varepsilon})$ and $\exp(k^{\varepsilon})$ approximation factors for the underlying worst-case lattice problems, for an arbitrary desired constant $\varepsilon > 0$. Let $B = \lambda^{\mathrm{poly}(\lambda)}$ be the bound from Corollary 1. For 1D-R-SIS we need to choose k sufficiently large primes $p_i = B \cdot \mathrm{poly}(\lambda) = \lambda^{\mathrm{poly}(\lambda)}$ to get an approximation factor of

$$B \cdot \mathrm{poly}(\lambda) = \lambda^{\mathrm{poly}(\lambda)}$$

for k-dimensional lattices. Therefore, we can choose a sufficiently large $k = \mathrm{poly}(\lambda)$ to make this factor $\exp(k^{\varepsilon})$. We then set

$$q = p \prod_{i=1}^{k} p_i = p \cdot \lambda^{k \cdot \mathrm{poly}(\lambda)} = \lambda^{\mathrm{poly}(\lambda)},$$

which corresponds to some $\lambda^{\mathrm{poly}(\lambda)}$ approximation factor for n-dimensional lattices. Again, we can choose a sufficiently large $n = \mathrm{poly}(\lambda)$ to make this factor $\exp(n^{\varepsilon})$.

4   Constraint-Hiding Constrained PRF

In this section we formally define constraint-hiding constrained PRFs (CHC-PRFs) and give a construction based on our shiftable PRF from Sect. 3.

4.1   Definition

Here we give the definition of CHC-PRFs, specializing the simulation-based definition of [15] to the case of a single constrained-key query.

Definition 3. *A constrained function is a tuple of efficient algorithms* (Setup, KeyGen, Eval, Constrain, CEval) *having the following interfaces (where the domain $\mathcal{X}$ and range $\mathcal{Y}$ may depend on the security parameter):*

- Setup($1^{\lambda}, 1^{\sigma}$), *given the security parameter λ and an upper bound σ on the size of the constraining circuit, outputs public parameters pp.*
- KeyGen(pp), *given the public parameters pp, outputs a master secret key msk.*
- Eval(pp, msk, x), *given the master secret key and an input $x \in \mathcal{X}$, outputs some $y \in \mathcal{Y}$.*

- Constrain(pp, msk, C), *given the master secret key and a circuit C of size at most σ, outputs a constrained key sk_C.*
- CEval(pp, sk_C, x), *given a constrained key sk_C and an input $x \in \mathcal{X}$, outputs some $y \in \mathcal{Y}$.*

Definition 4. *A constrained function is a constraint-hiding constrained PRF (CHC-PRF) if there is a PPT simulator $\mathcal{S}$ such that, for any PPT adversary $\mathcal{A}$ (that without loss of generality never repeats a query) and any $\sigma = \sigma(\lambda) = \text{poly}(\lambda)$,*

$$\{\mathsf{Real}_{\mathcal{A}}(1^\lambda, 1^\sigma)\}_{\lambda \in \mathbb{N}} \overset{c}{\approx} \{\mathsf{Ideal}_{\mathcal{A}, \mathcal{S}}(1^\lambda, 1^\sigma)\}_{\lambda \in \mathbb{N}}, \qquad (47)$$

where Real *and* Ideal *are the respective views of $\mathcal{A}$ in the experiments defined in Fig. 2.*

The above simulation-based definition simultaneously captures privacy of the constraining function, pseudorandomness on unauthorized inputs, and correctness of constrained evaluation on authorized inputs. The first two properties (privacy and pseudorandomness) follow because in the ideal experiment, the simulator must generate a constrained key without knowing the constraining function, and the adversary gets oracle access to a function that is uniformly random on unauthorized inputs.

For correctness, we claim that the real experiment is computationally indistinguishable from a modified one where each query x is answered as CEval(pp, sk_C, x) if x is authorized (i.e., $C(x) = 0$), and as Eval(pp, msk, x) otherwise. In particular, this implies that Eval$(pp, msk, x) = $ CEval(pp, sk_C, x) with all but negligible probability for all the adversary's authorized queries x. Indistinguishability of the real and modified experiments follows by a routine hybrid argument, with the ideal experiment as the intermediate one. In particular, the reduction that links the ideal and modified real experiments itself answers authorized queries x using CEval, and handles unauthorized queries by passing them to its oracle.

procedure Real$_{\mathcal{A}}(1^\lambda, 1^\sigma)$
   $C \leftarrow \mathcal{A}(1^\lambda, 1^\sigma)$
   $pp \leftarrow$ Setup(1^λ)
   $msk \leftarrow$ KeyGen(pp)
   $sk_C \leftarrow$ Constrain(pp, msk, C)
   $(pp, sk_C) \to \mathcal{A}$
   repeat
     $x \leftarrow \mathcal{A}$
     Eval$(pp, msk, x) \to \mathcal{A}$
   until $\mathcal{A}$ halts

(a) The real experiment

procedure Ideal$_{\mathcal{A}, \mathcal{S}}(1^\lambda, 1^\sigma)$
   $C \leftarrow \mathcal{A}(1^\lambda, 1^\sigma)$
   $(pp, sk) \leftarrow \mathcal{S}(1^\lambda, 1^\sigma)$
   $(pp, sk) \to \mathcal{A}$
   repeat
     $x \leftarrow \mathcal{A}$
     if $C(x) = 0$ **then**
       CEval$(pp, sk, x) \to \mathcal{A}$
     else
       $y \leftarrow \mathcal{Y}; y \to \mathcal{A}$
   until $\mathcal{A}$ halts

(b) The ideal experiment

Fig. 2. The real and ideal experiments.

4.2   Construction

We now describe our construction of a CHC-PRF for domain $\mathcal{X} = \{0,1\}^\ell$ and range $\mathcal{Y} = \mathbb{Z}_p^m$, which handles constraining circuits of size σ. It uses the following components:

- A pseudorandom function PRF = (PRF.KG, PRF.Eval) having domain $\{0,1\}^\ell$ and range $\mathbb{Z}_q^m$, with key space $\{0,1\}^\kappa$.
- The shift hiding shiftable function SHSF = (Setup, KeyGen, Eval, Shift, SEval, Sim) from Sect. 3, which has parameters q, B that appear in the analysis below.

For a boolean circuit C of size at most σ and some $k \in \{0,1\}^\kappa$ define the function $H_{C,k} \colon \{0,1\}^\ell \to \mathbb{Z}_q^m$ as

$$H_{C,k}(x) = C(x) \cdot \mathsf{PRF.Eval}(k,x) = \begin{cases} \mathsf{PRF.Eval}(k,x) & \text{if } U(C,x) = 1 \\ 0 & \text{otherwise.} \end{cases} \tag{48}$$

Notice that the size of (the binary decomposition of) $H_{C,k}$ is upper bounded by

$$\sigma' = \sigma + s + \mathrm{poly}(n, \log q), \tag{49}$$

where s is the circuit size of (the binary decomposition of) $\mathsf{PRF.Eval}(k, \cdot)$.

Construction 2. Our CHC-PRF with domain $\mathcal{X} = \{0,1\}^\ell$ and range $\mathcal{Y} = \mathbb{Z}_p^m$ is defined as follows:

- Setup($1^\lambda, 1^\sigma$): output $pp \leftarrow \mathsf{SHSF.Setup}(1^\lambda, 1^{\sigma'})$ where σ' is defined as in Eq. (49).
- KeyGen(pp): output $msk \leftarrow \mathsf{SHSF.KeyGen}(pp)$.
- Eval($pp, msk, x \in \{0,1\}^\ell$): compute $\mathbf{y}_x = \mathsf{SHSF.Eval}(pp, msk, x)$ and output $\lfloor \mathbf{y}_x \rceil_p$.
- Constrain(pp, msk, C): on input a circuit C of size at most σ, sample a PRF key $k \leftarrow \mathsf{PRF.KG}(1^\lambda)$ and output $sk_C \leftarrow \mathsf{SHSF.Shift}(pp, msk, H_{C,k})$.
- CEval(pp, sk_C, x): on input a constrained key sk_C and $x \in \{0,1\}^\ell$, output $\lfloor \mathsf{SHSF.SEval}(pp, sk_C, x) \rceil_p$.

4.3   Security Proof

Theorem 1. *Construction 2 is a constraint-hiding constrained PRF assuming the hardness of* $\mathsf{LWE}_{n-1,q,\chi}$ *and* $1D\text{-}R\text{-}SIS_{(z\sigma'+\tau+1)m,p,q,B}$ *(where z, τ are respectively the lengths of fresh GSW ciphertexts and secret keys as used in* SHSF*), the CPA security of the GSW encryption scheme, and that* PRF *is a pseudorandom function.*

Proof. Our simulator $\mathcal{S}(1^\lambda, 1^\sigma)$ for Construction 2 simply outputs $\mathsf{SHSF}.\mathcal{S}(1^\lambda, 1^{\sigma'})$. Now let $\mathcal{A}$ be any polynomial-time adversary. To show that $\mathcal{S}$ satisfies Definition 4 we define a sequence of hybrid experiments and show that they are indistinguishable. Before defining the experiments in detail, we first define a particular "bad" event in all but one of them.

Definition 5. *In each of the following hybrid experiments except H_0, each query x is answered as $\lfloor \mathbf{y}_x \rceil_p$ for some $\mathbf{y}_x$ that is computed in a certain way. Define* Borderline *to be the event that at least one such $\mathbf{y}_x$ has some coordinate in $\frac{q}{p}(\mathbb{Z} + \frac{1}{2}) + [-B, B]$.*

Hybrid H_0: This is the ideal experiment $\mathsf{Ideal}_{\mathcal{A}, \mathcal{S}}$.

Hybrid H_1: This is the same as H_0, except that on every unauthorized query x (i.e., where $C(x) = 1$), instead of returning a uniformly random value from $\mathbb{Z}_p^m$, we choose $\mathbf{y}_x \leftarrow \mathbb{Z}_q^m$ and output $\lfloor \mathbf{y}_x \rceil_p$.

Hybrid H_2: This is the same as H_1, except that we abort the experiment if Borderline happens.

Hybrid H_3: This is the same as H_2, except that we initially choose a PRF key $k \leftarrow \mathsf{PRF.KG}(1^\lambda)$ and change how unauthorized queries x (i.e., where $C(x) = 1$) are handled, answering all queries according to a slightly modified CEval. Specifically, for any query x we answer $\lfloor \mathbf{y}_x \rceil_p$ where

$$\mathbf{y}_x = \mathsf{SHSF.SEval}(pp, sk, x) - C(x) \cdot \mathsf{PRF.Eval}(k, x). \tag{50}$$

Hybrid H_4: This is the same as H_3, except that (pp, sk) are generated as in the real experiment. More formally we instantiate $pp \leftarrow \mathsf{SHSF.Setup}(1^\lambda, 1^{\sigma'})$, $msk \leftarrow \mathsf{SHSF.KeyGen}(pp)$ and compute $sk \leftarrow \mathsf{SHSF.Shift}(pp, msk, H_{C,k})$.

Hybrid H_5: This is the same as H_4, except that we answer all evaluation queries as in the Eval algorithm, i.e., we output $\lfloor \mathbf{y}_x \rceil_p$ where

$$\mathbf{y}_x = \mathsf{SHSF.Eval}(pp, msk, x). \tag{51}$$

Hybrid H_6: This is the same as H_5, except that we no longer abort when Borderline happens. Observe that this is exactly the real experiment $\mathsf{Real}_{\mathcal{A}}$.

We now prove that adjacent pairs of hybrid experiments are indistinguishable.

Claim 5. Experiments H_0 and H_1 are identical.

Proof. This follows directly from the fact that p divides q.

Claim 6. Assuming that $\text{1D-R-SIS}_{(z\sigma' + \tau + 1)m, p, q, B}$ is hard, we have $H_1 \overset{c}{\approx} H_2$. In particular, in H_1 the event Borderline happens with negligible probability.

Proof. Let $\mathcal{A}$ be an adversary attempting to distinguish H_1 and H_2. We want to show that in H_1 event Borderline happens with negligible probability. Let x be a query made by $\mathcal{A}$. If $C(x) = 1$ then $\mathbf{y}_x$ is uniformly random in $\mathbb{Z}_q^m$, so for any $i \in [m]$ we have

$$\Pr[(\mathbf{y}_x)_i \in \tfrac{q}{p}(\mathbb{Z} + \tfrac{1}{2}) + [-B, B]] \leq 2 \cdot B \cdot p/q = \text{negl}(\lambda). \tag{52}$$

If $C(x) = 0$, the claim follows immediately by the border-avoiding property of SHSF (Lemma 2).

Claim 7. If PRF is a pseudorandom function then $H_2 \overset{c}{\approx} H_3$.

Proof. We use any adversary $\mathcal{A}$ that attempts to distinguish H_2 from H_3 to build an adversary $\mathcal{A}'$ having the same advantage against the pseudorandomness of PRF. Here $\mathcal{A}'$ is given access to an oracle $\mathcal{O}$ which is either $\mathsf{PRF.Eval}(k, \cdot)$ for $k \leftarrow \mathsf{PRF.KG}(1^\lambda)$, or a uniformly random function $f \colon \{0,1\}^\ell \to \mathbb{Z}_q^m$. We define $\mathcal{A}'$ to proceed as in H_2 to simulate the view of $\mathcal{A}$, except that on each query x it sets

$$\mathbf{y}_x = \mathsf{SHSF.SEval}(pp, sk, x) - C(x) \cdot \mathcal{O}(x) \tag{53}$$

and answers $\lfloor \mathbf{y}_x \rceil_p$. Finally, $\mathcal{A}'$ outputs whatever $\mathcal{A}$ outputs. Clearly, if $\mathcal{O}$ is $\mathsf{PRF.Eval}(k, \cdot)$ then the view of $\mathcal{A}$ is identical to H_3, whereas if the oracle is $f(\cdot)$ then the view of $\mathcal{A}$ is identical to its view in H_2. This proves the claim.

Claim 8. Assuming the hardness of $\mathsf{LWE}_{n-1,q,\chi}$ and CPA-security of GSW, $H_3 \overset{c}{\approx} H_4$.

Proof. This follows immediately from the shift hiding property of SHSF, i.e., Lemma 1.

Claim 9. H_4 and H_5 are identical.

Proof. This follows by Corollary 1 and noticing that both experiments abort if Borderline happens.

Claim 10. Under the hypotheses of Theorem 1, we have $H_5 \overset{c}{\approx} H_6$.

Proof. This follows by combining all the previous claims and recalling that we have proved that Borderline happens with negligible probability in H_1.

This completes the proof of Theorem 1.

5   Privately Programmable PRF

In this section we formally define privately programmable PRFs (PP-PRFs) and give a construction based on our shiftable PRF from Sect. 3.

5.1   Definitions

We start by giving a variety of definitions related to "programmable functions" and privately programmable PRFs. In particular, we give a simulation-based definition that is adapted from [8].

Definition 6. *A* programmable function *is a tuple* (Setup, KeyGen, Eval, Program, PEval) *of efficient algorithms having the following interfaces (where the domain $\mathcal{X}$ and range $\mathcal{Y}$ may depend on the security parameter):*

– Setup$(1^\lambda, 1^k)$, *given the security parameter λ and a number k of programmable inputs, outputs public parameters pp.*
– KeyGen(pp), *given the public parameters pp, outputs a master secret key msk.*

- Eval(pp, msk, x), *given the master secret key and an input $x \in \mathcal{X}$, outputs some $y \in \mathcal{Y}$.*
- Program($pp, msk, \mathcal{P} = \{(x_i, y_i)\}$), *given the master secret key msk and k pairs $(x_i, y_i) \in \mathcal{X} \times \mathcal{Y}$ for distinct x_i, outputs a programmed key $sk_{\mathcal{P}}$.*
- PEval($pp, sk_{\mathcal{P}}, x$), *given a programmed key $sk_{\mathcal{P}}$ and an input $x \in \mathcal{X}$, outputs some $y \in \mathcal{Y}$.*

We now give several definitions that capture various functionality and security properties for programmable functions. We start with the following correctness property for *programmed* inputs.

Definition 7. *A programmable function is* statistically programmable *if for all $\lambda, k = \mathrm{poly}(\lambda) \in \mathbb{N}$, all sets of k pairs $\mathcal{P} = \{(x_i, y_i)\} \subseteq \mathcal{X} \times \mathcal{Y}$ (with distinct x_i), and all $i \in [k]$ we have*

$$\Pr_{\substack{pp \leftarrow \mathsf{Setup}(1^\lambda, 1^k) \\ msk \leftarrow \mathsf{KeyGen}(pp) \\ sk_{\mathcal{P}} \leftarrow \mathsf{Program}(pp, msk, \mathcal{P})}} [\mathsf{PEval}(pp, sk_{\mathcal{P}}, x_i) \neq y_i] = \mathrm{negl}(\lambda). \qquad (54)$$

We now define a notion of *weak* simulation security, in which the adversary names the inputs at which the function is programmed, but the outputs are chosen at random (and not revealed to the adversary). As before, we always assume without loss of generality that the adversary never queries the same input x more than once in the various experiments we define.

Definition 8. *A programmable function is* weakly simulation secure *if there is a PPT simulator $\mathcal{S}$ such that for any PPT adversary $\mathcal{A}$ and any polynomial $k = k(\lambda)$,*

$$\{\mathsf{RealWeakPPRF}_{\mathcal{A}}(1^\lambda, 1^k)\}_{\lambda \in \mathbb{N}} \overset{c}{\approx} \{\mathsf{IdealWeakPPRF}_{\mathcal{A}, \mathcal{S}}(1^\lambda, 1^k)\}_{\lambda \in \mathbb{N}}, \qquad (55)$$

where RealWeakPPRF *and* IdealWeakPPRF *are the respective views of $\mathcal{A}$ in the procedures defined in Fig. 3.*

procedure RealWeakPPRF$_{\mathcal{A}}(1^\lambda, 1^k)$
  $\{x_i\}_{i \in [k]} \leftarrow \mathcal{A}(1^\lambda, 1^k)$
  $\{y_i\}_{i \in [k]} \leftarrow \mathcal{Y}$
  $pp \leftarrow \mathsf{Setup}(1^\lambda, 1^k)$
  $msk \leftarrow \mathsf{KeyGen}(pp)$
  $sk \qquad\qquad\qquad\qquad \leftarrow$
  $\mathsf{Program}(pp, msk, \{(x_i, y_i)\})$
  $(pp, sk) \rightarrow \mathcal{A}$
  repeat
    $x \leftarrow \mathcal{A}$
    $\mathsf{Eval}(pp, msk, x) \rightarrow \mathcal{A}$
  until $\mathcal{A}$ halts

    (a) The real experiment

procedure
IdealWeakPPRF$_{\mathcal{A}, \mathcal{S}}(1^\lambda, 1^k)$
  $\{x_i\}_{i \in [k]} \leftarrow \mathcal{A}(1^\lambda, 1^k)$
  $(pp, sk) \leftarrow \mathcal{S}(1^\lambda, 1^k)$
  $(pp, sk) \rightarrow \mathcal{A}$
  repeat
    $x \leftarrow \mathcal{A}$
    if $x \notin \{x_i\}$ **then**
      $\mathsf{PEval}(pp, sk, x) \rightarrow \mathcal{A}$
    else
      $y \leftarrow \mathcal{Y}; y \rightarrow \mathcal{A}$
  until $\mathcal{A}$ halts

    (b) The ideal experiment

Fig. 3. The (weak) real and ideal experiments.

Similarly to Definition 4, the above definition simultaneously captures privacy of the programmed inputs given the programmed key, pseudorandomness on those inputs, and correctness of PEval on *non-programmed* inputs.

Definition 9. *A programmable function is a* weak privately programmable PRF *if it is statistically programmable (Definition 7) and weakly simulation secure (Definition 8).*

We now define a notion of (non-weak) simulation security for programmable functions. This differs from the weak notion in that the adversary specifies the programmed inputs *and* corresponding outputs, and the simulator in the ideal game is also given these input-output pairs. The simulator needs this information because otherwise the adversary could trivially distinguish the real and ideal experiments by checking whether $\mathsf{PEval}(pp, sk_{\mathcal{P}}, x_i) = y_i$ for one of the programmed input-output pairs (x_i, y_i). Simulation security itself therefore does not guarantee any privacy of the programmed inputs; below we give a separate simulation-based definition which does.

Definition 10. *A programmable function is* simulation secure *if there is a PPT simulator $\mathcal{S}$ such that for any PPT adversary $\mathcal{A}$ and any polynomial $k = k(\lambda)$,*

$$\{\mathsf{RealPPRF}_{\mathcal{A}}(1^\lambda, 1^k)\}_{\lambda \in \mathbb{N}} \stackrel{c}{\approx} \{\mathsf{IdealPPRF}_{\mathcal{A},\mathcal{S}}(1^\lambda, 1^k)\}_{\lambda \in \mathbb{N}}, \tag{56}$$

where Real *and* Ideal *are the respective views of $\mathcal{A}$ in the procedures defined in Fig. 4.*

We mention that a straightforward hybrid argument similar to one from [6] shows that simulation security implies that (KeyGen, Eval) is a pseudorandom function.

Finally, we define a notion of privacy for the programmed inputs. This says that a key programmed on adversarially chosen inputs and *random* corresponding outputs (that are not revealed to the adversary) does not reveal anything about the programmed inputs.

procedure $\mathsf{RealPPRF}_{\mathcal{A}}(1^\lambda, 1^k)$
   $\mathcal{P} = \{(x_i, y_i)\} \leftarrow \mathcal{A}(1^\lambda, 1^k)$
   $pp \leftarrow \mathsf{Setup}(1^\lambda, 1^k)$
   $msk \leftarrow \mathsf{KeyGen}(pp)$
   $sk_{\mathcal{P}} \leftarrow \mathsf{Program}(pp, msk, \mathcal{P})$
   $(pp, sk_{\mathcal{P}}) \rightarrow \mathcal{A}$
   repeat
      $x \leftarrow \mathcal{A}$
      $\mathsf{Eval}(pp, msk, x) \rightarrow \mathcal{A}$
   until $\mathcal{A}$ halts

(a) The real experiment

procedure $\mathsf{IdealPPRF}_{\mathcal{A},\mathcal{S}}(1^\lambda, 1^k)$
   $\mathcal{P} = \{(x_i, y_i)\} \leftarrow \mathcal{A}(1^\lambda, 1^k)$
   $(pp, sk_{\mathcal{P}}) \leftarrow \mathcal{S}(1^\lambda, \mathcal{P})$
   $(pp, sk_{\mathcal{P}}) \rightarrow \mathcal{A}$
   repeat
      $x \leftarrow \mathcal{A}$
      if $x \notin \{x_i\}$ **then**
         $\mathsf{PEval}(pp, sk_{\mathcal{P}}, x) \rightarrow \mathcal{A}$
      else
         $y \leftarrow \mathcal{Y}; y \rightarrow \mathcal{A}$
   until $\mathcal{A}$ halt

(b) The ideal experiment

Fig. 4. The real and ideal experiments

procedure
RealPPRFPrivacy$_\mathcal{A}(1^\lambda, 1^k)$
$\quad \{x_i\}_{i \in [k]} \leftarrow \mathcal{A}(1^\lambda, 1^k)$
$\quad \{y_i\}_{i \in [k]} \leftarrow \mathcal{Y}$
$\quad pp \leftarrow \mathsf{Setup}(1^\lambda, 1^k)$
$\quad msk \leftarrow \mathsf{KeyGen}(pp)$
$\quad sk$
$\mathsf{Program}(pp, msk, \{(x_i, y_i)\})$
$\quad (pp, sk) \rightarrow \mathcal{A}$

(a) The real experiment

$\leftarrow$

procedure
IdealPPRFPrivacy$_{\mathcal{A},\mathcal{S}}(1^\lambda, 1^k)$
$\quad \{x_i\}_{i \in [k]} \leftarrow \mathcal{A}(1^\lambda, 1^k)$
$\quad (pp, sk) \leftarrow \mathcal{S}(1^\lambda, 1^k)$
$\quad (pp, sk) \rightarrow \mathcal{A}$

(b) The ideal experiment

Fig. 5. The real and ideal privacy experiments

Definition 11. *A programmable function is* privately programmable *if there is a PPT simulator $\mathcal{S}$ such that for any PPT adversary $\mathcal{A}$ and any polynomial $k = k(\lambda)$,*

$$\{\mathsf{RealPPRFPrivacy}_\mathcal{A}(1^\lambda, 1^k)\}_{\lambda \in \mathbb{N}} \overset{c}{\approx} \{\mathsf{IdealPPRFPrivacy}_\mathcal{A}(1^\lambda, 1^k)\}_{\lambda \in \mathbb{N}}, \qquad (57)$$

where RealPPRFPrivacy *and* IdealPPRFPrivacy *are the respective views of $\mathcal{A}$ in the procedures defined in Fig. 5.*

We now give our main security definition for PP-PRFs.

Definition 12. *A programmable function is a* privately programmable PRF *if it is statistically programmable, simulation secure, and privately programmable.*

5.2 From Weak PP-PRFs to PP-PRFs

In this section we describe a general construction of a privately programmable PRF from any weak privately programmable PRF. Let $\Pi' = (\mathsf{Setup}, \mathsf{KeyGen}, \mathsf{Eval}, \mathsf{Program}, \mathsf{PEval})$ be a programmable function with domain $\mathcal{X}$ and range $\mathcal{Y}$, where we assume that $\mathcal{Y}$ is a finite additive group. The basic idea behind the construction is simple: define the function as the sum of two parallel copies of Π', and program it by programming the copies according to additive secret-sharings of the desired outputs. Each component is therefore programmed to uniformly random outputs, as required by weak simulation security.

Construction 3. We construct a programmable function Π as follows:

- $\Pi.\mathsf{Setup}(1^\lambda, 1^k)$: generate $pp_i \leftarrow \Pi'.\mathsf{Setup}(1^\lambda, 1^k)$ for $i = 1, 2$ and output $pp = (pp_1, pp_2)$.
- $\Pi.\mathsf{KeyGen}(pp)$: on input $pp = (pp_1, pp_2)$ generate $msk_i \leftarrow \Pi'.\mathsf{KeyGen}(pp_i)$ for $i = 1, 2$, and output $msk = (msk_1, msk_2)$.
- $\Pi.\mathsf{Eval}(pp, msk, x)$: on input $pp = (pp_1, pp_2)$, $msk = (msk_1, msk_2)$, and $x \in \mathcal{X}$ output
$$\Pi'.\mathsf{Eval}(pp_1, msk_1, x) + \Pi'.\mathsf{Eval}(pp_2, msk_2, x).$$

- $\Pi.\mathsf{Program}(pp, msk, \mathcal{P})$: on input $pp = (pp_1, pp_2)$, $msk = (msk_1, msk_2)$, k pairs $(x_i, y_i) \subset \mathcal{X} \times \mathcal{Y}$, first sample uniformly random $r_i \leftarrow \mathcal{Y}$ for $i \in [k]$, then output $sk_\mathcal{P} = (sk_1, sk_2)$ where

$$sk_1 \quad \leftarrow \Pi'.\mathsf{Program}(pp_1, msk_1, \mathcal{P}_1 = \{(x_i, r_i)\}) \tag{58}$$
$$sk_2 \leftarrow \Pi'.\mathsf{Program}(pp_2, msk_2, \mathcal{P}_2 = \{(x_i, y_i - r_i)\}). \tag{59}$$

- $\Pi.\mathsf{PEval}(pp, sk_\mathcal{P}, x)$: on input $pp = (pp_1, pp_2)$, $sk_\mathcal{P} = (sk_1, sk_2)$, and $x \in \mathcal{X}$ output

$$\Pi'.\mathsf{PEval}(pp_1, sk_1, x) + \Pi'.\mathsf{PEval}(pp_2, sk_2, x).$$

Theorem 2. *If Π' is a weak privately programmable PRF then Construction 3 is a privately programmable PRF.*

Proof. This follows directly from Theorems 3 and 4, which respectively prove the simulation security and private programmability of Construction 3, and from the statistical programmability of Π', which obviously implies the statistical programmability of Construction 3.

Theorem 3. *If Π' is a weak privately programmable PRF then Π is simulation secure.*

Due to space constraints, the (straightforward) proof of Theorem 3 is deferred to the full version.

Theorem 4. *If Π' is weakly simulation secure then Π is privately programmable.*

Proof. Let $\mathcal{S}'$ be the simulator algorithm for the weak simulation security of Π'. Our simulator $\mathcal{S}(1^\lambda, 1^k)$ for the private programmability of Π simply generates $(pp_i, sk_i) \leftarrow \mathcal{S}'(1^\lambda, 1^k)$ for $i = 1, 2$ and outputs $(pp = (pp_1, pp_2), sk = (sk_1, sk_2))$. To show that $\mathcal{S}$ satisfies Definition 12 we define the following hybrids and show that they are indistinguishable.

Hybrid H_0: This is the experiment $\mathsf{RealPPRFPrivacy}_\mathcal{A}$ from Fig. 5.
Hybrid H_1: This experiment is the same as the previous one, except that we generate $(pp_1, sk_1) \leftarrow \mathcal{S}'(1^\lambda, 1^k)$.
Hybrid H_2: This experiment is the same as the previous one, except that we generate $(pp_2, sk_2) \leftarrow \mathcal{S}'(1^\lambda, 1^k)$. Observe that this experiment is identical to the experiment $\mathsf{IdealPPRFPrivacy}_{\mathcal{A}, \mathcal{S}}$ from Fig. 5.

Claim 11. We have $H_0 \overset{c}{\approx} H_1$.

Proof. Let $\mathcal{A}$ be an adversary attempting to distinguish H_0 and H_1. We build an adversary $\mathcal{A}'$ against the weak simulation security of Π', which runs $\mathcal{A}$ internally. When $\mathcal{A}$ outputs $\{x_i\}$, $\mathcal{A}'$ also outputs $\{x_i\}$, receiving (pp_1, sk_1) in response. Then $\mathcal{A}'$ generates $pp_2 \leftarrow \Pi'.\mathsf{Setup}(1^\lambda, 1^k)$ and $msk_2 \leftarrow \Pi'.\mathsf{KeyGen}(pp_2)$, and chooses uniformly random $r_i \leftarrow \mathcal{Y}$ for $i \in [k]$. It then generates

$sk_2 \leftarrow \Pi'.\mathsf{Program}(pp_2, msk_2, \{(x_i, r_i)\})$. Finally it gives $(pp = (pp_1, pp_2), sk = (sk_1, sk_2))$ to $\mathcal{A}$. It is straightforward to see that if $\mathcal{A}'$ is in RealWeakPPRF (respectively, IdealWeakPPRF) then the view of $\mathcal{A}$ is identical to its view H_0 (resp., H_1). So by weak simulation security of Π', we have $H_0 \overset{c}{\approx} H_1$.

Claim 12. We have $H_1 \overset{c}{\approx} H_2$.

Proof. This is entirely symmetrical to the proof of Claim 11, so we omit it.

This completes the proof of Theorem 4.

5.3 Construction of Weak Privately Programmable PRFs

In this section we construct a weak privately programmable PRF from our shiftable function of Sect. 3. We first define the auxiliary function that the construction will use. For $\{(x_i, \mathbf{y}_i)\}_{i \in [k]} \subset \{0,1\}^\ell \times \mathbb{Z}_q^m$ where the x_i are distinct, define the function $H_{\{(x_i, \mathbf{w}_i)\}_{i \in [k]}} : \{0,1\}^\ell \to \mathbb{Z}_q^m$ as

$$H_{\{(x_i, \mathbf{w}_i)\}_{i \in [k]}}(x) \begin{cases} \mathbf{w}_i & \text{if } x = x_i \text{ for some } i, \\ \mathbf{0} & \text{otherwise.} \end{cases} \tag{60}$$

Notice that the circuit size of $H_{\{(x_i, \mathbf{w}_i)\}_{i \in [k]}}$ is upper bounded by some $\sigma' = \mathrm{poly}(n, k, \log q)$.

Construction 4. Our weak privately programmable PRF with input space $\mathcal{X} = \{0,1\}^\ell$ and output space $\mathcal{Y} = \mathbb{Z}_p^m$ uses the SHSF from Sect. 3 with parameters q, B chosen as in Sect. 3.4, and is defined as follows:

- Setup$(1^\lambda, 1^k)$: Output $pp \leftarrow \mathsf{SHSF.Setup}(1^\lambda, 1^{\sigma'})$.
- KeyGen(pp): Output $msk \leftarrow \mathsf{SHSF.KeyGen}(pp)$.
- Eval$(pp, msk, x \in \{0,1\}^\ell)$: Compute $\mathbf{y}_x = \mathsf{SHSF.Eval}(pp, msk, x)$ and output $\lfloor \mathbf{y}_x \rceil_p$.
- Program$(pp, msk, \mathcal{P})$: Given k pairs $(x_i, \mathbf{y}_i) \in \{0,1\}^\ell \times \mathbb{Z}_p^m$ where the x_i are distinct, for each $i \in [k]$ compute $\mathbf{w}_i$ as follows: choose $\mathbf{y}_i' \leftarrow \mathbb{Z}_q^m$ uniformly at random conditioned on $\lfloor \mathbf{y}_i' \rceil_p = \mathbf{y}_i$, and set

$$\mathbf{w}_i = \mathbf{y}_i' - \mathsf{SHSF.Eval}(pp, msk, x_i). \tag{61}$$

  Output $sk_\mathcal{P} \leftarrow \mathsf{SHSF.Shift}(pp, msk, H_{\{(x_i, \mathbf{w}_i)\}})$.
- PEval$(pp, sk_\mathcal{P}, x)$: output $\lfloor \mathsf{SHSF.SEval}(pp, sk_\mathcal{P}, x) \rceil_p$.

5.4 Security Proof

Theorem 5. *Construction 4 is a weak privately programmable PRF (Definition 9) assuming the hardness of* $\mathsf{LWE}_{n-1, q, \chi}$ *and* $\mathsf{1D\text{-}R\text{-}SIS}_{(z\sigma'+\tau+1)m, p, q, B}$ *(where z, τ are respectively the lengths of fresh GSW ciphertexts and secret keys as used in* SHSF*) and the CPA security of the GSW encryption scheme.*

Proof. The proof follows immediately by Theorems 6 and 7 below.

Theorem 6. *Assuming the hardness of $\mathsf{LWE}_{n-1,q,\chi}$ and $1D\text{-}R\text{-}SIS_{(z\sigma'+\tau+1)m,p,q,B}$ and the CPA security of the GSW encryption scheme, Construction 4 is weakly simulation secure.*

Proof. Our simulator $\mathcal{S}(1^\lambda, 1^k)$ for Construction 4 simply outputs $(pp, sk) \leftarrow \mathsf{SHSF}.\mathcal{S}(1^\lambda, 1^{\sigma'})$. Let $\mathcal{A}$ be any polynomial-time adversary. To show that $\mathcal{S}$ satisfies Definition 10 we define a sequence of hybrid experiments and show that they are indistinguishable.

Hybrid H_0: This is the simulated experiment $\mathsf{IdealWeakPPRF}_{\mathcal{A},\mathcal{S}}$ (Fig. 3).

Hybrid H_1: This is the same as the previous experiment, except that on query $x \in \{x_i\}$, instead of returning a uniformly random value from $\mathbb{Z}_p^m$, we choose $\mathbf{y}_x \leftarrow \mathbb{Z}_q^m$ and output $\lfloor \mathbf{y}_x \rceil_p$.

Hybrid H_2: This is the same as the previous experiment, except that we abort if the event Borderline happens, where Borderline is as in Definition 5.

Hybrid H_3: This is the same as the previous experiment, except that we initially choose uniformly random $\mathbf{w}_i' \leftarrow \mathbb{Z}_q^m$ for $i \in [k]$ and change how queries for $x \in \{x_i\}$ are answered (the "else" clause in $\mathsf{IdealWeakPPRF}_{\mathcal{A},\mathcal{S}}$): for $x = x_j$, we answer as $\lfloor \mathbf{y}_x \rceil_p$, where

$$\mathbf{y}_x = \mathsf{SHSF}.\mathsf{SEval}(pp, sk, x) - \mathbf{w}_j'. \tag{62}$$

Hybrid H_4: This is the same as the previous experiment, except that we generate pp and sk as follows: we generate $pp \leftarrow \mathsf{Setup}(1^\lambda, 1^k)$, $msk \leftarrow \mathsf{KeyGen}(pp)$ and $sk \leftarrow \mathsf{SHSF}.\mathsf{Shift}(pp, msk, H_{\{(x_i, \mathbf{w}_i')\}})$.

Hybrid H_5: This is the same as the previous experiment, except that we answer all queries as in the Eval algorithm, i.e., we output

$$\lfloor \mathsf{SHSF}.\mathsf{Eval}(pp, msk, x) \rceil_p. \tag{63}$$

Hybrid H_6: This is the same as the previous experiment, except that here we generate sk as in the real game. Specifically, for each $i \in [k]$ we choose a uniformly random vector $\mathbf{y}_i \leftarrow \mathbb{Z}_p^m$ and uniformly random $\mathbf{y}_i' \leftarrow \mathbb{Z}_q^m$ conditioned on $\lfloor \mathbf{y}_i' \rceil_p = \mathbf{y}_i$, and then set

$$\mathbf{w}_i = \mathbf{y}_i' - \mathsf{SHSF}.\mathsf{Eval}(pp, msk, x). \tag{64}$$

We then set $sk \leftarrow \mathsf{SHSF}.\mathsf{Shift}(pp, msk, H_{\{(x_i, \mathbf{w}_i)\}})$.

Hybrid H_7: This is the same as the previous experiment, except that we no longer abort when Borderline happens. Observe that this is the real experiment $\mathsf{IdealRealPPRF}_{\mathcal{A}}$ (Fig. 3).

The proofs of indistinguishability (either computational or statistical) for adjacent hybrids are straightforward, and are deferred to the full version for lack of space.

Theorem 7. *Construction 4 is statistically programmable.*

Proof. Fix any $\mathcal{P} = \{(x_i, \mathbf{y}_i)\}_{i \in [k]} \subset \mathcal{X} \times \mathcal{Y}$. We need to show that for any $i \in [k]$,

$$\Pr_{\substack{pp \leftarrow \mathsf{Setup}(1^\lambda, 1^k) \\ msk \leftarrow \mathsf{KeyGen}(pp) \\ sk_\mathcal{P} \leftarrow \mathsf{Program}(pp, msk, \mathcal{P})}} \left[\left\lfloor \mathsf{SHSF.SEval}(pp, sk_\mathcal{P}, x_i) \right\rceil_p \neq \mathbf{y}_i \right] = \mathrm{negl}(\lambda). \tag{65}$$

By Lemma 3 we have

$$\begin{aligned} \mathsf{SHSF.SEval}(pp, sk_\mathcal{P}, x_i) &\approx \mathsf{SHSF.Eval}(pp, msk, x_i) + H_{\{(x_i, \mathbf{w}_i)\}}(x_i) \\ &= \mathsf{SHSF.Eval}(pp, msk, x_i) + \mathbf{w}_i \\ &= \mathbf{y}_i', \end{aligned}$$

where the approximation hides some B-bounded error and the last equality holds because $\mathbf{w}_i = \mathbf{y}_i' - \mathsf{SHSF.Eval}(pp, msk, x_i)$. Because $\mathbf{y}_i'$ is chosen uniformly at random such that $\lfloor \mathbf{y}_i' \rceil_p = \mathbf{y}_i$, the probability that some coordinate of $\mathsf{SHSF.SEval}(pp, sk_\mathcal{P}, x_i)$ is in $\frac{q}{p}(\mathbb{Z} + \frac{1}{2}) + [-B, B]$ is at most $2mBp/q = \mathrm{negl}(\lambda)$, which establishes Eq. (65).

References

1. Ajtai, M.: Generating hard instances of lattice problems. Quaderni di Matematica **13**, 1–32 (2004). Preliminary version in STOC 1996
2. Banerjee, A., Peikert, C.: New and improved key-homomorphic pseudorandom functions. In: Garay, J.A., Gennaro, R. (eds.) CRYPTO 2014. LNCS, vol. 8616, pp. 353–370. Springer, Heidelberg (2014). https://doi.org/10.1007/978-3-662-44371-2_20
3. Banerjee, A., Peikert, C., Rosen, A.: Pseudorandom functions and lattices. In: Pointcheval, D., Johansson, T. (eds.) EUROCRYPT 2012. LNCS, vol. 7237, pp. 719–737. Springer, Heidelberg (2012). https://doi.org/10.1007/978-3-642-29011-4_42
4. Barak, B., Goldreich, O., Impagliazzo, R., Rudich, S., Sahai, A., Vadhan, S.P., Yang, K.: On the (im)possibility of obfuscating programs. J. ACM **59**(2), 6:1–6:48 (2012). Preliminary version in CRYPTO 2001
5. Boneh, D., Gentry, C., Gorbunov, S., Halevi, S., Nikolaenko, V., Segev, G., Vaikuntanathan, V., Vinayagamurthy, D.: Fully key-homomorphic encryption, arithmetic circuit ABE and compact garbled circuits. In: Nguyen, P.Q., Oswald, E. (eds.) EUROCRYPT 2014. LNCS, vol. 8441, pp. 533–556. Springer, Heidelberg (2014). https://doi.org/10.1007/978-3-642-55220-5_30
6. Boneh, D., Kim, S., Montgomery, H.: Private puncturable PRFs from standard lattice assumptions. In: Coron, J.-S., Nielsen, J.B. (eds.) EUROCRYPT 2017. LNCS, vol. 10210, pp. 415–445. Springer, Cham (2017). https://doi.org/10.1007/978-3-319-56620-7_15
7. Boneh, D., Lewi, K., Montgomery, H., Raghunathan, A.: Key homomorphic PRFs and their applications. In: Canetti, R., Garay, J.A. (eds.) CRYPTO 2013. LNCS, vol. 8042, pp. 410–428. Springer, Heidelberg (2013). https://doi.org/10.1007/978-3-642-40041-4_23

8. Boneh, D., Lewi, K., Wu, D.J.: Constraining pseudorandom functions privately. In: Fehr, S. (ed.) PKC 2017. LNCS, vol. 10175, pp. 494–524. Springer, Heidelberg (2017). https://doi.org/10.1007/978-3-662-54388-7_17

9. Boneh, D., Waters, B.: Constrained pseudorandom functions and their applications. In: Sako, K., Sarkar, P. (eds.) ASIACRYPT 2013. LNCS, vol. 8270, pp. 280–300. Springer, Heidelberg (2013). https://doi.org/10.1007/978-3-642-42045-0_15

10. Boyle, E., Gilboa, N., Ishai, Y.: Function secret sharing. In: Oswald, E., Fischlin, M. (eds.) EUROCRYPT 2015. LNCS, vol. 9057, pp. 337–367. Springer, Heidelberg (2015). https://doi.org/10.1007/978-3-662-46803-6_12

11. Boyle, E., Goldwasser, S., Ivan, I.: Functional signatures and pseudorandom functions. In: Krawczyk, H. (ed.) PKC 2014. LNCS, vol. 8383, pp. 501–519. Springer, Heidelberg (2014). https://doi.org/10.1007/978-3-642-54631-0_29

12. Brakerski, Z., Langlois, A., Peikert, C., Regev, O., Stehlé, D.: Classical hardness of learning with errors. In: STOC, pp. 575–584 (2013)

13. Brakerski, Z., Tsabary, R., Vaikuntanathan, V., Wee, H.: Private Constrained PRFs (and More) from LWE. In: Kalai, Y., Reyzin, L. (eds.) TCC 2017. LNCS, vol. 10677, pp. 264–302. Springer, Cham (2017). https://doi.org/10.1007/978-3-319-70500-2_10

14. Brakerski, Z., Vaikuntanathan, V.: Constrained key-homomorphic PRFs from standard lattice assumptions. In: Dodis, Y., Nielsen, J.B. (eds.) TCC 2015. LNCS, vol. 9015, pp. 1–30. Springer, Heidelberg (2015). https://doi.org/10.1007/978-3-662-46497-7_1

15. Canetti, R., Chen, Y.: Constraint-hiding constrained PRFs for NC^1 from LWE. In: Coron, J.-S., Nielsen, J.B. (eds.) EUROCRYPT 2017. LNCS, vol. 10210, pp. 446–476. Springer, Cham (2017). https://doi.org/10.1007/978-3-319-56620-7_16

16. Cohen, A., Holmgren, J., Nishimaki, R., Vaikuntanathan, V., Wichs, D.: Watermarking cryptographic capabilities. In: STOC, pp. 1115–1127 (2016)

17. Garg, S., Gentry, C., Halevi, S., Raykova, M., Sahai, A., Waters, B.: Candidate indistinguishability obfuscation and functional encryption for all circuits. In: FOCS, pp. 40–49 (2013)

18. Gentry, C., Sahai, A., Waters, B.: Homomorphic encryption from learning with errors: conceptually-simpler, asymptotically-faster, attribute-based. In: Canetti, R., Garay, J.A. (eds.) CRYPTO 2013. LNCS, vol. 8042, pp. 75–92. Springer, Heidelberg (2013). https://doi.org/10.1007/978-3-642-40041-4_5

19. Goldreich, O., Goldwasser, S., Micali, S.: How to construct random functions. J. ACM **33**(4), 792–807 (1986). Preliminary version in FOCS 1984

20. Gorbunov, S., Vaikuntanathan, V., Wee, H.: Predicate encryption for circuits from LWE. In: Gennaro, R., Robshaw, M. (eds.) CRYPTO 2015. LNCS, vol. 9216, pp. 503–523. Springer, Heidelberg (2015). https://doi.org/10.1007/978-3-662-48000-7_25

21. Gorbunov, S., Vaikuntanathan, V., Wichs, D.: Leveled fully homomorphic signatures from standard lattices. In: STOC, pp. 469–477 (2015)

22. Kiayias, A., Papadopoulos, S., Triandopoulos, N., Zacharias, T.: Delegatable pseudorandom functions and applications. In: CCS, pp. 669–684 (2013)

23. Kim, S., Wu, D.J.: Watermarking cryptographic functionalities from standard lattice assumptions. In: Katz, J., Shacham, H. (eds.) CRYPTO 2017. LNCS, vol. 10401, pp. 503–536. Springer, Cham (2017). https://doi.org/10.1007/978-3-319-63688-7_17

24. Micciancio, D., Peikert, C.: Trapdoors for lattices: simpler, tighter, faster, smaller. In: Pointcheval, D., Johansson, T. (eds.) EUROCRYPT 2012. LNCS, vol. 7237, pp. 700–718. Springer, Heidelberg (2012). https://doi.org/10.1007/978-3-642-29011-4_41

25. Regev, D.M.O.: Worst-case to average-case reductions based on Gaussian measures. SIAM J. Comput. **37**(1), 267–302 (2007). Preliminary version in FOCS 2004

26. Peikert, C.: Public-key cryptosystems from the worst-case shortest vector problem. In: STOC, pp. 333–342 (2009)

27. Peikert, C., Regev, O., Stephens-Davidowitz, N.: Pseudorandomness of Ring-LWE for any ring and modulus. In: STOC, pp. 461–473 (2017)

28. Regev, O.: On lattices, learning with errors, random linear codes, and cryptography. J. ACM **56**(6), 1–40 (2009). Preliminary version in STOC 2005

Learning with Errors and Extrapolated Dihedral Cosets

Zvika Brakerski[1], Elena Kirshanova[2(✉)], Damien Stehlé[2], and Weiqiang Wen[2]

[1] Weizmann Institute of Science, Rehovot, Israel
zvika.brakerski@weizmann.ac.il
[2] ENS de Lyon and Laboratoire LIP (U. Lyon, CNRS, ENS de Lyon,
INRIA, UCBL), Lyon, France
{elena.kirshanova,damien.stehle,weiqiang.wen}@ens-lyon.fr

Abstract. The hardness of the learning with errors (LWE) problem is one of the most fruitful resources of modern cryptography. In particular, it is one of the most prominent candidates for secure post-quantum cryptography. Understanding its quantum complexity is therefore an important goal.

We show that under quantum polynomial time reductions, LWE is equivalent to a relaxed version of the dihedral coset problem (DCP), which we call extrapolated DCP (eDCP). The extent of extrapolation varies with the LWE noise rate. By considering different extents of extrapolation, our result generalizes Regev's famous proof that if DCP is in BQP (quantum poly-time) then so is LWE (FOCS 02). We also discuss a connection between eDCP and Childs and Van Dam's algorithm for generalized hidden shift problems (SODA 07).

Our result implies that a BQP solution for LWE might not require the full power of solving DCP, but rather only a solution for its relaxed version, eDCP, which could be easier.

1 Introduction

The Learning With Errors problem $\text{LWE}_{n,q,\alpha}$ with parameters $n, q \in \mathbb{Z}$ and $\alpha \in (0, 1)$ consists in finding a vector $\mathbf{s} \in \mathbb{Z}_q^n$ from arbitrarily many samples $(\mathbf{a}_i, \langle \mathbf{a}_i, \mathbf{s} \rangle + e_i) \in \mathbb{Z}_q^n \times \mathbb{Z}_q$, where $\mathbf{a}_i$ is uniformly sampled in $\mathbb{Z}_q^n$ and e_i is sampled from $\mathcal{D}_{\mathbb{Z}, \alpha q}$, the discrete Gaussian distribution of standard deviation parameter αq (i.e., the distribution such that $\mathcal{D}_{\mathbb{Z}, \alpha q}(k) \sim \exp(-\pi k^2/(\alpha q)^2)$ for all $k \in \mathbb{Z}$). Since its introduction by Regev [28,29], LWE has served as a security foundation for numerous cryptographic primitives (see e.g. an overview in [24]). The cryptographic attractiveness of LWE stems from two particularly desirable properties. First, its algebraic simplicity enables the design of primitives with

Z. Brakerski—Supported by the Israel Science Foundation (Grant No. 468/14) and Binational Science Foundation (Grants No. 2016726, 2014276) and ERC Project 756482 REACT.

E. Kirshanova, D. Stehlé and W. Wen—Supported by ERC Starting Grant ERC-2013-StG-335086-LATTAC.

© International Association for Cryptologic Research 2018
M. Abdalla and R. Dahab (Eds.): PKC 2018, LNCS 10770, pp. 702–727, 2018.
https://doi.org/10.1007/978-3-319-76581-5_24

advanced functionalities, such as fully homomorphic encryption [8], attribute-based encryption for all circuits [14] and (single key) functional encryption [13]. Second, LWE is conjectured hard even in the context of quantum computations, making it one of the most appealing candidate security foundations for post-quantum cryptography [5]. Current quantum algorithms for LWE do not out-perform classical ones, but it is not clear whether this is inherent (for example, it is known that LWE is *easier* than the Dihedral Coset Problem under polynomial-time reductions, see below). In this work, we characterize the quantum hardness of LWE under polynomial-time reductions and show that it is computationally equivalent (up to small parameter losses) to a quantum problem closely related to the aforementioned Dihedral Coset Problem.

LWE, *Lattices and the Dihedral Coset Problem.* LWE is tightly connected to worst-case approximation problems over Euclidean lattices. In particular, LWE is an (average-case) instance of the Bounded Distance Decoding problem (BDD) (see, e.g., [21, Section 5.4]), but is also known to be as hard as *worst-case* BDD (with some polynomial loss in parameters) [29]. BDD is the problem of finding the closest lattice vector to a given target point which is promised to be very close to the lattice (formally, closer than λ_1/γ where λ_1 is the length of the shortest non-zero vector). Classical and quantum connections between BDD and other problems such as SIVP, GapSVP, uSVP are also known [7,20,23,29].

Regev [25,27] showed that uSVP, and therefore also BDD and LWE, are no harder to solve than the quantumly-defined Dihedral Coset Problem (DCP). An instance of $DCP_{N,\ell}$, for integer parameters N and ℓ, consists of ℓ quantum registers in superposition $|0, x_k\rangle + |1, x_k + s\rangle$, with a common $s \in \mathbb{Z}_N$ and random and independent $x_k \in \mathbb{Z}_N$ for $k \in [\ell]$. The goal is to find s (information theoretically $\ell = \mathcal{O}(\log N)$ is sufficient for this task [10]). We note that Regev considered a variant with unbounded number of registers, but where a fraction of them is faulty (a faulty state is of the form $|b, x_k\rangle$ for arbitrary $b \in \{0, 1\}, x_k \in \mathbb{Z}_N$). In our work, we assume a non-faulty formulation of DCP.

Still, it is quite possible that DCP is in fact much harder to solve than LWE. The best known algorithm for DCP, due to Kuperberg [17], runs in time $2^{\mathcal{O}(\log \ell + \log N / \log \ell)}$ which does not improve upon classical methods for solving LWE. Other variants of the problem were explored in [10,11], and of particular relevance to this work is a "vector" variant of the problem where $\mathbb{Z}_N$ is replaced with $\mathbb{Z}_q^n$ (i.e. s and x_k are now vectors). These problems behave similarly to DCP with $N = q^n$.

Finally, Regev showed that DCP can be solved given efficient algorithms for the subset-sum problem (which is classically defined), however in a regime of parameters that appears harder to solve than LWE itself.

Extrapolated DCP. The focus of this work is a generalization of the DCP problem, i.e. rather than considering registers containing $|0, x_k\rangle + |1, x_k + s\rangle$, we allow (1) x_i's and s be n-dimensional vectors, and (2) other than non-uniform distribution for amplitudes. We name this problem Extrapolated DCP (EDCP) as its input registers has more extrapolated states. To be more precise, $\text{EDCP}^{\ell}_{n,N,f}$, with parameters three integers n, N, ℓ and a function $f : \mathbb{Z} \mapsto \mathbb{C}$ with $\sum_{j \in \mathbb{Z}} j \cdot |f(j)|^2 < +\infty$, consists in recovering $\mathbf{s} \in \mathbb{Z}^n_N$ from the following ℓ states over $\mathbb{Z} \times \mathbb{Z}^n_N$:

$$\left\{ \frac{1}{\sqrt{\sum_{j \in \mathbb{Z}} |f(j)|^2}} \cdot \sum_{j \in \mathbb{Z}} f(j) |j, \mathbf{x}_k + j \cdot \mathbf{s}\rangle \right\}_{k \leq \ell},$$

where the $\mathbf{x}_k$'s are arbitrary in $\mathbb{Z}^n_N$.[1] Note that DCP is the special case of EDCP for $n = 1$ and f being the indicator function of $\{0, 1\}$.

In [9], Childs and van Dam consider a special case of EDCP where f is the indicator function of $\{0, \ldots, M - 1\}$ for some integer M, which we will refer to as uniform EDCP (or, $\text{U-EDCP}^{\ell}_{n,N,M}$).

Our Main Result. We show that up to polynomial loss in parameters, U-EDCP is equivalent to LWE. Thus we provide a formulation of the hardness assumption underlying lattice-based cryptography in terms of the (generalized) Dihedral Coset Problem.

Theorem 1 (Informal). *There exists a quantum polynomial-time reduction from* $\text{LWE}_{n,q,\alpha}$ *to* $\text{U-EDCP}^{\ell}_{n,N,M}$, *with* $N = q$, $\ell = \text{poly}(n \log q)$ *and* $M = \frac{\text{poly}(n \log q)}{\alpha}$. *Conversely, there exists a polynomial-time reduction from U-EDCP to* LWE *with the same parameter relationships, up to* $\text{poly}(n \log q)$ *factors.*

Our proof crucially relies on a special case of EDCP where f is a Gaussian weight function with standard deviation parameter r. We call this problem Gaussian EDCP (G-EDCP). We show that G-EDCP and U-EDCP are equivalent up to small parameter losses.

EDCP is analogous to LWE in many aspects. The decisional version of LWE (dLWE) asks to distinguish between LWE samples and random samples of the form $(\mathbf{a}, b) \in \mathbb{Z}^n_q \times \mathbb{Z}_q$ where both components are chosen uniformly at random. Similarly, we also consider the decisional version of EDCP, denoted by dEDCP. In $\text{dEDCP}_{n,N,f}$, we are asked to distinguish between an EDCP state and a state of the form

$$|j\rangle |\mathbf{x} \bmod N\rangle,$$

where j is distributed according to the function $|f|^2$, and $\mathbf{x} \in \mathbb{Z}^n_N$ is uniformly chosen. EDCP enjoys a reduction between its search and decisional variants via LWE.

---

[1] Note that the assumption on f implies, via Markov's inequality, that one may restrict the sum to a finite index set and obtain a superposition which remains within negligible ℓ_2 distance from the countable superposition above.

Related work. In [9], Childs and van Dam show that U-EDCP$^\ell_{1,N,M}$ reduces to the problem of finding all the solutions $\mathbf{b} \in \{0, \dots, M-1\}^k$ to the equation $\langle \mathbf{b}, \mathbf{x} \rangle = w \bmod N$, where $\mathbf{x}$ and w are given and uniformly random modulo N. They interpret this as an integer linear program and use lattice reduction, within Lenstra's algorithm [19], to solve it. This leads to a polynomial-time algorithm for U-EDCP$^\ell_{1,N,M}$ when $M = \lfloor N^{1/k} \rfloor$ and $\ell \geq k$, for any $k \geq 3$. Interestingly, finding small solutions to the equation $\langle \mathbf{b}, \mathbf{x} \rangle = w \bmod N$ is a special case of the Inhomogeneous Small Integer Solution problem [12] (ISIS), which consists in finding a small-norm $\mathbf{x}$ such that $\mathbf{B}\mathbf{x} = \mathbf{w} \bmod q$, with $\mathbf{B} \in \mathbb{Z}_q^{n \times m}$ and $\mathbf{w} \in \mathbb{Z}_q^n$ uniform (where q, n, m are integer parameters). A reduction from the homogeneous SIS (i.e., with $\mathbf{w} = \mathbf{0}$ and $\mathbf{x} \neq \mathbf{0}$) to LWE was provided in [31]. It does not seem possible to derive from it a reduction from EDCP to LWE via the Childs and van Dam variant of ISIS, most notably because the reduction from [31] does not provide a way to compute all ISIS solutions within a box $\{0, 1, \dots, M-1\}^k$.

It is not hard to see that, at least so long as M is polynomial, a solution to DCP implies a solution to EDCP$^\ell_{n,N,M}$. Therefore our result implies [25] as a special case. On the other extreme, our result also subsumes [9] since the LLL algorithm [18] can be used to solve LWE$_{n,q,\alpha}$ in polynomial time when $1/\alpha$ and q are $2^{\Theta(n)}$, which implies a polynomial-time algorithm for EDCP for $M = 2^{\Theta(\sqrt{n \log N})}$, significantly improving Childs and van Dam's $M = 2^{\varepsilon n \log N}$.

Finally, we observe that the LWE to U-EDCP reduction (and the uSVP to DCP reduction from [27]) can be adapted to a uSVP to U-EDCP reduction, as explained below. Combining this adaptation with the reduction from U-EDCP to LWE (via G-EDCP) provides a novel quantum reduction from worst-case lattice problems to LWE. However, it does not seem to have advantages compared to [29].

1.1   Technical Overview

As mentioned above, the hardness of LWE is essentially invariant so long as $n \log q$ is preserved, and therefore we restrict our attention in this overview to the one-dimensional setting. A crucial ingredient in our reduction is a weighted version of EDCP, denoted by G-EDCP and quantified by a Gaussian weight function $f_r(j) = \rho_r(j) = \exp(-\pi j^2/r^2)$, for some standard deviation parameter r. We refer to this problem as Gaussian EDCP (G-EDCP).

Reducing G-EDCP *to* LWE. Given an G-EDCP state as input, our reduction efficiently transforms it into a classical LWE sample with constant success probability. Thus, making only one query to the LWE oracle, we are able to solve G-EDCP. More precisely, the reduction input consists of a normalized state corresponding to $\sum_{j \in \mathbb{Z}_N} \rho_r(j) |j\rangle |x + j \cdot s \bmod N\rangle$, for some integers $r \ll N$. One can think of N as the LWE modulus and of r as the standard deviation parameter of the LWE error.

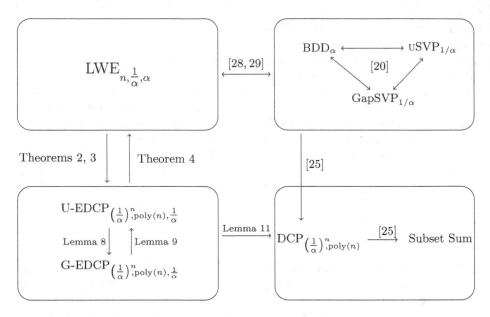

Fig. 1. Graph of reductions between the LWE problem (upper-left), worst-case lattice problems (upper-right), combinatorial problems (lower-right) and the Extrapolated Dihedral Coset problems (lower-left). Parameters α are given up to poly(n)-factors, where n is the dimension of the LWE problem. The same n stands for the lattice-dimension considered in problems of the upper-right corner. The subset-sum problem stated in the lower-right corner is of density ≈ 1 (in particular, the expected number of solutions is constant).

Our first step is to apply a quantum Fourier transform over $\mathbb{Z}_N$ to the second register. This gives us a quantum superposition of the form:

$$\sum_{a\in\mathbb{Z}_N}\sum_{j\in\mathbb{Z}_N} \omega_N^{a\cdot(x+j\cdot s)}\cdot \rho_r(j)\,|j\rangle\,|a\rangle.$$

where $\omega_N = \exp(2i\pi/N)$. We then measure the second register and obtain a value $\widehat{a}\in\mathbb{Z}_N$. This leaves us with the state:

$$\sum_{j\in\mathbb{Z}_N} \omega_N^{j\cdot\widehat{a}\cdot s}\cdot \rho_r(j)\,|j\rangle\,|\widehat{a}\rangle.$$

Note that $\widehat{a}$ is uniformly random over $\mathbb{Z}_N$, which at the end serves as the first component of LWE sample. The exponent of relative phase in current state has a form similar to the second component of LWE sample but without noise. Now we can benefit from the first register, which stores a superposition corresponding to a Gaussian distribution over $\mathbb{Z}_N$ with standard deviation r. Applying a second quantum Fourier transform over $\mathbb{Z}_N$ to the first register gives us a quantum superposition of the form:

$$\sum_{b\in\mathbb{Z}_N}\sum_{j\in\mathbb{Z}_N} \omega_N^{j\cdot(\widehat{a}\cdot s+b)} \cdot \rho_r(j)\,|b\rangle\,.$$

Now the second component of the LWE sample $\widehat{a}\cdot s+b$ is stored in the phase (up to a factor j). Omitting the exponentially small Gaussian tail, we assume the summation for j is taken over the integers. An application of the Poisson summation formula transfers $\widehat{a}\cdot s + b$ into a shift of the Gaussian distribution defined over $\mathbb{Z}$. In other words, the received state is exponentially close to the superposition:

$$\sum_{e\in\mathbb{Z}_N} \rho_{1/r}\left(\frac{e}{N}\right)\,|-\widehat{a}\cdot s+e\rangle\,.$$

Once we measure the state above, we obtain a value $-\widehat{a}\cdot s+e$, where $e \hookleftarrow \mathcal{D}_{\mathbb{Z},N/r}$. Together with already known $\widehat{a}$, this gives us an LWE sample:

$$(-\widehat{a}, -\widehat{a}\cdot s + e)\,.$$

In case the input state is of the form $|j\rangle\,|x \bmod N\rangle$, where j is distributed according to the function ρ_r^2, and $x \in \mathbb{Z}_N$ is uniformly chosen (the decisional case), the reduction outlined above outputs a uniform random pair (a,b) from $\mathbb{Z}_N\times\mathbb{Z}_N$. This gives a reduction from decisional version of G-EDCP to decisional version of LWE.

Reducing LWE *to G-EDCP.* Our reduction from LWE to G-EDCP follows the general design of Regev's reduction from uSVP to DCP [27], with several twists that enable simplifications and improvements. We note that this reduction is folklore,[2] although we could not find it described explicitly.

First, the use of LWE rather than uSVP allows us to avoid Regev's initial sub-reduction from uSVP to BDD, as LWE is a randomized variant of BDD. Indeed, if we consider m samples $(a_i, a_i \cdot s + e_i)$ from $\text{LWE}_{n,q,\alpha}$, then we have a BDD instance for the lattice $\Lambda = \mathbf{A}\mathbb{Z}_q + q\mathbb{Z}^m$ and the target vector $\mathbf{t} = \mathbf{b} + \mathbf{e} \in \mathbb{Z}^m$ with $\mathbf{b} \in \Lambda$ satisfying $\mathbf{b} = \mathbf{A}\cdot s \bmod q$.

As Regev's, our reduction proceeds by subdividing the ambient space $\mathbb{R}^m$ with a coarse grid, setting the cell width between $\|\mathbf{e}\|$ and $\lambda_1(\Lambda)$. We map each point $\mathbf{y} \in \mathbb{R}^m$ to a cell $\phi(\mathbf{y})$. By choice of the cell width, we have $\phi(\mathbf{c}_1) \neq \phi(\mathbf{c}_2)$ for any $\mathbf{c}_1 \neq \mathbf{c}_2$ in Λ. Also for any $\mathbf{c} \in \mathbb{R}^m$, the vectors $\mathbf{c}$ and $\mathbf{c}+\mathbf{e}$ are most likely mapped to the same cell, as $\mathbf{e}$ is short. This intuition fails if a border between two cells falls close to $\mathbf{c}$. This (rare but non-negligibly so) event is the source of the limitation on the number ℓ of DCP/EDCP states produced by the reduction. The space subdivision by a grid is illustrated in Fig. 2.

---

[2] https://groups.google.com/d/msg/cryptanalytic-algorithms/uhr6gGrVkIk/XxEv4u vEBwAJ.

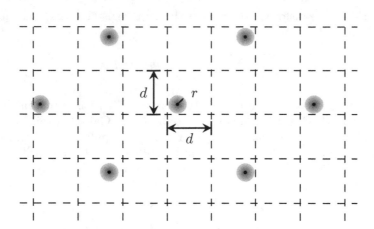

Fig. 2. A visualization of the space subdivision. Each radially shaded disk has width r, the upper bound of the error $\|\mathbf{e}\|$. Each cell has width d, chosen to be between $\|\mathbf{e}\|$ and $\lambda_1(L)/\sqrt{m}$. Note that the grid intersects the left-most disk, potentially leading to an error in the reduction.

Regev's reduction and ours differ in the way the grid is used to create the DCP/EDCP states. Let us first briefly recall the core of Regev's reduction. Let $\mathbf{B} = (\mathbf{b}_1, \ldots, \mathbf{b}_m)$ be a basis of Λ and subtract an appropriate combination of the $\mathbf{b}_i$'s from $\mathbf{t}$ to get $\mathbf{t}'$ so that the coordinates $\mathbf{x}'$ of the closest vector $\mathbf{b}' \in \Lambda$ to $\mathbf{t}'$ with respect to the $\mathbf{b}_i$'s are $\leq 2^m$ (this may be achieved using LLL [18] and Babai's nearest plane algorithm [1]). The first step is the creation of a superposition

$$\sum_{\substack{\mathbf{x} \in \mathbb{Z}^m \\ \|\mathbf{x}\|_\infty \leq 2^{2m}}} \left(|0, \mathbf{x}, \phi(\mathbf{Bx})\rangle + |1, \mathbf{x}, \phi(\mathbf{Bx} - \mathbf{t}')\rangle \right) =$$

$$|0\rangle \sum_{\substack{\mathbf{x} \in \mathbb{Z}^m \\ \|\mathbf{x}\|_\infty \leq 2^{2m}}} |\mathbf{x}, \phi(\mathbf{Bx})\rangle + |1\rangle \sum_{\substack{\mathbf{x} \in \mathbb{Z}^m \\ \|\mathbf{x}+\mathbf{x}'\|_\infty \leq 2^{2m}}} |\mathbf{x} + \mathbf{x}', \phi(\mathbf{Bx} - \mathbf{e})\rangle,$$

where the equality holds by a change of variable. By measuring the last register, with overwhelming probability this collapses to $|0\rangle |\mathbf{x}_k\rangle + |1\rangle |\mathbf{x}_k + \mathbf{x}'\rangle$, which corresponds to an m-dimensional DCP input state with modulus $2^{\mathcal{O}(m)}$. The whole process can be repeated multiple times using the same input vector $\mathbf{t}$, and results in different $\mathbf{x}_k$'s but a common $\mathbf{x}'$. Each iteration may fail because of an ill-placed cell delimitation, or if $\mathbf{x}_k + \mathbf{x}'$ has a coordinate whose magnitude is larger than 2^{2m}. This leads to a bounded number of correct DCP input states. Finally, m-dimensional DCP can be reduced to 1-dimensional DCP, with a significant modulus increase: the resulting modulus N is $2^{\mathcal{O}(m^2)}$.

Instead of using a superposition based on the coordinates with respect to a basis, we exploit the special form of $\Lambda = \mathbf{a}\mathbb{Z}_q + q\mathbb{Z}^m$ (w.l.o.g., assume 1-dimensional LWE, [7]). We start with the following superposition:

$$\sum_{x \in \mathbb{Z}_q} |0, x, \phi(\mathbf{a}x)\rangle + |1, x, \phi(\mathbf{a}x - \mathbf{t})\rangle = |0\rangle \sum_{x \in \mathbb{Z}_q} |x, \phi(\mathbf{a}x)\rangle + |1\rangle \sum_{x \in \mathbb{Z}_q} |x + s, \phi(\mathbf{a}x - \mathbf{e})\rangle .$$

We then measure the last register (classically known and omitted) and hopefully obtain a superposition $|0\rangle |x\rangle + |1\rangle |x + s\rangle$. This approach has several notable advantages. First, by using a grid over the torus $\mathbb{R}^m/q\mathbb{R}^m$, the only source of failure is the position of the cell delimitation (coordinates cannot spill over, they wrap around). Second, we directly end up with a DCP state, not a vectorial variant thereof. Third, and most importantly, the DCP modulus N is only q and not $2^{\mathcal{O}(m^2)}$. Note that m should be set as $\Omega(\log q)$ for s to be uniquely determined by the LWE samples. This improvement results in a much tighter reduction.

The improvement stems from the use of a small modulus q rather than large integer coordinates. It is possible to obtain such a small DCP modulus while starting from BDD (rather than LWE), by modifying Regev's reduction as follows. One may first reduce BDD to a variant thereof that asks to find the coordinates of the BDD solution modulo a small modulus q rather than over the integers. Such a reduction is presented in [29, Lemma 3.5]. One may then reduce this BDD variant to DCP as we proceed for LWE. Note that this transformation makes the BDD to DCP reduction from [27] iterative: the DCP oracle is called several times, and the input of an oracle call depends on the output of the previous oracle calls. This is akin to the phenomenon described in the *open questions* paragraph from [7].

A further difference between our reduction and the one from [27] is that we consider larger multiples of s in the input superposition to obtain a state of the form $\sum_j \rho_r(j) |j\rangle |x + js\rangle$, with $r \approx 1/\alpha$ (up to polynomial factors). This does not lead to any extra complication, but leads us to G-EDCP rather than DCP, which we crucially need to allow for a converse reduction. We conjecture that G-EDCP is strictly easier than DCP.

As Regev [26], we can also improve the resulting deviation parameter r of G-EDCP by a factor of $\sqrt{m}$ using balls' intersections rather than cube separation. We consider intersections of balls drawn around $\mathbf{a} \cdot s$ and its noisy shifts. The radius R of each ball is set to be the largest value such that the balls arising from different s (and their shifts) do not intersect. We are interested in the intersection area the balls drawn around $\pm s, \pm 2s$, etc. Following Regev [26], this area is large enough to guarantee that once we measure, we hit a point from the intersection of all the balls (see grey areas in Fig. 3).

The same algorithm provides a reduction from dLWE to dG-EDCP. Given a random sample $(\mathbf{a}, \mathbf{b}) \in \mathbb{Z}_q^m \times \mathbb{Z}_q^m$, it suffices to show that all the balls centered at $\mathbf{a}s + j\mathbf{b}$ for $s \in \mathbb{Z}_q$ and $j \in \mathbb{Z}$, do not intersect with each other. All the points considered above form the lattice $(\mathbf{a}|\mathbf{b})\mathbb{Z}_q + q\mathbb{Z}$, We argue analogously using

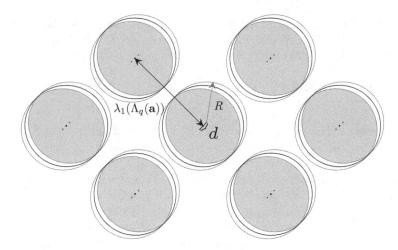

Fig. 3. A visualization of the balls' intersections. The lattice points (black dots) are of distance first minimum of lattice $\mathbf{a}\mathbb{Z}_q + q\mathbb{Z}$ to each other. The distance between the two furthest shifts $\|j\mathbf{e}\|$ (red dots) has an upper bound, denoted by d. Each ball has a radius R chosen to be (approximately) $\lambda_1(\Lambda_q(\mathbf{a}))/2$, where $\Lambda_q(\mathbf{a}) = \mathbf{a}\mathbb{Z}_q + q\mathbb{Z}$. Note that once the shaded gray area is measured, the reduction succeeds in outputting an G-EDCP sample. For the reduction to work with a constant success probability, the shaded area has to have a large enough proportion compared to the volume of the balls. (Color figure online)

the upper-bound on the minima of this lattice. As a result, the superposition collapses exactly to one of the balls, which gives a random sample of dG-EDCP.

1.2   Open Problems

Towards an alternative reduction from EDCP *to* LWE. In [9], Childs and van Dam obtain a state of the form

$$\sum_{a\in\mathbb{Z}_N} \sum_{\substack{\mathbf{j}\in\{0,\ldots,M-1\}^\ell \\ \langle\mathbf{j},\mathbf{y}\rangle = a \bmod N}} \omega_N^{a\cdot s} |\mathbf{j}\rangle .$$

for some uniform $\mathbf{y} \in \mathbb{Z}_N^\ell$. Note the uniform distribution of weights for $\mathbf{j}$. To recover s, the authors use the Pretty Good Measurement technique from [16] as was done in [2,3] for similar problems. Implementing this general technique to this particular setup requires the construction of a POVM with operators corresponding to superpositions of *all* the $\mathbf{j}$'s in $\{0,\ldots,M-1\}^\ell$ such that $\langle\mathbf{j},\mathbf{y}\rangle = a \bmod N$. As we already mentioned, a unitary operator that realizes such a POVM, uses a lattice-reduction technique as its main subroutine and, hence, works efficiently only for large values of M.

The question we do not address here is the interpretation of the POVM technique (and, possibly, a different reduction to LWE) for Gaussian-weighted superpositions. It might be simpler to obtain Gaussian $\mathbf{j}$'s rather than uniform from a cube, and hence it is possible that such a technique may lead to an improved reduction to LWE.

Hardness of EDCP *with more input states.* We show in this work that LWE and U-EDCP are computationally equivalent up to small parameter losses, when the number of U-EDCP states ℓ is polynomial. In these reductions, the U-EDCP bound M is within a polynomial factor of the LWE noise rate $1/\alpha$. When more states are available, U-EDCP is likely to become easier. For instance, with $M = 2$, the best known algorithms when ℓ is polynomially bounded are exponential. Oppositely, Kuperberg's algorithm [17] runs in time $2^{\widetilde{O}(\sqrt{\log N})}$ when $\ell = 2^{\widetilde{O}(\sqrt{\log N})}$. This suggests that there may be a U-EDCP self-reduction allowing to trade ℓ for M: Is it possible to reduce $\text{EDCP}_{N,\ell,M}$ to $\text{EDCP}_{N,\ell',M'}$ with $\ell' \leq \ell$, while allowing for $M' \geq M$?

2   Prerequisites

Notations. We use lower case bold letters to denote vectors and upper case bold to denote matrices. For a vector $\mathbf{x}$, we let $\|\mathbf{x}\|_\infty$ denote its ℓ_∞ norm and $\|\mathbf{x}\|$ denote its ℓ_2 norm. We let $\mathbb{Z}_N$ denote the cyclic group $\{0, 1, \cdots, N-1\}$ with addition modulo N. We assume we can compute with real numbers. All the arguments are valid if a sufficiently accurate approximation is used instead. For a distribution D, the notation $x \hookleftarrow D$ means that x is sampled from D. For a set S, we let $x \hookleftarrow S$ denote that x is a uniformly random element from S.

For any $r > 0$, we let $\rho_r(\mathbf{x})$ denote $\exp(-\pi\|\mathbf{x}\|^2/r^2)$, where $\mathbf{x} \in \mathbb{R}^n$ for a positive integer n. We let $\mathcal{D}_{\mathbb{Z},r}$ denote a Gaussian distribution over the integers with density function proportional to $\rho_r(\cdot)$. We let $\mathcal{D}_{\Lambda,r,\mathbf{c}}$ denote the Gaussian distribution over the n-dimensional lattice Λ (for a positive integer n), with standard deviation parameter $r \in \mathbb{R}$ and center $\mathbf{c} \in \mathbb{R}^n$. If $\mathbf{c} = \mathbf{0}$, we omit it. We let $\mathcal{B}_n(\mathbf{c}, R)$ denote the n-dimensional Euclidean ball of radius R centered at $\mathbf{c} \in \mathbb{R}^n$ and $\mathcal{B}_n$ denotes the n-dimensional Euclidean unit ball centered at $\mathbf{0}$. We use ω_N as a short-hand for $\exp(2\pi i/N)$.

For a lattice Λ with a basis $\mathbf{B}$, the parallelepiped $\mathcal{P}(\mathbf{B}) = \{\mathbf{Bx} : 0 \leq x_i \leq 1\}$ is a fundamental domain of Λ. We let $\lambda_1(\Lambda)$ (resp. $\lambda_1^\infty(\Lambda)$) denote the ℓ_2-norm (ℓ_∞-norm) of a shortest vector of Λ. We let $\Lambda^* = \{\mathbf{y} \in \mathbb{R}^n : \forall \mathbf{x} \in \Lambda, \langle \mathbf{x}, \mathbf{y}\rangle \in \mathbb{Z}\}$ denote the dual of a lattice Λ. We define the smoothing parameter $\eta_\varepsilon(\Lambda)$ as be the smallest r such that $\rho_{1/r}(\Lambda^*\backslash\{\mathbf{0}\}) \leq \varepsilon$ for an n-dimensional lattice Λ and positive $\varepsilon > 0$.

For $\mathbf{A} \in \mathbb{Z}_q^{m \times n}$, we define two lattices $\Lambda_q(\mathbf{A}) = \{\mathbf{Ax} \bmod q : \mathbf{x} \in \mathbb{Z}_q^n\}$ and $\Lambda_q^\perp(\mathbf{A}) = \{\mathbf{y} \in \mathbb{Z}_q^n \text{ s.t. } \mathbf{Ay} = \mathbf{0} \bmod q\}$.

We introduce a variable κ to relate all the parameters involved in the definitions below. Namely, n, q, etc. are actually functions in κ: $n(\kappa)$, $q(\kappa)$. We omit the variable κ for clarity.

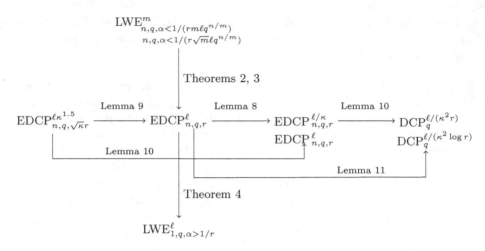

Fig. 4. Graph of reductions between the extrapolated Dihedral Coset Problem instantiated with uniform distribution over $\{0, 1, \ldots, r-1\}$ (the first and the third problems from the left) and ℓ-sample Gaussian EDCP with parameter r (the middle problem). We assume all the parameters n (the dimension), q (the modulus) and r are functions of a common parameter κ. The most relevant choice of such a relation one can keep in mind is when n, ℓ, q and r are poly(κ). One can trace the losses in the parameters (with respect to the number of samples ℓ and to r) once we move from one problem to another. Notice that some reductions may be performed in two ways. For example, using the self-reducibility property of EDCP (Lemma 10), we can bypass Gaussian EDCP and have a more sample-efficient reduction from EDCP with large r to an EDCP with smaller r. Similarly, Gaussian EDCP can be reduced to DCP either directly (Lemma 11) or via uniform EDCP.

The two central reductions that show equivalence between LWE and EDCP problems are on the vertical line. As for EDCP, the LWE parameters n, q, and α are functions of κ. We present two reductions from LWE to EDCP, the stronger one gives a tighter result for the error-parameter by a factor of $\sqrt{m}$.

Definition 1 (Search LWE). *Given a parameter κ, the input to the search $\mathrm{LWE}^m_{n,q,\chi}$ with dimension $n \geq 1$, modulus $q \geq 2$ and distribution χ over $\mathbb{Z}$, consists of $m \geq n$ many samples of the form $(\mathbf{a}, b) \in \mathbb{Z}^n_q \times \mathbb{Z}_q$, with $\mathbf{a} \hookleftarrow \mathbb{Z}^n_q$, $b = \langle \mathbf{a}, \mathbf{s} \rangle + e$ and $e \hookleftarrow \chi$, where $s \in \mathbb{Z}^n_q$ is uniformly chosen. We say that an algorithm solves the search $\mathrm{LWE}^m_{n,q,\chi}$ if it outputs $\mathbf{s}$ with probability poly$(1/(n \log q))$ in time poly$(n \log q)$.*

Definition 2 (Decision LWE). *Given a parameter κ, the decisional $\mathrm{LWE}^m_{n,q,\chi}$ with dimension $n \geq 1$, modulus $q \geq 2$ and distribution χ over $\mathbb{Z}$, asks to distinguish between $m \geq n$ many LWE samples and random samples of the form $(\mathbf{a}, b) \in \mathbb{Z}^n_q \times \mathbb{Z}_q$, with $\mathbf{a} \hookleftarrow \mathbb{Z}^n_q$, $b \hookleftarrow \mathbb{Z}_q$. We say that an algorithm solves the decisional $\mathrm{LWE}^m_{n,q,\chi}$ if it succeeds in distinguishing with probability poly$(1/(n \log q))$ in time poly$(n \log q)$.*

We let $\text{LWE}_{n,q,\alpha}^m$ (resp. $\text{dLWE}_{n,q,\alpha}^m$) denote search (resp. decisional) LWE problem with m samples of dimension n, modulus q, error distributed as $\mathcal{D}_{\mathbb{Z},\alpha q}$.

Definition 3 (Dihedral Coset Problem). *Given a parameter κ, the input to the DCP_N^ℓ with modulus N consists of ℓ states. Each state is of the form (normalization is omitted)*

$$|0\rangle |x\rangle + |1\rangle |(x+s) \bmod N\rangle,\tag{1}$$

stored on $1 + \lceil \log_2 N \rceil$ qubits, where $x \in \mathbb{Z}_N$ is arbitrary and $s \in \mathbb{Z}_N$ is fixed throughout all the states. We say that an algorithm solves DCP_N^ℓ if it outputs s with probability $\text{poly}(1/\log N)$ in time $\text{poly}(\log N)$.

Note that Regev in [25] defines the Dihedral Coset problem slightly differently. Namely, he introduces a failure parameter $f(\kappa)$, and with probability $\leq 1/(\log N(\kappa)^{f(\kappa)})$, we have a state of the form $|b\rangle |x\rangle$ for arbitrary $b \in \{0,1\}^n$ and $x \in \mathbb{Z}_N$. Such a state does not contain any information on s. Our definition takes 0 for the failure parameter. Conversely, Regev's definition is our Definition 3 with a reduced number of input states.

Now we define the problem which can be viewed as an extension of DCP. Analogous to LWE, it has two versions: search and decisional.

Definition 4 (Search Extrapolated Dihedral Coset Problem). *Given a parameter κ, the input to the search Extrapolated Dihedral Coset Problem $(\text{EDCP}_{n,N,D}^\ell)$ with dimension n, modulus N and a discrete distribution D, consists of ℓ input states of the form (normalization is omitted)*

$$\sum_{j\in\text{supp}(D)} D(j)|j\rangle |(\mathbf{x} + j\cdot\mathbf{s}) \bmod N\rangle,\tag{2}$$

where $\mathbf{x} \in \mathbb{Z}_N^n$ is arbitrary and $\mathbf{s} \in \mathbb{Z}_N^n$ is fixed for all ℓ states. We say that an algorithm solves search $\text{EDCP}_{n,N,D}^\ell$ if it outputs $\mathbf{s}$ with probability $\text{poly}(1/(n\log N))$ in time $\text{poly}(n\log N)$.

Definition 5 (Decisional Extrapolated Dihedral Coset Problem). *Given a parameter κ, the decisional Extrapolated Dihedral Coset Problem $(\text{dEDCP}_{n,N,D}^\ell)$ with modulus N and a discrete distribution D, asks to distinguish between ℓ many EDCP samples and ℓ many random samples of the form*

$$|j_k\rangle |\mathbf{x}_k \bmod N\rangle,\tag{3}$$

where $j_k \hookleftarrow D^2$ and $\mathbf{x}_k \in \mathbb{Z}_N^n$ is uniformly chosen for $1 \leq k \leq \ell$. We say that an algorithm solves $\text{dEDCP}_{n,N,D}^\ell$ if it distinguishes the two cases with probability $\text{poly}(1/(n\log N))$ in time $\text{poly}(n\log N)$.

Different choices of D give rise to different instantiations of EDCP. The two interesting ones are: (1) D is uniform over $\mathbb{Z}_M$ for some $M \in \mathbb{Z}$, which we further denote as $\text{U-EDCP}_{n,N,M}^\ell$ and (2) D is Gaussian $\mathcal{D}_{\mathbb{Z},r}$, which we further denote as $\text{G-EDCP}_{n,N,r}^\ell$. The former, named the generalized hidden shift problem, was already considered in [9]. The latter is central in our reductions. Correspondingly, we call the decisional version of G-EDCP by dG-EDCP.

Gaussian distribution on lattices. In the following, we recall some important properties of discrete Gaussian distribution.

Lemma 1. *For any $\kappa, r > 0$, we have $\rho_r(\mathbb{Z}\backslash[-\sqrt{\kappa}r, \sqrt{\kappa}r]) < 2^{-\Omega(\kappa)}\rho_r(\mathbb{Z})$.*

A proof can be found in Appendix A in the full version [6].

From Lemma 1, we can see that the tail of Gaussian distribution has only negligible proportion compared to the whole sum. We use this fact within a quantum superposition state. For a quantum superposition state with Gaussian amplitudes, the superposition corresponding to Gaussian distribution over full lattice and the one without Gaussian tail have exponentially small ℓ_2 distance.

Lemma 2 ([4, Lemma 1.5(ii)]). *For any n-dimensional lattice Λ and $\mathbf{u} \in \mathbb{R}^n$, it holds that*

$$\rho_r(\Lambda + \mathbf{u}\backslash\mathcal{B}(\mathbf{0}, \sqrt{n}r)) < 2^{-\Omega(n)}\rho_r(\Lambda).$$

Lemma 3 (Poisson Summation Formula). *For any n-dimensional lattice Λ and vector $\mathbf{u} \in \mathbb{R}^n$, it holds that*

$$\rho_r(\Lambda + \mathbf{u}) = \det(\Lambda^\star) \cdot r^n \cdot \sum_{\mathbf{x} \in \Lambda^\star} e^{2\pi i \langle \mathbf{x}, \mathbf{u} \rangle} \rho_{1/r}(\mathbf{x}).$$

The following Lemma is originally due to Grover-Rudolph [15] and was adapted to Gaussian distribution in [29].

Lemma 4 (Adapted from [29, Lemma 3.12]). *Given a parameter κ and an integer r, there exists an efficient quantum algorithm that outputs a state that is within ℓ_2 distance $2^{-\Omega(\kappa)}$ of the normalized state corresponding to*

$$\sum_{x \in \mathbb{Z}} \rho_r(x) |x\rangle.$$

The following two lemmata are well-known facts about lower-bounds on minimum of q-ary lattices.

Lemma 5. *Given a uniformly chosen matrix $\mathbf{A} \in \mathbb{Z}_q^{m \times n}$ for some positive integers q, m and n such that $m \geq n$, then we have $\lambda_1^\infty(\Lambda_q(\mathbf{A})) \geq q^{(m-n)/m}/2$ and $\lambda_1^\infty(\Lambda_q^\perp(\mathbf{A})) \geq q^{n/m}/2$ both with probability $1 - 2^{-m}$.*

Lemma 6. *Given a uniformly chosen matrix $\mathbf{A} \in \mathbb{Z}_q^{m \times n}$ for some positive integer q, m and n such that $m \geq n$, then we have $\lambda_1(\Lambda_q(\mathbf{A})) \geq \min\{q, \frac{\sqrt{m}q^{(m-n)/m}}{2\sqrt{2\pi e}}\}$ with probability $1 - 2^{-m}$.*

Reductions between EDCP variants. In the following, we show that the EDCP problem is analogue to the LWE problem in many aspects: (1) Gaussian-EDCP (G-EDCP$_{n,N,r}^{\ell'}$) and uniform-EDCP (U-EDCP$_{n,N,M}^{\ell}$) are equivalent, up to small parameter losses; (2) EDCP enjoys the self-reduction property as we show in Lemma 10. The main ingredient in both proofs is quantum rejection sampling due to Ozols et al. [22].

Lemma 7 ([22, Sect. 4]). *There is a quantum rejection sampling algorithm, which given as input*

$$\sum_{k=1}^{n} \pi_k \, |k\rangle \, |\eta_k\rangle \,,$$

for some probability π_k, outputs

$$\frac{1}{\|\mathbf{p}\|} \sum_{k=1}^{n} p_k \, |k\rangle \, |\eta_k\rangle \,.$$

for some $p_k \leq \pi_k$, with probability $\|\mathbf{p}\|^2 = \sum_{k=1}^{n} p_k^2$.

Lemma 8 (G-EDCP $\leq$ U-EDCP). *Let N, n and ℓ be integers greater than 1, r be any real number, and let $M = c \cdot r$ for some constant c such that M is an integer. Then there is a probabilistic reduction with run-time polynomial in κ, from G-EDCP$_{n,N,r}^{\ell}$ to U-EDCP$_{n,N,M}^{\mathcal{O}(\ell/\kappa)}$.*

Proof. We are given as input G-EDCP$_{n,N,r}^{\ell}$ states:

$$\left\{ \sum_{j\in\mathbb{Z}} \rho_r(j) \, |j\rangle \, |(\mathbf{x}_k + j \cdot \mathbf{s}) \bmod N\rangle \right\}_{k\leq\ell}.$$

Our aim is to find $\mathbf{s}$, given access to a U-EDCP$_{n,N,cr}^{\mathcal{O}(\ell/\kappa)}$ oracle for some constant c.

For each G-EDCP$_{n,N,r}$ sample, we proceed as follows. We let $sign(x)$ to denote the sign of x, its output is either 1 (for ' $+$ ') or 0 (for ' $-$ '). We first compute the sign of the first register and store it in a new register:

$$\sum_{j\in\mathbb{Z}} \rho_r(j) \, |j\rangle \, |(\mathbf{x} + j \cdot \mathbf{s}) \bmod N\rangle \, |sign(j)\rangle \,.$$

Second, we measure the third register. Note that we observe 1 with probability at least $1/2$, independently over all k's. If the observed value is 0, we discard the state. From states with the observed value 1, we obtain (up to normalization):

$$\sum_{j\in\mathbb{Z}_+} \rho_r(j) \, |j\rangle \, |(\mathbf{x} + j \cdot \mathbf{s}) \bmod N\rangle \,.$$

Using quantum rejection sampling (Lemma 7), we transform a G-EDCP$_{N,\ell,r}$ state into a U-EDCP$_{n,N,M}$ state of the form

$$\sum_{j\in[0,M-1]} |j\rangle \, |(\mathbf{x} + j \cdot \mathbf{s}) \bmod N\rangle \,.$$

with probability $\Omega(M\rho_r^2(c \cdot r)/r) = \Omega(1)$.

We repeat the above procedure until we obtain $\mathcal{O}(\ell/\kappa)$ many U-EDCP$_{n,N,M}$ states, which happens with probability $\geq 1 - 2^{-\Omega(\kappa)}$. We call the U-EDCP$_{n,N,M}^{\mathcal{O}(\ell/\kappa)}$ oracle to recover the secret $\mathbf{s}$ as the solution for the input G-EDCP$_{n,N,r}^{\ell}$ instance.

Lemma 9 (U-EDCP $\leq$ G-EDCP). *Let N, M, n and ℓ be integers greater than 1, r be any real number, such that $M = \sqrt{\kappa} \cdot r = \text{poly}(\kappa)$ is an integer. Then there is a probabilistic reduction with run-time polynomial in κ, from U-EDCP$_{n,N,M}^{\ell}$ to G-EDCP$_{n,N,r}^{\mathcal{O}(\ell/\kappa^{1.5})}$.*

Proof. We are given as input ℓ many U-EDCP$_{n,N,M}^{\ell}$ states:

$$\left\{ \sum_{j \in [0, M-1]} |j\rangle \, |(\mathbf{x} + j \cdot \mathbf{s}) \bmod N\rangle \right\}_{k \leq \ell}.$$

Our aim is to find $\mathbf{s}$, given access to a G-EDCP$_{n,N,r}^{\mathcal{O}(\ell/\kappa^{1.5})}$ oracle where $r = M/\sqrt{\kappa}$.

For each U-EDCP$_{n,N,M}$ state we proceed as follows. First, we symmetrize the uniform distribution by applying the function $f(x) = x - \lfloor (M-1)/2 \rfloor$ to the first register:

$$\sum_{j \in [0, M-1]} |j - \lfloor (M-1)/2 \rfloor\rangle \, |(\mathbf{x} + j \cdot \mathbf{s}) \bmod N\rangle = \sum_{j' \in \left[-\lfloor \frac{M-1}{2} \rfloor, \lceil \frac{M-1}{2} \rceil \right]} |j'\rangle \, |(\mathbf{x}' + j' \cdot \mathbf{s}) \bmod N\rangle,$$

where $j' = j - \lfloor (M-1)/2 \rfloor$, $\mathbf{x}' = \mathbf{x} + \lceil (M-1)/2 \rceil \cdot \mathbf{s}$.

Using rejection sampling (Lemma 7), with probability $\Omega(r/M) = \Omega(1/\sqrt{\kappa})$ we transform each U-EDCP$_{n,N,\lceil \frac{M-1}{2} \rceil}$ state into a G-EDCP$_{n,N,r}$ state:

$$\sum_{j' \in \left[-\lfloor \frac{M-1}{2} \rfloor, \lceil \frac{M-1}{2} \rceil \right]} \rho_r(j') \, |j'\rangle \, |(\mathbf{x}' + j' \cdot \mathbf{s}) \bmod N\rangle.$$

According to Lemma 1, the latter is within the ℓ_2 distance of $2^{-\Omega(\kappa)}$ away from the state

$$\sum_{j' \in \mathbb{Z}} \rho_r(j') \, |j'\rangle \, |(\mathbf{x}' + j' \cdot \mathbf{s}) \bmod N\rangle.$$

We repeat the above procedure until we obtain $\mathcal{O}(\ell/\kappa^{1.5})$ many G-EDCP$_{n,N,r}$ states, which happens with probability $\geq 1 - 2^{-\Omega(\kappa)}$. Then we can use the G-EDCP$_{n,N,r}^{\mathcal{O}(\ell/\kappa^{1.5})}$ oracle to recover the secret $\mathbf{s}$ as the solution to U-EDCP$_{n,N,M}^{\ell}$.

Next, we show the self-reducibility property for EDCP. We refer the reader to Appendix B in the full version [6] for the proof.

Lemma 10 (EDCP self-reduction). *Let N, n, and ℓ be integers greater than 1, r_1 and r_2 be such that $r_1 > r_2$ and $r_1/r_2 = \mathcal{O}(\kappa^c)$ for any constant c. Then there is a probabilistic reduction with run-time polynomial in κ, from G-EDCP$_{n,N,r_1}^{\ell}$ (resp. U-EDCP$_{n,N,r_1}^{\ell}$) to G-EDCP$_{n,N,r_2}^{\mathcal{O}(\ell/\kappa^{c+1})}$ (resp. U-EDCP$_{n,N,r_2}^{\mathcal{O}(\ell/\kappa^{c+1})}$).*

In the following, we give a reduction from Gaussian-EDCP to DCP. Thus uniform-EDCP can also be reduced to DCP in two ways: either via self-reduction, or via Gaussian-EDCP as the next lemma shows. This result is especially interesting when the parameter r (or M for the uniform-EDCP) is super-polynomially large, as in this case, Lemma 10 cannot be applied. Lemma below works with 1-dimensional EDCP. This is without loss of generality as we can combine our main result (equivalence of LWE and EDCP) with the result of Brakerski et al. [7] (equivalence of $\mathrm{LWE}_{n,q,\alpha}$ and $\mathrm{LWE}_{1,q^n,\alpha}$).

Lemma 11 (Gaussian-EDCP to DCP). *Let N and ℓ be arbitrary integers. Then there is a probabilistic reduction with run-time polynomial in κ, from $\mathrm{G\text{-}EDCP}^\ell_{1,N,r}$ to $\mathrm{DCP}_N^{\mathcal{O}(\ell/(\log r \cdot \kappa^2))}$ if $r \geq 3 \log N$, and from $\mathrm{G\text{-}EDCP}^\ell_{1,N,r}$ to $\mathrm{DCP}_N^{\mathcal{O}(\ell/(r \cdot \kappa))}$ otherwise.*

Proof. We are given as input ℓ many $\mathrm{G\text{-}EDCP}_{1,N,r}$ states:

$$\left\{ \sum_{j \in \mathbb{Z}} \rho_r(j) \, |j\rangle \, |(x_k + j \cdot s) \bmod N\rangle \right\}_{k \leq \ell}.$$

We show how to find s if we are given access to a $\mathrm{DCP}_N^{\mathcal{O}(\ell/(r \cdot \kappa))}$ oracle for $r < 3 \log N$, and a $\mathrm{DCP}_N^{\mathcal{O}(\ell/(\log r \cdot \kappa^2))}$ oracle otherwise.

• Case $r \geq 3 \log N$.

According to Lemma 8, we can transform ℓ many $\mathrm{G\text{-}EDCP}_{1,N,r}$ states into ℓ/κ many $\mathrm{U\text{-}EDCP}_{1,N,M'}$ states with $M' = 2c \cdot r + 1$ for some constant c losing a factor of κ samples. Assume we obtain ℓ/κ many $\mathrm{U\text{-}EDCP}_{1,N,M'}$ samples. For each such state, we symmetrize the interval $[0, M']$ as in the proof of Lemma 9. Then we receive a uniform distribution over $[-M, M]$ for $M = (M' - 1)/2$. We compute the absolute value of the first register and store it in a new register:

$$\sum_{j \in [-M,M]} |j\rangle \, |(\hat{x}_k + j \cdot s) \bmod N\rangle \, ||j|\rangle, \tag{4}$$

where $\hat{x}_k = x_k - M \cdot s$. We measure the third register and denote the observed value by v_k.

We make use of the two well-known facts from number theory. For proofs, the reader may consult [30, Chap. 5]. First, there exist more than $M/\log M$ many primes that are smaller than M. Second, N has at most $2 \log N/\log \log N$ prime factors. Thus there are at least $M/\log M - 2 \log N/\log \log N$ many numbers smaller than M that are co-prime with all prime factors of N.

From the above, with probability $\Omega(1/\log M) = \Omega(1/\log r)$, the observed value v_k is non-zero and co-prime with N. If this is not the case, we discard the state. Otherwise, we obtain (up to normalization):

$$|-v_k\rangle \, |(\hat{x}_k - v_k \cdot s) \bmod N\rangle + |v_k\rangle \, |(\hat{x}_k + v_k \cdot s) \bmod N\rangle.$$

We multiply the value in the second register by $v_k^{-1} \bmod N$:

$$|-v_k\rangle \, |(x_k' - s) \bmod N\rangle + |v_k\rangle \, |(x_k' + s) \bmod N\rangle \,,$$

where $x_k' = \hat{x}_k \cdot v_k^{-1}$.

Let $\bar{x}_k = x_k' - s \bmod N$ and $\bar{s} = 2 \cdot s \bmod N$. Rewrite the above state as:

$$|-v_k\rangle \, |\bar{x}_k\rangle + |v_k\rangle \, |(\bar{x}_k + \bar{s}) \bmod N\rangle \,.$$

As we know v_k classically, we uncompute the first register and obtain a DCP state:

$$|0\rangle \, |\bar{x}_k\rangle + |1\rangle \, |(\bar{x}_k + \bar{s}) \bmod N\rangle \,. \tag{5}$$

We repeat the above procedure until we obtain $\mathcal{O}(\ell/(\log r \cdot \kappa^2))$ many DCP_N states with probability $\geq 1 - 2^{-\Omega(\kappa)}$.

- Case that $r < 3 \log N$.

The first steps are identical to the proof for the case $r \geq 3 \log N$: Compute the absolute value of the first register to get a state as in (4) and measure the third register. Denote the observed value by v_k. Now we keep only those states, for which $v_k = 1$ was observed. Otherwise, we do not use the state. In case $v_k = 1$, we can easily transform the result to the state given in (5) analogously to the proof for $r \geq 3 \log N$.

Now we show that $v_k = 1$ occurs with probability $\Omega(1/r)$ independently over all k's. Indeed,

$$\Pr[v_k = 1] = \frac{\rho_r(1)^2 + \rho_r(-1)^2}{\sum_{j \in \mathbb{Z}} \rho_r(j)^2} \geq \frac{2 \cdot \rho_r(1)^2}{\int_{\mathbb{R}} \rho_r(x)^2 \mathrm{d}x + 1} = \frac{2 \cdot \exp(-\frac{2\pi}{r^2})}{\frac{r}{\sqrt{2}} + 1} = \Omega\left(\frac{1}{r}\right).$$

We repeat the above procedure until we obtain $\mathcal{O}(\ell/(r \cdot \kappa))$ many DCP_N states, which happens with probability $\geq 1 - 2^{-\Omega(\kappa)}$.

In both cases considered in this lemma, we can use the $\mathrm{DCP}_N^{\mathcal{O}(\ell/(r \cdot \kappa))}$ oracle and get the secret $\bar{s}$. There are at most 2 possible values s such that $\bar{s} = 2s \bmod N$: if there are 2 possibilities, we uniformly choose either, which decreases the success probability by at most a factor of 2.

3   Reduction from LWE to EDCP

In this section, we reduce $\mathrm{LWE}_{n,q,\alpha}^m$ to $\mathrm{G\text{-}EDCP}_{n,q,r}^\ell$, where $r \approx 1/\alpha$ up to a factor of $\mathrm{poly}(n \log q)$. Analogous to Regev's reductions from USVP to DCP, we present two versions of the reduction from LWE to G-EDCP. The second one is tighter with respect to the parameter losses. At the end of the section we show that using the same algorithm, one can reduce the decisional version of LWE to the decisional version of EDCP (see Definition 5).

3.1   First Reduction: Using Cube Separation

The main result of this section is the following theorem.

Theorem 2 (LWE $\leq$ EDCP). *Let (n, q, α) be LWE parameters and (n, q, r) be EDCP parameters. Given $m = n \log q = \Omega(\kappa)$ many $\mathrm{LWE}_{n,q,\alpha}$ samples, there exists a probabilistic quantum reduction, with run-time polynomial in κ, from $\mathrm{LWE}_{n,q,\alpha}^m$ to $\mathrm{G\text{-}EDCP}_{n,q,r}^\ell$, where $r < 1/(32 m \kappa \alpha \ell q^{n/m})$.*

The main step of our reduction is to partition the ambient space $\mathbb{R}^m$ with an appropriately chosen grid (cubes). This is analogous to Regev's reduction from uSVP to DCP [25]. Lemma 12 shows how we choose the width of the cell in our grid. Figure 2 gives a 2-dimensional example of such a grid.

Lemma 12. *For a constant $c \geq 8$, a matrix $\mathbf{A} \in \mathbb{Z}_q^{m \times n}$ is randomly chosen for integers q, n, $m = n \log q$, and $k \geq m$, consider a function*

$$g : (x_1, \cdots, x_m) \to (\lfloor x_1/z - w_1 \bmod \bar{q} \rfloor, \cdots, \lfloor x_m/z - w_m \bmod \bar{q} \rfloor),$$

where $z = q/c$ and $z \in [1/c, 1/2] \cdot \lambda_1^\infty(\Lambda_q(\mathbf{A}))$, $w_1, \ldots, w_m$ are uniformly chosen from $[0, 1)$, and $\bar{q} = q/z$. Then for any $\mathbf{x} \in \mathbb{Z}_q^n$, we have the following two statements.

- *For any $\mathbf{u} = \mathbf{A}\mathbf{x} + \mathbf{e}_1, \mathbf{v} = \mathbf{A}\mathbf{x} + \mathbf{e}_2$ where $\|\mathbf{e}_1\|_\infty, \|\mathbf{e}_2\|_\infty \leq \lambda_1^\infty(\Lambda_q(\mathbf{A}))/(2ck)$, with probability $(1 - 1/k)^m$, over the randomness of $w_1, \cdots, w_m$, we have $g(\mathbf{u}) = g(\mathbf{v})$.*
- *For any $\mathbf{u} = \mathbf{A}\mathbf{x} + \mathbf{e}_1, \mathbf{v} = \mathbf{A}\hat{\mathbf{x}} + \mathbf{e}_2$, where $\|\mathbf{e}_1\|_\infty, \|\mathbf{e}_2\|_\infty \leq \lambda_1^\infty(\Lambda_q(\mathbf{A}))/(2ck)$ and $\mathbf{x} \neq \hat{\mathbf{x}} \in \mathbb{Z}_q^n$, we have $g(\mathbf{u}) \neq g(\mathbf{v})$.*

Proof

- Proof for the first claim.

    Write $\mathbf{u} = \mathbf{A}\mathbf{x} + \mathbf{e}_1 \bmod q$ and $\mathbf{v} = \mathbf{A}\mathbf{x} + \mathbf{e}_2 \bmod q$ for some $\mathbf{x} \in \mathbb{Z}_q^n$ and $\|\mathbf{e}_1\|_\infty, \|\mathbf{e}_2\|_\infty \leq \lambda_1^\infty(\Lambda_q(\mathbf{A}))/(2ck)$.

    Let DIFF denote the event that $g(\mathbf{u}) \neq g(\mathbf{v})$, and, for all $i \leq m$, let DIFF_i denote the event that the iþ coordinates of $g(\mathbf{u})$ and $g(\mathbf{v})$ differ. Since we choose $w_1, \ldots, w_m$ independently and uniformly from $[0, 1)$, we can consider each of m dimension separately and view each $e_{1,i}/z + w_i$ and $e_{2,i}/z + w_i$ as random 1-dim. real points inside an interval of length 1. We have

$$\Pr_{w_i}[\mathrm{DIFF}_i] = \frac{|e_{1,i} - e_{2,i}|}{z} \leq \frac{z/k}{z} = \frac{1}{k},$$

where the inequality follows from the lower-bound on z. This implies

$$\Pr_{\mathbf{w}}[\mathrm{NO\ DIFF}] = \prod_{i \leq m} \left(1 - \Pr_{w_i}[\mathrm{DIFF}_i]\right) \geq \left(1 - \frac{1}{k}\right)^m.$$

- Proof for the second claim.

Write $\mathbf{u} = \mathbf{A}\mathbf{x} + \mathbf{e}_1 \bmod q$ and $\mathbf{v} = \mathbf{A}\widehat{\mathbf{x}} + \mathbf{e}_2 \bmod q$ for $\mathbf{x} \neq \widehat{\mathbf{x}} \in \mathbb{Z}_q^n$ and $\|\mathbf{e}_1\|_\infty, \|\mathbf{e}_2\|_\infty \leq \lambda_1^\infty(\Lambda_q(\mathbf{A}))/(2ck)$. Then we have

$$g(\mathbf{u}) = \left\lfloor \frac{1}{z} \cdot (\mathbf{A}\mathbf{x}) + \frac{1}{z} \cdot \mathbf{e}_1 + \mathbf{w} \bmod \bar{q} \right\rceil,$$

$$g(\mathbf{v}) = \left\lfloor \frac{1}{z} \cdot (\mathbf{A}\widehat{\mathbf{x}}) + \frac{1}{z} \cdot \mathbf{e}_2 + \mathbf{w} \bmod \bar{q} \right\rceil.$$

Now we show that $g(\mathbf{u})$ and $g(\mathbf{v})$ differ in at least 1 coordinate. This is the case if the arguments of the floor function differ by 1 in at least one coordinate, i.e., $\|\frac{1}{z}\mathbf{A} \cdot (\mathbf{x} - \widehat{\mathbf{x}}) + \frac{1}{z}(\mathbf{e}_1 - \mathbf{e}_2) \bmod \bar{q}\|_\infty \geq 1$.

Assume the contrary is the case. Note that due to our choice of $\mathbf{e}_i$ and $\bar{q}$, $\|\frac{1}{z}(\mathbf{e}_1 - \mathbf{e}_2) \bmod \bar{q}\|_\infty$ is either at most $1/k$ or at least $\bar{q} - 1/k$. Either way we have $\|\frac{1}{z}\mathbf{A}(\mathbf{x} - \widehat{\mathbf{x}}) \bmod \bar{q}\|_\infty < 1 + 1/k$ or $\|\frac{1}{z}\mathbf{A}(\mathbf{x} - \widehat{\mathbf{x}}) \bmod \bar{q}\|_\infty > \bar{q} - 1 + 1/k$. Due to the bounds on z and c, the former case is equivalent to

$$\|\mathbf{A}(\mathbf{x} - \widehat{\mathbf{x}}) \bmod \bar{q}\|_\infty < z + z/k \leq \lambda_1^\infty(\Lambda_{\bar{q}}(\mathbf{A}))\left(\frac{1}{2} + \frac{1}{2k}\right) \leq \lambda_1^\infty(\Lambda_{\bar{q}}(\mathbf{A})).$$

Hence, we have just found a vector in the lattice $\Lambda_{\bar{q}}(\mathbf{A})$ shorter than the minimum of the lattice. In the latter case when $\|\frac{1}{z}\mathbf{A} \cdot (\mathbf{x} - \widehat{\mathbf{x}}) \bmod \bar{q}\|_\infty > \bar{q} - 1/k + 1$, we obtain the same contradiction by noticing that $\Lambda_{\bar{q}}$ contains $\bar{q}$-ary vectors.

Proof (of Theorem 2). Assume we are given an $\mathrm{LWE}_{n,q,\alpha}^m$ instance $(\mathbf{A}, \mathbf{b}_0)$ with $\mathbf{b}_0 = \mathbf{A} \cdot \mathbf{s}_0 + \mathbf{e}_0 \bmod q$. Our aim is to find $\mathbf{s}_0$ given access to a $\mathrm{G\text{-}EDCP}_{n,q,r}^\ell$ oracle.

We first prepare a necessary number of registers in the state $|0\rangle$ and transform them to the state of the form (normalization omitted)

$$\sum_{\mathbf{s} \in \mathbb{Z}_q^n} |0\rangle \, |\mathbf{s}\rangle \, |0\rangle. \tag{6}$$

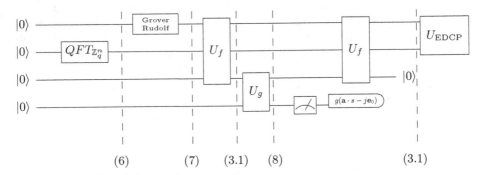

Fig. 5. Quantum circuit for our reduction LWE $\leq$ EDCP. All the global phases are omitted. The input registers are assumed to have the required number of qubits. Function f is defined as $U_f |j\rangle |s\rangle |0\rangle \to |j\rangle |s\rangle |\mathbf{As} - j\mathbf{b} \bmod q\rangle$. Function U_g is the embedding of function g described in Lemma 12, i.e. $U_g |\mathbf{x}\rangle |0\rangle \to |\mathbf{x}\rangle |\lfloor \mathbf{x}/z - \mathbf{w} \bmod \bar{q}\rceil\rangle$ for appropriately chosen $z, \mathbf{w}, \bar{q}$.

We use Lemma 4 to obtain a state within ℓ_2 distance of $2^{-\Omega(\kappa)}$ away from

$$\sum_{\mathbf{s} \in \mathbb{Z}_q^n} \left(\sum_{j \in \mathbb{Z}} \rho_r(j) \, |j\rangle \right) |\mathbf{s}\rangle \, |0\rangle . \tag{7}$$

According to Lemma 1, the state above is within ℓ_2 distance of $2^{-\Omega(\kappa)}$ away from[3]

$$\sum_{\substack{\mathbf{s} \in \mathbb{Z}_q^n \\ j \in \mathbb{Z} \cap [-\sqrt{\kappa} \cdot r, \sqrt{\kappa} \cdot r]}} \rho_r(j) \, |j\rangle \, |\mathbf{s}\rangle \, |0\rangle .$$

We evaluate the function $f(j, \mathbf{s}) \mapsto \mathbf{As} - j \cdot \mathbf{b} \bmod q$ and store the result in the third register. The next equality follows from a change of variable on s

$$\sum_{\substack{\mathbf{s} \in \mathbb{Z}_q^n \\ j \in \mathbb{Z} \cap [-\sqrt{\kappa} \cdot r, \sqrt{\kappa} \cdot r]}} \rho_r(j) \, |j\rangle \, |\mathbf{s}\rangle \, |\mathbf{As} - j \cdot \mathbf{As}_0 - j\mathbf{e}_0\rangle = \sum_{\substack{\mathbf{s} \in \mathbb{Z}_q^n \\ j \in \mathbb{Z} \cap [-\sqrt{\kappa} \cdot r, \sqrt{\kappa} \cdot r]}} \rho_r(j) \, |j\rangle \, |\mathbf{s} + j\mathbf{s}_0\rangle \, |\mathbf{As} - j\mathbf{e}_0\rangle .$$

Sample $w_1, \ldots, w_m$ uniformly from $[0, 1)$. Set $z = q/c$ for some constant $c \geq 8$, thus we have $z \in [1/c, 1/2] \cdot \lambda_1^\infty(\Lambda_q(\mathbf{A}))$, where the upper bound holds with probability $1 - 2^{-m} = 1 - 2^{-\Omega(\kappa)}$ (see Lemma 5).

For $\mathbf{x} \in \mathbb{Z}_q^m$, we define

$$g(\mathbf{x}) = (\lfloor (x_1/z - w_1) \bmod \bar{q} \rfloor, \ldots, \lfloor (x_m/z - w_m) \bmod \bar{q} \rfloor),$$

where $\bar{q} = q/z = c$. We evaluate the function g on the third register and store the result on a new register. We obtain

$$\sum_{\substack{\mathbf{s} \in \mathbb{Z}_q^n \\ j \in \mathbb{Z} \cap [-\sqrt{\kappa} \cdot r, \sqrt{\kappa} \cdot r]}} \rho_r(j) \, |j\rangle \, |\mathbf{s} + j \cdot \mathbf{s}_0\rangle \, |\mathbf{As} - j \cdot \mathbf{e}_0\rangle \, |g(\mathbf{As} - j \cdot \mathbf{e}_0)\rangle . \tag{8}$$

We measure the fourth register and do not consider it further. According to Lemma 1, we have $\|\mathbf{e}_0\|_\infty \leq \sqrt{\kappa} \alpha q$ with probability $\geq 1 - 2^{-\Omega(m)} = 1 - 2^{-\Omega(\kappa)}$. Recall that $r < 1/(32m\ell\kappa\alpha q^{n/m}) \leq 1/(4ck\kappa\alpha q^{n/m})$ for $c = 8$ and $k = m\ell$. Therefore, we have $\|\sqrt{\kappa} r \cdot \mathbf{e}_0\|_\infty \leq \lambda_1^\infty(\Lambda_q(\mathbf{A}))/(2ck)$. Then by Lemma 12, we obtain

$$\sum_{j \in \mathbb{Z} \cap [-\sqrt{\kappa} \cdot r, \sqrt{\kappa} \cdot r]} \rho_r(j) \, |j\rangle \, |\mathbf{s} + j \cdot \mathbf{s}_0\rangle \, |\mathbf{As} - j \cdot \mathbf{e}_0\rangle$$

for some $\mathbf{s} \in \mathbb{Z}_q^n$, with probability $(1 - 1/k)^m$ over the randomness of $\mathbf{A}$ and $w_1, \cdots, w_m$.

---

[3] Here we cut the tail of the Gaussian distribution on the first register. Otherwise, a measurement that follows leads to a state mixed with noisy vectors from different lattice points with large (unbounded) noise. However, it has ℓ_2 distance exponentially close to the state we consider in the current algorithm.

Finally, we evaluate the function $(j, \mathbf{s}, \mathbf{b}) \mapsto \mathbf{b} - \mathbf{As} + j \cdot \mathbf{b}_0$ on the first three registers, which gives $\mathbf{0}$. Discarding this $\mathbf{0}$-register, the state is of the form

$$\sum_{j \in \mathbb{Z} \cap [-\sqrt{\kappa} \cdot r, \sqrt{\kappa} \cdot r]} \rho_r(j) |j\rangle |\mathbf{s} + j \cdot \mathbf{s}_0\rangle .$$

According to Lemma 1, the above state is within ℓ_2 distance of $2^{-\Omega(\kappa)}$ away from

$$\sum_{j \in \mathbb{Z}} \rho_r(j) |j\rangle |\mathbf{s} + j \cdot \mathbf{s}_0\rangle .$$

We repeat the above procedure ℓ times, and with probability $(1 - \frac{1}{k})^{m\ell}$, we obtain ℓ many G-EDCP$_{n,q,r}^{\ell}$ states

$$\left\{ \sum_{j \in \mathbb{Z}} \rho_r(j) |j\rangle |\mathbf{x}_k + j \cdot \mathbf{s}_0\rangle \right\}_{k \le \ell} ,$$

where $\mathbf{x}_k \in \mathbb{Z}_q^n$.

Now we can call the G-EDCP$_{n,q,r}^{\ell}$ oracle with the above states as input and obtain $\mathbf{s}_0$ as output of the oracle.

3.2   An Improved Reduction: Using Balls' Intersection

Here we give an improved reduction from LWE to EDCP. Following the idea of Regev [25, Sect. 3.3], instead of separating the ambient space $\mathbb{Z}^m$ by cubes, we consider intersections of balls drawn around the points $\mathbf{As}$ and its shifts. Note that with this reduction we improve the upper-bound on r essentially by the factor of $\sqrt{m}$.

Theorem 3. (LWE $\le$ EDCP). *Let (n, q, α) be LWE parameters and (n, q, r) be EDCP parameters. Given $m = \Omega(\kappa)$ many LWE$_{n,q,\alpha}$ samples, there exists a quantum reduction, with run-time polynomial in κ, from LWE$_{n,q,\alpha}^m$ to G-EDCP$_{n,q,r}^{\ell}$, where $r < 1/(6\sqrt{2\pi}e\sqrt{m\kappa}\ell\alpha q^{n/m})$.*

We give an intuitive idea of how the reduction works. All the necessary lemmata and the full proof are given in Appendix B in the full version [6].

Informally, the reduction works as follows. Given an LWE instance $(\mathbf{A}, \mathbf{b} = \mathbf{As}_0 + \mathbf{e}_0) \in \mathbb{Z}_q^{m \times n} \times \mathbb{Z}_q^m$, for each $\mathbf{s} \in \mathbb{Z}_q^n$, we consider (in a superposition over all such $\mathbf{s}$) a lattice point $\mathbf{As}$ together with its small shifts of $\mathbf{As} - j\mathbf{e}_0$, where j's are drawn from a small interval symmetric around 0. So far this is exactly what we did in the first (weaker) reduction. Note that we receive a configuration of points in $\mathbb{Z}_q^m$ as depicted in Fig. 3. Note that contrary to Regev's reduction, where there is only one shift (i.e., the DCP case), our extrapolated version considers poly(κ) shifts thus leading us to the EDCP case.

Let us fix some **As** together with its shifts. Draw a ball around each shift of a maximal radius R such that there is no intersection between the shifts coming from different lattice points, i.e. there is no j, j' s.t. $\mathcal{B}(\mathbf{As} - j\mathbf{e}_0, R) \cap \mathcal{B}(\mathbf{As}' - j'\mathbf{e}_0, R) \neq \emptyset$ for any two $\mathbf{s}, \mathbf{s}'$ such that $\mathbf{s} \neq \mathbf{s}'$. To satisfy this condition, we can take R almost as large as the first minimum of the lattice $\Lambda_q(\mathbf{A})$ (again, see Fig. 3). With such an R, due to the fact that the shifts are small, the intersection of the balls drawn around the shifts is large enough (see Lemma 13 in Appendix B of the full version [6]). Hence, once we measure the register that 'stores' our balls, the resulting state collapses (with large enough probability) to a superposition of some **As** for *one* $\mathbf{s}$ and all its shifts. Informally, the higher this probability is, the tighter the parameters achieved by the reduction.

3.3   Reduction from dLWE to dEDCP

As a corollary to the above theorem, we show that the decisional LWE can be reduced to decisional EDCP. In fact, to establish the reduction, we use the same algorithm as for Theorem 3 (a weaker reduction given in Theorem 2 will work as well). Recall that in the proof, starting from an EDCP sample, we obtain an LWE sample with non-negligible probability. Corollary 1 below shows that in case we are given a tuple $(\mathbf{A}, \mathbf{b})$ drawn uniformly at random from $\mathbb{Z}_q^{m \times n} \times \mathbb{Z}_q^m$, the procedure described in Theorem 3 outputs a state of the form $|j\rangle\, |\mathbf{x} \bmod N\rangle$, a uniform counterpart to EDCP in the sense of Definition 5. A proof of the following corollary is given in Appendix B of the full version [6].

Corollary 1 (dLWE $\leq$ dEDCP). *Let (n, q, α) be valid dLWE parameters and (n, q, r) be valid dEDCP parameters. Given $m = \Omega(\kappa)$ many $\mathrm{LWE}_{n,q,\alpha}$ samples, there exists a quantum reduction, with run-time polynomial in κ, from $\mathrm{LWE}_{n,q,\alpha}^m$ to $\mathrm{G\text{-}EDCP}_{n,q,r}^\ell$, where $r < 1/(6\sqrt{2\pi}e\sqrt{m\kappa}\ell\alpha q^{(n+1)/m})$.*

4   Reduction from EDCP to LWE

In this section, we reduce $\mathrm{G\text{-}EDCP}_{n,N,r}^\ell$ to $\mathrm{LWE}_{n,N,\alpha}^\ell$, where $r \approx 1/\alpha$ up to a factor of $\mathrm{poly}(n \log N)$. Combined with the result of the previous section, this gives us equivalence between the two problems: LWE and EDCP, for both search and decisional variants.

Theorem 4 (EDCP $\leq$ LWE). *Let (n, N, r) be valid EDCP parameters and (n, N, α) with $r = \Omega(\sqrt{\kappa})$ be valid LWE parameters. Given $\ell = \Omega(\kappa)$ many $\mathrm{G\text{-}EDCP}_{n,N,r}$ samples, there exists a quantum reduction, with run-time polynomial in κ, from $\mathrm{G\text{-}EDCP}_{n,N,r}^\ell$ to $\mathrm{LWE}_{n,N,\alpha}^\ell$, where $\alpha = 1/r$.*

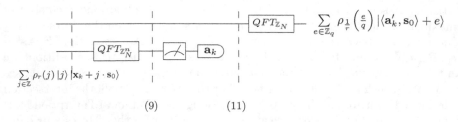

(9)   (11)

Fig. 6. Reduction from G-EDCP to LWE

Proof. Assume we are given ℓ many $\text{EDCP}_{n,N,r}$ instances

$$\left\{ \sum_{j\in\mathbb{Z}} \rho_r(j) \, |j\rangle \, |\mathbf{x}_k + j \cdot \mathbf{s}_0 \bmod N\rangle \right\}_{k\in[\ell]} .$$

Our aim is to find $\mathbf{s}_0$ given access to an $\text{LWE}^{\ell}_{n,N,\alpha}$ oracle.

For each input state, the quantum Fourier transform over $\mathbb{Z}_N^n$ is applied to the second register, which yields (without loss of generality, consider the kþ sample)

$$\sum_{\mathbf{a}\in\mathbb{Z}_N^n} \sum_{j\in\mathbb{Z}} \omega_N^{\langle \mathbf{a}, (\mathbf{x}_k + j \cdot \mathbf{s}_0)\rangle} \cdot \rho_r(j) \, |j\rangle \, |\mathbf{a}\rangle . \tag{9}$$

Then we measure the second register and let $\mathbf{a}_k$ denote the observed value. Note that each element of $\mathbb{Z}_N^n$ is measured with probability $1/N^n$ and that the distributions for different k's are independent. Omitting the global phase of each state, we obtain

$$\sum_{j\in\mathbb{Z}} \omega_N^{\langle \mathbf{a}_k, (j \cdot \mathbf{s}_0)\rangle} \cdot \rho_r(j) \, |j\rangle \, |\mathbf{a}_k\rangle . \tag{10}$$

We omit the second register as we know each $\mathbf{a}_k$ classically. Since $N \gg r$, from Lemma 1 it follows that the resulting state is within ℓ_2 distance of $2^{-\Omega(\kappa)}$ away from the state (note the change in the range for j)

$$\sum_{j\in\mathbb{Z}_N} \omega_N^{j \cdot \langle \mathbf{a}_k, \mathbf{s}_0\rangle} \cdot \rho_r(j) \, |j\rangle . \tag{11}$$

For each such an input state, the quantum Fourier transform over $\mathbb{Z}_N$ yields

$$\sum_{b\in\mathbb{Z}_N} \sum_{j\in\mathbb{Z}_N} \omega_N^{j \cdot (\langle \mathbf{a}_k, \mathbf{s}_0\rangle + b)} \cdot \rho_r(j) \, |b\rangle . \tag{12}$$

Once again we use Lemma 1 to argue that the state above is within ℓ_2 distance of $2^{-\Omega(\kappa)}$ away from the state

$$\sum_{b\in\mathbb{Z}_N} \sum_{j\in\mathbb{Z}} \omega_N^{j \cdot (\langle \mathbf{a}_k, \mathbf{s}_0\rangle + b)} \cdot \rho_r(j) \, |b\rangle .$$

Using the Poisson summation formula (Lemma 3) and changing the summation variable to $e \leftarrow N \cdot j + \langle \mathbf{a}_k, \mathbf{s}_0 \rangle + b$, the above state can be rewritten as

$$\sum_{b \in \mathbb{Z}_N} \sum_{j \in \mathbb{Z}} \rho_{1/r} \left(j + \frac{\langle \mathbf{a}_k, \mathbf{s}_0 \rangle + b}{N} \right) |b\rangle = \sum_{e \in \mathbb{Z}} \rho_{1/r} \left(\frac{e}{N} \right) |\langle \mathbf{a}_k', \mathbf{s}_0 \rangle + e \bmod N\rangle$$

where $\mathbf{a}_k' = -\mathbf{a}_k \bmod N$. Since $r = \Omega(\sqrt{\kappa})$, we can apply Lemma 1 to the above state (for a scaled $\mathbb{Z}$-lattice), and instead of the above state, consider the state that is within a $2^{-\Omega(\kappa)}$ ℓ_2-distance from it, namely:

$$\sum_{e \in \mathbb{Z}_N} \rho_{1/r} \left(\frac{e}{N} \right) |\langle \mathbf{a}_k', \mathbf{s}_0 \rangle + e\rangle. \tag{13}$$

Once we measure the state above, we obtain an LWE sample

$$(\mathbf{a}_k', \langle \mathbf{a}_k', \mathbf{s}_0 \rangle + e_k),$$

where $e_k \hookleftarrow \mathcal{D}_{\mathbb{Z}, N/r}$.

Now we can call the $\mathrm{LWE}_{n,N,\alpha}$ oracle for $\alpha = 1/r$ with the above states as input and obtain $\mathbf{s}_0$ as output of the oracle.

4.1   Reduction from dEDCP to dLWE

Similar to the previous section where as a corollary we show that dLWE can be reduced to dEDCP, we finish this section by a reverse reduction. Again we use exactly the same reduction algorithm as for the search versions (see Fig. 6). Thus it remains to show that we can obtain a uniform random sample $(\mathbf{a}, b) \in \mathbb{Z}_N^n \times \mathbb{Z}_N$ given as input a state of the form $|j\rangle |\mathbf{x} \bmod N\rangle$.

Corollary 2 (dEDCP $\leq$ dLWE). *Let (n, N, r) be valid dG-EDCP parameters and (n, N, α) be valid dLWE parameters. Given $\ell = \Omega(\kappa)$ many $\mathrm{EDCP}_{n,N,r}$ samples, there exists a quantum reduction, with run-time polynomial in κ, from dG-$\mathrm{EDCP}_{n,N,r}^{\ell}$ to dLWE$_{n,N,\alpha}^{\ell}$, where $\alpha = 1/r$.*

Proof. Assume we are given ℓ many samples of $\mathrm{EDCP}_{n,N,r}$ either of the form

$$\left\{ \sum_{j \in \mathbb{Z}} \rho_r(j) |j\rangle |\mathbf{x}_k + j \cdot \mathbf{s}_0\rangle \bmod N \right\}_{k \in [\ell]}$$

or of the form

$$\{ |j_k\rangle |\mathbf{x}_k \bmod N\rangle \}_{k \in [\ell]},$$

where $j_k \hookleftarrow \mathcal{D}_{\mathbb{Z}, r}^2$ and $\mathbf{x}_k \in \mathbb{Z}_N^n$ is uniform. Our aim is to distinguish between the above two forms given access to a dLWE$_{n,N,\alpha}$ oracle.

As explained above, we assume that random samples of EDCP are given. For each input state, after the quantum Fourier transform over $\mathbb{Z}_N^n$ on the second register, we obtain

$$\sum_{\mathbf{a} \in \mathbb{Z}_N^n} \omega_N^{\langle \mathbf{x}_k, \mathbf{a} \rangle} |j_k\rangle |\mathbf{a}\rangle.$$

Then we measure the second register and let $\mathbf{a}_k$ denote the observed value. Note that each element of $\mathbb{Z}_N^n$ is measured with probability $1/N^n$ and that the distributions for different k's are independent. Up to a global phase, we have

$$|j_k\rangle \, |\mathbf{a}_k\rangle \, .$$

We omit the second register which is known to us. According to Lemma 1, with probability $1 - 2^{-\Omega(\kappa)}$, the value stored in the first register is in the range $[-\lfloor N/2 \rfloor, \lceil N/2 \rceil - 1]$. Applying QFT over $\mathbb{Z}_N$ to the first register, we obtain

$$\sum_{b \in \mathbb{Z}_N} \omega_N^{j_k \cdot b} \, |b\rangle \, .$$

Once we measure the state above and let b_k denote the observed value. Note that each element of $\mathbb{Z}_N$ is measured with probability $1/N$ and that the distributions for different k's are independent. We obtain a sample

$$(\mathbf{a}_k, b_k) \, ,$$

where $(\mathbf{a}_k, b_k)$ are uniformly random from $\mathbb{Z}_N^n \times \mathbb{Z}_N$.

References

1. Babai, L.: On Lovász lattice reduction and the nearest lattice point problem. Combinatorica **6**, 1–13 (1986)
2. Bacon, D., Childs, A.M., van Dam, W.: From optimal measurement to efficient quantum algorithms for the hidden subgroup problem over semidirect product groups. In: Proceedings of FOCS, pp. 469–478. IEEE Computer Society Press (2005)
3. Bacon, D., Childs, A.M., van Dam, W.: Optimal measurements for the Dihedral hidden subgroup problem. Chicago J. Theor. Comput. Sci. (2006)
4. Banaszczyk, W.: New bounds in some transference theorems in the geometry of numbers. Math. Ann. **296**(4), 625–635 (1993)
5. Bernstein, D.J., Buchmann, J., Dahmen, E.: Post Quantum Cryptography, 1st edn. Springer, Heidelberg (2008). https://doi.org/10.1007/978-3-540-88702-7
6. Brakerski, Z., Kirshanova, E., Stehlé, D., Wen, W.: Learning with errors and extrapolated Dihedral cosets. CoRR, abs/1710.08223 (2017)
7. Brakerski, Z., Langlois, A., Peikert, C., Regev, O., Stehlé, D.: Classical hardness of learning with errors. In: Proceedings of STOC, pp. 575–584. ACM (2013)
8. Brakerski, Z., Vaikuntanathan, V.: Efficient fully homomorphic encryption from (standard) LWE. In: Proceedings of FOCS, pp. 97–106. IEEE Computer Society Press (2011)
9. Childs, A.M., van Dam, W.: Quantum algorithm for a generalized hidden shift problem. In: Procedings of SODA, pp. 1225–1232. SIAM (2007)
10. Ettinger, M., Høyer, P.: On quantum algorithms for noncommutative hidden subgroups. In: Meinel, C., Tison, S. (eds.) STACS 1999. LNCS, vol. 1563, pp. 478–487. Springer, Heidelberg (1999). https://doi.org/10.1007/3-540-49116-3_45
11. Friedl, K., Ivanyos, G., Magniez, F., Santha, M., Sen, P.: Hidden translation and translating coset in quantum computing. SIAM J. Comput. **43**(1), 1–24 (2014)

12. Gentry, C., Peikert, C., Vaikuntanathan, V.: Trapdoors for hard lattices and new cryptographic constructions. In: Proceedings of STOC, pp. 197–206. ACM (2008). http://eprint.iacr.org/2007/432.pdf

13. Goldwasser, S., Kalai, Y.T., Popa, R.A., Vaikuntanathan, V., Zeldovich, N.: Reusable garbled circuits and succinct functional encryption. In: Proceedings of STOC, pp. 555–564. ACM (2013)

14. Gorbunov, S., Vaikuntanathan, V., Wee, H.: Attribute-based encryption for circuits. In: Proceedings of STOC, pp. 545–554. ACM (2013)

15. Grover, L., Rudolph, T.: Creating superpositions that correspond to efficiently integrable probability distributions (2002). Draft https://arxiv.org/pdf/quant-ph/0208112v1

16. Hausladen, P., Wootters, W.K.: A 'pretty good' measurement for distinguishing quantum states. J. Mod. Opt. **41**(12), 2385–2390 (1994)

17. Kuperberg, G.: A subexponential-time quantum algorithm for the Dihedral hidden subgroup problem. SIAM J. Comput. **35**(1), 170–188 (2005)

18. Lenstra, A.K., Lenstra Jr., H.W., Lovász, L.: Factoring polynomials with rational coefficients. Math. Ann. **261**, 515–534 (1982)

19. Lenstra Jr., H.W.: Integer programming with a fixed number of variables. Math. Oper. Res. **8**(4), 538–548 (1983)

20. Lyubashevsky, V., Micciancio, D.: On bounded distance decoding, unique shortest vectors, and the minimum distance problem. In: Proceedings of CRYPTO, pp. 577–594 (2009)

21. Micciancio, D., Regev, O.: Lattice-based cryptography. In: Bernstein, D.J., Buchmann, J., Dahmen, E. (eds.) Post-Quantum Cryptography, pp. 147–191. Springer, Heidelberg (2009). https://doi.org/10.1007/978-3-540-88702-7_5

22. Ozols, M., Roetteler, M., Roland, J.: Quantum rejection sampling. ACM Trans. Comput. Theory **5**(3), 11:1–11:33 (2013)

23. Peikert, C.: Public-key cryptosystems from the worst-case shortest vector problem. In: Proceedings of STOC, pp. 333–342. ACM (2009)

24. Peikert, C.: A decade of lattice cryptography. Found. Trends Theor. Comput. Sci. **10**(4), 283–424 (2016)

25. Regev, O.: Quantum computation and lattice problems. In: Proceedings of the 43rd Symposium on Foundations of Computer Science, FOCS 2002, pp. 520–529. IEEE Computer Society (2002)

26. Regev, O.: New lattice-based cryptographic constructions. J. ACM **51**(6), 899–942 (2004)

27. Regev, O.: Quantum computation and lattice problems. SIAM J. Comput. **33**(3), 738–760 (2004)

28. Regev, O.: On lattices, learning with errors, random linear codes, and cryptography. In: Proceedings of STOC, pp. 84–93. ACM (2005)

29. Regev, O.: On lattices, learning with errors, random linear codes, and cryptography. J. ACM **56**(6), 34 (2009)

30. Shoup, V.: A Computational Introduction to Number Theory and Algebra. Cambridge University Press, Cambridge (2005)

31. Stehlé, D., Steinfeld, R., Tanaka, K., Xagawa, K.: Efficient public key encryption based on ideal lattices. In: Matsui, M. (ed.) ASIACRYPT 2009. LNCS, vol. 5912, pp. 617–635. Springer, Heidelberg (2009). https://doi.org/10.1007/978-3-642-10366-7_36

Rounded Gaussians
Fast and Secure Constant-Time Sampling for Lattice-Based Crypto

Andreas Hülsing[(✉)], Tanja Lange[(✉)], and Kit Smeets[(✉)]

Department of Mathematics and Computer Science,
Technische Universiteit Eindhoven, P.O. Box 513,
5600 MB Eindhoven, The Netherlands
andreas@huelsing.net, tanja@hyperelliptic.org, c.j.c.smeets@xept.nl

Abstract. This paper suggests to use rounded Gaussians in place of discrete Gaussians in rejection-sampling-based lattice signature schemes like BLISS or Lyubashevsky's signature scheme. We show that this distribution can efficiently be sampled from while additionally making it easy to sample in constant time, systematically avoiding recent timing-based side-channel attacks on lattice-based signatures.

We show the effectiveness of the new sampler by applying it to BLISS, prove analogues of the security proofs for BLISS, and present an implementation that runs in constant time. Our implementation needs no precomputed tables and is twice as fast as the variable-time CDT sampler posted by the BLISS authors with precomputed tables.

Keywords: Post-quantum cryptography · Lattice-based cryptography
Signatures · Gaussian sampling · BLISS
Constant-time implementations

1 Introduction

Lattice-based cryptography is a promising candidate for post-quantum cryptography. A key reason for this – especially from an applied point of view – is that it is known how to construct efficient signature *and* encryption/key-exchange schemes from lattice assumptions. As both primitives are needed for many applications this is an advantage as it allows for code reuse and relying on one sort of cryptographic hardness assumptions instead of two. For all other well-established candidate areas of post-quantum cryptography we only know how to construct efficient and confidence-inspiring signatures *or* encryption/key-exchange schemes.

This work was supported by the European Communities through the Horizon 2020 program under project number 645622 (PQCRYPTO) and project number 645421 (ECRYPT-CSA). Date: 2018.01.11. The full version is [14].

Permanent ID of this document: 7e89be5ae05d8b17a4d03e20a2c454e0.

M. Abdalla and R. Dahab (Eds.): PKC 2018, LNCS 10770, pp. 728–757, 2018.
https://doi.org/10.1007/978-3-319-76581-5_25

In this work we take a look at lattice-based signature schemes. The most efficient lattice-based signature scheme with a security reduction from standard lattice problems today is BLISS (Bimodal Lattice Signature Scheme) [11], designed by Ducas, Durmus, Lepoint and Lyubashevsky. BLISS is one of the few post-quantum schemes of which there already exists a production-level implementation. BLISS (or rather its subsequent improvement BLISS-b [10] by Ducas) is available in the open-source IPsec Linux library strongSwan [24].

BLISS builds on Lyubashevsky's signature scheme [16] which initiated the use of rejection sampling to make the signature distribution independent of the used secret key. In the most basic version of these schemes, a discrete Gaussian vector is added to a vector that depends on the secret key. The resulting vector follows a discrete Gaussian distribution that is shifted by a vector that depends on the secret key. To avoid leaking the secret key, a rejection step is executed that ensures that the output distribution is independent of the secret key, i.e. the outputs follow again a centered discrete Gaussian distribution.

The use of discrete Gaussian vectors to blind secrets is a very common approach in lattice-based cryptography. However, it is not trivial to sample from a discrete Gaussian efficiently. Over the last few years, many works have been published that deal with efficient sampling routines for discrete Gaussians, see e.g. [8, 11,12,19,21]. Despite the number of publications, none achieved constant-time sampling. At CHES 2016, Groot-Bruinderink, Hülsing, Lange, and Yarom [7] demonstrated that these sampling methods enable a cache attack on BLISS which recovers the secret key after less than 5000 signatures. While the attack is only implemented for two samplers, the appendix of the full version surveys other efficient samplers and shows for each of them that they have similar issues.

In [7], the authors already discuss straightforward approaches for achieving constant-time implementations of discrete Gaussian samplers, such as deterministically loading entire tables into cache or fixing the number of iterations for some functions by introducing dummy rounds. While such approaches might work for encryption schemes such as [5], signatures require much wider Gaussians to achieve security. Hence, the impact on efficiency of applying these countermeasures is larger, effectively rendering their use prohibitive.

A different way to deal with such attacks is to complicate the attack. Such a heuristic approach was proposed by Saarinen [22]. However, this approach does not fix the vulnerability, as shown by Pessl [18]; this only makes it harder to exploit it. In consequence, it starts a cat-and-mouse game of attack and fix.

Our contribution. To stop such a cat-and-mouse game before it fully starts, this work deals with ways to systematically fix the vulnerability. We propose to take a completely different approach by replacing discrete Gaussians by a different distribution, namely the *rounded Gaussian* distribution. This distribution shares the benefits of the discrete Gaussians that (slightly) shifted distributions are relatively close to centered distributions. However, the security analysis of using rounded Gaussians in Lyubashevsky's scheme and in BLISS is somewhat more involved than for discrete Gaussians as the probability density function of rounded Gaussians is the integral of a continuous Gaussian. Our main theoretical contribution is a proof that it is safe to replace the discrete Gaussian distribution by a rounded Gaussian distribution in these schemes, while the resulting rejection rates are identical.

As the name suggests, sampling from a rounded Gaussian is done by sampling from a continuous Gaussian and rounding the result to an integer. The Box-Muller method is an efficient way of computing samples of continuous Gaussians starting from uniformly random numbers, and all steps leading to rounded Gaussian samples are efficiently and easily computed in constant time. We present a constant-time implementation of rounded Gaussians suitable for the BLISS-I parameter set and show that it is more than twice as fast as a sampler based on cumulative distribution tables (CDT) as implemented by the authors of BLISS. The CDT sampler uses large precomputed tables to speed up sampling. Note that the CDT sampler is exactly the one that [7] broke at CHES 2016. Using rounded Gaussians brings better speed and better security. Another benefit of rounded Gaussians is that they can use the Box-Muller sampler (see Sect. 4.1) which naturally does not require any precomputed tables, hence can work with a small code base, and furthermore is extremely easy to implement.

We conclude our work with our second theoretical contribution – a proof that using rounded Gaussians, sampled using our Box-Muller implementation is secure. For this we provide a detailed analysis of the new sampler. We study the difference between (perfect) rounded Gaussians and implementations with finite precision p using statistical distance and Rényi divergence. We also compare the asymptotic results using these different measures. We instantiate the calculation for BLISS parameters and the precision achieved by our Box-Muller implementation to derive bounds on the allowable number of signatures per key pair.

Related work. Rounded Gaussians are not a new distribution, in fact they have been used in the initial proposals for learning with errors, but were replaced by discrete Gaussians to make proofs and protocols easier (the sum of two discrete Gaussians is a discrete Gaussian). See, e.g. Regev [20, p. 90] for an overview of distributions and [9] for an analysis of wrapped rounded Gaussians. Encryption schemes can be secure with narrow non-Gaussian distributions (NTRU/Frodo/New Hope) but signatures are much harder to protect, need much wider distributions (larger parameter σ), seemed to need discrete Gaussians, and so far were analyzed only for discrete Gaussians.

The work in this paper is based on Smeets' masters thesis [23]. After a first version of our paper was circulated we became aware of a recent paper by Micciancio and Walter [17] which has a new proposal to perform sampling of discrete Gaussians in constant time. The target of our paper is very different: Showing that rounded Gaussians can efficiently be sampled in constant time and that their use in signature schemes is safe.

Acknowledgements. The authors would like to thank Jacob Appelbaum for discussions about the implementation; Daniel J. Bernstein for help with the implementation, benchmarking, and many useful discussions; Leo Ducas for discussions about replacing discrete Gaussians in lattice-based signatures; and Marko Boon for discussions about the standard deviation of the rounded Gaussian distribution.

2   Preliminaries

Vectors, considered as column vectors, will be written in bold lower case letters; matrices will be written in upper case bold letters. For a vector $\mathbf{a} = (a_1, a_2, \ldots, a_n) \in \mathbb{R}^n$, the Euclidean norm is defined by $\|\mathbf{a}\| = \sqrt{\sum_{i=1}^{n} a_i^2}$. The ∞-norm is defined by $\|\mathbf{a}\|_\infty = \max(|a_1|, |a_2|, \ldots, |a_n|)$. The Hamming weight $\mathrm{wt}(\mathbf{a})$ is the number of non-zero positions in $\mathbf{a}$. For two vectors $\mathbf{a} = (a_1, a_2, \ldots, a_n)$ and $\mathbf{b} = (b_1, b_2, \ldots, b_n)$, both in $\mathbb{R}^n$, denote the inner product by $\langle \mathbf{a}, \mathbf{b} \rangle = \sum_{i=1}^{n} a_i b_i$.

In this paper we will be concerned with (discrete) probability functions. For a distribution h, we denote by $x \xleftarrow{\$} h$ that x is sampled according to h. For a set S we denote by $s \xleftarrow{\$} S$ that $s \in S$ is sampled uniformly at random from S.

We now cover some background on Gaussian distributions and signature schemes. We follow Lyubashevsky [16] closely and take definitions from there with minor modifications. Many lattice-based schemes use rejection sampling to massage one distribution to fit another. The following m-dimensional version which samples once from the provided distribution and outputs with a certain probability depending on both the target distribution and the sample is copied from Lemma 4.7 of the full ePrint version of [16].

Lemma 2.1 (Rejection Sampling). *Let V be an arbitrary set, and $h : V \to \mathbb{R}$ and $f : \mathbb{Z}^m \to \mathbb{R}$ be probability distributions. If $g_\mathbf{v} : \mathbb{Z}^m \to \mathbb{R}$ is a family of probability distributions indexed by $\mathbf{v} \in V$ with the property*

$$\exists M \in \mathbb{R} : \forall \mathbf{v} \in V : \Pr[Mg_\mathbf{v}(\mathbf{z}) \geq f(\mathbf{z}); \mathbf{z} \xleftarrow{\$} f] \geq 1 - \varepsilon,$$

then the distribution of the output of the following algorithm $\mathcal{A}$:

1: $\mathbf{v} \xleftarrow{\$} h$
2: $\mathbf{z} \xleftarrow{\$} g_\mathbf{v}$
3: output $(\mathbf{z}, \mathbf{v})$ with probability $\min\left(\frac{f(\mathbf{z})}{Mg_\mathbf{v}(\mathbf{z})}, 1\right)$

is within statistical distance ε/M of the distribution of the following algorithm $\mathcal{F}$:

1: $\mathbf{v} \xleftarrow{\$} h$
2: $\mathbf{z} \xleftarrow{\$} f$
3: output $(\mathbf{z}, \mathbf{v})$ with probability $1/M$.

Moreover, the probability that $\mathcal{A}$ outputs something is at least $(1 - \varepsilon)/M$.

2.1   Discrete Gaussian Distribution

The discrete Gaussian distribution is based on the continuous Gaussian distribution. The definition of the continuous Gaussian distribution, also called the Normal distribution, is given by:

Definition 2.1. *The continuous Gaussian distribution over $\mathbb{R}^m$ centered at some $\mathbf{v} \in \mathbb{R}^m$ with standard deviation σ is defined for $\mathbf{x} \in \mathbb{R}^m$ as the (joint) density $\rho_{\mathbf{v},\sigma}^m(\mathbf{x}) = \left(\frac{1}{\sqrt{2\pi\sigma^2}}\right)^m e^{\frac{-\|\mathbf{x}-\mathbf{v}\|^2}{2\sigma^2}}$.*

When $\mathbf{v} = \mathbf{0}$, we simply write $\rho_\sigma^m(\mathbf{x})$. The definition of the discrete Gaussian distribution is given by:

Definition 2.2. *The discrete Gaussian distribution over $\mathbb{Z}^m$ centered at some $\mathbf{v} \in \mathbb{Z}^m$ with parameter σ is defined for $\mathbf{x} \in \mathbb{Z}^m$ as $D_{\mathbf{v},\sigma}^m(\mathbf{x}) = \rho_{\mathbf{v},\sigma}^m(\mathbf{x})/\rho_\sigma^m(\mathbb{Z}^m)$, where $\rho_\sigma^m(\mathbb{Z}^m) = \sum_{\mathbf{z}\in\mathbb{Z}^m} \rho_\sigma^m(\mathbf{z})$.*

Note that the discrete Gaussian distribution is defined over all length-m integer vectors in $\mathbb{Z}^m$. However, samples with large entries have negligible probability. Implementations need to provision for the maximal size of coefficients and table-based sampling schemes would require a lot of storage to cover rarely used values and still not cover all possibilities. Therefore, a *tail cut* τ is used, meaning that only integers in $[-\tau\sigma, \tau\sigma]^m$ are sampled. Results about the necessary size of the tail cut can be found in [16] and Lemma A.2. In practice, τ is often chosen as $\sqrt{2\lambda \ln 2}$, where λ is the security level because that ensures a negligible loss in values.

2.2   Lyubashevsky's Signature Scheme

In 2012 Lyubashevsky [16] designed a signature scheme that uses an $m \times n$ matrix $\mathbf{S}$ with small coefficients as secret key and the following two matrices as public key: a random matrix $\mathbf{A} \in \mathbb{Z}_{2q}^{n\times m}, m = 2n$, and the $n \times n$ matrix $\mathbf{T} = \mathbf{AS}$ mod q, where q is an integer. The matrix $\mathbf{A}$ can be shared among all users, but the matrix $\mathbf{T}$ is individual. To sign a message, the signer picks a vector $\mathbf{y}$ according to the m-dimensional discrete Gaussian. Then $\mathbf{c} = H(\mathbf{Ay} \mod q, \mu)$, where $H(\cdot)$ is a hash function, and the potential signature vector $\mathbf{z} = \mathbf{Sc} + \mathbf{y}$ are computed.

The system then uses rejection sampling to shape the distribution of $\mathbf{z}$ to a centered discrete Gaussian, i.e., to decide whether to output the candidate signature $(\mathbf{z}, \mathbf{c})$. In terms of Lemma 2.1, h is the distribution of $\mathbf{Sc}, g_\mathbf{v}$ is the m-dimensional discrete Gaussian $D_{\mathbf{v},\sigma}(\mathbf{z})$ centered around $\mathbf{v} = \mathbf{Sc}$, and f is the m-dimensional centered discrete Gaussian $D_\sigma^m(\mathbf{z})$.

Because $D_\sigma^m(\mathbf{z})$ is independent of $\mathbf{S}$ the signatures do not leak information about the private key.

2.3   Bimodal Lattice Signature Scheme: BLISS

Ducas, Durmus, Lepoint and Lyubashevsky introduced the Bimodal Lattice Signature Scheme (BLISS) in [11]. BLISS is an improvement of Lyubashevsky's signature scheme described above in that signatures are smaller and generated faster. We only cover signature generation here as we are focusing on the use of the discrete Gaussian distribution. For a full description of BLISS, see [11].

BLISS uses a special hash function H mapping to $\{\mathbf{c} \in \{0,1\}^n | \mathrm{wt}(\mathbf{c}) = \kappa\}$ for κ some small constant. A simplified version of the BLISS signature algorithm is given in Algorithm 2.1.

Algorithm 2.1. Simplified BLISS Signature Algorithm using matrices

---

Input: Message μ, public key $\mathbf{A} \in \mathbb{Z}_{2q}^{n \times m}$ and secret key $\mathbf{S} \in \mathbb{Z}_{2q}^{m \times n}$
Output: A signature $(\mathbf{z}, \mathbf{c})$ of the message μ
1: $\mathbf{y} \leftarrow D_\sigma^m$
2: $\mathbf{c} \leftarrow H(\mathbf{Ay} \bmod 2q, \mu)$ // $\mathbf{c} \in \{0,1\}^n$, $\mathrm{wt}(\mathbf{c}) = \kappa$, κ small constant
3: Choose a random bit $b \in \{0,1\}$
4: $\mathbf{z} \leftarrow \mathbf{y} + (-1)^b \mathbf{Sc}$
5: Output $(\mathbf{z}, \mathbf{c})$ with probability $1 \Big/ \left(M \exp\left(-\frac{\|\mathbf{Sc}\|^2}{2\sigma^2}\right) \cosh\left(\frac{\langle \mathbf{z}, \mathbf{Sc} \rangle}{\sigma^2}\right) \right)$

Given a message μ, the signing algorithm first samples a vector $\mathbf{y}$ from the m-dimensional discrete Gaussian distribution D_σ^m. Then it computes the hash $\mathbf{c} \leftarrow H(\mathbf{Ay} \bmod 2q, \mu)$. It samples a random bit $b \in \{0,1\}$ and computes the potential signature $\mathbf{z} \leftarrow \mathbf{y} + (-1)^b \mathbf{Sc}$. Now that the signing algorithm has $\mathbf{z}$, it performs rejection sampling according to Lemma 2.1, i.e., it outputs the signature $(\mathbf{z}, \mathbf{c})$ with probability $1 \Big/ \left(M \exp\left(-\frac{\|\mathbf{Sc}\|^2}{2\sigma^2}\right) \cosh\left(\frac{\langle \mathbf{z}, \mathbf{Sc} \rangle}{\sigma^2}\right) \right)$, where M is some fixed positive real constant that is set large enough to ensure that this probability is at most 1 for all choices of $\mathbf{c}$. If the signature algorithm is unsuccessful, it restarts with a fresh $\mathbf{y}$ and continues until a signature is output.

Again, rejection sampling is used to force the distribution of the output $\mathbf{z}$ to be that of a centered Gaussian distribution (i.e., to be independent of $\mathbf{Sc}$).

The bulk of the time in one round of the signing algorithm using BLISS is spent in the first step in generating m samples from the one-dimensional Gaussian. The number of repetitions depends on M and the size of $\mathbf{Sc}$.

Bound on $\|\mathbf{Sc}\|$. The parameter σ of the discrete Gaussian distribution, the size of $\mathbf{Sc}$, and the rejection rate M control how much the distributions of the target distribution D_σ^m and the input distribution overlap, i.e., how small ε can be achieved. For BLISS the input distribution is a bimodal Gaussian distribution $0.5(D_{-\mathbf{Sc},\sigma}^m + D_{\mathbf{Sc},\sigma}^m)$. BLISS' authors show that rejection sampling can be used without error, i.e., $\varepsilon = 0$ is possible in Lemma 2.1 with resonable choices of σ and M. In later sections we require an upper bound on $\|\mathbf{Sc}\|$ for proofs. In [11] a new measure $N_\kappa(\mathbf{X})$ of $\mathbf{S}$, adapted to the form of $\mathbf{c}$, is presented.

Definition 2.3. *For any integer* κ, $N_\kappa : \mathbb{R}^{m \times n} \to \mathbb{R}$ *is defined as:*

$$N_\kappa(\mathbf{X}) = \max_{I \subset \{1,\ldots,n\}, \#I = \kappa} \sum_{i \in I} \left(\max_{J \subset \{1,\ldots,n\}, \#J = \kappa} \sum_{j \in J} W_{i,j} \right),$$

where $\mathbf{W} = \mathbf{X}^T \cdot \mathbf{X} \in \mathbb{R}^{n \times n}$.

With this definition, the authors of [11] show that for any $\mathbf{c} \in \{0, 1\}^n$ with $\mathrm{wt}(\mathbf{c}) \leq \kappa$, we have $\|\mathbf{Sc}\|^2 \leq N_\kappa(\mathbf{S})$ [11, Proposition 3.2]. In addition to the use of bimodal Gaussians, this upper bound lowers the parameter σ by a factor $\approx \sqrt{\kappa}/2$ compared to [16].

3   Rounded Gaussian Rejection Sampling

In this section we discuss the applicability of the *rounded Gaussian distribution* in rejection-sampling-based signature schemes. After giving a formal definition of the rounded Gaussian distribution, we provide proofs showing that it can be used to replace the discrete Gaussian distribution in Lyubashevsky's signature scheme and in BLISS. We show the analogies between the rounded Gaussian distribution and the discrete Gaussian distribution and we point out where the security reductions differ when rounded Gaussians are used in place of discrete Gaussians. In practice, the most important question is how the probability in Step 5 in Algorithm 2.1 (and the equivalent on in Lyubashevsky's scheme) needs to change if $\mathbf{y}$ is sampled according to the rounded Gaussian distribution instead of the discrete Gaussian distribution. Note, again, that this step determines the rejection rate, i.e. how many times the algorithm needs to restart sampling fresh randomness.

To simplify comparisons and show that rounded Gaussians can be used in place of discrete Gaussians we follow the presentation and structure from [16] and [11] very closely. The main difference is that the definition of rounded Gaussians requires integrals over an interval of length 1, while the definition of discrete Gaussians requires a division by the probability mass at all integers. We essentially have to prove the same lemmas that were shown for discrete Gaussians in [16] and [11] for rounded Gaussians. In the end closely analogous results hold but the analysis turns out far more complicated than in the discrete Gaussian setting because we have to deal with bounding integrals.

3.1   Rounded Gaussian Distribution

We now formally define the rounded Gaussian distribution. Intuitively, the rounded Gaussian distribution is obtained by rounding samples from a continuous Gaussian distribution to the nearest integer x_i. To compute the probability at an integer x_i, we compute the integral over the interval $(x_i - \frac{1}{2}, x_i + \frac{1}{2}]$.

Definition 3.1. *The* rounded Gaussian distribution *over $\mathbb{Z}^m$ centered at some $\mathbf{v} \in \mathbb{Z}^m$ with parameter σ is defined for $\mathbf{x} \in \mathbb{Z}^m$ as*

$$R_{\mathbf{v},\sigma}^m(\mathbf{x}) = \int_{A_\mathbf{x}} \rho_{\mathbf{v},\sigma}^m(\mathbf{s})d\mathbf{s} = \int_{A_\mathbf{x}} \left(\frac{1}{\sqrt{2\pi\sigma^2}} \right)^m \exp\left(\frac{-\|\mathbf{s} - \mathbf{v}\|^2}{2\sigma^2} \right) d\mathbf{s},$$

where $A_\mathbf{x}$ denotes the area defined by $\left[x_1 - \frac{1}{2}; x_1 + \frac{1}{2}\right) \times \cdots \times \left[x_m - \frac{1}{2}; x_m + \frac{1}{2}\right)$.

We point out that this gives us $\mathrm{vol}(A_{\mathbf{x}}) = 1$, since the volume of this area is equal to $|(x_1 + \frac{1}{2}) - (x_1 - \frac{1}{2})| \cdots |(x_m + \frac{1}{2}) - (x_m - \frac{1}{2})|$. Note that the parameter σ in the definition above is the standard deviation of the underlying continuous Gaussian and not the standard deviation σ' of the rounded Gaussian distribution, which is given by $\sigma' = \sqrt{\sigma^2 + \frac{1}{12} + \epsilon(\alpha)}$, where $\epsilon(\alpha)$ is some function of small value with mean 0.

3.2   Using Rounded Gaussians in Lyubashevsky's Scheme

The proofs by Lyubashevsky [16] for the discrete Gaussian distribution rely on several lemmas for which we prove analogous statements in Appendix A. The following lemma states that the centered rounded Gaussian $R_\sigma^m(\mathbf{z})$ and the shifted rounded Gaussian $R_{\mathbf{v},\sigma}(\mathbf{z})$ are almost always close, and Theorem 3.1 applies it to the rejection-sampling Lemma 2.1.

Lemma 3.1. *For any* $\mathbf{v} \in \mathbb{Z}^m$, *if* $\sigma = \omega(\|\mathbf{v}\|\sqrt{\log m})$, *then*

$$\Pr\left[R_\sigma^m(\mathbf{z})/R_{\mathbf{v},\sigma}^m(\mathbf{z}) = O(1); \mathbf{z} \xleftarrow{\$} R_\sigma^m\right] = 1 - 2^{-\omega(\|\mathbf{v}\|\sqrt{\log m})}.$$

This is proven in Appendix A.

Theorem 3.1. *Let* V *be a subset of* $\mathbb{Z}^m$ *in which all elements have norms less than* T, σ *be some element in* $\mathbb{R}$ *such that* $\sigma = \omega(T\sqrt{\log m})$, *and* $h : V \to \mathbb{R}$ *be a probability distribution. Then there exists a constant* $M = O(1)$ *such that the distribution of the following algorithm* $\mathcal{A}$:

1: $\mathbf{v} \xleftarrow{\$} h$
2: $\mathbf{z} \xleftarrow{\$} R_{\mathbf{v},\sigma}^m$
3: *output* $(\mathbf{z}, \mathbf{v})$ *with probability* $\min\left(\frac{R_\sigma^m(\mathbf{z})}{MR_{\mathbf{v},\sigma}^m(\mathbf{z})}, 1\right)$

is within statistical distance $2^{-\omega(\log m)}/M$ *of the distribution of the following algorithm* $\mathcal{F}$:

1: $\mathbf{v} \xleftarrow{\$} h$
2: $\mathbf{z} \xleftarrow{\$} R_\sigma^m$
3: *output* $(\mathbf{z}, \mathbf{v})$ *with probability* $1/M$.

Moreover, the probability that $\mathcal{A}$ *outputs something is at least* $(1 - 2^{-\omega(\log m)})/M$.

Proof. The proof of this theorem follows immediately from Lemma 3.1 and the general "rejection sampling" Lemma 2.1.   □

This theorem looks the same for rounded Gaussians and for discrete Gaussians; see Appendix A.1 for a detailed comparison of the results.

3.3   Using Rounded Gaussians in BLISS

In Sect. 3.2 we have shown that we can use the rounded Gaussian distribution in the rejection sampling scheme by Lyubashevsky [16]. In this section we show

how to apply the rounded Gaussian distribution to BLISS and that the same constant as in BLISS can be for rejection sampling.

BLISS randomly flips a bit to decide on adding or subtracting $\mathbf{Sc}$, i.e., for fixed $\mathbf{Sc}$, $\mathbf{z}^*$ is distributed according to the bimodal rounded Gaussian distribution $g_{\mathbf{Sc}}(\mathbf{z}^*) = \frac{1}{2}R^m_{\mathbf{Sc},\sigma}(\mathbf{z}^*) + \frac{1}{2}R^m_{-\mathbf{Sc},\sigma}(\mathbf{z}^*)$. To avoid leaking any information on the secret key $\mathbf{S}$ the scheme requires rejection sampling to change the bimodal Gaussian to a centered Gaussian $f(\mathbf{z}^*) = R^m_\sigma(\mathbf{z}^*)$. The probability to accept is given by $p_{\mathbf{z}^*} = f(\mathbf{z}^*)/Mg_{\mathbf{Sc}}(\mathbf{z}^*)$, where again M is chosen minimal such that this probability is ≤ 1 for all $\mathbf{z}^*$.

The results of this section are completely analogous to those in [11].

For any $\mathbf{z}^* \in \mathbb{Z}^m$, we have

$$
\begin{aligned}
\Pr[\mathbf{z} = \mathbf{z}^*] &= \tfrac{1}{2}R^m_{\mathbf{Sc},\sigma}(\mathbf{z}^*) + \tfrac{1}{2}R^m_{-\mathbf{Sc},\sigma}(\mathbf{z}^*) \\
&= \tfrac{1}{2}\left(\tfrac{1}{\sqrt{2\pi\sigma^2}}\right)^m \int_{A_{\mathbf{z}^*}} \exp\left(-\tfrac{\|\mathbf{x}-\mathbf{Sc}\|^2}{2\sigma^2}\right) + \exp\left(-\tfrac{\|\mathbf{x}+\mathbf{Sc}\|^2}{2\sigma^2}\right)d\mathbf{x} \qquad (1) \\
&= \exp\left(-\tfrac{\|\mathbf{Sc}\|^2}{2\sigma^2}\right)\left(\tfrac{1}{\sqrt{2\pi\sigma^2}}\right)^m \int_{A_{\mathbf{z}^*}} \exp\left(-\tfrac{\|\mathbf{x}\|^2}{2\sigma^2}\right)\cosh\left(\tfrac{\langle\mathbf{x},\mathbf{Sc}\rangle}{\sigma^2}\right)d\mathbf{x}.
\end{aligned}
$$

The desired output is the centered rounded Gaussian distribution $f(\mathbf{z}^*)$, since we need the centered property to avoid leaking $\mathbf{S}$. Thus by Theorem 3.1, we should accept the sample $\mathbf{z}^*$ with probability:

$$
\begin{aligned}
p_{\mathbf{z}^*} &= f(\mathbf{z}^*)/(Mg_{\mathbf{Sc}}(\mathbf{z}^*)) \\
&= \frac{\left(\frac{1}{\sqrt{2\pi\sigma^2}}\right)^m \int_{A_{\mathbf{z}^*}} \exp\left(-\|\mathbf{x}\|^2/(2\sigma^2)\right)d\mathbf{x}}{M\exp\left(-\|\mathbf{Sc}\|^2/(2\sigma^2)\right)\left(\frac{1}{\sqrt{2\pi\sigma^2}}\right)^m \int_{A_{\mathbf{z}^*}} \exp\left(-\|\mathbf{x}\|^2/(2\sigma^2)\right)\cosh\left(\langle\mathbf{x},\mathbf{Sc}\rangle/\sigma^2\right)d\mathbf{x}}.
\end{aligned}
$$

To compute a bound on M, we use Eq. (1) and that $\cosh(x) > 0$ for any x. This leads to the following upper bound:

$$
\begin{aligned}
p_{\mathbf{z}^*} &= \frac{\int_{A_{\mathbf{z}^*}} \exp\left(-\|\mathbf{x}\|^2/(2\sigma^2)\right)d\mathbf{x}}{M\exp\left(-\|\mathbf{Sc}\|^2/(2\sigma^2)\right)\int_{A_{\mathbf{z}^*}} \exp\left(-\|\mathbf{x}\|^2/(2\sigma^2)\right)\cosh\left(\langle\mathbf{x},\mathbf{Sc}\rangle/\sigma^2\right)d\mathbf{x}} \\
&\leq \frac{\int_{A_{\mathbf{z}^*}} \exp\left(-\|\mathbf{x}\|^2/(2\sigma^2)\right)d\mathbf{x}}{M\exp\left(-\|\mathbf{Sc}\|^2/(2\sigma^2)\right)\int_{A_{\mathbf{z}^*}} \exp\left(-\|\mathbf{x}\|^2/(2\sigma^2)\right)d\mathbf{x}} \\
&= 1/(M\exp\left(-\|\mathbf{Sc}\|^2/(2\sigma^2)\right)).
\end{aligned}
$$

Now M needs to be chosen large enough such that $p_{\mathbf{z}^*} \leq 1$. Note that the last inequality can only be used to estimate M, and not to define the probability. It suffices that $M = \exp\left(1/(2\alpha^2)\right)'$, where $\alpha > 0$ is such that $\sigma \geq \alpha\|\mathbf{Sc}\|$. We can use the upper bound $\|\mathbf{Sc}\|^2 \leq N_\kappa(\mathbf{S})$ as in Definition 2.3 to put $M = \exp(N_\kappa(\mathbf{S})/2\sigma^2)$; here κ denotes the sparsity of $\mathbf{c}$ in Algorithm 2.1. This is the same constant as in BLISS.

3.4   BLISS Security Reduction

The security proof as given in [11] works for the rounded Gaussian distribution with very little tweaking. This is due to the changes made in the proofs in Sect. 3.2 and Appendix A. All statements follow through when replacing the discrete Gaussian distribution with the rounded Gaussian distribution. We do not need to adjust the proofs for [11, Lemmas 3.3 and 3.5]. The proof for [11, Lemma 3.4] uses $\sigma \geq 3/\sqrt{2\pi}$ which comes from [16, Lemma 4.4]. Our corresponding result is Lemma A.2 which requires $\sigma \geq \sqrt{2/\pi}$. Next to that, we need to adjust the definitions of $f(\mathbf{z})$ and $g_{\mathbf{Sc}}(\mathbf{z})$ as above, such that these match the rounded Gaussian distribution.

4   Practical Instantiation

In this section we discuss how we can implement a sampler for the rounded Gaussian distribution. A very efficient and easy way to generate samples from the continuous Gaussian distribution is based on the Box-Muller transform. We state the algorithm and discuss an early rejection technique to prevent the computation of values which would later be rejected due to the tail cut. Finally, we analyze the output precision required for an implementation of the rounded Gaussian distribution.

4.1   Box-Muller Transform

We begin by reviewing the Box-Muller transform [6] which is used to create centered Gaussian distributed numbers with standard deviation $\sigma = 1$ from uniform random distributed numbers. The algorithm is given as Algorithm 4.1 below.

Algorithm 4.1. Box-Muller Sampling

Input: Two uniform numbers $u_1, u_2 \in (0, 1]$
Output: Two independent centered (continuous) Gaussian distributed numbers x_1, x_2
    with standard deviation $\sigma = 1$
1: $a \leftarrow \sqrt{-2 \ln u_1}$
2: $b \leftarrow 2\pi u_2$
3: $(x_1, x_2) \leftarrow (a \cos b, a \sin b)$
4: **return** (x_1, x_2)

4.2   Sampling Rounded Gaussians

We can now use the Box-Muller transform to create an algorithm for sampling according to the rounded Gaussian distribution. For applying rounded Gaussians to the signature scheme of BLISS, we need centered rounded Gaussians with parameter σ. This is done by scaling the output x_i for $i = 1, 2$ of the Box-Muller sampling scheme $z'_i = x_i \cdot \sigma$ and then rounding the nearest integer $z_i = \lfloor z'_i \rceil$.

4.3 Rejection Sampling of Signatures

At the end of Algorithm 2.1 we need to output $(\mathbf{z}, \mathbf{c})$ with probability

$$\frac{2 \int_{A_{\mathbf{z}^*}} \exp\left(-\|\mathbf{x}\|^2/(2\sigma^2)\right) d\mathbf{x}}{M \cdot \exp\left(-\|\mathbf{Sc}\|^2/(2\sigma^2)\right) \left(\int_{A_{\mathbf{z}^*}} \exp\left(-\frac{\|\mathbf{x}-\mathbf{Sc}\|^2}{2\sigma^2}\right) d\mathbf{x} + \int_{A_{\mathbf{z}^*}} \exp\left(-\frac{\|\mathbf{x}+\mathbf{Sc}\|^2}{2\sigma^2}\right) d\mathbf{x}\right)}$$

(see Sect. 3.2).

Each of the three integrals factors, i.e., can be computed as the product of one-dimensional integrals. Each one-dimensional integral is

$$\int_{z_i-1/2}^{z_i+1/2} \exp\left(\frac{-x_i^2}{2\sigma^2}\right) dx_i = \sigma\sqrt{\frac{\pi}{2}}\left(\text{erf}\left(\frac{z_i+1/2}{\sqrt{2\sigma^2}}\right) - \text{erf}\left(\frac{z_i-1/2}{\sqrt{2\sigma^2}}\right)\right),$$

i.e., a constant times a difference of two nearby values of the standard error function (erf).

5 Code Analysis and Benchmarks

This section provides details about our implementation. First we give a general overview over our implementation. Then we discuss the dependency between floating point precision and allowable number of signatures. We end with timings and a comparison to the BLISS CDT sampler.

5.1 Implementation Details

We have used the C++ vector class library VCL by Fog [13] for the implementation of the Box-Muller sampling and the rounded Gaussian sampling. This library offers optimized vector operations for integers, floating point numbers and booleans. We use `Vec8d`, which are vectors with 8 elements of double floating point precision. This means that we are only limited by the maximum size of the `double` type, i.e. values of at most 53 bits of precision.

According to [13], the trigonometric and logarithmic functions in VCL have constant runtime, i.e. there is no timing difference dependent on the input. This makes the library ideal for constant-time implementations. The square-root function $\text{sqrt}(\cdot)$ takes constant time, unless all 8 inputs are in $\{0, 1\}$, which can lead to a timing difference for the square root. However, this is unlikely to happen: the sqrt function is applied to $2 \ln u_1$ and the logarithm function is strictly positive and thus the case of input 0 cannot appear; the probability of sampling 8 consecutive values u_{1i} that all would evaluate $2 \ln u_{1i} = 1$ is negligible, since each u_{1i} is sampled from $(0, 1]$ with 53 bit precision, making this an event of probability at most $2^{-8 \cdot 53}$. Therefore we have chosen not to circumvent this problem in the implementation, even though one could also sacrifice a vector entry and force it to have a nontrivial square root computation.

Computing with floating-point numbers causes a drop in precision. While Fog states that operations in VCL lose at most one bit of precision with exception of several explicitly mentioned functions that can lose up to two bits of precision such as the trigonometric functions, a more careful analysis of the code shows that other operations keep (close to) the exact precision.

Sampling rounded Gaussians on top of VCL is only a few lines of code and the data paths are short (see the code listing in Appendix F of the full version [14]). The input of the code has 53 bits of precision and we loose at most 5 bits of precision, i.e. the output of the code has at least $p = 48$ bits of precision.

Remark 1. We were asked how to round floating point numbers in constant time. While VCL almost trivially rounds the entire vector in constant time, a bit more care is necessary if one wants to implement this on single values. To round $|A| < 2^{51}$ compute

$$(A + (2^{52} + 2^{51})) - (2^{52} + 2^{51})$$

in two arithmetic instructions or use assembly instructions.

5.2   Considerations Regarding the Precision

Samplers for discrete Gaussians typically require tables precomputed at a certain precision. This raises the question of how much a low-precision table can skew the distribution and whether this can lead to attacks. Similarly, floating-point computations, such as in our sampler, can slowly degrade precision.

An error in the computation of y results in a value y' which might be slightly larger or smaller than y. The magnitude of the error depends on the size of the value, e.g., values close to 0 have higher precision than larger values; in general the error of y is bounded by $|y|2^{-p}$.

When computing rounded Gaussians, most errors are insignificant because most erroneous values still get rounded to the correct integer. However, errors occurring close to the boundaries of the intervals $[z - \frac{1}{2}, z + \frac{1}{2}]$ can lead to wrong outputs. The interval of values that can possibly round to z is given by $[z - \frac{1}{2} - e_l, z + \frac{1}{2} + e_r)$, where the left boundary error satisfies $|e_l| \leq 2^{-p}|z - \frac{1}{2}|$ and the right boundary error satisfies $|e_r| \leq 2^{-p}|z + \frac{1}{2}|$.

We define success for the attacker to mean that he breaks the signature scheme or that he manages to distinguish between the implementation with precision p and a perfect implementation.

Most papers use the statistical distance (Definition B.1) to study the relative difference between two distributions. In [1] the authors showed that studying the Rényi divergence between the distributions can lead to better and tighter estimates.

In this section we work with the known precision $p = 48$ for our implementation and using the parameters for BLISS-I [11], we determine how many signatures an adversary $\mathcal{A}$ can observe before the Rényi divergence between the ideal implementation and the practical implementation becomes larger than some small constant c; this means, his chance of breaking the system is at most c times as high compared to the ideal implementation.

We also provide an analysis of the asymptotic behavior of the precision p compared to the standard deviation σ, the length m and the number of signatures q_s generated. The computations can be found in Appendix B. These results are naturally less tight because we prioritize readable formulas over best approximations. Accordingly, better results are obtained using numerical computations once one settles on concrete parameters. The asymptotic analysis is helpful in determining which distance or divergence to use.

To analyze the allowable number of signatures q_s before an attack could possibly distinguish the distributions, we look at the *Rényi divergence of order* ∞ as given in [1]:

Definition 5.1. *For any two discrete probability distributions P and Q, such that* $\mathrm{Supp}(P) \subseteq \mathrm{Supp}(Q)$, *the Rényi divergence of order* ∞ *is defined by*

$$\mathrm{RD}_\infty(P \parallel Q) = \max_{x \in \mathrm{Supp}(P)} \frac{P(x)}{Q(x)}.$$

In BLISS using rounded Gaussians we publish m independently sampled integers distributed according to the 1-dimensional rounded Gaussian distribution R_σ^1 to obtain an m-dimensional vector in R_σ^m. Next to that we assume q_s signing queries. This means a potential attacker can learn a vector of length mq_s with entries from the (imprecise) real-world sampler $R_\sigma'^1$. We want to determine the probability that an attacker can distinguish between a vector sampled from $R_\sigma^{mq_s}$ and $R_\sigma'^{mq_s}$.

By the probability preservation property (Lemma B.2) of the Rényi divergence, any adversary $\mathcal{A}$ having success probability ϵ on the scheme implemented with imprecise rounded Gaussian sampling has a success probability $\delta \geq \epsilon/\mathrm{RD}_\infty(R_\sigma'^{mq_s} \parallel R_\sigma^{mq_s})$ on the scheme implemented with the perfect rounded Gaussian. For a target success probability ϵ we have to choose $\delta \leq \epsilon/\exp(1)$ to have only a small, constant loss in tightness.

We need mq_s samples to create q_s signatures. By the multiplicative property of the Rényi divergence (Lemma B.1), we have $\mathrm{RD}_\infty(R_\sigma'^{mq_s} \parallel R_\sigma^{mq_s}) \leq \mathrm{RD}_\infty(R_\sigma'^1 \parallel R_\sigma^1)^{mq_s}$, so we can relate the divergence of the one-dimensional distributions to the mq_s dimensional one. The formula becomes

$$\mathrm{RD}_\infty(R_\sigma'^1 \parallel R_\sigma^1) =$$
$$\max_{z \in \mathrm{Supp}(R_\sigma'^1)} \left\{ \int_{z-\frac{1}{2}-e_l}^{z+\frac{1}{2}+e_r} \frac{1}{\sqrt{2\pi\sigma^2}} e^{-x^2/(2\sigma^2)} dx \; \Big/ \int_{z-\frac{1}{2}}^{z+\frac{1}{2}} \frac{1}{\sqrt{2\pi\sigma^2}} e^{-x^2/(2\sigma^2)} dx \right\}.$$

The BLISS-I parameters are $\sigma = 215, m = 2n = 1024$, and $\epsilon = 2^{-128}$, giving $\tau = \sqrt{2 \cdot 128 \ln(2)} = 13.32$, and we work with floating point precision $p = 48$. We compute RD_∞ numerically for the 1-dimensional case with Pari-GP with precision 200 digits, giving $\mathrm{RD}_\infty(R_\sigma'^1 \parallel R_\sigma^1) \approx 1.0000000000203563$. Recall we want $\mathrm{RD}_\infty(R_\sigma'^1 \parallel R_\sigma^1)^{mq_s} \leq \exp(1)$. For $m = 1024$ we get that $q_s = 2^{25}$ gives $2.01262 < \exp(1)$. This means that we can create 2^{25} signatures, i.e., 1 signature/min for over 60 years, securely with one key pair. Note also that the choice of $\exp(1)$ is kind of arbitrary and other constants would be suitable as well. Moreover, provable security continues to degrade slowly after these 2^{25} signatures. As far as we know, no attack is known that would use the distinguishability of the distributions.

Several papers, starting with [1], use Rényi divergence RD_a of order a to get much better results regarding the precision. We caution the reader that the relation $\delta > \epsilon^{a/(a-1)}/RD_a$, for $a = 2, \delta = 2^{-128}$ and constant $RD_a = 2$, means $\epsilon = 2^{-64}$, which is loose to the point of being meaningless. For the same looseness we could use constant 2^{64} in place of $\exp(1)$ in RD_∞ and sign 2^{88} times.

5.3 Implementation of Rejection Sampling of Signatures

There are many standard numerical techniques and libraries to efficiently compute the complementary error function $1 - \mathrm{erf}$ to high precision. We use the following constant-time mixture of standard techniques: for fixed s, the integral of e^{-x^2} for x ranging from $t-s/2$ to $t+s/2$ is e^{-t^2} (which we compute in constant time using VCL) times a quickly converging power series in t^2. For the constants $s = 1/\sqrt{2\sigma^2}$ relevant to BLISS-I through BLISS-IV, and for the entire range of t allowed by our tail cut, the truncation error after five terms of this power series is below the rounding error of double-precision floating-point computation.

Each of the three 1024-dimensional integrals is computed by the `bigintegral` function shown in Appendix G of the full version [14], which is implemented in just four lines of code, on top of the `erfdiff` function, which is implemented in just two lines of code, plus a few constants precomputed from σ. The rest of the code in Appendix G in [14] is for speeding up VCL's `exp` by replacing it with a streamlined `fastexp`; running a Monte-Carlo sanity check on `bigintegral`; and benchmarking `bigintegral`.

Each call to `bigintegral` takes just 7800 cycles on a Haswell CPU core using g++ 4.8.4 with standard compiler options (`-O3 -fomit-frame-pointer -std=gnu++11 -march=native -mtune=native -fabi-version=6`), and there are three integrals in the computation of rejection probabilities. (Dividing the integrals and comparing to a random number is equivalent to multiplying the random number by the denominator and comparing to the numerator, which takes constant time.) We save a lot more than these $3 \cdot 7800 = 23400$ cycles in the sampling step (see Table 5.1). Furthermore, the main point of the approach is to produce constant-time implementations, and our code is constant time.

There are only a small number of possible inputs to `erfdiff`. Specifically, each y_i is an integer in $[-\tau\sigma, \tau\sigma]$, and each entry of $\mathbf{Sc}$ is an integer bounded in absolute value by 3κ for BLISS-I and II and 5κ for BLISS-III and IV, so each `erfdiff` input is an integer bounded in absolute value by $\tau\sigma + 3\kappa$ or $\tau\sigma + 5\kappa$ respectively.

To compute the effects of approximating erf and working with finite-precision floating-point numbers we calculated the ratio of the result from our calculation (for all possible `erfdiff` inputs) to the exact solution, where we used Sage's arbitrary-precision `error_fcn` with 1000 bits of precision to very precisely compute the exact solution. The one-dimensional Rényi divergence RD_∞ of these distributions is defined as the maximum of these fractions.

For example, in $17\,\mathrm{s}$ on a $3.5\,\mathrm{GHz}$ Haswell core we calculate for BLISS-I that $\mathrm{RD}_\infty(\text{approx calculation} \| \text{exact calculation}) < 1 + 2^{-46}$.

Using that RD_∞ is multiplicative and $(1 + 2^{-46})^{2^{46}} < \exp(1)$ we get that for $m = 1024$ we can output 2^{36} signatures without the attacker gaining more than a factor of $\exp(1)$. This is more than the number in Sect. 5.2 so the approximation is sufficiently good.

5.4   Timings for Sampling Rounded Gaussians

Another property that needs to be compared between the rounded Gaussian distribution and the discrete Gaussian distribution is the time it takes to generate one signature. We compare our implementation to the CDT implementation from http://bliss.di.ens.fr/ which is a proof-of-concept, variable-time sampler for discrete Gaussians.

Both the discrete Gaussian and the rounded Gaussian can be used in the BLISS signature scheme as we have shown earlier. We now compare the time that it takes to generate $m = 1024$ samples by the two sampling schemes. We note that in a full implementation there are more steps to generate a signature, e.g., the rejection step. However, as said before, these steps are not the bottle neck and take approximately equal time for either sampling scheme; thus we do not include them in the analysis.

Our implementation starts by drawing random bits from `/dev/urandom` and then expanding them using ChaCha20 [3] to 8192 bytes of data. From that 128 vectors of 8 53-bit floating-point variables are initialized with randomness, corresponding to the initial u_i values in Algorithm 4.1. The rest of the implementation follows closely the description of that algorithm.

Both implementations have been compiled using `gcc` with `-O3`. The benchmarks have been run on a Haswell Intel(R) chip, i.e. Intel(R) Xeon(R) CPU E3-1275 v3 $3.50\,\mathrm{GHz}$. All values given in Table 5.1 are given in CPU cycles. We give the quartiles Q1 and Q3 and the median over $10\,000$ runs to show the statistical stability.

In Table 5.1 we can clearly see that the rounded Gaussian implementation is significantly faster than the discrete Gaussian implementation; the rounded Gaussian implementation needs noticeably less than half the number of CPU cycles compared to the discrete Gaussian implementation. We can also see that generating the randomness takes a significant part of the total CPU cycle count.

While the difference in speed is significant we would like to point out that the implementation we used for the discrete Gaussians is not fully optimized. It is hard to predict how much faster a better implementation would be and how much worse the performance would drop if countermeasures to achieve constant-time behavior were implemented.

Our motivation after [7] was to find an alternative to hard-to-secure discrete Gaussians, even if it was *slower* than current implementations. Our implementation shows that with less than 40 lines of code rounded Gaussians are at least fully competitive.

Table 5.1. CPU cycles analysis for the rounded Gaussian sampling scheme and discrete Gaussian sampling scheme with $m = 1024$ run on Intel(R) Xeon(R) CPU E3-1275 v3 3.50 GHz, stating median and quartiles for 10 000 runs.

Name of the scheme	Q1	Median	Q3
Rounded Gaussians (including generating randomness)	47532	47576	47616
Rounded Gaussians (without generating randomness)	27608	27672	27848
Discrete Gaussians (including generating randomness)	115056	116272	127170
Discrete Gaussians (without generating randomness)	77424	78136	78876

References

1. Bai, S., Langlois, A., Lepoint, T., Stehlé, D., Steinfeld, R.: Improved security proofs in lattice-based cryptography: using the Rényi Divergence rather than the statistical distance. In: Iwata, T., Cheon, J.H. (eds.) ASIACRYPT 2015. LNCS, vol. 9452, pp. 3–24. Springer, Heidelberg (2015). https://doi.org/10.1007/978-3-662-48797-6_1
2. Banaszczyk, W.: New bounds in some transference theorems in the geometry of numbers. Math. Ann. **296**(1), 625–635 (1993)
3. Bernstein, D.J.: The ChaCha family of stream ciphers. ChaCha, a variant of Salsa20 [4]. https://cr.yp.to/chacha.html
4. Bernstein, D.J.: The Salsa20 family of stream ciphers. In: Robshaw, M., Billet, O. (eds.) New Stream Cipher Designs. LNCS, vol. 4986, pp. 84–97. Springer, Heidelberg (2008). https://doi.org/10.1007/978-3-540-68351-3_8
5. Bos, J.W., Costello, C., Naehrig, M., Stebila, D.: Post-quantum key exchange for the TLS protocol from the ring learning with errors problem. In: IEEE Symposium on Security and Privacy, pp. 553–570. IEEE Computer Society (2015)
6. Box, G.E.P., Muller, M.E.: A note on the generation of random normal deviates. Ann. Math. Statist. **29**(2), 610–611 (1958)
7. Groot Bruinderink, L., Hülsing, A., Lange, T., Yarom, Y.: Flush, Gauss, and reload – a cache attack on the BLISS lattice-based signature scheme. In: Gierlichs, B., Poschmann, A.Y. (eds.) CHES 2016. LNCS, vol. 9813, pp. 323–345. Springer, Heidelberg (2016). https://doi.org/10.1007/978-3-662-53140-2_16
8. Buchmann, J.A., Cabarcas, D., Göpfert, F., Hülsing, A., Weiden, P.: Discrete Ziggurat: a time-memory trade-off for sampling from a Gaussian distribution over the integers. In: Lange et al. [15], pp. 402–417
9. Duc, A., Tramèr, F., Vaudenay, S.: Better algorithms for LWE and LWR. In: Oswald, E., Fischlin, M. (eds.) EUROCRYPT 2015, Part I. LNCS, vol. 9056, pp. 173–202. Springer, Heidelberg (2015). https://doi.org/10.1007/978-3-662-46800-5_8
10. Ducas, L.: Accelerating BLISS: the geometry of ternary polynomials. IACR Cryptology ePrint Archive, Report 2014/874 (2014). https://eprint.iacr.org/2014/874

11. Ducas, L., Durmus, A., Lepoint, T., Lyubashevsky, V.: Lattice signatures and bimodal Gaussians. In: Canetti, R., Garay, J.A. (eds.) CRYPTO 2013. LNCS, vol. 8042, pp. 40–56. Springer, Heidelberg (2013). https://doi.org/10.1007/978-3-642-40041-4_3. Full version: http://eprint.iacr.org/2013/383

12. Dwarakanath, N.C., Galbraith, S.D.: Sampling from discrete Gaussians for lattice-based cryptography on a constrained device. Appl. Algebra Eng. Commun. Comput. **25**(3), 159–180 (2014)

13. Fog, A.: VCL C++ vector class library (2016). Code and documentation www.agner.org/optimize

14. Hülsing, A., Lange, T., Smeets, K.: Rounded Gaussians – fast and secure constant-time sampling for lattice-based crypto. IACR Cryptology ePrint Archive, Report 2017/1025 (2017). https://eprint.iacr.org/2017/1025

15. Lange, T., Lauter, K., Lisoněk, P. (eds.): SAC 2013. LNCS, vol. 8282. Springer, Heidelberg (2014). https://doi.org/10.1007/978-3-662-43414-7

16. Lyubashevsky, V.: Lattice signatures without trapdoors. In: Pointcheval, D., Johansson, T. (eds.) EUROCRYPT 2012. LNCS, vol. 7237, pp. 738–755. Springer, Heidelberg (2012). https://doi.org/10.1007/978-3-642-29011-4_43

17. Micciancio, D., Walter, M.: Gaussian sampling over the integers: efficient, generic, constant-time. In: Katz, J., Shacham, H. (eds.) CRYPTO 2017, Part II. LNCS, vol. 10402, pp. 455–485. Springer, Cham (2017). https://doi.org/10.1007/978-3-319-63715-0_16

18. Pessl, P.: Analyzing the shuffling side-channel countermeasure for lattice-based signatures. In: Dunkelman, O., Sanadhya, S.K. (eds.) INDOCRYPT 2016. LNCS, vol. 10095, pp. 153–170. Springer, Cham (2016). https://doi.org/10.1007/978-3-319-49890-4_9

19. Pöppelmann, T., Ducas, L., Güneysu, T.: Enhanced lattice-based signatures on reconfigurable hardware. In: Batina, L., Robshaw, M. (eds.) CHES 2014. LNCS, vol. 8731, pp. 353–370. Springer, Heidelberg (2014). https://doi.org/10.1007/978-3-662-44709-3_20

20. Regev, O.: On lattices, learning with errors, random linear codes, and cryptography. J. ACM **56**(6) (2009). Article no. 34

21. Roy, S.S., Vercauteren, F., Verbauwhede, I.: High precision discrete Gaussian sampling on FPGAs. In: Lange et al. [15], pp. 383–401

22. Saarinen, M.-J.O.: Gaussian sampling precision and information leakage in lattice cryptography. IACR Cryptology ePrint Archive, Report 2015/953 (2015). https://eprint.iacr.org/2015/953

23. Smeets, K.: Securing BLISS-b against side-channel attacks lattice-based cryptography in a post-quantum setting. Master thesis at Technische Universiteit Eindhoven (2017)

24. strongSwan: strongSwan 5.2.2 released, January 2015. https://www.strongswan.org/blog/2015/01/05/strongswan-5.2.2-released.html

25. van Erven, T., Harremoës, P.: Rényi divergence and Kullback-Leibler divergence. IEEE Trans. Inf. Theory **60**(7), 3797–3820 (2014)

A   Proofs for Rounded Gaussian Rejection Sampling

In this section we provide the missing lemmas and proofs from Sect. 3. We follow the structure of the security proofs in [16] to show that we can use the rounded Gaussian distribution in Lyubashevsky's scheme. Similarly to [16], our main proof relies on several lemmas about the rounded Gaussian distribution over $\mathbb{Z}^m$.

The statements in the lemmas proven here differ slightly from those in [16] but serve analogous purposes.

First we look at the inner product of a rounded Gaussian variable with any vector in $\mathbb{R}^m$.

Lemma A.1. *For any fixed vector* $\mathbf{u} \in \mathbb{R}^m$ *and any* $\sigma, r > 0$, *we have*

$$\Pr[|\langle \mathbf{z} + \mathbf{y}, \mathbf{u} \rangle| > r; \mathbf{z} \xleftarrow{\$} R_\sigma^m] \leq 2e^{-\frac{r^2}{2\|\mathbf{u}\|^2 \sigma^2}},$$

where $\mathbf{y} \in \left[-\frac{1}{2}, \frac{1}{2}\right]^m$ *minimizes* $\exp\left(\frac{1}{\sigma^2}\langle \mathbf{z} + \mathbf{y}, \mathbf{u} \rangle\right)$.

Proof. Let $\mathbf{u} \in \mathbb{R}^m$ be fixed and let $\mathbf{y} \in \left[-\frac{1}{2}, \frac{1}{2}\right]^m$ be such that $\exp\left(\frac{1}{\sigma^2}\langle \mathbf{z} + \mathbf{y}, \mathbf{u} \rangle\right)$ is minimized. For any $t > 0$, we have for the expectation of $\exp\left(\frac{t}{\sigma^2}\langle \mathbf{z} + \mathbf{y}, \mathbf{u} \rangle\right)$, taken over all $\mathbf{z}$ sampled from R_σ^m:

$$
\begin{aligned}
E\left[\exp\left(\tfrac{t}{\sigma^2}\langle \mathbf{z} + \mathbf{y}, \mathbf{u} \rangle\right)\right] &= \exp\left(\tfrac{t}{\sigma^2}\langle \mathbf{y}, \mathbf{u} \rangle\right) E\left[\exp\left(\tfrac{t}{\sigma^2}\langle \mathbf{z}, \mathbf{u} \rangle\right)\right] \\
&= \exp\left(\tfrac{t}{\sigma^2}\langle \mathbf{y}, \mathbf{u} \rangle\right) \sum_{\mathbf{z} \in \mathbb{Z}^m} \Pr[\mathbf{z}] \exp\left(\tfrac{1}{\sigma^2}\langle \mathbf{z}, t\mathbf{u} \rangle\right) \\
&= \sum_{\mathbf{z} \in \mathbb{Z}^m} \int_{A_{\mathbf{z}}} \left(\tfrac{1}{\sqrt{2\pi\sigma^2}}\right)^m \exp\left(\tfrac{-\|\mathbf{x}\|^2}{2\sigma^2}\right) d\mathbf{x} \exp\left(\tfrac{1}{\sigma^2}\langle \mathbf{z} + \mathbf{y}, t\mathbf{u} \rangle\right) \\
&\leq \sum_{\mathbf{z} \in \mathbb{Z}^m} \int_{A_{\mathbf{z}}} \left(\tfrac{1}{\sqrt{2\pi\sigma^2}}\right)^m \exp\left(\tfrac{-\|\mathbf{x}\|^2}{2\sigma^2}\right) \exp\left(\tfrac{1}{\sigma^2}\langle \mathbf{x}, t\mathbf{u} \rangle\right) d\mathbf{x} \\
&= \sum_{\mathbf{z} \in \mathbb{Z}^m} \int_{A_{\mathbf{z}}} \left(\tfrac{1}{\sqrt{2\pi\sigma^2}}\right)^m \exp\left(\tfrac{-\|\mathbf{x} - t\mathbf{u}\|^2}{2\sigma^2}\right) \exp\left(\tfrac{t^2\|\mathbf{u}\|^2}{2\sigma^2}\right) d\mathbf{x} \\
&= \sum_{\mathbf{z} \in \mathbb{Z}^m} R_{t\mathbf{u},\sigma}^m(\mathbf{z}) \exp\left(\tfrac{t^2\|\mathbf{u}\|^2}{2\sigma^2}\right) \\
&= \exp\left(\tfrac{t^2\|\mathbf{u}\|^2}{2\sigma^2}\right),
\end{aligned}
$$

where the last equality follows from the fact that $\sum_{\mathbf{z} \in \mathbb{Z}^m} R_{t\mathbf{u},\sigma}^m(\mathbf{z}) = 1$ because it is the sum over the entire range of the probability density function. We proceed to prove the claim of the lemma by applying Markov's inequality first and then the above result. For any $t > 0$, we have:

$$
\begin{aligned}
\Pr\left[\langle \mathbf{z} + \mathbf{y}, \mathbf{u} \rangle > r\right] &= \Pr\left[\exp\left(\tfrac{t}{\sigma^2}\langle \mathbf{z} + \mathbf{y}, \mathbf{u} \rangle\right) > \exp\left(tr/\sigma^2\right)\right] \\
&\leq \left(E\left[\exp\left(t\langle \mathbf{z} + \mathbf{y}, \mathbf{u} \rangle/\sigma^2\right)\right]\right)/\left(\exp\left(tr/\sigma^2\right)\right) \\
&\leq \exp\left((t^2\|\mathbf{u}\|^2 - 2tr)/(2\sigma^2)\right).
\end{aligned}
$$

The function on the right assumes its maximum at $t = r/\|\mathbf{u}\|^2$, so we get $\Pr\left[\langle \mathbf{z} + \mathbf{y}, \mathbf{u} \rangle > r\right] \leq \exp\left(-r^2/(2\|\mathbf{u}\|^2\sigma^2)\right)$. Because the distribution is symmetric around the origin we also know $\Pr[\langle \mathbf{z} + \mathbf{y}, \mathbf{u} \rangle < -r] \leq \exp\left(-r^2/(2\|\mathbf{u}\|^2\sigma^2)\right)$. By applying the union bound to the two inequalities, we get the probability for $|\langle \mathbf{z} + \mathbf{y}, \mathbf{u} \rangle| > r$, which results in the claim of the lemma. □

Lemma A.2. *Under the conditions of Lemma A.1 we have:*

1. *For any* $k\sigma > 1/4(\sigma + 1), \sigma \geq 1, \Pr\left[|z| > k\sigma; z \xleftarrow{\$} R_\sigma^1\right] \leq 2e^{\frac{-\left(k - \frac{1}{2}\right)^2}{2}}$.

2. *For any* $\mathbf{z} \in \mathbb{Z}^m$ *and* $\sigma \geq \sqrt{2/\pi}, R_\sigma^m(\mathbf{z}) \leq 2^{-m}$.

3. *For any* $k > 1, \Pr\left[\|\mathbf{z}\| > k\sigma\sqrt{m}; \mathbf{z} \xleftarrow{\$} R_\sigma^m\right] < 2k^m e^{\frac{m}{2}(1 - k^2)}$.

Proof. Item 1 follows from Lemma A.1 by substituting $m = 1, r = k\sigma - \frac{1}{2}$ and $u = 1$. This gives

$$|z + y| = |z| - \frac{1}{2} > r = k\sigma - \frac{1}{2}.$$

In other words, $|z| > k\sigma$. Then we have for the upper bound of the probability:

$$2\exp\left(-\frac{r^2}{2\|u\|^2\sigma^2}\right) = 2\exp\left(-\frac{(k\sigma - \frac{1}{2})^2}{2\sigma^2}\right) \leq 2\exp\left(-\frac{(k - \frac{1}{2})^2\sigma^2}{2\sigma^2}\right),$$

where we use $-\left(k\sigma - \frac{1}{2}\right)^2 \leq -\left(k - \frac{1}{2}\right)^2\sigma^2$ for $\sigma \geq 1$ in the inequality. Note that for $0.44 < k < 1.89$ item 3 actually provides a better bound.

To prove Item 2, we write

$$R_\sigma^m(\mathbf{z}) = \left(\frac{1}{\sqrt{2\pi\sigma^2}}\right)^m \int_{A_\mathbf{z}} e^{-\|\mathbf{x}\|^2/(2\sigma^2)} d\mathbf{x}$$
$$\leq \left(\frac{1}{\sqrt{2\pi\sigma^2}}\right)^m \cdot \max_{\mathbf{x} \in A_\mathbf{z}} e^{-\|\mathbf{x}\|^2/(2\sigma^2)} \cdot \mathrm{vol}(A_\mathbf{z}) \leq \left(\frac{1}{\sqrt{2\pi\sigma^2}}\right)^m,$$

where the first inequality follows from the fact that integrating a continuous function on a bounded area is bounded from above by the maximum of the function on the area times the volume of the area. The second inequality follows from the fact that the volume of the area $A_\mathbf{z}$ is equal to 1 and $e^{-\|\mathbf{x}\|^2/(2\sigma^2)} \leq 1$ for all $\mathbf{x} \in A_\mathbf{z}$ for all $\mathbf{z} \in \mathbb{Z}^m$. Thus if $\sigma \geq \sqrt{2/\pi}$, we have $R_\sigma^m \leq 2^{-m}$.

For Item 3, we write the following:

$$\Pr\left[\|\mathbf{z}\| > k\sigma\sqrt{m}; \mathbf{z} \xleftarrow{\$} R_\sigma^m\right]$$
$$= \sum_{\mathbf{z} \in \mathbb{Z}^m, \|\mathbf{z}\| > k\sigma\sqrt{m}} \left(\frac{1}{\sqrt{2\pi\sigma^2}}\right)^m \int_{A_\mathbf{z}} e^{-\|\mathbf{x}\|^2/(2\sigma^2)} d\mathbf{x}$$
$$\leq \left(\frac{1}{\sqrt{2\pi\sigma^2}}\right)^m \sum_{\mathbf{z} \in \mathbb{Z}^m, \|\mathbf{z}\| > k\sigma\sqrt{m}} \left(\max_{\mathbf{x} \in A_\mathbf{z}} e^{-\|\mathbf{x}\|^2/(2\sigma^2)} \cdot \mathrm{vol}(A_\mathbf{z})\right) \tag{2}$$
$$\leq \left(\frac{1}{\sqrt{2\pi\sigma^2}}\right)^m \sum_{\mathbf{z} \in \mathbb{Z}^m, \|\mathbf{z}\| > k\sigma\sqrt{m}} e^{-\|\mathbf{z}+\mathbf{y}\|^2/(2\sigma^2)},$$

where $\mathbf{y} \in [-\frac{1}{2}, \frac{1}{2}]^m$ is chosen such that the maximum is attained, i.e. for each z_i we pick $y_i, i = 1, \ldots, m$ in the following way:

$$y_i = \begin{cases} -\frac{1}{2} & \text{if } z_i > 0, \\ 0 & \text{if } z_i = 0, \\ \frac{1}{2} & \text{if } z_i < 0. \end{cases} \tag{3}$$

We use the second part of a lemma by Banaszczyk [2, Lemma 1.5], saying that for each $c \geq 1/\sqrt{2\pi}$, lattice L of dimension m and $\mathbf{u} \in \mathbb{R}^m$, we have $\sum_{\mathbf{z} \in L, \|\mathbf{z}\| > c\sqrt{m}} e^{-\pi\|\mathbf{z}+\mathbf{u}\|^2} < 2\left(c\sqrt{2\pi e}e^{-\pi c^2}\right)^n \sum_{\mathbf{z} \in L} e^{-\pi\|\mathbf{z}\|^2}$, and put $\mathbf{u} = \mathbf{y}$. If we scale the lattice L by a factor of $1/s$ for some constant s, we have that for all s,

$$\sum_{\mathbf{z} \in L, \|\mathbf{z}\| > cs\sqrt{m}} e^{-\pi\|\mathbf{z}+\mathbf{y}\|^2/s^2} < 2\left(c\sqrt{2\pi e}e^{-\pi c^2}\right)^m \sum_{\mathbf{z} \in L} e^{-\pi\|\mathbf{z}\|^2/s^2}.$$

Setting $L = \mathbb{Z}^m$ and $s = \sqrt{2\pi}\sigma$, we obtain

$$\sum_{\mathbf{z} \in \mathbb{Z}^m, \|\mathbf{z}\| > c\sqrt{2\pi\sigma^2 m}} e^{-\|\mathbf{z}+\mathbf{y}\|^2/(2\sigma^2)} < 2\left(c\sqrt{2\pi e}e^{-\pi c^2}\right)^m \sum_{\mathbf{z} \in \mathbb{Z}^m} e^{-\|\mathbf{z}\|^2/(2\sigma^2)}.$$

Finally, by setting $c = k/\sqrt{2\pi}$ in the upper bound for the probability and applying it to Eq. (2), we get

$$\Pr\left[\|\mathbf{z}\| > k\sigma\sqrt{m}; \mathbf{z} \xleftarrow{\$} R_\sigma^m\right] < 2k^m e^{\frac{m}{2}(1-k^2)}\left(\frac{1}{\sqrt{2\pi\sigma^2}}\right)^m \sum_{\mathbf{z} \in \mathbb{Z}^m} e^{-\|\mathbf{z}\|^2/(2\sigma^2)}.$$

Note that $\left(\frac{1}{\sqrt{2\pi\sigma^2}}\right)^m \sum_{\mathbf{z} \in \mathbb{Z}^m} \exp(-\|\mathbf{z}\|^2/(2\sigma^2)) = 1$, since it is the probability density function $R_\sigma^m(\mathbf{z})$ summed over all possible values. Thus we have

$$\Pr\left[\|\mathbf{z}\| > k\sigma\sqrt{m}; \mathbf{z} \xleftarrow{\$} R_\sigma^m\right] < 2k^m e^{\frac{m}{2}(1-k^2)}.$$

$\square$

The following is the proof of Lemma 3.1 from Sect. 3.

Proof. By definition we have

$$\frac{R_\sigma^m(\mathbf{z})}{R_{\mathbf{v},\sigma}^m(\mathbf{z})} = \frac{\int_{A_\mathbf{z}} \rho_\sigma^m(\mathbf{x})d\mathbf{x}}{\int_{A_\mathbf{z}} \rho_{\mathbf{v},\sigma}^m(\mathbf{x})d\mathbf{x}} = \frac{\int_{A_\mathbf{z}} \exp(-\|\mathbf{x}\|^2/(2\sigma^2))d\mathbf{x}}{\int_{A_\mathbf{z}} \exp(-\|\mathbf{x}-\mathbf{v}\|^2/(2\sigma^2))d\mathbf{x}}$$

$$\leq \frac{\max_{\mathbf{x} \in A_\mathbf{z}} e^{-\|\mathbf{x}\|^2/(2\sigma^2)} \cdot \text{vol}(A_\mathbf{z})}{\min_{\mathbf{x} \in A_\mathbf{z}} e^{-\|\mathbf{x}-\mathbf{v}\|^2/(2\sigma^2)} \cdot \text{vol}(A_\mathbf{z})} = \frac{\exp(-\|\mathbf{z}+\mathbf{y}_1\|^2/(2\sigma^2))}{\exp(-\|\mathbf{z}-\mathbf{v}+\mathbf{y}_2\|^2/(2\sigma^2))},$$

where the inequality follows from the fact that integrating a continuous function on a bounded area is bounded from below by its minimum on the area times the volume of the area; $\mathbf{y}_1 \in \left[-\frac{1}{2}, \frac{1}{2}\right]^m$ is chosen such that the maximum is achieved for $\|\mathbf{z}+\mathbf{y}_1\|^2$, and $\mathbf{y}_2 \in \left[-\frac{1}{2}, \frac{1}{2}\right]^m$ is chosen such that the minimum is achieved for $\|\mathbf{z}-\mathbf{v}+\mathbf{y}_2\|^2$. In other words, $\mathbf{y}_1 \in \left[-\frac{1}{2}, \frac{1}{2}\right]^m$ is defined as in Eq. (3) and for $\mathbf{y}_2 \in \left[-\frac{1}{2}, \frac{1}{2}\right]^m$ we have for each $z_i - v_i, i = 1, \ldots, m$:

$$y_{2,i} = \begin{cases} -\frac{1}{2} & \text{if } z_i < v_i, \\ \frac{1}{2} & \text{if } z_i \geq v_i. \end{cases} \tag{4}$$

This results in the following formula:

$$\frac{e^{-\|\mathbf{z}+\mathbf{y}_1\|^2/(2\sigma^2)}}{e^{-\|\mathbf{z}-\mathbf{v}+\mathbf{y}_2\|^2/(2\sigma^2)}} \exp\left(\frac{(\|\mathbf{y}_2\|^2 - \|\mathbf{y}_1\|^2 + 2\langle\mathbf{z},\mathbf{y}_2-\mathbf{y}_1\rangle) - 2\langle\mathbf{z}+\mathbf{y}_2,\mathbf{v}\rangle + \|\mathbf{v}\|^2}{2\sigma^2}\right).$$

We want to combine $\|\mathbf{y}_2\|^2 - \|\mathbf{y}_1\|^2 + 2\langle\mathbf{z}, \mathbf{y}_2 - \mathbf{y}_1\rangle$ with the inner product $\langle\mathbf{z}+\mathbf{y}_2, \mathbf{v}\rangle$ into an inner product of the form $\langle\mathbf{z}+\mathbf{y}, \mathbf{v}+\mathbf{a}\rangle$ for some $\mathbf{a}$, where

$\mathbf{y} \in [-1/2, 1/2]^m$ minimizes $\langle \mathbf{z} + \mathbf{y}, \mathbf{v} + \mathbf{a} \rangle$, such that we can apply Lemma A.1, where we set $\mathbf{u} = \mathbf{v} + \mathbf{a}$. We can write

$$\|\mathbf{y}_2\|^2 - \|\mathbf{y}_1\|^2 + 2\langle \mathbf{z}, \mathbf{y}_2 - \mathbf{y}_1 \rangle = \sum_{i=1}^{m} \left(y_{2,i}^2 - y_{1,i}^2 + 2z_i \left(y_{2,i} - y_{1,i} \right) \right).$$

Using the definition of $y_{1,i}$ and $y_{2,i}$, for $i = 1, \ldots, m$ we get the following expression:

$$y_{2,i}^2 - y_{1,i}^2 + 2z_i \left(y_{2,i} - y_{1,i} \right) = \begin{cases} = -2z_i & \text{if } z_i < v_i \wedge z_i < 0, \\ = \frac{1}{4} & \text{if } z_i = 0, \\ = 2z_i & \text{if } z_i \geq v_i \wedge z_i > 0, \\ = 0 & \text{otherwise.} \end{cases} \tag{5}$$

To create an upper bound of the form $-2\langle \mathbf{z} + \mathbf{y}, \mathbf{a} \rangle$, where $\mathbf{y} \in \left[-\frac{1}{2}, \frac{1}{2} \right]^m$ minimizes $\langle \mathbf{z} + \mathbf{y}, \mathbf{v} + \mathbf{a} \rangle$, we need to determine an expression for $\mathbf{a}$, i.e. we determine a_i such that it fits Eq. (5). This gives us the following expressions for the coordinates $i = 1, \ldots, m$:

$$-2a_i z_i - 2a_i y_i = \begin{cases} -2a_i z_i + a_i & \text{if } z_i < 0, \\ -a_i & \text{if } z_i = 0, \\ -2a_i z_i - a_i & \text{if } z_i > 0. \end{cases} \quad \Rightarrow \quad a_i = \begin{cases} -\frac{2z_i}{-2z_i+1} & \text{if } z_i < 0, \\ -\frac{1}{4} & \text{if } z_i = 0, \\ -\frac{2z_i}{2z_i+1} & \text{if } z_i > 0. \end{cases}$$

Now we can write $\sum_{i=1}^{m} \left(y_{2,i}^2 - y_{1,i}^2 + 2z_i \left(y_{2,i} - y_{1,i} \right) \right) \leq -2\langle \mathbf{z} + \mathbf{y}, \mathbf{a} \rangle$, where $\mathbf{a}$ is chosen as above such that $-z_i a_i \leq 0$ and $|a_i| \leq 1$ for $i = 1, \ldots, m$ and $\mathbf{y}$ minimizes $\langle \mathbf{z} + \mathbf{y}, \mathbf{a} \rangle$. Given $\mathbf{y}_2$ and $\mathbf{y}$, we can write $\mathbf{y}_2 = \mathbf{y} + \mathbf{b}$, where we pick $b_i \in \{-1, 0, 1\}$ for $i = 1, \ldots, m$ such that the equation holds. Then we can write $2\langle \mathbf{z} + \mathbf{y}_2, \mathbf{v} \rangle = 2\langle \mathbf{z} + \mathbf{y}, \mathbf{v} \rangle + 2\langle \mathbf{b}, \mathbf{v} \rangle$. We have $|2\langle \mathbf{b}, \mathbf{v} \rangle| = \left| \sum_{i=1}^{m} 2b_i v_i \right| \leq 2\|\mathbf{v}\|^2$, because $b_i \in \{-1, 0, 1\}$, dependent on the value of z_i and v_i. Combining these bounds and applying them to the previous result, gives us

$$\exp \left(\left(\left(\|\mathbf{y}_2\|^2 - \|\mathbf{y}_1\|^2 + 2\langle \mathbf{z}, \mathbf{y}_2 - \mathbf{y}_1 \rangle \right) - 2\langle \mathbf{z} + \mathbf{y}_2, \mathbf{v} \rangle + \|\mathbf{v}\|^2 \right) / (2\sigma^2) \right)$$
$$\leq \exp \left(\left(-2\langle \mathbf{z} + \mathbf{y}, \mathbf{a} \rangle - 2\langle \mathbf{z} + \mathbf{y}, \mathbf{v} \rangle - 2\langle \mathbf{b}, \mathbf{v} \rangle + \|\mathbf{v}\|^2 \right) / (2\sigma^2) \right)$$
$$\leq \exp \left(\left(-2\langle \mathbf{z} + \mathbf{y}, \mathbf{v} + \mathbf{a} \rangle + 3\|\mathbf{v}\|^2 \right) / (2\sigma^2) \right).$$

Lemma A.1 tells us that $|\langle \mathbf{z} + \mathbf{y}, \mathbf{v} + \mathbf{a} \rangle| \leq \sigma\sqrt{2 \log m}\|\mathbf{v} + \mathbf{a}\|$ with probability at least $1 - 2^{-\log m}$ if $\mathbf{y}$ minimizes $\langle \mathbf{z} + \mathbf{y}, \mathbf{v} + \mathbf{a} \rangle$ and if $\mathbf{v} + \mathbf{a} \in \mathbb{Z}^m$. Since both conditions hold, we have

$$\exp \left(\frac{-2\langle \mathbf{z} + \mathbf{y}_2, \mathbf{v} + \mathbf{a} \rangle + 3\|\mathbf{v}\|^2}{2\sigma^2} \right) < \exp \left(\frac{2\sqrt{2 \log m}\|\mathbf{v} + \mathbf{a}\| + 3\|\mathbf{v}\|^2}{2\sigma^2} \right)$$
$$\leq \exp \left(\frac{\sqrt{2 \log m}\|\mathbf{v} + \mathbf{a}\|}{\sqrt{\log m}\|\mathbf{v}\|} + \frac{3\|\mathbf{v}\|^2}{2 \log m\|\mathbf{v}\|^2} \right) = \exp \left(\frac{3\|\mathbf{v}\| + 2\sqrt{2} \log m\|\mathbf{v} + \mathbf{a}\|}{2 \log m\|\mathbf{v}\|} \right) = O(1),$$

where the second inequality uses $\sigma = \omega(\|\mathbf{v}\|\sqrt{\log m})$ and the final equality uses $\|\mathbf{a}\|^2$ being small. $\square$

A.1   Comparison of Proofs for Rounded Gaussians vs. Discrete Gaussians

As we have mentioned at the beginning of this section, the theorems and proofs follow the line of the theorems and proofs of Lyubashevsky [16] closely. Here we give a quick overview of the changes made in the lemmas and theorems next to replacing the discrete Gaussian with the rounded Gaussian. We do not state in detail where the proofs differ, since we require different techniques to end up with similar results.

In Lemma A.1 we use $\langle \mathbf{z} + \mathbf{y}, \mathbf{u} \rangle$ with $\mathbf{y} \in \left[-\frac{1}{2}, \frac{1}{2} \right]^m$ minimizing $\exp\left(\frac{1}{\sigma^2} \langle \mathbf{z} + \mathbf{y}, \mathbf{u} \rangle \right)$ instead of the $\langle \mathbf{z}, \mathbf{u} \rangle$ that is used in [16, Lemma 4.3].

In Lemma A.2 we require for Item 1 that $k\sigma > 1/4(\sigma + 1)$ and $\sigma \geq 1$ instead of the $k > 0$ from [16, Lemma 4.4]. Next to that, we get that the probability $< \exp\left(\frac{-\left(k - \frac{1}{2} \right)^2}{2} \right)$ instead of the $< \exp\left(\frac{-k^2}{2} \right)$. For Item 2 we have $\sigma \geq \sqrt{2/\pi}$ instead of $\sigma \geq 3/\sqrt{2\pi}$. For Item 3 we have $2k^m e^{\frac{m}{2}(1-k^2)}$ instead of $k^m e^{\frac{m}{2}(1-k^2)}$.

Theorem 3.1 follows through directly based on the previous lemmas.

B   Rényi Divergence

An adversary wins if within q_s signing queries he can distinguish the perfect scheme and an implementation thereof or if he breaks the scheme with the perfect implementation. We will upper bound the success probability of any such adversary dependent on the precision used in the computation.

First we analyze the statistical distance (SD) and then Rényi divergences (RD) of order 1 and ∞ (Definition 5.1). Based on [1] we expect a lower precision requirement from the RD analysis. We use the definition of Rényi divergence as given in [1] and copy the relevant properties of RD from there; see [25] for a proof of the following lemmas and note that the definitions agree up to taking logarithms. For completeness we include the statistical difference.

Definition B.1. *The statistical distance $\Delta(P; Q)$ between two discrete probability functions P and Q is defined by*

$$\Delta(P; Q) = \frac{1}{2} \sum_{x \in V} |P(x) - Q(x)| ,$$

where $V = \mathrm{Supp}(P) \cup \mathrm{Supp}(Q)$ denotes the union of the support of P and the support of Q.

Definition B.2. *For any two discrete probability distributions P and Q, such that $\mathrm{Supp}(P) \subseteq \mathrm{Supp}(Q)$ the Rényi divergences of order 1 is defined by*

$$\mathrm{RD}_1(P \parallel Q) = \exp\left(\sum_{x \in \mathrm{Supp}(P)} P(x) \log \frac{P(x)}{Q(x)} \right) .$$

For RD the measures are related multiplicatively.

Lemma B.1 (Multiplicativity). *Let $a \in \{1, +\infty\}$. Let P and Q be two distributions with $\mathrm{Supp}(P) \subseteq \mathrm{Supp}(Q)$ of a pair of random variables (Y_1, Y_2) and let Y_1 and Y_2 be independent.*
Then we have: $\mathrm{RD}_a(P \parallel Q) = \mathrm{RD}_a(P_1 \parallel Q_1) \cdot \mathrm{RD}_a(P_2 \parallel Q_2)$.

We will use the following *probability preservation* property to quantify the probability of distinguishing the perfect rounded Gaussian distribution from the one implemented with finite precision.

Lemma B.2 (Probability Preservation). *Let P and Q denote distributions with $\mathrm{Supp}(P) \subseteq \mathrm{Supp}(Q)$. Let $A \subseteq \mathrm{Supp}(Q)$ be an arbitrary event. Then $Q(A) \geq P(A) / R_\infty (P \parallel Q)$.*

B.1   Precision for Rounded Gaussians

We now give a formal analysis linking the precision p of the implementation to the security level of the signature scheme. Computing with floating-point precision p means that the intermediate value x will be output with a certain *error* η. We can write this as $x' = x + \eta$, with $|\eta| \leq 2^{-p}x$. After this, x' is rounded to the nearest integer, i.e. $z = \lfloor x' \rceil$. Note that this implies that for computing the probability of sampling z only the interval changes from $[z - \frac{1}{2}, z + \frac{1}{2})$ to $[z - \frac{1}{2} - e_l, z + \frac{1}{2} + e_r)$, with $|e_l| \leq 2^{-p} \left| z - \frac{1}{2} \right|$ and $|e_r| \leq 2^{-p} \left| z + \frac{1}{2} \right|$. The tail cut forces $|z| \leq \tau\sigma$ and for $\tau = O(\sqrt{\lambda})$ Lemma A.2 implies that $\exp\left(\frac{-(\tau - \frac{1}{2})^2}{2\sigma^2}\right) \approx 2^{-\lambda}$, i.e. with all but negligible probability the sampled value lies within the tail bound. For all practical values $\lambda \ll 2^p$.

First we analyze the SD to gain a basic understanding of the precision needed for our sampler in BLISS. After this we analyze two different kinds of RD, since we expect that the required floating point precision will be smaller, because the bounds are tighter for other samplers. At the end of this section, we compare all of these bounds on the precision.

SD-based analysis. We follow [1] in assuming that any forging adversary $\mathcal{A}$ with success probability $\leq \delta$ on the scheme implemented with the perfect rounded Gaussian sampling has a success probability $\epsilon \leq \delta + \Delta(R'^{mq_s}_\sigma; R^{mq_s}_\sigma)$ against the scheme implemented with the truncated rounded Gaussian sampling, with $R^{mq_s}_\sigma$, i.e. the success probability ϵ on the truncated scheme is upper bounded by the success probability on the perfect scheme δ and the extra information we gain by comparing the distributions $R'^{mq_s}_\sigma$ and $R^{mq_s}_\sigma$. For a target success probability ϵ we have to choose $\delta \leq \epsilon/2$ for the success probability on the perfect scheme and we want to determine the lower bound on p such that $\Delta(R'^{mq_s}_\sigma; R^{mq_s}_\sigma) \leq \epsilon/2$.

By the union bound this means that we require $\Delta(R'_\sigma; R_\sigma) \leq \epsilon/(mq_s)$. We only look at values between the tail bounds, i.e. $z \in [-\tau\sigma, \tau\sigma]$, since any element lying outside of the tail bounds is rejected and thus not in the support of R'_σ. Next to that, we assume that $e_r, e_l \leq 2^{-p}\tau\sigma$, which is the worst case setting.

$$\Delta(R'^1_\sigma(z); R^1_\sigma(z))$$

$$= \frac{1}{2} \sum_{z=-\tau\sigma}^{\tau\sigma} \left| \int_{z-\frac{1}{2}-e_l}^{z+\frac{1}{2}+e_r} \frac{1}{\sqrt{2\pi\sigma^2}} e^{-x^2/(2\sigma^2)} dx - \int_{z-\frac{1}{2}}^{z+\frac{1}{2}} \frac{1}{\sqrt{2\pi\sigma^2}} e^{-x^2/(2\sigma^2)} dx \right|$$

$$\leq \frac{1}{2} \sum_{z=-\tau\sigma}^{\tau\sigma} \left| \int_{z-\frac{1}{2}-|e_l|}^{z-\frac{1}{2}} \frac{1}{\sqrt{2\pi\sigma^2}} e^{-x^2/(2\sigma^2)} dx + \int_{z+\frac{1}{2}}^{z+\frac{1}{2}+|e_r|} \frac{1}{\sqrt{2\pi\sigma^2}} e^{-x^2/(2\sigma^2)} dx \right|$$

$$\leq \frac{1}{2} \frac{1}{\sqrt{2\pi\sigma^2}} \left(\sum_{z=-\tau\sigma}^{-1} \left| |e_l| \exp\left(\frac{-(z-\frac{1}{2})^2}{2\sigma^2} \right) + |e_r| \exp\left(\frac{-(z+\frac{1}{2}+|e_r|)^2}{2\sigma^2} \right) \right| \right.$$

$$\left. + |e_l| + |e_r| + \sum_{z=1}^{\tau\sigma} \left| |e_l| \exp\left(\frac{-(z-\frac{1}{2}-|e_l|)^2}{2\sigma^2} \right) + |e_r| \exp\left(\frac{-(z+\frac{1}{2})^2}{2\sigma^2} \right) \right| \right)$$

$$\leq \frac{1}{2} \frac{2^{-p}\tau\sigma}{\sqrt{2\pi\sigma^2}} \left(\sum_{z=-\tau\sigma}^{-1} \left| \exp\left(\frac{-(z-\frac{1}{2})^2}{2\sigma^2} \right) + \exp\left(\frac{-(z+\frac{1}{2}+2^{-p}\tau\sigma)^2}{2\sigma^2} \right) \right| + 2 \right.$$

$$\left. + \sum_{z=1}^{\tau\sigma} \left| \exp\left(\frac{-(z-\frac{1}{2}-2^{-p}\tau\sigma)^2}{2\sigma^2} \right) + \exp\left(\frac{-(z+\frac{1}{2})^2}{2\sigma^2} \right) \right| \right)$$

$$\leq \frac{2^{-p}\tau\sigma}{\sqrt{2\pi\sigma^2}} \left(1 + \sum_{z=1}^{\tau\sigma} \left(\exp\left(\frac{-(z-\frac{1}{2}-2^{-p}\tau\sigma)^2}{2\sigma^2} \right) + \exp\left(\frac{-(z+\frac{1}{2})^2}{2\sigma^2} \right) \right) \right),$$

where we use in the second to last inequality the assumption that $|e_l|, |e_r| \leq 2^{-p}\tau\sigma$ and in the last inequality we note that for $z < 0$ we have $\exp\left(-\frac{(z-\frac{1}{2})^2}{2\sigma^2} \right) = \exp\left(-\frac{(|z|+\frac{1}{2})^2}{2\sigma^2} \right)$, which matches the term in the sum for $z > 0$. Similarly we have $\exp\left(-\frac{(z+\frac{1}{2}+2^{-p}\tau\sigma)^2}{2\sigma^2} \right) = \exp\left(-\frac{(|z|-\frac{1}{2}-2^{-p}\tau\sigma)^2}{2\sigma^2} \right)$. This means that we can group both sums under one sum running from 1 to $\tau\sigma$, which we need to multiply by 2 to compensate for having both distributions in one sum.

Note that this result looks like a rounded Gaussian centered around $\frac{1}{2}$ and a rounded Gaussian centered around $\frac{1}{2}+2^{-p}\tau\sigma$, except that all values for $z \leq 0$ are missing. Due to the symmetric property of the rounded Gaussian distribution, we know that both rounded Gaussians sum up to $\leq \frac{1}{2}$. This gives us:

$$\frac{2^{-p}\tau\sigma}{\sqrt{2\pi\sigma^2}} \left(1 + \sum_{z=1}^{\tau\sigma} \left(\exp\left(\frac{-(z-\frac{1}{2}-2^{-p}\tau\sigma)^2}{2\sigma^2} \right) + \exp\left(\frac{-(z+\frac{1}{2})^2}{2\sigma^2} \right) \right) \right)$$

$$\leq 2^{-p}\tau\sigma \left(\frac{1}{\sqrt{2\pi\sigma^2}} + \frac{1}{2} + \frac{1}{2} \right) = 2^{-p}\tau\sigma \left(\frac{1}{\sqrt{2\pi\sigma^2}} + 1 \right).$$

We require $2^{-p}\tau\sigma \left(\frac{1}{\sqrt{2\pi\sigma^2}} + 1 \right) \leq (\epsilon/2)/(mq_s)$. Note that $0 < \epsilon < 1$ and thus that $\log \epsilon < 0$. This means that a smaller ϵ requires a higher level of floating point precision. This is what we expect; if we want an adversary $\mathcal{A}$ to be less likely to be successful, we need to be more precise in our computations.

If we use the common setting $\epsilon = 2^{-\lambda}$, we get the precision requirement

$$p \geq \log\left(mq_s\tau\sigma \left(\sqrt{2\pi\sigma^2} + 1 \right) \right) + \lambda - \log\left(\sqrt{2\pi\sigma^2} \right) + 1. \tag{6}$$

RD$_1$-based analysis. According to [1], if $a = 1$ we have for an arbitrary event $A \subseteq \text{Supp}(Q)$ that $Q(A) \geq P(A) - \sqrt{\ln \text{RD}_1(P \parallel Q)/2}$, which is the probability preservation property (Lemma B.2) for $a = 1$. This means that we have $\delta \geq \epsilon - \sqrt{\ln \text{RD}_1\left(R'^{mq_s}_\sigma \parallel R^{mq_s}_\sigma\right)/2}$. We follow [1] in bounding the right-hand side by $\epsilon/2$. By the multiplicative property of the RD over the mq_s independent samples needed for signing q_s times, we get $\text{RD}_1\left(R'^{mq_s}_\sigma \parallel R^{mq_s}_\sigma\right) \leq \left(\text{RD}_1\left(R'^1_\sigma \parallel R^1_\sigma\right)\right)^{mq_s}$.

Recall that for the ln function we have $\ln(x) \leq x - 1$ for $x > 0$. Note that we are working with positive numbers, since probabilities lie between zero and one. If we only look at the elements between $-\tau\sigma$ and $\tau\sigma$, we know that they have a probability > 0. Now we compute the 1-dimensional case.

$$
\ln \text{RD}_1\left(R'^1_\sigma \parallel R^1_\sigma\right)
$$

$$
= \sum_{z \in \text{Supp}(R'^1_\sigma)} R'^1_\sigma(z) \ln\left(\frac{R'^1_\sigma(z)}{R^1_\sigma(z)}\right) \leq \sum_{z \in \text{Supp}(R'^1_\sigma)} R'^1_\sigma(z) \left(\frac{R'^1_\sigma(z)}{R^1_\sigma(z)} - 1\right)
$$

$$
\leq \sum_{z \in \text{Supp}(R'^1_\sigma)} \frac{1}{\sqrt{2\pi\sigma^2}} \int_{z-\frac{1}{2}-e_l}^{z+\frac{1}{2}+e_r} \exp\left(-\frac{x^2}{2\sigma^2}\right) dx \left(\frac{\int_{z-\frac{1}{2}-e_l}^{z+\frac{1}{2}+e_r} \exp\left(-\frac{x^2}{2\sigma^2}\right) dx}{\int_{z-\frac{1}{2}}^{z+\frac{1}{2}} \exp\left(-\frac{x^2}{2\sigma^2}\right) dx} - 1\right)
$$

$$
\leq \sum_{z \in \text{Supp}(R'^1_\sigma)} \frac{1}{\sqrt{2\pi\sigma^2}} \int_{z-\frac{1}{2}-e_l}^{z+\frac{1}{2}+e_r} \exp\left(-\frac{x^2}{2\sigma^2}\right) dx
$$

$$
\cdot \left(\frac{\int_{z-\frac{1}{2}-|e_l|}^{z-\frac{1}{2}} \exp\left(-\frac{x^2}{2\sigma^2}\right) dx + \int_{z+\frac{1}{2}}^{z+\frac{1}{2}+|e_r|} \exp\left(-\frac{x^2}{2\sigma^2}\right) dx}{\int_{z-\frac{1}{2}}^{z+\frac{1}{2}} \exp\left(-\frac{x^2}{2\sigma^2}\right) dx}\right).
$$

$$(7)$$

We now want to bound this equation. We first look at a bound in the case $z > 0$ for the following part of the equation:

$$
\int_{z-\frac{1}{2}-e_l}^{z+\frac{1}{2}+e_r} \exp\left(-\frac{x^2}{2\sigma^2}\right) dx \left(\frac{\int_{z-\frac{1}{2}-|e_l|}^{z-\frac{1}{2}} \exp\left(-\frac{x^2}{2\sigma^2}\right) dx + \int_{z+\frac{1}{2}}^{z+\frac{1}{2}+|e_r|} \exp\left(-\frac{x^2}{2\sigma^2}\right) dx}{\int_{z-\frac{1}{2}}^{z+\frac{1}{2}} \exp\left(-\frac{x^2}{2\sigma^2}\right) dx}\right)
$$

$$
\leq (1 + e_l + e_r) \exp\left(\frac{-\left(z-\frac{1}{2}-e_l\right)^2}{2\sigma^2}\right) \exp\left(\frac{\left(z+\frac{1}{2}\right)^2}{2\sigma^2}\right)
$$

$$
\cdot \left(|e_l| \exp\left(\frac{-\left(z-\frac{1}{2}-|e_l|\right)^2}{2\sigma^2}\right) + |e_r| \exp\left(\frac{-\left(z+\frac{1}{2}\right)^2}{2\sigma^2}\right)\right)
$$

$$
\leq (1 + e_r + e_l) \left(|e_l| \exp\left(\frac{-\left(z+\frac{1}{2}-2(1+|e_l|)\right)^2 + 2(1+|e_l|)^2}{2\sigma^2}\right) + |e_r| \exp\left(\frac{-\left(z-\frac{1}{2}-e_l\right)^2}{2\sigma^2}\right)\right).
$$

If we can find an equivalent bound like this for $z < 0$ and for $z = 0$, we can use the above formula to bound Eq. (7). For $z < 0$, we have the following equation that gives an upper bound:

$$\int_{z-\frac{1}{2}-e_l}^{z+\frac{1}{2}+e_r} \exp\left(-\frac{x^2}{2\sigma^2}\right) dx \left(\frac{\int_{z-\frac{1}{2}-|e_l|}^{z-\frac{1}{2}} \exp\left(-\frac{x^2}{2\sigma^2}\right) dx + \int_{z+\frac{1}{2}}^{z+\frac{1}{2}+|e_r|} \exp\left(-\frac{x^2}{2\sigma^2}\right) dx}{\int_{z-\frac{1}{2}}^{z+\frac{1}{2}} \exp\left(-\frac{x^2}{2\sigma^2}\right) dx}\right)$$

$$\leq (1 + e_l + e_r) \exp\left(\frac{-\left(z+\frac{1}{2}+e_r\right)^2}{2\sigma^2}\right) \exp\left(\frac{\left(z-\frac{1}{2}\right)^2}{2\sigma^2}\right)$$

$$\cdot \left(|e_l| \exp\left(\frac{-\left(z-\frac{1}{2}\right)^2}{2\sigma^2}\right) + |e_r| \exp\left(\frac{-\left(z+\frac{1}{2}+|e_r|\right)^2}{2\sigma^2}\right)\right)$$

$$\leq (1 + e_r + e_l) \left(|e_l| \exp\left(\frac{-\left(z+\frac{1}{2}+e_r\right)^2}{2\sigma^2}\right) + |e_r| \exp\left(\frac{-\left(z-\frac{1}{2}+2(1+|e_r|)\right)^2+2(1+|e_r|)^2}{2\sigma^2}\right)\right)$$

$$\leq (1 + e_r + e_l) \left(|e_l| \exp\left(\frac{-\left(|z|-\frac{1}{2}-e_r\right)^2}{2\sigma^2}\right)\right.$$

$$\left. + |e_r| \exp\left(\frac{-\left(|z|+\frac{1}{2}-2(1+|e_r|)\right)^2 + 2(1+|e_r|)^2}{2\sigma^2}\right)\right).$$

This means that we have the same result for $z > 0$ and $z < 0$, except that the e_l's change into e_r's and vice versa. Since $e_l, e_r \leq 2^{-p}\tau\sigma$, we end up with the following result for $z < 0$ and $z > 0$:

$$\int_{z-\frac{1}{2}-e_l}^{z+\frac{1}{2}+e_r} \exp\left(-\frac{x^2}{2\sigma^2}\right) dx \left(\frac{\int_{z-\frac{1}{2}-|e_l|}^{z-\frac{1}{2}} \exp\left(-\frac{x^2}{2\sigma^2}\right) dx + \int_{z+\frac{1}{2}}^{z+\frac{1}{2}+|e_r|} \exp\left(-\frac{x^2}{2\sigma^2}\right) dx}{\int_{z-\frac{1}{2}}^{z+\frac{1}{2}} \exp\left(-\frac{x^2}{2\sigma^2}\right) dx}\right)$$

$$\leq \left(1 + 2^{-p+1}\tau\sigma\right) 2^{-p}\tau\sigma \left(\exp\left(\frac{-\left(|z|-\frac{1}{2}-2^{-p}\tau\sigma\right)^2}{2\sigma^2}\right)\right.$$

$$\left. + \exp\left(\frac{-\left(|z|+\frac{1}{2}-2\left(1+2^{-p}\tau\sigma\right)\right)^2 + 2\left(1+2^{-p}\tau\sigma\right)^2}{2\sigma^2}\right)\right).$$

Now that we have found a bound for $z < 0$ and $z > 0$, we also need to find a bound for $z = 0$. If $z = 0$, we have

$$\int_{z-\frac{1}{2}-e_l}^{z+\frac{1}{2}+e_r} \exp\left(-\frac{x^2}{2\sigma^2}\right) dx \left(\frac{\int_{z-\frac{1}{2}-|e_l|}^{z-\frac{1}{2}} \exp\left(-\frac{x^2}{2\sigma^2}\right) dx + \int_{z+\frac{1}{2}}^{z+\frac{1}{2}+|e_r|} \exp\left(-\frac{x^2}{2\sigma^2}\right) dx}{\int_{z-\frac{1}{2}}^{z+\frac{1}{2}} \exp\left(-\frac{x^2}{2\sigma^2}\right) dx}\right)$$

$$\leq (1 + e_l + e_r) \exp\left(\frac{1}{8\sigma^2}\right) \left(|e_l| \exp\left(-\frac{1}{8\sigma^2}\right) + |e_r| \exp\left(-\frac{1}{8\sigma^2}\right)\right)$$

$$= (1 + e_l + e_r) \left(|e_l| + |e_r|\right) \leq \left(1 + 2^{-p+1}\tau\sigma\right) 2^{-p+1}\tau\sigma,$$

where we use $e_l, e_r < 2^{-p}\tau\sigma$ in the second inequality. Combining the result for $z = 0$ with the results for $z < 0$ and $z > 0$ gives us:

$$\ln \mathrm{RD}_1\left(R'^1_\sigma \,\|\, R^1_\sigma\right)$$

$$\leq \left(1 + 2^{-p+1}\tau\sigma\right) 2^{-p+1}\tau\sigma$$

$$+ \sum_{z \in \mathrm{Supp}(R'^1_\sigma), z > 0} \frac{1}{\sqrt{2\pi\sigma^2}} \left(1 + 2^{-p+1}\tau\sigma\right) 2^{-p+1}\tau\sigma \left(\exp\left(\frac{-\left(|z|-\frac{1}{2}-2^{-p}\tau\sigma\right)^2}{2\sigma^2}\right)\right.$$

$$\left. + \exp\left(\frac{-\left(|z|+\frac{1}{2}-2\left(1+2^{-p}\tau\sigma\right)\right)^2 + 2\left(1+2^{-p}\tau\sigma\right)^2}{2\sigma^2}\right)\right)$$

$$= \left(1 + 2^{-p+1}\tau\sigma\right) 2^{-p+1}\tau\sigma \left(1 + \sum_{z=0}^{\infty} \frac{1}{\sqrt{2\pi\sigma^2}} \left(\exp\left(\frac{-\left(z-\frac{1}{2}-2^{-p}\tau\sigma\right)^2}{2\sigma^2}\right)\right.\right.$$

$$\left.\left. + \exp\left(\frac{-\left(z+\frac{1}{2}-2\left(1+2^{-p}\tau\sigma\right)\right)^2 + 2\left(1+2^{-p}\tau\sigma\right)^2}{2\sigma^2}\right)\right)\right)$$

$$\leq \left(1 + 2^{-p+1}\tau\sigma\right) 2^{-p+1}\tau\sigma \left(2 + 2\exp\left(\frac{9}{4\sigma^2}\right)\right),$$

where we use in the last inequality that $\sum_{z=0}^{\infty} \frac{1}{\sqrt{2\pi\sigma^2}} \exp\left(\frac{-\left(z-\frac{1}{2}-2^{-p}\tau\sigma\right)^2}{2\sigma^2}\right) \leq 1$,

as this sums over parts of a Gaussian centered at $-1/2 - 2^{-p}\tau\sigma$. Similarly,

$\sum_{z=0}^{\infty} \frac{1}{\sqrt{2\pi\sigma^2}} \exp\left(\frac{-\left(z+\frac{1}{2}-2\left(1+2^{-p}\tau\sigma\right)\right)^2}{2\sigma^2}\right) \leq 1$ and $1 < (1 + 2^{-p}\tau\sigma) < \frac{3}{2}$, since $0 <$

$2^{-p}\tau\sigma < \frac{1}{2}$. We note that we could use the stronger bound $\tau\sigma < 2^{-p/2+1}$ here, which implies that we can use a smaller number in the exp function. However, the goal is to get rid of p with this equation and for this the current estimate is sufficient. This means that we can use the equation above to compute the floating point precision needed in the RD_1 setting. First we look at $\ln \mathrm{RD}_1(R'^{mq_s}_\sigma \| R^{mq_s}_\sigma)/2$, before we determine the precision p:

$$\ln \mathrm{RD}_1(R'^{mq_s}_\sigma \| R^{mq_s}_\sigma)/2 \leq mq_s \ln \mathrm{RD}_1(R'^1_\sigma \| R^1_\sigma)/2$$
$$\leq \frac{mq_s}{2}\left(1 + 2^{-p+1}\tau\sigma\right)2^{-p+1}\tau\sigma\left(2 + 2\exp\left(\frac{9}{4\sigma^2}\right)\right)$$
$$= mq_s\left(\left(2^{-p+1}\tau\sigma + \frac{1}{2}\right)^2 - \frac{1}{4}\right)\left(1 + \exp\left(\frac{9}{4\sigma^2}\right)\right).$$

If we now bound this expression by $\epsilon^2/4$ and determine p, we know that this p also holds in the setting $\sqrt{\ln \mathrm{RD}_1(R'^{mq_s}_\sigma \| R^{mq_s}_\sigma)/2} \leq \epsilon/2$. This results in:

$$mq_s\left(\left(2^{-p+1}\tau\sigma + \frac{1}{2}\right)^2 - \frac{1}{4}\right)\left(1 + \exp\left(\frac{9}{4\sigma^2}\right)\right) \leq \frac{\epsilon^2}{4}$$
$$\Leftrightarrow \left(2^{-p+1}\tau\sigma + \frac{1}{2}\right)^2 \leq \frac{\epsilon^2 + mq_s\left(1+\exp\left(\frac{9}{4\sigma^2}\right)\right)}{4mq_s\left(1+\exp\left(\frac{9}{4\sigma^2}\right)\right)}$$
$$\Leftrightarrow 2^{-p+1} \leq \frac{\sqrt{\epsilon^2 + mq_s\left(1+\exp\left(\frac{9}{4\sigma^2}\right)\right)} - \sqrt{mq_s\left(1+\exp\left(\frac{9}{4\sigma^2}\right)\right)}}{2\tau\sigma\sqrt{mq_s\left(1+\exp\left(\frac{9}{4\sigma^2}\right)\right)}}.$$

This means that we have as the floating point precision requirement

$$p \geq \log\left(\frac{\tau\sigma\sqrt{mq_s\left(1+\exp\left(\frac{9}{4\sigma^2}\right)\right)}}{\sqrt{\epsilon^2 + mq_s\left(1+\exp\left(\frac{9}{4\sigma^2}\right)\right)} - \sqrt{mq_s\left(1+\exp\left(\frac{9}{4\sigma^2}\right)\right)}}\right) + 2. \quad (8)$$

RD$_\infty$-based analysis. For $a = +\infty$, we follow [1] such that we have that any forging adversary $\mathcal{A}$ having success probability ϵ on the scheme implemented with imperfect rounded Gaussian sampling has a success probability $\delta \geq \epsilon/\mathrm{RD}_\infty(R'^{mq_s}_\sigma \| R^{mq_s}_\sigma)$ on the scheme implemented with the perfect rounded Gaussian, because of the multiplicative property of the RD, as given in Lemma B.1. If $\mathrm{RD}_\infty(R'^{mq_s}_\sigma \| R^{mq_s}_\sigma) \leq O(1)$, then $\delta = \Omega(\epsilon)$.

We need mq_s samples to create q_s signatures. By the multiplicative property of the RD, we have $\mathrm{RD}_\infty(R'^{mq_s}_\sigma \| R^{mq_s}_\sigma) \leq \mathrm{RD}_\infty(R'^1_\sigma \| R^1_\sigma)^{mq_s}$. We target $\delta \geq \epsilon/\exp(1)$. We first compute $R'^1_\sigma(z)/R^1_\sigma(z)$ from which the maximum will automatically follow:

$$\frac{R'^1_\sigma(z)}{R^1_\sigma(z)} = \left(\int_{z-\frac{1}{2}-e_l}^{z+\frac{1}{2}+e_r} \frac{1}{\sqrt{2\pi\sigma^2}}e^{-x^2/(2\sigma^2)}dx\right) \Big/ \left(\int_{z-\frac{1}{2}}^{z+\frac{1}{2}} \frac{1}{\sqrt{2\pi\sigma^2}}e^{-x^2/(2\sigma^2)}dx\right)$$
$$\leq 1 + \left(\int_{z-\frac{1}{2}-|e_l|}^{z-\frac{1}{2}}e^{-x^2/(2\sigma^2)}dx + \int_{z+\frac{1}{2}}^{z+\frac{1}{2}+|e_r|}e^{-x^2/(2\sigma^2)}dx\right) \Big/ \left(\int_{z-\frac{1}{2}}^{z+\frac{1}{2}}e^{-x^2/(2\sigma^2)}dx\right). \quad (9)$$

Now we need to find a lower bound for the integral in the denominator. We start by looking into the case $z > 0$. We have the following bounds:

$$\int_{z-\frac{1}{2}}^{z+\frac{1}{2}} e^{-x^2/(2\sigma^2)}dx \geq \int_{z-\frac{1}{2}}^{z-\frac{1}{2}+\frac{1}{z}} e^{-x^2/(2\sigma^2)}dx \geq \frac{1}{z}\exp\left(\frac{-(z-\frac{1}{2}+\frac{1}{z})^2}{2\sigma^2}\right)$$

$$= \frac{1}{z}\exp\left(\frac{-(z-\frac{1}{2})^2-2(z-\frac{1}{2})\frac{1}{z}-\frac{1}{z^2}}{2\sigma^2}\right) \geq \frac{1}{z}\exp\left(\frac{-(z-\frac{1}{2})^2}{2\sigma^2}\right)\exp\left(\frac{-1}{\sigma^2}\right), \quad (10)$$

where we use that $\frac{2}{z}(z-\frac{1}{2})+\frac{1}{z^2} \leq 2$ for $z \geq 1$ and $z \in \mathbb{Z}$. We bound the integrals in the numerator the same way as in the RD_1 analysis and combine this with the lower bound from Eq. (9):

$$1 + \left(\int_{z-\frac{1}{2}-|e_l|}^{z-\frac{1}{2}} e^{-x^2/(2\sigma^2)}dx + \int_{z+\frac{1}{2}}^{z+\frac{1}{2}+|e_r|} e^{-x^2/(2\sigma^2)}dx\right)\bigg/\left(\int_{z-\frac{1}{2}}^{z+\frac{1}{2}} e^{-x^2/(2\sigma^2)}dx\right)$$

$$\leq 1 + \left(|e_l|\exp\left(\frac{-(z-\frac{1}{2}-|e_l|)^2}{2\sigma^2}\right) + |e_r|\exp\left(\frac{-(z+\frac{1}{2})^2}{2\sigma^2}\right)\right)\bigg/\left(\frac{1}{z}\exp\left(\frac{-(z-\frac{1}{2})^2}{2\sigma^2}\right)\exp\left(\frac{-1}{\sigma^2}\right)\right)$$

$$= 1 + z\exp\left(\frac{1}{\sigma^2}\right)\exp\left(\frac{(z-\frac{1}{2})^2}{2\sigma^2}\right)\left(|e_l|\exp\left(\frac{-(z-\frac{1}{2}-|e_l|)^2}{2\sigma^2}\right) + |e_r|\exp\left(\frac{-(z+\frac{1}{2})^2}{2\sigma^2}\right)\right)$$

$$\leq 1 + z\exp\left(\frac{1}{\sigma^2}\right)\left(|e_l|\exp\left(\frac{|e_l|(2z-1-|e_l|)}{2\sigma^2}\right) + |e_r|\exp\left(\frac{-z}{\sigma^2}\right)\right)$$

$$\leq 1 + z\exp\left(\frac{1}{\sigma^2}\right)\left(|e_l|\exp\left(\frac{|e_l|z}{\sigma^2}\right) + |e_r|\right) \leq 1 + 2^{-P}(\tau\sigma)^2\exp\left(\frac{1}{\sigma^2}\right)\left(\exp\left(\frac{2^{-P}(\tau\sigma)^2}{\sigma^2}\right) + 1\right),$$

where we use in the last inequality that $|e_l|, |e_r| \leq 2^{-P}\tau\sigma$ and that $|z| \leq \tau\sigma$. We note that $2^{-P+1} \leq (\tau\sigma)^2$, which gives us

$$1 + 2^{-P}(\tau\sigma)^2\exp\left(\frac{1}{\sigma^2}\right)\left(\exp\left(\frac{2^{-P}(\tau\sigma)^2}{\sigma^2}\right) + 1\right) \leq 1 + 2^{-P}(\tau\sigma)^2\exp\left(\frac{1}{2\sigma^2}\right)\left(\exp\left(\frac{1}{2\sigma^2}\right) + 1\right)$$

$$\leq \exp\left(2^{-P}(\tau\sigma)^2\exp\left(\frac{1}{\sigma^2}\right)\left(\exp\left(\frac{1}{2\sigma^2}\right) + 1\right)\right).$$

We have found an upper bound for $R'^{mqs}_\sigma/R^{mqs}_\sigma$ if $z > 0$. We need to check if this bound works for any value of $z \in \mathbb{Z}$. First we look into the case $z < 0$. We want to find a similar bound as in Eq. (10). We have

$$\int_{z-\frac{1}{2}}^{z+\frac{1}{2}} e^{-x^2/(2\sigma^2)}dx \geq \int_{z+\frac{1}{2}+\frac{1}{z}}^{z+\frac{1}{2}} e^{-x^2/(2\sigma^2)}dx \geq \frac{1}{|z|}\exp\left(\frac{-(z+\frac{1}{2}+\frac{1}{z})^2}{2\sigma^2}\right)$$

$$= \frac{1}{|z|}\exp\left(\frac{-(z+\frac{1}{2})^2-2(z+\frac{1}{2})\cdot\frac{1}{z}-\frac{1}{z^2}}{2\sigma^2}\right) = \frac{1}{|z|}\exp\left(\frac{-(|z|-\frac{1}{2})^2-2(|z|-\frac{1}{2})\cdot\frac{1}{|z|}-\frac{1}{|z|^2}}{2\sigma^2}\right) \quad (11)$$

$$\geq \frac{1}{|z|}\exp\left(\frac{-(|z|-\frac{1}{2})^2}{2\sigma^2}\right)\exp\left(\frac{-1}{\sigma^2}\right),$$

which is the same expression as we had for $z > 0$. We note that the only difference between $z < 0$ and $z > 0$ is the e_l and the e_r, which we already have seen in the case of RD_1. Since we use $|e_l|, |e_r| \leq 2^{-P}\tau\sigma$, we can use the bound found for $z > 0$ also in the case $z < 0$. Now we check if this maximum also works for $z = 0$:

$$\frac{R'^1_\sigma(z)}{R^1_\sigma(z)} \leq \left(\int_{z-\frac{1}{2}-e_l}^{z+\frac{1}{2}+e_r} \frac{1}{\sqrt{2\pi\sigma^2}}e^{-x^2/(2\sigma^2)}dx\right)\bigg/\left(\int_{z-\frac{1}{2}}^{z+\frac{1}{2}} \frac{1}{\sqrt{2\pi\sigma^2}}e^{-x^2/(2\sigma^2)}dx\right)$$

$$\leq 1 + |e_r| + |e_l| \leq 1 + \frac{1}{2}\cdot2^{-P} + \frac{1}{2}\cdot2^{-P} = 1 + 2^{-P},$$

as we have seen in the computations for RD_1. Since this is less than the maximum, we can use the upper bound $\exp\left(2^{-p}(\tau\sigma)^2 \exp\left(\frac{1}{\sigma^2}\right)\left(\exp\left(\frac{1}{2\sigma^2}\right)+1\right)\right)$ to determine the floating point precision p needed.

We have $RD_\infty(R'^{mq_s}_\sigma \| R^{mq_s}_\sigma) \leq RD_\infty(R'^1_\sigma \| R^1_\sigma)^{mq_s}$ and want to find an expression for p from this. This results in the following equations:

$$RD_\infty(R'^{mq_s}_\sigma \| R^{mq_s}_\sigma) \leq RD_\infty(R'^1_\sigma \| R^1_\sigma)^{mq_s}$$
$$\leq \exp\left(2^{-p}(\tau\sigma)^2 \exp\left(\frac{1}{\sigma^2}\right)\left(\exp\left(\frac{1}{2\sigma^2}\right)+1\right)\right)^{mq_s}.$$

We set the floating point precision p such that

$$\exp\left(mq_s 2^{-p}(\tau\sigma)^2 \exp\left(\frac{1}{\sigma^2}\right)\left(\exp\left(\frac{1}{2\sigma^2}\right)+1\right)\right) \leq \exp(1).$$

This yields a precision argument

$$p \geq \log\left(mq_s(\tau\sigma)^2 \exp\left(\frac{1}{\sigma^2}\right)\left(\exp\left(\frac{1}{2\sigma^2}\right)+1\right)\right). \tag{12}$$

Recall that we assumed that $\tau\sigma \ll 2^{-p/2}$, i.e. $p > 2\log(\tau\sigma)$. We need to check if this is true for the result we got. We see that indeed we get

$$p \geq \log\left(mq_s(\tau\sigma)^2 \exp\left(\frac{1}{\sigma^2}\right)\left(\exp\left(\frac{1}{2\sigma^2}\right)+1\right)\right)$$
$$= 2\log(\tau\sigma) + \log\left(mq_s \exp\left(\frac{1}{\sigma^2}\right)\left(\exp\left(\frac{1}{2\sigma^2}\right)+1\right)\right) > 2\log(\tau\sigma),$$

since all the logarithms give a positive result.

Note that, as in the analysis of the discrete Gaussian in [1], Eq. (12) does not explicitly depend on ϵ. However, the dependency on ϵ is hidden in the security parameter λ, which is still dependent on ϵ.

Equation (12) eliminates the term ϵ from the floating point precision p, which was needed for the SD-based and the RD_1-based analyses. However, m, q_s and ϵ are dependent on λ, i.e. the resulting floating point precision p is not independent of ϵ, since it is not independent of λ.

We summarize the results in Table B.1. Before we can numerically compute this p, we need to know the value of m and against how many signing queries q_s we want to be protected.

Note that the precision plays different roles per sampler and implementation. In our sampling approach, each computation step has the potential to decrease the precision, but all considerations are worst-case considerations. The CDT sampler that we considered for comparison has a stored table of fixed precision. To compare the precision bounds as described in Table B.1 to the precision bounds found in [1] for BLISS-I we use the same values for the variables, that is, we use $\epsilon = 2^{-128}$, dimension $m = 1024, q_s = 2^{64}$ sign queries, $\sigma = 215$ and tail bound $\tau = \sqrt{(2 \cdot 128 \cdot \log(2))} = 13.32087377852$. The results can be found in Table B.2. Here we can see that rounded Gaussians need more precision than discrete Gaussians, but rounded Gaussians come with the advantage that they can easily be implemented in constant time and without table look ups, which

Table B.1. Comparison of the precision p to handle adversaries with success probability $\geq \epsilon$ making $\leq q_s$ signing queries to BLISS signature generation with Box-Muller transformation.

	Lower bound on the precision p
SD (Eq. (6))	$p \geq \log\left(mq_s\tau\sigma\left(\sqrt{2\pi\sigma^2}+1\right)\right) + \lambda - \log\left(\sqrt{2\pi\sigma^2}\right) + 1$
RD$_1$ (Eq. (8))	$p \geq \log\left(\dfrac{\tau\sigma\sqrt{mq_s\left(1+\exp\left(\frac{9}{4\sigma^2}\right)\right)}}{\sqrt{\epsilon^2+mq_s\left(1+\exp\left(\frac{9}{4\sigma^2}\right)\right)}-\sqrt{mq_s\left(1+\exp\left(\frac{9}{4\sigma^2}\right)\right)}}\right) + 2$
RD$_\infty$ (Eq. (12))	$p \geq \log\left(mq_s(\tau\sigma)^2\exp\left(\frac{1}{\sigma^2}\right)\left(\exp\left(\frac{\tau}{2\sigma}\right)+1\right)\right)$

Table B.2. Comparison of the precision p needed for BLISS-I implemented with rounded Gaussians and implemented with discrete Gaussians.

	Example p for rounded Gaussians	Example p for discrete Gaussians
SD	$p \geq 215$	$p \geq 207$
RD$_1$	$p \geq 346$	$p \geq 168$
RD$_\infty$	$p \geq 98$	$p \geq 79$

makes it suitable to use rounded Gaussians in practice for BLISS. Furthermore, the estimates are less tight because of the approximation of integrals and errors by their worst case value.

Note that the values in Table B.2 tell us the resulting precision needed. If we want to know the implementations precision, i.e. the precision before the implementation makes any changes, we need to compute how much precision is lost by the implementation. For our implementation of BLISS-I we have computed the loss of precision in Sect. 5.2.

Author Index

Printed in the United States
By Bookmasters